THE NEW YORK PUBLIC LIBRARY DESK REFERENCE

Fourth Edition

A STONESONG PRESS BOOK

HYPERION

New York

HYPERION
77 West 66th Street
New York, NY 10023-6298

The New York Public Library

The name *"The New York Public Library"* and the representation of the lion appearing in this Work are trademarks and the property of The New York Public Library, Astor, Lenox, and Tilden foundations.

Library of Congress Cataloging-in-Publication Data

ISBN: 0-7868-6846-5

Printed in the United States of America on acid-free paper.

A Stonesong Press Book

Hyperion books are available for special promotions and premiums. For details contact Hyperion Special Markets, 77 West 66th Street, 11th Floor, New York, New York, 10023, or call 212-456-0100.

Fourth Edition

10 9 8 7 6 5 4 3 2 1

Typesetting by Brad Walrod, High Text Graphics, Inc.

Four-color maps created by Netmaps, S.A.

To Alison

A Note from the Editors

Every attempt has been made to ensure that this publication is as accurate as possible and as comprehensive as space would allow. We are grateful to the many researchers, librarians, teachers, reference editors, and friends who contributed facts, figures, time, energy, ideas, and opinions. Our choice of what to include was aided by their advice and their voices of experience. The contents, however, remain subjective to some extent, because we could not possibly cover everything that one might look for in basic information. If errors or omissions are discovered, we would appreciate hearing from you, the user, as we prepare future editions. Please address suggestions and comments to The Stonesong Press, 11 East 47th Street, New York, NY 10017.

We hope you find our work useful.

CONTENTS

III THE WAY WE COMMUNICATE 389

12 SYMBOLS AND SIGNS 391

13 ALPHABETS AND WORDS 407

14 GRAMMAR AND PUNCTUATION 439

19 HOUSEHOLD TIPS 539

PREFACE

The New York Public Library, through its Research and Branch Libraries, provides free and open access to information on a scale unmatched by any other library in the world. Consisting of four major research libraries whose materials do not circulate and are used within their reading rooms—the Humanities and Social Sciences Library, The New York Public Library for the Performing Arts, the Schomburg Center for Research in Black Culture, and the Science, Industry and Business Library—and 85 neighborhood libraries with circulating collections throughout the Bronx, Manhattan, and Staten Island, it has more material than any other public library system in the nation.

The collections themselves reflect the profoundly democratic and all-encompassing nature of the Library. Numbering more than 50 million items, its holdings range from the most venerable monuments of human culture—such as the Gutenberg Bible and Jefferson's manuscript copy of the Declaration of Independence—to such icons of popular culture as 19th-century baseball cards, to the literary archives of Virginia Woolf, Jack Kerouac, and many others, to commonplace materials that document the everyday lives of otherwise anonymous people. The collections grow at a rate of approximately 10,000 items per week in dozens of languages. Over the years, the Library's holdings have played a vital role in the creation of innumerable works in the arts, science, literature, and history.

Founded in 1895, The New York Public Library officially opened the doors of its landmark building on Fifth Avenue on May 23, 1911, when on one day upwards of 50,000 visitors streamed past the guardian lions; today the Library system is visited and used annually by more than 15 million people, from neighborhood children and general readers to researchers and scholars from around the world. There are 1.7 million cardholders; over 6 million reference questions were answered last year, either in the libraries, by phone, or via the Internet. The Library's Telephone Reference service, augmented in 2002 by Ask Librarians Online, continues to provide quick, accurate information to thousands of users each year.

Today the global use of the Library's resources is dramatically increasing through access to catalogs and digitized collections via the Library's web site. An ongoing program to digitize primary source materials, both visual and textual, will make these unique items accessible from home. Additionally users have access to more than 300 electronic databases, some of which can also be used from home with a New York Public Library borrower's card.

Yet, as the Library embraces the technologies of the 21st century, the technology that has stood the test of time—the book—remains very much at the heart of what the Library does. Among these extraordinary collections are over 18 million books, a format that remains a convenient, easy-to-use tool for obtaining information. Back in 1989, when *The New York Public Library Desk Reference* was originally published, we felt that "a book fills a unique need for portability, individuality, and beauty." We still do. And it has been gratifying to find that this particular book seems to have filled the needs of our using public, as both a home and library reference.

Paul LeClerc
President, The New York Public Library

NOTE FROM THE NEW YORK PUBLIC LIBRARY

Like the first three editions, this fourth edition reflects the experience of librarians, professional researchers, and reference editors in handling a wide range of questions in many subject areas. It remains what it has been from its first publication—a compendium of basic information about a variety of subjects that allows readers to efficiently find answers to their questions. This edition has been thoroughly revised and updated to help the general reader handle the explosion of information that fills our 21st-century world. In response to many suggestions from users, and the impact of increased computer access to information, whole sections of the book have been rewritten and the popular easy-to-follow charts, graphs, and sidebars of the previous edition have been updated to include information through mid-2002. The index has been entirely reconceived, and hundreds of new text entries have been added to maintain the "browsabil-ity" factor that readers enjoy so much. Using as a criterion the works most likely to be available today in school and public libraries, all the bibliographies have been updated. Numerous web sites and phone numbers for further information are included. All of these tools can serve as a springboard for further inquiry by the reader.

Revising and updating a project such as this one is a major undertaking and has involved many people, including readers who have taken the time to write to us about omissions or errors in the earlier editions. Our special thanks to the staff of The Stonesong Press who have provided guidance and direction through all the editions.

Karen Van Westering
Director of the Publications Program
The New York Public Library

I

THE PHYSICAL WORLD

1

TIMES AND DATES

RECKONING DAYS AND HOURS

THE LENGTH OF THE DAY

The length of the *sidereal day* (Latin: *sider*—star) is determined by the rotation of the Earth, which causes the stars, to any observer, to appear to make one revolution each sidereal day from east to west. The length of a *true solar day* is determined by noting one passage of the Sun across the meridian of an observer and calculating the time that it takes for the Sun to cross the same point in the sky a second time. Because the Earth moves along its orbit around the Sun during the time it makes a single rotation, the solar day is slightly longer than the sidereal day (on average, by 3 minutes and 56 seconds of solar time).

The phrase "a red-letter day" dates from 1704, when holy days were marked in red letters on church calendars.

Over the course of a year (the time it takes the Earth to make one revolution around the Sun), the length of the true solar day varies because of (1) the eccentricity of the Earth's elliptical orbit and (2) the inclination of the equator (the plane running through the Earth's center and perpendicular to the Earth's axis of rotation) to the ecliptic (the plane of

the Earth's orbit). The uniform length of our 24-hour calendar day, the *mean solar day,* is based on the average length of the true solar day over a year.

HOW IS THE DAY SUBDIVIDED?

The division of the day into hours is an arbitrary standard, as is the uniform length of the hour. Different cultures divided their days in different ways. The ancient Egyptians, Greeks, and Romans had a 24-hour day, but they divided it into 10 hours of light, 10 hours of dark, and 1 hour each of dawn and dusk (the twilight hours), which meant that the length of the hours depended on the seasons. Only after the invention of mechanical clocks in the late Middle Ages (see the sidebar "Clocks—Measuring Time") did a need develop for days, hours, and smaller units of time of uniform length. The mean solar day, under the common system of solar time, is thus divided as follows:

1 mean solar day = 24 mean solar hours
1 mean solar hour = 60 mean solar minutes
1 mean solar minute = 60 mean solar seconds

One mean solar day is thus equal to 86,400 (= 24 × 60 × 60) mean solar seconds.

For civil purposes, the time when the Sun crosses the local meridian is defined as noon, the midpoint between successive noons is defined as midnight, and the standard measurement of the day is from

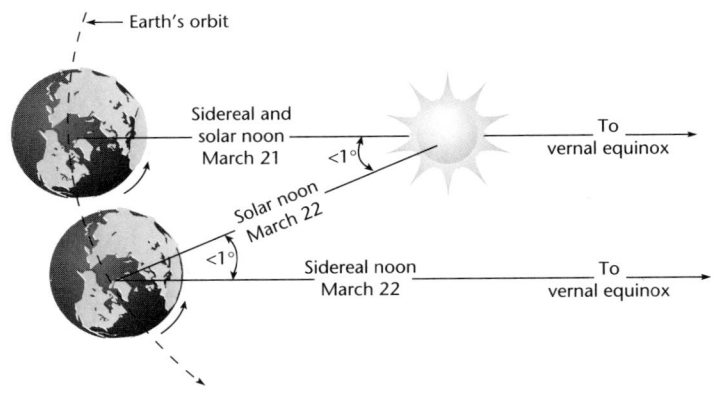

SIDEREAL AND SOLAR DAYS

midnight to midnight. (Some ancient peoples counted the day from dawn to dawn; others, such as the Jews, count their days from sunset to sunset.)

Under the 12-hour system of counting hours, the day is divided into two equal portions denoted by A.M. (before noon) and P.M. (after noon), derived from the Latin terms *ante meridiem* and *post meridiem*. The instant 4 hours and 15 minutes after midnight is designated 4:15 A.M.; the instant 5 hours and 23 minutes after noon is 5:23 P.M. According to the National Institute of Standards and Technology, confusion exists regarding 12 A.M., 12 P.M., noon, and midnight. The term *noon* is neither before or after noon—noon is noon; midnight is both 12 hours before noon and 12 hours after noon. It is best to refer to these times as noon and midnight instead of 12 A.M. and 12 P.M.

Clocks—Measuring Time

A Closer Look

The sundial may be the oldest device for measuring time, going back to the Fertile Crescent of about 2000 B.C. Its operation is based on the fact that the shadow of a fixed object will move around it from one side to the other as the Sun moves from east to west. Naturally, the duration of the hours marked off by a sundial changes according to the seasons of the year. Along with sundials, ancient peoples used water clocks that measured time by a constant rate of flow of water through a bowl-like device with an outlet. Sand flowing from one compartment into another also was used in late medieval Europe to measure time. These last two methods could be used at night; they also counted more uniform units of time.

With the invention of mechanical clocks, the hours became uniform. The first mechanical clocks appeared in Europe in the 14th century (mechanical timepieces existed in China at least two centuries earlier, though the Chinese never developed them highly). The earliest ones were driven by weights strung around a drum. As the weight fell, the mechanism was activated. Next came spring-driven clocks, although they had the disadvantage of running differently when the spring had just been wound and was in its most tense position and after it had unwound somewhat. The workings of all clocks depend on a motion or vibration that is constant and regular.

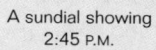

A sundial showing 2:45 P.M.

Circa 1581 the great Italian physicist Galileo (1564–1642) observed that the time it took for a pendulum to complete one total swing (called the period of oscillation) was almost independent of its magnitude—that is, how far it swung from side to side. He understood that this phenomenon could be used as a frequency mechanism for regulating a clock. In 1656, a Dutch physicist, Christian Huygens (1629–95), working independently, constructed the first pendulum clock. Pendulum clocks remained the most precise means of measuring time into the 20th century. Pendulums could be constructed to oscillate at specified frequencies once such factors as latitude, the pull of gravity, and weather and its effects on the materials used to make the clock had been compensated for.

With each swing of the pendulum, the escape wheel moves one notch as the pallet moves back and forth. Notch by notch, the escapement moves the clock's mechanism to a regular rhythm.

Pallet

Escapement

Escape wheel

Pendulum

Quartz clocks, introduced in the 1930s, improved on the pendulum, though only after years of development. By controlling the frequency of an electric circuit through the regular mechanical vibration of the quartz crystal, high degrees of constancy in vibration can be achieved, making a quartz clock even more accurate than a pendulum.

In the 1940s, atomic clocks were introduced. Their frequencies are based on the vibrations of certain atoms and molecules that vibrate the same number of times per second. Atomic clocks are constant to within a few seconds every 100,000 years. The fundamental unit of atomic time is the SI second.

Ship's Bell Time Signals

On most ships, a day consists of six 4-hour watches. The watches change at 8 A.M., noon, 4 P.M., 8 P.M., midnight, and 4 A.M. A chime indicates each half hour. During a 4-hour watch, one bell chimes at the first half hour, two bells at the second, and so on, up to eight, when the next watch begins and the sequence starts over again.

1 bell	12:30 or	4:30 or	8:30 A.M. or P.M.
2 bells	1:00	5:00	9:00
3 bells	1:30	5:30	9:30
4 bells	2:00	6:00	10:00
5 bells	2:30	6:30	10:30
6 bells	3:00	7:00	11:00
7 bells	3:30	7:30	11:30
8 bells	4:00	8:00	12:00

On many vessels, the ship's whistle is blown at noon. On some ships, 1 lightly struck bell announces 15 minutes before the change of watch.

A 24-hour system, which avoids repeating numbers and clearly distinguishes between midnight and noon, is used by the U.S. military and throughout continental Europe. Under this system, midnight (the beginning of the day) is designated 0000, the following noon is 1200, and the following midnight is 2400. (The designation 2400 of one day is the same instant of time as that of 0000 of the following day.) The times 4:15 A.M. and 5:23 P.M. are designated as 0415 and 1723 under this counting system.

UNIVERSAL AND STANDARD TIME

The mean solar time determined by the meridian that runs through Greenwich, England (where that country's Royal Observatory was originally located), is referred to as *Greenwich Mean Time, Zulu Time,* or *Universal Time.* The *Coordinated Universal Time* (UTC) is an atomic scale kept in agreement with Universal Time and is also known as the world time standard. Such precise times are especially useful for marine and air navigation and tracking of artificial satellites and space probes.

From Greenwich, too, longitudes are measured around the world. Greenwich, having a 0° longitude, is called the *prime meridian.*

Standard time, which for most localities differs from universal time by an integral number of hours, was created by international agreement in 1883 to avoid the continuous changes in mean solar time with longitude. Lines at every 15° longitude were drawn down a map of the Earth to create 24 international time zones. Within each zone, all localities keep the same standard time (i.e., the same minutes and seconds). The time in each zone differs from that in each neighboring zone by exactly 1 hour. (Because of political boundaries, the boundary lines between time zones often zigzag.) A few areas keep time that differs from universal time by a nonintegral number of hours (such an area might have, for example, a 30-minute difference from an adjoining zone).

According to legend, in 1364, Charles V wrongly corrected a clockmaker and told him to use the Roman numeral IIII instead of IV for the number four. Rather than offend the king, the clockmaker obeyed. That tradition is still used for some clocks today.

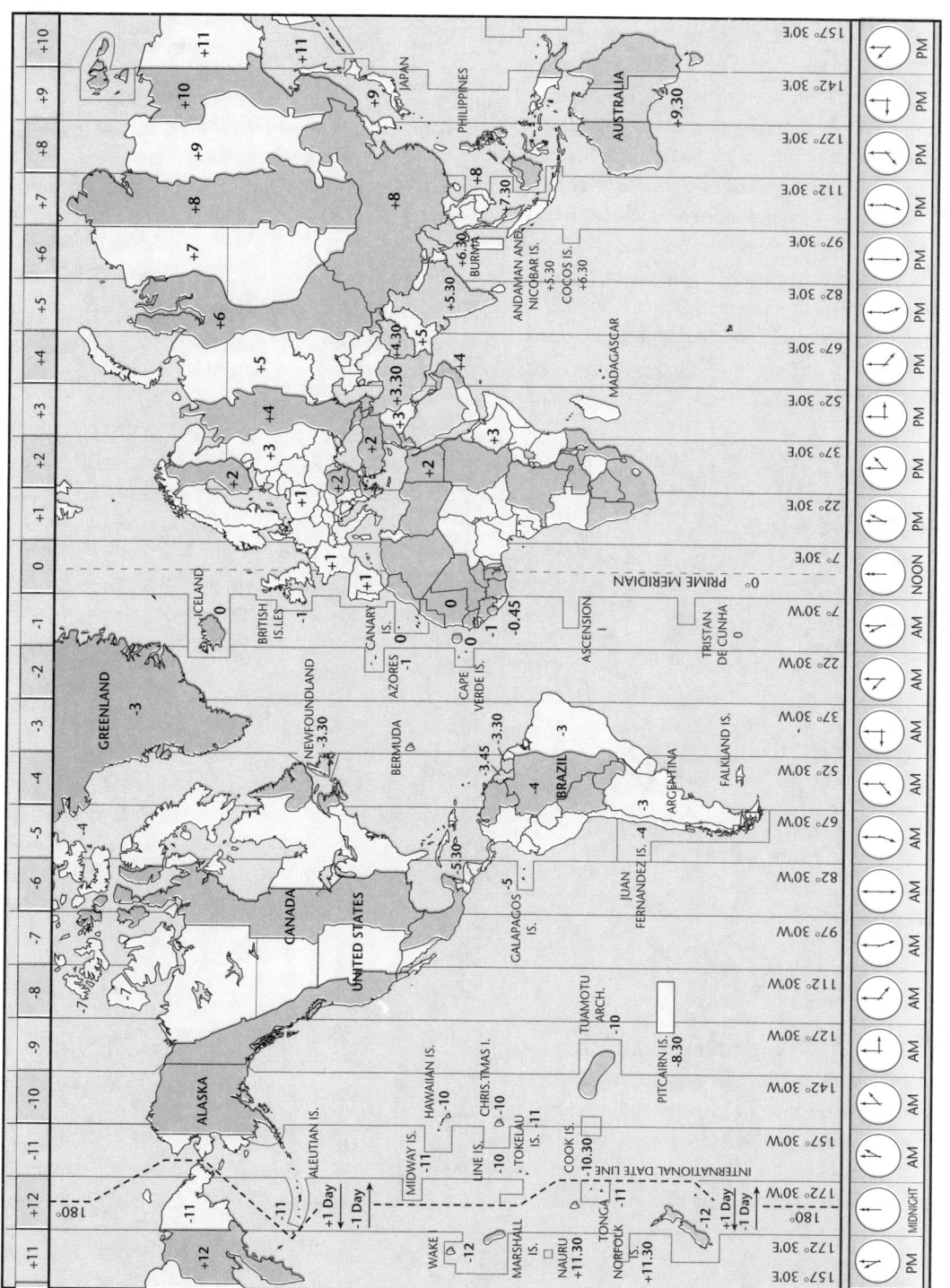

U.S. AND CANADIAN TIME ZONES

The continental United States has four standard time zones centered on the meridians 75° (Eastern Standard Time, or EST), 90° (Central Standard Time, or CST), 105° (Mountain Standard Time, or MST), and 120° (Pacific Standard Time, or PST) west of Greenwich; they are, respectively, 5, 6, 7, and 8 hours behind Universal Time. Alaska Standard Time is determined by the meridian at 135° west of Greenwich, and Hawaii-Aleutian Standard Time by the meridian at 150° west of Greenwich; they are 9 and 10 hours behind Universal Time. American Samoa and the Midway Islands use Samoan Standard Time, centered on the 165° W meridian and 11 hours behind Universal Time.

Canada has a total of six time zones: the four that apply to the continental United States and an additional two in the east. Atlantic Standard Time (which Puerto Rico and the U.S. Virgin Islands also keep) is determined by the meridian 60° west of Greenwich and is thus 4 hours behind Universal Time. Newfoundland Standard Time is determined by the meridian 52° 30′ west of Greenwich and is thus 3½ hours behind Universal Time.

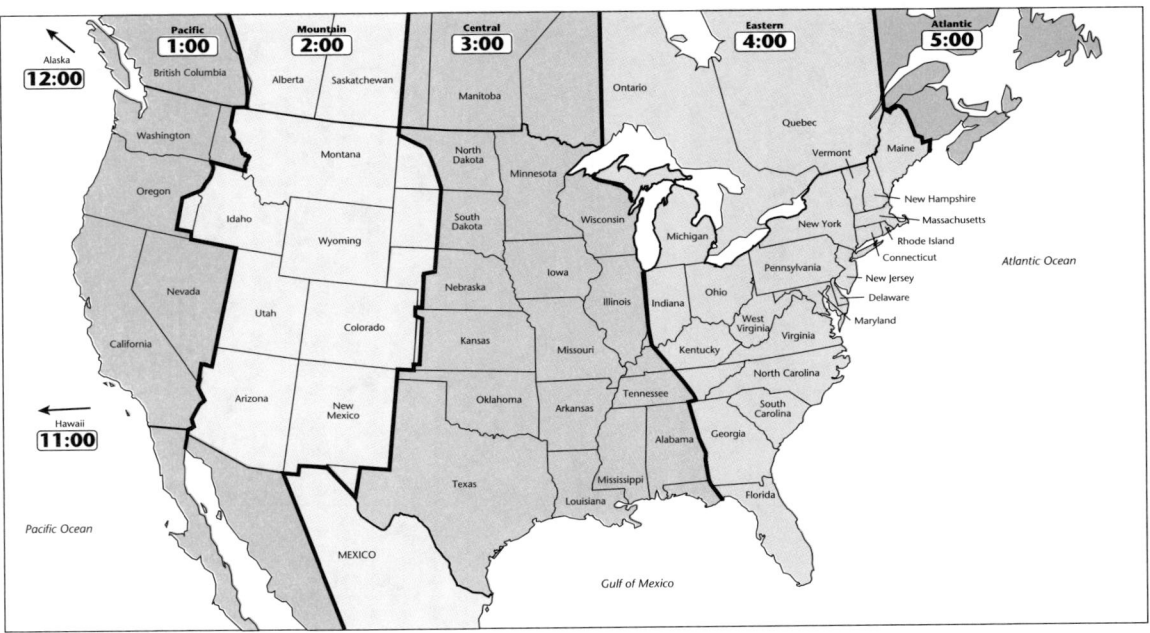

INTERNATIONAL DATE LINE

An imaginary line set at 180° longitude runs down the Earth. When someone crosses the line traveling to the west, one day is added—that is, Sunday on the east side of the line becomes Monday as one crosses westward. The line, of course, was fixed at the longitude exactly opposite Greenwich, England, on the other side of the Earth, but it zigzags for political reasons so that parts of countries do not find themselves on the wrong side—for instance, all of Siberia (west of the line), and all of Alaska (east of the line).

How does your Global Positioning Satellite (GPS) device work? Atomic clock timing signals from four or more Earth-orbiting satellites determine a user's position.

STANDARD TIME FOR MAJOR FOREIGN CITIES

The following list gives the time in cities around the world when it is noon Eastern Standard Time. An asterisk (*) indicates the morning of the following day.

Addis Ababa	8 P.M.	Geneva	6 P.M.	Ottawa	12 N
Alexandria	7 P.M.	Glasgow	5 P.M.	Panama	12 N
Amsterdam	6 P.M.	Halifax	1 P.M.	Paris	6 P.M.
Athens	7 P.M.	Hanoi	1 A.M.*	Prague	6 P.M.
Baghdad	8 P.M.	Havana	12 N	Quebec	12 N
Bangkok	12 M	Helsinki	7 P.M.	Rio de Janeiro	2 P.M.
Barcelona	6 P.M.	Ho Chi Minh City	1 A.M.*	Riyadh	8 P.M.
Beijing	1 A.M.*	Hong Kong	1 A.M.*	Rome	6 P.M.
Belfast	5 P.M.	Istanbul	7 P.M.	St. Petersburg	8 P.M.
Belgrade	6 P.M.	Jakarta	12 M	San Juan	1 P.M.
Berlin	6 P.M.	Jerusalem	7 P.M.	Santiago	1 P.M.
Bogotá	12 N	Johannesburg	7 P.M.	Seoul	2 A.M.*
Bombay	10:30 P.M.	Karachi	10 P.M.	Shanghai	1 A.M.*
Brasília	2 P.M.	Kuala Lumpur	1 A.M.*	Stockholm	6 P.M.
Brussels	6 P.M.	Lima	12 N	Sydney	4 A.M.*
Bucharest	7 P.M.	Lisbon	6 P.M.	Tangier	5 P.M.
Budapest	6 P.M.	Liverpool	4 P.M.	Teheran	8:30 P.M.
Buenos Aires	2 P.M.	London	5 P.M.	Tel Aviv	7 P.M.
Cairo	7 P.M.	Madrid	6 P.M.	Tokyo	2 A.M.*
Calcutta	10:30 P.M.	Managua	11 A.M.	Toronto	12 N
Calgary	10 A.M.	Manila	1 A.M.*	Tripoli	7 P.M.
Cape Town	7 P.M.	Marseilles	6 P.M.	Vancouver	9 A.M.
Caracas	1 P.M.	Mecca	8 P.M.	Venice	6 P.M.
Casablanca	5 P.M.	Melbourne	4 A.M.*	Vienna	6 P.M.
Copenhagen	6 P.M.	Mexico City	11 A.M.	Vladivostock	3 A.M.*
Delhi	10:30 P.M.	Montreal	12 N	Warsaw	6 P.M.
Dublin	5 P.M.	Moscow	8 P.M.	Winnipeg	11 A.M.
Edinburgh	5 P.M.	Munich	6 P.M.	Yangon	11:30 P.M.
Florence	6 P.M.	Naples	6 P.M.	Yokohama	2 A.M.*
Frankfurt	6 P.M.	Oslo	6 P.M.	Zurich	6 P.M.

TIME ADJUSTMENTS

DAYLIGHT SAVING TIME IN THE UNITED STATES

Daylight Saving Time is attained by advancing the clock 1 hour. In 1967, the Uniform Time Act went into effect in the United States. It proclaimed that all states, the District of Columbia, and U.S. possessions were to observe Daylight Saving Time starting at 2 A.M. on the last Sunday in April and ending at 2 A.M. on the last Sunday in October. Any state could exempt itself by law, and a 1972 amendment to the act authorized the states split by time zones to consider that split in exempting themselves. Non-Navaho sites in Arizona, Hawaii, part of Indiana, Puerto Rico, the Virgin Islands, Guam, and American Samoa are now exempt. (The Navaho Indian lands in Arizona do observe DST.) The Department of Transportation, which oversees the act, has modified some local zone boundaries in Alaska, Florida, Kansas, Michigan, and Texas over the past several years. Daylight Saving Time was extended by Congress during 1974 and 1975 to conserve energy, but the country then returned to the previous end-of-April to end-of-October system until 1987, when new legislation went into effect. The new bill, signed by President Ronald Reagan on July 8, 1986, moved the start of Daylight Saving Time up to the first

Sunday in April, but it did not change the end from the last Sunday in October.

INTERNATIONAL TIME ADJUSTMENTS

It is common throughout the world for clock time to be adjusted to use added daylight during summer.

Generally, Western Europe goes on daylight time on the last Sunday in March and changes back on the last Sunday in September. Most regions of the Commonwealth of Independent States stay on "advanced time" year-round. China, by government order, operates as one time zone even though it should, geographically, be in five different zones. For religious reasons, Israel is approximately 2 hours behind the rest of its time zone. Thus, the Sun may be setting there as early as 3:30 P.M.

Paraguay, Ireland, and the Dominican Republic adjust their clock time in winter instead of summer. Thus, their time is aptly known as winter time.

CALENDARS

NAMES OF THE DAYS

The names of the days in English derive from either ancient Latin or Saxon systems of naming days after gods or astrological planets.

English	Latin	Saxon
Sunday	Dies Solis (Sun)	Sun's Day
Monday	Dies Lunae (Moon)	Moon's Day
Tuesday	Dies Martis (Mars)	Tiw's Day
Wednesday	Dies Mercurii (Mercury)	Woden's Day
Thursday	Dies Jovis (Jupiter)	Thor's Day
Friday	Dies Veneris (Venus)	Frigg's Day
Saturday	Dies Saturni (Saturn)	Saterne's Day

DEFINITIONS OF A YEAR

A year can be defined in several ways.

The *tropical/equinoctial/solar/astronomical year* is the period (365 days, 5 hours, 48 minutes, and 46 seconds of mean solar time) spent by the Sun in making its apparent passage from vernal equinox to vernal equinox (defined in "The Seasons" section in this chapter).

The *sidereal year* is the period (365 days, 6 hours, 9 minutes, and 9.54 seconds) spent by the Sun in its apparent passage from a fixed star and back to the same position again. It is the true period of the Earth's revolution, and the difference in time between this and the tropical year is due to the precession of the equinoxes.

The *anomalistic year* is the period of time occupied by any planet in making one complete revolution from perihelion (the point in its orbit when it is closest to the Sun) to perihelion. For the Earth, this period is 365 days, 6 hours, 13 minutes, and 53 seconds. It is slightly longer than the sidereal year because of the extra time needed to reach an advancing perihelion, the lag being caused by the gravitational pull of the other planets.

Because the tropical year does not contain an integral number of days, the modern Gregorian *calendar year* (extending from January 1 to December 31) normally consists of 365 days (divided into 12 months). Because such a year is equivalent to 52 seven-day weeks plus one day, a given date normally advances by one day each year (for example, from Monday to Tuesday).

To avoid having the seasons move around the calendar, an extra leap day (February 29) is inserted in the calendar of a leap year, which thus has 366 days. A *leap year* is a year (e.g., 2004 and 2008) whose number is exactly divisible by 4, or, in case of the final year of a century, by 400. Thus, 1700, 1800, and 1900 were not leap years, but 2000 was.

A *fiscal year* is an accounting period of 12 months. The U.S. government's fiscal year (FY) ends on September 30; thus, its FY 2002 extends from October 1, 2001, to September 30, 2002. A business firm's fiscal year, however, may end on the last day of any month.

Some cultures have used or continue to use a *lunar year* (defined in "The Lunar Calendar" sidebar on the next page) of 12 lunar or synodic months.

The Lunar Calendar

A Closer Look

Calendars based on the movements of the moon and Sun have been used since ancient times. Whereas today most calendars are based on the solar year of 365.25 days, in ancient times the lunar calendar was the one most commonly used. Notches in bones dating from 15,000 to 10,000 B.C. have been discovered in what are now Israel and Jordan; their recordings of number sequences are thought to be the first lunar calendars.

In the lunar system, time is based on the number of days between two moons, or 29.5306 days, resulting in a lunar year of 354.3672 days. The lunar year is thus approximately 11 days shorter than the solar year.

The ancient Chinese synchronized their lunar calendar with the solar year by intercalating, or adding, extra months at fixed intervals on a 60-year cycle. This calendar, along with the modern Western one, is still used today in China.

The ancient Hebrews also intercalated months into the lunar calendar to keep it in agreement with the solar year. This calendar of 12 lunar months, with an intercalary month added seven times in every 19-year cycle, is used today in Israel and by Jews throughout the world for religious purposes.

The traditional lunar calendar, without regard to the solar year, is still used today by Muslims. In order to establish agreement between lunar and civil, or calendar, months, they intercalate 11 days in each 30 years.

THE SEASONS

The beginnings of the four seasons occur when the Sun reaches certain points in its apparent path around the Earth.

Spring in the Northern Hemisphere (fall or autumn in the Southern Hemisphere) begins at the *vernal equinox* (about March 21), when the Sun crosses the equator as it ascends from a southerly to a northerly declination (its angular distance north or south of the celestial equator). On this day, the hours of daylight and darkness are equal in length (approximately 12 hours each) everywhere on Earth.

Summer in the Northern Hemisphere (winter in the Southern Hemisphere) begins at the *summer solstice* (about June 21), when the Sun reaches its most northerly declination (approximately 23.5° N). On this day, locations in the Northern (Southern) Hemisphere have their maximum (minimum) number of hours of daylight.

Fall or autumn in the Northern Hemisphere (spring in the Southern Hemisphere) begins at the *autumnal equinox* (about September 21), when the Sun crosses the equator as it descends from a northerly to a southerly declination. On this day, the hours of

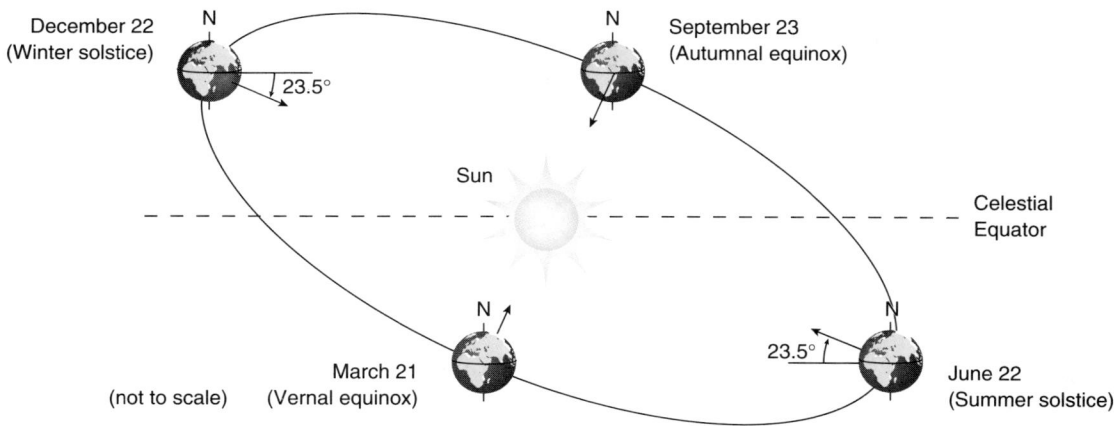

daylight and darkness are equal in length (approximately 12 hours each) everywhere on Earth.

Winter in the Northern Hemisphere (summer in the Southern Hemisphere) begins at the *winter solstice* (about December 21), when the Sun reaches its most southerly declination (approximately 23.5° S). On this day, locations in the Northern (Southern) Hemisphere have their minimum (maximum) number of hours of daylight.

THE DEVELOPMENT OF THE ROMAN/JULIAN/ GREGORIAN CALENDAR

According to legend, Romulus, one of the founders of the city of Rome, established the Roman calendar—most likely a version of the Greek lunar calendar—circa 738 B.C. King Numa Pompilius later added January at the beginning and February at the end to create a 12-month calendar year. In 46 B.C. Emperor Julius Caesar rejected the Roman lunar calendar in favor of a solar one, thus establishing a new dating system known as the Julian calendar. The solar year was made up of 365¼ days. A leap day was added every 4 years to maintain balance between the calendar and the seasons. However, because the Earth moves 11 minutes and 14 seconds faster every year than Caesar calculated, the calendar dates of the seasons regressed almost 1 day per century. In 1582 Pope Gregory XIII ordained that the calendar be decreased by 10 days that year and that no century year could be a leap year unless its date is evenly divisible by 400. (European nations adopted the Gregorian calendar at different dates, leading to some confusion regarding the 10 missing days in 1582.) See "Additional Sources of Information" at the end of this chapter to find out more about the development of the calendar.

Romulus 738 B.C.	King Numa Pompilius 713 B.C.	Council of Decemvirs 451 B.C.	Julius Caesar 47 B.C.	Augustus Caesar 8 B.C.	Gregory XIII Europe A.D. 1582 England A.D. 1752
Martius 31	Januarius 29	Januarius 29	Januarius 31	Januarius 31	January 31
Aprilis 30	Martius 31	Februarius 28	Februarius 29–30	Februarius 28–29	February 28–29
Maius 31	Aprilis 29	Martius 31	Martius 31	Martius 31	March 31
Junius 30	Maius 31	Aprilis 29	Aprilis 30	Aprilis 30	April 30
Quintilis 31	Junius 29	Maius 31	Maius 31	Maius 31	May 31
Sextilis 30	Quintilis 31	Junius 29	Junius 30	Junius 30	June 30
Septembris 31	Sextilis 29	Quintilis 31	Julius 31	Julius 31	July 31
Octobris 30	Septembris 29	Sextilis 29	Sextilis 30	Augustus 31	August 31
Novembris 31	Octobris 31	Septembris 29	Septembris 31	Septembris 30	September 30
Decembris 29	Novembris 29	Octobris 31	Octobris 30	Octobris 31	October 31
	Decembris 29	Novembris 29	Novembris 31	Novembris 30	November 30
	Februarius 28	Decembris 29	Decembris 30	Decembris 31	December 31
304 days	**355 days**	**355 days**	**348¼ days**	**365¼ days**	**365.2422 days**

PERPETUAL CALENDAR, 1775–2098

Look for the year you want in the following list. The number opposite each year is the number of the calendar on pages 14–17 to use for that year.

Year	No.	Year	No.	Year	No.	Year	No.	Year	No.
1775	1	1823	4	1871	1	1919	4	1967	1
1776	9	1824	12	1872	9	1920	12	1968	9
1777	4	1825	7	1873	4	1921	7	1969	4
1778	5	1826	1	1874	5	1922	1	1970	5
1779	6	1827	2	1875	6	1923	2	1971	6
1780	14	1828	10	1876	14	1924	10	1972	14
1781	2	1829	5	1877	2	1925	5	1973	2
1782	3	1830	6	1878	3	1926	6	1974	3
1783	4	1831	7	1879	4	1927	7	1975	4
1784	12	1832	8	1880	12	1928	8	1976	12
1785	7	1833	3	1881	7	1929	3	1977	7
1786	1	1834	4	1882	1	1930	4	1978	1
1787	2	1835	5	1883	2	1931	5	1979	2
1788	10	1836	13	1884	10	1932	13	1980	10
1789	5	1837	1	1885	5	1933	1	1981	5
1790	6	1838	2	1886	6	1934	2	1982	6
1791	7	1839	3	1887	7	1935	3	1983	7
1792	8	1840	11	1888	8	1936	11	1984	8
1793	3	1841	6	1889	3	1937	6	1985	3
1794	4	1842	7	1890	4	1938	7	1986	4
1795	5	1843	1	1891	5	1939	1	1987	5
1796	13	1844	9	1892	13	1940	9	1988	13
1797	1	1845	4	1893	1	1941	4	1989	1
1798	2	1846	5	1894	2	1942	5	1990	2
1799	3	1847	6	1895	3	1943	6	1991	3
1800	4	1848	14	1896	11	1944	14	1992	11
1801	5	1849	2	1897	6	1945	2	1993	6
1802	6	1850	3	1898	7	1946	3	1994	7
1803	7	1851	4	1899	1	1947	4	1995	1
1804	8	1852	12	1900	2	1948	12	1996	9
1805	3	1853	7	1901	3	1949	7	1997	4
1806	4	1854	1	1902	4	1950	1	1998	5
1807	5	1855	2	1903	5	1951	2	1999	6
1808	13	1856	10	1904	13	1952	10	2000	14
1809	1	1857	5	1905	1	1953	5	2001	2
1810	2	1858	6	1906	2	1954	6	2002	3
1811	3	1859	7	1907	3	1955	7	2003	4
1812	11	1860	8	1908	11	1956	8	2004	12
1813	6	1861	3	1909	6	1957	3	2005	7
1814	7	1862	4	1910	7	1958	4	2006	1
1815	1	1863	5	1911	1	1959	5	2007	2
1816	9	1864	13	1912	9	1960	13	2008	10
1817	4	1865	1	1913	4	1961	1	2009	5
1818	5	1866	2	1914	5	1962	2	2010	6
1819	6	1867	3	1915	6	1963	3	2011	7
1820	14	1868	11	1916	14	1964	11	2012	8
1821	2	1869	6	1917	2	1965	6	2013	3
1822	3	1870	7	1918	3	1966	7	2014	4

continues

Times and Dates

Perpetual Calendar, Continued

Year	No.	Year	No.	Year	No.	Year	No.	Year	No.
2015	5	2032	12	2049	6	2066	6	2083	6
2016	13	2033	7	2050	7	2067	7	2084	14
2017	1	2034	1	2051	1	2068	8	2085	2
2018	2	2035	2	2052	9	2069	3	2086	3
2019	3	2036	10	2053	4	2070	4	2087	4
2020	11	2037	5	2054	5	2071	5	2088	12
2021	6	2038	6	2055	6	2072	13	2089	7
2022	7	2039	7	2056	14	2073	1	2090	1
2023	1	2040	8	2057	2	2074	2	2091	2
2024	9	2041	3	2058	3	2075	3	2092	10
2025	4	2042	4	2059	4	2076	11	2093	5
2026	5	2043	5	2060	12	2077	6	2094	6
2027	6	2044	13	2061	7	2078	7	2095	7
2028	14	2045	1	2062	1	2079	1	2096	8
2029	2	2046	2	2063	2	2080	9	2097	3
2030	3	2047	3	2064	10	2081	4	2098	4
2031	4	2048	11	2065	5	2082	5		

Calendar 1

JANUARY
```
S  M  T  W  T  F  S
1  2  3  4  5  6  7
8  9 10 11 12 13 14
15 16 17 18 19 20 21
22 23 24 25 26 27 28
29 30 31
```

FEBRUARY
```
S  M  T  W  T  F  S
         1  2  3  4
5  6  7  8  9 10 11
12 13 14 15 16 17 18
19 20 21 22 23 24 25
26 27 28
```

MARCH
```
S  M  T  W  T  F  S
         1  2  3  4
5  6  7  8  9 10 11
12 13 14 15 16 17 18
19 20 21 22 23 24 25
26 27 28 29 30 31
```

APRIL
```
S  M  T  W  T  F  S
                  1
2  3  4  5  6  7  8
9 10 11 12 13 14 15
16 17 18 19 20 21 22
23 24 25 26 27 28 29
30
```

MAY
```
S  M  T  W  T  F  S
1  2  3  4  5  6
7  8  9 10 11 12 13
14 15 16 17 18 19 20
21 22 23 24 25 26 27
28 29 30 31
```

JUNE
```
S  M  T  W  T  F  S
            1  2  3
4  5  6  7  8  9 10
11 12 13 14 15 16 17
18 19 20 21 22 23 24
25 26 27 28 29 30
```

JULY
```
S  M  T  W  T  F  S
                  1
2  3  4  5  6  7  8
9 10 11 12 13 14 15
16 17 18 19 20 21 22
23 24 25 26 27 28 29
30 31
```

AUGUST
```
S  M  T  W  T  F  S
         1  2  3  4  5
6  7  8  9 10 11 12
13 14 15 16 17 18 19
20 21 22 23 24 25 26
27 28 29 30 31
```

SEPTEMBER
```
S  M  T  W  T  F  S
                1  2
3  4  5  6  7  8  9
10 11 12 13 14 15 16
17 18 19 20 21 22 23
24 25 26 27 28 29 30
```

OCTOBER
```
S  M  T  W  T  F  S
1  2  3  4  5  6  7
8  9 10 11 12 13 14
15 16 17 18 19 20 21
22 23 24 25 26 27 28
29 30 31
```

NOVEMBER
```
S  M  T  W  T  F  S
         1  2  3  4
5  6  7  8  9 10 11
12 13 14 15 16 17 18
19 20 21 22 23 24 25
26 27 28 29 30
```

DECEMBER
```
S  M  T  W  T  F  S
                1  2
3  4  5  6  7  8  9
10 11 12 13 14 15 16
17 18 19 20 21 22 23
24 25 26 27 28 29 30
31
```

Calendar 2

JANUARY
```
S  M  T  W  T  F  S
      1  2  3  4  5  6
7  8  9 10 11 12 13
14 15 16 17 18 19 20
21 22 23 24 25 26 27
28 29 30 31
```

FEBRUARY
```
S  M  T  W  T  F  S
            1  2  3
4  5  6  7  8  9 10
11 12 13 14 15 16 17
18 19 20 21 22 23 24
25 26 27 28
```

MARCH
```
S  M  T  W  T  F  S
            1  2  3
4  5  6  7  8  9 10
11 12 13 14 15 16 17
18 19 20 21 22 23 24
25 26 27 28 29 30 31
```

APRIL
```
S  M  T  W  T  F  S
1  2  3  4  5  6  7
8  9 10 11 12 13 14
15 16 17 18 19 20 21
22 23 24 25 26 27 28
29 30
```

MAY
```
S  M  T  W  T  F  S
      1  2  3  4  5
6  7  8  9 10 11 12
13 14 15 16 17 18 19
20 21 22 23 24 25 26
27 28 29 30 31
```

JUNE
```
S  M  T  W  T  F  S
               1  2
3  4  5  6  7  8  9
10 11 12 13 14 15 16
17 18 19 20 21 22 23
24 25 26 27 28 29 30
```

JULY
```
S  M  T  W  T  F  S
1  2  3  4  5  6  7
8  9 10 11 12 13 14
15 16 17 18 19 20 21
22 23 24 25 26 27 28
29 30 31
```

AUGUST
```
S  M  T  W  T  F  S
            1  2  3  4
5  6  7  8  9 10 11
12 13 14 15 16 17 18
19 20 21 22 23 24 25
26 27 28 29 30 31
```

SEPTEMBER
```
S  M  T  W  T  F  S
                  1
2  3  4  5  6  7  8
9 10 11 12 13 14 15
16 17 18 19 20 21 22
23 24 25 26 27 28 29
30
```

OCTOBER
```
S  M  T  W  T  F  S
      1  2  3  4  5  6
7  8  9 10 11 12 13
14 15 16 17 18 19 20
21 22 23 24 25 26 27
28 29 30 31
```

NOVEMBER
```
S  M  T  W  T  F  S
            1  2  3
4  5  6  7  8  9 10
11 12 13 14 15 16 17
18 19 20 21 22 23 24
25 26 27 28 29 30
```

DECEMBER
```
S  M  T  W  T  F  S
                  1
2  3  4  5  6  7  8
9 10 11 12 13 14 15
16 17 18 19 20 21 22
23 24 25 26 27 28 29
30 31
```

Calendar 3

JANUARY

S	M	T	W	T	F	S
		1	2	3	4	5
6	7	8	9	10	11	12
13	14	15	16	17	18	19
20	21	22	23	24	25	26
27	28	29	30	31		

FEBRUARY

S	M	T	W	T	F	S
					1	2
3	4	5	6	7	8	9
10	11	12	13	14	15	16
17	18	19	20	21	22	23
24	25	26	27	28		

MARCH

S	M	T	W	T	F	S
					1	2
3	4	5	6	7	8	9
10	11	12	13	14	15	16
17	18	19	20	21	22	23
24	25	26	27	28	29	30
31						

APRIL

S	M	T	W	T	F	S
	1	2	3	4	5	6
7	8	9	10	11	12	13
14	15	16	17	18	19	20
21	22	23	24	25	26	27
28	29	30				

MAY

S	M	T	W	T	F	S
			1	2	3	4
5	6	7	8	9	10	11
12	13	14	15	16	17	18
19	20	21	22	23	24	25
26	27	28	29	30	31	

JUNE

S	M	T	W	T	F	S
						1
2	3	4	5	6	7	8
9	10	11	12	13	14	15
16	17	18	19	20	21	22
23	24	25	26	27	28	29
30						

JULY

S	M	T	W	T	F	S
	1	2	3	4	5	6
7	8	9	10	11	12	13
14	15	16	17	18	19	20
21	22	23	24	25	26	27
28	29	30	31			

AUGUST

S	M	T	W	T	F	S
				1	2	3
4	5	6	7	8	9	10
11	12	13	14	15	16	17
18	19	20	21	22	23	24
25	26	27	28	29	30	31

SEPTEMBER

S	M	T	W	T	F	S
1	2	3	4	5	6	7
8	9	10	11	12	13	14
15	16	17	18	19	20	21
22	23	24	25	26	27	28
29	30					

OCTOBER

S	M	T	W	T	F	S
		1	2	3	4	5
6	7	8	9	10	11	12
13	14	15	16	17	18	19
20	21	22	23	24	25	26
27	28	29	30	31		

NOVEMBER

S	M	T	W	T	F	S
					1	2
3	4	5	6	7	8	9
10	11	12	13	14	15	16
17	18	19	20	21	22	23
24	25	26	27	28	29	30

DECEMBER

S	M	T	W	T	F	S
1	2	3	4	5	6	7
8	9	10	11	12	13	14
15	16	17	18	19	20	21
22	23	24	25	26	27	28
29	30	31				

Calendar 4

JANUARY

S	M	T	W	T	F	S
			1	2	3	4
5	6	7	8	9	10	11
12	13	14	15	16	17	18
19	20	21	22	23	24	25
26	27	28	29	30	31	

FEBRUARY

S	M	T	W	T	F	S
						1
2	3	4	5	6	7	8
9	10	11	12	13	14	15
16	17	18	19	20	21	22
23	24	25	26	27	28	

MARCH

S	M	T	W	T	F	S
						1
2	3	4	5	6	7	8
9	10	11	12	13	14	15
16	17	18	19	20	21	22
23	24	25	26	27	28	29
30	31					

APRIL

S	M	T	W	T	F	S
		1	2	3	4	5
6	7	8	9	10	11	12
13	14	15	16	17	18	19
20	21	22	23	24	25	26
27	28	29	30			

MAY

S	M	T	W	T	F	S
				1	2	3
4	5	6	7	8	9	10
11	12	13	14	15	16	17
18	19	20	21	22	23	24
25	26	27	28	29	30	31

JUNE

S	M	T	W	T	F	S
1	2	3	4	5	6	7
8	9	10	11	12	13	14
15	16	17	18	19	20	21
22	23	24	25	26	27	28
29	30					

JULY

S	M	T	W	T	F	S
		1	2	3	4	5
6	7	8	9	10	11	12
13	14	15	16	17	18	19
20	21	22	23	24	25	26
27	28	29	30	31		

AUGUST

S	M	T	W	T	F	S
					1	2
3	4	5	6	7	8	9
10	11	12	13	14	15	16
17	18	19	20	21	22	23
24	25	26	27	28	29	30
31						

SEPTEMBER

S	M	T	W	T	F	S
	1	2	3	4	5	6
7	8	9	10	11	12	13
14	15	16	17	18	19	20
21	22	23	24	25	26	27
28	29	30				

OCTOBER

S	M	T	W	T	F	S
			1	2	3	4
5	6	7	8	9	10	11
12	13	14	15	16	17	18
19	20	21	22	23	24	25
26	27	28	29	30	31	

NOVEMBER

S	M	T	W	T	F	S
						1
2	3	4	5	6	7	8
9	10	11	12	13	14	15
16	17	18	19	20	21	22
23	24	25	26	27	28	29
30						

DECEMBER

S	M	T	W	T	F	S
	1	2	3	4	5	6
7	8	9	10	11	12	13
14	15	16	17	18	19	20
21	22	23	24	25	26	27
28	29	30	31			

Calendar 5

JANUARY

S	M	T	W	T	F	S
				1	2	3
4	5	6	7	8	9	10
11	12	13	14	15	16	17
18	19	20	21	22	23	24
25	26	27	28	29	30	31

FEBRUARY

S	M	T	W	T	F	S
1	2	3	4	5	6	7
8	9	10	11	12	13	14
15	16	17	18	19	20	21
22	23	24	25	26	27	28

MARCH

S	M	T	W	T	F	S
1	2	3	4	5	6	7
8	9	10	11	12	13	14
15	16	17	18	19	20	21
22	23	24	25	26	27	28
29	30	31				

APRIL

S	M	T	W	T	F	S
			1	2	3	4
5	6	7	8	9	10	11
12	13	14	15	16	17	18
19	20	21	22	23	24	25
26	27	28	29	30		

MAY

S	M	T	W	T	F	S
					1	2
3	4	5	6	7	8	9
10	11	12	13	14	15	16
17	18	19	20	21	22	23
24	25	26	27	28	29	30
31						

JUNE

S	M	T	W	T	F	S
	1	2	3	4	5	6
7	8	9	10	11	12	13
14	15	16	17	18	19	20
21	22	23	24	25	26	27
28	29	30				

JULY

S	M	T	W	T	F	S
			1	2	3	4
5	6	7	8	9	10	11
12	13	14	15	16	17	18
19	20	21	22	23	24	25
26	27	28	29	30	31	

AUGUST

S	M	T	W	T	F	S
						1
2	3	4	5	6	7	8
9	10	11	12	13	14	15
16	17	18	19	20	21	22
23	24	25	26	27	28	29
30	31					

SEPTEMBER

S	M	T	W	T	F	S
		1	2	3	4	5
6	7	8	9	10	11	12
13	14	15	16	17	18	19
20	21	22	23	24	25	26
27	28	29	30			

OCTOBER

S	M	T	W	T	F	S
				1	2	3
4	5	6	7	8	9	10
11	12	13	14	15	16	17
18	19	20	21	22	23	24
25	26	27	28	29	30	31

NOVEMBER

S	M	T	W	T	F	S
1	2	3	4	5	6	7
8	9	10	11	12	13	14
15	16	17	18	19	20	21
22	23	24	25	26	27	28
29	30					

DECEMBER

S	M	T	W	T	F	S
		1	2	3	4	5
6	7	8	9	10	11	12
13	14	15	16	17	18	19
20	21	22	23	24	25	26
27	28	29	30	31		

Calendar 6

JANUARY

S	M	T	W	T	F	S
					1	2
3	4	5	6	7	8	9
10	11	12	13	14	15	16
17	18	19	20	21	22	23
24	25	26	27	28	29	30
31						

FEBRUARY

S	M	T	W	T	F	S
	1	2	3	4	5	6
7	8	9	10	11	12	13
14	15	16	17	18	19	20
21	22	23	24	25	26	27
28						

MARCH

S	M	T	W	T	F	S
	1	2	3	4	5	6
7	8	9	10	11	12	13
14	15	16	17	18	19	20
21	22	23	24	25	26	27
28	29	30	31			

APRIL

S	M	T	W	T	F	S
				1	2	3
4	5	6	7	8	9	10
11	12	13	14	15	16	17
18	19	20	21	22	23	24
25	26	27	28	29	30	

MAY

S	M	T	W	T	F	S
						1
2	3	4	5	6	7	8
9	10	11	12	13	14	15
16	17	18	19	20	21	22
23	24	25	26	27	28	29
30	31					

JUNE

S	M	T	W	T	F	S
		1	2	3	4	5
6	7	8	9	10	11	12
13	14	15	16	17	18	19
20	21	22	23	24	25	26
27	28	29	30			

JULY

S	M	T	W	T	F	S
				1	2	3
4	5	6	7	8	9	10
11	12	13	14	15	16	17
18	19	20	21	22	23	24
25	26	27	28	29	30	31

AUGUST

S	M	T	W	T	F	S
1	2	3	4	5	6	7
8	9	10	11	12	13	14
15	16	17	18	19	20	21
22	23	24	25	26	27	28
29	30	31				

SEPTEMBER

S	M	T	W	T	F	S
			1	2	3	4
5	6	7	8	9	10	11
12	13	14	15	16	17	18
19	20	21	22	23	24	25
26	27	28	29	30		

OCTOBER

S	M	T	W	T	F	S
					1	2
3	4	5	6	7	8	9
10	11	12	13	14	15	16
17	18	19	20	21	22	23
24	25	26	27	28	29	30
31						

NOVEMBER

S	M	T	W	T	F	S
	1	2	3	4	5	6
7	8	9	10	11	12	13
14	15	16	17	18	19	20
21	22	23	24	25	26	27
28	29	30				

DECEMBER

S	M	T	W	T	F	S
				1	2	3
4	5	6	7	8	9	10
11	12	13	14	15	16	17
18	19	20	21	22	23	24
25	26	27	28	29	30	31

Times and Dates

Calendar 7

JANUARY

S	M	T	W	T	F	S
						1
2	3	4	5	6	7	8
9	10	11	12	13	14	15
16	17	18	19	20	21	22
23	24	25	26	27	28	29
30	31					

FEBRUARY

S	M	T	W	T	F	S
		1	2	3	4	5
6	7	8	9	10	11	12
13	14	15	16	17	18	19
20	21	22	23	24	25	26
27	28					

MARCH

S	M	T	W	T	F	S
		1	2	3	4	5
6	7	8	9	10	11	12
13	14	15	16	17	18	19
20	21	22	23	24	25	26
27	28	29	30	31		

APRIL

S	M	T	W	T	F	S
					1	2
3	4	5	6	7	8	9
10	11	12	13	14	15	16
17	18	19	20	21	22	23
24	25	26	27	28	29	30

MAY

S	M	T	W	T	F	S
1	2	3	4	5	6	7
8	9	10	11	12	13	14
15	16	17	18	19	20	21
22	23	24	25	26	27	28
29	30	31				

JUNE

S	M	T	W	T	F	S
			1	2	3	4
5	6	7	8	9	10	11
12	13	14	15	16	17	18
19	20	21	22	23	24	25
26	27	28	29	30		

JULY

S	M	T	W	T	F	S
					1	2
3	4	5	6	7	8	9
10	11	12	13	14	15	16
17	18	19	20	21	22	23
24	25	26	27	28	29	30
31						

AUGUST

S	M	T	W	T	F	S
	1	2	3	4	5	6
7	8	9	10	11	12	13
14	15	16	17	18	19	20
21	22	23	24	25	26	27
28	29	30	31			

SEPTEMBER

S	M	T	W	T	F	S
				1	2	3
4	5	6	7	8	9	10
11	12	13	14	15	16	17
18	19	20	21	22	23	24
25	26	27	28	29	30	

OCTOBER

S	M	T	W	T	F	S
						1
2	3	4	5	6	7	8
9	10	11	12	13	14	15
16	17	18	19	20	21	22
23	24	25	26	27	28	29
30	31					

NOVEMBER

S	M	T	W	T	F	S
		1	2	3	4	5
6	7	8	9	10	11	12
13	14	15	16	17	18	19
20	21	22	23	24	25	26
27	28	29	30			

DECEMBER

S	M	T	W	T	F	S
				1	2	3
4	5	6	7	8	9	10
11	12	13	14	15	16	17
18	19	20	21	22	23	24
25	26	27	28	29	30	31

Calendar 8

JANUARY

S	M	T	W	T	F	S
1	2	3	4	5	6	7
8	9	10	11	12	13	14
15	16	17	18	19	20	21
22	23	24	25	26	27	28
29	30	31				

FEBRUARY

S	M	T	W	T	F	S
			1	2	3	4
5	6	7	8	9	10	11
12	13	14	15	16	17	18
19	20	21	22	23	24	25
26	27	28	29			

MARCH

S	M	T	W	T	F	S
				1	2	3
4	5	6	7	8	9	10
11	12	13	14	15	16	17
18	19	20	21	22	23	24
25	26	27	28	29	30	31

APRIL

S	M	T	W	T	F	S
1	2	3	4	5	6	7
8	9	10	11	12	13	14
15	16	17	18	19	20	21
22	23	24	25	26	27	28
29	30					

MAY

S	M	T	W	T	F	S
		1	2	3	4	5
6	7	8	9	10	11	12
13	14	15	16	17	18	19
20	21	22	23	24	25	26
27	28	29	30	31		

JUNE

S	M	T	W	T	F	S
					1	2
3	4	5	6	7	8	9
10	11	12	13	14	15	16
17	18	19	20	21	22	23
24	25	26	27	28	29	30

JULY

S	M	T	W	T	F	S
1	2	3	4	5	6	7
8	9	10	11	12	13	14
15	16	17	18	19	20	21
22	23	24	25	26	27	28
29	30	31				

AUGUST

S	M	T	W	T	F	S
			1	2	3	4
5	6	7	8	9	10	11
12	13	14	15	16	17	18
19	20	21	22	23	24	25
26	27	28	29	30	31	

SEPTEMBER

S	M	T	W	T	F	S
						1
2	3	4	5	6	7	8
9	10	11	12	13	14	15
16	17	18	19	20	21	22
23	24	25	26	27	28	29
30						

OCTOBER

S	M	T	W	T	F	S
1	2	3	4	5	6	7
8	9	10	11	12	13	14
15	16	17	18	19	20	21
22	23	24	25	26	27	28
29	30	31				

NOVEMBER

S	M	T	W	T	F	S
				1	2	3
4	5	6	7	8	9	10
11	12	13	14	15	16	17
18	19	20	21	22	23	24
25	26	27	28	29	30	

DECEMBER

S	M	T	W	T	F	S
						1
2	3	4	5	6	7	8
9	10	11	12	13	14	15
16	17	18	19	20	21	22
23	24	25	26	27	28	29
30	31					

Calendar 9

JANUARY

S	M	T	W	T	F	S
	1	2	3	4	5	6
7	8	9	10	11	12	13
14	15	16	17	18	19	20
21	22	23	24	25	26	27
28	29	30	31			

FEBRUARY

S	M	T	W	T	F	S
				1	2	3
4	5	6	7	8	9	10
11	12	13	14	15	16	17
18	19	20	21	22	23	24
25	26	27	28	29		

MARCH

S	M	T	W	T	F	S
					1	2
3	4	5	6	7	8	9
10	11	12	13	14	15	16
17	18	19	20	21	22	23
24	25	26	27	28	29	30
31						

APRIL

S	M	T	W	T	F	S
	1	2	3	4	5	6
7	8	9	10	11	12	13
14	15	16	17	18	19	20
21	22	23	24	25	26	27
28	29	30				

MAY

S	M	T	W	T	F	S
			1	2	3	4
5	6	7	8	9	10	11
12	13	14	15	16	17	18
19	20	21	22	23	24	25
26	27	28	29	30	31	

JUNE

S	M	T	W	T	F	S
						1
2	3	4	5	6	7	8
9	10	11	12	13	14	15
16	17	18	19	20	21	22
23	24	25	26	27	28	29
30						

JULY

S	M	T	W	T	F	S
	1	2	3	4	5	6
7	8	9	10	11	12	13
14	15	16	17	18	19	20
21	22	23	24	25	26	27
28	29	30	31			

AUGUST

S	M	T	W	T	F	S
				1	2	3
4	5	6	7	8	9	10
11	12	13	14	15	16	17
18	19	20	21	22	23	24
25	26	27	28	29	30	31

SEPTEMBER

S	M	T	W	T	F	S
1	2	3	4	5	6	7
8	9	10	11	12	13	14
15	16	17	18	19	20	21
22	23	24	25	26	27	28
29	30					

OCTOBER

S	M	T	W	T	F	S
		1	2	3	4	5
6	7	8	9	10	11	12
13	14	15	16	17	18	19
20	21	22	23	24	25	26
27	28	29	30	31		

NOVEMBER

S	M	T	W	T	F	S
					1	2
3	4	5	6	7	8	9
10	11	12	13	14	15	16
17	18	19	20	21	22	23
24	25	26	27	28	29	30

DECEMBER

S	M	T	W	T	F	S
1	2	3	4	5	6	7
8	9	10	11	12	13	14
15	16	17	18	19	20	21
22	23	24	25	26	27	28
29	30	31				

Calendar 10

JANUARY

S	M	T	W	T	F	S
		1	2	3	4	5
6	7	8	9	10	11	12
13	14	15	16	17	18	19
20	21	22	23	24	25	26
27	28	29	30	31		

FEBRUARY

S	M	T	W	T	F	S
					1	2
3	4	5	6	7	8	9
10	11	12	13	14	15	16
17	18	19	20	21	22	23
24	25	26	27	28		

MARCH

S	M	T	W	T	F	S
						1
2	3	4	5	6	7	8
9	10	11	12	13	14	15
16	17	18	19	20	21	22
23	24	25	26	27	28	29
30	31					

APRIL

S	M	T	W	T	F	S
		1	2	3	4	5
6	7	8	9	10	11	12
13	14	15	16	17	18	19
20	21	22	23	24	25	26
27	28	29	30			

MAY

S	M	T	W	T	F	S
				1	2	3
4	5	6	7	8	9	10
11	12	13	14	15	16	17
18	19	20	21	22	23	24
25	26	27	28	29	30	31

JUNE

S	M	T	W	T	F	S
1	2	3	4	5	6	7
8	9	10	11	12	13	14
15	16	17	18	19	20	21
22	23	24	25	26	27	28
29	30					

JULY

S	M	T	W	T	F	S
		1	2	3	4	5
6	7	8	9	10	11	12
13	14	15	16	17	18	19
20	21	22	23	24	25	26
27	28	29	30	31		

AUGUST

S	M	T	W	T	F	S
					1	2
3	4	5	6	7	8	9
10	11	12	13	14	15	16
17	18	19	20	21	22	23
24	25	26	27	28	29	30
31						

SEPTEMBER

S	M	T	W	T	F	S
	1	2	3	4	5	6
7	8	9	10	11	12	13
14	15	16	17	18	19	20
21	22	23	24	25	26	27
28	29	30				

OCTOBER

S	M	T	W	T	F	S
			1	2	3	4
5	6	7	8	9	10	11
12	13	14	15	16	17	18
19	20	21	22	23	24	25
26	27	28	29	30	31	

NOVEMBER

S	M	T	W	T	F	S
						1
2	3	4	5	6	7	8
9	10	11	12	13	14	15
16	17	18	19	20	21	22
23	24	25	26	27	28	29
30						

DECEMBER

S	M	T	W	T	F	S
	1	2	3	4	5	6
7	8	9	10	11	12	13
14	15	16	17	18	19	20
21	22	23	24	25	26	27
28	29	30				

Calendar 11

JANUARY

S	M	T	W	T	F	S
				1	2	3	4
5	6	7	8	9	10	11
12	13	14	15	16	17	18
19	20	21	22	23	24	25
26	27	28	29	30	31

MAY

S	M	T	W	T	F	S
					1	2
3	4	5	6	7	8	9
10	11	12	13	14	15	16
17	18	19	20	21	22	23
24	25	26	27	28	29	30
31

SEPTEMBER

S	M	T	W	T	F	S
	1	2	3	4	5
6	7	8	9	10	11	12
13	14	15	16	17	18	19
20	21	22	23	24	25	26
27	28	29	30

FEBRUARY

S	M	T	W	T	F	S
						1
2	3	4	5	6	7	8
9	10	11	12	13	14	15
16	17	18	19	20	21	22
23	24	25	26	27	28	29

JUNE

S	M	T	W	T	F	S
	1	2	3	4	5	6
7	8	9	10	11	12	13
14	15	16	17	18	19	20
21	22	23	24	25	26	27
28	29	30

OCTOBER

S	M	T	W	T	F	S
				1	2	3
4	5	6	7	8	9	10
11	12	13	14	15	16	17
18	19	20	21	22	23	24
25	26	27	28	29	30	31

MARCH

S	M	T	W	T	F	S
1	2	3	4	5	6	7
8	9	10	11	12	13	14
15	16	17	18	19	20	21
22	23	24	25	26	27	28
29	30	31

JULY

S	M	T	W	T	F	S
			1	2	3	4
5	6	7	8	9	10	11
12	13	14	15	16	17	18
19	20	21	22	23	24	25
26	27	28	29	30	31

NOVEMBER

S	M	T	W	T	F	S
1	2	3	4	5	6	7
8	9	10	11	12	13	14
15	16	17	18	19	20	21
22	23	24	25	26	27	28
29	30

APRIL

S	M	T	W	T	F	S
				1	2	3	4
5	6	7	8	9	10	11
12	13	14	15	16	17	18
19	20	21	22	23	24	25
26	27	28	29	30

AUGUST

S	M	T	W	T	F	S
						1
2	3	4	5	6	7	8
9	10	11	12	13	14	15
16	17	18	19	20	21	22
23	24	25	26	27	28	29
30	31

DECEMBER

S	M	T	W	T	F	S
	1	2	3	4	5
6	7	8	9	10	11	12
13	14	15	16	17	18	19
20	21	22	23	24	25	26
27	28	29	30	31

Calendar 12

JANUARY

S	M	T	W	T	F	S
				1	2	3
4	5	6	7	8	9	10
11	12	13	14	15	16	17
18	19	20	21	22	23	24
25	26	27	28	29	30	31

MAY

S	M	T	W	T	F	S
						1
2	3	4	5	6	7	8
9	10	11	12	13	14	15
16	17	18	19	20	21	22
23	24	25	26	27	28	29
30	31

SEPTEMBER

S	M	T	W	T	F	S
			1	2	3	4
5	6	7	8	9	10	11
12	13	14	15	16	17	18
19	20	21	22	23	24	25
26	27	28	29	30

FEBRUARY

S	M	T	W	T	F	S
1	2	3	4	5	6	7
8	9	10	11	12	13	14
15	16	17	18	19	20	21
22	23	24	25	26	27	28
29

JUNE

S	M	T	W	T	F	S
	1	2	3	4	5
6	7	8	9	10	11	12
13	14	15	16	17	18	19
20	21	22	23	24	25	26
27	28	29	30

OCTOBER

S	M	T	W	T	F	S
					1	2
3	4	5	6	7	8	9
10	11	12	13	14	15	16
17	18	19	20	21	22	23
24	25	26	27	28	29	30
31

MARCH

S	M	T	W	T	F	S
	1	2	3	4	5	6
7	8	9	10	11	12	13
14	15	16	17	18	19	20
21	22	23	24	25	26	27
28	29	30	31

JULY

S	M	T	W	T	F	S
				1	2	3
4	5	6	7	8	9	10
11	12	13	14	15	16	17
18	19	20	21	22	23	24
25	26	27	28	29	30	31

NOVEMBER

S	M	T	W	T	F	S
	1	2	3	4	5	6
7	8	9	10	11	12	13
14	15	16	17	18	19	20
21	22	23	24	25	26	27
28	29	30

APRIL

S	M	T	W	T	F	S
				1	2	3
4	5	6	7	8	9	10
11	12	13	14	15	16	17
18	19	20	21	22	23	24
25	26	27	28	29	30

AUGUST

S	M	T	W	T	F	S
1	2	3	4	5	6	7
8	9	10	11	12	13	14
15	16	17	18	19	20	21
22	23	24	25	26	27	28
29	30	31

DECEMBER

S	M	T	W	T	F	S
			1	2	3	4
5	6	7	8	9	10	11
12	13	14	15	16	17	18
19	20	21	22	23	24	25
26	27	28	29	30	31

Calendar 13

JANUARY

S	M	T	W	T	F	S
					1	2
3	4	5	6	7	8	9
10	11	12	13	14	15	16
17	18	19	20	21	22	23
24	25	26	27	28	29	30
31

MAY

S	M	T	W	T	F	S
1	2	3	4	5	6	7
8	9	10	11	12	13	14
15	16	17	18	19	20	21
22	23	24	25	26	27	28
29	30	31

SEPTEMBER

S	M	T	W	T	F	S
					1	2	3
4	5	6	7	8	9	10
11	12	13	14	15	16	17
18	19	20	21	22	23	24
25	26	27	28	29	30

FEBRUARY

S	M	T	W	T	F	S
	1	2	3	4	5	6
7	8	9	10	11	12	13
14	15	16	17	18	19	20
21	22	23	24	25	26	27
28	29

JUNE

S	M	T	W	T	F	S
			1	2	3	4
5	6	7	8	9	10	11
12	13	14	15	16	17	18
19	20	21	22	23	24	25
26	27	28	29	30

OCTOBER

S	M	T	W	T	F	S
						1
2	3	4	5	6	7	8
9	10	11	12	13	14	15
16	17	18	19	20	21	22
23	24	25	26	27	28	29
30	31

MARCH

S	M	T	W	T	F	S
		1	2	3	4	5
6	7	8	9	10	11	12
13	14	15	16	17	18	19
20	21	22	23	24	25	26
27	28	29	30	31

JULY

S	M	T	W	T	F	S
					1	2
3	4	5	6	7	8	9
10	11	12	13	14	15	16
17	18	19	20	21	22	23
24	25	26	27	28	29	30
31

NOVEMBER

S	M	T	W	T	F	S
		1	2	3	4	5
6	7	8	9	10	11	12
13	14	15	16	17	18	19
20	21	22	23	24	25	26
27	28	29	30

APRIL

S	M	T	W	T	F	S
					1	2
3	4	5	6	7	8	9
10	11	12	13	14	15	16
17	18	19	20	21	22	23
24	25	26	27	28	29	30

AUGUST

S	M	T	W	T	F	S
	1	2	3	4	5	6
7	8	9	10	11	12	13
14	15	16	17	18	19	20
21	22	23	24	25	26	27
28	29	30	31

DECEMBER

S	M	T	W	T	F	S
				1	2	3
4	5	6	7	8	9	10
11	12	13	14	15	16	17
18	19	20	21	22	23	24
25	26	27	28	29	30	31

Calendar 14

JANUARY

S	M	T	W	T	F	S
						1
2	3	4	5	6	7	8
9	10	11	12	13	14	15
16	17	18	19	20	21	22
23	24	25	26	27	28	29
30	31

MAY

S	M	T	W	T	F	S
1	2	3	4	5	6
7	8	9	10	11	12	13
14	15	16	17	18	19	20
21	22	23	24	25	26	27
28	29	30	31

SEPTEMBER

S	M	T	W	T	F	S
					1	2
3	4	5	6	7	8	9
10	11	12	13	14	15	16
17	18	19	20	21	22	23
24	25	26	27	28	29	30

FEBRUARY

S	M	T	W	T	F	S
	1	2	3	4	5
6	7	8	9	10	11	12
13	14	15	16	17	18	19
20	21	22	23	24	25	26
27	28	29

JUNE

S	M	T	W	T	F	S
			1	2	3
4	5	6	7	8	9	10
11	12	13	14	15	16	17
18	19	20	21	22	23	24
25	26	27	28	29	30

OCTOBER

S	M	T	W	T	F	S
1	2	3	4	5	6	7
8	9	10	11	12	13	14
15	16	17	18	19	20	21
22	23	24	25	26	27	28
29	30	31

MARCH

S	M	T	W	T	F	S
		1	2	3	4
5	6	7	8	9	10	11
12	13	14	15	16	17	18
19	20	21	22	23	24	25
26	27	28	29	30	31

JULY

S	M	T	W	T	F	S
					1
2	3	4	5	6	7	8
9	10	11	12	13	14	15
16	17	18	19	20	21	22
23	24	25	26	27	28	29
30	31

NOVEMBER

S	M	T	W	T	F	S
			1	2	3	4
5	6	7	8	9	10	11
12	13	14	15	16	17	18
19	20	21	22	23	24	25
26	27	28	29	30

APRIL

S	M	T	W	T	F	S
						1
2	3	4	5	6	7	8
9	10	11	12	13	14	15
16	17	18	19	20	21	22
23	24	25	26	27	28	29
30

AUGUST

S	M	T	W	T	F	S
	1	2	3	4	5
6	7	8	9	10	11	12
13	14	15	16	17	18	19
20	21	22	23	24	25	26
27	28	29	30	31

DECEMBER

S	M	T	W	T	F	S
					1	2
3	4	5	6	7	8	9
10	11	12	13	14	15	16
17	18	19	20	21	22	23
24	25	26	27	28	29	30
31

WORDS DESCRIBING PERIODS OF TIME

annually	yearly; occurring once every 12 months
biannually	occurring twice a year (at unequally spaced intervals)
bicentennial	relating to a period of 200 years
biennial	relating to a period of 2 years
bimonthly	occurring once every 2 months
biweekly	occurring once every 2 weeks
centennial	relating to a period of 100 years (1 century)
daily	occurring once every 24 hours
decennial	relating to a period of 10 years (1 decade)
diurnal	daily; of a day
duodecennial	relating to a period of 12 years
fortnightly	occurring once every 2 weeks
millennial	relating to a period of 1,000 years (1 millennium)
monthly	occurring once every 30 days (approximately)
novennial	relating to a period of 9 years
octennial	relating to a period of 8 years
perennial	occurring year after year
quadrennial	relating to a period of 4 years (1 olympiad)
quadricentennial	relating to a period of 400 years
quincentennial	relating to a period of 500 years
quindecennial	relating to a period of 15 years
quinquennial	relating to a period of 5 years
semiannually	occurring once every 6 months (at equally spaced intervals)
semicentennial	relating to a period of 50 years
semidiurnal	occurring twice a day
semimonthly	occurring twice a month
semiweekly	occurring twice a week
septennial	relating to a period of 7 years
sesquicentennial	relating to a period of 150 years
sexennial	relating to a period of 6 years
thrice weekly	occurring three times a week
triennial	relating to a period of 3 years
trimonthly	occurring once every 3 months
triweekly	occurring once every 3 weeks
undecennial	relating to a period of 11 years
vicennial	relating to a period of 20 years
weekly	occurring once every 7 days

A "jiffy" is an actual unit of time. It is ¹⁄₁₀₀ of a second.

MAJOR HOLIDAYS

AMERICAN

Dates marked with an asterisk (*) are the officially designated national holidays.

*January 1	New Year's Day
January 15	Martin Luther King Jr.'s Birthday
Third Monday in January	Martin Luther King Jr.'s Birthday (observed)
January 19	Robert E. Lee's Birthday (Southern states)
January 20	Inauguration Day
February 2	Groundhog Day
February 12	Lincoln's Birthday
February 14	Valentine's Day
February 22	Washington's Birthday
Third Monday in February	Washington's Birthday (observed as Presidents' Day)
March 17	St. Patrick's Day
March or April	Easter Sunday
April 1	April Fools' Day
April 14	Pan American Day
May 1	May Day
Second Sunday in May	Mother's Day
Third Saturday in May	Armed Forces Day
May 30	Memorial Day
*Last Monday in May	Memorial Day (observed)
June 3	Jefferson Davis's Birthday (Southern states)
June 14	Flag Day
Third Sunday in June	Father's Day
*July 4	Independence Day
*First Monday in September	Labor Day
September 17	Citizenship Day
Fourth Friday in September	Native American Day
October 12	Columbus Day
*Second Monday in October	Columbus Day (observed)
October 24	United Nations Day
October 31	Halloween
First Tuesday after the first Monday in November	Election Day
*November 11	Veterans' Day

Times and Dates

*Fourth Thursday in November	Thanksgiving Day	
*December 25	Christmas Day	

CANADIAN

January 1	New Year's Day
March or April	Good Friday
	Easter Monday
Last Monday before May 25	Victoria Day
July 1	Canada Day
First Monday in September	Labour Day
Second Monday in October	Thanksgiving Day
November 11	Remembrance Day
December 25	Christmas Day
December 26	Boxing Day

OTHER

January	Australia Day on the last Monday in Australia
January 1	New Year's Day throughout the Western world and in India, Indonesia, Japan, Korea, the Philippines, Singapore, Taiwan, and Thailand; founding of Republic of China (Taiwan)
January 2	Berchtoldstag in Switzerland
January 3	Genshi-Sai (First Beginning) in Japan
January 5	Twelfth Night (Wassail Eve or Eve of Epiphany) in England
January 6	Epiphany, observed by Catholics throughout Europe and Latin America
January 15	Adults' Day in Japan
January 20	St. Agnes' Eve in Great Britain
January 26	Republic Day in India
January–February	Chinese New Year and Vietnamese New Year (Tet)
February	Hamstrom on the first Sunday in Switzerland
February 3	Setsubun (Bean-throwing Festival) in Japan
February 5	Promulgation of the Constitution Day in Mexico
February 6	New Zealand Day in New Zealand
February 11	National Foundation Day in Japan
February 27	Independence Day in the Dominican Republic
March 1	Independence Movement Day in

	Korea; Constitution Day in Panama
March 8	International Women's Day in UN member nations
March 17	St. Patrick's Day in Ireland and Northern Ireland
March 19	St. Joseph's Day in Colombia, Costa Rica, Italy, and Spain
March 21	Benito Juarez's Birthday in Mexico
March 22	Arab League Day in Arab League countries
March 23	Pakistan Day in Pakistan
March 25	Independence Day in Greece; Lady Day (Quarter Day) in Great Britain
March 26	Fiesta del Arbol (Arbor Day) in Spain
March 29	Youth and Martyrs' Day in Taiwan
March 30	Muslim New Year in Indonesia
March–April	Carnival/Lent/Easter: The pre-Lenten celebration of Carnival (Mardi Gras) and the post-Lenten celebration of Easter are movable feasts widely observed in Christian countries.
April 1	Victory Day in Spain; April Fools' Day (All Fools' Day) in Great Britain
April 5	Arbor Day in Korea
April 6	Van Riebeeck Day in South Africa
April 7	World Health Day in UN member nations
April 8	Buddha's Birthday in Korea and Japan; Hana Matsuri (Flower Festival) in Japan
April 14	Pan American Day in the Americas
April 19	Declaration of Independence Day in Venezuela
April 22	Queen Isabella Day in Spain
April 23	St. George's Day in England
April 25	Liberation Day in Italy; ANZAC Day in Australia and New Zealand
April 26	Union Day in Tanzania
April 29	Emperor's Birthday in Japan
April 30	Queen's Birthday in The Netherlands; Walpurgis Night in Germany and Scandinavia
April–May	Independence Day in Israel

continues

Other Holidays, continued

May	Constitution Day on first Monday in Japan
May 1	May Day–Labor Day in the Commonwealth of Independent States and most of Europe and Latin America
May 5	Children's Day in Japan and Korea; Victory of General Zaragosa Day in Mexico; Liberation Day in The Netherlands
May 8	V-E Day in Europe
May 9	Victory over Fascism Day in the Commonwealth of Independent States
May 14	Independence Day in Paraguay
May 31	Republic Day in South Africa
June 2	Founding of the Republic Day in Italy
June 5	Constitution Day in Denmark; World Environment Day in UN member nations
June 6	Memorial Day in Korea; Flag Day in Sweden
June 8	Muhammad's Birthday in Indonesia
June 10	Portugal Day in Portugal
June 12	Republic Day in the Commonwealth of Independent States; Independence Day in the Philippines
mid-June	Queen's Official Birthday on second Saturday in Great Britain; Midsummer Celebrations in Sweden
June 16	Soweto Day in U.N. member nations
June 20	Flag Day in Argentina
June 29	Feast of Saints Peter and Paul in Chile, Colombia, Costa Rica, Italy, Peru, Spain, Vatican City, and Venezuela
July 1	Half-year Holiday in Hong Kong; Bank Holiday in Taiwan; Dominion Day in Canada
July 5	Independence Day in Venezuela
July 9	Independence Day in Argentina
July 10	Bon (Feast of Fortune) in Japan
July 12	Orangemen's Day in Northern Ireland
July 14	Bastille Day in France
mid-July	Feria de San Fermin during second week in Spain

July 17	Constitution Day in Korea
July 18	National Day in Spain
July 20	Independence Day in Colombia
July 21–22	National Holiday in Belgium
July 22	National Liberation Day in Poland
July 24	Simon Bolivar's Birthday in Ecuador and Venezuela
July 25	St. James' Day in Spain
July 28–29	Independence Day in Peru
August	Bank Holiday on first Monday in Fiji, Grenada, Guyana, Hong Kong, Ireland, and Malawi; Discovery Day on first Monday in Trinidad and Tobago; Independence Day on first Tuesday in Jamaica
August 1	Lammas Day in England; National Day in Switzerland
August 9	National Day in Singapore
August 10	Independence Day in Ecuador
August 14	Independence Day in Pakistan
August 15	Independence Day in India and Korea; Assumption Day in Catholic countries
August 16	National Restoration Day in the Dominican Republic
August 17	Independence Day in Indonesia
August 31	Independence Day in Trinidad and Tobago
September	Rose of Tralee Festival in Ireland
September 7	Independence Day in Brazil
September 9	Choxo-no-Sekku (Chrysanthemum Day) in Japan
September 14	Battle of San Jacinto Day in Nicaragua
mid-September	Sherry Wine Harvest in Spain
September 15	Independence Day in Costa Rica, Guatemala, and Nicaragua; Respect for the Aged Day in Japan
September 16	Independence Day in Mexico and Papua New Guinea
September 18–19	Independence Day in Chile
September 28	Confucius' Birthday in Taiwan
October	Thanksgiving Day in Canada on second Monday; Kruger Day in South Africa during second week
October 1	National Day in People's Republic of China; Armed Forces Day in Korea; National Holiday in Nigeria

October 2	Mahatma Gandhi's Birthday in India
October 3	National Day in the Federal Republic of Germany; National Foundation Day in Korea
October 5	Republic Day in Portugal
October 9	Korean Alphabet Day in Korea
October 10	Founding of Republic of China in Taiwan
October 12	Columbus Day in Spain and widely throughout Latin America
October 19	Ascension of Muhammad Day in Indonesia
October 20	Revolution Day in Guatemala; Kenyatta Day in Kenya
October 24	United Nations Day in UN member nations
October 26	National Holiday in Australia
October 28	Greek National Day in Greece
November 1	All Saints' Day, observed by Catholics in most countries
November 2	All Souls' Day in Ecuador, El Salvador, Luxembourg, Macao, Mexico, San Marino, Uruguay, and Vatican City
November 3	Culture Day in Japan
November 4	National Unity Day in Italy
November 5	Guy Fawkes' Day in Great Britain
November 11	Armistice Day in Belgium, French Guiana, and Tahiti; Veterans' Day in France; Remembrance Day in Canada and Bermuda
November 12	Sun Yat-sen's Birthday in Taiwan
November 15	Proclamation of the Republic Day in Brazil
November 19	National Holiday in Monaco
November 20	Anniversary of the Revolution in Mexico
November 23	Kinro-Kansha-No-Hi (Labor/ Thanksgiving Day) in Japan
November 30	National Heroes' Day in the Philippines
December 5	Discovery by Columbus Day in Haiti
December 6	Independence Day in Finland
December 8	Feast of the Immaculate Conception, widely observed in Catholic countries
December 10	Constitution Day in Thailand; Human Rights Day in UN member nations
mid-December	Nine Days of Posada during third week in Mexico
December 25	Christmas Day, widely observed in all Christian countries
December 26	St. Stephen's Day in Austria, Ireland, Italy, Liechtenstein, San Marino, and Switzerland; Boxing Day in Great Britain and Northern Ireland
December 28	National Day in Nepal
December 31	New Year's Eve throughout the world; Omisoka (Grand Last Day) in Japan; Hogmanay Day in Scotland

ADDITIONAL SOURCES OF INFORMATION

BOOKS

Barnett, Jo Ellen. *Time's Pendulum: From Sundials to Atomic Clocks, the Fascinating History of Timekeeping and How Our Discoveries Changed the World.* Harvest Books, 1999.

Blackburn, Bonnie, and Leofranc Holford-Strevens. *The Oxford Book of Days.* Oxford University Press, 2000.

Blaise, Clark. *Time Lord: Sir Sandford Fleming and the Creation of Standard Time.* Pantheon Books, 2001.

Chase, William D., and Helen M. Chase. *Chase's Annual Events.* Contemporary Books, annual.

Fitzpatrick, Gary L. *International Time Tables.* Scarecrow Press, 1990.

Landes, David S. *Revolution in Time: Clocks and the Making of the Modern World.* Harvard University Press, 1983.

Macey, Samuel L. *Encyclopedia of Time.* Garland, 1994.

———. *Time: A Bibliographic Guide.* Garland, 1991.

Mossman, Jennifer, ed. *Holidays and Anniversaries of the World.* Gale Research, 1990.

continues

Sobel, Dava. *Longitude: The True Story of a Lone Genius Who Solved the Greatest Scientific Problem of His Time.* Penguin, 1996.

Thompson, Sue Ellen, and Barbara W. Carlson. *Holidays, Festivals and Celebrations of the World Dictionary.* Omnigraphics, 1994.

Westrheim, Margo. *Calendars of the World.* Oneworld, 1993.

WEB SITES

http://timezoneconverter.com/
http://tycho.usno.navy.mil/tzones.html
(both give time around the world in various zones)

http://www.worldtime.com/
(interactive world atlas, information on local time)

http://www.time.gov
(to manually set your clock to the NIST's Universal Time Clock)

http://www.boulder.nist.gov/timefreq/service/time-computer.html
(to synchronize time on computers connected to the Internet, or via telephone for computers with analog modems)

2

WEIGHTS AND MEASURES

U.S. CUSTOMARY SYSTEM OF WEIGHTS AND MEASURES

The units of weights and measures commonly used today in the United States were derived during the colonial period from units used in Great Britain for many centuries.

LENGTH

1 nail (cloth)	=	2.25 inches		
1 palm	=	3 inches		
1 hand	=	4 inches		
1 span	=	6 inches		
1 quarter (cloth)	=	9 inches		
1 foot	=	12 inches		
1 pace	=	30 inches	=	2.5 feet
1 yard	=	36 inches	=	3 feet
1 fathom	=	6 feet	=	2 yards
1 rod	=	16.5 feet	=	5.5 yards
1 furlong	=	660 feet	=	220 yards
1 mile	=	5,280 feet	=	1,760 yards
1 nautical mile	=	6,076.1155 feet		

AREA

1 square foot	=	144 square inches		
1 square yard	=	9 square feet		
1 rood	=	10,890 square feet	=	40 square rods
1 acre	=	43,560 square feet	=	4 roods
1 square mile	=	640 acres		

VOLUME

1 cubic foot	=	1,728 cubic inches
1 cubic yard	=	27 cubic feet

CAPACITY (DRY MEASURE)

1 pint	=	33.6003125 cubic inches		
1 quart	=	67.200625 cubic inches	=	2 pints
1 gallon	=	268.8025 cubic inches	=	4 quarts
1 peck	=	537.605 cubic inches	=	2 gallons
1 bushel	=	2,150.42 cubic inches	=	4 pecks
1 cranberry barrel	=	5,876 cubic inches		
1 barrel	=	7,056 cubic inches		
1 cord-foot (wood)	=	16 cubic feet		
1 cord (wood)	=	128 cubic feet	=	8 cord-feet
1 freight ton	=	40 cubic feet		
1 register ton	=	100 cubic feet		

"Chemistry," "Mathematics," and "Physics" in chapter 4; "Standard Sizes Chart" in chapter 19
Go to

Six Quick Ways to Measure When You Don't Have a Ruler

1. Most credit cards are $3\frac{3}{8}$ inches by $2\frac{1}{8}$ inches.
2. Standard business cards are printed $3\frac{1}{2}$ inches wide by 2 inches long.
3. Floor tiles are usually manufactured in 12-inch by 12-inch squares.
4. U.S. paper currency is $6\frac{1}{8}$ inches wide by $2\frac{5}{8}$ inches long.
5. The diameter of a quarter is approximately 1 inch, and the diameter of a penny is approximately $\frac{3}{4}$ inch.
6. A standard sheet of paper is $8\frac{1}{2}$ inches wide by 11 inches long.

CAPACITY (LIQUID MEASURE)

1 fluid dram	=	60 minims		
1 teaspoon	=	80 minims		
1 tablespoon	=	240 minims	=	3 teaspoons
1 fluid ounce	=	480 minims	=	2 tablespoons
1 gill	=	4 fluid ounces		
1 cup	=	8 fluid ounces	=	2 gills
1 pint	=	16 fluid ounces	=	2 cups
1 quart	=	32 fluid ounces	=	2 pints
1 gallon	=	128 fluid ounces	=	4 quarts
1 barrel	=	31.5 gallons	=	7,276.5 cubic inches
1 petroleum barrel	=	42 gallons	=	9,702 cubic inches

MASS (AVOIRDUPOIS)

1 dram	=	27.34375 grains		
1 ounce	=	16 drams		
1 pound	=	16 ounces		
1 hundredweight	=	100 pounds		
1 ton	=	2,000 pounds	=	20 hundredweights

MASS (TROY AND APOTHECARY)

1 scruple	=	20 grains	
1 pennyweight	=	24 grains	
1 dram	=	60 grains	= 3 scruples
1 ounce	=	480 grains	= 8 drams
1 pound	=	12 ounces	

ANGLE

1 minute	=	60 seconds
1 degree	=	60 minutes
1 sign	=	30 degrees
1 octant	=	45 degrees
1 sextant	=	60 degrees
1 quadrant	=	90 degrees
1 semicircle	=	180 degrees
1 circle	=	360 degrees

METRIC SYSTEM OF MEASUREMENT

The metric system is a system of weights and measures, based on decimals, or units of ten, that was developed in the 1790s in revolutionary France and revised and refined several times since that period. In 1960, an international conference gave it the official name *Système International d'Unités* (International System of Units, or SI). Virtually all countries except the United States use this system.

On December 23, 1975, President Gerald R. Ford signed the U.S. Metric Conversion Act, declaring a national policy of encouraging voluntary conversion to the metric system. Federal agencies have made a transition to the metric system, but adoption elsewhere in the country has been more gradual than anticipated in 1975.

The coldest temperature ever recorded was at Vostock II, Antarctica, −128.6°F on July 21, 1983.

BASIC UNITS

The metric system includes seven basic units for different types of measurement.

The basic unit of length is the *meter (m)*, currently defined as the path traveled by light in a vacuum in 1/299,792.458 of a second.

The basic unit of mass is the *kilogram (kg)*, currently defined as the mass of a platinum-iridium cylinder preserved in a vault at Sèvres, near Paris, by the International Bureau of Weights and Measures.

The basic unit of time is the *second (sec)*, currently defined as the duration of 9,192,631,770 cycles of radiation given off by the element cesium 133 under certain conditions.

The basic unit of temperature is the *Kelvin (K)*, which is the same size as a Celsius degree. The lowest temperature possible in theory (absolute zero) is 273.16 degrees below zero Celsius. Thus, 0 K = −273.16°C. This unit is named after the British physicist Lord Kelvin (William Thomson; 1824–1907).

The basic unit of electric current is the *ampere (A)*, defined as the current that, if maintained in two straight parallel wires of infinite length and negligible cross section, and placed in a vacuum, will produce between the wires a force of 0.0000002 newton (defined in the following section) per meter of length. This unit is named after the French physicist André M. Ampère (1775–1836).

The basic unit of luminosity intensity is the *candela (cd)*, currently defined as the light given off by 1/600,000 square meters of a black body (a perfect radiator) at the freezing point of platinum under a pressure of 101,325 newtons per square meter.

The basic unit of substance is the *mole (mol)*, defined as the amount of substance equal to the molecular weight of that substance.

DERIVED UNITS

All other metric units are derived from the seven basic units defined in the preceding section.

One *newton (N)* is the force that imparts to a mass of one kilogram an acceleration of one meter per second. One *pascal (Pa)*, the unit of pressure, is one newton per square meter. One *joule (J)*, the unit of energy, is the work done by a force of one newton acting through a distance of one meter. These units are named after the English mathematician and philosopher Sir Isaac Newton (1642–1727); the French mathematician and philosopher Blaise Pascal (1623–62); and the English physicist James P. Joule (1818–89).

In electricity, one *coulomb (C)* is the electric charge transported through a conductor by a current of one ampere flowing for one second. One *volt (V)* is the electromotive force or difference in potential between two points in an electric field that requires one joule of work to move a positive charge of one coulomb from the point of lower potential to the point of higher potential. One *ohm* is the electrical resistance of a circuit in which an electromotive force of one volt maintains a current of one ampere. One *watt (W)*, equal to one joule per second, is the electrical power developed in a circuit by a current of one ampere flowing through a potential difference of one volt. These units are named after the French physicist Charles A. Coulomb (1736–1806), the Italian physicist Count Alessandro Volta (1745–1827), the German physicist Georg Simon Ohm (1787–1854), and the Scottish engineer and inventor James Watt (1736–1819).

METRIC PREFIXES

The metric, or SI, system is based on the decimal system and follows a consistent name scheme using the prefixes listed below. Multiples and submultiples always related to the power of 10 are combined with the basic metric units to provide the multiples and submultiples in the metric or SI system. For example, centi + meter = centimeter, meaning one one-hundredth of a meter.

Prefix	Symbol	Multiples	Equivalent	Prefix	Symbol	Multiples	Equivalent
exa	E	10^{18}	quintillionfold	deci	d	10^{-1}	tenth part
peta	P	10^{15}	quadrillionfold	centi	c	10^{-2}	hundredth part
tera	T	10^{12}	trillionfold	milli	m	10^{-3}	thousandth part
giga	G	10^{9}	billionfold	micro	μ	10^{-6}	millionth part
mega	M	10^{6}	millionfold	nano	n	10^{-9}	billionth part
kilo	k	10^{3}	thousandfold	pico	p	10^{-12}	trillionth part
hecto	h	10^{2}	hundredfold	femto	f	10^{-15}	quadrillionth part
deka	da	10	tenfold	atto	a	10^{-18}	quintillionth part

TABLES OF METRIC WEIGHTS AND MEASURES

LENGTH

10 millimeters (mm) = 1 centimeter (cm)
10 centimeters = 1 decimeter (dm)
10 decimeters = 1 meter (m)
10 meters = 1 dekameter (dam)
10 dekameters = 1 hectometer (hm)
10 hectometers = 1 kilometer (km)

The highest temperature ever recorded on Earth was 136°F on September 13, 1992, in Al ʼAzīzīyah, Libya

AREA

100 sq. millimeters (mm²) = 1 sq. centimeter (cm²)
10,000 sq. centimeters = 1 sq. meter (m²)
100 sq. meters = 1 are (a)
100 ares = 1 hectare (ha)
100 hectares = 1 sq. kilometer (km²)

"Cooking Equivalents and Substitutions" and "Champagne Bottle Sizes" in chapter 19
Go to

VOLUME

1,000 cu. millimeters (mm³) =
    1 cu. centimeter (cm³)
1,000 cu. centimeters = 1 cu. decimeter (dm³)
1,000 cu. decimeters = 1 cu. meter (m³)

CAPACITY (DRY AND LIQUID)

10 milliliters (ml) = 1 centiliter (cl)
10 centiliters = 1 deciliter (dl)
10 deciliters = 1 liter (l)
10 liters = 1 dekaliter (dal)
10 dekaliters = 1 hectoliter (hl)
10 hectoliters = 1 kiloliter (kl)

MASS

10 milligrams (mg) = 1 centigram (cg)
10 centigrams = 1 decigram (dg)
10 decigrams = 1 gram (g)
10 grams = 1 dekagram (dag)
10 dekagrams = 1 hectogram (hg)
10 hectograms = 1 kilogram (kg)
1,000 kilograms = 1 metric ton (t)

Weights/Measures

COMMON CONVERSION FACTORS

To Convert From	To	Multiply by	To Convert From	To	Multiply by
Acres	Hectares	0.40468586	Miles, square	Hectares	258.99881
Acres, square	Kilometers, square	0.004046856	Miles, square	Kilometers, square	2.5899881
Acres	Meters, square	4046.856	Miles, statute	Centimeters	160934.4
Centimeters	Meters	0.01	Miles, statute	Meters	1609.344
Centimeters, square	Meters, square	0.0001	Miles, statute	Kilometers	1.609344
Feet	Centimeters	30.48	Ounces, avoirdupois	Grams	28.349523
Feet	Meters	0.3048	Ounces, avoirdupois	Kilograms	0.028349523
Feet	Kilometers	0.0003048	Ounces, troy	Pounds, troy	0.083333
Feet, cubic	Liters	28.316847	Ounces, troy	Grams	31.10348
Feet, cubic	Meters, cubic	0.028316847	Pints, U.S. liquid	Millimeters	473.176473
Feet, square	Centimeters, square	929.0304	Pints, U.S. liquid	Liters	0.473176473
Feet, square	Meters, square	0.09290304	Pounds, avoirdupois	Grams	453.59237
Gallons, U.S. liquid	Liters	3.785412	Pounds, avoirdupois	Kilograms	0.45359237
Gallons, U.S. liquid	Meters, cubic	0.003785412	Pounds, avoirdupois	Quintals	0.0045359237
Grams	Ounces, troy	0.032151	Pounds, avoirdupois	Tons, metric	0.00045359237
Grams	Pounds, troy	0.002679			
Hectares	Kilometers, square	0.01	Pounds, troy	Ounces, troy	12
Hectares	Meters, square	10,000	Pounds, troy	Grams	373.2417216
Inches	Centimeters	2.54	Quarts, dry	Liters	1.101221
Inches	Meters	0.0254	Quarts, dry	Dekaliters	0.1101221
Inches, cubic	Milliliters	16.387064	Quarts, liquid	Milliliters	946.352946
Inches, cubic	Liters	0.016387064	Quarts, liquid	Liters	0.946352946
Inches, cubic	Meters, cubic	0.000016387064	Quintals	Tons, metric	0.1
Inches, square	Centimeters, square	6.4516	Ton-miles, long	Ton-kilometers, metric	1.635169
Inches, square	Meters, square	0.00064516	Ton-miles, short	Ton-kilometers, metric	1.4359972
Kilograms	Ounces, troy	32.15075	Tons, long	Kilograms	1016.047
Kilograms	Pounds, troy	2.679229	Tons, long	Tons, metric	1.016047
Kilograms	Tons, metric	0.001	Tons, metric	Quintals	10
Kilometers, square	Hectares	100	Tons, register	Meters, cubic	2.831685
Kilometers, square	Miles, square	0.3861	Tons, short	Kilograms	907.185
Liters	Milliliters	1000	Tons, short	Tons, metric	0.907185
Liters	Meters, cubic	0.001	Yards	Centimeters	91.44
Meters	Millimeters	1000	Yards	Meters	0.9144
Meters	Centimeters	100	Yards, cubic	Liters	764.5549
Meters	Kilometers	0.001	Yards, cubic	Meters, cubic	0.7645549
Meters, cubic	Liters	1000	Yards, square	Meters, square	0.836127
Meters, cubic	Tons, register	0.353147			
Miles, nautical	Kilometers	1.852			

A
Closer
Look

Mile/Kilometer Conversions			
Miles to Kilometers		**Kilometers to Miles**	
1	1.6	1	0.6
2	3.2	2	1.2
3	4.8	3	1.9
4	6.4	4	2.5
5	8.0	5	3.1
6	9.7	6	3.7
7	11.3	7	4.3
8	12.9	8	5.0
9	14.5	9	5.6
10	16.1	10	6.2
20	32.2	20	12.4
30	48.3	30	18.6
40	64.4	40	24.9
50	80.5	50	31.1
60	96.6	60	37.3
70	112.7	70	43.5
80	128.7	80	49.7
90	144.8	90	55.9
100	160.9	100	62.1
1,000	1,609.3	1,000	621.4

TEMPERATURE CONVERSIONS

The following can be used as general guidelines to tell the temperature in both Celsius and Fahrenheit.

0°C	Freezing point of water (32°F)
10°C	A warm winter day (50°F)
20°C	A mild spring day (68°F)
30°C	Quite warm—almost hot (86°F)
37°C	Normal body temperature (98.6°F)
40°C	Heat wave conditions (104°F)
100°C	Boiling point of water (212°F)

To convert degrees Fahrenheit to degrees Celsius, subtract 32 from the Fahrenheit temperature, multiply the difference by 5, and then divide the product by 9. To convert degrees Celsius to degrees Fahrenheit, multiply the Celsius temperature by 1.8 and add 32.

Absolute zero, the theoretically lowest temperature possible, is equal to −273°C and −459.4°F.

"Plant Cultivation" in chapter 3; "Wind Chill Factors" in chapter 4

Go to

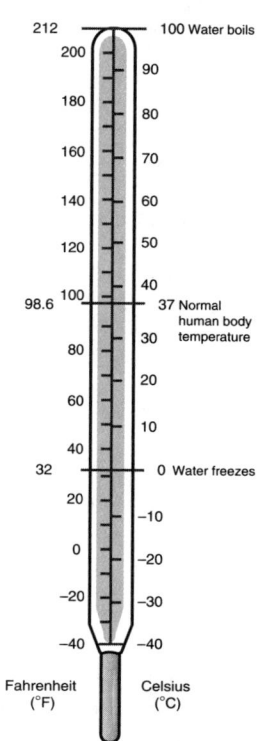

SPECIAL WEIGHTS AND MEASURES

astronomical unit (AU)   The unit of length used in astronomy equal to the mean distance of Earth from the Sun, or about 93 million miles.

bale   A large bundle of goods. In the United States, the approximate weight of a bale of cotton is 500 pounds.

board foot (fbm)   A measurement used in lumber: 144 cubic inches (12 inches by 12 inches by 1 inch).

bolt   Used in measuring cloth: 40 yards.

British thermal unit (Btu)   A unit of heat energy measured as the amount of heat required to raise the temperature of 1 pound of water from 60° to 61°F at a constant pressure of 1 standard atmosphere (the weight of the atmosphere at mean sea level). One Btu is equal to 1054.5 joules in the meter-kilogram-second system of measurements.

bundle   Two reams of paper.

caliber   The diameter of a bore of a gun, usually expressed in modern U.S. and British usage in hundredths or thousandths of an inch and typically written as a decimal fraction.

Without using precision instruments, Eratosthenes measured the radius of the Earth in the 3rd century B.C. and came within 1% of the value determined by today's technology.

carat   Originally the weight of a seed of the carob tree in the Mediterranean region, today it has two separate meanings: (1) 200 milligrams, or 3.086 grains troy, used for measuring the weight of gemstones; and (2) a measure of the amount of gold per 24 parts of gold alloy; in this sense, it also spelled *karat*. Thus, 24-carat gold is pure, and 18-carat gold is ¾ gold and ¼ other metal.

case   Four bundles of paper.

chain (ch)   A unit of length equal to 66 feet and usually divided into 100 links. Used in surveying.

decibel   A unit of relative loudness. The smallest amount of change that can be detected by the human ear is 1 decibel. A 20-decibel sound is 10 times as loud as a 10-decibel sound; a 30-decibel sound is 100 times as loud.

10 decibels	A light whisper
20 decibels	Quiet conversation
30 decibels	Normal conversation
40 decibels	Light traffic
50 decibels	A typewriter; loud conversation
60 decibels	A noisy office
70 decibels	Normal traffic; a quiet train
80 decibels	Raucous music; the subway
90 decibels	Heavy traffic; thunder
100 decibels	A plane at takeoff

The speed of sound is usually placed at 1,088 feet per second at 32°F at sea level.

ell (English)   1¼ yards or ¹⁄₃₂ bolt. Used for measuring cloth.

em   A printer's measure designating the square width of any given type size. The em of 10-point type is 10 points. An en is one-half of an em.

freight ton (measurement ton)   40 cubic feet of merchandise. Used for cargo freight.

gauge   A measure of shotgun bore diameter. Gauge numbers originally referred to the number per pound of round lead balls of a diameter equal to that of the bore. Today, an international agreement assigns millimeter measures to each gauge.

Gauge	Bore Diameter in mm
6	23.34
10	19.67
12	18.52
14	17.60
16	16.81
20	15.90

Weights/Measures

A Closer Look

Historic Weights and Measures

	Units	Location	Customary	Metric
Volume	amphora	Greece	10.3 gal.	38.8 l
		Rome	6.84 gal.	26 l
	bath	Israel	2.250 cu. in.	37 l
	ephah	Israel	1.1 bu.	40 l
	gallon, beer	England	282 cu. in.	4.62 l
	hekat	Israel	291 cu. in.	4.77 l
	tun	England	252 gal.	954 l
Weight	denarius	Rome	0.17 oz.	4.6 g
	dinar	Arabia	0.15 oz.	4.2 g
	drachma	Greece	0.154 oz.	4.36 g
	livre	France	1.08 lb.	490 g
	livre (demikilo)	France	1.10 lb.	500 g
	mite	England	0.05 grain	3.24 mg
	obol	Greece	11.2 grains	0.73 g
	pfund	Germany	1.1 lb.	500 g
	pound, tower:	England		
	12 oz.		5,400 grains	350 g
	15 oz.		6,750 grains	437 g
	16 oz.		7,200 grains	467 g
	shekel	Israel	0.5 oz.	14.1 g
	shekel, trade	Babylonia	0.3 oz.	8.37 g
Length	cubit	Greece	18.3 in.	46.5 cm
		Israel	21.8 in.	38.2 cm
		Rome	17.5 in.	44.4 cm
	hand	England U.S.	4 in.	10.2 cm
	stadion	Greece	622 ft.	190 m
	stadium	Rome	606 ft.	185 m

great gross   12 gross, or 1,728.

gross   12 dozen, or 144.

hand   A unit of measure equal to 4 inches. Used especially to measure the height of horses.

hertz   A unit of electromagnetic wave frequency equal to one cycle per second.

hogshead (hhd)   Two liquid barrels.

horsepower   The power needed to lift 33,000 pounds a distance of 1 foot in 1 minute (about 1½ times the power an average horse can exert) or to lift 550 pounds 1 foot in 1 second. Used to measure the power of steam engines, gasoline engines, etc.

"Words Describing Periods of Time" in chapter 1; "Food Weights and Measures" in chapter 19
Go to

knot   A unit for measuring the speed of ships. One knot is 1 nautical mile per hour, 10 knots is 10 nautical miles per hour, and so on.

league   Any of various units of distance from about 2.4 to 4.6 statute miles.

The length of the Mayflower *was measured in score-feet (1 score-foot is equal to 20 feet). After outliving its usefulness, the* Mayflower *was dismantled and rebuilt as a barn.*

light-year   A unit of length in interstellar astronomy equal to the distance that light travels in 1 year in a vacuum, or about 5,878,000,000,000 miles.

magnum   A large bottle of wine holding about ⅔ gallon.

parsec   The unit of measure for interstellar space equal to a distance having a heliocentric parallax of 1 second, or to 206,265 times the radius of Earth's orbit, or to 3.26 light-years, or to 19.2 trillion miles.

pica   One-sixth inch, or 12 points. Used to measure typographical material.

pipe   Two hogsheads. Used to measure wine and other liquids.

Early systems of measurement used body parts to calculate length. A cubit ran from elbow to middle fingertip. The distance from fingertip to fingertip of outstretched arms was a fathom.

point   0.013836 (approximately $\frac{1}{72}$) inch or $\frac{1}{12}$ pica. Used in printing to measure type size.

quintal   100,000 grams, or 220.46 pounds avoirdupois.

quire   24 or 25 sheets of paper.

ream   480 or 500 sheets of paper, or 20 quires.

ADDITIONAL SOURCES OF INFORMATION

ORGANIZATIONS AND SERVICES

National Institute of Standards and Technology
(formerly National Bureau of Standards)
Gaithersburg, MD, 20899
http://www.nist.gov

Standards Engineering Society
Miami, Florida 33176
http://www.ses-standards.org/

BOOKS

American Society for Testing and Materials. *Standard Practice for Use of International System of Units (SI): The Modernized Metric System.* ASTM, 1991.

Blocksma, Mary. *Reading the Numbers: A Survival Guide to the Measurements, Numbers, and Sizes Encountered in Daily Life.* Penguin, 1989.

Cook, James L. *Conversion Factors.* Oxford University Press, 1991.

Darton, Mike, and John Clark. *The Macmillan Dictionary of Measurement.* Macmillan, 1994.

The Economist Desk Companion: How to Measure, Convert, Calculate and Define Practically Anything. Henry Holt, 1994.

Fenna, Donald. *Elsevier's Encyclopedic Dictionary of Measures.* Elsevier, 1998.

Johnstone, William D. *For Good Measure.* NTC Publishing Group, 1996.

Sutcliffe, Andrea, ed. *Numbers: How Many, How Far, How Long, How Much.* HarperPerennial, 1996.

3

THE BIOLOGICAL WORLD

ANATOMICAL DRAWINGS OF THE HUMAN BODY

THE SKELETAL SYSTEM

FRONT VIEW

REAR VIEW

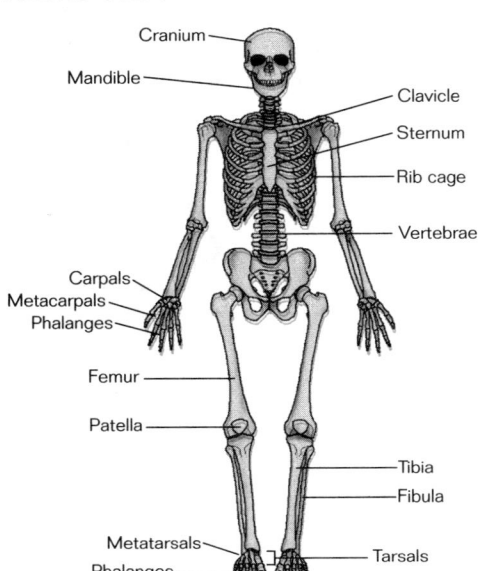

Cranium
Mandible
Clavicle
Sternum
Rib cage
Vertebrae
Carpals
Metacarpals
Phalanges
Femur
Patella
Tibia
Fibula
Metatarsals
Phalanges
Tarsals

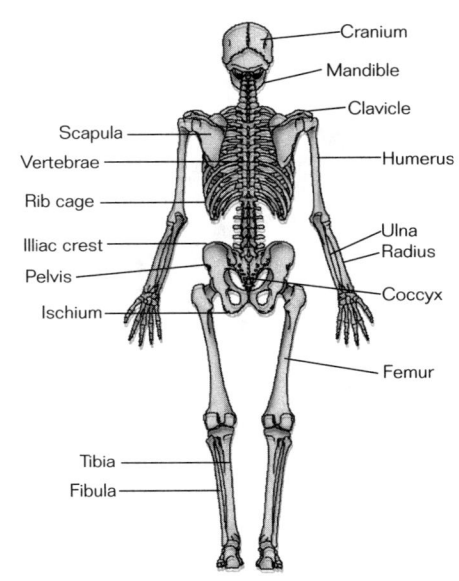

Cranium
Mandible
Clavicle
Scapula
Vertebrae
Humerus
Rib cage
Illiac crest
Pelvis
Ulna
Radius
Ischium
Coccyx
Femur
Tibia
Fibula

SKULL BONES

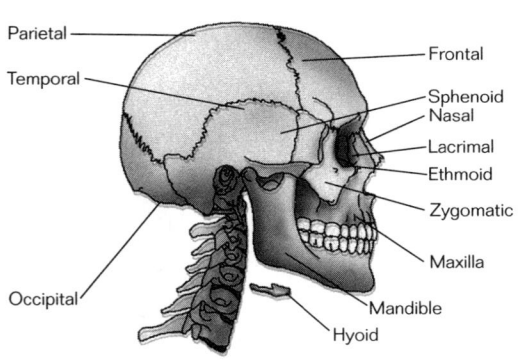

Parietal
Temporal
Frontal
Sphenoid
Nasal
Lacrimal
Ethmoid
Zygomatic
Maxilla
Occipital
Mandible
Hyoid

THE EYE

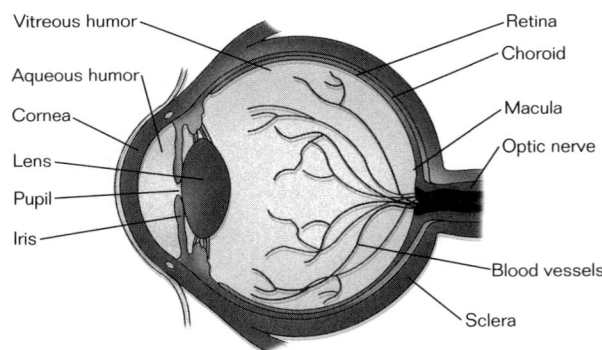

Vitreous humor
Aqueous humor
Cornea
Lens
Pupil
Iris
Retina
Choroid
Macula
Optic nerve
Blood vessels
Sclera

THE EAR

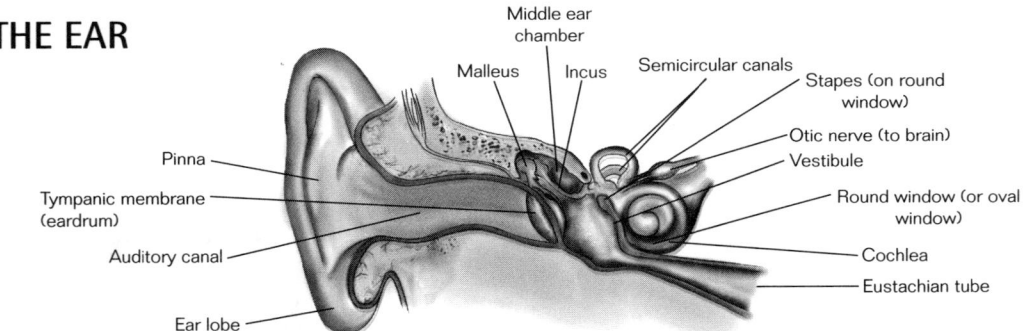

Middle ear chamber
Malleus
Incus
Semicircular canals
Stapes (on round window)
Otic nerve (to brain)
Vestibule
Round window (or oval window)
Cochlea
Eustachian tube
Pinna
Tympanic membrane (eardrum)
Auditory canal
Ear lobe

THE BRAIN
PARTS

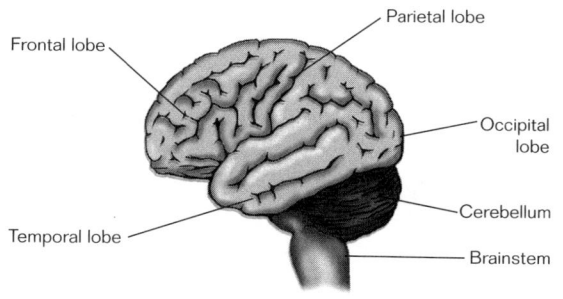

Frontal lobe

Parietal lobe

Occipital lobe

Cerebellum

Brainstem

Temporal lobe

FUNCTIONS

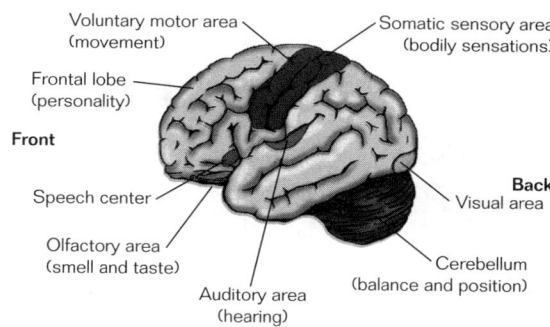

Voluntary motor area (movement)

Somatic sensory area (bodily sensations)

Frontal lobe (personality)

Front

Speech center

Back
Visual area

Olfactory area (smell and taste)

Cerebellum (balance and position)

Auditory area (hearing)

THE MUSCLE SYSTEM
FRONT VIEW

Superficial layer

Deep layer

Frontalis
Temporalis
Zygomaticus
Platysma
Deltoid
Pectoralis major
Serratus anterior
Biceps
Brachialis
Rectus abdominis
Brachioradialis
Obliquus externus
Gracilis
Sartorius
Rectus femoris
Vastus medialis
Vastus lateralis
Gastrocnemius
Tibialis anterior
Soleus

Orbicularis oculi
Masseter
Sternocleidomastoid
Trapezius
Pectoralis minor
Biceps
Intercostalis
Iliacus
Psoas major
Extensor digitorum communis
Adductor brevis
Adductor longus
Adductor magnus
Peroneus longus
Extensor digitorum longus

REAR VIEW

Deep layer

Superficial layer

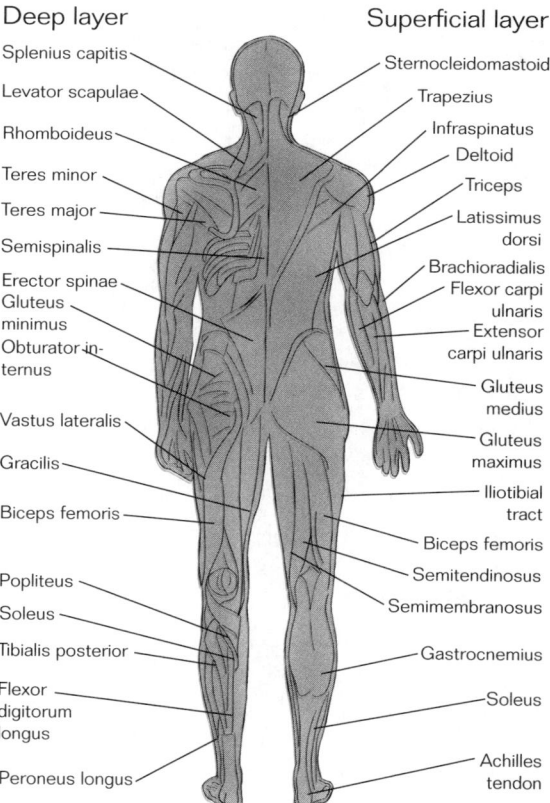

Splenius capitis
Levator scapulae
Rhomboideus
Teres minor
Teres major
Semispinalis
Erector spinae
Gluteus minimus
Obturator internus
Vastus lateralis
Gracilis
Biceps femoris
Popliteus
Soleus
Tibialis posterior
Flexor digitorum longus
Peroneus longus

Sternocleidomastoid
Trapezius
Infraspinatus
Deltoid
Triceps
Latissimus dorsi
Brachioradialis
Flexor carpi ulnaris
Extensor carpi ulnaris
Gluteus medius
Gluteus maximus
Iliotibial tract
Biceps femoris
Semitendinosus
Semimembranosus
Gastrocnemius
Soleus
Achilles tendon

Biological World

THE DIGESTIVE SYSTEM

THE RESPIRATORY SYSTEM

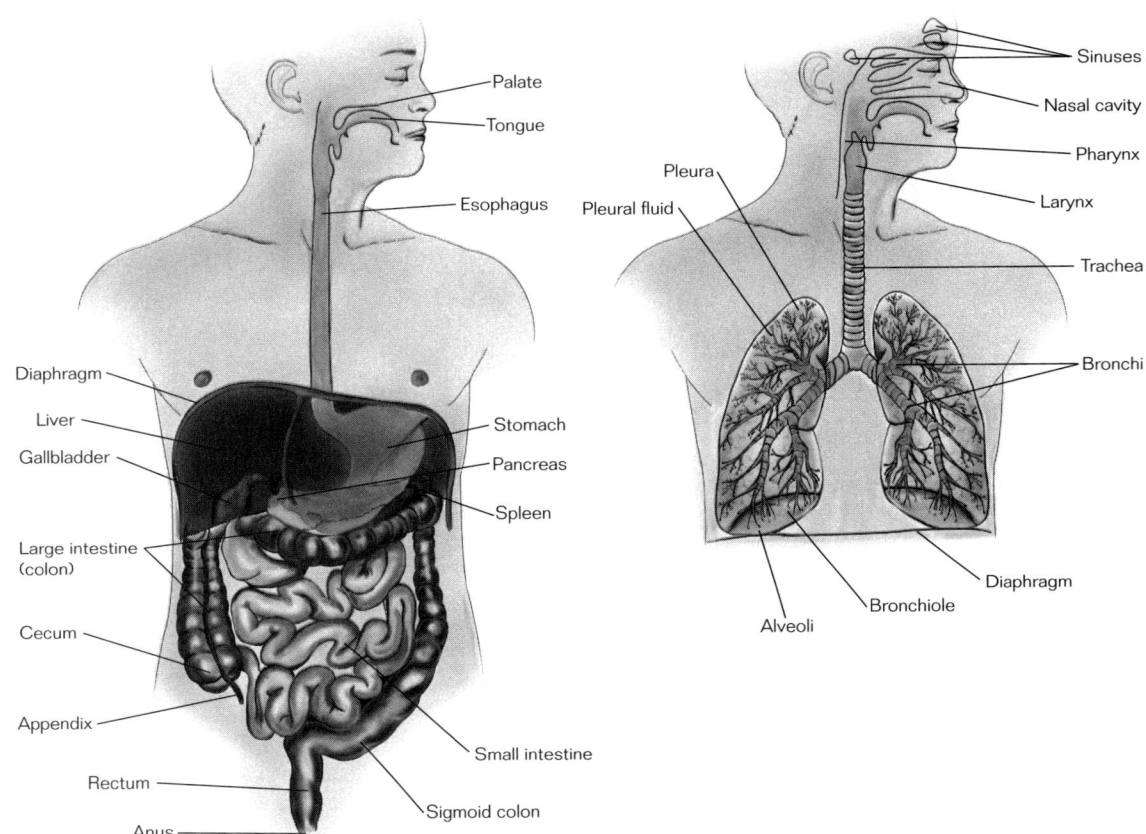

Palate
Tongue
Esophagus

Diaphragm
Liver
Gallbladder
Large intestine (colon)
Cecum
Appendix
Rectum
Anus

Stomach
Pancreas
Spleen
Small intestine
Sigmoid colon

Pleura
Pleural fluid

Sinuses
Nasal cavity
Pharynx
Larynx
Trachea
Bronchi
Diaphragm
Bronchiole
Alveoli

THE SCIENCE OF TAXONOMY

Taxonomy, or systematics, is the science of naming living organisms in a way that reflects their natural relationships. Taxonomic categories are arranged hierarchically, in a descending series of increasingly small ranks. The *taxa* (groups of related organisms; singular, *taxon*) most frequently used, from most to least in-

Taxonomic Level	Name	Distinguishing Feature
Kingdom	Animalia	Animal
Phylum	Chordata	Spinal cord
Subphylum	Vertebrata	Segmented backbone
Superclass	Tetrapoda	Four limbs
Class	Mammalia	Suckle young
Subclass	Theria	Live birth
Infraclass	Eutheria	Placenta
Order	Primates	Most highly developed
Superfamily	Hominoidea	Humanlike
Family	Hominidae	Two-legged
Genus	Homo	Human
Species	Sapiens	Modern human

clusive, are *kingdom, phylum* (plural, *phyla*), *class, order, family, genus* (plural, *genera*), and *species*; the names of plants often include *variety*. Although taxonomy dates from the days of Aristotle, in the 1700s Carolus Linnaeus developed the most familiar system: a binomial nomenclature assigning to each organism a two-word, always italicized Latin name designating its genus and species (for example, *Homo sapiens*). The table on page 36 shows the taxonomy of modern humans.

More recently, scientists are using classifications based on cladistics, which allows them to hypothesize relationships among organisms by examining their shared characteristics and evolutionary history. Simply put, cladistics groups together animals that share common traits and evolutionary history. However, not all scientists agree on cladistic classifications. Some do not agree with the interpretations of connections between groups; others believe multiple, new lineages can emerge from a single population at the same time. Thus, no universally accepted classification of life on Earth has emerged to date.

THE ANIMAL KINGDOM

The kingdoms of living organisms are divided into several phyla, classes, orders, and families. The examples below discuss vertebrates in terms of orders. Invertebrates are then discussed according to phyla.

THE ORDERS OF MAMMALS

More than one million different species of animals exist in the world. All animals with backbones, including humans, are chordates. That is, in the language of taxonomy, they belong to the phylum Chordata. Their subphylum is Vertebrata, meaning that their backbones are segmented. Mammals, members of the class Mammalia of vertebrate animals that includes humans, are the most highly advanced organisms on Earth. Warm-blooded and hairy, they have four-chambered hearts and relatively large brains. All but two species suckle their young.

The approximately 4,000 species of mammals are divided into 26 orders. Ten of these live in North America. Some orders include a wide range of animals; for example, shrews, lemurs, marmosets, monkeys, apes, and humans are all primates, one order of the class of mammals. Other orders are made up of only one sort of creature; order Chiroptera, for example, consists of 18 families of bats.

The Latin names of the orders of mammals given here are followed by their common names and the families that make up each order. Examples of the various types of animals included in each family also are given.

SUBCLASS PROTOTHERIA (MONOTREMES, OR EGG-LAYING ANIMALS)

Order Monotremata (egg-laying mammals)

These more primitive mammals make up the families *Tachyglossidae* (echidnas, also called spiny anteaters) and *Ornithorhynchidae* (platypuses).

SUBCLASS THERIA (ALL OTHER ORDERS OF LIVING MAMMALS)

INFRACLASS METATHERIA (MARSUPIALS)

Order Dasyuromorphia

This order has three families, two represented by a single living species. The Tasmanian tiger (family *Thylacinidae),* a larger carnivorous, wolflike animal, may in fact now be extinct. The numbat, or banded anteater (family *Myrmecobiidae)* feeds on ants and termites and has no pouch for carrying its young. The third family *(Dasyuridae)* are insectivorous and carnivorous marsupials, and include the marsupiak mice and the Tasmanian devil.

Order Didelphimorphia

This order includes the earliest marsupials known, dating from about 90 million years ago. Most are omnivorous (although some are fruit- or insect-eating) and most do not have pouches for carrying their young. Living forms include the Virginia opossum.

Order Diprotodontia

The families *Phascolarctidae* (koalas), *Vombatidae* (wombats), *Phalangeridae* (possums and cuscuses), *Petauridae* (gliders), and *Macropodidae* (kangaroo-like marsupials) are mainly herbivorous. The pygmy possums (family *Burramyidae*) and some gliders, on the other hand, are insectivorous. The honey possums (family *Tarsipedidae*), as their name implies, feed on pollen and nectar.

Order Microbiotheria (monito del monte)

This order has only one living species (family *Microbiotheridae*), a small pouched and insectivorous marsupial that constructs nests in thickets of bamboo in the beech forests of southern Chile and Argentina.

Order Notoryctemorphia (marsupial mole)

This order has only one living species (family *Notoryctidae*). Resembling the true moles and having large foreclaws and a tough leathery shield on its nose, it literally swims through Australian sand dunes.

Order Paucituberculata (shrew opossums)

There is only one family (*Caenolestidae*) of these small pouchless mammals, which are ground-dwelling and strongly insectivorous.

Koalas and humans are the only animals with unique prints. Koala prints cannot be distinguished from human fingerprints.

Order Peramelemorphia

This order includes the only marsupials—bandicoots (family *Peramelidae*) and the bilbies (family *Thylacomyidae*)—to have an advanced chorioallantoic placenta like those of the placental mammals. Small- to medium-sized, they use their elongate muzzles to feed chiefly on insects and other small animals.

INFRACLASS EUTHERIA (PLACENTALS)

Order Artiodactyla (even-toed hoofed animals)

Hoofed animals with an even number of toes include those that ruminate, or digest their food in four-chamber stomachs and chew cuds, and those that do not ruminate. Those that ruminate are the families *Girrafidae* (giraffes), *Cervidae* (deer, moose, reindeer, elk), *Antilocapridae* (pronghorn antelope), and *Bovidae* (cattle, bison, yaks, waterbucks, wildebeest, gazelles, springboks, sheep, musk oxen, goats). *Nonruminators* include the families Suidae (pigs), *Tayassuidae* (peccaries), *Hippopotamidae* (hippopotamuses), and *Camelidae* (camels, llamas).

Order Carnivora (meat eaters)

There are two suborders of these toe-footed creatures. They include the *Canidae* (wolves, dogs, jackals, foxes), *Ursidae* (bears, giant pandas), *Procyonidae* (coatis, raccoons, lesser pandas), and *Mustelidae* (martens, weasels, skunks, otters), which are all part of one superfamily characterized by long snouts and unretractable claws; and *Felidae* (cats, lions, cheetahs, leopards), *Hyaenidae* (hyenas), and *Viverridae* (mongooses, civets), all of which have retractable claws.

Order Cetacea (whales and porpoises)

Two suborders of order Cetacea are the toothed whales, which have regular conical teeth, and the baleen, or whalebone, whales, which have irregular whalebone surfaces instead of teeth. Toothed whales include the families *Physeteridae* (sperm whales), *Monodontidae* (narwhals, belugas), *Phocoenidae* (porpoises), and *Delphinidae* (dolphins, killer whales). Baleens are in the family *Eschrichtiidae* (gray whales), *Balaenidae* (right whales), or *Balaenoptridae* (fin-backed whales, humpback whales).

Order Chiroptera (bats)

There are two suborders of bats, the only mammals that can fly. Suborder *Megachiroptera* contains one family, the *Pteropodidae* (flying foxes, Old World fruit bats). Suborder *Microchiroptera* contains 17 families, including *Rhinopomatidae* (mouse-tailed bats), *Emballonuridae* (sheath-tailed bats), *Craseonycteridae* (hog-nosed or butterfly bats), *Noctilionidae* (bulldog or fisherman bats), *Nycteridae* (slit-faced bats), *Megadermatidae* (false vampire bats), and *Rhinolophidae* (horseshoe bats).

Order Dermoptera (colugos or flying lemurs)

These gliding tree mammals from Asia do not fly and are not lemurs, but they are known as flying lemurs, or family *Cynocephalidae.*

Order Hyracoidae (hyraxes, dassies)

Order Hyracoidae is one of three orders that has only one modern family remaining. *Procavia capensis* (the African rock hyrax) is one of nine living species in the family *Procaviidae.*

Order Insectivora (insect eaters)

The three members are the families *Talpidae* (moles), *Soricidae* (shrews), and *Erinaceidae* (hedgehogs).

Order Lagomorpha (pikas, hares, and rabbits)

Two families make up this order: *Ochotonidae* (pikas) and *Leporidae* (hares and rabbits of all sorts).

Order Macroscelidea (elephant shrews)

This order, represented by the family *Macroscelididae,* was once considered part of the order Insectivora. The elephant shrew has well-developed eyes and ears and a narrow, flexible, and elongate (but not retractable) trunklike snout that it uses to locate insect prey.

Order Perissodactyla (odd-toed hoofed animals)

The two suborders, Hippomorpha and Ceratomorpha, include creatures that have an odd number of toes. Families in this order are the *Equidae* (horses, donkeys, zebras), the *Tapiridae* (tapirs), and the *Rhinocerotidae* (rhinoceroses).

Order Pholidata (pangolins)

Family *Manidae* (pangolins) is the sole family in this order.

Order Pinnipedia (seals and walruses)

In the fin-footed order, there are *Otariidae* (eared seals, sea lions), *Odobenidae* (walruses), and *Phocidae* (earless seals).

Order Primates (primates)

The order to which people belong is divided into two suborders: the Prosimii, who have longer snouts than their relatives; and the Anthropoidae. The first group includes the families *Tupalidae* (tree shrew), *Lemuridae* (lemurs), *Daubentonlidae* (aye-ayes), *Lorisidae* (lorises, pottos), and *Tarsiidae* (tarsiers). The anthropoids include the families *Callitrichidae* (marmosets), *Cebidae* (New World monkeys), *Cercopithecidae* (baboons, Old World monkeys), *Hylobatidae* (gibbons), *Pongidae* (gorillas, chimpanzees, orangutans), and *Hominidae* (human beings).

Order Proboscidea (elephants)

Large enough to have an order all to itself is family *Elephantidae.*

Order Rodentia (gnawing mammals)

Order Rodentia, containing the most prolific mammals, includes three suborders. It takes in the families *Aplodontidae* (mountain beavers), *Sciuridae* (chipmunks, squirrels, marmots), *Cricetidae* (field mice, lemmings, muskrats, hamsters, gerbils), *Muridae* (Old World mice, rats), *Heteromyidae* (New World mice), *Geomyidae* (gophers), and *Dipodidae* (jerboas).

Order Scandentia (tree shrews)

This order, represented by the single family *Tupaiidae,* was once considered part of the order Insectivora. The squirrel-like tree shrew has a long snout and feeds mainly on insects and fruit.

Order Sirenia (dugongs and manatees)

The families *Trichechidae* (manatees) and *Dugongidae* (dugongs and other sea cows) make up the order Sirenia.

Order Tubulidentata (aardvarks)

Another mammal in an order by itself is family *Orycteropodidae.*

Order Xenarthra Edentata (toothless mammals)

Three families of mammals get by without teeth: *Dasypodidae* (armadillos), *Bradypodidae* (sloths), and *Myrmecophagidae* (hairy anteaters).

THE PHYLA OF INVERTEBRATES

Invertebrates are members of the animal kingdom with no spinal column, or backbone. They make up about 95 percent of all animal species. There are 20 phyla of invertebrates, the 2 largest being Arthropoda and Mollusca. Following are some of the phyla of invertebrates and descriptions of their members.

Phylum Annelida (segmented worms)

Also called annelid worms, this phylum includes earthworms, leeches, and marine worms. Annelid worms have soft bodies, are symmetrical, and can be anywhere from ¹⁄₃₂ of an inch (half a millimeter) to 10 feet (3 meters) in length.

Phylum Arthropoda (arthropods)

This is the largest phylum of invertebrates, as well as the one with the most creatures; almost 80 percent of all animal species are arthropods. Arthropods have segmented bodies covered by external skeletons, called *exoskeletons,* which are molted from time to time to allow for growth. Their appendages ("arms" and "legs") are paired. Among the animals in this phylum are spiders, horseshoe crabs, crustaceans, insects, and centipedes.

Phylum Coelenterata (coelenterates)

Mostly marine invertebrates, coelenterates have three-layered body walls, tentacles, primitive nervous systems, and special stinger cells to protect themselves. Animals in this phylum include jellyfish, sea anemones, and corals.

Phylum Echinodermata (echinoderms)

Another marine invertebrate, the echinoderm, lives on the floor of the sea. Echinoderms are headless and have tube feet and external skeletons just below the surface of the skin. They can regenerate virtually any part of their bodies. Starfish, sea urchins, sand dollars, and sea cucumbers are some of the members of this phylum.

"Major Zoos and Aquariums" in chapter 11; "Animal Highlights of the Most Popular National Wildlife Refuges" in chapter 24
Go to

Phylum Platyhelminthes (flatworms)

As their name implies, these organisms are basically flat, soft-bodied, and symmetrical. These very primitive creatures come in two varieties: an aquatic group that includes planarians and a parasitic one that counts flukes and tapeworms among its members.

Phylum Mollusca (mollusks)

Most mollusks live inside shells and reside in the water. They have soft, unsegmented bodies and a powerful foot that enables them to move around. Clams, oysters, scallops, bivalves, octopuses, and squid are mollusks.

Phylum Nematoda (roundworms)

These wormlike animals have an outer coat made of noncellular material and a fluid-filled chamber that separates their body walls from their insides. They live both in water and on land. Among their number are rotifers, nematodes, and horsehair worms.

Phylum Porifera (sponges)

Porifera is the most primitive multicellular phylum. Sponges live mostly in colonies in the water, attached to rocks. They are basically sacs taking in water through small holes; their skeletons are formed from hard substances that become stuck in their body walls.

EXTINCT ANIMALS

Extinction has happened to species and subspecies throughout the time creatures have lived on this planet. The most well-known cases involved the "great dying" of the dinosaurs some 50 to 75 million years ago.

If creatures great and small have in fact been dying off throughout the ages, why is there suddenly concern about animals becoming extinct? Isn't extinction part of the natural order of things?

The answer is no, at least not on the scale it has occurred in recent times. Over most of the past 300 years, the rate of extinction of species was about one per year. At present, the rate of species extinction is at least a thousand times as great as that. This biodepletion is most rapid in tropical forests, which, though they cover only 6 percent of the Earth's land surface, shelter at least 50 percent of all species.

The two hemispheres of a dolphin's brain operate independently. For 8 hours, the entire brain is awake. The left side then sleeps for 8 hours. When it wakes up, the right side sleeps for 8 hours. Thus the dolphin gets 8 hours of sleep without ever having to stop physically.

The cause of this rapid acceleration in the rate of extinctions is human activity. With some species, like the dodo, the extinction was unintentional: people introduced predators to the dodo's island home where previously there had been none. Other creatures, such as the Eastern buffalo, were purposely killed off by human beings who wanted to "make room" for themselves.

In the late 20th century and beyond, extinctions are more likely to be a result of human activity. Rural landfills take in urban garbage, open land is blacktopped, factories produce toxins as by-products, and engineers alter waterways. These activities all have a direct impact on the ecosystems that support animal life.

A major cause of the extinction of species in tropical forests is the number of impoverished farmers who are moving into and clearing the forests. Species also suffer from climatic change—the planetary warming from the buildup of carbon dioxide and other greenhouse gases in the global atmosphere.

Increased awareness of the fragile links of interdependence among all of Earth's creatures, and of the impact that human activities can have on those creatures, have led some to hope that the latest era of "great dying" may soon stop. It remains to be seen, however, if the forces already in motion can be stopped in time to save the hundreds of species that teeter on the brink of extinction.

Listed here are the popular names of those animals thought to be endangered or extinct at the end of the 20th century. Exact figures are difficult to determine because endangered species often make the transition to extinction quickly and without notice. Occasionally populations of animals thought to be extinct are discovered to be extant (in existence). In these lists, the number of individual species is in parentheses. If no number appears, one of that species is extinct—i.e., not all beavers are extinct, but one species is.

MAMMALS

Anoa (2)
Antelope, giant sable
Argali
Armadillo (2)
Ass (2)
Avahi
Aye-aye
Babirusa
Baboon, gelada
Bandicoot (5)
Banteng
Bat (13)
Bear (6)

Beaver
Bison, wood
Bobcat, Mexican
Bontebok
Camel, Bactrian
Caribou, woodland
Cat (9)
Chamois, Apennine
Cheetah
Chimpanzee (2)
Chinchilla
Civet, Malabar large-spotted
Cochito
Deer (22)

Dhole
Dibbler
Dog, African wild
Dolphin (2)
Drill
Dugong
Duiker, Jentink's
Eland, western giant
Elephant (2)
Ferret, black-footed
Fox (3)
Gazelle (10)
Gibbons
Goral

Biological World

continues

Gorilla
Hare, hispid
Hartebeest (2)
Hog, pygmy
Horse, Przewalski's
Huemul (2)
Hutia (4)
Hyena (2)
Ibex (2)
Impala, black-faced
Indri
Jaguar
Jaguarundi (4)
Kangaroo rat (6)
Kangaroo, Tasmanian forester
Koala
Kouprey
Langur (8)
Lechwe, red
Lemurs
Leopard (3)
Linsang, spotted
Lion, Asiatic
Loris, lesser slow
Lynx (2)
Macaque (5)
Manatee (3)
Mandrill
Mangabey (2)
Margay
Markhor (3)
Marmoset (4)
Marmot, Vancouver Island
Marsupial, eastern jerboa
Marsupial-mouse (2)
Marten, Formosian yellow-
    throated
Monkey (20)
Mountain Beaver, Point Arena
Mouse (19)
Muntjac, Fea's
Native-cat, eastern
Numbat
Ocelot
Orangutan
Oryx, Arabian
Otter (6)
Panda, giant

Pangolin, Temnick's ground
Panther, Florida
Planigale (2)
Porcupine, thin-spined
Possum (3)
Prairie Dog (2)
Pronghorn (2)
Pudu
Puma (3)
Quokka
Rabbit (4)
Rat (2)
Rat-kangaroo (5)
Rhinoceros (5)
Rice rat
Saiga, Mongolian
Saki (2)
Seal (5)
Sea-lion, Stellar
Seledang
Serow
Serval, Barbary
Shapo
Sheep, bighorn
Shou
Siamang
Sifakas
Sloth, Brazilian three-toed
Solenodon (2)
Squirrel (4)
Stag (2)
Suni, Zanzibar
Tahr, Arabian
Tamaraw
Tamarin (3)
Tapir (4)
Tarsier, Phillipine
Tiger (2)
Uakari
Urial
Vicuna
Vole (3)
Wallaby (6)
Whale (8)
Wolf (3)
Wombat, Queensland hairy-
    nosed

Woodrat (2)
Yak, wild
Zebra (3)

BIRDS

Akepa (2)
Akialoa (2)
Albatross (2)
Alethe, Thyolo
Blackbird, yellow-shouldered
Bobwhite, masked
Booby, Abbott's
Bristlebird (2)
Broadbill, Guam
Bulbul, Muritius olivaceous
Bullfinch, Sao Miguel
Bush-shrike, Uluguru
Bushwren, New Zealand
Bustard, great Indian
Cahow
Caracara, Audobon crested
Condor (2)
Coot, Hawaiian
Cotinga (2)
Crane (8)
Creeper (3)
Crow (3)
Cuckoo-shrike (2)
Curassow (3)
Curlew, Eskimo
Dove (2)
Duck (4)
Eagle (7)
Egret, Chinese
Eider, spectacled
Eider, Steller's
Elepaio, Oahu
Falcon (2)
Finch (2)
Flycatcher (4)
Fody (3)
Francolin, Djibouti
Freira
Frigatebird, Andrew's
Gnatcatcher, coastal California
Goose, Hawaiian
Goshawk, Christmas Island
Grackle, slender-billed

Grasswren, Eyrean
Grebe (2)
Greenshank, Nordmann's
Guan (2)
Guineafowl, white-breasted
Gull (2)
Hawk (4)
Hermit, hook-billed
Honeycreeper, crested
Honeyeater, helmeted
Hornbill, helmeted
Ibis (2)
Jay, Florida scrub
Kagu
Kakapo
Kestrel (2)
Kingfisher, Guam Micronesian
Kite (3)
Kokako
Lark, Raso
Macaw (3)
Magpie-robin, Seychelles
Malimbe, Ibadan
Malkoha, red-faced
Mallard, Mariana
Megapode (2)
Millerbird, Nihoa
Monarch, Tinian
Moorhen (2)
Murrelet, marbled
Nightjar, Puerto Rican
Nukupu'u
Nuthatch, Algerian
'O'o, Kauai
Ostrich (2)
'O'u
Owl (6)
Owlet, Morden's
Oystercatcher, Canarian black
Palila
Parakeet (10)
Parrot (15)
Parrotbill, Maui
Pelican, brown
Penguin, Galapagos
Petrel (2)
Pheasant (15)

Pigeon (6)
Piping-guan, black-fronted
Pitta, Koch's
Plover (3)
Pochard, Madagascar
Po'ouli
Prairie-chicken, Attwater's
  greater
Pygmy-owl, cactus ferruginous
Quail, Merriam's Montezuma
Quetzel, resplendent
Rail (6)
Rhea, lesser (incl. Darwin's)
Robin (3)
Rockfowl (2)
Roller, long-tailed ground
Scrub-bird, noisy
Shama, Cebu black
Shearwater, Newell's Townsend's
Shrike, San Clemente logger-
  head
Siskin, red
Sparrow (3)
Sparrowhawk, Anjouan Island
Starling (2)
Stilt, Hawaiian
Stork (2)
Sunbird, Marungu
Swiftlet, Mariana gray
Teal, Campbell Island flightless
Tern (3)
Thrasher, white-breasted
Thrush (5)
Tinamou, solitary
Towhee, Inyo California
Trembler, Martinique
Turaco, Bannerman's
Turtle dove, Seychelles
Vanga (2)
Vireo (2)
Wanderer, plain
Warbler (9)
Wattle-eye, banded
Weaver, Clarke's
Whipbird, western
White-eye (4)
Woodpecker (4)
Wren (2)

REPTILES

Alligator (2)
Anole, Culebra Island giant
Boa (6)
Caiman (6)
Chuckwalla, San Esteban Island
Crocodile (13)
Gavial
Gecko (4)
Iguana (17)
Lizard (7)
Monitor (4)
Python, Indian
Rattlesnake (2)
Sea turtle (6)
Skink (3)
Snake (8)
Tartaruga
Terrapin, river
Tomistoma
Tortoise (6)
Tracaja
Tuatara (2)
Turtle (22)
Viper, Lar Valley
Whipsnake, Alameda

AMPHIBIANS

Coqui, golden
Frog (5)
Guajon
Salamander (13)
Toad (7)

FISH

Ala balik
Ayumodoki
Blindcat, Mexican
Bonytongue, Asian
Catfish (3)
Cavefish (2)
Chub (14)
Cicek
Cui-ui
Dace (8)
Darter (17)
Gambusia (4)

continues

Goby, tidewater
Logperch (2)
Madtom (5)
Minnow (3)
Nekogigi (catfish)
Pikeminnow, Colorado
Poolfish, Pahrump
Pupfish (7)
Salmon (4)
Sculpin, pygmy
Shiner (8)
Silverside, Waccamaw
Smelt, delta
Spikedace
Spinedace (3)
Splittail, Sacramento
Springfish (3)
Steelhead
Stickleback, unarmored three-
    spine
Sturgeon (5)
Sucker (7)
Tango, Miyako
Temoleh, Ikan
Topminnow, Gila
Totoaba
Trout (6)
Woundfin

MOLLUSKS

Ambersnail, Kanab
Acornshell, southern
Bankclimber, purple
Bean (2)

Blossom (4)
Campeloma, slender
Catspaw (2)
Clubshell (4)
Combshell (3)
Elimia, lacy
Elktoe (2)
Fanshell
Fatmucket, Arkansas
Heelsplitter (2)
Higgins eye
Kidneyshell, triangular
Lampmussel, Alabama
Lilliput, pale
Limpet, Banbury Springs
Lioplax, cylindrical
Mapleleaf, winged
Marstonia, royal
Moccasinshell (4)
Monkeyface (2)
Mucket (2)
Mussel, oyster
Pearlshell, Louisiana
Pearlymussel (7)
Pebblesnail, flat
Pigtoe (9)
Pimpleback, orangefoot
Pocketbook (5)
Rabbitsfoot, rough
Riffleshell (2)
Ring pink
Riversnail, Anthony's
Rocksnail (3)
Shagreen, Magazine Mountain

Slabshell, Chipola
Snail (16)
Spinymussel (2)
Springsnail (4)
Stirrupshell
Three-ridge, fat
Wartyback, white
Wedgemussel, dwarf

INSECTS

Beetle (10)
Butterfly (23)
Dragonfly, Hine's emerald
Fly, Delhi Sands flower-loving
Grasshopper, Zayante band-
    winged
Ground beetle (2)
Mold beetle, Helotes
Moth (2)
Naucorid, Ash Meadows
Skipper (2)
Tiger beetle (2)
Harvestman (3)
Pseudoscorpion, Tooth Cave
Spider (8)

CRUSTACEANS

Amphipod (4)
Crayfish (4)
Fairy shrimp (5)
Isopod (3)
Shrimp (4)
Tadpole shrimp, vernal pool

PETS

Though a wide variety of animals are kept as pets, the overwhelming majority are dogs and cats. Veterinarians and other animal-care experts suggest a number of basic rules to be considered by everyone contemplating pet ownership.

CHOOSING A PET

Do research on the kind of animal you want to get. Make sure you have the ability and finances to house and feed the animal (especially relevant with large dogs) and to pay for its medical care. Don't buy animals as gifts. If the recipient is not willing and able

to care for the animal, it will be a disaster for all concerned.

When choosing a dog, don't base your choice on looks without considering the purpose for which it was bred (e.g., don't turn a hunting dog into a house dog). Make sure you have enough time to spend with a puppy. Puppies shouldn't be left alone for more than 3 or 4 hours. Make sure the puppy is bright and alert, though not hyperactive. Check for any signs of ill health and have the puppy examined by a veterinarian before accepting it. Don't separate a puppy from its mother and littermates before it is 6 weeks old.

Go to
"Traveling with Pets" in chapter 24

When choosing a kitten, try to see its parents and observe their temperament. If you get a kitten or cat from an animal shelter, ask the shelter staff about the animal's background. A kitten should respond to attention and not mind being held. It should have a healthy-looking coat, pink gums, and no evidence of any discharge from its eyes or ears. Obtain a certificate of vaccinations and have the kitten examined by a veterinarian.

TRAINING

Never hit your dog or yell at it—such an action will only make the dog afraid or resentful. Because the dog craves affection and approval, a firm "No!" or "Bad dog!" is more than enough. A quick tug on your dog's leash or collar, however, is permissible to discourage unwanted behavior, especially with larger dogs. Using your leg to push your dog off balance is acceptable to teach it not to jump on people.

Issue reprimands immediately so that your dog associates your displeasure with a specific offense. Dragging your dog to the scene after the fact does no good.

When toilet training your dog, don't put down pieces of newspaper indoors, which will only make the dog think it's all right to eliminate in the house. Take your dog out first thing in the morning, 15 minutes after each meal, after vigorous play, and just before bedtime. Praise your dog for eliminating outside. Don't allow your dog access to the entire house until it is properly trained.

All dogs should be obedience-trained so that they respond to five basic commands: heel, sit, down, stay, and come. This is especially important with large aggressive breeds such as Dobermans, Rottweilers, and German shepherds. Dogs should be praised when they respond properly, and training should be incorporated into your dog's daily routine so that it remains effective. If you can't handle the job yourself, seek professional help. Options include group obedience lessons, a private trainer, and board and training kennels.

When disciplining a kitten, say "No!" in a deep voice. Holding your kitten gently by the scruff of the neck, as its mother would do, is permissible. Squirting your cat with a spritz of water can be effective in discouraging unwanted behavior, but it must be done while the offense is being committed.

Cats instinctively bury their stools; thus, getting your cat to use a litter box should not be hard. If your kitten eliminates outside the box, putting the stool in there will usually convey the message. Use absorbent clay litters and remove the stools every day with a slotted spoon. Replace the litter every third day and wash the pan with hot water, soap, and chlorine bleach. Keep on using the same type of litter once your cat is used to it.

SPAYING AND NEUTERING

Experts advise pet owners against breeding their animals at home because of the medical expenses involved (immunizations for the litter and possible health problems on the mother's part during or after pregnancy) and because of the possibility of not finding homes for the offspring. More than 15 million dogs and cats are put down every year because of overpopulation.

Neutering does not change a male dog's personality or his instinct to protect his home and those he loves. It simply makes him less aggressive toward other male dogs and stops him from marking his territory with urine.

Female cats will go into heat every 2 to 3 weeks if they are not mated. If they are going to be spayed, it should be done before the first onset of heat. The procedure should not be performed, however, before the cat is 5 or 6 months old; it can also be done after sexual maturity.

Neutering male cats will prevent roaming, spraying, and fighting. The operation can be performed either at 5–6 months old or after sexual maturity.

Biological World

PETS AND CHILDREN

Cats generally mix well with children and will tolerate treatment from a child that they would not accept from an adult. Experts recommend, however, that kittens not be introduced into a household where there are very young children who may frighten the cat with loud noise or rough handling. Parents should wait until the child is old enough to understand the animal's needs and play an active role in caring for it.

Relations between dogs and children should be carefully considered. For pet owners with young children, experts recommend a choice of breeds known for their gentle disposition and patience. These breeds include the basenji, bassett hound, beagle, boxer, bulldog, collie, Dalmatian, springer spaniel, German shepherd, golden retriever, Great Dane, Irish setter, Labrador retriever, and standard poodle. Less desirable breeds include the Afghan hound, Chow Chow, dachshund, Doberman, miniature schnauzer, Rottweiler, Weimaraner, and most varieties of terrier.

When a new baby is introduced into a household that already has a dog, a number of steps can be taken to prepare the pet for this dramatic change:

1. As the birth of your child approaches, prepare your dog gradually for the reduced attention that he or she is bound to receive by gradually modifying the amount of time you spend with the dog.
2. Bring home an article of your baby's clothing from the hospital and let your dog get used to the scent.
3. Praise your dog when the baby is around, so it associates good things with the baby.
4. Closely supervise your baby when it begins to crawl and interact with your dog. The dog will not necessarily recognize the baby as a human and may feel threatened.

NUTRITION

Allergies, gastrointestinal disorders, kidney disease, cancer, and other pet ailments can be linked to junk in pet foods. (Some dog foods, for example, contain grain hulls and peanut shells.) The best bet is to buy premium brands with meat-based protein sources.

Don't mix brands of pet food together, because each brand has its own balance of proteins, vitamins, and minerals.

Avoid low-quality foods, many of which contain materials that pets will be unable to digest. These undigestible materials will pass right through the system without providing any nutritional benefit.

Avoid soft, moist, processed foods wrapped in cellophane. They have little nutritional value and cause a disease of the red blood cells in cats.

Don't overfeed pets. Veterinarians estimate that three of five dogs are overweight. Dogs should not be more than 20 percent over the ideal weight for their particular breed. High-quality, low-calorie food can help in this area.

PET STAINS

In addition to removing the stain itself, remove any lingering odor so that your pet is not drawn back to the spot and prompted to urinate there again. To do this, it is necessary to use an enzyme odor remover, which breaks down urine molecules into carbon dioxide and water. Ordinary household cleaners will often leave enough traces of odor for your pet's sensitive olfactory organs to detect.

See also "Stain Removal: Urine" in chapter 19.

IMMUNIZATION
DOGS

5–8 weeks	Canine distemper-measles, CPI (parinfluenza)
8–16 weeks	DHLPP (distemper, hepatitis, leptospirosis, parainfluenza, parvovirus)
14–16 weeks	Rabies
12 months and then annually	DHLPP
12 months and then every three months	Rabies

Each locality may have specific requirements for immunizations and frequency of booster shots, and dog owners should check with their veterinarians. In some areas, for example, vaccination against Lyme disease, coronavirus, and kennel cough may also be necessary. In general, keep your dog away from strange dogs before the vaccination series is complete.

CATS

Any age	Upper respiratory infections (2–3 vaccinations 2–4 weeks apart)
8–12 weeks	Distemper (2–3 vaccinations 2–4 weeks apart)
	Rabies (2 vaccinations 2–4 weeks apart)
	Feline leukemia (2 vaccinations 2–4 weeks apart; 1 vaccination 2–4 months later)
12 weeks or older	Distemper (1 vaccination, then a yearly booster shot)
	Rabies (1 vaccination, then a yearly booster shot; also a 3-year booster is available)
	Feline leukemia (1 vaccination, then a yearly booster shot)
	Upper respiratory infections (1 vaccination, then a yearly booster shot)

A stool sample should be checked whenever shots are given.

ANIMAL FIRST AID

Animals, like people, suffer medical problems. Emergency and nonemergency ailments and traumas require quick attention to prevent serious situations from turning into life-threatening ones.

The meow of a cat is actually two distinct sounds. The "me" is a friendly greeting, but the "ow" means "I'm willing to defend myself." Although cats often meow at humans, they rarely meow at other cats.

Some problems—bleeding that cannot be stopped or convulsions, for instance—require the immediate attention of an expert in veterinary medicine. Many other problems, however, can be treated by the animal's owner.

The following are some common animal ailments and injuries. The symptoms and treatments for each are described. As with any medical condition, if the symptoms persist or the animal's owner is unsure about the nature of the problem, professional assistance should be sought.

BROKEN BONES

Symptoms Some bone breaks show obvious symptoms: twisted or distorted limbs, or, in the case of a compound fracture, bone fragments sticking through the skin. Less apparent breaks cause great pain and discomfort. The animal will cry or bite when the affected area is touched; will lie around, often on the affected area; and will usually not walk, although in some cases it will walk despite the break, notably when the pelvis is broken. The fracture will not bear weight. Swelling of the affected area within 24 hours can be expected from any sort of fracture.

Treatment Treatment of compound fractures by a veterinarian should be sought as soon as possible. Other breaks should be treated by a veterinarian within 24 hours. Apply an ice pack or cold wet compress to the affected area; change regularly. Protect the animal from further injury by confining it to a small room. Apply a temporary splint to broken limbs to avoid further dislocation.

See also "Treatment for Health Emergencies: Fractures, Dislocations, and Sprains" in chapter 17.

BURNS

Symptoms All burns are painful to the touch. *Electrical burns* are the most serious and can cause heart attacks and death. The burned area will show seared flesh, reddened skin, lesions, and blisters. The animal may suffer respiratory distress; paleness or blueness, especially in lips, gums, and eyelid linings;

rigidity in limbs; glassy stare; collapse; and shock. *Thermal burns* cause a singed or charred area; the exposed skin is reddened or inflamed, and the wound is warm or hot to the touch. *Friction burns* are similar in appearance to thermal burns, but the skin is chafed or scraped and has bare spots; bare skin is rubbed raw, is reddish in color, and is irritated or inflamed. The trauma causing the friction burn may leave cuts, lacerations, or embedded foreign matter.

Treatment   Depending on the type and extent of the burn, it can often be treated at home. Electrical burns can stop an animal's heart and must be treated immediately by a veterinarian; if shock occurs, keep the animal warm with heating pads or hot water bottles and a blanket or heavy coat and seek veterinary treatment immediately. Thermal burns can be treated topically by applying the jellylike substance from an aloe plant, a solution made from Domeboro® (available at most pharmacies), or vitamin E oil. Friction burns can be treated in the same way as thermal burns; however, if foreign matter is embedded, or the burn does not respond to treatment, the animal should be taken to a veterinarian.

See also "Treatment for Health Emergencies: Burns" and "Electric Shock" in chapter 17 and "Home Remedies: Burns—First Degree" in chapter 18.

CAT DISEASES

Symptoms   Four major diseases affect the well-being of cats. *Cat distemper* induces high fever, lethargy, vomiting, and diarrhea; young kittens can develop distemper very quickly and will often die of it without exhibiting symptoms. *Rhinotracheitis* causes fever, sneezing, loss of appetite, and dehydration; additional symptoms can include discharge from eyes and nose, congestion, and swelling of membranes in the respiratory tract. *Calici virus* is characterized by sneezing and discharge from the eyes and nose; it may cause fever, lethargy, loss of appetite, dehydration, and ulcers on the tongue. *Pneumonitis* usually causes labored breathing, sneezing, coughing, snorting, wheezing, and listlessness; it

may induce a loss of body fluids and very high temperatures.

Treatment   Three of these diseases—cat distemper, rhinotracheitis, and calici virus—can be prevented by annual vaccinations. All four must be treated as quickly as possible by a veterinarian if symptoms are present. Professional treatment will, in most cases, effect a cure.

CONSTIPATION

Symptoms   The animal struggles or strains during a bowel movement without passing a stool, avoids food, and becomes nervous or irritated.

Treatment   Feed the animal brans, cereal foods, vegetables (peas, carrots, corn), or kibble; use infant-size glycerine suppositories or soap suppositories; give an enema if the animal will allow it; add a small amount of stool softener, such as Metamucil®, to food; give mineral oil or milk of magnesia, but dosages should depend on size and type of animal (consult a veterinarian).

See also "Home Remedies: Constipation" in chapter 18.

DENTAL DISORDERS

Symptoms   Tartar, a brown crust, appears on teeth, starting at the gum line; tooth enamel erodes, especially in cats; bone fragments, foreign matter, food particles, or hair accumulate on teeth; bad breath is present. *Throat* or *mouth infections* cause coughing and discharges from mouth or nose. *Gingivitis* develops when tartar or dirty teeth are untreated. *Uremia* can cause blackish tartar, bad breath, and extraordinary thirst.

Treatment   Clean the animal's teeth monthly with a mixture of one teaspoon salt or hydrogen peroxide to half a cup of water; apply to teeth with a cotton swab or soft toothbrush. Include hard food, such as kibble, in the animal's diet; provide hard things for the animal to chew on. Infections, gingivitis, or uremia should be treated by a veterinarian.

DIARRHEA

Symptoms   The animal passes liquid stool during bowel movement; there may be abnormal coloration of stool.

Treatment   Remove grease, oils, and milk from the animal's diet; avoid high-fiber foods, kibble, and dry catmeal (never give your cat any type of dog food). For dogs, feed the animal a mix of 1 part hamburger, drained of grease, and 1 part rice; cats digest 1 part cooked, minced chicken and 1 part rice best. If diarrhea results from ingestion of foreign matter (from teething or eating plants, soap, or other household materials), treat a dog with small doses of Kaopectate® or Pepto-Bismol®. (NEVER give a cat Pepto-Bismol or aspirin—both can be fatal.) If symptoms persist for more than 24 hours, or if blood is present in stool, consult a veterinarian.

DOG DISEASES

Symptoms   A number of conditions affect only dogs. *Canine distemper* causes severe diarrhea and may cause high fever, discharge from eyes and nose, thickening of foot pads, coughing, muscle contractions, convulsions, and pneumonia. *Infectious canine hepatitis* usually results in fever, lethargy, and congestion of the mucous membranes; it also can cause loss of appetite and insatiable thirst. *Leptospirosis* is characterized by high fever, lethargy, loss of appetite, congestion in the whites of the eyes, and possibly pain in walking, jaundice, vomiting, and diarrhea. *Infectious canine tracheobron-chitis (kennel cough)* causes high fever and severe dry coughing spasms.

Treatment   All four of these diseases can be prevented by annual vaccinations. If a dog is not vaccinated, early diagnosis of the symptoms of each disease is imperative. None of these diseases can be treated at home; take the dog to a veterinarian as soon as possible.

PARASITES, EXTERNAL

Symptoms   Fleas, ticks, lice, maggots, and mites are common external parasites that prey on animals. All cause animals to scratch excessively, which can lead to hair loss. *Fleas* are tiny brown insects that move through the animal's coat. *Ticks* are small, round, dark-colored insects with hard shells that attach themselves to an animal's skin. *Lice* are small, dark-gray insects that remain in one place on an animal's body. *Maggots* look like small worms. *Mites,* which are invisible to the unaided eye, characteristically cause skin and ear irritation.

Ringworm is a fungal disease that affects the outer layers of your pet's skin, nails, and hair. It gives off toxins that can damage the skin and hair and is highly contagious to pets and humans. Ringworm should be treated by a veterinarian.

Treatment   External parasites can be readily eliminated and controlled with commercially available powders, baths, sprays, and dips. Check the labels of such treatments carefully to be sure they are appropriate for use on your animal and that they will control the parasite in question. Fleas can be controlled with flea collars, sprays, powders, baths, or dips; treat animal and surrounding furniture and carpets to eliminate infestations. Ticks can be pulled off by hand; the animal should then be treated with spray, powder, or bath to eliminate unseen ticks; treat surrounding furniture and carpets to eliminate infestations. Lyme disease, which is spread by ticks, can be prevented by vaccination. Lice can be treated with the same potions that work on fleas and ticks. Maggots are an increasingly rare parasite that, if present, should be treated by a veterinarian. Mites can cause recurring mange in dogs, or other recurring skin conditions in other animals; any recurring condition should be treated by a veterinarian.

See also "Treatment for Health Emergencies: Insect Bites" in chapter 17.

PARASITES, INTERNAL

Symptoms   All internal parasites drain an animal's natural defenses, leaving it susceptible to infections and diseases. All are likely to cause loss of appetite and lethargy. *Tapeworms* leave visible, light-colored segments (that look like rice kernels in stools), around sleeping areas, under the animal's tail, or near its anus. *Roundworms* look like spaghetti; they are light yellow, 2 to 4 inches long, have slightly pointed ends, and can be seen in stools or vomit. *Hookworms* are almost invisible to the naked eye, but can cause diarrhea (often with blood present), cramps, pale gums and lips, a dry coat, a slight cough, and noticeable weight loss. *Whipworms* cause symptoms similar to those caused by hookworms, as well as possible inflammation of the colon. *Heartworms* block an animal's arteries, causing tiredness, listlessness, a poor coat, weight loss, and constant panting and coughing. *Coccidia* (one-celled protozoa) cause diarrhea, emaciation, and discharges from the animal's eyes and nose. *Toxoplasmosis* is a parasite that afflicts mostly cats; it frequently presents no symptoms at all.

Treatment An infestation of internal parasites is a debilitating condition that should be dealt with by a veterinarian. Preventive medications for heartworm are available.

RABIES

Symptoms Rabies—whose symptoms include fever, loss of appetite, and an inability to swallow that results in drooling—can cause encephalitis, convulsions, or paralysis. One type of rabies causes animals to attack anything that moves (cars, animals, people); another type causes only the other symptoms.

Treatment Prevention of rabies is possible through regular vaccinations. Once contracted, however, there is no effective treatment for rabies, and the animal will have to be destroyed.

See also "Treatment for Health Emergencies: Animal Bites" in chapter 17.

RESPIRATORY INFECTIONS

Symptoms Sneezing, coughing, runny eyes, swollen glands, difficulty swallowing, labored breathing, fever.

Treatment If symptoms such as sneezing, coughing, and runny eyes are present but the animal re-

mains active and eats normally, the condition is probably not serious, and no treatment is needed. A veterinarian should examine the animal if symptoms continue for a while, if the animal becomes lethargic and loses appetite, if there are discharges of pus from its nose, if congestion becomes heavy or labored breathing is continued, or if fever of more than 102°F is present.

SHOCK

Symptoms Weakness, collapse, pale or muddy-colored gums, fast heartbeat, difficulty breathing, no breathing, dilated pupils, low body temperature.

Treatment Keep the animal warm by applying heating pads or hot water bottles and wrapping the animal in heavy blankets or coats. Take the animal to a veterinarian at once.

SKIN PROBLEMS

Symptoms Localized skin conditions cause inflammation or irritation and may cause bald spots of red, raw, or discolored skin. More serious disorders such as moist eczema, wet dermatitis, or acute pruritis cause raw, oozing bald spots that may be damp to the touch or oozing pus. A lump on the animal's skin that does not go away within a few days may be a tumor. Other skin problems can cause dry, flaky skin; an oily coat; and constant biting, licking, or scratching. Symmetrical skin disorders affect both sides of an animal's body equally; a generalized condition affects the animal's whole body.

Treatment Bald patches of red or raw skin and damp, oozing hot areas should be treated by a veterinarian. Localized inflammation can be treated with soothing topical sprays and lotions. Dry skin or coat can be soaked several times a day with water or a solution made from Domeboro® tablets (available at most pharmacies); small quantities of oil added to the animal's food also will help. Itchiness can be corrected with a solution of 1 part Alpha-Keri® (available from most pharmacies) to 20 or 30 parts water applied with a spray bottle; repeat as needed. A well-balanced diet, with appropriate levels of vitamins, can maintain healthy skin. Any skin condition that does not go away, or that reappears after treatment, should be treated by a veterinarian.

SPRAINS

Symptoms   Sprains usually occur in the joints of an animal's limbs, causing rapid swelling. The affected area will be hot to the touch. The animal will not walk normally, if it walks at all.

Treatment   Apply cold compresses or ice packs gently to the swollen area; keep the area cool for a day or two, changing the compress or ice when necessary. Wrap the affected area snugly with cloth, gauze, or athletic bandages; secure the wrapping to be sure the animal does not scratch or bite it off. Keep the animal quiet, discourage activity, and avoid stairs. For sprains that heal and recur, apply hot towels or compresses; keep the injured area moist and warm for several days. If a sprain does not heal, or pain and swelling continue or are severe, see a veterinarian.

See also "Treatment for Health Emergencies: Fractures, Dislocations, and Sprains" in chapter 17 and "Home Remedies: Sprains and Strains" in chapter 18.

WOUNDS

Symptoms   *Cuts* can be recognized by the presence of smoothly separated tissue and possible bleeding. *Lacerations* result in jaggedly torn skin, bleeding, swelling, irritation, and black or blue discoloration of the skin. *Abrasions* rub or scrape away the outer layers of skin, causing pain, swelling, redness, and heat. *Bruises* or *contusions* leave black-and-blue tissue and swelling.

Treatment   Any serious wound should be treated by a veterinarian if the bleeding will not stop, if blood is gushing out, or if shock is present. For cuts that are bleeding, apply a pressure bandage (clean gauze or cloth wrapped around some padding) pressed firmly but gently against the wound; an ice bag, pressed firmly but gently on the area; or a tourniquet. After the bleeding has been controlled, clean the wound with hydrogen peroxide or Bactine®

and then dry it. Keep skin from wrinkling or bunching and then apply an antiseptic or antibiotic to a gauze square and wrap snugly in place. Change the dressing daily and keep the animal from removing it. Lacerations can be treated in the same way as cuts, but an ice bag must be used to reduce swelling and prevent further inflammation. Abrasions require the application of a soothing cream, ointment, or lotion (Solarcaine®, Nupercainal®, Unguentine® ointment, or calamine lotion); a bandage is not needed, but the animal must be kept from licking the treated area. Bruises and contusions are best treated with cold compresses or ice packs.

See also "Treatment for Health Emergencies: Abrasions" and "Black Eyes and Bruises" in chapter 17.

THE PLANT KINGDOM

ORDERS OF PLANTS

There are more than 130 orders of plants. The following list includes some of the most common or important plant orders. The Latin names of the orders of plants given here are followed by their common names. Examples of the various types of plants included in each order are also given.

ORDER ASTERALES

The members of this order belong to a single large family consisting of some 15,000 to 20,000 species. Asterales includes many popular garden ornamentals, such as asters, mums, dahlias, daisies, marigolds, sunflowers, and zinnias. Other members are common weeds, such as dandelions, ragweeds, and thistles. Lettuce and safflower are among the economically important members of Asterales. Distribution is worldwide.

ORDER BEGONIALES (BEGONIAS)

This order of flowering plants consists of organisms ranging from small plants to relatively large shrubs. They are distributed mainly in the tropics around the world, but are popular cultivated plants in subtropical and temperate climates as well. There are about 1,000 species of the familiar begonia.

ORDER BETULALES (BIRCHES)

This order of flowering trees and shrubs are dominant in northern temperate and Arctic regions. Many of these plants are economically important. Birches are major sources of cabinet woods, and alders are important soil-builders. Other members of this order include ironwoods, hornbeams, and hazelnuts.

ORDER CACTALES (CACTI)

Cacti are often spiny, fleshy stemmed plants characteristically found in arid and semiarid regions. They are native to the Americas, but are cultivated worldwide for their unusual shapes and striking blossoms.

Some species are useful economically, especially in Mexico and Central and South America. Familiar members of the order include prickly pears, barrel cacti, saguaro, cereus, and opuntia.

ORDER CORNALES (DOGWOODS)

The more than 3,700 members of this order display considerable variety in form. Most of its 10 families are woody flowering plants, mainly shrubs, but several species, such as the ivy, are climbers. Other notable members of the order include dogwoods, sour gums, ginsengs, and parsleys. They are distributed worldwide, but are chiefly found in northern temperate zones.

The oldest living thing in the world was found in 1998 on Australia's island state of Tasmania—a naturally cloned king's holly shrub thought to be 43,000 years old.

ORDER FABALES

This order is second only to the grasses (Poales) in economic importance. It includes a variety of food products, including beans, peanuts, and peas. Other members, such as alfalfa and clover, provide grazing for animals. More than 20,000 species belong to this order, which can be found worldwide, especially in temperate regions.

ORDER FAGALES (BEECHES)

This order consists exclusively of deciduous or evergreen shrubs and trees, which often form forests that cover wide areas. They are mainly distributed over the Northern Hemisphere. Common members of this order include beeches, oaks, and chestnuts.

ORDER GERANIALES (GERANIUMS)

About 4,000 species make up this order of flowering plants, which are chiefly tropical in distribution. The order displays considerable variety in size and shape, from small annual plants to trees of the tropical rainforest. Although the order has some value as ornamental plants, it is generally not an economically important plant group. The major exception is flax, the source of a fiber that has been used by humans since prehistoric times.

ORDER JUGLANDES (WALNUTS)

The members of this order are generally large forest trees, found primarily in temperate areas but also in subtropical zones. They are distributed throughout eastern North America, Central America, western South America, and eastern Asia. Walnuts, hickories, and pecans are useful not only for their edible nuts, but for their valuable wood.

ORDER LAURALES (LAURELS)

Members of this order can be found worldwide, with the greatest concentration in the tropics. They are woody, with a simple, alternating leaf structure. Several members of this order are economically useful, such as the avocado, cinnamon, and sassafras trees.

ORDER MAGNOLIALES (MAGNOLIAS)

All members of this order are woody; most are small flowering trees, although the tulip tree can reach a height of 150 feet (46 meters). They are mainly distributed throughout wet, tropical regions, but some species survive in temperate climates. Besides the tulip tree, other common members of this order include magnolias and nutmegs.

ORDER NYMPHAEALES (WATER LILIES)

Not surprisingly, the members of this order are aquatic plants. They are cultivated worldwide for their beauty, but their natural habitats are temperate and tropical regions. Most are perennials.

ORDER OLEALES (OLIVES)

The members of this important order of small, woody flowering plants can be found throughout the world, except in the polar regions. Several families—especially the lilacs, jasmines, privets, and forsythia—are popular ornamental plants. Ashes are a notable source of hardwood timber, while the olive is widely cultivated as a source of olives and olive oil.

ORDER PRIMULALES (PRIMROSES)

This order contains nearly 2,000 species of flowering plants. Two of its three families are entirely composed of trees and shrubs; some of these are climbers or epiphytes (plants that grow on other plants, and are not rooted in soil). The order is important because of its ornamental value. Representative members include cyclamen, primrose, and loosestrife.

ORDER ROSALES (ROSES)

Members of this order are among the most frequently encountered plants in temperate zones around the world. They are cultivated especially for their beauty and hardiness. Some of its members are valuable food plants, including apples, pears, peaches, apricots, and plums. Roses, flowering cherries, spirea, mountain ash, firethorn, and hawthorn are other familiar members of this order.

"Major Botanical Gardens and Arboretums" in chapter 11

Biological World

BOTANICAL NAMES OF PLANTS

The abbreviation "sp." following a genus indicates that the common name refers to all species of that genus.

Common Name	Botanical Name	Common Name	Botanical Name
Acacia, giraffe	*Acacia giraffae*	Asparagus, garden	*Asparagus officinalis*
Adder's-tongue	*Erythronium sibiricum*	Aspen, European	*Populus tremula*
	Ophioglossum vulgatum islandicum	quaking	*P. tremuloides*
		Aster	*Aster* sp.
Alder, European	*Alnus glutinosa*	Attalea	*Attalea funifera*
hazel	*A. rugosa*	Avocado, American	*Persea americana*
red	*A. ruba*	Balloon vine	*Cardiospermum halicacabum*
Alfalfa	*Medicago sativa*	Balsam, garden	*Impatiens balsamina*
Almond	*Prunus amygdalus*	Barley	*Hordeum vulgare*
Aloe	*Aloe* sp.	Bean, broad	*Vicia faba*
Amaryllis	*Amaryllis* sp.	kidney	*Phaseolus vulgaris*
Angelica	*Angelica polyclada*	sieva	*P. lunatus*
garden	*A. archangelica*	Beech, American	*Fagus grandifolia*
Apple	*Malus pumila*	European	*F. sylvatica*
	M. sylvestris	Beet, common	*Beta vulgaris*
Apricot	*Prunus armeniaca*	Birch, European white	*Betula pendula*
Arborvitae, eastern	*Thuja occidentalis*	paper	*B. papyrifera*
giant	*T. plicata*	sweet	*B. lenta*
Arum, East Asian	*Pinellia ternata*	white	*B. populifolia*
Ash, European	*Fraxinus excelsior*	yellow	*B. lutea*
green	*F. pennsylvanica*	Blackberry	*Rubus* sp.
white	*F. americana*	Bladderpod	*Lesquerella densipila*

continues

Botanical Names of Plants, Continued

Common Name	Botanical Name	Common Name	Botanical Name
Blood-lily, Katharine	*Haemanthus katharinae*	Cocklebur, oriental	*Xanthium orientale*
Blueberry, highbush	*Vaccinium corymbosum*	Coconut	*Cocos nucifera*
Brake, sword	*Pteris ensiformis*	Coffee, Arabian	*Coffea arabica*
Bryony, white	*Bryonia alba*	Coneflower, pinewoods	*Rudbeckia bicolor*
Buckwheat	*Fagopyrum sagittatum*	Coreopsis, goldenwave	*Coreopsis drummondii*
Buttercup, creeping	*Ranunculus repens*	lance	*C. lanceolata*
Cabbage	*Brassica oleracea*	plains	*C. tinctoria*
	B. oleracea capitata	Corn	*Zea mays*
Kerguelen	*Pringlea antiscorbutica*	Cornflower	*Centaurea cyanus*
Cacao	*Theobroma cacao*	Coronilla, crownvetch	*Coronilla varia*
Calotrope, fantan	*Calotropis procera*	Cosmos	*Cosmos* sp.
Capeberry, South African	*Myrica cordifolia*	Cotton, Levant	*Gossypium herbaceum*
Carpotroche	*Carpotroche brasiliensis*	Sea Island	*G. barbadense*
Carrot	*Daucus carota*	upland	*G. hirsutum*
Cashew	*Anacardium occidentale*	Coventry bells	*Campanula trachelium*
Castor bean	*Ricinus communis*	Cowpea	*Vigna glabra*
Catalpa, Chinese	*Catalpa ovata*	yard-long	*V. sesquipedalis*
northern	*C. speciosa*	common	*V. sinensis*
Cedar	*Cedrus* sp.	Crotalaria	*Crotalaria vitellina*
California incense	*Libocedrus decurrens*	Croton, purging	*Croton tiglium*
Celery, garden	*Apium graveolens dulce*	Cucumber	*Cucumis sativus*
wild	*A. graveolens*	Currant, European black	*Ribes nigrum*
Chaulmoogra tree	*Gynocardia odorata*	red	*R. sativum*
common	*Hydnocarpus anthelmintica*	Cypress, Arizona	*Cupressus arizonica*
wight	*H. wightiana*	bald	*Taxodium distichum*
Cherry, black	*Prunus serotina*	Dahlia	*Dahlia* sp.
mazzard	*P. avium*	Dandelion	*Taraxacum officinale*
pin	*P. pennsylvanica*	Daphne	*Daphne* sp.
Chestnut, Chinese	*Castanea mollissima*	Date	*Phoenix dactylifera*
common horse-	*Aesculus hippocastanum*	Davallia, Fiji	*Davallia fejeensis*
Chickpea, gram	*Cicer arietinum*	Desert willow	*Chilopsis linearis*
Chinaberry	*Melia azedarach*	Dock, curly	*Rumex crispus*
Chrysanthemum, corn	*Chrysanthemum segetum*	Dogbane	*Apocynum* sp.
Pyrenees	*C. maximum*	Dogwood, cornelian cherry	*Cornus mas*
Cinchona, ledgerbark	*Cinchona ledgeriana*	flowering	*C. florida*
Clarkia, rose	*Clarkia elegans*	Dollar plant	*Lunaria annua*
Clover, alsike	*Trifolium hybridum*	Douglas fir	*Pseudotsuga menziesii*
burdock	*T. lappaceum*	common	*P. taxifolia*
crimson	*T. incarnatum*	Eggplant	*Solanum melongena*
Egyptian	*T. alexandrinum*	garden	*S. melongena esculentum*
Persian	*T. resupinatum*	Elm, American	*Ulmus americana*
red	*T. pratense*	Endive	*Cichorium endivia*
strawberry	*T. fragiferum*	Erysimum, plains	*Erysimum asperum*
subterranean	*T. subterraneum*	Eucalyptus	*Eucalyptus* sp.
uckling	*T. dubium*	Euphorbia, snow-on-	*Euphorbia marginata*
yellow sweet	*Melilotus officinalis*	the-mountain	
white	*Trifolium repens*	False-cypress, Lawson's	*Chamaecyparis lawsoniana*
white sweet	*Melilotus alba*	nootka	*C. nootkatensis*
Clubmoss, common	*Lycopodium clavatum*		

Common Name	Botanical Name	Common Name	Botanical Name
Fern, common staghorn	*Platycerium bifurcatum*	reed canary	*Phalaris arundinacea*
common sword	*Nephrolepis exaltata*	Sudan	*Sorghum vulgare sudanense*
filmy	*Hymenophyllum atrovirens*	Hackberry, common	*Celtis occidentalis*
grape	*Botrychium virginianum*	Hart's-tongue	*Phyllitis scolopendrium*
holly	*Crytomium falcatum*	Hemlock, eastern	*Tsuga canadensis*
lady	*Athyrium filix-femina*	western	*T. heterophylla*
maidenhair	*Adiantum pedatum*	Hemp	*Cannabis sativa*
pine	*Anemia adiantifolia*	Hibiscus, kenaf	*Hibiscus cannabinus*
royal	*Osmunda regalis*	Hickory, shagbark	*Carya ovata*
tropical	*Gleichenia flabellata*	Holly, American	*Ilex opaca*
water	*Azolla pinnata*	English	*I. aquifolium*
wood	*Thelypteris normalis*	Hollyhock	*Althaea rosea*
Fescue, alta	*Festuca elatior arundinacea*	Horsetail, common	*Equisetum arvense*
meadow	*F. elatior*	Hyssop, hedge	*Gratiola sp.*
red	*F. rubra*	Indigo	*Indigofera sp.*
Fig	*Ficus carica*	Iris, blue flag	*Iris versicolor*
Filbert	*Corylus sp.*	German	*I. germanica*
Fir, cascades	*Abies amabilis*	grass	*I. graminea*
grand	*A. grandis*	Ironweed, kinka oil	*Vernonia anthelmintica*
noble	*A. procera*	Jacaranda	*Jacaranda sp.*
red	*A. magnifica*	Jimsonweed	*Datura stramonium*
white	*A. concolor*	Juniper, Savin	*Juniperus sabina*
Flax, common	*Linum usitatissimum*	Kale	*Brassica oleracea acephala*
Forget-me-not	*Myosotis sp.*	Kamala tree	*Mallotus philippinensis*
Foxglove, common	*Digitalis purpurea*	Knotweed, prostrate	*Polygonum aviculare*
Grecian	*D. lanata*	Lamb's quarter	*Chenopodium album*
Frenchweed	*Thlaspi arvense*	Larch, western	*Larix occidentalis*
Ginkgo	*Ginkgo biloba*	Larkspur, rocket	*Delphinium ajacis*
Gladiolus, common	*Gladiolus hortulanus*	Lemon	*Citrus limon*
horticultural		Lentil	*Lens culinaris*
Gooseberry, Chinese	*Actinidia chinensis*	Lespedeza, common	*Lespedeza striata*
Gourd, snake	*Trichosanthes sp.*	Korean	*L. stipulacea*
Grape, European	*Vitis vinifera*	wand	*L. intermedia*
fox	*V. labrusca*	Lettuce	*Lactuca sativa*
roundleaf	*Ribes rotundifolium*	Licania	*Licania rigida*
Grass, Bermuda	*Cynodon dactylon*	Lilac, common	*Syringa vulgaris*
buffalo	*Buchloe dactyloides*	Lily, regal	*Lilium regale*
Canada blue-	*Pao compressa*	Linden, American	*Tilia americana*
canary	*Phalaris canariensis*	Litsea	*Litsea sp.*
cocksfoot orchard	*Dactylis glomerata*	Locust, black	*Robinia pseudoacacia*
colonial bent-	*Argostis tenuis*	Lotus, East Indian	*Nelumbo nucifea*
common carpet-	*Axonopus affinis*	Lupine	*Lupinus arcticus*
crested wheat-	*Asgropyron cristatum*	tree	*L. angustifolius*
dallis	*Paspalum dilatatum*	Macadamia,	*Macadamia ternifolia*
desert wheat-	*Agropyron desertorum*	Queenslandnut	
Italian rye-	*Lolium multiflorum*	Magnolia, great-leaved	*Magnolia macrophylla*
Johnson	*Sorghum halepense*	southern	*M. grandiflora*
Kentucky blue-	*Poa pratensis*	Malope	*Malope trifida*
perennial rye-	*Lolium perenne*	Mango, common	*Mangifera indica*
quack	*Agropyron repens*		

continues

Botanical Names of Plants, Continued

Common Name	Botanical Name	Common Name	Botanical Name
Maple, red	*Acer rubrum*	Pecan	*Carya illinoensis*
silver	*A. saccharinum*	Peony, fernleaf	*Paeonia tenuifolia*
sugar	*A. saccharum*	Pepper, bush red	*Capsicum frutescens*
Marattia	*Marattia salicina*	Pepperwort	*Marsilea minuta*
Marbleseed, western	*Onosmodium occidentale*	Perilla, common	*Pefrilla frutescens*
Marigold	*Tagetes* sp.	Persimmon, common	*Diospyros virginiana*
winter cape	*Dimorphoteca aurantiaca*	Petunia	*Petunia* sp.
Meadowrue, Sierra	*Thalictrum polycarpum*	Phlox, Drummond	*Phlox drummondii*
Milkweed, common	*Asclepias syriaca*	Pine, Austrian	*Pinus nigra*
Millet, pearl	*Pennisetum glaucum*	eastern white	*P. strobus*
Morning glory, common	*Ipomoea purpurea*	jack	*P. banksiana*
orizaba	*I. orizabensis*	loblolly	*P. taeda*
Muskmelon	*Cucumis melo*	longleaf	*P. palustris*
Mustard, black	*Brassica nigra*	ponderosa	*P. ponderosa*
white	*B. hirta*	shore	*P. contorta*
Nasturtium	*Tropaeolum* sp.	shortleaf	*P. echinata*
Niger seed	*Guizotia abyssinica*	slash	*P. caribea*
Oak, black	*Quercus velutina*	sugar	*P. lambertiana*
English	*Q. robur*	western white	*P. monticola*
scarlet	*Q. coccinea*	Pineapple	*Ananas comosus*
southern red	*Q. falcata*	Pink, clove	*Dianthus caryophyllus*
white	*Q. alba*	Pistachio	*Pistacia* sp.
Oat, common	*Avena sativa*	Plum, garden	*Prunus domestica*
Okra	*Hibiscus esculentus*	Japanese	*P. salicina*
Olive	*Olea europaea sativa*	Podocarpus	*Podocarpus* sp.
common	*O. europaea*	Polypody, rock	*Polypodium virginianum*
Oncoba, gorli	*Oncoba echinata*	Pomegranate, common	*Punica granatum*
Onion, garden	*Allium cepa*	Poplar, eastern	*Populus deltoides*
Orange, sweet	*Citrus sinensis*	Mongolian	*P. suaveolens*
trifoliate	*Poncirus trifoliata*	yellow, or tulip tree	*Liriodendron tulipfera*
Palm, African oil	*Elaeis guineensis*	Poppy, corn	*Papaver rhoeas*
Pansy, wild	*viola tricolor*	opium	*P. somniferum*
Parinarium	*Parinarium* sp.	oriental	*P. orientale*
Parsley	*Petroselinum crispum*	Portulaca, common	*Portulaca grandiflora*
common curly	*P. latifolium*	Potato	*Solanum tuberosum*
Parsnip	*Pastinaca sativa*	Primrose, evening	*Oenothera biennis*
Pea, field	*Pisum sativum arvense*	Lemarck	*O. lamarckiana*
garden	*P. sativum*	Pumpkin	*Cucurbita pepo*
sweet	*Lathyrus odoratus*	Purslane, common	*Portulaca oleracea*
Peach	*Prunus persica*	Pycnanthus, akomu	*Pycnanthus kambo*
Peanut	*Arachis hypogaea*	Quillwort	*Isoetes braunii*
Pear	*Pyrun communis*	Radish, garden	*Raphanus sativus*
Peavine, flat	*Lathyrus sylvestris*		

Common Name	Botanical Name	Common Name	Botanical Name
Rape, bird	*Brassica campestris*	Sugarcane	*Saccharum officinarum*
winter	*B. napus*	Sumac	*Rhus* sp.
Red cedar, eastern	*Juniperus virginiana*	Sunflower, common	*Helianthus annuus*
Redtop	*Agrostis alba*	Sweetcane	*Saccharum spontaneum*
Redwood	*Sequoia sempervirens*	Sweetgum, American	*Liquidambar styraciflua*
Rhododendron, catawba	*Rhododendron catawbiense*	Sweet potato	*Ipomoea batatas*
Rhubarb, garden	*Rheum rhaponticum*	Sweet William	*Dianthus barbatus*
medicinal	*R. officinale*	Tallow wood	*Ximenia americana*
sorrel	*R. palmatum*		*X. caffra*
Rice	*Oryza sativa*	Tara vine	*Taraktogenos kurzii*
Rose, cabbage	*Rosa centifolia*	Tetradenia, Asian	*Tetradenia glauca*
Rubber, pará	*Hevea brasiliensis*	Timothy	*Phleum pratense*
Rutabaga	*Brassica napobrassica*	Tobacco	*Nicotiana glutinosa*
Rye	*Secale cereale*	common	*N. tabacum*
Safflower	*Carthamus tinctorius*	Tomato, common	*Lycopersicon esculentum*
Sage, garden	*Salvia officinalis*	Trefoil, bird's foot	*Lotus corniculatus*
scarlet	*S. splendens*	Tulip	*Tulipa* sp.
Salsify, vegetable-oyster	*Tragopogon porrifolius*	Tung oil tree	*Aleurites fordii*
Scammony, glorybind	*Convolvulus scammonia*	Tupelo, water	*Nyssa acquatica*
Scarlet runner	*Phaseolus coccineus*	Turnip	*Brassica rapa*
Sequoia, giant	*Sequoiadendron giganteum*	Vetch, common	*Vicia sativa*
	Sequoia gigantea	hairy	*V. villosa*
Sesame, oriental	*Sesamum indicum*	Hungarian	*V. pannonica*
Snapdragon, common	*Antirrhinum majus*	narrow leaf	*V. angustifolia*
Sorghum	*Sorghum bicolor*	one-flower	*V. articulata*
Soybean	*Glycine max*	purple	*V. benghalensis*
Spicebush, Japanese	*Lindera obtusiloba*	tiny	*V. hirsuta*
Spiderwort	*Tradescantia paludosa*	wooly pod	*V. dasycarpa*
Virginia	*T. virginiana*	Violet, field	*Viola arvensis*
Spikemoss	*Selaginella selaginoides*	Walnut, eastern black	*Juglans nigra*
Spinach	*Spinacia oleracea*	Waterlily	*Nymphaea alba*
Spruce, Norway	*Picea abies*	Watermelon	*Citrullus vulgaris*
red	*P. rubens*	Waterweed, Canadian	*Elodea canadensis*
Sitka	*P. sitchensis*	Wheat	*Triticum aestivum*
white	*P. glauca*	Willow, basket	*Salix viminalis*
Spurge, South American	*Sebastiania fruticosa*	big catkin	*S. gracilistyla*
Spurry, corn	*Spergula avensis*	black	*S. nigra*
Sterculia, hazel	*Sterculia foetida*	pussy	*S. discolor*
Stillingia	*Stillingia* sp.	white	*S. alba*
Stock, common	*Matthiola incana*	Yellow trumpet, Florida	*Stenolobium stans*
Strawberry, chiloe	*Fragaria chiloensis*	Yew, English	*Taxus baccata*
pine	*F. ananassa*	Pacific	*T. brevifolia*
Strophanthus	*Strophanthus glaber*	Yucca	*Yucca* sp.
arrow poison	*S. sarmentosus*	Zinnia, oblong leaf	*Zinnia angustifolia*

Biological World

GROUND COVERS

Common Name	Botanical Name
Sunlit Areas	
Pussytoes	*Antennaria neodioica* (1, 6)
Bearberry	*Arctostaphylos uva-ursi* (1, 2, 3, 6)
Cranberry cotoneaster	*Cotoneaster apiculata* (1)
Bearberry cotoneaster	*Cotoneaster dammeri* and *cultivars* (1)
Purpleleaf wintercreeper	*Euonymus colorata* (3, 4, 6)
Creeping juniper	*Juniperus horizontalis* and *cultivars* (6)
Japanese juniper	*Juniperus procumbens Nana* (4, 6)
Hall's honeysuckle	*Lonicera japonica Halliona* (3, 4, 6)
Pachistima	*Pachistima canbyi* (1, 2, 6)
Wineleaf cinquefoil	*Potentilla tridentata* (1, 2, 6)
Cinquefoil	*Potentilla verna Nana* (1, 5)
Stonecrop	*Sedum species* (5, 6)
Barren strawberry	*Waldsteinia ternata* (1, 3, 6)
Shade	
Carpet bugle	*Ajuga reptans* and *cultivars* (3, 4)
Lily of the valley	*Convallaria majalis* (4, 5)
Wintercreeper	*Euonymus fortunei* varieties (3, 4, 6)
English ivy	*Hedera helix* and *cultivars* (4, 6)
Plantain lily	*Hosta species* (5)
Lily turn	*Liriope spicata* (6)
Japanese spurge	*Pachysandra terminalis* (2, 6)
Periwinkle or myrtle	*Vinca minor* and *cultivars* (3, 6)

1. Requires well-drained soil
2. Requires acid soil
3. Good in sunlit areas or shade
4. Confine; may grow out of bounds
5. Herbaceous
6. Foliage retention in winter

VINES FOR SPECIAL USES

Common Name	Botanical Name
Five-leaf akebia	*Akebia quinata* (1, 2, 3, 4)
Virgin's-bower	*Clematis species* and *hybrids* (1, 2, 3, 4)
Wintercreeper	*Euonymus fortunei* (2, 3)
English ivy	*Hedera helix* and *cultivars* (2)
Climbing hydrangea	*Hydrangea petiolaris* (1, 2)
Boston ivy	*Parthenocissus tricuspidata* (2)
Japanese wisteria	*Wisteria floribunda* (1, 2, 3, 4)

1. Flowering
2. Wall cover
3. Screening
4. Trellis

Go to "Treatment for Health Emergencies: Poisoning: Plant Poisons" and "Poison Control Centers" in chapter 17

POISONOUS CULTIVATED AND WILD PLANTS

The following chart lists 50 poisonous plants. It tells which portions, or areas, of the plant are toxic, describes symptoms of the illnesses they cause, and indicates which plants are or may be fatal.

Plants	Toxic Portions	Symptoms of Illness; Degree of Toxicity
Autumn crocus	Bulbs	Nausea, vomiting, diarrhea; may be fatal.
Azalea	All parts	Nausea, vomiting, depression, breathing difficulty, prostration, coma; fatal.
Belladonna	Young plants, seeds	Nausea, twitching muscles, paralysis; fatal.
Bittersweet	Leaves, seeds, roots	Vomiting, diarrhea, chills, convulsions, coma.
Bleeding heart (Dutchman's-breeches)	Foliage, roots	Nervous symptoms, convulsions.
Buttercups	All parts	Digestive system injury.
Caladium	All parts	Intense burning and irritation of the tongue and mouth; can be fatal if the base of the tongue swells, blocking air passage of the throat.
Castorbean	Seeds, foliage	Burning in mouth, convulsions; fatal.
Cherry	Twigs, foliage	Gasping, excitement, prostration.
Daffodil	Bulbs	Nausea, vomiting, diarrhea; may be fatal.
Daphne	Berries (red or yellow)	Severe burns to mouth and digestive tract followed by coma; fatal.
Delphinium	Young plants, seeds	Nausea, twitching muscles, paralysis; fatal.
Dumbcane (Dieffenbachia)	All parts	Intense burning and irritation of the tongue and mouth; fatal if the base of the tongue swells, blocking air passage of the throat.
Elderberry	Roots	Nausea and digestive upset.
Elephant ear	All parts	Intense burning and irritation of the tongue and mouth; fatal if the base of the tongue swells, blocking air passage of the throat.
English holly	Berries	Severe gastroenteritis.
English ivy	Leaves, berries	Stomach pains, labored breathing, possible coma.
Foxglove	Leaves, seeds, flowers	Irregular heartbeat and pulse, usually accompanied by digestive upset and mental confusion; may be fatal.
Goldenchain	All parts, especially seeds	Excitement, staggering convulsions, coma; may be fatal.
Horse chestnut	All parts	Nausea, twitching muscles, sometimes paralysis.
Hyacinth	Bulbs	Nausea, vomiting, diarrhea; may be fatal.
Hydrangea	Buds, leaves, branches	Severe digestive upset, gasping, convulsions; may be fatal.
Iris	Freshly underground portions	Severe but not usually serious digestive upset.
Jack-in-the-pulpit	All parts, especially roots	Intense irritation and burning of the tongue and mouth.
Jimson weed (thorn apple; datura)	All parts	Abnormal thirst, distortion of vision, delirium, incoherence, coma; may be fatal.
Larkspur	Young plants, seeds	Nausea, twitching muscles, paralysis; fatal.
Laurel	All parts	Nausea, vomiting, depression, breathing difficulty, prostration, coma; fatal.
Lily of the valley	Leaves, flowers	Irregular heartbeat and pulse usually accompanied by digestive upset and mental confusion; may be fatal.
Mayapple	Unripe apples, leaves, and roots	Diarrhea, severe digestive upset.
Mistletoe	All parts, especially berries	Fatal
Monkshood	All parts, especially roots	Digestive upset and nervous excitement; juice in plant parts is fatal.

continues

Poisonous Cultivated and Wild Plants, Continued

Plants	Toxic Portions	Symptoms of Illness; Degree of Toxicity
Morning glory	Seeds	Large amounts cause severe mental disturbances; fatal.
Mushrooms, wild	All parts of many varieties	Fatal.
Narcissus	Bulbs	Nausea, vomiting, diarrhea; may be fatal.
Nightshade	All parts, especially unripe berries	Intense digestive disturbances and nervous symptoms; often fatal.
Oak	Foliage, acorns	Gradual kidney failure.
Oleander	All parts	Severe digestive upset, heart trouble, contact dermatitis; fatal.
Philodendron	All parts	Intense burning and irritation of the tongue and mouth; fatal if the base of the tongue swells, blocking air passage of the throat.
Poinsettia	All parts	Severe digestive upset; fatal.
Poison hemlock	All parts	Stomach pains, vomiting, paralysis of the central nervous system; may be fatal.
Poison ivy and oak	All parts	Intense itching, watery blisters, red rash.
Poppy	Foliage, roots	Nervous symptoms, convulsions.
Potato	Foliage, green parts of vegetable	Intense digestive disturbances, nervous symptoms.
Privet	Berries, leaves	Mild to severe digestive disturbances; may be fatal.
Rhododendron	All parts	Nausea, vomiting, depression, breathing difficulty, prostration, coma; fatal.
Rhubarb	Leaf blade	Kidney disorder, convulsions, coma; fatal.
Rosary pea	Seeds, foliage	Burning in mouth, convulsions; fatal.
Rue	All parts	Skin irritation; if ingested, vomiting, convulsions, may be fatal
Snowdrop	Bulbs	Vomiting, nervous excitement.
Tomato	Vines	Digestive upset, nervous disorders.
Wisteria	Seeds, pods	Mild to severe digestive disturbances.

PLANT CULTIVATION

WHEN TO PLANT

Seeds, seedlings, and young plants should be planted outdoors according to the instructions specific to their variety. Here are general guidelines on when to plant what.

Plant Type	Variety	Warmer Zones	Cooler Zones
Vegetables	tender	spring, summer	late spring
	hardy	fall, winter	spring, summer
Flowers	perennials	fall, winter, spring	spring, late summer
	annuals	year-round	spring, summer
	bulbs, tender	spring	spring
	bulbs, hardy	fall	fall
Woody Plants	shrubs	fall, winter, spring	spring, fall
	trees	fall, winter, spring	spring, fall

USDA HARDINESS ZONES

ALASKA

HAWAII

Range Average Annual Minimum
Temperatures for Each Zone

Zone	1	Below -50°F
Zone	2	-50° to -40°F
Zone	3	-40° to -30°F
Zone	4	-30° to -20°F
Zone	5	-20° to -10°F
Zone	6	-10° to 0°F
Zone	7	0° to 10°F
Zone	8	10° to 20°F
Zone	9	20° to 30°F
Zone	10	30° to 40°F
Zone	11	Above 50°F

FROST DATES

SPRING

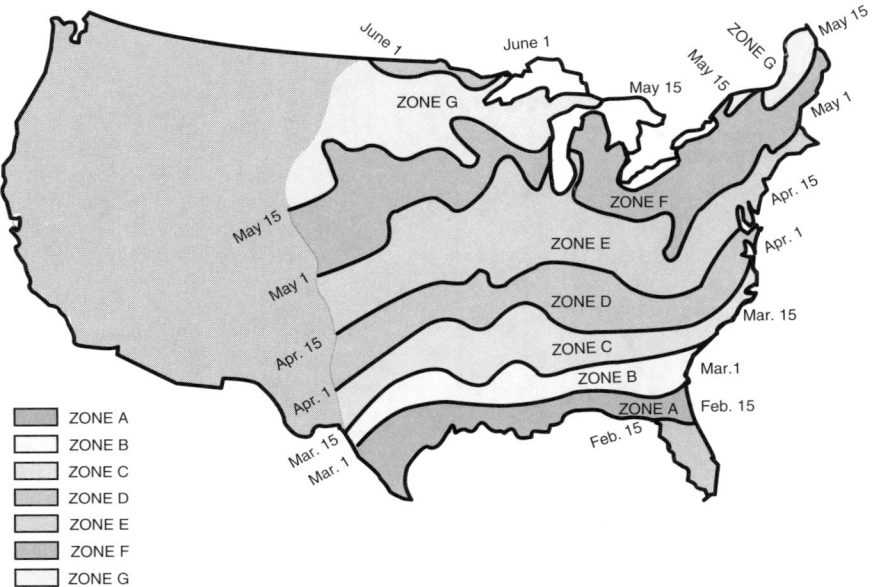

A zone map of the United States based on the average dates of the latest killing frost in spring east of the Rocky Mountains. Source: United States Department of Agriculture.

AUTUMN

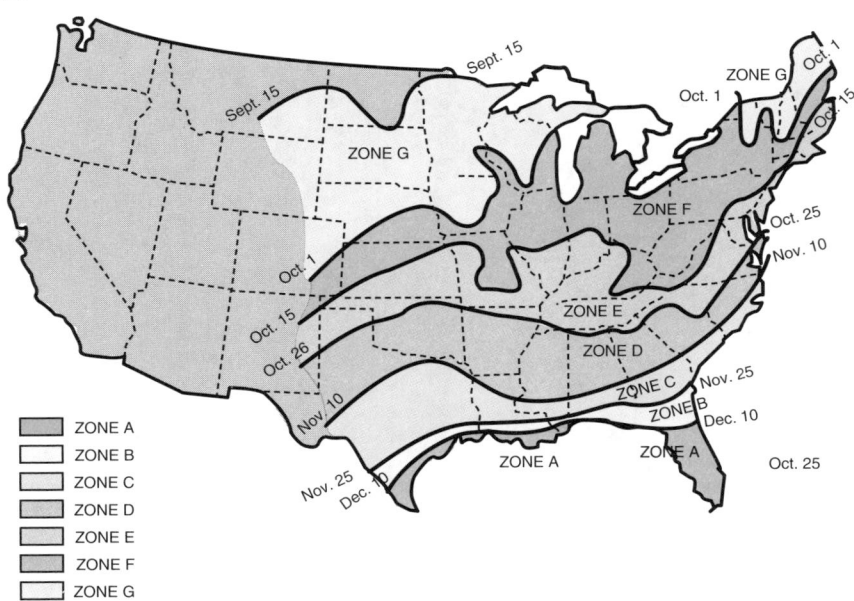

A zone map of the central and eastern part of the United States based on the average dates of the first killing frost in autumn. Source: United States Department of Agriculture.

GERMINATION TABLES

ANNUAL FLOWERS

Flower	Approximate Number of Days until Germination	Flower	Approximate Number of Days until Germination
Acrolinium	8–10	Gaillardia	12–15
Ageratum	7–11	Gomphrena	20–25
Alyssum, sweet	10–13	Helichrysum	5–10
Browallia	18–20	Larkspur	15–20
Cacalia	8–12	Lupine	25–30
Calendula	10–12	Marigold	5–8
California poppy	5–10	Nicotiana	20–25
Candytuft	6–9	Petunia	18–20
Canterbury bell	12–15	Phlox Drummondi	20–25
Celosia (coxcomb)	20–25	Pinks	5–8
Centaurea (ragged robin)	5–20	Portulaca	18–20
Chrysanthemum	6–8	Scabiosa	18–20
Cosmos	5–15	Snapdragon	20–25
Cynoglossum	11–15	Sweetpea	15–20
Flax	13–16	Verbena	8–10
Four-o'clock	12–15	Zinnia	5–8

VEGETABLE GARDEN PLANTS

Vegetable	Approximate Number of Days until Germination	Vegetable	Approximate Number of Days until Germination
Asparagus	21–28	Kohlrabi	6–8
Beans, bush	6–10	Lettuce	6–10
Beans, bush lima	6–10	Muskmelon	6–10
Beans, pole	6–10	Mustard	4–5
Beans, pole lima	7–12	Okra	15–20
Beets	7–10	Onion	8–12
Broccoli	6–10	Parsley	18–24
Brussels sprouts	6–10	Parsnip	12–18
Cabbage	6–10	Peas	6–10
Cabbage, Chinese	6–10	Pepper	10–14
Carrots	10–15	Pumpkin	6–10
Cauliflower	6–10	Radish	4–6
Celery	12–20	Rhubarb	12–14
Chard, Swiss	7–10	Rutabaga	4–7
Collards	6–10	Spinach	6–12
Corn, sweet	7–12	Squash, bush	6–10
Cress, garden	4–5	Squash, vine	6–10
Cucumber	6–8	Tomato	6–10
Eggplant	10–15	Turnip	4–7
Endive	8–12	Watermelon	8–12

Biological World

COMMON BIOLOGICAL TERMS

abaxial   Facing away from the stem or central axis of a plant or animal.

abiogenesis   A theory that living things can develop from nonliving material, as in spontaneous generation.

adaptation   The modification of an organism or part of an organism to adjust to new conditions or a new environment, as in adjustment of the eyes to bright light.

adenosine triphosphate (ATP)   A chemical compound present in all living cells that provides energy derived from food or sunlight for processes that require activity, such as contraction of a muscle or conduction of a nerve impulse.

The largest dinosaur egg ever discovered came from the Hypselosaurus. Measuring 1 foot by 10 inches, it had a liquid capacity of almost 6 pints.

appendage   A structure attached to a larger structure or part of an organism. Arms, legs, and other projections of body areas are examples of appendages.

ATP   *See* **adenosine triphosphate.**

bacteria   Tiny, one-celled plant organisms that are generally parasitic and lacking in chlorophyll. They are commonly involved in processes of fermentation and decay, and many species are the cause of diseases in humans and animals.

bladder   A saclike organ with a membranous wall that serves to collect or hold a fluid or gas. An example is the urinary bladder or the air bladder of marine animals.

blastula   A stage in the development of an embryo after the early phase of cell division when the cells form a hollow ball. The wall of the sphere is a single layer of cells, the blastoderm. The various organs, such as the gut, nervous system, and appendages, eventually evolve from cells of the blastula.

bud   An undeveloped appendage of an organism. A plant bud may develop into flowers or leaves while the bud of an animal embryo may become an arm, leg, or wing. Some bacteria and yeast cells reproduce by issuing buds, each of which becomes a new organism.

bug   Any of a large number of creeping or flying insects, mainly of the order Hemiptera. Examples of "true bugs" include bed bugs, cinch bugs, squash bugs, and giant water bugs.

calyx   A cuplike portion of a plant or animal organ. Examples include the sepals, or outermost parts of a flower, and the funnel-shaped part of a kidney that collects urine as it drains toward the bladder.

carnivore   Any meat-eating animal, particularly a member of the order Carnivora, which includes wolves, coyotes, bears, dogs, and cats.

cell   The basic structural unit of living things. It usually consists of a membranous wall containing protoplasm, a souplike mixture of proteins, enzymes, and other organic chemicals needed for survival and reproduction. Most cells also contain a nucleus that in turn holds the DNA molecules, or genetic material, that control the various cell functions.

chlorophyll   Any of nearly a dozen kinds of green pigments present in most plant cells. Chlorophylls are able to convert the energy from sunlight into carbohydrates, which plants form from carbon dioxide and water present in the environment. The carbohydrates in turn become a source of energy for animals and humans after the plant material is eaten.

chromosome   A rod-shaped unit of DNA present in the nucleus of a cell that is capable of reproducing itself. It contains a portion of the genetic or hereditary traits of the species it represents. The number of chromosomes and their shapes and sizes vary among different species and sexes within a species. Human males, for example, possess a Y-shaped chromosome that is not normally present in female cells and that governs masculine physical traits.

deoxyribonucleic acid (DNA)   A large molecule of nucleic acid found in the nuclei, usually in the chromosomes, of living cells. DNA controls such functions as the production of protein molecules in the cell and carries the template for reproduction of all the inherited characteristics of its particular species.

DNA   *See* **deoxyribonucleic acid.**

embryo   The young of a species at a very early stage of development, such as the rudimentary plant that bursts forth from a seed when it germinates, or the bird that has not yet hatched from its egg. In mammals, the embryo stage occurs after the cells of the blastula begin to specialize for the development of the fetus.

endogenous   Pertaining to factors influencing an organism that originate within that organism, as distinguished from *exogenous* factors, such as environmental influences, that originate on the outside.

evolution   The process by which a species of plants or animals gradually develops over a period of many generations from a simpler to a more complex form of organism. The traits of the simpler organism are often continued into the more complex form of the same organism, as can be observed in the brain and other structures of the human body.

exogenous   *See* **endogenous.**

fauna   The animal life of a region or period of history.

female   The sex of an animal that produces ova and bears offspring.

fermentation   A process whereby complex carbohydrates or other organic substances are converted to other chemicals by the action of enzymes produced by molds, yeasts, or bacteria. An example is the conversion of sugars to alcohol.

fertilization   The union of a male and a female reproductive cell resulting in the formation of a new organism. The term is also used to describe the process or enrichment of the soil for growing crops.

flora   The plant life of a region or period of history.

genitalia   The reproductive sex organs of a male or female of the species, particularly structures on the outside of the body.

genotype   *See* **phenotype.**

genus   A subdivision of a biological family. It is composed of a group of related species, such as the genus *Canis,* which includes various species of dogs.

gonads   The male and female reproductive organs.

haploid   Half the number of chromosomes ordinarily present in the nucleus of a cell. During reproduction, the offspring receives a haploid number of chromosomes from each parent, making a full, or diploid, set.

herbaceous   Herblike, usually used to describe a plant in which persistent woody tissue does not develop.

herbivore   An animal that feeds entirely or mainly on plant materials.

hormone   A chemical secretion of a gland or other tissue that triggers an action in another gland or tissue in a different part of the body.

immunity   A quality of being able to resist an infectious disease.

inbreeding   The mating of closely related individuals, as in self-pollinating plants or animals that are brothers and sisters.

joint   An area between two parts or segments of an organism, such as the junction of two separate bones of an animal or the node of a plant.

karyotype   The general appearance of a set of chromosomes of an individual. Karyotype may be used to determine sex, genetic defects, and other chromosome-related factors.

kernel   The entire grain or seed of a cereal plant.

larva   The young, immature form of an organism that undergoes a change in structure to become an adult. The caterpillar and the maggot are examples of larvae.

leaf   An outgrowth of a stem of a plant, usually green, in which many living functions, such as photosynthesis, respiration, and food and water storage, take place.

lipid   Any of a group of fatty substances, including oils and waxes, produced by plant or animal tissues. Lipids generally are insoluble in water, but they can be dissolved in alcohol, benzene, or similar organic solvents.

male   The sex of an animal that produces spermatozoa or of a plant that produces pollen.

mammal   A warm-blooded, air-breathing vertebrate of the class Mammalia, possessing hair and mammary glands.

Mendel's laws   A series of natural principles of heredity discovered by Gregor Mendel. They govern such factors as dominant and recessive traits resulting from the interaction of genes that are inherited in pairs.

metabolism   The chemical and energy changes associated with the consumption of food and oxygen, the production of heat, and the calories used in physical activity.

natural selection   A principle proposed by Charles Darwin to explain the ability of various species to adapt to changes in the environment. Called "survival of the fittest," the theory offered an explanation for the survival of some species and extinction of others.

neuron   The structural and functional unit of a nerve, including the cell body and its axon and dendrite fibers.

nucleus   A structure present in most plant and animal cells. It contains the chromosomes and ribonucleic acid (RNA) molecules that direct the cell's life functions.

osmosis   The diffusion of water through a semipermeable membrane from the side with a greater concentration of a solution to the side with a lesser concentration.

osseous   Pertaining to bones, as something composed of bone or resembling bone.

phenotype   The physical features or appearance of an individual, as distinguished from the genotype, or genetic composition of his or her cells. Two or more people with the same physical appearance may belong to the same phenotype.

pistil   The female sex structure of a plant, usually containing the ovary.

Protozoa   A phylum, or large group, of one-celled animals.

receptor   Any cell or group of cells that is the target of a stimulus, such as the retina of the eye.

regeneration   The ability of some plants and animals to restore or replace lost tissues or structures, such as a claw or feather.

stamen   The pollen-producing structure of a plant. It usually consists of an anther, the actual pollen producer, on the tip of a flower filament.

stimulus   An environmental influence, such as a chemical or physical irritant, that induces or brings about a response in a cell or organism.

symbiosis   A relationship in which two organisms live together for the mutual benefit of each.

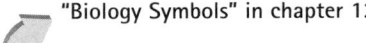

"Biology Symbols" in chapter 12

Go to

terrestrial   Pertaining to plant or animal life on land rather than in water.

tissue   A group of cells with similar structures and functions.

tropism   The involuntary response of an organism to a stimulus, such as the response of a plant to gravity or sunlight.

vacuole   Any of the spaces scattered about the protoplasm of a cell, usually containing fluid.

zygote   The fertilized egg cell of a plant or animal.

ADDITIONAL SOURCES OF INFORMATION

ORGANIZATIONS AND SERVICES

American Horticultural Society
7931 E. Boulevard Dr.
Alexandria, VA 22308

American Society for the Prevention of Cruelty to Animals
424 E. 92nd St.
New York, NY 10028

American Veterinary Medical Association
1931 North Meacham Rd., Suite 100
Schaumburg, IL 60173-4360

Garden Club of America
598 Madison Ave.
New York, NY 10022

Men's Garden Clubs of America
5560 Merle Hay Rd.
Des Moines, IA 50323

National Wildlife Federation
1412 16th St., NW
Washington, DC 20036

The Nature Conservancy
4245 North Fairfax Drive, Suite 100
Arlington, VA 22203-1606

Sierra Club
85 Second St., 2nd Floor
San Francisco, CA 94105-3441

BOOKS

Ackerman, J. *Chance in the House of Fate: A Natural History of Heredity.* Houghton Mifflin, 2001.

American Kennel Club Staff. *The Complete Dog Book.* 18th ed. Howell, 1992.

Bell, P.R., and A.R. Hemsley. *Green Plants: Their Origin and Diversity.* Cambridge University Press, 2000.

Bondwell, Sally. *The American Animal Hospital Association of Dog Health and Care.* Quill, 1996.

Burton, M., and R. Burton. *International Wildlife Encyclopedia.* Marshall Cavendish, 2002.

Burton, R., and S.W. Kress. *The Audubon Backyard Birdwatcher: Birdfeeders and Bird Gardens.* Thunder Bay Press, 1999.

Carlson, D.G. *Cat Owner's Home Veterinary Handbook.* Hungry Minds, 1995.

Cutler, K.D., ed. *Burpee: The Complete Vegetable & Herb Gardener: A Guide to Growing Your Garden Organically.* Hungry Minds, 1997.

Day, David. *The Doomsday Book of Animals: A Natural History of Vanished Species.* Viking Penguin, 1983.

Diamond, Jared. *Guns, Germs, and Steel: The Fates of Human Societies.* Norton, 1999.

Ehrlich, Paul R., David S. Dobkin, and Darryl Wheye. *Birds In Jeopardy: The Imperiled and Extinct Birds of the United States and Canada, Including Hawaii and Puerto Rico.* Stanford University Press, 1992.

Forshaw, J., ed. *Encyclopedia of Birds.* 2nd ed. Academic Press, 1998.

Giffin, J.M., et al. *The Dog Owner's Home Veterinary Handbook.* Hungry Minds, 1999.

Gould, E., ed. *Encyclopedia of Mammals.* 2nd ed. Academic Press, 1998.

Biological World

Lane, D., and N. Ewart. *A–Z of Dog Diseases & Health Problems: Signs, Diagnoses, Causes, Treatment.* Hungry Minds, 1997.

Grizimek, Bernhard, ed. *Encyclopedia of Animals.* 15 vols. McGraw-Hill, 1990.

MacDonald, D.W., ed. *The Encyclopedia of Mammals.* Checkmark Books, 1995.

Mackey, Betty, et al. *The Gardener's Home Companion.* Macmillan, 1991.

Niklas, K.J. *The Evolutionary Biology of Plants.* University of Chicago Press, 1997.

Peterson, Roger T. *Peterson's First Guide to Wildflowers.* Houghton Mifflin, 1986.

Riley, Laura, and William Riley. *Guide to the National Wildlife Refuges.* Macmillan, 1992.

Sussman, Les. *The American Animal Hospital Association Encyclopedia of Cat Health and Care.* Quill, 1996.

Pollan, M. *The Botany of Desire: A Plant's-Eye View of the World.* Random House, 2001.

Raven, P.H., et al. *Biology of Plants.* W.H. Freeman, 1998.

Siegal, M., ed. *The Cornell Book of Cats: A Comprehensive and Authoritative Medical Reference for Every Cat and Kitten.* Villard Books, 1997.

Taylor, Norman. *Taylor's Master Guide to Gardening.* Houghton Mifflin, 1994.

Weiner, J. *The Beak of the Finch: The Story of Evolution in Our Time.* Vintage, 1995.

WEB SITES

American Veterinary Medical Association
http://www.avma.org

Academy of Natural Sciences of Philadelphia
http://www.acnatsci.org

American Museum of Natural History
http://www.amnh.org

Cornell Laboratory of Ornithology
http://www.birds.cornell.edu

National Audubon Society
http://www.audubon.org

National Museum of Natural History, Smithsonian
http://mnh.si.edu

Nature Conservancy
http://nature.org

Sierra Club
www.sierraclub.org

The World Conservation Union
http://www.iucn.org

Biological World

4

THE PHYSICAL SCIENCES, MATH, AND TECHNOLOGY

ASTRONOMY

PHASES OF THE MOON

The Moon is the closest natural body to the Earth. Eight phases of the Moon are visible because the Moon has no light of its own. Its daylight side reflects the light of the Sun. As pictured below at the new moon, the dark side of the Moon is turned toward the Earth, and the Moon cannot be seen. The second phase is a waxing crescent moon, followed by a half moon, or first quarter. A waxing gibbous moon is then succeeded by a full moon. The Moon then begins to wane, through a waning gibbous moon, a third (or last) quarter moon, a waning crescent moon, and back to a new moon again. The cycle takes 27.3 days to complete.

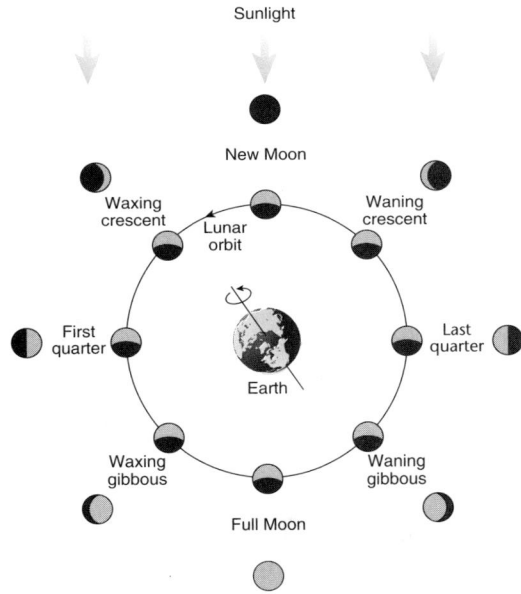

LUNAR AND SOLAR ECLIPSES

An eclipse occurs when a celestial body, such as the Earth or Moon, casts a shadow so that another celestial body seems to dim or disappear. As each of the celestial bodies is in constant motion with respect to the others, the alignment of the bodies is not always perfect. Totality during an eclipse rarely lasts more than a few minutes.

An eclipse of the Moon (lunar eclipse) occurs when the Sun, Earth, and Moon are in a straight line so that the Moon is in the shadow of Earth. It is visible from any point on the Earth facing the Moon at the time of the eclipse.

A total solar eclipse takes place when the Earth, Moon, and Sun are in alignment in such a way that the umbra of the shadow of the Moon reaches the Earth. (The *umbra* is the dark central part of the cone-shaped shadow projecting from the Moon to Earth during this phenomenon.) All the light of the Sun is blocked or eclipsed because of the Moon's position. The *penumbra* (the lighter shadow) shows a partial solar eclipse.

In an annular solar eclipse, the alignment is just the same as in a total solar eclipse, but the Moon is too far away from the Earth at the time for the umbra of the shadow to reach Earth. The circle of the Moon is not large enough to block our seeing the Sun, so a ring of light from the corona, or outer fringe, of the Sun can be seen surrounding the moon's circle.

The shadow of the Moon during a solar eclipse is visible only along an arc-shaped path on a portion of the Earth, and the shadow moves at a speed between 1,060 and 2,100 miles per hour, depending on the latitude of the shadow, the rotation of the Earth, and the speed of the Moon through its own orbit.

Because the Sun, Earth, and Moon travel in relatively predictable orbits, astronomers since the days of ancient Babylonia (700 B.C.) have been able to calculate the future dates on which the Sun, Earth, and Moon will once again be in alignment. Therefore, astronomers can forecast the time and place of eclipses many years in advance. For example, at regular intervals of 18 years, 9 to 11 days (depending on leap years), and 8 hours (a period of one saros), the Sun and Moon will return to the same orbital node relative to Earth. During one saros, there are usually 41 total or partial solar eclipses and 29 lunar eclipses, or an average of about 4 eclipses a year. But each successive solar eclipse is observed about 120 degrees to

Total Lunar Eclipse

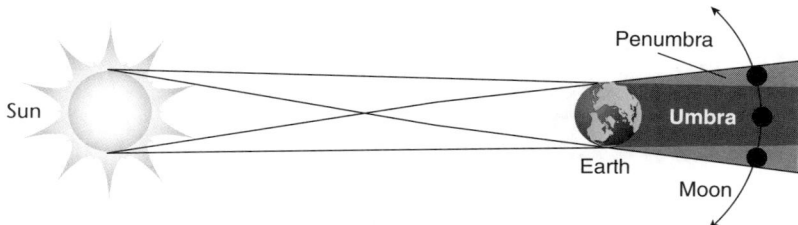

Annular Solar Eclipse

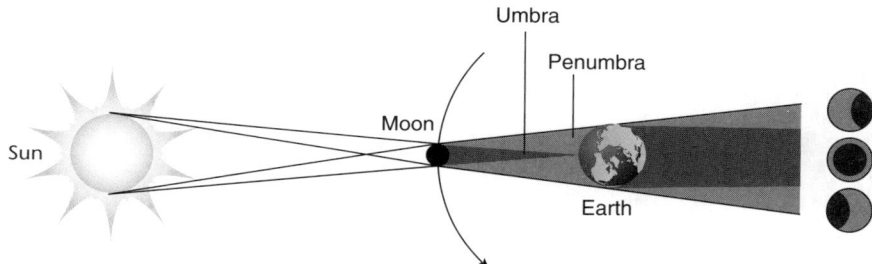

Total Solar Eclipse

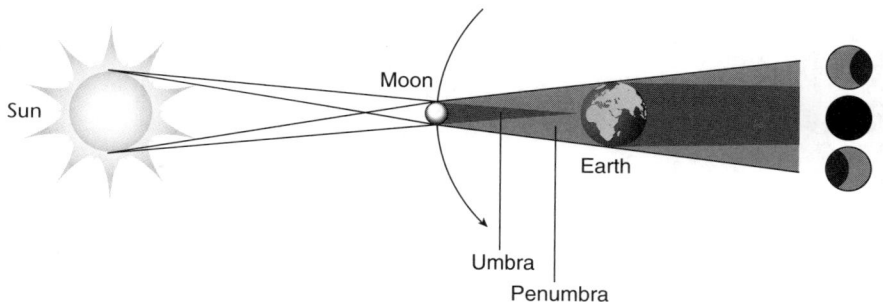

the west of the previous phenomenon and can be expected to recur at the same longitude on Earth after a period equivalent to three times the length of one saros. Each solar eclipse may affect an area only about 100 miles wide, and any given place on Earth can expect a total eclipse about once every 400 years.

"Reckoning Days and Hours" and "Calendars: The Seasons" in chapter 1

Go to

On rare occasions, sunlight can appear to be green. Known as a "green flash," this phenomenon occurs briefly when the Sun sets or rises on an extremely clear horizon. It is produced by the greater bending of green and blue rays as sunlight is refracted in the Earth's atmosphere.

Sciences

ALL LUNAR ECLIPSES, 1999–2020

Date	Mid-eclipse (Universal Time)	Type	Date	Mid-eclipse (Universal Time)	Type
1999 January 31	16:17	Penumbral	2010 June 26	11:38	Umbral
1999 July 28	11:34	Umbral	2010 December 21	08:17	Total
2000 January 21	04:43	Total	2011 June 15	20:12	Total
2000 July 16	13:56	Total	2011 December 10	14:32	Total
2001 January 9	20:21	Total	2012 June 4	11:03	Umbral
2001 July 5	14:55	Umbral	2012 November 28	14:33	Penumbral
2001 December 30	10:29	Penumbral	2013 April 25	20:07	Umbral
2002 May 26	12:03	Penumbral	2013 May 25	04:10	Penumbral
2002 June 24	21:27	Penumbral	2013 October 18	23:50	Penumbral
2002 November 20	01:46	Penumbral	2014 April 15	07:45	Total
2003 May 16	03:40	Total	2014 October 8	10:54	Total
2003 November 9	01:18	Total	2015 April 4	12:00	Total
2004 May 4	20:30	Total	2015 September 28	02:47	Total
2004 October 28	03:04	Total	2016 March 23	11:47	Penumbral
2005 April 24	09:55	Penumbral	2016 September 16	18:54	Penumbral
2005 October 17	12:03	Umbral	2017 February 11	00:44	Penumbral
2006 March 14	23:47	Penumbral	2017 August 7	18:20	Umbral
2006 September 7	18:51	Umbral	2018 January 31	13:30	Total
2007 March 3	23:21	Total	2018 July 27	20:22	Total
2007 August 28	10:37	Total	2019 January 21	05:12	Total
2008 February 21	03:26	Total	2019 July 16	21:31	Umbral
2008 August 16	21:10	Umbral	2020 January 10	19:10	Penumbral
2009 February 9	14:38	Penumbral	2020 June 5	19:25	Penumbral
2009 July 7	09:38	Penumbral	2020 July 5	04:30	Penumbral
2009 August 6	00:39	Penumbral	2020 November 30	09:43	Penumbral
2009 December 31	19:23	Umbral			

ALL SOLAR ECLIPSES, 1999–2020

Date	Type	Date	Type	Date	Type
1999 February 16	annular	2006 September 22	annular	2014 April 29	annular
1999 August 11	total	2007 March 19	partial	2014 October 23	partial
2000 February 5	partial	2007 September 11	partial	2015 March 20	total
2000 July 1	partial	2008 February 7	annular	2015 September 13	partial
2000 July 31	partial	2008 August 1	total	2016 March 9	total
2000 December 25	partial	2009 January 26	annular	2016 September 1	annular
2001 June 21	total	2009 July 22	total	2017 February 26	annular
2001 December 14	annular	2010 January 15	annular	2017 August 21	total
2002 June 10	annular	2010 July 11	total	2018 February 15	partial
2002 December 4	total	2011 January 4	partial	2018 July 13	partial
2003 May 31	annular	2011 June 1	partial	2018 August 11	partial
2003 November 23	total	2011 July 1	partial	2019 January 6	partial
2004 April 19	partial	2011 November 25	partial	2019 July 2	total
2004 October 14	partial	2012 May 20	annular	2019 December 26	annular
2005 April 8	partial	2012 November 13	total	2020 June 21	annular
2005 October 3	annular	2013 May 10	annular	2020 December 14	total
2006 March 29	total	2013 November 3	partial		

TOTAL ECLIPSES OF THE SUN, 1900–2000

Date	Approximate Duration (min:sec)	Course of Central Line
1900 May 28	2:10	Mexico, United States, Spain, North Africa
1901 May 18	6:17	Indian Ocean, Sumatra, Borneo, New Guinea
1903 September 21	2:02	Antarctica
1904 September 9	6:19	Pacific Ocean
1905 August 30	3:46	Canada, Spain, North Africa, Arabia
1907 January 14	2:24	Soviet Union, China
1908 January 3	4:20	Pacific Ocean
1908 December 23	0:12	South America, Atlantic Ocean, Indian Ocean
1909 June 17	0:24	Greenland, Russia
1910 May 9	4:14	Antarctica
1911 April 28	4:58	Pacific Ocean
1912 April 17	0:02	Atlantic Ocean, Europe, Russia
1912 October 10	2:02	Brazil, South Atlantic Ocean
1914 August 21	2:15	Greenland, Europe, Middle East
1916 February 3	2:36	Pacific Ocean, South America, Atlantic Ocean
1918 June 8	2:23	Pacific Ocean, United States
1919 May 29	6:50	South America, Atlantic Ocean, Africa
1921 October 1	1:52	Antarctica
1922 September 21	5:59	Indian Ocean, Australia
1923 September 10	3:37	Pacific Ocean, Central America
1925 January 24	2:32	Northeast United States, Atlantic Ocean
1926 January 14	4:11	Africa, Indian Ocean, Borneo
1927 June 29	0:50	England, Scandinavia, Arctic Ocean, Soviet Union
1928 May 19	—	(Umbra barely touched Antarctica)
1929 May 9	5:07	Indian Ocean, Malaya, Philippines
1930 April 28	0:01	Pacific Ocean, United States, Canada
1930 October 21	1:55	South Pacific Ocean
1932 August 31	1:45	Arctic Ocean, East Canada
1934 February 14	2:53	Borneo, Pacific Ocean
1936 June 19	2:31	Greece, Turkey, Soviet Union, Pacific Ocean
1937 June 8	7:04	Pacific Ocean, Peru
1938 May 29	4:04	South Atlantic Ocean
1939 October 12	1:32	Antarctica
1940 October 1	5:35	South America, Atlantic Ocean, Africa
1941 September 21	3:22	Soviet Union, China, Pacific Ocean
1943 February 4	2:39	Japan, Pacific Ocean, Alaska
1944 January 25	4:09	South America, Atlantic Ocean, Africa
1945 July 9	1:15	Canada, Greenland, Scandinavia, Soviet Union
1947 May 20	5:14	Argentina, Brazil, Central Africa
1948 November 1	1:56	Africa, Indian Ocean
1950 September 12	1:13	Arctic Ocean, Soviet Union, Pacific Ocean
1952 February 25	3:05	Africa, Arabia, Iran, Soviet Union

continues

Total Eclipses of the Sun, 1900–2000, Continued

Date	Approximate Duration (min:sec)	Course of Central Line
1954 June 30	2:35	United States, Canada, Scandinavia, Soviet Union
1955 June 20	7:08	Indian Ocean, Thailand, Pacific Ocean
1956 June 8	4:44	South Pacific Ocean
1957 October 23	—	(Umbra touched Antarctica)
1958 October 12	5:11	Pacific Ocean, Argentina
1959 October 2	3:01	Atlantic Ocean, Africa
1961 February 15	2:44	Europe, Soviet Union
1962 February 5	4:08	Borneo, New Guinea, Pacific Ocean
1963 July 20	1:40	Pacific Ocean, Alaska, Canada
1965 May 30	5:16	New Zealand, Pacific Ocean
1966 November 12	1:57	South America, Atlantic Ocean
1967 November 2	—	(Umbra touched Antarctica)
1968 September 22	0:40	Soviet Union
1970 March 7	3:28	Pacific Ocean, Mexico, Eastern United States
1972 July 10	2:36	Soviet Union, North Canada
1973 June 30	7:04	Atlantic Ocean, Central Africa, Indian Ocean
1974 June 20	5:08	Indian Ocean, Australia
1976 October 23	4:46	Africa, Indian Ocean, Australia
1977 October 12	2:37	Pacific Ocean, Colombia, Venezuela
1979 February 26	2:52	Northwest United States, Canada, Greenland
1980 February 16	4:08	Africa, Indian Ocean, India, China
1981 July 31	2:03	Soviet Union, Pacific Ocean
1983 June 11	5:11	Indian Ocean, New Guinea
1984 November 22	1:59	New Guinea, South Pacific Ocean
1985 November 12	1:59	Antarctica
1986 October 3	0:01	North Atlantic Ocean
1987 March 29	0:08	South Atlantic Ocean, Central Africa
1988 March 18	3:46	Sumatra, Borneo, Philippines
1990 July 22	2:33	Soviet Union, Pacific Ocean
1991 July 11	6:54	Hawaii, Mexico, South America
1992 June 30	5:20	South Atlantic Ocean
1994 November 3	4:15	Bolivia, Brazil, South Atlantic Ocean
1995 October 24	2:10	India, Southeast Asia, Indonesia
1997 March 9	2:50	Arctic Ocean, Russia
1998 February 26	4:08	Pacific Ocean, Venezuela, Atlantic Ocean
1999 August 11	2:23	Central Europe, Middle East, India

Sciences

Visitation Rights

A Closer Look

When the Luna 2 spacecraft—launched by the then-Soviet Union (now Russia) in 1959—impacted the surface of the Moon, exploration of other planetary bodies in our solar system began. Since that time, unmanned craft have visited all the planets except Pluto—and that may change in the near future.

Here is a brief list of the more famous flybys and landings on other planetary bodies:

Mercury   Mariner 10 was the first spacecraft to visit Mercury, making three flybys in 1974 and 1975 before running out of fuel.

Venus   In 1962, Mariner 2 became the first spacecraft to successfully fly by Venus. Twelve years later, Mariner 10 flew by Venus to gain a gravity assist to get to Mercury; on the way it took the first close-up images of cloud-shrouded Venus. Venera 7, launched by the Soviets, sent back surface data from Venus in 1970, becoming the first probe to do so; and by 1975, Venera 9 became the first spacecraft to land on the surface of another planet. (The spacecraft lasted only a few minutes, but was able to send back a few surface images). In 1978, Pioneer Venus made the first high-quality map of the planet. The Magellan spacecraft, launched in 1989, mapped 98 percent of the Venusian surface and 95 percent of the planet's gravity field. When its solar panels began to fail, engineers on Earth directed it into the Venusian atmosphere.

Mars   Mariner 4 took the first close-up images of the Martian surface in 1965. During a flyby of the planet in 1971, Mariner 9 became the first craft to orbit Mars and took the first close-up images of the Martian moons, Phobos and Deimos. Viking 1 was launched in 1975 and sent its lander to the Martian surface on July 20, 1976. Launched one month after Viking 1, Viking 2 released its lander to the surface in September 1976. Throughout the latter years of the twentieth-century, several Martian probes were lost, but the Mars Surveyor program, launched in 1996, successfully orbited Mars. The Mars Pathfinder (originally called the Mars Environmental Survey) was launched in 1996 and landed on the planet in July 1997. Renamed the Sagan Station after landing, the Pathfinder sent its surface rover, Sojourner, to record vital planetary data. Sojourner alllowed humans to have a mobile "telepresence" on the Martian surface.

Asteroids   The first close-up flyby of an asteroid occurred in 1991, when the Jupiter-bound Galileo spacecraft took images of asteroid Gaspra. In 1993, Galileo recorded the first images of a moon orbiting an asteroid when it showed Dactyl orbiting asteroid Ida. In 1996, the Near-Earth Asteroid Rendezvous (NEAR) spacecraft was launched. Renamed Shoemaker after geologist Eugene Shoemaker, it collected data for about a year, then was control-crashed into the asteroid.

Jupiter   Pioneer 10 was the first spacecraft to fly by Jupiter in 1973; Pioneer 11 followed a year later. (Pioneer 10 and 11 were also the first spacecraft to leave our solar system; both carrying a graphic message on a six-by-nine-inch gold anodized plaque.) Voyager 1, launched in 1977, flew past Jupiter in 1979; Voyager 2, launched a few weeks earlier than Voyager 1 in 1977, flew past the planet in 1979. (Both probes provided more data about the planets, moons, and rings of the visited planetary systems than ever before.) After its 1989 launch, the Galileo spacecraft reached Jupiter in 1995; it remains there through 2001 doing extensive study of the planet and its largest moons, Ganymede, Callisto, Europa, and Io.

Saturn   In 1979, Pioneer 11 became the first spacecraft to fly by Saturn. Voyager 1 flew past the planet in 1980; Voyager 2 flew by in 1981. Both probes revealed thousands of ringlets in Saturn's well-known rings, and seven additional satellites. NASA's Jet Propulsion lab could have directed Voyager 1 to Pluto but instead chose to send the probe to Titan, Saturn's largest moon. In 2004, the spacecraft Cassini—launched in 1977—is slated to orbit Saturn.

Uranus   Voyager 2 is the only spacecraft to fly by Uranus to date, doing so in 1986. It showed proof of rings around the planet and ten additional satellites. It also took close-up images of several moons, including Miranda, a satellite with a patchwork of various terrain.

Neptune   Voyager 2 flew by Neptune in 1989, the only probe to do so to date. It discovered active weather on the planet (including numerous large cloud features) and rings; it also recorded close-up images of Neptune's largest moon, Triton—a satellite complete with geysers.

Sciences

THE PLANETS

Planet	Mean Distance from Sun (millions of miles)	(millions of kilometers)	Sidereal Period of Revolution (years)	(days)	Moons	Diameter (miles)	(kilometers)	Period of Rotation (days)
Mercury	36	57.9	0.241	87.97	0	3,100	4,878	58.7
Venus	67	108.2	0.615	224.70	0	7,700	12,104	−243.0*
Earth	93	149.6	1.000	365.26	1	7,920	12,756	0.997
Mars	141	227.9	1.881	686.98	2	4,200	6,794	1.026
Jupiter	483	778.3	11.862		16	88,640	142,796	0.413
Saturn	886	1,427.0	29.46		18+	74,500	120,000	0.443
Uranus	1,782	2,869.6	84.01		21	32,000	52,400	−0.65*
Neptune	2,793	4,496.6	164.79		8	31,000	50,450	0.72
Pluto	3,670	5,913	247.7		1	1,500	2,400	6.387

*Both planets appear to have retrograde (opposite) rotation.

THE LIFE OF A STAR

A star begins its life by condensing out of the gases and dust that make up a nebula. Gravity causes the resulting globule to contract, thus heating up its center. When the temperature rises to a critical level, the mass starts to glow, becoming a protostar. The protostars with sufficient mass begin to convert hydrogen gas to helium by a nuclear reaction called fusion; those with insufficient mass become "failed stars," often called brown dwarf stars. If the star is successful at creating fusion, it enters its mature stages, in which it spends most of its life.

As the star ages, the core temperature rises enough so that the star becomes unstable. The core begins to deteriorate, while the outer layers swell out and cool, forming a red giant. At this stage, the typical star begins to shed its outer layers, creating a planetary nebula. When the outer layers have completely dissipated, only the tightly packed core, known as a white dwarf, remains.

If the star has a greater initial mass than an average star, however, the accelerated rate of core deterioration results in the star's sudden collapse, followed by a catastrophic explosion known as a supernova. Hypothetically, the superdense material forming at its core may not explode at all; instead, it could go on shrinking to form a black hole.

TYPES OF STARS

Not all stars are similar to our Sun. The differences are based on ages, size, formation, and structure of each star. The following is a brief list of the major stellar types.

black dwarfs   Stars in the latest stage of stellar life. After a star about the size of our Sun becomes a white dwarf, its energy is dissipated into space, and it is no longer luminous. Theoretically, the universe is not old enough to have formed any black dwarfs.

black holes   Theoretical regions of space that form when a massive star collapses. Because their gravitational field is so strong, light (photons) cannot escape—thus black holes can never really be seen. Black holes are inferred to exist by their gravitational effects on material falling into them. The binary star system Cygnus X-1 and the center of our own galaxy are thought to harbor black holes.

blue supergiants   The hottest, bluest, and most luminous stars. They are rare, and have large masses and low densities. Rigel in the constellation of Orion is a blue supergiant star.

hot subdwarfs   Stars with extremely high densities; they are also found at the center of most planetary nebulas, such as at the center of the Ring Nebula in the constellation Lyra.

A Closer Look

Understanding the Invisible

A black hole is a theoretical region of space in which the gravitational field is so strong that photon (light) particles cannot escape. To imitate a black hole's density, the Earth would have to be crushed to the size of a marble. Black holes are thought to be massive stars at the ends of their stellar lives. The problem with detecting a black hole is obvious. Because they don't produce or reflect light, seeing them in the inky black nighttime sky is impossible. Astronomers infer the presence of a black hole by the gravitational effects on the material falling into it.

J. Robert Oppenheimer and Hartland Snyder conceived the idea of a "black hole" in 1939 on the basis of Einstein's theory of general relativity. The idea was ignored, however, for several decades. One of the first possible black holes was found in the binary system Cygnus X-1, an X-ray source in the constellation of Cygnus. In 1994, astronomers using the Hubble Space Telescope noted that the region around the elliptical galaxy M87 in the Virgo Cluster was a possible black hole. In 1997, astronomers collected dramatic evidence for a supermassive black hole in NGC 4486B, a small elliptical satellite galaxy of M87. Many astronomers speculate that the core of our own Milky Way galaxy is a black hole. By the year 2001, astronomers claimed to have discovered more than 30 supermassive black holes in various galaxies. All the evidence is circumstantial; but if the effects in these regions are not caused by black holes, no alternative hypothesis is available.

---

neutron stars   The remains of a star with a mass between 1.4 and 3 solar masses. These stars collapse so violently that protons and electrons are rammed together to form neutrons. The mass of a neutron star is greater than the Sun, but a neutron star's size is only about 5 miles across *See also* **pulsars.**

novae   Usually associated with binary star systems, in which one of the stars is a white dwarf. As the mass from the companion star hits the white dwarf star, a fusion reaction occurs, and the star responds with a burst of brightness. Unlike the rare supernovae, novae appear once every few years.

pulsars   Thought to be rotating neutron stars. Their rotational speeds vary, from 642 times per second to once every 4 seconds. First discovered in 1967, pulsars send out radio waves in specific directions, much like a lighthouse beam of light sweeping around the sky.

red giants   Stars in the late stages of stellar life. They have low density and are brighter and larger than our Sun. Arcturus, in the constellation Boötes, is a red giant; it is predicted that our Sun will become a red giant at the end of its life, about 5 to 6 billion years from now.

red supergiants   The largest and brightest of stars, with a large mass and low density. Betelgeuse, in the constellation of Orion, is a red supergiant.

supernovae   Massive stars that undergo a gravitational collapse, then a gigantic explosion, blasting away the outer layers into space. The resulting gases spread out into space, with the core collapsing into a neutron star, or possibly a black hole. Seeing a supernova from Earth is rare. A supernova observed in the constellation of Taurus in 1054 produced the Crab Nebula; astronomer Johannes Kepler witnessed the last supernova seen in our Milky Way galaxy in 1604. Two more bright supernovae include one in 1987 in the Large Magellanic Cloud, a neighboring galaxy, and one in 1993 in the galaxy M81.

variable stars   Stars that change in brightness over time. There are numerous reasons for variability in stars: two stars eclipsing each other, explosions on the star, or a natural pulsation caused by an imbalance between the star's outer layer and core. Brightness can vary over the course of a day, a year, or several years.

white dwarfs   Stars at the end of stellar life. They form when a star depletes its thermonuclear energy, ceasing fusion. As the star collapses under its own weight, it becomes very dense. The gravitational energy is converted to heat, and the star continues to shine. The companion star of Sirius, in the constellation of Canis Major, is a white dwarf.

white holes   Theoretical stars that have properties opposite from those of black holes. Instead of pulling matter into them, white holes are regions in which matter spontaneously appears.

CONSTELLATIONS

THE 12 ZODIACAL CONSTELLATIONS

Aquarius, the Water-Bearer
Aries, the Ram
Cancer, the Crab
Capricornus, the Goat
Gemini, the Twins
Leo, the Lion
Libra, the Balance or Scales
Pisces, the Fish
Sagittarius, the Archer
Scorpius, the Scorpion
Taurus, the Bull
Virgo, the Virgin

THE 28 CONSTELLATIONS NORTH OF THE ZODIAC

Andromeda, the Chained Lady
Aquila, the Eagle
Auriga, the Charioteer
Boötes, the Herdsman
Camelopardalis, the Giraffe
Canes Venatici, the Hunting Dogs
Cassiopeia, the Lady in the Chair
Cepheus, the King
Coma Berenices, Berenice's Hair
Corona Borealis, the Northern Crown
Cygnus, the Swan
Delphinus, the Dolphin
Draco, the Dragon
Equuleus, the Colt
Hercules (Kneeling)
Lacerta, the Lizard
Leo Minor, the Lesser Lion
Lynx, the Lynx
Lyra, the Lyre
Ophiuchus, the Serpent Holder
Pegasus, the Winged Horse
Perseus, the Hero
Sagitta, the Arrow
Serpens, the Serpent
Triangulum, the Triangle
Ursa Major, the Greater Bear
Ursa Minor, the Lesser Bear
Vulpecula, the Fox

THE 48 CONSTELLATIONS SOUTH OF THE ZODIAC

Antlia, the Air Pump
Apus, the Bird of Paradise
Ara, the Altar
Caelum, the Engraver's Chisel
Canis Major, the Greater Dog
Canis Minor, the Lesser Dog
Carina, the Keel
Centaurus, the Centaur
Cetus, the Whale
Chamaeleon, the Chameleon
Circinus, the Pair of Compasses
Columba, (Noah's) Dove
Corona Australis, the Southern Crown
Corvus, the Crow
Crater, the Bowl
Crux, the (Southern) Cross
Dorado, the Gilthead or Swordfish
Eridanus, the River
Fornax, the Furnace
Grus, the Crane
Horologium, the Clock
Hydra, the Water-Serpent or Hydra (fem.)
Hydrus, the Water-Snake or Sea-Serpent (masc.)
Indus, the Indian
Lepus, the Hare
Lupus, the Wolf
Mensa, the Table Mountain
Microscopium, the Microscope
Monoceros, the Unicorn
Musca, the Fly
Norma, the Square or Rule
Octans, the Octant
Orion, the Hunter
Pavo, the Peacock
Phoenix, the Fabulous Bird
Pictor, the Painter's Easel
Piscis Austrinus, the Southern Fish
Puppis, the Stern
Pyxis, the (Ship's) Compass
Reticulum, the Net
Sculptor, the Sculptor's Shop
Scutum, the Shield
Sextans, the Sextant
Telescopium, the Telescope
Triangulum Australe, the Southern Triangle
Tucana, the Toucan
Vela, the Sails
Volans, the Flying Fish

THE 25 NEAREST STAR SYSTEMS

Components in the following table are referred to as A, B, or C in the case of multiple-star systems.

A *light-year* is the distance light travels in a year, equal to 5.88 trillion miles (9.46 trillion kilometers).

Rank	Name	Components	Constellation	Distance from Sun (light-years)
1a	Proxima Cantauri		Centauras	4.23
1b	Rigil Kentaurus	A & B	Centaurus	4.35
2	Barnard's Star		Ophiuchus	5.98
3	Wolf 359		Leo	7.80
4	Lalande 21185		Ursa Major	8.23
5	L 726-8	A & B	Cetus	8.57
6	Sirius	A & B	Canis Major	8.57
7	Ross 154		Sagittarius	9.56
8	Ross 248		Andromeda	10.33
9	Epsilon Eridani		Eridanus	10.67
10	Ross 128		Virgo	10.83
11	L 789-6	A, B, & C	Aquarius	11.08
12	Groomsbridge 34	A & B	Andromeda	11.27
13	Epsilon Indi		Indus	11.29
14	61 Cygni	A & B	Cygnus	11.30
15	BD +59° 1915	A & B	Draco	11.40
16	Tau Ceti		Cetus	11.40
17	Procyon	A & B	Canis Minor	11.41
18	Lacaille 9352		Piscis Austrinus	11.47
19	GJ 111		Cancer	11.83
20	GJ 1061		Horologium	12.06
21	L 725-32		Cetus	12.20
22	BD +05° 1668		Canis Minor	12.34
23	Lacaille 8760		Microscopium	12.61
24	Kapteyn's Star		Pictor	12.63
25	Krüger 60	A & B	Cepheus	12.95

COMMON ASTRONOMY TERMS

Additional terms are defined in the preceding astronomy sections.

aberration   The apparent displacement of a star owing to the orbital motion of Earth and the bending of light rays from the star. As the Earth travels around the Sun, the aberration causes the star to appear to trace an ellipse about its true position.

absorption nebula   A nebula seen in silhouette because it is absorbing or blocking light from behind. It is also called a dark nebula.

accretion   The process by which small particles coalesce by collisions or mutual gravitational pull, creating larger bodies. Accretion is suspected as a major process in the formation of the planets and satellites in any solar system.

albedo   The proportion of light reflected from a celestial body. The Moon reflects only about 7 percent of the sunlight falling on it, whereas the albedo of Venus is more than 70 percent, owing to its heavy cloud cover, which reflects a greater proportion of light.

altitude   Number of degrees above the horizon of an object on the celestial plane.

aphelion   The point in an object's orbit that is farthest from the Sun. *See also* **perihelion.**

Sciences

apogee   The point in the Moon's orbit (or any other orbiting body, such as an artificial satellite) when it is farthest from the Earth. *See also* **perigee.**

asterism   A pattern of stars that does not constitute one of the 88 official constellations. For example, the Big Dipper in the constellation of Ursa Major is an asterism.

The light that leaves the Sun takes 8 minutes to reach the Earth.

asteroid   A small, rocky object or minor planet that orbits the Sun. Most asteroids have orbits in the asteroid belt, located between the orbits of Mars and Jupiter. Others can be found throughout the solar system, including those that come close to the Earth, called near-Earth asteroids. More than 8,000 asteroids have been discovered, and it is likely thousands more exist undetected throughout the solar system. Most asteroids are leftovers from the formation of the solar system; others are debris from collisions between larger planetary bodies or remnants of extinct comets.

astrometry   The measure of the positions and apparent motions of celestial objects and the attempt to understand the factors that influence such movements.

astronomical unit   An astronomical distance, equal to the average distance from the Earth to the Sun, or about 93,000,000 miles (150,000,000 kilometers).

big bang model   A theory that describes the beginning of our universe as a titanic explosion. This explosion did not occur at a particular point in space, according to the theory, but rather was a transition from enormous density and temperature throughout all space to conditions of even lower density and lower temperature as space itself expanded. After the hypothetical explosion, the universe was swamped with energy in the form of radiant energy and various atomic particles. This phase was followed by a cooling and thinning out of the universe. It is believed that the universe is still expanding at this time.

binary star   Two stars that are gravitationally attracted to each other. *See also* **double star.**

celestial sphere   An imaginary sphere used to locate the positions and track the motions of all astronomical objects.

comet   A small object composed of rock, ice, and gases moving about the Sun in an elliptical orbit. A comet has three distinct components: the *nucleus,* made up of rock and ice; the *coma,* consisting of gases and dust; and the *tail,* formed when gases and dust spread out from the nucleus or coma. Short-period comets complete their orbits in less than 200 years; long-period comets may take thousands of years to revolve around the Sun, or may never return at all (parabolic orbit). Some astronomers believe that comets originate in the Oort cloud, a hypothetical region of space that lies outside the solar system.

corona   The outer envelope, or "atmosphere," of gas surrounding the Sun, possibly extending to the orbit of Earth. During an eclipse of the Sun, the corona may be visible around the edges of the Moon. It has a density that is about one-millionth that of the atmosphere of Earth.

cosmogony   The study of how the universe was formed.

cosmology   The study of the universe at large, of the distribution and behavior of the matter and energy in it, of the laws governing these factors, and of its origin and evolution.

dark matter   Matter that is thought to exist in the universe but has not yet been observed. It is based on measurements of unexplained gravitational effects on visible matter.

declination   On the celestial sphere, the coordinate analogous to latitude on the Earth. Declination is measured in degrees, minutes, and seconds of arc north (positive above the celestial equator) or south (negative below the celestial equator).

Doppler effect The phenomenon in which, as a source of waves (e.g., sound or light) and the observer move relative to each other, the emitted wavelength appears to change. In astronomy, Doppler shifts are used to determine the velocity and direction of distant objects. For example, light from a galaxy shifts to the red on the electromagnetic spectrum if the galaxy is moving away from the observer (red shift) and to the blue if the galaxy is moving toward the observer (blue shift).

double star Two stars that appear close together along a line of sight. Double stars may be an optical double, which are stars that just appear to be close as seen from Earth but are physically quite distant from one another; or true binaries, stars that are gravitationally bound to one another.

ecliptic The apparent path of the Sun in the sky as seen from Earth.

fireball A bright meteor, with an apparent magnitude ranging from about −5 to −20 (to compare, the Sun has an apparent magnitude of −26.7). Fireballs are sometimes seen during the day.

galaxy A large system of stars, usually containing between 1 million and 1 trillion stars, along with clouds of gas and dust. Galaxies are sometimes classified according to their shapes as spiral, elliptical, or irregular.

globular cluster A nearly spherical, dense cluster of hundreds of thousands to millions of stars.

gravitational collapse The contraction of a star when the pressure of thermonuclear reactions can no longer sustain the force of self-gravitation. Collapse occurs at the end of a star's life when its fuel of hydrogen and other elements is depleted. Depending on its original mass, the star may evolve into a white dwarf, a neutron star, or a black hole, or it may explode as a supernova.

inferior conjuction The passage of Mercury or Venus between the Earth and the Sun.

libration The effect that allows an observer on Earth to see about 59 percent of the Moon's surface, slightly more than would otherwise be visible. Because the Moon's rotation and orbital period are equal (on average), the Moon always keeps the same face to the Earth. Libration occurs because the Moon's elliptical orbit speed is not constant and its orbit is slightly tilted.

meteor A meteoroid that produces a streak of light as it enters the Earth's atmosphere and is vaporized by the resulting friction. This phenomenon is quite common when the Earth passes through swarms of meteoroids. The resulting meteor showers are usually associated with a specific constellation and time of year. Meteors are commonly called shooting or falling stars.

The Milky Way galaxy contains several hundred billion stars and is about 100,000 light-years across. Our solar system orbits the Milky Way once every 250 million years.

meteorite A meteor that passes through the outer layers of the Earth's atmosphere and strikes the planet's surface. The resulting explosive impact buries or disperses the meteorite, leaving a crater behind. The largest meteorite to fall to Earth so far is the more than 60-ton Hoba West meteorite, discovered in 1920 in Namibia, Africa.

meteoroid A small, solid particle of rock or other material that orbits the Sun, often along the same path as comets. Meteoroids form when a comet breaks up or leaves debris in its wake. Thousands of meteoroids traveling in closely grouped packs are called a swarm.

Milky Way The spiral galaxy in which our solar system is located. It contains about 200 billion stars, has a diameter of about 100,000 light-years, and is about 12 to 14 billion years old.

Sciences

nadir   The point directly below the observer, or 90 degrees below the horizon. *See also* **zenith.**

nebula   A concentration of gas and dust in the galaxy.

oblate   The shape of a planet or natural satellite that is not completely spherical but bulges in the center and is flattened at the poles. The shape is usually caused by rapid spinning or the gravitational pull from an accompanying moon. For example, rapidly rotating Jupiter is an oblate spheroid.

occulation   The crossing of one body in front of another, such as the Moon in front of a star, relative to an observer.

opposition   The point in a planet's orbit when it is 180 degrees from the Sun, usually as observed from Earth.

orbit   The path of an object around a central body; gravitational attraction keeps the bodies in orbit.

parallax   The change in the relative position of an object when viewed from different places; in astronomy, the closer the object, the greater the parallax.

perigee   The point where the Moon (or any other orbiting body, such as an artificial satellite) is closest in its orbit to the Earth. *See also* **apogee.**

perihelion   The point in the orbit of an object when it is closest to the Sun. *See also* **aphelion.**

perturbation   A local gravitational disturbance in the uniform motion of a body because of the gravitational influence of another object. For example, a comet orbiting the Sun can be perturbed by a close encounter with Jupiter, the solar system's largest planet, which influences the orbit of the comet.

planetesimals   Large rocky bodies more than one mile in diameter thought to have formed in the early solar system. Scientists theorize that planetesimals later accreted to form the rocky cores of the planets.

plasma   Matter in the form of electrically charged particles; the state in which most of the universe exists.

proper motion   The apparent angular motion of an object across the sky, determined as change in position with respect to the background star; caused by the star's true motion and the relative motion of the solar system.

quasar   A contraction of the word *quasi-stellar,* used to describe celestial objects with a starlike appearance. Quasars are the most distant objects known. They have large red shifts indicating great recessional velocities and emit energy that is more than a thousand times that of an average galaxy.

About half of the stars we can see are actually two stars that orbit each other.

radio telescope   An astronomical instrument used to collect, detect, and analyze radio waves from cosmic sources, such as radio galaxies, pulsars, and quasars.

revolution   The movement of an object around a central body.

right ascension   The angle of an object eastward from the vernal equinox, along the celestial equator; right ascension is measured in hours, minutes, and seconds.

rotation   The movement of a body as it turns on its axis.

scintillation   The twinkling of a star, planet, or other bright object in the sky. The rapid variations in brightness are caused as turbulence in the Earth's atmospheric layers, which cause random refraction of the light from the celestial body.

solar wind   A stream of particles, primarily protons and electrons, that constantly flows outward from the Sun.

space-time   A four-dimensional way of describing events and locations with three units of distance and one of time. Under the influence of gravity, space-time can actually warp and bend.

"Astronomers" in chapter 5; "Astronomy Symbols" in chapter 12

spectrum   Radiation (usually visible light) broken into its component wavelengths.

spectroscope   An instrument used to determine the spectrum or wavelength of a ray of light emanating from an object. A spectroscope is often used in astronomy.

star   A spherical celestial body consisting of a large mass of hot gas held together by its own gravity. It is self-luminating because of extensive internal nuclear reactions. Our Sun is a typical star.

superior conjunction   For a planet (Mercury or Venus) inside the Earth's orbit, the condition when the planet is behind the Sun, relative to the Earth.

syzygy   The condition when three celestial bodies are arranged in a straight line. Syzygy occurs during solar and lunar eclipses, when the Sun, Moon, and Earth are aligned.

terminator   The line separating sunlight and darkness on a planet or moon.

transit   The movement of a smaller object across the lighted face of a larger object, such as the movement of Mercury across the face of the Sun, or the moon Io across the face of the planet Jupiter.

universe   The entirety of all that is known to exist. The size of the observable universe is limited to the distance light has traveled since the Big Bang.

zenith   The point directly overhead from the observer, or 90 degrees above the horizon. *See also* **nadir.**

zodiacal light   A faint cone of light seen along the ecliptic at sunset, usually around the time of an equinox. It is caused by sunlight scattering small dust particles that possibly have an interplanetary origin.

CHEMISTRY

ELEMENTS AND THEIR SYMBOLS

Atomic Number	Symbol	Element	Atomic Number	Symbol	Element	Atomic Number	Symbol	Element
1	H	Hydrogen	22	Ti	Titanium	43	Tc	Technetium
2	He	Helium	23	V	Vanadium	44	Ru	Ruthenium
3	Li	Lithium	24	Cr	Chromium	45	Rh	Rhodium
4	Be	Beryllium	25	Mn	Manganese	46	Pd	Palladium
5	B	Boron	26	Fe	Iron	47	Ag	Silver
6	C	Carbon	27	Co	Cobalt	48	Cd	Cadmium
7	N	Nitrogen	28	Ni	Nickel	49	In	Indium
8	O	Oxygen	29	Cu	Copper	50	Sn	Tin
9	F	Fluorine	30	Zn	Zinc	51	Sb	Antimony
10	Ne	Neon	31	Ga	Gallium	52	Te	Tellurium
11	Na	Sodium	32	Ge	Germanium	53	I	Iodine
12	Mg	Magnesium	33	As	Arsenic	54	Xe	Xenon
13	Al	Aluminum	34	Se	Selenium	55	Cs	Cesium
14	Si	Silicon	35	Br	Bromine	56	Ba	Barium
15	P	Phosphorus	36	Kr	Krypton	57	La	Lanthanum
16	S	Sulfur	37	Rb	Rubidium	58	Ce	Cerium
17	Cl	Chlorine	38	Sr	Strontium	59	Pr	Praseodymium
18	Ar	Argon	39	Y	Yttrium	60	Nd	Neodymium
19	K	Potassium	40	Zr	Zirconium	61	Pm	Promethium
20	Ca	Calcium	41	Nb	Niobium	62	Sm	Samarium
21	Sc	Scandium	42	Mo	Molybdenum	63	Eu	Europium

continues

Elements and Their Symbols, Continued

Atomic Number	Symbol	Element	Atomic Number	Symbol	Element	Atomic Number	Symbol	Element
64	Gd	Gadolinium	80	Hg	Mercury	96	Cm	Curium
65	Tb	Terbium	81	Tl	Thallium	97	Bk	Berkelium
66	Dy	Dysprosium	82	Pb	Lead	98	Cf	Californium
67	Ho	Holmium	83	Bi	Bismuth	99	Es	Einsteinium
68	Er	Erbium	84	Po	Polonium	100	Fm	Ferium
69	Tm	Thulium	85	At	Astatine	101	Md	Mendelevium
70	Yb	Ytterbium	86	Rn	Radon	102	No	Nobelium
71	Lu	Lutetium	87	Fr	Francium	103	Lw	Lawrencium
72	Hf	Hafnium	88	Ra	Radium	104	Rf	Rutherfordium
73	Ta	Tantalum	89	Ac	Actinium	105	Db	Dubnium
74	W	Tungsten	90	Th	Thorium	106	Sg	Seaborgium
75	Re	Rhenium	91	Pa	Protactinium	107	Bh	Bohrium
76	Os	Osmium	92	U	Uranium	108	Hs	Hassium
77	Ir	Iridium	93	Np	Neptunium	109	Mt	Meitnerium
78	Pt	Platinum	94	Pu	Plutonium			
79	Au	Gold	95	Am	Americium			

The names of six recently created chemical elements, 104 through 109, were confirmed by the International Union of Pure and Applied Chemistry in 1998.

THE PERIODIC TABLE OF THE ELEMENTS

The Periodic Table of the Elements is a listing of the chemical symbols (and often many of their physical characteristics) of 109 elements. The first 92 elements occur in nature, with a few exceptions: astatine (atomic number 85), technetium (atomic number 43), and some other elements are artificial although their artificiality is debated. The remaining elements have been artificially created in laboratory particle accelerators. The chemical elements exist in a free state or combined with other elements.

In the Periodic Table, the elements are arranged in order of increasing atomic number from left to right and from top to bottom. The horizontal rows of elements are called *periods;* the vertical columns of related elements are called *groups*. Across the table, there is a general trend from metallic to nonmetallic elements; down a group, there is an increase in atomic size and in eletropositive behavior. The members of a group have similar behavior because of similarities in their electron configurations.

The first three periods are the short periods, containing elements with only *s* and *p* level electrons (the lowest energy levels) and having only up to 2 and 8 electrons, respectively. Period 1 consists of hydrogen (H) and helium (He) only, the two most abundant elements in the universe. Period 2 elements begin filling the second energy level, and the period ends with neon (Ne, atomic number 10). In Period 3, the third level is filled, ending with argon (Ar, atomic number 18).

Periods 4 and 5 are longer, each with 18 elements. Period 4 begins with potassium (K) followed by calcium (Ca). But after that, higher energy electrons (the *d* orbitals) begin to fill, giving the next elements in the center of the table characteristics unlike any of the previous elements. These elements, with their incomplete *d* subshell, are known as *transition* elements. This pattern repeats for Period 5 elements. Periods 6 and 7 contain 32 elements each. The Period 6 elements that follow lanthanum (La, atomic number 57) are called *lanthanoids*. This is also called the *rare earth series* and includes cerium (Ce) through lutetium (Lu). Period 7's transitional ele-

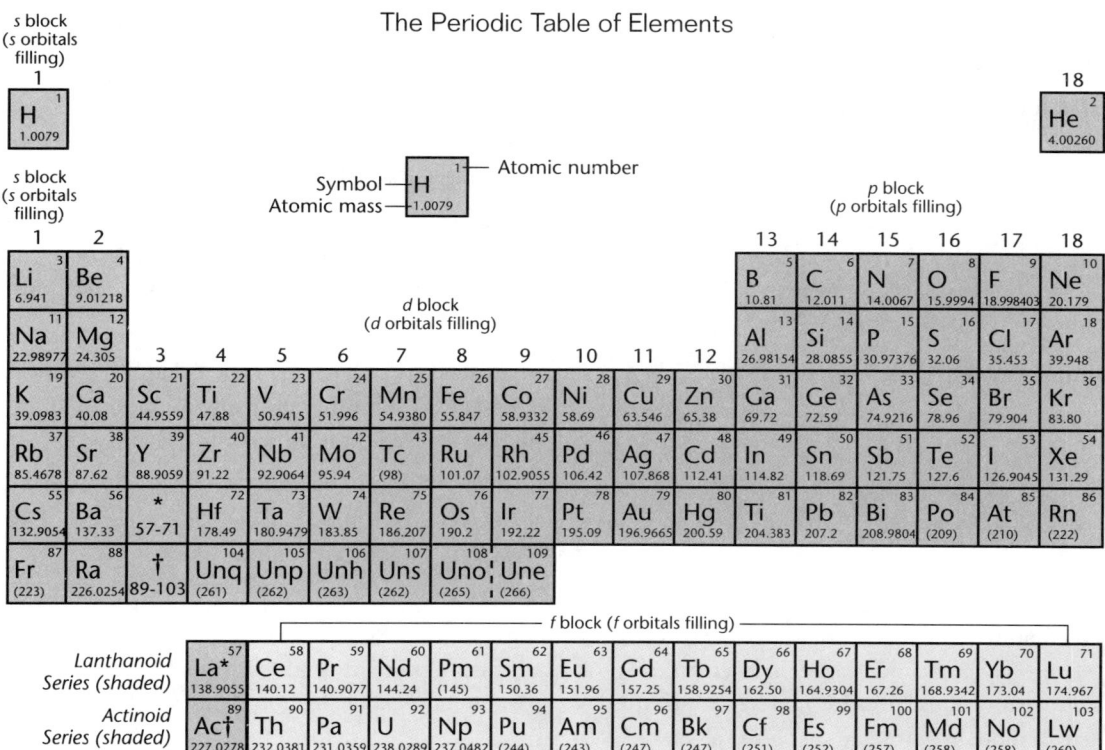

The Periodic Table of Elements

ments follow actinium (Ac, atomic number 89) and are called *actinoids*. This group includes thorium (Th) through lawrencium (Lw). Both of these groups are filling the *f* sublevel orbitals.

The Periodic Table can be divided into three basic groups: metals, nonmetals, and semimetals. In general, when you view the table, the metals are on the left, the nonmetals are on the extreme right, and the semimetals are in the center.

Metals make up the majority of the groups of elements. Most metals such as sodium (Na) are solid at room temperature, with mercury (Hg) being the only liquid metal. Metals have higher melting and boiling points because the atoms in the crystals are tightly packed together. In addition, their densities are high because the heavy nuclei are also tightly packed together. Metals have only a few (usually no more than four) valence electrons in the outermost shells. These are electrons that are often given up in a reaction, forming metallic, positive ions. Metals

(such as gold and copper) are generally good conductors of electricity. Elements of Group 1, including lithium, sodium, and potassium (but excluding hydrogen), are known as alkali metals; Group 2 metals, including magnesium and calcium, are the alkaline earth metals.

Nonmetals are usually dull in appearance, brittle, and not good electrical conductors. Many of the chemically active nonmetals are the halogens (Group 17), the group of elements that includes chlorine, bromine, and iodine. This group is highly reactive and electronegative and contains fluorine, the most highly electronegative element.

COMMON CHEMISTRY TERMS

Additional terms are defined in "Common Physics Terms" in this chapter.

acid A substance that, in liquid form, will turn blue litmus paper red, react with alkalis (bases) to form salts, and dissolve metals to form salts. On the pH scale of 0 to 14, acids register in numbers less than 7.

alcohol   Any of a group of organic compounds that contains a hydroxyl (OH) group. A common example is ethyl alcohol (C_2H_5OH).

alkali   Any compound that has chemical qualities of a base, such as reacting with acids to form salts. On the pH scale, alkalis register in numbers larger than 7.

anion   An ion with a negative electric charge.

base   An alkaline substance, either in molecular or ionic form, that will accept or receive a proton from another chemical unit. An example is a hydroxyl ion.

benzene ring   A common organic molecule structure consisting of a ring of six carbon atoms with an equal number of attached hydrogen atoms (C_6H_6). Many organic chemicals occur in a benzene ring format with various atoms or radicals substituted for one or more hydrogen atoms, as in toluene and xylene as variations of benzene.

bond   A strong electric force that holds atoms together in molecules, crystals, and other combinations. A molecular bond may depend on the attractive force of an electron whose orbit spans the outer shells of two or more component atoms. In double bonds, two pairs of electrons may be shared equally by adjacent atoms.

catalyst   A substance that accelerates a chemical reaction without becoming a part of the end product of the reaction. A catalyst can generally be recovered in its original form following the reaction.

compound   A substance formed by the combination of two or more chemical elements that cannot be separated from the combination by physical means. The constituent atoms, however, can usually be separated by means of chemical reactions.

"Chemists" in chapter 5; "Chemistry Symbols" in chapter 12; "Chemical Additives" in chapter 19
Go to

electrolyte   Any chemical, such as a mineral, that when melted or dissolved in water will show an electrical attraction or conduct an electric current.

electron   A negatively charged particle that moves in an orbit about the nucleus of an atom.

element   A substance composed of atoms with the same atomic number or the same number of protons in their nuclei. Examples include oxygen, hydrogen, carbon, and gold.

hydrocarbon   Any of a large group of chemical compounds consisting primarily of carbon and hydrogen atoms, usually associated with current or past life processes.

hydroxyl   Pertaining to the negatively charged OH (oxygen + hydrogen) radical in an organic compound.

inorganic chemistry   A branch of chemical science that deals primarily with elements and compounds that do not include hydrocarbons.

isotope   One of two or more atoms having the same atomic number but a different mass number due to the different number of neutrons in their nuclei. An example is zinc, which has isotopes with five different mass numbers ranging from 64 to 70. However, all of the isotopes have equal nuclear charges, orbital electrons, and chemical properties.

mass number   The atomic weight of an isotope, calculated from the numbers of protons and neutrons in the nucleus.

matter   Anything that has weight or fills space, such as a solid, liquid, or gas.

organic chemistry   A branch of chemistry that specializes in the composition, properties, and reactions of hydrocarbon compounds.

oxidation   Any chemical reaction that increases the number of oxygen atoms in a compound, or in which the positive valence is increased by a loss of electrons.

pH   A symbol for hydrogen ion activity of a substance as an expression of the negative logarithm of the concentration of hydrogen ions in moles per liter. Values of pH range from 0 to 14, with a pH of 7 representing acid-base neutrality. The degree of acidity increases as the number progresses toward zero, while alkalinity increases as the pH number approaches 14.

polymer   A huge molecule composed of repeating units of the same molecule. An example is polyethylene, formed by linking ethylene molecules into a giant chain.

reduction   A chemical reaction in which a substance gains electrons or loses part of its positive valence. Reduction generally occurs in a reaction that also involves oxidation.

solute   A substance that is dissolved in a solution.

solvent   The substance that represents the greatest proportion of parts of a solution when two or more substances, such as a solid and liquid, are mixed.

valence   A number that represents the combining power of an element, ion, or radical. The valence of hydrogen is +1, while the valence of oxygen is –2.

GEOLOGY AND GEOPHYSICS

LAYERS OF THE EARTH

Because the Earth's interior is inaccessible to observation, geologists have discerned its many layers by indirect methods. Earthquakes reveal the Earth's interior structure because certain seismic waves travel at varying speeds through materials of different densities. Other properties of the planet's interior can be inferred from magnetic, thermal, and gravitational characteristics.

CRUST

The Earth's outer solid *crust* surrounds the mantle. The crust makes up about 0.6 percent of the Earth's volume and 0.4 percent of its mass. Its overall thickness varies widely: beneath the oceans, the crust (mainly composed of basalt) ranges between 3 and

6.8 miles (5 to 11 kilometers) thick; beneath the continents, the crust (mostly light rocks such as granite) ranges between 12 and 40 miles (19 and 64 kilometers) thick.

The upper layer of the Earth is called the *lithosphere.* It includes the oceanic and continental crusts and part of the cooler, solid upper mantle.

MANTLE

The *mantle* makes up 84 percent of the Earth by volume and 67 percent by mass. It is about 1,802 miles (2,900 kilometers) thick and consists of silica, plus iron-, magnesium-, and other metal-rich minerals. The *Gutenberg discontinuity* separates the Earth's mantle from the outer core; the *Mohoovičić discontinuity* separates the uppermost portion of the mantle from the crust.

If the 4.6 billion years of Earth's existence were only a single day, the 40,000 years of human existence would cover only the last 2 seconds.

The hot plastic *asthenosphere,* part upper mantle and lower crust, separates the more brittle crust-mantle lithosphere above from the mesosphere below. Thought to be responsible for the movement of the lithospheric plates (crustal plates) that slowly "carry" the continents around the planet, the asthenosphere is about 186 miles (300 kilometers) thick. The more solid *mesosphere,* located below the asthenosphere, includes part of the upper mantle and all of the lower mantle.

CORE

The inner and outer *core* make up about 15 percent of the Earth by volume and 32 percent by mass. The *inner core* is about 800 miles (1,287 kilometers) thick; the *outer core* is about 1,400 miles (2,253 kilometers) thick. The inner core, thought to be solid, extends from the center of the Earth to the lower border of the outer core. The outer core, which appears to have characteristics of a liquid, extends to

Sciences

the Gutenberg discontinuity, the border between the mantle and outer core. Because of its extreme density, the entire core seems to be composed of mostly iron, with smaller amounts of other dense elements such as nickel. The pressure within the solid inner core reaches about 3 million atmospheres (1 atmosphere equals the atmospheric pressure at sea level); temperatures measure between 7,200 and 9,000°F (4,000 to 5,000°C)—nearly as hot as the Sun's surface. The heat is from the natural radioactive decay of uranium; it is also from dissipated heat from the Earth as it cooled after formation.

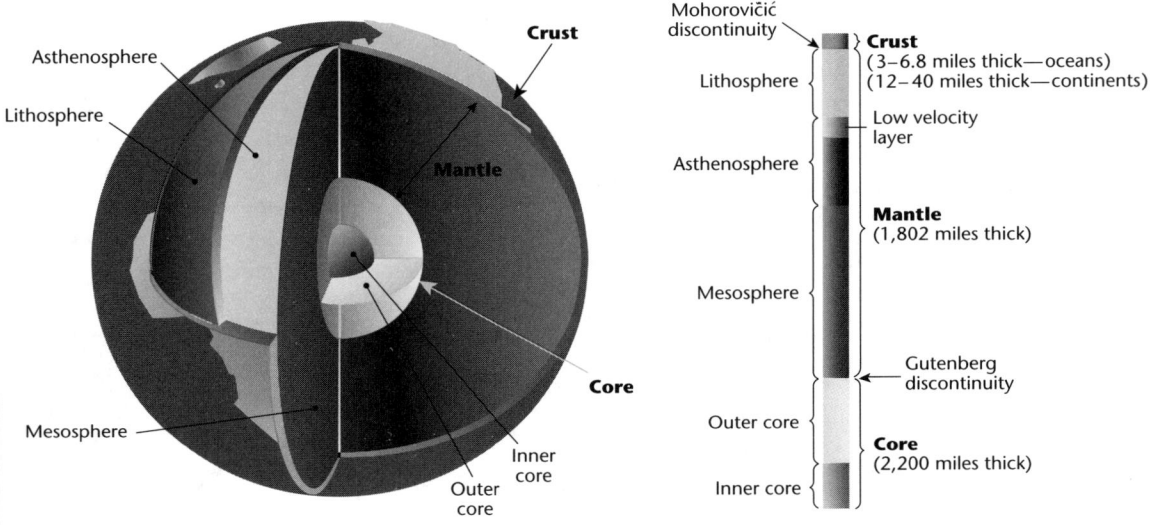

GEOLOGIC TIME SCALE

Age in Millions of Years	Era	Period or Epoch		Important Physical Events	Animal Life
.01 ±.5 ►	CENOZOIC	Quaternary	Holocene	Repeated extensions of ice caps in arctic and north temperate areas	Modern human beings
			Pleistocene	Continents generally elevated, mountains high, deserts widespread	Primitive man
13 ±1 ►		Tertiary	Pliocene	Mountain building in northwestern North America Deformation of Tethys geosyncline; Alps and Himalayas rise	Gorillas
25 ±1 ►			Miocene	Extensive erosion surfaces cut on Appalachians and Rockies Cool, dry climates over much of world	Whales, sabertooths
			Oligocene	Initiation of mountain building in Tethys geosyncline River and floodplain deposits begin on Great Plains	Apes, bats

MILLIONS OF YEARS BEFORE THE PRESENT

Age in Millions of Years	Era	Period or Epoch		Important Physical Events	Animal Life
36±2 ▶	CENOZOIC	Tertiary	Eocene	Climates warm and uniform; widespread jungles and forests	Alligators
58±2 ▶			Paleocene	Basins develop between ranges along Pacific Coast and Rockies	Kangaroos, birds, horses, camels, monkeys, elephants
65 ▶					
±2 ▶	MESOZOIC	Cretaceous		Mountain building in Rockies; seas invade much of western North America and cover Atlantic and Gulf coastal plains	Ancient birds, snakes, modern fish
135 ±5		Jurassic		Widespread mild, uniform climates Mountain building along Pacific Coast of North America Extensive marine invasions of southern and central Europe	Flying reptiles
180 ± ▶		Triassic		Fault basins in eastern North America Extensive deserts and dead seas develop in North America and Eurasia	Ichthyosaurs, tyrannosaurs
230 ±10 ▶	PALEOZOIC	Permian		Continents generally elevated Appalachian and Ural mountains complete their development Tethys geosyncline from Spain to India	Ammonites, finbacked reptiles
280 ±10 ▶		Carboniferous		Mountain building in southern North America and central Europe Extensive seas over much of interior North America	Amphibians, clams, lung fish
310 ±10 ▶		Devonian		Catskill delta built from New England mountains into New York and Pennsylvania Mountain building in northeastern North America Extensive submergence of geosynclines and interior of North America	Starfish
405 ±10 ▶		Silurian		Formation of Caledonian mountains in northwestern Europe Dead seas in Michigan, New York, Ohio, southeastern Canada Deltas and gravel beaches along eastern edge of Appalachian geosyncline	Sea scorpions, corals, sharks
425 ±10 ▶		Ordovician		Mountain building in northeastern North America Over 60 percent of North American continent covered by seas	Snails, jawless fish, echinoids
500 ±10 ▶		Cambrian		Climates generally mild and uniform Seas invade North American continent Geosynclines develop around edge of North America	Protozoans, trilobites

MILLIONS OF YEARS BEFORE THE PRESENT

continues

Geologic Time Scale, Continued

Age in Millions of Years	Era	Period or Epoch	Important Physical Events	Animal Life
c. 600 ▶			Fault basins in Lake Superior region	Jellyfish, flagellates, amoebas, worms, sponges
1,000 ▶			Deformation and mountain building through central North America	
2,000 ▶	PRECAMBRIAN		Geosynclines develop throughout central North America	
3,000 ▶			Extensive mountain building in Lake Superior region	
			Oldest dated rocks	
4,000 ▶			Probable origin of Earth from solar dust cloud	

This is only one interpretation of the geologic time scale. As scientists uncover more fossils and information about rock layers, the times, events, and animal life entries change.

PLATE TECTONICS

The theory of *plate tectonics* states that the lithosphere is divided into plates, or tabular blocks, that interact with each other over time. The crust and part of the solid upper mantle make up each crustal plate.

About 13 major crustal (lithospheric or tectonic) plates and many more small plates within the larger plates make up the Earth's crust, all moving in different directions and at various speeds (fractions of an inch per year). Most plates lie beneath a combination of ocean and continent; several lie only beneath ocean.

The true mechanism for the movement of the crustal plates is still unknown. Scientists theorize that convection in the upper mantle–lower crust, or asthenosphere, slowly "carries" the lithospheric plates around the planet; another theory states that convection in the mesosphere is transferred to the asthenosphere and moves the plates.

Crustal plates are created, are destroyed, and move past each other in a variety of ways.

"The Animal Kingdom" and "The Plant Kingdom" in chapter 3; "Major Zoos and Aquariums" and "Major Botanical Gardens and Arboretums" in chapter 11
Go to

Plate movement in ocean basins includes *seafloor spreading,* or diverging plates. A rift in the ocean floor constantly forms new crustal material—usually from volcanic action—and the ocean floor literally spreads apart. For example, the Mid-Atlantic Ridge is an area of seafloor spreading that splits the Atlantic Ocean; the plates move laterally about 1 inch (2.54 centimeters) per year. Shallow, substantial earthquakes are associated with diverging plates.

When one plate sinks under another, it is called *subduction,* with the subducting plate gradually breaking apart. The destructive plate margins where this occurs are called *subduction zones.* The surface expression of this activity takes the form of volcanic island areas associated with oceanic trenches, or a volcanic mountain region on an adjacent landmass. For example, the Japan Trench off the island of Honshu is the line where the Pacific plate subducts under the Eurasian plate. Some of the largest and deepest earthquakes are associated with subducting plates.

When two plates ram into one another, it is called *colliding plate boundaries,* causing the crust to buckle from intense pressure. For example, the Himalayas were formed by the collision of the Indo-Australian plate and the Eurasian plate. The Himalayas are still

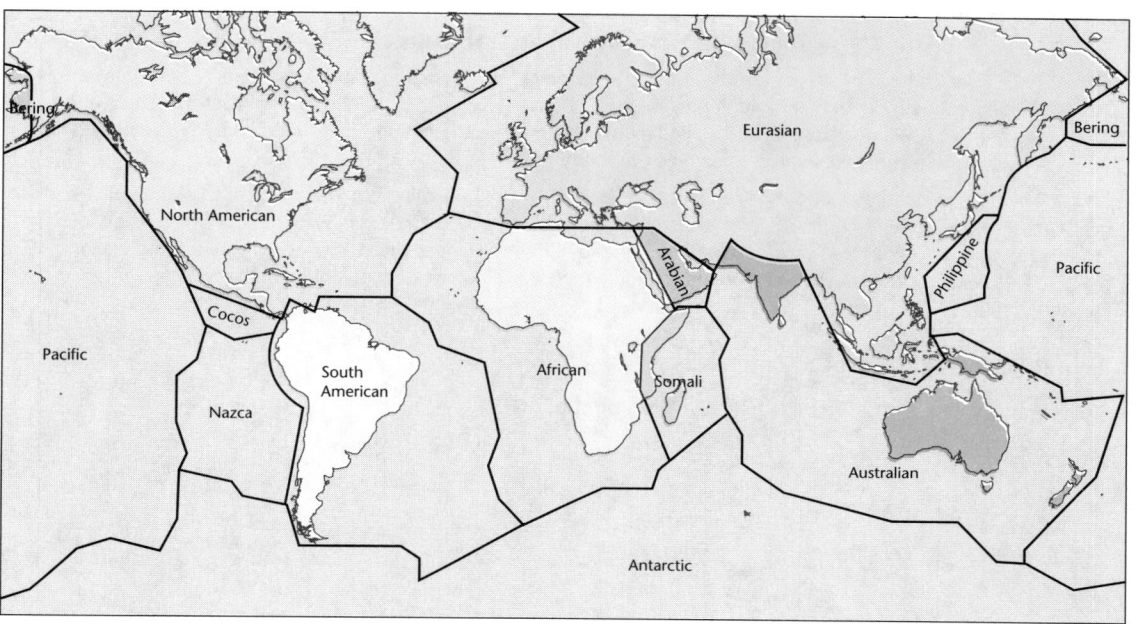

Crustal Plates Around the World (locations of crustal plates are approximate)

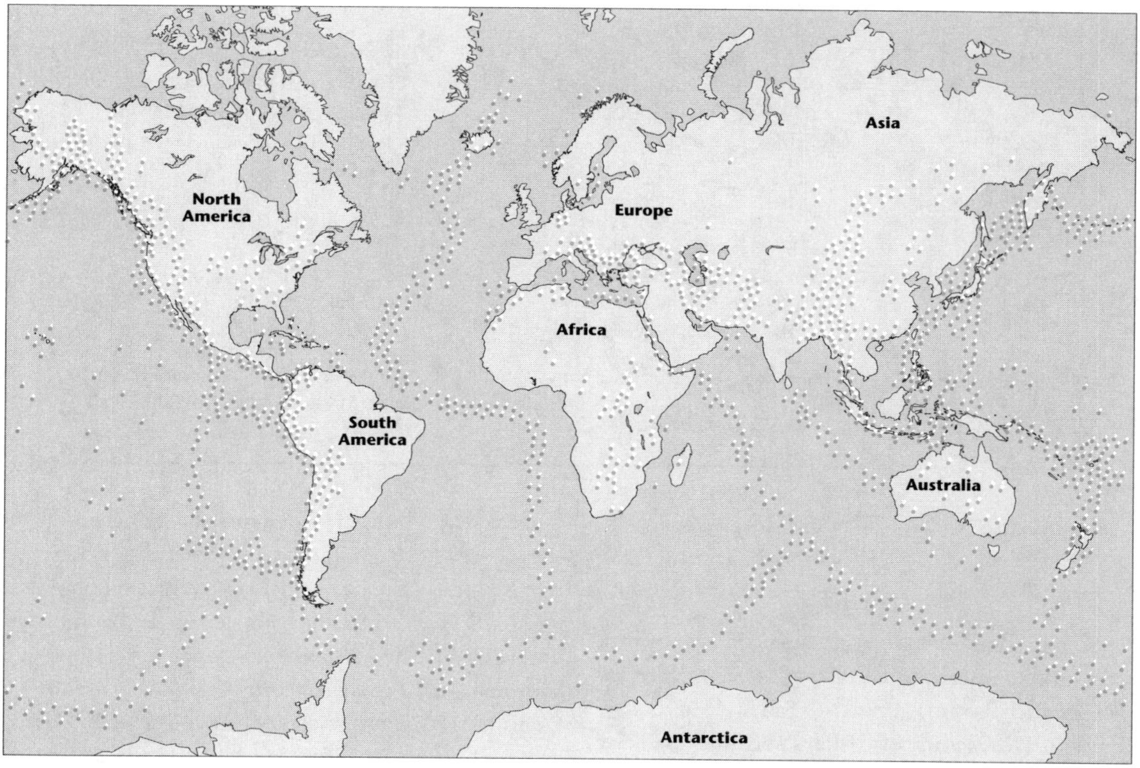

Major Earthquake and Volcanic Zones

Sciences

Measuring an Earthquake

A Closer Look

Two scales have gained notoriety in the past decades: the Mercalli Earthquake Intensity Scale and the Richter Scale. The first, although now rarely used, was developed by Italian seismologist Giuseppe Mercalli in 1902 and measures an earthquake's destructiveness. The scale was modified by American seismologists in the 1930s and is known as the Modified Mercalli Scale.

Modern technology has made the Mercalli scale obsolete, although the method is often used to fill in "seismic blanks" when there is an insufficient number of seismic instruments—especially in remote areas. The more prominent scale is the Richter Scale, developed in 1935 by Charles Richter. The scale is logarithmic, which means that each successive whole number represents a 10-fold increase in power. Each magnitude number represents the maximum amplitude of a seismic wave at a distance of 62 miles (100 kilometers).

Richter Scale of Earthquake Magnitude

Magnitude	Energy equivalent in weight of TNT	Example
1.0	170 grams	
1.5	900 grams	
2.0	5.9 kilograms	
2.5	28 kilograms	
3.0	179 kilograms	
3.5	450 kilograms	
4.0	5.5 metric tons	
4.5	29 metric tons	Denver, Colorado (1965)
5.0	181 metric tons	
5.3	455 metric tons	San Francisco, California (1957)
5.5	910 metric tons	
6.0	5.7×10^3 metric tons	
6.3	14.4×10^3 metric tons	Long Beach, California (1933)
6.5	28.7×10^3 metric tons	San Fernando, California (1971)
7.0	181×10^3 metric tons	
7.1	228×10^3 metric tons	El Centro, California (1940)
7.5	910×10^3 metric tons	
7.7	1811×10^3 metric tons	Kern County, California (1962)
8.0	5706×10^3 metric tons	
8.2	$11,421 \times 10^3$ metric tons	San Francisco, California (1906)
8.5	$28,711 \times 10^3$ metric tons	Anchorage, Alaska (1964)
9.0	$181,999 \times 10^3$ metric tons	

Thanks to new techniques and more precise instrumentation, seismologists now use their own version of an earthquake scale to measure quakes. But the Richter Scale is still used by the popular press, because so many readers are familiar with it.

rising because of that collision—about ⅕ inch (5 millimeters) per year. Deep, substantial earthquakes are associated with colliding plates.

When plates slide by each other and no plate is created or destroyed, it is called a *strike-slip plate margin* (or *transform fault*). For example, along the San Andreas Fault in California, the Pacific plate slides northwest past the North American plate. Shallow, substantial earthquakes are associated with transform boundary plates.

Crustal plates have moved across the planet for at least the past 600 million years. Scientists believe that a supercontinent called *Pangaea,* first proposed by Alfred Wegener in 1915, existed about 250 million years ago. By 180 million years ago, the supercontinent had broken up into *Gondwanaland,* or Gondwana (a hypothetical continent formed by the union of South America, Africa, Australia, India, and Antarctica), and *Laurasia* (composed of North

America and Eurasia). About 65 million years ago—at approximately the time of extinction of the dinosaurs—the two continents began to separate, slowly forming the familiar outlines of today's continents. Scientists estimate that in 50 million years, the west coast of North America will tear itself free from the mainland, Australia will move northward and collide with Indonesia, and Africa and Asia will split apart at the Red Sea.

See also "Earth's Layers" and "Earthquakes" in this chapter.

EARTHQUAKES

Earthquakes are considered one of the most deadly natural catastrophes that can affect human life. Most often, a quake occurs in an earthquake-prone zone where two tectonic plates meet, split, or slip by one another (*see* "Plate Tectonics," earlier in this chapter); the type of plate contact determines whether the earthquake will be shallow or deep. During the movement of these plates, intense forces overcome the friction between the plates. If the plates become "locked together," forces build up and eventually must give away—with the plates lurching into new positions and creating an earthquake. Other earthquakes form in association with volcanic regions, where the buildup of heat and pressure often triggers smaller tremors and localized quakes.

The *focus* is the point under the Earth's surface where the earthquake energy is released. The point on the surface just above the focus is called the *epicenter*. Most earthquake foci occur no more than 62 miles (100 kilometers) below the surface.

SOME IMPORTANT MINERALS AND THEIR USES

Mineral	Chemical Composition	Occurrence/ Important Producers	Uses
Arsenic	As	Chile, China, France, Sweden, Mexico, U.S.	Glassmaking, insecticides, preservatives
Beryl	$Be_3A_{12}Si_6O_{18}$	Brazil, South Africa, U.S.	Beryllium ore, gemstones
Borax	$Na_2B_4O_7 10H_2O$	Tibet, U.S.	Antiseptic, disinfectant, flux, soap, water softener
Calcite	$CaCO_3$	Worldwide*	Building stones, portland cement, quicklime, soil conditioner
Chromite	$FeCr_2O_4$	Brazil, Philippines, South Africa, Turkey, former USSR	Chemicals, chromium ore, refractories
Chrysotile (serpentine)	$Mg_3Si_2O_5(OH)_4$	Canada, Russia, U.S.	Asbestos
Copper	Cu	Canada, Chile, Russia, U.S.	Chemicals, electronics, metal alloys, wire
Corundum	Al_2O_3	Greece, India, Myanmar, Sri Lanka, Thailand, U.S.	Abrasives, bearings, gemstones
Diamond	C	Australia, Brazil, South Africa, U.S.	Drills, gemstones, industrial abrasives, jewelry, tools and dies
Dolomite	$CaMg(CO_3)_2$	Worldwide†	Building stones, cement productions, magnesium source, refractories
Emerald	$Be_3Al_2Si_6O_{18}$	Australia, Columbia, Rhodesia, U.S., former USSR	Gemstones
Fluorite	CaF_2	Germany, Mexico, U.S.	Chemicals, metallurgy, optics
Gold	Au	Australia, Canada, South Africa, U.S.	Coins, dentistry, electronics, jewelry
Graphite	C	Madagascar, Mexico, Sri Lanka, U.S.	Brake linings, electronics, lubricants, pencils

* Usually mined as limestone or marble.   † Usually mined as the rock dolomite.

continues

Some Important Minerals and Their Uses, Continued

Mineral	Chemical Composition	Occurrence/ Important Producers	Uses
Gypsum	$CaSO_4 \cdot 2H_2O$	Canada, France, Great Britain, Mexico, U.S.	Building materials, flux, plaster of paris, retardant (in cement)
Halite	$NaCl$	Worldwide	Chemical, rock salt
Hematite	Fe_2O_3	Brazil, Canada, U.S., Venezuela	Iron ore, pigment, polishing agent
Kaolinite	$Al_4Si_4O_{10}(OH)_2$	Worldwide/esp. England	Ceramics (esp. porcelain), paper (as coating)
Limonite	$Fe_2O_3 \cdot 3H_2O$	Worldwide/esp. U.S.	Iron ore, pigment
Magnesite	$MgCO_3$	Austria, China, U.S.	Cement production, chemicals, magnesium ore, refractories
Mercury	Hg	Mexico, Spain, U.S.	Barometers and thermometers, dentistry, electronics, lamps, medicines
Olivine	$(Mg,Fe)_2SiO_4$	Myanmar, U.S.	Gemstones, ornamental stone, refractories
Opal	SiO_2H_2O	Australia, Honduras, Mexico, U.S.	Gemstones
Platinum	Pt	Canada, South Africa, former USSR	Jewelry, catalytic converters, oil refining
Quartz	SiO	Worldwide	Building materials, electronics, gems, glass manufacture, jewelry, optics
Ruby	Al_2O_3	Myanmar, Sri Lanka, Thailand	Bearings, lasers, gemstones
Sapphire	Al_2O_3	Australia, Myanmar, Sri Lanka, Thailand, U.S.	Bearings, dies, gauges, gemstones
Siderite	$FeCO_3$	Germany, Great Britain	Iron ore
Silver	Ag	Canada, Mexico, Peru, U.S.	Coins, electronics, electroplating, jewelry, photography, silverware
Spinel	$MgAl_2O_4$	Myanmar, Sri Lanka, Thailand, U.S.	Gemstones
Sulfur	S	Worldwide/esp. Mexico, U.S.	Chemicals, explosives, fertilizers, sulfa drugs, sulfuric acid
Talc	$Mg_3Si_4O_{10}(OH)$	Brazil, France, Japan, U.S.	Ceramics, face powder, lubricants, paints, paper (as filler), sinks and countertops, talcum powder
Topaz	$Al_2SiO_4(F,OH)_2$	Brazil, Russia, U.S.	Gemstones
Uraninite	UO_2	Canada, South Africa, U.S.	Uranium ore (pitchblende)
Wolframite	$(Fe,Mn)WO_4$	Australia, England, Malay Peninsula, Myanmar, Portugal	Tungsten ore
Wollastonite	$CaSiO_3$	Finland, Italy, Romania, U.S.	Ceramics, paints (as filler)
Zircon	$ZrSiO_4$	Australia, Brazil, India, Sri Lanka, U.S.	Gemstones, zirconium ore

IGNEOUS, SEDIMENTARY, AND METAMORPHIC ROCKS

Igneous rocks are formed by the cooling and subsequent hardening of molten material. Intrusive igneous rocks are produced when magma hardens slowly underground. Extrusive igneous rocks result when lava, molten material that flows on the surface, solidifies quickly.

Sedimentary rocks form from the accumulation of eroded material that is transported and deposited by water, wind, or glaciers. Detrital sediments result when preexisting rock erodes; chemical sediments occur through precipitation in shallow marine environments.

Metamorphic rocks form when preexisting igneous or sedimentary rocks are transformed by external forces. Regional metamorphism alters rocks through heat and pressure. Contact metamorphism occurs when a magma intrusion heats the surrounding rock. Dynamic metamorphism is the product of tectonic forces, usually along thrust faults.

IGNEOUS, SEDIMENTARY, AND METAMORPHIC ROCKS

Name	Type	Texture	Mineral Composition
Igneous			
Andesite	Extrusive	Coarse grains/crystalline	Feldspar, pyroxene, mica
Anorthosite	Intrusive	Coarse grains/crystalline	Feldspar; traces of iron oxides, pyroxene, olivine
Basalt	Extrusive	Fine grains/crystalline	Feldspar, pyroxene, usu. magnetite
Gabbro	Intrusive	Coarse grains/crystalline	Feldspar, pyroxene, olivine, magnetite
Granite	Intrusive	Coarse grains/crystalline	Quartz, feldspar; mica, hornblende, muscovite often present
Obsidian	Extrusive	Glassy/crystalline	Silicate minerals, often quartz and feldspar
Pegmatite	Intrusive	Coarse grains/crystalline	Quartz, feldspar; mica or pyroxene often present
Porphyry	Intrusive	Medium grains/crystalline	Feldspar, quartz, olivine, or pyroxene embedded in dark-colored groundmass
Pumice	Extrusive	Fine grains/crystalline	Quartz, feldspar
Rhyolite	Extrusive	Fine grains/often glassy/crystalline	Quarty, alkali feldspars, light-colored
Sedimentary			
Breccia	Detrital	Coarse, angular grains	Cemented rock fragments; calcite or silica
Chalk	Chemical	Fine, rounded grains	Calcite
Chert	Chemical	Fine grains/crystalline	Silica
Clay	Detrital	Fine, angular grains	Clay minerals, quartz, feldspar, mica
Coal	Chemical	Fine-medium grains	Organic matter (high carbon content)
Conglomerate	Detrital	Coarse, rounded grains	Cemented rock fragments; silica, iron oxides, or calcite
Dolomite	Chemical	Fine-coarse grains/crystalline	Dolomite
Flint	Chemical	Fine grains/crystalline	Silica
Gypsum	Chemical	Crystalline	Gypsum
Limestone	Chemical	Fine-coarse, angular, or rounded grains	Calcite; lesser amounts of quartz, organic matter, or fossils often present
Sandstone	Detrital	Medium, angular or rounded grains	Quartz; lesser amounts of calcite, silica, iron oxides, feldspar, or mica
Shale	Detrital	Fine, angular grains	Clay minerals, mica, usu. organic matter or fossils
Siltstone	Detrital	Fine, angular grains	Quartz, calcite
Metamorphic			
Gneiss	Regional	Coarse grains/foliated, crystalline	Quartz, feldspar; garnet, hornblende, mica may be present
Marble	Contact	Coarse-fine grains/crystalline	Calcite or dolomite
Quartzite	Contact	Coarse grains/nonfoliated	Quartz
Schist	Regional	Medium grains/foliated	Quartz, feldspar, mica
Slate	Regional	Fine grains/foliated	Quartz, feldspar, mica, clay minerals

COMMON GEOLOGY AND CARTOGRAPHY TERMS

Additional terms are defined in the preceding geology and geophysics sections.

abyssal zone   A region of greatest ocean depth, generally greater than 328 feet (100 meters), including the deep-sea trenches. Biological activity is rare in the abyssal zone; light does not penetrate the water, as the depth and pressure are tremendous. The region represents about 96,525,000 square miles (250 million square kilometers) of Earth's surface.

age   An interval of geological time that indicates when a body of rock was formed in the surface of Earth. A group of ages forms an epoch.

alluvium   The sediment carried by rivers, including deposits from estuaries, lakes, and other freshwater bodies draining into a river. The particles of sediment are generally smaller than 0.000788 inch (0.02 millimeters), depending on such factors as valleyside slopes in the watershed, the distance carried downstream, and progressive wear on the particles as they move downstream.

barrier beach   An accumulation of sand, rock, and other material lying parallel to the coast but separated from it by a channel; a barrier beach measures from a few yards to a few miles in width. Large barrier beaches may be identified as barrier islands. They are formed by the action of waves but are usually vulnerable to overwashing or breaching during severe storms.

bathyal zone   A zone of ocean water ranging from about 656 to 3,281 feet (200 to 1,000 meters) in depth, generally located along continental slopes. Unlike the abyssal zone, light reaches the upper layer of the bathyal zone, and there is abundant biological activity in the water. The bathyal zone of the world covers a total of about 15,444,000 square miles (40 million square kilometers).

bed   The smallest division of stratified sedimentary rock, usually occurring as a relatively thin sheet of sedimentary material separating distinctively different layers above and below it. A bed often marks a particular event in geologic history, such as a volcanic eruption, and it may contain fossils that help identify its age.

Cambrian   The earliest period of the Paleozoic era, about 600 million years ago. Rocks formed at this period contain some of the earliest fossil remains of invertebrate animals.

"Major Science and Technology Museums and Their Special Collections" in chapter 11
Go to

continental drift   The shifting of continental landmasses from one location to another on the face of Earth, owing to seafloor spreading.

Coriolis effect   A force produced on objects moving on a north-south line on the surface of Earth because of the angular velocity of Earth as it rotates from west to east. Thus, a projectile fired directly southward from the North Pole would be deviated to the west. The Coriolis force affects mainly the flow of air in the atmosphere.

creep   The slowest mass movement of rock and soil on gentle slopes with angles of less than 20 degrees. The movement—usually fractions of an inch per year—is caused by freezing, thawing, wetting, drying, and the force of gravity. The effect can be observed in the tendency of telephone poles, tombstones, and other objects to change position (especially tilt) on gentle slopes over a period of years.

diagenesis   The process whereby sedimentary rock is formed from sediment because of compaction, reduced pore space between particles, and chemical reactions between molecules of the compressed particles and dissolved substances in moisture between the particles.

era   An interval of geological time composed of a group of periods.

estuary   The portion of a river that is affected by ocean tides above the mouth, with a resulting mixture of salt water and fresh water. Most estuaries are former valleys that were flooded by rising ocean levels after the last glacial event. The Hudson River is an example of an estuary.

fjord   A narrow sea inlet between mountain slopes. Most fjords were once glaciated valleys that became flooded by rising sea water after the last ice age. In some cases, the bottom of the fjord may be lower than the bottom of the sea at its opening into the fjord.

geology   The science of the structure and composition of Earth.

glacier   An accumulation of land ice that develops in the colder regions and higher latitudes of the Earth. It is formed by compaction of accumulated snow moving downslope from a source area because of the force of gravity. A glacier is usually confined within the limited space of a valley or basin. It may be gaining ice at the source but losing ice at a point where it melts while moving into warmer temperatures or a body of water.

intermittent stream   A stream, often in reference to desert areas, that carries water only part of the time, usually during a flash flood.

lava   *See* **magma.**

leaching   The action of water draining through soil layers carrying dissolved minerals or organic matter from the upper layers. Because leaching tends to remove alkaline substances, the soils eventually become acidic.

magma   Hot, molten material from deep underground, usually associated with volcanic eruptions. Magma that reaches the surface is called lava.

Mercator projection   A map in which the spherical Earth is projected as a cylinder onto a flat surface, resulting in straight-line bearings that are correct. Such a map is most commonly used for navigation charts, although the projection distorts the areas toward the North and South poles.

meridian   A line of longitude. It is formed by creating an imaginary line that approximates a semicircle around the Earth through both poles and at a right angle to the equator.

mesa   An isolated, flat-topped plateau with steep sides. Composed of limestone or hard sandstone, the mesa's top rock is usually more resistant to erosion than the underlying rock. Mesas eventually erode into buttes. Mesas are common in arid parts of the southwestern United States and Mexico.

metal   Any elementary substance, such as gold, copper, or silver, that is crystalline when solid and typically displays opacity, ductility, conductivity, and luster. Metals may be found in their natural state or in combination with other minerals, commonly called ores.

mid-ocean ridge   A ridge of volcanic mountains on the ocean floor, usually associated with seafloor spreading of crustal plates. These ridges occasionally rise above the surface and form volcanic islands such as Iceland, located on the Mid-Atlantic Ridge.

mineral   An inorganic compound naturally occurring in the Earth's crust and having a precise chemical formula and usually a crystalline structure. Minerals vary greatly in size, shape, color, and economic value. With the exception of natural glasses such as obsidian, they are the basic building blocks of rocks.

moraine   A mound or ridge of unstratified rock and dirt deposited by a glacier. Moraines may dam up melting glacier water, forming circular mountain lakes called tarns or long, narrow lakes such as those found in New York State's Finger Lakes region.

mountain   A naturally formed elevation that rises above the surrounding landmass and is higher than a hill, usually 2,000 feet (610 meters) or more. Mountains are formed by subduction (when a lithospheric plate dives under another plate) or by a collision between continental landmasses. The latter processes produced the Andes and the Himalayas, respectively. Volcanoes can also form singular or chains of mountains.

parallel   A line of latitude. It is formed by creating an imaginary line that runs parallel to the equator and connects places with the same latitude.

permafrost   A deep layer of soil that remains frozen during summer, despite the thawing of the ground above it. The result is in the poorly drained landscape typical of the arctic regions of Canada and northern Europe, especially the former Soviet Union.

plateau   A broad, flat land area raised sharply above the surrounding landscape on at least one side. They form where erosion-resistant rock rests on weaker rocks or soil.

Sciences

prime meridian   The line of zero degrees longitude that runs through Greenwich, England, and from which all other lines of longitude (meridians) are measured.

projection   In cartography, a systematic construction of intersecting coordinate lines on a flat surface, representing the meridians and parallels of the curved surface of the Earth. Each method of projection results in some distortion of the planet's features; *See* **Mercator projection** for an example.

relief   The variations in elevation and slope between the higher and lower parts of a given landscape. A map displaying these contour changes is called a relief map.

rock   an aggregate of minerals; generally classified as igneous, sedimentary, and metamorphic.

sand   Small, loose, granular substance formed by the disintegration of rock due to erosion. Consisting mostly of silicates, sand has a number of industrial uses, especially in abrasives and glassmaking.

scale   The ratio of the actual size of a place or region and its representation on a map.

seamount   An isolated submarine mountain that rises from the abyssal plain of the ocean floor but does not reach the surface of the water. Seamounts are volcanic in origin and may develop at points where the oceanic crustal plate passes over hot spots. Their existence may be an indirect proof of the theory of plate tectonics.

seismology   The study of the seismic waves generated by earthquakes or artificially produced vibrations of the Earth. Seismologists use these waves, measured on a seismograph, to locate petroleum reserves or to estimate the size and location of the Earth's plates.

soil   The layer of unconsolidated, fragmented, weathered rock mixed with organic material that makes up the topmost surface of the Earth.

stalactite   A columnar deposit, usually of calcium carbonate, hanging from the ceiling of a cave. It is formed by the precipitation of mineral-rich water and is often shaped like an icicle.

stalagmite   A columnar deposit, usually of calcium carbonate, that forms on a cavern floor. It is caused by the precipitation of mineral-rich water dripping from the ceiling.

stone   A concretion of mineral matter of indeterminate size and shape.

trench   A long, deep valley found on the ocean floor and bordering a subduction zone. Formed by the downward movement of one oceanic plate as it is consumed by another, a trench is associated with the creation of new oceanic crust. The Marianas Trench is the deepest in the world, measuring 36,201 feet (11,034 meters).

tundra   A vast, level, treeless plain characteristic of arctic and subarctic regions, especially in northern Europe, Asia, and North America. The top layer of the soil thaws each spring, while the base remains frozen, resulting in boggy areas. The dominant vegetation consists of mosses, lichens, and dwarf shrubs.

vent   An opening in the Earth's crust through which volcanic materials are violently expelled. Hydrothermal vents on ocean floors emit mineral-rich solutions that support a fantastic array of life, including tubeworms.

volcano   A vent in a mountain or the Earth's crust through which gases, rock fragments, and hot, molten lava are expelled from the Earth's interior. Volcanic eruptions usually occur along subduction zones or above hot spots, places where magma from the Earth's mantle upwells and melts through the crust.

water table   The irregular upper surface of underground water. It is usually highest beneath hills (though still farther below the surface) and about the same level as river channels in valleys.

weathering   The alteration or decomposition of rocks or soil by heat, cold, wind, precipitation, or chemical reactions, such as leaching, brought on by contact with the atmosphere.

METEOROLOGY

CLOUD TYPES

altocumulus (Ac)   Similar to cirrocumulus, with patches of small clouds occasionally separated by thin breaks. Although altocumulus clouds also may be identified by a "mackerel sky" pattern, they are lower, at around 10,000 feet, and the clumps of white or gray water droplets or ice crystals are larger. The clouds may develop directly overhead, depending on the temperature of the atmosphere, and may produce a shower.

altostratus (As)   Dull, drab gray or blue middle-level clouds that usually contain moisture in the form of water droplets. Altostratus clouds are often opaque, giving a "ground glass" view of the Sun or Moon behind them. They may be a source of virga, filaments of ice crystals or water droplets that fall toward Earth but evaporate before touching the ground.

cirrocumulus (Cc)   Loosely packed sheets of small white cloud segments at altitudes of around 18,000 to 20,000 feet, forming a "mackerel sky" resembling scales on a fish. The clouds may consist of ice crystals or water droplets or both. The patchy appearance is caused by vertical air currents at the cloud level, indicating a lack of stability and a possible approaching storm.

cirrostratus (Cs)   Translucent veils of white fibrous cloud that tend to occur at altitudes of around 20,000 feet or more. Cirrostratus clouds often cover the entire sky and may cause the appearance of halos or reflected images of the Sun or Moon. These clouds may signal an approaching storm.

cirrus (Ci)   Generally, the highest clouds, forming "mares' tails" at altitudes from 20,000 to 40,000 feet. The clouds may appear as delicate white filaments, featherlike tufts, or fibrous bands of ice crystals.

cumulonimbus (Cb)   Thunderstorm clouds that may vary considerably in altitude from ominously dark lower portions below 5,000 feet to white anvil-shaped tops that may reach upward to 50,000 feet. They contain large amounts of moisture, some of which may be in the form of hail. The cumulonimbus

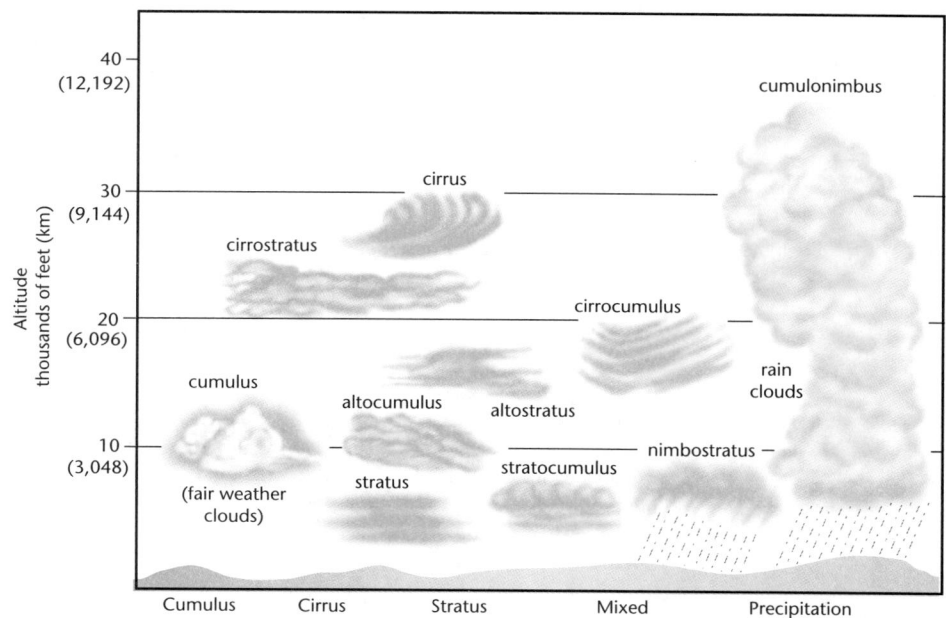

cloud may appear alone or as part of a wall of advancing storm clouds.

cumulus (Cu)   Low-level billowy clouds that are usually dark on the bottom while their tops resemble giant white cotton balls. A cumulus cloud may be relatively tall, extending from a base around 2,000 feet to a top near 10,000 feet above ground. It casts a dark shadow and may be a source of moisture but generally produces no more than a summer shower.

nimbostratus (Ns)   Low, dark rain clouds with ragged tops that have bottoms only a few hundred feet above ground and may range upward to an altitude of 3,000 feet. They obscure the Sun and are associated with continuous rain, sleet, or snow, but they are rarely accompanied by thunder or lightning.

stratocumulus (Sc)   Dark gray rolls of clouds that usually cover the entire sky at an altitude from 1,500 to 6,500 feet. The rounded segments may appear checkered or wavelike, and there may or may not be breaks of blue sky between segments. Stratocumulus clouds contain moisture but are usually not rain producers.

stratus (St)   Wispy foglike clouds that hover a few hundred feet above ground, sometimes obscuring hills or tall buildings. They may begin as ground fog and can be a source of drizzle.

BEAUFORT SCALE OF WIND FORCE

Beaufort Number	Knots	Description	Effect at Sea	Effect Ashore
0	Less than 1	Calm	Sea is like a mirror.	Smoke rises vertically.
1	1–3	Light air	Ripples with the appearance of a scale are formed but without foam crests.	Wind vanes are not moved, but wind direction is shown by smoke drift.
2	4–6	Light breeze	Small wavelets, still short but more pronounced, appear; crests have a glassy appearance but do not break.	Wind is felt on face; leaves rustle; ordinary vane is moved by wind.
3	7–10	Gentle breeze	Large wavelets appear; crests begin to break; foam is of glassy appearance, perhaps with scattered whitecaps.	Leaves and small twigs are in constant motion; wind extends light flag.
4	11–16	Moderate breeze	Small waves appear, becoming longer; there are fairly frequent whitecaps.	Dust and loose paper are raised; small branches are moved.
5	17–21	Fresh breeze	Moderate waves arise, taking a more pronounced long form; many whitecaps are formed (with chance of some spray).	Small trees in leaf begin to sway; crested wavelets form on island waters.
6	22–27	Strong breeze	Large waves begin to form; the white foam crests are more extensive everywhere (probably with some spray).	Large branches are in motion; whistling is heard in telegraph wires; umbrellas are used with difficulty.
7	28–33	Moderate gale (high wind)	Sea heaps up, and white foam from breaking waves begins to be blown in streaks along the direction of the wind; spindrift begins.	Whole trees are in motion; inconvenience is felt in walking against the wind.
8	34–40	Fresh gale	Moderately high waves of greater length appear; edges of crests break into spindrift. The foam is blown in well-marked streaks along the direction of the wind.	Twigs are broken off trees, and the wind generally impedes progress.

Beaufort Number	Knots	Description	Effect at Sea	Effect Ashore
9	41–47	Strong gale	High waves appear; dense streaks of foam arise along the direction of the wind; sea begins to roll; spray may affect visibility.	Slight structural damage occurs (chimney pots and slate removed).
10	48–55	Storm	Very high waves with long overhanging crests appear. The resulting foam in great patches is blown in dense white streaks along the direction of the wind. On the whole, the surface of the sea takes on a white appearance. The rolling of the sea becomes heavy and appears to come in shocks. Visibility is affected.	It is seldom experienced inland. Trees are uprooted; considerable structural damage occurs.
11	56–63	Violent storm	Exceptionally high waves appear. (Small and medium-size ships might for a long time be lost to view behind the waves.) The sea is completely covered with long white patches of foam lying along the direction of the wind. Everywhere the edges of the wave crests are blown into froth. Visibility is affected.	It is very rarely experienced and is accompanied by widespread damage.
12	Above 63 (above 72)	Hurricane	The air is filled with foam and spray. The sea is completely white with a driving spray; visibility is very seriously affected.	Devastation occurs.

WINDCHILL FACTOR

Windchill is based on the idea that moving air carries heat away from a warm body, making the temperature feel colder than the thermometer indicates. It was coined by Antarctic explorer Paul A. Siple in 1939, and the first windchill factor table was developed in 1945, measuring how long it would take water to freeze in a container 30 feet off the ground. In fall 2001, the National Weather Service issued a new windchill formula, based on experiments with humans and wind at about 5 feet off the ground. The new figures appear below, and the shaded area indicates temperatures that caused frostbite at exposures of 15 minutes or less.

Wind Speed (m.p.h.)	Thermometer Reading (°F)											
	30	25	20	15	10	5	0	−5	−10	−15	−20	−25
5	25	19	13	7	1	−5	−11	−16	−22	−28	−34	−40
10	21	15	9	3	−4	−10	−16	−22	−28	−35	−41	−47
15	19	13	6	0	−7	−13	−19	−26	−32	−39	−45	−51
20	17	11	4	−2	−9	−15	−22	−29	−35	−42	−48	−55
25	16	9	3	−4	−11	−17	−24	−31	−37	−44	−51	−58
30	15	8	1	−5	−12	−19	−26	−33	−39	−46	−53	−60
35	14	7	0	−7	−14	−21	−27	−34	−41	−48	−55	−62
40	13	6	−1	−8	−15	−22	−29	−36	−43	−50	−57	−64
45	12	5	−2	−9	−16	−23	−30	−37	−44	−51	−58	−65
50	12	4	−3	−10	−17	−24	−31	−38	−45	−52	−60	−67
55	11	4	−3	−11	−18	−25	−32	−39	−46	−54	−61	−68
60	10	3	−4	−11	−19	−26	−33	−40	−48	−55	−62	−69

Sciences

PHYSICS

BASIC FORMULAS AND LAWS OF PHYSICS

acceleration $a = (v_f - v_0)/t$, where a represents acceleration, v_f represents the final velocity, v_0 represents the initial velocity, and t represents the time.

acceleration of gravity $W = mg$, where W represents the force of weight, m represents the mass of the object, and g represents acceleration due to gravity (32 ft/sec^2).

centrifugal force $F = mv^2/r$, where F represents force, m represents the mass of a moving object, v represents its velocity, and r represents the radius of the orbit of the mass.

Coulomb's law $F = kQ_aQ_b/d^2$, where F represents the electrostatic force, k represents a constant of proportionality, Q_a and Q_b represent quantities of electrostatic charge, and d represents the distance between the charges.

electrical power $P = IV$, where P represents power, I represents electrical current, and V represents electric potential.

energy-matter relationship $E = mc^2$, where E represents energy, m represents mass, and c represents the velocity of light.

gravity inverse-square law $F = g\,Mm/r^2$, where F represents force, g represents the acceleration due to gravity, M and m represent the masses of two objects, and r represents the distance between the masses.

kinetic energy $KE = \frac{1}{2}mv^2$, where KE represents kinetic energy, m represents the mass of a moving object, and v represents the velocity.

light inverse-square law $I_1/I_2 = (d_2/d_1)^2$, where I_1 represents the light intensity at distance d_1 from the source and I_2 represents the intensity of light at distance d_2 from the source.

mass and weight relationship $m_1/m_2 = W_1/W_2$, where m_1 and m_2 represent two masses and W_1 and W_2 represent their respective weights.

momentum $p = mv$, where p represents momentum, m represents the mass of the object, and v represents velocity.

Newton's second law $F = ma$, where F represents force, m represents mass of the object, and a represents the acceleration.

Ohm's law $R = V/I$, where R represents electrical resistance, V represents electrical potential, and I represents electrical current.

potential energy $E = mgh$, where E represents potential energy, m represents the mass of an object, g represents the acceleration due to gravity, and h represents the distance to be traveled by m.

power $P = W/t$, where P represents power, W represents work, and t represents the time required to perform the indicated work.

velocity $v = d/t$, where v represents the velocity and d represents the distance traveled in time t.

wave equation $V = f\lambda$, where V represents the velocity of the wave, f represents its frequency, and λ represents the wavelength.

weight   *See* **acceleration of gravity**.

work $W = Fd$, where W represents work, F represents the applied force, and d represents the distance over which it is applied.

COMMON PHYSICS TERMS

acceleration   The rate of change of velocity with respect to time. It is calculated by subtracting the initial or starting velocity from the final velocity and dividing the difference by the time required to reach that velocity.

achromatic   An optical system that will transmit light without breaking it down into its component colors.

acoustics   The science of the production, transmission, and effect of sound waves.

action   The effect produced by a force, such as the force of a hammer hitting a nail; the action of the force is its effect, and the nail is driven into the wood.

adhesion   The tendency of matter to cling to other types of matter, due to intermolecular forces.

adiabatic   Pertaining to any activity that is not accompanied by a gain or loss of heat.

anode   The positive terminal of an electrical current flow. In a vacuum tube, electrons flow from a cathode toward an anode.

Bohr theory   A commonly accepted concept of the atom introduced by Niels Bohr in 1913. It holds that each atom consists of a small, dense, positively charged nucleus surrounded by negatively charged electrons that move in fixed, defined orbits about the nucleus, the total number of electrons normally balancing the total positive charge of particles in the nucleus.

Boyle's law   The principle that the volume of a gas times its pressure is constant at a fixed temperature.

cathode   The negative terminal of an electric current system. In a vacuum tube, the filament serves as the cathode or source of electrons that are emitted.

conduction   The transfer of heat by molecular motion from a source of high temperature to a region of lower temperature, tending toward a result of equalized temperatures.

convection   The mechanical transfer of heated molecules of a gas or liquid from a source to another area, as when a room is warmed by the movement of air molecules heated by a radiator.

Coulomb's law   The principle that an electrostatic force of attraction or repulsion between electrical charges is directly proportional to the product of the electrical charges and inversely proportional to the square of the distance between them.

deceleration   The decrease in velocity per unit time. It is also called negative acceleration.

density   The mass per unit volume of a material. Every material has a characteristic density.

energy   The ability or capacity to do work. There are numerous types of energy, including potential (stored), kinetic (from motion), heat, light, electrical, chemical, and nuclear energy. One form of energy can be transformed into another form, but energy normally is not created or destroyed.

entropy   A physical quantity that is the measurement of the amount of disorder in a system.

equilibrium   A state of balance between opposing forces or effects.

force   The influence on a body that causes it to accelerate, as expressed by the formula $F = ma$, where F is force, m is mass, and a is acceleration.

friction   The resistance to motion between two surfaces moving over each other. It is usually measured in terms of force and velocity.

heat   A form of energy that results from the disordered motion of molecules. As the motion becomes more rapid and disordered, the amount of heat is increased.

kinetic energy   Energy that is associated with the motion of an object.

mass   The measured amount of a material. All materials possess mass, and that mass never changes no matter where it resides in the universe.

mechanics   A branch of physics that deals with the motion of objects.

medium   The matter through which a wave travels. Sound waves need a medium; light waves do not need a medium and can travel through a vacuum.

particle   Anything small and discrete, such as a proton, neutron, atom, or molecule.

Sciences

phase   The state of matter of a material—either solid, liquid, gas, or plasma.

physical law   A description of a certain behavior in nature; for example, the idea that an object does not change its position until it is acted on by an outside force is a physical law.

Planck's law   Relates temperature to wavelength, stating that hotter objects radiate most at shorter wavelengths.

It is rumored that in the late 19th century, Australian meteorologist Clemet Wragge gave tropical storms that hit his continent the names of politicians' wives and other people he didn't like.

plasma   A hot, ionized (electrically charged) gas.

potential energy   Energy that is stored because of position or configuration, such as the gravitational energy of a weight that is positioned on the roof of a building.

power   The rate at which work is performed.

pressure   The force acting on a per-unit area of a surface.

radiation   The emission and propagation of radiant energy—either atomic, by radioactive substances, or spectral, as in light.

reaction   The effect opposite of an action. A reaction is equal to an action but is in the opposite direction. For example, when a stone strikes a wall, the wall does not move or change shape—it pushes back with a reaction that is equal to the action.

resistance   A force that opposes a change in motion or shape.

speed   The distance traveled divided by the time it takes to travel the distance.

strain   The change in a shape or size of a body caused by pressure and movement.

stress   Tension forces exerted on a body that tend to produce a deformation of that body.

surface tension   The property of a liquid in which the surface molecules show a strong inward attraction, forming an apparent membrane across the surface of the liquid.

thermodynamics   The study of the movement of heat from one body to another and the relations between heat and other forms of energy.

vacuum   In theory, it is the absence of matter; in space, a vacuum is where air or other gases are almost exhausted.

velocity   The speed with which an object travels over a specified distance during a measured amount of time.

vibration   The regular oscillation, backward and forward, of a material. For example, elastic vibrates, as do most fluids.

viscosity   The property of a liquid that makes it resist flow or any change in the arrangement of its molecules. The higher the viscosity, the "thicker" a liquid seems.

weight   The force on a body produced by the downward pull of gravity on it.

work   The force applied to an object times the distance over which it is applied. Work may be independent of the energy expended.

Additional terms are defined in "Common Chemistry Terms" in this chapter.

"Symbols Used in Science, Mathematics, and Technology" in chapter 12
Go to

Sciences

MATHEMATICS

BASIC RULES OF MATHEMATICS
ADDITION OF FRACTIONS

$$\frac{a}{b} + \frac{c}{d} = \frac{ad}{bd} + \frac{bc}{bd} = \frac{ad+bc}{bd}$$

$$\frac{2}{3} + \frac{4}{5} = \frac{2\times5}{3\times5} + \frac{3\times4}{3\times5} = \frac{10}{15} + \frac{12}{15} = \frac{10+12}{15} = \frac{22}{15} = 1\frac{7}{15}$$

SUBTRACTION OF FRACTIONS

$$\frac{a}{b} - \frac{c}{d} = \frac{ad}{bd} - \frac{bc}{bd} = \frac{ad-bc}{bd}$$

$$\frac{4}{5} - \frac{2}{3} = \frac{4\times3}{5\times3} - \frac{5\times2}{5\times3} = \frac{12}{15} - \frac{10}{15} = \frac{12-10}{15} = \frac{2}{15}$$

MULTIPLICATION OF FRACTIONS

$$\frac{a}{b} \times \frac{c}{d} = \frac{ac}{bd}$$

$$\frac{2}{5} \times \frac{7}{4} = \frac{2\times7}{5\times4} = \frac{14}{20} = \frac{14\div2}{20\div2} = \frac{7}{10}$$

DIVISION OF FRACTIONS

$$\frac{a}{b} \div \frac{c}{d} = \frac{a}{b} \times \frac{d}{c} = \frac{ad}{bc}$$

$$\frac{3}{4} \div \frac{2}{3} = \frac{3}{4} \times \frac{3}{2} = \frac{3\times3}{4\times2} = \frac{9}{8} = 1\frac{1}{8}$$

SOLVING FOR AN UNKNOWN NUMBER x, WHERE a, b, AND c ARE KNOWN NUMBERS

Unknown Multiplied by a Number

$$ax = b \qquad\qquad 5x = 10$$

$$\frac{ax}{a} = \frac{b}{a} \qquad\qquad \frac{5x}{5} = \frac{10}{5}$$

$$x = \frac{b}{a} \qquad\qquad x = 2$$

Number Added to an Unknown

$$x + a = b \qquad\qquad x + 7 = 10$$

$$x + a - a = b - a \qquad x + 7 - 7 = 10 - 7$$

$$x = b - a \qquad\qquad x = 3$$

Unknown in a Fraction

$$\frac{x}{a} = \frac{b}{c} \qquad\qquad \frac{x}{5} = \frac{3}{8}$$

$$xc = ab \qquad\qquad x \times 8 = 5 \times 3$$

$$x = \frac{ab}{c} \qquad\qquad x = \frac{5\times3}{8} = \frac{15}{8} = 1\frac{7}{8}$$

NUMBERS WITH EXPONENTS

$$a^1 = a$$

$$a^2 = a \times a$$

$$a^3 = a \times a \times a$$

$$a^n = a \times a \times \ldots \times a \ (n \text{ factors})$$

$$a^{-n} = \frac{1}{a^n}$$

$$a^x \times a^y = a^{x+y}$$

$$a^x \div a^y = a^{x-y}$$

Thus:

$$\frac{2^3}{3^2} = \frac{2\times2\times2}{3\times3} = \frac{8}{9}$$

$$10^{-3} = \frac{1}{10^3} = \frac{1}{1,000}$$

$$10^2 \times 10^3 = 10^{2+3} = 10^5 = 10 \times 10 \times 10 \times 10 \times 10 = 100,000$$

$$10^6 \div 10^4 = 10^{6-4} = 10^2 = 10 \times 10 = 100$$

If 111,111,111 is multiplied by itself, the result is all of the digits in ascending to descending order, or 12,345,678,987,654,321.

Sciences

DECIMAL AND PERCENT EQUIVALENTS OF COMMON FRACTIONS

A plus symbol (+) indicates that the decimal repeats.

Fraction	Decimal	Percent (%)	Fraction	Decimal	Percent (%)
1/64	0.015625	1.5625	1/2	0.5	50
1/32	0.3125	3.125	17/32	0.53125	53.125
1/16	0.0625	6.25	6/11	0.5454+	54.5454+
1/12	0.0833+	8.333+	5/9	0.5555+	55.5555+
1/11	0.0909+	9.0909+	9/16	0.5625	56.25
3/32	0.09375	9.375	4/7	0.571428+	57.1428+
1/10	0.1	10	7/12	0.5833+	58.3333+
1/9	0.1111+	11.1111+	19/32	0.59375	59.375
1/8	0.125	12.5	3/5	0.6	60
1/7	0.142857+	14.2857+	5/8	0.625	62.5
5/32	0.15625	15.625	7/11	0.6363+	63.6363+
1/6	0.1666+	16.6666+	21/32	0.65625	65.625
2/11	0.1818+	18.1818+	2/3	0.66666+	66.666+
3/16	0.1875	18.75	11/16	0.6875	68.75
1/5	0.2	20	7/10	0.7	70
7/32	0.21875	21.875	5/7	0.714285+	71.4285+
2/9	0.2222+	22.2222+	23/32	0.71875	71.875
1/4	0.25	25	8/11	0.7272+	72.7272+
3/11	0.2727+	27.2727+	3/4	0.75	75
9/32	0.28125	28.125	7/9	0.7777+	77.7777+
2/7	0.285714+	28.5714+	25/32	0.78125	78.125
3/10	0.3	30	4/5	0.8	80
5/16	0.3125	31.25	13/16	0.8125	81.25
1/3	0.33333+	33.333+	9/11	0.8181+	81.8181+
11/32	0.34375	34.375	5/6	0.8333+	83.3333+
4/11	0.3636+	36.3636+	27/32	0.84375	84.375
3/8	0.375	37.5	6/7	0.857142+	85.7142+
2/5	0.4	40	7/8	0.875	87.5
13/32	0.40625	40.625	8/9	0.8888+	88.8888+
5/12	0.4166+	41.6666+	9/10	0.9	90
3/7	0.428571+	42.8571+	29/32	0.90625	90.625
7/16	0.4375	43.75	10/11	0.9090+	90.9090+
4/9	0.4444+	44.4444+	11/12	0.9166+	91.6666+
5/11	0.4545+	45.4545+	15/16	0.9375	93.75
15/32	0.46875	46.875	31/32	0.96875	96.875

GEOMETRIC SHAPES AND THEIR AREA, CIRCUMFERENCE, AND VOLUME FORMULAS

In this section, π (pi) is the ratio of the circumference of a circle to its diameter. It is a transcendental number having a value to eight places of 3.14159265. For practical purposes, the value is 3.1416.

TWO-DIMENSIONAL SHAPES

circle   A continuous line or the plane bounded by such a line, in which every point of the line is equidistant from the central point lying on the plane. The complete distance along such a line is the circumference C of the circle. A circle is commonly described by its radius r—a straight line extending from the center of the circle to any point on the perimeter—and its diameter d—a straight line extending from a point on the perimeter, through the center, to a point on the perimeter on the other side of the circle (it is also expressed as twice the radius).

$$C = \pi d = 2\pi r \qquad \text{Area} = \pi r^2$$

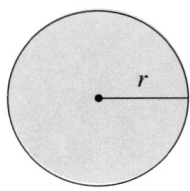

ellipse   The path of a point that moves so that the sum of its distances from two fixed points—the foci—is constant. An ellipse is commonly described by its semimajor axis *a* and its semiminor axis *b*.

$$\text{Area} = \pi ab$$

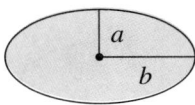

polygon   A closed plan figure bound by three or more straight lines.

rectangle   A four-sided polygon, bound by four straight lines at 90° angles, whose opposite sides are parallel to each other and are equal in length.

$$\text{Area} = (\text{length})(\text{width}) = lw$$

regular hexagon   A six-sided regular polygon.

$$\text{Area} = 2.59808a^2$$

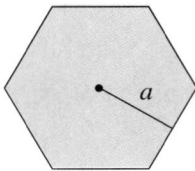

"Mathematics Symbols" in chapter 12; "Standard Sizes Chart" in chapter 19
Go to

regular octagon   An eight-sided regular polygon.

$$\text{Area} = 4.82843a^2$$

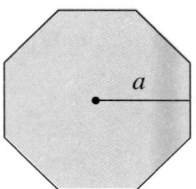

regular pentagon   A five-sided regular polygon.

$$\text{Area} = 1.72048a^2$$

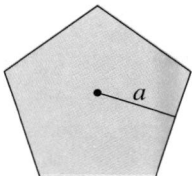

regular polygon   A polygon in which all sides are equal in length and all inside angles are equal.

square   A four-sided regular polygon. Its four inside angles are all 90°.

$$\text{Area} = a^2$$

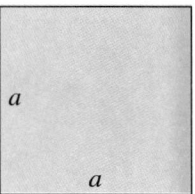

triangle   A three-sided polygon; its three inside angles always add up to 180°.

$$\text{Area} = \tfrac{1}{2}(\text{perpendicular height})(\text{base}) = \tfrac{1}{2}ab$$

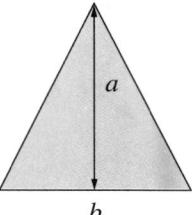

Sciences

THREE-DIMENSIONAL SHAPES

circular cylinder   A solid that has two equal-sided circular bases and a third side that joins the bases.

Volume = $\pi r^2 h$ Surface area = $2\pi rh + 2\pi r^2$

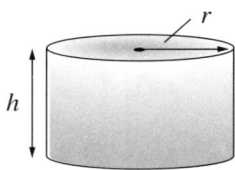

cube   A solid that has six square sides, with each at right angles to each adjacent side.

Volume = a^3 Surface area = $6a^2$

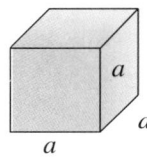

rectangular prism   A six-sided solid whose opposite sides are equal in length and parallel to each other. All junctions of its sides are at 90° angles.

Volume = lwh Surface area = $2hw + 2hl + 2lw$

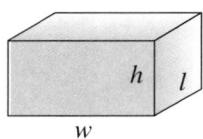

regular right pyramid   A solid figure having a polygonal base, the sides of which form the bases of triangular surfaces meeting at a common vertex point that is perpendicular to the center of the base and not in the same plane as the base.

Volume = $\frac{1}{3}h$(area of the base)

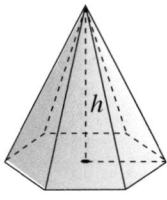

right circular cone   A flat-based, single-pointed solid formed by a rotating straight line that traces out a closed curve based from a fixed vertex point that is perpendicular to the center of the base and not in the same plane as the base.

Volume = $\frac{1}{3}\pi h r^2$ Surface area = $\pi r\sqrt{r^2 + h^2}$
($+ \pi r^2$ if the base is added)

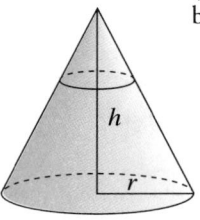

sphere   A solid that is bounded by a curved surface. Any point measured from the outside of the sphere to the center of the sphere is equal in distance.

Volume = $\frac{4}{3}\pi r^3$ Surface area = $4\pi r^2$

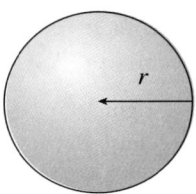

TRIANGLES
PYTHAGOREAN THEOREM

The square of the hypotenuse of a right-angled triangle is equal to the sum of the squares of the other two sides.

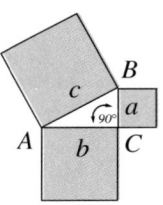

TRIGONOMETRIC FUNCTIONS

The standard abbreviation for each trigonometric function appears in parentheses after the name of the function.

cosecant (csc)   In a right triangle, the ratio of the length of the hypotenuse to the length of the side opposite to an acute angle (csc $A = c/a$); reciprocal of the sine function (csc $A = 1/\sin A$).

cosine (cos)   In a right triangle, the ratio of the length of the side adjacent to an acute angle to the length of the hypotenuse (cos $A = b/c$).

A googol is a 1 followed by 100 zeros. The name is said to have come from the 9-year-old nephew of the American mathematician Edward Kasner. A googolplex is the number 1 followed by a googol of zeros.

cotangent (cot or ctn)   In a right triangle, the ratio of the side adjacent to an acute angle to the length of the side opposite that angle (cot $A = b/a$); reciprocal of the tangent function (cot $A = 1/\tan A$).

secant (sec)   In a right triangle, the ratio of the length of the hypotenuse to the length of the side adjacent to an acute angle (sec $A = c/b$); reciprocal of the cosine function (sec $A = 1/\cos A$).

sine (sin)   In a right triangle, the ratio of the length of the side opposite an acute angle to the length of the hypotenuse (sin $A = a/c$).

tangent (tan)   In a right triangle, the ratio of the length of the side opposite an acute angle to the length of the side adjacent to that angle (tan $A = a/b$).

TRIGONOMETRIC FORMULAS

Law of Sines

In any triangle, $a/\sin A = b/\sin B = c/\sin C$

Right Triangles

$a = c \sin A = b \tan A$
$b = c \cos A = a \cot A$
$c = a \operatorname{cosec} A = b \sec A$

For All Triangles

$A + B + C = 180°$

Given two angles (A and B) and one side (b):
$a = b \times \sin A/\sin B$
$c = b \times \sin C/\sin B$

Given two sides (b and c) and one angle (A):
$a = (b^2 + c^2 - 2bc \cos A)$
$\sin B = b/a \sin A$

Given three sides (a, b, and c):
$\cos A = (b^2 + c^2 - a^2)/2bc$
$\sin B = b/a \times \sin A$

The only number not found in the Roman numeral system is zero.

ROMAN NUMERALS

1	I	70	LXX	1,910	MCMX
2	II	80	LXXX	1,920	MCMXX
3	III	90	XC	1,930	MCMXXX
4	IV	100	C	1,940	MCMXL
5	V	150	CL	1,950	MCML
6	VI	200	CC	1,960	MCMLX
7	VII	300	CCC	1,970	MCMLXX
8	VIII	400	CD	1,980	MCMLXXX
9	IX	500	D	1,990	MCMXC
10	X	600	DC	2,000	MM
15	XV	700	DCC	3,000	MMM
20	XX	800	DCCC	4,000	MMMM OR MV̄
25	XXV	900	CM	5,000	V̄
30	XXX	1,000	M	10,000	X̄
40	XL	1,500	MD	50,000	L̄
50	L	1,900	MCM or	100,000	C̄
60	LX		MDCCCC	1,000,000	M̄

COMPUTERS

PERSONAL COMPUTER COMPONENTS

PERSONAL COMPUTER COMPONENTS

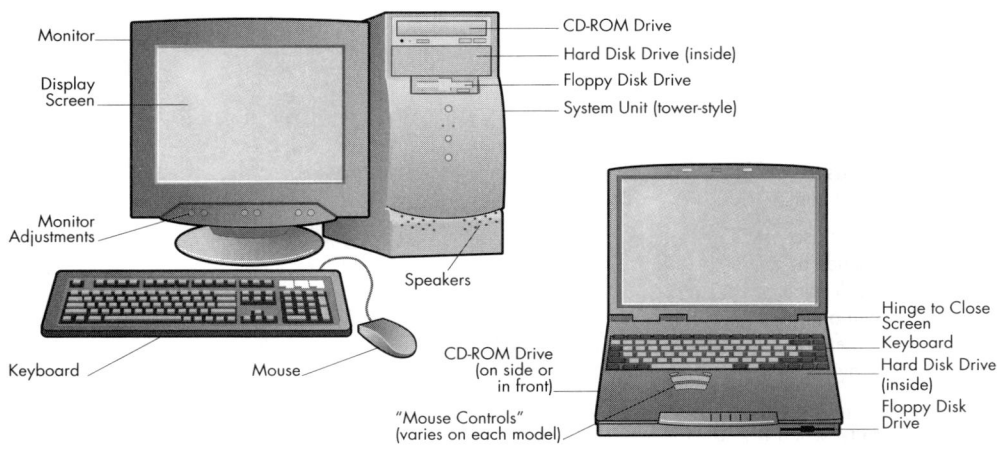

Monitor

Display Screen

Monitor Adjustments

Keyboard

Mouse

CD-ROM Drive

Hard Disk Drive (inside)

Floppy Disk Drive

System Unit (tower-style)

Speakers

CD-ROM Drive (on side or in front)

"Mouse Controls" (varies on each model)

Hinge to Close Screen

Keyboard

Hard Disk Drive (inside)

Floppy Disk Drive

NOTEBOOK COMPUTER COMPONENTS

MACs AND PCs

The computer market is now dominated by the PC (short for personal computer), which accounts for more than 90 percent of sales to homes and businesses. The first successful home computers, the PC and PC/XT models, were introduced in 1981 by the International Business Machines Corporation (IBM). In a short time, other manufacturers began marketing PCs. Known as IBM clones or IBM compatibles, these machines were powered by the same technology—the Intel microprocessor—as IBM's product. They could all use the same software and share the same data. Eventually, all IBM-compatible home computers became known as PCs, no matter which company manufactured them.

In 1984, Apple Computer added a new dimension to the home computer market when it introduced the Macintosh (Mac). Whereas PCs relied on complicated commands typed by the user, the Mac's operating system featured on-screen icons. Commands could be executed simply by positioning a pointer on an image and clicking a button. Because of this innovation, Macs were far less intimidating for novices and became extremely popular. Because

Macs and PCs used different microprocessors and different file formats, they required different software and could not share data.

With the introduction of Microsoft's Windows and IBM's OS/2 during the 1990s, the difference between PCs and Macs diminished considerably (although IBM's OS/2 operating system is no longer popular). Both these operating systems (and their updated versions) use the same icon-based graphical user interface (GUI) and point-and-click technology as the Mac does. As a result, the Mac has lost some of its allure, and Apple's position in the computer industry has declined. Mac devotees maintain, however, that their computers are still easier to use than PCs; artists and designers tend to prefer the Mac because of its enhanced graphics capabilities. PC and Mac computers continue to be upgraded with additional speed and memory. For example, more than six generations of PC processors have been developed—such as those that include the Intel Pentium chips, which have allowed computers to be that much faster than the previous generations. Users of PCs and Macs have no problem exchanging e-mail because the messages are routed through providers' host computers.

Growth of the Internet

A Closer Look

The Internet was originally a network of computers called the ARPnet (Advance Research Projects), a project managed by the United States Department of Defense's Advanced Research Project Agency (ARPA) for military and government purposes. Not long after its inception, various universities and other institutions with higher-end computers began their own networks and eventually merged with ARPnet to form the Internet.

The modern Internet is a huge network of electronic links between computers that span the world. Even though computers from all around the world use many different protocols (i.e., how a computer communicates with other computers), there is generally no problem with communication. The reason is that the connection between computers is processed through worldwide gateways that allow each protocol to be translated into a standard format. Thus, the computer user—with the right software and hardware—can receive text, and often sound and graphics, at his or her personal computer.

Because of the ease of use, millions of personal computer users are "on" the Internet, "surfing" for information from hundreds of thousands of university, library, commercial, and government databases (often using a connection called the World Wide Web, or WWW, that provides graphics, sound, and text to enhance the desired information); ordering items from online catalogs; sending electronic mail (e-mail); and creating their own home pages available for most Internet users to view. Even the most remote places can often connect to the Internet by using an Internet Service Provider (ISP), a link that usually provides a local access phone number to the Internet.

But the Internet is not infallible. It is often unable to handle a large number of users at once, creating a user bottleneck. For example, when the *Mars Pathfinder* space probe landed on Mars on July 4, 1997, millions of people tried to access the National Aeronautics and Space Administration's (NASA) server for images and information on the red planet. The system eventually overloaded, making it difficult to access NASA's home page and download information during the peak days of the Internet user activity.

INTERNET SEARCH ENGINES

With millions of Web sites in existence, finding information on the Internet would be a daunting task if not for the availability of search engines. A search engine is a Web site that uses special software (known as a robot) to comb the Internet and find nearly instantaneous matches for keywords typed by the searcher. (Yahoo! is sometimes referred to as a "links site" because it also provides a menu of hypertext links in a variety of broad categories, such as "Arts," "Education," "Science," and so on.) Each search engine has its own characteristics; a bit of experimentation will reveal which is best for a particular searcher's needs.

Alta Vista	http://www.altavista.digital.com
Excite	http://www.excite.com
Google	http://www.google.com
HotBot	http://www.hotbot.com
Infoseek	http://www.infoseek.com
Lycos	http://www.lycos.com
Northern Light	http://www.nlsearch.com
WebCrawler	http://www.webcrawler.com
Yahoo!	http://www.yahoo.com

NATIONAL INTERNET SERVICE PROVIDERS

National providers may offer a variety of services that include news, stock market updates, chat rooms, travel services, and online reference libraries. Some of the larger providers are listed here.

America Online	(800) 827-6364	http://www.aol.com
AT&T WorldNet	(800) 967-5363	http://www.att.com/worldnet
CompuServe	(800) 848-8199	http://www.compuserve.com
EarthLink	(800) 395-8425	http://www.earthlink.net
MCI Worldcom	(800) 550-0927	http://www.mci.com
Microsoft Network	(800) 373-3676	http://www.msn.com
Prodigy	800-776-3449	http://www.prodigy.com

National Internet service providers may or may not provide better connectivity and convenience than the numerous local providers throughout the country. (Check your local phone book's yellow pages for an ISP near you.) An online search for local providers can be conducted by using any search engine and the words "local ISPs."

COMMON COMPUTER TERMS

address   A location in the computer memory where a particular unit of data is stored. The address may be in the form of an identifying label, name, or number.

algorithm   A defined set of instructions or procedural steps that will lead to a logical conclusion for a specific problem.

The first electronic computer was about 80 feet long, weighed 30 tons, and had 17,000 tubes.

analog computer   A computer that measures a function or behavior involving continuously variable signals, such as signals representing current, voltage, or other factors. An analog computer is also able to respond immediately to changes in input. The output may be presented in the form of a tracing on a graph or a design on a TV picture tube.

analog-to-digital computer   A device that is able to convert continuous analog signals into digital data, or discrete numbers.

architecture   The design of a computer so that hardware and software interface effectively.

arithmetic/logic unit   The part of a computer that performs calculations and comparisons.

array   An arrangement of data in which each item may be identified by a key or subscript so that a computer program can be designed to examine and extract specific data. An example is a calendar array in which a particular day of the year can be identified.

ASCII   Acronym for *A*merican *S*tandard *C*ode for *I*nformation *I*nterchange, a uniform character code used by many computer systems so that data can be exchanged directly between various types of central and remote units and peripheral devices. Each alphabetic and numeric character requires a full byte.

assembler   A computer program designed to assemble machine code from symbolic code or source language.

assembly language   A machine-oriented computer-programming language that can be translated directly into machine instructions.

bandwidth   The amount of data that can be transmitted in a certain amount of time. It is usually expressed in bits per second (bps) or bytes per second.

BASIC   Acronym for *B*eginner's *A*ll-purpose *Sym*bolic *I*nstruction *C*ode, a program that is a standard language for most personal computers. It is designed for developing programs in a "conversational mode" for online use.

baud rate   The rate at which information is transmitted serially from a computer. It is expressed in terms of bits per second.

BBS   *See* **bulletin board system.**

binary   A numbering system based on twos (2s) rather than decimals (10s). Each element has a digit value of either zero (0) or one (1) and is known as a bit.

bit   An acronym constructed from the words *bi*nary digi*t*. It refers to a single digit of a binary number.

bootstrap (boot)   The process of initializing or loading the basic operating instructions into a computer.

browser   Short for Web browser, a software application used to find and display Web pages on the Internet. The most popular graphical browsers are Netscape Navigator and Microsoft Internet Explorer. Mosaic was one of the very first browsers and is still occasionally encountered.

buffer   A temporary storage area for data that helps compensate for differences in the speed of operations of two or more parts of a computer system, such as the central processing unit and a printer.

Sciences

"Libraries Online" and "Data Banks Available for Computer Research" in chapter 11

bug Any error or malfunction in a computer operation or program.

bulletin board system An electronic message center maintained by a newsgroup. Users can leave e-mail messages on the bulletin board and read messages left by others.

bus A group of wires through which data is sent from one part of the computer to another. Most personal computers have an internal bus that connects components to the Central Processing Unit (CPU) and main memory.

byte A set or unit of binary digits, usually eight bits, such as a division of a word. The storage capacity of a disk is usually given in megabytes.

cable modem A modem that operates over television coaxial cable lines. These lines offer a much wider bandwidth, allowing for faster access to the World Wide Web.

CD-ROM An abbreviation for *Compact Disk–Read Only Memory*. It is a large-storage compact disk that resembles a music CD and holds information that can be viewed on the computer screen but cannot be altered.

central processing unit (CPU) The part of the computer circuitry that actually handles the data processing and controls the storage, movement, and other basic computer functions. For personal computers, the terms *CPU* and *microprocessor* are used synonymously. A microprocessor is the single, large-scale integrated circuit on a fingernail-size silicon chip, and the heart of the CPU. *See* **microprocessor**.

character Any digit, letter, punctuation, or symbol, usually represented by a single byte of eight bits.

clock An electronic device that monitors, measures, or synchronizes various functions of a computer system.

COBOL An acronym formed from the words *CO*mmon *B*usiness *O*riented *L*anguage. A high-level programming language used for business applications.

command A part of a computer code that gives input/output instructions to the computer.

compiler A set of programs that compiles or converts a program into the machine language instructions used by a particular computer.

control data Computer information that helps organize data in key categories, such as sorting sequences.

control unit The part of the central processing unit that manipulates the sequences of operations according to the program instructions.

cookie A message sent from a Web server to a Web browser, usually to identify a user's preferences and requested pages.

CPU *See* **central processing unit.**

cursor A symbol appearing on a video display indicating the position where a user can add or delete characters.

cyberspace A slang term for the Internet and related spheres of digital communication. *See* **Internet**.

database A large file of organized information that may be updated and manipulated as needed.

data management system A set of commands used to search and retrieve content as well as to update and reference information from a database.

debug The process of removing errors or defects in software or hardware that cause malfunction of the computer.

diagnostic routine A program designed to trace the source of program errors or the cause of a computer malfunction.

digital computer A computer in which discrete numbers are used to express data and instructions.

direct access *See* **random access.**

disk (diskette) A circular plate coated with magnetic material that can be used to store computer data.

disk crash The malfunction of a disk, either a floppy disk or a hard drive. Generally, floppy disks crash because of physical damage to the disk. Hard drives crash because of physical damage (lightning strikes or being dropped), contamination (dust or liquids), or an unaligned head.

disk drive A device that is able to "read" data stored in magnetic material on a disk or to "write" data onto such a disk.

disk operating system A program that controls how the various parts of a computer interact; also known by its acronym, DOS.

domain The last part of a World Wide Web address that includes a main name and suffix. For example, "nypl.org" is a domain name. Standard top-level domains in the United States are *.com* (commercial), *.edu* (educational), *.gov* (government), *.mil* (military), *.org* (nonprofit organization), and *.net* (network). In 2000, seven new top-level domain names were added, the first since 1988. By 2002, *.aero* (air transportation industry), *.biz* (businesses), *.coop* (cooperatives), *.info* (information-based services), *.museum* (museums, archival institutions, and exhibitions), *.name* (individuals), *.pro* (accountants, lawyers, physicians, and other professionals) were operating or becoming operational. In addition, two-letter country code suffixes appear in some domain names.

DOS *See* **disk operating system.**

download To transfer a file from one computer to another.

DSL An acronym for *Digital Subscriber Lines.* These technologies use various ways to pack data onto copper wires and are used only for connections from telephone switching stations to a home or office—not between switching stations.

e-book an electronic version of a book. An e-book is a small computer—the size of a paperback or a notepad—with a screen that allows a user to read, save, highlight, bookmark, and annotate text.

e-mail A computer application that enables users to send messages to other computers anywhere on the Internet.

error message A message output by the computer, triggered by a program, indicating failure to follow a correct input/output routine, a hardware malfunction, or another problem that may cause the operation to discontinue.

execute Performance of an operation specified by a program routine or instruction.

FAQ Acronym for *Frequently Asked Questions.* A document that answers the most common queries about a particular subject. Almost all newsgroups post one or more FAQ lists.

fiber optic network A technology that uses glass (or plastic) threads (fibers) to transmit data. A fiber optic cable consists of a bundle of glass threads, each of which is capable of transmitting messages modulated into light waves.

file A collection of related data or information that is stored as a unit.

firewall A combination of hardware and software that protects a computer or a system of computers from Internet hackers—users who access the computer or system via the Internet without permission.

flame An insulting e-mail message or newsgroup posting. A series of flames and counterflames is often referred to as a flame war.

floppy disk *See* **disk.**

FORTRAN An acronym formed from the words *FOR*mula *TRAN*slator. It is a programming language used for mathematical and scientific operations.

FTP An acronym for *File Transfer Protocol*, the basic function that allows a computer to transfer files back and forth between other computers over the Internet.

generation Pertaining to a group of computers developed within the same time period and based on the model of an earlier product.

GIF An acronym for *Graphics Interchange Format*. A GIF is a graphic image in a file format often used to display images on the computer screen or used on Web pages on the Internet. They most often are seen as gray-scale graphics. *See* **JPEG.**

gigabyte A gigabyte is 1,024 megabytes; 1,024 gigabytes is a terabyte. Gigabytes are often used to measure the size (capacity) of a hard drive.

Gopher A text-only Internet site that contains a series of menus organized by subject matter. Created before the advent of the World Wide Web, Gopher sites function as electronic libraries, providing access to documents such as research papers and periodical articles.

GUI An acronym for *Graphical User Interface*, a system through which the user can interact with the computer by means of pictures and symbols called icons.

hard copy A copy of the output of a computer that has been produced on paper, as distinguished from the electronic copy of the same data on disk or tape.

hardware The physical equipment or devices, such as the central processing unit, of a computer system. *See also* **software.**

hexadecimal A system of whole numbers with a base of 16 used in certain computer operations. Hexadecimal coding uses numerals 0 to 16 with the first 10 digits represented by 0 through 9 and the next 6 digits represented by the letters *A* through *F*.

high-level language Any computer language in which each instruction corresponds to a group of machine code instructions. Examples include BASIC and COBOL.

home page A term that applies both to the first page loaded by an Internet browser and the main document for an organization, newsgroup, or individual user.

housekeeping Standard computer routines, such as deleting garbage or preliminary input/output functions, that are not directly related to a particular job.

HTML An abbreviation for *Hypertext Markup Language*, which is used to create documents on the World Wide Web. Hypertext is a method of connecting sites through text-based links rather than the menu-oriented systems used by Gopher sites. Clicking on a link (typically an underlined word or phrase) automatically calls a new area of the current document or calls up a different website.

http An abbreviation for *hypertext transfer protocol*, a common system for requesting and sending HTML documents on the Internet. It is the first element (http://) in all URL addresses on the World Wide Web.

hybrid computer A computer that is able to perform both analog and digital computing functions.

icon The graphic representation of a computer command.

input The information a computer receives from a keyboard, tape, or disk.

input/output (I/O) terminal A computer device that is capable of both receiving and retrieving data.

instruction A part of a program that directs a computer to perform a single specific function as part of a sequence of functions.

interface A device that serves as a link or common surface boundary between two different parts of a computer system.

Internet   A cooperatively run global collection of computer networks with a common addressing scheme. First created during the 1970s as a channel for information sharing among scientists, it has now become a worldwide communications medium.

Internet service provider (ISP)   A company that sells access to the Internet. In addition to the national online services, there are more than 100,000 local service providers in the United States.

interrupt   A temporary suspension of processing by a computer, caused by input or other activity by another part of the system.

I/O terminal   *See* **input/output (I/O) terminal.**

intranet   private network inside a company or organization that uses the same kinds of software as does the public Internet. However, access to an intranet is limited—usually it is only for the internal use of the organization that created it.

Java   A programming language that allows users to create applications, particularly multimedia applications that can run on several platforms without rewriting. Often used in Web sites.

joystick   A lever that is connected to a computer for use in moving the cursor from one point to another on a video display terminal.

JPEG   An acronym for *J*oint *P*hotographic *Ex*perts *G*roup. This is the name of the committee responsible for designing this photographic image-compression standard. JPEGs are usually photographs, stored as color or gray-scale digital images. *See* **GIF.**

K   An abbreviation for kilo and a symbol for 1,000 (actually 2^{10}, or 1,024); it is commonly used to indicate the storage capacity of a computer's memory. For example, a 64K memory has a theoretical capacity of $64 \times 1,024$, or 65,536 bytes or data storage locations.

keyboard   A device that encodes characters for a computer function by the pressing of keys. Pressing the keys formerly punched holes in cards that the computer read; now it more commonly provides a direct input of data to the computer.

label   A group of computer characters used to identify a file, record, or memory storage area.

LAN   *See* **network.**

language   A set of characters that can be used to form a meaningful set of words and symbols in writing instructions for a computer. Examples include ALGOL, BASIC, COBOL, and FORTRAN.

laptop   A small, portable computer that folds into a compact case. Laptop computers also frequently called notebook computers. Small size and light weight are priorities in laptop or notebook construction.

light pen   A photoelectric device connected to the cathode-ray tube of a display unit. It can be used by the operator to activate the computer to change or modify an image displayed by touching the pen to the screen.

listserv   An automated mailing list distribution system that allows a group of e-mail addresses to receive (and often send) e-mail to one another as a group.

local area network   *See* **network.**

machine language   A language composed of a set of numbers and symbols that can direct computer operations without the need for translation.

magnetic memory   A memory device that uses magnetic fields for storing data.

mainframe computer   A large professional computer system used by a major industry or government agency, as distinguished from a smaller minicomputer or microcomputer.

megabyte   A megabyte is 1,024 kilobytes; 1,024 megabytes is a gigabyte. A computer's random-access memory (RAM) is usually measured in megabytes.

memory   The ability of a computer to store and retrieve data.

menu   A list of commands in a program from which the user can choose to initiate an action.

message   A combination of characters or symbols used to communicate information between points of a computer system. *See also* **error message.**

metadata   Descriptions of how, when, and by whom a particular set of data was collected, and how the data is formatted. Metadata is essential for understanding information stored in data warehouses.

microcomputer   A small personal computer.

microprocessor   *See* **Central Processing Unit.**

minicomputer   A computer that is larger in capacity, flexibility, and cost than a microcomputer. It may commonly be used to control industrial processes.

modem   An acronym formed from the words *mo*dulator *dem*odulator. It is an electronic device that allows computer data to be carried over telephone lines.

mouse   A movable device attached to a computer that permits the operator to reposition the cursor on the video display terminal.

multimedia   Software applications that incorporate sound, video, and animation with text and graphics.

netiquette   A set of informal rules promoted by newsgroups. Principles of netiquette discourage such practices as flaming, spamming, and overlong postings that hog Internet resources. *See also* "Network Etiquette (Netiquette)" in chapter 16.

network   A group of two or more computers hooked together. A local area network (LAN) is a network of computers connected together, usually within the same building; a wide area network (WAN) is a network of computers connected together, usually over long distances by telephone lines or radio waves.

newsgroup   A Usenet discussion group dedicated to a particular subject.

offline   Pertaining to computer functions that are not under the direct control of a central processing unit or computer operator. The term is sometimes applied to hard copy or stored data.

online   Computer operations that are under the direct control of the central processing unit or operator.

operating system (OS)   Any program that controls how the various parts of a computer interact.

optical scanner   An electronic device that scans direct or reflected light from a surface, such as a printed page, and converts the signals to machine-readable inputs.

OS   *See* **operating system.**

output   The results of a computer operation, which may appear in the form of a printout or visual display.

PalmPilot™   A specific brand of palmtop computer. A palmtop is a very small computer that literally fits in the palm of one's hand. Compared to full-size computers, the power of a palmtop is severely limited, but palmtops are practical for certain functions such as phone books and calendars. Palmtops that use a pen rather than a keyboard for input are often called handheld computers or PDAs.

peripheral   Any device that is separate from but connected to the computer for the purpose of supplying input or output functions, such as a modem or printer.

personal digital assistant (PDA)   A handheld device that combines computing, telephone/fax, and networking features. A typical PDA can function as a cellular phone, fax sender, and personal organizer. Unlike laptops, they use a stylus rather than a keyboard for input.

primary memory   The part of the computer used as the main storage area for data or programs.

RAM   *See* **random-access memory.**

random access   The direct retrieval of data from a location in the computer memory without the need for sorting through sequential information.

Random-access memory (RAM)   A computer storage device that permits direct access to data independent of its location in the computer memory.

Read-only memory (ROM)   A type of computer memory that can be used to retrieve data for output only; new data cannot be written into it.

real time   Computer operations that permit rapid analyses of data so that decisions can be made immediately.

register   A part of the computer's central processing unit that stores information for future use. It may have specific uses, such as arithmetic functions or word processing. A computer may contain several different registers.

ROM   *See* **read-only memory.**

scanner   A device that scans a printed page and converts text and graphics into digital form. The data can then be incorporated into electronic documents.

serial processing   A type of computer function in which two or more programs are run in sequence rather than simultaneously.

server   A central computer that makes services available on a network.

Standard Generalized Markup Language (SGML)   A system for organizing and tagging elements of a document. SGML itself does not specify any particular formatting; rather, it specifies the rules for tagging elements. These tags can then be interpreted to format elements in different ways.

shareware   Copyrighted software programs that are distributed based on an honor system. Many shareware programs are free, but the author usually requests a small fee if the program is regularly used; the shareware can be copied for other computer users, but they too must pay a fee if the program is regularly used. Shareware cannot be sold by anyone but the author.

software   The programs or instructions used to operate a computer system, as distinguished from the hardware.

spam   In general, any unsolicited junk e-mail; or to use a newsgroup to send e-mail messages (typically advertisements) to a vast number of users without their permission.

storage capacity   The amount of data that can be stored in a computer memory. *See also* **K.**

surge protector   A device that protects software and hardware from sudden electrical surges. A surge protector is usually plugged into an electrical outlet; the computer is then plugged into the surge protector.

T-1 line   A dedicated phone connection supporting data rates of 1.544 Mbits per second. A T-1 line actually consists of 24 individual channels, each of which supports 64 Kbits per second. Each 64 Kbit/second channel can be configured to carry voice or data traffic.

terminal   An input/output device that allows an operator to control a computer. The terminal may consist of a keyboard and video display screen.

time sharing   A computer function of handling two or more tasks simultaneously, as when a mainframe computer is used to process operations of several remote terminals at the same time. Such a system depends on buffering and switching inputs and outputs for each terminal. This is done at such a high rate of speed that operators of individual terminals are unaware that others are sharing the same central processing unit.

track   A segment of a disk or other magnetic storage device that stores a fixed amount of data in a designated address for rapid retrieval.

Sciences

URL   Uniform Resource Locator. The addressing system for the World Wide Web. A typical URL would read http://www.nypl.org.

Usenet   A large, unedited Internet bulletin board that contains individual newsgroups.

virus   A destructive computer code inserted into an ordinary file or program. When downloaded, a virus will replicate itself within a user's computer system, often destroying data. As a protective measure, many computer users install antivirus software.

WAN (wide area network)   *See* **network.**

Web server   The outside computer that delivers Web pages to your computer. For example, if you entered the URL for the New York Public Library (http://www.nypl.org), the Web server for the library (nypl.org) would search for your query and send the requested page back to your browser.

Web site   A *Web site* is a location on the World Wide Web that contains a personal, commercial, or organizational home page.

word   A fixed number of bits processed by a computer as a single basic unit.

World Wide Web   The primary platform of the Internet. Created in 1989, the World Wide Web is a collection of files and databases linked by hypertext. It differs from older Internet applications in its ability to display graphics and multimedia in addition to text.

write   The process of recording data in a computer's memory.

write-protected disk   A computer disk designed to prevent altering the data stored on it.

SPACE EXPLORATION

MANNED SPACECRAFT

Apollo was the manned United States space program that eventually put 12 men on the Moon. The Apollo spacecraft included a command module for orbiting and a lunar module for landing on the Moon.

Gemini was the second series of United States manned missions, after the Mercury launches. The Gemini spacecraft seated two astronauts and was used to test rendezvous and docking maneuvers, human responses to weightlessness, extravehicular activity, and landing techniques.

Mercury was the first series of United States manned missions, including the first suborbital and orbital flights. These one-person crafts tested the feasibility of flight and monitored humans' reaction to space.

The *MIR* ("Peace") space station, built by the Soviet Union (now Russia), was the largest and longest-running permanent working space station. Launched in 1986, *MIR* was constructed of modules. It was used for extensive study of microgravity and other valuable space experiments. It was also the testing ground to determine the effects of the space environment on humans, and some cosmonauts stayed in the station for more than 400 days. Toward the end of its time in orbit, the station was host to an international crew of space travelers. Lack of funding, a host of technical problems, and a lowering orbit eventually caught up with the *MIR* project. In 2001, the Russian space agency officially closed the station, and sent the spacecraft plunging into the southern Pacific Ocean.

Skylab was the first and only United States space station, launched in 1973. It was not permanently manned but was visited by three separate crews of astronauts. In 1979, because of a technical problem, solar flares that caused atmospheric drag on the craft, and lack of funding (NASA was then concentrating on building a reusable shuttle), *Skylab* fell from orbit and burned up in the atmosphere.

Salyut was a series of seven Soviet space stations launched from 1971 to 1982. The addition of a second docking port—permitting the docking of a second *Soyuz* ferry, an unmanned *Progress* supply craft,

Sciences

and *Cosmos* modules—paved the way for the *MIR* space station.

The space shuttle is the reusable Earth-orbiting, manned vehicle used in the United States space program. There are four active shuttles (*Columbia, Discovery, Atlantis,* and *Endeavour*) in the fleet. Each shuttle can comfortably carry a crew of five to eight astronauts. Work done by the shuttle crews includes testing the reaction of humans in space, conducting Spacelab experiments, operating Earth-monitoring systems, and launching or capturing satellites into or from orbit. Currently, most space shuttle missions concentrate on ferrying astronauts, and shipping supplies and equipment to the Earth-orbiting International Space Station.

Voskhod, hastily developed by the Soviet Union, were actually *Vostok* craft modified to carry three persons. To make room, engineers removed the ejections that would be used in case of an aborted launch. The first extravehicular activity (EVA) was conducted during the second and last Voskhod mission in 1965.

Vostok ("east" in Russian) capsules, developed by the Soviet Union as their first manned spaceflight program, were one-person vehicles controlled from the ground.

HUMAN MISSIONS TO THE MOON

Mission	Launch Date	Crew	Comments
Apollo 8	December 21, 1968	Frank Borman James A. Lovell Jr. William A. Anders	First manned mission to orbit the Moon.
Apollo 10	May 18, 1969	Thomas P. Stafford John W. Young Eugene A. Cernan	Rehearsal for first landing; lunar module descended to within 2.2 miles (3.5 kilometers) of the Moon's surface.
Apollo 11	July 16, 1969	Neil A. Armstrong* Michael Collins† Edwin E. "Buzz" Aldrin Jr.*	First manned landing in Mare Tranquillitatis; Armstrong was the first human to walk on the Moon (July 20, 1969).
Apollo 12	November 14, 1969	Charles Conrad Jr.* Richard F. Gordon† Alan L. Bean*	Landed in Oceanus Procellarum.
Apollo 13	April 11, 1970	James A. Lovell Jr. John L. Swigert Jr. Fred W. Haise Jr	Never landed on the Moon; an accident en route required the craft to return after swinging around the far side of the Moon.
Apollo 14	January 31, 1971	Alan B. Shepard Jr.* Stuart A. Roosa† Edgar D. Mitchell*	Landed in Fra Mauro.
Apollo 15	July 26, 1971	David R. Scott* Alfred M. Worden† James B. Irwin*	Landed adjacent to the Imbrium Basin near Apennine Mountains.
Apollo 16	April 16, 1972	John W. Young* Thomas K. Mattingly II† Charles M. Duke Jr.*	Landed in highlands near Crater Descartes.
Apollo 17	December 7, 1972	Eugene A. Cernan* Ronald E. Evans† Harrison H. Schmitt*	Landed in Taurus Littrow Valley.

* Walked on Moon.   † Remained in command module, orbiting the Moon.

"Significant Inventions, Technological Advances, and Discoveries" in chapter 5
Go to

COMMON ENGINEERING TERMS

aggregate   A mixture of several materials. For example, an aggregate of gravel, mud, natural sand, and crushed stone is used for making concrete.

alloy   A substance that has metallic properties and consists of two or more elements; usually at least one is a metal.

alternator   A type of alternating-current generator.

ammeter   An instrument that measures the strength of an electric current in amperes.

annealing   The process of making glass, metal, or an alloy less brittle by exposing it to heating and then cooling.

cantilever   A beam or other horizontal member supported on only one end.

cathode   The negative terminal of an electric current system. In a vacuum tube, the filament serves as the cathode or source of electrons that are emitted.

cathode-ray tube   A tube in which an electron beam is directed across a fluorescent tube in order to generate images. CRTs are used in oscilloscopes, radar, television sets, and computer monitors.

circuit   A line of conductors and other electrical devices along which an electrical current flows. A closed circuit allows the current to travel through all devices. If the circuit is broken at some point so that the current cannot flow, it is called an open circuit.

coil   A turned wire used to introduce inductance into an electrical circuit.

current   The flow of electricity. Metals are good conductors of electric current.

diode   A tube with two electrodes; the main use of diodes is to keep the electric current flowing in one direction.

dynamo   A type of generator; usually a direct-current generator. It converts energy of mechanical motion into electric current. *See also* **alternator.**

elasticity   The ability of an object or material to return to its original size and shape, after being pushed or pulled by an outside force. For example, rubber is elastic.

electrode   A rod, plate, or wire that is used to conduct electric current out of or into any device.

electromagnet   A coil with a soft iron core that acts as a magnet when an electric current is passed through it.

electromotive force   The force that moves an electric current around a circuit. For example, a generator produces an electromotive force.

engine   A machine that applies power to do work. It converts various forms of energy into mechanical force and motion.

expansion joint   A space left in structures or roads that allows for the expansion and contraction of the material, caused by heating and cooling of the surrounding environment.

filament   A metallic wire that is heated in an incandescent lamp in order to produce light.

fuse   A safety device that protects a circuit from receiving too much current. The fuse's wire melts in response to too much electric current passing through it, thus breaking the circuit.

galvanometer   An instrument that detects, measures, and determines the direction of a small electric current.

gasket   A deformable material, usually a ring of plastic or metal, that is used to make a pressure-tight joint between two (usually stationary) parts.

generator   A machine that converts mechanical energy into electrical energy.

"Major Scientists and Engineers" in chapter 5
Go to

Sciences

girder   A large beam of wood, metal, or concrete, usually found in skyscrapers and other large buildings. It is used for structural support.

insulator   A device with high resistance to heat, electricity, or sound; for example, an electrical insulator prevents electricity from sending current to other objects.

lubricant   A substance applied to a surface to reduce friction.

machine   A device that helps to do work. Most machines either overcome a force or change the direction of the applied force.

microphone   A device that acts as a transformer and amplifier of sound waves into electric currents.

motor   A machine that converts electrical energy into mechanical energy.

oscilliscope   An instrument that produces an image of varying electrical voltages on a cathode-ray tube.

polymer   Large molecules made up of a series of molecular units, similar to beads on a string. Natural polymers include rubber, wool, and cotton; synthetic polymers include nylon and polythene. Polymers are often called giant molecules.

pulley   A wheel over which a rope, chain, or wire passes. Pulleys are used to ease the pulling of objects or lifting of heavy weights.

pulley system   An arrangement of two or more pulleys that form a machine.

radar (*radio detection and ranging*)   An instrument in which a cathode-ray tube receives reflected radio waves to detect distant objects.

radio   A system of transmitting sound signals (as electric impulses) through the air using electromagnetic waves.

receiver   A device that transforms radio waves and translates them mainly into sounds or pictures.

relay   A device that controls a large electrical current along another circuit by switching on or off. The relay uses a small electric current to control the larger current.

resistor   A device that resists an electric current.

rheostat   *See* **variable resistor.**

stator   A stationary machine part about which a rotor turns.

switch   A device that is used to switch parts of a circuit on or off. When the switch is on, the electric current is flowing through; when the switch is off, the electric current is cut off.

television   A system for transmitting video and audio signals using electromagnetic waves. A television uses a cathode-ray tube to produce images built from 625 constantly changing lines, each of which contains 400 small dots of light.

thermocouple   Shortened term for thermoelectric couple.

thermoelectricity   The production of an electric current directly from heat, or the reverse.

transformer   A device that changes the voltage of an alternating current. Transformers are used to modify the high voltage received from power lines so that it can be used by homes that require lower voltage for electrical devices.

tube (or valve)   An electrical device that allows electric current to flow in only one direction. Such devices are also referred to as diodes, triodes, etc., depending on the number of electrodes present.

variable resistor (or rheostat)   A device that variably resists an electrical current. The resistance can be changed by varying the contacts, allowing the resistor to slide around a length of wire.

voltmeter   An instrument that measures electromotive force or potential difference between two points, usually in volts.

ADDITIONAL SOURCES OF INFORMATION

ORGANIZATIONS AND SERVICES

American Association for the Advancement of Science
1200 New York Ave., NW
Washington, DC 20005
http://www.aaas.org

American Astronomical Society
200 Florida Ave., NW
Washington, DC 20009
http://www.aas.org

American Chemical Society
1155 16th St., NW
Washington, DC 20036
http://www.acs.org

American Geophysical Union
2000 Florida Ave., NW
Washington, DC 20009-1277
http://www.agu.org

American Institute of Physics
1 Physics Ellipse
College Park, MD 20740
http://www.aip.org

National Academy of Sciences
2101 Constitution Ave., NW
Washington, DC 20418
http://www.www4.nationalacademies.org/nas/nashome.nsf

National Aeronautics and Space Administration
300 E St., SW
Washington, DC 20546
http://www.nasa.gov

National Oceanic and Atmospheric Administration
14th St. and Constitution Ave., NW, Room 6013
Washington, DC 20230
http://www.noaa.gov

National Science Foundation
4201 Wilson Blvd.
Arlington, VA 22230
http://www.nsf.gov

National Technical Information Service
Department of Commerce
5285 Port Royal Rd.
Springfield, VA 22161
http://www.ntif.gov

National Weather Service Office of Public Affairs
1325 East-West Hwy.
Silver Spring Metro Center II
Silver Spring, MD 20910
http://www.nws.noaa.gov/pa

New York Academy of Sciences
2 E. 63rd St.
New York, NY 10021
http://www.nyas.org

Smithsonian Institution
1000 Jefferson Dr., SW
Washington, DC 20560
http://www.smithsonian.org/

MAGAZINES

Air & Space/Smithsonian
901 D Street, NW, 10th floor
Washington, DC 20024
http://www.airspacemag.com

Astronomy
21027 Crossroads Circle
P.O. Box 1612
Waukesha, WI 53187
http://www.astronomy.com

Discover Magazine
114 Fifth Ave.
New York, NY 10011
http://www.discover.com

Physics Today
One Physics Ellipse
College Park, MD 20740
http://www.aip.org/pt/

Popular Mechanics
224 W. 57th St.
New York, NY 10019
http://www.popularmechanics.com

Popular Science
2 Park Ave.
New York, NY 10016
http://www.popsci.com

Scientific American
415 Madison Ave.
New York, NY 10017
http://www.sciam.com

Sky & Telescope
P. O. Box 9111
Cambridge, MA 02178-9111
http://www.skypub.com

Sciences

Smithsonian Magazine
900 Jefferson Drive
Washington, DC 20560
http://www.smithsonianmag.si.edu

BOOKS

Abell, George O., et al. *Exploration of the Universe.* 6th ed. Saunders College, 1991.

Allaby, A., ed. *A Dictionary of Earth Sciences.* 2nd ed. Oxford University Press, 1999.

Beatty, J. Kelly, ed., et al. *The New Solar System.* 4th ed. Sky Publishing, 1999.

Clapham, Christopher. *The Concise Oxford Dictionary of Mathematics.* Oxford University Press, 1996.

Clarke, Donald, and Mark Dartford, eds. *The New Illustrated Science and Invention Encyclopedia: How It Works.* Marshall Cavendish, 1994.

Considine, Douglas, and Glenn D. Considine, eds. *Van Nostrand's Scientific Encyclopedia.* 8th ed., 2 vols. Van Nostrand Reinhold, 1997.

Curtis, Anthony R. *Space Almanac.* 2nd ed. Gulf, 1992.

Daintith, John, ed. *A Dictionary of Chemistry.* 3rd ed. Oxford University Press, 1996.

Dean, John A. *Lange's Handbook of Chemistry.* 14th ed. McGraw-Hill, 1996.

Dunlop, S. *A Dictionary of Weather.* Oxford University Press, 2001.

Hawking, Stephen. *A Brief History of Time: From the Big Bang to Black Holes.* Bantam, 1990.

Lambert, David, and the Diagram Group. *The Field Guide to Geology.* Facts on File, 1997.

Lide, David R., ed. *CRC Handbook of Chemistry and Physics: A Ready-Reference Book of Chemical and Physical Data.* 78th ed. CRC Press, 1997.

Ludlum, David, et al. *Clouds and Storms* (National Audubon Society Pocket Guide). Knopf, 1995.

Macaulay, David. *The Way Things Work.* Houghton-Mifflin, 1988.

McPhee, John. *Annals of the Former World.* Farrar, Straus & Giroux, 1998.

Parker, Sybil P., ed. *McGraw-Hill Encyclopedia of Science and Technology.* 8th ed. McGraw-Hill, 1997.

Pellant, Chris, *Rocks and Minerals.* Dorling Kindersley, 1992.

Pough, Frederick H. and Roger Tory Peterson. *Peterson's First Guide to Rocks and Minerals.* Houghton-Mifflin, 1991.

Ralston, Anthony, and Edwin D. Reilly, eds. *Encyclopedia of Computer Science.* 3rd ed. International Thompson, 1993.

Vernon, R.H. *The Rocks Beneath Our Feet.* Cambridge University Press, 2001.

Ward, P. D. *Rivers in Time: The Search for Clues to Earth's Mass Extinctions.* Columbia University Press, 2001.

Williams, Jack. *The Weather Book.* 2nd ed. Vintage, 1997.

Zukowsky, J., ed. *2001: Building for Space Travel.* Harry N. Abrams, 2001.

WEB SITES

Computer User High-Tech Dictionary
http://www.computeruser.com/resources/dictionary/dictionary.html

National Center for Atmospheric Research
http://www.ncar.ucar.edu/ncar/index.html

Natural Hazards Center
http://www.colorado.edu/hazards/

Online Encyclopedia Dedicated to Computer Technology
http://www.pcwebopedia.com

United States Army Corps of Engineers
http://www.usace.army.mil/

United States Geological Survey
http://www.usgs.gov

INVENTIONS AND
SCIENTIFIC DISCOVERIES

SIGNIFICANT INVENTIONS, TECHNOLOGICAL ADVANCES, AND SCIENTIFIC DISCOVERIES

Date	Invention/Advance/Discovery	Inventor/Origin
B.C.		
c. 12,000	Fire	Unknown
c. 5000	Woven cloth	Mesopotamia, Egypt
	Copper working	Rudna Glava, Yugoslavia
c. 3500	Wheeled vehicles	Sumeria, Syria
	Potter's wheel	Middle East
	Gold mining	Mesopotamia, Africa
	Sundial	Middle East
c. 3150	Irrigation	China, Egypt
c. 3000	Ox-drawn plow	Egypt
c. 2780	First step pyramid	Imhotep
c. 2700	Great Pyramid of Cheops	Cheops
c. 2640	Silk production	Si-ling Chi
c. 2500	Kite	China
	Cotton production	China, India
c. 1350	22-letter alphabet	Phoenicians
c. 1300	Musical notation	Ugarit, Syria
c. 700	First aqueduct	Sennacherib
570	Geographical and star charts	Anaximander of Miletus
430	Concept of atomic structure	Democritus
c. 400	Profession of medicine	Hippocrates
300	Deductive system of mathematics	Euclid
	Abacus	Asia, Middle East
c. 260	Theory that sun is the center of the solar system	Aristarchus
c. 250	Principles of the lever and other simple machines	Archimedes
c. 221	Beginning of the Great Wall of China	Shih Hwang-ti
c. 190	Ellipse and hyperbola	Appollonius
c. 140	Trigonometry	Hipparchus
	Wheel bearings	On a wagon found at Dejbjerg, Jutland
c. 85	Seed-planting machine	China
c. 40	Rotary winnowing machine	China

The Kite

A Closer Look

The kite is not only the earliest form of flying machine, but also one of the few ancient technological objects to be used continuously into modern times. There is evidence that kites were known in China as early as 2500 B.C., and they eventually came to be used for recreational, religious, and military purposes throughout Asia and the Pacific islands. Kites served a ceremonial function, for example, in Polynesian myth, in which gods were personified in kite form.

One of the first references to kites in Europe is found in the 1300s: A German book contains an illustration of soldiers using a kite to drop a bomb over the walls of an enemy castle. By the 1600s, kites had lost their military overtones, growing popular as toys for children. In 1752, Benjamin Franklin used a kite to show the electrical nature of lightning. During the nineteenth century, kites saved lives—shipwrecked boats would use them to carry lines to potential rescuers onshore.

Also in the 1800s, kites were important in early studies of aeronautics. Lawrence Hargrave of Australia was one of the first to try to make the kite into a flying machine, a forerunner of our modern glider.

Leonardo da Vinci

Modern science has its roots in the Italian Renaissance, and perhaps the most striking example of the "Renaissance Man" is Leonardo da Vinci (1452–1519). Although he is best known for his work as an artist, Leonardo's scientific contributions may rival his renowned *Mona Lisa*. In 1493, Leonardo sketched a design for a hovering machine that he called a "helix pteron," an early version of our modern helicopter. He designed and built the first swinging miter lock gates for canals. And he sketched the separation of traffic on two levels—a forerunner of modern road systems. In his scientific contributions, Leonardo was a precursor of two other Renaissance greats, Copernicus and Galileo.

Date	Invention/Advance/Discovery	Inventor/Origin
A.D.		
c. 80	Magnetism	China
c. 100	Paper making	China
c. 170	Function of the arteries	Galen
c. 180	Rotary fan	China
c. 230	Wheelbarrow	China
c. 500	Algebra	India
	Decimal system	India, Mesopotamia
c. 550	Water mill	Greece
580	Iron-chain suspension bridge	China
c. 600	Zero	India
640	Windmill	Persia
c. 700	Porcelain	T'ang dynasty
886	24-hour-day measurement system	Alfred the Great
c. 900	Moldboard plow	China
980	Canal locks	Ciao Wei-Yo
c. 1100	Rocket	China
1150	Paper mill	Spain
c. 1150	Gunpowder	China
1250	Magnifying glass	Roger Bacon
1260	Gun/cannon	Konstantin Anklitzen
1269	360° compass	Petrus Peregrinus de Maricourt
1280	Belt-driven spinning wheel	Hans Speyer
1285	Eyeglasses	Alessandro de Spina
1287	Nitric acid	Raymond Lully
1326	Metal cannon	Rinaldo di Villamagna
1335	Public striking clock	Palace Chapel of the Visconti, Milan, Italy
1360	Mechanical clock	Henri de Vick of Wurttemburg for King Charles V of France
1410	Wire	Rodolph of Nuremberg
1450	Printing press with movable type	Johann Gutenberg
1455	Cast-iron pipe	Castle of Dillenburgh, Germany
1474	Lunar nautical navigation	Regiomontanus
1489	Addition (+) and subtraction (−) signs in mathematics	Johann Widman
1493	Drawing of a flying machine	Leonardo da Vinci
1500	Portable clock	Peter Henlein
1520	Spirally grooved rifle barrel	August Kotter
1525	Portable shotgun (harquebus)	Marquis of Pescara

Inventions

continues

Significant Inventions, Technological Advances, and Scientific Discoveries, Continued

Date	Invention/Advance/Discovery	Inventor/Origin
c. 1535	Heliocentric planetary model	Copernicus
1538	Optic nerve	Constanzo Varolio
1540	Artificial limbs	Ambroise Parase
	Pistol	Camillo Vettelli
1550	Screwdriver	Gunsmiths and armorers (location unknown)
	Wrench	Unknown
	Ligature to stop bleeding during surgery	Ambroise Paré
1557	Enamel	Bernard Palissy
	Platinum	Julius Caesar Scaliger
1561	Dredger	Pieter Breughel
1565	Graphite pencil	Konrad Gesner
1569	Screw-cutting machine and ornamental turning lathe	Jacques Besson
1581	Pendulum motion	Galileo Galilei
1582	Modern calendar	Pope Gregory XIII and Christoph Clavius
1585	Time bomb	Dutch siege of Antwerp
1589	Hosiery-knitting machine	Rev. William Lee
1590	Compound microscope	Zacharias Jannsen
	Law of falling bodies	Galileo Galilei
1592	Wind-powered sawmill	Cornelius Corneliszoon
	Thermoscope (primitive thermometer)	Galileo Galilei
1597	Proportional compass (sector)	Galileo Galilei
1599	Silk-knitting machine	Rev. William Lee
1600	Wind-driven land vehicle	Simon Stevin
1603	Pantograph	Christoph Scheiner
1606	Surveying chain	Edmund Gunter
1609	Astronomical telescope	Galileo Galilei
	Laws of planetary motion	Johannes Kepler
1611	Coke (for iron)	Simon Sturtevant
	Rainbow theory	Johannes Kepler
1611	Double convex microscope	Johannes Kepler
1614	Logarithms	John Napier
1615	Solar-powered motor	Salomon de Caux
	Surveying by triangulation	Willebrord Snell von Roigen
1616	Function of the heart and complete circulation of the blood	William Harvey
	Medical thermometer	Santorio Santorii (Sanctorius)
1621	Rectilinear slide rule	William Oughtred
1630	Circular slide rule	Richard Delamain
1631	Multiplication ($\times$) sign	William Oughtred
	Vernier scale	Pierre Vernier
1637	Analytic geometry	René Descartes
1638	Micrometer	William Gascoigne
1642	Calculating machine	Blaise Pascal
1643	Barometer (Torricellian tube)	Evangelista Torricelli and Vincenzo Viviani
1647	Map of moon and star catalog	Helvius (Johannes Hewelcke)
1648	Hydrochloric acid	Johann Rudolph Glauber
	Concept of air pressure in barometers	Blaise Pascal
1650	Lymph glands	Olof Rudbeck

Date	Invention/Advance/Discovery	Inventor/Origin
1654	Air vacuum pump	Otto von Guericke
	Basic laws of probability	Blaise Pascal and Pierre de Fermat
1656	Pendulum clock	Christiaan Huygens
1658	Clock balance spring	Robert Hooke
	Red blood cells	Jan Swammerdam
1661	Wood (methyl) alcohol	Robert Boyle
1662	Boyle's law/gas pressure laws	Robert Boyle
	Statistical mathematics	Sir William Petty
1664	Hygrometer	Francesco Folli
1666	Principles of integral calculus	Isaac Newton
1667	Blood transfusion (lamb to boy)	Jean-Baptiste Denis
	Wind gauge	Christian Forner
1668	Reflecting telescope	Isaac Newton
1669	Phosphorus	Hennig Brand
1671	Silk-spinning machine	Edmund Blood
	Binary number system	Gottfried Wilhelm Leibnitz
1674	Tourniquet	Morel, France
1675	Calibrated foot ruler	Unknown
	Speed of light	Ole Römer
1676	Artificial water filtration	William Woolcott
1679	Pressure cooker	Denis Papin
1682	Halley's comet	Edmond Halley
1683	Bacteria	Anton van Leeuwenhoek
	Spermatozoa	Anton van Leeuwenhoek
1684	Theory of gravity	Isaac Newton
	Foundations of integral and differential calculus	Gottfried Leibniz
1694	Plant pollen	Rudolph Jakob Camerarius
1695	Epsom salts	Nehemiah Grew
	Periodicity of comet orbit	Edmond Halley
1699	Portable fire pump	Dumaurier Duperrier
1701	Machine seed drill	Jethro Tull
1702	Tidal pump	George Sorocold
	Boron/borax	Guillaume Homberg
1709	Coke smelting (iron)	Abraham Derby
	Anemometer	Wolfius
	Alcohol thermometer	Gabriel Fahrenheit
1711	Tuning fork	John Shore
1712	Steam engine	Thomas Newcomen
1716	True porcelain (Meissen)	Johann Friedrich Bottger
1717	Fahrenheit temperature scale	Gabriel Fahrenheit
1718	Mercury thermometer	Gabriel Fahrenheit
1719	Color printing	Jakob Christof Le Blon
1729	Aberration of light	Rev. James Bradley
1731	Octant (Hadley's quadrant)	John Hadley
1732	Copper-zinc alloy	Christopher Pinchbeck
	Threshing machine	Michael Menzies
1733	Arsenic	George Brandt
	Flint-glass lens	Chester Moor Hall
	Fly shuttle (weaving)	John Kay
1735	Plant classification system	Carl von Linnè (Carolus Linnaeus)

Inventions

continues

Significant Inventions, Technological Advances, and Scientific Discoveries, Continued

Date	Invention/Advance/Discovery	Inventor/Origin
1736	Scarlet fever	William Douglass
1740	Curare (drug)	Charles Marie de Lacondamine
1742	Crucible steel production	Benjamin Huntsman
	Celsius temperature scale	Anders Celsius
1743	Wool carding machine	David Bourne
	Compound lever	John Wyatt
1746	Leyden jar (prototype of electrical condenser)	Pieter van Musschenbroeck and E. G. von Kleist
1747	Scurvy cure	James Lind
1748	Sea quadrant	B. Cole
1750	Dyanometer	Gaspard de Prony
1751	Nickel	Axel Frederik Cronstedt
1752	Lightning conductor	Benjamin Franklin
1755	Iron-girder bridge	M. Garvin
1756	Carbon dioxide	Joseph Black
1757	Sextant	John Campbell
1758	Achromatic lens (for eyeglasses)	John Dolland
	Refracting telescope	John Dolland
1760	Screw manufacturing machine	Job and William Wyatt
	Cast-iron cog wheel	Carron Iron Works, Scotland
1761	Mass production of steel scissors	Robert Hinchliffe
	Medical percussion method (diagnostic technique)	Joseph Leopold Avenbrugger
1762	Fire extinguisher	Ambrose Godfrey
1764	Spinning jenny	James Hargreaves
1766	Hydrogen	Henry Cavendish
1768	Aerometer	Antoine Baumé
1769	Steam automobile	Joseph Cugnot
	Steam tractor	Joseph Cugnot
	Hydraulic spinning machine	Richard Arkwright
1770	Sulfur dioxide	Joseph Priestley
	Electric battery	John Cuthbertson
1772	Nitrogen	Daniel Rutherford
1774	Oxygen	Karl Wilhelm Scheele, Joseph Priestley, and Antoine-Laurent Lavoisier
	Ammonia	Joseph Priestley
	Barium	Karl Wilhelm Scheele
	Chlorine	Karl Wilhelm Scheele
	Manganese	Karl Wilhelm Scheele
1775	Chain-driven machine	Crane (England)
	Digitalis (as drug)	William Withering
1776	One-person submarine	David Bushnell
1777	Circular saw	Samuel Miller
	Iron boat	Yorkshire, England
1778	Mortise tumbler (lock)	Robert Barron
	Flush toilet	Joseph Bramah
	Molybdenum	Karl Wilhelm Scheele
1779	Glycerine	Karl Wilhelm Scheele
1780	Artificial insemination	Lazzaro Spallanzani
1781	Uranus	William Herschel

Inventions

Date	Invention/Advance/Discovery	Inventor/Origin
1782	Tellurium	Franz Joseph Müller
	Hot-air balloon	Joseph-Michel and Jacques-Étienne Montgolfier
1783	Hydrogen balloon	Jacques Alexandre Charles and the Robert brothers
	Tungsten	Don Fausto d'Elhuyar and Juan José d'Elhuyar
1784	Bifocal lenses	Benjamin Franklin
	Model helicopter	Launoy (France)
	Rope-spinning machine	Robert March
	Shrapnel shell	Henry Shrapnel
1785	Automatic gristmill	Oliver Evans
	Methane and ethylene	Claude Louis Berthollet
	Rule of electrical forces	Charles Coulomb
1786	Steamboat	John Fitch
1787	Roller bearings	John Garnett
	Power loom	Edmund Cartwright
1789	Uranium	Martin Heinrich Klaproth
	Zirconium	Martin Heinrich Klaproth
	Table of 31 chemical elements	Antoine Lavoisier
1790	Semaphore (visual telegraph)	Claude Chappé
	Cotton spinning and weaving machine (first U.S. patent)	William Pollard
1793	Cotton gin	Eli Whitney
	Astigmatism	Thomas Young
	Strontium	Thomas Charles Hope
	Daltonism (color blindness)	John Dalton
1794	Ball bearings	Philip Vaughan
1795	Hydraulic press	Joseph Bramah
1796	Lithography	Aloys Senefelder
	Smallpox vaccine	Edward Jenner
1797	Chromium	Louis Nicolas Vaquelin
	First parachute jump	André Jacques Garnerin
1798	Process of mass production	Eli Whitney
1799	Metric system	French Academy of Sciences
1800	Infrared light	William Herschel
	Method for storing electricity	Alessandro Volta
	Submarine (metal clad)	Robert Fulton
1801	Asteroid	Giuseppe Piazzi
	Niobium	Charles Hatchett
	Wave theory of light	Thomas Young
	Ultraviolet light	Johann Wilhelm Ritter (and William Hyde Wollaston)
1803	Modern atomic theory	John Dalton
	Iridium	Smithson Tennant
	Palladium and rhodium	William Hyde Wollaston
	Spray gun (aerosol medication)	Alan de Vilbiss
1804	Fishnet-making machine	Joseph Marie Charles Jacquard
	Food canning process	Nicolas Appert
1805	Mechanical silk loom	Joseph Marie Charles Jacquard
	Amphibious vehicle	Oliver Evans
	Morphine	Friedrich Wilhelm Adam Serturner

Inventions

continues

Significant Inventions, Technological Advances, and Scientific Discoveries, Continued

Date	Invention/Advance/Discovery	Inventor/Origin
1806	Beaufort wind scale	Francis Beaufort
	Carbon paper	Ralph Wedgwood
1807	Patent for gas-driven automobile	Isaac de Rivez
	Long-distance steamboat	Robert Fulton
	Potassium	Humphrey Davy
	Sodium	Humphrey Davy
	Sensory-motor nerve system	Charles Bell
1810	Homeopathy	Samuel Hahnemann
	Ammonia-soda reaction	Augustin Jean Fresnel
	Metronome	Dietrich Nikolaus Winkel
	Mowing machine	Peter Gaillard
1811	Avogadro's law	Amedeo Avogadro
	Iodine	Bernard Courteois
1813	Gun cartridge	Samuel Pauly
	Gas meter	Samuel Clegg
	Mine safety lamp	Humphrey Davy and George Stephenson
1814	Steam locomotive	George Stephenson
1816	Stethoscope	René Théophile and Hyacinthe Laënnec
	Phosphorus match	François Derosne
1817	Parkinson's disease	James Parkinson
	Lithium	John August Arfwedson
	Dental plate	Anthony A. Plantson
1818	Cadmium	Friedrich Strohmeyer
	Selenium	Johan Jakob Berzelius
	Hydrogen peroxide	Baron Louis-Jacques Thénard
	Strychnine	Pierre-Joseph Pelletier and Joseph-Bienaimé Caventou
	Geothermal energy experiment	F. de Larderel
1819	Dental amalgam	Charles Bell
	Dioptric system (for lighthouses)	Augustin Jean Fresnel
1820	Diphtheria	Pierre Fidèle Bretonneau
	Quinine	Pierre-Joseph Pelletier and Joseph-Bienaimé Caventou
	Electromagnetism	Hans Christian Oersted
1821	Caffeine	Pierre Joseph Pelletier
	Electric motor principle	Michael Faraday
	Heliotrope	Carl Friedrich Gauss
1822	Thermocouple	Thomas Johann Seebeck
1823	Electromagnet	William Sturgeon
1824	Galvanometer	André-Marie Ampère
	Magnetic pull	Dominique François Jean Arago
1825	Binocular telescope	J. P. Lemière
1826	Gas stove	James Sharp
1827	Aluminum	Friedrich Wohler
	Electrical resistance	George Simon Ohm
	Astigmatic lens	George Biddell Airy
	Microphone	Charles Wheatstone
	Trifocal lens	John Isaac Hawkins
	Water turbine	Benoît Fourneyron

Inventions

Date	Invention/Advance/Discovery	Inventor/Origin
1828	First differential gear for four-wheeled vehicle	Onésiphore Pecqueur
	Stethoscope with earpiece	Pierre Adolphe Poirry
	Cocoa	Conrad van Houten
	Beryllium	Friedrich Wohler
	Thorium	Johan Jakob Berzelius
1830	Vanadium	Nils Gabriel Sefstrom
	Thermostat	André Ure
	Friction match	Charles Sauria
	Lawn mower	Edwin Beard Budding
	Paraffin	Karl, Baron von Reichenbach
1831	Electric bell	Joseph Henry
	Reaping machine	Cyrus McCormick
	Electromagnetic induction	Michael Faraday
	Electromagnetic balance	Antoine César Becquerel
	Magnetic north pole	James Clark Ross
	Chloroform	Samuel Guthrie
1833	Differential calculating machine	Charles Babbage
	Creosote	Karl, Baron von Reichenbach
	Nervous reflex	Marshall Hall
1834	Galvanic cells (continuous electric light)	James Bowman Lindsay
1835	Automatic revolver	Samuel Colt
1836	Steam shovel	William Smith Otis
	Stroboscope	Joseph Antoine Ferdinand Plateau
	Combine harvester	H. Hoare and J. Hascall
	Acetylene	Edmund Davy
1837	Braille reading system	Louis Braille
	Daguerreotype	Louis Jacques Mandé Daguerre
	Electric telegraph	William Fothergill Cooke and Charles Wheatstone
	Electric motor	Thomas Davenport
	Morse code	Samuel F. B. Morse
1838	Plant cells	Matthias Jakob Schleiden
	Stereoscope	Charles Wheatstone
1839	Animal cells	Theodore Schwann
	Protoplasm	Jan Evangelista Purkinje
	Vulcanization of rubber	Charles Goodyear
	First fuel cell	William Robert Grove
1840	Ozone	Christian Friedrich Schonbein
	Chronoscope	Charles Wheatstone
	Electroplating	John Wright
1841	Incandescent lamp	Frederick de Moleyne
1842	Carbon electrode battery	Robert Wilhelm Eberhard von Bunsen
	Underwater telegraph cable	Samuel F. B. Morse
	Ether anesthesia	Crawford Williamson Long
1844	Nitrous oxide anesthesia	Horace Wells and Gardner Q. Colton
1845	Rotary printing press	Richard M. Hoe
	Giant telescope	William Parsons
1846	Sewing machine	Elias Howe
	Use of anesthetic gases in surgery	William Morton
	Neptune	Johann Gottfield Galle and Heinrich Ludwig d'Arrest

Inventions

continues

Significant Inventions, Technological Advances, and Scientific Discoveries, Continued

Date	Invention/Advance/Discovery	Inventor/Origin
1847	Nitroglycerine	Ascanio Sobrero
	Chloroform anesthesia	Jacob Bell and James Young Simpson
1850	Foucault's pendulum (proving Earth's rotation)	Jean Bernard Léon Foucault
1851	Doppler principle	Christian Doppler
	Absolute zero	Lord Kelvin (William Thompson)
	Odometer	William Grayson
	Ophthalmoscope	Herman von Helmholtz
	Flash photography	Henry F. Talbot
1852	Steam-powered airship	Henri Giffard
	Piloted glider	George Cayley
	Microfilm	John Benjamin Dancer
	Fluorescence	George Gabriel Stokes
1853	Hypodermic syringe	Charles Gabriel Pravaz and Alexander Wood
1854	Paleozoic fossils	Adam Sedgwick
1855	Spinal anesthesia	J. L. Corning (U.S.)
	Bunsen burner	Robert Wilhelm Eberhard von Bunsen
	Stopwatch	Edward Daniel Johnson
	Safety match	Johan Edvard Lundstrom
	Battlefield nursing care	Florence Nightingale
1857	Passenger elevator	Elisha G. Otis
1858	Cell replication theory	Rudolf Virchow
	Mobius band	August Mobius
	Atomic and molecular weights	Stanislao Cannizzaro
1859	Cathode rays	Julius Plucker
	Theory of evolution through natural selection	Charles Darwin
	Internal combustion engine (coal gas)	Joseph-Etienne Lenoir
	Technique for drilling oil wells	Edwin Drake
	Ironclad ship	France (*La Gloire*)
1860	Linoleum	Frederick Walton
	Snap button	John Newnham
	Cesium	Robert Wilhelm Eberhard von Bunsen and Gustav Robert Kirchoff
1861	Pneumatic drill	Germain Sommelier
	Speech center of brain	Pierre Paul Broca
1862	Machine gun	Richard Jordan Gatling
1863	The word *Phonograph* first used in a British patent to describe a device to record a keyboard sequence on paper tape	F. B. Fenby
	TNT	J. Wilbrand
	Sodium carbonate process	Ernest Solvay
1864	Electromagnetic wave transmission	Mahlon Loomis
	Pasteurization	Louis Pasteur
	Refutation of spontaneous generation	Louis Pasteur
	Nitroglycerine and dynamite explosives	Alfred Nobel
	Railroad sleeping car	George Pullman
1865	Electric arc welding	Henry Wilde
	Reinforced concrete	W. B. Wilkinson
	Yale cylinder lock	Linus Yale, Jr.

Date	Invention/Advance/Discovery	Inventor/Origin
1865 (cont'd)	Offset printing (web press)	William Bullock
	Genetics	Gregor Johann Mendel
1866	Transatlantic cable	Cyrus West Field, Samuel Canning, and Daniel Gooch
	Lip reading	Alexander Melville Bell
1867	Formaldehyde	August Wilhelm von Hofmann
	Barbed wire	Lucien B. Smith
	Introduction of antiseptic practices in hospitals	Joseph Lister
	Bicycle	Ernest Michaux
	Typewriter	Christopher Latham Sholes
1868	Margarine	Hippolyte Megé-Mouriès
	Stapler	Charles Henry Gould
	Plywood	John K. Mayo
	Helium (in Sun's chromosphere)	Edward Frankland and Joseph Normal Lockyer
1869	Periodic law	Dmitri Ivanovitch Mendeleyev
	Color photography	Charles Cros and Louis Ducos du Hauron
	Celluloid	John Wesley Hyatt and Isaiah Smith Hyatt
1871	Wind tunnel	Francis Herbert Wenham
1872	Hydroplane	Rev. Charles Meade Ramus
	Solar water distillation	Charles Wilson
1873	Direct current electric motor	Zénobe Théophile Gramme
	Electromagnetic radiation	James Clerk-Maxwell
1875	Mimeograph	Thomas Alva Edison
1876	Articulating telephone	Alexander Graham Bell
	Dewey decimal system	Melvil Dewey
	Carburetor (surface type)	Gottlieb Daimler
	Refrigerator	Karl Paul Gottfried von Linde
1877	Differential gear for tricycles	James Starley
	Switchboard	Edwin T. Holmes
	Four-cycle internal combustion engine	Nikolaus August Otto
	Phonograph	Thomas Alva Edison
	Liquid oxygen	Louis-Paul Cailletet and Raoul Pictet
1878	Cathode ray tube	William Crookes
	Milking machine	L. O. Colvin
	Electric alternator	Zénobe Théophile Gramme and Hippolyte Fontaine
	Carbon filament	Joseph Wilson Swann
1879	Arc lighting system	Edwin James Houston and Elihu Thomson
	Cash register	James J. Ritty
	Saccharin	Constantin Fahlberg and Ira Remsen
	Incandescent bulb patent	Thomas Alva Edison
1880	Hearing aid	R. G. Rhodes
	First successful roll film	George Eastman
	Inoculation	Louis Pasteur
1881	Interferometer	Albert A. Michelson
	Rechargeable battery	Camille Fauré
	Telephotography	Shelford Bidwell
1882	Induction coil	Lucien Gaulard and John Gibbs
	Commercial electric fan	Schuyler Skaats Wheeler
	Skyscraper	William Le Baron Jenny

Inventions

continues

Significant Inventions, Technological Advances, and Scientific Discoveries, Continued

Date	Invention/Advance/Discovery	Inventor/Origin
1882 *(cont'd)*	Three-wire system for transporting electrical power	Thomas Alva Edison
	Fountain pen	Lewis Edson Waterman
	Carburetor (float-feed spray)	Edward Butler
	Tuberculosis and cholera germs	Robert Koch
1883	Long-span suspension bridge (Brooklyn Bridge)	John Augustus Roebling
1884	Steam turbine	Charles Parsons
	Local anesthesia (cocaine)	K. Koller
	Gram bacteria test	Hans Christian Joachim Gram
1885	Ammonium picrate (explosive)	Eugène Turpin
	Gas-engine automobile	Gottlieb Daimler, Wilhelm Maybach, and Karl Friedrich Benz
1886	Aluminum electrolysis process	Paul Louis Toussaint Héroult and Charles Martin Hall
	Railway car brake	George Westinghouse
	Comptometer	Dorr Eugene Felt
	Linotype machine	Ottmar Mergenthaler
1887	Mach supersonic scale	Ernst Mach
	Contact lens	Eugen A. Frick
	Electrocardiogram	Augustus Desire Walker
1888	Alternating current motor	Nikola Tesla
	Cellulose photographic film	John Carbutt
	Monorail	Charles Lartigue
	Monotype	Tolbert Lanston
	Hand camera	George Eastman
	Gas-engine farm tractor	Charter Engine Co. (U.S.)
	Cotton picker	Angus Campbell
	Data-processing computer	Herman Hollerith
1889	Active molecules	Svante August Arrhenius
	Cordite	James Dewar and Frederick Augustus Abel
	Lysine (amino acid)	Edmund Drechsel
1890	Motion pictures	William Friese-Greene
	Electric subway train	London, England
1891	Electric motor car	William Morrison
	Silicon carbide	Eduard Goodrich Acheson
	Flashlight	Bristol Electric Lamp Co. (England)
	Aluminum boat	Escher Wyss & Co. (Switzerland)
	Zipper	Whitcomb L. Judson
	Diphtheria antitoxin	Emil Adolf von Behring and Shibasaburo Kitasato
1892	Cholera vaccine	Waldemar Mordecai Wolff Haffkine
	Phagocytes	Illya Mechnikov
	Vacuum flask (early thermos)	Sir James Dewar
	Viruses	Dmitri Iosifovich Ivanovsky
	Viscose rayon	C. F. Cross and E. J. Bevan
1893	Photoelectric cell	Julius Elster and Hans F. Geitel
	Electric toaster	Crompton & Co. (England)
	Diesel engine	Rudolf Diesel
1894	Argon gas	John William Strutt and William Ramsay
	Helium	William Ramsay
	Escalator	Jesse W. Reno

Date	Invention/Advance/Discovery	Inventor/Origin
1895	X rays	Wilhelm Konrad von Roentgen
	Electric hand drill	Wilhelm Fein
	Photographic typesetting	William Friese-Greene
	First public motion picture showing with on-screen projection	Louis Lumière and Auguste Lumière
	Wireless telegraph	Guglielmo Marconi
	Gas-engine motorcycle	Count Albert de Dion and Georges Bouton
1896	Electron	Joseph John Thomas
	Histidine (amino acid)	Albrecht Kossel and Sven A. Hedin
	Science of radioactivity	Henri Becquerel
1897	Conditioned reflexes	Ivan Petrovic Pavlov
	Cause of malaria (mosquito)	Ronald Ross
	Digestion physiology	Ivan Petrovic Pavlov
	Plasticine	William Harbutt
	Worm gear	Frederick W. Lanchester
1898	Antineuritic vitamin B	Christiaan Eijkman
	Krypton	William Ramsay and Morris William Travers
	Neon	William Ramsay and Morris William Travers
	Xenon	William Ramsay and Morris William Travers
	Vitamin-deficiency diseases	Christiaan Eijkman
	Loudspeaker	Horace Short
1899	Aspirin	Felix Hoffman
1900	Radon	Friedrich Ernst Dorn
	Tryptophan (amino acid)	Frederick Gowland Hopkins
	Paper clip	Johann Vaaler
	Alkaline battery	Thomas Alva Edison
	Tractor	Benjamin Holt
1901	Blood groups	Karl Landsteiner
	Valine and proline (amino acids)	Emil Hermann Fischer
	Electric typewriter	Thaddeus Cahill
	Vacuum cleaner	H. Cecil Booth
	Quantum theory	Max Karl Ernst Planck
1902	Hormones	William Maddock Bayliss and Ernest H. Starling
	Ionosphere	Arthur Edwin Kennelly and Oliver Heaviside
	Radium	Pierre Curie and Marie Curie
	Air conditioning	Willis H. Carrier
	Disc brakes	Frederick W. Lanchester
1903	First successful airplane flight	Orville Wright and Wilbur Wright
	Barbiturates	Emil Herman Fischer and Emil Adolf von Bering
1904	Diode vacuum tube	John Ambrose Fleming
1905	Theory of relativity	Albert Einstein
	Silicones	Frederic S. Kipping
	Chemical foam fire extinguisher	Alexander Laurent
	Hydraulic centrifugal clutch	Hermann Fottinger
1906	Crystal radio apparatus	H. H. C. Dunwoody
	Animated cartoon film	James S. Blackton and Walter Booth
	Motion-picture sound	Eugen Augustin Lauste
	Wasserman test (for syphilis)	August von Wasserman

Inventions

continues

Significant Inventions, Technological Advances, and Scientific Discoveries, Continued

Date	Invention/Advance/Discovery	Inventor/Origin
1907	Detergents (household)	Henkel et Cié (Germany)
	Upright vacuum cleaner (attached dust bag)	J. Murray Spangler
	Modern color photography	Louis Lumière
1908	Bakelite	Leo Henrik Baekeland
	Cellophane	Jacques E. Brandenberger
1909	Synthetic ammonia	Fritz Haber
	Typhus fever body louse	Charles Jules Henri Nicolle
	IUD (intrauterine device)	R. Richter
1910	Tumor virus	Francis Peyton Rous
	Gene theory of heredity	Thomas Morgan
	Neon lighting	Georges Claude
1911	Cosmic rays	Victor Franz Hess
	Theory of atomic structure	Ernest Rutherford and Niels Bohr
	Superconductivity	Heike Kamerlingh Onnes
	Binet intelligence test	Alfred Binet
	Calculating machine (full automatic multiplication and division)	Jay R. Monroe
	Monoplane	Léon Levasseur
1912	Diffraction of X rays	Max Theodor Felix von Laue
	Thiamine (vitamin B$_1$)	Casimir Funk
	Diesel locomotive	North British Locomotive Co. (England)
	Cabin biplane (airliner forerunner)	Igor Sikorsky
1913	Stainless steel	Harry Brearley
	Vitamin A	Thomas B. Osborne, Lafayette B. Mendel, Elmer V. McCollum, and M. Davis
	Isotope labeling	Georg von Hevesy and Friedrich A. Paneth
	Moving assembly line for mass production	Henry Ford
1914	Brassiere	Mary Phelps Jacob
	Leica 35mm camera	Oskar Barnack
	Tear gas	Dr. von Tappen
1915	Amplitude modulation (AM) radio	Hendrick Johannes van der Bijl and Raymond A. Heising
	British army tank	Walter Wilson and William Tritton
1917	VHF electromagnetic waves	Guglielmo Marconi
	SONAR detection system	Paul Langevin and Robert Boyle
1918	Vitamin D	Edward Mellanby
	Electric food mixer	Universal Co. (U.S.)
	Domestic refrigerator	Nathaniel Wales and E. J. Copeland
1920	Commercial radio broadcasts	Station KDKA, Pittsburgh, PA (U.S.)
1921	Insulin	Frederick G. Banting and Charles H. Best
	Hydraulic four-wheel brakes	Duesenberg Motor Co. (U.S.)
	Lie detector	John Larsen
	Wirephoto	Western Union Cables (U.S.)
1922	Vitamin E	Herbert McLean Evans
	Three-dimensional movies	Perfect Pictures (U.S.)
1924	Spin dryer	Savage Arms Corp.(U.S.)

Date	Invention/Advance/Discovery	Inventor/Origin
1925	Quantum mechanics	Max Born and Werner Karl Heisenberg
	Technetium and rhenium	Ida Eva Noddack, Walter Karl, and Friedrich Noddack
	Wave mechanics	Erwin Schrödinger
	Hi-fi radio loudspeaker	C. W. Rice and E. W. Kellogg
1926	Aerosol can	Erik Rotheim
	Synthetic rubber	I. G. Farben (Germany)
	Liquid-fueled rocket	Robert H. Goddard
	Television	John Logie Baird, C. F. Jenkins, and D. Mihaly
1927	Iron lung	Philip Drinker and Louis Shaw
	Pop-up toaster	Charles Strite
	First solo, nonstop transatlantic flight	Charles Lindbergh
	Uncertainty principle in physics	Werner Heisenberg
	Sex hormones	Bernhard Zondek and Selmar Ascheim
1928	Penicillin	Alexander Fleming
	Vitamin C	Albert von Nagyrapolt Szent-Györgyi
	Particles in visible light	Chandrasekhara Raman
	Geiger counter	Hans Geiger
	Teletype	Edward Ernst Kleinschmidt
	PVC (polyvinylchloride)	Carbide Corp., Carbon Chemical Corp., and Du Pont (U.S.)
	Tomography	Andre Bocage
1929	Electron microscope	Max Knoll and Ernst Ruska
	Coaxial cable	Bell Telephone Laboratories (U.S.)
	Brain-wave electroencephalograph	Hans Berger
	Frozen food	Clarence Birdseye
	First color television image transmission	Bell Telephone Laboratories (U.S.)
1930	Pluto	Clyde Tombaugh
	Pepsin	John Howard Northrop
	Cyclotron	Ernest O. Lawrence and N. E. Edlesfsen
	Polystyrene	I. G. Farben (Germany)
	TV electronic scanning suitable for the home	Philo T. Pharnsworth
1931	Neutrino	Wolfgang Pauli
	Radio astronomy	Karl Jansky
	Photographic exposure meter	J. Thomas Rhamstine
	Fiberglass	Owens Illinois Glass Co. (U.S.)
	Blood bank	Sergei Sergeivitch
	TWX (teletypewriter exchange)	Bell Telephone & Telegraph (U.S.)
	Electric razor	Jacob Schick
	Cathode-ray tube for television transmission	Vladimir Zworykin
1932	Neutron	James Chadwick
	Proton bombardment (lithium disintegration)	John Douglas Cockcroft and Ernest Thomas Sinton Walton
	Positron	Carl David Anderson and Patrick M. Stuart Blackett
	Deuterium (heavy hydrogen)	Harold Urey
	Defibrillator	William Bennett Kouwenhoven
	Nylon and neoprene	Wallace Carothers and Arnold Collins

Inventions

continues

Significant Inventions, Technological Advances, and Scientific Discoveries, Continued

Date	Invention/Advance/Discovery	Inventor/Origin
1933	Riboflavin (vitamin B_2)	Richard Kuhn
	Pantothenic acid	Roger J. Williams
	Frequency modulation (FM)	Edwin H. Armstrong
	Polyethylene	Reginald Gibson and E. W. Fawcett
1934	Cerenkov effect	Pavel Alekseevich Cerenkov
	Vitamin K	Carl Peter Henrik Dam and Edward Adelbert Doisy
	Progesterone	Adolf Friedrich Johann Butenandt
	Vitamin B_6	Albert von Nagyrapolt Szent-Györgyi
1935	Meson	Hideki Yakawa
	Electronic hearing aid	Edwin A. Steven
	Richter earthquake scale	Charles Francis Richter
1936	Jet engine	Frank Whittle and Hans von Ohain
	Helicopter (contra-rotating rotors)	Henrich Focke
	Plexiglas	I. G. Farben (Germany)
1937	Citric acid cycle	Hans Adolf Krebs
	Niacin	Conrad A. Elvehjem
	Radio telescope	Grote Reber
1938	Cortisone	Edward C. Kendall, Philip S. Hench, and Tadeus Reichstein
	Folic acid	P. L. Day
	Teflon	Roy Plunkett
	LSD	Albert Hofman and Arthur Stoll
	Pressurized airplane cabin	Transcontinental Airways, Boeing 307 Stratoliner
	Ballpoint pen	Lázló J. Biro and Georg Biro
	Fluorescent lighting	Arthur H. Compton and George Inman
	Photocopy machine	Chester Carlson
	First all-plastic hard contact lenses	T. Obrig and F. Muller
1939	Jet aircraft	Hans von Ohain
	Binary calculator	John Atanasoff and George R. Stibitz
	DDT	Paul Hermann Müller
	Microfilm camera	Elgin G. Fassel
	Betatron	Donald W. Kerst
	Concept of black hole	J. Robert Oppenheimer and Hartland S. Snyder
1940	Plutonium	Glenn Theodore Seaborg and Edwin Mattison McMillan
	Radar	Robert M. Page (word coined by S. M. Tucker)
	Automatic transmission	General Motors (U.S.)
	Cavity magnetron (radar tube)	John Randall
1941	Microwave radar	U.S. Radiation Laboratory
	Dacron	John R. Whinfield
	First color television system	Peter Goldmark
1942	First sustained and controlled release of nuclear energy	Enrico Fermi and team
	Vitamin H (biotin)	Vincent du Vigneaud
1943	Streptomycin	Selman A. Waksman
	Electronic computer	Max Newman and T. H. Flowers

Inventions

Date	Invention/Advance/Discovery	Inventor/Origin
1944	Americium	Glenn T. Seaborg and Albert Ghiorso
	Curium	Glenn T. Seaborg and Albert Ghiorso
	Sequence-controlled calculator	Howard Aiken
1945	Artificial kidney	Willem J. Kolff
	Atomic bomb	J. Robert Oppenheimer and Manhattan Project team
	Tupperware	Earl W. Tupper
	Vinyl floor covering	Du Pont (U.S.)
1946	Electronic vacuum tube computer (ENIAC)	John W. Mauchly and J. Presper Eckert
1947	Coenzyme A	Fritz A. Lipman
	Vitamin B_{12} as cure for pernicious anemia	Karl A. Folkers
	Radiocarbon dating	Willard Frank Libby
	Holography	Dennis Gabor
	Supersonic aircraft	Bell XS-1 (U.S.)
	First supersonic flight	Chuck Yeager
1948	Transistor	William Shockley, John Bardeen, and Walter H. Brattain
	Atomic clock	William F. Libby
	Cybernetics	Norbert Wiener
	Long-playing phonographic record (microgroove record)	Peter Goldmark
	Solid electric guitar	Leo (Clarence) Fender, "Doc" Kauffman, and George Fullerton
	Velcro	Georges de Mestral
	Corneal contact lenses	Kevin Tuohy
1949	Berkelium	Glenn T. Seaborg and Stanley G. Thompson
	Jet airliner	R. E. Bishop and team
1950	Chlorpromazine (tranquilizer)	Paul Charpentier
	Radioimmunoassay	Rosalyn Sussman Yalow
	Xerographic copying machine	Haloid Co. (U.S.)
1951	Oral contraceptive pill	Gregory Goodwin Pincus, Min Chuch Chang, John Rock, and Carl Djerassi
1952	Artificial heart valve	Charles A. Hufnagel
	Hydrogen bomb	Edward Teller and team
	Experimental videotape	John Mullin and Wayne Johnson
	Transistor radio	Sony (Japan)
1953	DNA (deoxyribonucleic acid)	Francis H. Compton Crick and James D. Watson
	Fermium	Albert Ghiorso and Stanley G. Thompson
	Measles vaccine	John F. Enders and Thomas Peebles
	Reperine (antidepressant drug)	Nathan S. Kline
	Reserpine (antihypertensive)	Nathan S. Kline
	Heart-lung machine	John H. Gibbon
1954	Regular broadcast of color television	National Broadcasting Co. (U.S.)
1955	Fiber optics	Narinder S. Kapany
	Mendelevium	Albert Ghiorso
	RNA synthesis	Severo Ochoa
	Ultrasound (to observe heart)	Leskell (U.S.)
	Polio vaccine (killed-virus)	Jonas Salk
	Felt-tip pen	Esterbrook (England)
	Stereo tape recording	EMI Stereosonic Tapes
	Hovercraft	Christopher S. Cockerell

continues

Inventions

Significant Inventions, Technological Advances, and Scientific Discoveries, Continued

Date	Invention/Advance/Discovery	Inventor/Origin
1956	Amniocentesis	St. Mary's Hospital (England)
	Human growth hormone	Choh Hao Li
	DNA synthesis with enzymes, nucleotides	Arthur Kornberg
	Methacrylate corneal contact lenses	Norman Bier
1957	BCS theory (superconductivity)	John Bardeen, Leon N. Cooper, and J. Robert Schrieffer
	Interferon (protein)	Alick Isascs and Jean Lindeman
	Mossbauer effect (gamma radiation)	Rudolph Ludwig Mossbauer
	Polio vaccine (live virus)	Albert S. Sabin
	Artificial satellite	*Sputnik* (USSR)
	FORTRAN (computer language)	John Backus and team for IBM (U.S.)
	Intercontinental ballistic missile	USSR
	Laser theory	Gordon Gould
	Artificial-heart pacemaker	Clarence Lillehie
1958	Laser	Charles A. Townes and Arthur L. Schawlow
	Communications satellite	*SCORE* (U.S.)
	ALGOL computer language	Switzerland
	Nobelium	Albert Ghiorso
	Van Allen radiation belts	James A. Van Allen
	Integrated circuit	Jack S. Kilby, Texas Instruments (U.S.)
1959	Tunnel diode	Sony, Japan, based on work by Leo Esaki
	Microwave radio system	Pacific Great Eastern Railway between Vancouver and Dawson Creek–Fort St. John, British Columbia, Canada
	COBOL computer language	Grace Murray Hopper
	Ion engine	Alvin T. Forrester
1960	Argon ion laser	D. R. Herriott, A. Javan, and W. R. Bennett at Bell Laboratories (U.S.)
	Vertical takeoff and landing aircraft	Frank Taylor and team at Short Brothers & Harland (Northern Ireland)
	Weather satellite	*TIROS* (U.S.)
	Muonium	Vernon W. Hughes and coworkers
1961	Manned space flight	*Vostok 1* (U.S.S.R.)
	Stereophonic radio broadcast	Zenith and General Electric Companies (U.S.)
	Valium	Hoffman-LaRoche Laboratories (Switzerland)
	Kenyapithecus wickeri (hominid)	Louis S. B. Leakey
1962	Minicomputer	Digital Corp. (U.S.)
	Robotics	Rand Corp. and IBM (U.S.)
	X-ray astronomical sources	Riccardo Giacconi
	Muon neutrino	Leon Max Lederman, Melvin Schwartz, and Jack Steinberger
1963	Cassette tapes	Philips Co. (The Netherlands)
	Quarks	Murray Gell-Mann and George Zweig
	Quasars	Marten Schmidt
1964	BASIC computer language	Thomas E. Kurtz and John G. Kemeny
	Carbon fiber	RAF Farnborough (England)
	Home-use transistor videotape recorder	Sony (Japan)
	Laser eye surgery	H. Vernon Ingram

Inventions

Quarks

A Closer Look

Murray Gell-Mann and George Zweig formulated the concept of quarks in 1963 to explain the large variety of new elementary particles, called hadrons, that were being discovered. (Protons and neutrons are two types of hadrons.) Quarks are hypothetical particles presumed to be the basic constituents of hadrons. Quarks come in various "flavors," such as up, down, strange, and charmed.

But Gell-Mann and Zweig's theory left unanswered the question of why no one had ever observed isolated quarks. One theory stated that hadrons are composed of strings of quarks that are bound together so tightly that an infinite amount of energy would be required to break the bonds.

The search for quarks continued, and in 1969 strong evidence of their existence was discovered at the Stanford Linear Accelerator Center (SLAC). Richard E. Taylor of SLAC, Henry W. Kendall of MIT, and Jerome I. Friedman of MIT shared the 1990 Nobel prize for this work.

Date	Invention/Advance/Discovery	Inventor/Origin
1965	Word processor	IBM (U.S.)
	Rubella vaccine	Paul D. Parkman and Harry M. Meyer, Jr.
1966	Integrated radio circuit	Sony (Japan)
	Noise reduction system for audiotapes	Ray M. Dolby
1967	Bubble memory prototype (computers)	A. H. Bobeck and team at Bell Telephone Laboratories (U.S.)
	Pulsars	Jocelyn Bell Burnell
1968	Holographic storage technique	Bell Telephone Laboratories (U.S.)
	Hemoglobin molecule structure (complete)	Max Ferdinand Perutz
1969	Manned moon landing	*Apollo 11* (U.S.)
	PASCAL computer language	Niklaus Wirth
	Videotape cassette	Sony (Japan)
	Jumbo jet airliner	Joe Sutherland and team at Boeing (U.S.)
	Antibody chemical and molecular structure	Rodney Robert Porter
1970	Bar code system	Monarch Marking (U.S.) and Plessey Telecommunications (England)
	Computer floppy disk	IBM (U.S.)
	Remote-controlled lunar vehicle	*Lunokhod 1* (USSR)
1971	Earth-orbiting space station	*Salyut 1* (USSR)
	Liquid crystal display (LCD)	Hoffmann-LaRoche Laboratories (Switzerland)
	Quartz digital watch	George Theiss and Willy Crabtree
1972	Video disk	Philips Co. (The Netherlands)
	Video game	Noland Bushnel
	Artificial hip	John Charnley
	Enkephalin (brain chemical)	John Hughes
	Antimatter particles	Yuri Dmitriyevich Prokoshkin and coworkers
	Black holes	Robert L. F. Boyd
	MRI (magnetic resonance imaging)	Raymond Damadian
	Switching technology for cell phones	Amos E. Joel at Bell Laboratories
1973	Computerized axial tomography (CAT scan)	Allan Macleod Cormac and Godfrey N. Hounsfield
	Microcomputer	Trong Truong
	Recombinant DNA	Paul Berg
1974	Nonimpact printing	Honeywell (U.S.)
	J/psi atomic particle	Burton Richter and Samuel Chao Chung Ting

Inventions

continues

Significant Inventions, Technological Advances, and Scientific Discoveries, Continued

Date	Invention/Advance/Discovery	Inventor/Origin
1975	Hybrid cells	Jack Lucy and Ted Cocking
	Monoclonal antibodies	César Milstein
	Betamax videotaping system	Sony (Japan)
	Video home system (VHS)	Matsushita/JVC (Japan)
1976	Charm subatomic particle	Stanford Linear Accelerator Center (U.S.)
	Mars space probe landings	*Viking I* and *Viking II* (U.S.)
1977	Upsilon particle	Leon Lederman
	Neutron bomb	U.S. military
	Space shuttle	NASA (U.S.)
	Alkyd paint	Winsor & Newton Ltd. (England)
1978	Cyclosporin A	Tony Allison and Roy Calne
	Human insulin	Genentech (U.S.)
	Charon (Pluto's moon)	James Walter Christy and Robert S. Harrington
	Test-tube baby	Patrick C. Steptoe and Robert G. Edwards
1979	Single-cell protein process	ICI Agricultural Division (England)
1980	Solar-powered aircraft	Paul MacCready
1981	Anti-interferon	Medical Research Council's Molecular Biology Laboratory (England)
	First official recognition of AIDS	Centers for Disease Control (U.S.)
	Silicon 32-bit chip	Hewlett-Packard, U.S.
	Nuclear magnetic resonance (NMR) scanner	Thorn-EMI Research Laboratories and Nottingham University (England)
1982	Abnormal cancer-causing genes	Robert Weinberg and Mariano Barbacid
	Artificial heart	Robert Jarvik
	Airborne observatory	NASA (U.S.)
1983	W and Z particles	Carlo Rubbia and Simon van der Meer
	Biopol (biodegradable plastic)	ICI Agricultural Division (England)
	Biosensors	Cambridge Life Sciences (England)
	Carbon-fiber aircraft wing	Great Britain
	512K dynamic access memory chip	IBM (U.S.)
1984	Gene cloning	National Institutes of Health (U.S.); Transgene (France); and Otago University (New Zealand)
	Genetically engineered blood-clotting factor	Genentech (U.S.)
	Compact disk player	Sony and Fujitsu Companies (Japan) and Philips Co. (The Netherlands)
	Megabit computer chip	IBM (U.S.)
	Isolation of virus believed to cause AIDS	Robert C. Gallo (U.S. National Cancer Institute); Luc Montagnier (Pasteur Institute, France); and Myron Essex (Harvard School of Public Health, U.S.)
1985	Cloned leprosy genes (for vaccines)	Ron Davis and coworkers
	Anxiety chemical (human brain)	Alessandro Guidotti and Erminio Costa
	CD-ROM (compact disc read-only memory)	Hitachi (Japan)
	Image digitizer	Optronics (England)
	Polymer electric conductor	Terje Skotheim and team at Brookhaven National Laboratory (U.S.)
	Soft bifocal contact lens	Sofsite Contact Lens Laboratory (U.S.)

Date	Invention/Advance/Discovery	Inventor/Origin
1985 *(cont'd)*	Positron emission tomography	Michael Phelps
	Publication of the first image from a positron transmission microscope	James Van House and Arthur Rich
	First baby born from frozen embryo	Australia
1986	DNA fingerprinting	Alec Jeffreys
	Diminished ozone shield	Susan Solomon at National Oceanic and Atmospheric Administration (U.S.)
	High-temperature superconductivity	Georg Bednorz and Karl Alex Müller
	Synthetic skin	G. Gregory Gallico, III
1987	Higher-temperature superconductivity	C. W. Chu, M. K. Wu, and coworkers
	Alzheimer's disease gene	National Institutes of Health (U.S.); University of Cologne (Germany)
	Gene-altered bacteria	Advanced Genetic Sciences (U.S.)
1988	Galaxy 12 billion light-years away	Simon J. Lilly
	Patented animal life	Philip Leder and Timothy Stewart
1989	Introduction of foreign gene into human patient	Steven A. Rosenberg and coworkers at National Institutes of Health (U.S.)
1991	Controlled nuclear fusion	Joint European Torus (Oxfordshire, England)
	X-ray research showing first photographs of the human brain recalling a word	Dr. Marcus Raichle and coworkers
1992	Fluctuations in cosmic background radiation	George Smoot
1994	Proof of Fermat's last theorem	Andrew John Wiles
1995	Decipherment of entire DNA sequence of living organism	Craig J. Venter and Hamilton Smith
1997	Cloning of adult animal	Ian Wilmut
	Atom laser	Wolfgang Ketterle
1998	Lunar Prospector discovers evidence of frozen water on the Moon	NASA
	Observations of supernovae suggest the expansion of the Universe is accelerating	Saul Perlmutter (Lawrence Berkeley National Lab) and Nicholar Suntzeff (Cerro Tololo Inter-American Observatory)
1999	Human stem cells found to have potential for treating incurable disease	James A. Thomson (University of Wisconsin), John D. Gearhart (Johns Hopkins University), Evan Y. Snyder (Harvard Medical School), Angelo L. Vescovi (National Neurological Institute), et al.
	Earliest life on Earth found to be 2.7 billion years old	Jochen Brocks, et. al. (University of Sydney)
	Cosmic ray bursts linked to collapse of massive stars	Shrinivas Kulkarni and Joshua Bloon (Caltech)
2000	Sequencing of the human genome accomplished	The Human Genome Project and Celera Genomics
	Potential first human ancestors to journey out of Africa found in Republic of Georgia	Reid Ferring, Carl Swisher, Susan Antòn, et al.
	NEAR Shoemaker spacecraft rendezvouses with the asteroid Eros	NASA
2001	First space "tourist" visits the International Space Station	Dennis Tito (U.S.)
	Sunken ancient Egyptian port city of Herakleion is rediscovered	Franck Goddio, leader of international mission

Inventions

MAJOR SCIENTISTS AND ENGINEERS

AEROSPACE ENGINEERS

Goddard, Robert Hutchings (1882–1945). American physicist who launched the first liquid-propellant rocket.

Sikorsky, Igor I. (1889–1972). Russian-born American aircraft designer responsible for the first multiengine airplane and the world's first true production helicopter.

Tsiolkovsky, Konstantin Eduardovich (1857–1935). Russian rocket pioneer and research scientist in aeronautics and astronautics who was one of the first to publish scientific papers about space flight.

The Wright brothers' historic flight covered a distance shorter than the length of today's space shuttle.

ASTRONOMERS

Aristotle (384–322 B.C.). Greek philosopher who developed many of the astronomical beliefs of his time, including the idea that the Earth was the center of the universe, into a cosmological system that dominated astronomy for nearly 1,800 years. He believed that everything in the universe was composed of four "basic elements"—earth, water, air, and fire.

Bode, Johann Elert (1747–1826). German astronomer who published the Titius-Bode Law in the late 1700s, a mathematical calculation that determines the distances to the planets in astronomical units.

Brahe, Tycho (1546–1601). Danish astronomer and one of the greatest astronomical observers before the advent of the telescope. His accurate measurements of planetary positions were the foundation for Johannes Kepler's formulation of the laws of planetary motion.

Cassini, Giovanni Domenico (1625–1712). Italian-born French astronomer who discovered several moons around Saturn and the dark division in Saturn's rings. He was the first of four generations of astronomers.

Copernicus, Nicolaus (1473–1543). Polish astronomer who revolutionized astronomy by proposing that the Sun, not the Earth, is the center of the solar system.

Eratosthenes of Cyrene (c. 276–c. 194 B.C.). Hellenic librarian and astronomer who was the first to estimate fairly accurately the circumference of the Earth.

Galileo Galilei (1564–1642). Italian astronomer and physicist who was the first to use a telescope for astronomical observations, discovering the moons around Jupiter and the phases of Venus.

Hale, George Ellery (1868–1938). American astrophysicist who discovered magnetic fields in sunspots and who secured funding for several large telescopes, including the 200-inch reflector on Palomar Mountain in California.

Halley, Edmond (1656–1742). British astronomer and physicist who determined the periodicity of the comet that bears his name.

Hawking, Stephen William (1942–   ). British theoretical physicist who is especially known for his theories on black holes and the origin and evolution of the universe.

Herschel, Sir John Frederick William (1792–1871). British astronomer, son of William Herschel, who made the first exhaustive study of the southern sky and made significant contributions to the development of photography.

Herschel, Sir William (1738–1822). German-born British astronomer who discovered the planet Uranus. He also founded modern stellar astronomy, discovered nearly 1,000 double stars, determined the general shape and size of the Milky Way, and published numerous catalogs of nebulae and clusters.

Go to "Astronomy," "Meterology," and "Space Exploration" in chapter 4; "Astronomy Symbols" and "Weather Symbols" in chapter 12

Hewish, Anthony (1924–). British radio astronomer whose work in radio scintillation led to the discovery of pulsars.

Hipparchus (c. 170–c. 120 B.C.). Greek astronomer and geographer who worked out the epicycle theory of the solar system, with the Earth at the center. He also discovered the precession of the equinox, calculated the length of a year within 6.5 minutes, and devised the first known star map.

Hoyle, Sir Fred (1915–). British astrophysicist who developed the steady-state hypothesis of the universe.

Hubble, Edwin Powell (1889–1953). American astronomer and cosmologist whose work demonstrated that the universe was expanding. He also formulated the Hubble constant, which measures the rate of expansion of the universe and is used to determine the age of the universe.

Jansky, Karl Guthe (1905–50). American radio engineer who, by discovering radio emissions from the Milky Way galaxy, founded the field of radio astronomy.

U.S. Army Lt. Thomas E. Selfridge was the first person to be killed in an airplane accident. The pilot of the flight was Orville Wright.

Jeans, Sir James Hopwood (1877–1946). British mathematician, astronomer, and physicist who was the first to propose that matter is continuously created throughout the universe. He also wrote numerous popular astronomy books.

Kepler, Johannes (1571–1630). German astronomer who formulated the three principal laws governing the motion and elliptical orbits of planetary bodies, thus eliminating the epicycle models that had governed astronomy for close to 2,000 years.

Kuiper, Gerard Peter (1905–73). Dutch-born American astronomer who studied lunar and planetary surface features. He discovered Mirända, a satellite of Uranus, and Nereid, a satellite of Neptune.

Laplace, Marquis Pierre Simon de (1749–1827). French mathematician, astronomer, and physicist who contributed extensively to celestial mechanics. Among other things, he established that the solar system has long-term stability. His nebular hypothesis postulated that the planets resulted from a primitive nebula that rotated around the sun.

Lowell, Percival (1855–1916). American astronomer who developed theories of life on Mars and predicted the existence of a ninth planet (Pluto, which would not be discovered until 1930).

Oort, Jan Hendrik (1900–92). Dutch astronomer who detected the rotation of the Milky Way galaxy and who postulated that a sphere of incipient cometary material, now called the Oort Cloud, surrounds the solar system far outside the orbit of Pluto.

Penzias, Arno (1933–). American astronomer who, with Robert Wilson (1936–), discovered the radio wave remnants of the Big Bang.

Piazzi, Giuseppe (1746–1826). Italian astronomer who discovered Ceres, the first asteroid (minor planet).

Ptolemy (Claudius Ptolemaeus) (c. A.D. 2nd century). Egyptian astronomer and encyclopedist who made extensive use of epicycles and other devices to achieve a fairly accurate match of observations with the idea that the Earth was the center of the universe. His achievement enabled the geocentric hypothesis to dominate astronomy for over a thousand years.

Sagan, Carl Edward (1934–96). American astronomer and exobiologist who increased public awareness and support of science through his popular writings and television presentations.

Schiaparelli, Giovanni Viginio (1835–1910). Italian astronomer who studied the planets and is known mostly for his report of *canali* (channels) on the planet Mars.

Shapley, Harlow (1885–1972). American astronomer who established the size and structure of our Milky Way galaxy.

Inventions

Shoemaker, Eugene (1928–97). American astro-geologist who established the meteoric nature of Meteor Crater in Arizona, helped map the Moon for the Apollo missions, and searched for asteroids that crossed the orbit of Earth.

Tombaugh, Clyde William (1906–97). American astronomer who discovered the planet Pluto in 1930.

Whipple, Fred Lawrence (1906–   ). American astronomer whose "dirty snowball" model of comet composition postulated that a cometary nuclei consists of a frozen mixture of water, carbon dioxide, ammonia, methane, and particles of dust, silicates, and other materials.

Wolszczan, Alex (1946–   ). Polish radio-astronomer, astrophysicist, and discoverer, along with Dale Frail of the National Radio Astronomy Observatory, of the first extrasolar planet, which was observed orbiting around pulsar PSR 1257+12 in the constellation Virgo.

BIOLOGISTS

Audubon, John James (1785–1851). French-American ornithologist and naturalist who is known for his bird drawings and paintings.

Bateson, William (1861–1926). British biologist who coined the term *genetics* (the causes and effects of heritable characteristics). He was a strong proponent of Gregor Mendel's work on heredity.

Borlaug, Norman Ernest (1914–   ). American agronomist and plant breeder who was one of the creators of the green revolution in agriculture. He won the Nobel Prize for peace in 1970 for his work on breeding "miracle" wheat for India and Mexico.

Burbank, Luther (1849–1926). American plant breeder who developed new varieties of many plants, including the Burbank potato, berries, and plums.

Carver, George Washington (c. 1860–1943). American agricultural researcher who developed new crop-rotation methods for conserving nutrients in soil and devised hundreds of new products from such crops as the peanut and sweet potato.

Cohen, Stanley H. (1922–   ). American biochemist who determined that DNA molecules could be cut, separated, and joined, thus paving the way for genetic engineering. He also worked on the mechanisms responsible for cell and organ growth.

Cuvier, Baron, Georges Léopold Chrétien Frédéric Dagobert (1769–1832). French comparative anatomist, paleontologist, and taxonomist who developed the first method of classifying mammals and founded the science of comparative anatomy. He was the first to propose that catastrophes were responsible for the extinction of species.

Darwin, Charles Robert (1809–82). British naturalist who revolutionized biology with his theory of evolution through the process of natural selection. He also provided geological evidence for evolution and made detailed observations of volcanoes and earthquakes.

de Vries, Hugo Marie (1848–1935). Dutch plant physiologist and geneticist who promoted the works of Gregor Mendel, which had been ignored for four decades. He also determined that mutations occur in organisms.

Lamarck, Jean Baptiste Pierre Antoine de Monet, Chevalier de (1744–1829). French naturalist who proposed an early theory of evolution. He was the first to distinguish between invertebrates and vertebrates, and he developed a classification system for invertebrates.

Leeuwenhoek, Anton van (1632–1723). Dutch microscopist who discovered numerous organisms, including protists, sperm (which he correctly assumed to be the source of reproduction), and bacteria.

Linnaeus, Carolus (Carl von Linné) (1707–78). Swedish naturalist who introduced certain classifications of organisms that are still in use today.

Go to "Major Zoos and Aquariums" and "Major Botanical Gardens and Arboretums" in chapter 11

Mendel, Gregor Johann (1822–84). Austrian monk and botanist who discovered the basic laws of heredity, based on his studies of pea plants.

Miller, Stanley Lloyd (1930–). American chemist who created a primitive atmosphere that demonstrated how amino acids might have been generated in the oceans of a primitive Earth.

Sachs, Julius von (1832–97). German botanist who greatly developed the field of plant physiology. He was the first to demonstrate that photosynthesis occurs in chloroplasts.

Theophrastus (c. 372–c. 287 B.C.). Greek botanist and philosopher who described some 500 species of plants.

Tull, Jethro (1674–1741). British agriculturist, writer, and inventor who invented a machine for planting seeds. He is best known for his suggestions on plant cultivation, such as the use of manure and hoeing around crops to remove weeds.

von Frisch, Karl (1886–1982). Austrian entomologist, ethnologist, and zoologist who studied the dance of bees, recorded their detailed movements, and determined that they were actually communicating.

Wallace, Alfred Russel (1823–1913). British naturalist who formulated a theory of evolution by natural selection independently of Charles Darwin.

CHEMISTS

Arrhenius, Svante August (1859–1927). Swedish physical chemist whose work established the basis for modern electrochemistry. He also developed the theory of panspermia, in which bacterial spores were thought to travel from space to Earth. He won the Nobel Prize for chemistry in 1903.

Avogadro, Lorenzo Romano Amedeo Carlo, count of Quaregna and Cerreto (1776–1856). Italian physicist and chemist who expanded on Gay-Lussac's law of combining volumes and determined the formula for water. He differentiated molecules from atoms and was the first to use the word *molecule*. He developed Avogadro's constant and is considered one of the founders of modern physical chemistry.

Boltzmann, Ludwig (1844–1906). Austrian scientist and inventor of statistical mechanics and the concept of probability, concepts used to connect the behavior and properties of atoms and molecules with those of larger substances.

Boyle, Robert (1627–91). Irish-born chemist and physicist who explored the characteristics of gases and developed Boyle's law, which states that pressure and volume are inversely proportional for a fixed mass of gas at constant temperatures.

Cannizzaro, Stanislao (1826–1910). Italian chemist who established the use of atomic weights in chemical formulas and calculations.

Cavendish, Henry (1731–1810). English chemist and physicist who discovered hydrogen and determined the mass of the Earth.

Crookes, Sir William (1832–1919). British chemist and physicist who discovered the element thallium (using the then-new method of spectroscopy), invented the radiometer, and investigated radioactivity.

Curie, Marie Sklodowska (1867–1934). Polish-born French chemist who isolated the radioactive elements radium (with her husband Pierre Curie and Gustav Bemont) and polonium (with Pierre Curie) and was the first person to win two Nobel Prizes (for physics in 1903 and for chemistry in 1911).

Curie, Pierre (1859–1906). French physicist who codiscovered radium and polonium and shared the Nobel Prize for physics in 1903. He also discovered the piezoelectric effect, in which certain substances produce a current as the result of pressure.

Dalton, John (1766–1844). British chemist and physicist who determined the law of partial pressures and formulated an atomic theory of matter.

"The Animal Kingdom" and "The Plant Kingdom" in chapter 3
Go to

Inventions

Davy, Sir Humphry (1778–1829). British chemist who established the important connection between electrochemistry and the elements, discovered the elements sodium and potassium, and invented a safety lamp for miners.

Hodgkin, Dorothy Crowfoot (1910–94). British chemist who determined the structure of vitamin B_{12} and analyzed the structure of penicillin. She won the Nobel Prize for chemistry in 1964.

Langmuir, Irving (1881–1957). American chemist who studied chemical reactions at high temperatures and low pressures, leading to the development of the gas-filled tungsten lamp. He also worked on thermal effects on gases, which led to using atomic hydrogen in welding torches. He won the Nobel Prize for chemistry in 1932.

An 11-year-old California boy mixed soda water powder with water, then accidentally left it on the back porch with the stirring stick still in it. The mixture froze during the night. His discovery later became known as the "popsicle."

Lavoisier, Antoine Laurent (1743–94). French chemist who was one of the first to quantify methods in chemistry. He determined the nature of combustion, noted the composition of the atmosphere, articulated the law of conservation of matter, and wrote the first modern chemistry book.

Mendeleev, Dmitri Ivanovich (1834–1907). Russian chemist who published the first periodic table of the elements in 1869.

Newlands, John Alexander Reina (1837–98). British chemist who was one of the first to determine periodicity in the properties of chemical elements.

Nobel, Alfred Bernhard (1833–96). Swedish chemist, engineer, and inventor of dynamite and several other explosives. His fortune endowed the Nobel Prizes.

Pauling, Linus Carl (1901–94). American chemist who applied quantum theory to molecular structures, establishing modern theoretical organic chemistry. He also determined the role of electrons in the formation of molecules and developed theories on ionic and covalent bonding, for which he won the Nobel Prize for chemistry in 1954. He was also awarded the Nobel Prize for peace in 1962 for his efforts to stop nuclear weapons testing.

Priestley, Joseph (1733–1804). British chemist and Presbyterian minister who first reported the discovery of oxygen. (Although Carl Scheele discovered the element earlier, he published his results after Priestley.)

Proust, Joseph Louis (1754–1826). French chemist who worked to measure the mass of each component of a compound. He formulated the law of constant proportions, which states that compounds always contain certain elements in the same proportion, regardless of the method of preparation.

Seaborg, Glenn Theodore (1912–99). American scientist. Codiscoverer of plutonium, he also discovered the transuranium elements through element 102 and identified more than 100 isotopes of a variety of elements.

Soddy, Frederick (1877–1966). English chemist who proposed the isotope theory of the elements and determined how radioactive elements break down. He won the Nobel Prize for chemistry in 1921.

Urey, Harold Clayton (1893–1981). American physical chemist whose pioneering isotope-separation methods enabled him to discover heavy water and deuterium (the heavy isotope of hydrogen). He also extensively studied the origin of the Earth and the other planets.

"Computers" in chapter 4; "Data Banks Available for Computer Research" in chapter 11
Go to

Inventions

COMPUTER SCIENTISTS

Babbage, Charles (1792–1871). British mathematician and inventor who developed one of the first early calculating machines, called the difference engine.

Hollerith, Herman (1860–1929). American inventor who developed the first electrically driven computer; it used punch cards to count the census.

Hopper, Grace Murray (1906–92). American computer programmer who helped invent COBOL, the computer language for business use.

Jacquard, Joseph Marie (1752–1834). French inventor who created the Jacquard loom; with this device, he programmed complicated carpet patterns onto punched cards.

Pascal, Blaise (1623–62). French mathematician, physicist, and religious philosopher who invented the first mechanical calculating machine and founded the modern theory of probabilities.

Turing, Alan Mathison (1912–54). British mathematician who developed the idea of a universal computer called the Turing machine, which could solve any type of mathematical problem by reducing it to coding in a given set of commands. (Bell Laboratories put his ideas into practice in 1939, by developing the first relay computer.)

Von Neumann, John (1903–57). Hungarian-born American mathematician who developed principles of design for digital computers and supervised the construction of the first stored-program computer.

EARTH SCIENTISTS AND ENVIRONMENTALISTS

Agassiz, Jean Louis Rodolphe (1807–73). Swiss-born American geologist and biologist who introduced the idea of the Ice Age, a period when ice sheets covered most of the Northern Hemisphere.

Agricola, Georgius (Georg Bauer) (1494–1555). German mineralogist who coined the word *fossil* but did not differentiate fossils from other types of rock.

Bjerknes, Vilhelm Friman Koren (1862–1951). Norwegian meteorologist who, with his son Jacob Aall Bonnevie Bjerknes (1897–1975), proved that the atmosphere was made up of air masses of different temperatures with sharp boundaries called fronts between them.

Today a desktop computer can store a million times more information than the first computer and is 50,000 times faster.

Brongniart, Alexandre (1770–1847). French geologist and paleontologist who pioneered the idea of using fossils to identify ages and layers of sedimentary rock.

Buys Ballot, Christoph Hendrik Diederik (1817–90). Dutch meteorologist who formulated the law for determining areas of low pressure based on observing the wind's direction.

Carson, Rachel Louise (1907–64). American ecologist and author of several scientific and popular publications concerning ecology and the environment, many of which inspired environmental protection policies.

Conybeare, William Daniel (1787–1857). British geologist and minister who synthesized the ideas of catastrophism (that geologic changes occur in brief bursts separated by long quiet periods) and progressivism (the biological theory that a series of creations yields organisms that are increasingly more complex).

Coriolis, Gustave-Gaspard (1792–1843). French physicist who, in 1835, first described the curving deflection of winds caused by the Earth's rotation, now called the Coriolis effect.

Cousteau, Jacques-Yves (1910–97). French oceanographer who developed the aqualung, underwater photography techniques, and the bathyscaph.

Inventions

He was also an author and filmmaker who increased public awareness of the diversity of ocean life and environmental problems of the oceans and the Earth.

Dana, James Dwight   (1813–95). American geologist and mineralogist who wrote the first standard reference books in geology and mineralogy.

Drake, Edwin Laurentine   (1819–80). American investor who drilled the world's first oil well in Titusville, Pennsylvania, in 1859. His work greatly advanced geological studies in the search for more oil.

Ewing, William Maurice   (1913–74). American oceanographer who made detailed maps of the sea bottom using refraction of waves caused by explosions (similar to sonar). He helped describe the Mid-Atlantic Ridge, an area of seafloor spreading that cuts through the Atlantic Ocean.

Gilbert, Grove Karl   (1843–1918). American geologist and geomorphologist who developed the foundations of 20th-century earth science. He contributed detailed descriptions of river and other geologic processes that became standards for his time.

Hadley, George   (1685–1768). English lawyer and climatologist who suggested that the Earth's rotation from west to east caused the trade winds to blow from the northeast in the Northern Hemisphere and from the southeast in the Southern Hemisphere.

Hall, Sir James   (1761–1832). British chemist and geologist who was one of the first scientists to use laboratory experiments to test geologic theories. He also showed that crystals form from melted rock.

Hess, Harry Hammond   (1906–1969). American geologist and discoverer of the phenomena of seafloor spreading, which expanded the theory of plate tectonics.

Humboldt, (Friedrich Wilhelm Heinrich) Alexander, Baron von   (1769–1859). Prussian scientific explorer who made detailed investigations of the Earth's magnetism, identified the Jurassic Period of geologic time, and explored the cold current running north along the Pacific coast of South America.

Hutton, James   (1726–97). Scottish natural philosopher who was the founder of modern geology and geomorphology. He was the first to propose the idea of uniformitarianism—that is, that all geologic features can be explained by rocks from the past.

Leakey, Louis Seymour Bazett   (1903–72) and **Leakey, Mary Nichol**   (1913–96). British anthropologists and husband-and-wife team who found some of the oldest humanoid fossils in the Olduvai Gorge, Africa, including members of the Australopithecines. Mary later found a 3.75-million-year-old humanoid fossil at Laetoli, Africa.

Leakey, Richard Erskine Frere   (1944–   ). Kenyan paleontologist, son of Louis and Mary Leakey. He found some of the oldest known humanoid fossils in Kenya, including a nearly complete fossil of a large *Homo erectus* (found with colleagues) in Kenya.

Leopold, Aldo   (1886–1948). American naturalist who was one of the first scientists to arouse public interest in wilderness conservation. He wrote *A Sand County Almanac* (1949).

Lyell, Sir Charles   (1797–1875). Scottish geologist whose *Principles of Geology* was one of the most influential works on geology. He shared James Hutton's belief that the present is the key to the past and held that fossils were the best guides to describing geologic rock layers. He was also one of the first to postulate that the Earth was millions of years old.

Maury, Matthew Fontaine   (1806–73). American hydrologist and oceanographer who wrote the first text of modern oceanography, detailing the trade winds and ocean currents.

Mohs, Friedrich   (1773–1839). German mineralogist who was the first to classify minerals based on hardness.

Muir, John   (1838–1914). British-born American naturalist who is noted for his work to gain popular and federal support of forest conservation.

Playfair, John   (1748–1819). Scottish mathematician, geologist, and philosopher who expanded on the work of his friend James Hutton. Playfair's law states that river tributaries are as deep as the surrounding major valley; he used this information to distinguish river valleys from glacial hanging valleys.

Pytheas (fl. 350 B.C.). Greek geographer and explorer who observed the strong Atlantic tides and correctly theorized that they were caused by the Moon.

Richter, Charles Francis (1900–85). American seismologist who developed a scale (the Richter scale) for measuring the intensity, or magnitude, of earthquakes.

Torricelli, Evangelista (1608–47). Italian mathematician and physicist who is considered the father of hydrodynamics. He proposed an experiment (later performed by his colleague Vincenzo Viviani) that demonstrated that atmospheric pressure determines the height a fluid will rise in a tube when it is inverted over a saucer of the same liquid. This idea led to the development of the barometer.

Wegener, Alfred Lothar (1880–1930). German geologist and meteorologist who suggested the idea of continental drift in 1912, noting that the coastlines of several continents fit roughly together into a supercontinent that he named Pangaea. His ideas were not accepted until the 1960s, when geomagnetic and oceanographic evidence established the theory of plate tectonics.

Werner, Abraham Gottlob (1750–1817). German mineralogist and geologist who developed the first systematic classification of minerals.

White, Gilbert (1720–93). British naturalist whose *Natural History and Antiquities of Selborne* was one of the first known works on ecology.

MATHEMATICIANS

Archimedes (c. 287–212 B.C.). Greek mathematician who is considered to be the greatest mathematician and engineer of ancient times. He derived the theory of the lever, discovered the principle of buoyancy, and developed methods for determining the volumes of geometric solids.

Bernoulli, Daniel (1700–82). Netherlands-born Swiss mathematician who is known for his pioneering work on hydrodynamics.

Cauchy, Baron Augustin Louis (1789–1857). French mathematician whose work concentrated on complex analysis. With the concepts of limit and continuity, he introduced rigor into the development of calculus.

Euclid (c. 330–c. 260 B.C.). Greek mathematician whose systematic proof of theorems in his *Elements of Geometry* formed the basis of most mathematical thought for the next 2,000 years.

Euler, Leonhard (1707–83). Swiss mathematician and physicist who was one of the founders of pure mathematics. The most prolific mathematician in history, he contributed to calculus, geometry, mechanics, and number theory.

Fermat, Pierre de (1601–65). French mathematician who helped lay the foundation for analytical geometry. He was also the founder of the modern theory of numbers.

Gauss, Karl Friedrich (1777–1855). German mathematician who worked on electricity and magnetism and on planetary orbits.

Hero of Alexandria (fl. 1st century A.D.). Greek mathematician and inventor who was best known for his formulation for the area of a triangle. He was also the inventor of the first known steam-powered engine.

Hypatia (c. 370–415). Egyptian mathematician and philosopher who was the first notable female mathematician.

Möbius, August Ferdinand (1790–1868). German mathematician who discovered the Möbius strip, a figure that has only one side and one edge. He also made major contributions to analytical geometry and topology.

"Geology and Geophysics" and "Mathematics" in chapter 4; "Symbols Used in Science, Mathematics, and Technology" in chapter 12

Go to

Inventions

Omar Khayya'm   (1048–?). Best known for his *Rubaiyat* (a collection of poetical quatrains), he was a Persian mathematician and astronomer who was the first to demonstrate that a cubic equation might have two roots. His work was a step toward the unification of algebra and geometry.

Pappus of Alexandria   (fl. 320 A.D.). Greek mathematician who wrote a compendium of eight books covering mathematical knowledge of his time.

The mother of Mike Nesmith (formerly of the rock group the Monkees) invented Liquid Paper.

Pythagoras   (c. 580–c. 500 B.C.). Greek mathematician and philosopher who is credited with the theorem on right-angled triangles named after him and founding the science of acoustics.

Russell, Bertrand Arthur William, Earl   (1872–1970). British philosopher and mathematician who had great influence in mathematical logic through the three-volume *Principia Mathematica* (1910, 1912, 1913) that he cowrote with Alfred North Whitehead.

Tartaglia (Niccolò Fontana)   (1500–57). Italian mathematician, topographer, and military scientist who provided an algebraic solution to cubic equations and produced that first translation of Euclid's *Elements* into a modern language (Italian).

MEDICAL SCIENTISTS

Avicenna   (980–1037). Persian physician whose encyclopedic *Canon of Medicine* was the authoritative treatise on medicine until the 17th century.

Banting, Sir Frederick Grant   (1891–1941). Canadian medical scientist who, along with John Richard Macleod (1876–1935), discovered insulin.

Bernard, Claude   (1813–78). French physiologist who introduced the concepts that the functions of the various organs within the body are closely interrelated and that the body maintains a constant internal environment despite external changes.

Blackwell, Elizabeth   (1821–1910). The first female physician in the United States. Her small practice in New York expanded into the New York Infirmary for Women and Children, which had an all-female staff.

Bowman, Sir William   (1816–92). British physician who founded histological anatomy and ophthalmic surgery. Working with a microscope, he made detailed descriptions of nerves, skin, and muscles. He also did major work on eye diseases.

Broca, Pierre Paul   (1824–80). French physician, anthropologist, and surgeon who was the first to identify the speech center in the brain.

Crick, Francis Harry Compton   (1916–   ). British molecular biologist who with James Watson discovered the double-helix structure of DNA, for which they shared the Nobel Prize for physiology or medicine in 1962.

Darwin, Erasmus   (1731–1802). British physician who developed ideas on animal causation and classification of disease. He also worked out a theory of biological evolution somewhat similar to the one his grandson, Charles Darwin, developed years later.

Ehrlich, Paul   (1854–1915). German physician, bacteriologist, and chemist who discovered numerous bacterial toxins and antitoxins; he was also the first to use chemotherapy in medicine. He shared the 1908 Nobel Prize for physiology or medicine with Ilja Mecnikov for their immunity studies.

Erasistratus of Chios   (c. 276–c. 194 B.C.). Greek anatomist and physician whose work was the most respected of his time. Studies by Herophilus of Chalcedon and Erasistratus laid the foundation for anatomy and physiology. He also was one of the first to discover that the brain was the center of intelligence.

Fleming, Sir Alexander   (1881–1955). British bacteriologist who discovered how the human body defends itself against bacterial infection. He also worked on eradicating syphilis. He shared the Nobel

Prize for physiology or medicine in 1945 with Sir Howard Florey and Ernst Chain for the discovery of penicillin.

Flourens, Jean Pierre Marie (1794–1867). French physician and anatomist who studied the physiology of the nervous system and the formation and growth of bones. He also discovered chloroform's anesthetic properties.

Franklin, Rosalind (1920–58). British crystallographer whose X-ray diffraction studies of DNA suggested a helical structure.

Freud, Sigmund (1856–1939). Austrian psychiatrist who laid the foundation for modern psychoanalysis. He introduced the concepts of ego, superego, and id and is known for his work on the interpretation of dreams.

Galen (c. 130–c. 200). Turkish-born physician who became one of the most famous and influential doctors of Rome. He developed a physiological model of the human body that was held as the standard for anatomy for centuries.

Harvey, William (1578–1657). British physician who discovered that heart pulsations caused blood to circulate around the body.

Hippocrates of Cos (c. 460–c. 370 B.C.). Greek physician who developed ideas that led to the Hippocratic oath. He started a school of medicine at Cos, where he encouraged the separation of medicine and religion.

Jenner, Edward (1749–1823). British physician who discovered the smallpox vaccine. He was also the founder of immunology and the pioneer of modern virology.

Jung, Carl Gustav (1875–1961). Swiss psychologist and psychiatrist who founded analytic psychology. His work contradicted many of the ideas of Sigmund Freud.

Koch, Robert (1843–1910). German physician, surgeon, and discoverer of the tuberculosis bacillus in 1882, and the cholera bacillus in 1883.

Pasteur, Louis (1822–95). French chemist and microbiologist who developed the germ theory of disease. He also developed the first vaccine against rabies and was the founder of microbiology.

Pavlov, Ivan Petrovich (1849–1936). Soviet physiologist who worked on blood circulation, digestion, and the physiology of the brain and nervous system. He is best known for his demonstration of the phenomenon of the conditioned reflex.

Ross, Sir Ronald (1857–1932). British physician responsible for discovering that malaria was transmitted by mosquitoes.

In 1809, Melitta Bentz invented the world's first drip coffeemaker by making a filter out of her son's notebook paper.

Sabin, Albert Bruce (1906–93). Polish-born American microbiologist who invented the first oral polio vaccine.

Salk, Jonas Edward (1914–95). American microbiologist who formulated the first successful polio vaccine, which was administrated by injection.

Stokes, William (1804–78). Irish physician who advanced the fields of cardiac and pulmonary disease.

Sydenham, Thomas (1624–89). English physician who was one of the founders of epidemiology. He was instrumental in describing numerous diseases, including measles and scarlet fever.

Watson, James Dewey (1928–   ). American biochemist who, with Francis Crick, discovered the double-helix structure of DNA, for which they shared the Nobel Prize for physiology or medicine in 1962.

Wilkins, Maurice (Hugh Frederick) (1916–   ). New Zealand–born British biophysicist who, with James Watson, Francis Crick, and Rosalind Franklin, discovered the structure of DNA. He shared the

---

A Closer Look

Schrödinger's Cat Paradox

The theory of quantum mechanics states that for a specific event, there is not one but numerous possible states that may exist simultaneously at a microscopic level. When we observe the event—that is, make a measurement—one of the states becomes "real" on our (macroscopic) level.

In 1935, Erwin Schrödinger published an essay dealing with paradoxes that were occurring in the then-new field of quantum mechanics. He sought to explain the influence of measurement on an event by using his now famous Schrödinger's Cat paradox. In this imaginary setting, a cat is placed in a sealed box with a flask of poisonous gas. The decay of a radioactive atom "triggers" a mechanism that shatters the flask and kills the cat. In the course of an hour, the atom may decay, triggering the gas, but also, with equal probability, it may not.

We open the box after an hour and observe the radioactive atom. Until that measurement is made, the cat exists in our sealed box in two probable states, dead or alive, based on the equal probability of whether or not the atom has decayed. This question is resolved by our observation; that is, one of the states becomes "real," and the cat is either ready for some milk or needs to be buried.

Although this is a thought experiment, in the late 1990s physicists at the National Institute of Standards and Technology (NIST) in Boulder, Colorado, succeeded in creating a "Schrödinger-cat-like state of matter" in a single beryllium atom. The researchers trapped the atom with nonuniform electric fields and cooled it to near standstill. Then laser pulses were used to vibrate the atom's electrons, creating a dual presence, as if two atoms existed in distinct locations at the same time. The two states were separated by a distance larger than the normal area of the atom. For a brief period, the atom appeared to exist in two places, or states, similar to Schrödinger's cat.

1962 Nobel Prize with Watson and Crick (Franklin died before the award was presented).

PHYSICISTS

Alvarez, Luis Walter   (1911–88). American physicist who won the Nobel Prize for physics in 1968 for his work in advancing the field of high-energy-particle physics. He developed the practical linear accelerator. Alvarez and his son Walter, along with several others, first proposed the theory that massive extinctions around the time of the boundary between the Cretaceous and Tertiary periods were caused by the impact of a large meteorite or asteroid.

Ampere, Andre Marie   (1775–1836). French physicist and mathematician who laid the foundation of the science of electrodynamics and determined that electric currents produce magnetic fields.

Becquerel, Antoine Henri   (1852–1908). French physicist who discovered the natural radioactivity produced by uranium.

Bohr, Niels Hendrik David   (1885–1962). Danish physicist who was the first to apply quantum theory to atomic structure and to note the connection between spectral lines and the energy levels of elec-trons. For his work with atoms, he was awarded the Nobel Prize for physics in 1922.

Celsius, Anders   (1701–44). Swedish astronomer who was the developer of the temperature scale that was named after him.

Chadwick, Sir James   (1891–1974). British physicist who discovered the neutron, for which he was awarded the Nobel Prize for physics in 1932.

Coriolis, Gaspard Gustave de   (1792–1843). French physicist who was first to coin the term *kinetic energy*. He was also the first to describe the effect (named after him) that deals with the apparent force on a moving object when observed from a rotating system. This Coriolis force governs the movement of atmospheric winds.

de Broglie, Prince Louis Victor Pierre Raymond (1892–1987). French physicist who discovered the wave nature of electrons and other particles. For this work, he won the Nobel Prize for physics in 1929.

Doppler, Christian Johann   (1803–53). Austrian physicist who discovered that a wave frequency changes when the source and observer are in motion relative to each other (the Doppler effect).

"Physics" in chapter 4; "Major Science
and Technology Museums and Their Special
Collections" in chapter 11 **Go to**

Dyson, Freeman (1923–). British physicist, educator, and author best known for his work on the possibility of extraterrestrial civilizations.

Einstein, Albert (1879–1955). German-born theoretical physicist who helped establish quantum theory (first put forth by Max Planck) by using it to describe photoelectric effects, work for which he was awarded the Nobel Prize for physics in 1921. He also developed the theories of special and general relativity.

Fahrenheit, Daniel Gabriel (1686–1736). Polish-born Dutch physicist who developed the temperature scale that was named after him. He invented a mercury thermometer.

Faraday, Michael (1791–1867). British physicist and chemist who proposed the idea of magnetic "lines of force," developed the first electric generator, and pioneered the study of low temperatures. He also discovered benzene.

Fermi, Enrico (1901–54). Italian-American physicist who produced the first controlled chain reaction in a nuclear reactor. He produced new radioactive isotopes by neutron bombardment, work for which he won the Nobel Prize for physics in 1938.

Feynman, Richard Phillips (1918–88). American theoretical physicist known for his work on the basic principles of quantum electrodynamics, for which he shared the Nobel Prize for physics in 1965.

Foucault, Jean Bernard Leon (1819–68). French physicist who invented the gyroscope, developed a method for demonstrating the rotation of the Earth (using a Foucault pendulum), and was the first to accurately determine the velocity of light.

Franklin, Benjamin (1706–90). American statesman and scientist who experimented with electricity and introduced the terms *positive* and *negative* to describe electric charge.

Gell-Mann, Murray (1929–). American physicist known for his work on the theory of elementary particles, including the postulation of fundamental building blocks he named "quarks."

Grimaldi, Francesco Maria (1618–63). Italian physicist who discovered optical diffraction and accepted the idea of waves of light. He also made one of the first lunar maps and started the tradition of naming the Moon's features after famous scientists.

Hertz, Heinrich Rudolf (1857–94). German physicist who discovered radio waves.

Joliot-Curie, Frédéric (1900–58) and **Irène** (1897–1956). French physicists who developed the first artificial radioactive substance, an isotope of phosphorus; for this work, they were awarded the Nobel Prize for chemistry in 1935. Irène was the daughter of chemists Marie and Pierre Curie.

Joule, James Prescott (1818–89). British physicist who measured the amount of heat produced by an electric current. He also determined that if a gas expands without performing work, its temperature falls.

Kelvin, Lord (William Thomson) (1824–1907). British theoretical and experimental physicist who proposed the absolute scale of temperature and the idea that mechanical energy tends to dissipate as heat, which Rudolf Clausius later developed into the concept of entropy.

Mach, Ernst (1838–1916). Austrian physicist who discovered that airflow becomes disturbed at the speed of sound. Mach numbers (which represent how fast a craft is traveling beyond the speed of sound) were named after him.

Maxwell, James Clerk (1831–79). British physicist who developed equations that served as a basis for the understanding of electromagnetism. He also determined that light is electromagnetic radiation, developed the kinetic theory of gases, and proved the particle nature of Saturn's rings.

Newton, Sir Isaac (1642–1727). English physicist and mathematician who invented calculus, determined the nature of white light, constructed the

Inventions

first reflecting telescope, and formulated the laws of motion and the theory of universal gravitation.

Ohm, Georg Simon (1789–1854). German physicist who determined the law (named after him) that states that electrical current is equal to the ratio of the voltage to the resistance.

Planck, Max Karl Ernst Ludwig (1858–1947). German physicist who developed the quantum theory to explain the nature of black-body radiation. He won the Nobel Prize for physics in 1918.

Roentgen, Wilhelm Conrad (1845–1923). German physicist who discovered X rays, for which he was awarded the Nobel Prize for physics in 1901.

Rutherford, Ernest, Lord (1871–1937). New Zealand–born British physicist who established the basic structure of the atom. He was also the first to change one element to another by an artificial nuclear reaction, for which he won the Nobel Prize for chemistry in 1908.

Schrödinger, Erwin (1887–1961). Austrian physicist who founded wave mechanics to describe the behavior of electrons in atoms. For this work, he shared the Nobel Prize for physics in 1933.

Tesla, Nikola (1856–1943). Serbian-American scientist and inventor responsible for the induction motor, rotating magnetic field principle, alternating-current power transmission, wireless communication, and numerous other electrical discoveries.

Thomson, William. *See* **Kelvin, Lord (William Thomson).**

Torricelli, Evangelista (1608–47). Italian physicist who used Galileo Galilei's ideas on the laws of motion to describe the motion of fluids.

Volta, Count Alessandro Giuseppe Antonio Anastasio (1745–1827). Italian physicist who built the first chemical battery and first produced electric current without using animal tissues.

Wilson, Charles Thomson Rees (1869–1959). British physicist who invented the Wilson Cloud Chamber, which revolutionized the study of particle physics by allowing the tracks of subatomic particles to be easily viewed.

ADDITIONAL SOURCES OF INFORMATION

BOOKS

Ballard, Robert D., and W. Hively. *The Eternal Darkness.* Princeton University Press, 2000.

Biographical Dictionary of Mathematicians. Scribner, 1991.

Biographical Dictionary of Scientists. Scribner, 1981.

Boyer, Carl. *History of Mathematics.* Wiley, 1991.

James, Peter. *Ancient Inventions.* Ballantine Books, 1995.

Macaulay, David. *The Way Things Work.* Houghton-Mifflin, 1988.

McNeil, Ian. *Encyclopedia of the History of Technology.* Routledge, 1990.

Messadie, Gerald. *Dictionary of Inventions.* NTC Publishing Group, 1998.

Pacey, Arnold. *Technology in World Civilization: A Thousand-Year History.* M.I.T. Press, 1990.

Strandh, Sigvard. *The History of the Machine.* A&W Publishers Inc., 1979.

Van Dulken, S., and A. Phillips. *Inventing the 20th Century: 100 Inventions That Shaped the World.* New York University Press, 2000.

WEB SITES

Nobel e-Museum
http://www.nobel.se/

Nobel Prize Internet Archive
http://www.almaz.com/nobel/

ScienceDaily Magazine
http://www.sciencedaily.com/

Scientific American
http://www.sciam.com

Inventions

II

THE WORLD OF IDEAS

6

PERFORMANCE AND ENTERTAINMENT ARTS

ILLUSTRATED LIST OF MUSICAL INSTRUMENTS

STRINGED INSTRUMENTS

The stringed instruments described below are divided into three classifications: plucked, hammered, and bowed. Other classifications are possible.

PLUCKED

guitar family   The guitar is a flat-backed stringed instrument of Spanish origin. It has a long, fretted neck and usually six strings, which are strummed or plucked with the fingers or a plectrum, or pick. Members of the guitar family include the banjo, which is strung with at least four but usually five strings and is generally played with the fingers, and the four-stringed ukulele, originally from Portugal but introduced into the Hawaiian Islands around 1879.

harp family   Originating in Mesopotamia and Egypt, the harp is an instrument with strings stretched vertically in an open triangular frame and played by plucking with the fingers. The modern harp usually has 46 strings and seven pedals that permit the playing of halftones.

harpsichord family   The harpsichord is a stringed instrument with one or more keyboards, also called manuals. The instrument has one or more strings for each key and produces tones when the strings are plucked with quills or leather points activated by the keys.

Guitar   Harp

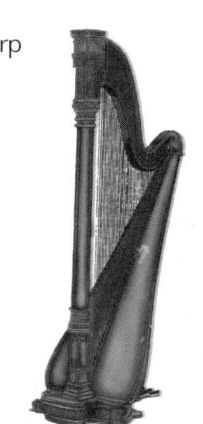

lute family   The lute is an ancient stringed instrument related to the guitar, with a large pear-shaped body, a fretted finger board, and a head with tuning pegs, which is often angled backward from the neck. The strings can be played with either a plectrum or the fingers.

Lute

lyre   Lyres come in many sizes. They are open, stringed instruments on a square or rectangular frame, played by plucking with the fingers. The lyre was used by the ancient Greeks to accompany singers and reciters.

zither   The zither is a flat-backed instrument usually having 30 to 40 strings stretched over a shallow horizontal soundboard. The instrument is played on a table or resting on the knees. It can be plucked with the fingers or played with a plectrum.

HAMMERED

clavichord   The clavichord, predecessor of the piano, is a stringed musical instrument with a rectangular keyboard. The strings are struck at various points from below by metal wedges, or tangents, attached directly to the key ends.

piano   This large keyboard instrument was introduced in Italy around 1700. Its steel wire strings sound when struck by covered hammers operated from the keyboard. In upright pianos, the strings are vertical; in wing-shaped pianos, they are horizontal.

BOWED

hurdy-gurdy   This instrument of the Middle Ages is shaped like a lute or viol but played by turning a crank attached to a rosined wheel that causes the strings to vibrate. The hurdy-gurdy is most often associated with traveling musicians of the 17th century.

viol family   Viols are stringed instruments played with a curved bow, characterized generally by six strings, frets, a flat back, and C-shaped sound holes. These instruments, used chiefly in the 16th and 17th centuries, vary in size from the treble viol to the bass viol.

violin family   These instruments were developed in the 17th century but became popular around 1700. They are played with a straight bow, are characterized by a rounded back and F-shaped sound holes, and have fretless fingerboards. The violin is the highest pitched of the family. The viola, slightly larger than the violin, is tuned a fifth lower. The larger violoncello, or more commonly called the cello, is a rich-toned bass instrument. The largest and deepest-toned of all the violins is the double bass.

Violin   Viola

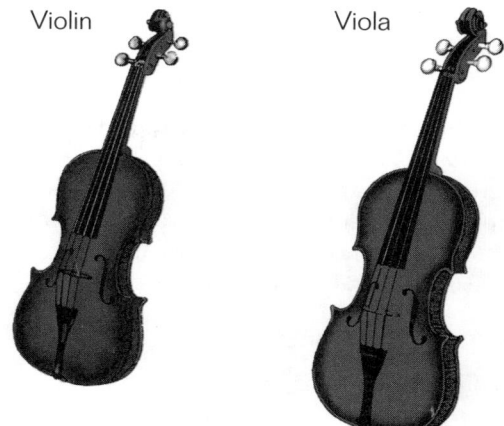

Double Bass

Violoncello

WIND INSTRUMENTS

Wind instruments are divided into three classifications: open mouthpiece, reed type, and brass type.

OPEN MOUTHPIECE

flute family   The flute is a high-pitched wind instrument consisting of a long slender tube, played by blowing across a hole near one end. The player can produce various tones by fingering the holes and keys along its length. Variations include the smaller piccolo and the larger alto flute and bass flute.

Flute

Piccolo

panpipes   Primitive and varied in form, the panpipe is made of a row or rows of reeds or tubes of gradual length and bound together. The player blows across the open upper ends to produce sound.

pipe organ   The pipe organ is a large wind instrument consisting of various sets of pipes. A keyboard controls the flow of air into the pipes, where sound is produced. Simple organs were widely used in religious services in 10th-century Europe. By the

Performance Arts

Middle Ages, portable and indoor tabletop organs were introduced.

recorder family   Unlike flutes, which are blown from the side, recorders are end blown. They have eight finger holes and a reedless mouthpiece. This instrument was popular from the Renaissance through the 18th century. Other members of the recorder family include the six-holed flagolet as well as the double and triple flagolets.

REED TYPE

bagpipe family   The bagpipe is a shrill-toned instrument with one double-reed pipe operated by finger stops and one or more drone pipes. The pipes are sounded by air forced with the arm from a leather bag, which is kept filled by the breath. The bagpipe is an ancient instrument, with Asian predecessors dating from the first millennium B.C.

bassoon family   This double-reed bass woodwind instrument dates from the Baroque musical period (1600–1750). It has a long, curved stem attached to the mouthpiece and is built in four joints: the wing, butt, long joint, and bell. The normal bassoon's range is two octaves lower than the oboe, and the contrabassoon sounds an octave further down.

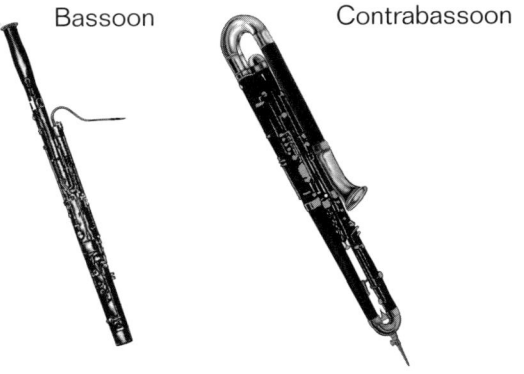

Bassoon   Contrabassoon

clarinet family   Clarinets are single-reed woodwind instruments with a long wooden or metal tube ending in a slightly flared bell. Orchestral types of clarinets have a variety of pitches, notably B-flat and A. The bass clarinet's tones are an octave lower than B-flat, and the E-flat clarinet is the sopranino.

A Clarinet   B-flat Clarinet

Bass Clarinet

oboe family   Oboes are double-reed orchestral instruments with a range of nearly three octaves and a high, penetrating, melancholy tone. The modern oboe has a flared bell. Another member of the oboe family is the English horn.

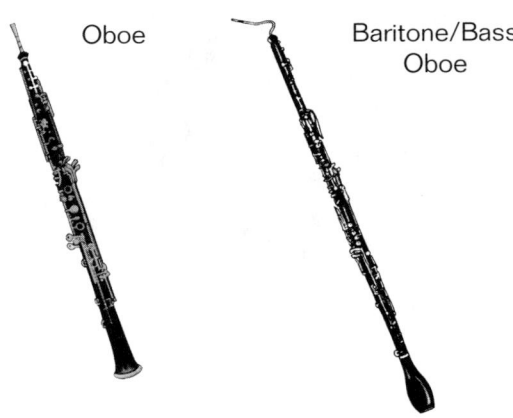

Oboe   Baritone/Bass Oboe

reed-organ family   The reed organ differs from the pipe organ in that it produces the tones with a set of free metal reeds. Other members of the reed-organ family include the harmonica and the accordion.

saxophone family   The saxophone is a single-reed, keyed woodwind instrument with a conical bore and metal body. The two principal categories of saxophone are orchestral and band. The band, or military, saxophones are the type most commonly seen, particularly the alto and tenor.

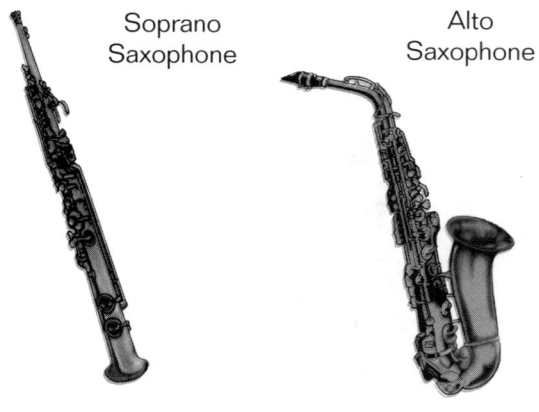

Soprano Saxophone

Alto Saxophone

Tenor Saxophone

Baritone Saxophone

BRASS TYPE

horn family   The term *horn* commonly designates an orchestral valved instrument with a flared end. The French horn is a circular instrument with three valves and a funnel-shaped mouthpiece.

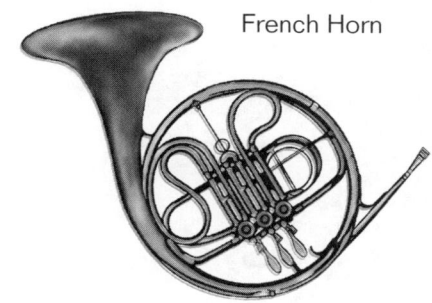

French Horn

saxhorn family   These valved brass-band instruments have a full, even tone and range in pitch from soprano to contrabass. Members of the saxhorn family include the alto horn, baritone, and euphonium.

trombone family   The trombone is a large brass wind instrument consisting of a long tube bent parallel to itself twice and ending in a bell mouth. The two types of trombones are the slide and the valve. The slide trombone produces different tones when the slide is moved in or out. The valve trombone is constructed, like the trumpet, with valves.

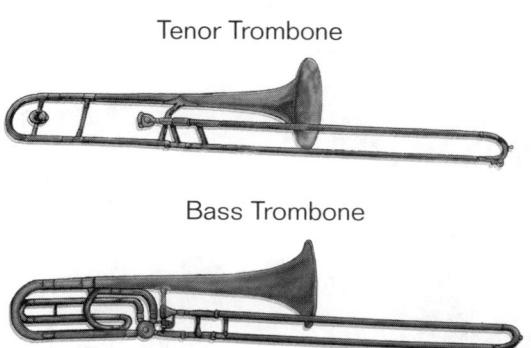

Tenor Trombone

Bass Trombone

Modern nanotechnology has allowed scientists to produce a guitar no bigger than a blood cell. The guitar is 10 micrometers long with 6 strings.

trumpet family   The trumpet consists of a tube in an oblong loop or loops, with a flared bell and, in today's version, three valves for producing changes in pitch. Other members of the trumpet family include the cornet and the bugle.

Flügelhorn

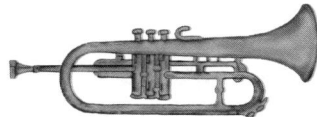

Cornet

Bugle

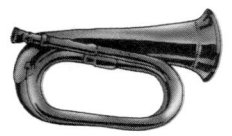

tuba family   This largest of the valved brass instruments has the lowest pitches in that group. The tuba consists of a conical bore and three to five valves. Various types of tubas include the sousaphone, double B-flat, double C, E-flat, and F.

Sousaphone   Tuba

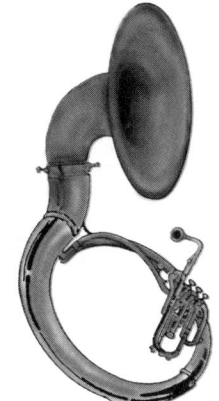

PERCUSSION INSTRUMENTS

Percussion instruments are divided into two classifications: definite pitch and indefinite pitch.

DEFINITE PITCH

glockenspiel   The glockenspiel consists of chromatically tuned, flat metal bars set in a frame. It is played with small hammers and produces bell-like tones.

kettledrum   Kettledrums consist of hollow hemispheres of copper or brass with a parchment head stretched across the top. The head can be tightened or loosened to change the pitch.

Kettledrum

tubular bells   An 18th-century invention, tubular bells are metal tubes of varying lengths hung vertically in a frame. They are struck with mallets and produce bell-like tones.

xylophone family   The xylophone consists of a series of wooden bars or other material graduated in length so that they sound the notes of the scale when struck with mallets.

INDEFINITE PITCH

bass drum   The bass drum is the largest and lowest-toned of the double-headed drums and lends itself to both marching bands and symphony orchestras.

castanets   These small, hollowed pieces of hard wood or ivory are held in the hand by a connecting cord and clicked together with the fingers to beat time to music.

cymbals Either handheld or mounted and struck with a stick, cymbals are circular, slightly concave brass plates that produce a variety of metallic sounds. Specific types of drum cymbals include the ride cymbal, hi-hats, and crash cymbals.

gong The gong is a slightly convex metallic disk that gives a loud resonant tone when struck with sticks or mallets. Flat gongs lack a definite pitch, but a knob, or boss, located at the gong's center lends it a specific pitch.

side drum or snare drum This instrument consists of a wooden or metal cylinder with two heads and wires, known as snares, strung across the bottom head for added vibration. The player strikes the upper head with sticks or wire brushes, which causes the snares to reverberate.

tambourine This instrument is a shallow, single-headed drum with jingling metal disks on the rim. The player shakes or hits the tambourine with the hand or sticks.

tenor drum This 19th-century invention is slightly deeper than the side drum and lacks snares. The tenor drum is a marching instrument usually played with felt-headed sticks.

triangle The triangle consists of a steel rod bent into a triangle shape, left open at one angle. It produces a high-pitched tinkling sound when struck with another steel rod.

ELECTRONIC INSTRUMENTS AND DEVICES

electric guitar The electric guitar's sounds are amplified by means of an electronic pickup that converts string vibrations into electric impulses. In the 1920s the body was hollow, but in the 1940s a solid body replaced the sound box with wood or fiberglass.

electronic organ The electronic organ consists of rotating tone wheels and fixed-pitch oscillators or vibrating reeds to generate sound like that of an acoustic organ.

Musical Instrument Digital Interface (MIDI) At its most basic form, the MIDI allows musicians to play multiple digital instruments from one mechanism. It transmits the information in a series of digital codes. The MIDI can be used for more complicated arrangements as well, such as connecting a variety of instruments to a master computer.

signal processor Electrified instruments transmit signal sounds to a number of devices (such as equalizers, pitch transposers, compressors, and limiters). These devices alter pitch, tone, and other components of the instrument, even making one musical instrument sound like another.

synthesizer This machine, equipped with a keyboard, contains filters, oscillators, and voltage-control amplifiers that are used to generate sounds

---

A Closer Look

The Makeup of a Symphony Orchestra

Strings	12 to 14 first violins, 10 to 12 second violins, 8 to 10 violas, 6 to 8 cellos, 4 to 6 double basses.
Woodwinds	2 flutes, 2 oboes, 2 clarinets, 2 bassoons.
Brass	2 trumpets, 2 or 4 horns, 2 or 3 trombones, 1 tuba.
Percussion	2 or 3 kettledrums and various instruments of definite pitch (glockenspiel, bells, xylophone) and indefinite pitch (snare drum, bass drum, cymbals, triangle).
Harps	1 or 2 (2 are called for more often than 1).

A larger orchestra would have this typical composition:

Strings	16 first violins, 14 second violins, 12 violas, 10 cellos, 8 double basses.
Woodwinds	2 flutes and piccolo, 2 oboes and English horn, 2 clarinets and bass clarinet, 2 bassoons and contrabassoon.
Brass	3 trumpets, 4 horns, 3 trombones, 1 tuba.
Percussion	As above.
Harps	As above.

Performance Arts

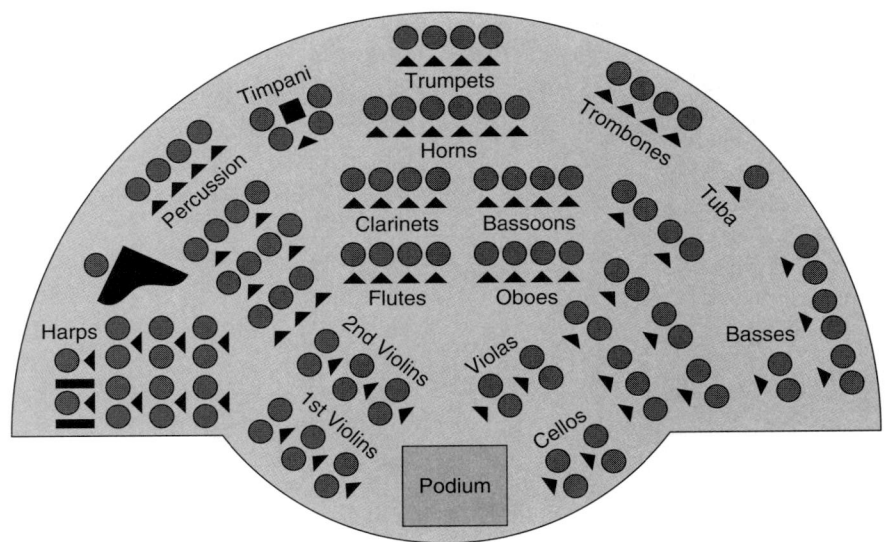

Instrument Positions in the Classic Orchestra

unobtainable from ordinary instruments or to imitate instruments and voices.

MAJOR COMPOSERS OF CLASSICAL MUSIC

AMERICAN

Amram, David (1930–   ), b. Pennsylvania. Composer and musical director of the New York Shakespeare Festival (1956–68) and the Lincoln Center Repertory Theater (1963–65). He has composed incidental music for plays, orchestra, opera, choral works, and jazz concerts.

Barber, Samuel (1910–81), b. Pennsylvania. Winner, two Pulitzer prizes, for the opera *Vanessa* (1958) and for *Piano Concerto No. 1* (1963). Known for their romantic style, his works also include two symphonies, the overture to *The School for Scandal* (1932) and the popular *Adagio for Strings* (1938).

Beach, Amy Marcy (1867–1944), b. New Hampshire. Composer whose symphonies, mass, and concerto were widely performed in the United States and abroad, particularly between 1893 and 1914. She was one of the first women composers in the United States to achieve wide respect and popularity. Her works include *Gaelic Symphony in E Minor,* *op. 32* (1896), *Piano Concerto in C Sharp Minor* (1899), and *Scottish Legend, op. 54* (1903).

Bernstein, Leonard (1918–90), b. Massachusetts. Conductor and music director of the New York Philharmonic (1958–69). He composed symphonies, songs, and ballets and is best known for his musicals, including *West Side Story* (1957). His world renown also stemmed from his ability to discuss music vividly and in a way intelligible to the musically uneducated person.

Blitzstein, Marc (1905–64), b. Pennsylvania. Pianist, composer, librettist. He was a student of Schoenberg. Among his most important works are orchestral variations; a piano concerto; operas, including the choral opera *The Cradle Will Rock* (1937); ballets; and film music.

Bloch, Ernest (1880–1959), b. Switzerland. Director of the Cleveland Institute of Music (1920–25) and the San Francisco Conservatory (1925–30). Influenced by his Jewish heritage, his works include symphonies, such as *Hivers-Printemps* (1905), *Israel* (1912–17), *America* (1926), *Voice in the Wilderness,* and *Evocations;* operas; chamber music; choral works; a piano sonata; songs; and *Avodath Hakodesh* (1933), a sacred service for Reform Judaism.

Cage, John (1912–92), b. California. Originator of controversial and experimental theories, performances, and compositions. He is best known for his experiments with random-chance music and for introducing performances with prepared piano. His works include the *Music of Changes* for piano (1951), derived from the ideas of *I Ching; Imaginary Landscape No. 4* for 12 radios tuned randomly (1951); and *4'33"* (1952), in which no sound is called for. Cage collaborated with dancer Merce Cunningham, artist Marcel Duchamp, and others.

All popular songs can be accompanied on a guitar using only three chords. Typical chords are G, C, and D7.

Copland, Aaron (1900–90), b. New York. Composer of three symphonies, a piano concerto, other orchestral works, chamber music, and ballets, including *Billy the Kid* (1938) and *Rodeo* (1942). The creator of a distinctly American music, Copland received the Pulitzer prize in 1945 for *Appalachian Spring* (1944).

Corigliano, John (1938–), b. New York. Composer whose lyrical and rhythmical expression is in the tradition of Bartók and Prokofiev. His works include *Kaleidoscope* (1959) for two pianos, *Violin Sonata* (1963), the score for the film *Altered States* (1981), and the opera *The Ghosts of Versailles* (1991).

Cowell, Henry Dixon (1897–1965), b. California. Pianist and composer of symphonies, an opera, and the piano concerto *Tales of Our Countryside* (1939). Cowell founded the New Musical Society (1927); he invented (with Leon Theremin) an electronic instrument called the "rhythmicon" and a method of playing the piano with forearm, elbow, and fist. His books on music include *New Musical Resources* (1930) and *Charles Ives and His Music* (1955).

Dello Joio, Norman (1913–), b. New York. Concert pianist, organist, and award-winning composer whose style reflects the influence of American jazz, Italian opera, and the neoclassicism of the early 1900s. His works include piano sonatas, chamber music, orchestral and choral pieces, and ballets. He

won the 1957 Pulitzer prize in music for his *Meditations on Ecclesiastes* for orchestra.

Gershwin, George (1898–1937), b. New York. Composer of music in a distinct blend of classical, popular, and jazz styles. Gershwin's works include numerous popular songs and musical comedies and more ambitious concert pieces: *Rhapsody in Blue* (1924), *An American in Paris* (1928), and the jazz opera *Porgy and Bess* (1935).

Hanson, Howard (1896–1981), b. Nebraska. Conductor and composer of romantic works, including symphonies, piano music, and the opera *Merry Mount* (1934). He served as director of the Eastman School of Music (1924–64) in Rochester, New York, and received the 1944 Pulitzer prize in music for his *Symphony No. 3, The Requiem* (1943).

Ives, Charles (1874–1954), b. Connecticut. Composer of advanced and innovative works and winner of the Pulitzer prize in 1947 for his *Symphony No. 3*. His compositions—including four symphonies, chamber and choral music, songs, and piano works—stressed American folk and popular music, jazz, military marches, patriotic songs, and revival hymns.

MacDowell, Edward (1860–1908), b. New York. Best known as a composer of piano works, MacDowell also wrote orchestral works, symphonic poems, and a suite that appropriates melodies of northern Native Americans. He was the first head of the department of music at Columbia University (1896–1904).

Menotti, Gian Carlo (1911–), b. Italy. Composer of ballets, a piano concerto, and some of the most popular operas of the mid–20th century. He won the 1950 Pulitzer prize for *The Consul* and the 1955 Pulitzer prize for *The Saint of Bleecker Street*. He founded the Festival of Two Worlds in Spoleto, Italy.

Moore, Douglas (1893–1969), b. New York. Composer of works noted for their use of the American vernacular, including the operas *The Devil and Daniel Webster* (1939) and *The Ballad of Baby Doe* (1956). He was the author of *Listening to Music* (1931) and *From Madrigal to Modern Music* (1942) and won the 1951 Pulitzer prize for *Giants of the Earth* (1951).

Performance Arts

Piston, Walter (1894–1976), b. Maine. Professor at Harvard and neoclassical composer of orchestral works, string quartets, sonatas, chamber music, and the ballet *The Incredible Flautist* (1938). Piston wrote studies of harmony and counterpoint. He won the Pulitzer prize in 1948 for his *Symphony No. 3* and in 1961 for his *Symphony No. 7.*

Schoenberg, Arnold (1874–1951), b. Austria. Originator of the revolutionary 12-tone system. The theory is exemplified in his works of 1921–33, including *Five Pieces* (1923) for piano and *Serenade* (1923) for seven instruments and bass baritone.

Schuman, William (1910–92), b. New York. President of the Juilliard School of Music (1945–61) and Lincoln Center (1962–69). Schuman composed ballets and concertos as well as chamber, orchestral, and choral works that featured energetic melodies, lively rhythms, and brilliant orchestrations. He was the winner of the first Pulitzer prize for music in 1943 for *A Free Song.*

Sessions, Roger (1896–1985), b. New York. Composer of intense, intellectual works, including eight symphonies, a violin concerto, piano works, organ pieces, and songs. His books include *Questions About Music* (1970). Sessions's most popular work is the orchestral suite *The Black Maskers* (1923), and he won the 1982 Pulitzer prize for *Concerto for Orchestra.*

Thomson, Virgil (1896–1989), b. Missouri. Music critic and composer. Based on early American hymns and folk songs, his works include two operas (with librettos by Gertrude Stein), a ballet, choral and chamber music, pieces for theater and film (among them *The River,* 1937), keyboard music, and songs. He wrote several books, including *The State of Music* (1939) and *Music, Right and Left* (1951). Thomson won the 1949 Pulitzer prize for the documentary *Louisiana Story.*

Varèse, Edgar (1883–1965), b. France. Founder and conductor of the New Symphony Orchestra, New York (1919), and founder of the International Composers Guild (1921). Varèse was a leading experimental composer of the early 1920s and wrote nontraditional works for orchestra with electronic music. His *Poème Electronique* (1958) is considered a major work in this field.

Zwilich, Ellen Taafe (1939–   ), b. Florida. Composer and first woman to receive the Pulitzer prize in music composition, in 1983, for her *Symphony No. 1.* Her works have been characterized as romantic with a lush Straussian flavor. Among her other works is *Trio for Piano, Violin, and Cello* (1987).

AUSTRIAN

Berg, Alban (1885–1935). Composer in Arnold Schoenberg's 12-tone system. Principal works are the opera *Wozzeck* (1925), the unfinished opera *Lulu* (1937), orchestral pieces, concertos, string quartets, *Lyric Suite* (1926–28), and a piano sonata.

Bruckner, Anton (1824–96). Organist and composer of romantic music. Much revised by his friends, his original compositions were published in 1929. Principal works include nine symphonies, choral works, and chamber music for string quintet.

The setting for the musical The Sound of Music *is Salzburg, Austria, which is also Mozart's birthplace.*

Czerny, Karl (1791–1857). Virtuoso pianist and composer of many works for piano. Best known for his technical studies, Czerny was a pupil of Beethoven and a teacher of Liszt.

Haydn, Franz Joseph (1732–1809). Consummate artist of the classical style in music, who has been called the "father of the symphony." Among his works are more than 100 symphonies, numerous concertos, 20 operas (five are lost), marionette operas, church music, string quartets, piano trios, keyboard sonatas and variations, songs, and 377 arrangements of Scottish and Welsh airs. His most famous works include *The Bird* quartet (1781), the oratorios *The Creation* (1798) and *The Seasons* (1801), and the *Surprise Symphony* (1791).

Haydn, Johann Michael (1737–1806). Brother of Franz Joseph Haydn and composer of oratorios and church music, symphonies, concertos, divertimenti, quintets, and other instrumental works.

Mahler, Gustav (1860–1911). Conductor of the Hamburg and Vienna operas and the Metropolitan Opera in New York. He composed nine symphonies, as well as songs, in a late Romantic style, including *Resurrection Symphony* (1894) and *Symphony of a Thousand* (1907).

Mozart, Wolfgang Amadeus (1756–91). Master of the classical style in all its forms of his time. Mozart began to compose and perform at age 6; at age 11 he had composed three symphonies and 30 other works and arranged some piano concertos of Johann Sebastian Bach. His principal works include the operas *The Marriage of Figaro* (1786), *Don Giovanni* (1787), and *The Magic Flute* (1791); chamber music; piano sonatas and fantasias; 50 symphonies; and church music, including the *Requiem* (1791). One of his most popular compositions is *A Little Night Music* (1787). Mozart's works are noted for their lyrical charm.

Schubert, Franz Seraph Peter (1797–1828). Composer of numerous symphonies, masses, quartets, and sonatas, but most notably of songs in the spirit of early romantic poetry. His works after 1823 consummate his lyrical, melodic style, as in the *No. 9 C Major Symphony* ("The Great") (1828); 22 piano sonatas, including the *Wanderer Fantasie* (1822); and the *Piano Trio in B-flat major* (1827) and *Piano Trio in E-flat major* (1827).

Strauss. Family of Viennese musicians. **Johann I** (1804–49) was the composer of waltzes famous throughout Europe. He was the father of **Johann II** (1825–99), who became his rival and who composed more than 400 waltzes, including *The Blue Danube* (1866) and *Tales from the Vienna Woods* (1868), as well as operettas. Johann II's brothers, **Josef** (1827–70) and **Eduard I** (1835–1916), were also successful composers and conductors.

Webern, Anton von (1883–1945). Editor, conductor, and composer in the 12-tone system of Arnold Schoenberg. Webern wrote a symphony for small orchestra, three cantatas, a string quartet, a concerto for nine instruments, songs, and other works. His major choral works include *Das Augenlicht* (1935), *First Cantata* (1939), and *Second Cantata* (1943).

BRITISH

Britten, (Edward) Benjamin (1913–76). Major 20th-century composer famous for his vocal music and operas. The latter include *Peter Grimes* (1945), *The Rape of Lucretia* (1946), *Billy Budd* (1951), *The Turn of the Screw* (1954), and *A Midsummer Night's Dream* (1960). Among his most popular works are *A Ceremony of Carols* (1942), *A Young Person's Guide to the Orchestra* (1945), and the *War Requiem* (1962).

Byrd, William (1543–1623). Organist and composer. A master of 16th-century polyphony, Byrd excelled in the composition of church music, including *Gradualia* (1605–07).

Delius, Frederick (1862–1934). Composer of orchestral works, including *Paris* (1899), *Appalachia* (1896), and *Brigg Fair* (1907); choral works, including *Sea Drift;* and the operas *A Village Romeo and Juliet* (1901) and *Fennimore and Gerda* (1910).

Dowland, John (c. 1563–1626). Lutenist and composer of the most important English collection of songs for the lute. His most famous work is *Lachrymae* (1605), a collection of dance pieces.

Elgar, Sir Edward (1857–1934). Composer best known for *Pomp and Circumstance,* a set of five marches; an adaptation of *Pomp and Circumstance* (1902) for the coronation of King Edward VII; *The Dream of Gerontius* (1900); *The Enigma Variations* (1899) for orchestra; and *Introduction and Allegro for Strings* (1905).

Gibbons, Orlando (1583–1625). Organist and composer of anthems, madrigals, chamber music, and keyboard pieces.

Holst, Gustav (1874–1934). Composer who combined an interest in folk music with a knowledge of Hindu scales and Sanskrit literature. His later music experimented with harmony and polytonality. Principal works include the operas *Savitri* (1908) and *The Perfect Fool* (1923); for orchestra, *The Planets* (1914–16) and *Egdon Heath* (1927); and for chorus, *Hymns from the Rig-Veda* (1910) and *Hymn for Jesus* (1917).

Morley, Thomas (1557–1602). Composer, theorist, and organist at St. Paul's Cathedral. Morley was

Performance Arts

granted a monopoly on music printing (1598) and wrote the first comprehensive treatise on composition in English (1597). He became known for his light songs, including canzonets, airs, and madrigals.

Purcell, Henry (c. 1659–95). Organist at Westminster Abbey and composer of music for more than 40 plays, including the first important English opera, *Dido and Aeneas* (1689), and *The Fairy Queen* (1692), a masque. He also wrote odes, songs, cantatas, church music, chamber music, and keyboard works.

Sullivan, Sir Arthur (1842–1900). Conductor, organist, and composer. His works include the grand opera *Ivanhoe* (1891); ballads; oratorios; cantatas, including *The Golden Legend;* church music; a symphony; songs; and works for piano. He is best known for light operas to librettos by W. S. Gilbert.

Tallis, Thomas (c. 1505–85). Organist and composer. He was granted a monopoly in music printing with William Byrd (1575). Tallis's works include church music and secular pieces for vocals and keyboard.

Vaughan Williams, Ralph (1872–1958). Composer noted for his adaptations of English folk music and Tudor church music. Principal compositions include *A London Symphony* (1913), *Norfolk Rhapsodies* (1906), and *The Lark Ascending* (1914), all for orchestra; *A Sea Symphony* (1910) and *Five Mystical Songs* (1911) for chorus; the operas *Hugh the Drover* (1914), *Riders to the Sea* (1937), and *The Pilgrim's Progress* (1951); and works for stage, chamber music, and songs.

FRENCH

Berlioz, Hector (1803–69). Conductor and composer of romantic works. Berlioz is best known for his genius with orchestration and his way of relating musical works to story ideas, as in the *Symphonie Fantastique* (1830). He also wrote the symphonic work *Harold in Italy* (1834), the opera *Damnation of Faust* (1846), and the oratorio *Childhood of Christ* (1850–54).

Bizet, Georges (1838–75). Composer best known for the operas *Carmen* (1875), *The Pearlfishers* (1863), *The Young Maid of Perth* (1867), and

Djmileh (1872). His *Symphony in C Major* (1868) is highly regarded. His music is melodic and tightly organized, with uncomplicated orchestral accompaniment.

Boulanger, Lili (1893–1918). Composer in an impressionist style. She composed more than 50 works in the genres of secular and sacred music, chorus with and without orchestra, cantatas, chamber music, songs, and an uncompleted opera. Boulanger is best known for her cantata *Faust et Hélène* (1913), for which she was awarded the Prix de Rome.

Boulez, Pierre (1925–   ). Composer of experimental works using the serial technique, including *Pli selon pli* (1962) and *Memoriales* (1975). Many of his compositions contain unusual rhythms with separate sounds. He served as music director of the New York Philharmonic (1971–77) and as director of L'Institut Recherche et Coordination Acoustique Musique until 1992.

Couperin, François (1668–1733). Member of a family of distinguished organists. Organist to the king at Versailles, he composed music for organ and harpsichord, instrumental ensembles, secular songs, and church music. He wrote a well-known textbook, *The Art of Playing the Harpsichord.*

Debussy, Claude (1862–1918). Composer noted for his impressionist style. Orchestral works include *La Mer* (1903–05) and *Nocturnes* (1893–99); piano works include *Clair de Lune* (1890), preludes, études, arabesques, and *The Children's Corner* (1906–08). Debussy also wrote choral works, an opera, and the well-known tone poem *Prelude to the Afternoon of a Faun* (1894).

Delibes, (Clément Philibert) Léo (1836–91). Composer of operas, including *Le Roi l'a dit* (1873) and *Lakmé* (1883), and ballets, including *Coppélia* (1870) and *Sylvia* (1876).

Dukas, Paul (1865–1935). Composer best known for the orchestral scherzo *Sorcerer's Apprentice* (1897), the opera *Ariane et barbe-Bleue* (1907), and the ballet *La Peri* (1912).

Fauré, Gabriel (1845–1924). Organist and composer who excelled in songwriting and an adventurous use of harmony. He wrote the operas

Prométhée (1900) and *Pénélope* (1913), orchestral music, chamber works, and piano and church music. Fauré was the teacher of Maurice Ravel.

Franck, César (1822–90). A teacher who influenced an entire generation of composers. Distinctive compositions include *Symphony in D Minor* (1888), the *Symphonic Variations* (1885) for piano and orchestra, *Prelude, Chorale, and Fugue* (1884), and the opera *Hulda* (1894).

Gounod, Charles (1818–93). Composer of the operas *Faust* (1859) and *Romeo and Juliet* (1867). Gounod also wrote church music, symphonies, and cantatas. His music includes elements of seriousness, melodrama, and sentimentality.

Honegger, Arthur (1892–1955). Founding member of the Parisian group "The Six" in 1916 with Erik Satie, Darius Milhaud, and Jean Cocteau. Rejecting romanticism and impressionism, Honegger is best known for the oratorio *King David* (1921) and for *Pacific 231* (1923) and *Joan of Arc at the Stake* (1935), both for orchestra.

Ibert, Jacques François Antoine (1890–1962). Ibert's colorful works include a suite for orchestra, *Escales* (1922); *Divertissement* (1930); music for theater and film; chamber music; and works for piano and organ. He served as director of the Académie de France in Rome (1937) and the Paris Opera (1955).

Lully, Jean-Baptiste (orig. Lulli, Giambattista) (1632–87). Lully composed for the comedy ballets of Molière and was the founder of the French opera *(tragédie lyrique)*. He also composed court ballets, divertissements, church music, and two instrumental suites. His best-known works include *Cadmus and Hermione* (1673), *Amadis de Gaule* (1684), and *Roland* (1685).

Massenet, Jules Emile Frédéric (1842–1912). Best known for his pop operas *Le Roi de Lahore* (1877), *Manon* (1884), *Werther* (1892), and *Le Jongleur de Notre-Dame* (1902). Massenet also wrote oratorios, orchestral works, concertos, and songs.

Messiaen, Olivier Eugène Prosper Charles (1908–92). Organist and composer of symphonic poems and works for piano, organ, and vocals. He became known for using birdcalls, electronic sounds, religious songs, and Oriental themes in his compositions. Messiaen helped form the group "Jeune France" in 1936 and wrote a treatise on composition. His works include the 10-movement symphony *Turangalila* (1949).

Milhaud, Darius (1892–1974). A member of the Parisian group "The Six," Milhaud composed works that combine jazz, polytonality, and Brazilian elements. He is well known for the opera *Christophe Colomb* (1930) and for ballets, including *Creation of the World* (1923).

Offenbach, Jacques (1819–80). Composer of 90 operettas, including the popular *Orpheus in the Underworld* (1858), *La Belle Hélène* (1864), and *La Vie Parisienne* (1866). His best work is thought to be *The Tales of Hoffmann,* which was unfinished at his death and later completed by Ernest Guiraud.

Poulenc, Francis (1899–1963). Member of the Parisian circle "The Six," Poulenc composed ballets, including *Les Biches* (1924); chamber music; a concerto for two pianos; songs; choral works; a cantata; and operas, among them *Dialogues of the Carmelites* (1957). He was noted for his vocal music featuring beautiful melodies and sensitive lyrics.

Rameau, Jean-Philippe (1683–1764). Theorist and important composer of French opera. His works include the operas *Castor et Pollux* (1737) and *Dardanus* (1739), the opera-ballet *Les Indes galantes* (1735), and the ballet-bouffon *Platée* (1745). His *Treatise of Harmony* (1722) laid the foundation for the modern theory of harmony.

Ravel, Maurice (1875–1937). Leading exponent of impressionism, who relied on the strong melodies and rich textures of 19th-century classical music. Ravel's principal works include *Rapsodie espagnole* (1908), *Daphnis and Chloe* (1912), and *Bolero* (1928), all for orchestra; and *Valses nobles et sentimentales* (1911) and *Gaspard de la nuit* (1908), both for piano.

Saint-Saëns, Charles Camille (1835–1921). Pianist and composer. Saint-Saëns began performing at age 10 and later composed symphonic poems under the influence of Franz Liszt; operas, including *Samson et Dalila* (1877); and concertos.

Satie, Erik (1866–1925). Composer noted for his ironic, humorous style and ranked as a leader in the development of modern music. Satie composed three ballets, including *Parade* (1917); operettas; a symphonic drama, *Socrates;* songs; and piano pieces.

GERMAN

Bach, Johann Sebastian (1685–1750). Baroque organist and composer; one of the greatest creators of Western music. Among his religious works are more than 200 cantatas, the *Mass in B Minor* (1733–49), and the *St. Matthew Passion* (1727). His other works include *The Well-Tempered Clavier* (1722), a collection of preludes and fugues; the Brandenburg concertos (1721); and many sonatas and suites. He had 20 children, 10 of whom survived, including **Wilhelm Friedemann** (1710–84), organist and composer; **Carl Philipp Emanuel** (1714–88), composer of religious music, symphonies, concertos, sonatas, and chamber music; **Johann Christoph Friedrich** (1732–95), composer; and **Johann Christian** (1735–82), composer of operas, chamber music, and church music.

Beethoven, Ludwig van (1770–1827). Considered one of the greatest composers of instrumental works, particularly symphonies, he is regarded as one of the founding fathers of musical romanticism. Beethoven was a student of Haydn, whose influence permeates his early works. By 1824 he had lost his hearing, but he continued to compose under the sponsorship of aristocratic patrons. His works include *Fidelio* (1805), an opera; a violin concerto and five piano concertos; the *Egmont* overture (1810); 32 piano sonatas, including the *Appassionata* (1804–05); 16 string quartets; the *Mass in D (Missa Solemnis)* (1818–23); and nine symphonies, the best known of which are the *Third (Eroica)* (1804), the *Fifth (Victory)* (1805), the *Sixth (Pastoral)* (1809), and the *Ninth (Choral)*. The *Ninth,* completed in 1823, is considered the greatest of his works.

Brahms, Johannes (1833–97). Developer of a romantic style that was both lyrical and classical. His principal works include four symphonies, two overtures, and two serenades for orchestra; two piano concertos, one violin concerto, and one concerto for violin and cello; *A German Requiem* (1857–68), his best-known choral work; piano solos, including variations on themes by Paganini, Handel, and Schumann; chamber music; rhapsodies; ballades; piano duets; waltzes; Hungarian dances; songs; folk song arrangements; and 11 choral preludes for organ.

Bruch, Max (1838–1920). Famous for his setting of the melody to the Jewish prayer *Kol Nidre* (1880) for cello and orchestra. His works also include three symphonies, three operas, an operetta, choral works, and chamber music.

Beethoven dedicated his third symphony, the Eroica, *to Napoleon but later tore it up when Napoleon crowned himself Emperor of France.*

Gluck, Christoph Willibald von (1714–87). Composer of more than 100 operas, among them *Orfeo ed Euridice* (1762) and *Alceste* (1767), which established a new style of Italian opera; 11 symphonies; instrumental trios; seven odes by Friedrich Klopstock for solo voice and keyboard; and a flute concerto.

Handel, George Frideric (1685–1759). Baroque composer most famous for the oratorio *Messiah* (1742). Trained in law and music in Germany, Handel produced his operas in Italy and London, incorporating German, Italian, and English styles. Among his works are many operas, including *Almira* (1705), *Ottone* (1723), and *Orlando* (1733); *Music for the Royal Fireworks* (1749) and *Water Music* (1717); suites for harpsichord; chamber music; and many Italian cantatas.

Hindemith, Paul (1895–1963). Composer, teacher, theorist, performer, and conductor who brought a neoclassical element to contemporary music. Early works, such as the opera *Murder, Hope of Women* (1921), reflect the expressionism of the period. Later works, including *Ludus Tonalis* (1942), exemplify his new theory of tonality expounded in *The Craft of Musical Composition* (1941, 1945). Hindemith was banned by the Nazis for his modernity. His best-known work is a symphony from his opera *Mathis the Painter* (1938).

Humperdinck, Engelbert (1854–1921). Composer of six operas, including the popular *Hansel and Gretel* (1893); incidental music; vocal works; and songs.

Mendelssohn, Felix (1809–47). Pianist, conductor, and composer of orchestral works, including five symphonies and the overture to *A Midsummer Night's Dream* (1826); choral works, including the oratorios *St. Paul* (1836) and *Elija* (1846); operas; incidental music; several collections of piano works; *Songs Without Words* (1832); and songs. His music contains smooth progressions in harmony accompanying melodies that are easy to sing.

Meyerbeer, Giacomo (1791–1864). Composer of operas in a spectacular style that influenced Richard Wagner. His works include *Robert le Diable* (1831), *Les Huguenots* (1836), and *Le Prophète* (1849).

Orff, Carl (1895–1982). Composer of stage works that combined instrumental singing, gestures, and dance, including the cantata *Carmina Burana* (1937); the opera *Der Mond* (1939); and musical plays. Orff developed a widely used system for teaching music to children.

Schumann, Clara Josephine Wieck (1819–96). Pianist and composer of piano works and songs. She was a renowned interpreter of music, particularly the works of her husband, Robert Schumann.

Schumann, Robert (1810–56). Composer of piano music, including sonatas and impromptus, and of orchestral works. His compositions include *Symphonic Études* (1834), *Fantasia in C Major* (1836), *Album for the Young* (1848), and *Piano Concerto in A Minor* (1845). The *Rhenish Symphony* (1850) combined classical and romantic elements.

Strauss, Richard (1864–1949). Composer of numerous operas, many with librettos by Hugo von Hofmannsthal, including the famous *Der Rosenkavalier* (1911); two ballets; tone poems for orchestra, including *Also Sprach Zarathustra* (1896); concertos; *Metamorphosen* (1945) for 23 solo strings; chamber music; songs; and piano works.

Wagner, Richard (1813–83). Composer of operas and architect of a theory of the "total" work of art, in which drama, spectacle, and music are fused.

Principal works include *Der Ring des Nibelungen* (1853–74), which was made up of four operas: *Das Rheingold* (1854), *Die Walküre* (1856), *Siegfried* (1857–69), and *Götterdämmerung* (1874); *Tristan and Isolde* (1859); and *Parsifal* (1882). Exiled for his role in the revolution of 1848, Wagner resettled in Bavaria in 1864, where he constructed his theater at Bayreuth.

Frideric Handel was known to have a fiery temper. During an argument with an opera singer, he picked her up by the waist and dangled her out of a two-story window.

Weber, Carl Maria von (1786–1826). Composer, conductor, pianist, critic, and virtual creator of romantic German opera. Principal works include the operas *Der Freischütz* (1821) and *Oberon* (1826), choral and orchestral pieces, piano sonatas, concertos, dances, and songs.

ITALIAN

Bellini, Vincenzo (1801–35). Composer of emotional and technically challenging operas, including *La Straniera* (1829), *La Sonnambula* (1831), *Norma* (1831), and *I Puritani* (1835).

Boccherini, Luigi (1743–1805). Cellist and composer. His principal compositions are for chamber music; he also wrote symphonies, concertos, and vocal music. His most popular works are his *Concerto in B-flat* (1770) for cello, and the minuet from his *String Quartet No. 3* (1771).

Boito, Arrigo (1842–1918). Poet and composer of operas, including *Mefistofele* (1868) and *Nerone* (1918). Boito is known chiefly for his librettos, notably for *Otello* (1887) and *Falstaff* (1893) by Giuseppe Verdi.

Cherubini, Maria Luigi (1760–1842). Composer of about 30 operas, among them the classic "rescue" opera *The Water Carrier* (1800); church music; string quartets; and piano sonatas. He served as director of the Paris Conservatory (1822).

Performance Arts

Clementi, Muzio (1752–1832). Pianist and composer of symphonies, piano sonatas, and piano studies, including *Gradus ad Parnassum* (1817).

Corelli, Arcangelo (1653–1713). Violinist and composer. His trio sonatas, solo violin sonatas, and concerti grossi established a style of composition for the violin.

Dallapiccola, Luigi (1904–75). Composer of 12-tone atonal music characterized by delicate counterpoint, lyrical line and textures, and subtle tone colors. He is most noted for his operas *The Prisoner* (1944) and *Odysseus* (1968), the oratorio *Job* (1950), and the *Christmas Concerto* (1956).

Donizetti, Gaetano (1797–1848). Prolific composer of operas. His best-known works included *Lucrezia Borgia* (1833), *La Favorite* (1840), and the comic operas *L'Elisir d'Amore* (1832) and *Don Pasquale* (1843).

Leoncavallo, Ruggiero (1858–1919). Composer of operas. His most successful was *Pagliacci* (1892). He wrote his own librettos, a ballet, and a symphonic poem.

Mascagni, Pietro (1863–1945). Opera composer and conductor. His most famous work is *Cavalleria Rusticana* (1890).

Monteverdi, Claudio (1567–1643). Ordained priest and composer of church music, including masses, vespers, and madrigals. He also wrote secular vocal music, at least 12 operas, and ballets. His works helped change the strict style of Renaissance music to the emotional style of the baroque movement. His *Orfeo* (1607) is called the first modern opera.

Palestrina, Giovanni Pierluigi da (Johannes Praenestinus) (c. 1525–94). Organist, choirmaster, and composer of church music, including masses, motets, and lamentations. He also wrote both sacred and secular madrigals.

Pergolesi, Giovanni Battista (1710–36). Composer of operas and comic intermezzos that became the prototype of the *opera buffa;* church music, including his renowned *Stabat Mater* (1736); and sonatas, which contributed to the development of the form.

Puccini, Giacomo (1858–1924). Composer of many operas with highly emotional melodies and orchestral brilliance. Best known are *La Bohème* (1896), *Tosca* (1900), and *Madame Butterfly* (1904). *Turandot* was completed after his death by Franco Alfano.

Respighi, Ottorino (1879–1936). Composer of operas, tone poems, and other orchestral works, chamber music, concertos, and songs. Among his most popular works are *The Fountains of Rome* (1917) and *The Pines of Rome* (1924), both symphonic poems.

Rossini, Gioacchino (1792–1868). Composer of operas. The best known are *William Tell* (1829) and *The Barber of Seville* (1816). Rossini also wrote cantatas, songs, piano pieces, and woodwind quintets.

Scarlatti, Alessandro (1660–1725). Conductor and the most prolific composer of Italian operas of his time. Besides composing about 80 operas, he wrote 20 oratorios, some 600 cantatas, 10 masses, a passion, motets, and other church music, chamber pieces, concertos, and works for harpsichord.

Scarlatti, (Giuseppe) Domenico (1685–1757). Son of Alessandro Scarlatti, and greatest Italian composer for harpsichord of his time. He wrote 550 pieces, now called sonatas, as well as concertos, operas, cantatas, masses, a *Stabat Mater,* and two *Salve Reginas.*

Tartini, Giuseppe (1692–1770). Violinist, teacher, composer, and theorist. He composed over 100 violin concertos and symphonies, solo sonatas, trio sonatas, and church music; published treatises on violin playing and acoustics; and established a violin school in Padua (1728).

Verdi, Giuseppe (1813–1901). Foremost composer of operas. His works are performed more often today than those of any other opera com-poser. They include *Rigoletto* (1851), *La Traviata* (1853), and the supreme *Otello* (1887) and *Falstaff* (1893). Verdi also composed church music, including the *Requiem* (1874), *Ave Maria* (1880), *Stabat Mater* (1898), and *Te Deum* (1898).

Vivaldi, Antonio (1678–1741). Violinist, composer, and ordained priest. Master of the Italian baroque, Vivaldi is best known for his instrumental music and the concertos *The Four Seasons* (1725). He also wrote church music, an oratorio, and nearly 50 operas.

RUSSIAN

Borodin, Aleksandr (1833–87). Composer and scientist. His works include three symphonies; *In the Steppes of Central Asia* (1880) for orchestra; string quartets; and the opera *Prince Igor* (1887), completed after his death by Nicolai Rimsky-Korsakov and Aleksandr Glazunov (1890).

Glinka, Mikhail (1804–57). Composer of two operas and other works. *A Life for the Czar* (1836) and *Ruslan and Ludmilla* (1842) established a Russian style against the conventions of Italian opera. Glinka introduced folk song into instrumental composition in the orchestral fantasia *Kamarinskaya.*

The Russian composer Aleksandr Borodin not only wrote the opera Prince Igor *but was also a professional chemist and the author of* On the Analogy of Arsenical with Phosphoric Acid.

Khachaturian, Aram (1903–78). Armenian composer whose works are distinguished for their incorporation of oriental folk elements. He is best known for the ballet *Gayane* (1942) and its popular "Sabre Dance" theme.

Mussorgsky, Modest (1839–81). Composer of operas and orchestral works. Mussorgsky is best known for his operas *Boris Godunov* (1868, 1874) and *Khovanschina* (1886), as well as for *Pictures at an Exhibition* (1874) for piano and *Night on Bald Mountain* (1860–66) for orchestra.

Prokofiev, Sergei (1891–1953). Composer, pianist, and conductor. His principal compositions are the operas *Love for Three Oranges* (1921) and *War and Peace* (1942); *Peter and the Wolf* (1936) and *Classical Symphony* (1918), both for orchestra and narrator; and seven symphonies, piano concertos, ballets, and piano sonatas.

Rachmaninoff, Sergei (1873–1943). Composer, pianist, and conductor whose works are filled with passion, power, and a feeling of melancholy. Rachmaninoff emigrated to the United States at age 17. His compositions include three operas; orchestral works, including the tone poem *Isle of the Dead* (1909); four concertos, including the *Second Piano Concerto* (1901); choral works; chamber music; and songs.

Rimsky-Korsakov, Nicolai (1844–1908). Composer of operas and orchestral works, including the popular symphonic suite *Scheherazade* (1888). His greatest works are the operas *Mlada* (1892), *Christmas Eve* (1895), *Sadko* (1898), and *The Golden Cockerel* (1907). His orchestration influenced the work of Igor Stravinsky and others.

Rubinstein, Anton (1829–94). Pianist and composer; founder of the Conservatory in St. Petersburg (1862). A representative of traditional Western ideas against the current of nationalism, he composed *Musical Portraits (Faust, Ivan the Terrible, Don Quixote)* for orchestra, 19 operas, 6 symphonies (including *The Ocean*), chamber music, 5 piano concertos, and other works.

Scriabin, Aleksandr (1872–1915). Composer and pianist. Scriabin experimented with esoteric harmonies related to theosophical ideas in *The Divine Poem* (1905) and *Poem of Ecstasy,* both for orchestra. He wrote sonatas, preludes, and *Prometheus* (1909–10), which includes the use of a "color organ" for slide projection.

Shostakovich, Dmitry (1906–75). Composer of chamber and symphonic works characterized by a bold, expressive modern style. Shostakovich alternated between political and satirical composition, later trying to bring his work closer to official prescriptions. His works include 15 symphonies, among them *May the First* (1930) and the outstanding *Ninth Symphony* (1940); operas; ballets, including *Lady Macbeth of Mtsensk* (1934) and revised in 1962 as *Katerina Ismailova;* piano works; sonatas; and 15 string quartets.

Stravinsky, Igor (1882–1971). Composer of the epochal ballets *The Firebird* (1910), *Petrouchka* (1911), and *Rite of Spring* (1913). Later works, such as *The Soldier's Tale* (1918), for narrator and instruments, and the ballet suite *Apollon Musagète* (1928) are more austere and neoclassical. Stravinsky settled in the United States in 1941, where he experimented with 12-tone composition, as in *Requiem Canticles* (1966).

Tchaikovsky, Peter Ilyich (1840–93). One of the most important Russian composers. His music is characterized by masterful orchestration and spirited yet often melancholy melodies. Tchaikovsky is best known for his ballet music, including *Swan Lake* (1876), *The Sleeping Beauty* (1889), and *The Nutcracker* (1892), and for his operas *Eugene Onegin* (1878) and *Queen of Spades* (1890). He also wrote symphonies, including the popular *Symphony No. 5* (1888), chamber music, and choral works, and he published books on harmony, autobiographical essays, and translations.

OTHER

Albéniz, Isaac (1860–1909). Spanish composer and pianist. Albéniz is known for his later piano works, notably *Iberia* (1906–09); he also wrote operas, including *The Magic Opal* (1893).

Bartók, Béla (1881–1945). Hungarian pianist and composer who studied and collected Hungarian folk music and developed a musical style that emphasized energetic rhythm, folk song scales, dissonance, and highly personal forms. His principal works include orchestral pieces; the opera *Duke Bluebeard's Castle* (1918); the ballet *The Wooden Prince* (1914–16); the pantomime *The Miraculous Mandarin* (1919, 1924, 1935); chamber music; piano works, including the *Mikrokosmos* (1926–37); and arrangements of folk songs. He emigrated to the United States in 1940.

Chávez, Carlos (1899–1978). Mexican composer of works using the idioms of Indian folk music, including *Xochipilli Macuilxochitl* (1940). Well-known works are the symphonic ode *Clio* (1969) and *Discovery* (1969).

Chopin, Frédéric François (1810–49). Polish composer and pianist. Called "the poet of the piano," he composed hundreds of pieces for that instrument, most notably two piano concertos and other pieces, including *Fantaisie-Impromptu* (1834).

Dvořák, Antonín (1841–1904). Czech composer of symphonies, operas, dances, and choral works in a nationalistic spirit and neoromantic style. His works include the *Symphonic Variations, Slavonic Rhapsodies,* and the opera *The Peasant Rogue* (1877). His best-known work, the *Symphony from the New World* (1893), contains elements of both Czech and American music.

Falla, Manuel de (1876–1946). Spanish composer and pianist. He published little but was the outstanding Spanish composer of his time. Principal works are the operas *La Vida Breve* (1905) and *El Retablo de Maese Pedro* (1923); the ballets *El Amor Brujo* (1915) and *The Three-Cornered Hat* (1919); and the *Fantasia Béticu* (1919) for piano.

Grainger, Percy Aldridge (1882–1961). Australian pianist and composer who settled in the United States in 1914. Head of the music department at New York University, he was known for his arrangements of traditional tunes from a variety of sources and for his interpretation of Edvard Grieg's piano music. His choral works include *Marching Song of Democracy* (1917) and *Tribute to Foster* (1930).

Granados, Enrique (1867–1916). Spanish pianist and composer, born in Cuba. Granados founded and directed the Academía Granados (1901) and composed seven operas, orchestral works, chamber music, a collection of *Tonadillas,* and *Goyescas* (1916), based on the paintings of Goya.

Grieg, Edvard (1843–1907). Norwegian composer, conductor, and pianist. Principal works include the overture *I Host* (1866), two suites from *Peer Gynt* (1876, 1888, 1891), *At a Southern Convent Gate* (1871) for chorus, and the 10-volume *Lyric Pieces* for piano.

Janáček, Leoš (1854–1928). Czech composer. Janáček wrote 10 operas, including *Jenufa* (1904); orchestral, choral, and piano works; chamber music; and songs. He published collections of Moravian folk music and a treatise on harmony.

Kodály, Zoltán (1882–1967). Hungarian composer and music educator whose works are distinguished by the influence of native folk music. His best-known works are the suites from *Háry János* (1927) and *Psalmus Hungaricus* (1923). Kodǎly developed a widely used method of teaching music.

Lasso, Orlando di (Roland de Lassus) (1532–94). Belgian composer. Among his many works are masses, motets, magnificats, and other church music. The complete edition of his nearly 2,000 works consists of 60 volumes.

Liszt, Franz (1811–86). Hungarian composer who spent time in Paris and Rome and is credited with developing the rhapsody as a form of serious music and employing the term *symphonic poem* for a composition. He was an unsurpassed virtuoso pianist and a composer of symphonies, including *Faust* (1857); piano concertos, études, and 19 *Hungarian Rhapsodies* (1839–85); choral pieces; fantasia and fugues for organ; and songs.

Nielsen, Carl (1865–1931). Danish composer of operas, symphonies, string quartets, piano pieces, and songs, including *Hymns amoris* (1896). Nielsen served as director of the Copenhagen Conservatory (1915–27).

Paderewski, Ignace (1860–1941). Polish pianist and composer. One of the most renowned pianists of modern times, in 1919 Paderewski was prime minister of Poland. He composed many piano works, the opera *Manru* (1901), a symphony, a concerto, and songs.

Sibelius, Jean (1865–1957). Finnish composer. Sibelius attempted a national music, as in *En Saga* (1892) and *Lemminkäinen's Homecoming* (1895), based on the Finnish epic *The Kalevala*. Notable works include *The Swan of Tuonela* (1893), *Finlandia* (1900), and *The Oceanides* (1914).

Smetana, Bedřich (1824–84). Czech composer whose nationalist music was based on folk songs and dances, as in the opera *The Bartered Bride* (1866). Smetana wrote his best instrumental works despite deafness, especially *The Moldau*, which is part of *My Country* (1879), and the string quartet *From My Life* (1876).

Villa-Lobos, Heitor (1887–1959). Brazilian composer and educator. His works show the influence of Indian music and Brazilian folk songs; they include five operas, six symphonies, symphonic poems, serenades, choral music, piano solos, and songs.

Wieniawski, Henri (1835–80). Polish violinist and composer. Among Wieniawski's compositions are two concertos and popular pieces, including *Légende.*

MAJOR JAZZ COMPOSERS AND PERFORMERS

Armstrong, Louis "Satchmo" (c. 1890–1971), b. Louisiana. Trumpeter and singer; first internationally known jazz soloist. He introduced the music of New Orleans to the world, inaugurated the style of improvisation, and was the first to record scat singing. His most influential recording may be "West End Blues" (1939), but his most famous is "Hello, Dolly" (1969).

Basie, William "Count" (1904–84), b. New Jersey. Pianist and bandleader. His brand of Kansas City jazz became the classic swing-band style, featuring spare keyboard playing with a precise four-beat rhythm section. He started the Barons of Rhythm in Kansas City, Missouri, in 1935 and then moved to New York in 1936. His hits include "Jumpin' at the Woodside" (1938) and "Stay Cool" (1946).

Beiderbecke, Bix (1903–31), b. Iowa. Cornetist, pianist, and composer. Famous for his solos, he was known as the first great white jazz musician. He advanced simple jazz into a more complex form built around improvisation and extended chords. His improvisations on "Singin' the Blues" (1927) were much admired and imitated.

Carter, Betty (1930–98), b. Michigan. Vocalist noted for her scat singing, humming, moaning, and extraordinary technique. She performed with the bands of Max Roach, Charlie Parker, Miles Davis, and others from the late 1940s through the late 1950s.

Christian, Charlie (c. 1916–42), b. Texas. A major contributor to the bebop movement, he was also among the first to capitalize on the sound of the electric guitar. He was admired for his innovative use of harmonic inversions, dissonance, and long strings of uninflected eighth notes. Major works include "Seven Come Eleven" (1939), "Gone with What Wind" (1940), and "Breakfast Feud" (1941).

Coleman, Ornette (1930–   ), b. Texas. Saxophonist and composer. He was a major influence on the avant-garde or "free-jazz" movement of the late 1950s and early 1960s, with a revolutionary style of breaking the restrictions of chords, ordinary harmony, bar lines, and tempered scales. Major recordings include "Something Else" (1958), "Congeniality" (1959), and "A Dedication to Poets and Writers" (1962).

Coltrane, John (1926–67), b. North Carolina. Tenor/soprano saxophonist, composer, and bandleader. His explosive style and angular melodic lines have influenced jazz musicians. He is credited with developing polytonality in modern jazz, and his quartet, which performed from 1960 to 1965, ranks among the best. His masterworks include "Giant Steps" (1959) and "A Love Supreme" (1964).

Davis, Miles (1926–91), b. Illinois. Trumpeter, composer, and bandleader. His lyrical and inventive playing made him a trendsetter for more than four decades. A major contributor to the bebop and cool forms of jazz, he pioneered the jazz-rock movement in the 1960s. His influential recordings include "Steamin'" (1956), "Kind of Blue" (1959), and "Bitches Brew" (1969).

Ellington, Edward Kennedy "Duke" (1899–1974), b. Washington, D.C. Pianist, composer, and bandleader. Nominated for a Pulitzer prize, he is considered the most important composer of big-band music. He wrote and arranged many jazz classics, popular songs, and blues or "mood" pieces. "Mood Indigo" (1930), "It Don't Mean a Thing (If It Ain't Got That Swing)" (1932), "Sophisticated Lady" (1933), and "In a Sentimental Mood" (1935) are among his many great recordings.

Evans, Bill (1929–80), b. New Jersey. Pianist, arranger, and composer whose soft harmonies, intricate voicing, and melodic improvising changed the sound of the piano in jazz. He earned national recognition for his playing in "Kind of Blue" (1959) with the Miles Davis Sextet.

Fitzgerald, Ella (1918–96), b. Virginia. Vocalist acclaimed for her pure tone, voice control, improvisation, and interpretation of ballads. Her first hit was "A Tisket, A Tasket" (1938), and she became world famous in 1946 when she sang with the *Jazz at the Philharmonic* concert series.

Gillespie, John Birks "Dizzy" (1917–93), b. South Carolina. Trumpeter and bandleader who pioneered the bebop movement in 1945 along with Charlie Parker. His Latin-influenced sound and virtuosity in upper-register playing are evident in his compositions "Salt Peanuts" (1945) and "A Night in Tunisia" (1946).

Goodman, Benny (1909–86), b. Illinois. Clarinetist and bandleader known as the "Pied Piper of Swing." He played with symphony orchestras and pioneered interracial bands. His best-known recordings include "After You've Gone" (1935) and "Moonglow" (1936).

Hancock, Herbie (1940–   ), b. Illinois. Pianist and composer whose highly individual keyboard style blends blues and bebop. He joined the Miles Davis Quintet in 1963 and helped expand the traditional jazz concept of the rhythm section and its relationship to the soloist. He contributed to the rock-jazz movement of the late 1960s and 1970s with his composition "Maiden Voyage" (1965).

Hawkins, Coleman (1904–69), b. Missouri. His powerful, original style and rich tone made him the dominant tenor saxophonist during the late 1930s and early 1940s. He played with Fletcher Henderson's orchestra (1923–43). His most celebrated recording is "Body and Soul" (1939).

Henderson, Fletcher (c. 1897–1952), b. Georgia. Bandleader, arranger, and trumpeter who pioneered the concept of the big band in the swing era. His best works include "Down South Camp Meeting" (1934), "Wrappin' It Up" (1934), and "King Porter Stomp" (1935).

Hines, Earl "Fatha" (c. 1903–83), b. Pennsylvania. Pianist and bandleader. He is known for his innovative "trumpet-style" single-note solos coupled with powerful rhythm and bass patterns. His best recordings include "A Monday Date" (1928) and "Skip the Gutter" (1928) with Louis Armstrong.

Holiday, Billie "Lady Day" (1915–59), b. Maryland. Vocalist famous for her melancholy improvisations of ballads and popular songs. She was discovered by record producer and critic John Hammond in 1933 and sang with Benny Goodman, Lester Young, Count Basie, and other great jazz musicians. She developed a large public following with her recordings of "Strange Fruit" (1939) and "Lover Man" (1944).

Joplin, Scott (1868–1917), b. Texas. Composer and pianist who popularized the early jazz form of ragtime. His composition "The Maple Leaf Rag" (c. 1899) became an instant hit. His works include 33 rags, about two dozen songs, and a ragtime opera.

Lewis, John A. (1920–2001), b. Illinois. Pianist and composer known for applying classical forms to jazz based on improvisation and carefully worked-out changes of tempo, key, meter, and instrumentation. He was one of the pioneers of cool jazz and founded the Modern Jazz Quartet. His noted works include "Bluesology" (1956) and "Between the Devil and the Deep Blue Sea" (1957).

Miller, Glenn (1904–44), b. Iowa. Trombonist, arranger, and star bandleader during the big-band swing era. His distinctive sound combined a clarinet and four saxophones. "In the Mood" (1939) and "String of Pearls" (1941) were among his many hit songs.

Mingus, Charlie (1922–79), b. Arizona. Double bassist, pianist, composer, arranger, and bandleader. He combined gospel and jazz forms to create a funky sound. He was the dominant bassist of the late 1950s and early 1960s. Best compositions include "Goodbye Pork Pie Hat" (1959) and "Better Git It in Your Soul" (1959).

Monk, Thelonious (1917–82), b. North Carolina. Pianist and composer noted for his spare style, slow tempo, and distinctive phrasing. Monk was a major contributor to bebop. "'Round About Midnight" (1947) and "Criss Cross" (1951) are among his many important compositions.

Morton, Ferdinand "Jelly Roll" (c. 1890–1941), b. Louisiana. Pianist, composer, and preeminent soloist who recorded about 175 sides and

piano rolls between 1923 and 1929. Combining blues, rags, and marches, he is considered the first important jazz composer. His influential works included "The Pearls" (1919), "Wolverine Blues" (1923), "Grandpa's Spells" (1923), and "Smokehouse Blues" (1926).

Parker, Charlie "Bird" (1920–55), b. Kansas. Alto saxophonist and composer whose virtuosity and inventive melodic lines made him a major influence in bebop. "Groovin' High" (1945) and "Out of Nowhere" (1948) are among his most innovative solos.

Reinhardt, Django (1910–53), b. Belgium. Considered the most important jazz guitarist. His swing style of playing was characterized by a full sound, strong rhythms, salvos of sixteenth notes, vibrato, and surprising melodic lines. Notable works include "Tiger Rag" (1934) and "Stardust" (1935).

Smith, Bessie (1894–1937), b. Tennessee. Vocalist considered the greatest of all the classic blues singers. She achieved the height of her fame in the 1920s pioneering jazz-oriented blues. Her best recordings include "Down-hearted Blues" (1923) and "Cold in Hand Blues" (1925).

Tatum, Art (1910–56), b. Ohio. Pianist known for his dazzling high-speed arpeggios and elaborate runs stretching the length of the keyboard. Tatum was the premier pianist of New York's Swing Street clubs from the 1930s through the 1950s. "Tea for Two" (1923), "Tiger Rag" (1933), and "Stompin' at the Savoy" (1953) are among his many great recordings.

Vaughan, Sarah "Sassy" (1924–90), b. New Jersey. Vocalist renowned for her operatic power, elegant phrasing, and extraordinarily wide range. She became popular while singing with Billy Eckstine's band in the mid-1940s. "Lover Man" (1945), recorded with Charlie Parker and Dizzy Gillespie, established her reputation.

Waller, Thomas "Fats" (1904–43), b. New York. Pianist, songwriter, and entertainer. Waller's jazz ragtime style of playing in the 1920s and 1930s made many of his songs jazz standards. His notable works, "Honeysuckle Rose" (1929) and "Ain't Misbehavin'"

Performance Arts

(1929), brought him fame as a satirical songwriter and entertainer.

Williams, Mary Lou (1910–81), b. Georgia. Pianist, arranger, and composer. Known as "the first great female instrumentalist in jazz," she created harmonically innovative arrangements ranging from swing to avant-garde. She arranged scores for the bands of Earl Hines, Benny Goodman, and Duke Ellington. Her most famous composition is "Zodiac Suite" (1945).

Young, Lester "Prez" (1909–59), b. Mississippi. Tenor saxophonist and premier soloist credited with transforming the "hot" jazz of the 1930s into the "cool" jazz of the 1940s and 1950s. His influential recordings include "Shoe Shine Boy" (1936), "Lady Be Good" (1936), and "Lester Leaps In" (1939).

COMMON MUSIC TERMS

a cappella Choral music without accompaniment (literally, "in the church style").

accelerando A direction to gradually increase the tempo.

accent The emphasis given to one tone over another.

accidental A sign used to indicate chromatic alteration; a sharp, double sharp, flat, double flat, or natural prefixed to a single note.

accompaniment Secondary instrument or background vocal added to the principal instrument or soloist.

acoustics The science of sound, which deals with intensity, quality, resonance, pitch, tone, and other qualities of sound.

adagietto A direction to play slightly faster than adagio.

adagio A direction to play slowly; between andante and largo.

adagissimo A direction to play very slowly.

"Music" under "Reference Works for General Information" in chapter 11; "Music Symbols" in chapter 12 — **Go to**

ad libitum A direction to interpret, improvise, or omit, according to the player's preference.

affetuoso A direction to play affectionately, with warmth.

agitato A direction to play in an agitated, restless, hurried manner.

air A tune or melody; the French 18th-century term for song; also, an instrumental piece whose melodic style is similar to that of a solo song.

alla breve A direction to play twice as fast as the notation signifies; ²⁄₂ instead of ⁴⁄₄.

allargando A direction to play slower, louder.

allegretto A direction to play with moderately quick movement; between andante and allegro.

allegro A direction to play quickly, briskly.

allemande A moderately slow dance of German origin.

allentando A direction to slow down.

alto The highest adult male voice or lowest female voice; also, a tenor violin or viola.

andante A direction to play in moderate tempo; "walking" speed; between allegretto and adagio.

andantino A direction to play in tempo slightly quicker than andante.

animato A direction to play with animation.

answer In a fugue, the second or fourth statement of the subject.

anthem A choral piece for use in church services.

appassionato A direction to play passionately.

appoggiatura An inharmonious note preceding a principal note, marked with a diagonal line through it, of short or long duration.

arabesque A lyrical piece in a fanciful style; a term used first by Schumann and later by Debussy.

aria An extended vocal solo in an opera or oratorio.

arioso A piece of recitative song, but more song-like.

arpeggio The technique of playing the notes of a chord successively rather than simultaneously.

ascending Moving upward on a musical scale.

assai A direction to play very quickly.

a tempo A direction to play in time, following a deviation from the regular tempo.

atonal Having no recognized tonal center or key.

aubade Morning music, in contrast to *serenade,* or evening music.

augmentation Presentation of a theme in notes of doubled value; the opposite of *diminution.*

auxiliary note Usually, a grace note one degree above or below a principal note.

ballad A narrative song, originally accompanied by dancing; also, an instrumental piece in ballad style.

bar line A line drawn vertically across the staff to divide into measures.

baritone The male voice between bass and tenor; also, any musical instrument intermediary between bass and tenor.

Baroque A term signifying the music composed between 1600 and 1750, characterized by homophonic texture with the uppermost part carrying the melody over the bass line; a search for affective expression; the development of new styles for various functions and new techniques, such as dissonance and tonality.

bass The lowest male voice, or lowest part in a musical composition; also, short for the double bass or bass tuba.

beat A unit of rhythm or time in a composition as indicated by the conductor's gesture; each unit of a measure with respect to accent.

bebop (bop) One of the principal styles of jazz developed in the early 1940s, characterized by complicated melody lines and chord patterns played at exceptional speed.

bel canto The Italian vocal techniques of the 18th century with an emphasis on beauty of sound and brilliance of performance rather than dramatic expression or romantic emotion.

berceuse A cradle song.

binary Musical form in which both main sections are repeated and where the first section characteristically is tonally not self-contained but demands a resolution in the second part (AB).

bolero A Spanish dance accompanied by castanets.

bowing A method of using the bow on stringed instruments as indicated by signs for down bow (∏) or up bow (V).

brace A vertical line used to join two or more staves.

As estimated today, a compact disc may last around 150 years if handled carefully.

buffa In the comic style.

buffo The singer of a comic part.

cadence A progression of chords that seems to move to a harmonic close or point of rest.

cadenza An ornamental passage near the end of a composition.

canon A contrapuntal composition in which the same melody is imitated by one or more voices overlapping in time in the same or related key.

cantata A vocal form from the Baroque period that consists of arias, recitatives, duets, and choruses. The term now refers to secular or sacred choral works accompanied by orchestra, similar to the oratorio but shorter.

canticle Religious song or chant.

canzona A form of Italian lyric poetry corresponding to the ode, set to music in a style similar to a madrigal, though simpler; also, an instrumental piece in the style of a song.

canzonet A vocal piece in a light vein, somewhat like a dance song, usually with instrumental accompaniment; a short instrumental piece.

capriccio A short composition in free form.

castrato A male singer castrated as a boy to maintain a soprano or alto voice range.

catch A humorous round for three or more voices.

chaconne A musical form based on a reiterated harmonic pattern.

chamber music Instrumental compositions performed by a small ensemble, with one player for each part.

chanson A song for solo voice or vocal ensemble; also, an instrumental piece of vocal character.

chant A sacred song, usually monophonic and in free rhythm and used in accordance with prescribed ritual. The chant is the oldest form of choral music.

chorale A psalm or hymn tune sung in church; also, a harmonization of a chorale melody.

chord The combination of three or more tones played at once. A *diatonic chord* uses only notes proper to the key. A *triad* is a chord of three notes in which the lowest is combined with the third and fifth above it. A *common chord* is a triad in root position. A *dominant chord* is founded on the dominant of the key. An *inverted chord* uses a tone other than the root as its lowest tone.

chromatic scale Consecutive series of notes that employ only a progression of semitones.

classical Term for the period and style of music from about 1700 to about 1830, characterized by regular, short, clearly articulated phrases combined with symmetrical patterns and textures. Haydn, Mozart, and Beethoven are its chief representatives.

clef A character that indicates the pitch of a particular line on a staff.

coda A passage that brings a piece or movement to a conclusion.

comma The small difference in pitch that occurs in the same note when obtained through different combinations of octaves, perfect fifths, and pure thirds.

common time Four-four (⁴⁄₄) time—that is, four quarter notes to a measure.

compound interval An interval that extends beyond an octave.

compound time Time in which each beat of the bar is divisible into three, in contrast to *simple time,* in which each is divisible into two.

concertmaster The leader of the first violins, next in rank to the conductor.

concerto A composition for solo instrument, usually with orchestral accompaniment.

concerto grosso A style of composition developed during the Baroque period (1600–1750) in which two groups of musicians, one large and one small, alternate in an echo effect.

concert pitch Pitch at which the piano and other nontransposing instruments play.

console The part of the organ from which the player controls the instrument—the keyboard, pedals, and so on—as distinguished from the pipes.

consonance Combination of pitches that produce little tension and are generally considered pleasing; opposite of dissonance.

consort A chamber ensemble; also, music written for such a group.

con spirito A direction to play in a lively manner.

continuo The bass, or lowest, line of a composition.

contralto The range of a low female voice; alto.

cool Style of modern jazz pioneered in the 1950s and 1960s, characterized by understated and emotionally subdued arrangements played by small ensembles.

counterpoint Music consisting of two or more melodic lines played simultaneously.

countersubject The contrasting motif to the subject of a fugue.

countertenor The male alto voice.

couplet Two lines having the same meter.

courante   A lively dance in triple time; also, the second part of a suite.

crescendo   A direction to increase the volume.

cut time   Another term for ½ meter.

da capo   A direction to repeat from the beginning.

decrescendo   A direction to decrease the volume.

descant   A different melody sung in a higher pitch and simultaneously with the main melodic line. It is the earliest form of polyphony, with contrasting motions between the parts.

The first composer to have one of his works performed in space was Dmitry Shostakovich.

descending   Moving downward on a musical scale.

development   The extension of a theme through contrapuntal elaboration, modulation, rhythmical variation, etc.

diatonic   Referring to minor and major scales that employ a particular combination of whole tones and half tones; the harmony and melodies that use only the pitches of a particular diatonic scale.

diminished chord   A chord in which the highest and lowest tones form a diminished interval.

diminished interval   A perfect or minor interval reduced by a semitone.

diminuendo   Diminishing; getting softer.

diminution   The breaking up of the notes in a melody into quick figures, as is done in variations.

dissonance   A combination of tones that are unresolved, jarring.

divertimento   An 18th-century form of instrumental chamber music having several short movements.

divertissement   A fantasia on well-known tunes.

divisi   In orchestral music, an indication that a group of players who play the same parts are to play two or more separate parts.

do   The first tone of a diatonic scale.

dolce   A direction to play softly, sweetly.

dolente, doloroso   Sorrowful.

dominant   The fifth tone of the major or minor diatonic scale.

dominant chord   A chord with the fifth pitch of a scale as its root.

doppio movimento   Twice as fast.

Dorian mode   A church mode represented on the white keys of a keyboard instrument by an ascending scale from D to D.

dot   Written after a note, an indication of the prolongation of its length by one-half; the double dot indicates by three-fourths. Above or below the note, the dot indicates staccato.

double stop   A chord of two notes played on a bowed string instrument, obtaining a two-part harmony.

doxology   In Christian worship, a hymn of praise to God.

duet   A composition for two players or two voices, with or without accompaniment.

duple   Two units to the measure, such as ²⁄₂, ²⁄₄, or ²⁄₈.

duration   The length of a tone.

dynamics   Varying and contrasting degrees of intensitiy or loudness.

eighth   A note whose value is one-eighth of a whole note.

enharmonic   Tones that have the same pitch when played on tempered instruments but that are different in notation, such as C (♯) and D (♭).

episode   The section of a fugue in which the main melody is not heard.

estinto   So soft that it can hardly be heard.

étude   A study; an exercise in technique.

exposition   The statement of the musical material on which a movement is based.

expression marks   Marks used to help the interpretation of a work; they are concerned with dynamics, tempo, and mood, and indicate forte, allegro, con spirito, etc.

fa   The fourth note of a diatonic scale.

falsetto   The false voice; an adult male voice in the alto and treble range.

fantasia   A piece in which the composition follows the fancy rather than any conventional form; of an improvisational character.

fermata   A symbol (◠) placed over the note to show that it is to be played longer than its normal duration.

fifth   The interval between the tonic and the fifth tone above it. In the key of C major, C to G is a fifth.

figuration   The extended use of a particular melodic or harmonic figure; the ornamental treatment of a passage.

finale   The last movement of a work of several movements—for example, the conclusion of a concerto or the last act of an opera.

flat   A sign (♭) indicating that the pitch is to be lowered by one semitone.

form   The pattern of design of a work; its basic elements are repetition, variation, and contrast in the areas of harmony, rhythm, and tone.

forte   A direction to play loudly.

fortissimo   A direction to play very loudly.

forza   A direction to play with force.

forzando   Strongly accenting.

fourth   The interval between the tonic and the fourth diatonic tone above it; in the key of C major, C to F is a fourth.

fugue   A composition in which three or more voices enter at different times and imitate the main melody in different ways according to a set pattern.

fundamental   Also called the tonic; the lowest tone of a chord when the chord is founded on that tone; also, the lowest note in the harmonic series.

funk (funky)   Style of African American music popular in the mid-1960s that combines soul and jazz. It is characterized by complex interlocking syncopated rhythm patterns in duple meter.

galop   A quick dance in ¾ time popular in the 19th century.

giocoso   Jocose; merry.

glee   A simple part song, generally for male voices.

glissando   The execution of rapid scales by sliding the finger rapidly across keys or strings.

grace note   An ornamental note not essential to the melody and not counted as part of the measure.

grandezza   Grandeur.

grave   A direction to play slowly, solemnly.

grazioso   A direction to play gracefully.

Gregorian chant   A style of church music for unaccompanied voices, without definite rhythm, in one of the eight church modes.

half note   A note having half the time value of a whole note and twice that of a quarter note.

harmonic   A tone whose frequency is an integral multiple of a single frequency known as the fundamental tone.

harmony   The simultaneously sounded pitches, as in chords.

homophonic   Single-voiced; music in which one melody or part is supported by chords; the opposite of *polyphonic*.

imitation   The use of the same or similar melodic material in different voices successively.

impresario   The conductor or manager of an opera or concert company.

impromptu   An improvised composition without fixed form.

incidental music   Music for performance during the action of a play or film.

interlude   A short piece played between the acts of a drama; the verses of a song, parts of a church service, or sections of a cantata.

intermezzo   A play with music performed between the acts of an opera or drama that gave rise to opera buffa; an interlude; a short movement in a symphony.

interval   The distance in pitch between two notes, harmonic if they are played together, melodic if they are played in succession. *Perfect interval:* the prime, fourth, fifth, and octave. *Major interval:* the second, third, sixth, and seventh of the major scale. *Minor interval:* a chromatic half step smaller than a major interval. *Augmented interval:* a chromatic half step larger than perfect and major. *Diminished interval:* A chromatic half step smaller than perfect and minor.

intonation   The degree of accuracy with which pitches are produced.

inversion   The transposition of the lower and upper notes of an interval. In an inverted chord, the lowest tone is not its root; an inverted melody is one in which its intervals are inverted.

Ionian mode   A mode of church music represented on the white keys of a keyboard by an ascending scale from C to C.

key   The main pitch or tonal center to which all of the composition's pitches are related.

key signature   Sharps or flats placed at the beginning of a composition to indicate its key.

la   The sixth tone of a diatonic scale.

largo   A direction to play broadly, more slowly than adagio but not as slowly as grave.

leading tone   The seventh degree or tone of the scale; a semitone below the tonic.

legato   A direction to play smoothly and continuously.

lento   A direction to play slowly, but not as slowly as largo.

libretto   The text of an opera or oratorio.

litany   A song of invocation to God.

madrigal   An unaccompanied song for three or more voices using counterpoint and imitation.

maestoso   A direction to play in a majestic, stately manner.

magnificat   Canticle of the Virgin Mary sung as part of the evening service in Reformed churches and at vespers in the Catholic church.

major   Applied to chords, intervals, scales, and keys; a standard in contrast to diminished, augmented, or minor.

major scale   A diatonic scale in which the half steps occur between the third and fourth and the seventh and eighth tones.

march   A composition usually in duple meter and in simple, strongly marked rhythms and regular phrases for a procession or parade.

mass   A musical setting of the liturgy of the Eucharist.

mazurka   A polkalike Polish folk dance in triple time with strong accents on the normally weak second and third beats.

measure   A unit of rhythm or musical time, indicated by bar lines.

Mozart's full name was Johannes Chrysostomus Wolfgangus Theophilus Mozart, but he is often known as "Amadeus," which means "beloved of God."

mediant   The third tone of a diatonic scale.

melody   A rhythmically organized succession of single tones that form a musical idea.

mensural music   A medieval term for music with definite note values, as distinguished from plainsong.

meter   A scheme of accents; a grouping of beats into units of measure.

mezzo   Medium, half; moderate.

mezzo-forte   A direction to play moderately loudly.

mezzo-soprano   The female voice between soprano and alto.

mi   The third tone in the diatonic scale.

middle C   The pitch represented by the first ledger line below the treble clef or the first above the bass clef.

minor   Intervals, scales, keys, and chords having intervals a semitone less than major.

minor scale   A diatonic scale having a minor third between the first and third tones and having several forms with different intervals above the fifth.

minuet   A slow, graceful dance of French origin in triple time; a composition in this rhythm.

mode   A selection of tones arranged in a scale that forms the basic tonal substance of a composition.

modulation   The change from one key to another through a succession of chords.

molto   Very.

monophony   Music consisting of a single melodic line without additional parts or accompaniment, as in plainsong or folk song.

mordent   An ornament played by quickly alternating a note with the note below it.

morendo   A fading away.

motet   An unaccompanied vocal composition with sacred lyrics from the 13th century.

motif   A short, significant melodic and/or rhythmic figure that recurs throughout a composition or section as a unifying element.

motion   The pattern of changing pitch levels in a melody.

natural   A musical symbol indicating the removal of a sharp or flat from a particular pitch.

nocturne   A musical composition in the romantic style, usually for piano, with an expressive melody over a broken-chord accompaniment.

note   A symbol used to express the relative time value of tones.

obbligato   An added melody, usually played by a solo instrument to enhance a vocal line.

octave   The distance between two pitches having the same name and located 12 half steps apart.

octet   A composition of eight parts or voices; also, the group of its performers.

opera   A drama set to music, in which words are sung in the form of recitatives, arias, and ensembles, usually accompanied by orchestra and generally performed with sets and costumes.

operetta   A light opera, usually humorous, with spoken dialogue, dances, and, almost unfailingly, a happy ending.

opus   A numbered musical work or composition.

oratorio   A musical setting of scriptural text set without costumes, scenery, or action.

orchestra   A large group of musicians who play together on various musical instruments, including strings, woodwinds, brass, and percussion.

overture   An introduction to a large composition such as an opera or oratorio; however, it can be independent or the predecessor of a symphonic poem.

parallel motion   The relative changes of pitches in two or more simultaneous voice-parts when the intervals separating them remain the same.

part   In orchestral or chamber music, the music or melodic line for a particular series of notes for voice or instrument.

partita   A set of related instrumental pieces; a series of variations or a suite.

part song   A 19th-century choral composition in the homophonic style in which the top part is the only carrier of the melody.

passion music   A musical setting for the story of the suffering and death of Christ.

pasticcio   An operatic medley of the 18th century made up of contributions of two or more composers.

pastorale   A musical composition suggestive of rural life.

pentatonic scale   A five-toned scale without semitones; the diatonic scale with fourth and seventh tones omitted.

phrase   A complete musical idea.

pianissimo   A direction to play very softly.

piano   A direction to play softly.

piano quartet   A term usually applied to quartets for piano, violin, viola, and cello.

piano quintet   A combination of piano with string quartet.

pitch   The perceived highness or lowness of a sound.

pizzicato   For violins and other bowed instruments, a direction that the string is to be picked with the finger.

plainsong   A nonmetrical chant in one of the church modes.

poco   Little.

polka   A lively dance in ²⁄₄ time that originated in Bohemia c. 1830.

polonaise   A Polish dance in ³⁄₄ time adopted as a musical form by Chopin.

polyphony   Contrapuntal music; a style in which two or more melodies are interwoven; the opposite of *homophony.*

prelude   An introductory movement complete in itself, as opposed to an introduction, which leads directly into the principal section; a short piano piece in one movement.

Roger Miller was inspired to write the classic song "King of the Road" when he saw a sign just west of Chicago that said, "Trailers for Sale or Rent."

program music   Music intended to depict a story or image.

progression   *Melodic:* the passage from tone to tone; *harmonic:* the passage from chord to chord.

quartet   A composition of four parts or voices; also, the performers of a four-part composition.

quintet   A composition of five voices or instruments; also, the performers of a five-part composition.

ragtime   Style of American music popular from about 1890 to the beginning of World War I, characterized by syncopated melodies set against a rhythmically strong bass.

re   The second tone of a diatonic scale.

recitative   A style of singing resembling dramatic speech.

refrain   Repeated lines that occur at the end of each stanza of a song or poem.

register   The range of a voice or instrument; a portion of the range of an instrument, as in upper register or lower register.

requiem   A mass for the dead; also, a musical setting for such a mass.

resolution   The progression from a dissonant tone or harmony to one that is consonant.

rest   A symbol indicating pause or silence.

rinforzando   A sudden accent on a single note or chord.

ritardando   A direction to slow the tempo gradually.

ritenuto   Immediate reduction in tempo.

romance   A short vocal or instrumental composition of a romantic character without fixed form.

rondo   A form of instrumental composition with a refrain that occurs at least three times in its original key between contrasting couplets.

root   The tonic of a triad or chord; the lowest tone, unless the chord is inverted.

round   A canon for three or more voices; the common name for a circle canon in which each singer returns from the conclusion of the melody to its beginning, repeating it.

scale   A series of tones arranged according to rising pitches.

scat   A technique of jazz singing that uses nonsense syllables for improvising vocal solos.

scherzo   A playful, humorous instrumental composition, usually in a rapid ¾ meter.

second   The interval between the tonic and the second tone of a diatonic scale; in the key of C major, C to D is a second.

semitone   One-half of a whole tone.

septet   A composition for seven voices or instruments.

sequence   Repetition of a short musical phrase at a different pitch.

serenade   An impromptu or unsolicited vocal or instrumental performance, often outdoors; an instrumental composition in several movements for a small group, between the symphony and the suite.

seventh   The interval between the tonic and the seventh tone of a diatonic scale; in the key of C major, C to B is a seventh.

sharp   A sign (♯) indicating that the pitch is to be raised by a half step.

si (or **ti**)   The seventh tone in a diatonic scale.

signature   A symbol placed on the staff at the beginning of a piece that shows the key and the meter.

sixth   The interval between the tonic and the sixth tone of a diatonic scale; in the key of C major, C to A is a sixth.

slur   A curved line over a series of notes that are to be played smoothly and continuously.

sol   The fifth tone of a diatonic scale.

solo   A piece performed either alone or with accompaniment.

sonata   An instrumental composition of three or four independent movements varying in mood, character, and tempo.

sonatina   A short, simple sonata.

soprano   The highest female or boy's voice; the treble.

sostenuto   Sustaining the tone to or beyond the nominal value.

sotto voce   In a low voice.

staccato   Direction to play notes in a distinct, detached manner.

staff   The five horizontal lines on and between which notes are written.

stretto   Compressed; in a fugue, the overlapping of subject and answer.

subdominant   The dominant below; the fourth tone of the diatonic scale, in the same relation to the key note from below as the dominant is from above.

subito   Suddenly.

subject   A melody or melody fragment that, because of its character, design, position, or treatment, is used in the basic musical form of a composition.

submediant   The sixth tone of a diatonic scale.

subtonic   The seventh tone of a diatonic scale; leading tone.

suite   An instrumental composition consisting of a series of movements or distinct compositions; originally, a cycle of dance tunes.

supertonic   The second tone of a diatonic scale.

symphonic poem   Originated by Franz Liszt, a large narrative orchestral work in one movement based on a nonmusical idea, either poetic or realistic.

symphony   A sonata for orchestra, usually in four contrasting movements.

syncopation   A rhythmic pattern that places emphasis on beats that are not normally accented, thus creating a catchy, lilting sound.

tempo   The speed at which a composition is played.

tenor   The highest natural adult male voice; also, the instrument of corresponding range.

ternary form   The form of a composition in three parts with repetition following one contrast (ABA).

texture   The way in which melody and harmony are combined to create layers of sound.

theme and variation   A musical form in which the theme is repeated and varied.

third   The interval between the tonic and the third tone of a diatonic scale; in the key of C major, C to E is a third.

ti (or **si**)   The seventh tone in a diatonic scale.

tie   A curved line that combines the duration of two notes of the same pitch.

time   Used synonymously with measure or rhythm.

time signature   The meter of a composition, shown by two numbers, one above the other; the lower tells the kind of note that represents one beat; the upper tells the number of these notes that make up a measure.

toccata   A composition popular in the 16th century, for organ or harpsichord, and resembling the capriccio.

tonal center   The tonic pitch around which a composition or scale is centered.

tone   A sound of definite duration and pitch; a note.

tone cluster   A group of notes played simultaneously with forearm, elbow, and fist in a method introduced by Henry Cowell.

tonic   The first tone of a diatonic scale; also called fundamental. In the key of C major, C is the tonic.

transposition   The rewriting or playing of a composition in a key other than the original one.

treble clef   G clef; indicates that the pitch G is located on the second line above middle C.

tremolo   Rapid repetition of a note to resemble trembling.

triad   A chord composed of a fundamental tone and the third and fifth above it.

trio   A composition for three parts or voices; the second part of a minuet or march.

triplet   A group of three notes played in the time value of two.

triple time   Time in which there are three beats to a measure.

Houseflies and car horns have something in common. Most American car horns beep in the key of F. The housefly also buzzes in the key of F.

turn   An embellishment consisting of a group of four or five notes that turn around the principal note.

tutti   Indications for passages for the whole orchestra as distinguished from those of the soloist.

twelve-tone music   A method of composition based on a chromatic scale of 12, rather than 8, tones, developed by Arnold Schoenberg.

unison   Equal pitch; performance of the same part by all voices.

variation   Development of a theme through a variety of forms; differences in rhythm, key, harmony, etc.

vivace   A direction to play in a lively manner.

voice   Vocal or instrumental part of a composition.

waltz   A dance in triple time performed by couples, which reached its peak of popularity during the 19th century; also, music in this rhythm.

whole note   The longest note in common use.

whole tone   An interval of a major second; the interval of two semitones.

BASIC POSITIONS FOR BALLET

FEET

1st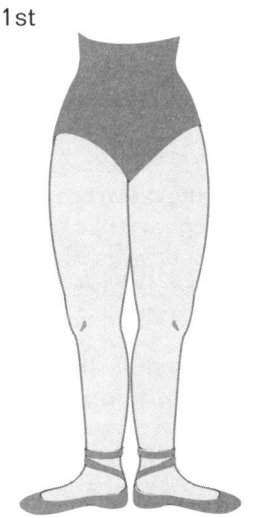

2nd

3rd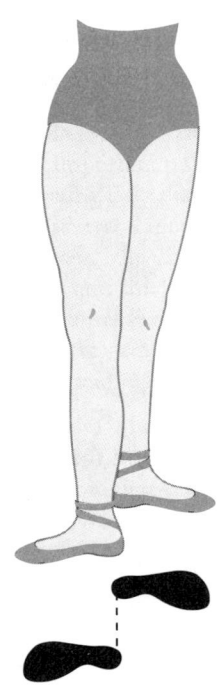

4th
open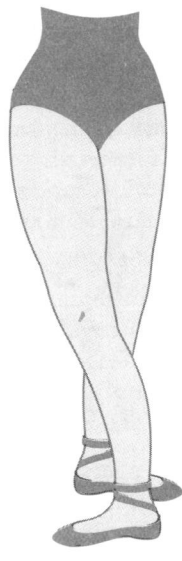

4th
crossed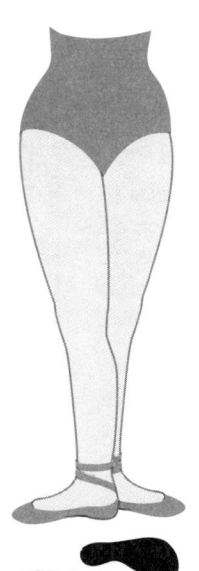

5th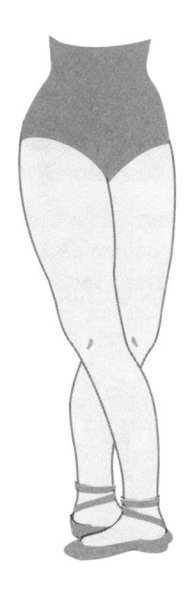

ARMS

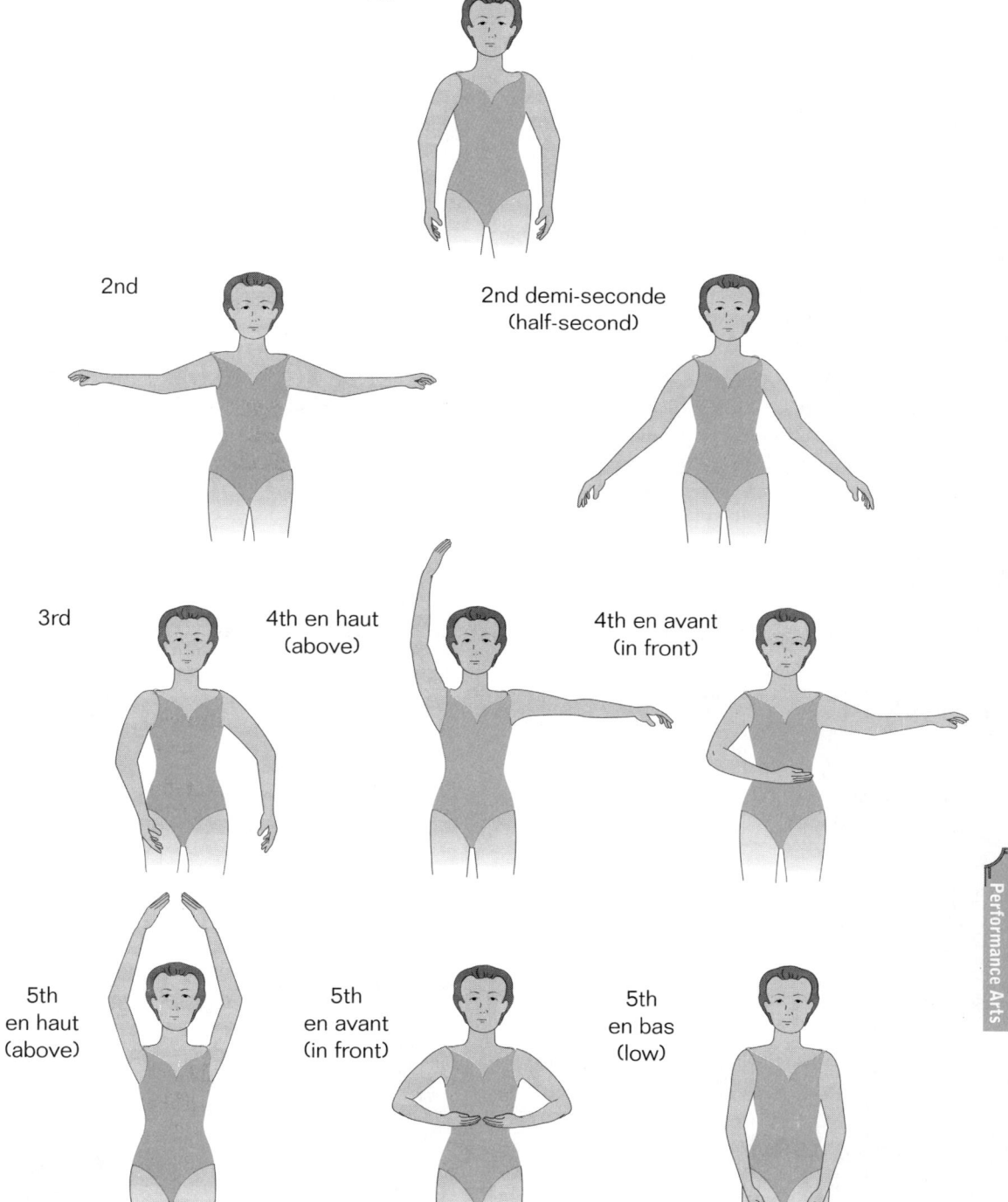

1st

2nd

2nd demi-seconde
(half-second)

3rd

4th en haut
(above)

4th en avant
(in front)

5th
en haut
(above)

5th
en avant
(in front)

5th
en bas
(low)

MAJOR DANCERS AND CHOREOGRAPHERS

AMERICAN

Ailey, Alvin   (1931–89). Choreographer noted for blending African, modern, and jazz elements, as seen in works such as *Revelations* (1960) and *Cry* (1971). His Alvin Ailey American Dance Theater was formed in 1958.

Arpino, Gerald   (1928–   ). Choreographer. Principal choreographer of the Joffrey Ballet, he became its artistic director in 1988. His sometimes trendy, energetic works include *Viva Vivaldi!* (1965) and *Trinity* (1970).

Astaire, Fred   (1899–1987). Actor and dancer in musical comedies on Broadway, such as *The Band Wagon,* and films, including *Top Hat* (1935) and *Shall We Dance?* (1937). Having started in vaudeville with his sister, Adele, Astaire later costarred with Judy Garland, Rita Hayworth, and Ginger Rogers. He was distinguished by his original and graceful tap dancing.

Balanchine, George   (1904–83). Russian-born American choreographer. Balanchine worked with Diaghilev's Ballets Russes (1924–29) and then came to America, founding the School of American Ballet in 1934. The New York City Ballet was created in 1948, with Balanchine as artistic director. He was an avatar of neoclassicism and the plotless ballet. Some of his major works, such as *Apollo* (1928) and *Agon* (1957), use the music of Stravinsky; other important works include *Serenade* (1934) and *Jewels* (1967).

Bujones, Fernando   (1955–   ). One of the few American dancers to base his career primarily on classical ballets, Bujones starred with the American Ballet Theater from 1975 to 1985 and then embarked on a career as a guest artist and choreographer. He is best known for his performances in *Don Quixote, La Bayadère, Swan Lake, Giselle,* and *La Sylphide.*

Castle, Vernon   (1887–1918) and **Irene** (1893–1969). Exhibition ballroom dancers whose elegance and style contributed to the spread of ballroom dancing before World War I. They created the Cas-

tle Walk and popularized the tango and other dances.

Cunningham, Merce   (1919–   ). Choreographer. He danced with Martha Graham's company, forming his own troupe in 1953, collaborating often with John Cage. His avant-garde and abstract works use isolated movements and the random ordering of dance movements. His works include *Summerspace* (1958) and the consecutively numbered *Events* (begun in 1964).

d'Amboise, Jacques   (1934–   ). Dancer and leading interpreter of the works of Balanchine during his years with the New York City Ballet (1949–84). He founded the National Dance Institute, which brings dance to New York City schoolchildren.

de Mille, Agnes   (1909–93). Choreographer. De Mille created ballets rooted in American folklore, such as *Rodeo* (1942) and *Fall River Legend* (1948). She also choreographed musicals for Broadway, including *Oklahoma!* (1943), and wrote *Dance to the Piper* (1952) and other books on dance.

Duncan, Isadora   (1877–1927). Dancer; one of the first figures in modern dance. Turning to ancient Greece for inspiration, she rejected the rigid system of ballet and created an expressive form of dance, which she performed dressed in a flowing tunic. Her works include *Marseillaise* (1915) and *Marche Slave* (1917).

Dunham, Katherine   (1912–   ). Choreographer and teacher. Through such works as the *Tropical Revues,* she was one of the first to bring African and Caribbean dance to the American stage. She also choreographed *Cabin in the Sky* (1940) for Broadway.

Farrell, Suzanne   (1945–   ). Dancer with the New York City Ballet (1961–69, 1975–89) and Ballets of the 20th Century (1970–75). One of the leading interpreters of the works of Balanchine, Farrell created important roles in such ballets as *Don Quixote* (1965).

Feld, Eliot   (1943–   ). Choreographer. He joined the American Ballet Theater in 1963, choreographing his first works, *Harbinger* and *At Mid-*

night (both 1967), there. In 1968, he formed the American Ballet company; and in 1974, the Feld Ballet.

Graham, Martha   (1894–1991). Choreographer. A leader of modern dance, she created a rigorous technique, which includes the contraction, a dramatic percussive movement based on the body's movement during intake and release of breath. Her works such as *Appalachian Spring* (1944) explore American roots; others, such as *Night Journey* (1947) and *Clytemnestra* (1958), draw on Greek mythology, exploring the psychology and passions of their protagonists.

Gregory, Cynthia   (1946–   ). Dancer. Noted for her virtuoso technique and majestic presence, she joined the San Francisco Ballet in 1961 and American Ballet Theater in 1965, where she was a principal dancer until 1991.

Holm, Hanya   (1898–1992).   German-born choreographer and teacher. A protégée of Mary Wigman, she started choreographing her own modern dance works in America, including *Trend* (1937). She also choreographed *Kiss Me Kate* (1948) and *My Fair Lady* (1956) for Broadway.

Horton, Lester   (1906–53). Dancer, choreographer, and teacher. A leader in modern dance and influenced by Native American dance, he formed the Lester Horton Dancers in 1934. Among his notable students was Alvin Ailey.

Humphrey, Doris   (1895–1958). A dancer with Denishawn, she left in 1927 to start a company with Charles Weidman. Her choreography is based on the principle of fall and recovery, which caters to the range of movement from balance to unbalance. Her works include *The Shakers* (1930) and *With My Red Fires* (1936).

Jamison, Judith   (1944–   ). Jamison joined the Alvin Ailey American Dance Theater in 1965 and became artistic director following Ailey's death in 1989. She has starred in numerous Ailey ballets, including *Cry, Maskela Language, Choral Dances,* and *Revelations.*

Joffrey, Robert   (1930–88). Choreographer. He formed his first company in 1954, and in 1956 he founded what became the Robert Joffrey Ballet. Joffrey's works include *Pas de Déesses* (1954) and *Astarte* (1967).

Jones, Bill T.   (1952–   ). The recipient of a MacArthur Fellowship in 1993, Jones is a postmodernist who performs only in his own works and those of his collaborators. These include *Negroes for Sale* (1972), *Stories, Steps, and Stomps* (1978), *War Between the States* (1993), and *You Walk* (2000).

Kelly, Gene   (1912–96). Actor, dancer, choreographer. In films such as *An American in Paris* (1952) and *Invitation to the Dance* (1956), he tried to make the choreography integral to the story and explored cinematic techniques for filming dance.

Kirkland, Gelsey   (1953–   ). Kirkland achieved stardom as a principal dancer with both the New York City Ballet and the American Ballet Theater. She is best known for partnering Mikhail Baryshnikov in *Hamlet Connotations, Awakening,* and *Theme and Variations.*

Kirstein, Lincoln   (1907–96). A promoter of American ballet, he brought George Balanchine to America and cofounded with him the School of American Ballet. He was general director of the New York City Ballet (1948–89) and wrote *Dance: A Short History of Classic Theatrical Dancing* (1935) and other books.

Limón, Jose   (1908–72). Born in Mexico, Limón is regarded as the most electrifying performer in modern dance history. He performed with the Humphrey/Weidman Group from 1930 until 1945, when he founded the Jose Limón Dance Company.

Martins, Peter   (1946–   ). Born in Denmark, he first danced with the Royal Danish Ballet (1965–1969). Martins then joined the New York City Ballet in 1970, becoming co–ballet master in chief in 1983 and ballet master in chief in 1990. Among his works, which follow in George Balanchine's neoclassical tradition, are *Calcium Night Light* (1977), *Eight Easy Pieces* (1979), *Ecstatic Orange* (1987), and *Jazz* (1993).

Mitchell, Arthur   (1934–   ). Dancer with the New York City Ballet from 1955. In 1968, he founded the Dance Theater of Harlem, the first black classical dance company.

Performance Arts

Nikolais, Alwin (1912–1993). Choreographer and founder of the Nikolais Dance Theater. His works, such as *Kaleidoscope* (1956), are theatrical productions in which dance, lighting, and sound play equal roles, forming abstract yet evocative patterns.

Robbins, Jerome (1918–98). Dancer and choreographer for the Ballet Theater (1941–44), where he choreographed *Fancy Free* (1944), and the New York City Ballet, where he was associate artistic director (1949–56) and later codirector (1983–90). His ballets combine the classical idiom with influences from jazz, modern, and social dance. Among his important works are *Goldberg Variations* (1971) and *Dances at a Gathering* (1969). His choreography for Broadway includes *West Side Story* (1957) and *Fiddler on the Roof* (1964).

Robinson, Bill (Bojangles) (1878–1949). Tap dancer who brought a new lightness to tap. Gaining renown with his appearance in the revue *Blackbirds* in 1928, he appeared in movies, including *The Little Colonel* with Shirley Temple.

St. Denis, Ruth (1879–1968). Dancer. Inspired by the Orient, her dances, such as *Radha* (1904) and *The Cobras* (1906), were both exotic and spiritual. In 1915, St. Denis founded Denishawn—the first school of modern dance—with her husband, Ted Shawn.

Shawn, Ted (1891–1972). Founder of Denishawn with Ruth St. Denis. In the 1930s, he started Men Dancers; with works such as *The Kinetic Molpai* (1935), he focused attention on male dancing. Shawn also founded the Jacob's Pillow Dance Festival.

Tallchief, Maria (1925–). Dancer with the Ballet Russe de Monte Carlo (1942–47) and the New York City Ballet (1948–1965). She founded the Chicago City Ballet and later was artistic director of the Lyric Opera of Chicago Ballet.

Taylor, Paul (1930–). Choreographer. He formed his own company in 1954, and his modern dance works are often characterized by humor. His works include *Arden Court* (1981), *Company B* (1991), *The Word* (1998), and *Dandelion Wine* (2000).

Tetley, Glen (1926–). At various times in his career, Tetley has danced and choreographed for Martha Graham, Jerome Robbins, and the American Ballet Theater. Among his best-known works are *Pierrot Lunaire* (1962), *Embrace Tiger and Return to Mountain* (1968), and *Sphinx* (1977).

Tharp, Twyla (1942–). Choreographer of idiosyncratic works that use ballet idiom to novel effect. She had her own modern dance company (1965–88) and then served as artistic associate with the American Ballet Theater (1988–91). Her works include *Deuce Coupe* (1973) and *Push Comes to Shove* (1976). She also choreographed the films *Hair* (1979) and *Amadeus* (1984). She founded the company Twyla Tharp Dance in 2000.

Villella, Edward (1936–). Dancer. As a member of the New York City Ballet (1957–79), he was noted for his virile dancing. He has been artistic director of the Miami City Ballet since 1985.

Weidman, Charles (1901–75). Dancer and choreographer. After dancing with Denishawn, he founded a company with Doris Humphrey in 1927 and later began his own company. His works, known for their humor, include *Flickers* and *And Daddy Was a Fireman*.

BRITISH

Ashton, Sir Frederick (1904–88). A pioneer of British ballet, he was chief choreographer of the Sadler's Wells (now Royal) Ballet from 1935, and its director from 1963 to 1970. His works, noted for their lyrical classicism, include *Symphonic Variations* (1946), *Les Patineurs* (1937), and *Ondine* (1958).

Dolin, Anton (1904–83). English dancer with Diaghilev's Ballets Russes (1924–29) and Ballet Theater. One of Britain's first danseurs nobles, in 1949 he founded the London Festival Ballet with Alicia Markova and served as artistic director.

Fonteyn, Dame Margot (1919–91). English dancer and prima ballerina assoluta of the Royal Ballet, which she joined in 1934 when it was the Vic Wells Ballet. Known for her musicality and refinement, she was the partner of Rudolf Nureyev after 1962; her major roles include Aurora in *Sleeping Beauty* and Juliet in *Romeo and Juliet*.

MacMillan, Kenneth (1929–92). The creator of more than 60 ballets, MacMillan was a bold innovator who expanded the dramatic and intellectual horizons of the dance, often grappling with social, psychological, and political themes. His masterworks include *The Burrow* (1958), *The Invitation* (1960), *Requiem* (1976), *Isadora* (1981), and *Valley of Shadows* (1983).

Markova, Dame Alicia (1910–). English dancer with the Ballets Russes (1925–29), Ballet Theater (1941–45), and other companies. Markova was one of the leading interpreters of *Giselle* and the first British ballerina of international renown.

Rambert, Dame Marie (1888–1982). Polish-born dancer, teacher, and ballet director. She advised Nijinsky on rhythm when he was choreographing *Le Sacre du Printemps* and later became one of the pioneers of modern British ballet, founding her Ballet Rambert in 1935.

Tudor, Antony (1908–87). English choreographer of ballets of psychological drama. He was associated with the American Ballet Theater (1939–49), then known as Ballet Theater, and later served as associate artistic director (1974–80). Among the ballets that exemplify his use of gesture to express character are *Lilac Garden* (1936) and *Pillar of Fire* (1942).

Valois, Dame Ninette de (1898–). A founder of modern British ballet. After dancing with the Ballets Russes (1923–26), she founded a school in London; and in 1931, a company, the Vic Wells Ballet, which became the Sadler's Wells Ballet and then the Royal Ballet. Her works include *The Rake's Progress* (1935) and *The Haunted Ballroom* (1934).

FRENCH

Béjart, Maurice (1927–). Choreographer. He founded the Ballet de l'Etoile in 1953, and later the Ballets of the 20th Century. In 1988, his troupe moved to Lausanne, Switzerland. Béjart's controversial works are highly theatrical and sometimes mystical; they include *Symphony for a Lonely Man* (1955) and *Ring Around the Ring* to Wagner (1991).

Camargo, Marie (1710–70). Dancer at the Paris Opera and rival of Marie Sallé, Camargo shortened the dancer's skirt to show her brilliant entrechats and other beats and eliminated the heels from her shoes for greater freedom of movement.

Noverre, Jean Georges (1727–1810). Choreographer and ballet reformer who tried with the *ballet d'action* to highlight the expressiveness of the ballet and integrate dance with drama. He wrote down his ideas in his *Letters sur la danse et sur les ballets.*

Perrot, Jules (1810–92). Dancer and ballet master of the Imperial Theater in St. Petersburg (1851–58). A leading dancer and choreographer of the Romantic era, he choreographed *La Esmeralda* and parts of *Giselle* (1841).

Petit, Roland (1924–). Founder of the Ballets de Paris de Roland Petit (1948) and director of the Ballet National de Marseilles since 1972. His story ballets combine high and popular art; his works include *Le Jeune homme et la mort* (1946) and *Le Loup* (1953).

Sallé, Marie (1707–56). Dancer with the Paris Opera (1727–40) and rival of Camargo. An advocate of the use of pantomime in ballet, Sallé was noted for her expressiveness and intelligence.

Vestris, Auguste (1760–1842). Dancer and teacher and illegitimate son of Gaetano. As premier danseur of the Paris Opera, he was noted for his exceptional elevation and virtuosity.

Vestris, Gaetano (1728–1808). Italian-born dancer and choreographer. Known as "the god of the dance," he became premier danseur of the Paris Opera in 1751 and cochoreographer in 1761. He was the first to discard the mask worn by dancers in performance.

RUSSIAN

Baryshnikov, Mikhail (1948–). A principal with the Kirov Ballet (1968–74), the Russian dancer defected to the West in 1974, joining the American Ballet Theater and serving as its director (1980–89). He then formed the White Oak Dance Project. His virtuosity and purity of classical style make him one of the leading male dancers of the period.

Danilova, Alexandra (1904–97). Russian-born dancer. Noted for her charm and elegance, she was a ballerina with the Ballets Russes (1927–29) and prima ballerina with the Ballet Russe de Monte Carlo (1938–52). She taught at the School of American Ballet (1964–89) and appeared in the film *The Turning Point* (1977).

Diaghilev, Sergei Pavlovich (1872–1929). Russian impresario and founder of the Ballets Russes (1909). He brought together leading choreographers, composers, and artists, from Fokine and Balanchine to Stravinsky and Picasso, whose collaborations revolutionized the ballet.

Eglevsky, Andre (1917–77). Russian-born dancer. A leading dancer with the Ballet Russe de Monte Carlo (1939–42), Ballet Theater (1942–43), and New York City Ballet (1951–58). He founded the Eglevsky Ballet Company in 1961.

Fokine, Michel (1880–1942). Russian-born choreographer for the Ballets Russes (1909–12, 1914–15). His emphasis on dramatic coherence and on the unity of the style of dance and decor with the subject matter revolutionized the ballet. His important works include *The Firebird* (1910) and *Petrouchka* (1911).

Ivanov, Lev (1834–1901). Russian choreographer. His most important ballets were *The Nutcracker* (1892) and the second and fourth acts of *Swan Lake* (1894).

Karsavina, Tamara (1885–1978). Russian dancer with the Ballets Russes and partner of Nijinsky. She created important roles in *The Firebird* and *Petrouchka* and wrote her autobiography, *Theatre Street*.

Lifar, Serge (1905–86). Russian dancer with the Ballets Russes (1923–29), where he created the title role in Balanchine's *Prodigal Son*. As director of the Paris Opera Ballet (1929–45, 1947–58), he reinvigorated French ballet, choreographing many works, including *Icare* (1935) and *Suite en blanc* (1943).

Makarova, Natalia (1940–). Russian dancer. A leading member of the Kirov Ballet (1959–70), she defected to the West, where she danced with the American Ballet Theater, the Royal Ballet, and other companies. She won a Tony for her performance in the musical *On Your Toes*.

Massine, Léonide (1895–1979). Russian-born dancer and choreographer with the Ballets Russes (1914–21, 1925–28) and the Ballet Russe de Monte Carlo (1932–42). His works include *Parade* (1917) and *Gaîté, Parisienne* (1938).

Nijinska, Bronislava (1891–1972). The sister of Vaslav Nijinsky, she also worked with the Ballets Russes as a dancer and innovative choreographer, incorporating sport and satire into ballet. Among her important ballets are *Les Noces* (1923) and *Les Biches* (1924).

Nijinsky, Vaslav (1889–1950). Polish-Russian dancer and choreographer with the Ballets Russes, creating important roles in Fokine's ballets, such as *Petrouchka*. Considered by many to be the greatest dancer of the 20th century, he also choreographed works such as *L'Après-midi d'un faune* (1912) and *Le Sacre du printemps* (1913), which were radical breaks with ballet tradition.

Nureyev, Rudolf (1938–93). Russian dancer with the Kirov Ballet. He defected to the West in 1961, where he often partnered Dame Margot Fonteyn with the Royal Ballet. A leading dancer of his time, he was noted for his virtuosity and animal sensuality. He was director of the Paris Opera from 1983 to 1989.

Pavlova, Anna Matveyevna (1881–1931). Russian ballerina. She danced briefly with the Ballets Russes and then toured with her own company, introducing ballet to people all over the world. An outstanding ballerina, she was known for her grace and lightness and the spiritual quality of her dancing.

Petipa, Marius (1818–1910). French-born dancer who became first ballet master of the Imperial Theater of St. Petersburg in 1862. Russian ballet reached its apogee under his direction. He was one of the leading choreographers in ballet history, and his works include *La Bayadère* (1877) and *The Sleeping Beauty* (1890).

Plisetskaya, Maya (1925–). Leading Russian ballerina with the Bolshoi Ballet, which she joined in

Performance Arts

1945. She is noted for her virtuosity and dramatic presence and for the pliancy of her arms.

Ulanova, Galina Sergeyevna (1910–   ). Russian dancer and teacher noted for her dramatic projection and lyricism. After joining the Kirov Ballet in 1928, she left to dance with the Bolshoi Ballet (1944–61), becoming the prima ballerina of Soviet ballet.

Youskevitch, Igor (1912–94). Russian-born dancer with the Ballet Russe de Monte Carlo (1938–44) and the Ballet Theater (1946–55). He was admired for his nobility and elegance and for his partnership with Alicia Alonso.

OTHER

Alonso, Alicia (1921–   ). Cuban dancer known for the purity of her classical style, particularly in the role of Giselle. After dancing with the American Ballet Theater and other companies, she founded the National Ballet of Cuba in 1959.

Bournonville, Auguste (1805–79). Danish choreographer. His Romantic works, such as *Napoli* (1842), form the core of the repertory of the Royal Danish Ballet.

Bruhn, Erik (1928–86). Danish-born dancer noted for his immaculate technique and nobility of style. After dancing with the American Ballet Theater and other companies, he was artistic director of the National Ballet of Canada (1983–86).

Cerrito, Fanny (1817–1909). Italian dancer, one of the leading ballerinas of the Romantic era. Noted for her strength and sensuous appeal, she created the leading role in *Ondine* (1843).

Elssler, Fanny (1810–84). Austrian daughter of an assistant to Franz Joseph Haydn, Elssler was one of the great ballerinas of the Romantic era, noted for her dramatic projection and earthiness. Her most famous dance was the Cachucha in *Le Diable boiteux* (1836).

Grisi, Carlotta (1819–99). Italian dancer with the Paris Opera. One of the great Romantic ballerinas, she created the title role in *Giselle,* whose libretto was written for her by Théophile Gautier.

Jooss, Kurt (1901–79). German choreographer whose theatrical works combined classical and modern modes of dance. His important works include *The Green Table,* a scathing indictment of war, and *Big City* (1932).

Taglioni, Marie (1804–84). Italian ballerina, the incarnation of the spiritual and lyrical ideal of the Romantic era. In the title role of *La Sylphide* (1832), she brought toe dancing to a new artistic level.

Wigman, Mary (1886–1973). German dancer and choreographer. The first major European modern dancer, Wigman choreographed somber works in an expressionist mode. Her works include *Totenmal* (1930).

COMMON DANCE TERMS

abstract dance   A plotless work composed of pure dance movements, although the composition may suggest a mood or subject.

adagio   Any dance to slow music; also, part of the classical pas de deux in ballet.

air, en l'   In ballet, a step done off the ground—for instance, tour en l'air, rond de jambe en l'air. It is the opposite of par terre.

allegro   A dance with a fast or moderate tempo.

allongé   In ballet, an elongated line; in particular, the horizontal line of an arabesque with one arm stretched front and the other back.

arabesque   In ballet, the extension of one leg straight in back at 90 degrees, with shoulders square; the position of the arms may vary.

assemblé   In ballet, a jump from one to both feet, usually landing in fifth position.

attitude   In ballet, a pose in which one leg is raised in back or in front with knee bent, usually with one arm raised.

balancé   A step that rocks from one foot to the other, usually in ¾ time.

ballet   From the Italian *balletto,* diminutive of *ballo,* "dance." Classical theatrical dancing based on the *danse d'école,* the rules and vocabulary that were codified around 1700 in France.

Performance Arts

ballet blanc   A ballet in which the women wear white tutus, such as the second and fourth acts of *Swan Lake.*

ballet d'action   A ballet with a plot, usually tragic, advocated by reformer Jean Georges Noverre, ballet master of the Paris Opera, to bring dramatic coherence to the performance of ballet.

ballet de cour, le (court ballet)   Spectacles for entertainment, usually with allegorical or mythological themes, performed by the aristocracy in the 16th and 17th centuries, combining music, recitatives, and mime.

ballo   Standard Italian dances and their music of the 15th and 16th centuries.

ballon   In ballet, the ability of a dancer to remain suspended in air during a jump; elasticity in jumping.

ballroom dances   Social dances usually performed by couples, including the fox-trot, waltz, tango, rumba, and cha cha.

bas, en   In ballet, low, as in placement of arms.

basic movement   In ballroom dance, a characteristic figure that remains constant.

basse danse   A solemn court dance usually in duple time, popular in the 15th and 16th centuries.

battement   A beating movement of the legs.

bourrée, pas de   A series of small, fast steps executed with the feet very close together.

brisé   In ballet, a jump off one foot that is "broken" by a beating of the legs in the air.

cabriole   In ballet, a leap in which the lower leg beats against the upper one at an angle, before the dancer lands again on the lower leg.

cachucha   A Spanish dance in ¾ or ⅜ time with castanets.

cakewalk   An African American dance in which couples strut and compete with high kicks and fast steps.

cambré   In ballet, a bend from the waist to the side or to the back.

cancan   Originating around 1830 as a social dance, by 1844 it had become a raucous dance performed in French music halls.

chassé   A sliding step in which one foot "chases" and displaces the other.

chat, pas de   Catlike leap in which one foot follows the other into the air, knees bent; the landing is in the fifth position.

ciseaux   A jump in which the legs open in second position in the air, resembling a scissors.

coda   In ballet, the third and final part of the classical pas de deux.

contraction   A basic movement in the technique of Martha Graham, based on breath inhalation and exhalation.

contredanse   Popular social dance during the 18th century; done in rows or circles, it may have derived from English country dancing.

corps de ballet   The members of a ballet company who do not perform solo.

country dance   Traditional English dance in which dancers form two facing lines.

croisée   In ballet, a position with the body at an oblique angle and the working leg crossing the line of the body.

danseur noble   A male dancer who performs the "princely" roles of the classical ballet, such as the Prince in *Swan Lake.*

dégagé   In ballet, shifting weight from one foot to the other.

développé   In ballet, an unfolding of the leg in the air.

écarté   In ballet, a position with one leg extended at an oblique angle while the body is also at an oblique angle.

effacé   In ballet, a position of the body at an oblique angle and partly hidden.

entrechat   A ballet movement in which the dancer repeatedly crosses his or her legs in the air.

épaulement   In ballet, the position of the torso from the waist up.

fandango   A lively Spanish dance in triple time performed with castanets or tambourines.

fermé   In ballet, a closed position of the feet.

five positions   In ballet, the basic positions of the feet. *First position:* feet in a straight line, heels touching. *Second position:* feet in a straight line, heels apart. *Third position:* one foot in front of the other, parallel to it, with heel of front foot in hollow instep of back foot. *Fourth position:* one foot in front of the other, parallel, but apart. *Fifth position:* one foot in front of the other, parallel, with heel in front foot touching toe of back foot. See illustrations on page 192.

flamenco   A Sevillian gypsy dance, possibly originating in India, also with Moorish and Arabian influences, originally accompanied by songs and clapping and later by the guitar, and characterized by its heelwork *(taconeo)*.

fondu   In ballet, a lowering of the body by bending the knee.

fouetté en tournant   A spectacular movement in which the dancer propels himself or herself around a supporting leg with rapid circular movements of the other leg while remaining in a fixed spot.

fox-trot   A social dance of American origin in duple time.

glissade   In ballet, a gliding step that usually connects two steps.

haut, en   In ballet, a position of the arms above the head.

jeté   In ballet, a leap from one leg to the other in which one leg is thrown to the side, front, or back. *Grand jeté:* a large leap forward.

jitterbug   A lively social dance popular during the 1930s; it originated at the Savoy Ballroom in Harlem in 1928, where it was known as the Lindy.

kabuki   A Japanese dance drama featuring stylized narrative choreographic movements.

mazurka   A Polish national dance in triple time with an accent on the second beat, characterized by proud bearing; clicking of heels; and *holubria,* a special turning step.

minuet   A slow and graceful dance, the most popular dance of the 18th century, characterized by symmetrical figures and elaborate curtsies and bows.

morris dance   An English folk dance that appeared in the 15th century, in which dancers wore bells on their legs and characters included a fool, a boy on a hobbyhorse, and a man in blackface.

ouvert   In ballet, an open position of the feet.

par terre   In ballet, steps performed on the floor. It is the opposite of en l'air.

pas de deux   A dance for two, usually a woman and a man. In its traditional form, it begins with an entrée and adagio, followed by solo variations for each dancer and a coda.

pavane   A grave, processional court dance popular in the 16th and 17th centuries.

penché   In ballet, leaning forward.

piqué   In ballet, stepping directly onto the point of a foot.

pirouette   A turn on one leg, with the toe of the other leg touching the knee of the turning leg.

plié   A bending of the knees in any of the five positions. *Demi plié:* a half bending of the knees, with heels on the floor. *Grand plié:* a full bending of the knees.

point   A position on the tip of the toes. *Demi-point:* a position on the balls of the feet.

polka   A Bohemian folk dance in duple time with a hop on the fourth beat. It became a popular ballroom dance in the mid–19th century.

port de bras   In ballet, the positions of the arms.

premier danseur   Principal male dancer.

promenade   In ballet, a slow turn of the body on the whole foot.

quadrille   A social dance popular in the 19th century. It was a square dance in five sections, each in a different time.

Performance Arts

reel   Popular in Britain, Ireland, and Scotland, it is a lively dance for two or more couples; also, the second part of the Virginia reel. The Highland fling is a variant.

relevé   In ballet, a rising with a spring movement to point or demi-point.

révérence   A ballet bow or curtsy in which one foot is pointed in front and the body leans forward.

spotting   A fixing of the eyes on one spot as long as possible during turns to avoid dizziness and to keep one's orientation.

square dance   An American folk dance with an even number of couples forming a square, two lines, or a circle. The dance consists of figures announced by a caller.

tango   A social dance in ⅔ time, which, after originating in Spain, developed in Argentina, where it was influenced by black dance style and rhythm.

tour en l'air   In ballet, a turn while jumping straight up in the air.

variation   Any solo performance in a ballet.

waltz   A social dance in ¾ time that became widely popular in the 19th century. It developed from the Landler, a German-Austrian turning dance.

MAJOR PLAYWRIGHTS

AMERICAN

Albee, Edward   (1928–   ). Playwright, producer, director. *Who's Afraid of Virginia Woolf?* (1962) made his reputation. Other works include *The Zoo Story* (1959), *A Delicate Balance* (1966), *Seascape* (1975), and *Three Tall Women* (1994).

Barry, Philip   (1896–1949). His most successful plays are witty and elegant comedies about the social elite. They deal with the true nature of love and marriage and with a quest for personal fulfillment. His works include *Holiday* (1929), *The Animal Kingdom* (1932), and *The Philadelphia Story* (1939).

Chayefsky, Paddy (Sidney)   (1923–81). Playwright and television writer and screenwriter. His most notable television plays, such as *Marty* (1953), and stage plays, such as *The Tenth Man* (1959), are

about the search for love as a source of spiritual redemption. His screenplays include *Network* (1976).

Guare, John   (1938–   ). Playwright known for satires and black comedies that explore American society, often within the context of family relationships. In addition to writing stage works such as *The House of Blue Leaves* (1971) and *Six Degrees of Separation* (1990), he also wrote the screenplay for *Atlantic City* (1980).

Hellman, Lillian   (1905–84). Dramatist. Her tightly constructed plays skillfully depict human perversity and evil. Among her best are *The Children's Hour* (1934), *The Little Foxes* (1939), and *Watch on the Rhine* (1941).

Henley, Beth   (1952–   ). Her dark, comedic plays contain elements of the Southern Gothic tradition. She is best known for *Crimes of the Heart* (1981), which won the Pulitzer prize.

Inge, William   (1913–1973). Playwright. His tightly constructed realistic dramas deal with small-town life in the American Midwest, giving form to the yearnings and the guilt of simple people. Among his best plays are *Come Back, Little Sheba* (1950), *Picnic* (1953), *Bus Stop* (1955), and *Dark at the Top of the Stairs* (1957).

Mamet, David   (1947–   ). Dramatist known for *American Buffalo* (1975). He was awarded the 1984 Pulitzer prize for *Glengarry Glenn Ross*, for which he also wrote the screenplay. Other works include *Speed the Plow* (1988), *Oleanna* (1992), and the screenplay for *Wag the Dog* (1998).

Miller, Arthur   (1915–   ). Outstanding contemporary dramatist. His concern with the moral problems of American society led him to probe the psychological causes of behavior. His classic *Death of a Salesman* (1949) won the Pulitzer prize; other plays include *The Crucible* (1953) and *A View from the Bridge* (1955).

Odets, Clifford   (1906–63). Leading playwright of the Group Theatre and the most important of the American social dramatists of the 1930s. His plays of social and political protest include *Waiting for Lefty* (1935) and *Awake and Sing* (1935). Among his other works are *Golden Boy* (1937), *The Big Knife* (1949), and *The Country Girl* (1951).

"Important Authors" in chapter 8 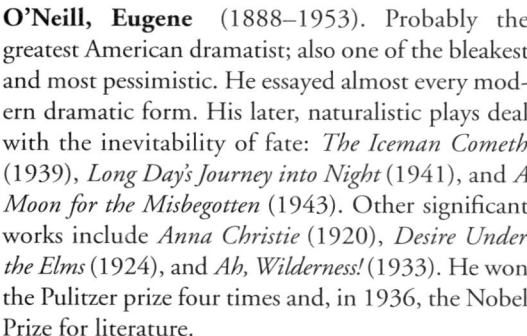 Go to

O'Neill, Eugene (1888–1953). Probably the greatest American dramatist; also one of the bleakest and most pessimistic. He essayed almost every modern dramatic form. His later, naturalistic plays deal with the inevitability of fate: *The Iceman Cometh* (1939), *Long Day's Journey into Night* (1941), and *A Moon for the Misbegotten* (1943). Other significant works include *Anna Christie* (1920), *Desire Under the Elms* (1924), and *Ah, Wilderness!* (1933). He won the Pulitzer prize four times and, in 1936, the Nobel Prize for literature.

Rabe, David (1940–). Dramatist known for his harsh view of American society. His best-known plays are *The Basic Training of Pavlo Hummel* (1973), *Streamers* (1976), and *Hurlyburly* (1984).

Saroyan, William (1908–81). Playwright and novelist. His essential theme is the triumph of child-like goodness over the corruption of a materialistic society. He won the Pulitzer prize for his classic *The Time of Your Life* (1939) but refused the award.

Shepard, Sam (1943–). Playwright and actor. Myth and reality clash in his plays, which explore the disintegration of American values and the chaos beneath. His works include *Operation Sidewinder* (1970); *Buried Child* (1978), which won a Pulitzer prize; and *Fool for Love* (1984).

Sherwood, Robert (1896–1955). Dramatist and biographer. His plays deal with the conflict between man's civilized values and his frequent descent into savagery. Among his best works are *The Petrified Forest* (1935), *Idiot's Delight* (1936), and *There Shall Be No Night* (1940).

Simon, Neil (1927–). Playwright and screenwriter. He has had more Broadway comedy hits than any other playwright. Among his well-known plays and musicals are *Barefoot in the Park* (1963); *The Odd Couple* (1965); *Sweet Charity* (1966); *The Sunshine Boys* (1972); *Brighton Beach Memoirs* (1983); and *Lost in Yonkers* (1991), which won the Pulitzer prize and Tony award.

Wasserstein, Wendy (1950–). Awarded the Pulitzer prize in 1989 for *The Heidi Chronicles,* Wasserstein focuses on the lives of modern women, their search for identity, and their attitude to the traditional roles projected for them.

Wilder, Thornton (1897–1975). Playwright, novelist, and essayist. His work is a celebration of human existence; he sees man and the universe as intimately related. His major plays are *Our Town* (1938), *The Skin of Our Teeth* (1942), which both won Pulitzer prizes, and *The Matchmaker* (1953).

Williams, Tennessee (1911–83). Probably the greatest American dramatist since Eugene O'Neill. His essential theme is the vulnerability of beauty to time and to a society dominated by violence. Among his most significant plays are *The Glass Menagerie* (1945); *A Streetcar Named Desire* (1947), which won a Pulitzer prize; *Summer and Smoke* (1948), *Cat on a Hot Tin Roof* (1955), which also won a Pulitzer; and *Night of the Iguana* (1961).

Wilson, August (1945–). One of the most acclaimed American dramatists. Wilson has chronicled the African American experience through each decade of the 20th century. He has won the Pulitzer prize twice, for *Fences* in 1987 and *The Piano Lesson* in 1990.

Wilson, Lanford (1937–). Dramatist and screenwriter whose works explore the conflict between traditional values and modern life. Among his best plays are *The Hot L Baltimore* (1973) and *Talley's Folly*, which won the Pulitzer prize in 1980.

BRITISH

Beaumont, Francis (c. 1584–1616). Jacobean dramatist, best known for his collaborations with John Fletcher. They developed a new form called "tragicomedy," which allowed for the treatment of serious themes without a tragic resolution. Their works include *Philaster* (1610) and *The Maid's Tragedy* (c. 1611). Beaumont alone wrote *The Knight of the Burning Pestle* (c. 1607), a burlesque of the historical romances of the time.

Churchill, Caryl (1938–). Playwright. Known for using experimental techniques, she examines contemporary society from a feminist and socialist point of view. Among her works are *Light Shining in Buckinghamshire* (1976), *Cloud Nine* (1981), and *Serious Money* (1982).

Coward, Noël   (1899–1973). Playwright, actor, composer, and director. His comedies present witty, stylish people acting in accordance with their unconventional morality and in league against more banal types. His best plays are *Private Lives* (1930), *Design for Living* (1930), and *Blithe Spirit* (1933).

Dekker, Thomas   (c. 1572–1632). Dramatist and pamphleteer. He centered his plays on contemporary life and merged Elizabethan romance with everyday realism, exhibiting sympathy for society's outcasts. His best plays are *The Shoemaker's Holiday* (1600), *The Honest Whore, Part I* (with Thomas Middleton, 1604; *Part II,* 1630), *Westward Ho!* (with John Webster, 1604), *The Roaring Girl* (with Middleton, 1607–08), and *The Witch of Edmonton* (with William Rowley and John Ford, 1621).

Eliot, Thomas Stearns (T. S.)   (1888–1965). Poet, critic, and playwright, born in America. He spearheaded a new interest in formal verse drama. His most admired play, *Murder in the Cathedral* (1935), derived its form from Greek tragedy, medieval morality plays, and church ritual. Other plays include *The Cocktail Party* (1949).

Fletcher, John   (1579–1625). Prolific and immensely popular playwright who collaborated with Francis Beaumont and many others, apparently including Shakespeare (*The Two Noble Kinsmen* [1613] and *Henry VIII* [1613]). Alone, Fletcher wrote two early tragedies, *Valentinian* (1610–14) and *Bonduca* (1609–14), and the comedies *Wit Without Money* (c. 1614) and *Rule a Wife and Have a Wife* (1624). He helped to lay the basis for the Restoration "comedy of manners."

Goldsmith, Oliver   (c. 1728–74). Irish-born essayist, poet, novelist, and comic playwright. He ridiculed the sentimental comedy of the time and promoted what he called "laughing comedy," designed to make us smile at our own follies. His comic masterpiece is *She Stoops to Conquer* (1773).

Hare, David   (1947–   ). Dramatist and screenwriter who often probes the political and moral condition of England and the world at large. In addition to writing plays such as *Slag* (1970), *Plenty* (1978), and *Pravda* (1985), he created the screenplay for *Strapless* (1990) and wrote *Licking Hitler* (1978) for British television.

Jonson, Ben   (1572–1637). Dramatist, poet, and literary critic. He developed the "comedy of humours," which featured characters dominated by one overruling passion. His masterpieces are *Volpone* (1605–06), *Epicoene* (1610), *The Alchemist* (1610), and *Bartholomew Fair* (1614).

Kyd, Thomas   (1558–94). Author of *The Spanish Tragedy* (1592), which introduced the theme of vengeance into Elizabethan drama; the "tragedy of revenge" became popular throughout the period. Kyd drew his inspiration from the Roman tragedies of Seneca.

Marlowe, Christopher   (1564–93). Poet and playwright who ushered in the great age of Elizabethan drama. His distinctive blank verse—called "Marlowe's mighty line"—established this verse style as a basic tool of Elizabethan playwrights. His masterpieces are *Tamburlaine the Great: Part I* (c. 1586–87; *Part II,* 1587), *Dr. Faustus* (c. 1588), *The Jew of Malta* (c. 1589), and *Edward II* (1591). Marlowe, often in trouble with the law, was murdered in 1593.

Middleton, Thomas   (c. 1570–1627). Jacobean dramatist with a dark and pessimistic vision of human corruption. In his comedies, the manners of the age are held up to scathing ridicule; his tragedies are remarkable for their penetrating psychological realism. His plays include *A Trick to Catch the Old One* (c. 1607), *A Chaste Maid in Cheapside* (1611), *The Changeling* (with William Rowley, 1622), and *Women Beware Women* (c. 1625).

Osborne, John   (1929–94). His work was fueled by a disgust for the quality of life in contemporary Britain. In the opening of his most famous play, *Look Back in Anger* (1956), his protagonist, Jimmy Porter, a working-class intellectual rebel, opens fire on the establishment. Among Osborne's other works are *The Entertainer* (1957), *Luther* (1961), and *Inadmissible Evidence* (1964).

Pinter, Harold   (1930–   ). Dramatist and actor. The motivation for the action in his plays is typically omitted; the characters evade real communication. The central motif is often two people in a room, involved in a seemingly commonplace situation that is gradually invested with menace, dread, and mystery. Pinter's language reproduces the inflections and rambling irrelevancy of everyday speech. His best plays include *The Birthday Party* (1958), *The Dumb Waiter* (1959), *The Homecoming* (1965), and *Betrayal* (1978).

Shakespeare, William (1564–1616). Elizabethan poet and dramatist. The most influential writer in English literature and perhaps the greatest dramatist of all time. His plays resonate with the full range of human emotion and experience. In his dramatic poetry, the English language reached perfection. As Ben Jonson wrote in his great tribute, "He was not of an age, but for all time!" Shakespeare wrote tragedies, comedies, and histories. His tragedies are *Titus Andronicus* (1594), *Romeo and Juliet* (c. 1595–96), *Julius Caesar* (1599), *Hamlet* (1602), *Othello* (1602–03), *Timon of Athens* (1604–05), *King Lear* (1605–06), *Macbeth* (1605–06), *Antony and Cleopatra* (1606–07), and *Coriolanus* (1607–10). His comedies are *The Comedy of Errors* (1591–94), *The Taming of the Shrew* (1593–94), *The Two Gentlemen of Verona* (1594–95), *Love's Labour's Lost* (1593–95), *A Midsummer Night's Dream* (1595–96), *The Merchant of Venice* (1596–97), *Much Ado About Nothing* (1598–99), *The Merry Wives of Windsor* (1598–99), *As You Like It* (1599–1600), *Twelfth Night* (1599–1600), *Troilus and Cressida* (1601–02), *All's Well That Ends Well* (1602–03), *Measure for Measure* (1603–04), *Pericles* (1606–08), *Cymbeline* (1609–10), *The Winter's Tale* (1610–11), and *The Tempest* (1611). The histories are *Henry VI: Part I* (1589–91), *Henry VI: Part II* (1590–91), *Henry VI: Part III* (1590–91), *Richard III* (1593), *Richard II* (1595), *King John* (1596–97), *Henry IV: Part I* (1597–98), *Henry IV: Part II* (1597–98), *Henry V* (1598–99), and *Henry VIII* (1613).

Shaw, George Bernard (1856–1950). Irish-born dramatist, journalist, critic, and Fabian socialist. His plays combine brilliant, incisive wit with a moral purpose: to expose the follies of the contemporary social order. He created a "drama of ideas," in which philosophical discussion becomes a theatrical event. Among his best-known works are *Arms and the Man* (1894), *Man and Superman* (1905), *Major Barbara*

(1905), *Pygmalion* (1912), *Heartbreak House* (1913–19), and *Saint Joan* (1923).

Sheridan, Richard Brinsley (1751–1816). Irish-born comic playwright, theatrical manager, and politician. Sheridan sought to restore a comedy of wit to the post-Restoration theater, which had been engulfed by middle-class moralizing. His masterpieces are *The Rivals* (1775) and *The School for Scandal* (1777).

Stoppard, Tom (1937–). Playwright, born in Czechoslovakia. Heavily influenced by Beckett and the Theatre of the Absurd, he is best known for *Rosencrantz and Guildenstern Are Dead* (1967), *The Real Inspector Hound* (1968), *Arcadia* (1993), and *The Invention of Love* (1997).

Tourneur, Cyril (1575–1626). Jacobean dramatist, author of two famous tragedies of revenge, both based on Senecan drama: *The Revenger's Tragedy* (1606–07: the authorship of this play is in dispute but is generally ascribed to Tourneur) and *The Atheist's Tragedy* (1607–11).

Webster, John (c. 1580–1634). Jacobean dramatist and creator of two outstanding tragedies, *The White Devil* (1609–12) and *The Duchess of Malfi* (1613–14). His vision was one of dark, brooding pessimism.

Wilde, Oscar (1854–1900). Irish-born playwright, novelist, poet, and aesthete. Famous for his epigrammatic wit and for his eccentricity in dress and lifestyle, Wilde used his satirical gifts to expose the shallowness and hypocrisy of Victorian society. His comic masterpiece is *The Importance of Being Earnest* (1895).

FRENCH

Anouilh, Jean (1910–87). Dramatist and screenwriter. His plays, which are laced with humor, deal with the impossibility of purity surviving in a world dominated by compromise. Among his best-known works are *Thieves' Carnival* (1932), *Antigone* (1944), *The Waltz of the Toreadors* (1952), and *The Lark* (1953).

Beckett, Samuel (1906–89). Playwright and novelist, born in Ireland. One of the originators of the Theatre of the Absurd, he mixes comedy with existential anguish to express the dilemma of 20th-century man. His major works include *Waiting for Godot* (1952) and *Endgame* (1957). He was awarded the 1969 Nobel Prize for literature.

Corneille, Pierre (1606–84). The first of the great French neoclassic dramatists. His early masterpiece, *Le Cid* (1637), was harshly criticized by the French Academy because it did not adhere to the "classical unities." All his later tragedies followed the rules. Other works include *Horace* (1640), *Cinna* (1640–41), and *Polyeuctes* (1641–42).

Genet, Jean (1919–86). Novelist and preeminent dramatist of the Theatre of the Absurd. In the face of the void, his deeply alienated characters assume inauthentic roles, which become ritualized. Genet's best plays include *The Maids* (1947), *The Balcony* (1956), and *The Blacks* (1959).

Giraudoux, Jean (1882–1944). Novelist and dramatist. Many of his plays are reinterpretations of Greek myth. Among his best works are *Tiger at the Gates* (1935) and *The Madwoman of Chaillot* (1946).

Hugo, Victor Marie (1802–85). Poet, novelist, playwright, and politician; he was the acknowledged leader of French Romanticism. The famous "battle" that disrupted the premiere of his tragedy *Hernani* (1830) marked a watershed in the history of the Romantic movement. Other plays include *The King Amuses Himself* (1832—the source for Verdi's *Rigoletto*), *Ruy Blas* (1838), and *The Burgraves* (1843).

Ionesco, Eugene (1912–94). Dramatist, born in Romania. One of the leading exponents of the Theatre of the Absurd. At the core of his work is the idea that human existence, language, and effort are essentially meaningless. His most famous plays are *The Bald Soprano* (1950), *The Lesson* (1951), and *Rhinoceros* (1959).

Molière (Jean Baptiste Poquelin) (1622–73). Actor, director, and theater manager. He took the stylized comic archetypes of the commedia dell'arte and made them human, while retaining the "flaw" that always led them to folly. The result was a new genre, "character comedy." His satires caused great controversy. His greatest plays are *The School for Wives* (1662), *Tartuffe* (1664), *The Misanthrope*

(1666), *The Miser* (1668), and *The Bourgeois Gentleman* (1670).

Racine, Jean (1639–99). Exemplar of French classicism and master of the Alexandrine line. The classical unities of time, place, and action provided an ideal framework for the concise action of his tragedies. His protagonists are usually driven by a single, dominant passion. His greatest works are *Andromache* (1667), *Bérénice* (1670), *Phèdre* (1676), and *Athalie* (1691).

Rostand, Edmund (1868–1918). Poet and dramatist, responsible for the brief revival of the romantic spirit in the era of naturalism. His one masterpiece, *Cyrano de Bergerac* (1897), is a tour de force of dramatic poetry.

Sartre, Jean-Paul (1905–80). Philosopher, novelist, essayist, and playwright. His dramas expound his existential philosophy: that man is essentially free, in a universe without God; and that he is defined by his own acts and is obliged to choose responsibly. Among his best-known works are *No Exit* (1944) and *Dirty Hands* (1948). Sartre won the Nobel Prize for literature in 1964.

GERMAN

Brecht, Bertolt (1895–1956). Playwright, poet, stage director, and theorist. He created "epic theater," the purpose of which was to make people first *think,* and only later feel, about what they were seeing. The technique he used was alienation—the creation of emotional distance between the spectator and the event. Paradoxically, his ironic dramas are deeply moving. Among his greatest plays are *In the Jungle of Cities* (1923), *The Threepenny Opera* (1928), *Galileo* (1938–39), *Mother Courage and Her Children* (1941), and *The Good Woman of Setzuan* (1943).

Buchner, Georg (1813–37). Three plays established Buchner as a seminal figure. His themes were distinctly modern: man's loneliness, his helplessness before the events of history and the conditions of society, and the absurdity of a world without God. Works by Buchner include *Danton's Death* (1835) and *Woyzeck* (1836).

GREEK

Aeschylus (525–456 B.C.). The originator of Greek tragedy as we know it. He added a second actor to the drama (thus making true stage dialogue possible), and he raised tragic diction to the level of grandeur. He explored themes of cosmic justice and the transmission of evil from generation to generation. He probably wrote some 90 plays, of which 7 survive complete, including *Prometheus Bound* (466–459 B.C.) and the trilogy *The Oresteia* (458 B.C.).

Aristophanes (c. 445–385 B.C.). The only surviving (and probably greatest) writer of Attic (ancient Athenian) old comedy. His freewheeling and joyous plays blend political satire, personal lampoon, portraits of domestic life, dance, music, and fantasy. Only 11 of his more than 40 plays survive, including *The Acharnians* (425 B.C.), *The Clouds* (423 B.C.), *The Wasps* (422 B.C.), *Peace* (422 B.C.), *The Birds* (414 B.C.), *Lysistrata* (411 B.C.), and *The Frogs* (405 B.C.).

Euripides (480–406 B.C.). Last of the great Greek tragedians. Influenced by the rationalism of the sophists, Euripides was distinctively modern. The depth of his characterization was new to the Attic stage, prefiguring psychological realism. His hatred of war was the mainspring of some of his best dramas. He wrote 92 plays, of which 19 survive, including *Alcestis* (438), *Medea* (431), *The Trojan Women* (415), *Electra* (413), *Iphegenia in Tauris* (412), *Orestes* (408), and *The Bacchae* (405).

Sophocles (c. 496–406 B.C.). The second of the great Greek tragedians. He introduced a third speaking actor, thus making possible more complex dramatic interactions. By creating self-contained works rather than the customary trilogies, he narrowed the focus to one solitary individual at the critical moment of his life, refusing to yield to time or circumstance. He wrote approximately 123 plays, of which 7 survive, including *Antigone* (c. 442–441 B.C.), *Oedipus Rex* (c. 430–426 B.C.), *Electra* (c. 409 B.C.), and *Oedipus at Colonus* (c. 404–401 B.C.).

IRISH

O'Casey, Sean (1880–1964). His plays present an antiheroic view of life, alternately tragic and comic. He mocked sentimental patriotism by looking at the brutality of war through the eyes of working-class Irish women. Among his best works are *The Shadow of a Gunman* (1923), *Juno and the Paycock* (1924), and *The Plough and the Stars* (1926).

Synge, John Millington (1871–1909). Poet and dramatist. His Irish peasant characters aspire to a wild life of freedom and fantasy, which they achieve in imagination as expressed through their powerful and poetic Irish idiom. Among his works are *In the Shadow of the Glen* (1903), *Riders to the Sea* (1904), and *The Playboy of the Western World* (1907). Synge was cofounder of the Abbey Theatre in Dublin, with William Butler Yeats and Lady Gregory.

ROMAN

Plautus (c. 251–184 B.C.). Popular comic playwright. His plays were based on Greek comedy and performed in Greek dress. A typical plot presents a young lover kept from his beloved by a stubborn father, a greedy pimp, or lack of money. A clever slave contrives an elaborate intrigue to unite the lovers, and the play follows the ups and downs of the scheme. Among his surviving works are *Pseudolus* (191 B.C.) and *The Menaechmi* (date unknown).

Seneca (4 B.C.–A.D. 65). Tragic playwright, stoic philosopher, and statesman. The form of his plays follows the conventions of Greek tragedy, but the content reflects his concern with the stoic absolutes of passion and reason. His plays deal with the triumph of evil in a single human soul and its devastating impact on the outer world. Nine of his plays survive, including *Agamemnon, Medea*, and *Phaedra* (dates unknown).

RUSSIAN

Chekhov, Anton Pavlovich (1860–1904). Great modern dramatist and short-story writer. He depicts the provincial aristocracy before the revolution, trapped in a stultifying environment and paralyzed by a lack of will. Stanislavsky's productions at the Moscow Art Theatre of Chekhov's greatest plays—*The Seagull* (1896), *Uncle Vanya* (1899), *The Three*

Sisters (1901), and *The Cherry Orchard* (1904)—made the Russian theater famous throughout the world.

Gorky, Maxim (Alexei Maximovich Peshkov) (1868–1936). Russian novelist, short-story writer, and playwright. Writing out of his own experience of poverty, he won international fame for his drama of the slums, *The Lower Depths* (1902).

SPANISH

Calderón de la Barca, Pedro (1600–81). Poet and last great playwright of the Spanish Golden Age. He wrote more than 200 full-length plays, as well as more than 70 one-act sacramental dramas, called "autos." In a time when the Spanish Empire was crumbling, his essential themes were faith and honor. Among his best-known plays are *The Phantom Lady* (1629), *Life Is a Dream* (1631–32), *Devotion to the Cross* (1633), *Secret Vengeance for Secret Insult* (1635), and *The Mayor of Zalamea* (1640–44).

García Lorca, Federico (1899–1936). Spanish poet and playwright, executed by Franco's soldiers soon after the outbreak of the Spanish Civil War. His poetic tragedies deal with the conflict between the individual and society—a conflict particularly bitter in Spain, where life was tightly regulated by an unyielding conservative moral code. His most famous plays are *Blood Wedding* (1933), *Yerma* (1934), and *The House of Bernarda Alba* (1936).

Molina, Tirso de (Gabriel Tellez) (c. 1571–1648). A disciple of Lope de Vega and the second great dramatist of the Spanish Golden Age. His most famous play is *The Trickster of Seville* (c. 1625), in which he created the great modern myth of Don Juan.

Vega Carpio, Lope de (1562–1635). Member of the Spanish Armada and the first great dramatist of the Spanish Golden Age. He established the *commedia* (new comedy) as the principal dramatic form in the Spain of his time. His works include *The Peasant in his Nook* (1611–15), *Fuenteovejuna* (1612), *The King's the Best Magistrate* (1620–23), and *The Knight from Olmedo* (1620–25).

OTHER

Ibsen, Henrik (1828–1906). Norwegian playwright. Generally credited with being the "father of modern drama," he demonstrated the power of psychological realism. His plays often present individuals in bitter conflict with the norms of society. His masterpieces include *Peer Gynt* (1867), *A Doll's House* (1879), *Ghosts* (1881), *An Enemy of the People* (1883), *The Wild Duck* (1884), and *Hedda Gabler* (1891).

Pirandello, Luigi (1867–1936). Italian dramatist and novelist, winner of the 1934 Nobel Prize for literature. The playwright par excellence of the conflict between illusion and reality, he depicts with eloquence the isolation of the individual from society and from himself. Among his best-known plays are *Right You Are—If You Think You Are* (1917), *Six Characters in Search of an Author* (1921), and *The Man with the Flower in His Mouth* (1923).

Strindberg, Johan August (1849–1912). Swedish playwright and seminal modern dramatist, best known for his intensely psychological plays about tormented male-female relationships. His later plays prefigure expressionism. Among his best-known works are *The Father* (1887), *Miss Julie* (1889), *The Dance of Death* (*Part I* and *Part II*—1900), and *A Dream Play* (1902).

MAJOR FILM DIRECTORS

AMERICAN

Capra, Frank (1897–1991), b. Sicily. A pioneer of screwball comedy with the Academy Award–winning *It Happened One Night* (1934), he is best known for fast-paced populist comedy-dramas such as *Mr. Deeds Goes to Town* (1936) and *Mr. Smith Goes to Washington* (1939) that show the triumph of the individual against the system. His Christmas fable *It's a Wonderful Life* (1946) is a television staple.

Coppola, Francis Ford (1939–), b. Michigan. In signature works *The Godfather* (1972) and *The Godfather, Part II* (1974), he fused his strengths—epic scale, operatic staging, and understanding of family conflict—into modern film tragedy. Other films, such as *Apocalypse Now* (1979), *Peggy Sue Got Married* (1986), and *The Godfather, Part III* (1990),

A Brief History of Film

Experiments in motion pictures began in the United States and Europe during the late 19th century. American inventor Thomas Alva Edison patented the first movie machine, the Kinetoscope, in 1891. Four years later, French inventors Louis and Auguste Lumière demonstrated the camera-projector called the *cinématographe*. American filmmaker Edwin S. Porter's eight-minute *The Great Train Robbery* (1903) launched the movies as mass entertainment.

American filmmakers soon became preeminent. Major studios were situated in New York, with D. W. Griffith the medium's most influential director. In dozens of films, he developed a grammar of shots and lighting effects to evoke audience emotion. His highly successful *The Birth of a Nation* (1915) pioneered the idea of film as art.

Between 1910 and 1920, American filmmaking shifted to Hollywood. Leading directors such as Cecil B. De Mille (*The Ten Commandments,* 1923), Ernst Lubitsch (*The Marriage Circle,* 1924), and John Ford (*The Iron Horse,* 1924) offered a variety of genres—epics, romantic comedies, and westerns. Mack Sennett pioneered film slapstick with the Keystone Cops and introduced English comic Charlie Chaplin. Portraying the forlorn "Tramp" in *The Kid* (1921), *The Gold Rush* (1925), and others, Chaplin became one of the first international movie stars.

Several other countries established themselves as filmmaking centers. Germany was the birthplace of the expressionist movement, embodied in Robert Weine's *The Cabinet of Dr. Caligari* (1919). In Russia, Sergei Eisenstein's *Potemkin* (1925) epitomized the idea of *montage*. France became a rich film source, with such humanistic directors as René Clair and Abel Gance.

The 1927 U.S. film *The Jazz Singer* introduced sound to movies, revolutionizing the industry worldwide. Genres requiring witty or action-oriented dialogue, such as gangster movies and screwball comedies, gained primacy, as did extravagant musicals. The American studios, including Metro-Goldwyn-Mayer, Paramount, and Warner Bros., honed a "studio system" that produced a steady stream of films and stars for Depression-era audiences seeking escape. American stars of the period included James Cagney, Bette Davis, Clark Gable, Cary Grant, and Katharine Hepburn. The system reached its apex in 1939, with dozens of now-classic films, including the Civil War epic *Gone with the Wind* (1939).

High artistic achievements marked European cinema during the years before WWII. Notable films included Jean Renoir's antiwar classic *Grand Illusion* (1937) and Leni Riefenstahl's Nazi paean *Triumph of the Will* (1935).

WWII and its aftermath also brought heightened realism to international filmmaking. Italian directors Roberto Rossellini and Vittorio De Sica ushered in neorealism with, respectively, *Open City* (1949) and *The Bicycle Thief* (1945). Countering the trend toward realism were such stylized, idiosyncratic filmmakers as Italy's Federico Fellini (*La Dolce Vita,* 1960) and Swedish psychological master Ingmar Bergman (*The Seventh Seal,* 1956).

In the 1950s and 1960s, a group of French directors (many of them film critics), initiated the *nouvelle vague* (new wave). This movement of quirky, original films included François Truffaut's *The Four Hundred Blows* (1959) and Jean-Luc Godard's *Breathless* (1960). German cinema reinvented itself after WWII with the varied social critiques of directors Werner Herzog, Wim Wenders, and Rainer Werner Fassbinder (*The Marriage of Maria Braun,* 1979).

Nonwestern cinema gained an international following after World War II through the works of Japanese directors Akira Kurosawa (*Rashomon,* 1950) and Yasujiro Ozu (*Tokyo Story,* 1953) and Indian filmmaker Satyajit Ray (*Pather Panchali,* 1955). National cinemas that have come to prominence since the 1970s include those of Australia and New Zealand, the former offering such filmmakers as Peter Weir and the latter, Jane Campion.

Changing tastes, decreasing film attendance, and corporate takeovers effectively destroyed the American studio system by the end of the 1960s. In its wake came increased experimentation and independence through filmmakers such as Stanley Kubrick, Robert Altman, Francis Ford Coppola (*The Godfather,* 1972) and Martin Scorsese (*Raging Bull,* 1980). In recent years, independent studios have grown in stature, becoming known for supporting high-quality original filmmaking such as Quentin Tarantino's *Pulp Fiction* (1994).

American films since the 1970s have been distinguished by the big-budget blockbuster. Primarily special-effects-laden fare, the blockbuster has been dominated by two directors: George Lucas and Steven Spielberg. Lucas's *Star Wars* (1977) and its sequels made hundreds of millions of dollars. With *Jaws* (1975) and *E.T.* (1982), Spielberg became the leading director of big-budget, high-tech films. However, director James Cameron's *Titanic* (1997) eclipsed all previous records for gross revenues and garnered 11 Academy Awards as well. Despite the success of blockbusters such as *The Matrix* (1999) and *Gladiator* (2000), small films like *Shakespeare in Love* (1998) and *Boys Don't Cry* (1999) surprised the industry by doing relatively well commercially.

Performance Arts

have varied in subject matter but share Coppola's ambitiousness.

De Mille, Cecil B. (1881–1959), b. Massachusetts. Specializing at first in spicy modern narratives, he became known as the master of religious and historical epics such as *The Ten Commandments* (1923; remade 1956). He is credited with helping to establish Hollywood as a film capital. His sweeping entertainments include *The Sign of the Cross* (1932), *Samson and Delilah* (1949), and *The Greatest Show on Earth* (1952).

Ford, John (1895–1973), b. Maine. The most celebrated and enduring American director, he combined strong storytelling and visual poetry in classic meditations on the country's conflict between frontier and civilization. Though successful in silents (*The Iron Horse,* 1924), he left his legacy in sound films. He won the Academy Award for best director for three films: *The Grapes of Wrath* (1940), *How Green Was My Valley* (1941), and *The Quiet Man* (1952). Other influential works include *Stagecoach* (1939), *My Darling Clementine* (1946), and *The Searchers* (1956).

Griffith, D. W. (1875–1948), b. Kentucky. A pioneer in shaping the medium, and American cinema's standard bearer, he infused cinematic power into basic techniques of camera use, editing, and lighting. His Civil War epic *Birth of a Nation* (1915) is a hallmark in the development of film as art. Other major films from his hundreds of works include *Intolerance* (1916), *Broken Blossoms* (1919) and *Orphans of the Storm* (1922). His career ended soon after the advent of sound film.

Hawks, Howard (1896–1977), b. Indiana. Prized for his storytelling ability and stylistic economy, he directed definitive works in several genres: gangster dramas (*Scarface,* 1932), screwball comedy (*Bringing Up Baby,* 1938; *His Girl Friday,* 1940), action films (*Only Angels Have Wings,* 1939), and westerns (*Red River,* 1948). He introduced actress Lauren Bacall in *To Have and Have Not* (1944), with Humphrey Bogart; insolent and fearless, the two actors embody the ideal Hawksian man and woman. He won an honorary Academy Award (1974).

Kubrick, Stanley (1928–99), b. New York. He left a career as a still photographer to become a cool,

meticulous maker of visually stunning films. His sardonic, often pessimistic works include *Paths of Glory* (1957), *Dr. Strangelove* (1964), *2001: A Space Odyssey* (1968), *A Clockwork Orange* (1971), and *Full Metal Jacket* (1987). He resided in Britain from the 1960s until his death.

Lang, Fritz (1890–1976), b. Austria. In Germany, his expressionist films *Dr. Mabuse* (1922), *Metropolis* (1927), and *M* (1931) conveyed tension and inexorable fate. He left Germany in 1933 after his film *The Testament of Dr. Mabuse* (1933) was banned by Nazis. He directed several films in Hollywood, many concerning injustice or corruption, including *Fury* (1936), *Hangmen Also Die* (1943), and *The Big Heat* (1953).

George Lucas was riding in a car with a friend when the car went over a bump. His friend said, "Oops, I just ran over a wookie back there." Thus was created the word that George later used in the Star Wars *films.*

Lubitsch, Ernst (1892–1947), b. Germany. With the wit, visual brevity, and sexual polish known as "the Lubitsch Touch," he directed scores of sophisticated comedies, musicals, and dramas in Germany and America. Many remain classics: *The Marriage Circle* (1924), *The Love Parade* (1929), *Monte Carlo* (1930), *Trouble in Paradise* (1932), *Ninotchka* (1939). He received an honorary Academy Award in 1937.

Scorsese, Martin (1942–), b. New York. Over decades of rough urban dramas, he has defined New York City as an underworld where denizens find resolution and redemption through violence. Notable New York films include *Mean Streets* (1973), *Taxi Driver* (1976), *GoodFellas* (1990), and *Raging Bull* (1980), hailed by some as the finest American film of the decade. Other films include *The Color of Money* (1986) and *The Age of Innocence* (1993). He is active in film preservation.

Soderbergh, Steven (1963–), b. Atlanta. Soderbergh received acclaim for his first feature, the independent film *Sex, Lies, and Videotape* (1989), which he both wrote and directed. Nominated for an Academy Award for Best Director for both *Erin Brokovich* and *Traffic* in 2000, he won for the latter.

Spielberg, Steven (1947–   ), b. Ohio. One of the most commercially successful directors in film history, he specializes in big-budget adventure or science-fiction films that include *Jaws* (1975), *Close Encounters of the Third Kind* (1977), *Raiders of the Lost Ark* (1981), *E.T.* (1982), and *Jurassic Park* (1993). He gained respect with the Holocaust drama *Schindler's List* (1993), which won an Academy Award for best picture, and *Saving Private Ryan* (1998).

Welles, Orson (1915–85), b. Wisconsin. His stunning first film *Citizen Kane* (1941) influenced generations of filmmakers in its structure, composition, and cinematography—and the audacity of its maker, who became a lifelong boy wonder. Although later films were often compromised by studio intervention or self-indulgence, many are exceptional: *The Magnificent Ambersons* (1942), *The Lady From Shanghai* (1948), and *Touch of Evil* (1958).

Wilder, Billy (1906–2002), b. Austria. Blending masterful timing, wit, and worldliness, he created some of Hollywood's smartest comedies and most cynical dramas. Notable works include *Double Indemnity* (1944), *Sunset Boulevard* (1950), *Stalag 17* (1953), *Sabrina* (1954), and *Some Like It Hot* (1959). *The Lost Weekend* (1945) and *The Apartment* (1960) won Academy Awards for best picture and director.

ASIAN

Chen Kaige (1952–   ), b. China. A major presence in post–Cultural Revolution filmmaking, he is known for his mix of high drama and emotional subtlety in such films as *Yellow Earth* (1984), *King of Children* (1987), and *Farewell My Concubine* (1993). His early cinematographer, Zhang Yimou, also became a noted director.

Kurosawa, Akira (1910–98), b. Japan. The humanistic filmmaker's ability to convey universal messages in works like *Drunken Angel* (1948) and *Rashomon* (1950) has bridged cultures and brought decades of worldwide appeal. His samurai films have been influential: *The Seven Samurai* (1954) inspired *The Magnificent Seven* (1960); *Hidden Fortress* (1958) informed the *Star Wars* trilogy. Other notable films include *Yojimbo* (1961) and pioneering Shakespeare adaptations, *Throne of Blood* (1957) and *Ran* (1985).

Lee, Ang (1954–   ), b. Taiwan. Ang Lee's 1993 film *The Wedding Banquet* was the first film from Taiwan to earn an Academy Award nomination for Best Foreign Language Film, and his work *Crouching Tiger, Hidden Dragon* (2000) was the first Asian film to win in that category. Lee's other works include *Eat Drink Man Woman* (1994), *Sense and Sensibility* (1995), and *The Ice Storm* (1997).

Ozu, Yasujiro (1903–63), b. Japan. With films like *The Flavor of Green Tea over Rice* (1952) and *Tokyo Story* (1953), he is renowned for his simply filmed, delicate dramas of middle-class family life. He is also praised in his country for capturing Japan's national sensibility. Other representative films include *Early Spring* (1956) and *Late Autumn* (1961).

Ray, Satyajit (1921–92), b. Calcutta. Acclaimed for his humanity and subtle cinematic style, he gained early success with *Pather Panchali* (1955), the first entry in his "Apu Trilogy," about a Bengali child. Other parts are *The Unvanquished* (1957) and *The World of Apu* (1958). Later, more thematically and cinematically daring films include *The Lonely Wife* (1964) and *Distant Thunder* (1973). He won an honorary Academy Award (1992).

BRITISH

Chaplin, Charles (1889–1977), b. England. The preeminent director and star of silent film immortalized his "Tramp" character in films including *The Tramp* (1915) and *The Kid* (1921). Cofounding the studio United Artists, he directed some of his finest works for it: *The Gold Rush* (1925), *City Lights* (1931), and *Modern Times* (1936). His increasingly serious sound films include *The Great Dictator* (1940), *Monsieur Verdoux* (1947), and *Limelight* (1952). Accused of Communist affiliations, he was denied reentry to the United States in 1952 and did not return for 20 years. He won special Academy Awards in 1927–1928 and 1972. He was knighted in 1975.

Performance Arts

Hitchcock, Alfred (1899–1980), b. England. Cinema's unmatched master of suspense built his international reputation in the 1930s with British thrillers *The Man Who Knew Too Much* (1934, remade 1956), *The 39 Steps* (1935), and *The Lady Vanishes* (1938). In Hollywood, his works became more lavish and cinematically refined, with top stars and crew. Some classic works include *Notorious* (1946), *Rear Window* (1954), *Vertigo* (1958), *North by Northwest* (1959), and *Psycho* (1960).

Lean, David (1908–91), b. England. He gained early notice with his literary adaptations *Brief Encounter* (1945) and *Great Expectations* (1946) but is most respected for his grand, ironic epics, notably *The Bridge on the River Kwai* (1957) and *Lawrence of Arabia* (1962). Blending human drama and 20th-century history, each won the Academy Award for best picture. Later films include *Doctor Zhivago* (1965) and *A Passage to India* (1984). He was knighted in 1984.

Powell, Michael (1905–90), b. England, and **Emeric Pressburger** (1902–88), b. Hungary. Successful filmmakers alone, they are renowned for their literate, visually stunning collaborations in the 1940s and 1950s. Among them are *The Life and Death of Colonel Blimp* (1943), *I Know Where I'm Going* (1945), *Black Narcissus* (1947), and the quintessential ballet film *The Red Shoes* (1948). Powell faced severe criticism following his study of a psychopath, *Peeping Tom* (1960).

FRENCH

Godard, Jean-Luc (1930–   ), b. France. Beginning with *Breathless* (1960), the former film critic influenced French New Wave and avant-garde filmmaking with his visually surprising, improvisational works. Acclaimed works of the period also include *The Little Soldier* (1960) and *Alphaville* (1965). By the late 1960s, he became more formless and didactic in works such as *Masculine Feminine* (1966) and *Weekend* (1968). After a hiatus, he turned to more humanistic filmmaking, with *First Name: Carmen* (1983) and others.

Renoir, Jean (1894–1979), b. France. Son of impressionist painter Auguste Renoir, he is unsurpassed at conveying the human condition through poetic, fluid filmmaking. The antiwar classic *Grand Illusion* (1937) and social meditation *The Rules of the Game* (1939) are considered his masterpieces. Other works include *Boudu Saved from Drowning* (1932), *Toni* (1935), and *The Crime of Monsieur Lange* (1936).

Truffaut, François (1932–84), b. France. Beginning with *The 400 Blows* (1959), he established himself as the central force of French New Wave. Tender and exuberant, his films are also renowned for their insight into human emotions. Among other major works are *Shoot the Piano Player* (1960), *Jules and Jim* (1961), and *The Wild Child* (1970). Notable books include *Hitchcock/Truffaut* (1983).

GERMAN

Fassbinder, Rainer Werner (1946–82), b. Germany. His spirited, iconoclastic dramas about modern German society made him a major force in rebuilding German cinema after World War II. A feverish worker, he made up to four films per year until his death at 36. Representative works include *Effi Briest* (1974), *Despair* (1978), *The Marriage of Maria Braun* (1979), and *Veronika Voss* (1982).

Murnau, F. W. (1888–1931), b. Germany. With *Nosferatu the Vampire* (1922) and *The Last Laugh* (1924), he refined a visually expressive style that influenced generations of filmmakers. His first U.S. work, *Sunrise* (1927), is considered one of the most beautiful works in film history. Other U.S. films include *Our Daily Bread* (1930) and *Tabu* (1931), codirected with Robert Flaherty.

Ophüls, Max (1902–57), b. Germany. Prizing *mise-en-scéne* above plot, he was a master of fluid camera work and lush decor with an otherworldly, baroque quality that suited his often romantic tales. Among his most acclaimed works are *Letter from an Unknown Woman* (1948), *La Ronde* (1950), *The Earrings of Madame De* (1953), and *Lola Montez* (1955). His son is filmmaker Marcel Ophüls.

ITALIAN

Antonioni, Michelangelo (1912–   ), b. Italy. A major force in postwar Italian cinema, he is noted for conveying the emotional void of modern existence in such works as *The Red Desert* (1964), *L'Avventura* (1960), *Blow-Up* (1966), and *The Pas-*

senger (1975). He is expert in using the physical world to communicate metaphysical and psychological states.

De Sica, Vittorio   (1902–74), b. Italy. With *Shoeshine* (1946) and *The Bicycle Thief* (1948), he made two pivotal (and Academy Award–winning) works of Italian neorealism. Other of his humane, varied works include *Umberto D* (1952); *The Condemned of Altona* (1962); *Yesterday Today and Tomorrow* (1963); and *The Garden of the Finzi-Continis* (1971); the last two winning foreign-film Academy Awards.

Fellini, Federico   (1920–93), b. Italy. Humanistic, sharply observed, and sensual, he is Italy's most beloved and acclaimed filmmaker. He gained international fame with the autobiographical *I Vitelloni* (1953) and followed with *La Strada* (1954), which won the Academy Award for best foreign film. Other milestone films include *The Nights of Cabiria* (1957) and *8½* (1963), also Academy Award winners for best foreign film; *La Dolce Vita* (1960); the psychological study *Juliet of the Spirits* (1965); and the playful *Amarcord* (1973).

OTHER

Almodóvar, Pedro   (1951–   ), b. Spain. Perhaps Spain's best-known modern filmmaker, Almodóvar's early films such as *Dark Habits* (1984) became cult hits. He gained international notoriety with *Women on the Verge of a Nervous Breakdown* (1988). *All About My Mother* (1999) won the Academy Award for Best Foreign Language Film.

Bergman, Ingmar   (1918–   ), b. Sweden. Early films *Smiles of a Summer Night* (1955) and *The Seventh Seal* (1957) won prizes at the Cannes Film Festival and established his ability to portray human relationships and explore religious and philosophical concerns, often crises of faith and personal detachment. Other works include *Wild Strawberries* (1957), *Persona* (1966), *Cries and Whispers* (1972), and *Fanny and Alexander* (1983).

Buñuel, Luis   (1900–83), b. Spain. A critical and cult favorite, he first demonstrated his outrageous visual style with the Surrealist classic *Un Chien andalou* (1928, with Salvador Dali). Later works incorporated fearless criticism of the Catholic church and other social institutions; among them are *L'Age d'or* (1930), *Los Olvidados* (1950), *Viridiana* (1961), and *That Obscure Object of Desire* (1977).

Eisenstein, Sergei   (1898–1948), b. Latvia. A seminal voice in formulating film language, he developed the practice of *montage* in works including *The Battleship Potemkin* (1925), *October/Ten Days That Shook the World* (1928), and *The General Line* (1929). Later works, such as *Alexander Nevsky* (1938), further refined its use. A noted film theorist, he wrote such books as *Film Sense* (1942) and *Film Form* (1949).

Sembène, Ousmane   (1923–   ), b. Senegal. The foremost filmmaker in sub-Saharan Africa, he established the region as a rich cinematic source from his first release, *Black Girl* (1966). It and other works, including *The Money Order* (1968), *The People* (1977), and *Camp de Thiaroye* (1988), explore conflicts between African and western cultures. From the 1960s, he has been a respected novelist and short story writer (*The Last of the Empire*, 1981).

THE ACADEMY AWARDS

The Academy Awards began in 1927. The awards for Best Supporting Actor and Best Supporting Actress were not included until 1936. The award for Best Foreign Film was added in 1956.

1927–28
Best Actor: Emil Jannings *(The Way of All Flesh)*
Best Actress: Janet Gaynor *(Seventh Heaven)*
Best Director: Frank Borzage *(Seventh Heaven);* Lewis Milestone *(Two Arabian Knights)*
Best Picture: *Wings*

1928–29
Best Actor: Warner Baxter *(In Old Arizona)*
Best Actress: Mary Pickford *(Coquette)*
Best Director: Frank Lloyd *(The Divine Lady)*
Best Picture: *Broadway Melody*

1929–30
Best Actor: George Arliss *(Disraeli)*
Best Actress: Norma Shearer *(The Divorcee)*
Best Director: Lewis Milestone *(All Quiet on the Western Front)*
Best Picture: *All Quiet on the Western Front*

1930–31

Best Actor: Lionel Barrymore *(A Free Soul)*
Best Actress: Marie Dressler *(Min and Bill)*
Best Director: Norma Taurog *(Skippy)*
Best Picture: *Cimarron*

1931–32

Best Actor: Frederic March *(Dr. Jekyll and Mr. Hyde)*; Wallace Berry *(The Champ)*
Best Actress: Helen Hayes *(The Sin of Madelon Claudet)*
Best Director: Frank Borzage *(Bad Girl)*
Best Picture: *Grand Hotel*

1932–33

Best Actor: Charles Laughton *(The Private Life of Henry VIII)*
Best Actress: Katharine Hepburn *(Morning Glory)*
Best Director: Frank Lloyd *(Cavalcade)*
Best Picture: *Cavalcade*

1934

Best Actor: Clark Gable *(It Happened One Night)*
Best Actress: Claudette Colbert *(It Happened One Night)*
Best Director: Frank Capra *(It Happened One Night)*
Best Picture: *It Happened One Night*

1935

Best Actor: Victor McLaglen *(The Informer)*
Best Actress: Bette Davis *(Dangerous)*
Best Director: John Ford *(The Informer)*
Best Picture: *Mutiny on the Bounty*

1936

Best Actor: Paul Muni *(The Story of Louis Pasteur)*
Best Actress: Luise Rainer *(The Great Ziegfeld)*
Best Supporting Actor: Walter Brennan *(Come and Get It)*
Best Supporting Actress: Gale Sondergard *(Anthony Adverse)*
Best Director: Frank Capra *(Mr. Deeds Goes to Town)*
Best Picture: *The Great Ziegfeld*

1937

Best Actor: Spencer Tracy *(Captains Courageous)*
Best Actress: Luise Rainer *(The Good Earth)*
Best Supporting Actor: Joseph Schildkraut *(The Life of Emile Zola)*
Best Supporting Actress: Alice Brady *(In Old Chicago)*
Best Director: Leo McCarey *(The Awful Truth)*
Best Picture: *The Life of Emile Zola*

1938

Best Actor: Spencer Tracy *(Boys Town)*
Best Actress: Bette Davis *(Jezebel)*
Best Supporting Actor: Walter Brennan *(Kentucky)*
Best Supporting Actress: Fay Bainter *(Jezebel)*
Best Director: Frank Capra *(You Can't Take It with You)*
Best Picture: *You Can't Take It with You*

1939

Best Actor: Robert Donat *(Goodbye Mr. Chips)*
Best Actress: Vivien Leigh *(Gone with the Wind)*
Best Supporting Actor: Thomas Mitchell *(Stagecoach)*
Best Supporting Actress: Hattie McDaniel *(Gone with the Wind)*
Best Director: Victor Fleming *(Gone with the Wind)*
Best Picture: *Gone with the Wind*

1940

Best Actor: James Stewart *(The Philadelphia Story)*
Best Actress: Ginger Rogers *(Kitty Foyle)*
Best Supporting Actor: Walter Brennan *(The Westerner)*
Best Supporting Actress: Jane Darwell *(The Grapes of Wrath)*
Best Director: John Ford *(The Grapes of Wrath)*
Best Picture: *Rebecca*

1941

Best Actor: Gary Cooper *(Sergeant York)*
Best Actress: Joan Fontaine *(Suspicion)*
Best Supporting Actor: Donald Crisp *(How Green Was My Valley)*
Best Supporting Actress: Mary Astor *(The Great Lie)*
Best Director: John Ford *(How Green Was My Valley)*
Best Picture: *How Green Was My Valley*

1942

Best Actor: James Cagney *(Yankee Doodle Dandy)*
Best Actress: Greer Garson *(Mrs. Miniver)*
Best Supporting Actor: Van Heflin *(Johnny Eager)*
Best Supporting Actress: Teresa Wright *(Mrs. Miniver)*
Best Director: William Wyler *(Mrs. Miniver)*
Best Picture: *Mrs. Miniver*

1943

Best Actor: Paul Lukas *(Watch on the Rhine)*
Best Actress: Jennifer Jones *(The Song of Bernadette)*
Best Supporting Actor: Charles Coburn *(The More the Merrier)*
Best Supporting Actress: Katina Paxinou *(For Whom the Bell Tolls)*
Best Director: Michael Curtiz *(Casablanca)*
Best Picture: *Casablanca*

1944

Best Actor: Bing Crosby *(Going My Way)*
Best Actress: Ingrid Bergman *(Gaslight)*
Best Supporting Actor: Barry Fitzgerald *(Going My Way)*
Best Supporting Actress: Ethel Barrymore *(None But the Lonely Heart)*

Best Director: Leo McCarey *(Going My Way)*
Best Picture: *Going My Way*

1945

Best Actor: Ray Milland *(The Lost Weekend)*
Best Actress: Joan Crawford *(Mildred Pierce)*
Best Supporting Actor: James Dunn *(A Tree Grows in Brooklyn)*
Best Supporting Actress: Anne Revere *(National Velvet)*
Best Director: Billy Wilder *(The Lost Weekend)*
Best Picture: *The Lost Weekend*

1946

Best Actor: Frederic March *(The Best Years of Our Lives)*
Best Actress: Olivia de Havilland *(To Each His Own)*
Best Supporting Actor: Harold Russell *(The Best Years of Our Lives)*
Best Supporting Actress: Anne Baxter *(The Razor's Edge)*
Best Director: William Wyler *(The Best Years of Our Lives)*
Best Picture: *The Best Years of Our Lives*

1947

Best Actor: Ronald Coleman *(A Double Life)*
Best Actress: Loretta Young *(The Farmer's Daughter)*
Best Supporting Actor: Edmund Gwenn *(Miracle on 34th Street)*
Best Supporting Actress: Celeste Holm *(Gentleman's Agreement)*
Best Director: Elia Kazan *(Gentleman's Agreement)*
Best Picture: *Gentleman's Agreement*

1948

Best Actor: Laurence Olivier *(Hamlet)*
Best Actress: Jane Wyman *(Johnny Belinda)*
Best Supporting Actor: Walter Huston *(Treasure of Sierra Madre)*
Best Supporting Actress: Claire Trevor *(Key Largo)*
Best Director: John Huston *(The Treasure of the Sierra Madre)*
Best Picture: *Hamlet*

1949

Best Actor: Broderick Crawford *(All the King's Men)*
Best Actress: Olivia de Havilland *(The Heiress)*
Best Supporting Actor: Dean Jagger *(Twelve O'Clock High)*
Best Supporting Actress: Mercedes McCambridge *(All the King's Men)*
Best Director: Joseph L. Mankiewicz *(A Letter to Three Wives)*
Best Picture: *All the King's Men*

1950

Best Actor: Jose Ferrer *(Cyrano de Bergerac)*
Best Actress: Judy Holliday *(Born Yesterday)*
Best Supporting Actor: George Sanders *(All About Eve)*
Best Supporting Actress: Josephine Hull *(Harvey)*
Best Director: Joseph L. Mankiewicz *(All About Eve)*
Best Picture: *All About Eve*

1951

Best Actor: Humphrey Bogart *(The African Queen)*
Best Actress: Vivien Leigh *(A Streetcar Named Desire)*
Best Supporting Actor: Karl Malden *(A Streetcar Named Desire)*
Best Supporting Actress: Kim Hunter *(A Streetcar Named Desire)*
Best Director: George Stevens *(A Place in the Sun)*
Best Picture: *An American in Paris*

1952

Best Actor: Gary Cooper *(High Noon)*
Best Actress: Shirley Booth *(Come Back, Little Sheba)*
Best Supporting Actor: Anthony Quinn *(Viva Zapata!)*
Best Supporting Actress: Gloria Grahame *(The Bad and the Beautiful)*
Best Director: John Ford *(The Quiet Man)*
Best Picture: *The Greatest Show on Earth*

1953

Best Actor: William Holden *(Stalag 17)*
Best Actress: Audrey Hepburn *(Roman Holiday)*
Best Supporting Actor: Frank Sinatra *(From Here to Eternity)*
Best Supporting Actress: Donna Reed *(From Here to Eternity)*
Best Director: Fred Zinnemann *(From Here to Eternity)*
Best Picture: *From Here to Eternity*

1954

Best Actor: Marlon Brando *(On the Waterfront)*
Best Actress: Grace Kelly *(The Country Girl)*
Best Supporting Actor: Edmond O'Brien *(The Barefoot Contessa)*
Best Supporting Actress: Eva Marie Saint *(On the Waterfront)*
Best Director: Elia Kazan *(On the Waterfront)*
Best Picture: *On the Waterfront*

1955

Best Actor: Ernest Borgnine *(Marty)*
Best Actress: Anna Magnani *(The Rose Tattoo)*
Best Supporting Actor: Jack Lemmon *(Mister Roberts)*
Best Supporting Actress: Jo Van Fleet *(East of Eden)*

Best Director: Delbert Mann *(Marty)*
Best Picture: *Marty*

1956

Best Actor: Yul Brynner *(The King and I)*
Best Actress: Ingrid Bergman *(Anastasia)*
Best Supporting Actor: Anthony Quinn *(Lust for Life)*
Best Supporting Actress: Dorothy Malone *(Written on the Wind)*
Best Director: George Stevens *(Giant)*
Best Picture: *Around the World in Eighty Days*
Best Foreign Film: *La Strada*

1957

Best Actor: Alec Guinness *(The Bridge on the River Kwai)*
Best Actress: Joanne Woodward *(The Three Faces of Eve)*
Best Supporting Actor: Red Buttons *(Sayonara)*
Best Supporting Actress: Miyoshi Umeki *(Sayonara)*
Best Director: David Lean *(The Bridge on the River Kwai)*
Best Picture: *The Bridge on the River Kwai*
Best Foreign Film: *The Nights of Cabiria*

1958

Best Actor: David Niven *(Separate Tables)*
Best Actress: Susan Hayward *(I Want to Live)*
Best Supporting Actor: Burl Ives *(The Big Country)*
Best Supporting Actress: Wendy Hiller *(Separate Tables)*
Best Director: Vincente Minnelli *(Gigi)*
Best Picture: *Gigi*
Best Foreign Film: *My Uncle*

1959

Best Actor: Charlton Heston *(Ben-Hur)*
Best Actress: Simone Signoret *(Room at the Top)*
Best Supporting Actor: Hugh Griffith *(Ben-Hur)*
Best Supporting Actress: Shelley Winters *(The Diary of Anne Frank)*
Best Director: William Wyler *(Ben-Hur)*
Best Picture: *Ben-Hur*
Best Foreign Film: *Black Orpheus*

1960

Best Actor: Burt Lancaster *(Elmer Gantry)*
Best Actress: Elizabeth Taylor *(Butterfield 8)*
Best Supporting Actor: Peter Ustinov *(Spartacus)*
Best Supporting Actress: Shirley Jones *(Elmer Gantry)*
Best Director: Billy Wilder *(The Apartment)*
Best Picture: *The Apartment*
Best Foreign Film: *The Virgin Spring*

1961

Best Actor: Maximillian Schell *(Judgment at Nuremberg)*
Best Actress: Sophia Loren *(Two Women)*
Best Supporting Actor: George Chakiris *(West Side Story)*
Best Supporting Actress: Rita Moreno *(West Side Story)*
Best Director: Jerome Robbins, Robert Wise *(West Side Story)*
Best Picture: *West Side Story*
Best Foreign Film: *Through a Glass Darkly*

1962

Best Actor: Gregory Peck *(To Kill a Mockingbird)*
Best Actress: Anne Bancroft *(The Miracle Worker)*
Best Supporting Actor: Ed Begley *(Sweet Bird of Youth)*
Best Supporting Actress: Patty Duke *(The Miracle Worker)*
Best Director: David Lean *(Lawrence of Arabia)*
Best Picture: *Lawrence of Arabia*
Best Foreign Film: *Sundays and Cybele*

1963

Best Actor: Sidney Poitier *(Lilies of the Field)*
Best Actress: Patricia Neal *(Hud)*
Best Supporting Actor: Melvyn Douglas *(Hud)*
Best Supporting Actress: Margaret Rutherford *(The V.I.P.s)*
Best Director: Tony Richardson *(Tom Jones)*
Best Picture: *Tom Jones*
Best Foreign Film: *8½*

1964

Best Actor: Rex Harrison *(My Fair Lady)*
Best Actress: Julie Andrews *(Mary Poppins)*
Best Supporting Actor: Peter Ustinov *(Topkapi)*
Best Supporting Actress: Lila Kedrova *(Zorba the Greek)*
Best Director: George Cukor *(My Fair Lady)*
Best Picture: *My Fair Lady*
Best Foreign Film: *Yesterday, Today and Tomorrow*

1965

Best Actor: Lee Marvin *(Cat Ballou)*
Best Actress: Julie Christie *(Darling)*
Best Supporting Actor: Martin Balsam *(A Thousand Clowns)*
Best Supporting Actress: Shelley Winters *(A Patch of Blue)*
Best Director: Robert Wise *(The Sound of Music)*
Best Picture: *The Sound of Music*
Best Foreign Film: *The Shop on Main Street*

1966

Best Actor: Paul Scofield *(A Man for All Seasons)*

Best Actress: Elizabeth Taylor *(Who's Afraid of Virginia Woolf?)*

Best Supporting Actor: Walter Matthau *(The Fortune Cookie)*

Best Supporting Actress: Sandy Dennis *(Who's Afraid of Virginia Woolf?)*

Best Director: Fred Zinnemann *(A Man for All Seasons)*

Best Picture: *A Man for All Seasons*

Best Foreign Film: *A Man and a Woman*

1967

Best Actor: Rod Steiger *(In the Heat of the Night)*

Best Actress: Katharine Hepburn *(Guess Who's Coming to Dinner)*

Best Supporting Actor: George Kennedy *(Cool Hand Luke)*

Best Supporting Actress: Estelle Parsons *(Bonnie and Clyde)*

Best Director: Mike Nichols *(The Graduate)*

Best Picture: *In the Heat of the Night*

Best Foreign Film: *Closely Watched Trains*

1968

Best Actor: Cliff Robertson *(Charly)*

Best Actress: Katharine Hepburn *(The Lion in Winter)*; Barbra Streisand *(Funny Girl)*

Best Supporting Actor: Jack Albertson *(The Subject Was Roses)*

Best Supporting Actress: Ruth Gordon *(Rosemary's Baby)*

Best Director: Sir Carol Reed *(Oliver!)*

Best Picture: *Oliver!*

Best Foreign Film: *War and Peace*

1969

Best Actor: John Wayne *(True Grit)*

Best Actress: Maggie Smith *(The Prime of Miss Jean Brodie)*

Best Supporting Actor: Gig Young *(They Shoot Horses Don't They?)*

Best Supporting Actress: Goldie Hawn *(Cactus Flower)*

Best Director: John Schlesinger *(Midnight Cowboy)*

Best Picture: *Midnight Cowboy*

Best Foreign Film: *Z*

1970

Best Actor: George C. Scott *(Patton;* refused*)*

Best Actress: Glenda Jackson *(Women in Love)*

Best Supporting Actor: John Mills *(Ryan's Daughter)*

Best Supporting Actress: Helen Hayes *(Airport)*

Best Director: Franklin Schaffner, Frank McCarthy *(Patton)*

Best Picture: *Patton*

Best Foreign Film: *Investigation of a Citizen Above Suspicion*

1971

Best Actor: Gene Hackman *(The French Connection)*

Best Actress: Jane Fonda *(Klute)*

Best Supporting Actor: Ben Johnson *(The Last Picture Show)*

Best Supporting Actress: Cloris Leachman *(The Last Picture Show)*

Best Director: William Friedkin *(The French Connection)*

Best Picture: *The French Connection*

Best Foreign Film: *The Garden of the Finzi-Continis*

1972

Best Actor: Marlon Brando *(The Godfather;* refused*)*

Best Actress: Liza Minnelli *(Cabaret)*

Best Supporting Actor: Joel Grey *(Cabaret)*

Best Supporting Actress: Eileen Heckart *(Butterflies Are Free)*

Best Director: Bob Fosse *(Cabaret)*

Best Picture: *The Godfather*

Best Foreign Film: *The Discreet Charm of the Bourgeoisie*

1973

Best Actor: Jack Lemmon *(Save the Tiger)*

Best Actress: Glenda Jackson *(A Touch of Class)*

Best Supporting Actor: John Houseman *(The Paper Chase)*

Best Supporting Actress: Tatum O'Neal *(Paper Moon)*

Best Director: George Roy Hill *(The Sting)*

Best Picture: *The Sting*

Best Foreign Film: *Day for Night*

1974

Best Actor: Art Carney *(Harry and Tonto)*

Best Actress: Ellen Burstyn *(Alice Doesn't Live Here Anymore)*

Best Supporting Actor: Robert De Niro *(The Godfather, Part II)*

Best Supporting Actress: Ingrid Bergman *(Murder on the Orient Express)*

Best Director: Francis Ford Coppola *(The Godfather, Part II)*

Best Picture: *The Godfather, Part II*

Best Foreign Film: *Amarcord*

1975

Best Actor: Jack Nicholson *(One Flew over the Cuckoo's Nest)*

Best Actress: Louise Fletcher *(One Flew over the Cuckoo's Nest)*

Best Supporting Actor: George Burns *(The Sunshine Boys)*

Best Supporting Actress: Lee Grant *(Shampoo)*
Best Director: Milos Forman *(One Flew over the Cuckoo's Nest)*
Best Picture: *One Flew over the Cuckoo's Nest*
Best Foreign Film: *Dersu Uzala*

1976

Best Actor: Peter Finch *(Network)*
Best Actress: Faye Dunaway *(Network)*
Best Supporting Actor: Jason Robards *(All the President's Men)*
Best Supporting Actress: Beatrice Straight *(Network)*
Best Director: John G. Avildsen *(Rocky)*
Best Picture: *Rocky*
Best Foreign Film: *Black and White in Color*

1977

Best Actor: Richard Dreyfuss *(The Goodbye Girl)*
Best Actress: Diane Keaton *(Annie Hall)*
Best Supporting Actor: Jason Robards *(Julia)*
Best Supporting Actress: Vanessa Redgrave *(Julia)*
Best Director: Woody Allen *(Annie Hall)*
Best Picture: *Annie Hall*
Best Foreign Film: *Madame Rosa*

1978

Best Actor: Jon Voight *(Coming Home)*
Best Actress: Jane Fonda *(Coming Home)*
Best Supporting Actor: Christopher Walken *(The Deer Hunter)*
Best Supporting Actress: Maggie Smith *(California Suite)*
Best Director: Michael Cimino *(The Deer Hunter)*
Best Picture: *The Deer Hunter*
Best Foreign Film: *Get Out Your Handkerchiefs*

1979

Best Actor: Dustin Hoffman *(Kramer vs. Kramer)*
Best Actress: Sally Field *(Norma Rae)*
Best Supporting Actor: Melvyn Douglas *(Being There)*
Best Supporting Actress: Meryl Streep *(Kramer vs. Kramer)*
Best Director: Robert Benton *(Kramer vs. Kramer)*
Best Picture: *Kramer vs. Kramer*
Best Foreign Film: *The Tin Drum*

1980

Best Actor: Robert De Niro *(Raging Bull)*
Best Actress: Sissy Spacek *(Coal Miner's Daughter)*
Best Supporting Actor: Timothy Hutton *(Ordinary People)*
Best Supporting Actress: Mary Steenburgen *(Melvin and Howard)*
Best Director: Robert Redford *(Ordinary People)*
Best Picture: *Ordinary People*
Best Foreign Film: *Moscow Does Not Believe in Tears*

1981

Best Actor: Henry Fonda *(On Golden Pond)*
Best Actress: Katharine Hepburn *(On Golden Pond)*
Best Supporting Actor: John Gielgud *(Arthur)*
Best Supporting Actress: Maureen Stapleton *(Reds)*
Best Director: Warren Beatty *(Reds)*
Best Picture: *Chariots of Fire*
Best Foreign Film: *Memphisto*

1982

Best Actor: Ben Kingsley *(Gandhi)*
Best Actress: Meryl Streep *(Sophie's Choice)*
Best Supporting Actor: Louis Gossett, Jr. *(An Officer and a Gentleman)*
Best Supporting Actress: Jessica Lange *(Tootsie)*
Best Director: Richard Attenborough *(Gandhi)*
Best Picture: *Gandhi*
Best Foreign Film: *To Begin Again*

1983

Best Actor: Robert Duvall *(Tender Mercies)*
Best Actress: Shirley MacLaine *(Terms of Endearment)*
Best Supporting Actor: Jack Nicholson *(Terms of Endearment)*
Best Supporting Actress: Linda Hunt *(The Year of Living Dangerously)*
Best Director: James L. Brooks *(Terms of Endearment)*
Best Picture: *Terms of Endearment*
Best Foreign Film: *Fanny and Alexander*

1984

Best Actor: F. Murray Abraham *(Amadeus)*
Best Actress: Sally Field *(Places in the Heart)*
Best Supporting Actor: Haing S. Ngor *(The Killing Fields)*
Best Supporting Actress: Dame Peggy Ashcroft *(A Passage to India)*
Best Director: Milos Forman *(Amadeus)*
Best Picture: *Amadeus*
Best Foreign Film: *Dangerous Moves*

1985

Best Actor: William Hurt *(Kiss of the Spider Woman)*
Best Actress: Geraldine Page *(The Trip to Bountiful)*
Best Supporting Actor: Don Ameche *(Cocoon)*
Best Supporting Actress: Angelica Houston *(Prizzi's Honor)*
Best Director: Sydney Pollack *(Out of Africa)*
Best Picture: *Out of Africa*
Best Foreign Film: *The Official Story*

1986

Best Actor: Paul Newman *(The Color of Money)*
Best Actress: Marlee Matlin *(Children of a Lesser God)*
Best Supporting Actor: Michael Caine *(Hannah and Her Sisters)*

Best Supporting Actress: Diane Wiest *(Hannah and Her Sisters)*
Best Director: Oliver Stone *(Platoon)*
Best Picture: *Platoon*
Best Foreign Film: *The Assault*

1987

Best Actor: Michael Douglas *(Wall Street)*
Best Actress: Cher *(Moonstruck)*
Best Supporting Actor: Sean Connery *(The Untouchables)*
Best Supporting Actress: Olympia Dukakis *Moonstruck)*
Best Director: Bernardo Bertolucci *(The Last Emperor)*
Best Picture: *The Last Emperor*
Best Foreign Film: *Babette's Feast*

1988

Best Actor: Dustin Hoffman *(Rain Man)*
Best Actress: Jodie Foster *(The Accused)*
Best Supporting Actor: Kevin Kline *(A Fish Called Wanda)*
Best Supporting Actress: Geena Davis *(The Accidental Tourist)*
Best Director: Barry Levinson *(Rain Man)*
Best Picture: *Rain Man*
Best Foreign Film: *Pelle the Conquerer*

1989

Best Actor: Daniel Day-Lewis *(My Left Foot)*
Best Actress: Jessica Tandy *(Driving Miss Daisy)*
Best Supporting Actor: Denzel Washington *(Glory)*
Best Supporting Actress: Brenda Fricker *(My Left Foot)*
Best Director: Oliver Stone *(Born on the Fourth of July)*
Best Picture: *Driving Miss Daisy*
Best Foreign Film: *Cinema Paradiso*

1990

Best Actor: Jeremy Irons *(Reversal of Fortune)*
Best Actress: Kathy Bates *(Misery)*
Best Supporting Actor: Joe Pesci *(GoodFellas)*
Best Supporting Actress: Whoopi Goldberg *(Ghost)*
Best Director: Kevin Costner *(Dances with Wolves)*
Best Picture: *Dances with Wolves*
Best Foreign Film: *Journey of Hope*

1991

Best Actor: Anthony Hopkins *(The Silence of the Lambs)*
Best Actress: Jodie Foster *(The Silence of the Lambs)*
Best Supporting Actor: Jack Palance *(City Slickers)*
Best Supporting Actress: Mercedes Ruehl *(The Fisher King)*

Best Director: Jonathan Demme *(The Silence of the Lambs)*
Best Picture: *The Silence of the Lambs*
Best Foreign Film: *Mediterraneo*

1992

Best Actor: Al Pacino *(Scent of a Women)*
Best Actress: Emma Thompson *(Howard's End)*
Best Supporting Actor: Gene Hackman *(Unforgiven)*
Best Supporting Actress: Marisa Tomei *(My Cousin Vinny)*
Best Director: Clint Eastwood *(Unforgiven)*
Best Picture: *Unforgiven*
Best Foreign Film: *Indochine*

1993

Best Actor: Tom Hanks *(Philadelphia)*
Best Actress: Holly Hunter *(The Piano)*
Best Supporting Actor: Tommy Lee Jones *(The Fugitive)*
Best Supporting Actress: Anna Paquin *(The Piano)*
Best Director: Steven Spielberg *(Schindler's List)*
Best Picture: *Schindler's List*
Best Foreign Film: *Belle Epoque*

1994

Best Actor: Tom Hanks *(Forrest Gump)*
Best Actress: Jessica Lange *(Blue Sky)*
Best Supporting Actor: Martin Landau *(Ed Wood)*
Best Supporting Actress: Diane Wiest *(Bullets over Broadway)*
Best Director: Robert Zemeckis *(Forrest Gump)*
Best Picture: *Forrest Gump*
Best Foreign Film: *Burnt by the Sun*

1995

Best Actor: Nicolas Cage *(Leaving Las Vegas)*
Best Actress: Susan Sarandon *(Dead Man Walking)*
Best Supporting Actor: Kevin Spacey *(The Usual Suspects)*
Best Supporting Actress: Mira Sorvino *(Mighty Aphrodite)*
Best Director: Mel Gibson *(Braveheart)*
Best Picture: *Braveheart*
Best Foreign Film: *Antonia's Line*

1996

Best Actor: Geoffrey Rush *(Shine)*
Best Actress: Frances McDormand *(Fargo)*
Best Supporting Actor: Cuba Gooding, Jr. *(Jerry Maguire)*
Best Supporting Actress: Juliette Binoche *(The English Patient)*
Best Director: Anthony Minghella *(The English Patient)*
Best Picture: *The English Patient*
Best Foreign Film: *Kolya*

1997

Best Actor: Jack Nicolson *(As Good as It Gets)*
Best Actress: Helen Hunt *(As Good as It Gets)*
Supporting Actor: Robin Williams *(Good Will Hunting)*
Supporting Actress: Kim Basinger *(L.A. Confidential)*
Best Director: James Cameron *(Titanic)*
Best Picture: *Titanic*
Best Foreign Film: *Character*

1998

Best Actor: Roberto Benigni *(Life Is Beautiful)*
Best Actress: Gwyneth Paltrow *(Shakespeare in Love)*
Supporting Actor: James Coburn *(Affliction)*
Supporting Actress: Judi Dench *(Shakespeare in Love)*
Best Director: Steven Spielberg *(Saving Private Ryan)*
Best Picture: *Shakespeare in Love*
Best Foreign Film: *Life is Beautiful*

1999

Best Actor: Kevin Spacey *(American Beauty)*
Best Actress: Hilary Swank *(Boys Don't Cry)*
Supporting Actor: Michael Caine *(The Cider House Rules)*
Supporting Actress: Angelina Jolie *(Girl Interrupted)*
Best Director: Sam Mendes *(American Beauty)*
Best Picture: *American Beauty*
Best Foreign Film: *All About My Mother*

2000

Best Actor: Russell Crowe *(Gladiator)*
Best Actress: Julia Roberts *(Erin Brockovich)*
Supporting Actor: Benicio Del Toro *(Traffic)*
Supporting Actress: Marcia Gay Harden *(Pollock)*
Best Director: Steven Soderbergh *(Traffic)*
Best Picture: *Gladiator*
Best Foreign Film: *Crouching Tiger, Hidden Dragon*

2001

Best Actor: Denzel Washington *(Training Day)*
Best Actress: Halle Berry *(Monster's Ball)*
Supporting Actor: Jim Broadbent *(Iris)*
Supporting Actress: Jennifer Connelly *(A Beautiful Mind)*
Best Director: Ron Howard *(A Beautiful Mind)*
Best Picture: *A Beautiful Mind*
Best Foreign Film: *No Man's Land (Bosnia and Herzegovina)*

Go to "Book Awards and Their Recipients" in chapter 8

ADDITIONAL SOURCES OF INFORMATION

BOOKS

MUSIC

Arnold, Denis, ed. *The New Oxford Companion to Music.* 2 vols. Oxford University Press, 1988.

Grout, Donald, and Claude V. Palisca. *A History of Western Music.* Norton, 2000.

Kerfeld, Barry. *The New Grove Dictionary of Jazz.* St. Martin's Press, 1994.

Sadie, Stanley, ed. *The New Grove Dictionary of Opera.* 4 vols. Groves Dictionaries of Music, 1998.

DANCE

Bremser, Martha, ed. *International Dictionary of Ballet.* St. James Press, 2001.

Bremser, Martha. *Fifty Contemporary Choreographers.* Routledge, 2000.

Mazo, Joseph. *Prime Movers: The Makers of Modern Dance in America.* Princeton Book Co., 2000.

McQuade, *The Schirmer Biographical Dictionary of Dance.* Macmillan, 1998.

STAGE AND FILM

Corey, Melinda, and George Ochoa. *The American Film Institute Desk Reference.* Dorling Kindersley, 2002.

Hartnoll, Phyllis, and Peter Found, eds. *The Concise Oxford Companion to the Theatre.* 2nd ed. Oxford University Press, 1992.

Katz, Ephraim. *The Film Encyclopedia.* 3rd ed. HarperPerennial, 1998.

Riggs, Thomas. *Contemporary Dramatists.* 6th ed. St. James Press, 1998.

Rubin, Don, Ousmane Diakhate, and Hansel Ndumbe Eyoh, eds. *The World Encyclopedia of Contemporary Theatre.* Routledge, 2000.

Tibbetts, John C., and James M. Welsh. *The Encyclopedia of Stage Plays into Film.* Facts on File, 2001.

7

THE VISUAL ARTS

MAJOR PAINTERS AND SCULPTORS

AMERICAN

Albers, Josef (1888–1976), b. Germany. Painter and designer, teacher at the Bauhaus, and director of the Yale School of Art. He is best known for his *Homage to the Square* series (begun 1949) and for his widely studied color theories.

Calder, Alexander (1898–1976), b. Pennsylvania. Sculptor best known for his mobiles and playful wire constructions of circuses, begun in 1926. Much of his later work is large, heavy sculpture, often for public areas.

Cassatt, Mary (1845–1926), b. Pennsylvania. Artist who spent much of her life in Paris, where she was allied with the Impressionists. She is best known for paintings of women with children, such as *The Bath* (1892), and for etchings, such as *The Letter* (1891).

Chicago, Judy (1939–   ), b. Chicago. A pioneer in feminist art and art education. Chicago's best-known work is *The Dinner Party* (1974–1979), a multimedia project dealing with women's history. Other important installations include *Womanhouse* (1971), *The Birth Project* (1984), and *The Holocaust Project* (1993).

Copley, John Singleton (1738–1815) b. Massachusetts. Painted portraits and historical subjects. His Boston portraits show a thorough knowledge of his New England models, and his talent as a draftsman and colorist produced pictures of aristocratic elegance and grace. His works include *Henry Pelham (Boy with a Squirrel)* (1765) and *Watson and the Shark* (1778).

Cornell, Joseph (1903–72), b. New York. His surrealist-influenced constructions are boxes filled with found objects and collaged images, arranged in privately symbolic ways. Some of the best-known examples are *Medici Slot Machine* (1942) and *Hôtel du Nord* (1953).

Davies, Arthur Bowen (1862–1928), b. New York. Member of The Eight and an organizer of the historic 1913 Armory Show. His symbolic, idyllic paintings include landscapes such as *Unicorns* (1906).

Davis, Stuart (1894–1964), b. Pennsylvania. Davis developed a distinctly American interpretation of cubism in his brightly colored paintings, such as *Hot Still-Scape for Six Colors* (1940) and *Colonial Cubism* (1954).

de Kooning, Willem (1904–97), b. The Netherlands. A leader of abstract expressionism in the United States, de Kooning is best known for his monumental, violently painted *Woman* series, begun in the early 1950s.

Demuth, Charles (1883–1935), b. Pennsylvania. One of the first to incorporate geometric shapes of modern technology into painting. His best-known work is *I Saw the Figure 5 in Gold* (1928).

Dove, Arthur Garfield (1880–1946), b. New York. In his paintings of abstracted natural forms, such as *Waterfall* (1925) and *Rise of the Full Moon* (1937), Dove was a forerunner of abstract expressionism.

Eakins, Thomas (1844–1916), b. Pennsylvania. An important portraitist, Eakins was criticized for innovations such as working from live nude models. His best-known works include *The Gross Clinic* (1875), which shows an operation in progress, and *Max Schmitt in a Single Scull* (1871).

Feininger, Lyonel (1871–1956), b. New York. Feininger, who taught at the Bauhaus (1919–32), developed a style of delicate architectural forms fractured by rays of light, as in *Church at Gelmeroda* (1936).

Frankenthaler, Helen (1928–   ), b. New York. Frankenthaler developed a technique of staining canvases with paint, creating sensuous abstract works such as *Mountains and Sea* (1952), a seminal work in this style, and *Arden* (1961).

Gorky, Arshile (1904–48), b. Armenia. An influence on abstract expressionism, Gorky painted abstract but often biomorphic forms in brilliant, glowing colors, as in *The Liver Is the Cock's Comb* (1944).

Henri, Robert (1865–1929), b. Ohio. Painter and influential teacher. As a member of The Eight, he was a leader in the rebellion against academic art. Henri is best known for his dramatic portraits, such as *Woman in Manteau* (1898), *Himself* (1913), and *Herself* (1913).

Holzer, Jenny (1950–   ), b. Ohio. A multimedia conceptual artist, Holzer brings provocative phrases to public attention via electronic message boards, posters, and web sites, among other things. Popular works include *Truisms* (1979–1983), *Survival Series* (1983–1985), and *Lustmord* (1997).

Hofmann, Hans (1880–1966), b. Germany. Founder of two U.S. art schools important in the development of abstract expressionism. Hofmann boldly manipulated violent, clashing colors, as in *Effervescence* (1944) and *The Gate* (1959).

Homer, Winslow (1836–1910), b. Massachusetts. One of the most prominent 19th-century American painters, Homer is best known for his dramatic seascapes, such as *West Point, Prout's Neck, Maine,* and *On a Lee Shore* (both 1900).

Hopper, Edward (1882–1967), b. New York. Hopper painted lonely street scenes, buildings, and interiors, giving careful attention to light and shade, as in *Nighthawks* (1942) and *Early Sunday Morning* (1930).

Indiana, Robert (1928–   ), b. Indiana. Pop artist best known for his bold and vivid signlike paintings and sculpture, such as the *Love* series (begun 1966).

Johns, Jasper (1930–   ), b. Georgia. A founder of pop art, Johns uses everyday signs, symbols, and objects—such as flags, targets, and beer cans—in his paintings and sculptures. An example is the painting *Three Flags* (1958).

Kline, Franz (1910–62), b. Pennsylvania. He painted large canvases with dynamic black and white brush strokes, as in *White Forms* (1955) and *Mahoning* (1956). His work exemplifies abstract expressionism.

Lichtenstein, Roy (1923–97), b. New York. Pop artist known for his paintings based on comic strips. Examples are *Masterpiece* (1962) and *Good Morning, Darling* (1964).

Louis, Morris (1912–62), b. Maryland. He used a technique of soaking poured paint through canvases, so that the canvas essentially became dyed by the paint. His work includes the *Veil* series (1954, 1958) and the *Unfurled* series (1960–61).

Moses, Grandma (Anna Mary Robertson Moses) (1860–1961), b. New York. A farmer's wife who began painting in her seventies. Her primitive, colorful works of farm life, such as *Sugaring-Off* (1943), achieved wide popularity.

Motherwell, Robert (1915–91), b. Washington. Painter, writer, and important theoretician of abstract expressionism. His works are characterized by amorphous shapes in austere colors; best known is the series *Elegy for the Spanish Republic,* begun in 1949.

Nevelson, Louise (1900–88), b. Russia. Sculptor known for her large works of painted wood, metal, and found objects. Examples are *Sky Cathedral* (1958) and *World* (1966).

If a statue of a horse has both front legs in the air, the rider died in battle. If the horse has one front leg in the air, the rider died as a result of battle. If the horse has all four legs on the ground, the rider died of natural causes.

Newman, Barnett (1905–71), b. New York. Painter whose works bridged abstract expressionism and the color field movement. His canvases are typically large planes of flat color with thin vertical stripes, such as *Onement I* (1948) and *Concord* (1949). He also produced sculpture.

Noguchi, Isamu (1904–88), b. California. Sculptor well known for his abstract works designed for architectural spaces, such as the sculpture garden for the UNESCO building in Paris (1958) and the entrance for the Museum of Modern Art in Tokyo (1969).

O'Keeffe, Georgia (1887–1986), b. Wisconsin. Painter whose most characteristic images are sculptural, organic forms such as bones and flowers. She lived in New Mexico and often used elements of the southwestern landscape, as in *Cow's Skull: Red, White, and Blue* (1931).

Oldenburg, Claes (1929–   ), b. Sweden. Leader of the pop-art movement, known for his giant sculptures of common objects, such as *Dual Hamburger* (1962) and *Lipstick* (1969).

Parrish, Maxfield (1870–1966), b. Pennsylvania. Creator of posters, magazine covers, and book illustrations in a distinctive, decorative style.

Pollock, Jackson (1912–56), b. Wyoming. A pioneer of abstract expressionism, Pollock developed a method called action painting. His canvases are typically large, with paint dripped, poured, and thrown in complex, dense rhythms, as in *Number 1* (1948), *Number 32* (1950), and *Blue Poles* (1953).

Prendergast, Maurice Brazil (1859–1924), b. Canada. Member of The Eight. He painted landscapes and figures in a colorful, decorative style influenced by the Nabis, as in *The Promenade* (1913).

Rauschenberg, Robert (1925–   ), b. Texas. His collagelike "combine paintings" appropriating everyday images and objects represent a transition between abstract expressionism and pop art. His work includes *Bed* (1955) and *Monogram* (1959).

Reinhardt, Ad (Adolph) (1913–67), b. New York. Associated with minimalism, Reinhardt began painting monochrome canvases by 1953. He is best known for his *Black Paintings,* begun in 1960.

Remington, Frederic (1861–1909), b. New York. Painter, sculptor, illustrator, and writer whose subject was life on the western plains. His works include the sculpture *Bronco Buster* (1895) and the painting *Evening on a Canadian Lake* (1905).

Rivers, Larry (1923–   ), b. New York. In his use of popular images from sources such as artworks and advertising, Rivers was a forerunner of pop art. His paintings include *Washington Crossing the Delaware* (1953) and the *Dutch Masters* series (1963). He has also done sculpture.

Rockwell, Norman (1894–1978), b. New York. Illustrator best known for his *Saturday Evening Post* covers (1916–63). His realistically drawn, popular works portray anecdotal scenes of small-town America. *The Four Freedoms* (1943) are among his most famous paintings.

Rothko, Mark (1903–70), b. Russia. Important figure in abstract expressionism. His canvases contain soft-edged, luminously colored rectangular forms. His work includes *No. 10* (1950) and a series of murals for an ecumenical chapel in Houston (1967–69).

Saint-Gaudens, Augustus (1848–1907) b. Ireland. A sculptor best known for his important public monuments and memorials, including the Adams Memorial in Washington, D.C.; several Lincoln sculptures in Chicago's Lincoln Park; the Shaw Memorial in Boston, Massachusetts; and the General Sherman, Peter Cooper, and Admiral Farragut monuments in New York City. He was active as a teacher throughout the 1890s and maintained a large studio in Cornish, New Hampshire.

Sargent, John Singer (1856–1925), b. Italy. Painter known for his vivid portraits of high society, such as *The Daughters of Edward D. Boit* (1882) and *Madame X* (1884). He also produced impressionistic watercolor landscapes.

Segal, George (1924–   ), b. New York. Sculptor known for his life-size plaster human figures in everyday environments, such as *Woman in Restaurant Booth* (1961) and *Cinema* (1963). Segal is associated with pop art.

Shahn, Ben (1898–1969), b. Lithuania. Versatile artist of social-realistic work that often tells a story without preaching. In the early 1930s, he did a series of 23 paintings based on the Sacco-Vanzetti trial.

Sheeler, Charles (1883–1965), b. Pennsylvania. Photographer and painter known for his depictions of industrial forms reduced to cool, formal simplification. His works include the paintings *Ballardvale Revisited* (1949) and *Steel-Croton* (1953).

Smith, David (1906–65), b. Indiana. Renowned abstract sculptor of welded metal forms. He worked on his large *Cubi* series from the late 1950s until his death.

Stella, Frank (1936–   ), b. Massachusetts. Abstract painter of large, colorful works on irregularly shaped canvases. Works such as *Empress of India* (1965) use series of angular stripes; later works such as *Guadalupe Island* (1979) exhibit sweeping arched forms and wildly exuberant colors.

Stuart, Gilbert (1775–1828) b. Rhode Island. Gilbert Stuart was America's leading portraitist of the Federal period, and he set a standard for portraiture. Best known for his portraits of George Washington, Stuart painted more than a thousand portraits of the next four presidents of the United States, governors, diplomats, merchants, and other leaders of the new nation, as well as their wives and children.

Sully, Thomas (1783–1872), b. England. A leading portraitist, especially of national figures. His most famous work is the historical painting *Washington's Passage of the Delaware* (1819).

Trumbull, John (1756–1843) b. Connecticut. John Trumbull's works include portraits, engravings, and historical paintings. He sought to capture the most important historical moments of the American Revolution. Among his many well-known works are *The Declaration of Independence* (1788) and the murals he painted for the rotunda of the Capitol (installed in 1826).

Warhol, Andy (1930–87), b. Pennsylvania. Leader of the pop art movement. His works are notable for the repetition of everyday images, such as Campbell's soup cans, and for figures from popular culture, such as Marilyn Monroe (both series begun 1962).

West, Benjamin (1738–1820), b. Pennsylvania. Working in both Neoclassical and Romantic styles, he produced paintings such as *The Death of General Wolfe* (1770) and *Death on a Pale Horse* (1802). West worked mainly in England and was a founder and president of the Royal Academy of Arts there.

Whistler, James Abbott McNeill (1834–1903), b. Massachusetts. Painter and graphic artist whose works show a brilliant sense of color and design. His paintings include *The White Girl: Symphony in White No. 1* (1862) and *The Artist's Mother: Arrangement in Gray and Black* (1871). His series of *Nocturnes* foreshadowed abstract art.

Wood, Grant (1891–1942), b. Iowa. Painter best known for his stern figures and stylized landscapes of the rural Midwest. *American Gothic* (1930) is a quintessential American work.

Wyeth, Andrew (1917–   ), b. Pennsylvania. Popular painter of rural landscapes and portraits in a meticulous, naturalistic style. His best-known work is *Christina's World* (1948). In 1986, Wyeth astonished the public with the appearance of a previously secret series, the *Helga* paintings.

BELGIAN/FLEMISH

Bruegel, Pieter, the Elder (c. 1525–69). Flemish painter of peasants at work and play, genre scenes, landscapes, and illustrations of proverbs. His paintings include *The Corn Harvest* (1565) and *The Peasant Wedding* (c. 1567).

Ensor, James (Baron) (1860–1949). Belgian painter and etcher. Ensor created innovative and grotesque compositions, such as *The Temptation of St. Anthony* (1887) and *The Entry of Christ into Brussels* (1888), opening the way for the surrealist movement.

Limbourg, Herman, Jean, and **Pol** (active 1380–1416). Flemish brothers who worked in France for the Duke of Berry. Their *Les Très Riches Heures du Duc de Berry* (1413–16) is an exquisite, colorful, illuminated manuscript, showing activities of daily life.

Magritte, René (1898–1967). A leading Belgian surrealist painter. His works, such as *The Key of Dreams* (1930) and *The Human Condition* (1934), are odd fantasies based on everyday situations, or plays on relationships between pictures and words.

Rubens, Peter Paul (1577–1640). The foremost Flemish artist and a major baroque figure. Working with great freedom and vitality, Rubens produced dynamic, monumental paintings. His works include *The Raising of the Cross* (1610–11), a series of allegorical paintings on the life of Marie de Médici (1622–25), and *The Judgment of Paris* (1638–39).

Van der Weyden, Rogier (c. 1400–64). Flemish painter. His religious works, such as *The Descent from the Cross* (1435) and *The Last Judgment* (c. 1450), combine monumentality with a profound sense of emotion. His penetrating portraits include *Francesco d'Este* (c. 1455).

Van Dyck, Sir Anthony   (1599–1641). A major Flemish baroque artist. Van Dyck's many portraits of the aristocracy include a number of Charles I of England (his royal patron from 1632 on) such as *Portrait of Charles I Hunting* (c. 1635). Van Dyck also painted religious works, such as *The Lamentation* (1634).

Van Eyck, Jan   (c. 1390–1441). A master of Flemish painting. In works such as the church altarpiece in Ghent (1426–32) and the *Arnolfini Wedding Portrait* (1434), Van Eyck achieved an unprecedented luminosity, intensity of color, and detail.

BRITISH

Bacon, Francis   (1909–92), b. Ireland. Painter of disturbing, hallucinatory images, as in *Three Studies at the Base of a Crucifixion* (1944) and his series based on Velázquez's *Pope Innocent X* portrait, begun in the 1950s.

Blake, William   (1757–1827). Painter, engraver, and poet. Blake, a mystic and visionary, created paintings and engravings for John Linnell's editions of the *Book of Job* (1821–26) and Dante's *Divine Comedy* (1824–27), and for his own poetic works in an unearthly, highly personal style.

Constable, John   (1776–1837). Leading English landscape painter. In works such as *The White Horse* (1819), *The Hay Wain* (1821), and *Salisbury Cathedral* (1827), he carefully observed natural phenomena and changes.

Gainsborough, Thomas   (1727–88). Portraitist and landscape painter. His well-known works include *Mr. and Mrs. Robert Andrews* (1748), *Mrs. Siddons* (1785), and his most famous painting, *The Blue Boy* (1770).

Hogarth, William   (1697–1764). Painter and engraver of satirical works, often on moral themes and told in a series of scenes, such as *The Rake's Progress* (1733–35) and *Marriage à la Mode* (1743–45).

Moore, Henry   (1898–1986). Sculptor whose abstract and figurative works are characterized by smooth organic shapes and hollows. His many public commissions include works for the Time-Life building in London (1952–53) and for Lincoln Center for the Performing Arts in New York City (1962–65).

Reynolds, Sir Joshua   (1723–92). Reynolds, first president of the Royal Academy of Arts, painted portraits of nearly every important figure of his day with great versatility. His works include *Commodore Keppel* (1753) and *Mrs. Siddons as the Tragic Muse* (1784).

Rossetti, Dante Gabriel   (1828–82). Painter and poet; one of the founders of the Pre-Raphaelite Brotherhood in 1848. His sensual and symbolic works include *The Annunciation* (1850) and *Beata Beatrix* (1864).

Turner, Joseph Mallord William   (1775–1851). The foremost English landscape painter. Turner depicted atmospheric effects with a style of shimmering light and luminous colors, as in *Calais Pier* (1803) and *The Grand Canal* (1835).

DUTCH

Bosch, Hieronymus (Jerom Bos)   (c. 1450–1516). Painter of bizarre and colorful religious allegories, filled with grotesque figures and animals and obscure symbolism. His works include *The Garden of Earthly Delights* (c. 1505–10) and *The Temptation of St. Anthony* (c. 1500).

The Dutch painter Rembrandt, often called the master of light and shade, painted almost 100 self-portraits.

Hals, Frans   (c. 1580–1666). He painted lively and naturalistic portraits and genre scenes in vivid, sparkling colors. His works include *The Banquet of the Officers of the St. George Militia* (1616) and *The Laughing Cavalier* (1624).

Mondrian, Piet   (1872–1944). A founder of the Stijl group and the magazine *Die Stijl*. Mondrian developed a geometric style known as "neoplasticism." Typical works consist of primary-color squares bounded by black outlines, as in *Composition in Yellow and Blue* (1929) and *Red, Yellow, and Blue Composition* (1930).

Rembrandt Harmenszoon van Rijn (1606–69). A master of the Dutch school, he produced some 600 paintings distinguished by their profound humanity, including *The Anatomy Lesson of Dr. Tulp* (1632), *The Blinding of Samson* (1636), and *The Night Watch* (1642). Rembrandt also painted nearly 100 self-portraits, dating from the 1620s to his last years.

Van Gogh, Vincent (1853–90). One of the most influential 19th-century artists. Many of van Gogh's vibrant, expressive paintings were produced in a 29-month period preceding his suicide. Among his most famous works are *The Potato Eaters* (1885), *The Night Café* (1888), *Starry Night* (1889), and a number of self-portraits.

Vermeer, Jan (Johannes) (1632–75). Vermeer mainly painted intimate interiors, often with solitary figures, depicting them with clarity and luminous, subtle colors. His work includes *Head of a Girl* (c. 1665), *Woman Weighing Pearls* (c. 1665), and *The Letter* (1666).

FLEMISH

See "Belgian/Flemish" above.

FRENCH

Arp, Jean (Hans) (1887–1966). Creator of abstract paintings, sculptures, and collages using organic forms, such as *Squares Arranged According to the Laws of Chance* (1916–17) and *Navel, Shirt, and Head* (1926). Arp was associated with dadaism and surrealism.

Bonnard, Pierre (1867–1947). A founder of the Nabis, Bonnard was a painter, lithographer, and illustrator. He excelled at domestic interiors with subtle lighting effects. His work includes *Bowl of Fruit* (1933).

Braque, Georges (1882–1963). A figure in fauvism and, with Picasso, a founder of cubism. Braque's works include the monumental *Nude* (1907–08) and *Woman with a Mandolin* (1937).

Cézanne, Paul (1839–1906). Postimpressionist painter. His works include *The Card Players* (1890–92), *Bathers* (1898–1905), and a series of increasingly abstracted, geometric landscapes of Mont Sainte-Victoire. Cézanne had a profound influence on modern art, especially cubism.

Chardin, Jean-Baptiste-Siméon (1699–1779). Painter of genre scenes and still lifes in a subtle, delicate, unsentimental style. His works include *Return from Market* (1739) and *Saying Grace* (c. 1740).

Corot, Jean-Baptiste Camille (1796–1875). Influential landscape painter whose delicately lit, carefully observed works include *View of the Forest of Fontainebleau* (1831) and *View of Avray* (c. 1840).

Courbet, Gustave (1819–77). The initiator of realism, Courbet was a revolutionary at odds with political authority and visual idealization. His paintings include *The Stone Breakers* (1849) and *The Artist's Studio* (1854–55).

Daumier, Honoré (1808–79). Painter, lithographer, and sculptor. A great social satirist, Daumier produced some 4,000 lithographs, such as *Rue Transnonain, 15 Avril, 1834* (1834) and *The Legislative Body* (1834).

David, Jacques-Louis (1748–1825). The leading neoclassical painter. David's work reflects his passion for the ideas of the French Revolution and for classical art. His paintings include *The Oath of the Horatii* (1784) and *The Death of Marat* (1793).

Degas, Edgar (1834–1917). Painter and sculptor. He exhibited with the impressionists, although his approach differed from theirs. His paintings, such as *The Bellini Family* (1858–59) and *The Glass of Absinthe* (1876), often use daring spatial innovations.

Delacroix, Eugène (1798–1863). The foremost French romantic painter. His exuberant, freely painted, and richly colored works include *The Death of Sardanapalus* (1827) and *Liberty Leading the People* (1830).

Dubuffet, Jean (1901–85). Painter and sculptor of semiabstract, primitive works. He often used mixed media such as asphalt, pebbles, and glass to enrich his paintings' surface. His works include the *Topographies* and *Texturologies* series (1957–59).

Duchamp, Marcel (1887–1968). Painter and sculptor. He created cubist works and also co-founded dadaism. His "ready-mades" are everyday objects exhibited as art. His works include the painting *Nude Descending a Staircase* (1912), the ready-made *Fountain* (1917), and the construction *The Bride Stripped Bare by Her Bachelors, Even* (1915–23).

Dufy, Raoul (1877–1953). Painter, illustrator, and decorator known for his fauvist landscapes, seascapes, and portraits of society, including *Riders in the Wood* (1931) and *Cowes Regatta* (1934).

Fragonard, Jean-Honoré (1732–1806). Rococo painter of playful, erotic scenes, done in delicate colors and free brushwork. His works include *The Swing* (1769) and four *Progress of Love* paintings (1771–73).

Gauguin, Paul (1848–1903). Postimpressionist painter. At age 35, he left his career and family to devote himself to painting; he developed a style called synthetism. His best-known works, using flat planes, solid figures, and bright colors, were done in Tahiti and include *Nevermore* (1897) and *Where Do We Come From? What Are We? Where Are We Going?* (1897).

Géricault, Théodore (Jean Louis André Théodore) (1791–1824). A founder of romanticism. His works, based on contemporary events, were done in a powerful, spontaneous style. They include *A Cavalry Officer* (1812) and *The Raft of the Medusa* (1819).

Ingres, Jean-Auguste-Dominique (1780–1867). A leading neoclassical painter, Ingres was also deeply influenced by Raphael. His works, including *La Grande Odalisque* (1814), *La Comtesse d'Haussonville* (1845), and *The Turkish Bath* (1859–62), are both rigidly academic and richly sensual.

Léger, Fernand (1881–1955). He created a distinctive style, characterized by flat planes of color and simplified forms based on the surfaces of machines. His paintings include *The City* (1919) and *Le Grand Déjeuner* (1921).

Lorrain, Claude (Claude Gellée, called Claude) (1600–82). In his influential landscape paintings, such as *The Embarkation of the Queen of Sheba*

(1648) and *The Expulsion of Hagar* (1668), he depicted atmospheric and lighting variations in a lyrical, sensitive style.

Maillol, Aristide (1861–1944). Sculptor, painter, and woodcut artist. His best-known works are his calm, monumental female nudes, such as *The Mediterranean* (c. 1901).

Manet, Édouard (1832–83). He introduced extraordinary thematic and technical innovations. His *Luncheon on the Grass* and *Olympia* (both 1863), both paintings of contemporary women, nude and unidealized, shocked viewers of the time. His works also include *A Bar at the Folies-Bergères* (1881).

Matisse, Henri (1869–1954). Painter, sculptor, and lithographer. Matisse, a leader of the Fauves, was a master of vivid color and line used in decorative, sensual patterns. His paintings include *La Joie de Vivre* (1905–06) and *The Dance* (1910).

Millet, Jean-François (1814–75). Realist painter associated with the Barbizon School. His unidealized scenes of peasant life include *The Sower* (1850) and *The Angelus* (1855–57).

Monet, Claude (1840–1926). A founder of impressionism and a major landscape painter. His works include many series of the same subject seen under different atmospheric and lighting conditions, such as haystacks (1891), the Rouen Cathedral (1892–94), and water lilies (1899–1926).

Morisot, Berthe (1841–95). The first woman to join the Impressionists. Morisot's paintings have a delicate, luminous style and smooth brushwork. Her works include *The Cradle* (1873) and *Young Woman at the Dance* (1880).

Pissarro, Camille (1830–1903), b. Virgin Islands. Impressionist painter who was also influenced by pointillism. His works include *Red Roofs* (1877) and *The Boulevard Montmartre at Night* (1897).

Poussin, Nicolas (1594–1665). Painter who developed the standard for French classical art, though he spent most of his life in Italy. His contemplative, precise works include *The Rape of the Sabine Women* (1636–37) and *The Holy Family on the Steps* (1648).

Renoir, Pierre Auguste (1841–1919). Impressionist painter of sensuous, joyous, light-filled works, such as *Moulin de la Galette* (1876), *The Bathers* (1884–87), and *Luncheon of the Boating Party* (1881).

Rodin, Auguste (1840–1917). Sculptor of unusual power and expression. Many of his most famous works, such as *The Thinker* (1879–1900) and *The Kiss* (1886–98), are enlarged figures from his great unfinished *Gates of Hell* (begun 1880). Other well-known works include *The Burghers of Calais* (1884–86) and *Balzac* (1892–97).

Rouault, Georges (1871–1958). Expressionist; also associated with the Fauves. His subjects, in paintings such as *Little Olympia* (1906), *Three Judges* (1913), and *Christ Mocked* (1932), were prostitutes, corrupt judges, and Christ.

Rousseau, Henri (1844–1910). Self-taught painter of naive, stylized, colorful works, often of jungle scenes, including *Sleeping Gypsy* (1897) and *The Dream* (1910).

Rousseau, Théodore (1812–67). A leading figure of the Barbizon School. His landscapes, such as *Descent of the Cattle* (1835), are full of gravity and intensity.

Seurat, Georges (1859–91). Painter who developed the pointillist or neoimpressionist technique of using small dots of pure color. His works include *Bathing at Asnières* (1883–84) and *A Sunday Afternoon on the Island of La Grande Jatte* (1885–86).

Toulouse-Lautrec, Henri de (1864–1901). Painter and lithographer. He depicted music halls, cabarets, and brothels in an unidealized, vivid way, as in *At the Moulin de la Galette* (1892) and *In the Parlor at the Rue des Moulins* (1894).

Vuillard, Édouard (1868–1940). Painter, lithographer, and member of the Nabis, known for his intimate interiors and interest in flat patterns, as in *Mother and Sister of the Artist* (c. 1893) and *Sitting Room with Three Lamps* (1899).

Watteau, Jean-Antoine (1684–1721). Rococo painter. In works such as *A Pilgrimage to Cythera* (1717) and *La Toilette* (1720), he depicted delicate, sensuous scenes in an exquisitely colored, lyrical manner.

GERMAN

Beckmann, Max (1884–1950). Expressionist painter. His highly personal style reflected the misery of contemporary events in Germany. His works include *The Night* (1918–19) and a series of nine triptychs, including *Departure* (1932–35).

Dürer, Albrecht (1471–1528). Painter, engraver, and most influential artist of the German school. Dürer is known for his technical mastery and his adoption of the principles of the Italian Renaissance. His works include the *Apocalypse* woodcuts (1498), the engraving *St. Jerome in His Study* (1514), and the painting *Four Apostles* (1526).

Ernst, Max (1891–1976). A founder of dadaism and surrealism. His grotesque, sometimes whimsical paintings include *Two Children Are Threatened by a Nightingale* (1924) and *The Temptation of St. Anthony* (1945).

Grosz, George (1893–1959). Painter known for his savage caricatures of post–World War I bourgeois society, such as *The Suicide* (1916) and *Eclipse of the Sun* (1926). He left Germany for the United States in 1933.

Grünewald, Mathias (Mathis Gothardt Neithardt) (c. 1475–1528). Religious painter of unusually expressive works, most frequently of the crucifixion of Christ. His masterpiece is the Isenheim altarpiece (1515).

Holbein, Hans, the Younger (c. 1497–1543). Outstanding portrait and religious painter of the Northern Renaissance. His works include *Sir Thomas More* (1527) and the *Madonna of the Burgomeister Meyer* (c. 1528).

Kollwitz, Käthe Schmidt (1867–1945). Graphic artist and sculptor whose works reflect her socialist and pacifist views. They include the etching series *Peasants' War* (1902–08) and the lithography series *The War* (1923) and *Death* (1934–35).

ITALIAN

Angelico, Fra (Guido or **Guidolino di Pietro,** also known as **Giovanni da Fiesole)** (c. 1400–55). Religious painter of great expressiveness; a master of graceful line and color. Among his works are the frescoes for San Marco in Florence, including *The Annunciation* (c. 1447), and scenes from the lives of saints Stephen and Lawrence in the Vatican (c. 1447–49).

Bellini, family of Renaissance painters. **Jacopo** (c. 1400–70) ran a workshop in Venice with his sons **Gentile** (1429–1507) and **Giovanni** (c. 1430–1516). Jacopo's work includes *The Madonna and Child with Lionello d'Este* (c. 1441). Gentile excelled at depicting contemporary Venetian ceremonies, as in *The Procession in the Piazza San Marco* (1496). Giovanni, probably the most talented, produced expressive works such as *St. Francis in Ecstasy* (c. 1475) and the San Zaccaria altarpiece (1505).

The most looked-at painting in the Louvre is Leonardo da Vinci's Mona Lisa.

Bernini, Giovanni Lorenzo (Gianlorenzo) (1598–1680). Sculptor, architect, painter, and leading baroque artist. His dramatic, masterful sculptures include *David* (1623) and *The Ecstasy of St. Theresa* (1645–52). Among his paintings is *Saints Andrew and Thomas* (1627).

Boccioni, Umberto (1882–1916). Painter, sculptor, and major figure of futurist art. His works include the painting *The City Rises* (1910) and the sculpture *Unique Forms of Continuity in Space* (1913).

Botticelli, Sandro (Alessandro di Mariano Filipepi) (c. 1444–1510). A favorite of the Medici, this Renaissance painter was a supreme colorist and master of the rhythmic line. He is known for his mythological scenes, such as *Primavera* (c. 1478) and *The Birth of Venus* (c. 1482). His religious works include *Madonna of the Magnificat* (c. 1485).

Canova, Antonio (1757–1822). Neoclassical sculptor. His graceful, polished works include the tomb of Pope Clement XIV (1783–87) and *Pauline Borghese as Venus* (1805–07).

Caravaggio, Michelangelo Merisi da (c. 1573–1610). An influential painter whose bold works are masterpieces of dramatic light and shadow, featuring figures with strong physical presence. They include *The Calling of St. Matthew* (c. 1598) and *The Conversion of St. Paul* (1600–01).

Carracci, family of painters. The brothers **Annibale** (1560–1609) and **Agostino** (1557–1602) and their cousin **Ludovico** (1555–1619) established an important academy of painting in Bologna. Annibale, the most talented, and Agostino painted richly sculptural, decorative frescoes for the Farnese Palace in Rome (1597–1600). Annibale also did landscape paintings, such as *Landscape with the Flight into Egypt* (1604).

Cellini, Benvenuto (1500–71). Sculptor, metalsmith, and author. His works include the gold and enamel saltcellar of Francis I (1540) and his masterpiece, the Mannerist *Perseus with the Head of Medusa* (1545–54).

Chirico, Giorgio de (1888–1978), b. Greece. Forerunner of surrealism. His best-known paintings are characterized by deep perspective, solitary figures, and objects used out of context. They include *Mystery and Melancholy of a Street* (1914) and *Disquieting Muses* (1916–17).

Correggio (Antonio Allegri) (c. 1494–1534). He painted graceful, delicately lit works, especially on mythological themes, such as *Jupiter and Io* (c. 1530), and illusionistic ceiling frescoes, such as *The Assumption of the Virgin* for the cathedral in Parma (1526–30).

da Vinci, Leonardo. *See* **Leonardo da Vinci.**

della Robbia, Florentine family of sculptors and ceramicists known for their enameled terra-cotta. **Luca** (c. 1400–82) founded a workshop; his works include *The Resurrection* and *The Ascension* (both late 1440s), for the Florence Cathedral. His nephew **Andrea** (1435–1525), best known for his medallions for the Foundling Hospital in Florence, continued the workshop with his sons, **Luca II, Giovanni,** and **Girolamo.**

Donatello (Donato di Niccolo di Betto Bardi) (c. 1386–1466). An innovative Renaissance artist, he developed a technique of shallow relief, *schiacciato*. Donatello's powerful and expressive sculptures include *David* (c. 1408), *St. George* (c. 1415), and *Mary Magdelene* (c. 1456).

Ghiberti, Lorenzo (1378–1455). Major early Renaissance sculptor. His two pairs of bronze doors for the Florence Baptistery, with their finely modeled scenes, are his masterpieces (1403–24 and 1425–52). His life-size bronzes include *St. John the Baptist* (1412–16) and *St. Matthew* (1419).

Giorgione (Giorgione da Castelfranco) (c. 1476–1510). His poetic and warmly colored works had a major influence on Venetian painting. They include *The Tempest* (c. 1500–10), *The Three Philosophers* (c. 1505–10), and *Sleeping Venus,* which was completed by Titian (c. 1510).

Giotto (Giotto di Bondone) (c. 1266–1337). Most important early Italian painter. His monumental figures and realistic treatment of pictorial space were major innovations. His works include the *Ognissanti Madonna* (c. 1310); frescoes in the Arena Chapel, Padua (finished 1313); and frescoes in the Bardi and Peruzzi chapels, Santa Croce, Florence (1320s).

Leonardo da Vinci (1425–1519). Painter, sculptor, architect, engineer, and scientist. His balanced, beautifully painted designs embody the High Renaissance; his studies of perspective and anatomy were also highly influential. His paintings include *The Virgin of the Rocks* (1483–85), *The Last Supper* (1495–98), and the *Mona Lisa* (1503–06).

Lippi. Family of Florentine painters. **Fra Filippo** (c. 1406–69) was an important early Renaissance artist whose works include *The Coronation of the Virgin* (1441) and the frescoes for the Prato cathedral (1452–65). His son, **Filippino** (c. 1457–1504), painted a fresco cycle for the Strozzi Chapel, Santa Maria Novella, Florence (1495–1502).

Mantegna, Andrea (1431–1506). Early Renaissance painter and engraver. His works show monumental forms and an interest in perspective. They include frescoes for the Ovetari Chapel in the Church of the Eremitani in Padua (1448–57), and the S. Zeno Altarpiece (1456–59).

Michelangelo Buonarroti (1475–1564). Sculptor, painter, architect, poet. The influence of this foremost Renaissance figure on Western art was supreme. His works, all in a heroic style, include the sculptures *Pietà* (1499), *David* (1501–04), *Moses* (1513–16), and the tombs of Lorenzo and Giuliano de Medici (1519–34). Also among his monumental works are the *Book of Genesis* frescoes (1508–12) on the Sistine Chapel's ceiling and the *Last Judgment* fresco (1534–41) on its altar wall.

When Michelangelo painted the scene of the last judgment in the Sistine Chapel, he put in hell those people he didn't like, including Pope Julius II, the man who forced him to paint the chapel.

Modigliani, Amedeo (1884–1920). Painter and sculptor. His style is characterized by an elongated, smooth line. Most of his works are portraits and female nudes, such as the paintings *Jeanne Hébuterne* (1919) and *Reclining Nude* (1919).

Piero della Francesca (c. 1420–92). Major Renaissance painter. His works are characterized by strong symmetricality and angularity and an interest in precise ratios of perspective. They include frescoes of *The Legend of the True Cross* in the Church of San Francesco, Arezzo (1452–64), and *The Flagellation of Christ* (c. 1456).

Pisano, family of sculptors. **Nicola** (c. 1220–84) worked in an elaborate, architectural style; his works include pulpits for the Pisa Baptistery (finished 1260) and Siena Cathedral (1265–68). His son, **Giovanni** (c. 1250–1314), created the decorative facade, Siena Cathedral (1284–96), and the pulpit, Pisa Cathedral (1302–10).

Raphael (Santi or **Sanzio)** (1483–1520). His exquisitely balanced paintings epitomize the High Renaissance. They include frescoes for the Vatican's Stanza della Segnatura, including *The School of*

Athens (finished 1511); *Galatea* (c. 1512); and *The Sistine Madonna* (1512).

Tintoretto (Jacopo Robusti) (1518–94). A great Venetian mannerist who employed dramatic lighting, coloring, and foreshortening. Among his paintings are a cycle in the Scuola di San Rocco in Venice, including an enormous *Crucifixion* (1564–87), and *The Last Supper* (1592–94).

Titian (Tiziano Vecellio) (c. 1490–1576). High Renaissance painter whose innovations, especially his expressive use of color, were influential. His works include *The Assumption of the Virgin* (1516–18), *Pope Paul III and His Grandsons* (1546), and the *Pietà* (1576).

Uccello, Paolo (c. 1396–1475). Florentine painter; early master of perspective. His colorful, decorative works, including three panels of *The Battle of San Romano* (c. 1455) and a cycle of frescoes for Santa Maria Novella, Florence (c. 1445), are notable for their foreshortening.

Veronese, Paolo (Paolo Caliari) (1528–88). Venetian painter whose large works depicting scenes of sumptuous ceremonies are distinguished by opulent colors. They include *The Marriage at Cana* (1562), *The Feast in the House of Levi* (1573), and decorative paintings for the Ducal Palace, Venice (1577–82).

Verrocchio, Andrea del (Andrea di Michele di Francesco di Cioni) (1435–88). Leading early Renaissance sculptor and painter. His sculptures include *The Doubting of Thomas* (1465); among his paintings is *The Baptism of Christ* (1472), in which he was assisted by his pupil, Leonardo da Vinci.

MEXICAN

Kahlo, Frida (1907–54). Painter of vivid works, especially self-portraits, conveying intense psychic and physical pain. They include *Frida and Diego Rivera* (1931) and *The Love Embrace of the Universe, the Earth (Mexico), Diego, Me and Señor Xolotl* (1949).

Orozco, José Clemente (1883–1949). Muralist whose monumental scenes contain humanitarian symbolism. His murals are in the New School for Social Research, New York City (1931), and Dartmouth College, New Hampshire (1932–34).

Rivera, Diego (1886–1957). A founder of the Mexican mural renaissance. His works pay homage to Mexico's history and workers. They include *The History of Mexico,* National Palace of Mexico City (1929–36), and a series at the Detroit Institute of Arts (1933).

Siqueiros, David Alfaro (1896–1974). One of the three great Mexican muralists. His dynamic brushwork reflects revolutionary themes. Siqueiros's murals include a series at the Plaza Art Center, Los Angeles (1932), and *The Liberation of Chile* at the Mexican School, Chillán, Chile (1942).

Tamayo, Rufino (1899–1991). A leading Mexican painter. His decorative works are influenced by cubism, fauvism, and themes from Mexican folklore. They include *Sleeping Musicians* (1950) and a series of murals at Smith College, Massachusetts (1943).

RUSSIAN

Chagall, Marc (1887–1985). Russian painter who lived mainly in France. His poetic, colorful, and symbolic works are often based on Jewish folklore. They include *I and the Village* (1911), *Self-Portrait with Seven Fingers* (1911), and murals for the Metropolitan Opera House, New York City (installed 1966).

Gabo, Naum (Naum Neemia Pevsner) (1890–1977). Russian-born American constructivist sculptor and theorist. His works include *Column* (1923) and *Kinetic Construction* (1920), a sculpture with a motor. In his *Realist Manifesto*, he proposed that concepts of time and space be included in art.

Kandinsky, Wassily (1866–1944). Russian painter, a founder of the avant-garde *Blaue Reiter* group, and a teacher at the Bauhaus. His series of *Compositions, Improvisations,* and *Impressions,* beginning in 1910, are often seen as the first purely abstract works.

Malevich, Kasimir Severinovich (1878–1935). Russian painter and founder of suprematism. He is known for his sparse geometric paintings, including

Black Square (1915) and the *White on White* series (c. 1918). He described his theories in the book *The Non-Objective World* (1915).

Tatlin, Vladimir Evgrafovich (1885–1953). Russian artist and a founder of constructivism. His works include the *Relief Constructions* series (begun 1913) and the *Corner Reliefs* (begun 1915).

SPANISH

Dalí, Salvador (1904–89). Surrealist painter who worked in a precise style. His hallucinatory images can be seen in *The Persistence of Memory* (1931), *Crucifixion* (1951), and *The Last Supper* (1955).

El Greco. *See* **Greco, El.**

Goya y Lucientes, Francisco Jose de (1746–1828). Highly original painter and graphic artist. His expressive works are often telling social satires. They include the paintings *Nude Maja* and *Clothed Maja* (both c. 1804) and *Charles IV and His Family* (1800); and etching series, such as *Los Caprichos* (1799) and *Disasters of War* (1810–14).

Greco, El (Domenikos Theotokopoulos) (1541–1614), b. Crete. Painter of dynamic scenes, often of religious ecstasy. His works, distinguished by elongated figures and vivid highlights, include *The Disrobing of Christ* (1577–79), *The Burial of Count Orgaz* (1586), and *View of Toledo* (1600).

Gris, Juan (José Victoriano González) (1887–1927). A developer of synthetic cubism, he used simple forms and a rhythmic style in his paintings and collages. His works include *Homage to Picasso* (1911–12), *The Violin* (1916), and *Violin and Fruit Dish* (1924).

Miró, Joan (1893–1983). Surrealist painter. He worked in a playful, lyrical style, with colorful, amoebic shapes. His works include *Harlequin's Carnival* (1924–25), *Dog Barking at the Moon* (1926), and ceramic murals for the UNESCO building, Paris (1955–58).

Murillo, Bartolemé Estéban (1618–82). Religious and portrait painter. Among his important works are a series for the Charity Hospital in Seville

(1671–73), portraits, and many depictions of the Immaculate Conception.

Picasso, Pablo (Pablo Ruiz y Picasso) (1881–1973). Painter, sculptor, graphic artist, ceramicist. He was an enormously versatile, original, and prolific artist. His *Les Desmoiselles d'Avignon* (1907) is a seminal cubist work. Other important paintings include *The Three Musicians* (1921) and *Guernica* (1937).

Ribera, Jusepe de (1591–1652). Baroque painter, mainly of religious scenes. His naturalistic yet mystical works include *The Martyrdom of St. Bartholomew* (c. 1630) and *The Mystic Marriage of St. Catherine* (1648).

Velázquez, Diego Rodríguez de Silva y (1599–1660). One of the greatest of Spanish painters. He was a master of shimmering tones and brilliant colors. His expressive works include *The Surrender of Breda* (1634–35), *Pope Innocent X* (1650), and *The Maids of Honor* (1656).

Zurbarán, Francisco de (1598–1664). Baroque painter. His works, mostly religious, combine severity with spiritual intensity. They include *The Apotheosis of St. Thomas Aquinas* (1631) and *St. Serapion* (1628).

OTHER

Brancusi, Constantin (1876–1957). Romanian sculptor whose economical, simple style was radically innovative. His works include *Bird in Space* (1919) and the immense *Endless Column,* erected in a park near his birthplace (1937).

Giacometti, Alberto (1901–66). Swiss sculptor and painter, known especially for his sculptures of elongated figures, such as *The Forest* (1950) and *Walking Man* (1960).

Klee, Paul (1879–1940). Swiss painter whose works, such as *Twittering Machine* (1922) and *Park Near L(ucerne)* (1938), combine theories of abstraction with playful childlike inventiveness. Klee was associated with the *Blaue Reiter* group.

Klimt, Gustav (1862–1918). Austrian painter; a founder of the Vienna Secession group and a figure of the art nouveau movement. His exotic, erotic, symbolic works include *Judith* (1909) and *The Kiss* (1907–08).

Kokoschka, Oskar (1886–1980). Austrian expressionist painter. He produced many portraits and landscapes, such as *Le Marquis de Montesquiou* (1909–10) and *Jerusalem* (1929–30), as well as a series of self-portraits.

Munch, Edvard (1863–1944). Leading Norwegian painter and graphic artist. He foreshadowed expressionism with his charged images of terror, despair, and isolation, as in the paintings *The Scream* (1893) and *Vampire* (1895).

Paik, Nam June (1932–), b. South Korea. A contemporary artist working primarily with video-related installations, sculptures, and performances. Paik has been instrumental in establishing video as an art form. As a student in Germany, Paik participated in the Fluxus Movement, combining music and performance. His video works include the installations and sculptures *TV Buddha* (1964), *Family of Robots* (1986), and *Megatron* (1995). He began experimenting with satellite technology in the late 1970s, as seen in *Wrap Around the World* (1988).

Phidias (Pheidias) (c. 500–432 B.C.). One of the greatest ancient Greek sculptors, although none of his original works survive. He sculpted the enormous *Athena Parthenos,* Athens (c. 447–439 B.C.); and the *Zeus,* Olympia, one of the Seven Wonders of the Ancient World (c. 435 B.C.).

Praxiteles (c. 370–330 B.C.). He was considered the greatest Greek sculptor of his time. His *Hermes with the Infant Dionysus* (c. 350–330 B.C.) is the only existing original work by an ancient master. He also sculpted the *Aphrodite of Cnidus* (c. 350–330 B.C.).

Schiele, Egon (1890–1918). Austrian expressionist painter and graphic artist who developed an angular, linear style. Many of his works are nudes, often in disturbing, erotic poses. His paintings include *The Embrace* (1917) and *Paris von Gütersloh* (1918).

ART MOVEMENTS AND STYLES

abstract expressionism   Movement in painting, originating in New York City in the 1940s. It emphasized spontaneous personal expression, freedom from accepted artistic values, surface qualities of paint, and the act of painting itself. Jackson Pollock, Willem de Kooning, Robert Motherwell, and Franz Kline are important abstract expressionists.

art deco   A design style prevalent during the 1920s and 1930s, characterized by a sleek use of straight lines and slender forms.

art nouveau   A decorative art movement that emerged in the late 19th century. Characterized by dense asymmetrical ornamentation in sinuous forms, it is often symbolic and of an erotic nature. Gustav Klimt worked in an art-nouveau style.

Ash Can School   Group of American artists active from 1908 to 1918. It included members of The Eight, such as Robert Henri and Arthur Davies; Edward Hopper was also part of the Ash Can group. Their work featured scenes of urban realism.

Barbizon School   An association of French landscape painters, c. 1840–70, who lived in the village of Barbizon and who painted directly from nature. Théodore Rousseau was a leader; Jean-Baptiste Corot and Jean-François Millet were also associated with the group.

baroque   A movement in European painting in the 17th and early 18th centuries, characterized by violent movement, strong emotion, and dramatic lighting and coloring. Giovanni Bernini, Michelangelo Caravaggio, and Peter Paul Rubens were among important baroque artists.

Byzantine   A style of the Byzantine Empire and its provinces, c. 330–1450. Appearing mostly in religious mosaics, manuscript illuminations, and panel paintings, it is characterized by rigid, monumental, stylized forms with gold backgrounds.

"Major Art Museums and Their Special Collections" in chapter 11

Go to

classicism   Refers to the principles of Greek and Roman art of antiquity with its emphasis on harmony, proportion, balance, and simplicity. In a general sense, classicism refers to art based on accepted standards of beauty.

color field painting   A technique in abstract painting developed in the 1950s. It focuses on the lyrical effects of large areas of color, often poured or stained onto the canvas. Barnett Newman, Mark Rothko, and Helen Frankenthaler painted in this manner.

conceptual art   A movement of the 1960s and 1970s that emphasized the artistic idea over the art object. It attempted to free art from the confines of the gallery and the pedestal.

constructivism   A Russian abstract movement founded by Vladimir Tatlin, Naum Gabo, and Antoine Pevsner, c. 1915. It focused on art for the industrial age. Tatlin believed in art with a utilitarian purpose.

cubism   A revolutionary movement begun by Pablo Picasso and Georges Braque in the early 20th century. It employs an analytic vision based on fragmentation and multiple viewpoints.

dadaism   A movement, c. 1915–23, that rejected accepted aesthetic standards. It aimed to create antiart and nonart, often employing a sense of the absurd.

The Eight   A group of American painters who united out of opposition to academic standards in the early 20th century. Members of the group were Robert Henri, Arthur Davies, Maurice Prendergast, William James Glackens (1870–1938), Ernest Lawson (1873–1939), Everett Shinn (1876–1953), John Sloan (1871–1951), and George Luks (1867–1933).

expressionism   Refers to art that uses emphasis and distortion to communicate emotion. More specifically, it refers to early-20th-century northern European art, especially in Germany, c. 1905–25. Artists such as Georges Rouault, Oskar Kokoschka, and Egon Schiele painted in this manner.

"Literary Movements, Periods, and Styles" in chapter 8

Go to

fauvism   From the French word *fauve,* meaning "wild beast." A style adopted by artists associated with Henri Matisse, c. 1905–08. They painted in a spontaneous manner, using bold colors.

folk art   Works of a culturally homogeneous people without formal training, generally according to regional traditions and involving crafts.

futurism   An Italian movement, c. 1909–19, that attempted to integrate the dynamism of the machine age into art. Umberto Boccioni was a futurist artist.

Gothic   A European movement beginning in France. Gothic sculpture emerged c. 1200; Gothic painting appeared later in the 13th century. The artworks are characterized by a linear, graceful, elegant style more naturalistic than that which had existed previously in Europe.

impressionism   A late-19th-century French school of painting. It focused on transitory visual impressions, often painted directly from nature, with an emphasis on the changing effects of light and color. Claude Monet, Pierre Renoir, and Camille Pissarro were important Impressionists.

mannerism   A style, c. 1520–1600, that arose in reaction to the harmony and proportion of the High Renaissance. Mannerism featured elongated and contorted poses, crowded canvases, and harsh lighting and coloring.

minimalism   A movement in American painting and sculpture that originated in the late 1950s. It emphasized pure, reduced forms and strict, systematic compositions.

Nabis   From the Hebrew word for "prophet." A group of French painters active in the 1890s who worked in a subjective, sometimes mystical style, stressing flat areas of color and pattern. Pierre Bonnard and Édouard Vuillard were members.

naive art   Artwork, usually paintings, characterized by a simplified style, nonscientific perspective, and bold colors. The artists are generally not professionally trained. Henri Rousseau and Grandma Moses worked in this style.

neoclassicism A European style of the late 18th and early 19th centuries. Its elegant, balanced works revived the order and harmony of ancient Greek and Roman art. Jacques-Louis David and Antonio Canova are examples of neoclassicists.

op art An abstract movement in Europe and the United States, begun in the mid-1950s, based on the effects of optical patterns. Josef Albers worked in this style.

Al Capp, the creator of **Li'l Abner,** *once said, "Abstract art is a product of the untalented, sold by the unprincipled to the utterly bewildered."*

photorealism A figurative movement that emerged in the United States and Britain in the late 1960s and 1970s. The subject matter, usually everyday scenes, is portrayed in an extremely detailed, exacting style. It is also called superrealism, especially when referring to sculpture.

pointillism A method of painting developed by Georges Seurat and Paul Signac (1863–1935) in the 1880s. It used dabs of pure color that were intended to mix in the eyes of viewers rather than on the canvas. It is also called divisionism or neoimpressionism.

pop art A movement that began in Britain and the United States in the 1950s. It used the images and techniques of mass media, advertising, and popular culture, often in an ironic way. Works of Andy Warhol, Roy Lichtenstein, and Claes Oldenburg exemplify this style.

postimpressionism A term coined by British art critic Roger Fry to refer to a group of 19th-century painters, including Paul Cézanne, Paul Gauguin, and Vincent van Gogh, who were dissatisfied with the limitations of impressionism. The term has since been used to refer to various reactions against impressionism, such as fauvism and expressionism.

Pre-Raphaelite Brotherhood A group of English painters formed in 1848. These artists attempted to recapture the style of painting preceding the Italian artist Raphael. They rejected industrialized England and focused on painting from nature, producing detailed, colorful works. Dante Rossetti was a founding member.

realism In a general sense, refers to objective representation. More specifically, a 19th-century movement, especially in France, that rejected idealized academic styles in favor of everyday subjects. Honoré Daumier, Jean-François Millet, and Gustave Courbet were realists.

Renaissance Meaning "rebirth" in French. Refers to Europe, c. 1400–1600. Renaissance art, which began in Italy, stressed the forms of classical antiquity, a realistic representation of space based on scientific perspective, and secular subjects. The works of Leonardo da Vinci, Michelangelo, and Raphael exemplify the balance and harmony of the High Renaissance (c. 1495–1520).

rococo An 18th-century European style, originating in France. In reaction to the grandeur and massiveness of the baroque, rococo employed refined, elegant, highly decorative forms. Jean-Honoré Fragonard worked in this style.

Romanesque A European style developed in France in the late 11th century. Its sculpture is ornamental, stylized, and complex. Some Romanesque frescoes survive, painted in a monumental, active manner.

romanticism A European movement of the late 18th to mid–19th century. In reaction to neoclassicism, it focused on emotion over reason and on spontaneous expression. The subject matter was invested with drama and usually painted energetically in brilliant colors. Eugène Delacroix, Théodore Géricault, Joseph Turner, and William Blake were Romantic artists.

suprematism A Russian abstract movement originated by Kasimir Malevich, c. 1913. It was characterized by flat geometric shapes on plain backgrounds and emphasized the spiritual qualities of pure form.

surrealism   A movement of the 1920s and 1930s that began in France. It explored the unconscious, often using images from dreams. It used spontaneous techniques and featured unexpected juxtapositions of objects. René Magritte, Salvador Dalí, Joan Miró, and Max Ernst painted surrealist works.

symbolism   A painting movement that flourished in France in the 1880s and 1890s in which subject matter was suggested rather than directly presented. It featured decorative, stylized, and evocative images.

COMMON ART TERMS

acrylic   Water-soluble paint made from pigments and a plastic binder.

aquatint   An etching technique in which a solution of asphalt or resin is used on the plate. Aquatint produces prints with rich, gray tones.

caricature   An artwork humorously exaggerating the qualities, defects, or peculiarities of a person or idea.

cartoon   A humorous sketch or drawing usually telling a story or caricaturing some person or action. In fine arts, a preparatory sketch or design for a picture or ornamental motif to be transferred to a fresco or tapestry.

carving   In sculpture, the cutting of a form from a solid, hard material such as stone or wood, in contrast to the technique of modeling.

casting   In sculpture, a technique of reproducing a work by pouring into a mold a substance such as plaster or molten metal, which then hardens.

chiaroscuro   The rendering of light and shade in painting; the subtle gradations and marked variations of light and shade for dramatic effect.

collage   A composition made of cut and pasted pieces of materials, sometimes with images added by the artist.

colors, complementary   Two colors at opposite points on the color scale—for example, orange and blue, green and red.

colors, primary   Red, yellow, and blue, the mixture of which will yield all other colors in the spectrum but which themselves cannot be produced through a mixture of other colors.

colors, secondary   Orange, green, and purple—colors produced by mixing two primary colors.

composition   The organization of forms and colors within an artwork.

drypoint   A technique of engraving, using a sharp-pointed needle, that produces a furrowed edge resulting in a print with soft, velvety lines.

encaustic   A painting technique using pigments dissolved in hot wax.

engraving   The art of producing printed designs through various methods of incising on wood or metal blocks, which are then inked and printed.

etching   The technique of producing printed designs through incising on a coated metal plate, which is then bathed in corrosive acid, inked, and printed.

figure   A representation of a human or an animal form.

foreshortening   Reducing or distorting in order to represent three-dimensional space as perceived by the eye, according to the rules of perspective.

fresco   Meaning "fresh" in Italian. The technique of painting on moist lime plaster with colors ground in water.

frieze   A band of painted or sculpted decoration, often at the top of a wall.

genre painting   A realistic style of painting in which everyday life forms the subject matter, as distinguished from religious or historical painting.

gesso   Ground chalk or plaster mixed with glue, used as a base coat for tempera and oil painting.

gouache   A method of watercolor painting, but prepared with a more gluey base, producing a less transparent effect.

"Common Music Terms" and "Common Dance Terms" in chapter 6

Go to

highlight   On a represented form, a point of most intense light.

impasto   Paint applied very thickly. It often projects from the picture surface.

landscape   Painting in which natural scenery is the subject.

lithography   A printing process in which ink impressions are taken from a flat stone or metal plate prepared with a greasy substance, such as an oily crayon.

modeling   In sculpture, the building up of form using a soft medium such as clay or wax, as distinguished from carving. In painting and drawing, using color and lighting variations to produce a three-dimensional effect.

monochrome   A painting or drawing executed in a single color.

monotype   A single print made from a metal or glass plate on which an image has been represented in paint, ink, etc.

mural   A large painting or decoration done on a wall.

oil   A method of painting with pigments mixed with oil, producing a vast range of light and color effects.

palette   A flat board used by a painter to mix and hold colors, traditionally oblong, with a hole for the thumb; also, a range of colors used by a particular painter.

pastel   A soft, subdued color; also, a drawing stick made of ground pigments, chalk, and gum water.

perspective   A method of representing three-dimensional volumes and spatial relationships on a flat surface to produce an effect similar to what is seen by the eye.

polychrome   Of many or various colors.

polyptych   In painting, a work made of several panels or scenes joined together. A diptych has two panels; a triptych, three.

primary colors   *See* **colors, primary.**

relief   In sculpture, the projection of an image or form from its background. Sculpture formed in this manner is described as high relief or low relief (bas-relief), depending on the degree of projection. In painting or drawing, the apparent projection of parts conveying the illusion of three dimensions.

secondary colors   *See* **colors, secondary.**

stenciling   A method of producing images or letters from sheets of cardboard, metal, or other materials from which forms have been cut away.

still life   The representation of inanimate objects in painting, drawing, or photography.

tempera   A painting technique using pigments mixed with egg yolk and water. Tempera produces clear, pure colors.

texture   The visual and tactile quality of a work of art based on the particular way the materials are handled; also, the distribution of tones or shades of a single color.

tone   The effect of the harmony of color and values in a work.

trompe l'oeil   Meaning "fool the eye" in French. In painting, the fine, detailed rendering of objects to convey the illusion that the painted forms are real and three-dimensional.

value   In painting, the degree of lightness or darkness in a color.

wash   In painting, a thin layer of translucent color.

watercolor   Painting in pigments suspended in water. It can produce brilliant colors and transparent effects.

woodcut   A print made by carving on a wood block, which is then inked and printed.

MAJOR ARCHITECTS

AMERICAN

Bulfinch, Charles (1763–1844), b. Massachusetts. He designed the first theater in New England, the Federal Street Theater (1794); the Massachusetts State House (1795–97); and the Massachusetts General Hospital (1818–23), all in Boston. In his completion of the design of the Capitol building, Washington, D.C. (1818–30), he achieved a model for state capitols throughout the country.

Burnham, Daniel Hudson (1846–1912), b. New York. Architect and city planner. With his partner, John Root, he designed the first major skeleton skyscraper, the Masonic Temple Building, Chicago (1892). Alone, Burnham designed the Flatiron Building, New York City (1903), and Union Station, Washington, D.C. (1903–07).

Fuller, (Richard) Buckminster (1895–1983), b. Massachusetts. Architect and engineer. His revolutionary designs, such as the geodesic dome, aimed at achieving the maximum effect with a minimal investment of materials.

Gehry, Frank O. (1929–   ) b. Canada. Educated in the U.S.A. Postmodern architect and designer known for dramatic sculptural buildings such as the Vitra Design Museum, Weil am Rhein, Germany (1987), the Rasin ("Fred and Ginger") Building, Prague, Czech Republic (1996), and the Guggenheim Museum, Bilbao, Spain (1997), along with numerous private homes.

Graves, Michael (1934–   ), b. Indiana. Postmodern architect. His influences range from classical Greece and Rome to the work of Le Corbusier. Graves's designs are known for their use of color and mix of delicacy and strength. They include the Fargo-Moorhead Cultural Center Bridge, Fargo, North Dakota, and Moorhead, Minnesota (1977); and the Public Services Building, Portland, Oregon (1980–82).

Gropius, Walter (1883–1969), b. Germany. A great modern functionalist. In 1919, he reorganized the Weimar School of Art into the Bauhaus. He designed the glass Fagus Factory, Alfeld (1911–12), and the Bauhaus buildings, Dessau (1925–26). His U.S. work includes the Pan American Building, New York City (1957). In 1946, he and young associates formed The Architects Collaborative (TAC), working together on buildings such as the United States Embassy, Athens (1956).

Hunt, Richard Morris (1827–95), b. Vermont. Architect. His work, which closely follows historical styles, exemplifies 19th-century eclecticism. He designed the Lenox Library (1870–77) and the Tribune Building (1873–76), both in New York City; and various mansions, such as those for the Vanderbilts in New York City and Newport, Rhode Island.

Jefferson, Thomas (1743–1826), b. Virginia. President, statesman, architect, and scientist. Jefferson, a self-taught architect, designed Monticello, his house near Charlottesville, Virginia (1768–82); the Virginia State Capitol in Richmond (1785–99); and the University of Virginia, Charlottesville (1817–26).

Jenney, William Le Baron (1832–1907), b. Massachusetts. Architect and engineer. His 10-story-high Home Insurance Building in Chicago (1884–85) is often considered to have been the first skyscraper. It was the first steel-framed office building.

Johnson, Philip Cortelyou (1906–   ), b. Ohio. He is noted for his glass-walled house in New Canaan, Connecticut (1949), and for the New York State Theater at Lincoln Center (1964), his collaboration with Mies van der Rohe on the Seagram Building (1958), and the American Telephone and Telegraph Building (1978–84), all in New York City. Johnson's writings include *The International Style* (1932), which he coauthored.

Kahn, Louis Isadore (1901–74), b. Estonia. Kahn designed the Yale University Art Gallery, New Haven (1951–53); the Kimbell Art Museum, Fort Worth (1966–72); and many housing projects, such as Carver Court Housing, Coatesville, Pennsylvania

(1941–43). The Richards Medical Research Building, University of Pennsylvania (1957–64), has been admired for its integration of form and function.

Latrobe, Benjamin Henry   (1764–1820), b. England. Considered the first professional architect in the United States, Latrobe produced some of the best monumental architecture of his time in classic revival style. His works include the Bank of Pennsylvania, Philadelphia (1799); and the Roman Catholic Cathedral, Baltimore, the first cathedral built in the United States (1805–18). He also worked on the Capitol, Washington, D.C. (1803–17).

Mies van der Rohe, Ludwig   (1886–1969), b. Germany. A director of the Bauhaus (1930–33) and a founder of modern architecture. His U.S. buildings, mainly unornamented skyscrapers, include Chicago's Lake Shore Drive Apartments (1948–51); the Chicago Federal Center (1959–73); and, with Philip Johnson, the Seagram Building, New York City (1958).

Pei, I(eoh) M(ing)   (1917–   ), b. China. He carefully integrates his expressive works with their surrounding environment. His buildings include the Mile High Center, Denver (1955); the John Hancock Tower, Boston (1973); the East Wing of the National Gallery of Art, Washington, D.C. (1978); a pyramidal addition to the Louvre museum, Paris (1989); and the Rock and Roll Hall of Fame in Cleveland, Ohio (1998).

Richardson, Henry Hobson   (1838–86), b. Louisiana. His monumental building, Trinity Church, Boston (1872–77), exemplifies the "Richardson romanesque" style. His work also includes the Marshall Field store, Chicago (1885–87).

Mills, Robert   (1781–1855), b. South Carolina. Mills, a classic revivalist, was appointed architect of public buildings in Washington, D.C. There, he built the Patent Office (1836–40), the Treasury (1836–42), and the Post Office (1839–42). In 1833, he designed the Washington Monument (built 1848–84).

Saarinen, Eero   (1910–61), b. Finland. Son of Eliel. His works, especially his domed constructions, are innovative. His projects include the Kresge Auditorium, Massachusetts Institute of Technology, Cambridge (1953–56); Dulles International Airport, Chantilly, Virginia (1958–62); and the Gateway Arch, St. Louis (1959–64). He also designed furniture, especially chairs.

Saarinen, (Gottlieb) Eliel   (1873–1950), b. Finland. Architect and city planner. He designed the National Museum (1902–04) in Helsinki, Finland. His work in the United States includes several buildings at the Cranbrook Foundation, where he was president of the Academy of Art; and, with his son, Eero, performance halls at the Berkshire Music Center in Tanglewood, Massachusetts (late 1930s–early 1940s). Saarinen's writings include *The City: Its Growth, Its Decay, Its Future* (1943).

Strickland, William   (1788–1854), b. New Jersey. Classic revivalist architect. His most original work is the Merchants' Exchange, Philadelphia (1832–34). Also in Philadelphia, he built the Second Bank of the United States (1818–24) and the U.S. Mint (1829–33). He was a founder and first president of the American Institution of Architects.

Sullivan, Louis Henry   (1856–1924), b. Massachusetts. Prominent in the development of modern architecture, Sullivan propounded the theory that form should follow function. He designed the Wainwright Building, St. Louis (1890–91); the Transportation Building at the World's Columbian Exposition, Chicago (1893); and the Stock Exchange in Chicago (1893–94).

Venturi, Robert   (1925–   ), b. Pennsylvania. Venturi uses architectural elements from popular culture in his work, which includes Guild House, Philadelphia (1962–66); the Humanities and Social Sciences Building, State University of New York, Purchase (1968–70); and the new building for the Seattle Art Museum (1991). His writings include *Complexity and Contradiction in Architecture* (1966).

Walter, Thomas Ustick   (1804–87), b. Pennsylvania. As government architect in Washington, D.C., from 1851 to 1865, he added the Senate and

House wings to the Capitol, built its central dome, and designed the interior of the Library of Congress. Walter was a founder and president of the American Institute of Architects.

White, Stanford (1853–1906), b. New York. Architect. He worked in partnership with Charles Follen McKim and William Rutherford Mead. White's accomplishments include the first Madison Square Garden (1887–91), the Washington Memorial Arch (1889–92), and the New York Herald Building (1890–95), all in New York City. White's buildings reflect his passion for graceful, decorative elements and rich ornamentation.

Wright, Frank Lloyd (1867–1959), b. Wisconsin. Architect. His innovative approach integrated modern technology into architectural aesthetics. He is especially known for his dramatic interior spaces. His buildings include the Larkin Building, Buffalo, New York (1904); the Imperial Hotel, Tokyo (1915–22); the Kaufmann house, "Fallingwater," Bear Run, Pennsylvania (1936–39); a Unitarian church, Madison, Wisconsin (1947); and the Guggenheim Museum, New York City (1959).

BRITISH

Adam, Robert (1728–92). Scottish architect. He designed, with his brother James, numerous public and private buildings in England and Scotland in a distinctive and decorative style that combines Palladian, Renaissance, and classical elements. Notable examples are Osterley Park (1761–80) and Syon House (1762–69), both in Middlesex, England.

Chambers, Sir William (1723–96), b. Sweden. His *Treatise on the Decorative Part of Civil Architecture* (1759) was a classic design text. He is known for Somerset House, London (begun 1776); and for decorative architecture in Kew Gardens, Surrey, England, especially the Chinese Pagoda (1763).

Jones, Inigo (1573–1652). One of the first great English architects. He broke from the Jacobean style, thus beginning the Renaissance and the Georgian periods in English architecture. His works include the Queen's House, Greenwich Palace, Kent (1616–35); and the royal banqueting hall, White-hall Palace, London (1619–22). Both employ Palladian principles.

Lutyens, Sir Edwin Landseer (1869–1944). The leading English architect of his time, Lutyens combined romantic and classical styles. His outstanding achievement is the plan of New Delhi, India, centering on the Viceroy's House (1912–31). Other works include war memorials, such as the Cenotaph in London (1919–20), and the British Embassy in Washington, D.C. (1927–28).

Mackintosh, Charles Rennie (1868–1928). Scottish architect, artist, and furniture designer. His interiors, such as those for four Glasgow tearooms (1896–1919), display a sumptuous art nouveau style. His buildings, such as the Glasgow School of Art (1896–99), are subtly proportioned.

Paxton, Sir Joseph (1803–65). Architect and horticulturist. His Great Conservatory, a greenhouse in Chatsworth, England (1836–40), served as a model for the glass Crystal Palace, which he built for the Great Exhibition of 1851 in London. Paxton's use of glass and iron in this building was a great technological innovation.

Pugin, Augustus Welby Northmore (1812–52). Architect, designer, and author. Pugin, a Gothic revivalist, worked on the interior and ornamentation of the Houses of Parliament (1844–52) and designed more than 65 churches, including Saint George's, London (1840–48). His writings, however, were more influential than his buildings.

Nash, John (1752–1835). Architect and city planner. Nash, a leader in the neoclassic Regency style, planned the layout of Regent Street and Regent's Park in London (built c. 1818), remodeled Buckingham Palace (1824–30), and worked on the "Indian"-style Royal Pavilion in Brighton (1815–21).

Smirke, Sir Robert (1781–1867). Classic revivalist architect. His best-known work is the main facade of the British Museum, London (1823–47). Other achievements include the Royal College of

Physicians (1822–25) and the General Post Office (1823–29), also in London. Upon his retirement, his brother Sydney Smirke (1798–1877) continued work on the British Museum (1854–57).

Soane, Sir John (1753–1837). Soane, a classic revivalist, developed a complicated and highly personal style. His works in London include the Bank of England (begun 1788), the Dulwich College Art Gallery (1811–14), and his own eccentric house at Lincoln's Inn Fields (1812–13), now a museum.

Vanbrugh, Sir John (1664–1726). Architect and dramatist. His buildings include Blenheim Palace, Oxfordshire (1705–16), which epitomizes the English baroque; and the Queen's Theatre in the Haymarket, London (1704–05). He designed theatrical, picturesque country houses, such as Seaton Delaval, Northumberland (begun 1720).

Wren, Sir Christopher (1632–1723). Astronomer, architect, and mathematician. His elegant and dignified designs were highly influential. He designed St. Paul's Cathedral, London (1675–1710), and 52 other London churches, including St. Mary-le-Bow (1671–80). Other works include the Sheldonian Theatre, Oxford (1664–69), and Trinity College Library, Cambridge (1679–84).

FRENCH

Garnier, Jean Louis Charles (1825–98). His principal work is the ornate Opéra in Paris, with its grand staircase (1861–75). He also designed the Casino at Monte Carlo (1878–81) and Bischofsheim's Observatory, Nice (1880–88).

Hardouin Mansart, Jules (1646–1708). Baroque architect. In 1699, he became chief architect of the royal buildings. Some of his major works are at the Palace of Versailles, including the Galerie des Glaces and the Grand Trianon (both 1678–89). In Paris, he designed the Church of the Invalides (1679–91) and the Place Vendôme (1698).

Labrouste, Henri (Pierre François Henri) (1801–75). He was one of the first to successfully use metal construction in architecture, as he did in the reading room of the Bibliothèque Sainte-Geneviève, Paris (1843–50). He also worked extensively on the Bibliothèque Nationale (1854–75).

Le Corbusier (Charles-Édouard Jeanneret) (1887–1965). b. Switzerland. His innovative buildings and writings express a revolutionary approach toward aesthetic and technological architectural problems. His works, reflecting industrial as well as sculptural influences, include the Villa Savoye, Poissy, France (1928–31); collaboration on the United Nations buildings, New York City (1947–53); and buildings for the new capital of the Punjab, Chandigarh, India (1951–65).

Ledoux, Claude Nicolas (1736–1806). This imaginative neoclassicist's buildings include the Pavilion de Louveciennes and the theater at Besançon in France (both 1771–73). He is known for his architectural treatise of 1804 and for his plans for Chaux, an ideal city for the workers of the salt mines of Arc-et-Senans, France.

ITALIAN

Alberti, Leone Battista (1404–72). Architect and painter. His treatise, *De Re Aedificatoria* (c. 1450), established architecture as an intellectual field. His works include the exteriors of the churches of San Francesco in Rimini (c. 1450–61) and Sant'Andrea in Mantua (c. 1470–72).

Bernini, Giovanni Lorenzo (Gian Lorenzo) (1598–1680). Major Italian baroque architect and sculptor. As architect of St. Peter's in Rome, he designed the ornate baldachin (canopy) under the dome (1624–33) and the monument for St. Peter's chair (1657–66). From 1656 to 1667, he worked on the piazza and colonnade in front of St. Peter's. His Cornaro Chapel, in the church of Santa Maria della Vittoria, Rome (1647–51), is a dynamic melding of sculpture and architecture.

Borromini, Francesco (1599–1667). Italian baroque architect. His influential designs for churches and palaces were complex and extravagant. His works include the churches of San Carlo alle Quattro Fontane (1634–41) and Sant'Ivo alla Sapienza (1642–60) and the completion of the church of Sant'Agnese, Piazza Navona (1653–57), all in Rome.

Bramante (Donato di Angelo di Antonio) (1444–1514). Leading Italian High Renaissance architect. He designed much of the church of Santa Maria presso San Satiro (c. 1480) and the east end of Santa Maria delle Grazie (c. 1492), both in Milan. His plans for St. Peter's, Rome (1505–06), though not fully carried out, were influential.

Brunelleschi, Filippo (1377–1446). The first great architect of the Italian Renaissance. His masterpiece is the celebrated ribbed octagonal dome for the Florence Cathedral (1420–36). His other works include the Foundling Hospital (1419) and the churches of San Lorenzo (begun c. 1420) and Santo Spirito (begun 1436), all in Florence.

da Vinci, Leonardo. *See* **Leonardo da Vinci.**

Giotto (Giotto di Bondone) (c. 1266–1337). Florentine architect and painter. In 1334, he was appointed architect of the Florence Cathedral. His main accomplishment is the multicolored bell tower called Giotto's Tower (begun 1334).

Leonardo da Vinci (1452–1519). Painter, sculptor, architect, engineer, and scientist. Around 1488, Leonardo did architectural work for the Milan Cathedral; he later worked on the reconstructions of cathedrals in Pavia and Piacenza. Beginning in 1506, he served as architect and engineer in Milan for Louis XII. In Rome, from 1513 to about 1515, he worked on several projects for the Vatican. Although most of Leonardo's designs were not executed, his architectural studies are of great historic importance.

Michelangelo Buonarroti (1475–1564). Italian Renaissance sculptor, painter, architect, and poet. Michelangelo's designs include the Medici Chapel (1520–34), where he powerfully combined architecture and sculpture, and the Laurentian Library (begun 1524), both at San Lorenzo, Florence. His work includes designs for St. Peter's (1546–64); its monumental dome, completed after Michelangelo's death, is based largely on his ideas.

Palladio, Andrea (1508–80). Italian Renaissance architect; a leading figure in Western architecture. Classical models were of extreme importance to him. He published a famous treatise in 1570. His works include rebuilding the Basilica at Vicenza, Italy (1549–80); many houses, including the Villa Barbaro, Maser, Italy (1554–58); and the Villa Rotunda, Vicenza (1567–70). In Venice, he built the churches of San Giorgio Maggiore (1560–80) and Il Redentore (1576–80).

Piranesi, Giovanni Battista (1720–1778). Architect and designer. Although he constructed few buildings—among them, Santa Maria del Priorato (1764) in Rome—his imaginative designs and theoretical writings were a major influence on European neoclassicism. His *Antichità Romane* (1756) and *Parere su l'Architettura* presented classical Rome as the creative foundation for a contemporary architecture.

OTHER

Aalto, Alvar (1898–1976). Finnish architect and furniture designer. The works of this leading 20th-century architect combine Finnish building traditions with modern techniques. They include the Municipal Library, Viipuri, Finland (1933–35); the Finnish Pavilion for the World's Fair, New York City (1939); and the undulating Baker House, Massachusetts Institute of Technology, Cambridge, Massachusetts (1946–49).

Behrens, Peter (1868–1940). German architect and industrial designer. His factory buildings, such as the A. E. G. Turbine Factory, Berlin (1908–09), show a simple, utilitarian approach. He is also known for the German Embassy, Leningrad (1911–12). Le Corbusier, Ludwig Mies van der Rohe, and Walter Gropius were his students.

Berlage, Hendrik Petrus (1856–1934). Pioneering modern Dutch architect. He is known for the redbrick Stock Exchange (1897–1903) and the Diamond Workers' Union Building (1899–1901), both in Amsterdam. He was also active in urban planning and furniture design.

Gaudí y Cornet, Antonio (1852–1926). Spanish architect whose colorful, sculptural, undulating style has similarities to art nouveau as well as surrealism.

His masterpiece is the unfinished Expiatory Church of the Holy Family, Barcelona (begun 1883; work still in progress). Other examples of his work are Parc Güell (1900–14) and Casa Battló (1904–06) in Barcelona.

Hoffmann, Josef Franz Maria (1870–1956). Austrian architect and decorator; a leader of the early-20th-century Viennese style. He is known for his use of rectilinear forms with delicate ornamentation, as in the Palais Stoclet, Brussels (1905–11).

Loos, Adolf (1870–1933). Austrian architect. His purity of form influenced the development of the modern functional style. His best-known works include the office and store building on Michaelerplatz and the Steiner House, both in Vienna (both 1910).

Mendelsohn, Erich (1887–1953). German architect. In Germany, he built the Herman and Co. hat factory, Luckenwalde (1921–23), and the sculptural Einstein Tower Observatory, Potsdam (1919–24). He designed several buildings in Israel, including the Hebrew University on Mount Scopus, Jerusalem (1937–39), and four synagogues in the United States.

Niemeyer, Oscar (1907–   ). Brazilian architect. Influenced by Le Corbusier, Niemeyer is a daring and original designer. He collaborated on the United Nations buildings, New York City (1947–53); directed the building of Brazil's new capital, Brasília (1950–60); and designed the Mondadori Headquarters in Milan (1968–75).

Wagner, Otto (1841–1918). Austrian architect. The most significant work by this pioneer of modern architecture is the Postal Savings Bank Office, Vienna (1904–12). He also designed stations for the Vienna Municipal Railway (1894–1901) and the church at Steinhof (1905–07). His writings, including *Modern Architecture* (1895), were influential.

ARCHITECTURAL MOVEMENTS AND STYLES

baroque A style that flourished in the 17th and early 18th centuries, characterized by exuberant decoration, curvaceous forms, and a grand scale generating a sense of movement; later developments within the movement show more restraint.

Bauhaus The style of the Bauhaus School, founded in Germany by Walter Gropius in 1919, emphasizing simplicity, functionalism, and craftsmanship.

Byzantine A style of the Byzantine Empire, dating from the 5th century. Its churches are characterized by masonry construction around a central plan, with domes, foliage patterns on stone capitals, and interiors decorated with mosaics and frescoes.

classical revival A movement in England and the United States in the late 18th and 19th centuries that looked to the traditions of Greek and Roman antiquity. Robert Mills, William Strickland, Sir Robert Smirke, and Sir John Soane participated in this movement.

classicism The architecture of Greek and Roman antiquity, distinguished by the qualities of simplicity, harmony, and balance; also, a later style that emphasizes these values.

Georgian The prevailing style of English architecture during the reigns of George I, II, and III (1714–1820), based on the principles of the Italian Renaissance architect Andrea Palladio.

Gothic A style employed in Europe during the 13th, 14th, and 15th centuries. It is characterized by the use of pointed arches and ribbed vaults, piers, and buttresses in the support of its stone construction. The style is exemplified in France by the Cathedral of Notre Dame in Paris and the cathedrals in Amiens and Chartres.

"Seven Wonders of the Ancient World" in chapter 26

Go to

Gothic revival   A movement in the United States and Britain in the late 18th and 19th centuries that returned to building styles of the Gothic period.

international style   A movement that developed in the 1920s, characterized by a regularized surface, a lightening of mass, and, often, large expanses of glass. Walter Gropius, Mies van der Rohe, and Le Corbusier worked in this style.

Norman   A building style created by the Normans (1066–c. 1200) based on the Italian romanesque and characterized by sparsely decorated masonry and the use of the round arch. The style was used principally in castles, churches, and abbeys of massive proportions.

postmodernism   A style that emerged in the 1970s characterized by references to and evocations of past architectural styles, particularly the classical tradition. It is frequently colorful and wittily ornamentative. Michael Graves works in this style.

Renaissance   A European style of the 15th and 16th centuries, beginning in Italy. Ancient Roman elements were adapted to contemporary uses, with attention to the principles of the architect Vitruvius and to existing ruins. Symmetry, simplicity, and exact mathematical relationships were emphasized.

A Hindu temple represents a mountaintop or the abode of the gods, while the inner part of the temple is the "womb" chamber, representing birth.

rococo   A style originating in France, c. 1720, developed out of baroque types and characterized by elegant, delicate ornamentation and refined use of different materials, such as stucco, metal, or wood, for an ethereal effect.

Romanesque   A style developed in Europe, c. 1050, characterized by heavy masonry and the use of the round arch, barrel and groin vaults, narrow openings, the vaulting rib, the vaulting shaft, and central and western towers.

Tudor   A style of English architecture prevalent during the reigns of the Tudors (1485–1558), transitional between Gothic and Palladian, with emphasis on country manors.

COMMON ARCHITECTURAL TERMS

abacus   A stone slab at the top of a classical column aiding the support of the architrave.

acropolis   The elevated stronghold in ancient Greek cities.

adobe   Sun-dried brick used in places with warm, dry climates, such as Egypt and Mexico; also, the structures built out of adobe bricks.

aisle   A passageway of a Christian church or a Roman basilica running parallel to the nave, separated from it by an arcade or colonnade.

ambulatory   A continuous aisle in a building, especially around the apse in a church.

apse   A semicircular area at the end of a church; in most churches it contains the altar.

arcade   A series of arches supported by columns or piers, or a passageway formed by these arches.

arch   A curved structure used to span an opening.

architrave   The lowest part of an entablature resting on the capital of a column.

continued, p. 248

ILLUSTRATIONS OF ARCHITECTURAL ELEMENTS

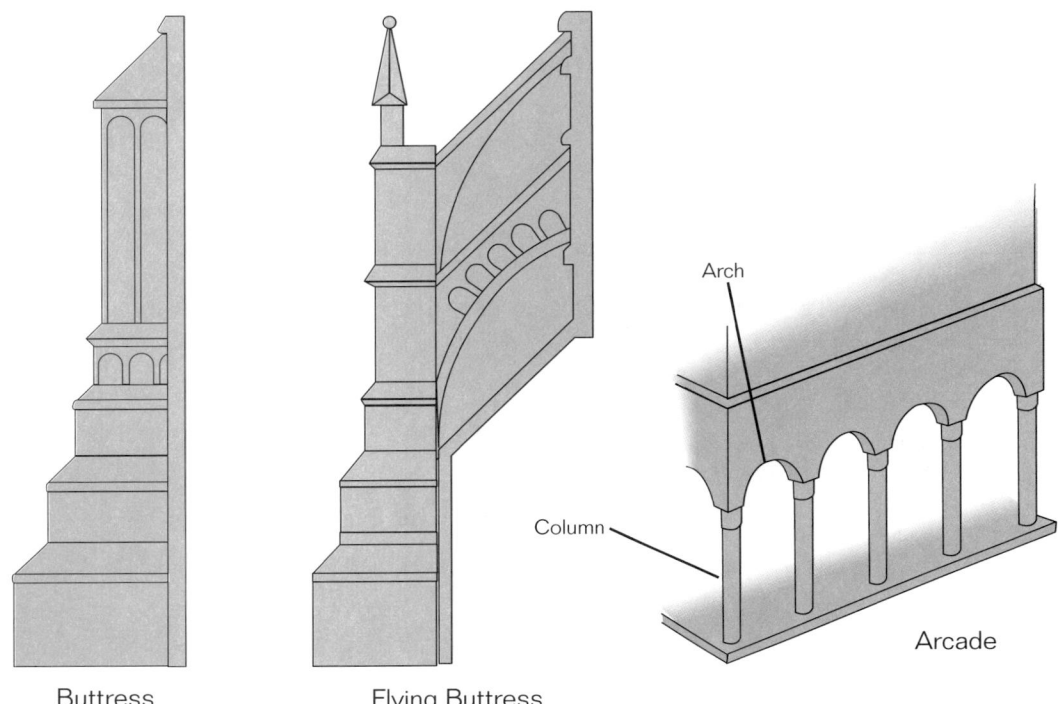

Buttress

Flying Buttress

Arch

Column

Arcade

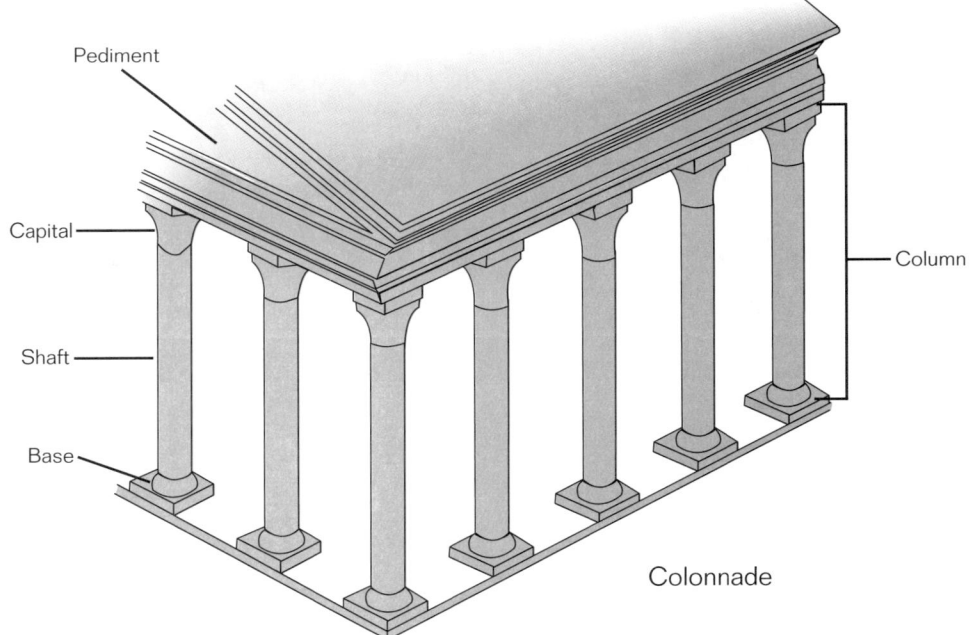

Pediment

Capital

Shaft

Base

Column

Colonnade

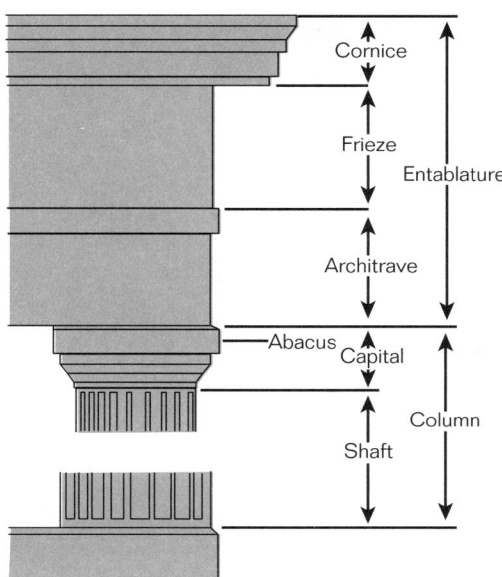

Column and Entablature

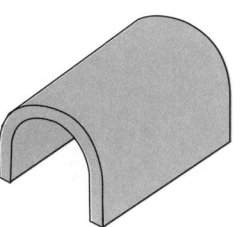

Barrel Vault

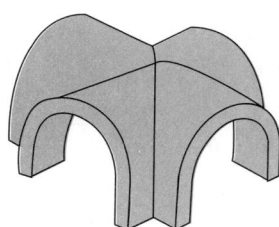

Groined Vault

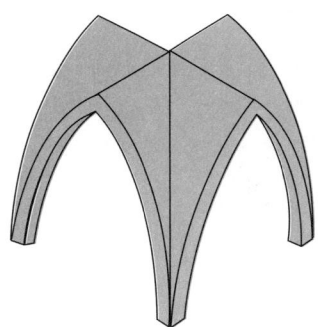

Ribbed Vault

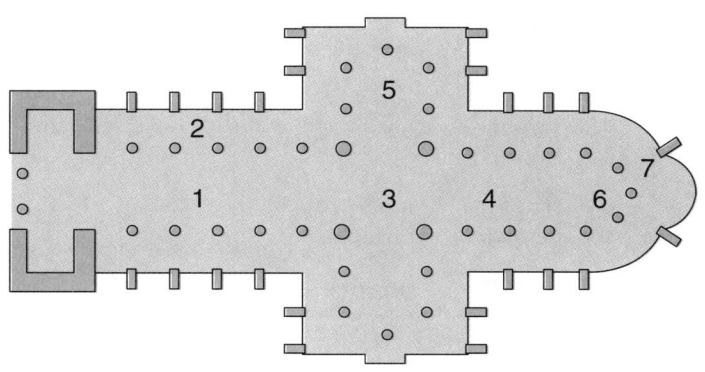

Church interior

1. Nave
2. Aisle
3. Crossing
4. Choir

5. Transept
6. Apse
7. Ambulatory

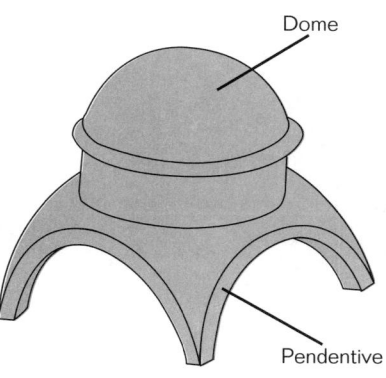

Vaulted Roof

ashlar Stones hewn, squared, and smoothed for use in building, as distinguished from rough building stones.

atrium In an ancient Roman house, a central room open to the sky, usually having a pool for the collection of rainwater. In churches, a front courtyard.

attic The story above the cornice of a building.

baldachin An ornamented canopy over an altar, tomb, or throne.

baptistery A part of a church or a separate building, often octagonal or round, in which baptisms take place.

basilica In ancient Roman architecture, a large oblong building, generally with double columns and a semicircular apse at one end. In Christian architecture, a church with a nave, apse, and aisles.

beam A long piece of heavy wood, steel, etc., used as a horizontal support in construction.

buttress A projecting support built into or against the external wall of a building, typically used in Gothic buildings. A flying buttress is an arch that transfers the thrust of a vault to a lower support.

campanile A bell tower, especially one that stands apart from any other building.

cantilever A horizontal projection, such as a balcony or beam, supported at one end only.

choir A square or rectangular area in a church between the apse and the crossing.

clerestory A row of windows in the upper part of a wall, especially in a church, to admit light below.

cloister In religious institutions, a courtyard with covered walks.

colonnade A row of columns, usually equidistant, supporting a beam or entablature.

column A cylindrical vertical support usually consisting of a base, shaft, and capital.

Composite Order A Roman order; its capital combines the Corinthian acanthus leaf decoration with volutes from the Ionic Order.

Corinthian Order The latest of the three Greek orders, similar to the Ionic, but with the capital decorated with carvings of the acanthus leaf.

cornice The upper part of an entablature, extending beyond the frieze; also, ornamental molding projecting along the top of a building or wall.

crossing In a church, the area where the transept and the nave intersect, usually emphasized by a dome or tower.

dome A vaulted roof of circular or polygonal shape.

Doric Order The first and simplest of the three Greek orders and the only one that normally has no base.

entablature The upper horizontal part of a classical order, between a capital and the roof; it consists of the architrave, frieze, and cornice.

facade Any important face of a building, usually the principal front with the main entrance.

forum The main public square of an ancient Roman city.

frieze The middle part of an entablature, often decorated with sculpture.

gargoyle A spout placed on the roof gutter of a Gothic building to carry away rainwater; usually carved in the shapes of fanciful animals and grotesque beasts.

Ionic Order Second of the three Greek orders. Its capital is decorated with spiral scrolls (volutes).

lantern   A small structure on top of a dome, tower, or roof, often open to admit light below.

lintel   *See* **post and lintel.**

loggia   A roofed gallery with an open arcade or colonnade on at least one side.

minaret   A slender, lofty tower with balconies, attached to a Muslim mosque.

module   The measurement by which parts of a building are related to one another. An example is the diameter of a column.

narthex   The transverse entrance hall of a church.

nave   In a Roman basilica, the central aisle. In a church, the main section extending from the entrance to the crossing.

obelisk   A tall, tapering, four-sided stone shaft with a pyramidal top.

ogive   The pointed arch used in Gothic architecture.

order   A term applied to the three styles of Greek columns and entablatures (Doric, Ionic, and Corinthian) and to the Roman Composite and Tuscan orders, developed from the original three orders.

pagoda   A multistoried building, typically Asian, forming a tower with upward curving roofs over the individual stories.

pediment   In a classical building, the triangular gable between the horizontal entablature and the sloping roof; in general, an architectural feature over a door or window.

pendentive   A curved triangle at the corners of a square or polygonal room, used at the opening of a dome.

pier   An upright masonry support.

pilaster   A flattened, shallow column or pier projecting from a wall. It usually has a base, shaft, and capital but is decorative rather than structural.

portico   A structure usually attached to a building, such as a porch, consisting of a roof supported by piers or columns.

post and lintel   A method of construction in which vertical beams (posts) are used to support a horizontal beam (lintel).

pyramid   A quadrilateral masonry mass with steeply sloping sides meeting at an apex; in ancient Egypt, pyramids were used as royal tombs.

relief   Moldings and ornamentation projecting from the surface of a wall.

spandrel   The triangular area between the sides of two adjacent arches.

spire   A tall, tapering, pointed roof on a tower, as in the top of a steeple.

tracery   Ornament of ribs, bars, etc., in panels or screens, as in the upper part of a Gothic window.

transept   A structure that forms the arms of a cross-shaped church.

turret   A small tower, usually starting at some distance from the ground, attached to a building such as a castle or fortress.

Tuscan Order   A Roman order resembling the Doric, but with a base and an unfluted shaft.

vault   An arched brick or stone ceiling or roof. The simplest form is the **barrel vault,** a single continuous arch; the **groined vault** consists of two barrel vaults joined at right angles; a **ribbed vault** has a web of ribs added to the groins.

volute   A spiral scroll used on Ionic and Corinthian capitals.

westwork   In German Romanesque, a monumental entrance to a church consisting of towers, with a chapel above.

ziggurat   In ancient Assyria and Babylonia, a tower in the shape of a stepped pyramid. It formed the base of a temple.

ADDITIONAL SOURCES OF INFORMATION

Boorstin, Daniel J. *The Creators: A History of Heroes of the Imagination.* Random House, 1992.

Fleming, John, et al. *Penguin Dictionary of Architecture and Landscape.* 5th ed. Penguin, 2000.

Hunt, William D., Jr. *Encyclopedia of American Architects.* McGraw-Hill, 1980.

Janson, H. W., and Anthony Janson. *History of Art.* 6th ed. Abrams, 2001.

Kostof, Spiro. *A History of Architecture: Settings and Rituals.* 2nd ed. Oxford University Press, 1995.

Marks, Claude. *World Artists, 1950–1980.* H. W. Wilson Co., 1984.

_____. *World Artists, 1980–1990.* H. W. Wilson Co., 1991.

Musgrove, John, ed. *A History of Architecture: Sir Banister-Fletcher's.* 19th ed. Butterworth, 1987.

Phaidon Encyclopedia of Art and Artists. Phaidon Press Ltd., 1978.

Piper, David. *Random House Library of Painting and Sculpture.* Random House, 1981.

8  LITERATURE

IMPORTANT AUTHORS

Any list of "important" authors is subject to debate. The following list is not all-inclusive but does include many authors who have made a substantial contribution to literature.

The titles and years of first publication of each author's major works are given. In those instances where an author is known by a pseudonym, he or she is listed by that pseudonym with the real name in brackets.

A dagger (†) indicates that the author was awarded a Nobel Prize in literature. For American authors, an asterisk (*) designates a book that was awarded a Pulitzer prize in literature, and a plus sign (+) indicates that the work was awarded a National Book Award.

The shortest complete two-word sentence in the English language is "I am." One-word sentences include "Do." and "Go."

AMERICAN

Agee, James (1909–55): *Let Us Now Praise Famous Men* (1941), **A Death in the Family* (1957), *Agee on Film* (1958, 1960)

Aiken, Conrad (1889–1973): *The House of Dust: A Symphony* (1920), **Selected Poems* (1924), *Conversation; or, Pilgrim's Progress* (1940), *The Soldier* (1944), *The Kid* (1947), *Ushant: An Essay* (1952)

Alcott, Louisa May (1832–88): *Little Women* (1868), *Little Men* (1871)

Algren, Nelson (1909–81): *The Man with the Golden Arm* (1949), *A Walk on the Wild Side* (1956)

Anderson, Sherwood (1876–1941): *Winesburg, Ohio* (1919), *The Triumph of the Egg* (1921)

Asimov, Isaac (1920–92): *I, Robot* (1950), *Foundation* series (1951, 1952, 1953, 1982, 1986, 1988, 1993)

Auchincloss, Louis [Stanton] (1917–): *Portrait in Brownstone* (1962), *Life, Law and Letters* (1979), *Diary of a Yuppie* (1987), *The Education of Oscar Fairfax* (1995)

Auden, W(ystan) H(ugh) (1907–73): *Spain* (1937), *For the Time Being* (1944), **The Age of Anxiety: A Baroque Eclogue* (1947), *The Dyer's Hand* (1962)

Audubon, John James (1785–1851): *The Birds of America* (1827–38)

Austin, Mary (1868–1934): *A Woman of Genius* (1912), *Earth Horizon* (1932)

Baldwin, James (1924–87): *Go Tell It on the Mountain* (1953), *Notes of a Native Son* (1955), *Nobody Knows My Name* (1961), *Another Country* (1962), *Just Above My Head* (1979)

Baraka, Imamu Amiri (formerly LeRoi Jones, 1934–): *Preface to a Twenty Volume Suicide Note* (1961), *Dutchman* (1964), *The Slave* (1964), *The Toilet* (1964), *Black Music* (1967), *Eulogies* (1996)

Barth, John (1930–): *The Sot-Weed Factor* (1960), *Giles Goat-Boy* (1966), *+Chimera* (1972)

Barthelme, Donald (1931–89): *Come Back, Dr. Caligari* (1964), *Snow White* (1967), *City Life* (1970), *Sixty Stories* (1981)

Bartlett, John (1820–1905): *Familiar Quotations* (1855)

Baum, L(yman) Frank (1856–1919): *The Wonderful Wizard of Oz* (1900)

Beattie, Ann (1947–): *Distortions* (1976), *Chilly Scenes of Winter* (1976), *Where You'll Find Me* (1986), *Picturing Will* (1989), *Perfect Recall: New Stories* (2001)

Bellow, Saul† (1915–): *Dangling Man* (1944), *+The Adventures of Augie March* (1953), *Henderson, the Rain King* (1959), *+Herzog* (1964), *+Mr. Sammler's Planet* (1970), **Humboldt's Gift* (1975), *The Dean's December* (1982), *More Die of Heartbreak* (1987), *It All Adds Up* (1994), *Ravelstein* (2000)

Benchley, Robert (1889–1945): *My Ten Years in a Quandary and How They Grew* (1936), *Benchley Beside Himself* (1943)

"Pseudonyms of Famous Authors" and "Book Awards and Their Recipients" in this chapter
Go to

Benét, Stephen Vincent (1898–1943): **John Brown's Body* (1928), **Western Star* (1943)

Benét, William Rose (1886–1950): **The Dust Which Is God* (1941)

Bierce, Ambrose (c. 1842–1914?): *Tales of Soldiers and Civilians* (1891), *Can Such Things Be?* (1893), *The Devil's Dictionary* (1911)

Bontemps, Arna (1902–73): *God Sends Sunday* (1931), *Sam Patch* (1951)

Boyle, Kay (1903–92): *Plagued by the Nightingale* (1931), *Death of a Man* (1936), *Thirty Stories* (1946), *The Underground Woman* (1975), *Fifty Stories* (1980)

Bradbury, Ray (1920–   ): *The Martian Chronicles* (1950), *The Illustrated Man* (1951), *Fahrenheit 451* (1953), *Something Wicked This Way Comes* (1962), *I Sing the Body Electric* (1969), *Green Shadows, White Whale* (1992)

Bradstreet, Anne (c. 1612–72): *The Tenth Muse Lately Sprung Up in America* (1650)

Brooks, Gwendolyn (1917–2000): **Annie Allen* (1949), *In the Mecca* (1968), *Family Pictures* (1970), *Children Coming Home* (1991)

Buck, Pearl S(ydenstricker)† (1892–1973): **The Good Earth* (1931), *My Several Worlds* (1954), *Imperial Woman* (1956)

Burroughs, Edgar Rice (1875–1950): *Tarzan of the Apes* (1914)

Burroughs, William S. (1914–97): *The Naked Lunch* (1959), *Cities of the Red Night* (1981)

Capote, Truman (1924–84): *Other Voices, Other Rooms* (1948), *The Grass Harp* (1951), *Breakfast at Tiffany's* (1958), *In Cold Blood* (1965)

Cather, Willa (1873–1947): *O Pioneers!* (1913), *The Song of the Lark* (1915), *My Ántonia* (1918), **One of Ours* (1922), *Shadows on the Rock* (1931)

Chandler, Raymond (1888–1959): *The Big Sleep* (1939), *Farewell, My Lovely* (1940), *The Long Goodbye* (1953)

Cheever, John (1912–82): *+The Wapshot Chronicle* (1957), *The Wapshot Scandal* (1964), *Falconer* (1977), **The Stories of John Cheever* (1978)

Chopin, Kate (1851–1904): *Bayou Folk* (1894), *The Awakening* (1899)

Cooper, James Fenimore (1789–1851): *The Spy* (1821), *The Pioneers* (1823), *The Pilot* (1823), *The Last of the Mohicans* (1826), *The Prairie* (1827), *The American Democrat* (1838), *The Pathfinder* (1840), *The Deerslayer* (1841)

Crane, Stephen (1871–1900): *Maggie: A Girl of the Streets* (1893), *The Red Badge of Courage* (1895), *The Black Riders* (1895), *The Monster* (1899)

cummings, e.e. [Edward Estlin] (1894–1962): *The Enormous Room* (1922), *&* (1925), *is 5* (1926), *50 Poems* (1940), *I x I* (1944), *Ninety-five Poems* (1958), *+Poems 1923–1954* (1955)

Dickinson, Emily (1830–86): *Poems* (1890), *Poems: Second Series* (1891), *Poems: Third Series* (1896), *The Single Hound* (1914)

Didion, Joan (1934–   ): *Slouching Towards Bethlehem* (1968), *The White Album* (1979), *Play It As It Lays* (1970), *Democracy* (1984), *The Last Thing He Wanted* (1996)

Dillard, Annie (1945–   ): **Pilgrim at Tinker Creek* (1974), *Teaching a Stone to Talk* (1982), *The Living* (1992), *Mornings Like This: Found Poems* (1995)

Doctorow, E(dgar) L(awrence) (1931–   ): *The Book of Daniel* (1971), *Ragtime* (1975), *Loon Lake* (1980), *+World's Fair* (1985), *Billy Bathgate* (1989), *City of God* (2000)

Dos Passos, John (1896–1970): *Manhattan Transfer* (1925), *The 42nd Parallel* (1930), *1919* (1932), *The Big Money* (1936)

Dreiser, Theodore (1871–1945): *Sister Carrie* (1900), *The Financier* (1912), *The Titan* (1914), *The "Genius"* (1915), *An American Tragedy* (1925)

Edel, Leon (1907–1997): **+Henry James: A Life* (5 vols., 1953–1972), *Bloomsbury: A House of Lions* (1979)

Eliot, T(homas) S(tearns)† (1888–1965): *Prufrock and Other Observations* (1917), *The Waste Land* (1922), *Murder in the Cathedral* (1935), *Four Quartets* (1943)

Ellison, Ralph (1914–94): +*Invisible Man* (1952), *Juneteenth* (1999)

Emerson, Ralph Waldo (1803–82): "Nature" (1836), "The American Scholar" (1837), *Essays: First Series* (1841), *Essays: Second Series* (1844), *The Conduct of Life* (1860)

Faulkner, William† (1897–1962): *Sartoris* (1929), *The Sound and the Fury* (1929), *As I Lay Dying* (1930), *Absalom, Absalom!* (1936), *The Hamlet* (1940), *Collected Stories* (1950), *+A Fable* (1954), *The Reivers* (1962)

Fitzgerald, F(rancis) Scott (1896–1940): *Tales of the Jazz Age* (1922), *The Great Gatsby* (1925), *Tender Is the Night* (1933), *The Last Tycoon* (1941)

Franklin, Benjamin (1706–90): *Poor Richard's Almanack* (1733–58), *Autobiography* (1791)

Frost, Robert (1874–1963): *North of Boston* (1914), *Mountain Interval* (1916), *New Hampshire* (1923), *Collected Poems* (1930), *A Further Range* (1936), *A Witness Tree* (1942), *In the Clearing* (1962)

Gardner, John (1933–82): *Grendel* (1971), *October Light* (1976)

Ginsberg, Allen (1926–97): *Howl* (1956), *Kaddish and Other Poems* (1961), *The Fall of America* (1973)

Hammett, Dashiell (1894–1961): *The Maltese Falcon* (1930), *The Thin Man* (1934)

Hawkes, John Clendennin Burne, Jr. (1925–1998): *The Lime Twig* (1961), *The Blood Oranges* (1970), *Whistle Jacket* (1989), *An Irish Eye* (1997)

Hawthorne, Nathaniel (1804–64): *Twice-Told Tales* (1837; enlarged 1842), *The Scarlet Letter* (1850), *The House of the Seven Gables* (1851)

Heinlein, Robert A. (1907–88): *Stranger in a Strange Land* (1962)

Heller, Joseph (1923–1999): *Catch-22* (1961), *Something Happened* (1974), *Good as Gold* (1979), *Closing Time* (1994)

Hellman, Lillian (1905–84): *An Unfinished Woman* (1969), *Pentimento* (1973), *Scoundrel Time* (1976)

Hemingway, Ernest† (1899–1961): *The Sun Also Rises* (1926), *A Farewell to Arms* (1929), *For Whom the Bell Tolls* (1940), *The Old Man and the Sea* (1952), *A Moveable Feast* (1964)

Henry, O. [William Sydney Porter] (1862–1910): *The Four Million* (1906), *The Trimmed Lamp* (1907), *Whirligigs* (1910)

Hersey, John [Richard] (1914–93): *A Bell for Adano* (1944), *Hiroshima* (1946), *The Wall* (1950)

Howells, William Dean (1837–1920): *The Rise of Silas Lapham* (1885)

Hughes, Langston (1902–67): *The Weary Blues* (1926), *The Ways of White Folks* (1934), *Shakespeare in Harlem* (1942), *Ask Your Mama* (1961)

Hurston, Zora Neale (1903–1960): *Mules and Men* (1935), *Their Eyes Were Watching God* (1937), *Dust Tracks on a Road* (1942)

Irving, Washington (1783–1859): *History of New York* (1809), *The Sketch Book of Geoffrey Crayon, Gent.* (1819–20), *Legends of the Alhambra* (1832)

Jackson, Shirley (1919–65): "The Lottery" (1948), *The Bird's Nest* (1954), *The Haunting of Hill House* (1959), *We Have Always Lived in the Castle* (1962)

James, Henry (1843–1916): *The American* (1877), *The Europeans* (1879), *Daisy Miller* (1879), *The Portrait of a Lady* (1881), *The Bostonians* (1886), *Embarrassments* (1896), *The Two Magics* (1898), *The Awkward Age* (1899), *The Ambassadors* (1903), *The Golden Bowl* (1904)

Jarrell, Randall (1914–65): +*The Woman at the Washington Zoo* (1960), *No Other Books* (2000)

Jong, Erica (1942–   ): *Fear of Flying* (1973), *Fanny* (1980), *Fear of Fifty* (1994)

Kerouac, Jack (1922–69): *On the Road* (1957), *The Dharma Bums* (1958), *Desolation Angels* (1965)

Kosinski, Jerzy (1933–91): *The Painted Bird* (1965), +*Steps* (1968), *Being There* (1970), *Cockpit* (1975), *The Hermit of 69th Street* (1988)

Lardner, Ring(old) (1885–1933): *You Know Me, Al* (1916), *How to Write Short Stories* (1924), *The Love Nest and Other Stories* (1926)

Lewis, Sinclair† (1885–1951): *Main Street* (1920), *Babbitt* (1922), *Arrowsmith (1925), *Dodsworth* (1929)

London, Jack (1876–1916): *The Call of the Wild* (1903), *The Sea-Wolf* (1904), *White Fang* (1906), *The Iron Heel* (1907), *Martin Eden* (1909)

Longfellow, Henry Wadsworth (1807–82): *Voices of the Night* (1839), *Ballads and Other Poems* (1841), *The Song of Hiawatha* (1855), *The Courtship of Miles Standish* (1858), *The Tales of a Wayside Inn* (1863)

Lowell, James Russell (1819–91): *A Fable for Critics* (1848)

Lowell, Robert (1917–77): *Land of Unlikeness* (1944), **Lord Weary's Castle* (1946), *Old Glory* (1964), *Dolphin (1973)

Lowry, Malcolm (1909–57): *Ultramarine* (1933), *Under the Volcano* (1947), *Hear Us O Lord from Heaven Thy Dwelling Place* (1961)

Mailer, Norman (1923–   ): *The Naked and the Dead* (1948), *An American Dream* (1965), **The Armies of the Night* (1968), **The Executioner's Song* (1979), *Ancient Evenings* (1983), *Tough Guys Don't Dance* (1984), *Harlot's Ghost* (1991), *The Gospel According to the Son* (1997)

Malamud, Bernard (1914–86): *The Natural* (1952), +*The Magic Barrel* (1958), *+*The Fixer* (1966), *The Tenants* (1971), *God's Grace* (1982)

McCarthy, Mary (1912–89): *The Groves of Academe* (1952), *Memories of a Catholic Girlhood* (1957), *The Group* (1963), *Intellectual Memoirs: New York, 1936–1938* (1992)

McCullers, Carson (1917–67): *The Heart Is a Lonely Hunter* (1940), *Member of the Wedding* (1946), *Clock Without Hands* (1961)

Melville, Herman (1819–91): *Typee* (1846), *Omoo* (1847), *White Jacket* (1850), *Moby-Dick* (1851)

Mencken, H(enry) L(ouis) (1880–1956): *The American Language* (1919, rev. 1921, 1923, 1936; suppl. 1945, 1948)

Michener, James (1907?–97): **Tales of the South Pacific* (1947), *Hawaii* (1959), *The Source* (1965), *The Drifters* (1971), *Chesapeake* (1978), *Mexico* (1992)

Miller, Henry (1891–1980): *Tropic of Cancer* (1934), *Tropic of Capricorn* (1939)

Mitchell, Margaret (1900–49): **Gone with the Wind* (1936)

Morrison, Toni [Chloe Anthony Wofford]† (1931–   ): *The Bluest Eye* (1970), *Sula* (1973), +*Song of Solomon* (1977), *Tar Baby* (1981), *Beloved (1987), *Jazz* (1992), *Paradise* (1998)

Oates, Joyce Carol (1938–   ): +*Them* (1969), *Bellefleur* (1980), *Black Water* (1992), *Broke Heart Blues* (1999), *Blonde* (2000)

Paine, Thomas (1737–1809): *Common Sense* (1776), *The Age of Reason* (1794–95)

Parker, Dorothy (1893–1967): *Laments for the Living* (1930), *After Such Pleasures* (1933), *Here Lies* (1942)

Percy, Walker (1916–90): +*The Moviegoer* (1961), *The Last Gentleman* (1966), *Love in the Ruins* (1971), *The Thanatos Syndrome* (1987), *Signposts in a Strange Land* (1991)

Plath, Sylvia (1932–63): *The Colossus* (1960), *The Bell Jar* (1963), *Ariel* (1965), *Collected Poems (1981)

Poe, Edgar Allan (1809–49): *Poems* (1831), *Tales of the Grotesque and Arabesque* (1840), *The Raven and Other Poems* (1845)

Porter, Katherine Anne (1890–1980): *Flowering Judas* (1930), *Pale Horse, Pale Rider* (1939), *Ship of Fools* (1962), *+*Collected Stories* (1965)

Pound, Ezra (1885–1972): *Cantos* (1925–60)

Pynchon, Thomas (1937–   ): *V.* (1963), *The Crying of Lot 49* (1966), +*Gravity's Rainbow* (1973), *Vineland* (1990), *Mason & Dixon* (1997)

Rand, Ayn (1905–82): *The Fountainhead* (1943), *Atlas Shrugged* (1957)

Roth, Philip (1933–   ): +*Goodbye, Columbus* (1959), *Portnoy's Complaint* (1969), *The Ghost Writer* (1979), *The Counterlife* (1986), *Patrimony* (1991), +*Sabbath's Theater* (1995), *American Pastoral* (1997), *The Human Stain* (2000)

Salinger, J(erome) D(avid) (1919–   ): *The Catcher in the Rye* (1951), *Franny and Zooey* (1961)

Sandburg, Carl (1878–1967): *Chicago Poems* (1916), *Cornhuskers* (1918), *Complete Poems* (1950)

Saroyan, William (1908–81): *The Daring Young Man on the Flying Trapeze* (1934), *The Human Comedy* (1943)

Sexton, Anne (1928–74): *Live or Die* (1966), *Love Poems* (1969)

Singer, Isaac Bashevis† (1904–91): *Satan in Goray* (1935), *The Family Moskat* (1950), *Gimpel the Fool* (1957), *The Spinoza of Market Street* (1961), *A Crown of Feather* (1973)

Stein, Gertrude (1874–1946): *Three Lives* (1909), *The Autobiography of Alice B. Toklas* (1933), *Yes Is for a Very Young Man* (1946)

Steinbeck, John† (1902–68): *Tortilla Flat* (1935), *Of Mice and Men* (1937), *The Grapes of Wrath* (1939), *East of Eden* (1952)

Stowe, Harriet Beecher (1811–96): *Uncle Tom's Cabin* (1852)

Styron, William (1925–   ): *Lie Down in Darkness* (1951), *The Confessions of Nat Turner* (1967), +*Sophie's Choice* (1979), *A Tidewater Morning* (1993)

Thoreau, Henry David (1817–62): "Civil Disobedience" (1849), *Walden* (1854)

Twain, Mark [Samuel Langhorne Clemens] (1835–1910): *The Innocents Abroad* (1869), *Roughing It* (1872), *The Adventures of Tom Sawyer* (1876), *The Adventures of Huckleberry Finn* (1884)

Tyler, Anne (1941–   ): *Dinner at the Homesick Restaurant* (1982), *The Accidental Tourist* (1985), *Breathing Lessons* (1988), *Saint Maybe* (1991), *Ladder of Years* (1995), *Back When We Were Grownups* (2001)

Updike, John (1932–   ): *Rabbit, Run* (1960), *The Centaur* (1963), *Couples* (1968), *+Rabbit Is Rich* (1981), *The Witches of Eastwick* (1985), *Rabbit at Rest* (1990), *Brazil* (1994), *Licks of Love* (2000)

Vonnegut, Kurt Jr. (1922–   ): *Cat's Cradle* (1963), *Slaughterhouse-Five; or The Children's Crusade* (1969), *Breakfast of Champions* (1973), *Timequake* (1994)

Walker, Alice (1944–   ): *Meridian* (1976), *+The Color Purple* (1982), *The Temple of My Familiar* (1989), *The Way Forward Is with a Broken Heart* (2000)

Warren, Robert Penn (1905–89): *All the King's Men* (1946), *Promises* (1957)

Webster, Noah (1758–1843): *An American Dictionary of the English Language* (2 vols., 1828)

Welty, Eudora (1909–2000): *The Bride of the Innisfallen* (1955), *The Optimist's Daughter* (1972), *One Writer's Beginnings* (1984)

Wharton, Edith (1862–1937): *The House of Mirth* (1905), *Ethan Frome* (1911), *The Age of Innocence* (1920)

White, E(lwyn) B(rooks) (1899–1985): *One Man's Meat* (1942), *Here Is New York* (1949), *Charlotte's Web* (1952), *The Elements of Style* (1959)

Whitman, Walt (1819–92): *Leaves of Grass* (1855), *Drum Taps* (1865)

Wilson, Edmund (1895–1972): *Axel's Castle* (1931), *The Wound and the Bow* (1941), *Patriotic Gore* (1962)

Wolfe, Thomas (1900–38): *Look Homeward, Angel* (1929), *Of Time and the River* (1935), *The Web and the Rock* (1939)

Wolfe, Tom [Thomas Kennerly Wolfe, Jr.] (1931–): *The Pump House Gang* (1968), *The Electric Kool-Aid Acid Test* (1968), +*The Right Stuff* (1979), *The Bonfire of the Vanities* (1987), *A Man in Full* (1998)

Wouk, Herman (1915–): **The Caine Mutiny* (1951), *Marjorie Morningstar* (1955), *The Winds of War* (1971), *War and Remembrance* (1978)

Wright, Richard (1908–60): *Native Son* (1940), *Black Boy* (1945), *The Outsider* (1953)

AFRICAN

Armah, Ayi Kwei (Ghanaian, 1939–): *The Beautyful Ones Are Not Yet Born* (1968), *Why Are We So Blest?* (1972)

Beti, Mongo [Alexandre Biyidi] (Cameroonian, 1932–2001): *Le Pauvre Christ de Bomba* (1956), *Mission Terminée* (1957), *Le Roi Miraculé* (1958)

Cavafy, C(onstantine) P. (Egyptian, 1863–1933): *The Complete Poems of Cavafy* (1961)

Gordimer, Nadine† (South African, 1923–): *A Guest of Honour* (1970), *Burgher's Daughter* (1979), *My Son's Story* (1990), *The House Gun* (1998)

Laye, Camara (Guinean, 1928–80): *The Dark Child* (1953), *The Radiance of the King* (1954), *The Guardian of the Word* (1978)

Mahfouz, Naguib† (Egyptian, c. 1911–): *Midaq Alley* (1947), *Cairo Trilogy* (1956-57), *Children of Gelbewi* (1959), *Echoes of an Autobiography* (1995)

Paton, Alan Stewart (South African, 1903–88): *Cry the Beloved Country* (1948)

Sembene, Ousmane (Senegalese, 1923–): *The Black Docker* (1956), *God's Bits of Wood* (1960), *The Money Order* (1965)

Senghor, Léopold Sédar (Senegalese, 1906–): *Shadow Songs* (1945), *Nocturnes* (1961)

Soyinka, Wole† (Nigerian 1934–): *The Forest of a Thousand Daemons* (1968), *Aké: The Years of Childhood* (1981), *The Beatification of Area Boy* (1996)

ASIAN

Bashō, Matsuo [Matsuo Munefusa] (Japanese, 1644–94): *The Narrow Road to the Deep North* (1689)

Chatterji, Bankim Chandra (Indian, 1838–94): *The Chieftain's Daughter* (1865), *Krishna Kanta's Will* (1878)

Confucius (Chinese, c. 551–479 B.C.): *The Analects*

Kawabata, Yasunari† (Japanese, 1899–1972): *Snow Country* (1948), *Thousand Cranes* (1952), *Beauty and Sadness* (1965)

Lao-tzu (Chinese, c. 6th century B.C.): *Tao-te-ching*

Li Bo (Chinese, 701–762): *Complete Works*

Mishima, Yukio (Japanese, 1925–70): *Confessions of a Mask* (1949), *The Sailor Who Fell from Grace with the Sea* (1963), *The Sea of Fertility* (4 vols., 1965–70)

Murasaki, Shikibu (Japanese, c. 978–1015?): *The Tale of the Genji* (c. 1014)

Natsume, Sōseki (Japanese, 1867–1916): *I Am a Cat* (1905–07), *The Three-Cornered World* (1907), *And Then* (1910)

'Omar Khayyám (Persian, 1048–1131): *Rubáiyát* (1859)

Rushdie, Salman (Indian, 1947–): *Midnight's Children* (1981), *Shame* (1983), *The Satanic Verses* (1988), *Haroun and the Sea of Stories* (1990), *The Moor's Last Sigh* (1995)

Tagore, Rabindranath† (Indian, 1861–1941): *Gitāñjāli: Song Offerings* (1912)

Tanizaki, Jun'ichirō (Japanese, 1886–1965): "The Tattooer" (1911), *The Makioka Sisters* (1943–48), *Diary of a Mad Old Man* (1961)

Cao Zhan [T'sao Chan] (Chinese, c. 1715–63): *Dream the of Red Chamber* (c. 1763)

AUSTRALIAN

Clavell, James [du Maresq]   (1924–94): *King Rat* (1962), *Tai-Pan* (1966), *Shogun* (1975), *Noble House* (1981), *Gai-Jin* (1993)

Franklin, Miles [Stella Maria Sarah Miles] (1879–1954): *My Brilliant Career* (1901), *Some Everyday Folk and Dawn* (1909), *All That Swagger* (1936)

Greer, Germaine   (1939–   ): *The Female Eunuch* (1970)

Hospital, Janette Turner   (1942–   ): *The Ivory Swing* (1982), *Borderline* (1985), *Isobars* (1990)

Keneally, Thomas (Michael)   (1935–   ): *The Chant of Jimmie Blacksmith* (1972), *Confederates* (1979), *Schindler's List* (1982), *Women of the Inner Sea* (1992), *A River Town* (1995), *The Great Shame* (1998)

Malouf, David   (1934–   ): *Johnno* (1975), *An Imaginary Life* (1978), *Harland's Half Acre* (1984), *Remembering Babylon* (1993), *Conversations at Curlow Creek* (1996)

McCullough, Colleen   (1937–   ): *Tim* (1974), *The Thorn Birds* (1977), *The First Man in Rome* (1990)

Moorehead, Alan [McCrae]   (1910–83): *Gallipoli* (1956), *The White Nile* (1960), *The Blue Nile* (1962), *Cooper's Creek* (1963)

Richardson, Henry Handel [Ethel Florence Lindesay Richardson Robertson]   (1870–1946): *Maurice Guest* (1908), *The Getting of Wisdom* (1910), *The Fortunes of Richard Mahoney* (trilogy; 1917–29)

Shute, Nevil [Nevil Shute Norway]   (1899–1960): *A Town Like Alice* (1950), *On the Beach* (1957), *Trustee from the Toolroom* (1960)

West, Morris L(anglo)   (1916–1999): *The Devil's Advocate* (1959), *The Shoes of the Fisherman* (1963), *The Tower of Babel* (1967), *Harlequin* (1974), *The Clowns of God* (1981), *Lazarus* (1990), *Vanishing Point* (1996)

BRITISH

Amis, Sir Kingsley   (English, 1922–95): *Lucky Jim* (1954), *Jake's Thing* (1978), *Old Devils* (1986)

Austen, Jane   (English, 1775–1817): *Sense and Sensibility* (1811), *Pride and Prejudice* (1813), *Emma* (1816), *Persuasion* (1818)

Belloc, (Joseph) Hilaire   (English, 1870–1953): *The Bad Child's Book of Beasts* (1896), *On Nothing* (1908), *Cautionary Tales for Children* (1907)

Blake, William   (English, 1757–1827): *Poetical Sketches* (1783), *Songs of Innocence* (1789), *The Marriage of Heaven and Hell* (c. 1790), *Songs of Innocence and Experience* (1794), *Milton* (1804–8)

Boswell, James   (English, 1740–95): *The Life of Samuel Johnson* (1791)

Brontë, Charlotte   (English, 1816–55): *Jane Eyre* (1847)

Brontë, Emily   (English, 1818–48): *Wuthering Heights* (1847)

Browning, Elizabeth Barrett   (English, 1806–61): *Sonnets from the Portuguese* (1850), *Aurora Leigh* (1857), *Last Poems* (1862)

Browning, Robert   (English, 1812–89): *Bells and Pomegranates* (1841–46), *Dramatic Lyrics* (1842), *Men and Women* (1855), *Dramatis Personae* (1864)

Burgess, Anthony   (English, 1917–93): *A Clockwork Orange* (1962), *Earthly Powers* (1980)

Burns, Robert   (Scottish, 1759–96): *Poems, Chiefly in the Scottish Dialect* (1786)

Byron, Lord [George Gordon]   (English, 1788–1824): *Childe Harold's Pilgrimage* (1812–18), *The Prisoner of Chillon* (1816), *Manfred* (1817), *Don Juan* (1819–24)

Carroll, Lewis [Charles Lutwidge Dodgson] (English, 1832–98): *Alice's Adventures in Wonderland* (1865), *Through the Looking-Glass* (1871)

Chaucer, Geoffrey   (English, c. 1343–1400): *The Canterbury Tales* (c. 1387)

Christie, Agatha (English, 1890–1976): *The Murder of Roger Ackroyd* (1926), *Murder on the Orient Express* (1933), *Death on the Nile* (1937)

Clarke, Sir Arthur C(harles) (English, 1917–   ): *Childhood's End* (1953), *2001: A Space Odyssey* (1968), *Rendezvous with Rama* (1973), *3001: The Final Odyssey* (1997)

Coleridge, Samuel Taylor (English, 1772–1834): *Lyrical Ballads* (1798), *Sybilline Leaves* (1817), *Biographia Literaria* (1817)

Isaac Asimov was not only a highly prolific author; he was also extremely versatile. He wrote over 400 books and is the only author to have a book in every major Dewey-decimal category.

Conrad, Joseph (English, 1857–1924): *The Nigger of the "Narcissus"* (1897), *Lord Jim* (1900), *Typhoon* (1903), *Nostromo* (1904), *Chance* (1914)

Defoe, Daniel (English, 1660–1731): *Robinson Crusoe* (1719), *Moll Flanders* (1722), *Roxanna* (1724)

Dickens, Charles (English, 1812–70): *Oliver Twist* (1838), *Nicholas Nickleby* (1839), *A Christmas Carol* (1843), *David Copperfield* (1850), *Bleak House* (1853), *A Tale of Two Cities* (1859), *Great Expectations* (1861)

Donne, John (English, 1572–1631): *Songs and Sonnets* (1633)

Doyle, Sir Arthur Conan (English, 1859–1930): *Study in Scarlet* (1887), *The Sign of the Four* (1890), *The Adventures of Sherlock Holmes* (1892), *The Valley of Fear* (1915), *The Case-Book of Sherlock Holmes* (1927)

Dryden, John (English, 1631–1700): *All for Love* (1677), *Absalom and Achitophel* (1681), *Mac Flecknoe* (1682)

Durrell, Lawrence (English, 1912–90): *The Alexandria Quartet* (1957–60)

Eliot, George [Mary Ann Evans] (English, 1819–80): *Silas Marner* (1861), *Middlemarch* (1872)

Fielding, Henry (English, 1707–54): *Joseph Andrews* (1742), *Tom Jones* (1749)

Forster, E(dward) M(organ) (English, 1879–1970): *A Room with a View* (1908), *Howards End* (1910), *A Passage to India* (1924)

Golding, Sir William† (English, 1911–93): *Lord of the Flies* (1954), *Free Fall* (1959), *Rites of Passage* (1980)

Hardy, Thomas (English, 1840–1928): *Far from the Madding Crowd* (1874), *The Return of the Native* (1878), *Tess of the D'Urbervilles* (1891), *Jude the Obscure* (1895)

Hopkins, Gerard Manley (English, 1844–89): *Poems* (1918)

Johnson, Samuel (English, 1709–84): *A Dictionary of the English Language* (1755)

Keats, John (English, 1795–1821): *Poems* (1817), *Endymion* (1818), *Lamia, Isabella, and The Eve of St. Agnes and Other Poems* (1820)

Kipling, Rudyard† (English, 1865–1936): *The Jungle Book* (1894), *The Second Jungle Book* (1895), *Captains Courageous* (1897), *Kim* (1901), *Just So Stories* (1902)

Lawrence, D(avid) H(erbert) (English, 1885–1930): *Sons and Lovers* (1913), *Women in Love* (1921), *Lady Chatterley's Lover* (1928)

Lessing, Doris (English, 1919–   ): *The Grass Is Singing* (1950), *The Children of Violence* (1952–69), *The Golden Notebook* (1962), *Under My Skin* (1994), *Walking in the Shade* (1997)

Malory, Sir Thomas (English, c. 1408–c. 1471): *Le Morte d'Arthur* (1485)

Marvell, Andrew (English, 1621–78): *Miscellaneous Poems* (1681)

Maugham, W(illiam) Somerset (English, 1874–1965): *Of Human Bondage* (1915), *Cakes and Ale* (1930), *The Summing Up* (1938), *The Razor's Edge* (1944)

Literature

Milton, John   (English, 1608–74): *Paradise Lost* (1667), *Paradise Regained* (1671)

Orwell, George [Eric Blair]   (English, 1903–50): *Animal Farm* (1945), *Nineteen Eighty-four* (1949)

Pope, Alexander   (English, 1688–1744): *An Essay on Criticism* (1711), "The Rape of the Lock" (1712)

Scott, Sir Walter   (Scottish, 1771–1832): *The Bride of Lammermoor* (1819), *Ivanhoe* (1819), *Kenilworth* (1821)

Mark Twain's Tom Sawyer *(1876) was the first published novel ever written on a typewriter.*

Shelley, Mary [Mary Wollstonecraft]   (English, 1797–1851): *Frankenstein, or the Modern Prometheus* (1818)

Shelley, Percy Bysshe   (English, 1792–1822): *Prometheus Unbound* (1820), "Adonais" (1821)

Spenser, Edmund   (English, c. 1552–99): *The Faerie Queene* (1590–96)

Stevenson, Robert Louis   (Scottish, 1850–94): *Treasure Island* (1883), *The Strange Case of Dr. Jekyll and Mr. Hyde* (1886)

Swinburne, Algernon Charles   (English, 1837–1909): *Atalanta in Calydon* (1865), *Poems and Ballads: First Series* (1866), *Poems and Ballads: Second Series* (1878)

Tennyson, Alfred (Lord)   (English, 1809–92): *Poems, Chiefly Lyrical* (1830), *Poems* (1832), *In Memoriam* (1850), *Maud, and Other Poems* (1855), *Idylls of the King* (1859–85)

Thackeray, William Makepeace   (English, 1811–63): *Vanity Fair* (1848), *Barry Lyndon* (1852)

Thomas, Dylan   (English-Welsh, 1914–53): *Eighteen Poems* (1934), *Twenty-Five Poems* (1936), *A Child's Christmas in Wales* (1955), *Under Milk Wood* (1954), *Adventures in the Skin Trade* (1955)

Trollope, Anthony   (English, 1815–82): *The Warden* (1855), *Barchester Towers* (1857)

Wells, H(erbert) G(eorge)   (English, 1866–1946): *The Time Machine* (1895), *The Island of Dr. Moreau* (1886), *The Invisible Man* (1897), *The War of the Worlds* (1898), *Tono-Bungay* (1909)

Woolf, Virginia   (English, 1882–1941): *Mrs. Dalloway* (1925), *To the Lighthouse* (1927), "A Room of One's Own" (1929)

Wordsworth, William   (English, 1770–1850): *Lyrical Ballads* (1798)

CANADIAN

Atwood, Margaret   (1939–   ): *The Circle Game* (1964), *Surfacing* (1972), *Life Before Man* (1979), *Bodily Harm* (1981), *The Handmaid's Tale* (1984), *Cat's Eye* (1988), *Alias Grace* (1996), *The Blind Assassin* (2000)

Connor, Ralph [Charles William Gordon]   (1860–1937): *Black Rock* (1898), *The Sky Pilot* (1899), *The Men from Glengarry* (1901), *Glengarry School Days* (1902)

Davies, Robertson   (1913–95): *A Mixture of Frailties* (1958), *Fifth Business* (1970), *The Rebel Angels* (1981), *What's Bred in the Bone* (1985), *The Lyre of Orpheus* (1988), *The Cunning Man* (1994)

Leacock, Stephen   (1869–1944): *Literary Lapses* (1910), *Nonsense Novels* (1911), *My Discovery of the West* (1937)

Montgomery, Lucy Maude   (1874–1942): *Anne of Green Gables* (1908), *Emily of New Moon* (1923), *The Blue Castle* (1926), *A Tangled Web* (1931), *Jane of Lantern Hill* (1937)

Munro, Alice   (1931–   ): *Dance of the Happy Shades* (1968), *Who Do You Think You Are?* (1978), *The Progress of Love* (1986), *The Love of a Good Woman* (1998)

Pratt, E. J.   (1882–1964): *The Witches' Brew* (1925), *Titans: Two Poems* (1926), *The Fable of the Goats and Other Poems* (1932), *The Titanic* (1935), *Brebeuf and His Brethren* (1940), *Towards the Last Spike* (1952)

Richler, Mordecai   (1931–2001): *A Choice of Enemies* (1957), *The Apprenticeship of Duddy Kravitz*

(1959), *Cocksure* (1968), *St. Urbain's Horseman* (1971), *Barney's Version* (1997)

Roberts, Sir Charles G. D. (1860–1943): *Orion, and Other Poems* (1880), *In Divers Tones* (1887), *Songs of the Common Day* (1893), *Earth's Enigmas* (1896), *The Vagrant of Time* (1927), *The Iceberg, and Other Poems* (1934), *Further Animal Stories* (1936)

Ross, Sinclair (1908–1996): *As for Me and My House* (1941), *The Well* (1958), *The Lamp at Noon and Other Stories* (1968), *Whir of Gold* (1970), *Sawbones Memorial* (1974)

FRENCH

Balzac, Honoré de (1799–1850): *The Human Comedy* (1842–53)

Baudelaire, Charles Pierre (1821–67): *Les Fleurs du Mal* (1857), *Petits Poèmes en Prose* (1869)

Breton, André (1896–1966): *Nadja* (1928), *Les Vases Communicants* (1932), *L'Amour Fou* (1937)

Camus, Albert† (1913–60): *The Stranger* (1942, rev. 1953), *The Myth of Sisyphus and Other Essays* (1942), *Caligula* (1944), *The Plague* (1947), *The Rebel* (1951), *The Fall* (1956), *The First Man* (1994)

Colette [Sidonie-Gabrielle Colette] (1873–1954): *Claudine* (1900–03), *The Vagabond* (1910), *Mitsou* (1919), *Chéri* (1920)

Dumas, Alexandre, père (1802–70): *The Count of Monte Cristo* (1844–45), *The Three Musketeers* (1844)

Flaubert, Gustave (1821–80): *Madame Bovary* (1857), *Sentimental Education* (1869)

Gide, André† (1869–1951): *The Immoralist* (1902), *Straight Is the Gate* (1909), *The Pastoral Symphony* (1919), *The Counterfeiters* (1926)

Hugo, Victor (1802–85): *The Hunchback of Notre-Dame* (1831), *Les Misérables* (1862)

Malraux, André (1901–76): *Man's Fate* (1933), *Man's Hope* (1937)

Maupassant, [Henri René Albert] Guy de (1850–93): *Boule de Suif* (1880), "La Maison Tellier" (1881), *Bel-Ami* (1885), *Pierre et Jean* (1888)

Mauriac, François† (1885–1970): *Genetrix* (1923), *Thérèse Desqueyroux* (1927), *The Desert of Love* (1925), *A Woman of the Pharisees* (1941)

Montaigne, Michel de (1533–92): *Essais* (1580)

Proust, Marcel (1871–1922): *Remembrance of Things Past* (7 vols., 1913–27)

Rabelais, François (c. 1494–1553): *Gargantua and Pantagruel* (1532–64)

Rimbaud, Arthur (1854–91): *A Season in Hell* (1873), *Illuminations* (1886)

Rostand, Edmond (1868–1918): *Cyrano de Bergerac* (1897)

Sand, George [Amandine-Aurore Lucile Dupin] (1804–76): *Indiana* (1832), *Lélia* (1833), *She and He* (1859)

Sartre, Jean-Paul† (1905–80): *Nausea* (1938), *The Flies* (1943), *Being and Nothingness* (1943), *No Exit* (1945)

Stendhal [Marie Henri Beyle] (1783–1842): *The Red and the Black* (1830), *The Charterhouse of Parma* (1839)

Tocqueville, Alexis de (1805–59): *Democracy in America* (2 vols., 1835; 2 supplementary vols., 1840), *The Old Regime and the Revolution* (1856)

Valéry, Paul (1871–1945): *Charmes* (1922)

Verne, Jules (1828–1905): *A Journey to the Center of the Earth* (1864), *Twenty Thousand Leagues Under the Sea* (1870), *Around the World in Eighty Days* (1873)

Voltaire [François-Marie Arouet] (1694–1778): *Candide* (1759)

Zola, Émile (1840–1902): *Thérèse Raquin* (1867), *Nana* (1880), *Germinal* (1885)

GERMAN

Böll, Heinrich† (1917–85): *Billiards at Half-past Nine* (1959), *The Clown* (1963), *Group Portrait with Lady* (1971), *The Lost Honor of Katharina Blum* (1974)

Literature

Goethe, Johann Wolfgang von (1749–1832): *Wilhelm Meister's Apprenticeship* (1795–96), *Faust,* Part I (1808) and Part II (1832)

Grass, Günter (1927–): *The Tin Drum* (1959), *The Flounder* (1977)

Grimm, Jacob (1785–1863) and **Grimm, Wilhelm** (1786–1859): *Grimm's Fairy Tales* (1812–15)

Hesse, Hermann† (1877–1962): *Siddhartha* (1922), *Steppenwolf* (1927)

Kafka, Franz (1883–1924): *Metamorphosis* (1915), *In the Penal Colony* (1919), *The Trial* (1925), *The Castle* (1926), *Amerika* (1927)

Mann, Thomas† (1875–1955): *Buddenbrooks* (1903), *Death in Venice* (1912), *The Magic Mountain* (1924)

Rilke, Rainer Maria (1875–1926): *The Book of Hours* (1905), *New Poems* (2 vols., 1907–08), *Duino Elegies* (1923), *Sonnets to Orpheus* (1923)

ITALIAN

Boccaccio, Giovanni (1313–75): *Decameron* (1349–53)

Calvino, Italo (1923–85): *The Path to the Nest of Spiders* (1947), *Cosmicomics* (1965), *Invisible Cities* (1972), *If on a Winter's Night a Traveler* (1979), *Mr. Palomar* (1985)

Dante Alighieri (1265–1321): *Divine Comedy* (c. 1314–21)

Manzoni, Alessandro (1785–1873): *The Betrothed* (1825–26)

Petrarch [Francesco Petrarca] (1304–74): *Rimes* (1350–74)

LATIN AMERICAN

Borges, Jorge Luis (Argentine, 1899–1986): *Ficciones* (1944), *Labyrinthe* (1962), *The Book of Sand* (1975)

Césaire, Aimé (West Indian, 1913–): *Return to My Native Land* (1939), *The Tragedy of King Christophe* (1963)

Fuentes, Carlos (Mexican, 1928–): *The Death of Artemio Cruz* (1962), *Distant Relations* (1980), *The Old Gringo* (1985), *Myself with Others* (1998)

García Márquez, Gabriel† (Colombian, 1928–): *One Hundred Years of Solitude* (1967), *The Autumn of the Patriarch* (1975), *Love in the Time of Cholera* (1985), *The General in His Labyrinth* (1989), *Of Love and Other Demons* (1994)

Guzmán, Martín Luis (Mexican, 1887–1976): *The Eagle and the Serpent* (1928), *Memorias de Pancho Villa* (4 vols., 1938–40)

Machado de Assis, Joaquim Maria (Brazilian, 1839–1908): *Epitaph of a Small Winner* (1891), *Philosopher or Dog?* (1891), *Dom Casmurro* (1899)

Márquez, Gabriel García. *See* **García Márquez, Gabriel.**

Naipaul, Sir V(idiadhar) S(urajprasad)† (Trinidadian, 1932–): *The Mystic Masseur* (1957), *A House for Mr. Biswas* (1961), *In a Free State* (1971), *India: A Million Mutinies Now* (1990)

Neruda, Pablo [Neftalí Ricardo Reyes Basoalto]† (Chilean, 1904–73): *Twenty Love Poems and a Story of Despair* (1924), *The Heights of Macchu Picchu* (1947), *Canto General* (1950), *Odes to Common Things* (1954)

Paz, Octavio† (Mexican, 1914–1998): *The Labyrinth of Solitude* (1950), *Sun Stone* (1957), *Salamandra* (1962)

Vargas Llosa, Mario (Peruvian, 1936–): *The Green House* (1966), *Conversation in the Cathedral* (1969), *The War of the End of the World* (1981), *The Notebooks of Don Rigoberto* (1997)

RUSSIAN

Blok, Aleksandr (1880–1921): *Verses About a Beautiful Lady* (1905), *The Puppet Show* (1906), *The Twelve* (1918)

Bulgakov, Mikhail (1891–1940): *The Master and Margarita* (1973)

Chekhov, Anton   (1860–1904): *Uncle Vanya* (1897), *The Seagull* (1897), *The Three Sisters* (1901), *The Cherry Orchard* (1904)

Dostoyevsky, Fyodor   (1821–81): *Notes from the Underground* (1864), *Crime and Punishment* (1867), *The Idiot* (1874), *The Possessed* (1872), *The Brothers Karamazov* (1880)

Gogol, Nikolai   (1809–52): *Arabesques* (1835), *Mirgorod* (1835), *The Inspector General* (1836), *Dead Souls* (1842)

Gorky, Maxim   (1868–1936): *Foma Gordeev* (1899), *The Lower Depths* (1902), *Mother* (1906)

The Yongle Dadian (thesaurus of the Chinese Yongle reign) is the longest book ever written, containing 22,937 chapters in 11,095 volumes. More than 2,000 Chinese scholars worked for five years to complete the book.

Mandelshtam, Osip   (1891–1938): *Kameny* (1913), *Tristia* (1922)

Nabokov, Vladimir   (1899–1977): *Lolita* (1955), *Pale Fire* (1962), *Speak, Memory* (1966)

Pasternak, Boris†   (1890–1960): *My Sister—Life, Summer, 1917* (1922), *Doctor Zhivago* (1957)

Pushkin, Aleksandr   (1799–1837): *Eugene Onegin* (1833)

Solzhenitsyn, Aleksandr†   (1918–   ): *One Day in the Life of Ivan Denisovich* (1962), *The Cancer Ward* (1968), *The Gulag Archipelago* (1973)

Tolstoy, Leo [Count Lev]   (1828–1910): *War and Peace* (1868–69), *Anna Karenina* (1878)

Turgenev, Ivan   (1818–83): *A Month in the Country* (1855), *A Sportsman's Sketches* (1852), *A Nest of Gentlefolk* (1859), *On the Eve* (1860), *Fathers and Sons* (1862), *Smoke* (1867)

OTHER EUROPEAN

Andersen, Hans Christian   (Danish, 1805–75): *Fairy Tales for Children* (1835–42), *Tales and Stories* (1839), *New Fairy Tales* (1843–47), *New Tales and Stories* (1858–67)

Blasco Ibañez, Vicente   (Spanish, 1867–1928): *Blood and Sand* (1898), *The Cabin* (1898), *The Mayflower* (1895), *Reeds and Mud* (1902), *The Four Horsemen of the Apocalypse* (1916)

Canetti, Elias†   (1905–94): *Auto-da-Fé* (1935), *Crowds and Power* (1960)

Čapek, Karel   (Czech, 1890–1938): *R.U.R.: Rossum's Universal Robots* (1920), *Tales from Two Pockets* (1932), *Hordubal* (1933), *Meteor* (1934), *An Ordinary Life* (1934)

Catullus   (Roman, c. 84–54 B.C.): verse

Cervantes [y Saavedra], Miguel de   (Spanish, 1547–1616): *Don Quixote* (1605–15), *Exemplary Stories* (1613)

Dinesen, Isak [Karen Dinesen, Baroness Blixen-Finecke]   (Danish, 1885–1962): *Seven Gothic Tales* (1934), *Out of Africa* (1937), *Winter's Tales* (1942), *Last Tales* (1957)

García Lorca, Federico   (Spanish, 1898–1936): *The Gypsy Ballads* (1928), *The Poet in New York* (1940)

Gombrowicz, Witold   (Polish, 1904–69): *Ferdydurke* (1937), *Pornografia* (1960)

Hamsun, Knut†   (Norwegian, 1859–1952): *Mysteries* (1892), *Hunger* (1899), *Growth of the Soil* (1917)

Hašek, Jaroslav   (Czech, 1883–1923): *The Good Soldier Schweik* (4 vols., 1921–23)

Homer   (Greek, c. 700 B.C.): *The Iliad, The Odyssey*

Joyce, James   (Irish, 1882–1941): *Dubliners* (1914), *Portrait of the Artist as a Young Man* (1916), *Ulysses* (1922), *Finnegan's Wake* (1939)

Ovid   (Roman, 43 B.C.–A.D. 17?): *Amores* (c. 16 B.C.), *Heroines, Metamorphoses*

Petronius Arbiter (Roman, ?–66): *Satyricon* (c. 50)

Plutarch (Greek, c. 46–120): *Moralia, Parallel Lives*

Sappho (Greek, c. 612–580 B.C.): verse

Swift, Jonathan (Irish, 1667–1745): *Gulliver's Travels* (1726)

Undset, Sigrid† (Norwegian, 1882–1949): *Kristin Lavransdatter* (1920–22), *The Master of Hestviken* (1925–27)

Vergil [Publius Vergilius Maro] (Roman, 70–19 B.C.): *Georgics* (30 B.C.), *Eclogues* (37 B.C.), *Aeneid* (29–19 B.C.)

Wilde, Oscar (Irish, 1854–1900): *The Picture of Dorian Gray* (1891), *The Importance of Being Earnest* (1895), *Salomé* (1896)

Yeats, William Butler† (Irish, 1865–1939): *The Wind Among the Reeds* (1899), *The Wild Swans at Coole* (1917), *The Winding Stair* (1929)

LITERARY MOVEMENTS, PERIODS, AND STYLES

Aestheticism A 19th-century European movement emphasizing aesthetic values over social or moral themes. Advocating "art for art's sake," leading aesthetes imbued their work with a flamboyant, nearly hedonistic quality. Charles Baudelaire and Oscar Wilde were among the movement's most notable figures.

Angry Young Men A group of English writers, chiefly from the working or middle classes, who became prominent in the 1950s. Their work, characterized by a bitter disillusionment with traditional English society, produced the figure of the antihero, one who rebels against the Establishment. The group's leaders included Kingsley Amis and John Osborne.

baroque Grandiose, ornate artistic style prevalent from the late 16th to the early 18th century. Initially associated with architectural forms, the term was later applied to the fine arts. In literature, the baroque style employed dramatic motifs and strong emotions in an attempt to expand the artistic vision.

Beat Generation A group of American writers whose work expressed their alienation from middle-class society during the 1950s and 1960s. Led by Jack Kerouac and Allen Ginsberg, they disdained conventional values, focusing instead on self-discovery through drugs, sexual experience, and exotic travel.

Bloomsbury Group A group of writers, artists, and intellectuals who held informal discussions in Bloomsbury, a section of London, throughout the early 20th century. Although individual members such as John Maynard Keynes (1883–1946), Lytton Strachey (1880–1932), and Virginia Woolf (1882–1941) were influential figures, the group produced no uniform moral or aesthetic principles.

The saying "The female of the species is more deadly than the male" comes from Rudyard Kipling's 1911 poem "The Female of the Species."

classical The period in which Greek and Roman literature flourished. Classical writers in Greek include Sophocles, Aeschylus, and Herodotus; in Latin, Vergil, Ovid, and Cicero, among many others.

classicism In a general sense, any literary style or movement that adheres to the principles of classical literature. In English literature, the term refers to the reaction of 18th- and 19th-century writers to romanticism. *See also* **Neoclassicism.**

Dadaism A European movement founded during World War I and devoted to the negation of traditional artistic values. Dadaists embraced nihilism, irrationality, and the absurd, often shocking their audiences. The movement's leaders included André Breton (1896–1966) and Tristan Tzara (1896–1963). Breton later broke with Tzara and founded *surrealism.*

Décadents A group originating in 19th-century France that emphasized the autonomy of art, the rejection of middle-class society, a sophisticated despair, and unconventional, often morbid experiences. Charles Baudelaire and Arthur Rimbaud were among the leading *décadents.*

Elizabethan   Pertaining to the drama and literature produced during the reign of Elizabeth I of England (1558–1603). The Elizabethan age saw the flowering of English literature, with its classical humanism and dazzling achievements in drama and verse forms. William Shakespeare, Christopher Marlowe, and Edmund Spenser were notable Elizabethans.

The Enlightenment   An intellectual movement in the late 17th and 18th centuries that sought the perfection of human society through applied reason. Rejecting conventional religious authority, its members postulated instead a rational unity of God, man, and nature. Jean-Jacques Rousseau and Voltaire were among its most influential thinkers.

Expressionism   An early-20th-century movement stressing individual expression and subjective truth as opposed to conventional forms and objective reality. Its followers used distorted imagery and narrative compression to depict violent emotions and the workings of the subconscious mind.

Futurism   A European movement (c. 1908–20) advocating the abandonment of conventional syntax and the uninhibited use of images drawn from the age of technology. Futurists exalted at the speed of modern life.

Gothic   In literature, the term applies to a specific form of the novel, popular in the late 18th and early 19th centuries, that featured supernatural horrors and violent events, often with a medieval setting.

Graveyard School   A preromantic movement of 18th-century British poets. Its members adopted a melancholy tone in their verses, which were usually set in graveyards or other gloomy locations.

Imagism   A movement in American and English poetry beginning around 1910. Borrowing freely from foreign verse techniques such as the *haiku* and *free verse,* it demanded precision in the use of imagery. Ezra Pound was influential within this movement.

Go to   "Art Movements and Styles" and "Architecture Styles and Movements" in chapter 7; "Philosophical Movements and Schools of Thought" in chapter 10

impressionism   In modern literature, the term refers especially to poems and novels that focus on the author's or character's inner life and subjective impressions. James Joyce, Thomas Mann, Marcel Proust, and Virginia Woolf employed impressionistic techniques, such as the stream of consciousness.

Irish Renaissance   A period of intense creative energy, beginning in the 19th century, aimed at the revival of Ireland's native culture. At the height of the movement, from 1900 to 1920, writers such as John Millington Synge and William Butler Yeats turned to traditional Irish folklore and themes for inspiration. The movement's influence continues to the present.

Jacobean   Pertaining to the literature produced during the reign of James I of England (1603–25). The period was one of great social upheaval. Reflecting the times, English literature rejected Elizabethan optimism for a darker, more cynical view of human affairs. William Shakespeare's greatest works were written in this period.

Lost Generation   A term coined by Gertrude Stein to describe a group of expatriate American writers who came into prominence after World War I (1914–18). Their work was characterized by disillusionment with postwar society. F. Scott Fitzgerald and Ernest Hemingway were among the group's notable figures.

metaphysical   Referring to a style of primarily 17th-century poetry emphasizing dramatic imagery, complex metaphors, and language in everyday use. John Donne is usually considered the greatest of the metaphysical poets.

modernism   A mid-20th-century (c. 1910–45) movement emphasizing a self-conscious break with past literary forms and the development of experimental techniques and fresh motifs. The Irish author James Joyce's use of interior monologue and myth as narrative structures typify modernism's concern with untried forms of expression.

naturalism   A late-19th-century and early-20th-century movement that rejected sentimentality, subjectivity, and preconceived notions of morality in art. Naturalist writers often chose their subjects from the lower depths of society, viewing their characters' sordid lives or tragic fates with scientific detachment. Thomas Hardy, Émile Zola, and Theodore Dreiser were among the leading naturalists.

Neoclassicism In European literature, the term refers to the emphasis placed on balance, restraint, clarity, and proportion in the works of late-17th-century and 18th-century writers such as Alexander Page, Jean Racine, Jonathan Swift, and Voltaire.

Parnassians Late-19th-century school of French poets. Reacting against the emotionalism and subjectivity of romanticism, they attempted to replicate the precision of plastic arts such as sculpture in their work. The objective poetry thus created was a precursor of the realistic novel and drama.

Pre-Raphaelites A group of poets and artists established in London in 1848. They asserted the superiority of nature in their work, rejecting formal or academic techniques in favor of sensual imagery and religious symbolism. Dante Gabriel Rossetti was one of its leaders.

realism Movement originating in the late 19th century that portrayed the details of everyday life in factual, objective language and without idealization. The author sought to let the story tell itself, devoid of sentiment and thematic manipulation. Honoré de Balzac, Gustave Flaubert, and Henrik Ibsen wrote in this manner.

Renaissance From the French word for "rebirth." It pertains to the literature produced in Europe from the mid–14th century to the end of the 16th century. Marked by a revival in classical values and learning, the period witnessed an outburst of creative activity unmatched in the history of western culture. Miguel de Cervantes, François Rabelais, and William Shakespeare were the leading figures of the period.

Romanticism Movement originating in 18th-century Europe as a reaction to Neoclassicism. Romantic works typically emphasized intense emotions, sensual imagery, and individualism and often featured lurid themes and sensational plots. Samuel Taylor Coleridge, Johann Goethe, and Jean-Jacques Rousseau are usually associated with this movement.

Socialist Realism A state-mandated literary style that writers were obligated to follow in the former Soviet Union (c. 1932–90). Under this doctrine, all literary works were to display the steady progress of Soviet society toward achieving the goals of socialism. In practice, it was a tool by which the state could control freedom of expression.

Sturm und Drang German phrase meaning "storm and stress." Nationalistic, late-18th-century German movement emphasizing dramatic story lines, turbulent emotions, and the individual's revolt against society. Johann Goethe's early work was written in this fashion.

Surrealism A movement founded in France in the 1920s. It attempted to express the workings of the subconscious mind through automatic writing and irrational, often juxtaposed imagery. André Breton was the movement's principal architect.

Symbolism A European movement originating with French poetry in the late 19th century. It sacrificed objective representation and realistic narrative techniques in favor of a pattern of images or symbols that conveyed the author's meaning. Joseph Conrad, Arthur Rimbaud, and Virginia Woolf employed symbolism in their writing.

Transcendentalism A 19th-century American movement centered in New England. It advocated reliance on personal conscience over the dictates of external authority or moral conventions. Ralph Waldo Emerson and Henry David Thoreau were among its leaders.

Victorian Pertaining to the drama and literature produced during the reign of Queen Victoria of England (1837–1901). Although associated with strict codes of moral conduct and social stagnation, the age witnessed a crisis in religious faith and growing social unrest. Joseph Conrad, Charles Dickens, George Eliot, George Bernard Shaw, and Oscar Wilde produced much of their greatest work during this period.

PSEUDONYMS OF FAMOUS AUTHORS

Real Name	Pseudonym or Pen Name
Brian W. Aldiss	Jael Cracken, Arch Mendicant, Peter Pica, John Runciman, C. C. Shackelton
Kingsley Amis	Robert Markham
Hans Christian Andersen	Villiam Christian Walter
Poul Anderson	A. A. Craig, Michael Karageorge, Winston P. Sanders
François-Marie Arouet	Voltaire
Isaac Asimov	Dr. A., Paul French, Dale E. George
Louis Auchincloss	Andrew Lee
Neftalí Ricardo Reyes Basoalto	Pablo Neruda
L. Frank Baum	Edith Van Dyne
Robert Benchley	Guy Fawkes
Marie Henri Beyle	Stendhal
Ambrose Bierce	Dod Grile
Eric Arthur Blair	George Orwell
Anne Brontë	Acton Bell, Lady Geralda, Olivia Vernon, Alexandria Zenobia
Charlotte Brontë	C. B., Currer Bell, Marquis of Douro, Genius, Lord Charles Wellesley
Emily Brontë	R. Acton, Ellis Bell
William S. Burroughs	William Lee
Barbara Cartland	Barbara Hamilton McCorquodale
Agatha Christie	Agatha Christie Mallowen, Mary Westmacott
Arthur C. Clarke	E. G. O'Brien, Charles Willis
Samuel Langhorne Clemens	Mark Twain
Michael Crichton	Jeffrey Hudson, John Lange
Edward Estlin Cummings	e. e. cummings
Karen Dinesen, Baroness Blixen-Finecke	Isak Dinesen
Charles Lutwidge Dodgson	Lewis Carroll
Amandine-Aurore-Lucile Dupin	George Sand
Mary Ann Evans	George Eliot
Howard Fast	E. V. Cunningham, Walter Ericson
Erle Stanley Gardner	A. A. Fair, Charles M. Green, Carleton Kendrake, Charles J. Kenny
Theodor Seuss Geisel	Theo Lesieg, Dr. Seuss
Edward St. John Gorey	Eduard Blutig, Mrs. Regera Dowdy, Redway Grode, O. Mude, Hyacinthe Phypps, Ogdred Weary, Dreary Wodge
Dashiell Hammett	Peter Collinson
Robert A. Heinlein	Anson MacDonald, Lyle Monroe, John Riverside, Caleb Saunders, Simon York
Eleanor Alice Burford Hibbert	Eleanor Burford, Philippa Carr, Elbur Ford, Victoria Holt, Kathleen Kellow, Jean Plaidy, Ellalice Tate
L. Ron Hubbard	Elron, Tom Esterbrook, Rene La Fayette, Capt. B. A. Northrop, Kurt von Rachen
Ford Herman Hueffer	Ford Madox Ford
E. Howard Hunt	John Baxter, Gordon Davis, Robert Dietrich, David St. John
LeRoi Jones	Imamu Amiri Baraka
Dean Koontz	David Axton, Brian Coffey, Deanna Dwyer, K. R. Dwyer, John Hill, Leigh Nichols, Andrew North, Richard Paige, Owen West, Aaron Wolfe
Józef Teodor Konrad Korzeniowski	Joseph Conrad
Louis LaMoore	Louis L'Amour, Tex Burns
T. E. Lawrence	J. H. Ross, T. E. Shaw
Manfred Lee and Frederic Dannay	Ellery Queen, Barnaby Ross
Salvatore A. Lombino	Hunt Collins, Evan Hunter, Richard Marsten, Ed McBain
Robert Ludlum	Jonathon Ryder, Michael Shepherd
James du Maresq	James Clavell
Alan McCrae	Alan Moorehead

continues

Real Name	Pseudonym or Pen Name
Kenneth Millar	John Ross Macdonald, Ross Macdonald
Edna St. Vincent Millay	Nancy Boyd
William Anthony Parker White	Theo Durrant
Nevil Shute Norway	Nevil Shute
Conor Cruise O'Brien	Donat O'Donnell
Dorothy Parker	Constant Reader
Eric Partridge	Vigilans
William Sydney Porter	O. Henry
William Saroyan	Sirak Goryan
Terry Southern	Maxwell Kenton
Irving Stone	Irving Tannenbaum
Gore Vidal	Edgar Box
Nathan Weinstein	Nathanael West
J. A. Wight	James Herriot
John Burgess Wilson	Anthony Burgess, Joseph Kell
Chloe Anthony Wofford	Toni Morrison
Willard Huntington Wright	S. S. Van Dine

POET LAUREATES

ENGLISH

In 1616, Ben Jonson was named England's first poet laureate; however, the title did not become an official royal office until 1668, when John Dryden assumed the honored post. Since that time, the office has been awarded for life. The poet laureate is responsible for composing poems for court and national occasions. At the time of each laureate's death, it is the duty of the prime minister to nominate successors from which the reigning sovereign will choose. It is the Lord Chamberlain who appoints the poet laureate by issuing a warrant to the laureate-elect. The life appointment is always announced in the *London Gazette*.

Laureateship	Poet	Birth and Death Dates
1668–88	John Dryden	1631–1700
1689–92	Thomas Shadwell	1643?–92
1692–1715	Nahum Tate	1652–1715
1715–18	Nicholas Rowe	1674–1718
1718–30	Laurence Eusden	1688–1730
1730–57	Colley Cibber	1671–1757
*1757–85	William Whitehead	1715–85
1785–90	Thomas Warton	1728–90
1790–1813	Henry James Pye	1745–1813
1813–43	Robert Southey	1774–1843
1843–50	William Wordsworth	1770–1850
†1850–92	Alfred, Lord Tennyson	1809–92
1896–1913	Alfred Austin	1835–1913
1913–30	Robert Bridges	1844–1930
1930–67	John Masefield	1878–1967
1968–72	Cecil Day-Lewis	1904–72
1972–84	Sir John Betjeman	1906–84
1984–98	Ted Hughes	1930–98
1999–	Andrew Motion	1952–

* The 1757 appointment was declined by Thomas Gray.   † The 1850 appointment was declined by Samuel Rogers.

AMERICAN

In 1986, Robert Penn Warren was named the first poet laureate of the United States. The American poet laureate is appointed annually by the Librarian of Congress.

Laureateship	Poet	Birth and Death Dates
1986–87	Robert Penn Warren	1905–89
1987–88	Richard Wilbur	1921–
1988–90	Howard Nemerov	1920–91
1990–91	Mark Strand	1934–
1991–92	Joseph Brodsky	1940–96
1992–93	Mona Van Duyn	1921–
1993–95	Rita Dove	1952–
1995–97	Robert Hass	1941–
1997–2000	Robert Pinsky	1940–
2001–	Billy Collins	1941–

BOOK AWARDS AND THEIR RECIPIENTS

NOBEL PRIZE FOR LITERATURE

The Swedish Academy in Stockholm annually awards this prize to a writer who "shall have produced in the field of literature the most outstanding work in an ideal direction." Recipients may be of any nationality.

2001 V. S. Naipaul, Great Britain
2000 Gao Xingjian, China
1999 Günter Grass, Germany
1998 José Saramago, Portugal
1997 Dario Fo, Italy
1996 Wisława Szymborska, Poland
1995 Seamus Heaney, Ireland
1994 Kenzaburo Oe, Japan
1993 Toni Morrison, U.S.
1992 Derek Walcott, West Indies
1991 Nadine Gordimer, South Africa
1990 Octavio Paz, Mexico
1989 Camilo José Cela, Spain
1988 Naguib Mahfouz, Egypt
1987 Joseph Brodsky, U.S.
1986 Wole Soyinka, Nigeria
1985 Claude Simon, France
1984 Jaroslav Seifert, Czechoslovakia
1983 William Golding, Great Britain
1982 Gabriel García Márquez, Colombia
1981 Elias Canetti, Bulgaria
1980 Czesław Miłosz, Poland–U.S.
1979 Odysseus Elytis, Greece
1978 Isaac Bashevis Singer, U.S.
1977 Vicente Aleixandre, Spain
1976 Saul Bellow, U.S.
1975 Eugenio Montale, Italy
1974 Eyvind Johnson, Sweden, and Harry Edmund Martinson, Sweden

1973 Patrick White, Australia
1972 Heinrich Böll, Federal Republic of Germany
1971 Pablo Neruda, Chile
1970 Aleksandr Solzhenitsyn, U.S.S.R.
1969 Samuel Beckett, Ireland
1968 Yasunari Kawabata, Japan
1967 Miguel Angel Asturias, Guatemala
1966 Samuel Joseph Agnon, Israel, and Nelly Sachs, Sweden
1965 Mikhail Sholokhov, U.S.S.R.
1964 Jean-Paul Sartre, France (declined the prize)
1963 Gorgios Seferis, Greece
1962 John Steinbeck, U.S.
1961 Ivo Andric, Yugoslavia
1960 Saint-John Perse, France
1959 Salvatore Quasimodo, Italy
1958 Boris Pasternak, U.S.S.R.
1957 Albert Camus, France
1956 Juan Ramón Jiménez, Spain
1955 Halldór Kiljian Laxness, Iceland
1954 Ernest Hemingway, U.S.
1953 Sir Winston Churchill, Great Britain
1952 François Mauriac, France
1951 Pär Lagerkvist, Sweden
1950 Bertrand Russell, Great Britain
1949 William Faulkner, U.S.
1948 T. S. Eliot, Great Britain
1947 André Gide, France
1946 Hermann Hesse, Germany *continues*

Nobel Prize for Literature *continued*

1945	Gabriela Mistral, Chile
1944	Johannes V. Jensen, Denmark
1943–1940	No Award
1939	Frans Eemil Sillanpää, Finland
1938	Pearl S. Buck, U.S.
1937	Robert Martin du Gard, France
1936	Eugene O'Neill, U.S.
1935	No Award
1934	Luigi Pirandello, Italy
1933	Ivan A. Bunin, Russia
1932	John Galsworthy, Great Britain
1931	Erik A. Karlfeldt, Sweden
1930	Sinclair Lewis, U.S.
1929	Thomas Mann, Germany
1928	Sigrid Undset, Norway
1927	Henri Bergson, France
1926	Grazia Deledda, Italy
1925	George Bernard Shaw, Great Britain
1924	Władysław S. Reymount, Poland
1923	William Butler Yeats, Ireland
1922	Jacinto Benavente, Spain
1921	Anatole France, France
1920	Knut Hamsun, Norway
1919	Carl F. G. Spitteler, Switzerland
1918	No Award
1917	Karl A. Gjellerup, Denmark, and Henrik Pontoppidan, Denmark
1916	Verner von Heidenstam, Sweden
1915	Romain Rolland, France
1914	No Award
1913	Rabindranath Tagore, India
1912	Gerhart Hauptmann, Germany
1911	Maurice Maeterlinck, Belgium
1910	Paul J. L. Heyse, Germany
1909	Selma Lagerlöf, Sweden
1908	Rudolf Eucken, Germany
1907	Rudyard Kipling, Great Britain
1906	Giusuè Carducci, Italy
1905	Henryk Sienkiewicz, Poland
1904	Frédéric Mistral, France, and José Echegaray, Spain
1903	Björnstjerne Björnson, Norway
1902	Theodor Mommsen, Germany
1901	René F. A. Sully-Prudhomme, France

PULITZER PRIZE IN LETTERS

Awarded by Columbia University in New York for distinguished work by an American author.

FICTION

2002	*Empire Falls* Richard Russo
2001	*The Amazing Adventures of Kavalier & Clay* Michael Chabon
2000	*Interpreter of Maladies* Jhumpa Lahiri
1999	*The Hours* Michael Cunningham
1998	*American Pastoral* Philip Roth
1997	*Martin Dressler: The Tale of an American Dreamer* Stephen Millhauser
1996	*Independence Day* Richard Ford
1995	*The Stone Diaries* Carol Shields
1994	*The Shipping News* E. Annie Proulx
1993	*A Good Scent from a Strange Mountain* Robert Olen Butler
1992	*A Thousand Acres* Jane Smiley
1991	*Rabbit at Rest* John Updike
1990	*The Mambo Kings Play Songs of Love* Oscar Hijuelos
1989	*Breathing Lessons* Anne Tyler
1988	*Beloved* Toni Morrison
1987	*A Summons to Memphis* Peter Taylor
1986	*Lonesome Dove* Larry McMurtry
1985	*Foreign Affairs* Alison Lurie
1984	*Ironweed* William Kennedy
1983	*The Color Purple* Alice Walker
1982	*Rabbit Is Rich* John Updike
1981	*A Confederacy of Dunces* John Kennedy Toole
1980	*The Executioner's Song* Norman Mailer
1979	*The Stories of John Cheever* John Cheever
1978	*Elbow Room* James Alan McPherson
1977	No Award
1976	*Humboldt's Gift* Saul Bellow
1975	*The Killer Angels* Michael Shaara
1974	No Award
1973	*The Optimist's Daughter* Eudora Welty
1972	*Angle of Repose* Wallace Stegner
1971	No Award
1970	*Collected Stories* Jean Stafford
1969	*House Made of Dawn* N. Scott Momaday
1968	*The Confessions of Nat Turner* William Styron
1967	*The Fixer* Bernard Malamud
1966	*The Collected Stories of Katherine Anne Porter* Katherine Anne Porter
1965	*The Keepers of the House* Shirley Ann Grau
1964	No Award
1963	*The Reivers* William Faulkner
1962	*The Edge of Sadness* Edwin O'Connor
1961	*To Kill a Mockingbird* Harper Lee
1960	*Advise and Consent* Allen Drury

1959	*The Travels of Jamie McPheeters* Robert Lewis Taylor
1958	*A Death in the Family* James Agee
1957	No Award
1956	*Andersonville* MacKinlay Kantor
1955	*A Fable* William Faulkner
1954	No Award
1953	*The Old Man and the Sea* Ernest Hemingway
1952	*The Caine Mutiny* Herman Wouk
1951	*The Town* Conrad Richter
1950	*The Way West* A. B. Guthrie, Jr.
1949	*Guard of Honor* James Gould Cozzens
1948	*Tales of the South Pacific* James A. Michener
1947	*All the King's Men* Robert Penn Warren
1946	No Award
1945	*A Bell for Adano* John Hersey
1944	*Journey in the Dark* Martin Flavin
1943	*Dragon's Teeth* Upton Sinclair
1942	*In This Our Life* Ellen Glasgow
1941	No Award
1940	*The Grapes of Wrath* John Steinbeck

1939	*The Yearling* Marjorie Kinnan Rawlings
1938	*The Late George Apley* John Phillips Marquand
1937	*Gone with the Wind* Margaret Mitchell
1936	*Honey in the Horn* Harold L. Davis
1935	*Now in November* Josephine Winslow Johnson
1934	*Lamb in His Bosom* Caroline Miller
1933	*The Store* T. S. Stribling
1932	*The Good Earth* Pearl S. Buck
1931	*Years of Grace* Margaret Ayer Barnes
1930	*Laughing Boy* Oliver LaFarge
1929	*Scarlet Sister Mary* Julia M. Peterkin
1928	*The Bridge of San Luis Rey* Thornton Wilder
1927	*Early Autumn* Louis Bromfield
1926	*Arrowsmith* Sinclair Lewis
1925	*So Big* Edna Ferber
1924	*The Able McLaughlins* Margaret Wilson
1923	*One of Ours* Willa Cather
1922	*Alice Adams* Booth Tarkington
1921	*The Age of Innocence* Edith Wharton
1920	No Award
1919	*The Magnificent Ambersons* Booth Tarkington
1918	*His Family* Ernest Poole

POETRY

2002	*Practical Gods* Carl Dennis
2001	*Different Hours* Stephen Dunn
2000	*Repair* C. K. Williams
1999	*Blizzard of One* Mark Strand
1998	*Black Zodiac* Charles Wright
1997	*Alive Together: New and Selected Poems* Lisel Mueller
1996	*The Dream of the Unified Field* Jorie Graham
1995	*Simple Truth* Philip Levine
1994	*Neon Vernacular* Yusef Komunyakaa
1993	*The Wild Iris* Louise Glück
1992	*Selected Poems* James Tate
1991	*Near Changes* Mona Van Duyn
1990	*The World Doesn't End* Charles Simic
1989	*New and Collected Poems* Richard Wilbur
1988	*Partial Accounts: New and Selected Poems* William Meredith
1987	*Thomas and Beulah* Rita Dove
1986	*The Flying Change* Henry Taylor
1985	*Yin* Carolyn Kizer
1984	*American Primitive* Mary Oliver
1983	*Selected Poems* Galway Kinnell
1982	*The Collected Poems* Sylvia Plath
1981	*The Morning of the Poem* James Schuyler
1980	*Selected Poems* Donald Justice
1979	*Now and Then: Poems 1976–1978* Robert Penn Warren
1978	*Collected Poems* Howard Nemerov
1977	*Divine Comedies* James Merrill
1976	*Self-Portrait in a Convex Mirror* John Ashbery
1975	*Turtle Island* Gary Snyder

1974	*The Dolphin* Robert Lowell
1973	*Up Country* Maxine Kumin
1972	*Collected Poems* James Wright
1971	*The Carrier of Ladders* William S. Merwin
1970	*Untitled Subjects* Richard Howard
1969	*Of Being Numerous* George Oppen
1968	*The Hard Hours* Anthony Hecht
1967	*Live or Die* Anne Sexton
1966	*Selected Poems* Richard Eberhart
1965	*77 Dream Songs* John Berryman
1964	*At the End of the Open Road* Louis Simpson
1963	*Pictures from Breughel* William Carlos Williams
1962	*Poems* Alan Dugan
1961	*Times Three: Selected Verse from Three Decades* Phyllis McGinley
1960	*Heart's Needle* W. D. Snodgrass
1959	*Selected Poems 1928–1958* Stanley Kunitz
1958	*Promises: Poems 1954–1956* Robert Penn Warren
1957	*Things of This World* Richard Wilbur
1956	*Poems, North & South* Elizabeth Bishop
1955	*Collected Poems* Wallace Stevens
1954	*The Waking* Theodore Roethke
1953	*Collected Poems 1917–1952* Archibald MacLeish
1952	*Collected Poems* Marianne Moore
1951	*Complete Poems* Carl Sandburg
1950	*Annie Allen* Gwendolyn Brooks
1949	*Terror and Decorum* Peter Viereck
1948	*The Age of Anxiety* W. H. Auden
1947	*Lord Weary's Castle* Robert Lowell
1946	No Award

continues

Pulitzer Prize, Poetry *continued*

1945	*V-Letter and Other Poems* Karl Shapiro		1929	*John Brown's Body* Stephen Vincent Benét
1944	*Western Star* Stephen Vincent Benét		1928	*Tristram* Edwin Arlington Robinson
1943	*A Witness Tree* Robert Frost		1927	*Fiddler's Farewell* Leonora Speyer
1942	*The Dust Which Is God* William Rose Benét		1926	*What's O'Clock* Amy Lowell
1941	*Sunderland Capture* Leonard Bacon		1925	*The Man Who Died Twice* Edwin Arlington Robinson
1940	*Collected Poems* Mark Van Doren		1924	*New Hampshire: A Poem with Notes and Grace Notes* Robert Frost
1939	*Selected Poems* John Gould Fletcher			
1938	*Cold Morning Sky* Marya Zaturenska		1923	*The Ballad of the Harp-Weaver and Other Poems* Edna St.Vincent Millay
1937	*A Further Range* Robert Frost			
1936	*Strange Holiness* Robert P. T. Coffin		1922	*Collected Poems* Edwin Arlington Robinson
1935	*Bright Ambush* Audrey Wurdemann		1921	No Award
1934	*Collected Verse* Robert Hillyer		1920	No Award
1933	*Conquistador* Archibald MacLeish		1919	*Old Road to Paradise* Margaret Widdemer and *Corn Huskers* Carl Sandburg
1932	*The Flowering Stone* George Dillon			
1931	*Collected Poems* Robert Frost		1918	*Love Songs* Sara Teasdale
1930	*Selected Poems* Conrad Aiken			

DRAMA

2002	*Topdog/Underdog* Susan Lori-Parks		1974	No Award
2001	*Proof* David Auburn		1973	*That Championship Season* Jason Miller
2000	*Dinner with Friends* Donald Margulies		1972	No Award
1999	*Wit* Margaret Edson		1971	*The Effect of Gamma Rays on Man-in-the-Moon Marigolds* Paul Zindel
1998	*How I Learned to Drive* Paula Vogel			
1997	No Award		1970	*No Place to Be Somebody* Charles Gordone
1996	*Rent* Jonathan Larson		1969	*The Great White Hope* Howard Sackler
1995	*The Young Man from Atlanta* Horton Foote		1968	No Award
1994	*Three Tall Women* Edward Albee		1967	*A Delicate Balance* Edward Albee
1993	*Angels in America: Millenium Approaches* Tony Kushner		1966	No Award
			1965	*The Subject Was Roses* Frank D. Gilroy
1992	*The Kentucky Cycle* Robert Schenkkan		1964	No Award
1991	*Lost in Yonkers* Neil Simon		1963	No Award
1990	*The Piano Lesson* August Wilson		1962	*How to Succeed in Business Without Really Trying* music and lyrics by Frank Loesser and book by Abe Burrows
1989	*The Heidi Chronicles* Wendy Wasserstein			
1988	*Driving Miss Daisy* Alfred Uhry			
1987	*Fences* August Wilson		1961	*All the Way Home* Tad Mosel
1986	No Award		1960	*Fiorello!* book by Jerome Weidman and George Abbott; music by Jerry Bock; lyrics by Sheldon Harnick
1985	*Sunday in the Park with George* music and lyrics by Stephen Sondheim; book by James Lapine			
			1959	*J. B.* Archibald MacLeish
1984	*Glengarry Glen Ross* David Mamet		1958	*Look Homeward Angel* Ketti Frings
1983	*'night, Mother* Marsha Norman		1957	*Long Day's Journey Into Night* Eugene O'Neill
1982	*A Soldier's Play* Charles Fuller		1956	*The Diary of Anne Frank* Albert Hackett and Frances Goodrich
1981	*Crimes of the Heart* Beth Henley			
1980	*Talley's Folly* Lanford Wilson		1955	*Cat on a Hot Tin Roof* Tennessee Williams
1979	*Buried Child* Sam Shepard		1954	*The Teahouse of the August Moon* John Patrick
1978	*The Gin Game* Donald L. Coburn		1953	*Picnic* William Inge
1977	*The Shadow Box* Michael Cristofer		1952	*The Shrike* Joseph Kramm
1976	*A Chorus Line* conceived, choreographed, and directed by Michael Bennett; book by James Kirkwood and Nicholas Dante; music by Marvin Hamlisch and lyrics by Edward Kleban		1951	No Award
			1950	*South Pacific* Richard Rodgers, book by Oscar Hammerstein II and Joshua Logan; lyrics by Hammerstein
			1949	*Death of a Salesman* Arthur Miller
1975	*Seascape* Edward Albee		1948	*A Streetcar Named Desire* Tennessee Williams

1947	No Award
1946	*State of the Union* Russell Crouse and Howard Lindsay
1945	*Harvey* Mary Chase
1944	No Award
1943	*The Skin of Our Teeth* Thornton Wilder
1942	No Award
1941	*There Shall Be No Night* Robert E. Sherwood
1940	*The Time of Your Life* William Saroyan
1939	*Abe Lincoln in Illinois* Robert E. Sherwood
1938	*Our Town* Thornton Wilder
1937	*You Can't Take It with You* Moss Hart and George S. Kaufman
1936	*Idiot's Delight* Robert E. Sherwood
1935	*The Old Maid* Zoë Akins
1934	*Men in White* Sidney Kingsley
1933	*Both Your Houses* Maxwell Anderson
1932	*Of Thee I Sing* book by George S. Kaufman and Morrie Ryskind; lyrics by Ira Gershwin
1931	*Alison's House* Susan Glaspell
1930	*The Green Pastures* Marc Connelly
1929	*Street Scene* Elmer L. Rice
1928	*Strange Interlude* Eugene O'Neill
1927	*In Abraham's Bosom* Paul Green
1926	*Craig's Wife* George Kelly
1925	*They Knew What They Wanted* Sidney Howard
1924	*Hell-Bent fer Heaven* Hatcher Hughes
1923	*Icebound* Owen Davis
1922	*Anna Christie* Eugene O'Neill
1921	*Miss Lulu Bett* Zona Gale
1920	*Beyond the Horizon* Eugene O'Neill
1919	No Award
1918	*Why Marry?* Jesse Lynch Williams

NATIONAL BOOK AWARD

The National Book Award was known as the American Book Award from 1980 to 1986. The award reverted to its original name in 1987.

FICTION

2001	*The Corrections* Jonathan Franzen
2000	*In America* Susan Sontag
1999	*Waiting* Ha Jin
1998	*Charming Billy* Alice McDermott
1997	*Cold Mountain* Charles Frazier
1996	*Ship Fever and Other Stories* Andrea Barrett
1995	*Sabbath's Theater* Philip Roth
1994	*A Frolic of His Own* William Gaddis
1993	*The Shipping News* E. Annie Proulx
1992	*All the Pretty Horses* Cormac McCarthy
1991	*Mating* Norman Rush
1990	*The Middle Passage* Charles Johnson
1989	*Spartina* John Casey
1988	*Paris Trout* Pete Dexter
1987	*Paco's Story* Larry Heinemann
1986	*World's Fair* E. L. Doctorow
1985	*White Noise* Don DeLillo
1984	*Victory over Japan* Ellen Gilchrist
1983	*The Color Purple* Alice Walker
1982	*Rabbit Is Rich* John Updike
1981	*Plains Song* Wright Morris
1980	*Sophie's Choice* William Styron
1979	*Going After Cacciato* Tim O'Brien
1978	*Blood Ties* Mary Lee Settle
1977	*The Spectator Bird* Wallace Stegner
1976	*J. R.* William Gaddis
1975	*Dog Soldiers* Robert Stone and *The Hair of Harold Roux* Thomas Williams
1974	*Gravity's Rainbow* Thomas Pynchon and *A Crown of Feathers and Other Stories* Isaac Bashevis Singer
1973	*Chimera* John Barth
1972	*The Complete Stories of Flannery O'Connor* Flannery O'Connor
1971	*Mr. Sammler's Planet* Saul Bellow
1970	*Them* Joyce Carol Oates
1969	*Steps* Jerzy Kosinski
1968	*The Eighth Day* Thornton Wilder
1967	*The Fixer* Bernard Malamud
1966	*The Collected Stories of Katherine Anne Porter* Katherine Anne Porter
1965	*Herzog* Saul Bellow
1964	*The Centaur* John Updike
1963	*Morte D'Urban* J. F. Powers
1962	*The Moviegoer* Walker Percy
1961	*The Waters of Kronos* Conrad Richter
1960	*Goodbye, Columbus* Philip Roth
1959	*The Magic Barrel* Bernard Malamud
1958	*The Wapshot Chronicle* John Cheever
1957	*Field of Vision* Wright Morris
1956	*Ten North Frederick* John O'Hara
1955	*A Fable* William Faulkner
1954	*The Adventures of Augie March* Saul Bellow
1953	*Invisible Man* Ralph Ellison
1952	*From Here to Eternity* James Jones
1951	*The Collected Stories of William Faulkner* William Faulkner
1950	*The Man with the Golden Arm* Nelson Algren

continues

Literature

National Book Award *continued*

NONFICTION

From 1964 to 1979, the category of general nonfiction was eliminated. Prizes were given instead in specialized categories, such as history, contemporary affairs, the sciences, and biography.

2001	*The Noonday Demon: An Atlas of Depression* Andrew Solomon	1985	*Common Ground: A Turbulent Decade in the Lives of Three American Families* J. Anthony Lukas
2000	*In the Heart of the Sea: The Tragedy of the Whaleship Essex* Nathaniel Philbrick	1984	*Andrew Jackson and the Course of American Democracy, 1833–1845* Robert V. Remini
1999	*Embracing Defeat: Japan in the Wake of World War II* John W. Dower	1983	*China: Alive in the Bitter Sea* Fox Butterfield
1998	*Slaves in the Family* Edward Ball	1982	*The Soul of a New Machine* Tracy Kidder
1997	*American Sphinx: The Character of Thomas Jefferson* Joseph Ellis	1981	*China Men* Maxine Hong Kingston
1996	*An American Requiem: God, My Father, and the War That Came Between Us* James Carroll	1980	*The Right Stuff* Tom Wolfe
		1963	*Henry James, Vol. II: The Conquest of London; Henry James, Vol. III: The Middle Years* Leon Edel
1995	*The Haunted Land: Facing Europe's Ghosts after Communism* Tina Rosenberg	1962	*The City in History: Its Origins, Its Transformations and Its Prospects* Lewis Mumford
1994	*How We Die: Reflections on Life's Final Chapter* Sherwin B. Nuland	1961	*The Rise and Fall of the Third Reich* William L. Shirer
1993	*United States: Essays 1952–1992* Gore Vidal	1960	*James Joyce* Richard Ellmann
1992	*Becoming a Man: Half a Life Story* Paul Monette	1959	*Mistress to an Age: A Life of Madame de Stael* J. Christopher Herold
1991	*Freedom* Orlando Patterson	1958	*The Lion and the Throne* Catherine Drinker Bowen
1990	*The House of Morgan: An American Banking Dynasty and the Rise of Modern Finance* Ron Chernow	1957	*Russia Leaves the War* George F. Kennan
1989	*From Beirut to Jerusalem* Thomas L. Friedman	1956	*An American in Italy* Herbert Kubly
		1955	*The Measure of Man* Joseph Wood Krutch
1988	*A Bright Shining Lie: John Paul Vann and America in Vietnam* Neil Sheehan	1954	*A Stillness at Appomattox* Bruce Catton
		1953	*The Course of an Empire* Bernard A. DeVoto
1987	*The Making of the Atom Bomb* Richard Rhodes	1952	*The Sea Around Us* Rachel Carson
1986	*Arctic Dreams* Barry Lopez	1951	*Herman Melville* Newton Arvin
		1950	*Ralph Waldo Emerson* Ralph L. Rusk

THE GREAT BOOKS: A READING LIST

These books and writings about our civilization are recommended by the Great Books Foundation. They are listed in alphabetical order by author.

Adams, Henry	*The Education of Henry Adams* (1907)
Aeschylus	*Agamemnōn* (458 B.C.)
Aristotle (4th century B.C.)	*Politics*
	"On Happiness" (excerpt from *Nicomachean Ethics*)
	"On Tragedy"
Augustine, St.	*The City of God* (413–26)
Bible	*Genesis*
	Exodus
	Job
	Ecclesiastes
	The Gospel of Mark
Burke, Edmund	*Reflections on the Revolution in France* (1790)
Chaucer, Geoffrey	*The Canterbury Tales* (after 1387)

Chekhov, Anton	*Rothschild's Fiddle* (1894)
	Uncle Vanya (1897)
Clausewitz, Karl von	"What Is War?" [excerpt from *On War* (1833)]
Conrad, Joseph	"Heart of Darkness" [story in *Typhoon and Youth* (1902)]
Dante, Alighieri	"The Inferno" [canticle in *Divine Comedy* (c. 1314–21)]
Darwin, Charles	"The Moral Sense of Man and the Lower Animals" [excerpts from *On the Origin of Species* (1859) and *The Descent of Man* (1871)]
Dewey, John	"The Virtues" [excerpt from *Ethics* (1908)]
	"Habits and Will" [excerpt from *Human Nature and Conduct* (1922)]
Diderot, Denis	*Rameau's Nephew* (posthumously published in 1805)
Dostoevsky, Fyodor	*Notes from the Underground* (1864)
Euripides (5th century B.C.)	*Medea* (431 B.C.)
	Iphigeneia at Aulis
Flaubert, Gustave	"A Simple Heart" (short story, c. 1850)
Freud, Sigmund	"On Dreams" [excerpt from *The Interpretation of Dreams* (1899)]
Gibbon, Edward	*The History of the Decline and Fall of the Roman Empire* (1776, 1781, 1787–88)
Goethe, Johann Wolfgang von	*Faust,* Part I (1808)
Gogol, Nikolai	"The Overcoat" [First part of novel *Dead Souls* (1842)]
Hamilton, Alexander; Jay, John; Madison, James	The Federalist (1787–88)
Herodotus (5th century B.C.)	"The Persian Wars" (excerpt from his *History*)
Hobbes, Thomas	*Origin of Government*
Homer (8th century B.C.)	*The Iliad*
Hume, David	"Of Personal Identity" [excerpt from *A Treatise on Human Nature* (1739–40)]
	"Of Justice and Injustice" [excerpt from *Essays, Moral and Political* (1741–42)]
James, Henry	*The Beast in the Jungle* (1903)
Kafka, Franz	*The Metamorphosis* (1915)
Kant, Immanuel	*Conscience*
	"First Principles of Morals" [excerpt from *Fundamental Principles of the Metaphysic of Ethics* (1785)]
Kierkegaard, Søren	"The Knight of Faith" [excerpt from *Fear and Trembling* (1843)]
Locke, John	"Of Civil Government" [excerpt from the second of his *Two Treatises of Government* (1690)]
Machiavelli, Niccolò	*The Prince* (1513)
Maimonides (12th century)	"On Evil" [excerpt from *Guide for the Perplexed*]
Marx, Karl	"Alienated Labour" [excerpt from *Das Kapital* (1867)]
Melville, Herman	*Billy Budd, Sailor* (1924)
Mill, John Stuart	*On Liberty* (1859)
	Utilitarianism (1863)
Molière	*The Misanthrope* (1666)
Montaigne, Michel de	"Of Experience" [Book III, Chapter 13 (1588) of his *Essays*]
Montesquieu, Baron de	"Principles of Government" [excerpt from *The Spirit of the Laws* (1748)]
Nietzsche, Friedrich	*Thus Spake Zarathustra* (1883–85)
Plato (4th century B.C.)	*The Republic*
	Symposium
	The Crito
	The Apology
Rousseau, Jean-Jacques	*The Social Contract* (1762)
Schopenhauer, Arthur	"The Indestructibility of Our Inner Nature" [excerpt from *The World as Will and Representation* (1818)]
Shakespeare, William	*Hamlet* (1601)
	Othello (1604)
	King Lear (1605–6)
	Anthony and Cleopatra (1607)
	The Tempest (c. 1611)

continues

The Great Books: A Reading List *continued*

Shaw, George Bernard	*Caesar and Cleopatra* (1901)
Simmel, Georg	"Individual Freedom" [excerpt from *The Philosophy of Money* (1900)]
Smith, Adam	*Inquiry into the Nature and Causes of the Wealth of Nations* (1776)
Sophocles (5th century B.C.)	*Antigone*
	Oedipus the King
Swift, Jonathon	*Gulliver's Travels* (1726)
Thoreau, Henry David	*Civil Disobedience* (1849)
Thucydides (5th century B.C.)	*History of the Peloponnesian War*
Tocqueville, Alexis de	"The Power of the Majority" [excerpt from *Democracy in America* (1835, 1840)]
Tolstoy, Count Leo Nikolayevich	*The Death of Ivan Ilych* (1886)
Weber, Max	*The Protestant Ethic and the Spirit of Capitalism* (1920)

THE NEW YORK PUBLIC LIBRARY'S BOOKS OF THE CENTURY

To commemorate the New York Public Library's centennial, librarians identified the following books as ones that played defining roles in history and culture from 1895 to 1995—the Library's first one hundred years.

LANDMARKS OF MODERN LITERATURE

Anton Chekhov	*Tri Sestry [The Three Sisters]* (1901)
Marcel Proust	*À la Recherche du Temps Perdu [Remembrance of Things Past]* (3 vols., 1913–27)
Gertrude Stein	*Tender Buttons: Objects Food Rooms* (1914)
Franz Kafka	*Die Verwandlung [The Metamorphosis]* (1915)
Edna St. Vincent Millay	*Renascence and Other Poems* (1917)
William Butler Yeats	*The Wild Swans at Coole* (1917)
Luigi Pirandello	*Sei Personaggi in Cerce d'Autore [Six Characters in Search of an Author]* (1921)
T. S. Eliot	*The Waste Land* (1922)
James Joyce	*Ulysses* (1922)
Thomas Mann	*Der Zauberberg [The Magic Mountain]* (1924)
F. Scott Fitzgerald	*The Great Gatsby* (1925)
Virginia Woolf	*To the Lighthouse* (1927)
Federico García Lorca	*Primer Romancero Gitano [Gypsy Ballads]* (1928)
Richard Wright	*Native Son* (1940)
William Faulkner	*The Portable Faulkner* (1946)
W. H. Auden	*The Age of Anxiety: A Baroque Eclogue* (1947)
Samuel Beckett	*En Attendant Godot [Waiting for Godot; A Tragicomedy in Two Acts]* (1952)
Ralph Ellison	*Invisible Man* (1952)
Vladimir Nabokov	*Lolita* (1955)
Jorge Luis Borges	*Ficciones [Fictions]* (1944; 2nd augmented edition, 1956)
Jack Kerouac	*On the Road* (1957)
Gabriel García Márquez	*Cien Años de Soledad [One Hundred Years of Solitude]* (1967)
Philip Roth	*Portnoy's Complaint* (1969)
Toni Morrison	*Song of Solomon* (1977)

NATURE'S REALM

Maurice Maeterlinck	*La Vie des Abeilles [The Life of the Bee]* (1901)
Marie Sklodowska Curie	*Traité de Radioactivité [Treatise on Radioactivity]* (1910)
Albert Einstein	*The Meaning of Relativity* (1922)
Roger Tory Peterson	*A Field Guide to the Birds* (1934)
Aldo Leopold	*A Sand County Almanac* (1949)
Konrad Z. Lorenz	*Er Redete Mit dem Vieh, den Vögeln und den Fischen: [King Solomon's Ring: New Light on Animal Ways]* (1949)

Rachel Carson	*Silent Spring* (1962)
United States Surgeon General	*Smoking and Health* [known as *The Surgeon General's Report*] (1964)
James Watson	*The Double Helix: A Personal Account of the Discovery of the Structure of DNA* (1968)
Edward O. Wilson	*The Diversity of Life* (1992)

PROTEST AND PROGRESS

Jacob Riis	*The Battle with the Slum* (1902)
W. E. B. Du Bois	*The Souls of Black Folk* (1903)
Upton Sinclair	*The Jungle* (1906)
Jane Addams	*Twenty Years at Hull-House* (1910)
Lillian Wald	*The House on Henry Street* (1915)
Lincoln Steffens	*The Autobiography of Lincoln Steffens* (1931)
John Dos Passos	*U.S.A.* (1937)
John Steinbeck	*The Grapes of Wrath* (1939)
James Agee and Walker Evans	*Let Us Now Praise Famous Men* (1941)
Lillian Smith	*Strange Fruit* (1944)
Paul Goodman	*Growing Up Absurd* (1960)
James Baldwin	*The Fire Next Time* (1963)
Malcolm X	*The Autobiography of Malcolm X* (1965)
Randy Shilts	*And the Band Played On* (1987)
Alex Kotlowitz	*There Are No Children Here* (1991)

COLONIALISM AND ITS AFTERMATH

Joseph Conrad	*Lord Jim* (1900)
Rudyard Kipling	*Kim* (1901)
Mohandas K. Gandhi	*Satyagraha [Non-Violent Resistance]* (1921–40)
E. M. Forster	*A Passage to India* (1924)
Albert Camus	*L'Étranger [The Stranger]* (1942)
	United Nations Charter (1945)
Alan Paton	*Cry, the Beloved Country* (1948)
Edward Steichen	*The Family of Man: The Photographic Exhibition Created by Edward Steichen for the Museum of Modern Art* (1955)
Chinua Achebe	*Things Fall Apart* (1958)
Frantz Fanon	*Les Damnés de la Terre [The Wretched of the Earth]* (1961)
Jean Rhys	*Wide Sargasso Sea* (1966)
Tayeb el-Salih	*Mawsim al-Hijra ila al-Shamal [Season of Migration to the North]* (1969)
V. S. Naipaul	*Guerrillas* (1975)
Buchi Emecheta	*The Bride Price* (1976)
Ryszard Kapuscinski	*Cesarz [The Emperor]* (1978)
Rigoberta Menchú	*Me Llamo Rigoberta Menchú y Así me Nació Conciencia [I, Rigoberta Menchú]* (1983)
Marguerite Duras	*L'amant [The Lover]* (1984)

MIND AND SPIRIT

Emile Durkheim	*Le Suicide: Étude de Sociologie [Suicide: A Study in Sociology]* (1897)
Sigmund Freud	*Die Traumdeutung [The Interpretation of Dreams]* (1899)
Havelock Ellis	*Studies in the Psychology of Sex* (1901–28)
William James	*The Varieties of Religious Experience: A Study in Human Nature* (1902)
Kahlil Gibran	*The Prophet* (1923)
Bertrand Russell	*Why I Am Not a Christian* (1927)
Margaret Mead	*Coming of Age in Samoa* (1928)
Jean-Paul Sartre	*L'Être et le Néant [Being and Nothingness]* (1943)

continues

Literature

Mind and Spirit *continued*

Benjamin Spock   *The Common Sense Book of Baby and Child Care* (1946)
The Holy Bible
Paul Tillich   *The Courage to Be* (1952)
Ken Kesey   *One Flew Over the Cuckoo's Nest* (1962)
Timothy Leary   *The Politics of Ecstasy* (1968)
Elisabeth Kübler-Ross   *On Death and Dying* (1969)
Bruno Bettelheim   *The Uses of Enchantment* (1976)

POPULAR CULTURE AND MASS ENTERTAINMENT

Bram Stoker   *Dracula* (1897)
Henry James   *The Turn of the Screw* (1898)
Arthur Conan Doyle   *The Hound of the Baskervilles* (1902)
Edgar Rice Burroughs   *Tarzan of the Apes* (1914)
Zane Grey   *Riders of the Purple Sage* (1912)
Agatha Christie   *The Mysterious Affair at Styles* (1920)
Dale Carnegie   *How to Win Friends and Influence People* (1936)
Margaret Mitchell   *Gone with the Wind* (1936)
Raymond Chandler   *The Big Sleep* (1939)
Nathanael West   *The Day of the Locust* (1939)
Grace Metalious   *Peyton Place* (1956)
Dr. Seuss   *The Cat in the Hat* (1957)
Robert A. Heinlein   *Stranger in a Strange Land* (1962)
Joseph Heller   *Catch-22* (1961)
Truman Capote   *In Cold Blood: A True Account of a Multiple Murder and Its Consequences* (1965)
Jim Bouton   *Ball Four: My Life and Hard Times Throwing the Knuckleball in the Big Leagues* (1970)
Stephen King   *Carrie* (1974)
Tom Wolfe   *The Bonfire of the Vanities* (1987)

WOMEN RISE

Edith Wharton   *The Age of Innocence* (1920)
Carrie Chapman Catt and   *Woman Suffrage and Politics: The Inner Story of the Suffrage Movement* (1923)
  Nettie Rogers Shuler
Margaret Sanger   *My Fight for Birth Control* (1931)
Zora Neale Hurston   *Dust Tracks on a Road* (1942)
Simone de Beauvoir   *Le Deuxième Sexe [The Second Sex]* (1949)
Doris Lessing   *The Golden Notebook* (1962)
Betty Friedan   *The Feminine Mystique* (1963)
Maya Angelou   *I Know Why the Caged Bird Sings* (1970)
Robin Morgan, editor   *Sisterhood Is Powerful: An Anthology of Writings from the Women's Liberation Movement* (1970)
Susan Brownmiller   *Against Our Will: Men, Women and Rape* (1975)
Alice Walker   *The Color Purple* (1982)

ECONOMICS AND TECHNOLOGY

Thorstein Veblen   *The Theory of the Leisure Class: An Economic Study of Institutions* (1899)
Max Weber   *Die protestantische Ethik und der Geist des Kapitalismus [The Protestant Ethic and the Spirit of Capitalism]* (1904)
Henry Adams   *The Education of Henry Adams* (1907)
John Maynard Keynes   *The General Theory of Employment, Interest and Money* (1936)
Friedrich A. von Hayek   *The Road to Serfdom* (1944)

Milton Friedman	*A Theory of the Consumption Function* (1957)
John Kenneth Galbraith	*The Affluent Society* (1958)
Jane Jacobs	*The Death and Life of Great American Cities* (1961)
Helen Leavitt	*Superhighway—Superhoax* (1970)
E. F. Schumacher	*Small Is Beautiful: A Study of Economics as if People Mattered* (1973)
Ed Krol	*The Whole Internet: User's Guide & Catalog* (1992)

UTOPIAS AND DYSTOPIAS

H. G. Wells	*The Time Machine* (1895)
Theodor Herzl	*Der Judenstaat [The Jewish State]* (1896)
L. Frank Baum	*The Wonderful Wizard of Oz* (1900)
J. M. Barrie	*Peter Pan* (1904)
Charlotte Perkins Gilman	*Herland* (1915)
Aldous Huxley	*Brave New World* (1932)
James Hilton	*Lost Horizon* (1933)
B. F. Skinner	*Walden Two* (1948)
George Orwell	*Nineteen Eighty-four* (1949)
Ray Bradbury	*Fahrenheit 451* (1953)
Ayn Rand	*Atlas Shrugged* (1957)
Anthony Burgess	*A Clockwork Orange* (1962)
Margaret Atwood	*The Handmaid's Tale* (1984)

WAR, HOLOCAUST, TOTALITARIANISM

Arnold Toynbee	*Armenian Atrocities: The Murder of a Nation* (1915)
John Reed	*Ten Days That Shook the World* (1919)
Siegfried Sassoon	*The War Poems* (1919)
Jaroslav Hašek	*Osudy Dobrého Vojáka Švejka za Světové Války [The Good Soldier Schweik]* (1921–23)
Adolf Hitler	*Mein Kampf* (1925–26)
Erich Maria Remarque	*Im Westen nichts Neues [All Quiet on the Western Front]* (1928)
Anna Akhmatova	*Rekviem [Requiem]* (1940)
Ernest Hemingway	*For Whom the Bell Tolls* (1940)
Arthur Koestler	*Darkness at Noon* (1940)
John Hersey	*Hiroshima* (1946)
Anne Frank	*Het Achterhuis [The Diary of a Young Girl]* (1947)
Winston Churchill	*The Gathering Storm* (1948)
Elie Wiesel	*La Nuit [Night]* (1958)
Mao Zedong	*Quotations from Chairman Mao* (1966)
Dee Alexander Brown	*Bury My Heart at Wounded Knee: An Indian History of the American West* (1970)
Aleksandr I. Solzhenitsyn	*Arkhipelag GULag, 1918–1956 [The Gulag Archipelago, 1918–1956: An Experiment in Literary Investigation]* (1973)
Michael Herr	*Dispatches* (1977)
Art Spiegelman	*Maus: A Survivor's Tale* (2 vols., 1986–91)

OPTIMISM, JOY, GENTILITY

Sarah Orne Jewett	*The Country of the Pointed Firs* (1896)
Helen Keller	*The Story of My Life* (1903)
G. K. Chesterton	*The Innocence of Father Brown* (1911)
Juan Ramón Jiménez	*Platero y yo [Platero and I]* (1917)
George Bernard Shaw	*Pygmalion* (1913)
Emily Post	*Etiquette in Society, in Business, in Politics, and at Home* (1922)
P. G. Wodehouse	*The Inimitable Jeeves* (1923)
A. A. Milne	*Winnie-the-Pooh* (1926)

continues

Optimism, Joy, Gentility *continued*

Willa Cather	*Shadows on the Rock* (1931)
Irma S. Rombauer	*The Joy of Cooking: A Compilation of Reliable Recipes with a Casual Culinary Chat* (1931)
J. R. R. Tolkien	*The Hobbit* (1937)
Margaret Wise Brown	*Goodnight Moon* (1947)
Harper Lee	*To Kill a Mockingbird* (1960)
Langston Hughes	*The Best of Simple* (1961)
Elizabeth Bishop	*The Complete Poems* (1969)

FAVORITES OF CHILDHOOD AND YOUTH

Beatrix Potter	*The Tale of Peter Rabbit* (1901)
Betty Smith	*A Tree Grows in Brooklyn* (1943)
C. S. Lewis	*The Lion, the Witch and the Wardrobe* (1950)
J. D. Salinger	*The Catcher in the Rye* (1951)
E. B. White	*Charlotte's Web* (1952)
Ezra Jack Keats	*The Snowy Day* (1962)
Maurice Sendak	*Where the Wild Things Are* (1963)
Patricia MacLachlan	*Sarah, Plain and Tall* (1985)

COMMON LITERARY TERMS

allegory   A story with an underlying meaning symbolized by the characters and action.

alliteration   The repetition of the same sounds—usually initial consonants of words or of stressed syllables—in any sequence of neighboring words.

allusion   A reference to a familiar person or event, often from literature.

anachronism   A chronological error in literature that places a person, event, or object in an impossible historical context.

anagram   A word or phrase created by transposing the letters of another word.

analogy   The relation of one thing to something familiar.

antagonist   The major character opposing a hero or a protagonist.

anthropomorphism   The assigning of human characteristics and feelings to animals and other nonhuman things.

anticlimax   Something that works against a climax, such as humor; a sudden descent from the lofty to the trivial.

antihero   A protagonist lacking in heroic qualities like courage, idealism, and honesty.

antithesis   A rhetorical figure in which sharply opposing ideas are expressed within a balanced grammatical structure.

assonance   The close repetition of similar vowel sounds.

autobiography   The story of one's life as written by oneself.

ballad   A poem, often meant to be sung, that tells a story.

bathos   A sudden descent from the lofty to the ordinary or ridiculous.

belles-lettres   Literature. Currently, lighter writings or appreciative essays on the beauties of literature.

bibliography   A list of books on a similar subject or by a given author or authors.

biography   The story of someone's life as written by another.

blank verse Unrhymed poetry, especially poetry written in iambic pentameter.

cacophony Discordant sounds, sometimes used in poetry for effect.

cadence The natural rhythm of language determined by its inherent alternation of stressed and unstressed syllables.

caesura A pause or break in a line of verse.

climax The point of high emotional intensity at which a story or play reaches its peak.

conceit A fanciful image, especially an elaborate or startling analogy.

couplet Two successive lines of poetry, usually rhymed.

dénouement Literally, the "unknotting": the final unraveling of the plot following the climax.

diction The choice and arrangement of words in a literary work.

doggerel Crudely written poetry.

elegy A poetic lament.

epic An extended narrative poem, exalted in style and heroic in theme.

epistolary novel A novel written in the form of correspondence.

essay A short written work of nonfiction, usually on one topic.

euphony Harmonious sounds, often used in poetry for effect.

fable A prose or poetic story that illustrates a moral.

fiction Narrative writing drawn from the imagination of the author rather than from history or fact.

foot A group of syllables forming a metrical unit.

free verse A poem without regular meter or line length.

genre A literary type or class.

haiku An unrhymed poem form, originated by the Japanese, consisting of three lines of five, seven, and five syllables that record the essence of a moment.

hero A character, often the protagonist, who exhibits qualities such as courage, idealism, and honesty.

high comedy Comedy that is characterized by intellect or wit.

historical novel A narrative that places fictional characters or events in historically accurate surroundings.

hyperbole A deliberate overstatement.

iamb A metrical foot that contains one short or unstressed syllable preceding one long or stressed syllable.

iambic pentameter Poetry consisting of five parts per line, each part having one short or unstressed syllable and one long or stressed syllable.

imagery Figurative language used to evoke particular mental pictures.

irony An expression of a meaning that contradicts the literal meaning.

literature Novels, stories, poems, and plays of high standards that entertain, inform, stimulate, or provide aesthetic pleasure.

low comedy Humorous material that employs physical actions or jokes of questionable taste.

malapropism A mistaken substitution of one word for another that sounds similar, generally with humorous effect.

metaphor A figure of speech in which two unlikely objects are compared by identification or by the substitution of one for the other.

meter The pattern of stressed and unstressed syllables in poetry.

motif A theme, character, or verbal pattern that recurs in literature or folklore.

myth A legend, usually made up in part of historical events, that helps define the beliefs of a people and that often has evolved as an explanation for rituals and natural phenomena.

nonfiction   A historically accurate narrative.

novel   A long work of fictional prose.

novella   A short novel; also, the early tales or short stories of French and Italian writers.

ode   A lyric poem marked by strong feelings and an involved style.

onomatopoeia   Formation of a word by imitating the natural sound associated with the object or action involved; the use of words that are so named.

oxymoron   A figure of speech that employs two contradictory terms. For examples, *see* "Oxymoron: Pairings of Contradictory or Incongruous Words" in chapter 13.

palindrome   A word, a sentence, or a group of sentences (sometimes in verse) that reads the same backward and forward. For examples, *see* "Palindromes" in chapter 13.

parable   A short story that illustrates a moral.

paradox   An apparently contradictory statement that contains a truth that reconciles the contradiction.

parody   A humorous, often exaggerated imitation of a serious literary work.

pathetic fallacy   The assigning of human attributes to nature.

pathos   An element that evokes feelings of pity, tenderness, and sympathy.

personification   The assigning of human attributes to abstractions, objects, and other nonhuman things.

plot   The organization of individual incidents in a narrative or play.

poem   A rhythmic expression of feelings or ideas, often using metaphor, meter, and rhyme.

poetic license   The practice of violating rules, expectations, or conventions to achieve a desired effect.

prologue   An introductory speech or monologue, given by an actor or actress before a play, which helps to set the stage for what is to come.

prose   Literary expression not marked by rhyme or metrical regularity.

prose poem   A prose composition that exhibits the rhythms of verse

protagonist   The main character of a play, novel, or story, usually the hero.

pun   A humorous and often clever play on words in which one word evokes another with a similar sound but a different meaning.

refrain   A phrase or verse that is repeated throughout a poem or song.

rhetorical question   A question put forth to achieve an effect or make a point, to which an answer is not expected.

rhyme   The repetition of similar or identical sounds at the ends of lines of verse.

rhythm   The pattern of stressed and unstressed syllables in a line of poetry or prose.

satire   Ridicule of human vice or folly; the work in which it is contained.

short story   A brief work of narrative prose.

simile   A comparison of two unlike things that usually employs *like* or *as*.

soliloquy   A dramatic monologue meant to convey the thoughts of a character in a play.

sonnet   A poem consisting of fourteen iambic pentameter lines with a rigidly prescribed rhyming scheme.

spondee   A type of metrical foot with two stressed syllables.

spoonerism   The transposition of the initial sounds of two or more words, often with humorous results. Named for a Professor Spooner of Oxford, who was famous for such transpositions.

style   An author's individual method and tone.

subplot   A secondary plot in a story.

symbol   In literature, something that stands for, or means, something else.

theme   The central idea or thesis of a work.

trochee   A metrical foot that contains one long or stressed syllable preceding one short or unstressed syllable.

verse   Lines of writing arranged in metrical patterns, or a single such line.

ADDITIONAL SOURCES OF INFORMATION

BOOKS

Andrews, William L., ed. *The Oxford Companion to African American Literature.* Oxford University Press, 1997.

Baldick, Chris. *The Concise Oxford Dictionary of Literary Terms.* Oxford University Press, 1991

Baldwin, Neil, and Diane Osen, eds. *The Writing Life: National Book Award Authors.* Random House, 1995

Bauer, Andrew. *The Hawthorn Dictionary of Pseudonyms.* Hawthorn Books, 1971.

Beckson, Karl, and Arthur Ganz. *Literary Terms: A Dictionary.* Farrar, Straus & Giroux, 1989.

Bede, Jean-Albert, and William B. Edgerton, eds. *Columbia Dictionary of Modern European Literature.* Columbia University Press, 1980.

Beetz, Kirk H., ed. *Beacham's Encyclopedia of Popular Fiction.* Beacham, 1996.

Benson, Eugene, and William Toye, eds. *The Oxford Companion to Canadian Literature.* 2nd ed. Oxford University Press, 1997.

Connolly, S. J., ed. *The Oxford Companion to Irish Literature.* Oxford University Press, 1999.

Contemporary Authors. 188 vols. Gale, 1962–2000.

Contemporary Authors: New Revision Series. 94 vols. Gale, 1962–2000.

Contemporary Literary Criticism. 137 vols. Gale, 1973–2000.

Cuddon, J. A. *Dictionary of Literary Terms and Literary Theory.* Blackwell, 1998.

Davidson, Cathy N., and Linda Wagner-Martin, eds. *The Oxford Companion to Women's Writing in the U.S.* Oxford University Press, 1995.

Drabble, Margaret, ed. *The Oxford Companion to English Literature.* Rev. 6th ed. Oxford University Press, 2000.

Frye, Northrop, Sheridan Baker, and George Perkins. *The Harper Handbook to Literature.* 2nd ed. HarperCollins, 1997.

Garland Henry and Mary, eds. *The Oxford Companion to German Literature.* 3rd ed., Oxford University Press, 1997.

Harmon, William, and Clarence Hugh Holman, *A Handbook to Literature.* 8th ed. Simon & Schuster, 1999.

Hart, James D. *The Oxford Companion to American Literature.* 6th ed. Oxford University Press, 1995.

Howatson, Margaret, and Ian Chilvers, eds. *The Oxford Companion to Classical Literature*, 3rd ed. Oxford University Press, 1993.

Levi, Anthony, ed. *Guide to French Literature.* 2 vols. St. James Press, 1994.

Moss, Joyce, and George Wilson, eds. *Literature and its Times.* 5 vols. Gale, 1997.

Murphy, Bruce, ed. *Benet's Readers Encyclopedia of American Literature.* 4th ed. HarperCollins, 1996.

National Book Foundation. *The National Book Awards: Forty-eight years of Literary Excellence: Winners and Finalists, 1950–1998.* National Book Foundation, 1998.

Ousby, Ian. *The Cambridge Guide to Literature in English*, 2nd ed. Cambridge University Press, 1994.

Padgett, Ron, ed. *World Poets.* 3 vols. Scribners, 2000.

Parini, Jay, et al. eds. *American Writers.* 4 vols. and 8 supplements. Scribners, 1974–2001.

Parini, Jay, et al. eds. *British Writers.* 8 vols. and 6 supplements. Scribners, 1974–2001.

Parker, Peter, ed. *A Reader's Guide to the 20th Century Novel.* Oxford University Press, 1995.

Preminger, Alex, and T. V. F. Brogan. *The New Princeton Encyclopedia of Poetry and Poetics.* Princeton University Press, 1996.

Serafin, Steven, ed. *The Encyclopedia of World Literature in the 20th Century.* 4 vols. St. James Press, 1999.

Skillion, Anne, ed. *The New York Public Library Literature Companion.* Free Press, 2001.

Sole Jr., Carlos A., and Maria I. Abreu, eds. *Latin American Writers.* 3 vols. Macmillan, 1989.

Stade, George, ed. *European Writers.* 3 vols. Scribners, 1992.

Wakeman, John, et al. eds. *World Authors.* 9 vols. H. W. Wilson, 1975–2000.

Wilde, William L., ed. *The Oxford Companion to Australian Literature,* 2nd ed. Oxford University Press, 1995.

WEB SITES
** Indicates subscription-based web sites

American National Biography**
http://www.anb.org

The American Verse Project
http://www.hti.umich.edu/a/amverse/

Bibliomania
http://www.bibliomania.com/

Electronic Poetry Center
http://www.epc.buffalo.edu/

Electronic Text Center, University of Virginia Library
http://etext.lib.virginia.edu

Literature Online
Bartleby.com

Literature Resource Center**
http://www.galenet.com/

MLA International Bibliography**
http://www.mla.org/publications/bibliography.htm

The On-Line Books Page
http://digital.library.upenn.edu/books/

Online Literary Criticism Collection
http://www.ipl.org/ref/litcrit

The Perseus Digital Library
http://www.perseus.tufts.edu

Project MUSE: Scholarly Journals Online**
http://muse.jhu.edu/

Virtual Reference Library
http://www.bl.uk/collections/resources/humanities/vrlnew.html

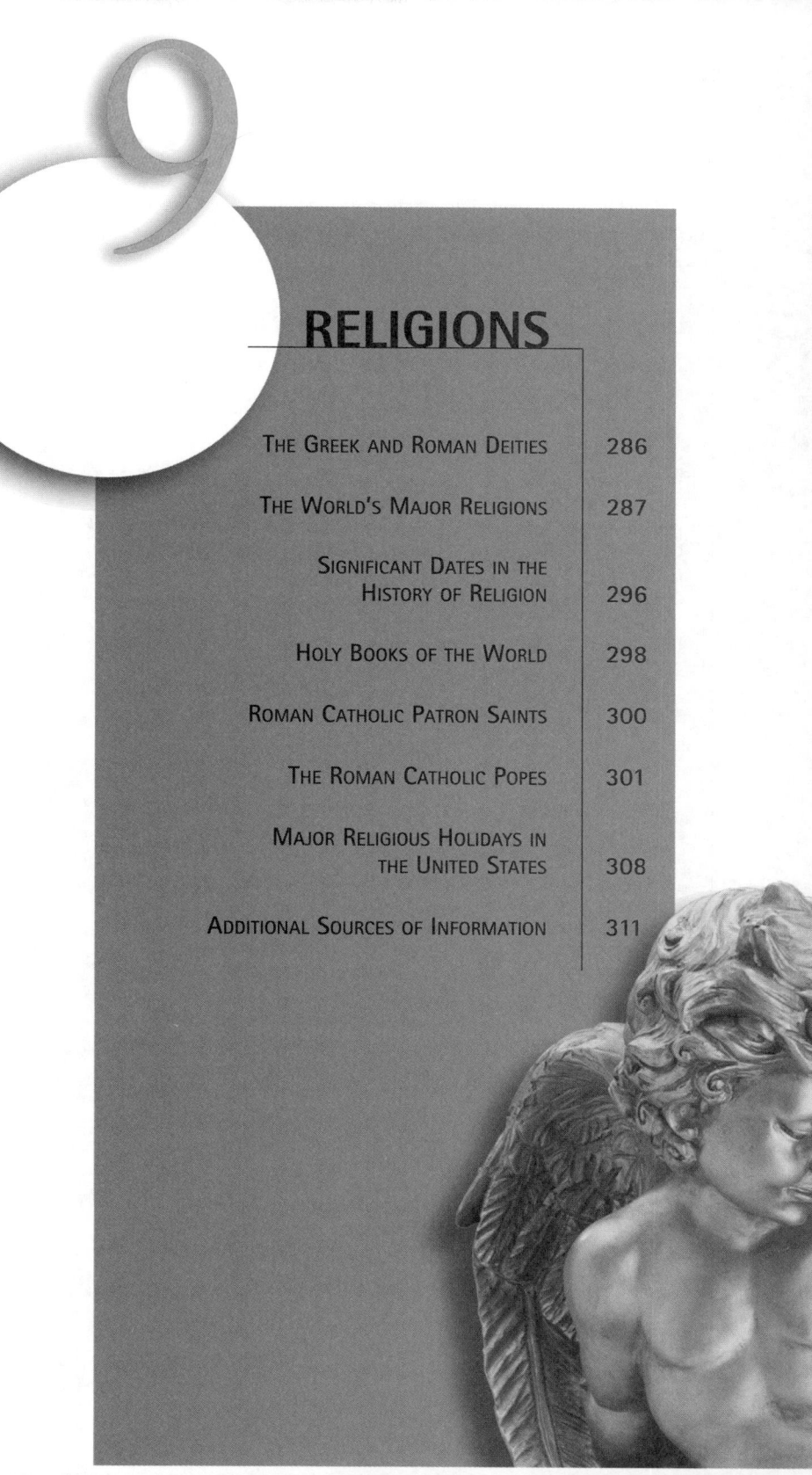

RELIGIONS

THE GREEK AND ROMAN DEITIES

The myths of the gods and goddesses of ancient Greece and Rome have had a lasting impact on Western thought. They have played an essential role in the development of the arts, philosophy, psychology, literature, and religion. The following list gives the names of these ancient deities as well as the spheres of influence ascribed to them.

Greek	Roman	Sphere of Influence
Adonis	——	Symbolizes the death of nature each autumn and its rebirth in the spring
Aeolus	——	God of the winds
Aphrodite	Venus	Goddess of love and beauty
Apollo	——	God of beauty, youth, poetry, music, prophecy, and archery
Ares	Mars	God of war
Artemis	Diana	Goddess of the hunt, moon, and nature
Asclepius	Aesculapius	God of medicine
Athena	Minerva	Goddess of wisdom
Chaos	——	God of the shapeless void that preceded creation of the Earth
Cronus	Saturn	Leader of the Titans who ruled the heavens after overthrowing his father, Uranus
Demeter	Ceres	Goddess of the earth, grain, and harvests
Dionysus	Bacchus (Liber)	God of wine
Dis (Hades)	Pluto	God of the underworld
Eos	Aurora	Goddess of dawn
Eris	Discordia	Goddess of strife and discord
Eros	Cupid (Amor)	God of love
Fates	Fates	Three sisters—Clotho, Lachesis, and Atropos (called Nona, Decuma, and Morta by the Romans)—who spun the thread of human destiny and cut it with their shears when they pleased
Flora	——	Goddess of flowers
Furies	Furies	Three goddesses, their heads (Eumenides) topped by serpents, who punished those who escaped human justice
Gorgons	——	Three winged sisters—Euryale, Medusa, and Stheno—the sight of whom turned mortals to stone
Graces	Graces	Three sisters—Aglaia, Euphrosyne, and Thalia—who were goddesses of banquets, dances, social enjoyments, and the arts
Hebe	Juventas	Goddess of youth
Hephaestus	Vulcan	God of fire
Hera	Juno	Sister and wife of Zeus; queen of the goddesses
Herakles	Hercules	Son of Zeus; greatest of Greek heroes, who performed 12 labors and was eventually granted immortality
Hermaphroditus	——	Son of Hermes and Aphrodite who was joined forever to the nymph of the fountain of Salmacis, creating one body with the sexual characteristics of both males and females
Hermes	Mercury	Messenger of the gods; patron of thieves
Hestia	Vesta	Goddess of the hearth
Hygeia	——	Goddess of health
Hymen	——	God of marriage
Hypnus	Somnus	God of sleep
——	Janus	Porter of heaven, who opens the year; also god of gates and doors, with two opposing faces
——	Lares	Spirits of ancestors who watch over homes and cities
——	Lemures	Spirits of the dead, both good and bad

Greek	Roman	Sphere of Influence
Metis	Prudence	First wife of Zeus, who helped him become king of gods; personification of prudence
Morpheus	———	God of dreams
Muses	Camenae	Nine sisters, daughters of Zeus, who are goddesses of the arts and sciences: Clio (history), Euterpe (lyric poetry), Thalia (comedy), Melpomene (tragedy), Terpsichore (dance), Erato (erotic poetry), Polyhymnia (sacred poetry), Urania (astronomy), and Callipe (epic poetry; chief of the Muses)
Nemesis	———	Goddess of vengeance
Nike	Victoria	Goddess of victory
Nymphs	———	Nature spirits who oversee water, trees, mountains, valleys, and particular locations
Nyx	Nox	Goddess of night
Pan	Faunus	God of flocks and shepherds
Persephone	Proserpine	Goddess of the underworld; symbol of the death of nature each autumn and its rebirth each spring
Plutus	———	God of wealth
———	Pomona	Goddess of fruit and gardens
Poseidon	Neptune	God of the oceans
Priapus	———	God of fertility
Psyche	Psyche	Goddess of the soul, who was united with Eros, or Cupid
Rhea	Ops	Goddess of fertility, wife of Cronus; mother of the Olympian gods and goddesses Demeter, Hades, Hera, Hestia, Poseidon, and Zeus
———	Romulus	Founder of the city of Rome; raised by a wolf with his twin brother, Remus
Satyrs	Satyrs	Field and forest gods with goats' feet and horns who represent nature's bounty and lust
Selene	Luna	Goddess of the moon
Sirens	———	Sea nymphs whose singing enchanted those who heard it
Thanatos	Mors	God of death
Titans	Titans	Sons and daughters of Uranus, who took power when Cronus overthrew their father: Atlas, Coeus, Crius, Dione, Epimetheus, Hyperion, Iapetus, Leto, Maia, Mnemosyne, Oceanus, Ophion, Pallas, Phoebe, Prometheus, Rhea, Tethys, Themis, and Thia
Tyche	Fortuna	Goddess of fortune or fate
Uranus	———	God of heaven; father of the Titans
Zeus	Jupiter (Jove)	Chief god of Olympus; ruler of heaven, who wielded thunder and lightning

——— indicates no corresponding deity in this culture.

THE WORLD'S MAJOR RELIGIONS

Religious beliefs are an intrinsic aspect of virtually every society that has ever existed. Many of these beliefs are organized and codified, often based on the teachings and writings of one or more founders. Other belief systems are less rigid in their external structures and may be transmitted orally from one generation to the next, either by family members or by religious leaders within the community.

While all religious beliefs are of vital importance to those who hold them, the less formalistic belief systems—variously referred to as animist or tribal religions, and adhered to by peoples all over the world—are not covered in this section.

BAHA'I

Baha'i has nearly 7 million followers worldwide and 750,000 followers in the United States. It was founded by Mirza Husayn 'Ali Nuri, who took the name Bahá'u'lláh (Glory of God) while in exile in Baghdad. Bahá'u'lláh's coming had been foretold by Mirza Ali Muhammad, known as al-Bab, who founded Babism in 1844, from which the Baha'i faith grew. The central tenets of the Baha'i faith are the oneness of God, the oneness of humanity, and the common foundation of all religion. Baha'ists also believe in the equality of men and women, universal education, world peace, and the creation of a world federal system of government.

BUDDHISM

Buddhism has 354 million followers worldwide and 2 million followers in the United States. It was founded by Siddhartha Gautama, known as the Buddha (Enlightened One), in southern Nepal in the 6th and 5th centuries B.C. The Buddha achieved enlightenment through meditation and gathered a community of monks to carry on his teachings. Buddhism teaches that meditation and the practice of virtuous and moral behavior can lead to Nirvana, the state of enlightenment. Before achieving Nirvana, however, one is subject to repeated lifetimes that are good or bad depending on one's actions *(karma)*. The doctrines of the Buddha describe temporal life as featuring "four noble truths": Existence is a realm of suffering; desire, along with the belief in the importance of one's self, causes suffering; achievement of Nirvana ends suffering; and Nirvana is attained only by meditation and by following the path of righteousness in action, thought, and attitude.

CONFUCIANISM

A faith with 6 million followers worldwide (the number of followers in the United States is uncertain), Confucianism was founded by Confucius, a Chinese philosopher, in the 6th and 5th centuries B.C. Confucius's sayings and dialogues, known col-lectively as the *Analects,* were written down by his followers. Confucianism, which grew out of a strife-ridden time in Chinese history, stresses the relationship between individuals, their families, and society, based on *li* (proper behavior) and *jen* (sympathetic attitude). Its practical, socially oriented philosophy was challenged by the more mystical precepts of Taoism and Buddhism, which were partially incorporated to create neo-Confucianism during the Sung dynasty (A.D. 960–1279). The overthrow of the Chinese monarchy and the Communist revolution during the 20th century have severely lessened the influence of Confucianism on modern Chinese culture.

HINDUISM

Hinduism has 760 million followers worldwide and 950,000 followers in the United States, Hinduism developed from indigenous religions of India in combination with Aryan religions brought to India c. 1500 B.C. and codified in the Veda and the Upanishads, the sacred scriptures of Hinduism. Hinduism is a term used broadly to describe a vast array of sects to which most Indians belong. Although many Hindus reject the caste system—in which people are born into a particular subgroup that determines their religious, social, and work-related duties—Hinduism classifies society at large into four groups: the Brahmins or priests, the rulers and warriors, the farmers and merchants, and the peasants and laborers. The goals of Hinduism are release from repeated reincarnation through the practice of yoga, adherence to Vedic scriptures, and devotion to a personal guru. Various Hindu deities are worshiped at shrines. The divine trinity, representing the cyclical nature of the universe, is made up of Brahma the creator, Vishnu the preserver, and Shiva the destroyer.

ISLAM

Islam has 1.1 billion followers worldwide and 5.6 million followers in the United States. It was founded by the prophet Muhammad, who received the holy scriptures of Islam, the Koran, from Allah (God) c. A.D. 610. Islam (Arabic for "submission to

God") maintains that Muhammad is the last in a long line of holy prophets, preceded by Adam, Abraham, Moses, and Jesus. In addition to being devoted to the Koran, followers of Islam (Muslims) are devoted to the worship of Allah through the Five Pillars: the statement "There is no god but God, and Muhammad is his prophet"; prayer, conducted five times a day while facing Mecca, the birthplace of Muhammad and the holy city of the Islamic world (Mecca is the capital of the Hejaz region of Saudi Arabia); the giving of alms; the keeping of the fast of Ramadan during the ninth month of the Muslim year; and the making of a pilgrimage to Mecca at least once, if possible. The two main divisions of Islam are the Sunni and the Shiite. The Wahabis are the most important Sunni sect; the Shiite sects include the Assassins, the Druses, and the Fatimids, among countless others.

JUDAISM

Stemming from the descendants of Judah in Judea, Judaism was founded c. 2000 B.C. by Abraham, Isaac, and Jacob. It has 14 million followers worldwide and 5.5 million followers in the United States. Judaism espouses belief in a monotheistic God, who is creator of the universe and who leads His people, the Jews, by speaking through prophets. His word is revealed in the Hebrew Bible (or Old Testament), especially in that part known as the Torah. The Torah also contains, according to rabbinic tradition, a total of 613 biblical commandments, including the Ten Commandments, which are explicated in the Talmud. Jews believe that the human condition can be improved, that the letter and the spirit of the Torah must be followed, and that a Messiah will eventually bring the world to a state of paradise. Judaism promotes community among all people of Jewish faith, dedication to a synagogue or temple (the basic social unit of a group of Jews, led by a rabbi), and the importance of family life. Religious observance takes place both at home and in the temple. Judaism is divided into three main groups who vary in their interpretation of those parts of the Torah that deal with personal, communal, international, and religious activities: the Orthodox community, which views the Torah as derived from God and therefore absolutely binding; the Reform movement, which follows primarily its ethical content; and the Conservative Jews, who follow most of the observances set out in the Torah but allow for change in the face of modern life. A fourth group, Reconstructionist Jews, rejects the concept of the Jews as God's chosen people, yet maintains rituals as part of the Judaic cultural heritage.

ORTHODOX CHURCH

With 214 million followers worldwide and over 4.2 million followers in the United States, the Orthodox Church is the third-largest Christian community in the world. It began its split from the Roman Catholic Church in the 5th century; the break was finalized in 1054. The followers of the Orthodox Church are in fact members of many different denominations, including the Church of Greece, the Church of Cyprus, and the Russian Orthodox Church. Orthodox religion holds biblical Scripture and tradition, guided by the Holy Spirit as expressed in the consciousness of the entire Orthodox community, to be the source of Christian truth. It rejects doctrine developed by the Western churches. Doctrine was established by seven ecumenical councils held between 325 and 787 and amended by other councils in the late Byzantine period. Relations between the Orthodox churches and Roman Catholicism have improved since Vatican Council II (1962–65).

PROTESTANTISM

Protestantism is a form of Christian faith. It includes any member of the various Christian churches established as a result of the Reformation, the 16th-century religious movement that aimed at reforming the Roman Catholic Church. The following is a list of major Protestant denominations and their beliefs.

"Holy Books of the World" in this chapter and "Religion Symbols" in chapter 12 Go to

MAJOR PROTESTANT DENOMINATIONS IN THE UNITED STATES

Denomination	Founder	Followers	Tenets
Amish Mennonites	Founded in Switzerland in the 1500s after secession from the Zurich state church; the followers of Jacob Ammann broke from the other Mennonites in Switzerland and Alsace in 1693; most Amish Mennonites emigrated to Pennsylvania in the 18th century when others rejoined the main Mennonite group.	80,000 Amish Mennonites; 200,000 Mennonites primarily located in the United States.	The Bible is the sole rule of faith; beliefs are outlined in the *Dordrecht Confession of Faith* (1632); Mennonites shun worldly ways and modern innovation (education and technology); the sacraments are adult baptism and communion.
Baptists	Founded by John Smyth in England in 1609 and Roger Williams in Rhode Island in 1638.	36 million in the United States; 38 million worldwide.	No creed; authority stems from the Bible; most Baptists oppose the use of alcohol and tobacco; baptism is by total immersion.
Church of Christ	Organized by Presbyterians in Kentucky in 1804 and in Pennsylvania in 1809.	1.6 million in the United States; 3 million worldwide.	The New Testament is believed in, and what is written in the Bible is followed without elaboration; rites are not ornate; baptism is of adults.
Church of England	King Henry VIII of England broke with the Roman Catholic Church; he issued the Act of Supremacy in 1534, which declared the king of England to be the head of the Church of England.	300,000 in the Anglican Orthodox Church in North America; 27 million worldwide.	Supremacy of the Bible is the test of doctrine; emphasis is on the most essential Christian doctrines and creeds; the *Book of Common Prayer* is used; the Church of England is part of the Anglican Communion, which is represented in the United States mainly by the Episcopal Church.
Disciples of Christ	Founded on the American frontier at the beginning of the 19th century as a means of cutting through doctrinal disputes to achieve Christian unity.	937,000, mostly in the United States.	Rigorous adherence to the New Testament as the basis of Christian faith; literal interpretation of the Bible; rejection of ecclesiastical institutions except for the congregation.

Denomination	Founder	Followers	Tenets
Episcopal Church	U.S. offshoot of the Church of England; it installed Samuel Seabury as its first bishop in 1784 and held its first General Convention in 1789, creating an independent church.	2.5 million in the United States; 70 million worldwide; 75 million worldwide are part of the Anglican Communion.	Worship is based on the *Book of Common Prayer* and interpretation of the Bible; services
Lutheran Church	Based on the writings of Martin Luther, who broke (1517–21) with the Roman Catholic Church and led the Protestant Reformation; the first Lutheran congregation in North America was founded in 1638 in Wilmington, Delaware; the first North American regional synod was founded in 1748 by Heinrich Melchior Mühlenberg.	9 million in the United States; 63 million worldwide.	Faith is based on the Bible and the Augsburg Confession (written in 1530); salvation comes through faith alone; services include the Lord's Supper communion; Lutherans are mostly conservative in religious and social ethics; infants are baptized; the church is organized in synods; the two largest synods in the United States are the Evangelical Lutheran Church in America and the Lutheran Church Missouri Synod.
Mennonites	*See* Amish Mennonites.		
Methodist Church	Reverend John Wesley began evangelistic preaching within the Church of England in 1738; a separate Wesleyan Methodist Church was established in 1791; the Methodist Episcopal Church was founded in the United States in 1784.	13.5 million in the United States; 26 million worldwide.	The name derives from the founders' desire to study religion "by rule and method" and follow the Bible interpreted by tradition and reason; worship varies by denomination within Methodism (the United Methodist Church is the largest congregation); the church is perfectionist in social dealings; communion and the baptism of infants and adults are practiced.

continues

Religions

Major Protestant Denominations in the United States, Continued

Denomination	Founder	Followers	Tenets
Pentecostal churches	The churches grew out of the "holiness movement" that developed among Methodists and other Protestants in the first decade of the 20th century.	10.6 million in the United States; 200 million worldwide.	Baptism in the Holy Spirit, speaking in tongues, faith healing, and the second coming of Jesus are believed in; of the various Pentecostal churches, the Assemblies of God is the largest; a perfectionist attitude toward secular affairs is common; services feature enthusiastic sermons and hymns; adult baptism and communion are practiced.
Presbyterian Church	Grew out of Calvinist churches of Switzerland and France; John Knox founded the first Presbyterian church in Scotland in 1557; the first presbytery in North America was established by Irish missionary Francis Makemie in 1706.	3.7 million in the United States; 50 million worldwide.	Faith is in the Bible; the sacraments are infant baptism and communion; the church is organized as a system of courts in which clergy and lay members (presbyters) participate at local, regional, and national levels; services are simple, with emphasis on the sermon.
Reformed churches	The churches trace their origin to the Swiss Reformation in the 16th century. The first Reformed church in the United States was founded by Alexander Whitaker in Virginia in 1611.	2 million in United States; number of followers worldwide is uncertain.	Confirmation of the Trinity and the humanity and divinity of Christ; belief in the justification of grace through faith.
Seventh-Day Adventist Church	Grew out of the teachings of William Miller in the 1840s; formally founded in North America in 1863.	775,000 in the United States; 8 million worldwide.	The Bible is the only creed; the second coming of Jesus is emphasized; members abstain from alcoholic beverages and tobacco; baptism and communion are practiced.
United Church of Christ	Formed in 1957 by the union of the General Council of Congregational Christian Churches with the Evangelical and Reformed Churches.	1.5 million, mostly in the United States.	Belief in the Bible is guided by the *Statement of Faith* (written in 1959); the church is organized by congregations, which are represented at a general synod that set policy; services are simple, with emphasis on the sermon; infant baptism and communion are practiced.

OTHER CHRISTIAN–BASED RELIGIONS AND ORGANIZATIONS

Religion/Org.	Founder	Followers	Tenets
The Church of Jesus Christ of Latter-Day Saints (Mormons)	Joseph Smith, in the 1820s, found golden tablets with *The Book of Mormon* inscribed on them; church headquarters were established in upstate New York in 1830, then in Ohio in 1831; after two more attempts to establish a permanent home for the church (the second resulting in Smith's death at the hands of a mob), Salt Lake City, Utah, was founded in 1847 under the leadership of Brigham Young.	4.7 million in the United States; 7.7 million worldwide.	Faith is based on the Bible, *The Book of Mormon, The Doctrine and Covenants,* and *The Pearl of Great Price,* all of which are considered scripture; stress is placed on revelation through the connection of spiritual and physical worlds and through proselytizing; members abstain from alcohol and tobacco and believe in community self-reliance; public services are conservative; there is baptism, laying on of hands, and communion; a secret temple holds other cermonies, including baptism for the dead.
Jehovah's Witnesses	Founded by Charles T. Russell in the United States in the late 19th century.	945,000 in the United States; 4 million worldwide.	Belief is in the imminent second coming of Christ and the potential salvation of mortal souls during the millennium; all members are ministers who proselytize their faith with door-to-door missionary work; members refuse service in the armed forces, will not salute national flags or participate in politics, will not accept blood transfusion (but will accept all other forms of medical treatment), and discourage smoking, drunkenness, and gambling.

continues

Other Christian–Based Religions and Organizations, Continued

Religion/Org.	Founder	Followers	Tenets
Religious Society of Friends (Quakers)	George Fox in England in the 17th century began preaching against organized churches, professing a doctrine of the Inner Light.	100,000 in the United States; 300,000 worldwide.	Reliance is on the Inner Light, the voice of God's Holy Spirit experienced within each person; meetings are characterized by quiet meditation without ritual or sermon; Quakers are active in peace, education, and social welfare movements; they refuse to bear arms or take oaths; earlier schisms are still reflected in three main affiliations of Friends.
Unitarian Universalist Association	The denomination resulted from the merger in 1961 of the Universalist Church of America (organized in 1779) and the American Unitarian Association (founded in 1825).	200,000 in the United States; 330,000 worldwide.	Members profess no creed; strong social, ethical, and humanitarian concerns are manifest in the search for religious truth through freedom of belief; theists, humanists, and agnostics are accepted in religious fellowship; efforts are aimed at the creation of a worldwide interfaith religious community; many members come from other denominations and religions.

ROMAN CATHOLICISM

The Roman Catholic Church, with 1.1 billion followers worldwide and 62 million followers in the United States, is the largest Christian church in the world. It claims direct historical descent from the church founded by the apostle Peter. The pope in Rome is the spiritual leader of all Roman Catholics. He administers church affairs through bishops and priests. Members accept the gospel of Jesus Christ and the teachings of the Bible, as well as the church's interpretations of these. God's grace is conveyed through the seven sacraments, especially the Eucharist or communion that is celebrated at mass, the regular service of worship. The other six sacraments are baptism, confirmation, penance, holy orders, matrimony, and anointing of the sick. Redemption through Jesus Christ is professed as the sole method of obtaining salvation, which is necessary to ensure a place in heaven after life on earth.

New York's Cathedral of St. John the Divine, begun in 1892, is only now nearing completion. Taking more than 100 years to construct, it will be the largest cathedral in the world when finished.

Religions

"Roman Catholic Patron Saints" and "The Roman Catholic Popes" in this chapter Go to

ROSICRUCIANISM

Rosicrucianism, a modern movement begun in 1868 by R. W. Little, claims ties to an older Society of the Rose and Cross that was founded in Germany in 1413 by Christian Rosencreuz. The number of its followers is uncertain. The Ancient Mystical Order Rosae Crusis (AMORC) was founded in San Jose, California, in 1915 by H. Spencer Lewis. The Rosicrucian Brotherhood was established in Quakertown, Pennsylvania, by Reuben Swinburne Clymer in 1902. Both sects could be classified as either fraternal or religious organizations, although they claim to empower members with cosmic forces by unveiling secret wisdom regarding the laws of nature.

SHINTO

Shinto, with 2.8 million followers worldwide (the number of followers in the United States is uncertain), is the ancient native religion of Japan, established long before the introduction of writing to Japan in the 5th century A.D. The origins of its beliefs and rituals are unknown. Shinto stresses belief in a great many spiritual beings and gods, known as *kami,* who are paid tribute at shrines and honored by festivals, and reverence for ancestors. Although Shinto has no overall dogma, adherents are expected to remember and celebrate the *kami,* support the societies of which the *kami* are patrons, remain pure and sincere, and enjoy life.

TAOISM

Both a philosophy and a religion, Taoism was founded in China by Lao-tzu, who is traditionally said to have been born in 604 B.C. Its number of followers is uncertain. It derives primarily from the *Tao-te-ching,* which claims that an ever-changing universe follows the Tao, or path. The Tao can be known only by emulating its quietude and effortless simplicity; Taoism prescribes that people live simply,

spontaneously, and in close touch with nature and that they meditate to achieve contact with the Tao. Temples and monasteries, maintained by Taoist priests, are important in some Taoist sects. Since the Communist revolution, Taoism has been actively discouraged in the People's Republic of China, although it continues to flourish in Taiwan.

Madalyn Murray O'Hair, the renowned atheist who opposed prayer in schools, mysteriously disappeared on September 28, 1995, along with her son Jon Garth and adopted family member Robin Murray. In April 2001, David R. Waters was sentenced to 20 years in prison for his role in their abduction and murder.

ZOROASTRIANISM

An ancient religion that influenced both Judaism and Christianity, Zoroastrianism arose in Persia (modern-day Iran) as early as the 6th century B.C. Based mainly on a Persian text known as the *Avesta,* Zoroastrianism rejected the worship of multiple gods, adhering to belief only in Ahura Mazda, the "Wise Lord." With the advent of the Sasanid dynasty in the 3rd century A.D., Zoroastrianism became Persia's state religion, but it declined dramatically after the Islamic conquest of the 8th century. The remaining Zoroastrian believers eventually made their way to western India, where they are now known as Farsis, or Parsees. Numbering about 300,000 worldwide and 20,000 in the United States, they still adhere to tenets of the ancient religion. Among other beliefs, they revere the forces of nature, particularly fire, as expressions of Ahura Mazda's divine power.

SIGNIFICANT DATES IN THE HISTORY OF RELIGION

B.C.

c. 2000	Abraham, founder of Judaism, is alive.
c. 13th century	Moses, Hebrew lawgiver, is alive.
c. 1100–c. 500	The Vedas, sacred texts of the Hindus, are compiled.
604	Traditional birth date of Lao-tzu, founder of Taoism.
588	Traditional date of Zoroaster's revelation.
c. 563–c. 483	Buddha, founder of Buddhism, is alive.
551–479	Confucius, founder of Confucianism, is alive.
c. 200	The *Bhagavad Gita,* important Hindu text, is written.
6 or 4	Jesus of Nazareth, founder of Christianity, is born.

A.D.

33?	The Crucifixion and death of Jesus Christ.
64?	Peter, disciple of Jesus and, according to tradition, first bishop of Rome, dies.
c. 70–c. 100	First four books of the New Testament—Matthew, Mark, Luke, and John—are written.
5th century	Two Buddhist sects—Zen and Pure Land (or Amidism)—are established.
c. 570–632	Muhammad the prophet—whose teachings, recorded in the Koran, form the basis of Islam—is alive.
622	Muhammad flees persecution in Mecca and settles in Yathrib (later Medina); the first day of the lunar year in which this event, known as the Hegira, takes place marks the start of the Muslim era.
936	Traditional date of the arrival from Iran of the first Parsees (followers of Zoroastrianism) in India.
1054	Catholic Pope Leo IX condemns the patriarch of Constantinople, finalizing the split between the Orthodox Church and the Roman Catholic Church.
c. 1224–74	Saint Thomas Aquinas, Italian philosopher and Roman Catholic theologian, is alive.
1309–77	The Roman Catholic papacy is seated in Avignon, France.
1483–1546	Martin Luther, leader of the Protestant Reformation in Germany and author of "95 Theses" (1517) is alive.
1491–1556	Ignatius Loyola, founder of the Jesuit Order of Roman Catholic priests, is alive.
1509–64	John Calvin, leader of the Protestant Reformation in France, is alive.
1549	The first Christian mission in Japan is established.
1582	Jesuit Matteo Ricci is the first missionary to be sent to China.
1620	Plymouth Colony in North America is founded in December by 102 English Puritan separatists, known as Pilgrims.

One of the Dead Sea scrolls, the "Copper" scroll, lists 64 underground hiding places in Israel that supposedly contain gold, silver, aromatics, and manuscripts. These are believed to be treasures from the Temple at Jerusalem that were hidden for safekeeping.

1624–91	George Fox, English founder of the Protestant Society of Friends (the Quakers), is alive.
1703–91	John Wesley, English founder of the Protestant movement that later became the Methodist Church, is alive.
1869–70	The first Roman Catholic Vatican Council, at which the dogma of papal infallibility is promulgated, is convened by Pope Piux IX.
1869–1948	Mohandas K. Gandhi, Indian spiritual and political leader who helped his country achieve independence from Britain and sought rapprochement between Hindus and Muslims, is alive.

1933–45	The systematic persecution and attempted extermination of European Jews by Adolf Hitler's Nazi party, known as the Holocaust, takes place.
1948	The independent Jewish state of Israel is declared.
1962–65	The second Roman Catholic Vatican Council, at which changes were made in the liturgy and greater participation in services by lay church members was encouraged, is convened by Pope John XXIII and concluded by Pope Paul VI.

The Ten Commandments

A Closer Look

During their exodus from the land of Egypt, Moses led the people of Israel to Mount Sinai, where God issued to Moses the Ten Commandments. These commandments form the foundation of both Jewish and Christian morality. The following is from Exodus, chapter 20; the bold numbers indicate the verse number (the Ten Commandments also appear, with slightly different wording, in Deuteronomy 5:6–21).

1. **2** I am the Lord thy God, which have brought thee out of the land of Egypt, out of the house of bondage,

2. **3** Thou shalt have no other gods before me.

   4 Thou shalt not make unto thee any graven image, or any likeness of any thing that is in heaven above, or that is in the earth beneath, or that is in the water under the earth.

   5 Thou shalt not bow down thyself to them, nor serve them; for I the Lord thy God am a jealous God, visiting the iniquity of the fathers upon the Children unto the third and fourth generation of them that hate me; **6** And showing mercy unto thousands of them that love me, and keep my commandments.

3. **7** Thou shalt not take the name of the Lord thy God in vain; for the Lord will not hold him guiltless that taketh his name in vain.

4. **8** Remember the sabbath day, to keep it holy, **9** Six days shalt thou labor, and do all thy work; **10** But the seventh day is the sabbath of the Lord thy God; in it thou shalt not do any work, thou, nor thy son, nor thy daughter, nor thy manservant, nor thy maidservant, nor thy cattle, nor thy stranger that is within thy gates; **11** For in six days the Lord made heaven and earth, the sea, and all that in them is, and rested the seventh day; wherefore the Lord blessed the sabbath day, and hallowed it.

5. **12** Honor thy father and thy mother; that thy days may be long upon the land which the Lord thy God giveth thee.

6. **13** Thou shalt not kill.

7. **14** Thou shalt not commit adultery.

8. **15** Thou shalt not steal.

9. **16** Thou shalt not bear false witness against thy neighbor.

10. **17** Thou shalt not covet they neighbor's house, thou shalt not covet thy neighbor's wife, nor his manservant, nor his maidservant, nor his ox, nor his ass, nor anything that is thy neighbor's.

HOLY BOOKS OF THE WORLD

The Analects   A collection of Confucius's teachings thought to have been recorded by his students. They are considered the only sayings that can reliably be attributed to him.

Bhagavad Gita   A Sanskrit poem that is part of the Indian epic known as the *Mahabharata*. It describes, in a dialogue between Lord Krishna and Prince Arjuna, the Hindu path to spiritual wisdom and the unity with God that can be achieved through *karma* (action), *bhakti* (devotion), and *jnana* (knowledge). The *Bhagavad Gita* was probably written sometime between 200 B.C. and A.D. 200.

Five Classics   Five works traditionally attributed to Confucius that form the basic texts of Confucianism. They are the *Spring and Autumn Annals,* a history of Confucius's native district; the *I Ching* (or *Book of Changes*), a system of divining the future; the *Book of Rites,* which outlines ceremonies and describes the ideal government; the *Book of History;* and the *Book of Songs,* a collection of poetry. Together they promulgate a system of ethics for managing society based on sympathy for others, etiquette, and ritual. Although the dates of these books are uncertain, they were probably written before the 3rd century B.C.

Koran   (Arabic, **al-Qur'ân**) The primary holy book of Islam. It is made up of 114 *suras,* or chapters, which contain impassioned appeals for belief in God, encouragement to lead a moral life, portrayals of damnation and beatitude, stories of Islamic prophets, and rules governing the social and religious life of Muslims. Believers maintain that the Koran contains the verbatim word of God, revealed

to the prophet Muhammad through the angel Gabriel. Some of the *suras* were written during Muhammad's lifetime, but an authoritative text was not produced until c. A.D. 650.

The shortest verse in the Bible is "Jesus wept" (John 11:35).

New Testament   The second portion of the Christian Bible, which contains 27 books that form the basis of Christian belief. These books include the sayings of Jesus; the story of his life and work; the death and resurrection of Jesus now celebrated as Easter; the teachings and writings of the apostles; and instruction for converting nonbelievers and for performing baptisms, blessings, and other rituals. The New Testament is believed to have been written c. A.D. 100, some 70 to 90 years after the death of Jesus.

Old Testament   The Christian name for the Hebrew Bible. It is the sacred scripture of Judaism and the first portion of the Christian Bible. According to Jewish teachings, it is made up of three parts: *the Law* (also known as the Torah or Pentateuch), consisting of the first five books (Genesis, Exodus, Leviticus, Numbers, and Deuteronomy), which de-

---

A Closer Look

The Seven Canonical Hours

Psalms 118:164 states: "Seven times a day I praise you." These hours were designated as matins and lauds, prime, terce, sext, nones, vespers, and compline.

A Closer Look

The Four Horsemen of the Apocalypse

The Book of Revelation, attributed to John the Apostle, refers to four horsemen who will ride forth bringing hardships to the earth.

Pestilence	Rides a white horse and carries a bow and a crown
War	Rides a red horse and swings a great sword
Famine	Rides a black horse and carries scales
Death	Rides a pale horse and has Hades close behind

THE BOOKS OF THE BIBLE

The Old Testament		The New Testament	
Genesis	Nahu	Matthew	I Peter
Exodus	Habakkuk	Mark	II Peter
Leviticus	Zephaniah	Luke	I John
Numbers	Haggai	John	II John
Deuteronomy	Zachariah	Acts	III John
Joshua	Malachi	Romans	Jude
Judges	Psalms	I Corinthians	Revelation
I Samuel	Proverbs	II Corinthians	
II Samuel	Job	Galatians	
I Kings	The Song of Songs	Ephesians	
II Kings	Ruth	Philippians	
Isaiah	Lamentations	Colossians	
Jeremiah	Ecclesiastes	I Thessalonians	
Ezekiel	Esther	II Thessalonians	
Hosea	Daniel	I Timothy	
Joel	Ezra	II Timothy	
Amos	Nehemiah	Titus	
Obadiah	I Chronicles	Philemon	
Jonah	II Chronicles	Hebrew	
Micah		James	

scribes the origins of the world, the covenant between the Lord and Israel, the exodus and entry into the promised land, and the various rules governing social and religious behavior; *the Prophets,* including the former prophets (Joshua, Judges, I and II Samuel, I and II Kings) and the latter prophets (Isaiah, Jeremiah, Ezekiel, and the 12 minor prophets), which describes the history of the Israelites, the stories of heroes, kings, judges, and wars, and the choosing of David as leader of the Israelites; and *the Writings* (including Psalms, Job, Song of Solomon, and Ruth, among others), which describes the reactions of the people to the laws and covenants, as well as prayers and praises of the covenant. Some books of the Old Testament regarded as sacred by the Jews are not accepted as such by Christians; among Christians there are differences between Roman Catholics and Protestants about the inclusion of some books, the order of the books, and the original sources used in translating them. Scholars generally agree that the Old Testament was compiled from c. 1000 B.C. to c. 100 B.C.

Talmud   A compilation of Jewish oral law and rabbinical teachings that is separate from the scriptures of the Hebrew Bible, or Old Testament. The Talmud is made up of two parts: the *Mishna,* which is the oral law itself, and the *Gemara,* which is a commentary on the *Mishna.* The Talmud contains both a legal section (the *Halakah*) and a portion devoted to legends and stories (the *Aggada*). The authoritative Babylonian Talmud was compiled in the 6th century.

Tao-te-ching (The Way and Its Power)   The basic text of the Chinese philosophy and religion known as Taoism. It is made up of 81 short chapters or poems that describe a way of life marked by quiet effortlessness and freedom from desire. This state is thought to be achieved by following the creative, spontaneous life force of the universe, called the Tao. The book is attributed to Lao-tzu, but it was probably a compilation by a number of writers over a long period of time.

Upanishads   The basis of Hindu religion and philosophy that form the final portion of the *Veda.* The 112 Upanishads describe the relationship of the

Brahman, or universal soul, to the *atman,* or individual soul; they also provide information about Vedic sacrifice and yoga. The original texts of the Upanishads come from various sources and were written beginning c. 900 B.C.

Veda   The sacred scripture of Hinduism. Four Vedas make up the *Samhita,* a collection of prayers and hymns that are considered to be revelations of eternal truth written by seer-poets inspired by the gods. The *Rig-Veda,* the *Sama-Veda,* and the *Yajur-Veda* are books of hymns; the *Atharva-Veda* compiles magic spells. These writings maintain that the *Brahman,* or Absolute Self, underlies all reality and can be known by invoking gods through the use of hymns

or mantras. The Vedic texts were compiled between c. 1000 B.C. and c. 500 B.C., making them the oldest known group of religious writings.

A Closer Look

The Twelve Apostles

The twelve men who were chosen to be the missionaries of Christ's word were Peter, Andrew, James (the Greater), John, Thomas, James (the Less), Jude (or Thaddaeus), Philip, Bartholomew, Matthew, Simon, and Judas Iscariot (who was replaced by Mathias). St. Paul is also considered an apostle.

ROMAN CATHOLIC PATRON SAINTS

Protector of	Saint(s)	Protector of	Saint(s)
Accountants	Matthew	Cripples	Giles
Actors	Genesius	Dancers	Vitus
Aviators	Joseph of Cupertino	Deaf	Francis de Sales
Altar boys	John Berchmans	Dentists	Apollonia
Architects	Thomas	Desperate situations	Jude
Art	Catherine of Bologna	Domestic animals	Antony
Artists	Luke	Dying	Joseph
Astronomers	Dominic	Ecologists	Francis of Assisi
Athletes	Sebastian	Editors	John Bosco
Authors	Francis de Sales	Emigrants	Frances Xavier Cabrini
Bakers	Elizabeth of Hungary	Eyes	Lucy and Odilia
Bankers	Matthew	Falsely accused	Raymund Nonnatus
Barren women	Antony of Padua	Farmers	Isidore the Farmer
Beggars	Martin of Tours	Fathers	Joseph
Blind	Raphael	Searchers for lost objects	Anthony
Bookbinders	Peter Celestine	Firefighters	Florian
Bookkeepers	Matthew	Fire prevention	Catherine of Siena
Booksellers	John of God	Fishermen	Andrew
Bowels	Erasmus		Peter
Boy Scouts	George	Foundlings	Holy Innocents
Bricklayers	Stephen	France	Joan of Arc
Brides	Nicholas of Myra	Funeral directors	Joseph of Arimathea
Broadcasters	Archangel Gabriel	Gardeners	Adelard
Builders	Vincent Ferrer	Girls	Agnes
Cabdrivers	Fiacre	Glassworkers	Luke
Cancer victims	Peregrine Laziosi	Gravediggers	Antony the Abbot
Carpenters	Joseph	Grocers	Michael
Charitable societies	Vincent de Paul	Hairdressers	Martin de Porres
Childbirth	Gerard Majella	Heart patients	John of God
Children	Nicholas of Myra	Homeless	Margaret of Cortona
Church	Joseph	Hospitals	Camillus de Lellis
Comedians	Vitus		John of God
Cooks	Martha	Hotel keepers	Amand

Protector of	Saint(s)	Protector of	Saint(s)
Hungary	Stephen	Printers	Augustine
Invalids	Roch		Genesius
Ireland	Patrick		John of God
Jewelers	Eligius	Prisoners	Dismas
Journalists	Francis de Sales	Radio workers	Gabriel
Laborers	Isidore	Rheumatism	James the Greater
Lawyers	Thomas More	Sailors	Brendan
	Yves		Erasmus
Learning	Ambrose	Scholars	Brigid
Librarians	Jerome	Scientists	Albert the Great
Lovers	Valentine	Sculptors	Four Crowned Martyrs
Mariners	Nicholas of Tolentine	Secretaries	Genesius
Married women	Monica	Servants	Martha
Mentally ill	Dympna	Sick	John of God
Messengers	Gabriel		Camillus de Lellis
Midwives	Raymund Nonnatus	Skaters	Lidwina
Missions	Francis Xavier	Skiers	Bernard
	Thérèse of Lisieux	Social justice	Joseph
	Leonard of Port Maurice	Social workers	Louise de Marillac
Mothers	Monica	Soldiers	George
Musicians	Cecelia		Martin of Tours
	Gregory		Michael the Archangel
Nurses	Agatha	Students	Catherine of Alexandria
	Camillus de Lellis		Thomas Aquinas
	John of God	Surgeons	Cosmas and Damian
Orators	John Chrysostom		Luke
Orphans	Jerome Emiliani	Tax collectors	Matthew
Painters	Luke	Teachers	Gregory
Pawnbrokers	Nicholas of Myra		John Baptist de la Salle
Philosophers	Justin	Television	Clare of Assisi
Physicians	Cosmas and Damian	Theologians	Alphonsus Liguori
	Luke		Augustine
Plasterers	Bartholomew	Throat	Blaise
Poets	David	Travelers	Christopher
Police officers	Michael	United States	The Immaculate
Poor	Antony of Padua		Conception
Postal workers	Gabriel	Vintners	Amand
Preachers	Catherine of		Urban
	Alexandria		Vincent
	John Chrysostom	Vocations	Alphonsus
Pregnant women	Gerard Majella	Widows	Paula
Priests	John Vianney	Women in labor	Anne
		Writers	Francis de Sales
		Youth	Aloysius Gonzaga

THE ROMAN CATHOLIC POPES

The religious head of the Roman Catholic Church is known as the pope or the bishop of Rome. He is elected by the College of Cardinals, who as a group rank next to the pope in ecclesiastical authority. New popes are elected upon the death or retirement of a current pope. To be elected, a new pope must be named on two-thirds of the ballots cast, and each member of the College of Cardinals must vote. Once elected, a pope must be asked by the dean of cardinals if he accepts the post. If he does, he is then asked to choose a name. The custom of a pope changing his name upon election originated shortly before the year 1000.

The following table includes all the popes of the Roman Catholic Church, beginning with St. Peter the Apostle, who is traditionally considered to be the first pope because of his appointment by Jesus and his role in organizing the church. Also included (in brackets) are the so-called antipopes, those who were elected or claimed to be pope at various times during church history but whose positions were later invalidated. The table gives the names of the popes, the years of their papacies, and the original names of those who changed their names upon election. Alternative spellings of names are given in parentheses.

ROMAN CATHOLIC POPES

Pope	Reign	Original Name
St. Peter the Apostle	died c. 64	Symeon (Simon)
St. Linus	c. 66–c. 78	
St. Anacletus (Cletus)	c. 79–c. 91	
St. Clement I	c. 91–c. 100	
St. Evaristus	c. 100–c. 109	
St. Alexander I	c. 109–c. 116	
St. Sixtus I	c. 116–c. 125	
St. Telesphorus	c. 125–c. 136	
St. Hyginus	c. 136–c. 142	
St. Pius I	c. 142–c. 155	
St. Anicetus	c. 155–c. 166	
St. Soter	c. 166–c. 174	
St. Eleutherius (Eleutherus)	c. 174–189	
St. Victor I	189–198	
St. Zephyrinus	198–217	
St. Callistus I (Calixtus)	217–222	
[St. Hippolytus]	217–235	
St. Urban I	222–230	
St. Pontianus (Pontian)	July 21, 230–September 29, 235	
St. Anterus	November 21, 235–January 3, 236	
St. Fabian	January 10, 236–January 20, 250	
St. Cornelius	March 251–June 253	
[Novatian]	March 251–c. 258	
St. Lucius I	June 25, 253–March 5, 254	
St. Stephen I	May 12, 254–August 2, 257	
St. Sixtus II	August 30, 257–August 6, 258	
St. Dionysius	July 22, 260–December 26, 268	
St. Felix I	January 3, 269–December 30, 274	
St. Eutychian	January 4, 275–December 7, 283	
St. Gaius (Caius)	December 17, 283–April 22, 296	
St. Marcellinus	June 30, 296–c. 304	
St. Marcellus I	November/December 306–January 16, 308	
St. Eusebius	April 18, 310–October 21, 310	
St. Miltiades (Melchiades)	July 2, 311–January 11, 314	
St. Silvester I	January 31, 314–December 31, 335	
St. Mark	January 18, 336–October 7, 336	
St. Julius I	February 6, 337–April 12, 352	
Liberius	May 17, 352–September 24, 366	
[Felix II]	c. 355–November 22, 365	
St. Damasus I	October 1, 366–December 11, 384	

Pope	Reign	Original Name
[Ursinus]	September 366–November 367	
St. Siricius	December 384–November 26, 399	
St. Anastasius I	November 27, 399–December 19, 401	
St. Innocent I	December 22, 401–March 12, 417	
St. Zosimus	March 18, 417–December 26, 418	
St. Boniface I	December 28, 418–September 4, 422	
[Eulalius]	December 27, 418–April 3, 419	
St. Celestine I	September 10, 422–July 27, 432	
St. Sixtus III	July 31, 432–August 19, 440	
St. Leo I	August/September 440–November 10, 461	
St. Hilary (Hilarus)	November 19, 461–February 29, 468	
St. Simplicius	March 3, 468–March 10, 483	
St. Felix III (II)	March 13, 483–March 1, 492	
St. Gelasius I	March 1, 492–November 21, 496	
Anastasius II	November 24, 496–November 19, 498	
St. Symmachus	November 22, 498–July 19, 514	
[Lawrence]	November 22, 498–February 499; 501–506	
St. Hormisdas	July 20, 514–August 6, 523	
St. John I	August 13, 523–May 18, 526	
St. Felix IV (III)	July 12, 526–September 22, 530	
Boniface II	September 22, 530–October 17, 532	
[Dioscorus]	September 22, 530–October 14, 530	
John II	January 2, 533–May 8, 535	Mercury
St. Agapitus I	May 13, 535–April 22, 536	
St. Silverius	June 8, 536–November 11, 537	
Vigilius	c. 538–June 7, 555	
Pelagius I	April 16, 556–March 3, 561	
John III	July 17, 561–July 13, 574	Catelinus
Benedict I	June 2, 575–July 30, 579	
Pelagius II	November 26, 579–February 7, 590	
St. Gregory I	September 3, 590–March 12, 604	
Sabinian	September 13, 604–February 22, 606	
Boniface III	February 19, 607–November 12, 607	
St. Boniface IV	September 15, 608–May 8, 615	
St. Deusdedit I (Adeodatus I)	October 19, 615–November 8, 618	
Boniface V	December 23, 619–October 25, 625	
Honorius I	October 27, 625–October 12, 638	
Severinus	May 28, 640–August 2, 640	
John IV	December 24, 640–October 12, 642	
Theodore I	November 24, 642–May 14, 649	
St. Martin I	July 5, 649–June 17, 653	
St. Eugene I	August 10, 654–June 2, 657	
St. Vitalian	July 30, 657–January 27, 672	
Adeodatus II	April 11, 672–June 17, 676	
Donus	November 2, 676–April 11, 678	
St. Agatho	June 27, 678–January 10, 681	
St. Leo II	August 17, 682–July 3, 683	
St. Benedict II	June 26, 684–May 8, 685	
John V	July 23, 685–August 2, 686	

Religions

continues

Roman Catholic Popes, Continued

Pope	Reign	Original Name
Conon	October 21, 686–September 21, 687	
[Theodore]	687	
[Paschal]	687	
St. Sergius I	December 15, 687–September 9, 701	
John VI	October 30, 701–January 11, 705	
John VII	March 1, 705–October 18, 707	
Sisinnius	January 15, 708–February 4, 708	
Constantine	March 25, 708–April 9, 715	
St. Gregory II	May 19, 715–February 11, 731	
St. Gregory III	March 18, 731–November 28, 741	
St. Zachary (St. Zacharius)	December 3, 741–March 15, 752	
Stephen (II) unconsecrated	March 22 or 23, 752–March 25 or 26, 752	
Stephen II (III)	March 26, 752–April 26, 757	
St. Paul I	May 29, 757–June 28, 767	
[Constantine]	July 5, 767–August 6, 768	
[Philip]	July 31, 768	
Stephen III (IV)	August 7, 768–January 24, 772	
Adrian I (Hadrian I)	February 1, 772–December 25, 795	
St. Leo III	December 26, 795–June 12, 816	
Stephen IV (V)	June 22, 816–January 24, 817	
St. Paschal I	January 24, 817–February 11, 824	
Eugene II	February 824–August 827	
Valentine	August 827–September 827	
Gregory IV	September 827–January 25, 844	
[John]	January 844	
Sergius II	January 844–January 27, 847	
St. Leo IV	April 10, 847–July 17, 855	
Benedict III	September 29, 855–April 17, 858	
[Anastasius (Bibliothecarius)]	August 855–September 855	
St. Nicholas I	April 24, 858–November 13, 867	
Adrian II (Hadrian II)	December 14, 867–November or December 872	
John VIII	December 14, 872–December 16, 882	
Marinus I	December 16, 882–May 15, 884	
St. Adrian III (St. Hadrian III)	May 17, 884–September 885	
Stephen V (VI)	September 885–September 14, 891	
Formosus	October 6, 891–April 4, 896	
Boniface VI	April 896	
Stephen VI (VII)	May 896–August 897	
Romanus	August 897–November 897	
Theodore II	November 897	
John IX	January 898–January 900	
Benedict IV	May/June 900–August 903	
Leo V	August 903–September 903	
[Christopher]	September 903–January 904	
Sergius III	January 29, 904–April 14, 911	
Anastasius III	c. June 911–c. August 913	
Lando	c. August 913–c. March 914	
John X	March 914–May 928	

Pope	Reign	Original Name
Leo VI	May 928–December 928	
Stephen VII (VIII)	December 928–February 931	
John XI	February or March 931–December 935 or January 936	
Leo VII	January 3, 936–July 13, 939	
Stephen VIII (IX)	July 14, 939–October 942	
Marinus II	October 30, 942–May 946	
Agapetus (Agapitus) II	May 10, 946–December 955	
John XII	December 16, 955–May 14, 964	Octavian
Leo VIII	December 4, 963–March 1, 965	
Benedict V	May 22, 964–June 23, 964	
John XIII	October 1, 965–September 6, 972	
Benedict VI	January 19, 973–July 974	
[Boniface VII]	June 974–July 974	Franco
	August 984–July 20, 985	
Benedict VII	October 974–July 10, 983	
John XIV	December 983–August 20, 984	Peter Canepanova
John XV	August 985–March 996	
Gregory V	May 3, 996–February 18, 999	Bruno
[John XVI]	February 997–May 998	John Philagathos
Silvester II	April 2, 999–May 12, 1003	Gerbert
John XVII	May 16, 1003–November 6, 1003	John Sicco
John XVIII	December 25, 1003–July 1009	John Fasanus
Sergius IV	July 31, 1009–May 12, 1012	Peter
Benedict VIII	May 17, 1012–April 9, 1024	Theophylact
[Gregory]	1012	
John XIX	April 19, 1024–October 20, 1032	Romanus
Benedict IX	October 21, 1032–September 1044	Theophylact
	March 10, 1045–May 1, 1045	
	November 8, 1047–July 16, 1048	
Silvester III	January 20, 1045–March 10, 1045	John of Sabina
Gregory VI	May 1, 1045–December 20, 1046	John Gratian
Clement II	December 24, 1046–October 9, 1047	Suidger
Damasus II	July 17, 1048–August 9, 1048	Poppo
St. Leo IX	February 12, 1049–April 19, 1054	Bruno
Victor II	April 13, 1055–July 28, 1057	Gebhard
Stephen IX (X)	August 2, 1057–March 29, 1058	Frederick of Lorraine
[Benedict X]	April 5, 1058–January 24, 1059	John Mincius
Nicholas II	December 6, 1058–July 19 or 26, 1061	Gerard
Alexander II	September 30, 1061–April 21, 1073	Anselm
[Honorius II]	October 28, 1061–May 31, 1064	Peter Cadalus
St. Gregory VII	April 22, 1073–May 25, 1085	Hildebrand
[Clement III]	June 25, 1080	Guibert
	March 24, 1084–September 8, 1100	
Victor III	May 24, 1086	Daufer (Daufari)
	May 9, 1087–September 16, 1087	
Urban II	March 12, 1088–July 29, 1099	Odo (Eudes)
Paschal II	August 13, 1099–January 21, 1118	Rainerius

Religions

continues

Roman Catholic Popes, Continued

Pope	Reign	Original Name
[Theodoric]	September 1100–January 1101	
[Albert (Adalbert)]	1101	
[Silvester IV]	November 18, 1105–April 12, 1111	Maginulf
Gelasius II	January 24, 1118–January 29, 1119	John of Gaeta
[Gregory VIII]	March 8, 1118–April 1121	Maurice Burdinus
Calistus II	February 2, 1119–December 14, 1124	Guido
Honorius II	December 21, 1124–February 13, 1130	Lamberto of Ostia
[Celestine II]	December 15–16, 1124	Teobaldo Boccapecci
Innocent II	February 14, 1130–September 24, 1143	Gregorio Papareschi
[Anacletus II]	February 14, 1130–January 25, 1138	Pietro Pierleoni
[Victor IV]	March 1138–May 29, 1138	Gregorio Conti
Celestine II	September 26, 1143–May 8, 1144	Guido of Citta di Castello
Lucius II	March 12, 1144–February 15, 1145	Gherardo Caccianemicic
Eugene III	February 15, 1145–July 8, 1153	Bernardo Pignatelli
Anastasius IV	July 8, 1153–December 3, 1154	Corrado
Adrian IV (Hadrian IV)	December 4, 1154–September 1, 1159	Nicholas Breakspear
Alexander III	September 7, 1159–August 30, 1181	Orlando (Roland) Bandinelli
[Victor IV]	September 7, 1159–April 20, 1164	Ottaviano
[Paschal III]	April 22, 1164–September 20, 1168	Guido of Crema
[Calistus III]	September 1168–August 29, 1178	Giovanni
[Innocent III]	September 29, 1179–January 1180	Lando
Luicius III	September 1, 1181–November 25, 1185	Ubaldo Allucingoli
Urban III	October 25, 1185–October 20, 1187	Umberto Crivelli
Gregory VIII	October 21, 1187–December 17, 1187	Alberto de Morra
Clement III	December 19, 1187–March 1191	Paolo Scolari
Celestine III	March/April 1191–January 8, 1198	Giacinto Bobo
Innocent III	January 8, 1198–July 16, 1216	Lotario
Honorius III	July 18, 1216–March 18, 1227	Cencio Savelli
Gregory IX	March 19, 1227–August 22, 1241	Ugo (Ugolino)
Celestine IV	October 25, 1241–November 10, 1241	Goffredo da Castiglione
Innocent IV	June 25, 1243–December 7, 1254	Sinibaldo Fieschi
Alexander IV	December 12, 1254–May 25, 1261	Rinaldo, Count of Segni
Urban IV	August 29, 1261–October 2, 1264	Jacques Pantaléon
Clement IV	February 5, 1265–November 29, 1268	Guy Foulques
Gregory X	September 1, 1271–January 10, 1276	Tedaldo Visconti
Innocent V	January 21, 1276–June 22, 1276	Pierre of Tarentaise
Adrian V (Hadrian V)	July 11, 1276–August 18, 1276	Ottobono Fieschi
John XXI	September 8, 1276–May 20, 1277	Pedro Juliñao (Peter of Spain)
Nicholas III	November 25, 1277–August 22, 1280	Giovanni Gaetano
Martin IV	February 22, 1281–March 28, 1285	Simon de Brie (Brion)
Honorius IV	April 2, 1285–April 3, 1287	Giacomo Savelli
Nicholas IV	February 22, 1288–April 4, 1292	Girolamo Masci
St. Celestine V	July 5, 1294–December 13, 1294	Pietro del Morrone
Boniface VIII	December 24, 1294–October 11, 1303	Benedetto Caetani
Benedict XI	October 22, 1303–July 7, 1304	Niccolò Boccasino
Clement V	June 5, 1305–April 20, 1314	Bertrand de Got
John XXII	August 7, 1316–December 4, 1334	Jacques Duèse
[Nicholas V]	May 12, 1328–July 25, 1330	Pietro Rainalducci

Pope	Reign	Original Name
Benedict XII	December 20, 1334–April 25, 1342	Jacques Fournier
Clement VI	May 7, 1342–December 6, 1352	Pierre of Rosier d'Engleton
Innocent VI	December 18, 1352–September 12, 1362	Étienne Aubert
Urban V	September 28, 1362–December 19, 1370f	Guillaume de Grimoard
Gregory XI	December 30, 1370–March 27, 1378	Pierre Roger de Beaufort
Urban VI	April 8, 1378–October 15, 1389	Bartolomeo Prignano
[Clement VII]	September 20, 1378–September 16, 1394	Robert of Cambrai
Boniface IX	November 2, 1389–October 1, 1404	Pietro Tomacelli
[Benedict XIII]	September 28, 1394–July 26, 1417	Pedro de Luna
Innocent VII	October 17, 1404–November 6, 1406	Cosimo Gentile de'Migliorati
Gregory XII	November 30, 1406–July 4, 1415	Angelo Correr
[Alexander V]	June 26, 1409–May 3, 1410	Pietro Philarghi (Peter of Candia)
[John XXIII]	May 17, 1410–May 29, 1415	Baldassare Cossa
Martin V	November 11, 1417–February 20, 1431	Oddo Colonna
[Clement VIII]	June 10, 1423–July 26, 1429	Gil Sanchez, Muñoz
[Benedict XIV]	November 12, 1425–?	Bernard Garnier
Eugene IV	March 3, 1431–February 23, 1447	Gabriele Condulmaro
[Felix V]	November 5, 1439–April 7, 1449	Amadeus VIII, Duke of Savoy
Nicholas V	March 6, 1447–March 24, 1455	Tommaso Parentucelli
Callistus III	April 8, 1455–August 6, 1458	Alfonso de Boria (Borgia)
Pius II	August 19, 1458–August 15, 1464	Enea Silvo Piccolomini
Paul II	August 30, 1464–July 26, 1471	Pietro Barbo
Sixtus IV	August 9, 1471–August 12, 1484	Francesco della Roverre
Innocent VIII	August 29, 1484–July 25, 1492	Giovanni Battista Cibò
Alexander VI	August 11, 1492–August 18, 1503	Rodrigo de Borja y Borja (Borgia)
Pius III	September 22, 1503–October 18, 1503	Francesco Todeschini
Julius II	November 1, 1503–February 21, 1513	Giuliano dell Rovere
Leo X	March 11, 1513–December 1, 1521	Giovanni de' Medici
Adrian VI (Hadrian VI)	January 9, 1522–September 14, 1523	Adrian Florensz Dedal
Clement VII	November 19, 1523–September 25, 1534	Giulio de' Medici
Paul III	October 13, 1534–November 10, 1549	Alessandro Farnese
Julius III	February 8, 1550–March 23, 1555	Giovanni Maria Ciocchi del Monte
Marcellus II	April 9, 1555–May 1, 1555	Marcello Cervini
Paul IV	May 23, 1555–August 18, 1559	Giampietro Carafa
Pius IV	December 25, 1559–December 9, 1565	Giovanni Angelo edici
St. Pius V	January 7, 1566–May 1, 1572	Michele Ghislieri
Gregory XIII	May 14, 1572–April 10, 1585	Ugo Boncompagni
Sixtus V	April 24, 1585–August 27, 1590	Felice Peretti
Urban VII	September 15, 1590–September 27, 1590	Giambattista Castagna
Gregory XIV	December 5, 1590–October 16, 1591	Niccolò Sfondrati
Innocent IX	October 29, 1591–December 30, 1591	Giovanni Antonio Achinetti
Clement VIII	January 30, 1592–March 5, 1605	Ippolito Aldobrandini
Leo XI	April 1, 1605–April 27, 1605	Alessandro Ottaviano de' Medici
Paul V	May 16, 1605–January 28, 1621	Camillo Borghese
Gregory XV	February 9, 1621–July 8, 1623	Alessandro Ludovisi
Urban VIII	August 6, 1623–July 29, 1644	Mafeo Barberini
Innocent X	September 15, 1644–January 1, 1655	Giambattista Pamfili
Alexander VII	April 7, 1655–May 22, 1667	Fabio Chigi
Clement IX	June 20, 1667–December 9, 1669	Giulio Rospigliosi

Religions

continues

Roman Catholic Popes, Continued

Pope	Reign	Original Name
Clement X	April 29, 1670–July 22, 1676	Emilio Altieri
Innocent XI	September 21, 1676–August 12, 1689	Benedetto Odescalchi
Alexander VIII	October 6, 1689–February 1, 1691	Pietro Ottoboni
Innocent XII	July 12, 1691–September 27, 1700	Antonio Pignatelli
Clement XI	November 23, 1700–March 19, 1721	Giovanni Francesco Albani
Innocent XIII	May 8, 1721–March 7, 1724	Michelangelo dei Conti
Benedict XIII	May 27, 1724–February 21, 1730	Pietro Francesco Orsini
Clement XII	July 12, 1730–February 6, 1740	Lorenzo Corsini
Benedict XIV	August 17, 1740–May 3, 1758	Prospero Lorenzo Lambertini
Clement XIII	July 6, 1758–February 2, 1769	Carlo della Torre Rezzonico
Clement XIV	May 18, 1769–September 22, 1774	Lorenzo Ganganelli
Pius VI	February 15, 1775–August 29, 1799	Giovanni Angelo Brachi
Pius VII	March 14, 1800–July 20, 1823	Luigi Barnab à Chiaramonte
Leo XII	September 28, 1823–February 10, 1829	Annibale Sermattei della Genga
Pius VIII	March 31, 1829–November 30, 1830	Francesco Saverio Castiglione
Gregory XVI	February 2, 1831–June 1, 1846	Bartolomeo Albert Cappellari
Pius IX	June 16, 1846–February 7, 1878	Giovanni Maria Mastai-Ferretti
Leo XIII	February 20, 1878–July 20, 1903	Gioacchino Vincenzo Pecci
St. Pius X	August 4, 1903–August 20, 1914	Giuseppe Melchiorre Sarto
Benedict XV	September 3, 1914–January 22, 1922	Giacomo Della Chiesa
Pius XI	February 6, 1922–February 10, 1939	Ambrogio Damiano Archille Ratti
Pius XII	March 2, 1939–October 9, 1958	Eugenio Maria Giuseppe Pacelli
John XXIII	October 28, 1958–June 3, 1963	Angelo Giuseppe Roncalli
Paul VI	June 21, 1963–August 6, 1978	Giovanni Battista Montini
John Paul I	August 26, 1978–September 28, 1978	Albino Luciani
John Paul II	October 16, 1978–	Karol Wojtyla

MAJOR RELIGIOUS HOLIDAYS IN THE UNITED STATES

January 6	*Feast of the Epiphany* (Christian) marks the arrival of the Three Wise Men who sought the newborn baby Jesus and the Twelfth Night, or end, of the Christmas season.
February 2	*Candlemas* (Christian) celebrates the presentation of the Christ child in the temple and the purification of the Blessed Virgin Mary 40 days after she gave birth to Jesus; mostly observed in Roman Catholic, Orthodox, and Anglican churches.
February or March	*Purim* (Jewish), the Feast of Lots, memorializes Queen Esther's prevention of the annihilation of the Persian Jews; it is a celebratory festival of food, entertainment, and costumes held on the 14th day of the lunar month of Adar or Adar II.
	Shrove Tuesday (Christian), or Mardi Gras, is the last day before Lent; it is celebrated by eating rich foods forbidden during Lent and by carnivals in such cities as New Orleans, Rio de Janeiro, and Nice.
February, March, or April	*Lent* (Christian) is a 40-day period of fasting and penitence in preparation for Easter. It begins on Ash Wednesday in Western churches and on the Monday 41 days before Easter in the Orthodox Church.

March or April	*Passover* (Jewish), or Pesach, commemorates the time when Moses led the Jews out of Egypt; it is celebrated for seven days by Reform and Israeli Jews and for eight days by Orthodox and Conservative Jews, starting on the 14th day of the lunar month Nisan with a meal of remembrance called a seder.
	Palm Sunday (Christian) celebrates Jesus' triumphal ride into Jerusalem and the start of Holy Week; it is observed the Sunday before Easter.
	Maundy Thursday (Christian), the Thursday before Easter, marks the Last Supper, the Agony in the Garden, and the arrest of Jesus.
	Good Friday (Christian), the Friday before Easter, commemorates Jesus' Crucifixion.
	Holy Saturday (Christian), the Saturday before Easter, is observed primarily in Roman Catholic, Orthodox Eastern, and Anglican churches.
	Easter Sunday (Christian) celebrates the day Jesus Christ rose from the dead.
May or June	*Ascension Day* (Christian) celebrates Christ's ascent to heaven; it is held 40 days after Easter.
	Shavuot (Jewish) celebrates the harvest of grain while also observing the receipt of the Ten Commandments by Israel; it is held for one day by Reform and Israeli Jews or for two days by Orthodox and Conservative Jews, starting the sixth day of the lunar month of Sivan.
	Pentecost (Christian), or Whitsunday, marks the descent of the Holy Spirit on the Apostles; it is held 50 days after Easter.
August 15	*The Assumption of the Blessed Virgin Mary* (Roman Catholic and Orthodox) is the principal feast day in honor of Mary, celebrating her assumption, body and soul, into heaven after her death.
September or October	*Rosh Hashanah* (Jewish) marks the start of the new year with solemn prayer and the blowing of the shofar, a ram's horn; it is observed for one day by Reform and Israeli Jews or for two days by Orthodox and Conservative Jews, starting the first day of the lunar month of Tishri.
	Yom Kippur (Jewish), the Day of Atonement, is a day of fasting and repentance for the previous year's sins; it concludes the 10 days of penitence that began on Rosh Hashanah; it is observed on the 10th day of the lunar month of Tishri.
	Sukkoth (Jewish), the Feast of the Tabernacles, is an autumn harvest festival that recalls the wandering of the Jews in the wilderness; it is celebrated for eight days (seven in Israel) starting on the 15th day of the lunar month of Tishri.
Sunday nearest October 31	*Reformation Sunday* (Protestant) celebrates the day Martin Luther nailed his "95 Theses" to a church door, heralding the start of the Protestant Reformation.

Go to "Major Foreign Holidays" in chapter 1; "Seven Wonders of the Ancient World" in chapter 26

continues

Major Religious Holidays, continued

November 1	*All Saints' Day* (Christian) is the feast day honoring all martyrs and the Virgin Mary; it is celebrated by Roman Catholic, Orthodox, and Anglican churches; it is also known as All Hallow's Day and is preceded by Halloween on October 31.
Sunday nearest November 30	*Advent* (Christian) is the period of repentance through Christmas Eve preparation for the anniversary of the birth of Christ.
December	*Hanukkah* (Jewish), the Festival of Lights, is marked by the lighting of eight candles in a menorah; it commemorates the restoration of traditional worship and the rededication of the temple in Jerusalem after the victory of the Jews over the troops of the Syrian emperor Antiochus; it is held for eight days beginning on the 25th day of the lunar month of Kislev.
December 8	*Feast of the Immaculate Conception* (Roman Catholic) honors the Virgin Mary's state of freedom from original sin from the time of her conception.
December 9	*Feast of the Conception of St. Anne* (Orthodox) celebrates the conception of the Virgin Mary.
December 25	*Christmas Day* (Christian) celebrates the birth of Jesus Christ; in many Western countries, it has become a nonsectarian winter holiday.
_____*	First day of Muharram, the first month, (Islamic) celebrates the hegira of Muhammad to Medina. The beginning of the Islamic year.
_____*	*Ramadan* (Islamic) is a month of fasting to celebrate the revelation of the Koran. It is the ninth month of the Islamic calendar.
_____*	*Eid-al-Fitr* (Islamic) is one of the two main festivals of Islam; this holiday concludes the month of Ramadan and is a day of thanksgiving for the blessings of Ramadan. Large early-morning worship services are followed by small private celebrations. It is held on the first day of Shawwal, the tenth month.
_____*	*Eid-al Adha* (Islamic), the Feast of Sacrifice, is the second of the two main festivals of Islam; it follows the day of pilgramage, or Haj; it is traditionally celebrated with a large prayer services and commemorates Abraham's willingness to sacrifice his son Ismael to Allah. Because an animal was substituted for Ismael, animals are sometimes sacrificed and their meat given to the needy. It is held on the tenth day of the twelfth month, Thw al-Hijjah.

* The Islamic calendar works on a lunar cycle; annual holidays thus advance about 10 days a year on the solar calendar. It takes Ramadan, for example, 36 years to move around the entire solar year.

ADDITIONAL SOURCES OF INFORMATION

BOOKS

Achtemeier, Paul J., ed. *HarperCollins Bible Dictionary.* HarperCollins, 1996.

Armstrong, Karen. *A History of God, The 4000-Year Quest of Judaism, Christianity, and Islam.* Ballantine, 1994.

Cairns, Alan. *Dictionary of Theological Terms.* Evangelical Press, 1998.

Cavendish, Richard, ed. *Man, Myth and Magic: The Illustrated Encyclopedia of Mythology, Religion and the Unknown.* Rev. 94 ed. Marshall Cavendish, 1994.

Danielou, Alain. *The Myths and Gods of India.* Inner Traditions, 1992.

DuBois, Thomas, ed. *Encyclopedia of World Mythology.* 3 vols. ABC-CLIO, 2001.

Eliade, Mircea, ed. *The Encyclopedia of Religion.* 16 vols. Macmillan, 1993.

Esposito, John L., ed. *The Oxford History of Islam.* Oxford University Press, 2000.

Fisher-Schreiber, Ingrid, et al., eds. *The Encyclopedia of Eastern Philosophy and Religion.* Shambhala, 1994.

Freedman, David Noel, ed. *Eerdman's Dictionary of the Bible.* Eerdman's Publishing, 2000.

Johnston, Willim M., ed. *Encyclopedia of Monasticism.* Fitzroy, 2000.

Jordon, Michael. *The Encyclopedia of Gods.* Facts on File, 1993.

Kelly, J. N. D. *The Oxford Dictionary of Popes.* Oxford University Press, 1989.

Kolatch, Alfred J. *The Jewish Book of Why/The Second Jewish Book of Why.* Jonathan David Publications, 1989.

Melton, J. Gordon, ed. *The Encyclopedia of American Religions.* 6th ed. Gale, 1998.

Mercatante, Anthony S., ed. *The Encyclopedia of World Myth and Legend.* Facts on File, 1988.

Metzger, Bruce M., and Michael D. Coogan, eds. *The Oxford Companion to the Bible.* Oxford University Press, 1998.

Newsner, Jacob, et al., eds. *Encyclopedia of Judaism.* Continuum, 1998.

Parrinder, Geoffrey, ed. *World Religions: From Ancient History to the Present.* Facts On File, 1988.

Peters, F. E. *Judaism, Christianity, and Islam.* 3 vols. Kazi, 1996.

Queen, Edward L., et al., eds. *The Encyclopedia of American Religious History.* 2 vols. Facts on File, 1996.

Smart, Ninia. *Atlas of the World's Religions.* Oxford University Press, 1999.

Smith, Jonathan Z., ed. *The HarperCollins Dictionary of Religion.* HarperCollins, 1995.

Suzuki, Shunryu. *Zen Mind, Beginner's Mind.* John Weatherhill, 1986.

Telushkin, Joseph. *Jewish Literacy: The Most Important Things to Know About the Jewish Religion, Its People, Its History.* William Morrow, 1991.

Terry, Michael. *Reader's Guide to Judaism.* Fitzroy, 2000.

Ware, Timothy, and Kallistos Ware. *The Orthodox Church.* 2nd ed. Penguin, 1992.

WEB SITES

Comparative Analysis of Major World Religions
www.comparativereligion.com

Divine Digest
www.divinedigest.com

Adherents of World Religions
www.adherents.com

PHILOSOPHY

MAJOR WORLD PHILOSOPHERS

Abelard, Peter (1079–1142). French philosopher. One of the most influential medieval logicians and theologians. Around 1113, while teaching theology in Paris, Abelard fell in love with his student Heloise, whom he secretly married; he was condemned for heresy a few years later because of his nominalist views. He wrote *Sic et Non.*

Anaxagoras (c. 500–428 B.C.). Greek pre-Socratic philosopher who is said to have made Athens the center of philosophy and to have been Socrates's teacher; he rejected the four-elements theory of Empedocles and posited instead an infinite number of unique particles of which all objects are composed.

Anaximander (c. 611–547 B.C.). Greek pre-Socratic thinker who believed the universal substance to be "the boundless" or "the indefinite," rather than something resembling familiar objects. Unlike Thales (his teacher) and Anaximenes, he did not believe that a single element underlies all things.

Anaximenes (6th century B.C.). One of the pre-Socratics and an associate of Anaximander. He agreed with Thales that one type of substance underlies the diversity of observable things. Anaximenes believed that air was that universal substance and that all things are made of air in different degrees of density.

Anselm, St. (1033–1109). Italian monk and Scholastic theologian who became archbishop of Canterbury. St. Anselm founded Scholasticism, integrated Aristotelian logic into theology, and believed that reason and revelation are compatible. He is most famous for his influential ontological argument for God's existence.

Aquinas, St. Thomas (1225–74). The greatest thinker of the Scholastic School. His ideas, in 1879, were made the official Catholic philosophy. He incorporated Greek ideas into Christianity by showing Aristotle's thought to be compatible with church doctrine. In Aquinas's system, reason and faith (revelation) form two separate but harmonious realms whose truths complement rather than oppose one another. He presented influential philosophical proofs for the existence of God. His works include *Summa Theologica* (1267–1273) and *On Being and Essence.*

Aristotle (384–322 B.C.). Greek philosopher, scientist, logician, and student of many disciplines. Aristotle studied under Plato and became the tutor of Alexander the Great. In 335, Aristotle opened the Lyceum, a major philosophical and scientific school in Athens. He emphasized the observation of nature and analyzed all things in terms of "the four causes." In ethics, he stressed that virtue is a mean between extremes and that a person's highest goal should be the use of his or her intellect. Most of Aristotle's works were lost to Christian civilization from the 5th through the 12th centuries. Among his writings are *Metaphysics, Politics,* and *Rhetoric.*

Augustine of Hippo, St. (354–430). The greatest of the Latin church fathers and possibly the most influential Christian thinker after St. Paul. St. Augustine emphasized a person's need for grace. His *Confessions* and *The City of God* were highly influential.

Averroes (1126–98). Spanish-born Arabian philosopher, lawyer, and physician whose detailed commentaries on Aristotle were influential for over 300 years. He emphasized the compatibility of faith and reason but believed philosophical knowledge to be derived from reason. The church condemned his views.

Avicenna (980–1037). Islamic medieval philosopher born in Persia. His Neoplatonist interpretation of Aristotle greatly influenced medieval philosophers, including St. Thomas Aquinas. Avicenna was also a physician; his writings on medicine were important for nearly 500 years.

Ayer, Alfred Jules (1910–89). British proponent of logical positivism. Maintaining that philosophical arguments have no validity unless they can be verified by empirical means, Ayer proposed linguistic analysis as the essential method of philosophic investigation. His most influential work is *Language, Truth, and Logic* (1936).

Bacon, Sir Francis (1561–1626). English statesman, essayist, and philosopher. He was one of the great precursors of the tradition of British empiricism and of belief in the importance of scientific method. He emphasized the use of inductive reasoning in the pursuit of knowledge.

Bentham, Jeremy (1748–1832). English philosopher and lawyer and one of the founders of utilitarianism. Bentham was a highly influential reformer of the British legal, judicial, and prison systems. He is the author of *Introduction to the Principles of Morals and Legislation* (1789).

Berkeley, George (1685–1753). Irish philosopher and an Anglican bishop; one of the British empiricists. Berkeley held to a "subjective idealism." He believed that everything that exists is dependent on being perceived by a mind. According to this view, material objects are simply collections of sensations or "ideas" in the mind of a person or of God. His works include *Essay Toward a New Theory of Vision* (1709) and *A Treatise Concerning the Principles of Human Knowledge* (1710).

Boethius (c. 475–535). Roman statesman, philosopher, and translator of Aristotle, whose *Consolation of Philosophy* (written in prison) was widely read throughout the Middle Ages; it showed reason's role in the face of misfortune and was the link between the ancient philosophers and the Scholastics.

Buber, Martin (1878–1965). German-Israeli philosopher influenced by Jewish mysticism and existentialism, a major force in 20th-century Jewish thought and philosophy of religion. His *I and Thou* (1923) held that God and man can have a direct and mutual "dialogue."

Comte, Auguste (1798–1857). French founder of positivism and social reformer. Comte put forth a "religion of humanity" that replaced the notion of God with the notion of humankind as a whole. He invented the term *sociology*.

Democritus (c. 460–370 B.C.). Greek philosopher who proposed a mechanistic theory of the world that required no supernatural forces, only the constant motion of the indestructible atoms of which everything is composed. He held that perception is an unreliable source of knowledge and that knowledge can be obtained through reason only.

Derrida, Jacques (1930–   ). French philosopher and founder of deconstructionism, which challenges traditional Western concepts of meaning. In the view of deconstructionists, language refers only to language, and all written works may have innumerable meanings independent of the author's intention.

Descartes, René (1596–1650). French philosopher and scientist, considered the father of modern philosophical inquiry. Descartes tried to extend mathematical method to all knowledge in his search for certainty. Discarding the medieval appeal to authority, he began with "universal doubt," finding that the only thing that could not be doubted was his own thinking. The result was his famous "*Cogito, ergo sum,*" or "I think, therefore I am." His major works are the *Discourse on Method* (1637) and *Meditations on First Philosophy* (1641).

Dewey, John (1859–1952). Leading American philosopher, psychologist, and educational theorist. Dewey developed the views of Charles S. Peirce (1839–1914) and William James into his own version of pragmatism. He emphasized the importance of inquiry in gaining knowledge and attacked the view that knowledge is passive.

Diderot, Denis (1713–84). Materialist thinker of the French Enlightenment and originator of the *Encyclopédie* (1751–72).

Diogenes (c. 400–325 B.C.). Greek founder of cynicism who rejected social conventions and supposedly lived in a tub in defiance of conventional comforts.

Empedocles (c. 495–435 B.C.). Greek pre-Socratic philosopher who believed the universe to consist of four elements: air, fire, water, and earth. Empedocles held that the interaction between love and hate causes the mixing of the elements.

Engels, Friedrich (1820–95). German socialist thinker and historian and the cofounder of Marxism. He was Marx's lifelong collaborator and coauthor of the *Communist Manifesto* (1848) and an originator of the philosophy of dialectical materialism.

Epictetus (c. 50–138). Stoic moral philosopher who established a school of philosophy after being freed as a slave. His *Manual* teaches that only by detaching ourselves from what is not in our power can we attain inward freedom.

Epicurus (341–270 B.C.). Founder of the Epicurean philosophy and a follower of Democritus, the greatest ancient philosopher of atomism. Virtually all of Epicurus's writings are lost.

Foucault, Michel (1926–84). French philosopher and historian of ideas whose major works analyze the origin and growth of social institutions. In *Madness and Civilization* (1961), Foucault explores society's response to mental illness; *Discipline and Punish* (1975) examines the treatment of criminals.

Hegel, Georg Wilhelm Friedrich (1770–1831). German philosopher whose idealistic system of metaphysics was highly influential. It was based on a concept of the world as a single organism developing by its own inner logic through trios of stages called "thesis, antithesis, and synthesis" and gradually coming to embody reason. Hegel held the monarchy to be the highest development of the state. His works include *The Science of Logic* (1812, 1813, 1816) and *Phenomenology of Mind* (1807).

Heidegger, Martin (1889–1976). German philosopher who studied with Husserl. Heidegger's own philosophy, which was influenced by Kierkegaard, emphasized the need to understand "being," especially the unique ways that humans act in and relate to the world. He wrote *Being and Time* (1927).

Heraclitus (c. 535–475 B.C.). Pre-Socratic philosopher opposed to the idea of a single ultimate reality. Heraclitus believed that all things are in a constant state of change.

Hobbes, Thomas (1588–1679). English materialist and empiricist; one of the founders of modern political philosophy. In *Leviathan* (1651), Hobbes argued that because men are selfish by nature, a powerful absolute ruler is necessary. In a "social contract," men agree to give up many personal liberties and accept such rule.

Hume, David (1711–76). British empiricist whose arguments against the proofs for God's existence are still influential. In his *Treatise of Human Nature* (1739–40), Hume held that moral beliefs have no basis in reason, but are based solely on custom.

Husserl, Edmund (1859–1938). German philosopher who founded the phenomenology movement. He aimed at a completely accurate description of consciousness and conscious experience. His works include *Logical Investigations* (1900–01) and *Ideas Pertaining to a Pure Phenomenology and Phenomenological Philosophy* (1913).

James, William (1842–1910). American philosopher and psychologist, one of the founders of pragmatism, and one of the most influential thinkers of his era. James viewed consciousness as actively shaping reality, defined truth as "the expedient" way of thinking, and held that ideas are tools for guiding our future actions rather than reproductions of our past experiences. His writings include *The Will to Believe* (1897) and *Pragmatism* (1907).

Kant, Immanuel (1724–1804). German philosopher, possibly the most influential of modern times. He synthesized Leibniz's rationalism and Hume's skepticism into his "critical philosophy": in *The Critique of Pure Reason* (1781), Kant wrote that ideas do not conform to the external world, but rather the world can be known only insofar as it conforms to the mind's own structure. In *The Critique of Practical Reason* (1788), Kant claimed that morality requires a belief in God, freedom, and immortality,

How to Argue Logically

A
Closer
Look

We like to think that we speak logically all the time, but we are aware that we sometimes use illogical means to persuade others of our point of view. In the heat of an impassioned argument, or when we are afraid our disputant has a stronger case, or when we don't quite have all the facts we'd like to have, we are prone to engage in faulty processes of reasoning, using arguments we hope will appear sound.

Such defective arguments are called *fallacies* by philosophers who, starting with Aristotle, have cataloged and classified these fallacious arguments. There are now over 125 separate fallacies, most with their own impressive-sounding names, many of them in Latin.

Some arguments have easily recognizable defects. For instance, in the *argument ad hominem,* a person's views are criticized because of a logically irrelevant personal defect: "You can't take Smith's advice on the stock market; he's a known philanderer." In the *genetic fallacy,* something is mistakenly reduced to its origins: "We know that emotions are nothing more than physiology; after all, medical research has shown emotions involve the secretion of hormones." Another illogical argument is named for the erroneous thinking a wagering person may fall prey to, the *gambler's fallacy* (also called the *Monte Carlo fallacy*): "I'm betting on heads; it's got to come up since we've just had nine straight tails."

Some fallacies may not be recognized as erroneous reasoning because they are such commonly used forms of argument. For instance, if we say, "I'm sure my cold is due to the weather; I started sneezing right after it went from 60 degrees to 31 degrees in three hours," we are committing the fallacy with the Latin name of *post hoc ergo propter hoc* ("after this, therefore because of this"). Many a political argument exemplifies the fallacy of *arguing in a circle:* "Only wealthy men are capable of leading the country; after all, leadership can be learned only if you have had money to exercise power." Many prejudicial or stereotypical arguments commit the *fallacy of division,* or of applying to the part what may be true of the whole: "North Dakota has wide-open spaces; because Jack's farm is there, it must be quite large." The converse of this is the *fallacy of composition,* where properties of the parts are erroneously attributed to the whole: "Every apple on this tree is rotten; therefore, the tree itself is hopelessly diseased."

It may be a surprise to realize that some widely accepted forms of argument are just as fallacious as the most logically defective reasoning. When we appeal to the beliefs or behavior of the majority to prove the truth of something, we are committing the *fallacy of consensus gentium:* "Imbibing alcohol cannot be bad for people, because all cultures studied have used alcohol." Or consider the person who argues that "Tragedy is the highest form of literature; after all, didn't Aristotle consider it such?" This is a form of the *fallacy of arguing from authority.* There is also the *fallacy of ignoratio elenchus,* which has nothing to do with ignorance; its name means that the point made is irrelevant to the issue at hand, as in the untenable view of a lawyer who says, "Ladies and gentlemen of the jury, you cannot convict my client of manslaughter while driving under the influence; after all, advertisements for alcohol exist everywhere in our culture."

Philosophy

although these can be proved neither scientifically nor by metaphysics. Finally, in his *Foundations of the Metaphysic of Morals* (1785), he presented the concept of the categorical imperative.

Kierkegaard, Søren   (1813–55). Danish philosopher, religious thinker, and extraordinarily influential founder of existentialism. Kierkegaard held that "truth is subjectivity," that religion is an individual matter, and that man's relationship to God requires suffering. He wrote *Either/Or* (1843) and *Fear and Trembling* (1843).

Leibniz, Gottfried Wilhelm   (1646–1716). German philosopher, diplomat, and mathematician; one of the great minds of all time. Leibniz was an inventor (with Sir Isaac Newton) of calculus and a forefather of modern mathematical logic. He held that the entire universe is one large system expressing God's plan. His writings include *New Essays on Human Understanding* (1703–04).

Locke, John   (1632–1704). Highly influential founder of British empiricism. In his *Essay Concerning Human Understanding* (1690), Locke wrote that all ideas come to mind from experience and that none are innate. He also held that authority derives solely from the consent of the governed, a view that deeply influenced the American Revolution and the writing of the U.S. Constitution. His *Two Treatises on Government* (1690) express his political thought.

Lucretius   (c. 99–55 B.C.). Roman Epicurean philosopher and poet. In *De Rerum Natura* (On the Nature of Things), Lucretius depicted the entire world, including the soul, as composed of atoms.

Machiavelli, Niccolò   (1469–1527). Italian Renaissance statesman and political writer. In *The Prince* (1513), one of the most influential political books of modern times, Machiavelli argues that any act of a ruler designed to gain and hold power is permissible. The term *Machiavellian* is used to refer to any political tactics that are cunning and power-oriented.

Maimonides (Moses ben Maimon)   (1135–1204). Spanish-born medieval Jewish philosopher and thinker. Maimonides tried to synthesize Aristotelian and Judaic thought. His works, such as *Guide for the Perplexed*, had enormous influence on Jewish and Christian thought.

Marcus Aurelius   (121–180). Roman emperor from A.D. 161 and a proponent of the Stoic philosophy. His *Meditations* held that death is as natural as birth and that the world is rational and orderly. Although a great humanitarian, Marcus Aurelius persecuted the Christians of his time.

Marx, Karl   (1818–83). German revolutionary thinker, social philosopher, and economist. His ideas, formulated with Friedrich Engels, laid the foundation for 19th-century socialism and 20th-century communism. Although Marx was initially influenced by Georg Hegel, he soon rejected Hegel's idealism in favor of materialism. His *Communist Manifesto* (1848) and *Das Kapital* (1867) are among the most important writings of the last 200 years.

Mill, John Stuart   (1806–73). English empiricist philosopher, logician, economist, and social reformer. His *System of Logic* (1843) described the basic rules for all scientific reasoning. As a student of Jeremy Bentham, he elaborated on utilitarian ethics; in *On Liberty* (1859), he presented a plea for the sanctity of individual rights against the power of any government.

Montesquieu, Baron de (Charles-Louis de Secondat)   (1689–1755). French political philosopher, influenced by John Locke. In *Spirit of the Laws* (1748), Montesquieu put forth the theory of separation of powers that strongly influenced the writing of the U.S. Constitution.

Moore, G. E. (George Edward)   (1873–1958). British philosopher who emphasized the "common sense" view of the reality of material objects. In ethics, Moore held that goodness is a quality known directly by moral intuition and that it is a fallacy to try to define it in terms of anything else.

More, Sir Thomas   (1478–1535). A leading Renaissance humanist and statesman; Lord Chancellor of England. More was beheaded for refusing to accept the king as head of the church. Influenced by Greek thinking, he believed in social reform and drew a picture of an ideal peaceful state in his *Utopia* (1516).

Nietzsche, Friedrich Wilhelm   (1844–1900). German philosopher, philologist, and poet. As a moralist, he rejected Christian values and championed a "Superman" who would create a new, life-affirming, heroic ethic by his "will to power." His works include *Thus Spake Zarathustra* (1883–85) and *Beyond Good and Evil* (1886).

Parmenides   (fl. c. 500 B.C.). The founder of Western metaphysics. This pre-Socratic thinker held that "being" is the basic substance and ultimate reality of which all things are composed and that motion, change, time, difference, and reality are illusions of the senses.

The Greek philosopher Epicurus believed that the only evil in the world was pain.

Pascal, Blaise (1623–62). French philosopher, mathematician, scientist, and theologian. His posthumous *"Pensées"* ("Thoughts") argues that reason is by itself inadequate for man's spiritual needs and cannot bring man to God, who can be known only through mystic understanding.

Plato (c. 428–348 B.C.). Athenian father of Western philosophy and student of Socrates, after whose death he traveled widely. Upon returning to Athens, Plato founded an academy, where he taught until he died. His writings are in the form of dialogues between Socrates and other Athenians. Many of Plato's views are set forth in *The Republic* (c. 370 B.C.), where an ideal state postulates philosopher kings, specially trained at the highest levels of moral and mathematical knowledge. Plato's other works analyzed moral virtues, the nature of knowledge, and the immortality of the soul. His views on cosmology strongly influenced the next 2,000 years of scientific thinking.

Plotinus (205–270). Egyptian-born founder of Neoplatonism, who synthesized the ideas of Plato and other Greek philosophers. Plotinus believed all reality is caused by a series of outpourings (called emanations) from the divine source. Although not himself a Christian, he was a major influence on Christianity.

Pythagoras (c. 582–507 B.C.). Greek philosopher, mathematician, and mystic; founder of a religious brotherhood that believed in the immortality and the transmigration of the soul. Pythagoras may have been the first thinker to assert that numbers constitute the true nature of all things; he also may have coined the term *philosophy*.

Quine, Willard Van Orman (1908–   ). A leading American linguistic philosopher, Quine has explored the connections between language and logic and made important contributions to set theory.

Among his best-known works are *Word and Object* (1960) and *Theories and Things* (1981).

Rawls, John (1921–   ). American philosopher whose major work, *A Theory of Justice* (1971), revived interest in political theory. Rawls has attempted to provide a modern philosophical foundation for the idea of the social contract, first developed by John Locke and Jean Jacques Rousseau.

Rousseau, Jean-Jacques (1712–78). Swiss-French thinker, born in Geneva. Rousseau has been enormously influential in political philosophy, educational theory, and the romantic movement. In *The Social Contract* (1762), he viewed governments as being expressions of the people's "general will," or rational people's choice for the common good. Rousseau emphasized a person's natural goodness.

Russell, Bertrand (1872–1970). English philosopher and logician influential as an agnostic and a pacifist. Early work with Alfred North Whitehead gave birth to modern logic; they coauthored *Principia Mathematica* (3 vols., 1910–13). Russell changed his views numerous times but always sought to establish philosophy, especially epistemology, as a science.

Ryle, Gilbert (1900–76). British philosopher who was a leader in linguistic analysis. Ryle's work related grammar and word usage to the principles of logic. His main work, *The Concept of Mind* (1949), challenged Descartes's distinction between mind and body, arguing that the mind is a set of capacities belonging to the body.

Santayana, George (1863–1952). Spanish-born American philosopher and poet; a student of William James. Santayana attempted to reconcile Platonism and materialism, studied how reason works, and found "animal faith," or impulse, to be the basis of reason and belief. Among his works are *The Sense of Beauty* (1896) and *The Life of Reason* (5 vols., 1905–06).

Sartre, Jean-Paul (1905–80). French philosopher, novelist, and dramatist; one of the founders of existentialism. Sartre was a Marxist through much of his life. He held that man is "condemned to be free" and to bear the responsibility of making free choices. His primary philosophical work was *Being and Nothingness* (1943).

Schopenhauer, Arthur (1788–1860). German post-Kantian philosopher who held that although irrational will is the driving force in human affairs, it is doomed not to be satisfied. He believed that only art and contemplation could offer escape from determinism and pessimism. Schopenhauer strongly influenced Friedrich Nietzsche, Sigmund Freud, Leo Tolstoy, Marcel Proust, and Thomas Mann. He wrote *The World as Will and Representation* (1818).

Scotus, John Duns (c. 1266–1308). Scottish-born Scholastic philosopher who tried to integrate Aristotelian ideas into Christian theology. Scotus emphasized that all things depend not just on God's intellect but on divine will as well. He wrote *On the First Principle.*

Smith, Adam (1723–90). Scottish philosopher and economist. The author of *An Inquiry into the Nature and Causes of the Wealth of Nations* (1776), he believed that if government left the marketplace to its own devices, an "invisible hand" would guarantee that the results would benefit the populace. Smith has had enormous influence on economists into the present day.

Socrates (c. 470–399 B.C.). Athenian philosopher who allegedly wrote down none of his views, supposedly from his belief that writing distorts ideas. His chief student, Plato, is the major source of knowledge about his life. Socrates questioned Athenians about their moral, political, and religious beliefs, as depicted in Plato's dialogues; his questioning technique, called dialectic, has greatly influenced Western philosophy. In 399 B.C., he was brought to trial on charges of corrupting the youth and religious heresy. Sentenced to die, he drank poison.

Spinoza, Benedict (Baruch) (1623–77). Dutch-born philosopher expelled from the Amsterdam Jewish community for heresy in 1656; he was attacked by Christian theologians 14 years later. In *Ethics Demonstrated in Geometrical Order* (1677), Spinoza

presents his views in a mathematical system of deductive reasoning. A proponent of monism, he held—in contrast to Descartes—that mind and body are aspects of a single substance, which he called God or nature.

Thales of Miletus (c. 636–546 B.C.). Regarded as the first Western philosopher, this pre-Socratic monist thinker is said to have believed that the fundamental principle of all things, or universal substance, is water. All of his writings are lost.

Unamuno, Miguel de (1864–1936). The major Spanish philosopher of his time. Unamuno criticized philosophic abstractions such as "man" for ignoring concrete men. He held that reason by itself is virtually useless and cannot reveal the basic fact of human immortality. He wrote *The Tragic Sense of Life in Men and Nations* (1913).

Voltaire (François Marie Arouet) (1694–1778). French philosopher, essayist, and historian; one of the major thinkers of the Enlightenment. A Deist who was anti-Christian, Voltaire widely advocated tolerance of liberal ideas and called for positive social action. His novel *Candide* (1759) is a parody of the optimism of Gottfried Leibniz.

Whitehead, Alfred North (1861–1947). British philosopher and mathematician who worked with Bertrand Russell. Whitehead tried to integrate 20th-century physics into a metaphysics of nature.

William of Ockham (Occam) (c. 1285–1349). Franciscan monk and important English theologian and philosopher. In his nominalism, he opposed much of the thought of St. Thomas Aquinas and of medieval Aristotelianism; he also rejected the pope's power in the secular realm.

Wittgenstein, Ludwig (1889–1951). Austrian-born philosopher who spent the last 20 years of his life in England. Wittgenstein was one of the most influential philosophers of the 20th century, primarily through his emphasis on the importance of the study of language. His *Tractatus Logico-Philosophicus* (1921) influenced analytic philosophy. His later views emphasized that philosophic problems are often caused by linguistic confusions.

Zeno of Elea (c. 490–430 B.C.). Pre-Socratic philosopher and disciple of Parmenides. Zeno argued that motion, change, and plurality are logical absurdities and that only an unchanging being is real. His four arguments against motion (Zeno's paradoxes) attempted to demonstrate logically that the notions of time and motion are erroneous.

Zeno (of Citium) the Stoic (c. 334–262 B.C.). Greek philosopher born in Cyprus; the founder of Stoicism.

PHILOSOPHICAL MOVEMENTS AND SCHOOLS OF THOUGHT

analytical philosophy An influential 20th-century movement whose major proponents include Bertrand Russell, Ludwig Wittgenstein, and such logical positivists as Rudolph Carnap (1891–1970) and Willard Van Orman Quine. This school of thought emphasizes restating philosophical problems in highly structured terms based on modern logic.

anthroposophy The philosophy of Rudolf Steiner (1861–1925), an Austrian-born thinker who held that cultivating man's spiritual development is humanity's most important task. His followers founded a large number of schools worldwide based on his philosophy.

Aristotelianism A system of thought originating with the teachings of Aristotle (4th century B.C.), who held that knowledge originates in experience and observation, from which comes an understanding of the universal. His teachings and writings were influential in the Western world until the fall of Rome, when all but his writings on logic were lost to Christian civilization in Europe. His empiricism was embraced by medieval thinkers, especially St. Thomas Aquinas. Aristotle's works were preserved in Syrian and Arabic cultures and were revived in the West at the end of the 12th century.

British empiricism The empiricism of John Locke, George Berkeley, and David Hume in the 17th and 18th centuries. They shared the axiom that our knowledge of the world derives from experience or sensation rather than from reason. This view was opposed to rationalism, as well as to the Platonic notion of Forms as the source of knowledge.

British idealism (neo-Hegelianism) The philosophy of Georg Hegel as followed in England and Scotland in the mid–19th century. The most prominent members of this school were Thomas Hill Green (1836–82), Bernard Bosanquet (1848–1923), and Francis Herbert Bradley (1846–1924). They were united in their opposition to empiricism and utilitarianism and in their emphasis on mind and spirit as primary.

Cambridge Platonists A group of 17th-century English philosophers and theologians who tried to provide Christian theology with a philosophical defense based on Platonic and Neoplatonic theories. Ralph Cudworth (1617–88) was the most prominent member.

Cartesianism The views of René Descartes as interpreted by 17th-century rationalistic, dualistic, and theistic philosophers. They held that the search for knowledge and certainty can be based on logical analysis and mathematical principles. Nicolas Malebranche (1638–1715) was the most prominent of Descartes's followers.

Cynics A school of Greek philosophers founded in the 4th century B.C. by Diogenes. According to legend, Diogenes walked around night and day with a lighted lantern seeking an honest man but could not find one. The Cynics held that virtue was the only good and that happiness was to be attained only by living in a simple state of nature with as few desires and needs as possible. They advocated moderation, self-discipline, and training of the mind as well as the body.

Cyrenaics A school of philosophy of the 4th century B.C. in Athens, founded by Cyrene, a disciple of

Socrates. Cyrenaics believed that only momentary feelings of pleasure or pain can be known; they held that the good life is one that maximizes pleasure derived from satisfying one's bodily desires. Unlike the Epicureans, the Cyrenaics focused on physical sensation and the primacy of personal experience. *See also* **hedonism.**

deism A philosophical viewpoint appearing in England in the 17th and 18th centuries and in France in the 18th century. Deists held that although God created the universe and its laws, He then removed Himself from any ongoing interaction with the material world.

dialectical materialism The philosophy of Karl Marx and many of his followers. It holds that matter is the primary reality and that it obeys the dynamic laws of change. The most fundamental of these laws is that progress occurs through conflict and struggle between opposing forces (thesis and antithesis), such as between different classes and between capitalism and communism. Essentially deterministic, this philosophy maintains that individuals have no influence over the course of history. *See also* **Marxism.**

Eleatics A school of pre-Socratic philosophers (5th century B.C.) from Elea in southern Italy, of whom Parmenides and Zeno of Elea are the best known. The Eleatics denied the reality of what is known to the senses, holding that the ultimate reality is an undifferentiated and unchanging "being."

Encyclopedists A group of 18th-century French writers who combined to produce an encyclopedia of philosophy, art, and science (1751–65), edited by Denis Diderot and Jean d'Alembert (1717–83). The work was skeptical about religion and advocated liberal, democratic political views. At the time, it was the largest compendium of human knowledge that had ever been produced.

Enlightenment (Age of Reason) A mainly 18th-century European philosophical movement. Its thinkers strove to make reason the ruler of human life; they believed that all people could gain knowledge and liberation. They sought the perfection of human society through applied reason. Rejecting conventional religious and secular authority, this movement substituted tolerance, humanism, and positive social action by the state. Major Enlightenment figures include Voltaire, Jean-Jacques Rousseau, Denis Diderot, and Baron de Montesquieu in France; David Hume in England; and Gotthold Ephraim Lessing (1729–81) and Johann Gottfried von Herder (1744–1803) in Germany. *See also* **philosophes.**

Epicureanism An ethical doctrine established in Greece in the 3rd century B.C. Based on the teachings of Epicurus, it maintained that pleasure is the highest good and that pleasure can only be attained through a life of virtuous conduct. Epicureans sought mental pleasures over bodily ones.

existentialism A philosophy of the 19th and 20th centuries. The dogma holds that because there are no universal values, a person's essence is not predetermined but is based only on free choice; a person is in a state of anxiety because of his or her realization of free will; and there is no objective truth. Major existentialists were Søren Kierkegaard, Friedrich Nietzsche, Jean-Paul Sartre, Martin Heidegger, Karl Jaspers (1883–1969), and the religious existentialists Martin Buber and Gabriel Marcel (1889–1973).

hedonism The ethical doctrine holding that pleasure is the highest or the only good in life, and that a person should strive for pleasure and the avoidance of pain. In ancient Greece, the Cyrenaics emphasized physical sensation, while the Epicureans stressed the importance of simple living and virtuous moral conduct. The utilitarians in the 19th century were also proponents of hedonism.

Hegelianism (neo-Hegelianism) A school of thought associated with Georg Hegel in the 19th and early 20th centuries, especially in England, America, France, and Italy. Francis Herbert Bradley (1846–1924), Josiah Royce (1855–1916), and Benedetto Croce (1866–1952) were prominent members; they emphasized the importance of spirit and the belief that ideas and moral ideals are fundamental.

intuitionism Any philosophy holding that intuition is the basis of knowledge or of philosophy. French philosopher Henri Bergson (1859–1941)

A Closer Look

Famous Philosophical Quotes

Aristotle	"Man is by nature a political animal."
Sir Francis Bacon	"Knowledge is power."
Jeremy Bentham	"The greatest happiness of the greatest number is the foundation of morals and legislation."
Confucius	"Hold faithfulness and sincerity as first principles."
René Descartes	"*Cogito, ergo sum*" (Latin for "I think, therefore I am").
Ralph Waldo Emerson	"Nature is a mutual cloud, which is always and never the same."
Friedrich Engels	"The state is not 'abolished,' it withers away."
Georg Hegel	"What experience and history teach us is this—that people and governments have never learned anything from history, or acted on principles deduced from it."
Thomas Hobbes	"The life of man [in a state of nature is], solitary, poor, nasty, brutish, and short."
Immanuel Kant	"Happiness is not an ideal of reason but of imagination."
John Locke	"No man's knowledge here can go beyond his experience."
Niccolò Machiavelli	"God is not willing to do everything, and thus take away our free will and that share of glory which belongs to us."
Karl Marx	"The proletarians have nothing to lose [in this revolution] but their chains. They have a world to win. Workers of the world, unite!"
	"Religion is the opium of the people."
	"The class struggle necessarily leads to the dictatorship of the proletariat."
John Stuart Mill	"Liberty consists in doing what one desires."
Friedrich Nietzsche	"I teach you the Superman. Man is something to be surpassed."
Thomas Paine	"Suspicion is the companion of mean souls, and the bane of all good society."
Plato	"The life which is unexamined is not worth living."
Jean-Jacques Rousseau	"Man was born free, and everywhere he is in chains."
Bertrand Russell	"It is undesirable to believe a proposition when there is no ground whatever for supposing it true."
Seneca	"Even while they teach, men learn."
Socrates	"There is only one good, knowledge, and one evil, ignorance."
Voltaire	"If God did not exist, it would be necessary to invent Him."

was a prominent advocate. In particular, intuitionism refers to a British school of thought that maintains that all ethical knowledge rests on moral intuition.

linguistic philosophy (linguistic analysis) The 20th-century school of thought whose key tenet is that philosophical problems are best approached by asking questions about the use of words and by analyzing how language works in specific social contexts.

logical positivism A 20th-century school founded in the 1920s in Europe that was extremely influential for American and English philosophers. It attempted to introduce mathematical and scientific methodology into philosophy. It rejected metaphysical speculation in favor of a vigorous analysis of experience and language, without which understanding is not possible. The school advocated the principle of verifiability, according to which all statements that could not be validated empirically were meaningless. Logical positivism held that this principle showed that all of metaphysics, religion, and ethics were incapable of being proved either true or false. *See also* **Vienna Circle.**

Manichaeanism A religious-philosophical doctrine that originated in Persia in the 3rd century A.D. and reappeared throughout the next 1,300 years. It holds that the entire universe, especially human life, is a struggle between the opposing forces of good and evil (light and darkness).

Bertrand Russell said, "The point of philosophy is to start with something so simple as not to seem worth stating, and to end with something so paradoxical that no one will believe it."

Marxism The political, economic, and philosophical theories developed by Karl Marx and Friedrich Engels in the second half of the 19th century. The philosophical side of Marxism is called dialectical materialism; it emphasizes economic determinism. *See also* **dialectical materialism.**

Miletian School The pre-Socratics from Miletus in Greece—Thales and his two best-known pupils, Anaximander and Anaximenes.

Neoplatonism A school of philosophy that flourished from the 2nd to the 5th centuries A.D. It was founded by Plotinus and was influential for the next thousand years.

nihilism An extremist movement in 19th-century Russia. *Ethical nihilism* is the theory that morality cannot be justified in any way and that all moral values are, therefore, meaningless and irrational. *Political nihilism* is the social philosophy that society and its social, political, and economic popularized institutions are so corrupt that their complete destruction is desirable. Nihilists may, therefore, advocate violence and even terrorism in the name of overthrowing what they believe to be a corrupt social order. The term *nihilism* was first popularized in *Fathers and Sons* (1862) by the Russian novelist Turgenev.

Ordinary Language Philosophy The 20th-century school advocating that we can best understand and resolve philosophic problems by analyzing how people other than philosophers ordinarily use language and the presuppositions underlying such use; the school holds that everyday language is adequate for philosophy. Ludwig Wittgenstein, Gilbert Ryle, and John L. Austin (1911–60) were the most influential members of this school.

personalism A term applied to any philosophy that makes personality (whether of people, God, or spirit) the supreme value or the source of reality. Personalism as a movement flourished in England and America in the 19th and 20th centuries. Personalists are usually idealists.

phenomenology A 20th-century school founded by Edmund Husserl and an important influence on existentialism. This school developed its own philosophical "method" of using intuition for describing consciousness and experience. Phenomenologists claim that this method can be used to study the inherent qualities of phenomena as they appear to the mind. They attempt to classify and describe all phenomena without resorting to universal concepts or preconceived notions of reality. The focus is on the phenomena, not on how it is perceived.

philosophes Term applied to 18th-century French Enlightenment thinkers such as Jean-Jacques Rousseau, Denis Diderot, and Voltaire.

Platonism Thoughts and writings developed in the 4th century B.C. in Athens by Plato, the greatest student of Socrates. Platonism's chief tenet is that the ultimate reality consists of unchanging, absolute, eternal entities called Ideas or Forms; all earthly physical objects are not truly real but merely partake in the Forms.

pragmatism An American philosophy developed in the 19th century by Charles Sanders Peirce (1839–1914) and William James and elaborated on in the 20th century by John Dewey. Its central precepts are that thinking is primarily a guide to action and that the truth of a concept or idea could be determined only by testing it against experimental results and practical consequences.

Pre-Socratics   Name given to all Greek "theorists of nature" or philosophers who lived before Socrates. Major pre-Socratics include Anaximander, Pythagoras, and Thales.

Pythagoreans   Followers of Pythagoras. The group flourished until about 400 B.C. and were influential in philosophy, religion, mathematics, and science. They strongly influenced the thinking of Plato and Neoplatonists.

Scholasticism   A movement (c. 9th century–17th century), especially at the medieval universities, that attempted to reconcile Christian dogma with the empiricism of Aristotle. Its adherents used highly analytical logical and linguistic methods of argumentation, especially with respect to the problem of universals. Aquinas, the movement's greatest thinker, demonstrated that faith and reason were separate but compatible ideas; his teachings were accepted by the Catholic church.

17th-century rationalists   A broad term referring to the rationalism shared by René Descartes, Gottfried Leibniz, and Benedict Spinoza. It held that reason and deduction could provide knowledge of the world independent of experience.

Sophists   Wandering teachers in the 4th and 5th centuries B.C. in ancient Greece who taught any subjects that their paying students wished to learn, from grammar to public speaking. They were strongly ridiculed by Plato, who held that they were less interested in truth than in pleasing their students for a fee.

Stoicism   A Greek school founded by Zeno in the 3rd century B.C. Stoics held that people should submit to natural law and that a person's chief duty is to conform to his destiny. They also believed the soul to be another form of matter, and thus not immortal. Stoics rejected material comfort and advocated freedom from earthly passions and desires. They

viewed reality as materialistic and defined the organizing principle of the universe as force, or God.

Thomism   The philosophical and theological system developed by St. Thomas Aquinas in the 13th century. Specifically, it refers to Aquinas's synthesis of philosophy and theology, in which reason seeks knowledge through experiment and observation, while faith seeks understanding through divine revelation. The two are thus never in conflict; rather, both come from God. Thomism is accepted as a vital doctrine in the Roman Catholic Church.

transcendentalism   A 19th-century movement developed in New England and expounded by Ralph Waldo Emerson (1803–82) and Henry David Thoreau (1817–62). It maintains that beyond our material world of experience is an ideal spiritual reality that can be grasped intuitively. It advocates a reliance on personal conscience, based on perception and experience, over the dictates of external authority or moral conventions.

utilitarianism   A theory of morality formulated in the 19th century and holding that all actions should be judged for rightness or wrongness in terms of their consequences; thus, the amount of pleasure people derive from those consequences becomes the measure of moral goodness. Jeremy Bentham believed that happiness was the sole consequence by which actions should be judged. John Stuart Mill equated morality with the attainment of the maximum good for the greatest number of people. *See also* **principle of utility** under "Common Philosophical Terms."

Vienna Circle   A major school of logical positivism founded by Moritz Schlick (1882–1936) in the 1920s. It was known for its hostility to metaphysics and theology and for its belief that physics is the model for all knowledge of the world. Other leading members of the school were Rudolph Carnap (1891–1970) and Otto Neurath (1882–1945).

Go to "Major World Philosophers" and "Common Philosophical Terms" in this chapter

Philosophy

Young Hegelians   A group of thinkers in Germany in the first half of the 19th century whose views strongly influenced Karl Marx. They were followers of Georg Hegel who believed that the political conditions under which they lived were irrational. They held that the goal of philosophy should be to promote a revolution of ideas and critical thinking about the world. Ludwig Feuerbach (1804–72) was the most important of the Young Hegelians.

COMMON PHILOSOPHICAL TERMS

Entries in this glossary include basic terms and concepts used by philosophers, branches of philosophy, and "isms" that describe various philosophical attitudes, beliefs, doctrines, positions, precepts, theories, and viewpoints.

absolutism   The doctrine that there is one explanation of all reality—the absolute—that is unchanging and objectively true. Absolutists (such as G. W. F. Hegel) hold that this absolute, such as God or mind, is eternal and that in it all seeming differences are reconciled.

aesthetics (esthetics)   The philosophical study of art, or of beauty in general. It attempts to systematically answer such questions as, What is beauty? How do we evaluate works of art? Are aesthetic judgments objective or subjective? How does art embody truth and convey knowledge? How does beauty in art relate to beauty in nature?

agnosticism   The belief that it is impossible to know whether God exists, or to have any other theological knowledge. Thomas H. Huxley (1825–95) and Bertrand Russell were influential agnostics.

altruism   The ethical theory that morality consists of concern for and the active promotion of the interests of others. Altruists strongly disagree with the doctrine of egoism, which states that individuals act only in their own self-interest.

analytic statement   A statement true by definition, such as "All triangles have three sides."

anarchism   A political philosophy that advocates the abolition of an organized state as the ruling government. Its advocates believe that individuals should be free to organize themselves in the ways that best enable them to fulfill their needs and ideals. The Russian thinker Mikhail Bakunin (1814–76) was an influential anarchist.

angst   A German word meaning anxiety, anguish, or dread. The term was used by Martin Heidegger and other adherents of existentialism to express their belief that anxiety characterizes the human condition and that dread arises from our realization that we are totally responsible for all of our choices.

a posteriori knowledge   Knowledge based on or derived from sensory experience.

a priori knowledge   Knowledge acquired by the mind or reasoning alone, without any specific basis in experience—for instance, 2 + 2 = 4.

argument   An attempt to relate one set of statements, called the premises or the starting point, to another set, called the conclusion or the end point, by valid means. Arguments are either inductive or deductive. *See also* **syllogism.**

asceticism   The view that attention to the body's needs is evil, an obstacle to moral and spiritual development, and displeasing to God. According to this view, humans are urged to withdraw into an inner spiritual world to reach the good life.

associationism   A philosophical theory of the mind that holds that all mental states can be analyzed as separate component items and that all mental activity can be explained by the combining and recombining of these items, often called ideas. David Hume and John Stuart Mill were prominent advocates of this view. *See also* **association of ideas.**

association of ideas (laws of association)   The principles by which the mind connects ideas. Aristotle included similarity, contrast, and closeness; David Hume held the basic laws to be resemblance, closeness in time or place, and causality. Hume and

John Stuart Mill are the two most prominent philosophers who emphasized association as the basic principle of the mind. *See also* **associationism.**

Followers of conservative Franciscan philosopher Duns Scotus were called Dunsmen or Duncemen. Resisting more progressive forms of learning, they became regarded as dull or stupid. Hence, the term dunce.

atheism   The rejection of the belief in God. Some atheists have held that there is nothing in the world that requires a God in order to be explained. Atheism is not the same as agnosticism, which holds that we can have knowledge neither of the existence nor of the nonexistence of God.

atomism   The theory that reality is composed of simple and indivisible units (atoms) that are completely separate from and independent of one another. Philosophers have differed as to the nature of atoms; for instance, the Greek thinkers Leucippus and Democritus (5th century B.C.) held that the atoms are different-shaped bits of matter.

bad faith   Term used by Jean-Paul Sartre for self-deception and the deception of others caused by denying one's freedom of choice and one's responsibility for making decisions.

becoming   That which changes from one form to another, or, in Plato, that which is known only by experience and exists only temporarily. *See also* **being.**

being   Frequently used in metaphysics to contrast with appearance or nonexistence; often synonymous with unchanging substance, ultimate reality, God, infinity, or all that exists. Aristotle held that being is the subject matter of metaphysics. *See also* **becoming.**

Go to   "Philosophical Movements and Schools of Thought" and "Major World Philosophers" in this chapter

bioethics   A branch of philosophy that studies ethical issues that arise from conflicts between human rights and medical and biological research and the technology they use. Areas of concern are genetic manipulation, euthanasia, and brain control.

Buridan's ass   A story, falsely attributed to the 14th-century thinker John Buridan, in which an ass, faced with two equally desirable bales of hay, starves to death because he cannot find a good reason for preferring one bale to the other.

categorical imperative   Immanuel Kant's term for the binding moral law, which dictates that one should act only according to a maxim that could serve as a universal law—for instance, to treat humanity as an end and never only as a means.

cause   Whatever is responsible for change, action, or motion. Historically, Aristotle's analysis of cause falls into four types: material cause, the substance a thing is made of; formal cause, the design of the thing; efficient cause, the maker of the thing; and final cause, its purpose or function. David Hume argued that all knowledge of cause comes from our actual experience of observed regularities.

certainty   According to René Descartes, a condition of knowing that anything is true; various types of statements—for example, 1 + 1 = 2, or all widows are female—have certainty.

chain of being   An idea, originating with Plato and very influential in Western thought into the Renaissance, that all possible things are realized in the world in an ordered chain of diminishing complexity and richness, from God down to the tiniest, humblest bit of matter. The view captures the concept of the universe as an ordered hierarchy.

conceptualism   The doctrine, intermediate between nominalism and realism, that general ideas, such as the idea of man or of redness, exist explicitly in the human mind as concepts and implicitly in the minds of all people. These concepts are not arbitrary ideas, but reflect the similarities between particular things.

Philosophy

cosmogony   A theory or story about the origin of the universe, either scientific or mythological. Cosmogonies are also called creation myths.

cosmology   The systematic study of the origin and structure of the universe as a whole. Such philosophers as Plato, Aristotle, and Immanuel Kant considered cosmology to be a metaphysical speculation; today cosmology is a branch of the physical sciences.

counterexample   A specific fact that refutes or negates a generalization; for instance, a black swan is a counterexample to the statement "All swans are white."

deductive reasoning   Reasoning from a general statement to a particular or specific example; for example, "All cats are mortal; William is a cat; therefore, William is mortal." *See also* **syllogism.**

deontology   The ethical philosophy that makes duty the basis of all morality. According to deontological theorists, such as Immanuel Kant, some acts —such as keeping a promise or telling the truth— are moral obligations regardless of their consequences.

determinism   The view that every event has a cause and that everything in the universe is absolutely dependent on and governed by causal laws. Because determinists believe that all events, including human actions, are predetermined, determinism is typically thought to be incompatible with free will.

dialectic   A term with different meanings for different philosophers. It derives from the Greek word meaning "to converse" and is used to describe

---

A Closer Look

More Than Just Philosophers

Before knowledge was as specialized as it is today, many of the greatest philosophers followed their other interests while creating or studying philosophical systems. They did groundbreaking work in areas as far afield from philosophy proper as geometry, zoology, literary criticism, and calculus.

Perhaps Aristotle was the model for some of these thinkers, because he was regarded not only in his own time but also throughout most of the Middle Ages as a universal genius whose knowledge on any subject he had written on could hardly be questioned. His nonphilosophical writings were astonishingly broad; even a partial list of his subjects, which include physics, zoology, botany, sociology, political theory, and economics, is testimony to one of the greatest minds of all time.

Even medicine and the law were not too far afield for some of the great philosophers. Avicenna, Averroes, and John Locke were trained in medicine; Avicenna's *Canon of Medicine* was the most influential medieval medical treatise. And Jeremy Bentham, a founder of utilitarianism, was one of the most influential jurists and lawyers of the 19th century; his work deeply influenced reform of the British penal, judicial, and parliamentary systems.

History, too, is a philosopher's domain. *History of England,* not his philosophy books, brought David Hume success and renown in mid-18th-century England.

Both mathematics and logic were fruitfully developed by philosophers when they were not writing philosophical works. Gottfried Leibniz is the coinventor of calculus, along with Sir Isaac Newton; Blaise Pascal is one of the founders of the modern theory of probability; and Descartes invented analytical geometry almost singlehandedly.

Logic, although now a separate discipline, was a part of philosophy until the late 19th century. Aristotle was the founder of logic, but many other philosophers have invented or organized entire sections of the field. John Stuart Mill formulated the "rules" of scientific experimentation that are now called Mill's methods; and Bertrand Russell and Alfred North Whitehead wrote *Principia Mathematica,* probably the most important work in modern logic.

The list of philosophers engaged in other fields is seemingly endless. Examples include Friedrich Nietzsche, whose *On the Birth of Tragedy* is a classic in Greek studies and literary criticism; William James, whose *Principles of Psychology* deeply influenced decades of thinking in that field; and John Dewey, the father of the American progressive education movement.

Socrates's method of teaching by question-and-answer technique. Plato used the word to mean the study of the Forms. To Immanuel Kant, it meant a method of criticizing claims of knowledge going beyond experience. Georg Hegel means by it the necessary pattern of thinking.

doubt   According to René Descartes, the argument that nothing can be considered true unless it can never be doubted under any conditions. Descartes doubted everything "systematically" to find out if anything is indubitable; his "*Cogito, ergo sum*" ("I think, therefore I am") survived his test.

dualism   Any philosophical theory holding that the universe consists of, or can only be explained by, two independent and separate forces, such as matter and spirit, the forces of good and evil, or the supernatural and natural. *See also* **mind-body problem.**

duty   According to many ethical theories, the basis of the virtuous life. The Stoics held that man has a duty to live virtuously and according to reason; and Immanuel Kant held that his categorical imperative is the highest law of duty, no matter what the consequences.

egocentric predicament   The belief that each of us is limited to, and by, our unique pattern of perceptions. Any knowledge of the world outside our minds would thus be colored by our perceptions. *See also* **solipsism.**

egoism   The ethical theory that each person should forward his or her own self-interest. Egoists sometimes argue that this is not selfishness, but that self-interest is compatible with helping others as well. Some egoists also argue that, psychologically speaking, human beings always in fact seek their own well-being.

élan vital   *See* **vitalism.**

empirical   Based on experience, observation, or facts—in short, describing any knowledge derived from or validated by sensory experience.

empiricism   The view that all knowledge of the world derives solely from sensory experience, using

observation and experimentation if needed; empiricism also holds that reason on its own can never provide knowledge of reality unless it also utilizes experience. Empiricism suggests that any concept of the physical world is nothing more than a generalization derived from particular circumstances.

epistemology   The branch of philosophy that studies how knowledge is gained, how much we can know, and what justification there is for what is known.

eschatology   In theology, the study of "final things," such as death, resurrection, immortality, the second coming of Christ, and the day of judgment.

essence   That which makes a specific thing what it is and not something else; its nature. While the Greek philosophers viewed essence and substance as basically the same, St. Thomas Aquinas and the philosophy of Scholasticism held that even nonexistent things have natures or essences distinguishable from the fact of their existence.

esthetics   *See* **aesthetics.**

euthanasia   The act of allowing a terminally ill person to freely choose when and how he or she will die; mercy killing.

fatalism   The belief that "what will be will be," because all past, present, and future events have already been predetermined by God or another all-powerful force. In religion, this view may be called predestination; it holds that whether our souls go to heaven or hell is determined before we are born and is independent of our good deeds.

Forms   According to Plato, the eternal, unchanging, immaterial, and perfect archetypes of which all existing things are merely imperfect copies; also called Ideas.

four elements   According to many early Greek philosophers, the four basic constituents of the physical world: earth, air, fire, and water.

free will   The theory that human beings have freedom of choice or self-determination; that is, that

Philosophy

given a situation, a person could have done other than what he did. Philosophers have argued that free will is incompatible with determinism. *See also* **indeterminism.**

golden mean　The ethical doctrine, originating with Aristotle, that virtuous actions fall exactly between too much of some quality, such as impulsive behavior, and too little of it, such as timidity. It is associated with ethics calling for moderation.

"Peanuts" creator Charles M. Schulz once quipped, "There's a difference between a philosophy and a bumper sticker."

golden rule　The fundamental moral rule of most religions, especially Christianity, that states, "Do unto others as you would have others do unto you."

greatest happiness principle　*See* **principle of utility; utilitarianism** under "Philosophical Movements and Schools of Thought."

Hobson's choice　A choice offered without any real alternative—therefore, not really a choice at all.

humanism　Any philosophic view that holds that humankind's well-being and happiness in this lifetime are primary and that the good of all humanity is the highest ethical goal. Twentieth-century humanists tend to reject all beliefs in the supernatural, relying instead on scientific methods and reason. The term is also used to refer to Renaissance thinkers, especially in 15th-century Italy, who emphasized the revival of classical studies, or the humanities, and knowledge and learning not based on religious sources.

idealism　A term applied to any philosophy holding that mind or spiritual values, rather than material things or matter, are primary in the universe.

immortality　The view that the individual soul is eternal, and thus survives the death of the body it resides in. *See also* **transmigration of souls.**

indeterminism　The view that there are events that do not have any cause; many proponents of free will believe that acts of choice are capable of not being determined by any physiological or psychological cause.

inductive reasoning　Any process of reasoning from something particular to something general, or from a part to a whole. Inductive reasoning can be valid or invalid.

innate ideas　Ideas that are inborn and part of the mind at birth, rather than based on specific experiences. René Descartes believed there are "clear and distinct" ideas that are innate and that form the basis of all knowledge. Plato believed that knowledge of the Forms derives from innate ideas.

instrumentalism　A theory that holds that ideas and concepts should be regarded as tools or instruments to be used in specific situations. As such, they cannot be described as true or false, but only as effective or ineffective. This theory was first put forth by John Dewey.

justice　According to most philosophers, starting with Plato, the harmonious balance between the rights of the various members of a society. Justice is usually understood as including such social virtues as fairness, equality, and correct and impartial treatment.

language, philosophy of　*See* **philosophy of language.**

language game　A concept introduced by Ludwig Wittgenstein, who drew an analogy between how we use language and how we play games: Both have rules and moves that make sense only in the context of a particular game. Wittgenstein and his followers used this concept to point out that philosophers frequently try to make moves in one context that make sense only in another, as when they try to verify religious statements as if they were a part of science.

logic　The study of the rules and the nature of reasoning and of valid or sound patterns of thought. Aristotle classified many of the rules of reasoning. In the late 19th and early 20th centuries, logic was advanced into a branch of mathematics. Currently, mathematical logic is a growing field independent of philosophy. *See also* **syllogism.**

materialism   The theory that holds that the nature of the world is dependent on matter, or that matter is the only fundamental substance; thus, spirit and mind either do not exist or are manifestations of matter. Prevalent throughout the history of western civilization, this theory appeared as early as the 4th century B.C. in the teachings of Democritus, and it formed the basis for dialectical materialism, the philosophical doctrine underlying communism.

mathematical logic   *See* **logic.**

mathematics, philosophy of   *See* **philosophy of mathematics.**

mechanism   The philosophical theory that states that living organisms, including humans, are complex machines, because they are composed of matter.

metaethics   A branch of philosophy that analyzes ethics. It is concerned with such issues as, How are moral decisions justified? What is the foundation of any ethical view? What language is used to state moral beliefs?

metaphysics   The branch of philosophy concerned with the ultimate nature of reality and existence as a whole. Metaphysics also includes the study of cosmology and philosophical theology. Aristotle produced the first "system" of metaphysics.

metempsychosis   *See* **transmigration of souls.**

mind   *See* **philosophy of mind.**

mind-body problem   A central problem of modern philosophy that originated with René Descartes. It asks how the mind and the body are related.

monad   According to Leibniz, the ultimate and indivisible unit of all existence. Monads are not material, like atoms; each monad is self-activating, a unique center of force. All monads are in a "preestablished harmony" with each other and with God, the supreme monad.

monism   A term introduced in the 18th century to describe any theory that explains all phenomena by a single unifying principle or that reduces everything in the universe to one fundamental substance, energy, or force. In Georg Hegel, this concept can be seen in his vision of the world as a single organism, developing through a dialectical process. Benedict Spinoza held that mind and spirit are aspects of single entity, which he called God or nature.

mysticism   Any philosophy whose roots are in mystical experiences, intuitions, or direct experiences of the divine. In such experiences, the mystic believes that his or her soul has temporarily achieved union with God. Mystics believe reality can be known only in this manner, not through reasoning or everyday experience.

myth of Er   A parable at the end of Plato's *Republic* about the fate of souls after bodily death; according to Plato, the soul must choose wisdom in the afterlife to guarantee a good life in its next cycle of incarnation.

natural law   The theory that there is a higher law than the humanmade laws put forth by specific governments. This law is universal, unchanging, and a fundamental part of human nature. Advocates of this view believe that natural law can be discovered by reason alone. The theory originated with the Stoics and was elaborated on by St. Thomas Aquinas, among others.

natural rights   Certain freedoms or privileges that are held to be an innate part of the nature of being a human being and that cannot be denied by society. These are different from civil rights, which are granted by a specific nation or government. Philosophers have differed on which rights are natural, but usually included are life, liberty, equality, equal treatment under the law, the pursuit of happiness, and equality of opportunity. John Locke's influential views on natural rights inspired the writers of the U.S. Constitution.

A
Closer
Look

God's Existence—Proofs For

While theology may take God's existence as absolutely necessary on the basis of authority, faith, or revelation, many philosophers—and some theologians—have thought it possible to demonstrate by reason that there must be a God.

St. Thomas Aquinas, in the 13th century, formulated the famous "five ways" by which God's existence can be demonstrated philosophically:

1. *The "unmoved mover" argument.* We know that there is motion in the world; whatever is in motion is moved by another thing; this other thing also must be moved by something; to avoid an infinite regression, we must posit a "first mover," which is God.
2. *The "nothing is caused by itself" argument.* For example, a table is brought into being by a carpenter, who is caused by his parents. Again, we cannot go on to infinity, so there must be a first cause, which is God.
3. *The cosmological argument.* All physical things—even mountains, boulders, and rivers—come into being and go out of existence, no matter how long they last. Therefore, because time is infinite, there must be some time at which none of these things existed. But if there were nothing at that point in time, how could there be anything at all now, because nothing cannot cause anything? Thus, there must always have been at least one necessary thing that is eternal, which is God.
4. *Objects in the world have differing degrees of qualities such as goodness.* But speaking of more or less goodness makes sense only by comparison with what is the maximum goodness, which is God.
5. *The teleological argument (argument from design).* Things in the world move toward goals, just as the arrow does not move toward its goal except by the archer's directing it. Thus, there must be an intelligent designer who directs all things to their goals, and this is God.

Two other historically important "proofs" are the ontological argument and the moral argument. The former, made famous by St. Anselm in the 11th century and defended in another form by René Descartes, holds that it would be logically contradictory to deny God's existence. St. Anselm began by defining God as "that [being] than which nothing greater can be conceived." If God existed only in the mind, He then would not be the greatest conceivable being, for we could imagine another being that is greater because it would exist both in the mind and in reality, and that being would then be God. Therefore, to imagine God as existing only in the mind but not in reality leads to a logical contradiction; this proves the existence of God both in the mind and in reality.

Immanuel Kant rejected not only the ontological argument but the teleological and cosmological arguments as well, based on his theory that reason is too limited to know anything beyond human experience. He did argue, however, that religion could be established as presupposed by the workings of morality in the human mind ("practical reason"). God's existence is a necessary presupposition of there being any moral judgments that are objective, that go beyond mere relativistic moral preferences; such judgments require standards external to any human mind—that is, they presume God's mind.

---

naturalism   A philosophic view stating that all there is in reality is what the physical and human sciences (for example, physics or psychology) study and that there is no need to posit any supernatural forces or being, such as God, mind, or spirit.

naturalistic fallacy   A belief of many 20th-century philosophers in England and the United States that it is invalid to infer any statements of morality (for example, "Men ought to act kindly") from factual statements (for example, "Kindness is a natural quality"). The notion tries to derive *ought* from *is* and was first described by David Hume.

necessary and contingent truth   Terms used by philosophers to contrast two types of statements, such as "All widowers are male," which is necessarily true, and "All widowers are over 20 years old," which may be true but is not necessarily true.

nominalism   A doctrine, prevalent in the Middle Ages, that maintained that ideas and objects exist only in the particular instance, not as abstract concepts or forms. In opposition to realism, it held that all universals are merely names and have no existence of their own.

God's Existence—Arguments Against

A Closer Look

Arguments against God's existence have been given by philosophers, atheists, and agnostics. Some of these arguments find God's existence incompatible with observed facts; some are arguments that God does not exist because the concept of God is incoherent or confused. Others are criticisms of the proofs offered *for* God's existence.

One of the most influential and powerful "proofs" that there is no God proceeds from "The Problem from Evil." This argument claims that the following three statements cannot *all* be true: (a) evil exists; (b) God is omnipotent; and (c) God is all-loving. The argument is as follows:

- If God can prevent evil, but *doesn't,* then He isn't all-loving.
- If God intends to prevent evil, but *cannot,* then He isn't omnipotent.
- If God *both* intends to prevent evil and is capable of doing so, then how can evil exist?

Another argument claims that the existence of an all-knowing God is incompatible with the fact of free will—that humans do make choices. If God is omniscient, He must know beforehand exactly what a person will do in a given situation. In that case, a person is not in fact free to do the alternative to what God knows he or she will do, and free will must be an illusion. To take this one step further, if one chooses to commit a sin, how can it then be said that one sinned freely?

David Hume provided powerful critiques of the main arguments for God's existence. Against the cosmological argument (Aquinas's third argument), Hume argued that the idea of a necessarily existing being is absurd. He stated, "Whatever we can conceive as existent, we can also conceive as nonexistent." Hume also asked why the ultimate source of the universe could not be the entire universe itself, eternal and uncaused, without a God?

Hume also criticized the argument from design (Aquinas's fifth argument). In particular, he emphasized that there is no legitimate way we can infer the properties of God as the creator of the world from the qualities of His creation. For instance, Hume questioned how we can be sure that the world was not created by a team; or that this is not one of many attempts at creations, the first few having been botched; or, on the other hand, that our world is not a poor first attempt "of an infant deity who afterwards abandoned it, ashamed of his lame performance."

non sequitur   A Latin phrase meaning "it does not follow"; any argument where the conclusion drawn has not even the slightest connection to the premises offered.

objectivism   The view that there are moral truths that are valid universally and that it is wrong to knowingly gain pleasure from causing another pain.

obligation   In ethics, a moral necessity to do a specific deed. Some ethicists, following Immanuel Kant, hold that moral obligations are absolute. *See also* **categorical imperative.**

Ockham's razor   A principle attributed to the 14th-century English philosopher William of Ockham. It states that entities should not be mul-

tiplied beyond necessity, or that one should choose the simplest explanation, the one requiring the fewest assumptions and principles.

ontology   A branch of metaphysics that studies the nature of existence or reality, as such, as opposed to specific types of existing entities.

operationalism (operationism)   A philosophy of science according to which any scientific concept must be definable in terms of concrete, observable activities or the operations to which it refers.

optimism   The philosophic attitude that this is the best of all possible worlds, that hope and joy are justified, and that all things are ordered for the best. According to optimists, such as Gottfried Leibniz, evil either is an illusion or will be compensated for by an even greater good.

pantheism   The belief that God and the universe are identical; among modern philosophers, Benedict Spinoza is considered to be a pantheist.

particulars   *See* **universals.**

Pascal's wager   An argument made by Blaise Pascal for believing in God. Pascal said that either the tenets of Roman Catholicism are true or they are not. If they are true, and we wager that they are true, then we have won an eternity of bliss; if they are false, and death is final, what has the bettor lost? On the other hand, if one wagers against God's existence and turns out to be wrong, there is eternal damnation.

pessimism   The philosophic attitude holding that hope is unreasonable, that a person is born to sorrow, and that this is the worst of all possible worlds. Arthur Schopenhauer's philosophy is an example of extreme pessimism.

phenomenalism   The doctrine that the only knowledge we can ever have is of appearances, and thus that we can never know the nature of ultimate reality. Major adherents of the philosophy were John Stuart Mill and some members of the Vienna Circle.

philosopher king   In Plato's *Republic,* a philosopher trained by formal study in disciplines including mathematics and philosophy. Plato emphasized that philosopher kings' leadership would be shown by their ability to see the Forms, or universal ideals. *See also* **Forms.**

philosophy of language   The area of philosophic study whose subject matter is the nature and workings of language. Detailed discussions of such topics as meaning, reference, grammar, and symbols infuse this branch of philosophy.

philosophy of mathematics   A branch of philosophy that studies such questions as, What are mathematical statements about? Why is mathematics true? How do we come to have mathematical knowledge? Why is mathematics so useful in studying reality?

philosophy of mind   The area of philosophy that studies the mind, consciousness, and mental functions such as thinking, intention, imagination, and emotion. It is not one specific branch of philosophy, but rather an aspect of most traditional branches, such as metaphysics, epistemology, and aesthetics.

philosophy of religion   A branch of philosophy concerned with such questions as, What is religion? What is God? Can God's existence be proved? Is there immortality? What is the relationship between faith, reason, and revelation? Is there a divine purpose in the world?

philosophy of science   The branch of philosophy that studies the nature of science. It is particularly concerned with the methods, concepts, and assumptions of science, as well as with analyzing scientific concepts such as space, time, cause, scientific law, and verification.

physicalism   A theory about knowledge that originated within the Vienna Circle. It holds that all factual statements can be reduced to observations of physical objects and events. *See also* **operationalism.**

Plato's cave   An analogy in Plato's *Republic* between reality and illusion. The main image is of people who see on the walls of a cave only the shadows of the real objects moving around outside the cave. When these people leave the cave and see the real objects, they cannot, upon returning to the cave, convince those who have never left of the reality of the objects.

pluralism   The view that there are more than two kinds of fundamental, irreducible realities in the universe, or that there are many separate and independent levels of reality.

political philosophy   The branch of philosophy that studies a person as a political animal. It is concerned with such questions as, What obligations do I have to my government? How is political power justified? Under what conditions is war justified? It also studies the nature of property, justice, freedom, liberty, and political rights.

positivism   A theory originated by French philosopher Auguste Comte. It holds that all knowledge is defined by the limits of scientific investigation; thus, philosophy must abandon any quest for knowledge of an ultimate reality or any knowledge beyond that offered by science.

predestination   *See* **fatalism.**

premises   *See* **argument.**

principle (or law) of noncontradiction   Dating back to Aristotle, this universally accepted "law of thought" has two parts: A statement cannot be both true and false; nothing can both have a quality, like red, and not have it, at the same time.

The long sought-after philosopher's stone was believed by alchemists to have the power to change base metals into silver or gold.

principle of sufficient reason   The philosophical doctrine of Leibniz that asserts that for every fact there is a reason for its being the way it is rather than another way, even though we may not know that reason.

principle of utility (greatest happiness principle)   The basic tenet of utilitarianism. It states that the highest ethical good provides the greatest happiness for the greatest number of people.

psychologism   A view of philosophy holding that all philosophic concepts and problems are explainable based on psychological principles and that they should be treated by some form of psychological analysis. Advocates of this view may disagree on the type of psychological approach that is appropriate.

QED   Latin for *quod erat demonstrandum* ("that which was to be demonstrated"). This abbreviation is often used right before or after stating a conclusion, as a synonym for *therefore, thus,* or *as was to be shown.*

rationalism   A doctrine holding that reason or thinking alone, without recourse to observation or experience, can apprehend basic truths. The notion of innate, universal concepts is naturally associated with this theory. René Descartes, Gottfried Leibniz, Benedict Spinoza, and Georg Hegel were all essentially rationalists in their approach to the foundations of knowledge.

realism   The major medieval and modern view, other than nominalism, on the problem of universals. *Extreme realism,* which is close to Plato's theory of Forms, holds that universals exist independently of both particular things and the human mind; *moderate realism,* put forth by St. Thomas Aquinas, holds that universals exist as ideas in God's mind, through which He creates things.

reincarnation   *See* **transmigration of souls.**

relativism   The precept that people's ideas of right and wrong vary considerably from place to place and time to time; therefore, there are no universally valid ethical standards.

religion, philosophy of   *See* **philosophy of religion.**

science, philosophy of   *See* **philosophy of science.**

sensationalism   An empiricist theory of knowledge that holds that sensations are both the source of all knowledge and the ultimate verification of any statements. Thomas Hobbes originated the view; Étienne Condillac (1715–1880) and Ernst Mach (1838–1916) developed it.

sense data   The sensory qualities or feelings we experience directly, such as shapes, colors, and smells, without any interpretation of the material objects that may be causing them. Some empiricists and sensationalist philosophers make sense data the foundation of all factual knowledge.

skepticism   The philosophic theory that no certain knowledge can be attained by humans. Broadly speaking, skepticism states that all knowledge should be questioned and tested—for instance, by the scientific method.

social contract   That concept of an agreement between people, or between people and government or ruler, in which it is agreed that some personal liberties will be given up in exchange for the security of stable political rule. The term is used in the political philosophy of Thomas Hobbes, John Locke, and Jean-Jacques Rousseau to justify a form of political authority.

solipsism   The theory that one cannot know anything other than his or her own thoughts, feelings, or perceptions; therefore, other people and the real world must be projections of one's own mind with no existence in and of themselves. *See also* **egocentric predicament.**

spiritism   A term referring to the belief that spirits of the dead communicate with the living—for instance, at seances or through a medium.

spiritualism   The view that the ultimate reality in the universe is the spirit. Advocates of this view may disagree about the nature of the spirit.

state of nature   A term used by 17th- and 18th-century social philosophers such as Thomas Hobbes, John Locke, and Jean-Jacques Rousseau. It referred to the condition of humans without political organization, or before government.

subjectivism   The theory that all moral values are completely dependent on the personal tastes, feelings, or inclinations of the individual and have no source of validity outside such human subjective states of mind.

substance   A changeless, self-subsistent entity, not dependent on anything else, that underlies being in all its forms. It has been identified with God, mind, matter, and self-contained ultimate realities. *See also* **monad.**

supernaturalism   The belief that there are forces, energies, or beings beyond the material world—such as God, spirit, or occult forces—that affect events in our world.

syllogism   A kind of deductive reasoning or argument. As defined by Aristotle, it was considered the basis of reasoning for over two thousand years. In every syllogism, there are two statements (premises) from which a conclusion follows necessarily. Syllogisms are of three basic logical types, as illustrated by the following examples. *See also* **argument.**

1. If a broom is new, it sweeps clean; the broom is new; therefore, it sweeps clean.
2. Either the horse is male or female; the horse is not female; therefore, it is male.
3. All philosophers are men; all men are mortal; therefore, all philosophers are mortal.

synthetic statement   A factual statement describing a state of affairs, such as "Triangles are used in architectural studios."

tabula rasa   A Latin phrase meaning "blank slate," used by John Locke to describe the state of the human mind at birth. Locke believed there are no innate ideas and that the mind gets all of its ideas from experience.

tautology   Any statement that is necessarily true merely because of its meaning, such as "Bachelors are unmarried males" or "Every green object is colored." *See also* **necessary and contingent truth.**

teleological ethics   In contrast with deontological ethics, this moral theory holds that whether an action is morally right depends solely on its expected consequences.

transcendent   Beyond the realm of sense experience. In many religious views, God is held to be transcendent.

transmigration of souls (metempsychosis; reincarnation)   The belief that the same soul can, in different lifetimes (incarnations), reside in different bodies, human or animal. While typically a part of most Eastern religions, the doctrine came into Western philosophy from Pythagoras and his contemporaries in the 6th century B.C. and especially through Plato.

universals   The properties, or the abstract or general words, that apply to many individual things, called particulars. Redness, for instance, is a universal that applies to all red things.

utopianism The belief in the possibility or desirability of not just a better but a perfect society. The term derives from Sir Thomas More's *Utopia* (1516), which depicts an ideal state. Utopian states also appear in the writings of Plato and Sir Francis Bacon.

vitalism The theory that living organisms are inherently different from inanimate bodies; thus, life cannot be explained fully by materialistic theories as it is based on a vital force that is unlike other physical forces. Aristotle, Hans Driesch (1867–1941), and Henri Bergson (1859–1941) were prominent vitalists. In Bergson's view, the élan vital is the evolutionary force in organisms that propels life to achieve higher levels of structure.

will to believe A phrase made famous by William James. He held that in the absence of decisive evidence, the mind may create belief in order to act, often resulting in discovery. He also maintained that believing in such situations is a human right that should not be backed away from.

will to power The view, expounded by Friedrich Nietzsche, that power is the chief motivating force in human nature. The view was influential in 20th-century psychology and social science.

ADDITIONAL SOURCES OF INFORMATION

ORGANIZATIONS AND SERVICES

The Philosophy Documentation Center (P.O. Box 7147, Charlottesville, VA 22906) is a key source of information. Its publications include U.S. and international directories of philosophers, consciousness studies, and bibliographies. In conjunction with the InteLex Corporation, the PDC offers an online service that provides subscription-based access to dozens of philosophy journals. The PDC and InteLex currently operate Past Masters®, an online database containing the complete works of 30 philosophers ranging from Anselm to Wittgenstein. The PDC home page can be accessed at http://www.pdcnet.org.

BOOKS

Blackburn, Simon. *The Oxford Dictionary of Philosophy.* Oxford University Press, 1996.

Christian, James. *Philosophy: An Introduction to the Art of Wondering.* 7th ed. Harcourt Brace, 1998.

Collinson, Diane, ed. *Biographical Dictionary of 20th-Century Philosophers.* Routledge, 1996.

The Concise Routledge Encyclopedia of Philosophy. Routledge, 2000.

Copleston, Frederick C. *History of Philosophy.* 9 vols. Image, 1994.

Craig, Edward. *The Routledge Encyclopedia of Philosophy.* 10 vols. Routledge, 1998.

Deutsch, Eliot, and Ron Bontekoe, eds. *A Companion Guide to World Philosophies.* Blackwell, 1997.

Durant, Will. *The Story of Philosophy.* Pocket Books, 1991.

Edwards, Paul, ed. *The Encyclopedia of Philosophy.* 4 vols. Free Press, 1973.

Ferm, Vergilius. *A History of Philosophical Systems.* Ayer, 1977.

Gregory, Richard L. *The Oxford Companion to the Mind.* Oxford University Press, 1987.

Jaspers, Karl. *The Great Philosophers.* 4 vols. Harcourt Brace, 1993.

Lacey, A. R. *A Dictionary of Philosophy.* 3rd ed. Routledge, 1996.

Lineback, Richard, ed. *The Philosopher's Index.* 34 vols. Philosopher's Information Center, 1967–2001.

Magill, Frank N., ed. *Masterpieces of World Philosophy.* HarperCollins, 1990.

O'Connor, D. J. *A Critical History of Western Philosophy.* Free Press, 1985.

Reese, William L., ed. *Dictionary of Philosophy and Religion: Eastern and Western Thought.* 2nd ed. Humanities Press, 1996.

Runes, Dagobert D., ed. *Dictionary of Philosophy.* Littlefield, 1984,

Philosophy

Russell, Bertrand. *A History of Western Philosophy.* Routledge, 1993.

Scharfstein, Ben-Ami. *A Comparative History of World Philosophy.* State University of New York Press, 1998.

Solomon, Robert C., and Kathleen M. Higgins. *A Short History of Philosophy.* Oxford University Press, 1996.

Urmson, James O. *A Concise Encyclopedia of Western Philosophy and Philosophers.* 3 rd ed. Hyman, 1990.

Warburton, Nigel. *Philosophy: Basic Readings.* Routledge, 1999.

Weiner, Philip P., ed. *Dictionary of the History of Ideas: Studies of Selected Pivotal Ideas.* 5 vols. Scribners, 1985.

WEB SITES

The Internet Encyclopedia of Philosophy
http://www.utm.edu/research/iep

Meta-Encyclopedia of Philosophy
http://www.ditext.com/encyc/frame.html

Philosophy in Cyberspace
http://www-personal.monash.edu.au/~dey/phil

Stanford Encyclopedia of Philosophy
http://plato.stanford.edu

Philosophy

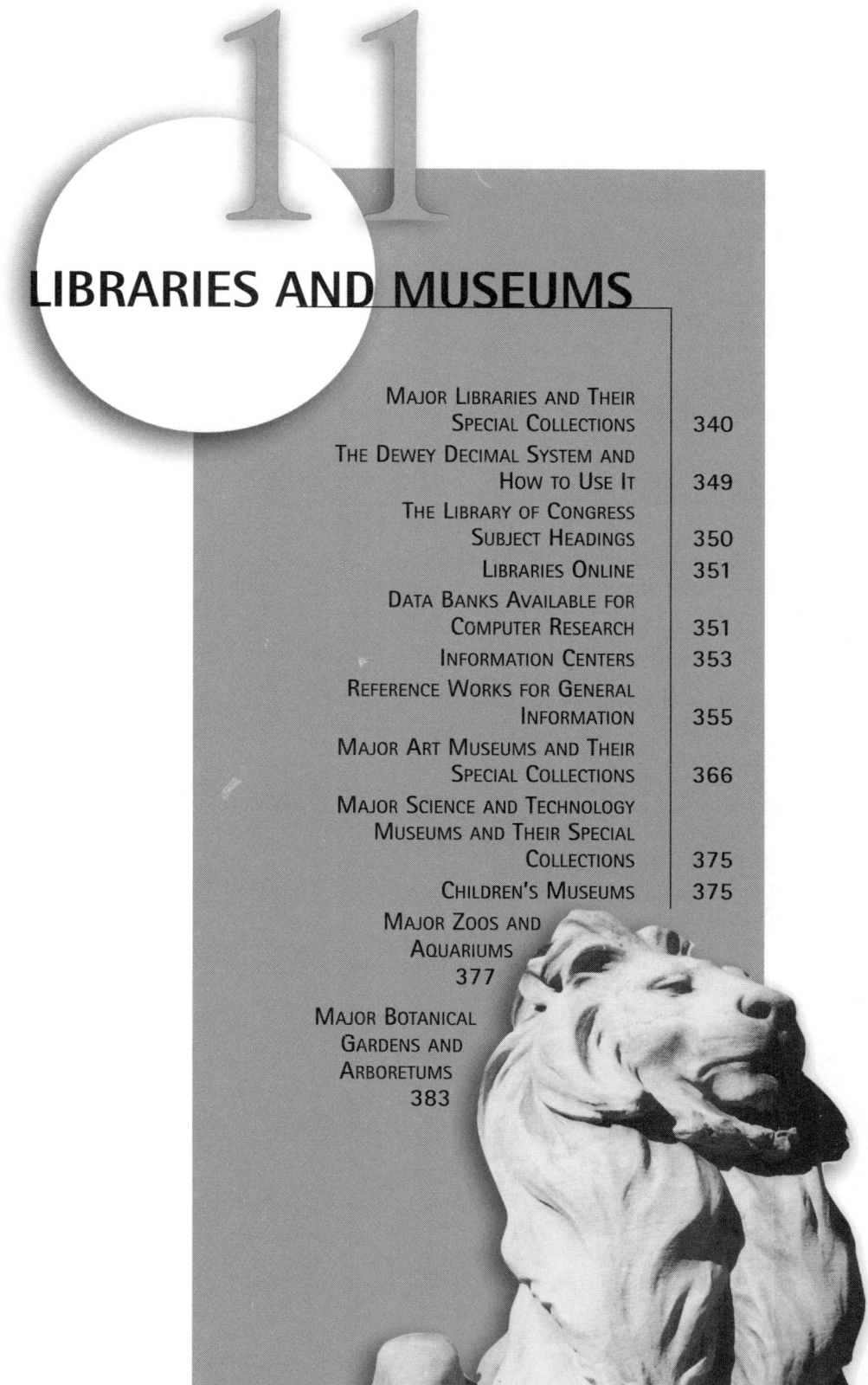

11

LIBRARIES AND MUSEUMS

MAJOR LIBRARIES AND THEIR SPECIAL COLLECTIONS

UNITED STATES

Arizona

University of Arizona Library
P.O. Box 210055
1510 E. University
Tucson, AZ 85721
520-621-2101
http://www.library.arizona.edu/

Established in 1891, the University of Arizona has more than 3.7 million volumes, with special collections on photography as an art form, fine arts, drama, private presses, Southwestern Americana, Arizona, science history, science fiction, and Mexican colonial history.

American libraries are used by two-thirds of the population but are financed with less than 1% of tax dollars.

California

County of Los Angeles Public Library, Administration
7400 E. Imperial Hwy.
Downey, CA 90241
562-940-8415
http://www.colapublib.org/

Founded in 1912, this library system contains more than 5.5 million volumes, with special collections on Afro-American studies, Asian-Pacific studies, California, multimedia, mountaineering, Hispanic-Americans, Native Americans, and poetry. The collection is dispersed among 114 community, mobile, and institutional libraries.

Los Angeles Public Library System
630 W. Fifth St.
Los Angeles, CA 90071
213-228-7515
http://www.lapl.org/

Founded in 1872, this public library system has 62 branches with more than 6.1 million volumes. Its special collections are on California studies, children's literature, cooking, genealogy, Native American studies, modern languages, orchestral scores, U.S. patents, and standards and specifications.

Stanford University Libraries & Academic Information Resources
Green Library Information Center
557 Escondido Mall
Stanford, CA 94305
650-725-1064
http://www.sul.stanford.edu/

Founded in 1892, Stanford's libraries contain 5.4 million volumes. Its special collections cover transportation, music, science, California, Irish literature, engineering mechanics, children's literature, Chicano studies, theater, and Hebraica and Judaica.

University of California, Berkeley
245 Doe Library
Berkeley, CA 94720
510-642-3773
http://www.lib.berkeley.edu/

Founded in 1871, this library contains more than 8.1 million volumes. Special collections include the letters, literary manuscripts, and scrapbooks of Samuel Clemens (Mark Twain Collection) and Recollections of Persons Who Have Contributed to the Development of the West (Regional Oral History Office).

University of California Los Angeles Library
11334 University Research Library
P.O. Box 951575
Los Angeles, CA 90095
310-825-1201
http://www.library.ucla.edu/

Founded in 1919, the University of California Los Angeles Library has holdings of more than 6.4 million books. It has special collections on British Commonwealth history, contemporary Western writers, early English children's books, folklore, Latin American studies, Mazarinades, mountaineering, and Western Americana.

University of Southern California
Edward L. Doheny Memorial Library
University Park
3550 Trousdale Parkway
Los Angeles, CA 90089-0182
213-740-2543
http://www.usc.edu/library/

Founded in 1880, the University of Southern California has more than 2.7 million volumes, with a number of independent departmental libraries whose subject matter ranges from architecture and fine arts to gerontology. Its special collections include Native American ethnopharmacology, American literature, cinema, dentistry, international relations, Latin American studies, and philosophy.

Colorado

University of Colorado, Boulder
University Libraries Campus Box 184
Boulder, CO 80309-0184
303-492-7511
http://www.colorado.edu/

Founded in 1876, the University of Colorado maintains holdings of more than 2 million volumes, with special collections on juvenile literature, the history of silver, mountaineering, and Western U.S. history.

Connecticut

Yale University Library
120 High St.
P.O. Box 208240
New Haven, CT 06520
203-432-1818
http://www.library.yale.edu/

The second largest university library in the United States, Yale has 10.5 million volumes in its collection. Its rare books total more than 500,000. Yale's special collections are numerous; they include works by James Boswell, the Aaron Burr family, Daniel Defoe, John Dryden, James Joyce, D. H. Lawrence, the Lindbergh family, Marcus Aurelius, H. L. Mencken, Napoleon, Mark Twain, and Edith Wharton. Founded in 1701, the Yale Library has more than 50 subjects of special strength, including Babylonian tablets, futurism, legal thought, playing cards, sporting books, urban and regional planning, and Western Americana.

District of Columbia

Folger Shakespeare Library
201 E. Capitol St., SE
Washington, DC 20003-1094
202-544-4600
http://www.folger.edu/

Opened in 1932, the Folger Shakespeare Library houses the world's largest collection of Shakespeare's printed works. The collection includes approximately 280,000 books and manuscripts; 27,000 paintings, drawings, engravings and prints; and musical instruments, costumes, and films.

The Library of Congress
101 Independence Ave., SE
Washington, DC 20540
202-707-5000
http://lcweb.loc.gov/

The nation's largest single library, the Library of Congress, established in 1800, contains over 80 million items, including about 20 million books and pamphlets. Its collections include over 1 million volumes on Hispanic and Portuguese culture, the largest collection of Russian literature outside Russia, and a collection from the Kennedy Center Performing Arts Library. Special collections include books for the blind and physically handicapped, cartography, folk music, law books, manuscripts, microforms, motion pictures, music, the Orient, prints and photographs, and more than half a million rare books. The library's first priority is service to the Congress of the United States. It also registers creative work for copyright and provides services to both the public and libraries throughout the country.

Florida

University of Florida Libraries
204 Library West
Gainesville, FL 32611
352-392-0342
http://www.uflib.ufl.edu/

Founded in 1905, this system contains more than 3 million volumes, with special collections on Florida history, Latin America, Judaica, aerial photographs, coastal engineering, New England literature, Brazilian law, and Florida newspapers.

Georgia

University of Georgia Libraries
Main Library
Jackson St.
University of Georgia
Athens, GA 30602
706-542-3251
http://www.libs.uga.edu/

Founded in 1800, this library system contains more than 3.3 million volumes, with special collections on music, theater, Georgia, Confederate imprints, Georgia authors, 19th- and 20th-century politics, and Georgia newspapers.

Hawaii

Hawaii State Library System
Office of the State Librarian
465 S. King St.
Honolulu, HI 96813
808-586-3704
http://www.hcc.hawaii.edu/hspls/hslov.html

Founded in 1852, Hawaii's libraries contain more than 3.4 million volumes, with a special collection devoted to Hawaiian history.

Illinois

Chicago Public Library
400 S. State St.
Chicago, IL 60605
312-747-4999
http://cpl.lib.uic.edu/CPL.html

Founded in 1872, Chicago's libraries offer more than 11.5 million volumes with special collections of national, U.S., foreign, and trade bibliographies; Chicago information; foreign-language encyclopedias; Abraham Lincoln papers; miniature books; early American newspapers; and World War I and II posters.

Northwestern University Library
1935 Sheridan Rd.
Evanston, IL 60208
847-491-7658
http://www.library.nwu.edu/

Founded in 1856, Northwestern holds more than 3 million volumes and bound periodicals, with special collections on Africa, architecture, contemporary music scores, feminism, German classics, Italian futurism, manuscripts, and printing.

University of Chicago Libraries
1100 E. 57th St.
Chicago, IL 60637
773-702-7874
http://www.lib.uchicago.edu/

The University of Chicago, founded in 1891, contains more than 5.8 million volumes. It maintains special collections of English Bibles, Lincolniana, modern poetry, anatomical illustrations, and Kentucky and Ohio River Valley history; children's books; early theology and Bible criticism; German fiction, 1790–1850; and books on ophthalmology.

University of Illinois Library at Urbana–Champaign
1408 W. Gregory Dr.
Urbana, IL 61801
217-333-0790
http://www.library.uiuc.edu/

This library's collection includes more than 8.1 million volumes, with special collections on American humor and folklore, freedom of expression, 16th- and 17th-century Italian drama, 19th-century publishing, Carl Sandburg, and H. G. Wells. Founded in 1868.

Indiana

Indiana University at Bloomington
Main Library
1320 East 10th St.
Bloomington, IN 47405

812-855-3403
http://www.indiana.edu/~libweb/index.php3

Founded in 1824, Indiana University has amassed a collection of more than 5.7 million volumes, with special collections of English and American literature, 19th-century British plays, English history, scientific and medical history, the works of Aristotle, and 19th-century French opera.

Iowa

University of Iowa Libraries
Main Library
100 Main Library
Iowa City, IA 52242
319-335-5299
http://www.lib.uiowa.edu/

Established in 1855, Iowa's libraries contain more than 3.6 million volumes, with special collections on Leigh Hunt and his friends, Abraham Lincoln, American Indians, Iowa authors, typography, the Union Pacific Railroad, editorial cartoons, the French Revolution, and the history of medicine.

Kansas

University of Kansas Libraries
Watson Library
1425 Jay Hack Blvd.
Lawrence, KS 66045
785-864-3956
http://www.lib.ukans.edu/

Established in 1866, the University of Kansas libraries contain in excess of 2.9 million volumes, with special collections on Anglo-Saxons, botany, children's books, Chinese classics, Colombia, the Continental Renaissance, economics, historical cartography, Irish history and literature, Kansas history, poetry, opera, ornithology, sound recordings, travel, and women.

Maryland

Enoch Pratt Free Library
400 Cathedral St.
Baltimore, MD 21201
410-396-5430
http://www.pratt.lib.md.us/

Founded in 1886, Enoch Pratt's collection of 2.3 million volumes has a special H. L. Mencken section and a Maryland history collection.

Johns Hopkins University
Milton S. Eisenhower Library
3400 N. Charles St.
Baltimore, MD 21218

410-516-8325
http://www.library.jhu.edu/

Established in 1876, Johns Hopkins has more than 2.4 million volumes, with special collections on economics, Lord Byron, French drama, modern German drama, German literature, sheet music, slavery, and trade unions.

Massachusetts

Boston Public Library
700 Boylston St.
Boston, MA 02116
617-536-5400
http://www.bpl.org/

Founded in 1852, the Boston library system is believed to be the oldest free municipal library system supported by taxation anywhere in the world. It has 6.3 million volumes, with the following special collections: the library of John Quincy Adams; military science, history, and the Civil War; astronomy, mathematics, and navigation; Robert and Elizabeth Browning; Daniel Defoe; drama; genealogy; government documents; heraldry; music; patents; Christian Science; the Sacco-Vanzetti papers; Walt Whitman; and World War I.

Harvard University Library
Wadsworth House
1341 Massachusetts Ave.
Cambridge, MA 02138
617-495-3650
http://hul.harvard.edu/

With more than 13 million volumes, the Harvard Library, founded in 1638, is the largest university library in the United States. Its special collections are numerous. They include the Trotsky archive; the Theodore Roosevelt Collection; and works by such authors as Dante, T. S. Eliot, Faulkner, Goethe, Kipling, Longfellow, Milton, Petrarch, Rousseau, Shakespeare, Steinbeck, and Thomas Wolfe. Some of its branches are located outside Massachusetts, such as the Harvard Library in New York and the Dumbarton Oaks Research Library and Collection in Washington, D.C. Others specialize in topics ranging from music to divinity and include Harvard's famed law library and the fine arts library at the Fogg Art Museum.

Massachusetts Institute of Technology (MIT) Libraries
Office of the Director
Room 14S-216
Cambridge, MA 02139-4307
617-253-5651
http://libraries.mit.edu

Founded in 1862, MIT's library holdings total approximately 2.4 million volumes, with special collections devoted to the early history of aeronautics, architecture and planning, civil engineering, 19th-century U.S. glass manufacturers, early works in mathematics and physics, shipbuilding and naval history, and spectroscopy.

University of Massachusetts at Amherst
W. E. B. DuBois Library
P.O. Box 34710
Amherst, MA 01003-4710
413-545-0284
http://www.library.umass.edu/

Founded in 1865, this university system maintains holdings in excess of 2.6 million volumes, with special collections on slavery and antislavery pamphlets; county atlases of New England, New York, and New Jersey; and the French Revolution.

Michigan

Detroit Public Library
5201 Woodward Ave.
Detroit, MI 48202
313-833-1000
http://www.detroit.lib.mi.us/

Founded in 1865, Detroit's library contains more than 2.7 million volumes, with special collections on automotive history, labor history, and black music, dance, and drama.

In the 10th century, the Grand Vizier of Persia took his entire library with him wherever he went. The 117,000-volume library was carried by camels trained to walk in alphabetical order.

Michigan State University Library
100 Library
East Lansing, MI 48824
517-353-8700
http://www.lib.msu.edu

Established in 1855, Michigan State has holdings of more than 3.9 million volumes, with special collections on American popular culture, American radical history, apiculture, cookery, criminology, fencing, illuminated manuscripts in facsimile, natural science, and veterinary history.

Library Administration
University of Michigan
818 Hatcher South
Ann Arbor, MI 48109-1205
734-764-9356
http://www.lib.umich.edu/

Founded in 1817, the University of Michigan's libraries contain nearly 6 million volumes, the fifth-largest collection in the country. The system consists of 18 collections located around campus. Major facilities include a medical and a fine-arts library. Separately administered are a library of Americana, a law library, a business-administration library, and the Gerald R. Ford Presidential Library.

Wayne State University Libraries
Dean of Libraries
3100 David Adamany
Undergraduate Library
5155 Gullen Mall
Detroit, MI 48202
313-577-4023
http://www.lib.wayne.edu/index.html

Wayne State has more than 2.9 million volumes, with special collections on 19th-century Spanish history, social studies, women and the law, law, and children and young people.

Minnesota

University of Minnesota Libraries–Twin Cities
499 O. Meredith Wilson Library
309 19th Ave. South
Minneapolis, MN 55455
612-624-4520
http://www.lib.umn.edu/

Founded in 1851, this university system contains more than 5.2 million volumes, with special collections on American and English literature, the history of quantum physics, ballooning, dime novels, information processing, Sherlock Holmes, children's literature, performing arts, private presses, August Strindberg, and the history of biology and medicine.

Missouri

Kansas City Public Library
311 E. 12th St.
Kansas City, MO 64106
816-701-3400
http://www.kcpl.lib.mo.us/

Founded in 1873, this library's collection numbers more than 2 million volumes, with special collections on black history and Missouri Valley history and genealogy.

Linda Hall Library of Science, Engineering and Technology
5109 Cherry St.
Kansas City, MO 64110-2498
816-363-4600
http://www.lhl.lib.mo.us/

Founded in 1946, the Linda Hall Library's holdings include more than 1 million volumes, with special collections in scientific journals; research monographs; conference and symposium proceedings; engineering standards and specifications; patent specifications and trademarks; unclassified NASA, Department of Energy, and government contractor reports; and geological maps.

St. Louis University Libraries
St. Louis University
3650 Lindell Blvd.
St. Louis, MO 63108
314-977-3100
http://www.slu.edu/libraries/

Founded in 1818, this system contains more than 1.2 million bound volumes and government documents. Libraries on campus include a divinity library, a library of the School of Social Service, a law library, and a medical library.

University of Missouri–Columbia
Administrative Offices
104 Ellis Library
Columbia, MO 65201-5149
573-882-4701
http://web.missouri.edu/~elliswww/

Established in 1839, this library holds more than 2.7 million volumes, with special collections devoted to American best-sellers, criminal law, philosophy, World War I and II posters, cartoons, and Fourth of July orations.

Washington University Libraries
P.O. Box 1061
One North Brookings Dr.
St. Louis, MO 63130
314-935-5400
http://library.wustl.edu/

Founded in 1853, this system maintains more than 3 million volumes, with special collections on German language and literature, Romance languages and literature, classical archeology and numismatics, architecture, musicology, history of the Russian Revolution and the Soviet Union, American and New York Stock Exchange reports, printing, and early history of communications-semantics.

New Jersey

Princeton University Library
Firestone Library
One Washington Rd.
Princeton, NJ 08544
609-258-4820
http://libweb.princeton.edu

This university was founded as the College of New Jersey, Elizabeth, in 1746. The principal building in its library system is the Harvey S. Firestone Memorial Library, constructed in 1948. Princeton has approximately 4.7 million volumes, with special collections devoted to the Brontës, Disraeli, aeronautics, American historical manuscripts, chess, civil rights, coins, Emily Dickinson, emblem books, fishing and angling, graphic arts, Mormon history, mountaineering, papyrus manuscripts, publishing, sports, women, and famous individuals.

Rutgers, The State University of New Jersey
University Libraries
169 College Ave.
New Brunswick, NJ 08901
732-932-7505
http://www.libraries.rutgers.edu

Established in 1766, this venerable library contains more than 2.9 million volumes. It has a special collection of New Jersey public-sector collective-bargaining contracts.

New York

Brooklyn Public Library System
Grand Army Plaza
Brooklyn, NY 11238
718-230-2100
http://www.brooklynpubliclibrary.org/

Founded in 1896 and consolidated with the Brooklyn Library in 1902, the library system now has 58 branches with a total of more than 4.1 million books. Special collections cover Brooklyn history, chess and checkers, the Civil War, costumes, fire protection, and Walt Whitman.

Columbia University
University Libraries
535 W. 114th St.
New York, NY 10027
212-854-2247
http://www.columbia.edu/cu/lweb/

Founded in 1761, Columbia offers more than 6.9 million volumes, with special collections on anatomy, architecture, cancer research, fine arts, physiology, and plastic surgery.

Cornell University Libraries
201 Olin Library
Cornell University
Ithaca, NY 14853
607-255-3393
http://campusgw.library.cornell.edu/

With approximately 5.8 million volumes, the Cornell libraries include special collections on Southeast Asia, civil engineering, medical dissertations, field recordings, early-16th-century music, beekeeping, food and beverages, and labor history.

New York Public Library
Astor, Lenox & Tilden Foundations
476 Fifth Ave.
New York, NY 10018
212-930-0800
http://www.nypl.org

Established in 1895 by the consolidation of the Astor and Lenox libraries and the Tilden Trust, the New York Public Library, encompassing 85 neighborhood branches and 4 research centers with noncirculatory collections, contains more than 50 million cataloged items: books, manuscripts, microfilm, prints, maps, recordings, photographs, and sheet music. Among its special collections are ones on black history and culture; performing arts; English and American literature; bindings and illustrated books; Japanese prints; tobacco; early Bibles including the Gutenberg; maps, photographs and prints; Jewish, Oriental, Slavonic cultures, and U.S. history and genealogy.

New York State Library
State Education Department, Cultural Education
  Center
Empire State Plaza
Albany, NY 12230
518-474-5930
http://www.nysl.nysed.gov/

Founded in 1818, New York State's library contains more than 2.3 million volumes, with special collections on Dutch colonial records, New York State political and social history, and the Shakers.

New York University
Elmer Holmes Bobst Library
70 Washington Sq. South
New York, NY 10012
212-998-2505
http://www.nyu.edu/library/bobst

Established in 1831, New York University's holdings total approximately 4 million volumes, with special collections on Lewis Carroll, Robert Frost, rare Judaica and Hebraica, mathematics, and the history of dentistry.

Libraries

Queens Borough Public Library System
89-11 Merrick Blvd.
Jamaica, NY 11432
718-990-0700
http://www.queenslibrary.org/

Organized in 1896, this library system contains more than 7.2 million books and has 62 branches. It maintains special collections of Long Island history and genealogy and a collection of over 1.5 million pictures.

State University of New York at Buffalo
University Libraries
433 Capen Hall
Buffalo, NY 14260
716-645-2967
http://ublib.buffalo.edu/libraries/

Founded in 1922, the State University libraries hold more than 2.3 million volumes, with special collections of poetry, the works of J. Frank Dobie, New York State governors' autographs, and books on science and engineering and the history of medicine.

Syracuse University Libraries
E. S. Bird Library
222 Waverly Ave.
Syracuse, NY 13244
315-443-2573
http://libwww.syr.edu/

Established in 1871, Syracuse University has holdings of more than 2.6 million volumes, with special collections on Stephen Crane, Loyalists in the American Revolution, economic history, Margaret Bourke-White, Rudyard Kipling, and cartoonists; science-fiction books and manuscripts; and the papers of Averell Harriman, Dorothy Thompson, and Benjamin Spock.

University of Rochester
Rush Rhees Library
Room 236
Rochester, NY 14627
716-275-4461
http://www.lib.rochester.edu/

Founded in 1850, the Rochester library's holdings include more than 2.3 million volumes, with special collections on 19th- and 20th-century public affairs, 19th-century botany and horticulture, American literature, regional history, and Leonardo da Vinci.

North Carolina

Duke University
William R. Perkins Library
P.O. Box 90193
Durham, NC 27708

919-660-5800
http://www.lib.duke.edu/reference/index.htm

Founded in 1838, Duke's library contains more than 4.5 million volumes, with special collections on American almanacs, architecture, city directories, Samuel Taylor Coleridge, Confederate imprints, Ralpho Waldo Emerson, Latin American history, manuscripts, the Methodist Church, newspapers, the Philippines, utopias, and Wesleyana.

University of North Carolina at Chapel Hill
Walter Royal Davis Library
Campus Box 3900
Chapel Hill, NC 27514
919-962-1301
http://www.lib.unc.edu/davis.html

Founded in 1795, North Carolina's library contains more than 4.2 million volumes, with special collections on North Carolina and Southern history.

Ohio

Cleveland Public Library
325 Superior Ave.
Cleveland, OH 44114
216-623-2800
http://www.cpl.org/

Founded in 1869, the Cleveland Public Library contains 2.5 million volumes. Its special collections are devoted to folklore, the Orient, and chess.

Ohio State University Libraries
William Oxley Thompson Memorial Library
1858 Neil Ave.
Columbus, OH 43210
614-292-6151
http://www.lib.ohio-state.edu

Established in 1873, Ohio State offers approximately 4 million volumes and bound periodicals. Special collections include those on the American Association of Editorial Cartoonists, American fiction to 1925, American sheet music, Australia, daguerreotypes and ambrotypes, dance notation, Reformation history, and science-fiction magazines.

Public Library of Cincinnati and Hamilton County
800 Vine St.
Library Square
Cincinnati, OH 45202
513-369-6900
http://www.cincinnatilibrary.org

Founded in 1853, Cincinnati's library has more than 3.5 million volumes, with 139,337 maps and special collections on local history, genealogy, theology, art, music, theater, and oral history.

Oklahoma

University of Oklahoma
University Libraries
410 W. Brooks St.
Room 212 NW
Norman, OK 73019-6030
405-325-2611
http://www.libraries.ou.edu

Founded in 1895, the University of Oklahoma's library holds more than 2.2 million volumes, with special collections devoted to early science, Western history, Native American papers, political speeches, theater, film, and dance.

Pennsylvania

Carnegie Library of Pittsburgh
4400 Forbes Ave.
Pittsburgh, PA 15213
412-622-3100
http://www.clpgh.org/clp/

Founded in 1895, the Carnegie Library collection contains more than 2.4 million volumes, with approximately 69,000 in foreign languages. It maintains special collections on architecture and design, the Atomic Energy Commission, cartoons, local history, U.S. patents, World War I, and 19th-century American and German music journals.

Free Library of Philadelphia
1901 Vine St.
Philadelphia, PA 19103
215-686-5322
http://www.library.phila.gov

Founded in 1891, the Free Library contains 6.7 million volumes and bound periodicals, with special collections on orchestral music, common law, automobile history, Americana, cuneiform tablets, Charles Dickens, Edgar Allan Poe, Beatrix Potter, Arthur Rackham, theater, and maps (including over 130,000 single-sheet maps, atlases, and geographies).

Pennsylvania State University
Dean's Office
Pattee/Paterno Library
510 Paterno Library
University Park, PA 16802
814-865-0401
http://www.libraries.psu.edu/

Established in 1857, Penn State's library has approximately 2 million volumes, with special collections on

American sociology, anthropology, art, architecture, Australia, Bibles, black literature, the Columbus family papers, English literature, photography, Pennsylvania, science fiction, surrealism, and the United Steelworkers of America.

University of Pennsylvania Libraries
Van Pelt Library
3420 Walnut St.
Philadelphia, PA 19104-6206
215-898-7555
http://www.library.upenn.edu/vanpelt/

Founded in 1749, the University of Pennsylvania's libraries hold more than 4.2 million volumes, with special collections on church history, the Spanish Inquisition, canon law, witchcraft, Shakespeare, alchemy and chemistry, Aristotle, Bibles, Jonathan Swift, Sanskrit manuscripts, Theodore Dreiser, Washington Irving, and the Spanish Golden Age of literature, as well as Benjamin Franklin imprints.

University of Pittsburgh
University Libraries
3960 Forbes Ave.
Pittsburgh, PA 15260
412-648-7710
http://www.pitt.edu/NewPittInfo/libraries.html

Founded in 1873, the University of Pittsburgh has holdings of more than 3.3 million volumes, with special collections on ballet, 19th- and 20th-century American and English theater, popular culture, early history and travel, children's literature, "Mr. Rogers' Neighborhood" videos, and ethnic organizations.

South Carolina

University of South Carolina
Thomas Cooper Library
1322 Greene St.
Columbia, SC 29208
803-777-3142
http://www.sc.edu/library/

Founded in 1801, South Carolina's system contains more than 2.3 million volumes, with special collections on archeology, ornithology, aerial photography, and rare medical books.

Texas

Dallas Public Library
1515 Young St.
Dallas, TX 75201
214-670-1400
http://www.dallaslibrary.org

Libraries

Founded in 1901, Dallas's library contains over 3 million volumes. Special collections cover business histories; children's literature; classical literature; classical recordings; Dallas black history; and diaries and manuscripts on dance, fashion, genealogy, grants, printing, and Texas.

Houston Public Library

500 McKinney Ave.
Houston, TX 77002
713-247-2700
http://www.hpl.lib.tx.us/hpl/index.html

Founded in 1901, the Houston Public Library has more than 4.1 million volumes, with special collections of Bibles; books on the Civil War, genealogy, Texas, and petroleum; Salvation Army posters; early Houston photographs; early printing and illuminated manuscripts; juvenile literature; and sheet music.

University of Texas at Austin
General Libraries

21st St. and Speedway St.
PCL 3.200
Austin, TX 78713
512-495-4350
http://www.lib.utexas.edu/

Founded in 1883, this university library system serves a student body of more than 46,000. With more than 7 million books and bound periodicals, its holdings are divided among individual libraries devoted to Asia; film; the Middle East; Latin America; public affairs; architecture and planning; chemistry; classics; engineering; fine arts; geology; physics, mathematics, and astronomy; science; business research; humanities; population research; and law. Its special collections cover Southern history, Canada, British Commonwealth literature, the U.S. Volleyball Association, and oral histories.

Utah

University of Utah
Marriott Library

295 South 1500 E.
Salt Lake City, UT 84112
801-581-8558
http://www.lib.utah.edu/

Founded in 1850, Utah's library contains in excess of 2 million volumes, with special collections on the Middle East, Western Americana, and the history of medicine.

Virginia

University of Virginia
Alderman Library

PO Box 400113
Charlottesville VA 22904-4113

804-924-3026
http://www.lib.virginia.edu/

Established in 1819, Virginia's library holds more than 4.1 million books and bound periodicals, with special collections devoted to American literature, the American Revolution, Americana, the Civil War and Reconstruction, political cartoons, Ceylon, classical studies, Stephen Crane, Oliver Cromwell, John Dos Passos, evolution, William Faulkner, finance, Robert Frost, Gothic novels, Bret Harte, Nathaniel Hawthorne, international law, Washington Irving, Thomas Jefferson, modern art, Mark Twain, typography and printing, Virginia, voyages and travels, and Walt Whitman.

Washington

University of Washington Libraries

Allen Library, Room 482
P.O. Box 352900
Seattle, WA 98195
206-543-1760
http://www.lib.washington.edu/

Founded in 1862, this university's holdings exceed 5.3 million volumes, with special collections devoted to East Asia, fisheries, forest resources, oceanography, and the Pacific Northwest.

Wisconsin

Milwaukee Public Library

814 W. Wisconsin Ave.
Milwaukee, WI 53233
414-286-3000
http://www.mpl.org/

Founded in 1878, the Milwaukee Public Library has more than 2.3 million volumes, with special collections on the Great Lakes, H. G. Wells, British and American authors, genealogy, and cookbooks.

University of Wisconsin–Madison
General Library System and Memorial Library

728 State St.
Madison, WI 53706
608-262-3193
http://www.library.wisc.edu/

The University of Wisconsin has amassed a collection of more than 4.5 million volumes since its founding in 1850. Special collections include those on alchemy, American gifts, bookplates, Brazilian positivism, Buddhism, children's literature, C. S. Lewis's letters, Calvinist theology and Dutch history, chess, Early American women authors, history of chemistry, medieval history, Mexican pamphlets, Polish literature and history, Tibetan studies, Mark Twain, and Welsh theology.

CANADA

Alberta

University of Alberta
5-02 Cameron Library
Edmonton, Alberta T6G 2J8
780-492-3790
http://libits.library.ualberta.ca/library.html

Established in 1909, Alberta's university system contains more than 3.7 million volumes, with special collections on literature, Native Americans, Victorian book arts, western Canada, and theology and canon law.

Ontario

University of Toronto Library System
130 Saint George St.
Toronto, Ontario M5S 1A5
416-978-8450
http://library.utoronto.ca/

Founded in 1827, the University of Toronto has holdings of more than 8 million volumes, with extensive sections of sheet music, films, slides, maps, and photographs. Its special collections include those on Shakespeare, the history of science, Darwin, Victorian natural history, ornithology, medical and related sciences, Italian plays, juvenile drama, Canada, and Canadian authors.

British Columbia

University of British Columbia Library
1956 Main Mall
Vancouver, British Columbia V6T 1Z1
604-822-3310
http://www.library.ubc.ca/

Established in 1915, British Columbia's library holds more than 3.5 million volumes, with special collections on Pacific Northwest history, Canada, the Orient, the history of science, English literature, and Canadian and Japanese maps.

Quebec

McGill University Libraries
3459 McTavish St.
Montreal, Quebec H3A 1Y1
514-398-4744
http://www.library.mcgill.ca/

Founded in 1821, this university system serves an enrollment of about 24,000 students and has holdings of 1.6 million volumes. Its special collections cover architecture, William Blake, Canada, entomology, early geology, the history of science and medicine, natural history and ornithology, printing, Shakespeare, and 16th- and 17th-century tracts.

THE DEWEY DECIMAL SYSTEM AND HOW TO USE IT

Melvil Dewey (1851–1931) believed in organization. Even as a child, he was busy devising a way to arrange his family's pantry to make it more efficient. Before his system of classifying library books was adopted, many libraries relied on systems that filed books by size or color—cumbersome and not very useful methods at best. While working as a librarian at Amherst College, Dewey developed a system that is used by most school and small public libraries today. Published anonymously in 1876, his classifications divide nonfiction books into 10 broad categories:

000–099	General works (encyclopedias and similar works)
100–199	Philosophy (how people think and what they believe)
200–299	Religion (including mythology and religions of the world)
300–399	Social sciences (folklore and legends, government, manners and customs, vocations)
400–499	Language (dictionaries, grammars)
500–599	Pure science (mathematics, astronomy, chemistry, nature study)
600–699	Technology (applied sciences—aviation, building, engineering, homemaking)
700–799	Arts (photography, drawing, painting, music, sports)
800–899	Literature (plays, poetry)
900–999	History (ancient and modern, geography, travel)

Each of these sections is further divided for accuracy in classification. For example, the numbers 500–599 cover the pure sciences, such as astronomy, chemistry, mathematics, paleontology, and physics. Each of these areas has its own division and section number. All books on mathematics are assigned numbers in the 510 to 519 range; mathematics is then broken down into types, such as algebra, arithmetic, and geometry. Geometry's specific number is 513, which can be subdivided through the use of decimal points to provide 10 basic categories. Additional digits can be added, creating an ever more precise categorization system.

Libraries

Cataloging in Publication Data

On the copyright page of most books, under the heading "Cataloging in Publication Data," are numbers and abbreviations that help librarians index new acquisitions for the card catalog. These data can be helpful to readers as well. A typical entry is shown below with an explanation of each part of the entry:

Library of Congress Cataloging in Publication Data

[Author]   McLanathan, Richard B. K.
[Title]   World art in American museums.
[Possible subject card   1. Art—United States—Guidebooks.   2. Art museums—United States—
headings, in order   Guidebooks.   3. Museums—United States—Guidebooks.   4. Art—Canada—
of importance]   Guidebooks.   5. Art—museums—Guidebooks.   6. Museums—Canada—
[Library of Congress   Guidebooks.
No.]   1. Title.
             N510.M34   1983   708.13 *[Dewey Decimal No.]*
             ISBN 0-385-18515-4 *[International Standard Book Number: country number; publisher number; title number; and check digit. The ISBN was started by the British in 1967 and adopted in the United States a year later.]*

Books are arranged alphabetically within each classification by the first letters of the author's last name. Therefore, a library that has several books on American history of the colonial period will assign the same basic number (973.2) to all the books and shelve them alphabetically.

Dewey's aim was to create a system that would be simple enough for even casual users to understand, but complex enough to meet a library's expanding needs. His system was developed to meet the needs of many libraries. A second popular system was created to fit the requirements of a specific library, the Library of Congress. This system, now in wide use, is even more detailed and has the advantage of being able to accommodate growth of knowledge in unexpected areas.

THE LIBRARY OF CONGRESS SUBJECT HEADINGS

The Library of Congress Classification System is used in most large public and university libraries today. A Library of Congress (LC) number contains three lines: a letter at the top, a number in the middle, and a letter/number combination at the bottom.

The Library of Congress went through several systems before devising its own method. Because the Library of Congress contains almost every book ever published in the United States, as well as valuable tapes and research materials, it needs a highly flexi-

ble system. The Library of Congress Classification System contains 21 classes:

A	General works
B	Philosophy, psychology, and religion
C	Auxiliary sciences of history
D	History: general and outside the Americas
E	History: America (general) and United States (general)
F	History: United States (local), Canada, Central and South America, Caribbean
G	Geography, anthropology, recreation
H	Social sciences
J	Political science
K	Law
L	Education
M	Music
N	Fine arts
P	Language and literature
Q	Science
R	Medicine
S	Agriculture
T	Technology
U	Military science
V	Naval science
Z	Bibliography and library science

Each of these classes can be divided into a subclass with the addition of a second letter. With the addition of numbers, the category becomes even more specific. The flexibility of the system becomes apparent when one sees that the alphabet permits 26 subdivisions of any one class. Each of the subdivisions can be broken down further by using the numbers 1 to 9999.

Librarians recommend that researchers turn to Subject Headings Used in the Dictionary Catalog of the Library of Congress for assistance. Because the LC system groups related topics together, a researcher may discover unexpected, related avenues to pursue.

Cataloging in Publication Data might also include information on a book's illustrator, whether a book has an index or bibliography, and number of pages.

LIBRARIES ONLINE

Internet links to more than 2,000 libraries (as well as various information services) in more than 70 countries can be found on the Lib Web SunSITE (http://sunsite.berkeley.edu/Libweb). Especially noteworthy among library home pages is the Library of Congress site (http://www.loc.gov). The site provides access to the Library of Congress catalog and catalogs of other libraries, allows users to call up information on a wide variety of subjects, and contains links to other Internet sites. It also offers access to the American Memory collection, which contains both multimedia presentations and documents; THOMAS, a survey of all the legislation pending before Congress; and text and graphics from current and recent Library of Congress exhibitions.

In addition to the various libraries' home pages, the Internet also offers a number of virtual libraries—collections of electronic documents and hypertext links—that exist solely in cyberspace:

Internet Public Library
http://www.ipl.org

Carrie: A Full-Text Electronic Library
http://www.ukans.edu/carrie/carrie_main.html

CyberStacks
http://www.public.iastate.edu/~CYBERSTACKS

Library Gazebo Kiosk
http://www.netins.net/showcase/gazebo/kiosk.html

Public Libraries with Internet Services
http://sjcpl.lib.in.us

WebCATS: Library Catalogues on the Web
http://www.lights.com/webcats

The Virtual Library
http://thorplus.lib.purdue.edu/vlibrar/index.html

DATA BANKS AVAILABLE FOR COMPUTER RESEARCH

CompuServe Interactive Services, Inc.
Customer Service Department
P.O. Box 28650
Jacksonville, FL 32226-8650
800-848-8990
http://www.compuserve.com

> This fee-based online system offers forums for users of various computers, with electronic editions of newspapers and computer magazines, an international newswire, conferences, and message boards. CompuServe provides remote computing services, a videotex information service, and a value-added network service, as well as games, entertainment, and personal finance services.

DIALOG Information Services, Inc.
Headquarters
11000 Regency Parkway
Suite 10
Cary, NC 27511

California Offices
3460 Hillview Ave.
Palo Alto, CA 94304

New York Offices
622 3rd Ave.
10th Floor
New York, NY 10017
800-334-2564
415-858-2700
http://www.dialog.com

> This fee-based online system provides access to approximately 280 databases, making it possible to search through thousands of newspapers, general-interest and trade magazines, and other publications in seconds. It includes databases compiled by Dun & Bradstreet, Moody's Investor's Service, and Standard & Poor's.

Dow Jones News/Retrieval
P.O. Box 300
Princeton, NJ 08534-0300
609-520-4000
http://www.bis.dowjones.com

> This fee-based online computer service offers an interactive information service with up-to-the-minute news and information to the business and financial community. Stories from the Wall Street Journal, Barron's, and the Dow Jones News Service appear as quickly as 90 seconds after filing and go back as far as 90 days. Dow Jones also offers online stock trading and portfolio management services.

Libraries

Getting Started in Genealogy

The search for a greater understanding of our ancestors has boomed in the United States since the American Bicentennial celebration and the publication of Alex Haley's immensely popular *Roots*. Genealogists lament that too many of us live in historical vacuums, unable to name more than a generation or two of our closest relatives. To help you join this search for a history that extends beyond the last few generations, experts offer several tips:

1. Begin with your closest family members, recording basic information that is already known to you and working backward. This part of the investigation can be quite far-reaching if you contact distant relatives and check sources that they suggest. You may be fortunate enough to have access to family Bibles, letters, and diaries. Vital records such as birth and death certificates can yield a wealth of information at this stage.

2. Consult popular references for research techniques. Some of the best follow.
   - Andereck, Paul A., and Richard A. Pence. *Computer Genealogy: A Guide to Research Through High Technology.* Ancestry Publishing, 1991.
   - Beard Field, Timothy. *How to Find Your Family Roots.* McGraw-Hill, 1977.
   - Cerny, Johni, and Wendy Elliot. *The Library: A Guide to the LDS Family History Library.* Ancestry Publishing, 1988. The book is an explanatory guide to the largest single collection of genealogical works, run by the Church of Jesus Christ of Latter Day Saints.
   - Doane, Gilbert Harry, and James B. Bell. *Searching for Your Ancestors: The How and Why of Genealogy.* 6th ed. University of Minnesota Press, 1992. This introductory guide to genealogical research covers techniques and sources for locating genealogical data.
   - Eakle, Arlene, and Johni Cierny. *The Source: A Guidebook of American Genealogy.* Ancestry Publishing, 1984. The book is a compilation of resources, research techniques, and record sources.
   - Kurzweil, Arthur. *From Generation to Generation.* Schocken Books, 1982. This volume addresses genealogical techniques and subjects particular to Jewish family history, from locating information on European shtetls to Sephardic research.

3. Check out the libraries. Extensive genealogical collections exist at the Library of Congress, the New York Public Library, the Los Angeles Public Library, the Newberry Library in Chicago, and the Allen County Public Library in Fort Wayne, Indiana. Specialized libraries, such as the famed Genealogical Library of the Church of Jesus Christ of Latter-Day Saints in Salt Lake City, Utah, can be extremely helpful. This particular library offers more than 1.3 million reels of microfilm of all types of documents useful to genealogists. Also visit or contact local libraries in areas where your ancestors are known to have lived.

4. Consider contacting the following organizations, which have extensive genealogical records:

American Family Records Association
P.O. Box 15505
Kansas City, MO 64106
816-373-6570

Ellis Island
http://www.ellisisland.org

Genealogical Libraries on the WWW
http://genealogy.org

Federation of Genealogical Societies
http://www.fgs.org

Jewish Genealogical Society
P.O. Box 6398
New York, NY 10128
212-330-8257

Library of Congress
Local History and Genealogy Reading Room
1st Street and Independence Avenue
Washington, DC 20540
202-707-5000
http://lcweb.loc.gov

National Archives and Records Administration
Consultant's Office
7th Street and Pennsylvania Avenue, NW
Washington, DC 20408
202-501-5402
http://www.nara.gov

National Genealogical Society
4527 17th St., N
Arlington, VA 22207
703-525-0050
http://www.genealogy.org/~ngs/

A Closer Look

Major Genealogical Libraries

Burton Collection, Detroit Public Library, 5201 Woodward Ave., Detroit, MI 48202

Dallas Public Library, 1515 Young St., Dallas, TX 75201

Daughters of the American Revolution Library, 1776 D St., NW, Washington, DC 20006 (to be used with the Library of Congress and National Genealogical Society Library, 4527 17th St. N, Arlington, VA 22207)

Genealogical Society Library, 50 E. N. Temple St., Salt Lake City, UT 84150

Los Angeles Public Library, 630 W. 5th St., Los Angeles, CA 90071

Newberry Library, 60 W. Walton St., Chicago, IL 60610

New England Genealogical Society, 101 Newbury St., Boston, MA 02116

New York Historic Genealogical and Biographical Society, 122–6 E. 58th St., New York, NY 10022

New York Public Library, 5th Avenue and 42nd Street, New York, NY 10018

Allen County Public Library, 301 W. Wayne St., Fort Wayne, IN 46802

State Historical Society of Wisconsin, 816 State St., Madison, WI 53706

Western Reserve Historical Society, 10825 East Blvd., Cleveland, OH 44106

Lexis-Nexis
9332 Springboro Pike
Miamisburg, OH 45342
800-444-3333
800-843-6476 (LEXIS-NEXIS EXPRESS)
http://www.lexisnexis.com

This legal, news, and business information service provides online access to more than 73,000 databases containing more than 1 billion separate documents. Areas covered include statutes, legal cases, and online law libraries; national and international news summaries from leading U.S. newspapers and magazines and worldwide wire services; company records and analysts' reports; and access to corporate financial data from the EDGAR system of the U.S. Securities and Exchange commission. Nonsubscribers can use LEXIS-NEXIS EXPRESS to conduct specific searches for a onetime fee.

Ovid Technologies
333 Seventh Ave.
New York, NY 10001
800-950-2035
212-563-3006
http://www.ovid.com

Ovid provides online access to bibliographic and full-text databases for academic, biomedical, and scientific research. Its clients represent Canada, Latin America, Europe, the Middle East, and Africa, as well as the United States.

Questel-Orbit
8000 Westpark Dr.
Suite 130
McLean, VA 22102
800-456-7248
703-442-0900
http://www.questel.orbit.com

This international online information company specializes in patent, trademark, scientific, chemical, and business information covering the United States and the world.

WILSONLINE
The H. W. Wilson Company
950 University Ave.
Bronx, NY 10452
800-367-6770
718-588-8400
http://www.hwwilson.com

WILSONLINE provides online access to The Readers' Guide to Periodical Literature, the Business Periodicals Index, the Index to Legal Periodicals, the Education Index, and numerous other periodical resources. It is used widely by corporations, government agencies, libraries, schools, and universities. Its database covers more than 3,000 periodicals and 500,000 books.

INFORMATION CENTERS

American Crafts Council Library
72 Spring St.
6th Floor
New York, NY 10012
212-274-0630
http://www.craftcouncil.org

Questions about the history of crafts or about learning how to pursue a particular craft, such as weaving or pottery, are answered. Calls may be made Tuesday through Friday between 10 A.M. and 5 P.M., EST.

Libraries

American Museum of Natural History Library

79th Street and Central Park West
New York, NY 10024
212-769-5400
http://library.amnh.org

Founded in 1869, this special library has 400,000 volumes devoted to subjects ranging from anthropology to travel and expedition, with sections on biology, ethnology, entomology, geology, herpetology, history of science, ichthyology, living and fossil invertebrates, mammalogy, mineralogy, museology, ornithology, and paleontology. Its special collections are devoted to astronomical instruments, rare books and manuscripts, rare films, and many other areas. The museum's librarians offer assistance in all areas.

Consumer Information Center

Pueblo, CO 81009
719-948-4000
http://www.pueblo.gsa.gov/

This federal government agency provides a wide selection of free publications such as its monthly National Consumer Buying Alert and guides to solar energy, tire buying, nutrition, budgeting, housing, and gardening. Write for a free catalog or specify your area of interest.

Educational Resources Information Center (ERIC)

AskERIC
2277 Research Blvd.
MS 4M
Rockville, MD 20850
800-LET-ERIC
202-219-2289
http://www.eric.ed.gov

The National Institute of Education within the U.S. Department of Education sponsors ERIC, the educational information system, to provide literature pertaining to various aspects of education. General questions about education are also answered. If a computer search is necessary, a charge will be imposed; otherwise, the information is free. ERIC also provides referrals to other organizations, including its own clearinghouses on adult, career, and vocational education; counseling and personnel services; educational management; elementary and early childhood education; handicapped and gifted children; higher education; information resources; junior colleges; languages and linguistics; reading and communications skills; rural education and small schools; science, mathematics, and environmental education; social studies/social science education; teacher education; tests, measurements, and evaluation; and urban education. Calls are accepted between 8 A.M. and 5:30 P.M., EST, weekdays.

"Federal Information Centers" in chapter 22   **Go to**

Museum of Television and Radio

25 W. 52nd St.
New York, NY 10019
Scheduled Activities: 212-621-6800
General: 212-621-6600
http://www.mtr.org
and
465 N. Beverly Dr.
Beverly Hills, CA 90210
Scheduled Activities: 310-786-1025

Founded in 1976, this museum has collected more than 10,000 radio and 8,000 TV tapes from the 1920s to the present and 2,400 radio scripts, with 1,600 available on microfiche. Its staff is knowledgeable about all aspects of broadcasting and has access to a thousand-volume library of books and magazines.

The National Archives and Records Administration

700 Pennsylvania Ave., NW
Washington, DC 20408-0001
202-501-5402
http://www.nara.gov

This federal government agency is responsible for keeping the permanent records of the U.S. government. Its holdings include maps, photographs, films, U.S. Census records, and all types of correspondence generated and received by government officials. The archives also contain ship passenger records dating as far back as 1820 and military records from the Revolutionary War. Some of its holdings occasionally overlap those of the Library of Congress. Call between 8:45 A.M. and 5:15 P.M., EST, weekdays.

United Nations Publications

2 United Nations Plaza, DC2-853
New York, NY 10017
800-253-9646
http://www.un.org/publications

This international organization's publications cover a wide range of topics, including human rights, public finance, atomic energy, treaties, and international statistics. The UN makes materials available in hardbound and paperback books, pamphlets, bulletins, periodicals, and official records—all in English, and frequently also in Spanish, French, and Russian. Write for a catalog and details of current offerings.

United States Military Academy Library

Bldg. 757
Corner of Thayer and Cullum
West Point, NY 10996-1711
914-938-3833
http://www.usma.edu

Libraries

Founded in 1802, the academy's library contains 400,000 volumes pertaining to the history of the military as well as government documents.

REFERENCE WORKS FOR GENERAL INFORMATION

The following lists are not meant to be comprehensive but are intended to serve as wide-ranging sources for the subjects. A library will provide further reference materials and works on each of the subjects.

GENERAL REFERENCE WORKS

American Reference Books Annual. Libraries Unlimited, 1970–.

This annual volume covers 1,300 to 1,800 new titles each year, reviewing about 300 categories of reference books. The most recent works in many disciplines are listed.

Bartlett's Familiar Quotations: A Collection of Passages, Phrases and Proverbs Traced to Their Sources in Ancient and Modern Literature. 16th ed. Little Brown, 1992.

This work lists more than 22,500 familiar and world-famous quotations along with a 600-page keyword subject index.

Books in Print. Bowker, 1947–.

This annual listing of books now in print or slated for publication by January 31 of the following year currently contains well over 700,000 titles.

Carruth, Gorton, ed. *The Volume Library.* The Southwestern Company, 1917–.

This two-volume, 2.5-million-word family encyclopedia is revised annually. It covers subjects of interest to students and their families and is illustrated and thoroughly indexed.

Encyclopaedia Britannica. 15th ed. Encyclopaedia Britannica, 2002.

A major comprehensive reference tool for any library.

Encyclopedia Britannica CD. Encyclopedia Britannica.

An easily accessed CD reference with extensive cross-referencing and yearly updates.

Ethridge, James M., ed. *The Directory of Directories: An Annotated Guide to Business and Industrial Directories, Professional and Scientific Rosters, and Other Lists and Guides of All Kinds.* 2nd ed. Information Enterprises, 1982.

The work lists 5,200 directories with categories such as business, education, and leisure, providing full details on each publication.

Garraty, John A., and Mark C. Carnes, eds. *American National Biography.* Oxford University Press, 1999.

Expands on the coverage of the *Dictionary of American Biography.* Includes 17,450 scholarly essays on eminent Americans.

Guinness Book of Records. Bantam, 1955–; Facts On File, 1991–.

An annual guide to "the biggest, largest, longest, most" all-time records.

Information Industry Market Place: An International Directory of Information Products and Services. Bowker, 1978.

This international directory describes information collection centers, database and abstract publishers, information brokers, support services and suppliers, conferences, associations, periodicals, and reference books.

Parry, Melanie, ed. *Chambers' Biographical Dictionary.* 6th ed. Larousse, 1997.

Introduced in 1897, Chambers' currently lists more than 17,500 biographies spanning the history of the world.

Readers' Guide to Periodical Literature. H. W. Wilson, 1900–.

The Readers' Guide provides a quick overview of current events through indexing of 174 general-interest U.S. magazines in a range of subject areas.

Sheehy, Eugene P., ed. *Guide to Reference Books.* American Library Association, 1986.

> Found on nearly every reference librarian's basic bookshelf, Sheehy's *Guide* is grouped into five main categories: general reference works; humanities; social and behavioral sciences; history and area studies; and science, technology, and medicine.

Who's Who in America. Marquis Who's Who, 1899–.

> The individuals listed in Who's Who provide the data to be included, so entries vary in completeness and accuracy. The work includes biographical details on approximately 72,000 Americans and others prominently linked to America.

World Almanac and Book of Facts. Newspaper Enterprise Association, 1868–.

> A handy and easy-to-use reference, the World Almanac is updated annually. It provides statistics and factual data on economic, educational, industrial, political, religious, and social issues.

ANTHROPOLOGY AND ETHNOLOGY

Ember, Melvin, and David Levinson, eds. *American Immigrant Cultures: Builders of a Nation.* Macmillan, 1997.

> Includes descriptive profiles and historical information on 161 ethnic groups of the United States. Covers cultural characteristics, detailed immigration and settlement histories, language, economic patterns, housing, religion, major holidays, marriage, family and kinship, relations with other ethnic groups, as well as discrimination. Maps and statistics.

Galens, Judy, Sheets, Anna J., and Young, Robyn V., eds. *Gale Encyclopedia of Multicultural America,* Gale, 1995.

> Informative and fascinating look at ethnic and racial populations of the United States, describing their history, assimilation, language, and religion, among other topics.

Glazer, Nathan, and Daniel P. Moynihan, eds. *Ethnicity: Theory and Experience.* Harvard University Press, January 1989.

> A classic collection of articles dealing with sociological theory as well as ethnic experience in the United States. First published 1975; updated.

Hunter, David E., and Philip Whitten, eds. *Encyclopedia of Anthropology.* Harper & Row, 1976.

> The first English-language encyclopedia in anthropological studies, this volume is compact, comprehensive, and accessible. It includes some 1,400 articles on pertinent topics, supplemented by generous illustrations, maps, diagrams, and photographs.

Lehman, Jeffrey, ed. *Gale Encyclopedia of Multicultural America: Primary Documents.* Gale 1999.

> Companion to the *Gale Encyclopedia of Multicultural America,* this volume is composed of 210 primary documents from 90 different U.S. groups, representing each ethnic group listed in the encyclopedia.

APPLIED ARTS

Boger, Louise A. *The Dictionary of Antiques and Decorative Arts.* Rev. ed. Scribner, 1979.

> This volume is international in scope, with short articles and illustrations covering furniture, glass, ceramics, styles, terms, and biographies.

Kovel, Ralph, and Terry Kovel. *Kovel's Antiques and Collectibles Price List.* Crown, annual.

> This book includes prices for more than 50,000 antiques and collectible items.

Kovel, Ralph, and Terry Kovel. *Kovel's Know Your Antiques.* Crown, 1990.

> This guide offers tips on how to recognize and evaluate any antique, large or small, like an expert. It covers pottery, porcelain, silver, pewter, furniture, pressed and cut glass, prints, bottles, ironware, tinware, letters, sheet music, autographs, books, magazines, and more. This volume also provides advice about caring for

antiques and recognizing frauds as well as bibliographies for each specialty.

Kovel, Ralph M., and Kovel, Terry. *Kovel's Know Your Collectibles.* Crown Publishing Group, May 1992.

> This guide advises on what collectible objects are likely to increase in value and how to preserve, protect, and sell them. It covers ceramics, pottery, furniture, glass, toys, print advertisements, and many other items, with bibliographies for each major specialty.

Liman, Ellen. *The Collecting Book.* Penguin, 1980.

> This book thoroughly describes individual collecting areas such as advertising memorabilia, comic books, tobacco items, clothing, boxes and tins, pottery, glass, and toys. It includes chapters on buying, preserving, and displaying collectibles, as well as numerous black-and-white photographs and extensive references to related publications and organizations.

ART AND ARCHITECTURE

American Art Directory. Bowker, 1898–.

> A biennial guide to the thousands of art councils, museums, art libraries, and art schools in the United States, Canada, and abroad.

Artist's Market. Writer's Digest, 1974–.

> This annual publication details names, addresses, contacts, payments, and other data for 4,000 purchasers of cartoons, illustrations, and photographs. It is considered a standard in its field.

Bell, Doris L. *Contemporary Art Trends: A Guide to Sources, 1960–1980.* Scarecrow Press, 1981.

> This work identifies 41 contemporary art trends with listings of appropriate books and museum catalogs. It also contains a listing of 200 contemporary art journals and a bibliography.

Carley, Rachel. *The Visual Dictionary of American Domestic Architecture.* H. Holt & Co., 1994.

> Chronologically presents the many styles of American houses, through clearly labeled black

and white illustrations of materials, structures, and design elements.

Hamlin, Talbot. *Architecture Through the Ages.* Putnam, 1953.

> This excellent college text offers a survey history from the social point of view. Indexed and illustrated.

Mayer, Ralph. *The HarperCollins Dictionary of Art Terms and Techniques.* HarperCollins, 1992.

> This book defines more than 3,200 terms used in the fields of ceramics, drawing, painting, printmaking, and sculpture.

Libraries in the U.S. issue more cards than VISA, have more children enrolled in summer programs than Little League, and have more visitors each week than all museums and zoos combined.

Musgrove, John, ed. *Sir Bannister Fletcher's A History of Architecture.* 19th ed. Butterworth, 1987.

> This comprehensive view of architectural history has been revised and expanded to include worldwide coverage. It is extensively illustrated, with glossary, index, and bibliographies appended to each chapter.

Phaidon Dictionary of Twentieth-Century Art. 2nd ed. Dutton, 1977.

> This concise and thorough survey covers international art movements and artists in depth from 1900.

Placzek, Adolph K., ed. *Macmillan Encyclopedia of Architects.* 4 vols. Free Press, 1982.

> This volume offers a social and historical view of architecture through the ages, from ancient to modern times, in Europe, the Middle East, and North America.

Wilkes, Joseph A., and Robert T. Packard. *Encyclopedia of Architecture: Design, Engineering and Construction.* Wiley, 1990.

This five-volume work addresses the history of Western architecture over the past 200 years and covers 500 different topics, with 3,000 photographs. Each article was prepared by experts in the field.

ASTRONOMY

Eicher, David J. *The Universe from Your Backyard: A Guide to Deep Sky Objects from Astronomy Magazine.* Cambridge University Press, 1988.

A useful guide for all amateur astronomers.

Hoskin, Michael, ed. *The Cambridge Illustrated History of Astronomy.* Cambridge University Press, 1997.

Beautifully illustrated history of astronomy and astronomers.

Moore, Patrick, ed. *The International Encyclopedia of Astronomy.* Orion, 1987.

This popular reference work condenses difficult concepts into readable prose. No prior knowledge of astronomy is assumed. More than 2,500 entries include several major essays by experts in various fields as well as shorter articles. Illustrated in full color.

Muirden, James. *The Amateur Astronomer's Handbook.* 3rd ed. Harper, 1982.

This is an excellent guide for beginners who want to select equipment and set up their own observatories. It includes celestial charts and tables of eclipses and planetary positions.

Pasachoff, Jay M. *Contemporary Astronomy.* 4th ed. CBS College Publishing, 1989.

This textbook is perfect for beginners who have no background in mathematics or physics, presenting astronomical concepts in clear, colloquial English.

BUSINESS

Brownstone, David M., and Gorton Carruth. *Where to Find Business Information: A World Guide for Everyone Who Needs the Answers to Business Questions* (A Hudson Group Book). 2nd ed. Wiley, 1982.

More than 5,000 English-language publications from around the world are listed and briefly described, with concentration on current periodical publications and services, especially magazines, newsletters, computerized databases, printouts, and microforms. The compendium deals with all subjects of interest to business.

Business Periodicals Index: A Cumulative Subject Index to Periodicals in the Fields of Accounting, Advertising, Banking and Finance, General Business, Insurance, Labor and Management, Marketing and Purchasing, Office Management, Public Administra-tion, Taxation, Specific Businesses, Industries, and Trades. H. W. Wilson, 1958–.

This monthly index provides data on approximately 250 periodicals and certain U.S. government documents.

Consumers Index to Product Evaluations and Information Sources. Pierian Press, 1973–. Quarterly; annual cumulation.

A quarterly guide to consumer magazine articles in 14 subject areas.

Consumer Reports Buying Guide. Consumers Union, 1936–.

Issued annually as the December issue of Consumer Reports, this guide is a starting point for a comparative analysis of all types of products. It contains test results, brand and model ratings and rankings, and general buying advice on products as diverse as stereos and orange juice. It also provides a subject index to evaluations from the previous five years of Consumer Reports.

Dow Jones Irwin Business Almanac. Dow Jones-Irwin, 1977–.

This annual almanac provides business, financial, and tax statistics. It includes a short business directory and a review of the previous year's significant business news.

Dun and Bradstreet Million Dollar Directory. Dun and Bradstreet, 1959–.

This annual directory offers alphabetical listings of industries and businesses with a net worth of at least $1 million. It includes the name, address, corporate officers, Standard Industrial Classification (SIC) number, approximate sales, and number of employees for approximately 39,000 U.S. companies.

Dun and Bradstreet's Guide to Your Investments. Crowell, 1973–.

An introductory guide for amateur stock-market investors, this annual explains basic concepts for all types of investments: common and preferred stocks, bonds, real estate, stock options, small business investment companies, and formula investing.

Fortune World Business Directory. Time, Inc., 1957–.

Taken from the annual listing in the May issue of Fortune magazine ranking the 500 largest U.S. industrial corporations, this directory includes the "Fortune 500" plus the 50 largest banks.

Franchise Opportunities Handbook. U.S. Bureau of Industrial Economics and Minority Business Development Agency, 1972–.

One of the best publications on franchising, this annual guide provides details on equity capital needed to buy specific franchises, available training, and support services.

Help: (Washington): The Useful Almanac. Everest House, 1977–.

This annual almanac offers up-to-date information for consumers. It is arranged topically, with material on health, real estate, nutrition, energy, education, insurance, and numerous other subjects.

Moody's Handbook of Common Stocks. Moody's Investors Service, 1965–.

Described as a quick-reference tool, Moody's quarterly publishes data on approximately 1,000 stocks, outlining capitalization, earnings, and the projected outlook for each.

Standard and Poor's Register of Corporations, Directors and Executives. Standard and Poor's, 1928–.

A standard in the field, Standard and Poor's Register offers three volumes each year with current information on about 46,000 U.S. and Canadian companies. The volumes include biographies of executives as well as separate listings of newly added individuals and companies, obituaries for the previous year, and complete data on each company.

Standard Directory of Advertisers. National Register Publishing, 1907–.

This annual directory lists over 17,000 companies that advertise nationally through various media. The directory provides details on officers and sales personnel, product lines, advertising agencies, and media.

Thomas Register of American Manufacturers and Thomas Register Catalog File. Thomas Publications, 1905–.

This annual authoritative listing of manufacturers is grouped by more than 70,000 product classifications. Its 17 volumes contain lists of products and services; company names, addresses, and phone numbers; names of executives; and ratings. Also included are a brand-name index and company catalogs.

U.S. Master Tax Guide. Commerce Clearing House, 1917–.

Using information on the Internal Revenue Code regulations and court and tax court decisions, this annual handbook covers all aspects of preparing federal income taxes for corporations, estates and trusts, individuals, and partnerships. It is considered a standard in its field.

COMMUNICATIONS

Barnouw, Eric, ed. *International Encyclopedia of Communications.* 4 vols. Oxford University Press, 1989.

This comprehensive, illustrated four-volume encyclopedia covers the entire spectrum of communications studies. Most articles are followed by brief bibliographies, and the work is extensively cross-referenced.

Brown, Les. *Les Brown's Encyclopedia of Television.* Visible Ink Press, 1992.

This reference work covers television terminology, notable television programs, and profiles of important television personalities, including actors, directors, producers, and writers.

Representative American Speeches Series. H. W. Wilson, 1967–.

This annual publication includes selected major speeches with biographical notes on the speaker.

Writers Market: Where to Sell What You Write. Writer's Digest, 1929–.

An essential annual reference for freelance writers that gives the pertinent data on more than 4,500 publishers of books, periodicals, audiovisual materials, greeting cards, plays, and other materials. It includes basics of copyright law and authors' rights.

EDUCATION

American Universities and Colleges. Walter de Gruyter, 2001.

This comprehensive directory provides information about the structure of higher education in the United States, as well as complete details on each of the more than 1,700 institutions granting baccalaureate or higher degrees.

Durnin, Richard G. *American Education: A Guide to Information Sources.* Gale, 1982.

This bibliography covers books relating to American education, with 107 topical chapters listing works on childhood through higher education. Most works included are recent publications, but classic works also are described.

Passow, Harry A., ed. *Dictionary of Education.* Greenwood, 2002.

This volume offers definitions of technical and professional terms and concepts in all areas of education.

The World of Learning. Europa Publications, 1947–.

This annual directory of international institutions includes educational and scientific institutions and organizations listed by country.

ETHNIC STUDIES
See **Anthropology and Ethnology.**

FILM

Halliwell, Leslie, and John Walker, eds. *Halliwell's Film and Video Guide.* HarperCollins (published annually).

This regularly revised comprehensive work covers a wide range of popular film lore.

Katz, Ephraim. *The Film Encyclopedia.* 4th ed. HarperInformation, 2001.

This volume covers directors, producers, actors, composers, and screenwriters, as well as major studios and film centers; it does not list individual movies.

GEOGRAPHY AND TRAVEL GUIDES

Rand McNally Comprehensive World Atlas. 2nd ed. Rand McNally, 1991.

This atlas includes 350 color maps and map inserts, with individual maps of each U.S. state and Canadian province. It also provides a list of 1980 census totals for about 20,000 U.S. political subdivisions. The main index contains 82,000 entries.

Rand McNally Road Atlas, latest edition. United States, Canada, and Mexico. Rand McNally.

This annual publication offers maps of all 50 states, each Canadian province, Central America, Mexico, and Puerto Rico, plus a 23,000-item place-name index. It also includes information on population, national park areas, mileage, recreational and historical sites, area codes, time zones, and how to compute miles per gallon.

Merrian-Webster's Geographical Dictionary. 3rd ed. Merriam-Webster, 1997.

This work presents basic geographic, demographic, economic, and historical notes on world countries, regions, cities, and natural features, with maps.

HISTORY

Barraclough, Geoffrey, ed. *The Times Concise Atlas of World History.* 4th ed. Hammond, 1995.

Seven sections detail the history of the world, beginning with "The World of Early Man" and concluding with "The Age of Global Civilizations." This work contains approximately 600 maps and illustrations depicting the rise and fall of major civilizations, as well as significant religious and historical events.

Barzun, Jacques, and Henry F. Graff. *The Modern Researcher.* 6th ed. Harcourt Brace, 2002.

This essential reference stresses historical research and provides methodologies useful to those in the humanities and social sciences.

Carruth, Gorton. *The Encyclopedia of American Facts & Dates.* 10th ed. HarperCollins, 1997.

This chronologically arranged encyclopedia of American history has become a standard reference book for students and others seeking basic information. It covers explorations, treaties, battles, politics, literature, and science, among other topics.

LAW

Black, Henry Campbell, and Bryan Garner, eds. *Black's Law Dictionary,* 7th ed. West Group, 1999.

A standard reference in the field, Black's gives detailed definitions in all aspects of law, including criminal procedure, estate planning, accounting, taxes, and commercial transactions.

Cohen, Morris L., and Robert C. Berring. *How to Find the Law.* 9th ed. West, 1989.

A basic text for law students, as well as a helpful tool for the layman investigating resources and methodologies of legal research.

LINGUISTICS

Guinagh, Kevin, ed. *Dictionary of Foreign Phrases and Abbreviations.* 3rd ed. H. W. Wilson, 1982.

This dictionary contains definitions for more than 5,000 French, German, Greek, Italian, Latin, and Spanish abbreviations, phrases, quotations, and proverbs that appear in the English language. Similar expressions are cross-referenced.

Merriam-Webster's Collegiate Dictionary. 10th ed. Merriam-Webster, 1998.

Almost 160,000 entries are offered, with pronunciations, functional labels, inflected forms, word histories, usage, and word divisions. Also included is the first known date of use for each word. The dictionary contains sections with biographical and geographical entries, foreign words and phrases, degree-granting colleges and universities, signs and symbols, and a style manual.

Roget's International Thesaurus. 6th ed. HarperInformation, 2001.

Topical listings of more than 250,000 words are provided, with an alphabetical index for easy use.

Strunk, William, and E. B. White. *The Elements of Style.* 4th ed. Macmillan, 1999.

A classic book noted for its simplicity and directness, *Elements* consists of only five chapters: "Elementary Rules of Usage," "Elementary Principles of Composition," "A Few Matters of Form," "Words and Expressions Commonly Misused," and "An Approach to Style."

Webster's New World College Dictionary. 4th ed. Wiley, 1999.

This authoritative dictionary provides over 150,000 entries, with in-depth etymologies, pronunciations, foreign expressions, a syllabification system, and over 11,000 Americanisms.

Libraries

LITERATURE

Drabble, Margaret, ed. *The Oxford Companion to English Literature.* 6th ed. Oxford University Press, 2000.

> Entries on English fiction, authors, and literary schools and movements are presented.

France, Peter, ed. *The New Oxford Companion to Literature in French.* Oxford University Press, 1995.

> *The New Oxford Companion to Literature in French* is a new work rather than a revision of the old *Companion to French Literature.* Coverage is extended to francophone writing throughout the world.

Garland, Henry, and Mary Garland. *The Oxford Companion to German Literature.* 3rd ed. Oxford University Press, 1997.

> German writers and their works, with cultural and historical background, are provided.

Gassner, John, and Edward Quinn, eds. *The Readers' Encyclopedia of World Drama.* Dover Publications, 2002.

> The book has entries on playwrights, critics, national dramatic literatures, and histories. Emphasis is on drama as literature.

Granger, Edith. *The Columbia Granger's Index to Poetry in Anthologies. 12th ed.* Columbia University Press, 2002.

> This standard work is indexed by title, first line, author, and subject.

Hart, James D. *Oxford Companion to American Literature.* 6th ed. Oxford University Press, 1995.

> This volume has entries on American fiction, authors, and literary schools and movements.

Harvey, Paul, and J. E. Heseltine. *The Oxford Companion to French Literature.* Oxford University Press, 1969.

> This volume covers authors and their works, with survey articles, terms, and movements from the Middle Ages to 1939.

Howatson, Margaret C., and Ian Chilvers. *Concise Oxford Companion to Classical Literature.* Oxford University Press, 1993.

> This comprehensive guide has entries on authors, characters, plots, literary forms, and cultural and historical background. A chronological table and maps are included.

MLA International Bibliography of Books and Articles on the Modern Languages and Literatures. Modern Language Association of America, 1921–. Annual.

> This useful reference covers articles and books in English, French, German, Spanish, Italian, Portuguese, Rumanian, and other languages.

Sader, Marion, ed. *The Reader's Adviser 6 Vol. Set.* 14th ed. Greenwood, 1993.

> This basic guide to literature covers the best in English and American fiction, poetry, essays, biographies, and other areas in the fields of reference, history, philosophy, and science.

MEDICAL SCIENCE

American Medical Association Family Medical Guide. 3rd ed. Charles R. Clayman, ed. 1994.

> This layperson's handbook features articles on diseases and disorders, diagnostic charts, and an index of drugs and medications.

Berkow, Robert, ed. *The Merck Manual of Medical Information.* Merck & Company, 1997.

> Written for the general reader, this version of *The Merck Manual of Diagnosis and Therapy* is comprehensive and easy-to-use.

Komaroff, Anthony, and Harvard Medical School. *The Harvard Medical School Family Health Guide.* Simon & Schuster, 1999.

> This family health guide covers symptoms, disorders, diseases, health maintenance, and information about the U.S. health care system. Includes more than 900 illustrations and full-color photographs.

Physicians' Desk Reference to Pharmaceutical Special-ties and Biologicals. Medical Economics, 1947–.

> This compendium, commonly referred to as the PDR, is a standard reference work for physicians and other health professionals. It offers details on dosage, contraindications, side effects, precautions, and undesirable interactions of pharmaceutical products.

The New Wellness Encyclopedia. Staff of the University of California, Berkeley, Wellness Letter, eds. Houghton Mifflin, 1995.

> This comprehensive guide focuses on preventive health through good eating, exercise, and risk reduction for disease.

MUSIC

Abraham, Gerald. *The Concise Oxford History of Music.* Oxford University Press, 1985.

> This scholarly survey of Western music from ancient to modern times is presented chronologically. It describes the musical styles of each period and region, with extensive bibliographies.

Garland Encyclopedia of World Music. Garland Publishing, 1998.

> Sweeping overview of the indigenous musical forms of the world's peoples, described in essay-style articles.

Grout, Donald J. *A History of Western Music.* 5th ed. Norton, 1996.

> This standard one-volume history of music is used in thousands of colleges and graduate schools. This illustrated volume contains a bibliography, chronology, and glossary.

Havlice, Patricia Pate. *Popular Song Index.* 3rd ed. Scarecrow Press, 1989.

> Hundreds of songbooks from the second half of the 20th century, including children's songs, folk songs, hymns, and popoular music, are anthologized.

Sadie, Stanley, ed. *The New Grove Dictionary of Music and Musicians.* Reprint ed. 20 vols. Grove's Dictionaries of Music, 1995.

> This comprehensive dictionary includes entries and articles on composers, performers, theorists, music publishers, scholars, terminology, genres, and orchestras, with exhaustive bibliographies.

MYTHOLOGY, FOLKLORE, AND POPULAR CUSTOMS

Bulfinch, Thomas. Illustrated by Giovannie Caselli. *The Illustrated Bulfinch's Mythology: The Age of Fable, the Age of Chivalry, and the Legends of Charlemagne.* Hungry Minds, 1997.

> The classic work on mythology, Bulfinch's summarizes Greek, Roman, Norse, Arthurian, and other myths, with notes on the Iliad, the Odyssey, and the Aeneid.

Mercatante, Anthony. *The Facts On File Encyclopedia of World Mythology and Legend.* Facts On File, 1988.

> This comprehensive reference covers world mythologies in thematic, biographical, and narrative essays.

Thompson, Stith. *The Folktale.* University of California Press, 1977.

> Considered a standard in the field, this work discusses the form and development of folk stories, with summaries of the most popular folktales of Europe, western Asia, and the Native North Americans. It also covers various methods of researching and studying folktales and folklore.

PHILOSOPHY

Borchert, Donald M. *Encyclopedia of Philosophy (Supplement).* Gale, 1996.

> A companion to the eight-volume *Encyclopedia of Philosophy* published by Macmillan.

Encyclopedia of Philosophy, 8 vols. Macmillan, 1973.

> An excellent scholarly reference, this eight-volume encyclopedia contains hundreds of articles relevant to political science as well as philosophy and biographies of scores of key figures such as Aristotle, Darwin, Hobbes, Jefferson, Locke, Machiavelli, Malthus, Marx, Mill, Plato, and Rousseau.

Libraries

Magill, Frank N., ed. *Masterpieces of World Philosophy: More Than 100 Classics of the World's Greatest Philosophers Analyzed and Explained.* HarperCollins, 1990.

This book contains more than 100 synopses and commentaries on key figures in Eastern and Western philosophy, including analyses of important influences on their development.

POLITICAL SCIENCE

Andriot, Laurie. *Internet Blue Pages: The Guide to Federal Government Web Sites.* 2nd ed. Information Today, 2000.

This wide-ranging guide to online information from the U.S. federal government is organized by agency. Comprehensive entries describe and list the function or purpose of each agency, its URLs, and links from various agency home pages.

Baum, Lawrence. *The Supreme Court.* 7th ed. Congressional Quarterly, 2000.

This overview of the Supreme Court explains its processes and discusses the justices, as well as examining policy-making influence and impact on government and individuals.

Congressional Quarterly's Guide to Congress. Latest ed. Congressional Quarterly.

This accurate, nonpartisan guide to the history, power, structure, and workings of Congress includes the texts of the Articles of Confederation, Constitution, Declaration of Independence, and important preconstitutional documents.

Klingemann, Hans-Dieter, and Robert E. Goodin, eds. *A New Handbook of Political Science.* Oxford University Press, 1998.

Containing contributions from 42 internationally known political scientists, this handbook covers the development of political science in the last quarter of the 20th century.

Roberts, Henry M., and William J. Evans, Daniel H. Honemann, and Thomas J. Balch. *Robert's Rules of Order: Newly Revised.* 10th ed. Perseus Publishing, 2000.

This completely revised edition provides the authoritative guide to parliamentary procedure.

Washington Information Directory. Congressional Quarterly, 1975–.

This annual publication describes 5,000 congressional, executive, and nongovernmental agencies, committees, and organizations. It is considered an indispensable guide to both official and unofficial Washington.

RECREATION AND SPORTS

Fortin, Francois, ed. *Sports: The Complete Visual References.* Firefly Books, 2000.

Illustrates and describes approximately 120 sports, including new sports. Summarizes history, equipment, playing fields, and techniques of each sport covered.

Levinson, David, and Karen Christensen, eds. *Encyclopedia of World Sport: From Ancient Times to the Present.* 3 vols. ABC-CLIO, 1996.

Comprehensive set covering the history of sport.

Robert, Markel, ed. *Women's Sports Encyclopedia.* Holt, 1997.

A comprehensive history of women in sports, including hundreds of biographies, world records to 1997, and a timeline dating from Ancient Greece.

RELIGION

Adams, Charles J., ed. *A Reader's Guide to the Great Religions.* 2nd ed. The Free Press, 1977.

Through bibliographic essays, this work covers major religions as well as ancient beliefs, religions of Mexico and Central and South America, the Sikh religion, and the Jains. It includes a subject index and an index of authors, compilers, translators, and editors for the serious researcher.

Attwater, Donald, and Catherine R. John. *Penguin Dictionary of Saints.* 3rd ed. Penguin, 1996.

This book provides brief biographical sketches of the best-known saints. The selections are worldwide but emphasize those in Great Britain.

Brandon, S. G. F., ed. *Dictionary of Comparative Religions.* Macmillan, 1978.

> Thorough and concise, this volume defines anthropology, iconography, philosophy, and the psychology of primitive, ancient, Asian, and Western religions. Articles describe practices and philosophies of specific religions, with terminology for each and pertinent bibliographies.

The Illustrated Bible Dictionary. 3 vols. Tyndale House, 1980.

> Comprehensive and well organized, this dictionary is based on the revised standard version. It offers definitions from all aspects of books of the Bible; major works and doctrines; and history, geography, customs, and cultures of biblical times. Extensive photographs, charts, diagrams, cross-references, and a useful index are included.

Kohlenberger, John R., and Richard E. Whitaker. *The Analytical Concordance to the New Revised Standard Version of the New Testament.* William B. Eerdmans Publishing, 1997.

> This massive work contains both a concordance and an index-lexicon. Entries give the English word followed by a subtitle line with three elements: definition, Greek word, and an English transliteration of the Greek word. Included are complete listings of each passage in which the subject word appears, with an explanation of its use in context.

SCIENCE AND TECHNOLOGY

Allin, Craig W. ed. *Encyclopedia of Environmental Issues.* 3 vols. Salem Press, 2000.

> Covers a wide range of environmental issues in 475 articles.

Chen, Ching-Chih. *Scientific and Technical Information Sources.* 2nd ed. MIT, 1986.

> Although the book is primarily a guide for science and technology librarians, it is a useful guide to relevant sources for the layperson.

The Cutting Edge: An Encyclopedia of Advanced Technologies. Oxford University Press, 2000.

> This volume contains 102 signed, cross-referenced entries, describing each technology's development and direction, as well as the opinions it provokes.

McGraw-Hill Encyclopedia of Science and Technology. 7th ed. McGraw-Hill, 1996.

> This 20-volume compendium continues to be the basic reference source covering important topics from earliest times to the present. Annual updates are available.

Walker, Peter, ed. *Chambers Dictionary of Science and Technology.* Larousse Kingfisher Chambers, 1999.

> A revision and expansion of a classic work, the *Chambers Dictionary* provides 45,000 understandable, alphabetical definitions of terms used in a variety of scientific disciplines.

SOCIAL SCIENCE

Baltes, Paul B., and Neil J. Smelser, eds. *International Encyclopedia of the Social and Behavioral Sciences.* Elsevier Science, 2001.

> This scholarly summary of the social sciences includes signed articles on numerous specific topics, as well as hundreds of biographies.

Calhoun, Craig J. ed. *Dictionary of the Social Sciences.* Oxford University Press, February 2001.

> Includes terms from anthropology, sociology, political science, economics, human geography, and cultural studies.

See also **Anthropology and Ethnology; Political Science;** and **Sociology.**

SOCIOLOGY

Barnes, Harry Elmer, and Howard Becker. *Social Thought from Lore to Science.* 3rd ed. Peter Smith, 1990.

> This is a three-volume encyclopedic inventory of the history of sociology.

Libraries

Directory of Counseling Services. International Association of Counseling Services, 1969–.

> This annual publication lists members of the American Personnel and Guidance Association who offer public and private counseling dealing with education, family, marriage, personal problems, rehabilitation, and vocational guidance.

STATISTICS AND DEMOGRAPHY

Bureau of the Census Catalog. U.S. Bureau of the Census, 1946–.

> This catalog provides listings of all published and unpublished material (tape, cards, or microform) created by the Census Bureau during the period covered.

Kotz, Samuel, and Normal L. Johnson, eds. *Encyclopedia of Statistical Sciences,* 9 vols. Wiley, 1982–1988; updates 1997-8.

> Information on many topics in statistical his-tory and application of statistical methods is presented in this nine-volume work, intended primarily for readers who seek more information than general references can offer.

United Nations Statistical Yearbook. United Nations, 1949–.

> This annual publication is considered the best source for international statistics. It offers data on such topics as agriculture, balance of payments, communications, construction, energy, population, transport, and wages and prices in 150 countries and territories.

THEATER AND PERFORMING ARTS

Cohen, Selma, ed. *International Encyclopedia of Dance.* 6 vols. Oxford University Press, 1998.

> Scholarly and groundbreaking work on dance around the world.

Hatnoll, Phyllis, ed. *The Oxford Companion Guide to World Theatre.* 4th ed. Oxford University Press, 1983.

> Articles on all aspects of theater are included, from history to theater architecture, technical the-

ater, terminology, and experimental theater. Also included are articles on national dramatic literature, plays, actors, playwrights, and teachers.

Hughes, Catherine. *American Theater Annual.* Gale Research, 1976–.

> All plays opening on and off Broadway during the year are listed, with details of cast members, opening and closing dates, plot summaries, and review excerpts.

Koegler, Horst. *The Concise Oxford Dictionary of Ballet.* 2nd ed. Oxford University Press, 1982.

> This book contains more than 5,000 alphabetically arranged entries covering all areas of ballet: choreographers, composers, dancers, history, schools and companies, and basic definitions.

Notable Names in the American Theater. James T. White, 1976.

> This major work is divided into nine sections covering administrators, agents, archivists, authors, casting directors, composers, conductors, critics, designers, directors, educators, historians, lyricists, performers, playwrights, producers, and teachers.

Theatre World. Crown, annual.

> This theater yearbook gives a complete pictorial and statistical record of each Broadway season from 1944–45 to the present.

MAJOR ART MUSEUMS AND THEIR SPECIAL COLLECTIONS

Internet links to numerous museums can be found on the Virtual Library Museums Pages, supported by the International Council of Museums. The organization's home page can be accessed at http://icom.org/vlmp.

UNITED STATES

Arizona
University Art Museum
Arizona State University Art Collections
Nelson Fine Arts Center and Matthews Center
Arizona State University
P.O. Box 872911
Tempe, AZ 85287-2911

480-965-2787 (ARTS)
http://asuartmuseum.asu.edu

Founded in 1950, Arizona State's collection includes American paintings of the 18th and 19th centuries; a fine print collection with Rembrandts, Whistlers, and Dürers; fine Americana and decorative arts, particularly pottery; European painting and sculpture; Latin American arts; and crafts.

California

California Palace of the Legion of Honor
100 34th Ave.
San Francisco, CA 94121
415-750-3600

M. H. deYoung Museum
75 Tea Garden Dr.
Golden Gate Park
San Francisco, CA 94118
415-750-3600

These museums are run by a joint administration, although they are not located near each other. Founded in 1924 and 1895, respectively, each museum has extensive collections. The deYoung includes the Hearst collection of Flemish Gothic tapestries; fine primitive pre-Columbian artifacts; Northwest Coast Native American, African, and Oceanic arts collections; and Renaissance and Baroque art. The California Palace is noted for its 18th-century French furniture and decorative arts; its French paintings, including those of Monet, Renoir, Fragonard, Boucher, Manet, and Corot; Rodin sculptures; and an extraordinary collection of prints and drawings of all periods.

J. Paul Getty Museum
1200 Getty Center Dr.
Los Angeles, CA 90049
310-440-7300

The world's best-endowed museum, the Getty was created in 1953. This popular museum is housed in a re-creation of the 1st century B.C. Villa dei Paryri at Herculaneum, complete with elaborate gardens. The Getty has acquired extraordinary classical collections, including illuminated manuscripts and French decorative arts.

Huntington Library, Art Collections, and Botanical Garden
1151 Oxford Rd.
San Marino, CA 91108
626-405-2100
http://www.huntington.org

In the Huntington complex, established in 1919, a beautiful garden setting enhances the extraordinary

collections of 18th-century British paintings, including Gainsborough's Blue Boy and Lawrence's Pinkie; Renaissance bronzes and 18th-century marbles; early editions of Shakespeare and Chaucer in the extensive library; and prints and drawings. The setting includes a Japanese garden and 16th-century samurai's house.

Los Angeles County Museum of Art
5905 Wilshire Blvd.
Los Angeles, CA 90036
323-857-6111
http:// www.lacma.org/

Established in 1910, this museum houses a general collection in three pavilions surrounded by a sculpture garden with works from Rodin's time to the present. Its acquisitions include early Near and Middle Eastern antiquities; Roman, Greek, Western, and modern art; Far Eastern collections; textiles; costumes; Indian arts; pottery; Italian mosaics; pre-Columbian, African, and Oceanic arts; and 19th- and 20th-century American and European paintings.

A researcher at the Smithsonian Museum removed a lens from the compound eye of a half-billion-year-old trilobite (a marine invertebrate animal), attached it to a microscope, and took a photograph of a building.

Norton Simon Museum
411 W. Colorado Blvd.
Pasadena, CA 91105
646-449-6840
http://nortonsimon.org

Established in 1924 as the Pasadena Museum of Modern Art, this museum has developed worldwide prominence through the loans of collector Norton Simon. His collections include European art from the Renaissance to recent times, with Old Masters of the highest quality.

Colorado

The Denver Art Museum
100 W. 14th Avenue Pkwy.
Denver, CO 80204-2788
720-865-5000
http://www.denverartmuseum.org

The Denver Art Museum is noted for its collection of primitive African, Oceanic, American, Native American, and Northwest Indian arts; its Peruvian art; its collection of the arts of China, Japan, Korea, India, Southeast Asia, Tibet, and the Middle and Near East; period rooms; Impressionist, post-Impressionist, and modern paintings; prints, drawings, and photographs; and the Neusteter Institute of Fashion, Costume, and Textiles.

Connecticut

The New Britain Museum of American Art

56 Lexington St.
New Britain, CT 06052-1412
860-229-0257
www.nbmaa.org

The New Britain Collection, established in 1903, focuses on outstanding American paintings from colonial times to the present. It includes Hudson River School painters and the Low memorial collection of American illustration, with N. C. Wyeth classics.

Yale Center for British Art

P.O. Box 208280
New Haven, CT 06520
203-432-2800

This collection of British watercolors, drawings, paintings, books, and prints is the largest of its kind outside Great Britain. Established in 1977, the center was the gift of Paul Mellon, a lifelong collector of British art.

Yale University Art Gallery

P.O. Box 208271
New Haven, CT 06520-8271
203-432-0600
http://www.yale.edu/artgallery

This outstanding world art collection has been built up since the gallery's founding in 1832. It includes the Jarves collection of early Italian paintings; collections of American silver, painting, and decorative arts; modern art; Greek and Roman vases; manuscripts; prints and drawings; and primitive arts.

Delaware

Delaware Art Museum

2301 Kentmere Pkwy.
Wilmington, DE 19806
302-571-9590
http://www.delart.org

The Delaware Art Museum, founded in 1912, specializes in American paintings, with examples by Hudson River School painters such as John Sloan, Howard Pyle, and the Wyeth family. There is an extensive collection of English pre-Raphaelites, a research library on American arts, and prints and drawings.

Henry Francis Du Pont Winterthur Museum

Route 52
Winterthur, DE 19735
302-888-4600

Founded in 1930, Winterthur has an outstanding collection of American furniture, furnishings, and decorative arts from the colonial period to the mid–19th century. Period rooms display extensive collections of ceramics, glass, Chinese porcelain, fabrics, lighting fixtures, and carpets.

District of Columbia

Arthur M. Sackler Gallery, Smithsonian Institution

1050 Independence Ave., SW
Washington, DC 20560
202-357-4880
http://www.asia.si.edu

This gallery contains a permanent collection of Asian art, including ancient works from China, the Indian subcontinent, and Southeast Asia as well as scrolls and other work by notable 20th-century painters.

Freer Gallery of Art, Smithsonian Institution

1050 Independence Ave., SW
Washington, DC 20560
202-357-4880
http://www.asia.si.edu

Established in 1906, the Freer has one of the world's best collections of Oriental art and a comprehensive collection of Whistler paintings (his close friend Charles Freer gathered the collection and donated it).

Hirshhorn Museum and Sculpture Garden, Smithsonian Institution

P.O. Box 37012
Hirshhorn Museum and Sculpture Garden
MRC Code 350
Washington, DC 20013-7012
202-357-3091
http://www.hirshhorn.si.edu

Created in 1966 to specialize in modern art, the Hirshhorn's collection is so vast that only a small portion can be displayed at any time.

National Gallery of Art

6 Constitution Ave.
Washington, DC 20565
202-737-4215
http://www.nga.gov

The National Gallery was endowed by Andrew Mellon in 1937 and continues to benefit from his children's donations. It includes paintings and sculptures of all schools of Western art, decorative arts, and drawings and prints, with all the classic masters represented.

Smithsonian American Art Museum, Smithsonian Institution

Washington, DC 20560-0970
202-275-1500
http://www.nmaa.si.edu

Housed in the historic Greek Revival Old Patent Office, the museum has a definitive collection of American arts, including graphic and decorative arts, from colonial times to the present.

The J. Paul Getty museum is the richest in the world. It paid $22 million for Fra Bartolommeo's The Rest on the Flight Into Egypt with Saint John the Baptist.

Hawaii

Honolulu Academy of Arts

900 S. Beretania St.
Honolulu, HI 96814
808-532-8787
http://www.honoluluacademy.org

The academy, founded in 1927, has a general collection representing everything from ancient Near Eastern and Mediterranean arts to European and American arts. Medieval art, the Michener Collection of Japanese prints, Monet's Water Lilies, and the arts of Africa, Oceania, and the Americas are also included.

Illinois

The Art Institute of Chicago

11 South Michigan Ave.
Chicago, IL 60603
312-443-3600
http://www.artic.edu

Founded in 1879, the Art Institute of Chicago has excellent collections in all areas of art. It is noted for the works of Old Masters, Impressionists, and American and Far Eastern artists; graphics; and Thorne miniature rooms. Famed works include Seurat's *Sunday Afternoon on the Island of la Grande Jatte,* Rembrandt's *Young Girl at an Open Half-Door,* and Mary Cassatt's *The Bath.*

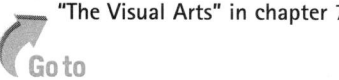

"The Visual Arts" in chapter 7

Oriental Institute Museum
University of Chicago

1155 E. 58th St.
Chicago, IL 60637
Museum Office: 773-702-9502
http://www.oi.uchicago.edu

Founded in 1919, the Oriental Institute houses a top collection of archeology and art of the ancient Near East, Babylonia, Egypt, early Christian cultures, and Islamic civilization.

Indiana

Indianapolis Museum of Art

1200 W. 38th St.
Indianapolis, IN 46208
317-923-1331
http://www.ima-art.org

Noted for its Chinese, primitive, and American art, this museum, founded in 1883, has an outstanding general collection of Old Masters, Turner watercolors, and European and American decorative arts.

Kansas

Wichita Art Museum

619 Stackman Dr.
Wichita, KS 67203
316-268-4921
http://www.wichitaartmuseum.org

Established in 1935, this museum's outstanding collection is noted for its American paintings, sculptures, prints, and drawings.

Kentucky

J. B. Speed Art Museum

2035 S. Third St.
Louisville, KY 40208
502-634-2700
http://www.speedmuseum.org

This extensive collection, founded in 1925, includes European painting, sculpture, and decorative arts from the Middle Ages to the present; French and Flemish tapestries; and Kentuckiana.

Maryland

The Baltimore Museum of Art

10 Art Museum Dr.
Baltimore, MD 21218
410-396-6300
http://www.artbma.org

Best known for its classic modern collections, this outstanding museum, established in 1914, displays contemporary drawings, period rooms illustrating stylistic development in Maryland, Old Masters paintings, and Far Eastern art.

Walters Art Gallery

600 N. Charles St.
Baltimore, MD 21201
410-547-9000
http://www.thewalters.org

Assembled by father and son, the Walters Art Gallery opened in 1931 with exquisite medieval treasures and Byzantine and Islamic art; early Christian liturgical vessels, Renaissance enamels, and jewelry; paintings from various periods; and Greek, Roman, and Etruscan art.

Massachusetts

Fogg Art Museum

32 Quincy St.
Harvard University
Cambridge, MA 02138
617-495-9400

With the largest and most extensive art collection of any university in the United States, the Fogg, opened in 1895, is particularly noted for its drawings and prints of all periods. It also has a fine collection of Chinese sculptures, stones and bronzes, jades, and ceramics.

Isabella Stewart Gardner Museum

280 The Fenway
Boston, MA 02115
617-566-1401
http://www.gardnermuseum.org

This personal collection, founded in 1900, covers a wide range of world art, with masterpieces such as Titian's *The Rape of Europa,* Giotto's *Presentation of the Child Jesus in the Temple,* and Botticelli's *Madonna of the Eucharist.*

Museum of Fine Arts

465 Huntington Ave.
Boston, MA 02115
617-267-9300
http://www.mfa.org

This collection, founded in 1870, includes masterpieces from around the world. It is noted for its Far Eastern, ancient, Egyptian, Greek, and Roman collections; its Old Masters, Impressionist, and post-Impressionist works; and its American paintings and decorative arts. It also has American silver, prints and drawings, ancient musical instruments, and ship models. Famed works include Paul Revere's Liberty Bowl,

Renoir's *Le Bal…Bougival,* and a Greek marble *Head of Aphrodite.*

Michigan

The Detroit Institute of Arts

5200 Woodward Ave.
Detroit, MI 48202
313-833-7900
http://www.dia.org

Founded in 1885, this institute is renowned for its comprehensive collection of world arts, especially its Old Master paintings of northern Europe, French 18th-century decorative arts, art of the ancient world, period rooms, prints and drawings, and American arts since colonial times.

Henry Ford Museum and Greenfield Village

20900 Oakwood Blvd.
Dearborn, MI 48124
313-271-1620
http://www.hfmgv.org

Described as a "Disneyland of Americana," the indoor/outdoor facilities, established in 1929, of the museum and village offer demonstrations of crafts and manufacturing techniques that complement its extensive collections of arts, crafts, artifacts, and technology. Activities include everything from antique car rallies to country fairs on its 14 acres.

Minnesota

The Minneapolis Institute of Arts

2400 Third Ave. S.
South Minneapolis, MN 55404
612-870-3000
http://www.artsmia.org

This outstanding general collection is strongest in European paintings from Old Masters to the present. Founded in 1912, the institute also houses the Pillsbury Collection of Chinese bronzes, Japanese prints and paintings, textiles, and photographs.

Walker Art Center

725 Vineland Pl.
Minneapolis, MN 55403
612-375-7600
http://www.walkerart.org

Founded in 1879, this museum contains contemporary art, including paintings, sculpture, drawings, and prints. Its renowned Minneapolis Sculpture Garden is a 7½-acre urban garden featuring 40 sculptures and a conservatory with horticultural displays.

Libraries

Missouri

Nelson-Atkins Museum of Art
4525 Oak St.
Kansas City, MO 64111
816-561-4000
http://www.Nelson-Atkins.org

This museum contains prestigious collections of European and American art as well as a renowned Oriental Collection.

The St. Louis Art Museum
One Fine Arts Dr.
St. Louis, MO 63110
314-721-0067
http://www.slam.org

Founded in 1881, the St. Louis Art Museum contains a comprehensive collection of art. Among its more than 35,000 works are important pre-Columbian and German Expressionist collections.

New Jersey

Princeton University Art Museum
Princeton, NJ 08544
609-258-3788
http://www.princetonartmuseum.org/

Opened in 1882, this comprehensive collection contains a wide spectrum of world art, including Chinese paintings and bronzes, classical antiquities, and French paintings and sculptures.

New Mexico

The University of New Mexico
Center for the Arts
University Art Museum
Room 1017
Albuquerque, NM 87131
505-277-4001
http://unmartmuseum.unm.edu

Established in 1963, the museum has important collections of 19th- and 20th-century prints and photographs and American paintings of the 20th century, with emphasis on artists who worked in New Mexico.

New York

Albany Institute of History and Art
125 Washington Ave.
Albany, NY 12210
518-463-4478
http://www.albanyinstitute.org

Founded in 1791, the institute's collection focuses on the fine and decorative arts of Albany and Hudson River artists, with portraits, silver, furniture, and period rooms.

The Brooklyn Museum of Art
200 Eastern Pkwy.
Brooklyn, NY 11238
718-638-5000
http://www.brooklynart.org

The Brooklyn Museum was founded in 1823 and has amassed comprehensive collections of Egyptian and classical arts; American arts; European and American graphics; and pre-Columbian, African, Native American, and other primitive arts.

The Cloisters
799 Fort Washington Ave.
Fort Tryon Park, NY 10040
212-923-3700
http://www.metmuseum.org

A branch of the Metropolitan Museum devoted exclusively to medieval art, the Cloisters opened in 1938 and incorporates four medieval cloisters, an arcade, a chapel, and exhibition rooms. The museum features 12th- and 13th-century Byzantine and Romanesque art from France and Spain.

Cooper-Hewitt, National Design Museum, Smithsonian Institution
2 E. 91st St.
New York, NY 10128
212-849-8300
http://ndm.si.edu/

Established in 1897, the Cooper-Hewitt is housed in the Carnegie mansion. Its excellent collection of decorative arts includes furniture, fabrics, wallpaper, ceramics, drawings, prints, architecture and design publications, and metalwork. It boasts the world's largest collection of Winslow Homer drawings and sketches by other late-19th-century artists.

The Frick Collection
One E. 70th St.
New York, NY 10021
212-288-0700
http://www.frick.org

The former home of Henry Clay Frick, built in 1914 as an 18th-century model, still has most of its original furnishings intact, including excellent European paintings from the 14th through the 18th centuries.

Guggenheim Museum
See **Solomon R. Guggenheim Museum.**

Libraries

The Jewish Museum

1109 Fifth Ave.
New York, NY 10128
212-423-3200
http://www.jewishmuseum.org

This preeminent U.S. collection numbers over 23,000 objects spanning 4 millennia, ranging from ancient Eastern Mediterranean archeological artifacts to contemporary art and including paintings, sculpture, ceramics, textiles, wood, metalwork, photography, drawings, prints, coins, medals, and broadcast materials. A permanent exhibit, The Jewish Experience, spans 4,000 years of history and culture.

The Metropolitan Museum of Art

1000 Fifth Ave.
New York, NY 10028
212-879-5500
http://www.metmuseum.org

One of the world's major museums, founded in 1870, the Metropolitan houses definitive collections covering about 5,000 years of art. A few of the highlights include medieval armor collections, Tiffany stained-glass windows, the complete Temple of Dendur, extensive painting collections, sculpture, decorative arts, and a re-creation of a classic Ming dynasty Chinese garden court.

The Museum of Modern Art

11 W. 53rd St.
New York, NY 10019
212-708-9480
http://www.moma.org

Begun in 1929, this exceptional collection traces the evolution of art from the Impressionist period forward. It represents a variety of disciplines, including drawings and prints, industrial design, architecture, paintings, sculpture, and decorative arts.

The Solomon R. Guggenheim Museum

1071 Fifth Ave.
New York, NY 10128
212-423-3500
http://www.guggenheim.org

Founded in 1937, this excellent collection of modern drawings, prints, paintings, and sculpture emphasizes abstract and nonobjective subjects. It is housed in a stunning Frank Lloyd Wright building.

Whitney Museum of American Art

945 Madison Ave.
New York, NY 10021
212-570-3600
http://www.whitney.org/index.shtml

Opened in 1966, the Whitney houses New York's largest collection of 20th-century art, with changing exhibitions of drawings, paintings, sculpture, and architecture. It shows contemporary avant-garde film and video and holds the Biennial of Contemporary American Art, a showcase of the best recent work.

Ohio

Cincinnati Art Museum

953 Eden Park Dr.
Cincinnati, OH 45202
513-721-5204
http://www.cincinnatiartmuseum.org

Founded in 1886, this major museum has an excellent, comprehensive general collection noted for its Near Eastern and American arts, Old Masters, medieval art, musical instruments, and drawings and prints.

Cleveland Museum of Art

11150 East Blvd.
Cleveland, OH 44106
216-421-7340
http://www.clevelandart.org

This excellent museum, founded in 1913, has a wide-ranging collection representing the artistic accomplishments of cultures throughout the world. It is recognized for one of the best Far Eastern collections and for its medieval art, Old Masters, classical antiquities, and American arts from the colonial time forward.

The Toledo Museum of Art

2445 Monroe St.
Toledo, OH 43620
and
P.O. Box 1013
Toledo, OH 43697
419-255-8000
http://www.toledomuseum.org

This museum is a renowned cultural center for art and music, featuring extensive collections of glass, European and American paintings, sculpture, and decorative arts. Collections range from ancient Egypt, Greece, and Rome through the Middle Ages and the Renaissance to contemporary Europe and America.

Oklahoma

Gilcrease Museum

1400 Gilcrease Museum Rd.
Tulsa, OK 74127
918-596-2700
http://www.gilcrease.org

This exceptional art collection, founded in 1942, captures the saga of America from prehistoric to modern times; the Gilcrease's art of the Old West is rivaled only by that of the Smithsonian. The institute also has maps, books, documents, artifacts, and manuscripts.

Oregon

Portland Art Museum
1219 SW Park Ave.
Portland, OR 97205
503-226-2811
http://www.portlandartmuseum.org

The Portland, founded in 1892, focuses on Native American arts of the Northwest. It also includes a unique collection of Cameroon art, pre-Columbian arts, Renaissance painting and sculpture, Ethiopian crosses, and European and American painting and sculpture.

Pennsylvania

The Carnegie Museum of Art
4400 Forbes Ave.
Pittsburgh, PA 15213
412-622-3131
http://www.cmoa.org/

This museum, founded in 1896, displays art from around the world, including American art since the colonial period; ancient and classical art; African, pre-Columbian, and Native American art; and European painting, sculpture, and decorative arts from the Renaissance forward. Works by Van Gogh, Cézanne, and Monet are included.

Pennsylvania Academy of the Fine Arts
118 N. Broad St.
Philadelphia, PA 19102
215-972-7600
http://www.pafa.org

Founded in 1805, the Pennsylvania Academy offers an excellent collection of American art from the 18th century to the present, with major works by Thomas Eakins, Charles Willson Peale, and William Rush.

Philadelphia Museum of Art
P.O. Box 7646
Philadelphia, PA 19101
215-763-8100
http://www.philamuseum.org

This museum, established in 1876, is noted for its masterpieces from the 12th to the 19th centuries; Barberini tapestries designed by Rubens; arms and armor; glass; European and American period rooms; folk, dec-

orative, and primitive art; and the Stieglitz Center collection of photographs.

The University Museum of Archaeology and Anthropology, University of Pennsylvania
33rd and Spruce Sts.
Philadelphia, PA 19104
215-898-4000
http://www.museum.upenn.edu/

Founded in 1887, the museum is renowned for its worldwide acquisitions of ancient and primitive art, its collection of Native American gold, and the largest grouping of West African art in the Americas. It has sponsored more than 275 expeditions to gather outstanding artifacts from the ancient Near, Middle, and Far East; Southeast Asia; the Mediterranean; the Pacific; Europe; Africa; and the Americas.

Texas

Amon Carter Museum
3501 Camp Bowie Blvd.
Fort Worth, TX 76107
817-738-1933
http://www.cartermuseum.org

Housed since its founding in 1961 in an impressive building designed by Philip Johnson, this museum concentrates on American paintings and sculptures from the 19th century forward, specializing in the works of the Old West. It also has a fine print collection and excellent Remingtons and Russells.

Kimbell Art Museum
3333 Camp Bowie Blvd.
Fort Worth, TX 76107
817-332-8451
http://www.kimbellart.org

Noted for its masterpieces from around the world, this collection, founded in 1972, ranges from 12th-century panel paintings to J. M. W. Turner landscapes, Gainsboroughs, and Goyas.

The Museum of Fine Arts
1001 Bissonet
P.O. Box 6826
Houston, TX 77265-6826
713-639-7300
http://www.mfah.org

This wide-ranging collection of world art, established in 1900, is especially strong in contemporary art; pre-Columbian and Native American art; Old Masters; and later European and American paintings and sculptures.

Libraries

Virginia

Virginia Museum of Fine Arts
2800 Grove Ave.
Richmond, VA 23221-2466
804-340-1400
http://www.vmfa.state.va.us

This museum, which opened its doors in 1936, features important collections of British sporting art and French Impressionist and post-Impressionist art, American paintings since World War II, and art nouveau and art deco objects; a collection of Russian imperial Easter eggs by Fabergé; and one of the nation's leading collections of art from India, Nepal, and Tibet.

Wisconsin

Elvehjem Museum of Art, University of Wisconsin
800 University Ave.
Madison, WI 53706
608-263-2246
http://www.lvm.wisc.edu

Established in 1962, this is one of the three largest university museums in the United States. Its wide-ranging collection of world art dates back to ancient times, with fine examples of classical coins and marbles; American painting, sculpture, and decorative arts from the 18th century forward; Indian miniatures; and Socialist Realist (propagandist) paintings from Russia.

CANADA

Alberta

The Glenbow Museum
130 9th Ave., SE
Calgary, Alberta T2G 0P3
403-268-4100
http://www.glenbow.org

This museum features exhibits on military history, mineralogy, and western Canadian history. These include artifacts from Indian and Inuit peoples as well as the Hudson Bay Company and the Canadian Pacific Railroad. The art gallery features works by historical and contemporary western Canadian artists, including Francis N. Hopkins, Emily Carr, John Hall, Ron Moppett, and Chris Cran.

BRITISH COLUMBIA

The Royal British Columbia Museum of Anthropology
675 Belleville St.
Victoria, British Columbia V8W 9W2
250-356-7226
http://www.royalbcmuseum.bc.ca

The Royal British Columbia Museum displays a range of exhibitions depicting the accomplishments of native peoples, the achievements of early explorers and settlers, and British Columbia's natural heritage and archeological past. It includes a 14-foot-high woolly mammoth and a native Indian penitentiary.

Ontario

Art Gallery of Hamilton
123 King St. West
Hamilton, Ontario L8P 4S8
905-527-6610
http://www.artgalleryofhamilton.com

A major North American museum, this gallery was established in 1914. It is noted for its collection of Canadian art; 20th-century British and American painting, sculpture, drawings, and prints; and French Impressionist works.

Museum of Civilization
100 Laurier Street
P.O. Box 3100, Station B
Gatineau, Quebec J8X 4H2
817-776-7000
http://www.civilization.ca

Opened in 1845, this museum specializes in history and folk culture, with excellent collections of the arts and crafts of Native Americans, particularly Eskimos and Northwest Coast Indians.

Museum of Nature
Victoria Memorial Museum Building
240 McLeod St.
P.O. Box 3443, Station D
Ottawa, Ontario K1P 6P4
613-556-4700
http://www.nature.ca

Formerly part of the Museum of Civilization, the Museum of Nature contains one of the world's largest and finest natural history collections. Comprised of 24 major science collections of more than 10 million specimens, the museum's holdings cover four billion years of Earth history.

National Gallery of Canada
P.O. Box 427, Station A
Ottawa, Ontario K1N 9N4
613-990-1985
http://www.national.gallery.ca

With more than 40,000 works, this museum contains the largest collection of Canadian art in the world and includes painting, sculpture, prints, drawings, photographs, video, film, and Inuit art.

Libraries

Royal Ontario Museum
100 Queens Park Crescent
Toronto, Ontario M5S 2C6
416-586-5549
http://www.rom.on.ca

From suits of armor to suits by Chanel, from totem poles to monstrous dinosaurs, the ROM is the largest museum in Canada. It is one of the world's few multi-disciplinary museums combining art, archeology, and science. The museum features a planetarium, as well as a prominent display of historical and contemporary ceramic art.

MAJOR SCIENCE AND TECHNOLOGY MUSEUMS AND THEIR SPECIAL COLLECTIONS

American Museum of Natural History
Central Park West at 79th St.
New York, NY 10024
212-769-5000
http://www.amnh.org

One of the world's largest natural history museums, opened in 1869, it has exceptional collections on Native Americans, Eskimos, dinosaurs, wildlife, minerals, and fossil specimens.

The Field Museum of Natural History
1400 South Lake Shore Dr.
Chicago, IL 60605
312-922-9410
http://www.fieldmuseum.org

Founded in 1893, the Field Museum contains definitive collections on anatomy, anthropology, costumes, ethnology, geology, Native American artifacts, science, textiles, and zoology. Among its highlights is Sue, the world's largest and most complete *Tyrannosaurus Rex* skeleton.

Franklin Institute Science Museum and Planetarium
222 North 20th St.
Philadelphia, PA 19103
215-448-1200
http://www.fi.edu

Founded in 1824, this comprehensive museum offers collections featuring science, history, industry, technology, aeronautics, astronomy, space exploration, and stamps and coins.

"The Physical Sciences, Mathematics, and Technology" in chapter 4 **Go to**

Museum of Science
Science Park
Boston, MA 02114
617-589-0100
http://www.mos.org

Founded in 1830, this science and technology museum includes collections of mineral and plant specimens, mounted animals, and exhibits on human physiology. Interactive exhibits demonstrate the principles of electricity as well as the inner workings of computers. The planetarium features rotating shows relating to space.

National Air and Space Museum, Smithsonian Institution
Seventh St. and Independence Ave., SW
Washington, DC 20560
202-357-2700
http:// www.nasm.si.edu

Founded in 1946, this museum houses a definitive collection of aeronautical and astronautical items; aircraft and spacecraft; and instruments, equipment, art, uniforms, and personal memorabilia related to air and space.

The Royal Tyrrell Museum
P.O. Box 7500
Drumheller, Alberta T0J 0Y0
Canada
403-823-7707
http://www.tyrrellmuseum.com

Canada's only museum devoted to paleontology features hands-on displays and computer simulations covering 4.5 billion years of Earth's history. Forty full dinosaur skeletons make up the world's largest exhibit of complete dinosaurs.

CHILDREN'S MUSEUMS

There are more than 90 museums located throughout the United States devoted to children. Although most museums offer at least a few special programs for children, those listed here focus almost exclusively on young visitors. For additional information, see the listing "Children's and Junior Museums" in The Official Museum Directory, published annually by the American Association of Museums.

Libraries

Brooklyn Children's Museum
145 Brooklyn Ave.
Brooklyn, NY 11213
718-735-4400
http://www.brooklynkids.org

Founded in 1899, this was the world's first children's museum. Its teaching collection includes more than 50,000 items, with exhibits on cultural history, natural history, and technology. It houses a greenhouse, a steam engine, and a gristmill. Children may attend workshops in school classes or groups. A portable loan collection and children's resource library is also available.

Capital Children's Museum
800 Third St., NE
Washington, DC 20002
202-675-4120
http://www.ccm.org

Founded in 1974, Capital Children's International Hall has a hands-on exhibit on Mexico where children learn to make their own tortillas, weave, and do other Mexican arts and crafts. Additional facilities include a living room, metric exhibit, simple machines display, communications exhibit, and futuristic center.

Children's Museum
300 Congress St.
Boston, MA 02210
617-426-6500
http://www.bostonkids.org

Located on Boston's picturesque waterfront, Children's Museum was founded in 1913. It offers special collections of Native American and Japanese art; Americana; games, toys, dolls, and dollhouses; and bird, insect, shell, and mineral specimens. The Exhibit Center presents participatory and cased exhibitions on child development, natural history, science and technology, careers, handicaps, and cross-cultural understanding. Its Resource Center makes available over 10,000 books, games, and other items.

Children's Museum of Manhattan
The Tisch Building
212 W. 83rd St.
New York, NY 10024
(212) 721-1234
http://www.cmom.org

Founded in 1979, this museum features hands-on, participatory exhibits related to science, nature, and art. A center for media and performing arts includes a television production and editing studio where children create their own television programs. Children contribute their art, toys, and found objects to the museum's rotating exhibits.

The Eugene Field House and St. Louis Toy Museum
634 S. Broadway
St. Louis, MO 63102
314-421-4689
http://www.eugenefieldhouse.org

Founded in 1936, this museum is housed in the birthplace of Eugene Field. It contains a collection of antique toys and dolls, along with a library on the works of Field.

The Exploratorium
3601 Lyon St.
San Francisco, CA 94123
415-563-7337
http://www.exploratorium.edu

Housed in the Palace of Fine Arts, this science museum offers 500 participatory exhibits and artworks illustrating the physical nature of the world and the sensory mechanisms through which we perceive it. Founded in 1969, it hosts field trips, concerts, lectures, and school groups.

Children's Museum of Los Angeles
205 S. Broadway
Suite 608
Los Angeles, CA 90012
213-687-8801
http://www.childrensmuseumla.org

Children participate in a variety of activities at this museum in such places as Sticky City, with giant foam blocks for construction fun; City Streets, with city vehicles and street signs; TV Studios, where children create their own news broadcasts; and Workshop Place, which fosters creativity in arts and crafts.

Please Touch Museum
210 N. 21st St.
Philadelphia, PA 19103
215-963-0667
http://www.pleasetouchmuseum.org

Founded in 1976, the Please Touch Museum issues a children's newspaper and offers special exhibits on cultural artifacts of daily life, folk art and sculpture, natural science, technology, musical instruments, games, registered toys, costumes, masks, foot gear, and hats.

MAJOR ZOOS AND AQUARIUMS

Zoos, or zoological gardens, are private or public parks where animals of all sorts are exhibited and studied.

Most major cities throughout the world have zoos. Zoos vary widely in scale and type, from petting zoos that allow contact between children and animals to primate research centers to amusement parks that put on shows with trained animals.

Aquariums are facilities with tanks (usually with glass sides) and pools for keeping live water animals and plants.

The following list of major zoos and aquariums in the United States and Canada is arranged by state and province. The name, address, phone number, and Web site of each are given, and, where available, the facility's specialty.

Links to Web sites for many other U.S. zoos and aquariums are provided at

http://www.mindspring.com/~zoonet/www_virtual_lib/zoos.html

UNITED STATES

Alabama

Birmingham Zoo
2630 Cahaba Rd.
Birmingham, AL 35223
205-879-0409
http://www.birminghamzoo.com/

Arizona

Arizona-Sonora Desert Museum
2021 N. Kinney Rd.
Tucson, AZ 85743
520-883-1380
http://www.desertmuseum.org
Specialty: natural history of the Arizona-Sonora desert

Phoenix Zoo
455 N. Galvin Pkwy.
Phoenix, AZ 85008
602-273-1341
http://www.phoenixzoo.org

Arkansas

Little Rock Zoo
1 Jonesboro Dr.
Little Rock, AR 72205
501-666-2406
http://www.littlerockzoo.com/

California

Chaffee Zoo (formerly Fresno Zoo)
894 West Belmont Ave.
Fresno, CA 93728
559-498-2671
http://www.chaffeezoo.org

The Los Angeles Zoo
5333 Zoo Dr.
Los Angeles, CA 90027-1498
213-666-4650
http://www.lazoo.org/

Marine World Six Flags
2001 Marine World Pkwy.
Vallejo, CA 94589
707-643-ORCA
http://www.sixflags.com

Oakland Zoo
9777 Golf Links Rd.
P.O. Box 5238
Oakland, CA 94605
510-632-9525
http://www.oaklandzoo.org/

San Diego Zoo
P.O. Box 120551
San Diego, CA 92112
619-234-3153
http://www.sandiegozoo.org/

San Francisco Zoo
1 Zoo Rd.
San Francisco, CA 94132-1098
415-753-7080
http://www.sfzoo.org
Specialties: primates, cats, endangered species

Santa Ana Zoo
1801 E. Chestnut Ave.
Santa Ana, CA 92701
714-836-4000
http://santaanazoo.org/
Specialty: primates

Sea World San Diego
Sea World of California
500 Sea World Dr.
San Diego, CA 92109
619-226-3901
http://www.seaworld.com
Specialties: trained marine mammals, waterfowl, fish

Steinhart Aquarium at California Academy of Sciences
Golden Gate Park
San Francisco, CA 94118
415-750-7145
http://www.calacademy.org

Birch Aquarium
Scripps Institute of Oceanography
University of California
9500 Gilman Dr., 0207
La Jolla, CA 92093
858-534-FISH
http://www.aquarium.ucsd.edu
Specialties: marine fish and invertebrates of southern California

Colorado
Cheyenne Mountain Zoological Park
4250 Cheyenne Mountain Zoo Rd.
Colorado Springs, CO 80906
719-475-9555
http://www.cmzoo.org
Specialties: primates, large felids (giraffes), hoofed mammals

Denver Zoo
2300 Steele St.
Denver, CO 80205
303-376-4800
http://www.denverzoo.org/
Specialties: waterfowl, North American hoofed mammals

Connecticut
Beardsley Zoo
1875 Noble Ave.
Bridgeport, CT 06610
203-394-6565
http://www.beardsley.zoo.com
Specialty: fauna of North and South America

Mystic Aquarium/Institute for Exploration
55 Coogan Blvd.
Mystic, CT 06355-1997
860-572-5955
http://www.mysticaquarium.org

District of Columbia
National Zoological Park
Smithsonian Institution
3001 Connecticut Ave., NW
Washington, DC 20008
202-673-4800
http://www.natzoo.si.edu/

Florida
Busch Gardens
P.O. Box 9158
Tampa, FL 33674
813-987-4800
http://www.buschgardens.com
Specialties: African hoofed mammals, parrots

Palm Beach Zoo at Dreher Park
1301 Summit Blvd.
West Palm Beach, FL 33405-2494
561-547-WILD
http://www.palmbeachzoo.org
Specialties: South American and South Floridian animals

Jacksonville Zoological Park
8605 Zoo Parkway
Jacksonville, FL 32218
904-757-4463
http://www.jaxzoo.org

Marineland of Florida
9600 Ocean Shore Blvd.
St. Augustine, FL 32080-8613
904-460-1275
http://www.marineland.net
Specialties: marine mammals, marine theme displays

Miami Metrozoo
12400 SW 152nd St.
Miami, FL 33177-1499
305-251-0400
http://www.zsf.org

Georgia
Zoo Atlanta
800 Cherokee Ave.
Atlanta, GA 30315
404-624-5600
http://www.zooatlanta.org
Specialties: amphibians, reptiles, giant apes

Hawaii
Honolulu Zoo
151 Kapahulu Ave.
Honolulu, HI 96815-4096

808-971-7171
808-926-3191
http://www.honoluluzoo.org
Specialty: Galapagos tortoise

Waikiki Aquarium
University of Hawaii
2777 Kalakaua Ave.
Honolulu, HI 96815
808-923-9741
http://waquarium.otted.hawaii.edu/
Specialty: aquatic life of Hawaii and the tropical Pacific

Illinois

**Chicago Zoological Park
(Brookfield Zoo)**
3300 Golf Rd.
Brookfield, IL 60513
708-485-0263
800-201-0784
http://www.brookfieldzoo.org
Specialties: Tropic World, Seven Seas

John G. Shedd Aquarium
1200 S. Lake Shore Dr.
Chicago, IL 60605
312-939-2435
http://www.sheddnet.org

Lincoln Park Zoological Gardens
2201 N. Clark St.
Chicago, IL 60614
312-742-2000
http://www.lpzoo.com/
Specialties: primates, South American mammals

Indiana

Fort Wayne Children's Zoo
3411 Sherman Blvd.
Fort Wayne, IN 46808
260-427-6800
http://www.kidszoo.com/

Indianapolis Zoo
1200 W. Washington St.
Indianapolis, IN 46222
317-630-2001
http://www.indyzoo.com

Mesker Park Zoo
2421 Bement Ave.
Evansville, IN 47712
812-428-0715
Specialty: large geographic exhibits

Kansas

Topeka Zoological Park
635 SW Gage Blvd.
Topeka, KS 66606-2066
785-272-5821
785-272-7042
http://www.topekazoo.org

Kentucky

Louisville Zoological Garden
1100 Trevilian Way
P.O. Box 37250
Louisville, KY 40213
502-459-2181
http://www.louisvillezoo.org

Louisiana

Audubon Aquarium of the Americas
P.O. Box 4327
New Orleans, LA 70178
800-774-7394
http://www.audoboninstitute.org/aoa/

Audubon Park & Zoological Garden
P.O. Box 4327
New Orleans, LA 70178
866-IT'S-A-ZOO
http://www.audoboninstitute.org/zoo/

BREC's Baton Rouge Zoo
3601 Thomas Rd.
Baker, LA 70807
504-775-3877
http://www.brzoo.org

Maryland

Baltimore Zoo
Druid Hill Park
Baltimore, MD 21217
410-366-LION
410-396-7102
http://www.baltimorezoo.org

National Aquarium in Baltimore
Pier 3, 501 E. Pratt St.
Baltimore, MD 21202
410-576-3800
http://www.aqua.org

Massachusetts

New England Aquarium
Central Wharf
Boston, MA 02110
617-973-5200

http://www.neaq.org/
Specialties: marine fish, invertebrates of the world

Zoo New England
Franklin Park Zoo
One Franklin Park Rd.
Boston, MA 02121
617-541-5466
http://www.zoonewengland.com/

Michigan

Detroit Zoological Park
8450 West Ten Mile Rd.
P.O. Box 39
Royal Oak, MI 48068-0039
248-398-0900
http://www.detroitzoo.org/
Specialties: polar bears, penguins

Potter Park Zoological Gardens
1301 S. Pennsylvania Ave.
Lansing, MI 48912
517-483-4221
517-483-4074
http://www.potterparkzoo.org

Minnesota

Lake Superior Zoological Gardens
7210 Fremont St.
Duluth, MN 55807
218-733-3777
http://www.lszoo.org

Minnesota Zoo
13000 Zoo Blvd.
Apple Valley, MN 55124
952-431-9200
952-431-9500
http://www.mnzoo.com/

St. Paul's Como Zoo
1250 Kaufman Drive North
St. Paul, MN 55103-1060
651-645-1014
651-487-8200
http://www.stpaul.gov/depts/parks/comopark/index.
  html/html
Specialties: large mammals

Mississippi

Jackson Zoological Park
2918 W. Capitol St.
Jackson, MS 39209
601-352-2585
http://techlink.net/jacksonzoo/

Missouri

Kansas City Zoological Gardens
6800 Zoo Dr.
Kansas City, MO 64132
816-513-5700
http://www.kansascityzoo.org

St. Louis Zoo
One Government Dr.
St. Louis, MO 63110-1935
314-781-0900
http://www.stlzoo.org/

Nebraska

Folsom Children's Zoo
1222 South 27th St.
Lincoln, NE 86502
402-475-6741
http://www.lincolnzoo.org

Omaha's Henry Doorly Zoo
3701 S. 10th St.
Omaha, NE 68107
402-773-8401
http://www.omahazoo.org
Specialties: largest cat complex in North America

New Jersey

Turtle Back Zoo
560 Northfield Ave.
West Orange, NJ 07052
973-731-5800
http://www.turtlebackzoo.com
Specialty: turtles

New Mexico

Rio Grande Zoological Park
903 10th St., SW
Albuquerque, NM 87102
505-764-6200
http://www.cabq.gov/biopark/zoo
Specialty: hoofed mammals

New York

Buffalo Zoological Gardens
300 Parkside Ave.
Buffalo, NY 14214-1999
716-837-3900
http://www.buffalozoo.org

**Central Park Wildlife Conservation Center
(formerly Central Park Zoo)**
830 Fifth Avenue
New York, NY 10021

212-861-6030
http://www.wcs.org/home/zoos/centralpark

**Aquarium for Wildlife Conservation
(formerly New York Aquarium)**
West 8th St. and Surf Ave.
Brooklyn, NY 11224
718-265-FISH
http://www.wcs.org/home/zoos/nyaquarium

**International Wildlife Conservation Park
(formerly Bronx Zoo)**
185th St. and Southern Blvd.
Bronx, NY 10460
718-367-1010
http://www.wcs.org/home/zoos/bronxzoo

Staten Island Zoo
614 Broadway
Staten Island, NY 10310
718-442-3100
http://www.statenislandzoo.org
Specialty: reptiles

North Carolina
North Carolina Zoological Park
4401 Zoo Parkway
Asheboro, NC 27203
800-488-0444
910-879-7000
http://www.nczoo.org/
Specialty: African wildlife

North Dakota
Dakota Zoo
Dakota Zoological Society
P.O. Box 711
Bismarck, ND 58502
701-223-7543
http://www.dakotazoo.org
Specialty: North American fauna

Ohio
Cincinnati Zoo & Botanical Garden
3400 Vine St.
Cincinnati, OH 45220
513-281-4700
http://www.cincyzoo.org/
Specialties: insects, amphibians, great apes, cats

Cleveland Metroparks Zoo
3900 Wildlife Way
Cleveland, OH 44109
216-661-6500
http://clemetzoo.com/
Specialties: Geoffroy's tamarin, white stork

Columbus Zoo and Aquarium
9990 Riverside Dr.
Powell, OH 43065
http://www.colszoo.org/
Specialties: gorillas, reptiles, cichlids

Toledo Zoo
P.O. Box 140130
Toledo, OH 43614-0801
419-385-5721
http://www.toledozoo.org/

Oklahoma
Oklahoma City Zoological Park
2101 NE 50th St.
Oklahoma City, OK 73111
405-424-3344
http://www.okczoo.com

Tulsa Zoo and Living Museum
6421 E. 36th St. North
Tulsa, OK 74115-2121
918-669-6600
Specialties: North American animals, plants, earth
  sciences

Oregon
Oregon Zoo
4001 SW Canyon Rd.
Portland, OR 97221
503-226-1561
http://www.zooregon.org/
Specialties: elephants, chimpanzees

Pennsylvania
Philadelphia Zoological Garden
3400 W. Girard Ave.
Philadelphia, PA 19104-1196
215-243-1100
http://www.phillyzoo.org/
Specialties: waterfowl, great apes, reptiles

Pittsburgh Zoo & Aquarium
One Wild Place
Pittsburgh, PA 15206
412-665-3640
800-474-4966
http://zoo.pgh.pa.us

Rhode Island
Roger Williams Park Zoo
1000 Elmwood Ave.
Providence, RI 02907-3600
410-785-3510
http://www.rwpzoo.org

South Carolina

Riverbanks Zoological Park and Botanical Gardens
500 Wildlife Pkwy.
P.O. Box 1060
Columbia, SC 29202
803-779-8717
http://www.riverbanks.org/

South Dakota

Great Plains Zoo and Delbridge Museum
805 S. Kiwanis Ave.
Sioux Falls, SD 57104
605-367-7003
http://www.gpzoo.org
Specialty: animals of the North American Great Plains

Tennessee

Knoxville Zoological Gardens
P.O. Box 6040-3500
Knoxville, TN 37914-0040
865-637-5331
http://www.knoxville-zoo.org/
Specialties: large cats, African elephants, red pandas,
    Southern white rhinoceros

Memphis Zoo
2000 Prentiss Place
Memphis, TN 38112
901-276-WILD
http://www.memphiszoo.org/
Specialties: aquatic animals, rare ruminants

Texas

Abilene Zoological Gardens
2070 Zoo Lane
Nelson Park
Abilene, TX 79602
915-676-6085
http://www.abilenetx.com/zoo/zoo.htm

Caldwell Zoo
2203 Martin Luther King Blvd.
Tyler, TX 75710
903-593-0121

Dallas Aquarium
P.O. Box 150113
Dallas, TX 75315-0113
214-670-8443
http://www.dallas-zoo.org

Dallas Zoo
Fair Park
650 South R.L. Thornton Fwy.

Dallas, TX 75203
214-670-5656
http://www.dallas-zoo.org

Fort Worth Zoo
1989 Colonial Pkwy.
Fort Worth, TX 76110
817-871-7050
http://www.fortworthzoo.com

Gladys Porter Zoo
500 Ringgold St.
Brownsville, TX 78520
956-546-7187
http://www.gpz.org/

Houston Zoological Gardens
1513 N. MacGregor
Houston, TX 77030
713-523-5888
http://www.houstonzoo.org

San Antonio Zoological Garden and Aquarium
3903 N. St. Mary's St.
San Antonio, TX 78212
210-734-7184
http://www.sazoo-aq.org/
Specialties: antelope, waterfowl, whooping cranes

Utah

Utah's Hogle Zoo
2600 E. Sunnyside Ave.
Salt Lake City, UT 84108
801-582-1631
http://www.xmission.com/~hoglezoo/

Virginia

Virginia Zoo
3500 Granby St.
Norfolk, VA 23504
757-624-9937
http://www.virginiazoo.org

Washington

Seattle Aquarium
1483 Alaskan Way, on Pier 59
Seattle, WA 98010
206-386-4300
http://www.seattleaquarium.org

Woodland Park Zoological Gardens
601 North 59th St.
Seattle, WA 98103
206-684-4880
http://www.zoo.org/

Libraries

Wisconsin
Henry Vilas Zoo
702 S. Randall Ave.
Madison, WI 53715-1665
608-266-4732
http://www.vilaszoo.org/

Milwaukee County Zoological Gardens
10001 W. Blue Mound Rd.
Milwaukee, WI 53226
414-771-5500
http://www.milwaukeezoo.org/

Racine Zoological Garden
2131 N. Main St.
Racine, WI 53402
626-636-9189
http://www.racinezoo.org

CANADA
Alberta
Calgary Zoo, Botanical Garden & Prehistoric Park
1300 Zoo Road NE
Calgary, Alberta Canada T2E 7V6
403-232-9300
http://www.calgaryzoo.ab.ca/

British Columbia
Stanley Park Zoological Gardens
Stanley Park
Vancouver, British Columbia V6G 1Z4
604-257-8400
http://www.city.vancouver.bc.ca/parks/3.htm

Vancouver Public Aquarium
Stanley Park
P.O. Box 3232
Vancouver, British Columbia V6B 3X8
604-659-3474
http://www.vanaqua.org
Specialties: marine mammals, fishes and invertebrates of
the Northeast Pacific

Manitoba
Assiniboine Park Zoo
The Zoological Society of Manitoba
54 Zoo Drive
Winnipeg, Manitoba R3P 2N8
204-982-0660 (Zoological Society)
204-986-2327 (Zoo info)
http://www.zoosociety.com
Specialty: Nearctic animals

Ontario
Toronto Zoo
361A Old Finch Ave.
Scarborough, Ontario M1B 5K7
416-392-5900
http://www.torontozoo.com/

Quebec
Biodôme de Montréal
4777, Pierre de Coubertin
Montréal, Québec H1V 1B3
514-868-3000
http://www.biodome.qc.ca

**Jardin Zoologique de Quebec and Aquarium
de Quebec**
8173 avenue du Zoo
Charlesbourg, Québec G1G 4G4
418-622-0313
http://www.aquarium.qc.ca/

Société Zoologique de Granby
Horace Boivin Pavilion
525, rue St-Hubert
Granby, Québec J2G 5P3
401-372-9113
877-GRANBY-ZOO
http://www.zoodegranby.com

MAJOR BOTANICAL GARDENS AND ARBORETUMS

Botanical gardens are places where collections of plants and trees are kept for exhibition and scientific study. Arboretums are places where many kinds of trees and shrubs are grown for exhibition or study.

The following list of major botanical gardens and arboretums in the United States is arranged by state.

Addresses, phone numbers, and Web sites of numerous other botanical gardens and arboreta that are members of the American Association of Botanical Gardens and Arboreta are listed at http://www.mobot.org/AAGBA/member-list.html.

Alabama
Birmingham Botanical Gardens
2612 Lane Park Rd.
Birmingham, AL 35523
205-414-3900
http://www.bbgardens.org/

Libraries

Arizona

Desert Botanical Garden
1201 N. Galvin Pkwy.
Papago Park
Phoenix, AZ 85008
480-941-1225
http://www.dbg.org

California

Balboa Park
1549 El Prado
San Diego, CA 92101
619-239-0512
http://www.balboapark.org

**Huntington Library, Art Collections, and
   Botanical Gardens**
1151 Oxford Rd.
San Marino, CA 91108
626-405-2100
http://www.huntington.org/

J. Paul Getty Museum and Gardens
The Getty Center
1200 Getty Center Drive
310-440-7300
http://www.getty.edu

Strybing Arboretum and Botanical Gardens
9th Ave. at Lincoln Way
Golden Gate Park
San Francisco, CA 94122
415-661-1316
http://www.strybing.org/

Villa Montalvo Arboretum
15400 Montalvo Rd.
Saratoga, CA 95070
408-961-5800
http://www.willamontalvo.org

Colorado

Denver Botanic Gardens
909 York St.
Denver, CO 80206
303-331-4000
http://www.botanicgardens.org/

Connecticut

Glebe House Museum and Gertrude Jekyll Garden
Hollow Rd.
Woodbury, CT 06798
203-263-2855

Harkness Memorial State Park
275 Great Neck Rd.
Waterford, CT 06385
860-443-5725
http://dep.state.ct.us/rec/parks/harkhist.htm

Delaware

Nemours Mansion and Gardens
P.O. Box 109
1600 Rockland Rd.
Wilmington, DE 19899
302-651-6912
http://www.nemours.org

Henry Francis du Pont Winterthur Museum
Rte. 52
Winterthur, DE 19735
800-448-3883
http://www.winterthur.org

District of Columbia

Dumbarton Oaks
1703 32nd St., NW
Washington, DC 20007
202-339-6410
http://www.doaks.com

Gardens of the Washington National Cathedral
Massachusetts and Wisconsin aves.
Washington, DC 20016-5098
202-537-6200
http://www.cathedral.org

United States Botanical Garden
245 First St., SW
Washington, DC 20024-3021
202-226-4082
202-225-8333 (information recording)
http://www.nationalgarden.org

United States National Arboretum
3501 New York Ave., NE
Washington, DC 20002-1958
202-245-2726
http://www.usna.usda.gov

Florida

Edison and Ford Winter Estates
2350 McGregor Blvd.
Ft. Myers, FL 33901
941-334-3614
http://www.edison-ford-estate.com

Fairchild Tropical Garden
10901 Old Cutler Rd.
Miami, FL 33156-4299
305-667-1651
http://www.fairchildgarden.org

Cypress Gardens
2641 South Lake Summit Drive
Winter Haven, FL 33884
863-3242111
http://www.cypressgardens.com

Alfred B. Maclay State Gardens
3540 Thomasville Rd.
Tallahassee, FL 32308
850-487-4115
http://www.floridastateparks.org

Georgia
Atlanta Botanical Garden
1345 Piedmont Ave.
Atlanta, GA 30309
404-876-5859
http://www.atlantabotanicalgarden.org

Callaway Gardens
U.S. Highway 27
P.O. Box 2000
Pine Mountain, GA 31822-2000
706-663-2281
800-255-5292
http://www.callawaygardens.com

The State Botanical Garden of Georgia
2450 S. Milledge Ave.
Athens, GA 30605
706-542-1244
http://www.uga.edu/botgarden

Hawaii
Foster Botanic Garden
180 N. Vineyard Blvd.
Honolulu, HI 96817
808-522-7066
http://www.co.honolulu.hi.us/parks/hbg/fbg.htm

Hoomaluhia Botanical Garden
45-680 Luluku Road
Kaneohe, HI 96744
808-233-7323
http://www.co.honolulu.hi.us/parks/hbg/hmbg.htm

Wahiawa Botanical Garden
1396 California Avenue
Wahiawa, HI 96786
808-621-7321
http://www.co.honolulu.hi.us/parks/hbg/wbg.htm

Idaho
Idaho Botanical Gardens
2355 N. Penitentiary Rd.
P.O. Box 2140
Boise, ID 83701
208-343-8649
http://www.idahobotanicalgarden.org/

Illinois
Garfield Park Conservatory
300 N. Central Park Ave.
Chicago, IL 60624-1996
312-746-5100
http://www.garfield-conservatory.org/

Lincoln Park Conservatory
2391 N. Stockton Dr.
Chicago, IL 60614-3419
312-742-7736
http://chicagoparkdistrict.com

Indiana
Indianapolis Museum of Art Gardens
1200 W. 38th St.
Indianapolis, IN 46208
317-920-2660
http://www.ima-art.org/

Iowa
Des Moines Botanical Center
909 E. River Dr.
Des Moines, IA 50316
515-323-8900
http://www.botanicalcenter.com/

Kansas
Botanica
The Wichita Gardens
701 Amidon
Wichita, KS 67203
316-264-0448
http://www.botanica.com

Louisiana
Audubon Louisiana Nature Center
P.O. Box 4327
5700 Read Blvd.
New Orleans, LA 70178
504-246-5672
http://www.auduboninstitute.org/lnc/index.htm

Maine

Asticou Azalea Garden
Asticou Way
Mount Desert Island
Northeast Harbor, ME 04662
207-276-5040
http://www.acadiamagic.com/Asticou2.html

Maryland

Hampton National Historic Site
535 Hampton Lane
Towson, MD 21286
410-823-1309 x226
http://www.nps.gov/hamp/index.htm

Massachusetts

Arnold Arboretum
125 Arborway
Jamaica Plain, MA 02130-3519
617-524-1718
http://www.arboretum.harvard.edu

Berkshire Botanical Garden
P.O. Box 826
Intersection Routes 102 and 183
Stockbridge, MA 01262
413-298-3926
http://www.berkshirebotanical.org/

Stanley Park
400 Western Ave.
Westfield, MA 01086
413-568-9312
http://www.stanleypark.org

Michigan

Anna Scripps Whitcomb Conservatory
Belle Island Botanical Society
Belle Isle Greenhouse
Detroit, MI 48207
313-852-4064
hhtp://www.bibsociety.org

Matthaei Botanical Garden
University of Michigan
1800 Dixboro Rd.
Ann Arbor, MI 48105-9406
313-998-7061
http://www.lsa.umich.edu/mbg

Missouri

Missouri Botanical Garden
P.O. Box 299
St. Louis, MO 63166-0299
800-642-8842
http://www.mobot.org/welcome.html

New Hampshire

Aspet
Saint-Gaudens National Historic Site
R.R. 3, P.O. Box 73
Cornish, NH 03745
603-675-2175

New Jersey

Deep Cut Park Horticultural Center
352 Red Hill Rd.
Middletown, NJ 07748
732-842-4000
http://www.monmouthcountyparks.com/parks/deepcut/
   horticultural_center.html

Frelinhuysen Arboretum
53 E. Hanover Ave.
Morristown, NJ 07962-1295
201-326-7600
http://www.morrisig.com/vgreen/arbor.htm

The Rutgers Gardens
Cook College, Rutgers University
122 Ryders Lane
New Brunswick, NJ 08901
732-932-8451
http://aesop.rutgers.edu/~rugardens/

New Jersey Botanical Garden
Morris Rd.
Ringwood, NJ 07458
973-962-7527
http://www.state.nj.us/travel/virtual/gardens/botanical.
   html

New Mexico

Living Desert Zoo and Gardens
P.O. Box 100
Carlsbad, NM 88221
505-887-5516
http://www.emnrd.state.nm.us/nmparks/PAGES/parks/
   desert/desert.htm

New York

Brooklyn Botanic Garden
1000 Washington Ave.
Brooklyn, NY 11225-1099

718-623-7200
http://www.bbg.org/

New York Botanical Garden
Bronx River Parkway @ Fordham Road
200th St. and Kazimiroff Blvd.
Bronx, NY 10458-5126
718-817-8700
http://www.nybg.org

Vanderbilt Mansion National Historic Site
4097 Albany Post Rd.
Hyde Park, NY 12538
845-229-9115
http://www.nps.gov/vama

North Carolina

Botanical Gardens at Asheville
151 W. T. Weaver Blvd.
Asheville, NC 28804
828-252-5190
http://www.ahevillbotanicalgardens.org

Sarah P. Duke Memorial Gardens
418 Anderson Street
P.O. Box 90341 Duke University
Durham, NC 27708-0341
919-684-3698
http://www.hr.duke.edu/dukegardens/dukegardens.html

North Carolina Botanical Garden
CB 3375, Totten Center
University of North Carolina at Chapel Hill
Chapel Hill, NC 27599-3375
919-962-0522
http://www.unc.edu/depts/ncbg

North Dakota

International Peace Garden
R.R. 1, Box 116
Dunseith, ND 58329
701-263-4390
http://www.peacegarden.com

Ohio

Dawes Arboretum
7770 Jacksontown Rd., SE
Newark, OH 43056-9380
800-44DAWES
740-323-2355
http://www.dawesarb.org

Cleveland Botanical Garden
11030 East Blvd.
Cleveland, OH 44106

216-721-1600
http://cbgarden.org/

Holden Arboretum
9500 Sperry Rd.
Kirtland, OH 44094-5172
440-946-4400
http://www.holdenarb.org

Oklahoma

Will Rogers Garden Exhibition Building
3400 NW 36th St.
Oklahoma City, OK 73112
405-943-0827

Oregon

Berry Botanic Garden
11505 SW Summerville Ave.
Portland, OR 97219
503-636-4112
http://www.berrybot.org/

Pennsylvania

Historic Bartram's Garden
54th Street and Lindbergh Boulevard
Philadelphia, PA 19143
215-729-5281
http://www.bartramsgarden/index.html

Longwood Gardens
Route 1
P.O. Box 501
Kennet Square, PA 19348-0501
610-388-1000
http://www.longwoodgardens.org/

Morris Arboretum of the University of Pennsylvania
100 Northwestern Avenue
Philadelphia, PA 19118
215-247-5777
http://upenn.edu/arboretum/

Phipps Conservatory and Botanical Gardens
One Schenley Park
Pittsburgh, PA 15213-3830
(412) 622-6914
http://www.phipps.conservatory.org/

Tyler Arboretum
515 Painter Rd.
Media, PA 19063
610-566-5431
http://www.tylerarboretum.org

Rhode Island

Hammersmith Farm
Bellevue Ave.
Newport, RI 02840
401-846-7346

South Carolina

Brookgreen Gardens
P.O. Box 3368
Pawleys Island, SC 29585-3368
843-235-6000
800-849-1931
http://www.brookgreen.com

Magnolia Plantation and Gardens
3550 Ashley River Rd.
Charleston, SC 29414
843-571-1266
800-367-3517
http://magnoliaplantation.com

Tennessee

Memphis Botanic Garden
750 Cherry Rd.
Memphis, TN 38117
901-685-1566
http://www.memphisbotanicgarden.com

Rock City Gardens
See Rock City, Inc.
1400 Patten Rd.
Lookout Mountain, GA 30750
706-820-2531
http://www.seerockcity.com/

Texas

Dallas Arboretum and Botanical Garden
8525 Garland Rd.
Dallas, TX 75218
214-327-8263
http://www.dallasarboretum.org/

Fort Worth Botanic Garden
3220 Botanic Garden Blvd.
Fort Worth, TX 76107
817-871-7686
http://www.fortworthgov.org/pacs/botgarden/

Samuel Grand Park Garden
6200 E. Grand Ave.
Dallas, TX 75223
214-670-1383

Virginia

Monticello
Home of Thomas Jefferson
P.O. Box 316
Charlottesville, VA 22902
434-984-9800
434-984-9822
http://www.monticello.org/

Mount Vernon Estate and Gardens
P.O. Box 110
Mount Vernon, VA 22121
703-780-2000
http://www.mountvernon.org/

Pavillion Gardens
University of Virginia
P.O. Box 400305
Charlottesville, VA 22903
434-924-7969
http://www.virginia.edu/uvatours/gardens/

Washington

Washington Park Arboretum
University of Washington
P.O. Box 358010
Seattle, WA 98195-8010
206-543-8800
http://depts.washington.edu/wpa/

Wisconsin

Mitchell Park Horticultural Conservatory
"The Domes"
524 S. Layton Blvd.
Milwaukee, WI 53215
414-649-9800
http://www.countyparks.com/horticulture/

Olbrich Botanical Gardens
3330 Atwood Ave.
Madison, WI 53704
608-246-4550
http://www.olbrich.org

III

THE WAY WE COMMUNICATE

12

SYMBOLS AND SIGNS

SYMBOLS USED IN SCIENCE, MATHEMATICS, AND TECHNOLOGY

ASTRONOMY SYMBOLS

SOLAR SYSTEM OBJECTS

☉	the Sun
☾, ☽	the Moon
☿	Mercury
♀	Venus
⊕, ♁	Earth
♂	Mars
♃	Jupiter
♄	Saturn
♅, ♅	Uranus
♆	Neptune
♇	Pluto
☄	comet
①, ②, ③, etc.	asteroids in the order of their discovery

PHASES OF THE MOON

●	new moon
☽, ☽	first quarter
○	full moon
☾, ☾	last quarter

STELLAR OBJECTS

*	fixed star
α, β, γ, etc.	stars (of a constellation) in the order of their brightness: the Greek letter is followed by the Latin genitive of the name of the constellation

ASPECTS AND NODES

☌	conjunction: with reference to bodies having the same longitude, or right ascension
□	quadrature: being 90° apart in longitude, or right ascension
☍	opposition: being 180° apart in longitude, or right ascension
☊	ascending node
☋	descending node

PHYSICAL CHARACTERS

A	albedo
D	diameter
M	mass
R	radius

"Astronomy" in chapter 4

Go to

UNITS OF MEASUREMENT

A.U.	astronomical unit
l.y.	light-year
pc	parsec
h, ^{h}	hours [5h *or* 5^h]
m, ^{m}	minutes of time [5m *or* 5^m]
s, ^{s}	seconds of time [16s *or* 16^s]
°	degrees of arc
′	minutes of arc
″	seconds of arc

DIRECTIONS

+	toward the zenith; toward the north celestial, ecliptic, or galactic pole
−	toward the nadir; toward the south celestial, ecliptic, or galactic pole
γ	vernal equinox

ORBITAL ELEMENTS

a	mean distance, semimajor axis
e	eccentricity of orbit
i	inclination to the ecliptic
P	sidereal period of revolution or rotation
Ω	longitude of ascending node
ω	argument of perihelion

COORDINATES

h	altitude
A	azimuth
δ	declination
α, R.A.	right ascension
β	celestial latitude
λ	celestial longitude
b	galactic latitude
l	galactic longitude

OTHER SYMBOLS

Δ	distance from earth
π	parallax
ø	geographical or astronomical latitude

Although the @ has no name in the United States (it's just called the "at symbol"), other countries call it "monkey's tail," "little snail," "cat's tail," or "spider monkey."

BIOLOGY SYMBOLS

♃	perennial herb
♂ , ♂	male organism or cell; staminate plant or flower
♀	female organism or cell; pistillate plant or flower
☿	perfect, or hermaphroditic, plant, or flower
○	individual, especially female, organism

□	individual, especially male, organism
×	crossed with; hybrid
+	wild type
P	parental generation
F	filial generation; offspring
F_1, F_2, F_3, etc.	offspring of the first, second, third, etc., filial generation

Go to
"The Biological World" in chapter 3

CHEMISTRY SYMBOLS

+	"and," "plus," or "together with," used between the symbols of reacting substances in chemical equations; when placed above a symbol or to its right as a superscript, the plus sign indicates a unit charge of positive electricity; the sign also indicates dextrorotation
—	single bond, used between the symbols of elements or groups that form a compound; when placed above a symbol or to its right as a superscript, the dash indicates a unit charge of negative electricity; it also signifies levorotation or the removal of a part from a compound
•	separates parts of a compound considered loosely joined (free radical)
⬡	benzene ring
=	"forms" or "results in," used between the symbols of reacting substances in chemical equations; a double bond; two unit charges of negative electricity when placed above a symbol or to its right as a superscript

≡	triple bond or triple negative charge
:	unshared pair of electrons; sometimes a double bond
⦙	triple bond
( )	groups or radicals within a compound
[ ]	with parentheses, shows certain radicals; in coordination formulas, shows relationship to the central atom
⌒ *or* ⌣	unites attached atoms or groups in structural formulas for cyclic compounds
→	gives, passes over to, or leads to; reaction direction
⇌	is in equilibrium with; forms and is formed from; reversible reaction
↓	precipitation of a substance
↑	gas expelled
≡ , ⇌	is equivalent to; used in equations to show how much of one substance will react with a given amount of another so that no excess of either remains
<	bivalent element
>	bivalent radical

Go to
"Chemistry" in chapter 4

ELECTRONICS SYMBOLS

BATTERIES

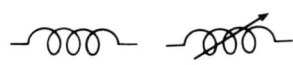

Single Cell   Multicell

CAPACITORS

Fixed   Variable

HEADSETS

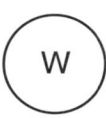

Single   Double

INDUCTORS

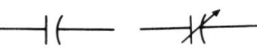

Fixed   Variable

INSTRUMENTS

Ammeter   Ohmeter   Voltmeter   Wattmeter

Symbols/Signs

LAMPS

Neon   Filament

RECTIFIERS

Half Wave   Full Wave

RESISTORS

Fixed   Variable

TRANSFORMERS

Air Core   Iron Core

VACUUM-TUBE TRIODES

Directly Heated
Cathode   Indirectly Heated
Cathode

WIRES

Connected   Not Connected

OTHER SYMBOLS

Alternating Cur-
rent Source   Antenna   Ground   Spark Gap   Single Throw
Switch

MATHEMATICS SYMBOLS

"Special Units of Measurement" in **Go to** chapter 2

OPERATION

+	plus; positive
−	minus; negative
~	difference
×	multiplied by
÷	divided by
±	plus or minus
∓	minus or plus
!	factorial
Σ	summation of
Π	product
√	square root
∛	cube root
∜	fourth root
ⁿ√	nth root
$\lvert b \rvert$	absolute value of b, magnitude of b

GROUPING

( )	parentheses	
[ ]	brackets	indicate that the quantities enclosed by them are to be taken together
{ }	braces	

RELATION

=	equal to
≠	not equal to
≡	identical with; congruent to (in number theory)
≈	nearly equal to
>	greater than
>>	much greater than
<	less than
<<	much less than
≧ or ≥	greater than or equal to
≦ or ≤	less than or equal to
≯	not greater than
≮	not less than
∝	varies directly as; is proportional to
:	is to; the ratio of
::	proportion
÷	geometrical proportion

FUNCTIONS

$f(x)$	function
log	logarithm
ln	natural logarithm

CONSTANTS

e	base (2.718) of natural logarithms
π	pi (3.1416)
∞	infinity
i	imaginary unit ($\sqrt{-1}$)

GEOMETRY

$\angle$	angle
$\llcorner$	right angle
$\perp$	perpendicular
$\parallel$	parallel
○ *or* ⊙	circle
⌒	arc of a circle
○	ellipse
$\varnothing$	diameter
△	triangle
□	square
▭	rectangle
⊞	cube
▱	rhomboid
°	degree
′	minute
″	second
≅	congruent to (in geometry)
m	slope
r	radius
d	diameter

SET THEORY AND LOGIC

∪	union
∩	intersection
∧ *or* ф	empty set; null set
∈	is an element of
∉	is not an element of
∴	therefore
∵	since
⊢	is deducible from

CALCULUS

d	differential of
∂	partial differential
$\int$	integral
$\oint$	contour integral
lim	limit

Fractions and Decimals

%	percent

"Mathematics" in chapter 4; "First Aid" **Go to**
(chapter 17); "Heath and Nutrition"
(chapter 18)

MEDICINE AND PHARMACOLOGY SYMBOLS

Å	angstrom unit		in d.	daily
Ā,ĀĀ, āā, āa	of each		lot.	a lotion
			ⓜ	heart murmur
a.c.	before meals		♏, ♏	minim
ad	up to; so as to make		μ	micron
add.	let there be added; add		μμ	micromicron
ad lib.	at pleasure; as needed or desired		mod. praesc.	in the manner prescribed
agit.	shake		O., o.	a pint
aq.	water		ol.	oil
b. (i.) d.	twice daily		oz.	ounce
c̄	with		p.c.	after meals
cap.	take; capsule		pil.	pill(s)
coch.	a spoonful		p.r.n.	as circumstances may require
d.	give		pulv.	powder
dil.	dilute *or* dissolve		Px	past history
Dx	diagnosis		q. (i.) d.	four times daily
fldxt.	fluid extract		q.l.	as much as you please
ft.	make		q.s.	as much as will suffice
ft. mist.	let a mixture be made		q.v.	as much as you like
ft. pulv.	let a powder be made		℞	take: used at the beginning of a prescription
gr.	a grain		rep.	let it be repeated
gtt.	drops		Rh+	positive blood factor
H.	hour		RH-	negative blood factor
haust.	a draft		♂	$\frac{1}{1000}$ of a second
Hx	history			

continues

s̄	without	t. (i.) d.	three times daily
S, Sig.	write: used in prescriptions to indicate the directions to be placed on the label of the medicine	ut dict.	as directed
		w/v	weight in volume
		℥	ounce
sol.	solution	f℥	fluidounce
s.o.s.	if necessary	ℨ	dram
s̄s̄	one half	fℨ	fluidram
tab.	tablet	℈	scruple

PHYSICS SYMBOLS

α	alpha particle	*e*	electronic charge of electron
Å	angstrom unit	*E*	electric field
β	beta ray	*G*	conductance; weight
γ	gamma radiation	*h*	Planck's constant
ε	electromotive force	*H*	enthalpy
η	efficiency	*L*	inductance
Λ	equivalent conductivity; permeance	*n*	index of refraction
λ	wavelength	*P*	momentum of a particle
μ	magnetic moment	*R*	universal gas constant
v	frequency	*S*	entropy
ρ	density; specific resistance	*T*	absolute temperature; period
σ	conductivity	*V*	electrical potential; frequency
φ	luminous flux; magnetic flux	*W*	energy
φ	fluidity	*X*	magnification; reactance
Ω	ohm	*Y*	admittance
B	magnetic induction; magnetic field	*Z*	impedance
c	speed of light		

 Go to

"Physics" and "Meteorology" in chapter 4

WEATHER SYMBOLS

FRONTS

Warm

Cold

Occluded

Stationary

GROUND VISIBILITY

Fog (Light)

Fog (Heavy)

Haze

Visibility Reduced by Smoke

PRECIPITATION

Drizzle

Rain Showers

Hail Showers

Sleet

Snow

Snow (Drifting, Slight to Moderate)

Symbols/Signs

SKY CONDITIONS

Clear Sky

Cloudy (Partly)

Cloudy (Completely Overcast)

STORMS

Lightning

Thunderstorm

Tornado

Tropical Storm

Hurricane

Sandstorm or Dust Storm

WIND SPEEDS

Calm

Approx. 1 mph (1 knot)

Approx. 6 mph (5 knots)

Approx. 12 mph (10 knots)

Approx. 58 mph (50 knots)

CULTURAL SYMBOLS

MUSIC SYMBOLS

o	whole note	𝄾	eighth rest	¢	[²⁄₂] time
♩	half note	𝄿	sixteenth rest	𝄴	[⁶⁄₈] time
♩.	dotted half note	𝅀	thirty-second rest	𝄞	treble, or G, clef
♩	quarter note	𝅁	sixty-fourth rest		
♪	eighth note	♯	sharp	𝄢	bass, or F, clef
♬	sixteenth note	X	double sharp	𝄡	alto, or C, clef
	thirty-second note	♭	flat		measure
	sixty-fourth note	♭♭	double flat		final bar
	whole rest	♮	natural		repeat
	half rest	¾	¾ time		repeat measure
𝄽	quarter rest	C	⁴⁄₄ time	D.C.	repeat from the beginning

p	piano (soft)	*ff*	fortissimo (very loud)		tie
pp	pianissimo (very soft)	<	crescendo	∿	trill
f	forte (loud)	>	decrescendo		

"Common Music Terms" in chapter 6; "Major World Religions" in chapter 9 Go to

RELIGION SYMBOLS

BUDDHISM

Buddha

Lotus

The Wheel

CHRISTIANITY

Celtic Cross

Latin Cross

Orthodox Cross

Agnus Dei

Chi Rho

Descending Dove; Holy Spirit

HINDUISM

Mandala

Om

Shiva

ISLAM

Star and Crescent

JUDAISM

Menorah

Star of David

Ten Commandments

SHINTO

Torii

TAOISM

Water: Life-Giving Source

Yin-Yang

ZODIAC SIGNS

Symbols		Sign	Planet	Element	Personality Traits
		Aries The Ram Mar. 21–Apr. 19	Mars	fire	bold, impulsive, confident, independent
		Taurus The Bull Apr. 20–May 20	Venus	earth	patient, determined, stubborn, devoted
		Gemini The Twins May 21–June 21	Mercury	air	ambitious, alert, intelligent, temperamental
		Cancer The Crab June 22–July 22	Moon	water	moody, sensitive, impressionable, sympathetic
		Leo The Lion July 23–Aug. 22	Sun	fire	noble, generous, enthusiastic, temperamental
		Virgo The Virgin Aug. 23–Sept. 22	Mercury	earth	intellectual, methodical, placid, tactless
		Libra The Scales Sept. 23–Oct. 23	Venus	air	just, sympathetic, orderly, persuasive, sociable
		Scorpio The Scorpion Oct. 24–Nov. 21	Mars	water	loyal, philosophical, willful, domineering
		Sagittarius The Archer Nov. 22–Dec. 21	Jupiter	fire	practical, imaginative, mature, just
		Capricorn The Goat Dec. 22–Jan. 19	Saturn	earth	ambitious, blunt, loyal, persistent
		Aquarius The Water Carrier Jan. 20–Feb. 18	Uranus	air	unselfish, generous, idealistic, original
		Pisces The Fishes Feb. 19–Mar. 20	Neptune	water	sympathetic, sensitive, timid, methodical

Symbols/Signs

"Astronomy: Constellations" in chapter 4

Go to

The swastika predates Hinduism and is considered an auspicious sign in India. It is the symbol painted on each toe in drawings of Buddha's footprint. It was also used by Native Americans.

BIRTHSTONES AND FLOWERS

Month	Birthstone	Flower
January	garnet	snowdrop
February	amethyst	primrose
March	aquamarine or bloodstone	violet
April	diamond	daisy
May	emerald	hawthorn
June	pearl, alexandrite, or moonstone	rose
July	ruby	water lily
August	sardonyx or peridot	poppy
September	sapphire	morning glory
October	opal or tourmaline	hops
November	topaz	chrysanthemum
December	turquoise or lapis lazuli	holly

Go to "Botanical Names of Plants" in chapter 3; "Some Important Minerals and Their Uses" in chapter 4

SYMBOLS TO GUIDE THE TRAVELER

MAP AND CHART SYMBOLS

BOUNDARIES

| International | Provincial or State | County | Township | Incorporated Village |

CITIES AND TOWNS

Capital City   Urban Area   Town or Village

CULTURAL, HISTORICAL, AND RECREATIONAL SYMBOLS

Point of Interest   Campsite   Winter Sports Area   State Monuments, Memorials, and Historical Sites   Ruins   National Wildlife Refuge   Ranger Station

Symbols/Signs

HYDROGRAPHIC FEATURES

   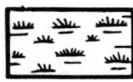 

Intermittent River | Intermittent Lake | Freshwater Lake: Reservoir | Marsh: Swamp | Dams | Falls

NATURAL FEATURES

Glaciers and Ice Shelves | Passes | Elevation Above Sea Level

ROADS AND RAILROADS

Superhighway | Superhighway Under Construction | Dual Highway | Main Road | Secondary Road

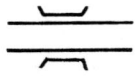 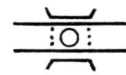 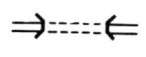  

Bridge and Road | Drawbridge and Road | Tunnel and Road | Railroad Track, Single | Railroad Tracks, Two or More | Railroad Station

DISTRESS SIGNALS

The symbols below, used for ground-to-air communication, may be made of strips of fabric or parachutes, pieces of wood, tree branches, stones, or any other material.

I	II	X	F	⩘	K
Need Doctor	Need Medicine	Cannot Proceed	Need Food and Water	Need Weapons	Indicate Direction
↑	▷	⸳⸳	⬟	LL	L
Going This Way	Aircraft Damaged	Attempting Take Off	Safe to Land	All Well	Need Fuel and Oil
N	Y	JL	W	▢	⁝
No	Yes	Don't Understand	Need Engineer	Need Compass and Map	Need Signal Lamp

INTERNATIONAL ROAD SIGNS

 Curve

 Intersection

 Opening Bridge

 Road Works

 Tunnel

 Pedestrian Crossing

 Watch Out for Children

 Animals Crossing

 Road Narrows

 Slippery Road

 Danger

 No Entry

 Road Closed

 Closed to Motor Vehicles

 Closed to Motorcycles

 Closed to Pedestrians

 No Left Turns

 No U-Turns

 Overtaking Prohibited

 Speed Limit

 End of All Restrictions

 Yield

 Stop

 Direction to Follow

 Traffic Circle

 Parking

 Hospital

 Mechanical Help

 Telephone

 Filling Station

 Camping Site

 Caravan Site

 Youth Hostel

Symbols/Signs

SYMBOLIC ALPHABETS
SEMAPHORE CODE

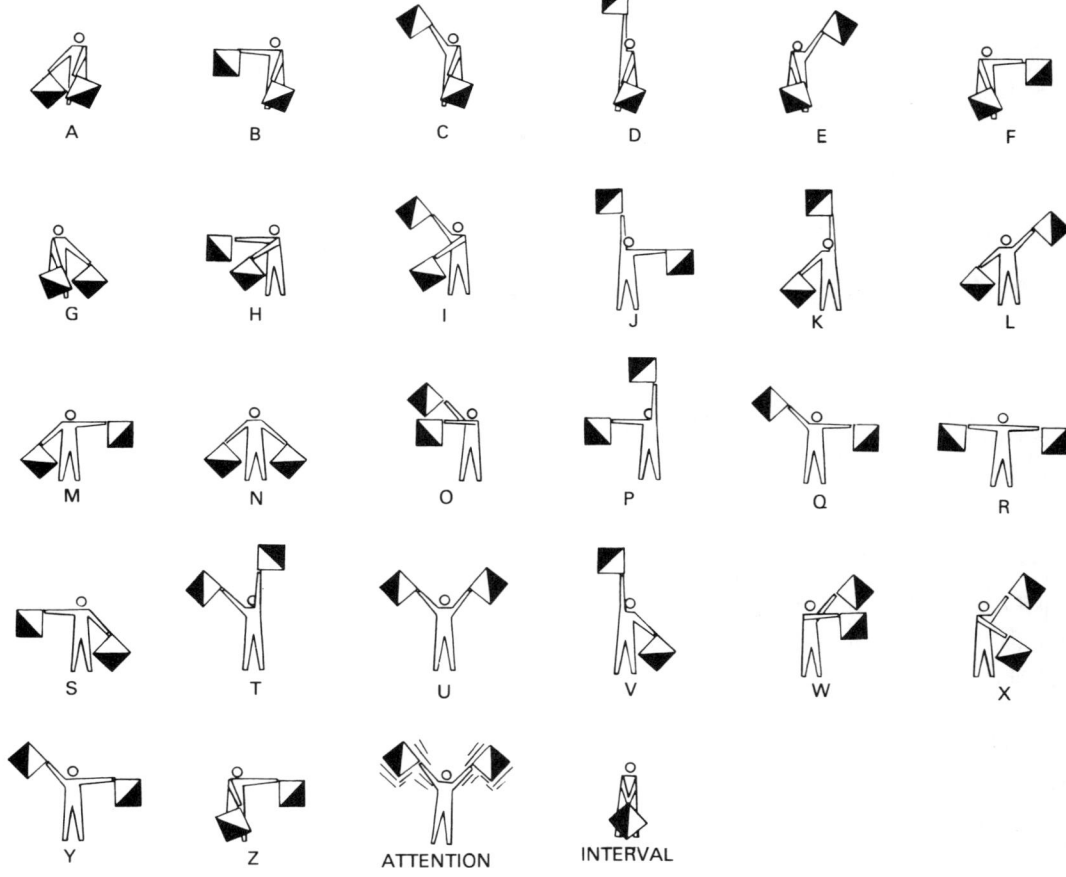

INTERNATIONAL RADIO ALPHABET AND MORSE CODE

A	Alpha	·—	**P**	Papa	·——·	**4**	four	····—
B	Bravo	—···	**Q**	Quebec	——·—	**5**	five	·····
C	Charlie	—·—·		(kaybec)		**6**	six	—····
D	Delta	—··	**R**	Romeo	·—·	**7**	seven	——···
E	Echo	·	**S**	Sierra	···	**8**	eight	———··
F	Foxtrot	··—·	**T**	Tango	—	**9**	nine	————·
G	Golf	——·	**U**	Uniform	··—	**10**	ten	—————
H	Hotel	····	**V**	Victor	···—	**.**	period	·—·—·—
I	India	··	**W**	Whiskey	·——	**,**	comma	——··——
J	Juliet	·———	**X**	X ray	—··—	**?**	question	··——··
K	Kilo	—·—	**Y**	Yankee	—·——		mark	
L	Lima	·—··	**Z**	Zulu	——··	**;**	semicolon	—·—·—·
	(leema)		**1**	one	·————	**:**	colon	———···
M	Mike	——	**2**	two	··———	**-**	hyphen	—····—
N	November	—·	**3**	three	···——	**'**	apostrophe	·————·
O	Oscar	———						

SIGN LANGUAGE

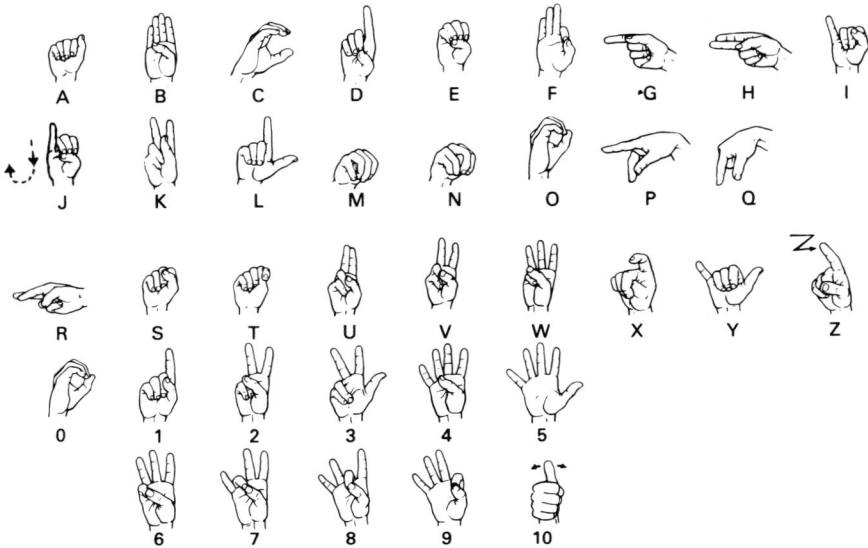

BRAILLE ALPHABET, NUMBERS, AND PUNCTUATION

Between 1826 and 1837, Louis Braille, a blind Frenchman, developed a system of printing and writing for the blind that uses raised dots representing letters, numbers, and punctuation.

The six dots of the Braille cell are arranged and numbered:

1 • • 4
2 • • 5
3 • • 6

The capital sign, dot 6,

1 • • 4
2 • • 5
3 • ● 6

placed before a letter makes a capital letter.

The number sign, dots 3, 4, 5, 6,

1 • ● 4
2 • ● 5
3 ● ● 6

placed before the characters a–j, makes the numbers 1 through 0. For example: <u>a</u> preceded by the number sign is 1, <u>b</u> is 2, etc.

George Washington was a Freemason and adopted the pyramid (a symbol of knowledge and wisdom) and the all-seeing eye of God as national emblems. They are still found on dollar bills.

The system illustrated on the next page is Standard English Braille—Grade 1 (letters, numerals, and punctuation). Grade 2 Braille additionally makes use of approximately 300 contractions (combinations of cells to shorten the lengths of a word). Grade 3 Braille, rarely used, employs additional contractions.

Go to "Telecommunications Device for the Deaf (TDD)" and "Books for Blind and Physically Handicapped Persons" in chapter 22

Symbols/Signs

a	b	c	d	e	f	g	h	i	j
1	2	3	4	5	6	7	8	9	0

k	l	m	n	o	p	q	r	s	t

u	v	w	x	y	z

comma	colon	semicolon	period	exclamation point	parenthesis
,	:	;	.	!	( )

question mark	hyphen	apostrophe	left quotation mark	right quotation mark
?	–	'	"	"

BUSINESS AND MONETARY SYMBOLS

A/C, a/c	account; account current	P/A	power of attorney
A/O, a/o	account of	P/C, p/c	prices current; petty cash
B/D	bank draft	P/N	promissory note
B/E	bill of exchange	w/	with
B/L	bill of lading	W/B	waybill
B/P	bills payable	w/o	without
B/R	bills receivable	@	at/per/priced at
B/V	book value	#	number, pounds
C/D	carried down; certificate of deposit	%	percent/per hundred
C/N	circular note; credit note	¢	cent
C/O	care of; carried over; cash order	$	dollar
d/d	delivered	DM	deutsche mark
D/O	delivery order	€	euro
G/A	general average	F	franc
L/C, l/c	letter of credit	L	lira
M/D, m/d	month's date	£	pound
N/S, n/s	not sufficient funds	R	ruble
o/c	overcharge	₨	rupee
O/S	out of stock	Y, ¥	yen

PROOFREADERS' MARKS

∧	Insert material as indicated in margin
✗	Delete
stet	Restore deleted material; let it stand (in text, use dots to indicate what is to be restored)
⌒	Close up; print as one word
⌒̃	Delete and close up
tr	Transpose (in text, indicate how to change order of)
(*sp*)	Spell out
#	Insert space
eq #	Space evenly
hr #	Insert hair space
⊡	Insert or indent one em space
⌐	Move up
⊔	Move down
⊐	Move to the right
⊏	Move to the left
⊐⊏	Center
‖	Align vertically
=	Align horizontally; straighten type
9	Turn over inverted letter
wf	Wrong font
×	Broken type; reset
¶	Begin a new paragraph
no ¶	Do not begin a new paragraph; run paragraphs together
(/)	Insert parentheses
[/]	Insert brackets
⌃	Insert comma
;/	Insert semicolon
:/	Insert colon
⊙	Insert period
?	Insert question mark
|·|·|	Insert ellipses
∛	Insert apostrophe (or single quotation mark)
❧ ❧	Insert quotation marks
|=|	Insert hyphen
⊥	Insert em dash
⊥	Insert en dash
∨	Insert superscript or superior
∧	Insert subscript or inferior
cap	Capitalize lowercase letter
lc	Lowercase capital letter
s.c.	Set in SMALL CAPITALS (in text, indicate by double underline)
rom	Set in roman type
bf	Set in **boldface** type
ital	Set in *italic* type

"Diacritical Marks" in chapter 13; "Grammar and Punctuation" (chapter 14); and "Network Etiquette (Netiquette)" in chapter 16
Go to

SMILEYS

Smileys, also known as emoticons, or emotional icons, are faces viewed sideways that are added to online messages in order to convey feelings.

:-)	Happy	8-|	In suspense
:-(	Sad	|-|	Asleep (indicates boredom)
;-)	Winking	:-&	Tongue-tied
:-t	Cross	:-#	Lips are sealed
:-o	Surprised	:-\	Undecided

ADDITIONAL SOURCES OF INFORMATION

BOOKS

Becker, Udo, ed. *The Continuum Encyclopedia of Symbols.* Continuum International, 2000.

Biedermann, Hans. *Dictionary of Symbolism.* Peter Smith, 1990.

Chevalier, Jean, et al., eds. *A Dictionary of Symbols.* Penguin, 1997.

Dreyfuss, Henry, ed. *Symbol Sourcebook: An Authoritative Guide to International Graphic Symbols.* Van Nostrand Reinhold, 1984.

Jean, Georges. *Signs, Symbols, and Ciphers.* Abrams, 1998.

Juliann, Nadia. *The Mammoth Dictionary of Symbols.* Carroll & Graf, 1995.

Lehner, Ernst. *Symbols, Signs, and Signets.* Peter Smith, 1990.

Mattia, Fioretta. *Elsevier's Dictionary of Acronyms, Initialisms, Abbreviations and Symbols.* Elsevier, 1997.

Tresidder, Jack. *Symbols and Their Meanings.* Friedman/Fairfax, 2000.

WEB SITES

The American Sign Language Browser
http://commtechlab.msu.edu/sites/aslweb

Encyclopedia of Symbols
http://www.symbols.com

National Federation for the Blind's Braille Page
http://www.nfb.org/brailco.htm

13

ALPHABETS AND WORDS

ALPHABETIZATION

There are two ways of alphabetizing a list of words, terms, or names. In both cases, the compiler of the list compares the first letters of the entries, then the second letters, and so forth. In a word-by-word list, the first word of each entry is considered, then the second, and third if necessary; hyphens are ignored. A letter-by-letter list is considered without regard for whether the entry consists of one word or more than one; spaces and hyphens are ignored.

The following list is arranged according to the word-by-word system:

> sea
> Sea Side Heights
> seafood
> seagull
> seal
> seaside
> season ticket
> seasoning
> second best
> second name
> secondary

Here is the same list compiled under the letter-by-letter system:

> sea
> seafood
> seagull
> seal
> seaside
> Sea Side Heights
> seasoning
> season ticket
> secondary
> second best
> second name

Either method of alphabetization is acceptable, as long as it is scrupulously adhered to. Although some lists may be better served by one approach or the other, neither is considered more correct.

ACRONYMS

Acronyms are pronounceable formations made by combining the initial letters or syllables of a string of words. Some abbreviations look like acronyms but are listed as abbreviations because they are not pro-

nounced as words; for example, CIA (usually pronounced "C-I-A") and DAR (usually pronounced "D-A-R"). A few acronyms may be pronounced either as words ("REM") or as abbreviations ("R-E-M"). Acronyms marked with an asterisk (*) have been generally accepted and used as common words.

Acronym	Stands for
ABEND	**ab**normal **end**
ACE	**A**merican **C**ouncil on **E**ducation
ACTION	**A**merican **C**ouncil **t**o **I**mprove **O**ur **N**eighborhoods
AFTRA	**A**merican **F**ederation of **T**elevision and **R**adio **A**rtists
AID	**A**gency for **I**nternational **D**evelopment
AID	**A**merican **I**nstitute of **D**ecorators
AID	**A**rmy **I**ntelligence **D**epartment
AIDS	**a**cquired **i**mmune **d**eficiency **s**yndrome
AIIM	**A**ssociation for **I**nformation and **I**mage **M**anagement
ALCOA	**Al**uminum **Co**mpany of **A**merica
ALGOL	**alg**orithmic **o**riented **l**anguage
ALIBI	**a**daptive **l**ocation of **i**nternetworked **b**ases of **i**nformation
ALINK	**a**ctive **link**
AMEX	**Am**erican **Ex**press Company
AMEX	**Am**erican Stock **Ex**change
AMVETS	**Am**erican **Vet**erans of World War II
ANSI	**A**merican **N**ational **S**tandards **I**nstitute
ARC	**A**IDS-**r**elated **c**omplex
ARCO	**A**tlantic **R**ichfield **Co**mpany
ASCAP	**A**merican **S**ociety of **C**omposers, **A**uthors, and **P**ublishers
ASCII	**A**merican **S**tandard **C**ode for **I**nformation **I**nterchange
AWACS	**a**irborne **w**arning **a**nd **c**ontrol **s**ystem
AWOL, awol*	**a**bsent **with**out **l**eave
BAM	**B**rooklyn **A**cademy of **M**usic
BAM	**b**asic **a**ccess **m**ethod
BART	**B**ay **A**rea **R**apid **T**ransit
BASIC	**B**eginner's **A**ll-purpose **S**ymbolic **I**nstruction **C**ode (computer language)
BASS	**B**ass **A**nglers **S**portsman **S**ociety
BIB	**B**ureau of **I**nternational **B**roadcasting
BIOS	**b**asic **i**nput/**o**utput **s**ystem
bit*	**bi**nary digi**t**
BIZNET	American **B**us**i**ness **Net**work (database)
BOLD	**b**ibliographic **o**n-line **d**isplay (document retrieval system)
CAB	**C**ivil **A**eronautics **B**oard
CAD	**c**omputer-**a**ided **d**esign
CARE	**C**ooperative for **A**merican **R**elief **E**verywhere

Acronym	Stands for
CAT (scan)	computerized axial tomography
CD-ROM	compact disk–read only memory
CLASSMATE	Computer Language to Aid and Stimulate Scientific, Mathematical and Technical Education
CODEC	coder/decoder
COMSAT	Communications Satellite Corporation
CONOCO	Continental Oil Company
CONUS	Continental United States
CORE	Congress of Racial Equality
COSMIC	Computer Software Management and Information Center
CURE	Citizens United for Racial Equality
DAM	Dayton Art Museum
DAM	Denver Art Museum
DELCO	Dayton Engineering Laboratory Company
DEW	distant early warning
DISCO	Defense Industrial Security Clearing Office
DOS	disk operating system
EARS	Electronic Airborne Reaction System
EARS	Electronically Agile Radar System
EARS	Emergency Airborne Reaction System
ELECTRA	Electrical, Electronics and Communications Trade Association
ENDEX	Environmental Data Index
EPCOT®	Experimental Prototype Community of Tomorrow
EXIMBANK	Export-Import Bank of the United States
FAQ	frequently asked questions
FEDLINK	Federal Library Information Network
FEW	Federally Employed Women
FICA	Federal Insurance Contributions Act (Social Security)
FLIP	Flexible Loan Insurance Program
FLIP	floating instrument platform
GAAP	generally accepted accounting principles
GAG	Graphic Arts Guild
GARB	Garment and Allied Industries Requirements Board
GATT	General Agreement on Tariffs and Trade
GENIE	General Electric Network for Information Exchange
GEO	Geostationary Earth Orbit
GEOS	graphic environment operating system
GILS	Government Information Locator Service
GIPSY	general information processing system

Acronym	Stands for
GLAAD	Gay and Lesbian Alliance Against Defamation
GOES	Geostationary Operational Environmental Satellite
GRAD	graduate resume accumulation and distribution
GUPCO	Gulf Petroleum Corporation
HALF	Human Animal Liberation Front
HART	Honolulu Area Rapid Transit
HEAL	Health Education Assistance Loans
HUD	(Department of) Housing and Urban Development
IMAX®	Maximum Image
INLAW	infantry laser weapon
INTELSAT	International Telecommunications Satellite Consortium
INTERMARC	International Machine-Readable Catalog
INTERPOL	International Criminal Police Organization
INTERTELL	International Intelligence Legion
JAG	judge advocate general
JOBS	Job Opportunities in the Business Sector
JUMPS	Joint Uniform Military Pay System
LAN	local area network
laser*	light amplification by stimulated emission of radiation
LEAP	Loan and Educational Aid Program
LEM	lunar excursion module
LILCO	Long Island Lighting Company
LORAN	Long-range Navigation
MACOM	major army command
MAD	mutually assured destruction
MADD	Mothers Against Drunk Driving
MARC	machine-readable cataloging
maser*	microwave amplification stimulated emission of radiation
MASH	mobile army surgical hospital
MOMA	Museum of Modern Art (New York)
NAFTA	North American Free Trade Agreement
NAM	network access machine
NAM	National Association of Manufacturers
NAPA	National Automotive Parts Association

A Closer Look

Recurrent Letters of the Alphabet

The letters of the alphabet in the order of their normal recurrence from most frequent to least frequent: E, T, A, O, I, N, S, H, R, D, L, U, C, M, P, F, Y, W, G, B, V, K, J, X, Z, Q.

Alphabets

Acronym	Stands for
NAPA	National Police Officers' Association of America
NARAD	Navy Research and Development
NARCO	United National Narcotics Commission
NASA	National Aeronautics and Space Administration
NASCAR	National Association of Stock Car Auto Racing
NASDAQ	National Association of Securities Dealers Automatic Quotation
NATO	North Atlantic Treaty Organization
NECCO	New England Confectionery Company
NOAA	National Oceanographic and Atmospheric Administration
NOMAD	navy oceanographic and meteorological device
NORAD	North American Defense Command
NOW	National Organization for Women
NOW	negotiable order of withdrawal (a NOW account is a savings account on which checks can be drawn)
OASIS	Overseas Access Service for Information Systems
ODECO	Ocean Drilling and Exploration Company
ODESY	On-Line Data Entry System
OPEC	Organization of Petroleum Exporting Countries
OSHA	Occupational Safety and Health Administration
OXFAM	Oxford Famine Relief
PAC	Pacific Air Command
PAC	political action committee
PATCO	Port Authority Transit Corporation
PATH	Port Authority Trans-Hudson
PEN	Poets, Playwrights, Editors, Essayists, and Novelists
PEST	People for Environmentally Sustainable Transport
PET	parent effectiveness training
PET	positron emission tomography
PIN	personal identification number
PIN	Police Information Network
PIM	personal information manager
PIRG	public interest research group
POSIX	Portable Operating System Interface for Computer Environments
PUSH	People United to Serve Humanity
radar*	radio detecting and ranging
RAM	random access memory
READ	real-time electronic access and display

Acronym	Stands for
RIF	Reading Is Fundamental
ROM	read-only memory
SAC	Strategic Air Command
SADD	Students Against Drunk Driving
SAFE	system for automated flight efficiency
SAG	Screen Actors Guild
SALT	Strategic Arms Limitation Talks
SAM	surface-to-air missile
SAP	system access protocol
SARA	Superfund Amendments and Reauthorization Act (1986)
SCOPE	Scientific Committee on Problems of the Environment
SCOR	Scientific Committee on Oceanic Research
SCOSTEP	Scientific Committee on Solar-Terrestrial Physics
scuba*	self-contained underwater breathing apparatus
SEATO	Southeast Asia Treaty Organization
SEP	simplified employee pension
snafu*	situation normal—all fouled up
sonar*	sound navigation ranging
START	Strategic Arms Reduction Talks
SUNOCO	Sun Oil Company
SWAK	sealed with a kiss
SWAT	Special Weapons and Tactics
TAC	Tactical Air Command
TIROS	Television and Infra-Red Observation Satellite
UNESCO	United Nations Educational, Social, and Cultural Organization
UNICEF	United Nations International Children's Emergency Fund
VISTA	Volunteers in Service to America
WAC	Women's Army Corps
WAIS	wide area information server
WAN	wide area network
WARMER	World Action for Recycled Material and Energy from Rubbish
WASP	white Anglo-Saxon Protestant
WATS	Wide Area Telecommunications Service
WAVES	Women Accepted for Volunteer Emergency Service (navy)
WHO	World Health Organization
WISE	World Information Systems Exchange
WORM	write once–read many
WUDO	Western European Defense Organization
yuppie*	young urban professional
zip*	zone improvement plan (code)

COMMON ABBREVIATIONS

An abbreviation is a shortened form of a word or phrase. Some abbreviations, such as Mr. and Mrs., always substitute for the longer form. Abbreviations are not limited to, but frequently are used for, titles, academic degrees, organizations, measurements, and scientific words. An asterisk (*) indicates a frequently used abbreviation that is incorrect according to the scientific metric notation system.

Abbr.	Stands for
1GL	first-generation language
2DR	two-door
2GL	second-generation language
2WD	two-wheel drive
3GL	third-generation language
4DR	four-door
4GL	fourth-generation language
4WD	four-wheel drive
a	acre
AA	Alcoholics Anonymous
AAA	American Automobile Association
ABC	American Broadcasting Company
ABM	antiballistic missile
AC	alternating current
ACLU	American Civil Liberties Union
ACT	American College Test
AD, A.D.	*anno domini* (Latin, in the year of our Lord)
A/D	analog to digital
ADA	American Dental Association
addn.	addition
addnl.	additional
adm.	administration, administrative
AEC	Atomic Energy Commission
AEF	American Expeditionary Force (World War I)
aet.	*aetatis* (Latin, of age, aged)
AF	air force
AFB	air force base
AFC	American Football Conference
AFDC	Aid to Families with Dependent Children
AFL	American Football League
AFL-CIO	American Federation of Labor and Congress of Industrial Organizations
Afr.	Africa, African
AFT	American Federation of Teachers
AFTP	Anonymous File Transfer Protocol
agcy.	agency
agt.	agent
AH, A.H.	*anno Hegirae/anno Hebraico* (Latin, in the year of the Hegira/Latin, in the Hebrew year)

Abbr.	Stands for
AHL	American Hockey League
AI	artificial intelligence
AIA	American Institute of Architects
aka, a.k.a.	also known as
AKC	American Kennel Club
AL	American League
AM	amplitude modulation
A.M.	*anno mundi* (Latin, in the year of the world)
A.M., AM, a.m.	*ante meridiem* (Latin, before noon)
AMA	American Medical Association
AMU	atomic mass unit
anon.	anonymous
AP	Associated Press
A/P	accounts payable
APA	American Psychological Association
APB	all points bulletin
APO	army post office (overseas)
appl.	applied
approx.	approximately
appt.	appointment
Apr.	April
APR	annual percentage rate
apt.	apartment
A/R	accounts receivable
ARV	American Revised Version
ASAP	as soon as possible (pronounced "A-S-A-P" or "A-SAP")
assn.	association
asoc.	associate
asst.	assistant
AST	Alaska Standard Time
AT&T	American Telephone and Telegraph Company
ATM	automated/automatic teller machine
ATTN, attn.	attention
atty.	attorney
ATV	all-terrain vehicle
Aug.	August
AV	audiovisual
AV	Authorized Version
AVR	automatic voice recognition
b.	born
B and B, B&B	bed and breakfast
B and E	breaking and entering
BBB	Better Business Bureau

Go to "Weights and Measures" in chapter 2; "Symbols and Signs" in chapter 12; "Abbreviated Titles That Follow Names" in chapter 15

Alphabets

Abbr.	Stands for
BBC	British Broadcasting Corporation
bbl.	barrel(s)
BC, B.C.	before Christ
BC, B.C.E.	before the Christian era
bef.	before
bf, b.f.	boldface
BLT	bacon, lettuce, and tomato
BMOC	big man on campus
BP	blood pressure
B.P.O.E.	Benevolent and Protective Order of Elks
BR	bedroom
BSA	Boy Scouts of America
bu.	bushel
BV, BVM	Blessed Virgin, Blessed Virgin Mary
b/w	black and white
BX	base exchange (commissary)
BYOB	bring your own beer/ booze/bottle
C	centigrade, Celsius
c., ca.	*circa* (Latin, about)
calc.	calculate, calculated
Cantab.	*Cantabrigiensis* (Latin, of Cambridge)
caps	capital letters
CATV	community antenna television, *now called* cable television
CBS	Columbia Broadcasting System
cc	cubic centimeter
cc, CC	carbon copy
CCC	Civilian Conservation Corps
CCU	cardiac/coronary/critical care unit
CD	certificate of deposit
CDC	Centers for Disease Control
CDT	Central Daylight Time
CEO	chief executive officer
cf.	*confer* (Latin, compare)
CFO	chief financial officer
CIA	Central Intelligence Agency
cm	centimeter
c/o	in care of
COD	cash on delivery
COO	chief operating officer
CP	Communist Party
CPA	certified public accountant
cpi	characters per inch
CPI	consumer price index
CPR	cardiopulmonary resuscitation
CPU	central processing unit
CSA	Confederate States of America
CST	Central Standard Time
cu.	cubic
DAR	Daughters of the American Revolution
dB	decibel
DB	database
d/b/a	doing business as

Abbr.	Stands for
DC	District of Columbia
DC	direct current
Dec.	December
dept.	department
dist.	district
div.	division
DMV	Department (Division) of Motor Vehicles
DMZ	demilitarized zone
DNA	deoxyribonucleic acid
DOA	dead on arrival
DOB	date of birth
doz.	dozen
Dr.	Doctor
D.S.M.	Distinguished Service Medal
D.S.O.	Distinguished Service Order
DST	Daylight Saving Time
DTs	*delerium tremens* (Latin, trembling delirium)
DUI	driving under the influence
DVD	digital video disc
DWI	driving while intoxicated
ED	emotional disability, emotionally disabled
EDS	Electronic Data Systems
EEO	equal employment opportunity
e.g.	*exempli gratia* (Latin, for example)
eng.	engineering
Eng.	English
engr.	engineer
engr.	engraved
EPA	Environmental Protection Agency
ERA	earned run average
ESP	extrasensory perception
esp.	especially
EST	Eastern Standard Time
et al.	*et alii, et aliae, et alia* (Latin, and others)
etc.	*et cetera* (Latin, and others of the same kind; and so forth)
ex.	example
exch.	exchange
ext.	extension
f., F	female, feminine
f., ff.	and following
F	Fahrenheit
FAA	Federal Aviation Administration
fax	facsimile
FBI	Federal Bureau of Investigation
FCC	Federal Communications Commission
FDA	Food and Drug Administration
FDIC	Federal Deposit Insurance Corporation
Feb.	February

Go to   "Cooking Measurement Abbreviations" in chapter 19; "Airline Codes, Toll-Free Numbers, and Web Sites" and "Airport Codes" in chapter 24

Abbr.	Stands for
fed.	federal
FHA	Federal Housing Administration
fig.	figure
FM	frequency modulation
f.o.b., FOB	free on board
fr.	from
Fr.	French
Fri.	Friday
FRM	fixed rate mortgage
FRS	Federal Reserve System
ft.	foot
f/t	full time
FTC	Federal Trade Commission
f/x	special effects
FWD	front-wheel drive
FYI	for your information
G	giga (metric prefix meaning 1,000,000,000)
GAO	General Accounting Office
G.A.R.	Grand Army of the Republic
GED	General Educational Development (tests)
GED	general equivalency diploma
Gk.	Greek
GMAT	Graduate Management Admission Test
GMT	Greenwich Mean Time
GNP	gross national product
GOP	Grand Old Party (Republican party)
gov., govt.	government
G.P.	general practitioner
GPA	grade point average
GPO	Government Printing Office
GRE	Graduate Record Examination
GSA	General Services Administration
GSA	Girl Scouts of America
GSO	general staff officer
GUI	graphical user interface
HEW	(Department of) Health, Education, and Welfare
H.M.S.	His/Her Majesty's Ship
hp	horsepower
HQ	headquarters
hr.	hour
HR	home run
H.R.	House of Representatives
H.R.H.	His/Her Royal Highness
HS	high school
ht., hgt.	height
HTML, html	hypertext markup language
HVAC	heating, ventilating, and air conditioning
ibid.	*ibidem* (Latin, in the same place)
I.B.M.	International Business Machines Corporation

Abbr.	Stands for
ICBM	intercontinental ballistic missile
ICC	Interstate Commerce Commission
ICF	intermediate care facility
ICU	intensive care unit
i.e.	*id est* (Latin, that is)
IGY	International Geophysical Year
IHS	Jesus (Greek contraction)
ILGWU	International Ladies' Garment Workers' Union
IMO	in my opinion
in.	inch
INRI	*Iesus Nazarenus Rex Iudaeorum* (Latin, Jesus of Nazareth, King of the Jews)
INS	Immigration and Naturalization Service
I.O.U.	I owe you
I.Q.	intelligence quotient
IRA	individual retirement account
IRA	Irish Republican Army
IRS	Internal Revenue Service
ISBN	international standard book number
ISO	International Organization for Standardization
Jan.	January
Jr.	Junior
k	karat
k	kilo (metric prefix meaning 1,000)
K	Kelvin
kb (K*, KB*)	kilobyte
kbps (KBps*)	kilobytes per second
kg	kilogram
KGB	*Komitet Gosudarstvennoi Bezopasnosti* (Russian, State Security Committee)
kHz	kilohertz
KJV	King James Version
km	kilometer
kW (kw*)	kilowatt
kWh (kwh*)	kilowatt-hour
l	liter
lat.	latitude
Lat.	Latin
lb.	pound
lc, l.c.	lowercase
L.C.	Library of Congress
LCD	liquid crystal display
LD	learning disability, learning disabled
LDS	Latter-Day Saints
LED	light-emitting diode
LMT	Local Mean Time
long.	longitude
LSAT	Law School Admission Test

Abbr.	Stands for
ltr.	letter
m	meter
m., M	male, masculine
M	mega (metric prefix meaning 1,000,000)
Mac	Macintosh computer
Mar.	March
max.	maximum
MB	megabyte (1,024 kilobytes)
MBps	megabytes per second
MC, emcee	master of ceremonies
mg	milligram
mgr.	manager
MHz	megahertz
mi.	mile
min.	minimum, minute
ml	milliliter
mm	millimeter
mo.	month
M.O.	money order
M.O.	*modus operandi* (Latin, mode of operation)
Mon.	Monday
MP, M.P.	Military Police
mph	miles per hour
MRI	magnetic resonance imaging
ms., mss.	manuscript, manuscripts
MSG	monosodium glutamate
MVP	most valuable player
MYOB	mind your own business
N/A	not applicable
NAACP	National Association for the Advancement of Colored People
N.B.	*nota bene* (Latin, note well)
NBA	National Basketball Association
NBC	National Broadcasting Company
NCAA	National Collegiate Athletic Association
NCO	noncommissioned officer
NEA	National Education Association
NEA	National Endowment for the Arts
NFL	National Football League
NHL	National Hockey League
NIH	National Institutes of Health
NL	National League
NLRB	National Labor Relations Board
NMHA	National Mental Health Association
non seq.	*non sequitur* (Latin, it does not follow)
NOS	not otherwise specified
Nov.	November
NR	not rated

Abbr.	Stands for
NRA	National Recovery Administration
NRA	National Rifle Association
NRC	National Research Council
NRC	Nuclear Regulatory Commission
N.S.	New Style
NSA	National Security Agency
NSC	National Security Council
NSF	National Science Foundation
NSF	not sufficient funds
NTSB	National Transportation Safety Board
Oct.	October
OCR	optical character recognition
op. cit.	*opere citato* (Latin, in the work cited)
O.S.	Old Style
OT	occupational therapy
OT, o/t	overtime
OTC	over-the-counter (non-prescription)
Oxon.	*Oxoniensis* (Latin, of Oxford)
oz.	ounce
PA (system)	public address (system)
p and h	postage and handling
P&I	principal and interest
P&L	profit and loss
PB&J	peanut butter and jelly
PBS	Public Broadcasting Service
PC	personal computer
PCB	polychlorinated biphenyl
PDA	public display of affection
PDR	*Physicians Desk Reference*
PDT	Pacific Daylight Time
PE	physical education
perp.	perpetrator
pk.	peck
P.M., PM, p.m.	*post meridiem* (Latin, after noon)
P.M.	prime minister
PMS	premenstrual syndrome
pmt.	payment
PO	post office
POB	post office box
POE	place of employment
POV	point of view
POW, PW	prisoner of war
ppb	parts per billion
ppm	parts per million
ppt	parts per thousand
prep., prep	preparatory
Pres.	President
prev.	previous
PRN	*pro re nata* (Latin, for an occasion that has written—as needed)
pro tem.	*pro tempore* (Latin, for the time being)
P.S., PS	postscript

Go to "Two-Letter State and Territory Abbreviations," "Geographic Directional Abbreviations," and "Street Designators (Street Suffixes)" in chapter 25

Alphabets

Abbr.	Stands for
PSA	public service announcement
psi	pounds per square inch
PST	Pacific Standard Time
psych	psychology
pt.	pint
p/t	part-time
PTA	Parent-Teacher Association
PX	post exchange (commissary)
QA	quality assurance
Q&A	questions and answers
Q.E.D.	*quod erat demonstrandum* (Latin, which was to be demonstrated)
QMHP	qualified mental health professional
qt.	quart
qty.	quantity
q.v.	*quod vide* (Latin, which see)
R&B	rhythm and blues
R&D	research and development
RBC	red blood cells, red blood cell count
rbi	run batted in
RDA	recommended daily allowance
REM	rapid eye movement (pronounced "R-E-M" or "REM")
RFD	rural free delivery
RIP, R.I.P.	*requiescat in pace* (Latin, rest in peace)
RNA	ribonucleic acid
ROTC	Reserve Officers' Training Corps (pronounced "R-O-T-C" or "ROTC")
rpm	revolutions per minute
RR	railroad
R and R	rest and relaxation
RSV	Revised Standard Version
R.S.V.P., RSVP	*repondez s'il vous plait* (French, respond if you please)
rtw	ready to wear
Rx	prescription
S&H	shipping and handling
S-M, S and M	sadism and masochism
SASE	self-addressed stamped envelope
SAT	Scholastic Aptitude Test
Sat.	Saturday
SBA	Small Business Administration
SBS	sick building syndrome
sc, s.c.	small capitals
SCLC	Southern Christian Leadership Conference
SDI	Strategic Defense Initiative
SDS	Students for a Democratic Society
sec.	seconds
SEC	Securities and Exchange Commission
Sen.	Senate
Sept.	September
seq.	*sequentes* (Latin, the following)
SNF	skilled nursing facility

Abbr.	Stands for
SOS	international Morse code distress signal (dot dot dot dash dash dash dot dot dot), often wrongly thought to stand for "Save Our Ship"; however, the letters do not stand for words
SPCA	Society for the Prevention of Cruelty to Animals
SPQR	*senatus populusque romanus* (Latin, the Senate and the Roman people)
sq.	square
Sr.	Senior
SRO	standing room only
SSA	Social Security Administration
SSN	Social Security number
Sun.	Sunday
SUV	sport utility vehicle
T	ton
TA	teaching assistant
TA	transactional analysis
TB	tuberculosis
TBA, tba	to be announced
TD	touchdown
TDD	telecommunications device for the deaf
temp.	temporary
TF	task force
TGIF	thank God it's Friday
Thurs.	Thursday
TIA	transient ischemic attack
TLC	tender loving care
TM	trademark
TM	transcendental meditation
TMJ	temporomandibular joint
TNT	trinitrotoluene
TOEFL	Test of English as a Foreign Language
TSS	toxic shock syndrome
TTY	teletypewriter
Tues.	Tuesday
TVA	Tennessee Valley Authority
uc, u.c.	uppercase
UFO	unidentified flying object
UHF	ultra high frequency
UK	United Kingdom
UN	United Nations
UPI	United Press International
US, USA	United States, United States of America
USA	United States Army
USAF	United States Air Force
USCG	United States Coast Guard
USDA	United States Department of Agriculture
USIA	United States Information Agency
USMC	United States Marine Corps
USN	United States Navy
USO	United Service Organization

Alphabets

Abbr.	**Stands for**
USS	United States Ship
USSR	Union of Soviet Socialist Republics
v., vs.	versus
VA	Veterans Administration
VCR	video cassette recorder
VD	venereal disease
VFW	Veterans of Foreign Wars
VHF	very high frequency
VIP	very important person
viz.	*videlicet* (Latin, namely)
VP	Vice President
W	watt
WB	World Bank
WBC	white blood cells/white blood cell count
WC	water closet (toilet)
WCTU	Women's Christian Temperance Union
Wed.	Wednesday
wk.	week
WNBA	Women's National Basketball Association
WP	word processing
WPA	Works Progress Administration
WTO	World Trade Organization
WWW	World Wide Web
WYSIWYG	what you see is what you get
Xmas	Christmas
XO	executive officer
yd.	yard
YTD	year to date
YMCA	Young Men's Christian Association
YMHA	Young Men's Hebrew Association
YWCA	Young Women's Christian Association
YWHA	Young Women's Hebrew Association
yr.	year

COMMONLY MISUSED WORDS

accept	to receive; to answer affirmatively
except	to leave out (verb); with the exclusion of (preposition)
affect	to influence; to pretend
effect	a result, an influence, an impression (noun); to bring about (verb)
antagonist	an adversary
protagonist	the leading character
anxious	worried, uneasy
eager	impatiently desirous
bathos	triteness, sentimentality
pathos	sympathy
brake	to reduce speed
break	to separate; to collapse; to destroy
capital	a city that is a seat of government; money; an uppercase letter
capitol	the building in which a legislature meets
compare	to examine differences and similarities
contrast	to examine differences
diagnosis	the identification of a disease or situation
prognosis	a prediction of the likely course of a disease or situation
dinner	the main meal of the day, at noontime or in the evening
supper	the evening meal
dyeing	coloring with dye
dying	ceasing to live
emigrate	to leave a country to live elsewhere
immigrate	to enter a country to live there
flair	skill, talent
flare	a bright light; an outburst
gorilla	an ape
guerrilla	a member of an irregular military force
hole	a space, a void
whole	complete, intact
illegible	cannot be read because of bad printing or handwriting
unreadable	uninteresting, not worth reading
ingenious	brilliant, clever
ingenuous	simple, naive
its	belonging to it
it's	it is
lay	to put; to set down
lie	to rest in a horizontal position; to make an untrue statement
liable	responsible; likely
libel	a defamatory statement
majority	more than half
plurality	more votes than any other candidate; the margin of victory
notable	worthy, impressive
notorious	widely known and ill-regarded
peace	harmony; the absence of war
piece	part of a whole
personal	intimate; having to do with a specific person
personnel	the employees of a company or organization

Alphabets

pray	to address a deity; to implore
prey	a victim
principal	main (adjective); the person in charge (noun)
principle	a moral rule; a law
put (some-one) down	to criticize or disparage someone
put (some-one) on	to mislead someone, especially in a joking way
recollect	to remember
re-collect	to collect again
sail	fabric that catches the wind to propel a boat (noun); to ride in a boat, especially one that is wind-powered (verb)
sale	a discounted offering; the act of selling
stationary	not moving
stationery	writing materials
talk to	to address others
talk with	to converse together
viral	having to do with a virus
virile	manly
whose	of which; of who
who's	who is
your	belonging to you
you're	you are

SPELLING GUIDELINES

Many words in American English are spelled just as they sound. That is, a long *a* sound is often spelled with an *a*. Aside from the old saw "*i* before *e* except

after *c*, unless sounded as *a* as in *neighbor* and *weigh*," there are few easy ways of remembering the intricacies of correct spelling. The following table shows the ways in which various sounds common in English words can be spelled.

Sound	Spellings
a	s**a**t, mer**i**ngue, s**a**lmon, l**au**gh
ah	f**a**ther, **au**nt, c**a**lm, s**e**rgeant, Afrik**aa**ns
aw	s**aw**, c**au**ght, **o**rder, **ou**ght, w**a**lk
ay	f**a**de, **ae**robic, pl**ai**n, c**ay**, br**ea**k, n**ei**gh, wh**ey**, r**e**gime
ch	**c**ello, **ch**ip, ques**ti**on, na**t**ure
e	**a**ny, gu**e**ss, l**eo**pard, fri**e**nd, br**ea**d
ee	m**e**, s**ee**, l**ea**, sk**i**, **ei**ther, **Ae**sop, ver**y**, bel**ie**ve, ph**oe**nix
er	**ear**th, j**er**k, st**ir**, t**ur**n, auth**or**, mart**yr**
f	**f**all, tele**ph**one, rou**gh**
ih	h**i**t, **E**nglish, w**o**men, b**u**sy, cabb**a**ge, b**ui**ld, carr**ia**ge, s**ie**ve
i	**i**ce, sl**y**, g**ey**ser, h**igh**, b**uy**, d**ie**, papa**ya**, **eye**
j	**j**am, le**dg**e, trage**d**y
k	**k**elp, **ch**aracter, sla**ck**, a**c**re, a**q**ua, a**cc**ount
n	**n**ap, **kn**ow, **pn**eumonia, **gn**aw
oh	b**o**ne, **oa**t, s**ou**l, **oh**, f**o**lk, br**oo**ch, cr**ow**, th**ou**gh, bur**eau**, l**oa**d
oo	d**o**, l**oo**, bl**ew**, s**ue**, y**ou**, cr**ui**se
ow	c**ow**, b**ou**gh, s**au**erkraut, f**ou**nd
sh	pu**sh**, o**c**ean, **ch**auffeur, spe**ci**al, fa**sc**ist, ti**ss**ue, compul**si**on, na**ti**on, vi**ci**ous, no**xi**ous, nau**se**ous, **s**ure
uh	**u**p, **o**ven, tr**ou**ble, w**a**s, d**oe**s
v	lo**v**e, o**f**
z	**x**ylophone, **z**ebra, vi**s**ible
zh	re**g**ime, divi**s**ion, bra**z**ier

COMMONLY MISSPELLED WORDS

abscess	all right	attendance	buoyant	changeable
accept/except	already	attorney	bureau	chaperon(e)
accessory	amateur	auxiliary	burglar	chauffeur
accidentally	analogous			chief
accommodate	antarctic	banana	calendar	cinnamon
accompany	antecedent	baptize	cantaloupe	circuit
accrue	apparent	bargain	capital/capitol	circumference
acknowledgment	appearance	battalion	cashmere	cocoa
acquaintance	arctic	bazaar	caterpillar	colonel/kernel
acquire	argument	beginning	ceiling	commitment
address	arithmetic	believe	cellar	committee
affect/effect	asparagus	benign	cemetery	compliment/
aisle/isle	asthma	biscuit	cereal/serial	complement
allege	athletic	bizarre	chamois	comptroller
		bookkeeper	chandelier	

Alphabets

concede
conceive
conscientious
conscious
consensus
consignment
convenient
coquette
corduroy
correspondent
cough
counterfeit
crucifixion

debt
definite
dependent
design
desirable
desperately
dessert/desert
devise
diaphragm
diarrhea
dictionary
diphtheria
disappear
disappoint
dispel
dissatisfied

effect/affect
eighth
embarrass
embezzle
environment
equipped
erroneous
especially
etiquette
exaggerate
exceed
excel
existence
expense

familiar
fascinate

fatigue
February
fiancé
fiancée
financier
foreclosure
forehead
foreign
foreword/forward
formerly/formally
forth/fourth
forty
fragile
freight

gauge
gingham
glacier
government
grammar
grease
guarantee
guess
guest

handkerchief
harass
height
heir
hemorrhage
hygiene
hypocrisy

idol/idle
incite/insight
independence
indict
indispensable
infinitesimal
irresistible
isthmus
its/it's

judgment

khaki

laboratory
larynx

laugh
league
library
license
licorice
literature
lose/loose
lying

mackerel
maintenance
malign
maneuver
manual
mathematics
mattress
medicine
minuscule
mischief
missionary
misspell
misstate
molasses
mortgage
mosquitoes

necessary
neighbor
niece
noticeable
nuisance

obedience
occasion
occur
occurred
occurrence
o'clock
offense
omitted

parallel
parliament
perseverance
phenomenon
physician
plaid
pneumonia

politically
porcelain
possess
potatoes
prairie
precede/proceed
preferred
principle/principal
privilege
probably
protégé
protégée
pseudonym
psychology
ptomaine

quiet/quite

rarefy
raspberry
receipt
receive
recess
recognize
recommend
reference
remittance
rendezvous
repellent
repentance
reservoir
résumé
reverence
rhythm
ridiculous

sacrilege
sacrilegious
sandwich
satire/satyr
scissors
secretary
seize
separately
siege
sieve
similar
sincerely

soliloquy
special
squirrel
stationary/
    stationery
straight/strait
strengthen
succeed
success
suit/suite
superintendent
supersede
susceptible
synagogue
syringe

tariff
temperance
tenement
than/then
their/there/they're
threshold
to/too/two
tobacco
tomatoes
tragedy
transferred
truly
Tuesday

usually

vaccinate
vacuum
villain
vinegar

warrant
Wednesday
weird
wholly
whose/who's
withhold

yolk
your/you're

zephyr

"American English and British English: Punctuation Differences" in chapter 14

Go to

*No other words in the English
language rhyme with the words*
month, orange, silver, *or* purple.

Alphabets

PHONETIC SYMBOLS

VOWELS

iy	beat	ʌ	but
ɪ	bit	ə	banana, sister
ɛ	bet	aɪ	by
æ	bat	aʊ	bound
ɑ	box, car	ɔɪ	boy
ɔ	bought, horse	ɝ	burn
oʷ	bone	ɪər	beer
ʊ	book	ɛər	bare
uʷ	boot	ʊər	tour

CONSONANTS

ŋ	velar nasal—si**ng**
θ	dental fricative—**th**ing
ð	dental fricative—**th**is
ʃ	postalveolar fricative—**sh**ort
ʒ	postalveolar fricative—mea**s**ure
tʃ	palatal fricative—it**ch**
dʒ	palatal fricative—**j**ust
ɹ	dental/alveolar/postalveolar approximant—bi**r**d
ɻ	retroflex tap (or flap)—wri**t**er
ʔ	glottal plosive—pause between vowels in **cooperate**

AMERICAN ENGLISH AND BRITISH ENGLISH: SPELLING AND NAME DIFFERENCES

It has been said that the United States and Great Britain are two nations divided by a single language. This is true in a number of ways. In the first place, spellings of the same words can be decidedly different. The following list shows some common examples of the variances between American and British spellings.

American	British
center	centre
check (money)	cheque
color	colour
curb	kerb
defense	defence
gray	grey
honor	honour
inquire	enquire
jail	gaol
jewelry	jewellery
labor	labour
organization	organisation
pajamas	pyjamas
peddler	pedlar

American	British
pretense	pretence
program	programme
realize	realise
recognize	recognise
theater	theatre

The two versions of the English language also diverge when it comes to the names for many everyday objects and events. It is easy for a visitor from across the Atlantic to provoke amusement from the natives by calling a cloth used to wipe one's mouth a *napkin* in England, or by asking an American waiter for the *W.C.* The following is a list of some common American terms and their counterparts in the United Kingdom.

American	British
apartment	flat
bathroom	toilet, W.C., or loo
Big Dipper	the Plough
candy	sweets
checkers	draughts
closet	cupboard
corn	maize
cracker	biscuit
diaper	nappy
drugstore	chemist's
elevator	lift
faucet	tap
gas, gasoline	petrol
hood (of car)	bonnet
line	queue
napkin	serviette
oven	cooker
round-trip ticket	return ticket
suspenders	braces
truck	lorry
trunk (of car)	boot
underpass	subway
undershirt	vest
vacation	holiday

DIACRITICAL MARKS

´	acute accent (as in *café*)
˘	breve (pronunciation symbol that indicates a short vowel)
¸	cedilla (as in *François*)
^	circumflex (as in *château*)
¨	diaeresis or umlaut (as in *Köln*)
`	grave accent (as in *à la carte*)
¯	macron (pronunciation symbol that indicates a long vowel)
~	tilde (as in *São Tomé*)

Alphabets

THE INDO–EUROPEAN FAMILY OF LANGUAGES

"CENTUM" LANGUAGES

"SATEM" LANGUAGES

Languages in parentheses are obsolete.

INDO-EUROPEAN

*The precise relationship of Anatolian to Indo-European is still subject to question, but evidence indicates that a relationship exists and that characteristics of the "Centum" languages appear in Hittite.

GREEK
- (Medieval Greek)
- (Ancient Greek)
- Modern Greek

CELTIC
- Breton
- (Cornish)
- Welsh
- Scottish Gaelic
- Irish Gaelic
- (Manx)

ITALIC
- (Gaulish)
- (Osco-Umbrian)
- Latin
  - Romanian
  - Italian
  - Rhaeto-Romanic
  - French
  - Provençal
  - Spanish
  - Catalan
  - Portuguese

GERMANIC
- North Germanic
  - Swedish
  - Danish
  - Norwegian
  - Icelandic
- East Germanic (Gothic)
- West Germanic
  - High German
    - Modern High German
    - Yiddish
  - Low German
    - Afrikaans
    - Dutch
    - Flemish
    - Modern Low German
    - Frisian
    - English

(TOCHARIAN)

(ANATOLIAN)*
- (Hittite)

Albanian

Armenian

Slavic
- West Slavic
  - Polish
  - Czech
  - Slovak
- South Slavic
  - Bulgarian
  - Slovenian
  - Serbo-Croatian
- East Slavic
  - Ukrainian
  - Russian

Baltic
- (Old Prussian)
- Latvian
- Lithuanian

INDO-IRANIAN
- Iranian
  - (Old Persian)
  - Persian
  - (Avestan)
  - Pashto
- Indo-Aryan
  - (Sanskrit)
    - Bengali
    - Punjabi
    - Hindi
    - Urdu
    - Marathi
    - Gujarati
    - Romany
  - Dard
    - Languages of Kashmir and the upper Indus

FREQUENTLY USED FOREIGN WORDS AND PHRASES

KEY TO ABBREVIATIONS

A	Arabic	Gr	German	It	Italian	Sp	Spanish
Fr	French	H	Hebrew	L	Latin	R	Russian
Gk	Greek	Hw	Hawaiian	lit.	literally	Y	Yiddish

Word/Phrase	**Meaning**
à bas (Fr)	down with
ab initio (L)	from the beginning
ab ovo usque ad mala (L)	from soup to nuts (lit., "from the egg to the apples")
ab urbe condita (L)	from the founding of the city (Rome, 753 B.C.)
a cappella (It)	in the church style (vocally)
adagio (It)	slowly
ad astra per aspera (L)	to the stars through difficulties
ad eundum (L)	to the same degree
ad hoc (L)	for a particular purpose (lit., "to this")
ad infinitum (L)	without end
ad libitum (L)	ad lib, freely (lit., "to pleasure")
ad nauseam (L)	to the point of disgust
aere perennius (L)	more durable than bronze
aficionado (Sp)	enthusiast, fan
alea jacta est (L)	the die is cast
alfresco (It)	in the open air
allegro (L)	fast, lively
alma mater (L)	old school (lit., "fostering mother")
aloha (Hw)	greeting or farewell
amor con amor se paga (Sp)	one good turn deserves another (lit., "love is repaid with love")
amor vincit omnia (L)	love conquers all
ancien régime (Fr)	the old regime (pre–French revolution)
anno domini; A.D. (L)	in the year of the Lord
annus mirabilis (L)	wonderful year
a posteriori (L)	inductive (lit. "from what comes after")
après moi, le déluge (Fr)	after me, the deluge
a priori (L)	deductive (lit., "from what comes before")
arma virumque cano (L)	I sing of arms and the man (Virgil)
ars gratia artis (L)	art for art's sake
ars longa, vita brevis (L)	art is long, life is short
au contraire (Fr)	on the contrary
au courant (Fr)	up to date, contemporary
au naturel (Fr)	nude, plain
aurea mediocritas (L)	golden mean
autre temps, autre mœurs (Fr)	other times, other customs
avant-garde (Fr)	forward, advanced; vanguard
ave atque vale (L)	hail and farewell
beau geste (Fr)	noble gesture
beau idéal (Fr)	highest ideal
bête noire (Fr)	someone or something strongly detested (lit., "black beast")
billet doux (Fr)	love letter
Blitzkrieg (Gr)	lightning war
bon marché (Fr)	inexpensive (lit., "good market")
bon mot (Fr)	clever turn of phrase
bonne chance (Fr)	good luck

Alphabets

Word/Phrase	Meaning
bon vivant (Fr)	partygoer; one who enjoys life
bon voyage (Fr)	good journey
campesino (Sp)	peasant, farmer
canard (Fr)	insult, hoax (lit., "duck")
carpe diem (L)	seize the day
carte blanche (Fr)	free hand, no restrictions (lit., "white card")
cause célèbre (Fr)	scandal; notorious incident
caveat emptor (L)	let the buyer beware
c'est la vie (Fr)	that's life
ceteris paribus (L)	other things being equal
chacun á son gout (Fr)	each to his own taste
chef d'œuvre (Fr)	masterpiece
cherchez la femme (Fr)	look for the woman
chutzpah (Y)	gall, daring
ciao (It)	good-bye, so long
circa (c., ca.) (L)	about, approximately
cogito ergo sum (L)	I think, therefore I am
cognoscenti (It)	intellectuals; those in the know
comédie de mœurs (Fr)	comedy of manners
comme ci comme ça (Fr)	so-so, neither good nor bad
comme il faut (Fr)	proper, appropriate
con mucho gusto (Sp)	with pleasure
corpus delicti (L)	evidence (lit., "body of the crime")
coup de grâce (Fr)	final blow
coup d'état (Fr)	overthrow of government
cui bono? (L)	to whose benefit?
cul de sac (Fr)	dead end (lit., "end of the bag")
cum grano salis (L)	with a grain of salt
de capo (It)	from the top
déclassé (Fr)	fallen in social standing
décolletage (Fr)	low-cut style
de facto (L)	in fact
de gustibus non est disputandum (L)	there is no arguing about taste
de jure (L)	in law
demimonde (Fr)	underworld; other side of the tracks
de mortuis nil nisi bonum (L)	of the dead [say nothing] but good
Deo gratias (L)	thanks be to God
Deo volente (L)	God willing
dernier cri (Fr)	the last word
déshabillé (Fr)	carelessly or scantily dressed
deus ex machina (L)	desperate or contrived solution (lit., "god from the machine")
dolce far niente (It)	sweet idleness
Doppelgänger (Gr)	phantom double
Drang nach Osten (Gr)	drive toward the east
dum spiro spero (L)	while there's life, there's hope
élan vital (Fr)	vital force
embarras de richesses (Fr)	embarrassment of riches
enfant terrible (Fr)	prodigy
en passant (Fr)	in passing; by the way
entre nous (Fr)	privately, between us
épater le bourgeois (Fr)	shock the middle class
e pluribus unum (L)	from many, one
ersatz (Gr)	fake, imitation
et cetera (etc.) (L)	and others

Word/Phrase	Meaning
Eureka! (Gk)	I've found it!
ex cathedra (L)	with high authority (lit., "from the chair")
exempli gratia (e.g.) (L)	by way of example
ex post facto (L)	after the fact
fait accompli (Fr)	accomplished fact
faute de mieux (Fr)	for want of something better
faux pas (Fr)	social error (lit., "false step")
femme fatale (Fr)	alluring, dangerous woman
fin de siècle (Fr)	end of century; decadent
flagrante delicto (L)	caught in the act (lit., "with the crime blazing")
gaudeamus igitur (L)	let us therefore rejoice
glasnost (R)	openness
gnothi seauton (Gk)	know yourself
gonif (Y)	thief
goy (Y)	gentile
habeas corpus (L)	writ requiring a court appearance (lit., "[that] you have the body")
haut monde (Fr)	high society
hoi polloi (Gk)	common people, mob
homo lupus homini (L)	man is a wolf to man
honi soi qui mal y pense (Fr)	shame to him who thinks evil of it
hubris (Gk)	overweening pride, arrogance
idée fixe (Fr)	fixed idea, obsession
id est (i.e.) (L)	that is
infra dignitatem (infra dig.) (L)	beneath one's dignity
in loco parentis (L)	in the place of parents
in medias res (L)	in the middle of things
in vino veritas (L)	in wine, truth
ipso facto (L)	by the fact itself
joie de vivre (Fr)	good spirits, exuberance (lit., "joy of living")
jus gentium (L)	law of nations
kamikaze (J)	suicide pilot (lit., "divine wind")
klutz (Y)	clumsy person
kvetch (Y)	complain, carp
la belle dame sans merci (Fr)	the beautiful woman without mercy
laissez-faire (Fr)	noninterference (lit., "let [people] do [as they wish]")
lapsus linguae (L)	slip of the tongue
Lebensraum (Gr)	living room; elbow room
lèse majesté (Fr)	treason
l'état, c'est moi (Fr)	I am the state
lingua franca (L)	common language (lit., "French tongue")
macher (Y)	big shot
magnum opus (L)	major work
mañana (Sp)	tomorrow
manqué (Fr)	failed
maven (Y)	expert, authority
mazel tov (Y)	congratulations
mea culpa (L)	my fault
memento mori (L)	reminder of death
mens sana in corpore sano (L)	a sound mind in a sound body
meshuggah (Y)	crazy
mirabile dictu (L)	amazingly (lit., "remarkable to say")
modus operandi (M.O.) (L)	method of operation
morituri te salutamus (L)	we who are about to die salute you
mutatis mutandis (L)	with the needed changes made

Alphabets

Word/Phrase	Meaning
ne plus ultra (L)	the best
n'est-ce pas? (Fr)	isn't that true?
noblesse oblige (Fr)	the responsibility of noble birth
nom de plume (Fr)	pen name
non sequitur (L)	something that does not follow
nosh (Y)	nibble, eat
nota bene (N.B.) (L)	note well
nunc aut nunquam (L)	now or never
obiter dictum (L)	something said in passing; a peripheral comment
o tempora, o mores! (L)	o the times, o the customs!
panem et circenses (L)	bread and circuses
par excellence (Fr)	above all, preeminently
par exemple (Fr)	for example
pari passu (L)	at an equal pace
parvenu (Fr)	newcomer, upstart; noveau riche
passim (L)	here and there
per diem (L)	by the day
per favore (It)	please
persona non grata (L)	unwanted person
pièce de résistance (Fr)	showpiece item
pied à terre (Fr)	in-town apartment; temporary lodging
plus ça change, plus c'est la même chose (Fr)	the more things change, the more they are the same
pons asinorum (L)	insoluble problem (lit., "bridge of asses")
por favor (Sp)	please
prego (It)	please; you're welcome
prima facie (L)	on the face of it; at first sight
primus inter pares (L)	first among equals
prix fixe (Fr)	fixed price
pro bono publico (L)	for the public good
que será será (Sp)	what will be will be
quid pro quo (L)	fair exchange; tit for tat
quién sabe? (Sp)	who knows?
quod erat demonstrandum (Q.E.D.) (L)	as has been demonstrated
quod vide (q.v.) (L)	which see (used as cross-reference)
raison d'être (Fr)	reason for being
rara avis (L)	rarity (lit., "rare bird")
reductio ad absurdum (L)	reduction to absurdity (in logical argument)
répondez s'il vous plaît (R.S.V.P.) (Fr)	respond if you please
requiescat in pace (R.I.P.) (L)	rest in peace
salaam aleicham (A)	peace
sancta sanctorum (L)	holy of holies
sangfroid (Fr)	aplomb; composure
savoir faire (Fr)	social savvy (lit., "to know what to do")
schadenfreude	pleasure taken in problems of others
schlemiel (Y)	unlucky person, loser
schmaltz (Y)	excessive sentimentality
schtick (Y)	gimmick; a performer's idiosyncracy
semper fidelis (L)	always faithful
shalom (H)	greeting or farewell (lit., "peace")
sic (L)	thus
sic semper tyrannis (L)	thus always to tyrants
sic transit gloria mundi (L)	thus passes the glory of the world

Word/Phrase	Meaning
sine qua non (L)	something indispensable (lit., "without which not")
sotto voce (It)	softly (lit., "in a soft voice")
status quo (L)	current state of affairs
Sturm und Drang (Gr)	storm and stress
sui generis (L)	one of a kind, unique
tabula rasa (L)	clean slate (lit., "erased tablet")
tant mieux (Fr)	all the better
tant pis (Fr)	all the worse
tempus fugit (L)	time flies
terra firma (L)	solid ground
terra incognita (L)	unknown territory
tête-à-tête (Fr)	intimate conversation (lit., "head to head")
tout de suite (Fr)	immediately
tout le monde (Fr)	everyone
tovarish (R)	comrade
trompe l'œil (Fr)	illusionary art or decor (lit., "fool the eye")
vade mecum (L)	handbook, guide (lit., "go with me")
vaya con Dios (Sp)	go with God
veni, vedi, vici (L)	I came, I saw, I conquered
verboten (Gr)	forbidden
verbum sapienti sat (L)	a word to the wise is enough
volte-face (Fr)	about-face, reversal
vox clamantis in deserto (L)	a voice crying in the desert
vox populi, vox Dei (L)	the voice of the people is the voice of God
Wanderjahr (Gr)	year of travel
Wanderlust (Gr)	desire to travel
Weltanschauung (Gr)	philosophy, outlook
Weltschmerz (Gr)	world-weariness (lit., "world pain")
Wunderkind (Gr)	prodigy
yenta (Y)	gossip or busybody
Zeitgeist (Gr)	spirit of the times

A Closer Look

Common Phrases in Major World Languages

English	French	German	Italian	Spanish	Chinese	Japanese
Hello/ good day	Bonjour	Guten Tag	Buon giorno	Hola/ Buenos días	Ni hao	Kon-nichiwa
Please	S'il vous plaît	Bitte	Per favore	Con su permiso/ por favor	Qíng	Douzo
Thank you	Merci	Danke	Grazie	Gracias	Xiè xiè	Arigatou
Excuse me/ pardon me	Excusez-moi/ pardon	Entschuldigen Sie	Mi scusi	Discúlpeme	Qíng ràng	Gomennasai/ shitsurei shimasu
Yes	Oui	Ja	Sì	Sí	Shì	Hai
No	Non	Nein	No	No	Bú shì	Iie
Good-bye/ so long	Au revoir/ à bientôt	Auf Wiedersehen	Arrivederci	Adiós/ hasta la vista	Zài jiàn	Sayounara

Alphabets

GREEK PREFIXES AND SUFFIXES

PREFIXES

Prefix	Meaning in English	Prefix	Meaning in English	Prefix	Meaning in English
a	not	chole, cholo	bile	ergo	work
acantho	spiny, thorny	chondro	cartilage	erythro	red
acous	hearing	choreo	dance	ethno	race, nation
acro	top, tip	choro	country	eu	good
adeno	gland	chrom(at)o	color	ex	out
aero	air, gas	chrono	time	exo	outside, external
allo	other	chryso	gold	galacto	milk
amphi	both, around	cleisto	closed	gam(o)	copulation, together
amylo	starch	clino	slope	gastro	stomach
an	not	cocci	berry-shaped	geo	earth, land
ana	again, thorough, thoroughly	coela	stomach	geronto	old age
		conio	dust	glosso	tongue
andro	man	copro	excrement	gluc, glyc	sweet
anem(o)	wind	cosmo	universe	glypto, glyph	carving
anthropo	man	cranio	skull		
anti	against	cryo	cold	gnath(o)	jaw
apo	away	crypto	hidden	gon(o)	reproduction (sexual)
arch(i)	chief	cteno	comb, rake		
arche(o), archae(o)	old, ancient	cymo	wave	grapho	writing
		cysto	bladder	gymno	nude, naked
arthro	joint	cyto	cell	gynec(o), gynaec(o)	woman
aster, astro	star	dactylo	finger		
atmo	vapor	deca	ten	haemato	blood
auto	self	dendro	tree	hagio	holy
azo	nitrogen	dermo, dermato	skin	halo	salt, sea
baro	weight			haplo	simple
batho, bathy	deep	deutero	second	hecto	hundred
		di(s)	apart	helico	spiral
biblio	book	dia	through	helio	sun
bio	life	dino	terrible	hema	blood
blepharo	eyelid	diplo	double	hemi	half
bracchio	arm	dodeca	twelve	hepato	liver
brachy	short	dyna, dynamo	force, power	hepta	seven
branchio	gills			hetero	different
broncho	throat	dys	evil, difficult	hexa	six
caco	evil	echino	spiny	histo	tissue
cardio	heart	ecto	outside, external	hodo	path, way
carpo	fruit	ef	out	holo	whole, complete
cath, cato	down, thorough, thoroughly	ele, em, en	in, into	homeo	similar, like
		encephalo	brain	homo	same
ceno	common	ennea	nine	hydro	water
cephalo	head	entero	gut	hyeto	rain
cero	wax	ento	inside, interior	hygro	wet
chilo	lip	entomo	insect	hylo	matter
chiro	hand	eo	dawn, early	hymeno	membrane
chloro	green	eph, epi	on	hyper	above

Prefix	Meaning in English	Prefix	Meaning in English	Prefix	Meaning in English
hypno	sleep	onto	being	pyo	pus
hypo	under	oo	egg	pyro	fire
hypso	high	ophio	snake	rheo	flow
hystero	womb	opthalm(o)	eye	rhino	nose
iatro	medicine	ornitho	bird	rhizo	root
ichthyo	fish	oro	mouth	sacchro	sugar
iso	equal	ortho	straight	sapro	decompose
kerato	horn	osteo	bone	sarco	flesh
kinesi,	movement	oto	ear	scato	excrement
kineto		oxy	sharp	schisto,	split
lepto	slender	pachy	thick	schizo	
leuko	white	paleo,	ancient, old	sclero	hard
litho	stone	palaeo		seleno	moon
logo	word, oral	pan	all	sidero	iron
lyo, lysi	dissolving	para	close, beside	somato	body
macro	large	patho	suffering, disease	speleo	cave
malaco	soft	pedo	child	spermato	seed
mega,	great	penta	five	sphygmo	pulse
megalo		peri	around, very	splanchno	guts
melano	black	petro	stone	stato	position
mero	part	phago	eating	stauro	cross
meso	middle	phlebo	vein	steno	short, narrow
meta	beyond, after,	phono	sound	stereo	solid
	changed	photo	light	stomato	mouth
metro	measure	phreno	brain	stylo	pillar
micro	small	phyco	seaweed	sy, syl,	with
miso	hatred	phyllo	leaf	sym, syn	
mono	one, single	phylo	species	tachy	rapid
morpho	shape	physio	nature	tauto	same
myelo	spinal cord	phyto	plant	tele	distant
mylo	fungus	picro	bitter	teleo	final
myo	muscle	piezo	pressure	telo	distant, final
necro	dead body	pleuro	side (of body)	thalasso	sea
neo	new	pluto	riches	thanato	death
nepho	cloud	pneumato	breath, spirit	theo	god
nephro	kidney	pneumo	lung	thermo	heat
neuro	nerve	polio	gray matter	thio	sulfur
noso	sickness	poly	many	toco	child, birth
noto	back (of body)	pro	before, forward	topo	place
nycto	night	proto	first	toxico	poison
octa, octo	eight	pseudo	false	trachy	rough
odonto	tooth	psycho	mind, spirit, soul	xeno	foreign
oligo	few	psychro	cold	zoo	living
ombro	rain	ptero	wing	zygo	double
oneiro	dream				

The Hawaiian alphabet has only 12 letters: the five vowels and the consonants H, K, L, M, N, P, *and* W.

Alphabets

SUFFIXES

Suffix	Meaning in English	Suffix	Meaning in English	Suffix	Meaning in English
algia	pain	iasis	disease	phany	manifestation
androus	man	iatrics, iatry	medical treatment	phobe, phobia	fear
archy	rule, government	itis	inflammation		
biosis	life	kinesis	movement	phone, phony	sound
blast	bud	lepsy	seizure, fit		
branch	gills	lith	stone	phyllous	leaf
carpous	fruit	logy	science of, list	phyte	plant
cele	hollow	lysise, lyte	dissolving	plasia, plasis	growth
cephalic, cephalous	head	machy	battle, fight		
		mancy, mantic	foretelling	plasm	matter
chrome	color			plast	cell
coccous	berry-shaped	mania(c)	craving	plegia	paralysis
cracy, crat	rule, government	mere, merous	part	plerous	wing
dendron	tree			rrhagia, rrhagic, rrhea	flow
derm	skin	meter, metry	measure		
drome, dromous	run (race)	morphic, morphous	shape	saur	lizard
emia	blood			scope, scopy	observation
gamy	marriage	mycete	fungus	sect, section	cutting
gen(ous), geny, gony	giving birth to, bearing	nomy	science of, law of	soma, some	body
		odont	tooth	sophy	wisdom
gnathous	jaw	odynia	pain	sperm, spermous	seed
gnomy, gnosis	knowledge	oid	like, similar		
		oma	tumor	stichous	row
gon	angle	opia	eye, sight	stome, stomous	mouth
gonium	seed	opsia	sight		
gram, graph(y)	writing	opsis	appearance	taxis, taxy	order
		pathy	suffering, disease	tomy	cutting
hedral, hedron	side, sided	phage, phagous	eating	trophy	feed
				tropous, tropy	turned

LATIN PREFIXES AND SUFFIXES

PREFIXES

Prefix	Meaning in English	Prefix	Meaning in English	Prefix	Meaning in English
a, abs	from	brevi	short	cruci	cross
ac, ad, af, ag, al, an, ap, as, at	to, toward	calci	lime	cupro	copper, bronze
		centi	hundred	de	not, down
		cerebro	brain	deci	tenth
alti, alto	high	cervico	neck	demi	half
ambi	both	circum	around	denti	tooth
ante	before	cirro	curl	di(s)	apart
api	bee	cis	near, on the near side of	digit(i)	finger
aqui	water	co, col, com, con,	with, thorough,	dorsi, dorso	back (of body)
arbori	tree	cor	thoroughly	e, ec, ef	out
audio	hearing			equi	equal
avi	bird	contra	against	ex	out
bacci	berry	costo	rib	extra	outside, external

Prefix	Meaning in English	Prefix	Meaning in English	Prefix	Meaning in English
febri	fever	ob, oc	against	re	again
ferri, ferro	iron	octa, octo	eight	recti	straight
fissi	split	oculo	eye	reni	kidney
fluvio	river	of, op	against	retro	backward
gemmi	bud	oleo	oil	sacro	dedicated
igni	fire	omni	all	sangui	blood
il, im, in	not, against, in, into, on	oro	mouth	se	apart
		ossi	bone	sebi, sebo	fatty
inguino	groin	ovi, ovo	egg	septi	seven
inter	between	pari	equal	sidero	star
intra, intro	inside, interior	per	through, very	somni	sleep
ir	not, against, in, into, on	pinni	fin, web	spiro	breath
		pisci	fish	stelli	star
juxta	close, near, beside	plano	flat	sub, suc, suf, sum, sup	under
labio	lip	plumbo	lead (metal)		
lacto	milk	pluvio	rain		
ligni	wood	post	after	super, supra	above
luni	moon	pre	before	terri	land, earth
magni	great	preter	beyond	trans	through, on the far side of
mal(e)	bad, evil	primi	first		
multi	many	pro	for, forward	ultra	beyond
naso	nose	pulmo	lung	uni	one, single
nati	birth	quadri	four	vari(o)	different
nocti	night	quinque	five		

SUFFIXES

Suffix	Meaning in English	Suffix	Meaning in English	Suffix	Meaning in English
cidal, cide	kill	fugal, fuge	run away from	pennale	wing
fid	split	grade	walking	vorous	eating

COMMON CROSSWORD-PUZZLE WORDS

Certain words frequently appear in crossword puzzles. Following is a list of such words, particularly ones not used regularly in everyday speech. Many of these words will be recognized by avid crossword-puzzle solvers. People new to crosswords will find familiarity with the list helpful in checking and building a crossword vocabulary.

Word	Meaning	Word	Meaning	Word	Meaning
aalii	tree; wood	adit	mine entrance	Aire	French river
Aare	Swiss river	adze	shaping tool	ait	river island
abbé	monk; cleric	Aeolus	Greek god of wind	alae	winglike part
abele	white poplar	aga	Muslim chief	alar	winged
abet	aid; assist	agar	moss; culture medium	alef	Hebrew letter
abou	father (Arabic)	agee	awry; askew	alen	Danish length
acer	maple genus	agha	Muslim leader	Aleut	Alaskan Indian
Acre	Israeli city	agora	assembly	Alma	Crimean river
acta	deeds	Agra	site of Taj Mahal	aloe	bitter herb; lily
Adah	wife of Lamech	aile	winged (heraldry)	alop	askew
Adak	Alaskan island	Aino, Ainu	Japanese aborigine	ama	cup; candlenut
Adar	Jewish month			amah	Oriental nurse

Alphabets

continues

Common Crossword–Puzzle Words, Continued

Word	Meaning	Word	Meaning	Word	Meaning
ameer	Arab chieftain	axil	leaf angle	cava	pepper shrub; vein
amir	Arab chieftain	axon	nerve-cell process	Cayuga	Iroquoian tribe
Amos	biblical prophet	Baal	god; idol	cere	wax; wrap
ana	collection; anthology	baft	astern	Ceres	grain goddess
anas	duck genus	Bahia	Brazilian state; bay	Clare	Irish county
ani	blackbird; cuckoo	baht	Siamese coin	Clio	muse of history
anil	indigo shrub	Baku	Caspian harbor	Comus	god of mirth
anile	old-womanish; feeble	Bali	Indonesian island	Coos	Oregon tribe
anion	ion; particle	Balt	Lett; Lithuanian	copa	Spanish measure
anise	fragrant seed	banc	judge's bench	cor	heart; brightest star
anoa	wild Celebes ox	bane	evil; scourge	corium	dermis; layer
ans	Belgian commune	bani	Romanian money	cos	lettuce
ansa	loop; handle	Bann	Irish river	Cree	Indian tribe
ante	poker stake; before	Barre	Vermont city	Crimea	Russian peninsula
anti	opposed	Baya	Bantu tribe	cuir	leather (French)
A one	first-rate; tops	Beda	Arabian city	cull	choose; assort
apa	wallaba tree	beka	biblical money;	cuya	Cuban timber tree
apis	bee; Egyptian sacred		Hebrew weight	dace	carplike fish
	bull	Belem	Brazilian city	Dade	Florida county
apod	footless	Benares	Indian city	dado	groove
Apollo	sun god	Bera	Arabian city	Dail	Irish parliament
Aral	Soviet sea	berm	bank; lodge	daler	Dutch money
Aran	Irish island	Berne	Swiss city	Davos	Swiss resort
Ares	Greek god of war	bes	ancient Roman weight	Dee	English river
aria	opera solo	besa	Abyssinian money	dhai	midwife
aril	seed covering	besant	old French money	dhak	East Indian dye tree
artel	union; cooperative	bezant	circle (heraldry)	dhal	lentil
arum	cuckoopint; flowerin	bhar	Indian weight	dhan	cattle; property
	plant	bilk	cheat	dhow	Oriental sailing ship
Asgard	abode of Norse gods	binh	Annam weight	dinar	Bulgarian or Yugoslav
Astarte	Phoenician love goddess	bisse	snake (heraldry)		money
atap	palm; nipa	Blanc	peak in Alps	dop	diamond holder
ates	sweetsop	boa	feathered scarf; con-	dopp	dip
Atka	Aleutian tribe		strictor	Duma	Russian council
atle	Tamarisk salt tree	bole	friable clay	durn	gatepost
Atli	Norse king	bolo	knife; machete	dyad	pair
Aton	Egyptian solar deity	Bonn	West German city	Dyak	Borneo tribe
atri	Italian commune	brae	Scottish hillside	dyne	unit of force
Attica	Greek district; New	brut	dry wine	ebon	black
	York State prison	cabal	secret group; junta	Edda	Icelandic saga; Norse
Attu	Alaskan island	Caen	French city		prose
Aude	French river	Caddo	Indian tribe	ede	Dutch commune
Auk	diving bird	cadi	Muslim judge	Eder	German river
aune	French length	Cain	Abel's brother	Edo	Tokyo
aux	French commune	calp	limestone	Eger	German river
avav	pepper shrub; hum-	cam	gear	Ela	highest note; Guido's
	mingbird	Carib	South American		note
avocet	bird; plover		Indian	Elam	biblical kingdom
awn	beard on grain	carr	pool	élan	dash; ardor

A Closer Look

Oxymoron: A Pairing of Contradictory or Incongruous Words

bittersweet	home office	passive aggressive
clearly confused	jumbo shrimp	randomly organized
cruel kindness	linear curve	same difference
definite maybe	liquid gas	sweet sorrow
eloquent silence	nonalcoholic beer	taped live
idiot savant	nondairy creamer	war games
genuine imitation	old news	working vacation
good grief	open secret	

Word	Meaning	Word	Meaning	Word	Meaning
Elbe	German river	Faroe	Danish islands	grao	Portuguese weight
Elia	Lamb pen name; Kazan	fass	Austrian measure	gulden	Dutch money
Elul	Jewish month	faun	satyr; Roman half goat	Hades	Greek underworld
emir	Muslim chieftain	Faunus	rural deity	hadj	pilgrimage
emu	ostrichlike bird	fels	Indian money	haft	handle
Enna	Sicilian city	fete	festival	ha ha	laugh; sunken fence
Enns	Austrian river	fiat	command; decree	haka	dance
Enos	Seth's son	fief	feudal estate	Hamar	city in Norway
ente	grafted (heraldry)	fils	son (French)	Hamite	biblical tribe
ento	inner (prefix)	flak	antiaircraft bursts	Han	river in China
Enyo	Ares' mother	flan	custard	hart	stag
Eolus	Colorado mountain	flay	skin	hemo	blood (prefix)
epee	fencing blade	fosse	moat; pit	Hera	queen goddess
ephah	Hebrew measure	Frey	Norse god	Herat	Afghanistan city
epi	finial; spire	Frigg	Odin's wife	Hermes	Greek god
Erda	Norse earth goddess	gad	rove	Herod	biblical ruler
eri	silkworm	Gael	Celt	Herr	Mister (German)
Eris	goddess of discord	gam	mouth; leg	Hesse	German state
Erlau	Hungarian commune	gaol	prison	Hilo	Hawaiian city
ern	sea eagle	gar	needle fish	hin	Hebrew measure
erne	sea eagle; Irish river	gard	French department	Hiram	biblical ruler
Erse	Gaelic	gare	railway station (French)	hiro	Japanese length
esker	glacial ridge			Hler	Norse god
esne	serf	Gaspé	Canadian peninsula	hoar	frost
esse	existence; abstract being	gata	shark	hod	brick tray; coal scuttle
		Gaza	biblical city	Hood	Oregon mountain
Este	Italian commune	Gerd	Frey's wife	hora	Israeli dance
Estes	Colorado park	Geri	Odin's wolf	Horeb	biblical mountain
estop	prevent by law	ghat	range; pass	Hosea	biblical prophet
et al.	and others (Latin abbreviation)	gila	lizard	Hoth	Norse god
		Gilead	biblical mountain	huk	Philippine guerrilla
etui	vanity case; needle case	gnu	antelope; wildebeest	hula	Hawaiian dance
evoe	bacchanals' cry	Goa	former Portuguese colony	Hun	barbarian; vandal
ewer	pitcher			Hydra	nine-headed monster
exe	English river	Golo	Bantu tribe	iamb	verse foot
fane	temple	Goshen	biblical land of plenty	ibex	wild goat
fanon	cape; orale	gowl	monster	ibid.	same place (abbreviation)
faro	card game	gradus	ancient Roman length		
		graf	German count	ibis	wading bird

Alphabets

continues

Palindromes

A Closer Look

A palindrome can be a single word, a verse, a sentence, a series of sentences, or a number that reads the same forward and backward. People have been creating palindromes in all languages since at least as early as the third century B.C. Palindromic sentences often become jokes when meanings are ascribed to them and when punctuation is added. For example, the two best-known English palindromes are "Able was I ere I saw Elba," which was not written by but could have been uttered by Napoleon, and "Madam, I'm Adam," which is fun to think of as the first introduction. Note that "madam" alone is a palindromic word, but sentences are more amusing:

Enid and Edna dine.
A man, a plan, a canal, Panama!
Draw, O Caesar, erase a coward.

Al lets Dell call Ed Stella.
Dennis sinned.
Ma is a nun, as I am.

Naomi, did I moan?
Niagara, O roar again!
He lived as a devil, eh?

And here is a palindromic conversation between two owls:

"Too hot to hoot!"
"Too hot to woo!"
"Too wot?"
"Too hot to hoot!"
"To woo!"
"Too wot?"
"To hoot! Too hot to hoot!"

Common Crossword-Puzzle Words, Continued

Word	Meaning	Word	Meaning	Word	Meaning
Ibo	West African tribe	itea	Virginia willow	Kano	Nigerian walled city
ici	here (French)	ixia	iris	kaph	Hebrew letter
icon	religious image	jako	parrot	Kara	Arabian sea
Ida	Asia Minor range;	jama	tunic	kava	Polynesian beverage
	Crete mountain	jami	mosque	kawa	Pepper shrub
Idas	killer of Castor	jann	genie	kela	Arabian weight
ideo	idea (prefix)	jara	palm	keno	lotto; bingolike game
ides	Roman date	Jebu	West African tribe	Kent	English county
iglu	Eskimo hut	Jehu	biblical ruler	kepi	military cap
ilex	holly	Jena	German city	kerf	notch
ilia	hipbones	jeté	ballet jump	khat	Turkish length
imam	caliph	jhow	Tamarisk shrub	Kiel	German canal
immi	Swiss measure	jib	triangular sail	Kiev	Russian city
Indus	Indian river	jilt	cheat; reject	kil	monk's cell; Irish
inee	arrow poison	jinn	demon		church; kilometer
Inez	Don Juan's mother	Joad	English philosopher		(abbreviation)
Inga	shrub genus	Joshua	biblical ruler	kiln	oven
Iole	Hercules' captive	Jove	chief Roman god	Kiowa	Indian tribe
Iona	Scottish isle	juba	African dance	kipe	basket
Ionia	Asia Minor district	Jung	psychiatrist	kiri	Kaffir war club
iota	Greek letter; bit	Juno	Roman queen of gods	kiwi	flightless bird
Irra	Babylonian god	junu	charm	Kobe	Honshu port
Isar	Bavarian river	jura	French department	Koko	Lord High Executioner
Iser	Czech river	kabul	Indian river	kola	nut
Isere	French river	kadi	judge	kopek	Russian money
Isis	Egyptian goddess; sister	Kafir	Bantu tribe	koss	Indian length
	and wife of Osiris	kana	Japanese writing	kraal	enclosure

Word	Meaning	Word	Meaning	Word	Meaning
kris	dagger	marl	clay-filled soil	nipa	drink; East Indian palm
Krishna	Hindu god	Maui	Hawaiian island	oast	kiln; oven
krona	Icelandic money	Mayo	Irish county; mayonnaise	obi	Oriental sash
Kronos	Titan	Mede	ancient Persian	obit	death notice
kudu	African antelope	Medusa	Gorgon	oca	edible tuber
Kurd	Turkish tribe	mega	great (prefix)	octo	eight (prefix)
kvas	Russian sour beer	meld	declare, in cards	oda	harem room
lac	resin	Melos	Aegean island	odea	music hall
lact	milk (prefix)	merl	blackbird	Order	Baltic river
Lagos	capital of Nigeria	Metz	French city	oeuf	egg (French)
lait	milk (French)	mil	wire measure	ogee	arch; molding
lama	Buddhist monk; Tibetan priest	Milo	Greek Island	Okie	migratory worker
Lamech	biblical patriarch	Minos	Greek king	okra	gumbo
lar	gibbon	moa	flightless bird; ostrich	ola	palm leaf
lath	strip of wood	Moab	biblical tribe	olay	palm leaf
lave	bathe	moho	honey-eating bird	olio	medley
lea	meadow	mohr	gazelle	olla	jar; meat dish
Leda	Castor's mother; swan	mojo	voodoo charm	Olor	swan genus
lees	dregs	moki	New Zealand raft	Omei	China mountains
Lena	Asian river	Moro	Philippine Muslim	omni	all (prefix); Atlanta arena
Lenape	Indian tribe	Mors	Roman god of death	Omsk	Russian city
Leto	Apollo's mother	Morta	goddess of fate	oner	individual; corker
Levi	Jacob's son; Hebrew tribe	Muir	Alaska glacier	onus	burden
Leyte	Pacific island	mumm	disguise	opah	colorful fish
libra	Mexican weight	nacre	mother-of-pearl	ope	unlock (poetic)
Lido	Adriatic resort	nae	no (Scottish)	orca	killer whale
limn	portray	Nahor	biblical patriarch	Orel	Russian port
limu	edible seaweed	naif	lustrous	orle	heraldic bearing
Linz	Austrian city	Namur	Belgian commune	Orly	French airport
liss	fleur-de-lis	nard	anoint; spice	orne	French department
lobo	timber wolf	neap	tide	ort	morsel; leftover
loch	Scottish lake	neb	beak; nose	osier	willow tree
Loki	Norse god	Nebo	biblical mountain	Ossa	Greek mountain
loup	half-mask (French)	née	born (French)	otic	pertaining to the ear
luff	sail into wind	Nene	English river; Hawaiian bird	Otoe	Oklahoma tribe
Luna	moon goddess	nep	catnip	oyez	attention; court cry
Lys	Belgian river	Nereid	sea nymph	paal	Javanese length
Maas	Dutch river	ness	promontory	pac	boot, moccasin
mage	magician	Nestor	Greek king	paca	rodent
Maia	Hermes' mother	neve	glacier; snow	padre	priest; cleric
Main	German river	newt	eft	pala	Indian weight
mani	peanut	nez	nose (French)	palp	tentacle; feeler
mano	hand grinding stone	nimb	halo	Panay	Philippine island

continues

The word posh *is supposedly an acronym for "port outward, starboard home." The term was coined to describe how rich people, traveling by sea to the Indies, avoided getting the morning sun on their side of the ship.*

Alphabets

Common Crossword-Puzzle Words, Continued

Word	Meaning	Word	Meaning	Word	Meaning
pard	leopard	sari	Indian dress	tapa	bark cloth
parr	young fish	sego	edible bulb	Tara	Irish capital; plantation in *Gone With the Wind*
pas	dance step	sera	antitoxins; evening (Italian)		
pavis	shield; cover			tare	biblical weed; allowance
Pelée	Martinique volcano	serac	glacial ridge; white cheese	tarn	lake; pool
pelu	hardwood tree			taro	edible root
peri	fairy	sere	dry; parched	tat	make lace; crochet
phon	loudness	serif	part of printer's letter	tec	detective
phot	light unit	seta	bristle	tela	membrane; tissue
pica	type measure	Seth	biblical patriarch; Adam's son	tele	from a distance (prefix)
Pico	Azores volcano			tern	gull
rale	rattle; breathing noise	shay	carriage	Terra	earth goddess
Rama	incarnation of Vishnu	Shem	biblical patriarch	Thalia	one of the Graces
rame	branch	shiv	knife	Thetis	Achilles' mother
rana	Indian prince	Sikh	Hindu soldier	tia	aunt (Spanish)
rani	Indian queen	sine	trigonometry function	tic	spasm
rati	Indian weight	sire	lord; father; beget	tio	uncle (Spanish)
Remi	ancient people of Gaul	Siva	Hindu god	Tioga	New York county
rena	rockfish	skag	part of a ship's keel	toga	Roman cloak
ret	soak flax	skew	twist	tole	lacquered metalware
rete	network	Skye	Hebrides island	Toltec	Mexican tribe
Rhea	Titan; Cronus's wife	sloe	plum; blackthorn	tome	large volume
Rhus	sumac genus	Smee	Captain Hook's assistant; pintail duck	tong	Chinese secret society
ria	narrow inlet; estuary			tor	craggy hill; pea
rial	Iranian coin	snee	dirk; knife	tort	civil wrong
rien	nothing (French)	soir	evening (French)	torte	rich cake
Riga	Baltic city	Sol	sun god	tret	waste allowance
rime	frost	sora	marsh bird	Triton	Greek god of sea
ripa	riverbank	Spad	biplane; nail	Truk	Island in Carolines
rom	gypsy husband	Spes	Roman goddess of hope	tsar	Russian despot
rood	crucifix			tsun	Chinese length
Rosa	shrub genus	Sri	Hindu goddess	tun	vat; cask
Ross	Antarctic sea	SRO	box-office sign	tutu	New Zealand shrub, ballet skirt
roti	roasted (French)	stere	dry measure		
rotl	Muslim weight	stet	let it stand	tyro	novice
Ruhr	German river; industrial area	stile	wall step; set of steps	über	over (German)
		stoa	portico	uca	crab
rune	mysterious sign; old alphabet character	suet	hard fat	uke	ukulele
		Suva	Fiji capital	ule	rubber tree
rupee	Indian money	Taal	Afrikaans	ulex	spine shrub
Saar	European river	Tabor	biblical mountain	Ulm	German city
Sac	Algonquin Indian; pouch	tabu	forbidden	ulna	elbow bone
		tace	body armor	unde	wavy; lined (heraldry)
sago	starch; pudding	tael	Oriental weight	ungula	hoof; claw
samp	cereal; maize; pudding	tamp	pack; ram	Ural	Russian river; range
sans	without (French)	Taos	New Mexico town	Urd	Norse goddess of destiny

The word dude *was coined by Oscar Wilde and his friends. It is a combination of the words* duds *and* attitude.

Word	Meaning	Word	Meaning	Word	Meaning
urde	key-shaped (heraldry)	vivo	lively (music)	yaba	cabbage tree
Uri	Swiss commune	viz	namely	yak	ox
Uria	Bathsheba's husband	voce	voice (Italian)	Yalu	Korean river
ursa	bear	vole	rodent	yamp	tuber
urus	ox; aurochs	WAC	female GI	yapa	palm-leaf mat
Ute	Colorado Indian	Waco	Texas city	yegg	burglar
Utu	Babylonian god	wadd	black ocher	Yemen	Arabian state
uvea	iris layer	wadi	dry riverbed	yen	Japanese money; urge
uvic	grapelike	wale	cloth ridge	yin	Chinese weight
Vaal	South African river	wang	Dutch East Indies weight	Ymir	Norse giant
vair	heraldic tincture	weft	web; yarn	Yser	Belgian river
vale	valley; glen; farewell	weir	fish trap	zak	Dutch measure
vari	diverse (prefix)	wen	cyst; old English letter	zany	nutty; crazy
vasa	ducts	woad	dyestuff	Zara	Italian province
Veda	Hindu bible	Wodan	Norse god	zee	final letter; zed
vega	meadow	Woden	Norse god	Zen	Buddhist sect
veld	South African grassland	Wotan	Norse god	zero	nothing; cipher
Venus	Roman goddess of love	xema	Arctic gull	zeta	Greek letter
vert	green	Xenia	Ohio city	Zeus	chief Olympian god
Vesta	goddess of hearth	xeno	foreign (prefix)	Zion	hill; heaven
Vishnu	Hindu god	xeres	wine; sherry	Zulu	Bantu tribe
vita	life (Latin)	Xosa	Kaffir tribe	Zuni	Pueblo Indian
vite	quick (French)	Xtian	Christian	zwei	two (German)

There are nine different ways to pronounce the letters ough. *All are contained in the sentence "A rough-coated, dough-faced, thoughtful ploughman strode through the streets of Scarborough; after falling into a slough, he coughed and hiccoughed."*

Go to "94 Acceptable Two-Letter Scrabble® Words" in chapter 23

Alphabets

FOREIGN ALPHABETS

GREEK

Forms	Name	Latin†
Α α	alpha	a (ā)
Β β	beta	b
Γ γ	gamma	g, n
Δ δ	delta	d
Ε ε	epsilon	e
Ζ ζ	zeta	zd, z
Η η	eta	ē
Θ θ	theta	th*
Ι ι	iota	i
Κ κ	kappa	k
Λ λ	lambda	l
Μ μ	mu	m
Ν ν	nu	n
Ξ ξ	xi	x
Ο ο	omicron	o
Π π	pi	p
Ρ ρ	rho	r, hr
Σ σ ς	sigma	s
Τ τ	tau	t
Υ υ	upsilon	u (u, ü)
Φ φ	phi	ph*
Χ χ	chi	ch*
Ψ ψ	psi	ps
Ω ω	omega	ō

ARABIC

Form	Name	Latin†
ا	alif	
ب	bā	b
ت	tā	t
ث	thā	th
ج	jīm	j
ح	ḥā	ḥ
خ	khā	kh
د	dāl	d
ذ	dhāl	dh
ر	rā	r
ز	zāy	z
س	sīn	s
ش	shīn	sh
ص	ṣād	ṣ
ض	ḍād	ḍ
ط	ṭā	ṭ
ظ	ẓā	ẓ
ع	'ayn	'
غ	ghayn	gh
ف	fā	f
ق	qāf	q
ك	kāf	k
ل	lām	l
م	mīm	m
ن	nūn	n
ه	hā	h
و	wāw	w
ي	yā	y

HEBREW

Forms	Name	Latin†
א	aleph	
ב	beth	b
ג	gimel	g
ד	daleth	d
ה	he	h
ו	vav	v
ז	zayin	z
ח	het	ch (H)
ט	teth	ṭ
י	yod	y
כ ך	kaf	k, ch
ל	lamed	l
מ ם	mem	m
נ ן	nun	n
ס	samekh	s
ע	ayin	'
פ ף	pe	p, f
צ ץ	sadhe	ts
ק	koph	q
ר	resh	r
שׂ	sin	ś
שׁ	shin	sh
ת	tav	t

CYRILLIC

Forms	Latin†
А а	a
Б б	b
В в	v
Г г	g
Д д	d
Е е	(y) e
Ж ж	zh
З з	z
И и Й й	j (i, ī)
К к	k
Л л	l
М м	m
Н н	n
О о	o
П п	p
Р р	r
С с	s
Т т	t
У у	u
Ф ф	f
Х х	kh
Ц ц	ts
Ч ч	ch
Ш ш	sh
Щ щ	shch
Ъ ъ	"
Ы ы	y
Ь ь	'
Э э	e
Ю ю	yu
Я я	ya

Gamma is transliterated as *n* when it precedes *kappa, xi, chi,* or another *gamma; upsilon* is transliterated as *u* when it is the final element in a diphthong. The *sigma* form ς is used only in final position.

*The letters *th, ph,* and *ch* represent strongly aspirated stops, *t, p,* and *k,* respectively.

The forms shown are of the letters in isolation. They may vary when used in words. The letter *alif* does not have a sound.

Pronunciation of vowels in letter names: *ā* = *a* in *father, ī* = *i* in *machine, ū* = *u* in *rule.*

The second form (and the second transliteration) of a letter when shown is used at the end of a word only. Vowels are shown by a system of subscript and superscript dots; the symbols shown are consonants. The letter *aleph* does not have a sound.

The Cyrillic alphabet is used for writing various Slavic languages, including Russian.

† The columns headed "Latin" show the letters used when these alphabets are transliterated into the Latin alphabet. The sounds represented by these letters are similar to the standard sounds in English. Diacritics indicate that the sound is somewhat different from the English sound represented by the letter shown; for any great difference the sound is shown in parentheses after the letter.

ADDITIONAL SOURCES OF INFORMATION

BOOKS

The American Heritage Book of English Usage. Houghton Mifflin, 1996.

Axtell, Roger E. *Do's and Taboos of Using English Around the World.* Wiley, 1995.

Ayto, John. *The Oxford Dictionary of Slang.* Oxford University Press, 2000.

Bonk, Mary Rose. *Acronyms, Initialisms, and Abbreviations Dictionary.* 27th ed. 3 vols. Gale, 2000.

Chapman, Robert L., et al., eds. *Dictionary of American Slang.* HarperCollins, 1998.

Chapman, Robert L., ed. *Roget's International Thesaurus.* 5th ed. HarperCollins, 1992.

The Chicago Manual of Style. 14th ed. University of Chicago Press, 1993.

Donadio, Stephen, et al., eds. *The New York Public Library Book of 20th Century American Quotations.* The Stonesong Press/Warner Books, 1992.

Edmunds, David. *The Oxford Reverse Dictionary.* Oxford University Press, 1999.

Ehrlich, Eugene. *The Highly Selective Dictionary for the Extraordinarily Literate.* HarperCollins, 1997.

_____. *The Highly Selective Thesaurus for the Extraordinarily Literate.* HarperCollins, 1994.

_____. *Veni Vidi Vici: Conquer Your Enemies, Impress Your Friends with Everyday Latin.* HarperPerennial, 1995.

Firmage, Richard. *Alphabet: The Story of One of Civilization's Greatest Inventions.* Bloomsbury, 2000.

Funk, Charles Earle. *A Hog on Ice and Other Curious Expressions.* HarperCollins, 1985.

Glazier, Stephen. *Word Menu.* Random House, 1998.

Heifetz, Josefa. *The Word Lover's Dictionary: Unusual, Obscure, and Preposterous Words.* Carol Publishing, 1996.

Hoad, T. F. *The Concise Oxford Dictionary of English Etymology.* Oxford University Press, 1993.

Jones, Daniel. *English Pronouncing Dictionary.* 15th ed. Cambridge University Press, 1997.

Kemp, Peter, consultant ed. *The Oxford Dictionary of Literary Quotations.* Oxford University Press, 2000.

Knowles, Elizabeth M., ed. *The Oxford Dictionary of Phrase, Proverb, and Quotation.* Oxford University Press, 1997.

Knowles, Elizabeth, and Julia Eliot. *The Oxford Dictionary of New Words.* Oxford University Press, 1999.

The word facetiously *has all the vowels, including* y, *in order.*

Laird, Charlton, and the editors of Webster's New World dictionaries. *Webster's New World Thesaurus.* Macmillan, 1997.

Lighter, J. E. *Random House Dictionary of American Slang.* 2 vols. Random House, 1997.

McArthur, Tom. *The Concise Oxford Companion to the English Language.* Oxford University Press, 1998.

McCutcheon, Marc. *Descriptionary: A Thematic Dictionary.* 2nd ed. Facts on File, 2000.

Preston, Charles, and Barbara Ann Kipfer. *The USA Today Crossword Puzzle Dictionary.* The Stonesong Press/Hyperion, 1996.

Pulliam, Tom. *The New York Times Crossword Puzzle Dictionary.* Times Books, 1997.

Robinson, Andrew. *The Story of Writing.* Thames and Hudson, 1999.

Room, Adrian. *The Cassell Dictionary of Word Histories.* Cassell, 2000.

Strunk, William, Jr., and E. B. White. *The Elements of Style.* 4th ed. Macmillan, 1999.

Sutcliffe, Andrea, ed. *The New York Public Library Writer's Guide to Style and Usage.* The Stonesong Press/HarperCollins, 1994.

Alphabets

Urdang, Laurence. *The New York Times Dictionary of Misunderstood, Misused, and Mispronounced Words.* Black Dog and Leventhal, 2001.

Webster's New World College Dictionary. 4th ed. Simon & Schuster, 1999.

Zinsser, William. *On Writing Well: An Informal Guide to Writing Nonfiction.* 6th rev. ed. Harper-Collins, 1998.

WEB SITES

The CMU Pronouncing Dictionary
Maintained by Kevin Lonzo, Robotics Institute, Carnegie Mellon University.
http://www.speech.cs.cmu.edu/cgi-bin/cmudict

Evolution of Alphabets
The development of alphabets in animation.
http://www.wam.umd.edu/~rfradkin/alphapage.html

The Evolution of Languages
Exploratorium magazine site explains where languages come from.
http://www.exploratorium.edu/exploring/language

The King's English
Online edition (copyright by the Trustees of Columbia University) of the 2nd edition of the book by Henry Watson Fowler and Francis George Fowler (copyright 1908 by the Clarendon Press).
http://www.bartleby.com/116/101.html

Merriam-Webster Online
Includes a searchable dictionary and thesaurus and other helpful language information links (copyright Merriam-Webster).
http://www.m-w.com/

The World Wide Web Acronym and Abbreviation Server
A searchable database of acronyms and abbreviations.
http://www.ucc.ie/info/net/acronyms/acro.html

Yahoo!—Reference: Dictionaries: Language
List of links to online dictionaries in many languages (copyright by Yahoo! Inc.).
http://www.yahoo.com/Reference/Dictionaries/Language/

Alphabets

14

GRAMMAR AND PUNCTUATION

Writing is a slow, painstaking process, and like playing tennis or the violin, it requires practice, practice, practice. The purpose of writing—and this is obviously true of language itself—is to communicate ideas. To communicate effectively, writers follow the general concepts of grammar, putting words and sentences together in a customary manner so that they can be readily understood. A person can be a good writer without being an expert in grammar, but some knowledge of the rules of language usage can promote confidence in speech and writing and a better understanding of language as a tool for imparting information.

This is not to say that everyone must write the same sentence to communicate the same concept. On the contrary, American English is so varied that it is possible to express the same basic idea in any number of ways. And each of those ways can be equally correct.

A very difficult sentence to punctuate is That that is is that that is not is not. *The correct punctuation is:* That that is, is; that that is not, is not.

What makes a variety of different sentences equally valid is grammar. Grammar is a set of rules that defines the ways words can and cannot be used. These rules are not arbitrarily imposed on the language by English teachers or grammarians; they have, instead, grown out of the language itself and can be observed in action in the everyday speech and writing of those who grew up speaking and writing it.

Much of grammar is intuitive and can be understood by anyone who has spoken American English for any length of time, even without a knowledge of the rules. For instance, the sentence *You be not home go yet* is readily recognized as incorrect even without knowledge of the rules of word order.

But because American English is a complex and difficult language, it is sometimes helpful to have the rules at hand in case logic and intuition fail. What follows, then, are the basics of grammar, spelling, punctuation, and alphabetization for American English. The information presented here is by no means exhaustive, and because language is a constantly changing thing, there can never be a "final word" as to what is correct and what is incorrect. As E.B. White wrote in his classic guide to writing well, *The Elements of Style*, "Writing is an act of faith, not a trick of grammar." Still, this guide should help provide a start in understanding grammar, usage, and punctuation.

THE PARTS OF SPEECH

The parts of speech define the ways words can be used in various contexts. Every word in the English language functions as at least one part of speech; many words can serve, at different times, as two or more parts of speech, depending on the context.

adjective   A word or combination of words that modifies a noun (*blue-green, central, half-baked, temporary*).

adverb   A word that modifies a verb, an adjective, or another adverb (*slowly, obstinately, much*).

article   Any of three words used to signal the presence of a noun. *A* and *an* are known as indefinite articles; *the* is the definite article.

conjunction   A word that connects other words, phrases, or sentences (*and, but, or, because*).

interjection   A word, phrase, or sound used as an exclamation and capable of standing by itself (*oh, Lord, damn, my goodness*).

noun   A word or phrase that names a person, place, thing, quality, or act (*Fred, New York, table, beauty, execution*). A noun may be used as the subject of a verb, the object of a verb, an identifying noun, the object of a preposition, or an appositive (an explanatory phrase coupled with a subject or object).

preposition   A word or phrase that shows the relationship of a noun to another noun (*at, by, in, to, from, with*).

pronoun   A word that substitutes for a noun and refers to a person, place, thing, idea, or act that was mentioned previously or that can be inferred from the context of the sentence *(he, she, it, that)*.

verb A word or phrase that expresses action, existence, or occurrence *(throw, be, happen)*. Verbs can be transitive, requiring an object *(her* in *I met her)*, or intransitive, requiring only a subject *(The sun rises)*. Some verbs, like *feel,* are both transitive *(Feel the fabric)* and intransitive *(I feel cold,* in which *cold* is an adjective and not an object).

MODIFIERS

There are two basic types of modifiers: single-word modifiers, which are generally adverbs or adjectives; and phrases, which are usually introduced by prepositions. Modifiers should be placed as close as possible to the words they modify to ensure clarity.

Adjectives, which modify nouns, often precede the nouns they modify. They serve to restrict, characterize, or further define the nouns immediately following. Thus, *great* in the sentence *You did a great job* is an adjective modifying the noun *job.*

Nouns can also be used to modify nouns. They, too, appear immediately before the noun being modified, and only their position in the sentence indicates that they are acting as modifiers rather than nouns. The noun *telephone* works as a modifier of the noun *booth* when it appears in the phrase *a telephone booth.*

When two or more adjectives each modify the noun independently, they are separated by commas *(a silly, cheerful mood)*. When the first adjective modifies an idea expressed by the combination of the second adjective and the noun, no comma is used *(a pretty oil painting)*. In some cases, two or more adjectives are combined, often with a hyphen, so that they function as a single adjective. In these compound adjectives, the first term modifies the second, which modifies the noun *(a high-flying airplane)*.

Adverbs modify verbs, adjectives, or other adverbs or phrases. They can often be recognized by their characteristic *-ly* ending. When modifying verbs, adverbs generally appear immediately after the verbs *(quickly* in the sentence *He walked quickly through*

the room). When used to modify an adjective, the adverb will immediately precede the adjective *(a swiftly moving deer)*; such compounds are not hyphenated.

In ancient Rome, authors did not punctuate their writing. It was up to the reader to insert the punctuation he felt was proper.

Phrases that modify nouns are often introduced by prepositions and immediately follow the nouns they modify. An example of a modifying phrase is *in the corner* in the sentence *The dog in the corner wagged her tail.* While useful in defining the nouns to which they are attached, modifying phrases are not as important to the sentence in the way a subject, verb, and object are. Such phrases can be essential or nonessential. In the sentence *The dog in the corner wagged her tail,* the phrase *in the corner* is essential because it identifies *which* dog wagged her tail. Clauses that modify nouns or pronouns contain a subject and a verb and can be either essential or nonessential. When they are introduced by relative pronouns (such as *who, what, that, which,* and *whose*), they are known as relative clauses. An example is *who wants to know* in the sentence *Anyone who wants to know can get the information.* Relative clauses are also known as dependent clauses because they cannot stand alone.

SENTENCE STRUCTURE

Individual words, even once their parts of speech are identified, do not communicate very much by themselves. They must be combined in such a way that they can convey meaning. This is done by forming sentences that combine words that have meaning in and of themselves (nouns, verbs, adjectives, adverbs, and pronouns) with those that are solely functional (conjunctions, prepositions, interjections, and articles).

Three main types of sentences can be constructed from these parts. Statements are sentences that tell of a fact, an occurrence, or an opinion; they provide information *(My daughter is almost three years old)*. Questions are sentences that seek out information *(How old is your daughter?)*. Commands are sentences that make a demand *(Tell your daughter to keep her hands off the cookies)*. In addition, there are exclamations *(You're a fool!)*, answers to questions *(Fine, thank you)*, sounds or cries *(Yipes!)*, and calls to others *(Yoo-hoo, Buzzy!)*.

SIMPLE SENTENCES

Every sentence includes two basic components, the subject and the predicate. The subject is what the sentence is about, and the predicate is what the sentence says about the subject:

The car	*has a flat tire.*
(subject)	(predicate)

Often, the subject performs an action upon the predicate *(Herb kicked the ball)*. A sentence may have a compound subject (**Ducks and geese** *fly south for the winter*), a compound predicate *(We **had dinner and went dancing**)*, or both.

The predicate contains at least one verb and sometimes one or more objects; the verb expresses the action of the sentence, and the object is the recipient of the action. Two types of sentences, however, do not contain objects. In sentences that have linking verbs (whose sole function is to connect subject and predicate), the predicate describes the subject with a predicate (identifying) noun or a predicate adjective *(My favorite food is **spinach**; I feel **happy**)*. When the verb is intransitive (it does not act upon anything), it takes no object, and the predicate consists solely of action *(The coyotes **howled**)*.

Transitive verbs, however, take one of two types of objects. Direct objects are the recipients of the verb's action *(Mary scrambled **eggs**)*, and indirect objects describe to or for whom the action occurs *(I loaned **Jackie** my sweater)*. Indirect objects always precede direct objects in a sentence.

COMPOUND, COMPLEX, AND COMPOUND-COMPLEX SENTENCES

These three types of sentences are made up of two or more clauses, each of which contains a subject and a predicate. An independent, or main, clause can stand on its own as a complete sentence, but a dependent, or subordinate, clause cannot. A compound sentence consists of two or more independent clauses *(Jane enjoyed scuba diving, but her husband preferred golf)*. A complex sentence has one independent clause and one or more dependent clauses:

When I arrived at the office,	*I found the memo on my desk.*
(dependent)	(independent)

Compound-complex sentences combine the two:

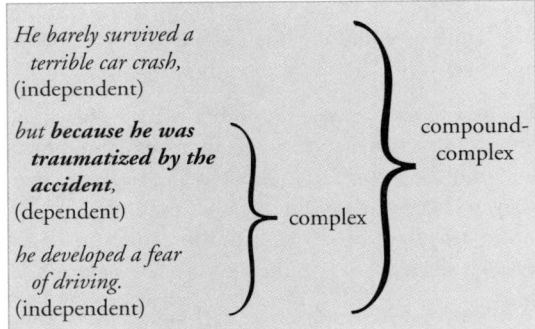

Dependent clauses may function as adjectives *(The woman **who gave the speech** was a famous athlete)*, as adverbs *(We walked along the beach **as the sun was setting**)*, or as nouns *(She was disappointed **that she could not attend the party**)*. Dependent clauses that are essential to the meaning of a sentence are called restrictive clauses *(The tree **that grew in the courtyard** was planted a century ago)*. Those that are not essential are called nonrestrictive clauses *(His mother, **who recently had a face-lift**, is quite vain)*.

Sentences may also use prepositional phrases in the role of adjectives *(The machine **in the factory** ran day and night)* or adverbs *(**After several years**

abroad, *Chris was ready to come home*). A prepositional phrase is made up of a preposition (*over, at, with, during*) and its object (*Meet me* **in St. Louis**).

See also "Modifiers" earlier in this chapter.

SUBJECT–VERB AGREEMENT

The verb generally follows the subject in statements (*We* **are** *happy*). It is often the first word in commands (**Come** *over here,* in which the subject *You* is understood, though not written). The verb precedes the subject in questions (**Am** *I blue?*). The verb and the subject must agree in number if the verb is one that can show number. Verbs that show number are the conjugations of *to be* and the third-person singular present tense form of verbs, which usually end in *-s* (*he* **shops,** but *they* **shop** for plural form). Both the subject and verb must be either singular (*I am*) or plural (*we are*).

A few subjects pose particularly tricky problems of subject-verb agreement. *Either* and *neither* are frequently misconstrued as plural subjects, although they should always be paired with singular verbs (*Neither of us is ready*). Other subjects, such as *none* and *pair,* can be used in singular or plural constructions, depending on their meaning. For instance, when *none* means "not one," it is singular (*None of the guests is here*); when it means "not any," it is plural (*None are more beautiful than a rose*).

Compound subjects can also pose agreement difficulties. Most of the time, a compound subject is plural (*Paul and Carol are ready for vacation*). But when a compound subject expresses a thought or concept that is definitely singular, it should be followed by a singular verb (*Hitting a ball and driving it over the outfield wall is a skill few can master*).

TENSE, VOICE, AND MOOD

Verbs not only define the action of a sentence but also describe the nature of that action through tense, voice, and mood.

Verbs have six tenses that characterize the timing of the action. The present tense indicates an action as now taking place (*I* **see**; *She* **goes**) or a state or condition as now existing (*The plums* **are** *ripe*); an action that is habitual (*He* **speaks** *with an accent*); or an action that is always the same (*The clock* **strikes** *twelve at noon*). The past tense indicates an action completed or in progress in the past but not continuing into the present (*I* **saw**; *She* **went**; *He* **spoke**) or a state or condition in existence at a former time (*The plums* **were** *ripe*). The future tense, always formed with *shall* or *will,* indicates an action that will occur in the future (*I* **shall see**; *She* **will go**; *He* **will speak**) or a state that will exist in the future (*The plums* **will be** *ripe*).

The present perfect tense, always formed with *have* or *has,* indicates an action or state as completed at the time of speaking but not at any definite time in the past (*I* **have seen** *him many times*; *She* **has gone** *to the conference*; *He* **has spoken** *often before*) or an action or state that occurred in the past and continues in the present (*The plums* **have been** *ripe for days*). The past perfect, always formed with *had,* indicates an action or state as completed before a specified or implied time in the past (*I* **had seen** *the movie before it was reviewed*; *She* **had gone** *home before the announcement was made*; *He* **had spoken** *before the bell rang*; *The plums* **had been** *ripe long before they were picked*). The future perfect tense, always formed with *shall have* or *will have,* indicates an action as completed or a state as having ended in relation to a specified time in the future (*I* **shall have seen** *the video before it must be returned*; *She* **will have gone** *before her brother arrives*; *He* **will have spoken** *before the break for lunch*; *By the time they are picked, the plums* **will have been** *ripe for several days*). Each tense has a progressive form, formed by combining with verb *to be* and adding the *-ing* suffix, which is used to indicate that the action or state expressed by the verb is continuing (*I* **have been walking** *for hours*).

Most verbs are made into past tense by adding the *-ed* suffix, regardless of whether the verb's action is performed by the subject (*I* **walked** *to the store*) or on the subject (*My dog* **was walked**). But as the examples in the preceding paragraph indicate, a number of verbs are made into other tense forms in ways that follow no general rule at all. The only rule that can be applied is the age-old maxim "When in doubt, consult a dictionary."

In every tense, verbs take one of two voices—active or passive—that indicate whether the subject of a sentence is the doer or receiver of the action. The active voice makes the subject the doer *(The children saw everything in the museum)*; the passive voice makes the subject the recipient of the action *(The children will be seen by a doctor)*.

F. Scott Fitzgerald once said, "Cut out all those exclamation marks. An exclamation mark is like laughing at your own jokes."

Likewise, in every tense, verbs also have one of three moods. A verb's indicative mood is used to make a statement or ask a question *(I see every one of his movies; Did you see his latest film?)*. The imperative mood makes a request or command *(See if you can*

fix this; See here!). In the subjunctive mood, a verb expresses a thought that is not fact at the time the sentence is spoken or written *(If they could see me now, they'd be amazed; It remains to be seen if the business will be a success)*.

VERBALS

In the form of verbals, verbs function not only as words of action but also as adjectives, nouns, or adverbs. Verbals cannot serve as the verb in the predicate of a sentence because they are incomplete forms of the verb. They can, however, be modified by adverbs just as verbs are. There are three types of verbals: participles, gerunds, and infinitives.

Participles combine the work of a verb and an adjective and end with the *-ing* or *-ed* suffix. Present participles, which express present or continuing action or state of being, end with *-ing* and take the active voice *(The boy is **growing**; It turned into an **exciting** game)*. Past participles, which express completed action or a time or state gone by, end

---

Four Common Grammatical Problems

A
Closer
Look

Double Negative   Do not use two negative words to express a single negative statement.

WRONG:	I **don't** owe Amy **no** money.	
RIGHT:	I **don't** owe Amy any money.	
RIGHT:	I owe Amy **no** money.	

Dangling Participial Phrase   A participial phrase modifies the first noun or pronoun following the comma that ends the participial phrase.

WRONG:	Sitting in the living room, a loud **knock** on the door was heard by Ellen.
RIGHT:	Sitting in the living room, **Ellen** heard a loud knock on the door.

Split Infinitive   Do not place an adverb between the parts of an infinitive.

WRONG:	I try **to** often **visit** Laura.
RIGHT:	I try **to visit** Laura often.

Parallel Structure   When parts of a sentence are parallel in meaning, place them in parallel or similar constructions.

WRONG:	Her morning consisted of a leisurely breakfast and strolling downtown.
RIGHT:	Her morning consisted of **a** leisurely breakfast and **a** stroll downtown.

Or:

WRONG:	We are responsible for choosing the costumes and that they should all be the correct size.
RIGHT:	We are responsible for **choosing** the costumes and **making sure** that they are all the correct size.

with *-ed* and take the passive voice *(He was **thrilled** to be there; She admired the **polished** brass)*. The perfect participle links the present participle with the word *having* and takes the active voice *(**Having worn out their welcome,** our houseguests finally left)*.

Gerunds function as nouns and end with *-ing*. They may be used and modified just like ordinary nouns in simple and complex grammatical structures *(**Eating** all those nachos was not a good idea; The dog's **barking** kept me awake all night; She loved nothing more than **throwing** a party)*.

Almost always accompanied by the word *to,* the infinitive may be used as a noun, an adjective, or an adverb. In its noun form, the infinitive resembles the gerund *(Mark liked **to work** alone)*. As an adjective, it modifies a noun *(It was her dream **to visit** Borneo)*; and as an adverb, it modifies a verb *(The engine struggled **to turn** over)*. For the sake of style, the *to* is sometimes dropped from the infinitive *(I feel the earth [to] **move** under my feet)*.

PUNCTUATION

Punctuation helps to make sense of the various parts constituting a sentence. It shows where to pause or stop, defines possession and contraction, sets off nonessential modifiers and asides, indicates excitement or interrogation, clarifies incompletion or continuation, and denotes dialogue and special terms.

TERMINATING PUNCTUATION

Four punctuation marks that can signal the end of a sentence are the period (.), the question mark (?), the exclamation point (!), and the ellipsis (. . .).

The **period** is used at the end of any sentence that is not a question or an exclamation. It shows that a sentence is finished and is followed by a space and a capital letter beginning the next sentence.

The **question mark** is used to terminate a sentence that is a question *(How much do you think this is worth?)*, to terminate a question within quoted dialogue *("Do you like my haircut?" he asked)*, or to terminate a question within a sentence *(Will the Orioles lose every game this year? is the question on the minds of fans everywhere)*. The question mark is not used to set off indirect questions *(Everyone wants to know whether the Orioles will continue losing)*.

The **exclamation point** terminates sentences that convey excitement *(What a finish that play has!)* or are emphatic *(Leave me alone!)*. It can also be used to terminate individual words used as interjections *(You'll get here today? Terrific!)*, even when an interjection is within a sentence *(Take four parts gin, add one part vermouth, and, behold! you have a martini)*.

Ancient Greek texts had no punctuation and no spaces between words.

The **ellipsis** indicates that one or more words are missing. When used at the end of a complete sentence, an ellipsis is made up of four dots *(I had hoped to go. . . .)*. Four dots indicate that although what's there makes a complete sentence, one or more words have been omitted from the end of the sentence. A four-dot ellipsis can also indicate the omission of one or more sentences. When the middle portion of a sentence has been omitted, a three-dot ellipsis is used.

PAUSE PUNCTUATION

The punctuation marks that can indicate a pause are the comma (,), the semicolon (;), the colon (:), the dash (—), and the ellipsis (. . .).

Commas are used to separate two main clauses set apart by a conjunction, such as *and, but,* or *or (I'd hoped to be done this afternoon, but I'm not sure that's possible)*. Commas can separate shorter clauses that do not have a conjunction between them *(I work, I sleep, I work some more)*. They are also used to set off all manner of words and phrases, such as adverbial clauses *(When he was finished, he set down his knife)*; transitional expressions *(Her remarks, on the other hand, were uncalled for)*; conjunctions *(We are often late; however, we must be back by five o'clock)*; illustrative expressions *(They were confused; that is, they*

Grammar

felt bewildered and afraid); and nonrestrictive clauses *(Your writing, although it is quite good, is not what we're looking for).*

In addition, commas are used to separate a series of words or phrases *(Hope, charity, and faith were not enough to sustain her);* to set off direct address *(You know, son, that's a good idea);* to set a direct quotation apart from the speaker *("Don't quote me," he said);* and to set off a question being asked about the previous part of the sentence *(It was fun, wasn't it?).*

Finally, commas indicate the inference of a word not stated, especially one used earlier in the sentence *(For us it's money; for them, food);* set off the parts of an address, place name, or date *(They went to London, England, to conduct research; She arrived on Monday 25, 1998);* and separate a name from a title following it *(Paul Fargis, President).*

The **semicolon** signals a more complete stop than is indicated by the comma. It is used to separate parts of a sentence that contain commas *(Our organization runs on the dedication, concern, and compassion of its staff; the generosity, moral support, and wisdom of its directors; and the gratitude, hope, and joy expressed by those it serves).* A semicolon can also join clauses that are not connected by a coordinating conjunction *(They left for London yesterday; I am leaving today)* as well as those joined by conjunctive adverbs *(It's easy to lie; however, lying is a bad habit to get into).*

The **colon** represents the closest thing to the full stop indicated by a period. It can mark the separation of an enumerated list or extract from the rest of a text *(The Ten Commandments:)* or can introduce an appositive *(She wanted only one thing: sleep)* or series *(It's easy to list the things money won't buy: love, health, happiness, and peace).* The colon also precedes an illustrative or explanatory phrase; many style guides recommend beginning such phrases with capital letters if they can function as sentences in and of themselves *(His Excellency demands satisfaction: He will expect you on the dueling field at dawn).*

Colons are frequently used in contexts other than sentences. They can separate book titles from their subtitles *(Curious Customs: The Stories Behind 296 Popular American Rituals);* set off the salutation in business correspondence *(Dear Mr. President:)* and the labels in memoranda *(To:);* and separate the elements of time *(8:45),* ratios *(3:5 mix of boys to girls),* and biblical references *(Deuteronomy 1:5).*

Watch out for spell checkers! If you ran the following sentence through your computer's spell checker, it would tell you that nothing was wrong: I have bin trying too improve my spelling for sum time now cents my secretary always says that it isn't two grate.

The **dash,** known as the em dash to compositors and editors, represents an abrupt shift within a sentence. It separates a clause or phrase from the rest of the sentence, whether for emphasis *(You want—my god, you need—an expert)* or to introduce a parenthetical remark *(He hopes to turn a profit—something I can't see happening anytime soon—within six months).* Dashes also are used to separate quoted material from its author *("I still find the Strunkian wisdom a comfort"—E. B. White).*

The **ellipsis** is used in dialogue to indicate faltering speech *("We want . . . that is . . . ").*

BRACKETS AND PARENTHESES

Brackets [ ] are specialized tools for setting off material from the rest of the text. They can be used with editorial comments: The *main point [emphasis mine] has been missed;* or as parentheses within parentheses: *It is hoped (some might say prayed [even atheists pray sometimes]) that she will pull through.* Brackets should not be used when simple paren-theses will do.

Parentheses ( ) are used to set off explanatory words and phrases that demand more of a break than is shown by commas and less than that indicated by dashes: *We can't bear it (or so we believe); to surround numbers when enumerating points in a sentence: He hopes (1) to be employed and (2) to make lots of money;* to give abbreviations: *American Telephone & Telegraph (AT&T);* and to indicate potential plurals or other alternatives: *Please tell us which course(s) of action you wish to take.*

APOSTROPHES, SINGLE QUOTATION MARKS, AND DOUBLE QUOTATION MARKS

Apostrophes are used to indicate a contraction *(didn't)* or a possessive by adding *'s* to most words *(Mr. Marx's humor);* an apostrophe alone is added to form the possessive of plurals *(the kittens' tails).* Apostrophes also appear in shortened forms of the year *(the '80s)* and for plurals of numbers, letters, and terms *(She received two A's and three B's).*

Single quotation marks are used for quotes within quotes *("'I'm not sure,' is what I think he said," she responded)* and for titles and special terms mentioned in dialogue *("She said she doesn't read the 'His' column anymore," he told his buddy).*

Charlotte Brontë and William Wordsworth asked their publishers to correct the punctuation in their manuscripts.

Double quotation marks are used for direct quotations and dialogue *("What was she up to?" he asked);* to set off special terms *(soldiers are sometimes called "grunts");* and to indicate the titles of stories, articles, songs, book chapters, radio shows, poems, and lectures.

Punctuating a sentence that contains quotation marks can be tricky. Commas used to set off quoted material from the speaker are placed within the quotation marks *("I hope it's finished," she said).* A period is also placed within the quotation marks *("We're done.").* A question mark or exclamation point ending a sentence that ends in a quotation mark is placed within the quotation marks too *("Will you marry me?").* However, when quoted material is used in a question, but is not itself a question, the question mark is placed outside *(Do you think he really meant "till death do us part"?).*

AMERICAN ENGLISH AND BRITISH ENGLISH: PUNCTUATION DIFFERENCES

As if confusion about spelling and word choice were not enough, (see "American English and British English: Spelling and Name Differences" in Chapter 13), there are also punctuation differences between American and British English. Although American English always uses double quotation marks to indicate speech, British English, especially in older texts, usually uses single quotation marks. A few more recent British publications use double quotation marks.

In both American and British English, periods and commas at the end of a quote come before the closing quotation marks when the quote is a full sentence (or a full sentence broken up by a connecting phrase such as *he said*):

> *"When you come to meet me," she explained hastily, "please bring the blue folders."*

In American English, the placement of periods and commas remains the same even when the quote is a sentence fragment. But in British English, periods and commas punctuating sentence fragments are placed outside quotation marks.

AMERICAN ENGLISH: *She described the party as "a sumptuous affair," and said that she arrived home "long after midnight."*

BRITISH ENGLISH: *She described the party as "a sumptuous affair", and said that she arrived home "long after midnight".*

ADDITIONAL SOURCES OF INFORMATION

The American Heritage Book of English Usage. Houghton Mifflin, 1996.

Castle, Lana R. *Style Meister: The Quick-Reference Custom Style Guide.* Castle Communications, 1999.

The Chicago Manual of Style. 14th ed. University of Chicago Press, 1993.

Fowler, H. W. *Dictionary of Modern English Usage.* 3rd ed. Rev. by R. W. Burchfeld. Wordsworth Editions, 1997.

Garner, Bryan A. *A Dictionary of Modern American Usage.* Oxford University Press, 1998.

Greenbaum, Sidney. *The Oxford English Grammar.* Oxford University Press, 1996.

Kramer, Melinda G., et al. *Prentice-Hall Handbook for Writers.* Prentice-Hall, 1995.

Maggio, Rosalie. *Talking About People: A Guide to Fair and Accurate Language.* Oryx Press, 1997.

Martin, Phyllis. *Word Watcher's Handbook: A Deletionary of the Most Abused and Misused Words.* iUniverse.com, 2000.

MLA Handbook for Writers of Research Papers. 4th ed. Modern Language Association, 1999.

The New York Public Library Writer's Guide to Style and Usage. HarperCollins, 1994.

Strunk, William, Jr., and E. B. White. *The Elements of Style.* 4th ed. Allyn & Bacon, 2000.

Words into Type. 3rd ed. Prentice-Hall, 1986.

Zinsser, William. *On Writing Well: An Informal Guide to Writing Nonfiction.* Rev. ed. HarperReference, 1998.

Grammar

15

LETTERS AND
FORMS OF ADDRESS

PERSONAL LETTERS

The popularity of electronic mail has reversed the slow demise of letter writing in the United States. Many people who never write personal letters email friends and associates on a daily basis. Email can be used to invite friends or coworkers to a casual gathering, such as an office picnic or a drinks party. Birthday and holiday cards can be emailed, as can thank-you notes and casual correspondence. There are, however, several situations in which a personal letter or announcement mailed in the traditional way is expected or required. Birth or death announcements, wedding invitations, and thank-you notes for wedding, christening, and bar or bat mitzvah presents require a more formal presentation than email can provide. Thank-you notes to the host or hostess of a party or to someone who has done a favor are not required, but they will make the writer's gratitude clear and warm the heart of the person who gets them.

Other occasions demand notes or letters as well. The death of someone in a friend's family is one such event, especially if you cannot express your condolences personally at a wake or during *shiva*. A letter of condolence need not be long and involved, but it should be a personal, handwritten note, not just a printed sympathy card.

Every time you lick a stamp, you consume $^1/_{10}$ *calorie.*

Formal invitations require a written response. Wedding invitations are the most common kind of formal invitation that people receive. While response cards are frequently included with wedding invitations, a personal response in addition to or in place of the response card will be greatly appreciated.

When a friend or family member has something important to celebrate—a promotion or graduation, or receipt of an award or other honor—a congratulatory note will make the celebration even happier. Even the briefest of notes adds a warmth that cannot be conveyed by a phone call.

Personal letter writing can also be done for no good reason at all. Or, rather, you may write letters to friends and family simply to keep in touch with them and to let them know that you are thinking of them. These are perhaps the most enjoyable letters to receive.

The U.S. Postal Service delivers mail to 134 million addresses, including 20 million post office boxes. About 1 million new addresses are added each year.

Personal letters, while not requiring a strict format, do have a few guidelines. The date should be written at the top, either in the center or the right-hand corner. The salutation, which may be a bit warmer than it would for a business letter ("My dearest Jeanne,"), should be followed by a comma instead of a colon.

The body or text of a personal letter is, of course, a highly personal matter. It should be written with less of an eye to what would be stylistically or grammatically correct and more of an eye to expressing feelings and thoughts. A personal letter should sound like you, and techniques that would be out of place in a business letter, such as using dashes, ellipses, and sentence fragments, can be employed in personal correspondence.

Closings for personal letters are also a matter of choice. "Love," is appropriate for those you do love; "Fondly," or "All my best," or "Affectionately," might be right for friends. As with the rest of the letter, the closing should express your own feelings.

BUSINESS PROTOCOL AND FORMS OF ADDRESS

BUSINESS LETTERS

Like business phone calls, business letters should be brief and to the point. The first line below the letterhead should include the date, with the name, company, and address of the recipient appearing two lines below it at the left margin. Two lines below the address, the salutation is given.

"Business Etiquette" in chapter 16; "U.S.
Postal Service" in chapter 25   **Go to**

If the recipient is known personally, he or she can be greeted by first name ("Dear Fred:"). If the recipient is known casually or not at all, use Mr. or Ms. ("Dear Mr. Burrows:" or "Dear Ms. Johnston:"). When the addressee is unknown, "Dear Sir or Madam:" or something like "Dear Sales Manager:" can be used.

The first paragraph of a business letter should clearly explain the purpose of writing. It should be straightforward and concise. If the letter is being written at the suggestion of someone else, this should be stated in the first paragraph along with the reason for writing.

The length of a business letter is determined by what needs to be said. If a reply is desired, the last paragraph should simply state, "I look forward to hearing from you at your earliest convenience." A response by a specific date should not be demanded unless there is a good reason for doing so.

Appropriate closings for a business letter include "Best wishes," "Sincerely," "Sincerely yours," or "Yours truly." Informal closings like "Yours," or "Cheers," should not be used. The signature can be either your full name ("Henry Wiggins") or, if the writer and the recipient are well acquainted, a first name alone ("Henry"). The writer's full name and company title should be typed below the signature unless they appear at the top of the letterhead.

HOW TO PREPARE A RÉSUMÉ

Along with a cover letter, a résumé is the first impression a prospective employee makes on a potential employer. Therefore, it is important that the résumé provide as much relevant information as possible about the person being described in it: you. Send a cover letter and résumé to a specific person. The correct spelling of their name is imperative. Close the cover letter by requesting an interview and state the intention to call in a week or two. It is also important that the résumé be kept brief—no more than one full side of a sheet of 8½-by-11-inch paper.

A résumé must be neatly typed, with at least a ¾-inch margin on both sides, top, and bottom. Single-space all information in the résumé, leaving one line of space between blocks of information. Use underlining, capital letters, small capitals, bold or italic type, and bullets or asterisks to highlight important information.

Begin a résumé with your name, address, and home and business telephone numbers. They can be laid out on the page in any way you find visually pleasing, so far as space allows. Do not include your age, marital status, or other personal facts.

Many résumés then list a career goal, such as "Career goal: Systems engineer responsible for monitoring, maintaining, and improving plant facilities" or "Objective: Position as illustrator/designer with opportunity to create book jackets from concept through mechanicals." Including a career goal is a good tactic if you are looking for a specific type of job; however, job hunters who would consider any of several possible careers are better off omitting any specific career goal.

The glue on Israeli postage stamps is certified kosher.

Most résumés then present a chronological outline of work experience, starting with one's current or most recent job and working backward. For each job listed, the important duties and skills involved should be outlined or described. Depending on how much "real world" experience you have, relevant high school or college employment, internships, and part-time work can be included. Such a portion of a typical résumé might look like the one on page 452.

This section is followed by one outlining your educational background, again from your most recent experience backward. List the date, school or course attended, and certificate or diploma obtained. Depending on the extent of your work experience, you may want to give a more detailed description of your

---

Work Experience

1999–present	Vice President, Marketing, *eTech.com*
	Responsible for developing, implementing, and overseeing marketing of all services provided by this Internet technology company.
	—Created company's first five-year marketing plan —Developed continuing training program for sales force —Increased client billings by 25 percent
1996–1999	Marketing Director, *Numbercrunch, Inc.*

---

higher education. If you are a college student, you may want to list your high school and any pertinent coursework or special achievements.

In the last part of your résumé, list any work you have done with civic or charitable organizations and any awards or certificates of recognition you have received. Place these under an appropriate heading, such as "COMMUNITY SERVICE." If you have no such background, leave this section out of your résumé.

Finally, it is unnecessary to write "References available upon request" at the bottom of a résumé. Anyone looking at it will assume you can provide references and will ask for them if and when they are needed.

When submitting an electronic résumé, preserve formatting by sending it as an Adobe .pdf (portable document file), which is the standard for sharing electronic documents. The recipient will need the Acrobat Reader to view it, but it is freely available from Adobe and widely used. When emailing a résumé to a career-placement site or a company's web site, be sure to list computer skills, and to include an email address and/or Web address.

SPOKEN AND WRITTEN FORMS OF ADDRESS

This section gives the correct forms of address for U.S. government officials, diplomats, UN officers, religious leaders, royalty, the British peerage, and mil-itary personnel. For each personage, the table on pages 453–457 gives the appropriate form or forms to be used in letter addresses, in letter salutations, in direct conversation, and in more formal introductions.

In Elizabethan England, a person of higher social standing was addressed as Goodman or Goodwife. A lower member of a clerical order was called Sir Priest.

In diplomatic and other public circles, "Sir" is generally considered an acceptable alternative to the formal address in both written and spoken greetings; this greeting does not apply to religious or titled persons. The use of "Madam" or "Ma'am" for a female addressee is less customary but still acceptable, especially for high officeholders ("Madam Governor"). This rule also holds for high officials of foreign countries.

For greetings in which "Mr." is used, the feminine equivalent may be "Madam" or, less formally, "Mrs.," "Miss," or "Ms."

Go to "American English and British English: Spelling and Name Differences" in chapter 13; "American English and British English: Punctuation Differences" in chapter 14

continues

Person	Letter Address	Letter Greeting	Spoken Greeting	Formal Introduction
Government Officials—Federal				
President of the United States	The President The White House 1600 Pennsylvania Avenue, NW Washington, DC 20500 president@whitehouse.gov	Dear Mr. (*or* Madam) President	Mr. (*or* Madam) President	The president *or* the president of the United States *or* President Jones
Former President	The Honorable John J. Jones Address	Dear Mr. (*or* Mrs., Ms.) Jones	Mr. (*or* Mrs., Ms.) Jones	Former president John J. Jones
Vice President	The Vice President Executive Office Building Washington, DC 20501 vice.president@whitehouse.gov	Dear Mr. (*or* Madam) Vice President	Mr. (*or* Madam) vice president	The vice president *or* the vice president of the United States *or* Vice President Jones
Cabinet members	The Honorable John (*or* Jane) Jones The Secretary of	Dear Mr. (*or* Madam) Secretary	Mr. (*or* Madam) secretary	The Secretary of _____, John (*or* Jane) J. Jones
Attorney General	The Honorable John (*or* Jane) Jones The Attorney General U.S. Department of Justice 950 Pennsylvania Avenue, NW Washington, DC 20530-0001 AskDOJ@usdoj.gov	Dear Mr. (*or* Madam) Attorney General	Mr. (*or* Madam) attorney general	The attorney general, John (*or* Jane) J. Jones
Chief Justice	The Chief Justice The Supreme Court One First Street, NE Washington, DC 20543	Dear Mr. (*or* Madam) Justice *or* Dear Mr. (*or* Madam) Chief Justice	Mr. (*or* Madam) chief justice	The chief justice *or* Chief Justice Jones
Associate Justice	Mr. Justice Jones *or* Madam Justice Jones The Supreme Court One First Street, NE Washington, DC 20543	Dear Mr. (*or* Madam) Justice	Mr. (*or* Madam)	Mr. (*or* Madam) Justice Jones *or* Justice Jones
Senator	The Honorable John (*or* Jane) Jones United States Senate Washington, DC 20510	Dear Senator Jones	Senator Jones	Senator Jones from Montana
Speaker of the House	The Honorable John (*or* Jane) Jones Speaker of the House of Representatives United States House of Representatives Washington, DC 20515	Dear Mr. (*or* Madam) Speaker	Mr. (*or* Madam) speaker	The speaker of the House of Representatives

Forms of Address

Continued

Person	Letter Address	Letter Greeting	Spoken Greeting	Formal Introduction
Representative	The Honorable John (*or* Jane) Jones United States House of Representatives Washington, DC 20515	Dear Mr. (*or* Mrs., Ms.) Jones	Mr. (*or* Mrs., Ms.) Jones	Representative Jones from New Jersey
Diplomats and Consuls				
U.S. Ambassador	The Honorable John (*or* Jane) Jones Ambassador of the United States American Embassy Address	Dear Mr. (*or* Madam) Ambassador	Mr. (*or* Madam) ambassador	The American ambassador *or* The ambassador of the United States of America
Consul	John (*or* Jane) Jones, Esq. American Consul Address	Dear Mr. (*or* Mrs., Ms.) Jones	Mr. (*or* Mrs., Ms.) Jones	Mr. (*or* Mrs., Ms.) Jones
Foreign Ambassador	His (*or* Her) Excellency John (*or* Jane) Johnson Ambassador of _____ Address	Excellency *or* Dear Mr. (*or* Madam)	Mr. (*or* Madam) ambassador	The Ambassador of _____ Ambassador
United Nations Officials				
Secretary-General of the United Nations	His Excellency Milo Jones Secretary-General of the United Nations United Nations Plaza New York, NY 10017	Excellency *or* Dear Mr. Secretary-General	Mr. Jones *or* the secretary-general	The secretary-general of the United Nations
U.S. Representative to the United Nations	The Honorable John (*or* Jane) Jones United States Permanent Representative to the United Nations United Nations Plaza New York, NY 10017	Dear Mr. (*or* Madam) Ambassador	Mr. (*or* Madam) ambassador	The United States representative to the United Nations
Foreign Heads of State				
Premier	His (*or* Her) Excellency John (*or* Amelia) Smith Premier of _____	Excellency *or* Dear Mr. (*or* Madam) Premier	Your excellency	The premier of _____

continues

Forms of Address

Person	Letter Address	Letter Greeting	Spoken Greeting	Formal Introduction
President of a republic	His (*or* Her) Excellency John (*or* Amelia) Smith President of _____	Excellency *or* Dear Mr. (*or* Madam) President	Your Excellency	President Smith
Prime minister	His (*or* Her) Excellency John (*or* Amelia) Smith	Excellency *or* Dear Mr. (*or* Madam) Prime Minister	Mr. (*or* Madame) prime minister	The prime minister of _____
Government Officials—State and Local				
Governor	The Honorable John (*or* Jane) Jones Governor of _____ State Capitol Address	Dear Governor Jones	Governor *or* Governor Jones	Governor Jones *or* The governor of _____ (only used outside his or her state)
State representative (includes assembly person, delegate)	The Honorable John (*or* Jane) Jones Address	Dear Mr. (*or* Mrs., Ms.) Jones	Mr. (*or* Mrs., Ms.) Jones	Mr. (*or* Mrs., Ms.) Jones
State senator	The Honorable John (*or* Jane) Jones Address	Dear Senator Jones	Senator Jones	Senator Jones
Justice of State Supreme Court	The Honorable John (*or* Jane) Jones Justice Division Supreme Court of the State of _____ Address	Dear Justice Jones	Mr. *or* Madam Justice Jones *or* Justice Jones	Mr. (*or* Madam) Justice Jones *or* Justice Jones
Mayor	The Honorable John (*or* Jane) Jones His (*or* Her) Honor the Mayor City Hall Address	Dear Mayor Jones	Mayor Jones *or* Mr. (*or* Madam) Mayor *or* Your Honor	Mayor Jones *or* The Mayor
Religious Officials*				
The Pope	His Holiness the Pope *or* His Holiness Pope John XII Vatican City Rome, Italy	Your Holiness *or* Most Holy Father	Your Holiness *or* Most Holy Father	His Holiness the Holy Father *or* the Pope *or* the Pontiff
Cardinal	His Eminence John Cardinal Jones, Archbishop of _____ Address	Your Eminence *or* Dear Cardinal Jones	Your Eminence *or* Cardinal Jones	His Eminence Cardinal Jones

* If the cleric holds a doctorate in divinity, it is customary to add the designation D.D. after his or her name in the letter address.

Continued

Person	Letter Address	Letter Greeting	Spoken Greeting	Formal Introduction
Bishop (Catholic)	The Most Reverend John Jones, Bishop (or Archbishop) of _____ Address	Your Excellency or Dear Bishop (Archbishop) Jones	Your Excellency or Bishop (Archbishop) Jones	Bishop (Archbishop) Jones
Monsignor	The Reverend Monsignor James Harding Address	Right Reverend and dear Monsignor or Dear Monsignor Harding	Monsignor Harding or Monsignor	Monsignor Harding
Priest	The Reverend John Jones Address	Reverend Father or Dear Father Jones	Father or Father Jones	Father Jones
Brother	Brother John or Brother John Jones	Dear Brother John or Dear Brother	Brother or Brother John	Brother John
Sister	Sister Mary Luke Address	Dear Sister Mary Luke or Dear Sister	Sister Mary Luke or Sister	Sister Mary Luke
Protestant Clergy	The Reverend John (or Jane) Jones	Dear Reverend Jones	Reverend Jones	The Reverend John Jones
Bishop (Episcopal)	The Right Reverend John Jones Bishop of _____ Address	Dear Bishop Jones	Bishop Jones	The Right Reverend John Jones, Bishop of Detroit
Rabbi	Rabbi Arthur (or Anne) Milgrom Address	Dear Rabbi Milgrom	Rabbi Milgrom or Rabbi	Rabbi Arthur Milgrom
Foreign Royalty and Nobility				
King or Queen	His (Her) Majesty King (Queen) _____ Address (letters traditionally are sent to reigning monarchs not directly but via the private secretary)	Your Majesty	Your Majesty or Sir or Madam	Varies depending on titles, holdings, etc.
Other royalty	His (Her) Royal Highness, the Prince (Princess) of _____ Address	Your Royal Highness or	Your Royal Highness or Sir Madam	His (Her) Royal Highness, the Duke (Duchess) of Gloucester
Duke/Duchess	His/Her Grace, the Duke/Duchess of _____	My Lord Duke/Madam or Dear Duke/Duchess of _____	Your Grace or Duke/Duchess	His/Her Grace, the Duke/Duchess of Bridgeport
Marquess/ Marchioness	The Most Honorable the Marquess/Marchioness of Bridgeport	My Lord/Madam or Dear Lord/Lady Bridgeport	Lord/Lady Bridgeport	Lord/Lady Bridgeport
Earl	The Right Honorable the Earl of Franklin	My Lord or Dear Lord Franklin	Lord Franklin	Lord Franklin

Person	Letter Address	Letter Greeting	Spoken Greeting	Formal Introduction
Countess (wife of an earl)	The Right Honorable the Countess of Franklin	Madam *or* Dear Lady Franklin	Lady Franklin	Lady Franklin
Viscount/ Viscountess	The Right Honorable the Viscount/Viscountess Tyburn	My Lord/Lady *or* Dear Lord/Lady Tyburn	Lord/Lady Tyburn	Lord/Lady Tyburn
Baron/Baroness	The Right Honorable Lord/ Lady Austin	My Lord/Madam *or* Dear Lord/Lady Austin	Lord/Lady Austin	Lord/Lady Austin
Baronet	Sir John Jones, Bt.	Dear Sir *or* Dear Sir John	Sir John	Sir John Jones
Wife of Baronet	Lady Jones	Dear Madam *or* Dear Lady Jones	Lady Jones	Lady Jones
Knight	Sir John Jones	Dear Sir *or* Dear Sir John	Sir John	Sir John Jones
Wife of knight	Dear Madam or Dear Lady Jones	Dear Lady Jones	Lady Jones	Lady Jones

Military Personnel

For commissioned officers in the U.S. armed services, the full rank is used as a title only in addressing letters and in formal introductions: one writes to Major General Ann Jones, U.S. Army, and introduces her as Major General Jones. In greetings, the full rank is shortened to General: "Dear General Jones." Similar acceptable shortened greetings follow.

For enlisted personnel, a similar principle applies. Sergeants—whether staff sergeants, gunnery sergeants, or first sergeants—are greeted simply as "Sergeant"; privates first class are referred to as "Private"; and, in the navy and Coast Guard, chief petty officers are referred to as "Chief." Other noncommissioned officers are greeted by their ranks although, informally, lower grades may be referred to generically as "Soldier" or "Sailor."

The universal terms of respect that lower ranks must use when addressing senior officers are "Sir" and "Madam." These terms are not applied to noncommissioned officers, however; the appropriate affirmative response to a sergeant, for example, is "Yes, Sergeant."

Service	Full Rank	Greetings
Army, Air Force, Marines	General of the army	General
	Lieutenant General	General
	Brigadier General	General
	Lieutenant Colonel	Colonel
	First Lieutenant	Lieutenant
	Second Lieutenant	Lieutenant
Navy, Coast Guard	Fleet Admiral	Admiral
	Vice Admiral	Admiral
	Rear Admiral	Admiral
	Lieutenant Commander	Commander
	Lieutenant, Junior Grade	Lieutenant

GRADES AND RANKS FOR U.S. MILITARY PERSONNEL

COMMISSIONED OFFICERS

Grade	Air Force, Army, and Marine Corps	Navy and Coast Guard
O–10	General	Admiral
O–9	Lieutenant general	Vice admiral
O–8	Major general	Rear admiral (upper half)
O–7	Brigadier general	Rear admiral (lower half)
O–6	Colonel	Captain
O–5	Lieutenant colonel	Commander
O–4	Major	Lieutenant commander
O–3	Captain	Lieutenant
O–2	First lieutenant	Lieutenant (junior grade)
O–1	Second lieutenant	Ensign
Special grades[1]	General of the air force	Fleet admiral
	General of the army	

[1] Five-star commissioned officers. The marine corps does not have a special grade for commissioned officers. No five-star generals are living at this time.

WARRANT OFFICERS

Grade	All Services
W-5	Chief warrant officer
W-4	Chief warrant officer
W-3	Chief warrant officer
W-2	Chief warrant officer
W-1	Warrant officer

Roman Catholic cardinals place the word Cardinal *between their first and last names to show humility; for example, Timothy Cardinal Manning.*

ENLISTED PERSONNEL

Grade	Air Force	Army	Marine Corps	Navy and Coast Guard
E-9	Chief master sergeant	Sergeant major	Sergeant major Master gunnery sergeant	Master chief petty officer
E-8	Senior master sergeant	First sergeant Master sergeant	First sergeant Master sergeant	Senior chief petty officer
E-7	Master sergeant	Sergeant first class	Gunnery sergeant	Chief petty officer
E-6	Technical sergeant	Staff sergeant	Staff sergeant	Petty officer first class
E-5	Staff sergeant	Sergeant	Sergeant	Petty officer second class
E-4	Senior airman	Corporal	Corporal	Petty officer third class
E-3	Airman first class	Private first class	Lance corporal	Seaman
E-2	Airman	Private	Private first class	Seaman apprentice
E-1	Airman basic	Private	Private	Seaman recruit
Special grades[1]	Chief master sergeant of the air force	Sergeant major of the army	Sergeant major of the marine corps	Master chief petty officer of the navy

[1] Senior enlisted advisers. Each branch of service has only one adviser.

ABBREVIATED TITLES THAT FOLLOW NAMES

An abbreviated title can tell more about a person than his or her name. It identifies a rank or position, membership in a monastic or secular order, academic degree, or military or civil honor. The following list includes some familiar as well as some obscure abbreviated titles.

Abbreviation Title

A.B.	*Artium Baccalaureus* (Latin, Bachelor of Arts)
A.M.	*Artium Magister* (Latin, Master of Arts)
A.R.A.	Associate of the Royal Academy
A.S.	Associate of Science
B.A.	Bachelor of Arts
Bart., Bt.	Baronet
B.C.S.W.	Board-Certified Social Worker
B.D.	Bachelor of Divinity
B.S.	Bachelor of Science
B.S.S.	Bachelor of Social Science
C.P.A.	Certified Public Accountant
C.S.W.	Certified Social Worker
D.A.	District Attorney
D.B.	*Divinitatis Baccalaureus* (Latin, Bachelor of Divinity)
D.C.	Doctor of Chiropractic
D.D.	*Divinitatis Doctor* (Latin, Doctor of Divinity)
D.D.S.	Doctor of Dental Surgery
D.O.	Doctor of Osteopathy
D.S.O.	Distinguished Service Order
D.V.M.	Doctor of Veterinary Medicine
Esq.	Esquire
F.R.S.	Fellow of the Royal Society
J.D.	*Juris Doctor* (Latin, Doctor of Law, Doctor of Jurisprudence), *Jurum Doctor* (Latin, Doctor of Laws)
J.P.	Justice of the Peace
Kt.	Knight
L.H.D.	*Litterarum Humaniorum Doctor* (Latin, Doctor of Humanities)
Litt.D.	*Litterarum Doctor* (Latin, Doctor of Letters)
LL.B.	*Legum Baccalaureus* (Latin, Bachelor of Laws)
LL.D.	*Legum Doctor* (Latin, Doctor of Laws)

"Acronyms" and **"Common Abbreviations"** in chapter 13
Go to

L.P.N.	Licensed Practical Nurse
M.A.	Master of Arts
M.B.A.	Master of Business Administration
M.D.	*Medicinae Doctor* (Latin, Doctor of Medicine)
M.Div.	Master of Divinity
M.Ed.	Master of Education
M.P.	Member of Parliament
M.S.	Master of Science
M.S.W.	Master of Social Work
N.P.	Notary Public
Ph.B.	*Philosophiae Baccalaureus* (Latin, Bachelor of Philosophy)
Ph.D.	*Philosophiae Doctor* (Latin, Doctor of Philosophy)
Ph.G.	Graduate in Pharmacy
Psy.D.	Doctor of Psychology
R.	*Rex, Regina* (Latin, King, Queen)
R.N.	Registered Nurse
R.Ph.	Registered Pharmacist
S.B.	Bachelor of Science
S.J.	Society of Jesus
S.M.	Master of Science
S.T.B.	*Sacrae Theologiae Baccalaureus* (Latin, Bachelor of Sacred Theology)

ADDITIONAL SOURCES OF INFORMATION

Blumenthal, Lassor A. *The Art of Letter Writing.* Perigee, 1986.

Bly, Robert W. *The Encyclopedia of Business Letters, Fax Memos, and E-Mail.* Career Press, 1999.

Booher, Dianna. *E-Writing: 21st Century Tools for Effective Communication.* Pocket Books, 2001.

De Vries, Mary A. *The New American Handbook of Letter Writing.* Signet, 2000.

Holberg, Andrea, ed. *Forms of Address: A Guide for Business and Social Use.* Rice University Press, 1994.

McCaffree, Maryjane, and Pauline Innis. *Protocol: The Complete Handbook of Diplomatic, Official and Social Usage.* Rev. ed. Devon, 1999.

Swartz, Oretha D. *Service Etiquette.* 4th ed. Naval Institute Press, 1988.

IV

DAILY LIFE

16

ETIQUETTE

Images of raised pinkies and white gloves may come readily to mind, but etiquette is as much a system of ethics as it is one of manners. All the niceties of social intercourse can be reduced down to the Golden Rule: "Do unto others as you would have others do unto you." (In her 1922 classic primer on etiquette, Emily Post redefined this dictum as "Keep your hands to yourself.") Courtesy is essential in any social situation, be it a business meeting, a lunch with co-workers, or a family reunion and, once learned, good manners can become so thoroughly ingrained that their observance becomes a matter of instinct rather than a conscious duty.

The Chinese philosopher Confucius taught his disciples that courtesies "when they are practiced with all the heart" lead to moral excellence.

This chapter details the basic rules for smoothing personal contacts and developing tact and good manners. It is hardly exhaustive—a great many books have been written on planning and organizing a wedding, for instance—and it does not cover the moral, psychological, or social implications of etiquette. But the chapter does describe what can be expected to occur when one participates in certain social activities and what is expected of those who participate.

WEDDING ETIQUETTE

Because weddings vary greatly in their level of formality and style, each component of a wedding—from the invitations to the reception—is flexible. The rule of thumb is that the various elements that make up a wedding should be compatible. That is, if a formal, evening church wedding is held, it should be preceded by formal, engraved invitations and followed by a formal, sit-down dinner; likewise, a wedding held in an open field in the countryside would call for an informal dining arrangement, perhaps a buffet.

INVITATIONS AND ANNOUNCEMENTS

Wedding invitations, like weddings themselves, come in two basic varieties: formal and informal. A formal, traditional invitation is engraved or printed in black ink on high-quality white or ivory paper. The size of the paper is either 5-by-7 inches, folded in half before being put in an envelope, or 4-by-5 inches, inserted into an envelope without folding.

The wording of a formal wedding invitation is written in the third person, and the date and time are written out in full. A typical example might read:

> Mr. and Mrs. Henry Appleton
> request the honor of your presence
> at the marriage of their daughter
> Carol June
> to
> Mr. Alan Hart
> Saturday, the fourth of February
> at eleven o'clock
> St. Albert's Church
> Bayonne, New Jersey

The invitation to the wedding ceremony itself can also invite the recipient to a reception afterward. If all those receiving invitations to the reception are not invited to the ceremony, or vice versa, a separate invitation to the reception is printed and, for those invited to both events, included with the wedding invitation. The reception invitation or the combined invitation should include the instructions "R.S.V.P."

Traditionally, the invitation is covered with a piece of tissue paper and enclosed with the reception invitation (and a response card and its envelope, if desired) in an inner envelope. The names of those invited, including a couple's children if they are also invited, are written out in full on the inner envelope. This inner envelope is then enclosed in an outer envelope that bears the handwritten names of all invited and their address, without abbreviations. Modern custom allows the bride's parents to forgo using an inner envelope altogether when sending out invitations.

Other enclosures that may be sent with the wedding invitation include cards designating reserved pews, "At-Home" cards that announce when the bride and groom will return from their honeymoon and where they will reside, and maps or other travel information.

Nontraditional, informal invitations can be designed and printed or handwritten in whatever style or form the bride and groom desire. African traditions, for instance, can be integrated into African American weddings by including Kinte colors and Adrinke symbols on the invitations.

Wedding announcements usually are sent to people who would like to know about the wedding but who would not be expected to attend. They use the same paper and printing as the invitations. The wording is also similar, although the parents of both the bride and the groom are often mentioned and the words *announce the marriage of* replace *request the honor of your presence at the marriage of.* Wedding announcements are sent out the day of, or shortly after, the wedding.

Response to a wedding invitation is dictated by the type of invitation. A formal invitation traditionally is answered with a third-person, handwritten note that might read:

> Mr. and Mrs. Harold Sloane
> accept with pleasure (or regret they will be
> unable to attend)
> Mr. and Mrs. Appleton's
> kind invitation for
> Saturday, the fourth of February.

Of course, if a response card is enclosed, it may simply be filled out and returned. If the invitation is less formal, a handwritten response in more standard, informal English is correct.

SHOWERS

Bridal or wedding showers can be given by any close friend of the bride. They should not be given by a member of the bride's immediate family.

There is no set rule for the number of showers that can be held before a wedding, although only members of the wedding party are invited to more than one shower. Nor is there a hard-and-fast rule for the types of parties they should be; serving anything from coffee and cake to cocktails to a light supper is appropriate.

Unless it is a surprise shower, the guest list is drawn up by the bride (or the bride and groom if both are to be present). The host for the party should set the limit on the number of guests. Guests invited to the shower should also be invited to the wedding, unless the wedding is to be very small.

"Etiquette" means, literally, "warning sign" as in "Keep off the Grass." When Louis XIV's gardener complained that the nobles were ignoring such warnings, the king ordered them to observe "the etiquettes." This term soon meant the rules for deportment at court.

Everyone attending a shower is expected to bring a present, which is opened at the party. The host or another friend of the bride should keep a list of who gave what, so that thank-you notes can be sent later on.

BACHELOR DINNER

Several days before the wedding, a bachelor dinner can be given for the groom. It is usually held in a private room of a restaurant and hosted by the best man or the ushers, although a groom may give his own bachelor dinner.

Generally, the men drink and eat a great deal. At some point in the evening, the groom toasts his bride-to-be. It is rarely appropriate to break the glasses after such a toast, although this was once the custom. The only important rule regarding bachelor dinners is that they should not be held the night before the wedding, so that there is adequate time for the groom to recover from the festivities.

REHEARSAL DINNER

The wedding rehearsal takes place the day before the wedding and is usually followed by a dinner party, or "rehearsal dinner." Customarily, the groom's parents host this dinner party, but it can be given by the bride's family or a close friend of the couple. Those invited include the members of the bridal party, immediate family, out-of-town family members who have been invited to the wedding, and the person performing the ceremony. Seating for rehearsal dinners may be arranged at one long table or, to fit more guests, at a U-shaped table. (See illustrations on next page.)

Etiquette

Best man   Bride   Groom   Maid of honor

Groom's father

Groom's mother

Bride's mother   Honored guest   Clergy or person performing service   Bride's father

Rehearsal Dinner—Seating Arrangement at One Long Table

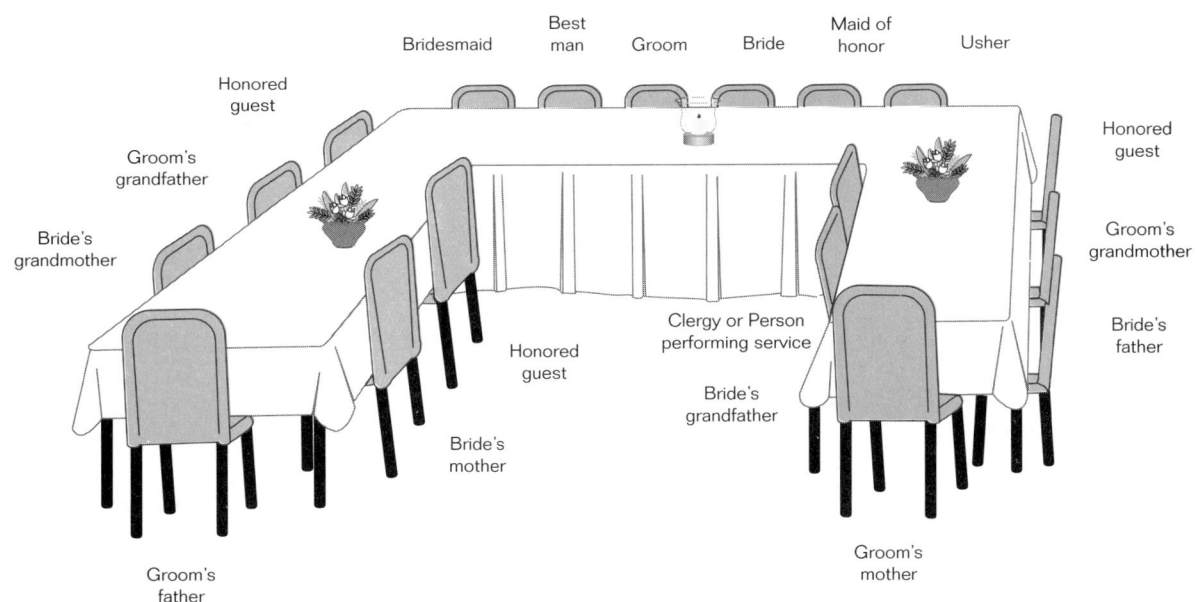

Bridesmaid   Best man   Groom   Bride   Maid of honor   Usher

Honored guest

Groom's grandfather

Bride's grandmother

Honored guest

Honored guest

Groom's grandmother

Bride's father

Clergy or Person performing service

Bride's grandfather

Bride's mother

Groom's father

Groom's mother

Rehearsal Dinner—Seating Arrangement at a U-shaped Table

CEREMONY

The wedding ceremony itself can be as formal or informal as the bride and groom wish it to be. For most weddings to which guests are invited, and especially church and synagogue weddings, a prescribed series of events will take place.

First comes the processional. In Christian and Reform Jewish weddings, the ushers come down the aisle first, arranged in height order, followed by any junior ushers. They are followed by junior bridesmaids, then bridesmaids, in height order, with the shortest first. Then comes the maid or matron of honor, the flower girls, the ring bearer, and, finally, the bride, holding the right arm of her father. The groom and the best man wait at the front of the room with the clergy.

Orthodox and Conservative Jewish processionals are led by the ushers, who are followed by the bridesmaids. Next come the rabbi and cantor followed by the best man and then the groom, accompanied by his mother and father. The maid of honor is next; she is followed by the bride, who walks between her mother and father.

The guests stand during the processional and remain standing until the clergy has asked them to sit, usually after opening remarks or a prayer. Once at the front of the room, the bride's father (or parents) steps back or to one side, and the groom steps forward to meet his bride. Bride and groom stand next to each other holding hands or with her hand on his arm, if they wish.

In Protestant ceremonies, the father of the bride gives her away before sitting down in the first pew. In Roman Catholic ceremonies, the father of the bride sits with his wife as soon as the bride is delivered to the groom. Orthodox and Conservative Jewish ceremonies require that the parents of the bride and groom remain at the front of the room; if there is space, they stand under the marriage canopy, known as a *chuppah*.

The actual events of the wedding ceremony differ widely among various denominations. African American couples sometimes include a symbolic jumping-of-the-broom in the ceremony in remembrance of enslaved African men and women jumping over a broomstick to symbolize their commitment during a time when they were forbidden by law to marry. Most Christian services include a blessing of the ring or rings. (If the bride is wearing an engagement ring, she should put it on her right hand for the service and then place it outside the wedding band afterward.) Orthodox Jewish services are mostly in Hebrew, and two glasses of wine are shared by the couple before the groom breaks the goblet at the end of the ceremony.

The recessional for Christian and Reform Jewish weddings is led by the bride and groom. They are followed by the flower girl, the best man and maid or matron of honor, and the ushers and bridesmaids; a line of bridesmaids follows the bride and a line of ushers follows the groom. Orthodox and Conservative Jewish recessionals are led by the bride and groom, followed by the bride's parents, the groom's parents, the maid of honor with the best man, the flower girl, and the rabbi and cantor. Bridesmaids and ushers bring up the rear. In Orthodox ceremonies, all the men are on one side, and all the women on the other.

RECEPTION

The style of the reception will follow the style of the rest of the wedding. Ordinarily, photographs are taken immediately after the ceremony; they are ordered and paid for by the bride's family.

A receiving line greets guests as they come into the room. The line consists of the mothers of the bride and groom, the wedded couple, the maid of honor, and, at the discretion of those involved, the fathers of the couple, the bridesmaids, the best man, and the ushers.

Formal receptions have assigned tables for those attending. The bridal party will generally be at the head table, and a parents' table will be nearby. Other guests should be assigned to tables with people whose company they will enjoy.

Almost all receptions include a toast to the bride and groom, which is proposed by the best man. The groom should reply with thanks after the toast has

Etiquette

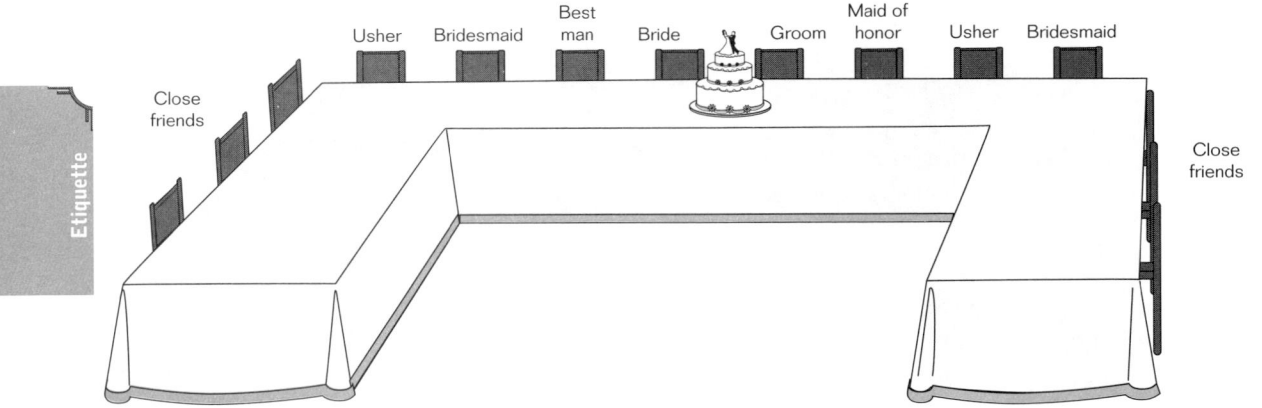

Reception—Seating Arrangement at Head Table

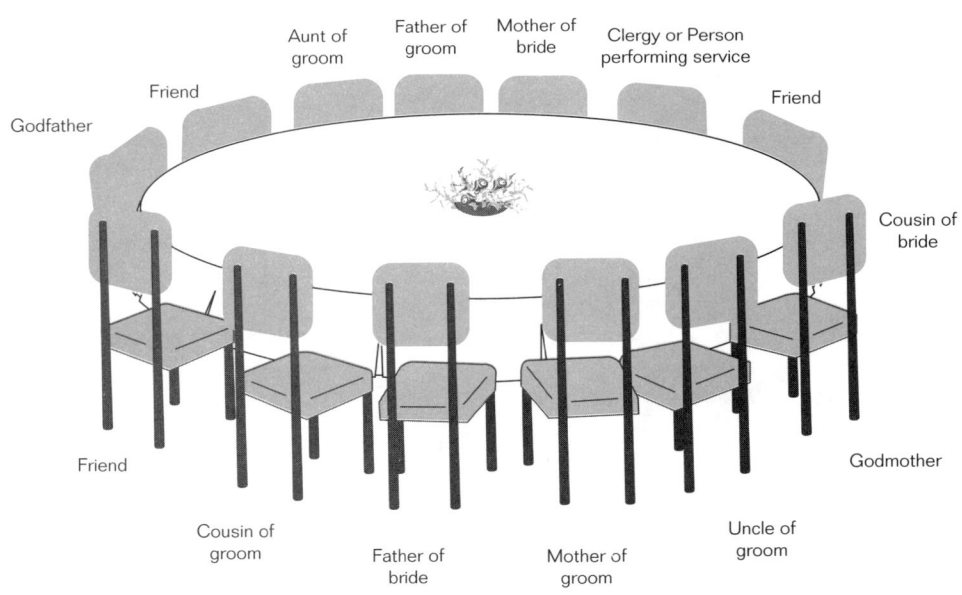

Reception—Seating Arrangement at Parents' Table

been drunk and offer a toast to his bride; other toasts may be offered as well. The toasts can be followed by dancing or a meal, if one is to be served. The wedding cake is cut just before dessert, or shortly before the bride and groom leave the reception if it is not a formal dinner. The bride cuts the first slice, with the help of her new husband, from the bottom tier of the cake, and the couple offer each other a bite. The top layer of the cake, with its decorations, is removed and saved for the bride and groom, while the remainder is cut up and served to the guests.

At the reception's end, the bride usually will toss her bouquet from stairs or a landing, turning her back and throwing it over her shoulder to her bridesmaids or other female friends; the one who catches it is supposed to marry next. Then the newlyweds change clothes, say good-bye to their families, and, led by the best man, leave in a shower of confetti, rose petals, rice, or birdseed.

GIFTS AND THANK-YOU NOTES

Gifts can be sent to the address on the At-Home card, if one is enclosed with the invitation, or to the home of the bride's mother. They also can be brought to the reception. Custom dictates that a wedding gift can be given to the bride and groom within the first year of their marriage. A note should be included explaining why the gift was delayed. Among some people, money is an appropriate wedding gift; it is usually presented to the bride in an

---

A Closer Look

Division of Wedding Expenses

Today, the groom and his family often offer to share some of the wedding expenses that traditionally have been borne by the bride's family. This is a significant change of custom, as the costs of traditional weddings have become too prohibitive for many families to absorb. If the groom's family does not offer to share expenses, however, the bride's family should plan a wedding in accordance with their means.

The traditional division of expenses is listed below. In addition to the change noted above, it should be kept in mind that there are numerous exceptions and variations depending on religion, ethnicity, or local custom. Many items may be omitted without diminishing the ceremony in any way.

Expenses Paid by Bride's Family

Bridal consultant, if needed
Invitations and announcements
Flowers for the church and receptions, bouquets for the bridesmaids, bouquet for bride (sometimes given by groom)
Music for the ceremony, including organist or choir fee
Transportation of bridal party to church or synagogue and reception
Bride's presents to her bridesmaids
Bride's present to groom (optional)
Groom's wedding ring
Sexton's fee (church fee)
Accommodations for out-of-town bridesmaids
All expenses of reception, including music

Expenses Paid by Bridesmaids

Dress and accessories
Transportation to and from town of wedding
Gift to the couple and contribution to a gift from all bridesmaids to the bride

Expenses Paid by Groom's Family

Bride's rings, both engagement and wedding
Groom's present to bride (optional)
Groom's presents to ushers and best man
Groom's boutonniere and boutonnieres for ushers
Ties and gloves for the ushers
Clergy member's fee; tips to altar boys
Corsages for immediate members of both families and bride's going-away corsage
Accommodations for out-of-town ushers
Bachelor dinner (optional, and often given by ushers)
Rehearsal dinner (optional, but becoming more standard)
Honeymoon

Expenses Paid by Ushers

Transportation to and from town of wedding
Rental of wedding attire
Gift to the couple and contribution to a gift from all ushers to the groom
Bachelor dinner (optional, and often given by groom)

Expenses Paid by Out-of-Town Guests

Transportation and accommodations
Gift to the couple

envelope, which she will place in a special purse or in a box or basket put out for this purpose. Envelopes, and usually gifts as well, are not opened until after the reception.

Thank-you notes should be handwritten and should mention the gift that was given. They should be sent shortly after the couple's honeymoon is over.

ANNIVERSARY GIFTS

Etiquette authorities differ on the appropriate gifts to be presented on the occasion of individual wedding anniversaries. The following list represents a modern consensus, with the eight oldest and most traditional gifts indicated in *italic*.

1	*Paper* or plastic
2	Cotton or calico
3	Leather
4	Linen, silk, or synthetics (rayon, nylon)
5	*Wood*
6	Iron
7	Copper, wool, or brass
8	Bronze or electrical appliances
9	Pottery
10	*Tin* or aluminum
11	Steel
12	Silk or linen
13	Lace
14	Ivory
15	*Crystal* or glass
20	*China*
25	*Silver*
30	Pearls
35	Coral or jade
40	Rubies or garnets
45	Sapphires or tourmalines
50	*Gold*
55	Emeralds or turquoise
60	*Diamonds* or gold
75	Diamonds or gold

BUSINESS ETIQUETTE

The business world is extraordinarily demanding and extremely competitive. In it, there are really only a few criteria on which members will be judged: competence, initiative, leadership, and how well one gets along with others. In this last area, manners play a crucial role, for individuals must be able to present themselves well and deal well with others if they wish to succeed in business.

APPOINTMENTS

Business life requires that people meet each other face-to-face to conduct transactions or exchange information. To do so, they schedule appointments. The first rule regarding business appointments is that they should be kept if at all possible; failing to show up for an appointment will be taken as a sign of uninterest, carelessness, and lack of professionalism. If an appointment cannot be kept, it should be canceled as far in advance as possible. If an individual is unavoidably delayed, he or she should telephone the host or have someone else make the call.

When greeting a person who has a severe loss of vision, always identify yourself. When talking to a person in a wheelchair, try to sit down so that you are at eye level. Never shout at a person with a hearing impairment; shouting inhibits lip reading and distorts the sounds amplified by hearing aids.

When guests are shown into the office where the appointment will take place, the host should rise from his or her desk, shake hands, and greet them; if the host and guests have not met before, they should introduce themselves. The guests should be offered seats, and the host should either sit back down at the desk or sit with the visitors. Coffee or tea may be offered by the host but should not be requested by the guests.

Any business meeting should get to the business at hand as quickly as possible. It is just as important to listen as it is to talk, not simply to be polite but to get the most out of the meeting. It is also important not to interrupt others during meetings. Taking notes during a business meeting is acceptable.

The host usually will conclude a business meeting, either by making remarks that sum up the discussion or by suggesting outright that everything pertinent has now been discussed. It is important for guests to pick up on such cues, gather their belongings, thank the host, shake hands, and leave. A follow-up letter, thanking the host for the meeting and outlining whatever was agreed upon at the meeting, should be sent by the next business day.

ENTERTAINMENT

Business entertaining generally takes place in an office; over breakfast, lunch, or dinner at a restaurant; or over drinks after work. The purpose of business entertaining is to conduct business in a congenial setting that is less formal than an office.

The person initiating business entertainment acts as the host. That person is responsible for deciding on the setting, making reservations, and paying the bill. The site chosen for entertaining a client or colleague should be appropriate to the person being invited and the nature of the business relationship; a prestigious restaurant would be right for entertaining a major client, while drinks at a clubby bar might be a good choice for entertaining a vendor who regularly sells supplies to the company.

Regardless of the setting, it should be kept in mind that business is the main purpose of the get-together. The host should endeavor to bring up the business at hand before the guest becomes impatient. However, business discussions should not interfere with the pleasure of enjoying the meal.

In 1907, President Theodore Roosevelt set a world record for handshaking by shaking hands with 8,513 people at a New Year's Day White House presentation.

The host should pick up the check when it is brought to the table, look it over, and pay it. Because business entertaining should give both parties more or less equal status, it makes no difference whether the host is a man or a woman. There is no reason for a guest even to show a pretense of wanting to pick up the check; the guest can express his or her thanks to the host as she or he is leaving.

GIFTS

Gift giving is not at all unusual among people who work together. Bosses often give gifts to employees for birthdays, Christmas, or Secretaries' Day; staff members may give the boss a present for holidays or birthdays; office colleagues sometimes give each other gifts; and executives can give presents to clients or vendors.

Such gifts are generally not lavish, although the type of gift is dictated by the nature of the relationship. Bosses tend to give larger presents to their employees than staff members give to the boss. Gifts to colleagues reflect the degree of friendship between them. Clients or vendors give and receive gifts appropriate to the amount of business transacted and the longevity of the relationship.

Business gifts should be less personal than gifts for a friend. A date book or similar office accessory, costume jewelry, a tie, or a bottle of wine makes a good, inexpensive business gift. More lavish presents, like theater tickets, food baskets, or a case of wine, can be given to long-standing clients or employees.

THE TELEPHONE

For many companies, the telephone is an essential tool for conducting business. Proper telephone manners can make it an effective tool.

Many people think that having a secretary or assistant place calls will enhance the image of an executive. In fact, having others place calls for oneself is an inconvenience, both for the secretary or assistant who must place the call and for the person receiving the call, who must wait for the executive to get on the line. People in business should place their own phone calls.

When the call goes through, the caller should identify himself or herself by name and company; if the nature of the call is not readily apparent, the caller should volunteer this information. With some companies, this process will have to be repeated two or three times—with the switchboard operator, a secretary, and the person being called.

Etiquette

Go to
"Business Letters" in chapter 15

A caller should not take offense if asked to identify the reason for the call, although this type of questioning is often a thinly disguised way of keeping a boss insulated from people he or she does not want to receive calls from. Screening phone calls is acceptable, but not if the caller is then asked to hold the line and finally is told that the person being called is not available. As with placing calls, the most convenient and polite way of dealing with incoming calls is to answer them yourself; if you are too busy to answer the phone yourself, a secretary should keep the interrogation of a caller to a minimum.

People answering business phones should identify themselves and ask if they can help the caller. They should be attentive, organized, and unhurried. If answering someone else's phone, they should be ready to take a message.

Business phones should not be used for personal calls. If a personal call must be made, or if one is received, it should be kept as brief as possible. Similarly, business calls should be kept brief and to the point. Chattiness and rudeness are always to be avoided in business telephone calls.

NETWORK ETIQUETTE (NETIQUETTE)

Just as social and business etiquette involves the use of good manners and consideration for others, network etiquette, or "netiquette," follows conventions on how people should conduct themselves when using a computer network or the Internet. Here are a few tips to keep in mind once you're online and surfing the Internet.

- When composing electronic mail, you must choose words carefully. Sending e-mail is not a secure procedure; because there is no control over where e-mail goes after it's sent, anyone could be reading your message.
- Unlike face-to-face or telephone conversations, computer communications make facial expressions or verbal emphasis difficult to convey. In addition, type styles are not transmitted well— if at all. If used for emphasis, they will some-

times produce an unreadable garbled message on the recipient's end. Instead of using italic or boldface to add emphasis, you can use *asterisks* or write in UPPERCASE. Avoid using uppercase too often in messages you send on the Internet because it is the equivalent of shouting. "Smileys" or "emoticons" are faces viewed sideways that are added to online messages to convey feelings: :) stands for a smile, :(stands for a frown, and ;) stands for a wink. "Smileys" are discussed in Chapter 12.

- While surfing the Net, a person cannot be judged by his age, weight, sex, or color, but a person can and will be judged by the quality of his or her writing. Correct spelling and grammar count.
- You may never see or meet the people you communicate with, so it's easy to be rude. Remember that you are interacting with other people, not simply with a computer screen.

PARTIES

GENERAL ASPECTS

Parties come in all shapes and sizes. They can be held for holidays, anniversaries, housewarmings, birthdays, weddings, or farewells, or just to have some friends over. Parties range from sit-down dinners in banquet halls to tea and cookies in living rooms. But whatever the size or style of the party, certain aspects need to be tended to make it a success.

INVITATIONS

Invitations can be given in writing, in person, or by telephone, or e-mail depending on the sort of party they are for. Engraved invitations are sent for formal parties, such as weddings and anniversary parties. Less formal events require less formal invitations; handwritten notes on personal stationery or printed invitation cards with blanks that can be filled in can be used. Invitations to small informal parties can be issued by telephone or by e-mail. Invitations should be sent out about three weeks before a party.

R.S.V.P.s

Your invitation should include a request that guests respond if you want to know in advance who will be coming. A formal invitation can include a response card or just "R.S.V.P." Informal invitations can include a statement like "Unless we hear otherwise, we'll expect you on the third" or "Please let us know if you can make it." Telephone invitations will usually get immediate responses; however, if you are invited by telephone and do not know whether you can attend, it is acceptable to put off a response. In any case, it is important to respond to an invitation as quickly as possible so that the hosts can plan accordingly.

ATTIRE

Formal events call for certain types of attire, especially for men. *White tie* is the most formal evening attire and includes a white tie, wing collar, and tailcoat. *Black tie* is the more common evening wear and includes a tuxedo, a bow tie, and a white, soft shirt. When the occasion calls for *semiformal* attire, that usually means a sport coat, shirt, tie, and nice slacks for men, and a dress or pantsuit for women.

Every aspect of a Japanese tea ceremony, from the tea bowls to the flowers and food, is carefully chosen by the host and should be complimented by his or her guests.

FORMAL DINNER PARTIES
SEATING ARRANGEMENTS

The host and hostess, as well as any guests of honor, are the people around whom seating arrangements are set at more formal dinner parties. The host and hostess will usually sit at either end of the table; a male guest of honor sits at the hostess's right and a female guest of honor at the host's right. Other guests are told where to sit by the host and hostess,

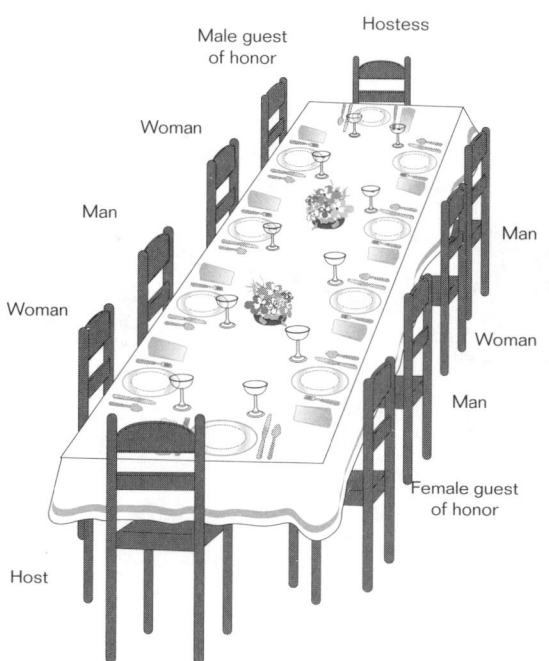

Formal Dinner Party—Seating Arrangement

either personally or by using place cards. Although it is customary to alternate men and women at a sit-down dinner, this practice can be ignored if there are more members of one sex than of the other. Husbands and wives can be seated together or separated. Obviously, buffet dinner parties, cocktail parties, and other informal get-togethers do not require any sort of specific seating arrangement; guests can be expected to fend for themselves.

TABLEWARE

A place setting at a formal dinner party can be somewhat intimidating to guests unfamiliar with such events. The arrangement of plates, glasses, and utensils is fairly standard, however, and fairly easy to deal with, as illustrated on the next page.

The basic setting should be in place when the guests sit down. A service plate is in the center, usually with the napkin on top of it. Flanking the plate will be the flatware: a dessert or salad fork to the immediate

a Oyster or shellfish fork
b Soup spoon
c Fork and knife for fish
d Fork and knife for meat

e Fork and knife for salad and cheese
f Sherry glass (with soup)
g White wineglass (with fish)
h Red wineglass (with meat)

i Water goblet
j Champagne glass (with dessert)
k Butter plate and knife

Formal Dinner Party—Place Setting

a Water goblet
b Wine glass
c Coffee cup and saucer
d Coffee spoon

e Soup spoon
f Dessert spoon
g Knife
h Dessert or salad fork

i Dinner fork
j Salad plate
k Butter plate and knife

Informal Dinner Party—Place Setting

Etiquette

left of the plate; a dinner fork to the left of it; and a fish fork, if needed, on the outside. To the right of the plate are, from closest to farthest, the salad knife; the meat knife; the fish knife; a soup or fruit spoon (or both); and, if shellfish is being served, a shellfish fork. Utensils are used in order from the outside in.

Glasses are placed above the knives to the right of the plate. There will be a water goblet and, extending to the right from there, a champagne glass, one or two wineglasses, and a sherry glass.

In addition to the service plate, a butter plate is placed above the forks, to the left of the service plate. The butter knife is set across the butter plate.

Formal etiquette dictates that a soup bowl must always be tipped away from, never toward, the diner.

SERVING

Food at a formal dinner party is usually served by hired help. Guests are served from the left, and plates are cleared from the right. The female guest of honor is served first; if there is no guest of honor, women are served before men or, if this is hard to manage, a woman is served the first plate with the other guests served in order. The hostess is served last. Warmed dinner plates are usually brought out just before the entree is served. A clean service plate should be brought out for each of the other courses.

INFORMAL DINNER PARTIES

If the dinner party is less formal and fewer courses are served, the basic place setting is arranged with fewer utensils. (See illustration on preceeding page.)

DEATHS AND FUNERALS

Plans for death should be discussed with family and loved ones before such plans are likely to be needed. A person's desires regarding the sort of funeral held, disposal of the body by burial or cremation, and donation of organs need to be known. Practical matters—where to find insurance papers, the will, bills, bank accounts, safety deposit boxes, or investment holdings—also should be dealt with in advance.

FUNERAL ARRANGEMENTS

Funeral directors provide a variety of services and handle the details of funeral arrangements, such as placement of a death notice in the newspaper; selection of a coffin; and travel to church, synagogue, and graveyard. Many of these arrangements can be made in advance or at the time of death. The death notice includes the deceased's name and date of death, the names of immediate family members who survive, and the place and time of the wake and funeral if the funeral is not private.

WAKES

Traditionally, wakes were held at the dead person's home, but today wakes are usually held at a funeral home. They are strictly a Christian phenomenon; Jews sit *shiva* during a seven-day period of mourning and remembrance immediately after burial. Anyone may attend a wake, unless it is kept private. The hours and days are set and usually appear in the death notice in the newspaper. Nonfamily members should sign the guest book provided at the funeral home, stay just long enough to express sympathy to the bereaved family, and then leave. Expressions of sympathy are best if they come from the heart; when at a loss for what to say, a simple "I'm sorry" is enough. Standing, kneeling, or praying at the coffin is optional.

FLOWERS

Sending flowers is a customary way of expressing sympathy, especially if attendance at the wake or funeral is not possible. They can be sent to the funeral home or the church along with a card. Flowers are not appropriate for Jewish funerals or if the death notice requests donations to charity instead.

FUNERAL SERVICES

Unless specified as private in the death notice, funeral services can be attended by anyone. They should be viewed not as an obligation but as an opportunity to publicly bid farewell to the person who died and to show concern for the survivors. Religious affiliation is unimportant; one may attend a

Etiquette

funeral service regardless of faith. It is important to speak to the bereaved family at the funeral service; if sympathy has already been expressed at the wake, a positive comment about the service, the eulogy, or the church or synagogue would be appropriate.

BURIAL

For Jews, burial takes place within 24 hours, or as quickly as possible. Christians are buried two or more days after death. Close friends and family members are generally the only people expected to attend the actual interment.

A reception generally is held after the burial. The funeral director or a family member will invite those present to attend. It can be held at the home of a relative or at a catering hall or restaurant. Food and drink are provided by the bereaved family or arranged for by them.

LETTERS OR CALLS OF CONDOLENCE

Letters or calls of condolence are appropriate in lieu of attendance at a wake or funeral service. They should be brief and should focus on memories of the dead person, sympathy for the survivors, and offers of help to the survivors. Avoid pity in such communications or visits, and make clear that a response is not expected soon.

AFTER BURIAL

It is important to be available to the grieving family after all ceremonies are over. If the family is Jewish, they will sit *shiva* for seven days; it is appropriate to drop by and bring food but not flowers. If the family is Christian, stop by a few days later to listen and talk. Whatever the religious affiliation, friends who are willing to listen and talk to bereaved family members are highly valued at this time.

ADDITIONAL SOURCES OF INFORMATION

Ford, Charlotte, and Jacqueline Demontravel. *21st-Century Etiquette*. Lyons Press, 2001.

Lauter, Peter. *Wireless Etiquette: A Guide to the Changing World of Instant Communication*. Omnipoint Communications, 1999.

Martin, Judith. *Miss Manners' Guide to Domestic Tranquillity: The Authoritative Manual for Every Civilized Household, However Harried*. Three Rivers Press, 2000.

Miller, Samantha. *E-Mail Etiquette*. Warner Books, 2000.

Pincus, Marilyn, and Letitia Baldrige. *Everyday Business Etiquette*. Barrons, 1996.

Post, Elizabeth. *Emily Post's Etiquette*. 16th ed. HarperCollins, 1997.

Post, Peggy. *Emily Post's Entertaining: A Classic Guide to Adding Elegance and Ease to Any Festive Occasion*. HarperReference, 1998.

_____. *Emily Post's Wedding Etiquette*. Harper Information, 2000.

Spizman, Robyn Freedman. *The Perfect Present: The Ultimate Gift Guide for Every Occasion*. Crown, 1998.

Stewart, Marjabelle Young. *Commonsense Etiquette: A Guide to Gracious, Simple Manners for the Twenty-First Century*. Griffin, 1999.

Tuckerman, Nancy, and Nancy Dunnan. *The Amy Vanderbuilt Complete Book of Etiquette*. 1st ed. Doubleday, 1995.

Von Drachenfels, Suzanne. *The Art of the Table: A Complete Guide to Table Setting, Table Manners and Tableware*. Simon & Schuster, 2000.

Woodward, Chiquita, *It's Just What I Always Wanted! More than 2,000 Imaginative and Unique Gifts*. Hyperion, 1999.

17

FIRST AID

LIFESAVING PROCEDURES

The American Medical Association recommends that when a person is injured or becomes suddenly ill one should ***immediately call for medical help.*** After help is summoned, priority should be given to these objectives:

1. Maintain breathing and circulation
2. Prevent loss of blood
3. Prevent further injury
4. Prevent shock

MAINTAINING BREATHING AND CIRCULATION

When breathing stops, the victim has enough oxygen in the blood and other tissues to sustain life for only a few minutes. Any delay in restoring the flow of oxygen to the brain and other body organs can result in death or permanent damage. Start artificial respiration and manual external cardiac massage immediately if the person is not breathing. Basic cardiopulmonary resuscitation (CPR)—mouth-to-mouth breathing and external cardiac massage—does not require equipment. It can be done by only one or two rescuers, but having more rescuers increases the chances for success.

If you are not directly involved in the rescue effort, you can help by calling a doctor, an emergency medical service (EMS), or the police or fire department. But rescuers should not wait for professional support to arrive. Seconds count. Rescue may involve

A Closer Look

First Aid

Methods of Cardiopulmonary Resuscitation (CPR)

Mouth-to-Mouth Breathing

Step 1: If there are no signs of breathing or there is no significant pulse, place one hand under the victim's neck and gently lift. At the same time, push with the other hand on the victim's forehead. This will move the tongue away from the back of the throat to open the airway. If available, a plastic "stoma," or oropharyngeal airway device, should be inserted now.

Step 2: While maintaining the backward head tilt position, place your cheek and ear close to the victim's mouth and nose. Look for the chest to rise and fall while you listen and feel for breathing. Check for about 5 seconds.

Step 3: Next, while maintaining the backward head tilt, pinch the victim's nose with the hand that is on the victim's forehead to prevent leakage of air, open your mouth wide, take a deep breath, seal your mouth around the victim's mouth, and blow into the victim's mouth with four quick but full breaths. For an infant, give gentle puffs and blow through the mouth *and* nose and do not tilt the head back as far as for an adult.

If you do not get an air exchange when you blow, it may help to reposition the head and try again.

If there is still no breathing, give one breath every 5 seconds for an adult and one gentle puff every 3 seconds for an infant until breathing resumes.

If the victim's chest fails to expand, the problem may be an airway obstruction. Mouth-to-mouth respiration should be interrupted briefly to apply first aid for choking. See the "Choking" subsection in "Treatment for Health Emergencies."

Step 1   Step 2   Step 3

continues

Methods of Cardiopulmonary Resuscitation (CPR), continued

Cardiac Massage

Check the carotid artery pulse. If there is no pulse, begin external cardiac massage by squeezing the heart between the sternum (breastbone) and the spinal column. To begin external cardiac massage, take a position facing the victim and uncover his or her chest. Find the bottom (xiphoid process) of the breastbone and place your index and middle fingers next to it to mark the location. Next, place the heel of your other hand on the sternum, just above the xiphoid process. Remove your first hand and place it on the second, interlocking the fingers. Holding your arms straight, rock back and forth from the hips and press downward so the sternum is depressed between one and two inches. Do not press on the xiphoid process and do not exert enough pressure to cause internal injuries to the liver or other organs in the area.

If possible, mouth-to-mouth breathing and external cardiac massage should be combined at a rate of 12 breath cycles and 60 chest compressions per minute. If at least two rescuers are available, one should perform mouth-to-mouth breathing while the other does chest compressions.

Check frequently for signs of a carotid artery pulse, a return of normal skin coloring, or signs of spontaneous breathing. Even if normal breathing returns, remain ready to resume CPR if necessary and until a doctor or other professional medical help arrives.

Mouth-to-Nose Breathing

When mouth-to-mouth breathing is not feasible, mouth-to-nose breathing can be performed in a similar manner by placing your mouth over the victim's nose and holding his or her lips closed between the thumb and forefinger.

For Small Children

If the victim is a small child, your mouth can be placed over both the nose and mouth. Be careful about extending the neck of an infant because soft tissues in the neck may obstruct the upper airway if the head is tilted too far.

External cardiac massage for a small child should be done with the pressure of two thumbs or two fingers, and compression should be limited to a depth of only one-half to one inch, depending on the size of the child.

For Drowning Victims

If drowning is the cause, do not wait until the victim can be transported to shore or placed on a flat surface to begin CPR. Mouth-to-mouth artificial respiration can be started while the victim is in a boat or is floating in the water. See the "Choking" and "Drowning" subsections in "Treatment for Health Emergencies" later in this chapter.

---

three related actions: opening an airway to the lungs, restoring breathing, and restoring circulation.

First, place the victim on his or her back on a hard, flat surface, such as the floor. If breathing has stopped because of poisonous gas or lack of oxygen, move the victim quickly to fresh air before beginning CPR.

Second, examine the victim closely for possible injuries or other obstacles that would interfere with CPR action. Check for a pulse in the carotid artery, on either side of the neck beneath the chin. Try to get the attention of the victim by talking, pinching, or tapping. If there is no response, assume that the person is unconscious. Look, listen, and feel for any signs of air moving in or out of the victim's lungs.

PREVENTING LOSS OF BLOOD

Heavy bleeding, or hemorrhaging, is a life-threatening emergency. Bleeding from a large artery can result in death in less than five minutes. As with maintaining breathing and circulation, immediate action is needed. Notify a doctor, an emergency medical service (EMS), the police, or the fire department. If the victim can be moved safely and quickly, take him or her to a nearby hospital emergency room.

COVERING THE WOUND

Unless there are injuries or other conditions that might interfere, keep the victim lying down with the bleeding part of the body raised higher than the rest of the body. If the bleeding is external, as from an open wound, place a clean cloth, handkerchief, pad, or similar object directly over the wound and press firmly, with both hands if necessary.

If blood soaks through the cloth, add more cloth and keep pressing, but do not take off the original pad or cloth until the bleeding is under control. Ice placed directly over the wound may help reduce the blood flow by causing constriction of the blood vessel that is the source of blood loss.

There are four basic blood types: A, B, O, and AB. The most common is type O, present in 40% to 60% of the population.

Apply firm pressure to the pressure point (see **Pressure Points** below) to control blood flow to the wound. If possible, apply pressure to the pressure point with one hand while your other hand presses a pad over the wound. Do not apply a tourniquet unless there is no other way to stop the loss of blood. A tourniquet can result in the death of tissues in an arm, leg, hand, or foot and may lead to amputation.

Pressure Points

A Closer Look

Fingers usually can be applied without worsening a victim's condition to control bleeding at a pressure point. There are a half-dozen pressure points where bleeding from an artery can be stopped or reduced by pressing the artery against a bone located next to it.

Neck, Mouth, or Throat

To stop bleeding from the neck, mouth, or throat area, apply pressure at a point near the base of the neck where an artery passes alongside the trachea, or windpipe. Place the thumb of the hand against the back of the victim's neck and the fingers on the neck just below the larynx, or Adam's apple. Then push the fingers against the artery.

Lower Arm

An artery supplying the lower arm passes by the bone of the upper arm about halfway along the upper arm. Pressing the artery against the arm bone can stop bleeding from nearly any point beyond.

Upper Arm

A pressure point for controlling the loss of blood in the area of the upper arm, shoulder, or armpit should be found where an artery passes over the outer surface of the top rib. Place the thumb in the position shown (the top rib is indicated in the drawing) and the fingers over the shoulder so that they press against the area behind the collarbone. Apply pressure to the artery crossing the top rib.

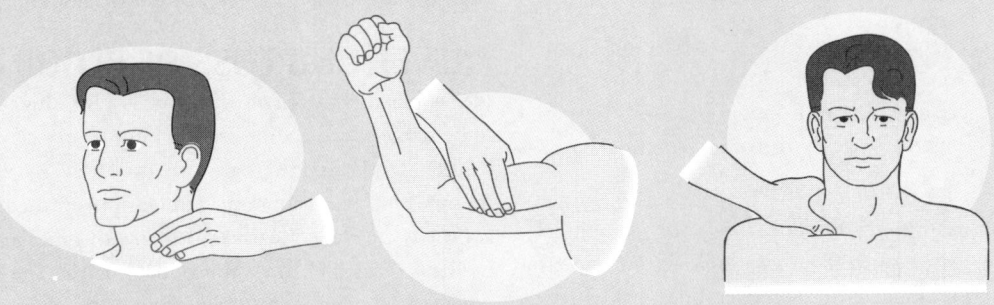

Neck, Mouth, or Throat   Lower Arm   Upper Arm

continues

Pressure Points, continued

Head Below Eye and Above Jawbone

Bleeding from an artery supplying the area of the face below the level of the eye usually can be controlled by finding the pressure point on the artery that crosses the edge of the jawbone.

Head Above Eye Level

For bleeding above the level of the eye, the rescuer should be able to find a pressure point where an artery passes over one of the skull bones in front of the upper portion of the ear, as shown in the drawing.

Leg or Foot

To stop bleeding from a leg or foot, apply pressure at a point in the area of the groin where the femoral artery passes over one of the bones of the pelvis, as shown in the drawing. If the blood flow slackens or stops, you can assume you have found the pressure point.

If at first you do not find the exact pressure point location, try again. The locations may vary somewhat with different body builds. You will know when you find the correct place, because bleeding will diminish or stop. As when a tourniquet is used, remember to release pressure at intervals to allow some blood to flow to deprived tissues. Do not continue compressing an artery if bleeding stops.

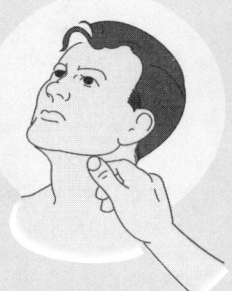

Head Below Eye and
Above Jawbone

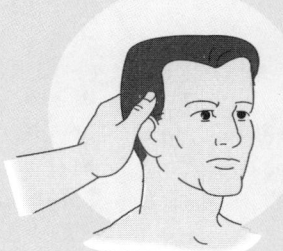

Head Above Eye Level

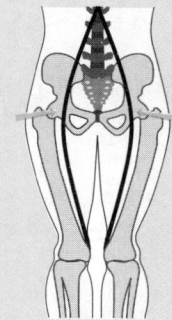

Leg or Foot

GENERAL CARE OF THE VICTIM

Heavy bleeding leads to symptoms of shock: thirst, cold and clammy skin, dizziness, and falling blood pressure. Keep the victim flat and covered with a blanket or coat. Also, maintain body temperature by making sure the victim is not lying on a cold or damp surface. Do not use the shock position if you suspect the victim has a head, neck, or back injury and cannot be moved.

Go to "Anatomical Drawings of the Human Body" in chapter 3; "Medicine and Pharmacology Symbols" in chapter 12

Unless the victim is unconscious or suffering from an abdominal wound, allow him or her to drink water or other beverages as needed; blood loss requires replacement of fluids. Do not give a wounded person alcoholic beverages, which would have the effect of increasing fluid depletion.

If the victim has suffered an open abdominal or chest wound and professional medical help is not immediately available, cover any protruding organs with a clean damp cloth held in place with a bandage or by hand pressure.

An open chest wound may result in a lung collapse unless the wound can be covered quickly with a gauze or cloth pad held in place by a firm bandage to prevent air from moving in or out of the lung. If a gauze pad is not available, make a pad from plastic sheeting, aluminum foil, or other clean material to form an airtight seal. If a bandage is not available, use a belt to hold the pad in place. Do not touch an open wound except as necessary to apply pressure or a pad or other dressing. Never try to explore a wound to locate fragments of metal, glass, or other debris that may have caused the injury.

An ice-cream headache is triggered when cold food or drink hits the roof of the mouth. The pain peaks in about 25 to 60 seconds, and skin temperature on the forehead falls almost 2 degrees Fahrenheit.

ADVISING DOCTORS AND EMS PERSONNEL

If a tourniquet is applied to stop the loss of blood from an arm or leg so seriously damaged that it may have to be amputated, be sure to advise the doctor or emergency medical service (EMS) personnel who will eventually take charge. Better yet, attach a note or write a message with lipstick on the victim's forehead that a tourniquet has been used. Do not assume that a hospital emergency-room doctor or intern many miles away will be aware that a tourniquet or any other special first-aid measures may have been applied at the scene of the accident.

PREVENTING FURTHER INJURY

First aid in an emergency should be limited to no more than is necessary to save a life or prevent further injury. In most cases, do not move an injured person from an accident site before a doctor, emergency personnel, or police or fire personnel arrive. An exception is a situation, such as a building fire or potential explosion, in which the lives of the rescuers as well as the victims could be in danger. If there is an injury to the neck or spine, a victim should not be moved until a stretcher or other carrying device that provides firm support is available. Improper

movement of the victim could cause a broken or dislocated bone that may damage an internal organ or pinch or sever a vital nerve trunk and result in death or permanent disability.

If the victim appears to have a head injury, movement should be delayed until a doctor has examined the person. Even then, any movement should be supervised by a physician. Do not move the head, or other body parts, if there is bleeding from the nose, mouth, or ears. If the victim is unconscious, you must assume that he or she has a head injury.

Never assume that an unconscious, disoriented, or apparently incoherent person is drunk. The victim may have suffered a head injury in a fall, a physical assault, or an accident. There are numerous causes of impaired consciousness, including brain hemorrhage, concussion, carbon-monoxide poisoning, epilepsy, encephalitis, diabetic coma, hypoglycemia, heart trouble, psychiatric disorders, and barbiturates or other medications. Never give alcoholic beverages to an accident victim, and never offer fluids of any kind to a person who is unconscious or semiconscious or who has internal injuries.

PREVENTING SHOCK

Shock can be expected at any accident scene. It is a common, natural reaction to any severe physical or psychological injury. Generally, shock results from an automatic change in a person's blood circulation, as nature suddenly diverts blood to the vital organs in an effort to ensure the victim's survival. This natural reaction, however, can lead to death through circulatory collapse.

Shock prevention is next in priority to maintaining respiration and control of bleeding. Watch for—but do not wait for—the common shock signs: (1) a weak, rapid pulse, (2) skin that is cold and moist with "cold sweat," (3) dilated pupils or eyes that appear "vacant," (4) restless or abnormally anxious behavior, (5) nausea or thirst, (6) faintness and weakness. If the person becomes quiet and slips into unconsciousness, shock has already progressed beyond the first stages.

First Aid

First-Aid Kits

Many people are confused about the meanings of terms, such as bandages and dressings, used by health professionals. Dressings are held in place by bandages. A *dressing* can be anything placed over an open wound to control bleeding, absorb blood or secretions, and prevent infectious agents from entering the body through the wound. The best kind of dressing is a piece of sterile gauze, but in an emergency, any clean material may become a dressing—even a sheet, a piece of plastic, or a newspaper. Fluffy materials, such as cotton wool, however, should not be used because the loose fibers will stick to body tissues.

A *bandage* is a strip of muslin, gauze, or other material used to hold a compress or dressing in place. A *roller bandage* is a long strip of cloth that can be used as a dressing or compress as well as a bandage. A *triangular bandage* is one cut from a square of cloth along a diagonal line. A *compress* is a square of fabric, generally of flannel or wool, used to apply heat, cold, or medications to the skin.

An ideal family first aid kit should contain the following:

12 4-by-4-inch sterile dressings in sealed envelopes	1 pair of needle-nose pliers
12 2-by-2-inch sterile dressings in sealed envelopes	1 eyedropper
	1 set of measuring spoons
2 15-foot-long roller bandages, 1 inch wide	12 wooden tongue blades (for finger splints)
2 15-foot-long roller bandages, 2 inches wide	12 wood splints, 12–18 inches long
	1 bar of antiseptic soap
1 roll of adhesive tape	1 package of salt
4 triangular bandages with safety pins	1 package of baking soda
1 clean bedsheet	1 package of aspirin tablets
2 small bath towels	1 package of antihistamine tablets
2 large bath towels	1 package of anti-motion-sickness tablets
1 pair of blunt-nose scissors	1 large package of adhesive bandages, assorted sizes
1 pair of tweezers	1 package of paper cups

A usual first-aid measure for shock is to position the victim so that the head is lower than the rest of the body, thus allowing gravity to pull blood toward the brain. An exception may be necessary if the victim has a head injury and cannot be moved.

Keep the victim warm and protected from the weather. Providing too much warmth, however, can lead to sweating with loss of vital body fluids and redirection of the blood flow from the vital organs to the surface of the body. Fluids may be given to a shock victim under certain circumstances—if the person is conscious, does not have internal injuries, and can swallow. Fluids can be vital for the survival of a victim who has suffered burns. It is better to give fluids in the early stages of shock, because fluids may not be absorbed from the digestive system later. If the accident site is some distance from the nearest hospital or doctor's office, small amounts of warm water or tea may be offered. But do not offer fluids if emergency service personnel or other professional help are nearby and the victim is likely to be anesthetized for surgery. If a physician is available, by telephone or otherwise, let the doctor make the final decision about fluids for accident victims.

Some persons at an accident scene may suffer only minor cuts and bruises but experience psychological shock. The signs and symptoms are the same as for victims with serious physical injuries. Time and personnel permitting, psychological shock cases should receive the same care for their shock symptoms as the severely injured. If those with psychological shock are allowed to slip into unconsciousness with possible circulatory failure, their condition will obviously complicate the overall rescue effort.

TREATMENT FOR HEALTH EMERGENCIES

ABRASIONS

A minor break in the skin, such as one caused by scraping or rubbing against a rough surface, should be washed with soap and water and treated with mild antiseptic, such as hydrogen peroxide. Then cover the abrasion with a sterile gauze dressing held in place with a bandage. If signs of infection appear, consult a doctor.

ANIMAL BITES

Animal bites, whether from a pet or a wild animal, can cause a puncture wound, a laceration, or an avulsion, in which part of the flesh is torn away. First aid should be directed toward control of bleeding and protecting the wound from infection until it can be examined by a doctor. Unless the wound is extremely painful or bleeding profusely, clean it with soap and water and cover it with a sterile dressing before taking the victim to a doctor's office or hospital emergency room.

Many animal bites require a tetanus shot and, if the animal is identified as being rabid, additional protection against rabies. In most communities, local health authorities require notification of any serious animal bite.

BLACK EYES AND BRUISES

Black eyes and bruises are actually a type of closed wound in which blood from a damaged vessel in the soft tissues has leaked into a space beneath the skin. Apply ice or a cold compress to reduce the swelling and control the further loss of blood under the skin. In most cases, the pool of blood will be reabsorbed and the skin color will return to normal.

BOILS AND BLISTERS

A *boil* is a tender, often painful, pus-filled swelling of the skin. A boil is also known as a *furuncle*, and a group of furuncles is a *carbuncle*. Boils should be treated quickly and carefully to prevent the spread of a more serious infection and the formation of a scar. A boil around the nose or face can be particularly serious and should be treated with antibiotics by a doctor. Most other boils should be treated with moist heat to cause spontaneous rupture and drainage. The pus contains staphylococcus bacteria and should not be allowed to spread the infection.

Blisters are fluid-filled skin eruptions that may be caused by allergy, injury, sunburn, insect bites, infection, friction, irritation, or drug reaction. Correcting the cause is important if the cause is an infection, allergy, or drug reaction. Most ordinary blisters can be treated with a mild antiseptic and a protective dressing. Do not puncture a blister. If the blister is accidentally broken, treat it as a wound.

BURNS

Burns can be caused by contact with heat, chemicals, electricity, or radiation. One of the effects is "burn shock," in which body fluid is diverted from normal blood flow to the brain, heart, and other vital organs to the burned area of the body. Burn shock is the same as physical or psychological shock and can even follow severe sunburn. Small thermal burns, as those caused from fire, steam, or touching a hot object, usually result in pain, a reddened skin area, and blisters. In many cases, the burn can be treated with ice or cold water. Do not try to open a blister. It can be protected by a pad held in place with a loose bandage.

In addition to all of the riches found in King Tut's tomb, archaeologists also found a personal first-aid kit that included bandages and a finger sling.

Never apply ointments or grease, including butter or margarine, baking soda, or other household substances, to a burned skin area.

A severe or extensive thermal burn requires professional care in a hospital. A doctor and/or emergency personnel should be summoned. While waiting for professional medical care, the victim should be made to lie down with the head and chest lower than the legs (shock position). Cover the burned area with a clean cloth to exclude air. Infection is a common complication if the skin is broken. If the victim is conscious and can swallow, provide adequate non-alcoholic liquids to drink. Because of burn shock, body tissues require fluid replacement. See "Lifesaving Procedures: Preventing Shock" earlier in this chapter.

FIRST- AND SECOND-DEGREE BURNS

First-degree burns are marked by redness or other skin discoloration, pain, and swelling. An ordinary sunburn is typical of a first-degree burn. These burns generally are treated as small thermal burns and usually will heal with the application of cold water followed by a dry dressing.

Second-degree burns are often the result of exposure to flame, scalding liquids, or a very severe sunburn. The skin is usually reddish, mottled, and damaged, with signs of body fluid loss. These burns are treated as extensive thermal burns, requiring professional medical care.

THIRD-DEGREE BURNS

Third-degree burns are marked by damage to tissues beneath the skin. The area may resemble a second-degree burn at first, but it quickly progresses to a whitish or charred coloration. Third-degree burns often result from contact with high-voltage electricity, steam, or boiling water, or from an accident in which the person is trapped in burning clothing. A third-degree burn is a true medical emergency. While ice or cold water may be used as a first-aid measure for first- or second-degree burns, nothing should be applied to a third-degree burn. Do not even remove clothing from burn areas. Burn areas can be covered temporarily, however, with sterile dressings, clean sheets, or even plastic garment bags. Do not put plastic materials over facial burns.

If the third-degree burn victim is conscious and not vomiting, small amounts of fluid should be offered.

The recommended beverage is lukewarm water containing a teaspoon of salt and one-half teaspoon of baking soda per quart of liquid, to be sipped at a rate of one ounce every four or five minutes while waiting for professional medical help.

The first known dentists were the Etruscans, who in 700 B.C. carved false teeth from mammals' teeth and created partial bridges that could be used to eat.

CHEMICAL BURNS

Chemical burns, either acid or alkali, are generally corrosive reactions that tend to affect the skin, eyes, and digestive tract. They usually result from spills, leaks, and splashes. A strong acid or alkali can cause permanent tissue damage. An alkali burn may be more serious than an acid burn because an acid usually is neutralized by contact with body tissues, whereas an alkali can continue causing damage until it is neutralized by another substance or washed away with copious amounts of water.

As a result, all chemical burns should be flooded—not merely rinsed—with water. It is usually important to remove contaminated clothing, which tends to absorb the chemical and hold it next to the skin, exacerbating the damage. Water flooding should continue while clothing is being removed. If possible, insert a hose under the clothing to inject water between the skin and the contaminated fabric.

CHOKING

Obstruction of the airways leading to the lungs can be caused by food, candy, chewing gum, or other objects accidentally inhaled. If air is unable to reach the lungs, the body's oxygen supply can become exhausted in a few minutes, resulting in death.

(*Note:* A person whose windpipe [trachea] is blocked cannot talk but must make those around aware that he or she is choking, using sign language or any other means so that first aid can be given immediately.)

First Aid

There are two accepted ways of giving first aid to a choking person.

1. The Heimlich maneuver, which consists of a series of thrusts to the upper abdomen. Stand behind the victim and put your arms around his or her upper abdomen so that your hands can be clasped in a fist at the bottom of the victim's breastbone. Then quickly push your fist upward into the victim's chest, putting pressure on the lungs so that any air in them will be squeezed backward up into the windpipe, pushing the obstruction into the mouth. The Heimlich maneuver may have to be repeated six or more times to dislodge a foreign body in the throat. If the victim is pregnant or very obese, the rescue pressure should be directed through the chest rather than the abdomen.

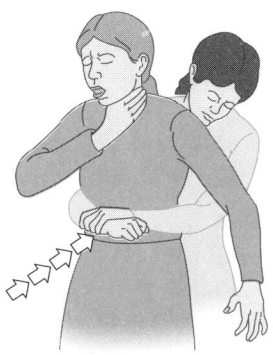

2. Firm blows over the spinal column between the shoulder blades. Stand behind the choking person and help him or her lean over, using one hand on the victim's chest to lend support.

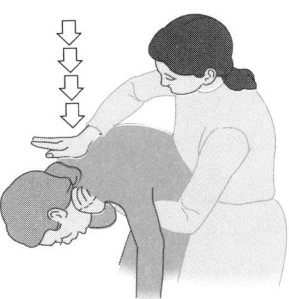

Then hit high on the back with the heel of your hand. Four or more back blows may be needed to dislodge the object in the windpipe.

CONCUSSIONS

A concussion can result from a head injury and may be accompanied by a brief or longer period of unconsciousness. The victim may experience headache, blurred vision, or other signs of nervous system damage and may lapse into a coma. The victim, even if conscious, should be treated as an unconscious person. Keep the person quiet and warm, watch for signs of shock, and help maintain breathing if necessary while awaiting arrival of a doctor or emergency medical service (EMS) personnel.

CONVULSIONS

A convulsion, or seizure, involves a disturbance of the nervous system that affects the muscles of movement. The person experiencing a convulsive seizure will lose consciousness and may have uncontrollable twitching of the muscles, or the muscles may become rigidly contracted. There are different kinds of seizures and many possible causes. In general, however, first aid should be aimed at keeping the victim safe until the seizure ends naturally. Keep calm and reassure other people who may be nearby. Clear the area of anything hard or sharp to lessen the chance of the victim hurting themselves. Remove glasses, if any, and loosen any tight neckware. Cushion the head and turn the person gently onto their side to help keep the airway open. You should not place anything in the victim's mouth, or restrain their movements, during or after the seizure. Meanwhile, keep track of the time; if the seizure lasts more than five minutes, or if the person has more than one seizure after another, summon a doctor or EMS personnel.

DROWNING

Drowning is a form of asphyxiation due to an inability of the victim to get oxygen into the lungs. It may also be complicated by inhalation of fluid into the lungs. First aid for a drowning victim requires

CPR procedures to maintain breathing and circulation. Do not waste time trying to squeeze water out of the lungs, particularly if the accident occurred in freshwater. If the victim has been in seawater, try to keep the body positioned with the head and chest lower than the abdomen and legs to assist fluid drainage from the lungs. See the "Methods of Cardiopulmonary Resuscitation (CPR)" sidebar earlier in this chapter.

ELECTRIC SHOCK

Severe electric shock can be caused by contact with ordinary electric lines in a home, office, or factory, as well as by high-voltage lines or a lightning bolt. An electric charge can have a number of effects on the body, including muscular contractions or seizures, paralysis of the lungs, abnormal heart function, bone fractures, thermal burns, and changes in blood chemistry.

Saving a person from further injury or death by electrocution should be done carefully so that the rescuer does not also become a victim. The electric shock victim first must be safely separated from contact with the electricity by turning the electricity off or by removing a wire or electric appliance with an insulated tool, such as a dry stick. In some cases, it may be easier to throw a loop of rope or cloth about the victim's arm or leg and drag him or her away from the source of electricity. However, do not go within 20 feet of a person who is being electrocuted by high-voltage electrical currents until the power is turned off. If the victim is alive but unconscious, summon a doctor or EMS personnel. If breathing has stopped or there is no pulse, begin CPR immediately while awaiting the arrival of medical professionals.

FRACTURES, DISLOCATIONS, AND SPRAINS

Fractures, dislocations, and sprains generally will require the use of splints and, for arm injuries, slings to prevent movement. Splints can be made with wood, pillows, or rolled-up newspaper, if necessary. See illustrations on page 488.

A *fracture* is a broken bone. If medical help is not available, these emergency treatment methods should be followed:

- Call an ambulance.
- While waiting for professional medical help, prevent movement by splinting the injury in the position in which you found it. No attempt should be made to try to reset a broken bone.
- If the broken bone punctures the skin, control the bleeding with direct pressure. Cover the wound with sterile dressing and secure it in place. See the "Pressure Points" sidebar under "Preventing Loss of Blood" earlier in the chapter.
- Keep the person warm and watch closely for signs of shock.

A *dislocation* is an injury in which a bone is displaced from its proper position at a joint. Suspect a dislocation if the injured part is swollen or visibly out of shape, or if the person is in intense pain and cannot put weight on the injured part. If medical help is not available, these emergency methods should be followed:

- Without an X ray, it is difficult to tell whether a bone is dislocated or fractured, so treat the injury as if a fracture has occurred. To prevent movement, splint the joint in the position in which you found it. Do not try to correct the dislocation yourself. See "Preventing Shock" earlier in the chapter.
- Take the person to an emergency room for an X ray and examination.

"Health and Nutrition" in chapter 18
Go to

Leg Splint

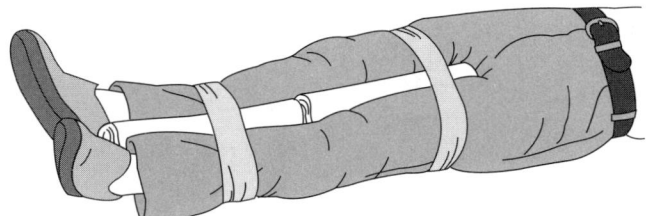

Arm Splint

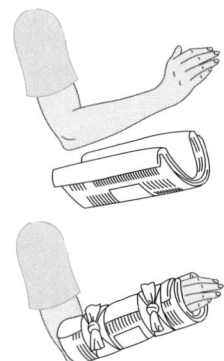

Splint and Sling Combinations

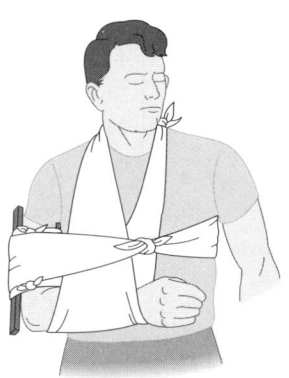

Sprain Treatment

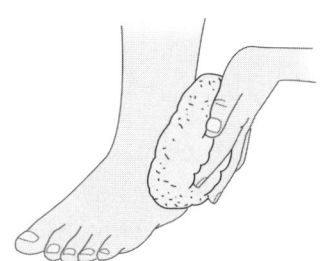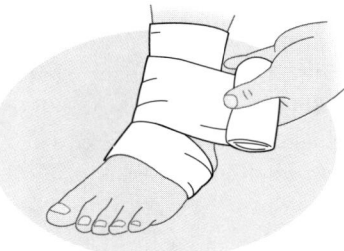

TREATMENT OF SPRAINS

A *sprain* is an injury to the ligaments. It occurs when a ligament or muscle is wrenched or twisted outside its normal range of movement and ligaments are torn. For a serious sprain, which may be indistinguishable from a fracture, treat the injury as if a fracture has occurred. For less severe, less painful sprains, follow these emergency methods:

- Do not let the person stand on or use the injured body part.
- Apply ice and compress the injury to decrease swelling.
- Support and immobilize the sprain with an elastic bandage.
- Keep the sprain elevated with either a pillow or sling.

FROSTBITE

The most common cold-weather injury is frostbite. Severe cold can constrict the blood vessels, thereby reducing the normal flow of warm blood to the exposed tissues. The symptoms usually include a very cold feeling in the exposed skin area followed by a loss of feeling. The skin may appear flushed or red at first, but later it becomes white or a grayish yellow. Because of the loss of feeling, the victim is often unaware of the danger of frostbite.

The victim should be taken into a warm environment, and all tight or wet clothing in the affected body area should be removed. The frostbitten area should be immersed in warm—but not extremely hot—water (experts recommend a water temperature of around 105°F).

You can offer the victim hot coffee, tea, cocoa, or soup, but smoking should be avoided because it has an effect similar to that of cold, causing constriction of blood vessels. Do not rub the frostbitten tissues. If bleeding, swelling from fluid accumulation, or other complications develop after the exposed areas have thawed, notify a doctor immediately.

HEAT CRAMPS, HEAT EXHAUSTION, HEATSTROKE

Prolonged exposure to high temperatures can lead to several life-threatening health problems. The most serious effects are heat exhaustion and heatstroke. *Heat cramps* are usually in the form of painful muscle spasms caused by excessive sweating and loss of body salt. The skin may be hot and dry or cool and clammy. In most cases, heat cramps can be treated with food and liquid containing sodium chloride (ordinary table salt).

Heat exhaustion, or heat prostration, is due to loss of body fluid. It is marked by nausea, weakness, excessive sweating, and faintness. The skin is pale and clammy, the pulse is weak, and the victim may show signs of shock. The loss of body fluid results in loss of blood volume and, in turn, a deficiency of oxygenated blood reaching the brain. Have the victim lie flat with the head down and give him or her small sips of cool, slightly salted liquids every few minutes. Do not give the victim too much fluid too rapidly.

Heatstroke, or sunstroke, is the most serious type of heat injury. It may begin suddenly with headache, dizziness, and fatigue. The skin is hot, dry, and flushed, and the pulse is extremely rapid. The victim can develop a very high fever of around 105°F, experience convulsions, or become unconscious. Unless first aid is given immediately, the person may suffer circulatory collapse and die. Cool the body by wrapping the victim in wet clothing or bedding. Use snow or ice, if available, or immerse the person in cool water while awaiting the arrival of an emergency medical service (EMS) crew or a physician. Check the victim's temperature every 10 minutes to make sure the body temperature does not fall too rapidly. Hypothermia, or excessively cold body temperature, could complicate the condition.

INSECT BITES

Bites or stings of ants, bees, hornets, wasps, yellow jackets, mosquitoes, and other insects usually result in the injection of substances under the skin of the person attacked. The body's reaction may vary from mild itching to a severe form of shock, depending on the venom or other foreign protein injected and the sensitivity of the person to the substance. Some hypersensitive persons can experience an extreme allergic reaction, known as *anaphylactic shock*, marked by breathing difficulty or circulatory failure within a few minutes after a bite or sting. Such individuals require special prescription drugs that should be carried when they expect to be near stinging or biting insects.

For most people who experience insect bites and stings, first aid may require only the application of ice or a cold compress to slow the rate of venom absorption. If the insect leaves its stinger in the skin, remove it with care, as the venom sac usually is still attached and should not be squeezed.

Ticks and other insects that may cling to the skin may require application of a petroleum product or similar irritant in order to remove them. In addition to causing local pain, swelling, and irritation, bites of ticks and other insects can result in serious infections requiring hospitalization.

NOSEBLEEDS

Nosebleeds are usually caused by rupture of the numerous capillaries in the soft tissues near the tip of the nose. A nosebleed may be started by an injury, high blood pressure, physical activity, or sudden change in atmospheric pressure, as may occur in traveling from sea level to a mountaintop. First aid requires keeping the victim quiet and in a seated position with the head leaning forward. Apply pressure to the outside of the bleeding nostril, or insert gauze pads in one or both nostrils and squeeze the outside of the nose toward the midline. Also, apply ice or a cold compress to the nose and surrounding areas of the face. If the nose continues to bleed, notify a doctor.

POISONING

A poison is anything that may be injurious to health or dangerous to life if it is swallowed, inhaled, or touched by the skin. Common sources of poisons include contaminated foods, carbon-monoxide gas, cleaning products and solvents, certain household plants, pesticides, and medicines.

In any case of a swallowed poison, the container of food or other substance should be saved, with the label and any remaining contents, so that doctors or poison control center personnel can recommend the most rapid and effective treatment.

First aid for most cases of swallowed poisons depends on the type of substance involved and the condition of the victim. Do not try to induce vomiting in any poisoning victim if he or she is unconscious or having convulsions.

"Directory of Poison Control Centers" in this chapter; **"Poisonous Cultivated and Wild Plants"** in chapter 3; **"Disposal of Hazardous Household Chemicals"** in chapter 19

CORROSIVE POISONS

Do not induce vomiting if the victim may have swallowed a corrosive substance, such as an acid or alkali, or has a burning pain in the mouth or throat. Examples of corrosive substances are toilet-bowl cleaners, drain cleaners, lye, washing soda, and chlorine bleach.

- Do not attempt to "neutralize" swallowed acids or alkalis.
- Do not use activated charcoal for swallowed corrosive poisons.
- Do give the victim adequate amounts of milk or water.
- Do begin CPR if breathing stops.

FOOD POISONING

Food poisoning may be caused by enterotoxins, or poisons produced by bacteria that may or may not still be in the food. Symptoms usually include nausea and vomiting, cramps, diarrhea, fever, and headache, which may begin minutes to hours after the food has been eaten.

First aid in most cases includes bed rest, preferably close to a bathroom, and avoidance of any food or beverage until vomiting has stopped. When vomiting has ended, the victim should be offered sweetened tea or soft drinks and strained broth or bouillon with a little salt added. It is important to replace the body fluids and electrolytes (minerals) lost in vomiting or diarrhea.

In addition to vomiting, cramps, or diarrhea, symptoms of poisoning may include loss of consciousness, confusion or disorientation, an unusual odor on the breath, pain or a burning sensation in the mouth or throat, and stains or discoloration in or about the mouth from the leaves or berries of poisonous plants.

If the symptoms are severe, with signs of shock or the presence of blood or mucus in the diarrhea, a doctor should be notified.

A potentially fatal form of food poisoning that does not always cause vomiting or diarrhea is botulism. It is caused by a bacteria-produced poison, usually found in home-canned or processed foods. Botulism attacks the nervous system. The victim may feel no symptoms for a day or two and then experience visual problems, dry mouth and swallowing difficulty, and constipation as the poison gradually paralyzes various organ systems. Immediate hospitalization is needed to prevent the spread of the paralyzing effects to the respiratory system.

INHALED POISONS

A common type of inhaled poison is carbon-monoxide gas, as produced by a car or truck engine in a confined area or by a faulty furnace or fireplace. The first symptoms are usually headache, yawning, breathing difficulty, dilated pupils, dizziness, faintness, ringing in the ears (tinnitus), nausea, and heart palpitations, followed by loss of consciousness. A distinctive sign is a cherry-red coloring of the mucous membranes. Persons with a light complexion may show a similar bright red coloring of the skin.

In the 16th century, people believed that a piece of red coral would stop bleeding, cure madness, and protect against curses.

First aid requires fresh air and oxygen. Give mouth-to-mouth resuscitation until an emergency medical service (EMS) unit can arrive to provide 100-percent oxygen by mask. Do not give any stimulants, but keep the victim warm and as quiet as possible.

In rescuing a person from an inhaled poison, such as smoke or carbon monoxide, protect yourself against becoming a victim of the same dangerous situation. Be sure that oxygen is available by opening doors or windows of an enclosed space. If possible, carry an independent air supply if you must enter a confined or overheated area to rescue a victim of inhaled poisons. Alternatively, place a wet cloth over your nose and mouth. When a second res-

cuer is present, tie a rope around your waist and give the other end to the second rescuer, who can pull you to safety if you also are overcome by poisonous fumes.

NONCORROSIVE POISONS

Most medicines, such as aspirin, may be noncorrosive poisons. Generally, the doctor may recommend that you try to induce vomiting if the person has swallowed a noncorrosive poison that is not a petroleum distillate product. If you do not know whether the swallowed substance is corrosive or noncorrosive—or even if it is actually poisonous—call a poison control center.

To induce vomiting, use syrup of ipecac (1 tablespoon for a child; 2 tablespoons for an adult) when it is available. The syrup of ipecac should be followed with one or more 8-ounce glasses of water.

If the person does not vomit within 15 minutes after one dose of syrup of ipecac, repeat the dose.

If syrup of ipecac is not available, use soapy water or a handwashing liquid detergent dissolved in water, or place the handle of a spoon or your finger at the back of the victim's throat. If the victim is a child, hold the child with the head lower than the hips while you induce vomiting. This position will reduce the chance of vomit entering the lungs.

Save a sample of the vomit so that it can be analyzed in a medical laboratory.

PETROLEUM DISTILLATES

For swallowed petroleum distillates, such as gasoline, kerosene, lighter fluid, paint thinner, or furniture polish, call the nearest poison control center or hospital emergency room immediately for specific instructions. The exact type and amount of the poison may determine the treatment. Some products contain more than one kind of poison.

Symptoms may include coughing, choking, cyanosis (blue skin), breath holding, a burning sensation in the stomach, lethargy, coma, convulsions, and spontaneous vomiting.

- Do not induce vomiting. There is a great risk that some of the vomited poison may enter the lungs; some hydrocarbon products are more than a hundred times as poisonous in the lungs as in the digestive tract.
- Do, if recommended by a doctor, give the person a glass of milk to dilute the poison and reduce stomach irritation.

PLANT POISONS

The major contact poison plants in North America are poison ivy, poison oak, and poison sumac. They are usually identified by their clusters of three shiny leaflets. Signs and symptoms of contact with these plants include itching skin and blisters. These are effects of a poisonous resin in the leaves. Some first-aid relief can be had by diluting and washing away the resin with a strong laundry soap and water. Follow-up treatments can include moistened dressings, starch baths, or oatmeal baths to relieve the itching. Do not break the blisters. If the blisters are oozing and crusting, exposing them to dry air may give some relief. More serious adverse effects can result from chewing the leaves of poison ivy or inhaling the smoke of plants being burned. Swallowing or inhaling the resin causes painful swelling of the lining of the throat, accompanied by fever and weakness. The symptoms may require professional medical treatment.

A study of American coins and currency revealed the presence of bacteria, including staphylococcus, E. coli, and klebsiella, on 18% of the coins and 7% of the bills.

SNAKEBITES

Most snakebites should be treated like those of any wild animal. If the bite is from a poisonous snake, the symptoms may vary according to the type of snake and its venom. But most poisonous snake bites will be followed immediately by an intense pain and a feeling of numbness in the bite area. The bite

of a pit viper, such as a rattlesnake, cottonmouth, or copperhead, is often identified by fang punctures about one-half inch apart. Such a bite may also produce swelling. Other snakebites may or may not leave fang marks. A wound from the bite of a coral snake may show a chewing action of the snake's jaws.

In general, a snakebite victim should remain still. Any body movement will tend to increase the spread of venom. If the bite is in an arm or leg, the limb should be immobilized and kept lower than the level of the heart. If a hospital or other medical facility is less than 30 to 40 minutes away, the victim should be delivered there for professional care as quickly as possible. Other first-aid measures are suggested only for cases in which a doctor or hospital is not easily available.

A constriction band should be tied around the arm or leg a few inches above the bite and between the bite and the heart. The bite may be washed with soap and water and covered with a sterile dressing. Ice or a cold compress can be applied, but not directly over the bite. As in any other serious injury, the victim should be monitored closely for signs of shock. In some cases, an incision can be made in the bite area for removal of some of the venom by suction. Incision and suction, however, should be performed only if a doctor is not available and immediately after the bite has been inflicted. The person making the incision should be aware that when cutting into an arm or leg, there is a high risk of causing permanent damage to nerves, blood vessels, muscles, or other tissue.

DIRECTORY OF POISON CONTROL CENTERS

Following is a list of poison control centers and state offices that can refer you to local poison control centers. Also, check your local phone directory for nearby centers or call 800-222-1222, a national poison control number that will route your call to the nearest available center in the United States.

UNITED STATES

Alabama

Alabama Poison Center
205-345-0600
800-462-0800 (Alabama only)

Regional Poison Control Center
The Children's Hospital of Alabama
205-939-9201
205-933-4050
800-292-6678 (Alabama only)

Alaska

Anchorage Poison Center
Providence Hospital Pharmacy
907-261-3193
800-478-3193 (Alaska only)

Arizona

Arizona Poison and Drug Information Center
Arizona Health Sciences Center
520-626-6016
800-362-0101 (Arizona only)

Samaritan Regional Poison Center
Good Samaritan Regional Medical Center
602-253-3334
800-362-0101 (Arizona only)

Arkansas

Arkansas Poison and Drug Information Center
University of Arkansas for Medical Sciences
501-686-5540
800-376-4766 (Arkansas only)

California

California Poison Control System
800-876-4766 (800-8-POISON) (California only)

Colorado

Rocky Mountain Poison and Drug Center
303-629-1123

Connecticut

University of Connecticut Health Center
203-674-3056
800-343-2722 (Connecticut only)

Delaware

The Poison Control Center
215-386-2100

District of Columbia

National Capital Poison Center
202-625-3333

Florida

The Florida Poison Information Center
Tampa General Hospital
813-256-4444
800-282-3171 (Florida only)

Georgia

Georgia Poison Center
Hughes Spalding Children's Hospital
404-616-9000
800-282-5846 (Georgia only)

Hawaii

Hawaii Poison Center
808-941-4411

Idaho

Idaho Poison Center
208-334-4570
800-632-8000 (Idaho only)

Illinois

BroMenn Poison Control Center
BroMenn Regional Medical Center
309-454-6666

Regional Poison Control Center
Rush-Presbyterian-St. Luke's Medical Center
312-942-5969
800-942-5969

Indiana

Indiana Poison Center
317-929-2323
800-382-9097 (Indiana only)

Iowa

Poison Information Center
515-241-6254
800-362-2327 (Iowa only)

Kansas

Mid-American Poison Control Center
University of Kansas Medical Center
913-588-6633
800-332-6633 (Kansas only)

Kentucky

Kentucky Regional Poison Center
Kosair Children's Hospital
502-589-8222
800-722-5725 (Kentucky only)

Louisiana

Louisiana Drug and Poison Information Center
Northeast Louisiana University
318-362-5393
800-256-9822 (Louisiana only)

Maine

Maine Poison Control Center
207-871-2950
800-442-6305 (Maine only)

Maryland

Maryland Poison Center
410-528-7701
800-492-2414 (Maryland only)
    For DC suburbs, see **District of Columbia**

Massachusetts

Massachusetts Poison Control System
617-232-2120
800-682-9211

Michigan

Blodgett Regional Poison Center
800-632-2727 (Michigan only)

Poison Control Center
Children's Hospital of Michigan
313-745-5711
800-764-7661

Minnesota

Hennepin Regional Poison Center
Hennepin County Medical Center
612-347-3141
Pet line: 612-337-7387

Minnesota Regional Poison Center
St. Paul-Ramsey Medical Center
612-221-2113

Mississippi

Mississippi Regional Poison Control Center
University of Mississippi Medical Center
601-354-7660

Missouri

Regional Poison Center
Cardinal Glennon Children's Hospital
314-772-5200
800-366-8888

Montana

Rocky Mountain Poison and Drug Center
303-629-1123

Nebraska

The Poison Center
402-390-5555
800-955-9119 (Nebraska and Wyoming only)

Nevada

Rocky Mountain Poison and Drug Center
303-629-1123 (Southern Nevada)

Washoe Medical Center
702-328-4129 (Northern Nevada)

New Hampshire

New Hampshire Poison Information Center
Dartmouth Hitchcock Medical Center
603-650-8000
800-562-8236 (New Hampshire only)

New Jersey

New Jersey Poison Information and Education System
800-764-7661

New Mexico

New Mexico Poison and Drug Information Center
University of New Mexico
505-843-2551
800-432-6866 (New Mexico only)

New York

Central New York Poison Control Center
SUNY Health Science Center
315-476-4766
800-252-5655

Finger Lakes Regional Poison Center
University of Rochester Medical Center
716-275-5151
800-333-0542

Hudson Valley Poison Center
Phelps Memorial Hospital Center
914-336-3030
800-336-6997

New York City Poison Control Center
N.Y.C. Department of Health
212-340-4494

Western New York Regional Poison Control Center
Children's Hospital of Buffalo
716-878-7654, 7655, 7856, 7857

North Carolina

Carolinas Poison Center
704-355-4000
800-848-6946

Duke Poison Control Center
North Carolina Regional Center
919-684-8111
800-672-1697 (North Carolina only)

North Dakota

North Dakota Poison Information Center
701-234-5575
800-732-2200 (North Dakota, Minnesota and South
Dakota only)

Ohio

Central Ohio Poison Center
614-228-1323
800-682-7625

Cincinnati Drug & Poison Information Center
and Regional Poison Control System
513-558-5111
800-872-5111 (Ohio only)

Oklahoma

Oklahoma Poison Control Center
405-271-5454
800-522-4611 (Oklahoma only)

Oregon

Oregon Poison Center
Oregon Health Sciences University
503-494-8968
800-452-7165 (Oregon only)

First Aid

A Closer Look

The Signs and Signals of Heart Attacks and Strokes

Heart-Attack Warning Signs

- Uncomfortable pressure, fullness, squeezing, or pain in the center of the chest lasting two minutes or more
- Spreading of pain to shoulders, neck, or arms
- Severe pain, dizziness, fainting, sweating, nausea, or shortness of breath

Not all of these signals are always present. Don't wait! Get help immediately.

Stroke Warning Signs

- Sudden, temporary weakness or numbness of the face, arm, and leg on one side of the body
- Temporary loss of speech, or trouble speaking or understanding speech
- Temporary dimness or loss of vision, particularly in one eye
- Unexplained dizziness, unsteadiness, or sudden falls

Many major strokes are preceded by "little strokes," warning signals, like the above, experienced days, weeks, or months before the more severe event.

In Case of Emergency

- If you are having chest discomfort that lasts for two minutes or more, call the emergency medical service (EMS) in your area.
- If you can get to a hospital faster by car, have someone drive you.

Before an Emergency

- Find out which hospitals in your area offer 24-hour emergency cardiac care.
- Select in advance the facility nearest your home and office, and tell your family and friends so that they will know what to do.
- Keep a list of emergency rescue service numbers next to your telephone and in a prominent place in your pocket, wallet, or purse.

Pennsylvania

Central Pennsylvania Poison Center
University Hospital
717-531-6111
800-521-6110

Pittsburgh Poison Center
412-681-6669

The Poison Control Center (greater Philadelphia
metropolitan area)
215-386-2100
800-722-7112

Rhode Island

Rhode Island Poison Center
401-444-5727

South Carolina

Palmetto Poison Center
College of Pharmacy
University of South Carolina
803-765-7359
800-922-1117 (South Carolina only)

South Dakota

McKennan Poison Control
605-336-3894
800-952-0123 (South Dakota only)

Tennessee

Middle Tennessee Regional Poison Center
Vanderbilt University Medical Center
615-936-2034
800-288-9999

Texas

North Texas Poison Center
800-746-7661

Texas Poison Control Network at Galveston
The University of Texas Medical Branch
409-765-1420 (Galveston)
713-654-1701 (Houston)
800-764-7661 (Texas only)

Utah

Utah Poison Control Center
801-581-2151
800-456-7707 (Utah only)

Vermont

Vermont Poison Center
802-658-3456

Virginia

Blue Ridge Poison Center
University of Virginia
804-924-5543
800-451-1428

Georgetown University Hospital
202-625-3333

Virginia Poison Center
Virginia Commonwealth University
804-828-9123
800-552-6337 (Virginia only)

Washington

Washington Poison Center
Children's Hospital and Medical Center
206-526-2121
800-732-6985 (Washington only)

West Virginia

West Virginia Poison Center
304-348-4211
800-642-3625 (West Virginia only)

Wisconsin

Poison Center
Children's Hospital of Wisconsin
414-266-2222
800-815-8855 (Wisconsin only)

Poison Center
University Hospital
608-262-3702
800-815-8855 (Wisconsin only)

Wyoming

The Poison Center
402-390-5555
800-955-9119 (Wyoming and Nebraska only)

First Aid

CANADA

British Columbia
B. C. Drug and Poison Information Centre
604-682-5050
800-567-8911

Ontario
Ontario Regional Poison Control Centre
The Hospital for Sick Children
416-813-5900
800-268-9017 (Ontario only)

Nova Scotia and Prince Edward Island
Poison Information Centre
902-428-8161 (Nova Scotia)
800-565-8161 (Prince Edward Island)

Quebec
Quebec Poison Control Center
418-656-8090

ADDITIONAL SOURCES OF INFORMATION

ORGANIZATIONS AND SERVICES
American College of Emergency Physicians
P.O. Box 619911
Dallas, TX 75261-9911
800-798-1822
http://www.acep.org

American Medical Association
515 N. State St.
Chicago, IL 60610
312-464-5000
http://www.ama-assn.org

American National Red Cross
17th and D Sts., NW
Washington, DC 20006
703-206-6000
http://www.redcross.org/index.html

National Association of Emergency Medical Technicians
102 W. Leake St.
Clinton, MS 39056-4252
800-346-2368
http://www.naemt.org

National Safety Council First Aid Institute
1121 Spring Lake Drive
Itasca, IL 60143
800-621-6244
http://www.nsc.org

BOOKS

Brown, Andrew J. *First Aid: Principles and Practices.* Macmillan, 1987.

Clayman, Charles. *The American Medical Association Family Medical Guide.* 3rd ed. Random House, 1994.

Handal, Kathleen. *The American Red Cross First Aid and Safety Handbook.* Little Brown, 1992.

Jagoda, Andy, *The Good Housekeeping Family First Aid Book.* ACMD Publishing Book, Hearst Books, 2000.

Thygerson, Alton L. *National Safety Council First Aid Handbook.* Jones and Bartlett Publishers, 1995.

Zydio, Stanley, and James A. Hill. *The American Medical Association Handbook of First Aid and Emergency Care.* Random House, 1990.

First Aid

18

HEALTH AND NUTRITION

QUESTIONS TO ASK YOUR DOCTOR

"I wish I'd asked the doctor about that" is a common lament after routine checkups and more serious consultations as well. Ambiguous symptoms that may indicate illness, such as pain, changes in emotional stability, or changes in eating or sleeping habits, should be reported. Your physician may need to be reminded of important facts about your family history, previous health problems, and other factors that can affect diagnosis and treatment. Many professionals suggest making a list of health-related questions/concerns before seeing the doctor. Consider the following for inclusion in your list.

At routine checkups—individual concerns related to problems experienced since the last visit:

- I have been experiencing _____ [headaches, back pain, unexplained drowsiness, trouble sleeping, dizziness, etc.]. What could that mean? What do you recommend?
- I have a family history of _____ [heart disease, diabetes, high blood pressure, breast cancer, etc.]. Could my symptoms indicate that I am developing a problem?

Other general areas of concern:

- What are my cholesterol levels? What should they be? What do my numbers mean?
- What is my blood pressure? What should it be? What do my numbers mean?
- Do I need medication? How long will I need to take it?
- Do I need to make any major lifestyle changes [stop smoking, modify activities, stop/start/change exercise program, change diet, etc.]?

When X rays, blood tests, or other types of tests are recommended:

- Why do I need to have this test? What will the results tell you?
- Are there any risks involved in having this test performed?

- When and how will I get the results? Depending on the results, what treatment or other tests may be recommended?
- Will the test be painful? How long will it take?
- How should I prepare for the test? Can it be scheduled early in the morning if overnight fasting is required? What about other medications I am taking? Should I take them while fasting for the test? Can I drink water to swallow my pills? [If you are diabetic or take any medication that must be taken with food or liquid, remind the doctor of your situation and get specific instructions, especially when consulting a specialist who is not your regular physician.]
- How much will the test cost?

When immunization or nonsurgical treatment is recommended:

- What are the benefits of this treatment?
- Are there any risks involved with this treatment? What physical or emotional side effects can I expect?
- Are there other treatments with fewer side effects or risks that I should consider?
- What will this treatment cost?
- How can I tell if the treatment is working?

About medication:

- What are the risks/benefits associated with this medication?
- How will this medication interact with prescriptions I am already taking? Should I avoid alcohol or certain foods?
- Please explain exactly how this medication is to be taken. In the morning or night? With food or milk, or on an empty stomach? What if I forget to take it?
- Is this medication expensive? Would a generic prescription be as effective?
- How will I know if the medication is working? What problems should I call you about?

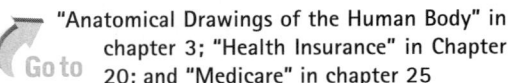

"Anatomical Drawings of the Human Body" in chapter 3; "Health Insurance" in Chapter 20; and "Medicare" in chapter 25

Go to

Health/Nutrition

Shelf Life of Medicine

A Closer Look

Pharmacists generally do not mark containers with expiration dates, although the containers usually show the dates of the original prescriptions. If a prescription drug is more than one year old but is not in its original container clearly showing the expiration date, it should be replaced. First-aid creams in tubes usually have expiration dates marked on the tubes, but the dates are generally hard to see. After the components separate, the creams should not be used. Vitamins and minerals will keep for a long time if protected from heat, moisture, and light. A good rule of thumb about the shelf life of drugs is "When in doubt, throw it out." Following is a list of the shelf life of some common drugs.

Cold tablets	1–2 years
Laxatives	2–3 years
Minerals	6 years or more
Nonprescription painkiller tablets	1–4 years
Prescription antibiotics	2–3 years
Prescription antihypertension tablets	2–4 years
Travel sickness tablets	2 years
Vitamins	6 years or more

If surgery is recommended:

- What procedure are you recommending? [Ask for details about the procedure.]
- Why do I need this operation?
- Are there other types of treatment available? If so, what are they?
- What are the benefits of having the procedure?
- What are the risks involved in this procedure?
- What is the prognosis if I choose not to have surgery?
- Who will perform the operation? What experience do you (does she/he) have with this type of procedure?
- I'd like to get a second opinion. Is there someone you'd recommend that I see?
- What type of anesthesia will be used? What are the risks involved? Are there alternatives?
- Will this be performed as inpatient or outpatient surgery? [If what seems to be a major procedure will be performed on an outpatient basis, ask further questions.] How long will I be in the hospital?
- Where will the procedure be performed? Is there a good success rate for this operation at that hospital? [A hospital may have high success rates with a procedure performed there frequently, whereas another medical center nearby has less success because that type of surgery is not often scheduled.]
- How much will the surgery cost? What is your fee? [Also check with your insurance company to see how much of the cost will be covered and how much your own cost will be.]
- How should I prepare for the surgery? Can it be scheduled early in the morning if overnight fasting is required?
- What about regular medications I am taking? Should I take them before surgery? Can I drink water to swallow my pills? What about after surgery? Will I take my regular medications as usual? Should I bring my prescriptions to the hospital with me? [If you take medication for chronic conditions such as diabetes or mental/emotional illness, be sure to discuss these issues with both the surgeon and your regular physician. If new orders for your regular medications are to be written in the hospital and you will be there for an extended stay, take a list of your prescriptions with you. Once there, ask what you are being given. If the amounts or medications are unfamiliar, check with your doctor.]
- How much pain can I expect after the operation? How long will it last? Will I need medication for pain during the recovery period?

Health/Nutrition

- How long will my recovery period be? Will I need special care at home after I leave the hospital?
- Should I expect to have an emotional reaction following my surgery? What support groups or coping methods do you recommend?
- After I leave the hospital, what symptoms should I call to report? When will a follow-up visit be scheduled?
- Will there be any restrictions on my activities [driving, climbing stairs, lifting, bending, sexual intercourse, etc.]? How long will it be before I can return to work?
- What should I tell my family about the surgery?

THE PATIENT'S BILL OF RIGHTS

The provision of a written statement of patient rights has become standard practice in many health-care in-stitutions in recent years. Such documents typically emphasize the health provider's intention to treat each patient with respect, to acknowledge the patient's right to refuse treatment/make decisions concerning treatment, to provide the best available treatment regardless of an individual's ability to pay for care, and to keep each patient's medical information confidential. The issues of a person's right to self-determination (decisions concerning treatment and the right to refuse treatment) and the protection of confidential medical records are usually central. A list of the patient's responsibilities concerning care usually follows the enumeration of rights.

An example of a typical patient's bill of rights is the following document that is now law in Florida.

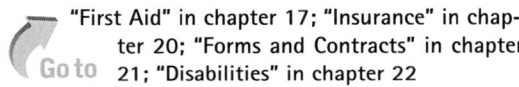 "First Aid" in chapter 17; "Insurance" in chapter 20; "Forms and Contracts" in chapter 21; "Disabilities" in chapter 22

The Patient's Bill of Rights

Each health-care facility or provider shall observe the following standards:

Individual Dignity

1. The individual dignity of a patient must be respected at all times and upon all occasions.
2. Every patient who is provided health-care services retains certain rights to privacy, which must be respected without regard to the patient's economic status or source of payment for his care. This patient's rights to privacy must be respected to the extent consistent with providing adequate medical care to the patient and with the efficient administration of the health-care facility or provider's office. However, this subparagraph does not preclude necessary and discreet discussion of a patient's case of examination by appropriate medical personnel.
3. A patient has the right to a prompt and reasonable response to a question or request. A health-care facility shall respond in a reasonable manner to the request of a patient's health-care provider for medical services to the patient. The health-care facility shall also respond in a reasonable manner to the patient's request for other services customarily rendered by the health-care facility to the extent such services do not require the approval of the patient's health-care provider or are not inconsistent with the patient's treatment.
4. A patient in a health-care facility has the right to retain and use personal clothing or possessions as space permits, unless for him to do so would infringe upon the right of another patient or is medically or programmatically contraindicated for documented medical, safety, or programmatic reasons.

Information

1. A patient has the right to know the name, function, and qualifications of each health-care provider who is providing medical services to the patient. A patient may request such information from his responsible provider or the health-care facility in which he is receiving medical services.

2. A patient in a health-care facility has the right to know what patient support services are available in the facility.

3. A patient has the right to be given by his health-care provider information concerning diagnosis, planned course of treatment, alternatives, risks, and prognosis, unless it is medically inadvisable or impossible to give this information to the patient, in which case the information must be given to the patient's guardian or a person designated as the patient's representative. A patient has the right to refuse this information.

4. A patient has the right to refuse any treatment based on information required by this paragraph, except as otherwise provided by law. The responsible provider shall document any such refusal.

5. A patient in a health-care facility has the right to know what facility rules and regulations apply to patient conduct.

6. A patient has the right to express grievances to a health-care provider, a health-care facility, or the appropriate state licensing agency regarding alleged violations of patients' rights. A patient has the right to know the health-care provider's or health-care facility's procedures for expressing a grievance.

7. A patient in a health-care facility who does not speak English has the right to be provided an interpreter when receiving medical services if the facility has a person readily available who can interpret on behalf of the patient.

Financial Information and Disclosure

1. A patient has the right to be given, upon request, by the responsible provider, his designee, or a representative of the health-care facility full information and necessary counseling on the availability of known financial resources for the patient's health care.

2. A health-care provider or a health-care facility shall, upon request, disclose to each patient who is eligible for Medicare, in advance of treatment, whether the health-care provider or the health-care facility in which the patient is receiving medical services accepts assignment under Medicare reimbursement as payment in full for medical services and treatment rendered in the health-care provider's office or health-care facility.

3. A health-care provider or a health-care facility shall, upon request, furnish a patient, prior to provision of medical services, a reasonable estimate of charges for such services. Such reasonable estimate shall not preclude the health-care provider or health-care facility from exceeding the estimate or making additional charges based upon changes in the patient's condition or treatment needs.

4. A patient has the right to receive a copy of an itemized bill upon request. A patient has a right to be given an explanation of charges upon request.

Access to Health Care

1. A patient has the right to impartial access to medical treatment or accommodations, regardless of race, national origin, religion, physical handicap, or source of payment.

2. A patient has the right to treatment for any emergency medical condition that will deteriorate from failure to provide such treatment.

Health/Nutrition

continues

The Patient's Bill of Rights, Continued

> **Experimental Research**
>
> In addition to the provisions of s. 766.103, a patient has the right to know if medical treatment is for purposes of experimental research and to consent prior to participation in such experimental research. For any patient, regardless of ability to pay or source of payment for his care, participation must be a voluntary matter; and a patient has the right to refuse to participate. The patient's consent or refusal must be documented in the patient's care record. [Florida statutes chapter 381 (026).]

APPROXIMATE DATES OF CHILDBIRTH

Find the date of the last menstrual period in the top line (lightface type) of the pair of lines. The dark number (boldface type) in the line below will be the expected day of delivery.

Jan	1 2 3 4 5 6 7 8 9 10 11 12 13 14 15 16 17 18 19 20 21 22 23 24 25 26 27 28 29 30 31	
Oct	**8 9 10 11 12 13 14 15 16 17 18 19 20 21 22 23 24 25 26 27 28 29 30 31 [1 2 3 4 5 6 7**	**Nov**
Feb	1 2 3 4 5 6 7 8 9 10 11 12 13 14 15 16 17 18 19 20 21 22 23 24 25 26 27 28	
Nov	**8 9 10 11 12 13 14 15 16 17 18 19 20 21 22 23 24 25 26 27 28 29 30 [1 2 3 4 5**	**Dec**
Mar	1 2 3 4 5 6 7 8 9 10 11 12 13 14 15 16 17 18 19 20 21 22 23 24 25 26 27 28 29 30 31	
Dec	**6 7 8 9 10 11 12 13 14 15 16 17 18 19 20 21 22 23 24 25 26 27 28 29 30 31 [1 2 3 4 5**	**Jan**
Apr	1 2 3 4 5 6 7 8 9 10 11 12 13 14 15 16 17 18 19 20 21 22 23 24 25 26 27 28 29 30	
Jan	**6 7 8 9 10 11 12 13 14 15 16 17 18 19 20 21 22 23 24 25 26 27 28 29 30 31 [1 2 3 4**	**Feb**
May	1 2 3 4 5 6 7 8 9 10 11 12 13 14 15 16 17 18 19 20 21 22 23 24 25 26 27 28 29 30 31	
Feb	**5 6 7 8 9 10 11 12 13 14 15 16 17 18 19 20 21 22 23 24 25 26 27 28 [1 2 3 4 5 6 7**	**Mar**
June	1 2 3 4 5 6 7 8 9 10 11 12 13 14 15 16 17 18 19 20 21 22 23 24 25 26 27 28 29 30	
Mar	**8 9 10 11 12 13 14 15 16 17 18 19 20 21 22 23 24 25 26 27 28 29 30 31 [1 2 3 4 5 6**	**Apr**
July	1 2 3 4 5 6 7 8 9 10 11 12 13 14 15 16 17 18 19 20 21 22 23 24 25 26 27 28 29 30 31	
Apr	**7 8 9 10 11 12 13 14 15 16 17 18 19 20 21 22 23 24 25 26 27 28 29 30 [1 2 3 4 5 6 7**	**May**
Aug	1 2 3 4 5 6 7 8 9 10 11 12 13 14 15 16 17 18 19 20 21 22 23 24 25 26 27 28 29 30 31	
May	**8 9 10 11 12 13 14 15 16 17 18 19 20 21 22 23 24 25 26 27 28 29 30 31 [1 2 3 4 5 6 7**	**June**
Sept	1 2 3 4 5 6 7 8 9 10 11 12 13 14 15 16 17 18 19 20 21 22 23 24 25 26 27 28 29 30	
June	**8 9 10 11 12 13 14 15 16 17 18 19 20 21 22 23 24 25 26 27 28 29 30 [1 2 3 4 5 6 7**	**July**
Oct	1 2 3 4 5 6 7 8 9 10 11 12 13 14 15 16 17 18 19 20 21 22 23 24 25 26 27 28 29 30 31	
July	**8 9 10 11 12 13 14 15 16 17 18 19 20 21 22 23 24 25 26 27 28 29 30 31 [1 2 3 4 5 6 7**	**Aug**
Nov	1 2 3 4 5 6 7 8 9 10 11 12 13 14 15 16 17 18 19 20 21 22 23 24 25 26 27 28 29 30	
Aug	**8 9 10 11 12 13 14 15 16 17 18 19 20 21 22 23 24 25 26 27 28 29 30 31 [1 2 3 4 5 6**	**Sept**
Dec	1 2 3 4 5 6 7 8 9 10 11 12 13 14 15 16 17 18 19 20 21 22 23 24 25 26 27 28 29 30 31	
Sept	**7 8 9 10 11 12 13 14 15 16 17 18 19 20 21 22 23 24 25 26 27 28 29 30 [1 2 3 4 5 6 7**	**Oct**

PRECAUTIONS DURING PREGNANCY

Good nutrition and prenatal medical care are essentials for maternal well-being and delivery of a healthy baby. It is also important to be aware of lifestyle habits, environmental hazards, and communicable diseases that may adversely affect the developing child. The following is a list of known risk factors for pregnancy. Consult your doctor for specifics if you are pregnant and have been exposed to one of these hazards.

ALCOHOL

Research has shown that heavy drinking during pregnancy leads to greatly increased chances of a child with fetal alcohol syndrome or some other birth defect. It is not known whether occasional social drinking is harmful to a developing fetus, so most doctors recommend against any alcohol consumption during pregnancy.

CAFFEINE

Excessive use during pregnancy may cause a baby's birth weight to be a little lower than average. Low birth weight is associated with increased vulnerability to infection and disease. Caffeine is found in tea, coffee, chocolate, some cola drinks, and some over-the-counter medications.

CHEMICALS

Prolonged exposure to lead, arsenic, formaldehyde, mercury, benzene, or ethylene oxide (or inhalation of their fumes) may increase the chances of having a miscarriage.

CHICKEN POX (VARICELLA)

When a pregnant mother develops chicken pox, the fetus has a 25 percent chance of also becoming infected. A small number of infants affected develop birth defects, including scars, eye problems, poor growth, an underdeveloped limb, small head size, delayed development, and/or mental retardation. The fetus is most at risk if the mother develops chicken pox between the eighth and twentieth weeks of pregnancy. Infection shortly before delivery can cause serious problems for the newborn, but the baby can be treated with a vaccine to prevent/lessen chicken pox's effects. The vaccine is not recommended during pregnancy, however, as its effects on the developing fetus are not yet clear.

DRUGS AND MEDICATIONS

Drug use during pregnancy can result in addicted infants who experience painful, life-threatening withdrawal symptoms after birth. In addition, some drugs and prescription and nonprescription medications may cause birth defects or complications during pregnancy and childbirth. Always consult your physician regarding pregnancy and medication usage.

"Disposal of Hazardous Household Go to Chemicals" in chapter 19; "Average Cost of Raising a Child" in chapter 20; and "Family Planning in chapter 22

FIFTH DISEASE (ERYTHEMA INFECTIOSUM)

Fifth disease is caused by a virus and occurs most often in children from ages 4 to 14. Symptoms include a mild fever, sore throat, flulike aches or pains, a bright red rash on the face, and a bumpy rash on other parts of the body. Adults often have no noticeable symptoms and children may not show symptoms until several weeks after infection. Contracting fifth disease in pregnancy (especially during the first half) can cause miscarriage, stillbirth, or heart problems if the fetus is also infected.

HOT TUBS, SAUNAS, AND STEAM BATHS

Research indicates that an increase in the mother's core body temperature may cause developmental abnormalities in the fetus, premature labor, or both. Hot showers or baths at home are okay, but saunas, steam baths, and immersion above the hips in hot tubs should be avoided.

MEASLES

Pregnant women who contract red measles (rubella) may have an increased risk of miscarriage or delivering an infant with low birth weight. Infection with German measles during pregnancy is known to put the fetus at risk for development of birth defects.

RADIATION

Avoid X rays of the abdomen whenever possible during pregnancy. X rays of the head, mouth, and extremities are permissible if medical staff are aware of your condition and take proper precautions. Also avoid environmental areas where excess radiation may be present, as prenatal exposure to radiation can cause birth defects.

Health/Nutrition

SMOKING

Research has shown that heavy smoking (more than a pack of cigarettes per day) results in smaller babies with increased vulnerability to infection and illness. Smoking during pregnancy also increases the risk of miscarriage or stillbirth. As with the use of alcohol, it is not known whether any level of smoking is completely safe for the developing fetus, so it is best to stop smoking completely before becoming pregnant.

TOXOPLASMOSIS

Toxoplasmosis is a parasitic infection usually contracted by eating undercooked infected meat, raw eggs, or unpasturized milk; handling infected soil; or handling cat litter from an outdoor cat that is infected. About 40 percent of women who become infected during pregnancy will pass the infection on to their unborn infants. Fetal infections may interfere with development of the brain, eyes, heart, kidneys, blood, liver, or spleen.

IMMUNIZATION SCHEDULE FOR INFANTS, CHILDREN, AND ADULTS

The following information is based on U.S. Preventive Services Task Force Recommendations.

Children Under 10 Years Old

Immunizations	Frequency
DTaP or DTP (Diptheria/ tetanus/pertussis[1])	5 immunizations: at 2, 4, and 6 mos., between 12–18 mos.; and once between 4–6 yrs.
Polio	4 immunizations: at 2, 4, between 6–18 mos., 4–6 yrs.
MMR (Measles, mumps, rubella)	2 immunizations: between 12–15 mos. and 4–6 yrs. If missed, give by ages 11–12.
H. influenzae[2] type B (hib)	3 or 4 immunizations, depending on the vaccine: at 2, 4, and 6 mos. and between 12–15 mos.
Hepatitis B	3 or 4 immunizations: at birth, 1, 2, and 12 mos.; or between 0–2 mos., 1–2 mos. later, and between 6–18 mos.
Varicella[3]	1 immunization: between 12–18 mos., or anytime for older children with no previous immunization and no history of chicken pox

A Closer Look

Flu Shots

Influenza, or flu, is a viral disease, thought to be spread by airborne particles from an infected person's respiratory tract. Risk of transmission is especially high in winter, when people tend to stay indoors and when temperature and humidity are low. Vaccines against influenza are available; however, because the flu virus mutates rapidly, new strains appear each year, rendering immunizations against previous years' strains ineffective. Vaccines are administered as an injection in the upper arm.

Who should get a flu shot every year?

- People over the age of 65
- Residents of long-term care facilities
- People with serious illnesses, especially chronic respiratory disease, cardiopulmonary disease, kidney disease, diabetes, or anemia
- Medical and nursing home personnel

Ages 11 to 24

Immunizations	**Frequency**
Tetanus-diphtheria (Td)	1 booster between 11–16 yrs. and then periodically [4]
Hepatitis B	If not previously immunized, 3 immunizations: at current (next) visit, 1 mo. later, and 6 mos. later
MMR	1 immunization: between 11–12 yrs. if second dose was not received at 4–6 yrs.
Varicella	1 immunization: between 11–12 yrs. if susceptible to chicken pox
Rubella	1 immunization: after 12 yrs. for females who are not pregnant

Ages 25 to 64

Rubella	1 immunization: recommended for all females of childbearing age vaccination history
Tetanus-diphtheria (Td)	1 booster every 10 yrs., or as recommended [4]

Ages 65 and Older

Tetanus-diphtheria (Td)	1 booster every 10 yrs., or as recommended [4]
Pneumonia	1 immunization: administered one time to all people whose immune systems have not been compromised [4]
Influenza	1 immunization: annually

[1] Whooping cough   [2] Influenza (the flu)   [3] Chicken pox   [4] Discuss with your physician

For more information, call the Centers for Disease Control's National Immunization Information Hot Line at 800-232-2522 (English) or 800-232-0233 (Spanish), or visit the Web site at http://www.cdc.gov/nip.

EXPECTED NUMBER OF DEATHS AT GIVEN PERIODS OF LIFE PER 100,000 INFANTS BORN ALIVE

Period of Life (Birthday to Birthday)	Number of Deaths During Interval	Number of Persons Remaining (Alive) at End of Interval
At birth	N/A	100,000
Birth to age 1	721	99,279
1 to 5	138	99,141
5 to 10	88	99,053
10 to 15	109	98,944
15 to 20	349	98,595
20 to 25	469	98,126
25 to 30	478	97,648
30 to 35	586	97,062
35 to 40	795	96,267
40 to 45	1,132	95,135
45 to 50	1,644	93,491
50 to 55	2,397	91,094
55 to 60	3,652	87,442
60 to 65	5,511	81,931
65 to 70	7,732	74,199
70 to 75	10,565	63,634
75 to 80	13,111	50,523
80 to 85	15,986	34,537
85 and above	34,537	0

Source: U.S. National Center for Health Statistics, *National Vital Statistical Report* (Vol. 48, No. 11, July 24, 2000).

Health/Nutrition

LIFE EXPECTANCY BY RACE, SEX, AND AGE

EXPECTATION OF LIFE IN YEARS

Exact Age in Years	All Races Both Sexes	Male	Female	White Both Sexes	Male	Female	Black Both Sexes	Male	Female
0	76.7	73.8	79.5	77.3	74.5	80.0	71.3	67.6	74.8
1	76.3	73.4	79.0	76.8	74.0	79.4	71.4	67.7	74.8
5	72.4	69.5	75.1	72.9	70.1	75.5	67.6	63.9	70.9
10	67.4	64.6	70.2	67.9	65.2	70.6	62.6	59.0	66.0
15	62.5	59.7	65.2	63.0	60.2	65.6	57.7	54.1	61.1
20	57.7	55.0	60.3	58.2	55.5	60.8	53.0	49.5	56.2
25	53.0	50.3	55.5	53.4	50.8	55.9	48.4	45.1	51.4
30	48.2	45.7	50.6	48.6	46.1	51.0	43.8	40.6	46.7
35	43.5	41.0	45.8	43.9	41.5	46.2	39.3	36.2	42.0
40	38.8	36.4	41.1	39.2	36.8	41.4	34.9	31.9	37.5
45	34.3	31.9	36.4	34.6	32.3	36.7	30.6	27.7	33.1
50	29.8	27.6	31.8	30.1	27.9	32.0	26.6	23.9	28.8
55	25.5	23.5	27.4	25.7	23.7	27.6	22.8	20.4	24.8
60	21.5	19.6	23.2	21.6	19.7	23.3	19.3	17.1	21.0
65	17.8	16.0	19.2	17.8	16.1	19.3	16.1	14.3	17.4
70	14.3	12.8	15.5	14.4	12.8	15.6	13.0	11.5	14.1
75	11.3	10.0	12.2	11.3	10.0	12.2	10.5	9.2	11.3
80	8.6	7.5	9.2	8.5	7.5	9.1	8.2	7.1	8.7
85	6.3	5.5	6.7	6.3	5.4	6.6	6.3	5.5	6.6
90	4.7	4.1	4.9	4.5	4.0	4.7	4.8	4.3	4.9
95	3.5	3.0	3.6	3.3	2.9	3.4	3.7	3.4	3.7
100	2.6	2.3	2.7	2.4	2.2	2.4	2.8	2.7	2.8

RECOMMENDED WEIGHTS

DETERMINING YOUR BODY MASS INDEX (BMI)

Height	Weight 100	110	120	130	140	150	160	170	180	190	200	210	220	230	240	250
5'0"	20	21	23	25	27	29	31	33	35	37	39	41	43	45	47	49
5'1"	19	21	23	25	26	28	30	32	34	36	38	40	42	43	45	47
5'2"	18	20	22	24	26	27	29	31	33	35	37	38	40	42	44	46
5'3"	18	19	21	23	25	27	28	30	32	34	35	37	39	41	43	44
5'4"	17	19	21	22	24	26	27	29	31	33	34	36	38	39	41	43
5'5"	17	18	20	22	23	25	27	28	30	32	33	35	37	38	40	42
5'6"	16	18	19	21	23	24	26	27	29	31	32	34	36	37	39	40
5'7"	16	17	19	20	22	23	25	27	28	30	31	33	34	36	38	39
5'8"	15	17	18	20	21	23	24	26	27	29	30	32	33	35	36	38
5'9"	15	16	18	19	21	22	24	25	27	28	30	31	32	34	35	37
5'10"	14	16	17	19	20	22	23	24	26	27	29	30	32	33	34	36
5'11"	14	15	17	18	20	21	22	24	25	26	28	29	31	32	33	35
6'0"	14	15	16	18	19	20	22	23	24	26	27	28	30	31	33	34
6'1"	13	15	16	17	18	20	21	22	24	25	26	28	29	30	32	33
6'2"	13	14	15	17	18	19	21	22	23	24	25	26	27	29	30	31
6'3"	12	14	15	16	17	19	20	21	22	24	25	26	27	28	29	30
6'4"	12	13	15	16	17	18	19	21	22	23	24	26	27	28	29	30

Interpretation Under 18.5 = Underweight; 18.5–24 = Normal; 25–29 = Overweight; 30 and over = Obese

To estimate your body mass index (BMI), first identify your weight (to the nearest 10 pounds) in one of the columns across the top. Then move your finger down the column until you come to the row that represents your height. Inside the square where your weight and height meet is a number that is an estimate of your BMI. For example, if you weigh 160 pounds and are 5'7", your BMI is 25.

HEIGHT AND WEIGHT CHARTS FOR CHILDREN

DESIRABLE WEIGHTS IN POUNDS FOR BOYS 5 TO 18 YEARS OLD

Height (in inches)	Age (in years)													
	5	6	7	8	9	10	11	12	13	14	15	16	17	18
38	34	34												
39	35	35												
40	36	36												
41	38	38	38											
42	39	39	39	39										
43	41	41	41	41										
44	44	44	44	44										
45	46	46	46	46	46									
46	47	48	48	48	48									
47	49	50	50	50	50	50								
48		52	53	53	53	53								
49		55	55	55	55	55	55							
50		57	58	58	58	58	58	58						
51			61	61	61	61	61	61	61					
52			63	64	64	64	64	64	64					
53			66	67	67	67	67	68	68					
54				70	70	70	70	71	71	72				
55				72	72	73	73	74	74	74				
56				75	76	77	77	77	78	78	80			
57					79	80	81	81	82	83	83			
58					83	84	84	85	85	86	87			
59						87	88	89	89	90	90	90		
60						91	92	92	93	94	95	96		
61							95	96	97	99	100	103	106	
62							100	101	102	103	104	107	111	116
63							105	106	107	108	110	113	118	123
64								109	111	113	115	117	121	126
65								114	117	118	120	122	127	131
66									119	122	125	128	132	136
67									124	128	130	134	136	139
68										134	134	137	141	143
69										137	139	143	146	149
70										143	144	145	148	151
71										148	150	151	152	154
72											153	155	156	158
73											157	160	162	164
74											160	164	168	170

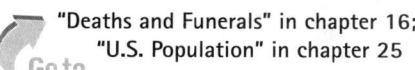
"Deaths and Funerals" in chapter 16; "U.S. Population" in chapter 25

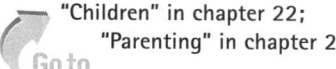
"Children" in chapter 22; "Parenting" in chapter 22

Go to   Go to

DESIRABLE WEIGHTS IN POUNDS FOR GIRLS 5 TO 18 YEARS OLD

Height (in inches)	Age (in years)													
	5	6	7	8	9	10	11	12	13	14	15	16	17	18
38	33	33												
39	34	34												
40	36	36	36											
41	37	37	37											
42	39	39	39											
43	41	41	41	41										
44	42	42	42	42										
45	45	45	45	45	45									
46	47	47	47	48	48									
47	49	50	50	50	50	50								
48		52	52	52	52	53	53							
49			54	55	55	56	56							
50			56	57	58	59	61	62						
51			59	60	61	61	63	65						
52			63	64	64	64	65	67						
53			66	67	67	68	68	69	71					
54				69	70	70	71	71	73					
55				72	74	74	74	75	77	78				
56					76	78	78	79	81	83				
57					80	82	82	82	84	88	92			
58						84	86	86	88	93	96	101		
59						87	90	90	92	96	100	103	104	
60						91	95	95	97	101	105	108	109	111
61							99	100	101	105	108	112	113	116
62							104	105	106	109	113	115	117	118
63								110	110	112	116	117	119	120
64								114	115	117	119	120	122	123
65								118	120	121	122	123	125	126
66									124	124	125	128	129	130
67									128	130	131	133	133	135
68									131	133	135	136	138	138
69										135	137	138	140	142
70										136	138	140	142	144
71										138	140	142	144	145

HOME REMEDIES

The following should not be considered medical advice and is prepared for informational purposes only. Always consult a professional health-care practitioner for medical problems. Do not give aspirin to children under the age of 15 unless directed by a physician.

"Treatment for Health Emergencies" and "Directory of Poison Control Centers" in chapter
Go to 17

ALLERGIES, SEASONAL

Symptoms   Watery eyes, stuffy nose, coughing. *Asthma* symptoms include a wheezing/hacking cough that may get worse at night, causes a tight feeling in the chest, and is often accompanied by panicky feelings of being unable to breathe. See your doctor if you experience these symptoms.

Remedies   Drink plenty of fluids to flush your system of allergens. Avoid strenuous exercise, especially if it causes asthmatic wheezing (see your doctor). Sleep with your head/chest elevated to facilitate breathing. Don't smoke or wear cologne, and avoid others who do. Keep your home and office dust-free (vacuum with a special filter, if necessary). Stay away from known irritants, such as smoke, perfumes, animals, and outdoor activities. Over-the-counter antihistamines and analgesics usually provide some relief, but remember that antihistamines cause drowsiness, and follow package directions carefully. Decongestants can provide temporary relief, but nasal congestion may return when use is discontinued. Horseradish and red/cayenne pepper can also be used as decongestants, either by adding them to food or by placing a small pinch under the nostrils or on the tongue. Get plenty of rest, and see your doctor if symptoms persist.

BACK PAIN FROM MUSCLE STRAIN

Symptoms   Pain that occurs when you move the affected portion of your back, which may ache and be sore to the touch; swelling and bruising may be present in severe cases. (Always call your doctor about sudden, unexpected back pain that occurs for no reason or about pain that moves from one body part to another, is severe, lasts more than 2 to 3 days, or is accompanied by fever or vomiting.)

Remedies   Rest in bed to take pressure off the back and allow it to heal. Take analgesics, such as aspirin, ibuprofen, naproxen sodium, or acetaminophen. If there is swelling or bruising, apply a cold pack (ice in a plastic bag wrapped in a towel) for 20 minutes and then remove the pack for 20 minutes, repeating this process for 2 to 3 hours.

BURNS, FIRST-DEGREE

Symptoms   A feeling of heat with pain and reddening but no blistering. If signs of infection (fever, chills, swelling, increased redness, or pus in the burned area) develop, seek medical attention. (Always see a doctor for more serious burns or any that cover a large area of the body.)

Remedies   Hold the burned area under cold tap water for 5 to 10 minutes to stop the burn process and reduce the amount of skin damage. (Don't apply ice or ice water, which can further damage the skin.) Leave the burn uncovered and keep it elevated, if possible. Use a dry, sterile dressing if necessary. Do not rub butter or salve onto the burn, as this can cause more damage. Analgesics may be taken orally to relieve pain, but experts advise against using local anesthetic sprays or ointments, as these can slow the healing process and may cause allergic reactions. *See also* "Treatment for Health Emergencies: Burns" in chapter 17.

COLDS, SORE THROATS, AND COUGHS DUE TO COLDS

Symptoms   Sneezing, runny nose, slight fever (101°F or less). Call a doctor if any of the following symptoms develop: a bright red sore throat; wheezing or difficulty breathing; irritability; lethargy; confusion/delirium; earache; visible pus deposits in the throat; enlarged/tender neck glands; persistent dry cough; cough that produces thick yellow-green or gray phlegm; a bad odor from the throat, nose, or ears; or a fever of over 103°F (104°F in a child under 12, 100.5°F in an infant less than two months old, or 102°F in an adult over 60).

Remedies   Bed rest if feverish; plenty of fluids; analgesics for aches and pains; chicken soup; foods and drinks rich in vitamin C.

Influenza was so named by 15th-century Italians because they thought the disease was caused by the influence of the stars and planets.

CONSTIPATION

Symptoms   Hard, small, dry bowel movements (usually fewer than three times a week); pain and difficulty having bowel movements; feeling bloated and uncomfortable; an urge to defecate but inability to do so.

Remedies   Drink plenty of water (8 to 10 glasses per day) and exercise regularly. Eat foods containing plenty of fiber, such as beans, whole grain and bran cereals, fresh fruits, and vegetables (such as asparagus, brussels sprouts, cabbage, and carrots). Respond immediately to the urge to have a bowel movement—putting it off is one of the major causes of constipation, especially in busy, stressed people. Adults and children may become constipated from a reluctance to defecate in public bathrooms (at school or work) because of lack of privacy or time constraints. If this is a problem, try eating fruit or cereal an hour before bedtime and setting the alarm to rise 30 minutes earlier than usual. Eat a high-fiber breakfast soon after getting out of bed. Then shower, dress, and prepare for the day. The extra fiber, early breakfast, and morning time to spare will facilitate the occurrence of bowel movements before leaving home for the day. Keep in mind that bowel movements are a very individual matter; some people normally have more than one a day, but for others, three or four times a week is the norm. Laxatives, stool softeners, and enemas should be used rarely and with great caution, as they are habit-forming. If you become dependent on such products, gradually reduce the amount used while making healthy lifestyle changes; abrupt withdrawal can cause serious problems. Extreme constipation can result in intestinal blockage—a very serious matter—so it is important to check with your doctor if constipation is a long-standing problem or causes major discomfort.

FLU (INFLUENZA)

Symptoms   Headache, general aches and pains, fatigue, chills, fever up to 104°F, burning sensation in the eyes, dry cough. Symptoms may resemble a cold but are more severe and develop faster; the person seems to get sick very quickly. People over age 65 and those with chronic illnesses should receive annual influenza immunizations, as complications from the flu can be severe.

Remedies   Bed rest, analgesics for aches and pains, and warm fluids. Use over-the-counter medications

to reduce symptoms if desired, but be sure to follow directions carefully. Decongestants can provide temporary relief, but nasal congestion may return when use is discontinued. Horseradish and red/cayenne pepper can also be used as decongestants, either by adding them to food or placing a small pinch under the nostrils or on the tongue.

HEADACHES

Symptoms   Generalized pain in the head or neck area. (Seek medical attention for pain that is localized on one side of the face or head; sudden, severe headaches of any type; persistent pain accompanied by nausea, high fever, or other symptoms; pain resulting from an injury or blow to the head or face; or pain accompanied by disorientation, drowsiness, or confusion.)

Remedies   Relax in a quiet area. Eat a nutritious meal if your stomach is empty. Take analgesics to relieve pain. Apply heat to relax tense muscles in the neck and shoulders. Use ice packs on the head itself. Wipe the brow and neck with vinegar. Some headaches respond well to aspirin and hot coffee; others are made worse by caffeine. If headaches are frequent, try to identify their cause (stress, hunger, menstrual cycle, certain foods) and work to remove it.

HICCUPS

Symptoms   Quick, jerky inhalations accompanied by a peculiar noise, caused by a spasmodic jerking of the diaphragm muscle. Hiccups usually stop within a few minutes but can continue for hours, days, or weeks. Sometimes the condition even requires hospitalization because they disturb sleep and preclude normal respiration. Call your health-care provider if hiccups continue more than 1 day.

Remedies   Regular, rhythmic breathing. The diaphragm muscle is not under voluntary control, but forcing yourself to breathe in a very regular pattern should get it back into a normal rhythm. Take deep enough breaths so that the diaphragm area (center of the lower rib cage down to the waist) moves in and out; quick shallow breaths that move only the upper chest will not solve the problem. (Avoid very deep, too-slow breaths, as these may cause hyperventilation.) If the hiccups do not respond within a minute or two, wait 5 minutes and try again. If you still have no success, try holding your breath. Breathe out until you have emptied your lungs as much as possible and then hold it as long as you can without becoming really uncomfortable. Then take a deep breath and hold it (again, only until you begin to feel uncomfortable). Breathe normally for a few minutes to see if the hiccups subside; then repeat.

HYPERVENTILATION

Symptoms   Dizziness, shortness of breath, chest pain or tightness, numbness/tingling of the extremities or around the mouth. In most cases, there is no obvious breathing irregularity—that is, one cannot tell that the hyperventilating person is breathing too deeply or too fast.

Remedies   Until medical attention is available, hold a paper bag over the mouth and nose, crumpling the edges so that little air can escape. Exhale into the bag and then inhale while still holding it over the mouth and nose. Repeat this procedure until symptoms subside (sometimes it takes several minutes).

(*Note:* The symptoms of hyperventilation are also symptoms of some life-threatening medical conditions. Also, frequent/chronic hyperventilation can cause serious complications. Therefore, it is recommended that you seek medical attention immediately if any of the symptoms described here are present, even if hyperventilation is suspected.)

INDIGESTION

Symptoms   Mild abdominal discomfort soon after eating; feeling "too full" after a heavy meal.

Remedies   Drink ½ cup of tepid water mixed with 1 tablespoon of vinegar, 1 tablespoon of lemon juice, or the juice of one freshly squeezed lime.

INSECT BITES

Symptoms   Localized pain, itching, swelling. (If allergic symptoms such as all-over itching, a rash, or breathing difficulties occur, seek emergency medical attention immediately.)

Remedies   For bee stings, a drop of ammonia applied directly to the wound will often stop the pain and prevent swelling; alternatively, use an antihistamine gel or ointment. If bites are numerous, you may want to take an over-the-counter antihistamine orally to reduce discomfort, but remember that such products usually make you drowsy. *See also* "Treatment for Health Emergencies: Insect Bites" in chapter 17.

On his first voyage to the South Pacific, Captain Cook lost almost half of his crew to scurvy (caused by lack of vitamin C). Once the cause of scurvy was discovered, lemon juice was issued on all British navy ships.

INSOMNIA

Symptoms   Inability to fall or stay asleep at night despite feeling tired and in need of rest, resulting in daytime drowsiness and fatigue. Symptoms may include feelings of anxiety, obsessive thinking or planning, or excessive worrying when trying to fall asleep.

Remedies   Get plenty of exercise in the late afternoon or early evening, but avoid strenuous workouts just before bedtime. Don't take naps during the day. Set a regular bedtime and stick to it (at least until difficulties are resolved), and also set a regular time to wake up. A light snack before bedtime may be helpful, but don't overdo it. Try wheat germ, brown rice, celery, milk, turkey, bananas, figs, yogurt, or tuna snacks because they are rich in tryptophan, an amino acid that promotes sleep. Avoid potatoes, cheese, chocolate, tomatoes, and spinach, all of which contain tryamine, a stimulant. If you smoke, try to cut down—nicotine is a powerful stimulant. Work to reduce other chemical/nutritional stimulants, too, such as iced tea, colas, and coffee. Decrease alcohol consumption and review all medications (prescription and over-the-counter) for their side effects. If you have been taking any form of sleep aid, your body needs time to adjust to falling asleep on its own. If anxiety or stress is keeping you awake, spend time relaxing before going to bed. Soak in a warm bath, gaze into the fireplace, or listen to music by candlelight (gazing at a lighted candle can actually make you sleepy). Once in bed, try not to dwell on your problems. Take some deep, slow breaths, and think soothing thoughts. If you do not fall asleep within 15 or 20 minutes, get out of bed and go into another room. Engage in a relaxing activity until you feel sleepy, and then go back to bed and try again.

PREMENSTRUAL SYNDROME (PMS)

Symptoms   Feeling bloated, out of sorts, irritable, and/or depressed.

Remedies   Make a calendar charting menstrual periods and PMS symptoms over several months and use it to predict the next episode. Cut down on salty foods, chocolate, and caffeine for a day or two prior to anticipated onset. Try to reschedule stressful events that occur during periods of PMS; avoid highly emotional situations and postpone major decisions until hormone levels return to normal. Get plenty of rest, exercise, and good nutrition. When PMS symptoms occur, drink plenty of water to reduce water retention and flush impurities from the system. Take diuretics only on the advice of a physician, as overuse can cause serious medical problems.

RASHES, PLANT-ALLERGY

Symptoms   Redness and/or small bumps accompanied by itching, usually after contact with plants such as poison oak or poison ivy.

Remedies   Calamine lotion may provide some relief, but an over-the-counter antihistamine gel or ointment will work better. Taking oral antihistamines may be necessary, especially at bedtime, to avoid scratching and infecting the area. Rashes due to contact with such plants may persist for weeks, are easily spread and infected by scratching, and are difficult to cure at home. If symptoms are still present in 2 to 3 days, see your doctor. *See also* "Poisonous Cultivated and Wild Plants" in chapter 3; "Treatment for Health Emergencies: Poisoning: Plant Poisons" in chapter 17.

RASHES, HEAT

Symptoms   Redness and a burning sensation when skin is touched.

Remedies   Take a cool (not cold) bath; apply cool compresses wet with a solution of baking soda and water, or apply calamine lotion. Leave the area open to the air if possible to avoid irritation, and stay out of the heat. If rash persists, see your doctor.

(*Note:* Some rashes are symptoms of illnesses such as infection or food allergies. If you do not know what may have caused a rash, see your doctor, especially if symptoms persist.)

If you burn your mouth when eating spicy foods, instead of reaching for water, eat something sweet.

SPRAINS AND STRAINS OF THE ANKLE, FOOT, HAND, WRIST, OR ELBOW

Symptoms   Pain and swelling of the injured limb (full range of motion still present; limb still capable of bearing weight). Seek medical attention if the skin is broken, the limb cannot move normally in all directions, numbness/blue discoloration occurs, or bones seem out of place and are painful when pressed.

Remedies   Elevate the injured limb to reduce swelling. Apply an ice pack to the injured area for

20 minutes; then remove the pack for 20 minutes. Repeat this cycle until swelling stops or improves. Rest the limb as much as possible to prevent further injury, and keep it elevated. After the first few days, applying heat to the area will promote healing, but do not apply heat initially as this can make swelling worse. You may wrap the injured limb loosely in a stretch bandage for support and comfort. Analgesics may be taken for the pain. See your doctor if symptoms are still present after 5 days. *See also* "Treatment for Health Emergencies: Fractures, Dislocations, and Sprains" in chapter 17.

STREP THROAT

Symptoms   Redness and pain or burning sensation when swallowing. If neck glands are swollen or tender, see your doctor. Strep throat symptoms include white pus areas in the back of the throat; fever; sometimes headaches, stomach pain, or a rash on the body. (However, these symptoms do not always indicate strep throat, and one may have strep throat without experiencing these symptoms.) Consult your physician if symptoms of strep throat appear, if pain is severe, or if a sore throat persists more than 2 to 3 days.

Remedies   Cut down on smoking, rest your voice, and use a humidifier or vaporizer to moisten the air. (Smoking, excessive vocalizing, and too-low humidity can cause or aggravate coughs and sore throats.) Throat soothers include gargling with salt water several times a day (½ to 1 teaspoon of salt in a cup of warm water), hot tea with lemon and honey, and medicated throat lozenges. (Plain lemon drops work well, too; the sourness stimulates the production of saliva to moisten your throat.) Analgesics may be taken to relieve pain.

LOOKING FOR SIGNS OF BREAST CANCER

It is important for you to know the signs of breast cancer, because most breast cancers are discovered by women themselves, not their doctors. If you discover any of the signs of breast cancer, see your doctor immediately. It is a frightening experience to find a lump or another possible cancer sign, but you should know that 8 of 10 lumps are *not* cancerous. Many women have naturally lumpy breasts. But your doctor should determine whether a lump or other sign is actually cancer or a harmless condition.

To find out how many calories it takes to maintain your current weight, multiply your weight by 15.

ASK FOR A BREAST EXAM

Don't be embarrassed. Asking your doctor or nurse for a breast examination as part of an office visit is one good way to learn what is normal for your breasts. But examination by a doctor is not enough—you, too, should examine your breasts monthly. Ask your doctor or nurse to teach you breast self-examination to be sure you are practicing it correctly.

PRACTICE BREAST SELF-EXAMINATION

Breast self-examination is an important key to early diagnosis. Along with regular examination by your physician, monthly self-examination can give you peace of mind because it helps you know how your breasts normally feel.

Knowing the normal feel of your breasts makes it easier to notice any changes early, when treatment is most effective. To examine your breasts correctly, you should follow the six steps described page 516.

WHEN TO EXAMINE YOUR BREASTS

Every month! If you menstruate, the best time to practice breast self-examination is 2 or 3 days after the end of your period, when your breasts are least likely to be tender or swollen. If you no longer menstruate, choose a day such as your birth date. That way, you will remember to do it every month.

HOW TO PERFORM A BREAST SELF-EXAMINATION

1. Stand before a mirror. Inspect both breasts for anything unusual, such as any discharge from the nipples or puckering, dimpling, or scaling of the skin.

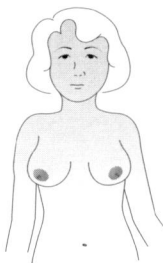

2. Watching closely in the mirror, clasp hands behind your head and press hands forward. This step and step 3 are designed to emphasize any changes in the shape or contour of your breasts. As you do them, you should be able to feel your chest muscles tighten.

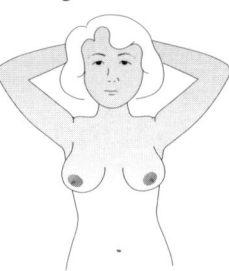

3. Press hands firmly on hips and bow slightly toward the mirror as you pull your shoulders and elbows forward.

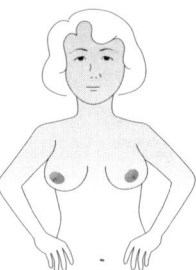

Note: Some women do the next part of the exam in the shower: Fingers glide over soapy skin, making it easy to concentrate on the texture underneath.

4. Raise your left arm. Use a few fingers of your right hand to explore your left breast firmly, carefully, and thoroughly. Beginning at the outer edge, press the flat part of your fingers in small circles, moving the circles slowly around the breast. Gradually work toward the nipple. Be sure to cover the entire breast. Pay special attention to the area between the breast and the armpit, including the armpit itself. Feel for any unusual lump or mass under the skin.

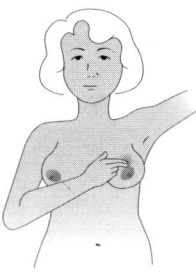

5. Gently squeeze the nipple and look for a discharge. Repeat the exam on your right breast.

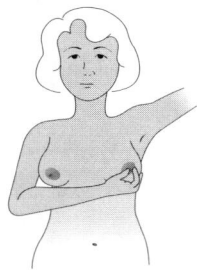

6. Repeat steps 4 and 5 lying down. Lie flat on your back with your left arm over your head and a pillow or folded towel under your left shoulder. This position flattens the breast and makes it easier to examine. Use the same circular motion described earlier. Repeat on your right breast.

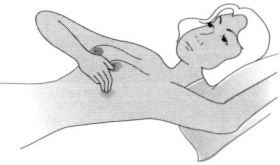

WHEN TO GET A MAMMOGRAM

The National Cancer Institute, the American College of Radiology, and the American Cancer Society recommend regular mammograms for women over 40, either annually, or once every 2 years, depending on a woman's age and medical history. Detection through mammography screening can lead to early treatment, adding years to the lives of women receiving such treatment.

Unfortunately, only a little more than a third of American women follow these guidelines. Of the 34 million women who do not get mammograms as recommended, about 4 million are expected to contract breast cancer at some point.

The ventriloquist Paul Winchell was not only the voice of Tigger in the Winnie the Pooh films, he also invented an early form of the artificial heart. He donated the patent for his life-saving device to the University of Utah.

Consult your physician for more information about whether it is time for you to get a mammogram.

INFECTIOUS DISEASES AND HOW THEY ARE SPREAD

Disease	Agent	Transmission
AIDS (acquired immune deficiency syndrome)	Virus	Contact of body fluid (semen, blood, vaginal secretions) with that of an infected person. Sexual contact and sharing of unclean paraphernalia for intravenous drugs are the most common means of transmission.
Blastomycosis	Fungus	Inhaling contaminated dust
Botulism	Bacteria	Consuming contaminated food
Chicken pox	Virus	Direct or indirect contact with infected person
Common cold	Virus	Direct or indirect contact with infected person
Diphtheria	Bacteria	Direct contact with infected person
Encephalitis	Virus	Mosquito bite
Gonorrhea	Bacteria	Sexual contact
Hepatitis	Virus	Direct or indirect contact with infected person
Herpes simplex	Virus	Direct contact with infected person
Histoplasmosis	Fungus	Inhaling contaminated dust
Hookworm	Nematode	Contact with contaminated soil
Infectious mononucleosis	Virus	Direct or indirect contact with infected person
Influenza	Virus	Direct or indirect contact with infected person
Lyme disease	Bacteria	Deer tick bite
Malaria	Protozoa	Mosquito bite
Measles	Virus	Direct or indirect contact with infected person
Mumps	Virus	Direct or indirect contact with infected person
Pertussis (whooping cough)	Bacteria	Direct or indirect contact with infected person
Poliomyelitis	Virus	Direct contact with infected person
Rubella (German measles)	Virus	Direct or indirect contact with infected person
Scarlet fever	Bacteria	Direct or indirect contact with infected person
Spotted fever	Rickettsia	Tick bite
Syphilis	Bacteria	Sexual contact
Tapeworm	Nematode	Consuming infected meat or fish
Toxoplasmosis	Protozoa	Consuming raw meat; contact with contaminated soil
Trichomoniasis	Protozoa	Sexual contact
Typhus	Rickettsia	Lice, flea, tick bite
Yellow fever	Virus	Mosquito bite

Health/Nutrition

DENTAL CARE

Dental-care professionals offer the following advice to maintain healthy teeth that will last a lifetime:

1. Have regular dental checkups.
2. Limit the amount of sugary foods you eat, and brush teeth immediately after eating sweets.
3. Brush teeth at least twice daily with a fluoride toothpaste.
4. Use a toothbrush with rounded bristles and be sure it is not too hard. Look for one that has American Dental Association (ADA) approval. And get a new toothbrush every 3 to 4 months —worn-down bristles do not clean your teeth well.
5. Floss regularly—at least once per day.
6. Drink fluoridated water (available in about half of the cities and towns in the United States). For added protection, especially if fluoridated water is not available, your dentist may prescribe a fluoridated gel, rinse, or tablet. Fluoride drops can be used for infants.
7. Follow other recommendations from your dentist concerning tooth and gum care.

A Closer Look — Osteopathy

Osteopathic physicians (D.O.s) are licensed to perform surgery, prescribe medication, and specialize in all areas of medicine from neurosurgery to psychiatry. Their approach to treatment emphasizes the importance of body mechanics and manipulative methods to detect and correct faulty structure and function. Noninvasive therapies are used whenever possible, with the goal of restoring the body to health by freeing it to heal itself. Osteopaths are specially trained in manual treatment of musculoskeletal disorders. They can specialize in sports medicine as well as pediatrics, general practice, or obstetrics/gynecology. They utilize generally accepted physical, pharmacological, and surgical methods of diagnosis.

For more information, contact the American Osteopathic Association's Public Relations Department, 142 E. Ontario St., Chicago, IL 60611 (telephone: 800-621-1773 or 312-280-5800), or see its Web site at http://www.aoa-net.org

A Closer Look — Chiropractic

Chiropractic is based on the idea that the structure of the human body, particularly the spinal column, has a profound effect on the functioning of all systems and organs of the body. Manipulation of the spine is perhaps the best-known type of chiropractic treatment. Its purpose is to align misplaced vertebrae to relieve unhealthy pressure on the nerves connecting the brain and body, thus restoring all functions to health. Doctors of Chiropractic (D.C.s) base their diagnoses on information collected via physical examination, patient history, X rays, magnetic resonance imagings (MRIs), laboratory tests, and other traditional diagnostic tools. Their whole-person approach may include physiological therapeutics—such as heat or massage, acupuncture, trigger point therapy, and counseling on stress management and lifestyle issues—as well as spinal and extravertebral manipulations. Treatment does not include pharmaceutical or surgical interventions, but nutritional counseling is often provided, as chiropractic doctors receive intensive education in all aspects of healthy nutrition.

For more information, contact the American Chiropractic Association, 1701 Clarendon Blvd., Arlington, VA 22209 (telephone: 800-986-4636; fax: 703-243-2593), or stop by the Chiropractic Online service at Web site http://www.amerchiro.org/.

Fluoride is a mineral that is present in most water to some extent. The water-fluoridation process used in the United States since 1945 is a means of ensuring that everyone receives the benefits of enough fluoride to prevent the tooth decay that seemed inevitable before its implementation. Fluoride is important to oral health for several reasons:

- It helps to deactivate the bacteria that cause tooth decay.
- It is an essential part of the repair process as tooth enamel rebuilds small areas of decay before large cavities form.
- It makes tooth enamel more resistant to the acid formed by bacteria.

Fluoride is most effective on the smooth surfaces of the teeth and least effective on the chewing surfaces on the back teeth (molars). Regular brushing and

Homeopathy

A Closer Look

The homeopathic approach to health care treats the whole person—body, mind, and spirit. One of its basic principles is the Law of Similars, which advocates stimulation of the body's own defense system by ingesting minute amounts of a substance that produces the same symptoms as the illness. (Homeopathic physicians point out that this approach is similar to the process of immunization used in conventional medicine.) The second basic principle is the use of minimum dosage to produce effective results. This concept is based on many practitioners' experience that use of an extreme dilution of the required substance (reducing the amount of substance to 1 part in 10,000 or even 100,000) produces better results than a stronger dosage. In addition to these foundations for treatment, homeopathic practitioners believe that symptoms of illness are often the body's own defense at work, and that treatment based on suppressing symptoms may interfere with the body's own healing process.

Health-care providers who practice homeopathy may be identified by one or more of these sets of initials:

RSHom (NA)	Member of the Registered Society of Homeopaths in North America
DHANP	Diplomate of the Homeopathic Association of Naturopathic Physicians
DHt	Diplomate of Homeotheraputics
CCH	Certified in Classical Homeopathy

For more information, contact The National Center for Homeopathy, 801 N. Fairfax St., Ste. 306, Alexandria, VA 22314 (telephone: 703-548-7790; fax: 703-548-7792; e-mail: info@homeopathic.org), or visit the center's Web site at http://www.homeopathic.org

flossing also help to prevent tooth decay by removing bacteria-containing plaque (an invisible sticky coating on teeth) that produces cavity-causing acid.

To protect teeth further against decay, plastic sealants are now widely used and recommended. The application is a simple one: the teeth are cleaned and wiped completely dry, and the substance is painted onto the tooth surface. The resulting coating (which may be clear or tinted) can last as long as 10 years, protecting teeth from the bacteria that cause decay. Many dentists now recommend that a sealant be applied to children's teeth immediately after the adult teeth appear, before any decay begins to occur.

For detailed information on preventive dental care and specific problems, see your dentist. Or contact the American Dental Association, 211 E. Chicago Ave., Chicago, IL 60611 (telephone: 312-440-2500; fax: 312-440-2800), or visit the ADA's Web site at http://www.ada.org/.

Go to "Living Will" in chapter 20; "Aging" in chapter 22; "Social Security" in chapter 25

LIVING WILLS

One of the most controversial issues in society today is a person's right to decide whether to live or die. With the enormous advances in medical care during recent decades, many more families are being asked to make difficult choices about life-sustaining measures for loved ones who are critically ill and unable to make their own decisions. Senior citizens, nursing-home patients, those who are seriously ill, and members of the public at large are now encouraged to record their thoughts by executing living wills. When properly prepared and executed, a living will can speak for someone who no longer has the ability to speak for herself.

Many states have legislation in place regarding the right of terminally ill persons or family members to decide to withhold life-sustaining measures, and the law in your state may not be as conservative or liberal as you would prefer. But laws are changing constantly in this field. Experts in the field suggest executing a living will that not only conforms to state legislative guidelines, but also includes information that may be of value in the future if state laws change.

Health/Nutrition

There are numerous resources available for anyone desiring to create a living will. Check the reference section of your public library for handbooks containing sample living wills for every state with current legislation, and generic forms for states without such laws. Or contact one of the organizations listed below for information on creating living wills and related legal issues.

Choice in Dying
1035 30th Street, NW
Washington, DC 20007
202-338-9790
Fax: 202-338-0242
http://www.choices.org

Death with Dignity National Center
11 Dupont Circle, NW, Suite 202
Washington, DC 20036
202-969-1669
Fax: 202-969-1668
http://www.deathwithdignity.org

Euthanasia Research & Guidance Organization (ERGO)
24829 Norris Lane
Junction City, OR 97448-9559
Messages and Fax: 541-998-1873
e-mail: ergo@efn.org
http://www.finalexit.org

TEN LEADING CAUSES OF DEATH

The table at right ranks the causes of death by age group according to mortality rates. Cause of death corresponds to classifications in the *International Classification of Diseases*; however, abbreviated forms have been used for reasons of space.

"Statistics and Demography" under "Reference Works for General Information" in **Go to** chapter 11

| Rank | Age Groups | | |
	<1	1–4	5–9
1	Congenital Anomalies (6,212)	Unintentional Injury & Adverse Effects (1,935)	Unintentional Injury & Adverse Effects (1,544)
2	Short Gestation (4,101)	Congenital Anomalies (564)	Malignant Neoplasms (487)
3	SIDS (2,822)	Homicide & Legal Intervention (399)	Congenital Anomalies (198)
4	Maternal Complications (1,343)	Malignant Neoplasms (365)	Homicide & Legal Intervention (170)
5	Respiratory Distress Syndrome (1,295)	Heart Disease (214)	Heart Disease (156)
6	Placenta Cord Membranes (961)	Pneumonia & Influenza (146)	Pneumonia & Influenza (70)
7	Perinatal Infections (815)	Septicemia (89)	Chronic Lower Respiratory Disease* (54)
8	Unintentional Injury & Adverse Effects (754)	Perinatal Period (75)	Benign Neoplasms (52)
9	Intrauterine Hypoxia (461)	Cerebro-vascular (57)	Cerebro-vascular (35)
10	Pneumonia & Influenza (441)	Benign Neoplasms (53)	HIV (29)

* Bronchitis, Emphysema, Asthma

Age Groups							
10–14	15–24	25–34	35–44	45–54	55–64	65+	All Ages
Unintentional Injury & Adverse Effects (1,710)	Unintentional Injury & Adverse Effects (13,349)	Unintentional Injury & Adverse Effects (12,045)	Malignant Neoplasms (17,022)	Malignant Neoplasms (45,747)	Malignant Neoplasms (87,024)	Heart Disease (605,673)	Heart Disease (724,859)
Malignant Neoplasms (526)	Homicide & Legal Intervention (5,506)	Suicide (5,365)	Unintentional Injury & Adverse Effects (15,127)	Heart Disease (35,056)	Heart Disease (65,068)	Malignant Neoplasms (384,186)	Malignant Neoplasms (541,532)
Suicide (317)	Suicide (4,135)	Homicide & Legal Intervention (4,565)	Heart Disease (13,593)	Unintentional Injury & Adverse Effects (10,946)	Chronic Lower Respiratory Disease* (10,162)	Cerebro-vascular (139,144)	Cerebro-vascular (158,448)
Homicide & Legal Intervention (290)	Malignant Neoplasms (1,699)	Malignant Neoplasms (4,385)	Suicide (6,837)	Liver Disease (5,744)	Cerebro-vascular (9,653)	Chronic Lower Respiratory Disease* (97,896)	Chronic Lower Respiratory Disease* (112,584)
Congenital Anomalies (173)	Heart Disease (1,057)	Heart Disease (3,207)	HIV (5,746)	Cerebro-vascular (5,709)	Diabetes (8,705)	Pneumonia & Influenza (82,989)	Unintentional Injury & Adverse Effects (97,835)
Heart Disease (170)	Congenital Anomalies (450)	HIV (2,912)	Homicide & Legal Intervention (3,567)	Suicide (5,131)	Unintentional Injury & Adverse Effects (7,340)	Diabetes (48,974)	Pneumonia & Influenza (91,871)
Chronic Lower Respiratory Disease* (98)	Chronic Lower Respiratory Disease* (239)	Cerebro-vascular (670)	Liver Disease (3,370)	Diabetes (4,386)	Liver Disease (5,279)	Unintentional Injury & Adverse Effects (32,975)	Diabetes (64,751)
Pneumonia & Influenza (51)	Pneumonia & Influenza (215)	Diabetes (636)	Cerebro-vascular (2,650)	HIV (3,120)	Pneumonia & Influenza (3,856)	Nephritis (22,640)	Suicide (30,575)
Cerebro-vascular (47)	HIV (194)	Pneumonia & Influenza (531)	Diabetes (1,885)	Chronic Lower Respiratory Disease* (2,828)	Suicide (2,963)	Alzheimer Disease (22,416)	Nephritis (26,182)
Benign Neoplasms (32)	Cerebro-vascular (178)	Liver Disease (506)	Pneumonia & Influenza (1,400)	Pneumonia & Influenza (2,167)	Septicemia (2,093)	Septicemia (19,012)	Liver Disease (25,192)

Source: Centers for Disease Control

Health/Nutrition

COMBINING FORMS OF MEDICAL TERMS

Prefix	Meaning of Prefix	Example	Prefix	Meaning of Prefix	Example
a-, ab-, an-	away, lack of, without	astigmatism	galact-	milk	galactose
acro-	extremity, end	acroparesthesia	gastro-	stomach	gastroenteric
adeno-	gland	adenous	gloss-	tongue	glossitis
adreno-	adrenal gland	adrenocortex	hemi-	half	hemiplegic
aero-	gas, air	aerophagia	hepato-	liver	hepatocolic
allo-	different, another	allorhythmia	hydro-	water	hydrocephalic
ambi-	both, both sides	ambidextrous	hyper-	above, beyond	hyperacidity
antero-	before, in front of	anterograde	hypo-	below, less	hypoglycemia
anti-	against	antiseptic	ileo-	end of small intestine	ileocolic
arterio-	artery	arteriospasm	ilio-	flank, upper hip bone	iliopelvic
arthro-, arthr-	joint	arthritis	infra-	below, inferior	infraorbital
bacterio-	bacteria	bacteriological	inter-	between	interdigital
blephari-	eyelash, eyelid	blepharitis	intra-	within	intrauterine
brady-	slow	bradycardia	kerat-	cornea, hard tissue	keratoid
broncho-	windpipe	bronchospasm	laryngo-, larying-	voice box	laryngitis
cardio-	heart, heart region	cardiovascular			
cephalo-	head	cephalometry	leuko-, leuk-	white	leukocyte
cerebro-	brain	cerebrovascular	mega-	abnormally large	megacolon
cervico-	neck	cervicobrachial	mela-	black	melanin
chole-	bile	cholecystis	myelo-, myel-	marrow, nerve sheath	myelination
chondro-	cartilage	chondroblastoma	myo-	muscle	myospasm
chromo-	color	chromogen	neo-	new	neoplasm
chylo-	lymph	chylomicron	nephro-, nephr-	kidney	nephritis
contra-	against, opposite	contraindication	neuro-, neuri-, neur-	nerve	neuritis
costo-	rib	costochondral			
cyst-	bladder, sac	cystitis	osteo-	bone	osteoarthritis
dacryo-	tears	dacryocystitis	peri-, pneumo-	around or about the lungs or air	pericardial pneumonia
derma-	skin	dermatitis			
dextro-	right side	dextromanual	sacro-	sacrum (triangular bone above tailbone)	sacroiliac
dys-	abnormal, bad, painful	dysentery			
encephalo-, encephal-	brain	encephalitis	sero-	serum, blood	serofibrous
			tachy-	rapid	tachycardia
endo-	inside	endocardium	thrombo-	blood clot	thrombosis
entero-	intestines	enterospasm	tracheo-	windpipe	tracheotomy
ep-, epi-	at, over, upon	epiglottis	utero-	uterus, womb	uterotomy
ex-, exo-	out, outside	excrement	vaso-	blood vessel	vasodilator
fibrino-	threadlike	fibrinogen	ventro-	belly, abdominal	ventroptosia
fibro-	fiber, fibrous	fibrocystic	zymo-	enzyme, fermentation	zymocide

"Common Biological Terms" in chapter 3; "Medical Science" under "Reference Works for General Information" in chapter 11; "Medicine and Pharmacology Symbols" in chapter 12

Go to

Health/Nutrition

RECOMMENDED DAILY (OR DIETARY) ALLOWANCES

In the following tables, heights and weights are medians of the U.S. population and are not meant to suggest ideal height-to-weight ratios.

PROTEINS

	Age (years)	Weight (pounds)	Heights (inches)	Protein (grams)
Males	11–14	99	62	45
	15–18	145	69	59
	19–24	160	70	58
	25–50	174	70	63
	51+	170	68	63
Females	11–14	101	62	46
	15–18	120	64	44
	19–24	128	65	46
	25–50	138	64	50
	51+	143	63	50
Pregnant				65
Nursing				62–65

FAT-SOLUBLE VITAMINS

	Age (years)	Weight (pounds)	Height (inches)	Vitamin A (IUs*)	Vitamin D (IUs)	Vitamin E (IUs)
Males	11–14	99	62	1,000	10	10
	15–18	145	69	1,000	10	10
	19–24	160	70	1,000	10	10
	25–50	174	70	1,000	5	10
	51+	170	68	1,000	5	10
Females	11–14	101	62	800	10	8
	15–18	120	64	800	10	8
	19–24	128	65	800	10	8
	25–50	138	64	800	5	8
	51+	143	63	800	5	8
Pregnant				800	10	10
Nursing				1,200–1,300	10	11–12

*IUs = International Units

Go to "Cooking Equivalents and Substitutions," "Cooking Times and Serving Sizes," "Chemical Additives," and "Beverages" in chapter 19

Health/Nutrition

WATER–SOLUBLE VITAMINS

	Age (years)	Weight (pounds)	Height (inches)	Vitamin C (mg*)	Folate (mcg)	Niacin (mg)	Riboflavin (mg)	Thiamin (mg)	Vitamin B6 (mg)	Vitamin B12 (mg)
Males	11–14	99	62	50	150	17	1.5	1.3	1.7	2.0
	15–18	145	69	60	200	20	1.8	1.5	2.0	2.0
	19–24	160	70	60	200	19	1.7	1.5	2.0	2.0
	25–50	174	70	60	200	19	1.7	1.5	2.0	2.0
	51+	170	78	60	200	15	1.4	1.2	2.0	2.0
Females	11–14	101	62	50	150	15	1.3	1.1	1.4	2.0
	15–18	120	64	60	180	15	1.3	1.1	1.5	2.0
	19–24	128	65	60	180	15	1.3	1.1	1.6	2.0
	25–50	138	64	60	180	15	1.3	1.1	1.6	2.0
	51+	143	63	60	180	13	1.2	1.0	1.6	2.0
Pregnant				70	400	17	1.6	1.5	2.2	2.2
Nursing				90–95	260–280	20	1.7–1.8	1.6	2.1	2.6

*mg = milligrams

MINERALS

	Age (years)	Weight (pounds)	Height (inches)	Calcium (mg)	Phosphorus (mg)	Iodine (mg)	Iron (mg)	Magnesium (mg)	Zinc (mg)
Males	11–14	99	62	1,200	1,200	150	12	270	15
	15–18	145	69	1,200	1,200	150	12	400	15
	19–24	160	70	1,200	1,200	150	10	350	15
	25–50	174	70	800	800	150	10	350	15
	51+	170	68	800	800	150	10	350	15
Females	11–14	101	62	1,200	1,200	150	15	280	12
	15–18	120	64	1,200	1,200	150	15	300	12
	19–24	128	65	1,200	1,200	150	15	280	12
	25–50	138	64	800	800	150	15	280	12
	51+	143	63	800	800	150	10	280	12
Pregnant				1,200	1,200	175	30*	320	15
				1,200	1,200	200	15	355	16–19

*A pregnant woman often requires iron supplement tablets because of the difficulty of providing an adequate iron intake in an otherwise balanced diet.

ACTIVITIES AND THE CALORIES THEY CONSUME

Activity		Calories Expended per Hour*				
		Person weighing:				
		100 lbs.	125 lbs.	150 lbs.**	175 lbs.	200 lbs.
Rest and light activity	Lying down or sleeping	53	67	80	93	107
	Sitting	67	83	100	117	133
	Typing	73	92	110	128	147
	Driving	80	100	120	140	160
	Standing	93	117	140	163	187
	Housework	120	150	180	210	240
	Shining shoes	123	154	185	216	247
Moderate activity	Bicycling (5½ mph)	140	175	210	245	280
	Walking (2½ mph)	140	175	210	245	280
	Gardening	147	183	220	257	293
	Canoeing (2½ mph)	153	192	230	268	307
	Golf (foursome)	167	208	250	292	333
	Lawn mowing (power mower)	167	208	250	292	333
	Fencing	200	250	300	350	400
	Rowing a boat (2½ mph)	200	250	300	350	400
	Swimming (¼ mph)	200	250	300	350	400
	Calisthenics	200	250	300	350	400
	Walking (3¼ mph)	200	250	300	350	400
	Badminton	200	250	350	350	400
	Horseback riding (trotting)	200	250	350	350	400
	Square dancing	200	250	350	350	400
	Volleyball	233	250	350	350	400
	Roller skating	233	292	350	408	467
	Stacking heavy objects (boxes, logs)	233	292	350	408	467
Vigorous activity	Baseball pitching	240	300	360	420	480
	Ditch digging (hand shovel)	267	333	400	467	533
	Ice-skating (10 mph)	267	333	400	467	533
	Chopping or sawing wood	267	333	400	467	533
	Bowling (continuous)	267	333	400	467	533
	Tennis	280	350	420	490	560
	Aerobic dancing	300	375	450	525	600
	Waterskiing	320	400	480	560	640
	Hill climbing (100 feet per hour)	327	408	490	572	653
	Basketball	333	417	500	583	667
	Football	333	417	500	583	667
	Jogging (5 mph)	367	458	550	642	733
	Skiing (10 mph)	400	500	600	700	800
	Squash and handball	400	500	600	700	800
	Bicycling (13 mph)	440	550	660	770	880
	Rowing (machine)	480	600	720	840	960
	Scull rowing (race)	560	700	840	980	1,120
	Running (10 mph)	600	750	900	1,050	1,200

* All figures are approximate, as individual differences in metabolism and how activities are performed affect energy expenditure.

** To approximate your own caloric usage, divide the figure under the "Person weighing 150 pounds" column by 150 to get the approximate caloric expenditure per pound, and then multiply the result by your own body weight.

Health/Nutrition

VITAMIN/MINERAL FOOD CHART (BEST FOOD SOURCES FOR EACH VITAMIN AND MINERAL)

Consult your physician before taking vitamin or mineral dietary supplements or giving them to children. Follow medical advice and label directions carefully, and keep both prescription and nonprescription supplements out of the reach of children. Overdoses can be harmful or fatal.

VITAMINS

Vitamin	Chief Functions	Results of Deficiency	Characteristics
Vitamin A Provitamin, carotene	Essential for maintaining the integrity of epithelial membranes; helps maintain resistance to infections; necessary for the formation of rhodopsin and prevention of night blindness	**Mild:** Retarded growth; increased susceptibility to infection; abnormal function of gastro intestinal, genitourinary, and respiratory tracts due to altered epithelial membranes; dry, shriveled, thickened skin, sometimes pustule formation; night blindness **Severe:** Xerophthalmia, a characteristic eye disease, and other local infections	Fat-soluble; not destroyed by ordinary cooking temperatures; destroyed by high temperatures when oxygen is present; marked capacity for storage in liver *Note:* Excessive intake of carotene, from which vitamin A is formed, may produce yellow discoloration of the skin (carotenemia).
Thiamin Vitamin B$_1$	Important role in carbohydrate metabolism; essential for maintenance of normal digestion and appetite; essential for normal functioning of nervous tissue	**Mild:** Loss of appetite; impaired digestion of starches and sugars; colitis, constipation, or diarrhea; emaciation **Severe:** Nervous disorders of various types; loss of coordinating power of muscles; beriberi; paralysis	Water-soluble; not readily destroyed by ordinary cooking temperature; destroyed by exposure to heat, alkali, or sulfites; not stored in body
Riboflavin Vitamin B$_2$	Important in formation of certain enzymes and in cellular oxidation; normal growth; prevention of cheilosis and glossitis	Impaired growth; lassitude and weakness; cheilosis; glossitis; atrophy of skin; anemia; photophobia; cataracts	Water-soluble; alcohol-soluble; not destroyed by heat in cooking unless with alkali; unstable in light, especially in presence of alkali
Niacin Nicotinic acid Nicotinamide Antipellagra vitamin	As the component of two important enzymes, it is important in glycolysis, tissue respiration, and fat synthesis; nicotinic acid but not nicotinamide causes vasodilation and flushing; prevents pellagra	Pellagra; gastrointestinal disturbances; mental disturbances	Soluble in hot water and alcohol; not destroyed by heat, light, air, or alkali; not destroyed in ordinary cooking
Vitamin B$_{12}$ Cyanoco-balamin	Produces remission in pernicious anemia; essential for normal development of red blood cells	Pernicious anemia	Soluble in water or alcohol; unstable in hot alkaline or acid solutions

Good Sources	Recommended Daily Allowances	
Natural: Animal fats (butter, cheese, cream, egg yolk, whole milk); fish liver oil; liver; vegetables (green leafy, especially escarole, kale, and parsley; and yellow, especially carrots) **Artificial:** Concentrates in several forms; irradiated fish oils	Males 11 yrs. and older Females 11 yrs. and older Pregnant females Lactating females Children Infants	1,000mg retinol equivalents 800mg retinol equivalents 1,000mg retinol equivalents 1,200mg retinol equivalents 400–700mg retinol equivalents 400mg retinol equivalents
Natural: Widely distributed in plant and animal tissues but seldom occurs in high concentration, except in brewer's yeast; other good sources are whole-grain cereals, peas, beans, peanuts, oranges, heart, liver, kidney, many vegetables and fruits, and nuts **Artificial:** Concentrates from yeast; rice polishings; wheat germ	Males 11 yrs. and older Females 11 yrs. and older Pregnant females Lactating females Children Infants	1.2–1.5mg 1.0–1.1mg 1.4–1.6mg 1.5–1.7mg 0.7–1.2mg 0.3–0.5mg
Eggs, green vegetables, liver, kidney, lean meat, milk, wheat germ, dried yeast, enriched foods	Males 11 yrs. and older Females 11 yrs. and older Pregnant females Lactating females Children Infants	1.4–1.8mg 1.2–1.3mg 1.6mg 1.7–1.8mg 0.8–1.2mg 0.4–0.5mg
Yeast, lean meat, fish, legumes, whole-grain cereals and peanuts, enriched foods	Males 11 yrs. and older Females 11 yrs. and older Pregnant females Lactating females Children Infants	16–19 mg 13–15 mg 17 mg 20 mg 9–16 mg 6–8 mg
Liver, kidney, dairy products; most of vitamin required by humans is synthesized by intestinal bacteria	Males 11 yrs. and older Females 11 yrs. and older Pregnant females Lactating females Children Infants	3 mcg 3 mcg 4 mcg 5 mcg 2–5mcg 1–2mcg

Health/Nutrition

continues

Vitamins, Continued

Vitamin	Chief Functions	Results of Deficiency	Characteristics
Vitamin C Ascorbic acid	Essential to formation of intracellular cement substances in a variety of tissues including skin, dentin, cartilage, and bone matrix; important in healing of wounds and fractures of bones; prevents scurvy; facilitates absorption of iron	**Mild:** Lowered resistance to infections; joint tenderness; susceptibility to dental caries, pyorrhea, and bleeding gums **Severe:** Hemorrhage; anemia; scurvy	Soluble in water; easily destroyed by oxidation, and heat hastens the process; lost in cooking, particularly if water in which food was cooked is discarded; loss is greater if cooked in iron or copper utensils; quick-frozen foods lose little; stored in the body to a limited extent
Vitamin D	Regulates absorption of calcium and phosphorus from the intestinal tract; antirachitic	**Mild:** Interferes with utilization of calcium and phosphorus in bone and teeth formation; irritability; weakness **Severe:** Rickets may be common in young children; osteomalacia in adults	Soluble in fats and organic solvents; relatively stable under refrigeration; stored in liver; often associated with vitamin A
Vitamin E Alpha tocopherol	Normal reproduction in rats; prevention of muscular dystrophy in rabbits and sheep	Red blood cell resistance to rupture is decreased	Fat soluble; stable to heat in absence of oxygen
Vitamin B$_6$ Pyridoxine	Essential for metabolism of tryptophan; needed for utilization of certain other amino acids	Dermatitis around eyes and mouth; neuritis; anorexia; nausea and vomiting	Soluble in water and alcohol; rapidly inactivated in presence of heat, sunlight, or air
Folate (Folic acid)	Essential for normal functioning of hematopoietic system	Anemia	Slightly soluble in water; easily destroyed by heat in presence of acid; decreases when food is stored at room temperature *Note:* A large dose may prevent the appearance of anemia in a case of pernicious anemia but still permits neuro-logical symptoms to develop.

* IUs = International Units

Good Sources	Recommended Daily Allowances	
Natural: Abundant in most fresh fruits and vegetables, especially citrus fruit and juices and tomatoes **Artificial:** Ascorbic acid; cevitamic acid	Males 11 yrs. and older	50–60mg
	Females 11 yrs. and older	50–60mg
	Pregnant females	80 mg
	Lactating females	100mg
	Children	45mg
	Infants	35mg
	The infant diet is likely to be deficient in vitamin C unless orange or tomato juice or another form is added.	
Butter, egg yolks, fish liver oils, fish having fat distributed through the flesh, (such as salmon, tuna fish, herring) sardines, liver, oysters, yeast, and foods irradiated with ultraviolet light; formed in the skin by exposure to sunlight; artificially prepared forms exist	Males 11 yrs. and older	200–400 IU*
	Females 11 yrs. and older	200–400 IU*; after age 22, none except during pregnancy or lactation
	Pregnant females	400–600 IU*
	Lactating females	400–600 IU*
	Children	400 IU*
	Infants	400 IU*
Lettuce and other green, leafy vegetables, wheat germ oil, margarine, rice	Males 11 yrs. and older	8–10mg
	Females 11 yrs. and older	8mg
	Pregnant females	10mg
	Lactating females	11mg
	Children	10–15 IU*
	Infants	5 IU*
Blackstrap molasses, meat, cereal grains, wheat germ	Males 11 yrs. and older	1.8–2.2mg
	Females 11 yrs. and older	1.8–2.2mg
	Pregnant females	2.6mg
	Lactating females	2.5mg
	Children	0.9–1.6mg
	Infants	0.3–0.6mg
Glandular meats; yeast; green, leafy vegetables	Males 11 yrs. and older	400mcg
	Females 11 yrs. and older	400mcg
	Pregnant females	800mcg
	Lactating females	500mcg
	Children	100–300mcg
	Infants	30–45mcg

MINERALS

Mineral	Chief Functions	Results of Deficiency
Calcium (Ca++)	Necessary for formation of bones and teeth; functioning of nerves and muscles; blood clotting; activation of enzymes that convert food to energy	Rickets (soft, deformed bones) and poor growth in children; osteoporosis in adults; muscle cramps
Iodine (I-)	Necessary for normal thyroid function; regulates oxidation in cells	Disturbance in thyroid function (hypothyroidism); in infants, stunting and mental retardation (cretinism)
Iron* (Fe++)	Necessary for production of hemo-globin and myoglobin (structures that enable oxygen to be carried in blood and stored in muscles)	Fatigue; weakness; headaches; shortness of breath; iron-deficiency anemia
Phosphorus (PO₄)	Necessary for formation of bones and teeth; activation of enzymes that convert food to energy; maintenance of body's proper chemical balance; nerve/muscle function	Weakness; pain in bones (deficiency is rare)
Magnesium (Mg++)	Essential to bone growth and production of cells and genetic material; cofactor in enzymatic release of energy; regulates neuromuscular sensitivity	Muscle cramps and weakness; twitching; confusion; (deficiency most often seen in alcoholics and people taking diuretics or dehydrated from prolonged diarrhea)

*At least 110,000 cases of accidental overdose of iron pills in children under 6 have been reported. Some were hospitalized and at least 35 died. From 1988 to 1992, children's deaths due to iron poisoning accounted for almost ⅙ of all children's poisoning deaths reported to poison control centers. (The number/percentage is increasing, probably due to the increased use of iron supplements among

Good Sources	Recommended Daily Allowances		
Milk and milk products; dark-green, leafy vegetables; broccoli; oysters; tofu; bone meal	Males and females	11–24 yrs.	1,200mg
		21 yrs. and older	800mg
	Pregnant/Lactating females		1,200mg
	Children	1–10 yrs.	800mg
	Infants	birth–6 mos.	400mg
		7 mos.–1 yr.	600mg
Seafood, iodized salt (in micrograms)	Males and females	11 yrs. and older	150mcg
	Pregnant females		25mcg
	Lactating females		50mcg
	Children	1–3 yrs.	70mcg
		4–6 yrs.	90mcg
		7–10 yrs.	120mcg
	Infants	birth–6 mos.	40mcg
		7 mos.–1 yr.	50mcg
Red meat and liver; egg yolks; green leafy vegetables; dried apricots; acidic foods prepared in cast-iron pots; whole-grain breads and cereals	Males	11–18 yrs.	12mg
		19 yrs. and older	10mg
	Females	11–50 yrs.	15mg
		51+ yrs.	10mg
	Pregnant females		30mg
	Lactating females		15mg
	Children	1–10 yrs.*	10mg
	Infants	birth–6 mos.*	6mg
		7 mos.–1 yrs.*	10mg
Milk and milk products; egg yolks; meat, poultry, and fish; whole-grain breads and cereals; beans; nuts	Males and females	11–24 yrs.	1,200mg
		25–51+ yrs.	800mg
	Pregnant/lactating females		1,200mg
	Children	1–10 yrs.	800mg
	Infants	birth–6 mos.	300mg
		7 mos.–1 yr.	500mg
Green, leafy vegetables; nuts; beans; whole-grain breads and cereals; oysters; scallops	Males	11–14 yrs.	270mg
		15–18 yrs.	400mg
		19 yrs. and older	350mg
	Females	11–14 yrs.	280mg
		15–18 yrs.	300mg
		19 yrs. and older	280mg
	Pregnant females		320mg
	Lactating females with infants	1–6 mos.	355mg
		7 mos.–1 yr.	340mg
	Children	1–3 yrs.	80mg
		4–6 yrs.	120mg
		7–10 yrs.	170mg
	Infants	birth–6 mos.	40mg
		7 mos.–1 yr.	60mg

adults.) New federal labeling/packaging regulations went into effect in July 1997 to address the issue; however, parents must be aware of this danger. Ingestion of as few as five tablets/200mg has caused death in children; immediate medical attention is required for any incident of known or possible overdose. Iron poisoning can also be harmful to adults.

continues

Minerals, Continued

Mineral	Chief Functions	Results of Deficiency
Potassium (K+)	Essential to regulation of fluid balance; aids in natural impulse transmission and muscle contraction	Muscle weakness; cardiac arrest; kidney damage (deficiency most often seen in people taking diuretics or dehydrated from prolonged diarrhea)
Selenium (Se)	Necessary for prevention of fat and body chemical breakdown	Deficiency almost unknown in humans, can cause cardiomyopathy
Sodium (Na+)	Necessary to maintenance of fluid balance	Deficiency rare in U.S.; sodium loss due to extremely heavy perspiration (usually in athletes) can cause muscle cramps, weakness, headache
Zinc (Zn++)	Essential element in enzymes necessary for digestion	Wounds slow to heal; loss of taste/appetite; stunted growth and sexual development in children

Health/Nutrition

Good Sources	Recommended Daily Allowances		
Bananas, citrus fruits, dried fruits; deep yellow vegetables; potatoes; beans; milk; whole grain breads and cereals	Males and females (including pregnant or lactating)	19–51+ yrs.	2,000mg
	Children	1 yr.	1,000mg
		2–5 yrs.	1,400mg
		6–9 yrs.	1,600mg
		10–18 yrs.	2,000mg
	Infants	birth–6 mos.	500mg
		7 mos.–1 yr.	700mg
Chicken; egg yolks; seafood; whole-grain breads and cereals; mushrooms, onions, and garlic	Males	11–14 yrs.	40 mcg
		15–18 yrs.	50 mcg
		19–51+ yrs.	70 mcg
	Females	11–14 yrs.	45 mcg
		15–18 yrs.	50 mcg
		19–51+ yrs.	65 mcg
	Pregnant females		65 mcg
	Lactating females		75 mcg
	Children	1–6 yrs.	20 mcg
		7–10 yrs.	30 mcg
	Infants	birth–6 mos.	10 mcg
		7 mos.–1 yr.	15 mcg
Table salt; processed foods; milk; drinking water (some locations)	Males and females	19–51+ yrs.	500mg
	Children	1 yr.	225mg
		2–5 yrs.	300mg
		6–9 yrs.	400mg
		10–18 yrs.	500mg
	Infants	birth–6 mos.	120mg
		7 mos.–1 yr.	200mg
Beef, liver; oysters/shellfish; yogurt; wheat germ; beans; fortified cereals	Males	11 yrs. and older	15mg
	Females	11 yrs. and older	12mg
	Pregnant females		30mg
	Lactating females		15mg
	Children 1–10 yrs.		10mg
	Infants birth–1 yr.		5mg

ALCOHOL CONSUMPTION

The effects of drinking alcoholic beverages depend in part on the amount of actual ethyl alcohol consumed and one's body weight. The level of alcohol in the blood is calculated in terms of milligrams (1 milligram = $\frac{1}{28,350}$ of an ounce) of pure alcohol per deciliter (1 deciliter = 3.5 fluid ounces) of blood. This is usually expressed as mg/dl. Twelve ounces of beer, 4 ounces of wine, or a 1.5-ounce shot of 80-proof whiskey, gin, or vodka contain approximately the same amount of ethyl alcohol: 8 grams, or 8,000 mg.

Blood alcohol concentrations often are expressed as a percentage of blood, as 0.05 percent for 50 milligrams of alcohol per deciliters of blood. It is recommended that drinkers keep their blood alcohol concentration (BAC) below 0.04 percent.

Depending on body weight and other factors, it takes the average adult nearly 1 hour for his or her liver to metabolize (break down) 8 grams of alcohol. Alcohol tends to accumulate in the blood because it is absorbed faster than it is metabolized.

Alcohol is absorbed through the membranes of the mouth and esophagus, from the stomach, and from the intestines. The rate of absorption is affected by proteins, fats, and carbohydrates in the digestive tract, which can slow absorption; by carbonation in drink mixers, which increases absorption; by the amount of water added to dilute the alcoholic beverage or the water or soft drinks consumed between alcoholic beverages; and by the presence of congeners (chemicals such as methyl alcohol, tannins, and histamines) present in the type of alcoholic beverage being consumed. The health of the drinker is also important, as a healthy liver metabolizes alcohol more efficiently.

> "Precautions During Pregnancy: Alcohol" in this chapter; "Beverages" in chapter 19
> Go to

A blood level of 20 to 30 mg/dl (the equivalent of 0.02 to 0.03 percent, or one or two drinks for an average adult) causes central nervous system changes in behavior, coordination, and ability to think clearly. Because alcohol is an anesthetic, the drinker may not notice the changes in his or her own behavior.

At a blood level of 50 mg/dl (0.05 percent), the drinker may experience sedation or a tranquilized feeling. Between 50 and 150 mg/dl (0.05 to 0.15 percent), there is a definite loss of coordination.

A concentration of 80 to 100 mg/dl (0.08 to 0.10 percent) is considered evidence of "legal intoxication" in many states, even though the alcohol level may be estimated by a breath test rather than actual blood analysis.

At blood levels between 150 and 200 mg/dl (0.15 and 0.20 percent), a person is obviously intoxicated and may show signs of delirium.

At levels between 300 and 400 mg/dl (0.30 and 0.40 percent), the drinker usually loses consciousness.

At levels above 500 mg/dl (0.50 percent), the heart and respiration become so depressed that they cease to function, and death follows.

DRINKING AND DRIVING

It is unsafe to drink and drive; in addition, many states have very strict driving-while-intoxicated (DWI) laws. The table on the next page is intended as a general guideline of at least how long to wait after imbibing before driving a motor vehicle. Note that it may take more than a night's sleep; a 115-pound person who has had 5 drinks in one evening may still be impaired the next morning, 13 hours later. The time varies, however, from person to person, and the best rule is "Don't drink and drive."

In the table, one drink equals 1½ ounces of liquor (86 proof), or 4 ounces of wine or champagne, or 12 ounces of beer.

WAITING PERIOD BEFORE DRIVING AFTER DRINKING

Body Weight	1 Drink	2 Drinks	3 Drinks	4 Drinks	5 Drinks	6 Drinks
100–119 pounds	0 hours	3 hours	6 hours	10 hours	13 hours	16 hours
120–139 pounds	0 hours	2 hours	5 hours	8 hours	10 hours	12 hours
140–159 pounds	0 hours	2 hours	4 hours	6 hours	8 hours	10 hours
160–179 pounds	0 hours	1 hour	3 hours	5 hours	7 hours	9 hours
180–199 pounds	0 hours	0 hours	2 hours	4 hours	6 hours	7 hours
200–219 pounds	0 hours	0 hours	2 hours	3 hours	5 hours	6 hours
Over 219 pounds	0 hours	0 hours	1 hour	3 hours	4 hours	6 hours

ADDITIONAL SOURCES OF INFORMATION

ORGANIZATIONS AND SERVICES

Alcoholics Anonymous
General Service Office
P.O. Box 459 Grand Central Station
New York, NY 10163
212-870-3400
http://www.alcoholics-anonymous.org

Alzheimer's Association
919 N. Michigan Ave., Ste. 1100
Chicago, IL 60611-1676
800-272-3900 (24-hour line) or 312-335-8700
http://www.alz.org/

The American Academy of Allergy, Asthma, & Immunology
611 E. Wells St.
Milwaukee, WI 53202
800-822-2762 (24-hour referral line)
http://www.aaaai.org

American Academy of Neurology
1080 Montreal Ave.
St. Paul, MN 55116
651-695-1940
http://www.aan.com

American Academy of Ophthalmology
655 Beach St.
San Francisco, CA 94109
415-561-8500
http://www.eyenet.org

American Cancer Society
1599 Clifton Rd., NE
Atlanta, GA 30329-4251
800-227-2345
http://www.cancer.org

American Chronic Pain Association
P.O. Box 850
Rocklin, CA 95677
916-632-0922
Fax: 916-632-3208

American Diabetes Association
1701 N. Beauregard St.
Alexandria, VA 22311
800-232-3472
Fax: 703-549-6995
http://www.diabetes.org

American Heart Association
Nation's Capital Affiliate
5535 Wisconsin Ave., NW, Ste. 940
Washington, DC 20015-2030
202-686-6888
Fax: 202-686-6162
http://americanheart.org

American Lung Association
1740 Broadway
New York, NY 10019-4374
212-315-8700
http://www.lungusa.org

American Medical Association
515 N. State St.
Chicago, IL 60610
312-464-5000
http://www.ama-assn.org/

American Optometric Association
243 N. Lindbergh Blvd.
St. Louis, MO 63141
314-991-4100
http://www.aoanet.org

American Speech-Language-Hearing Association
10801 Rockville Pike
Rockville, MD 20852
800-498-2071
TTY: 301-897-0157
Fax: 301-897-7355
http://www.asha.org

Health/Nutrition

Hot Lines and Information Services

A Closer Look

AIDS Hot Line	800-342-AIDS
Alzheimer's Disease and Related Disorders Association	800-621-0379
Cancer Hot Line	800-4-CANCER
Depression Hot Line	800-551-0008
Dial-a-hearing screening test	800-222-EARS
Medicare Hot Line	800-638-6833
Shriner's Hospital free children's hospital care referral line	800-237-5055

Arthritis Foundation
1330 W. Peachtree St.
Atlanta, GA 30309
800-283-7800 (24-hour recording) or 404-872-7100
http://www.arthritis.org

The Center for Nutrition Policy and Promotion
U.S. Department of Agriculture
1120 20th St., NW, Ste. 200, North Lobby
Washington, DC 20036
202-418-2312
Fax: 202-208-2321
http://www.usda.gov/cnpp

Center for Science in the Public Interest
Nutrition Action Healthletter
1875 Connecticut Ave., NW, Ste. 300
Washington, DC 20009
202-332-9110
Fax: 202-265-4954
http://www.cspinet.org

Centers for Disease Control and Prevention (CDC)
1600 Clifton Rd., NE
Atlanta, GA 30333
404-639-3311
http://www.cdc.gov/

CDC National Prevention Information Network
P.O. Box 6003
Rockville, MD 20849-6003
800-458-5231
TTY: 800-243-7012
e-mail: info@cdcnpin.org
http://www.cdcnpin.org

National Association of People With AIDS (NAPWA)
1413 K St., NW, Ste. 700
Washington, DC 20005
202-898-0414
Fax: 202-898-0435
http://www.napwa.org

National Cancer Institute
Public Inquiries Office
Bldg. 31, Room 10A03
31 Center Drive, MSC 2580
Bethesda, MD 20892
301-435-3848
http://www.nci.nih.gov/
http://www.cancernet.nci.nih.gov/

National Council on Alcoholism and
Drug Dependence
20 Exchange Place, Suite 2902
New York, NY 10005
800-622-2255 or 212-269-7797
Fax: 212-269-7510
http://www.ncadd.org/

National Institute of Child Health and
Human Development
Public Information and Communications Branch
Bldg. 31, Room 2A-32
31 Center Dr., MSC 2425
Bethesda, MD 20892-2425
301-496-5133
http://www.nichd.niv.gov/

National Institutes of Health
Bethesda, MD 20892
301-496-1776
Fax: 301-402-0601
http://www.nih.gov/

National Library of Medicine
8600 Rockville Pike
Bethesda, MD 20894
888-346-3656 or 301-594-5983
DOCLINE Service Desk: 800-633-5666
http://www.nlm.nih.gov/

National Women's Health Network
514 10th St., NW, Ste. 400
Washington, DC 20004
202-347-1140
http://www.womenshealthnetwork.org/

The President's Council on Physical Fitness and Sports
200 Independence Ave., SW, Ste. 738-H
Washington, DC 20201
202-690-9000
http://www.fitness.gov/

SMOKENDERS, Inc.
901 NW 133rd St., #A
Vancouver, WA 98685
800-828-4357

MAGAZINES

Natural Health
Box 1200
Brookline Village, MA 02147
http://www.naturalhealthmagazine.com

Prevention
Men's Health
33 E. Minor St.
Emmaus, PA 18098
http://www.prevention.com

Weight Watchers Magazine
360 Lexington Ave.
New York, NY 10017
http://www.weight-watchers.com

BOOKS

Alcoholics Anonymous. Alcoholics Anonymous World Services, 2001.

Cancer Research Institute HelpBook: What to Do When Cancer Strikes. (To order, send $2 postage and handling to Cancer Research Institute HelpBook, P.O. Box 5199, FDR Station, New York, NY 10150-5199, or call 800-992-2623.)

The Complete Food Count Guide. Editors of *Consumer Guide* with the Nutrient Analysis Center, Chicago Center for Clinical Research. Publications International, 1996.

Dupont, Robert L., and John P. McGovern. *A Bridge to Recovery: An Introduction to 12-Step Programs.* American Psychiatric Press, 1994.

Fries, James F., M.D. *Arthritis: A Comprehensive Guide to Understanding Your Arthritis.* 3rd ed. Addison-Wesley, 1990.

Garrison, Robert H., Jr., and Elizabeth Somer. *The Nutrition Desk Reference.* 3rd ed. Keats, 1997.

Greif, Judith, and Beth Ann Golden. *AIDS Care at Home: A Guide for Caregivers, Loved Ones, and People with AIDS.* Wiley, 1994.

Herbert, Victor, and Genell J. Subak-Sharpe, eds. *The Mount Sinai School of Medicine Complete Book of Nutrition.* St. Martin's Press, 1990.

Klesges, Robert C., and Margaret DeBon. *How Women Can Finally Stop Smoking.* Hunter House, 1994.

Komaroff, Anthony L., ed. *Harvard Medical School Family Health Guide.* Simon & Schuster, 1999.

Larson, David E., ed. *The Mayo Clinic Family Health Book.* 2nd ed. William Morrow, 1996.

Morgentaler, Abraham. *The Male Body: A Physician's Guide to What Every Man Should Know About His Sexual Health.* Fireside, 1993.

Northrup, Christiane. *Women's Bodies, Women's Wisdom: Creating Physical and Emotional Health and Healing.* Bantam Books, 1994.

Wexler, Nancy, Wesley J. Smith, and Ron Normon. *Mama Can't Remember Anymore: How to Manage the Care of Aging Parents.* Partners Publishing, 1997.

Yudofsky, Stuart C., Robert E. Hales, and Tom Ferguson. *What You Need to Know About Psychiatric Drugs.* American Psychiatric Press, 1991.

Health/Nutrition

19

HOUSEHOLD TIPS

FOOD

Properly preparing, storing, and cooking food is vital to a healthy, well-run household. The tips below provide information commonly needed in the kitchen.

COOKING EQUIVALENTS AND SUBSTITUTIONS

COMMON KITCHEN MEASURES

pinch (a few grains) = less than ⅛ teaspoon
3 teaspoons = 1 tablespoon
2 tablespoons = 1 fluid ounce
4 tablespoons = ¼ cup
5 tablespoons + 1 teaspoon = ⅓ cup
16 tablespoons = 1 cup
1 cup = ½ pint or 8 fluid ounces
2 cups = 1 pint
2 pints = 1 quart
4 quarts = 1 gallon
2 dry pints = 1 dry quart
8 dry quarts = 1 peck
4 pecks = 1 bushel

COOKING MEASUREMENT ABBREVIATIONS

Measure	Abbreviation
degrees Celsius	°C
degrees Fahrenheit	°F
fluid ounce	fl. oz.
gram	g
kilogram	kg
liter	l
milligram	mg
milliliter	ml
ounce	oz.
pint	pt.
pound	lb.
quart	qt.
tablespoon	tbsp.
teaspoon	tsp.

Go to "Recommended Daily (or Dietary) Allowances" and "Activities and the Calories They Consume" in chapter 18

METRIC COOKING MEASURE EQUIVALENTS

Customary	Metric
1 teaspoon	4.9 milliliters
1 tablespoon	14.8 milliliters
1 ounce (dry)	28.35 grams
1 fluid ounce	29.57 milliliters
1 cup	236.6 milliliters
1 pint	473.2 milliliters
1 quart	946.4 milliliters
0.9 quart (dry)	1 liter
1.06 quarts (liquid)	1 liter
1 pound	454 grams
2.2 pounds	1 kilogram
32° Fahrenheit (freezing point)	0° Celsius
212° Fahrenheit (boiling point)	100° Celsius

FOOD WEIGHTS AND MEASURES

Bread

1-pound loaf	12 to 16 slices
1 slice	½ cup soft or ¼ cup dry bread crumbs

Dairy

1 pound cheese	4 to 5 cups, shredded
1 pound cottage cheese	2 cups
3 ounces cream cheese	6 tablespoons
8 ounces cream cheese	1 cup
1 pound butter	2 cups (4 sticks)
1 quart milk	4 cups
1 pound instant nonfat dry milk	5 quarts liquid skim milk
13-ounce can evaporated milk	1⅔ cups
½ pint cream	1 cup
1 cup heavy cream	2 cups, whipped

Eggs

3 to 4	1 cup
8 to 10 whites	1 cup
12 to 14 yolks	1 cup
1 yolk	2 tablespoons

Flour

1 pound all-purpose flour	4 cups, sifted
1 pound cake flour	4¾ to 5 cups, sifted
1 pound whole-wheat flour	3½ to 3¾ cups, unsifted
1 pound cornmeal	3 cups

"U.S. Customary System of Weights and Measures" and "Metric System of Measurements" in chapter 2

Fruit

juice of 1 medium lemon	2 to 3 tablespoons
juice of 1 medium orange	⅓ to ½ cup
grated rind of medium orange	1 tablespoon
1 apple	1 cup, sliced
1 pound apples	3 cups, pared and sliced
3 to 4 bananas (1 pound)	1¾ cups, mashed
1 pound cherries	2 cups, pitted
1 pound cranberries	2 cups
1 pound grapes	2½ cups, seeded
1 pound raisins	2½ cups
1 pound cut candied fruit	3 cups
1 pound finely cut dates	1½ cups

Meat and Poultry

1 pound ground cooked meat	5 cups
1 pound diced cooked meat	5 cups
3½-pound chicken	3 cups diced, cooked

Nuts

1 pound almonds in shell	1¼ cups, shelled
1 pound pecans in shell	2 cups, chopped
1 pound walnuts in shell	1½ to 1¾ cups, chopped
¼ pound chopped nuts	about 1 cup

Sweeteners and Flavorings

1 pound confectioners' sugar	3½ cups
1 pound brown sugar	2¼ to 2½ cups, firmly packed
1 pound granulated sugar	2 cups
1 pound honey, molasses, or syrup	1⅓ cups or syrup
1 pound cocoa	4 cups
1 ounce unsweetened chocolate	1 square
6-ounce package chocolate chips	1 cup

Vegetables

1 whole bay leaf	¼ teaspoon, crushed
1 pound split peas	2½ cups
1 large green pepper	1 cup, diced
¼ pound sliced mushrooms (1¼ cups)	¼ to ½ cup, cooked
1 medium onion	½ cup, chopped
1 pound potatoes (3 medium)	2½ cups, sliced
1 pound green beans (3 cups)	2½ cups, cooked
1 pound cabbage	2½ cups, cooked
1 pound carrots	2½ cups, diced, or 2 cups, cooked
1 medium bunch celery	4½ cups, chopped
1 pound tomatoes (3 medium)	1½ cups, cooked

FOOD SUBSTITUTIONS

Ingredient	Substitution
Baking powder (1 teaspoon)	¼ teaspoon baking soda + ½ teaspoon cream of tartar
Baking powder (1¼ teaspoons)	½ teaspoon baking soda + 2 tablespoons vinegar
Black pepper	White pepper or paprika
Bouillon (1 cup)	1 bouillon cube dissolved in 1 cup hot water
Bread crumbs (1 cup)	¾ cup cracker crumbs
Butter (1 cup)	1 cup margarine *or* 1 cup vegetable shortening *or* ⅞ cup lard
Buttermilk or sour milk (1 cup)	1 cup yogurt *or* 1 cup whole milk + 1 tablespoon lemon juice *or* 1 tablespoon vinegar *or* 1¾ teaspoons cream of tartar
Carrots	Parsnips *or* baby white turnips
Chocolate Semisweet (1⅔ ounces)	1 ounce unsweetened chocolate + 4 teaspoons sugar
Unsweetened (1 ounce—1 square)	3 tablespoons cocoa powder + 1 tablespoon shortening
Cream, heavy (1 cup)	⅞ cup buttermilk *or* yogurt + 3 tablespoons butter
Croutons	Cubes of crustless white bread sautéed in butter
Curry powder	Turmeric plus cardamom, ginger powder, and cumin
Dry mustard	Prepared mustard
Egg, for thickening or baking	2 egg yolks

Household Tips

continues

Ingredient	Substitution
Flour	
All-purpose, for thickening (1 tablespoon)	1½ teaspoons cornstarch *or* 1½ teaspoons arrowroot *or* 1 tablespoon quick-cooking tapioca
All-purpose, for bread baking (1 cup)	Up to ½ cup bran, whole-wheat flour, *or* cornmeal + enough all-purpose flour to fill cup
Cake (1 cup sifted)	1 cup minus 2 tablespoons all-purpose flour
Fresh herbs (1 tablespoon)	⅓ to ½ teaspoon dried herbs
Honey (1 cup)	1¼ cups sugar + ¼ cup liquid, *or* 1 cup molasses
Lemon juice	Vinegar *or* lime juice *or* white wine
Mushrooms, fresh (1 pound)	6 oz. canned
Olive oil	Vegetable oil
Onion, chopped (1 cup)	1 tablespoon instant minced onion, reconstituted
Parsley	Chervil
Scallions	Green or white onions, *or* onion powder to taste
Shallots	2 parts onion + 1 part garlic
Sugar, brown (1 cup)	1 cup granulated sugar + 1 tablespoon molasses
Sugar, granulated (1 cup)	1¾ cups confectioners' sugar *or* 1 cup molasses + ½ teaspoon baking soda
Tomato sauce (2 cups)	¾ cup tomato paste + 1 cup water
Wine vinegar	Cider vinegar with a little red wine or white distilled vinegar with a little white wine
Yeast, active dry (1 tablespoon— 1 package)	1⅗-ounce cake yeast

KOSHER SUBSTITUTIONS

According to Jewish dietary laws, certain food items, such as pork products, shellfish, and some cuts of beef, are not allowed to be eaten. Also, meat and dairy products are not to be eaten at the same time. Below is a list of ingredients that may be problematic in preparing a kosher dish. On the right are acceptable replacements for these items.

Ingredient	Substitution
Butter	In pastry: all-vegetable margarine or vegetable shortening
	To sauté vegetables: all-vegetable margarine
	To fry meat or poultry: equal parts rendered chicken fat and oil; oil; equal parts oil and all-vegetable margarine
Ham or bacon	Used as flavoring: an equal quantity of anchovies, mushrooms, or pungent vegetables
Milk or cream	In chicken stew, soup, or sauce: for each ½ cup, ½ cup chicken stock mixed with 1 egg yolk and 1 teaspoon cornstarch
	In pancakes: an equal quantity of water, 1 tablespoon oil for each cup of flour, and twice as many eggs
Shellfish	An equal amount of firm fish that has both fins and scales

LOW-FAT SUBSTITUTIONS

Without changing your diet, you can significantly reduce your intake of fat by making the following substitutions for basic ingredients:

Ingredient	Substitution
Baker's chocolate, unsweetened	For each ounce, ¼ cup cocoa powder + 2 tsp. margarine
Butter	On vegetables and popcorn: butter substitute such as Butter Buds
	For sautéing onions and garlic: nonstick cooking spray and broth in a nonstick pan
	To prevent burning: chicken broth
Crème fraiche	Plain low-fat yogurt

Ingredient	Substitution
Eggs	For scrambled eggs and omelettes: egg substitute such as Egg Beaters
	For baking: 2 egg whites for 1 egg; 3 egg whites *or* 1 egg and 1 white for 2 eggs
Heavy cream	For whipped cream: substitute Cool Whip *or* low-fat whipped cream in a spray can
	For cooking: replace ½ cup cream with 1 tbsp. Butter Buds combined with ⅓ cup skim milk
Roux	Use cornstarch, arrowroot, or pureed vegetables, *or* make the roux with 1 tbsp. Butter Buds and ⅓ cup skim milk instead of the butter
Sour cream	Plain low-fat yogurt *or* 1 cup low-fat cottage cheese combined with 2 tbsp. skim milk and 1 tbsp. lemon juice in the blender
Whole milk	Skim *or* low-fat milk

Only tom (male) turkeys gobble. Hen turkeys make a clicking noise.

COOKING TIMES AND SERVING SIZES

When cooking meat, poultry, fish, and shellfish, the oven temperatures and cooking time used depends on the size of the serving.

OVEN TEMPERATURE SETTINGS

175° to 225°F	Warm
250° to 275°F	Very slow
300° to 325°F	Slow
350° to 375°F	Moderate
400° to 425°F	Hot
450° to 475°F	Very hot

ROASTING MEAT AND POULTRY

Recommended oven temperatures are given in parentheses. Use a meat thermometer to monitor internal temperatures.

To Roast Chicken (375°F)

Chickens weighing between 2 and 4 pounds can be roasted for 30 minutes per pound. Add 15 minutes to the total roasting time if the chicken is stuffed. When the chicken is done, a meat thermometer inserted in the thickest part of the thigh will read 190°F; a thermometer inserted in the stuffing will read 165°F. Estimate ½ pound per serving.

To Roast Beef (325°F)

Cut	Weight in Pounds	Minutes per Pound	Internal Temperature (°F)
Standing rib	4–8		
rare		20–25	140
medium		25–30	160
well-done		30–35	170
Rolled rib	5–7		
rare		30–35	140
medium		35–40	160
well-done		40–45	170
Rib eye	4–6		
rare		20	140
medium		22	160
well-done		24	170
Sirloin tip	3½–4	35–40	160
Tenderloin (roast at 425°F)			
whole	4–6	10	140
half	2–3	20	140

Household Tips

To Roast Lamb (325°F)

Cut	Weight in Pounds	Minutes per Pound	Internal Temperature (°F)
Leg	5–8	30–35	175–180
Shoulder	4–6	30–35	175–180
Cushion shoulder	3–5	30–35	175–180
Rib (rack)	4–5	40–45	175–180
Rolled shoulder	3–5	40–45	175–180
Crown roast	4–6	40–45	175–180

To Roast Pork (350°F)

Although human cases of trichinosis have greatly declined since 1950, pork should always be cooked to an internal temperature of at least 160° F, the temperature at which trichinosis parasites are killed.

Cut	Weight in Pounds	Minutes per Pound	Internal Temperature (°F)
Loin, center	3–5	20–22	160–170
Loin, half	5–7	22–25	160–170
Loin, rolled	3–5	25–30	160–170
Sirloin	3–4	25–30	160–170
Crown	4–6	20–22	160–170
Picnic shoulder	5–8	20–22	160–170
Rolled shoulder	3–5	22–25	160–170
Fresh ham (leg)			
whole	10–14	20–22	160–170
half	5–7	22–25	160–170
Spareribs	3	30	160–170

To Roast Ham and Other Cured Pork (325°F)

Cut	Weight in Pounds	Minutes per Pound	Internal Temperature (°F)
Whole ham	10–14		
uncooked		20	160
fully cooked		10	130
Half ham	5–7		
uncooked		25	160
fully cooked		15	130
Picnic shoulder	5–8	30	170
Rolled shoulder	2–4	40	170

To Roast Veal (325°F)

Cut	Weight in Pounds	Minutes per Pound	Internal Temperature (°F)
Leg	5–8	25–30	170
Loin	4–6	30–35	170
Rib (rack)	3–5	35–40	170
Rolled rump	3–5	40–45	170
Rolled shoulder	4–6	40–45	170

To Roast Duck or Goose (325°F)

Roast duck or goose about 30 minutes per pound. Estimate 1 pound per serving.

To Roast Turkey (325°F)

Turkey is done when a meat thermometer inserted in the thickest part of the thigh reads 185°F, or when a thermometer inserted in the stuffing reads 165°F. Plan on ½ pound per serving.

Ready-to-Cook Weight in Pounds	Total Number of Hours
4–8	3–4
8–12	4–4½
12–16	4½–5
16–20	6–7½
20–24	7½–9

BROILING MEAT AND POULTRY

To Broil Steak (place 2 inches from preheated oven broiler)

For a 1-inch-thick sirloin, porterhouse, T-bone, or ribeye:

Rare	5 minutes each side
Medium	7 minutes each side
Well-done	10 minutes each side

For a 1½-inch-thick sirloin, porterhouse, T-bone, or ribeye:

Rare	6 minutes each side
Medium	8 minutes each side
Well-done	12 minutes each side

For filet mignon, decrease the cooking time by 1 minute on each side. When grilling steak over hot charcoals, have the grill 3 inches from the fire and cook the meat 1 minute less on each side.

To Broil Lamb (place 2 inches from preheated oven broiler)

1-inch chops or patties	about 6 minutes on each side
1½-inch chops	9 minutes on each side
2-inch chops	11 minutes on each side

To Broil Pork (place 2 inches from preheated oven broiler)

Chops (¾ to 1 inch thick), shoulder steaks (½ to ¾ inch thick), and patties (1 inch thick) should be broiled about 11 minutes on each side.

For all boneless meat, allow ⅓ to ½ pound per serving; if the meat contains bone, estimate ½ to ¾ pound per serving.

Carving a Turkey

Before carving a turkey or other whole bird, allow it to rest breast side up on a platter outside the oven for 10 to 20 minutes, depending on size. This allows the juices to settle into the meat. While the bird is resting, make sure your carving knife (not serrated) is very sharp, and assemble a second large platter and a long two-tined carving fork.

1. Pierce the knee joint with the fork and bend the leg away from the body. Slice between the thigh and body to expose the hip joint, and then work the knife between the ball and socket to cut the leg from the body. Separate the thigh from the drumstick, slice the meat from each, and arrange on the serving platter. Repeat for the other leg.
2. Pierce the meaty part of the wing with the fork and pull the wing away from the body. Cut between the body and the wing, then through the wing joint to remove the wing from the body. Cut the wing in half at the joint and add the pieces to the serving platter, or remove the meat from the wing and arrange for serving.
3. Starting near the neck, slice the breast lengthwise across the grain of the meat. Continue removing slices until you reach the breastbone, and then turn the bird around and repeat for the second breast. Place the slices on the serving platter and enjoy.

COOKING FISH AND SHELLFISH

To Cook Fish

Fish can be cooked at either a very high temperature for a short time or a low temperature for a longer period. Following are general guidelines:

Baked	10 minutes at 500°F
Broiled	15 minutes
Deep-fried	2 minutes at 370°F
Pan-fried	10 minutes
Poached	10 minutes per pound
or steamed	

Allow ¾ to 1 pound of whole fish per serving, ½ pound per serving of dressed fish, fillets, and steaks.

To Cook Shellfish

There are many ways to cook shellfish. Here are just a few.

Starting with boiling water, drop in seafood and let it simmer as follows:

Shrimp	5 minutes
Crab	20 minutes
Lobster	20 to 40 minutes

Clams and mussels can be steamed until their shells just open.

Shrimp, scallops, clams, and oysters can be deep-fried at 370°F for about 3 minutes.

Allow the following quantities per serving:

1 quart unshelled soft-shell clams
1 to 2 crabs
1 small lobster or 1 pound unshelled lobster
6 to 8 oysters
⅔ cup or ⅓ pound shelled scallops
¼ pound unshelled shrimp

COOKING TIMES FOR FRESH VEGETABLES

Vegetable	Amount per Serving	Cooking Time (in minutes)*
Artichoke	1 whole	30–40
Asparagus	5–7 stalks	10–15
Beans (green and wax)	⅓ pound	5–10
Beans (lima)	¾ pound	20–25
Beets	⅓ pound	35–45, whole
Broccoli	½ pound	10–15
Brussels sprouts	⅓ pound	5–10
Cabbage	⅓ pound	5
Carrots	⅓ pound	10–15
Cauliflower	⅓ pound	20–25, whole; 10–15, flowerets
Corn	1–2 ears	5
Eggplant	¼ medium, sliced, broiled, or sautéed	5–10
Mushrooms	¼ pound, caps or sliced and sautéed	5
Onions	⅓ pound	20–30, whole
Peas	½ pound	5–10
Peppers (green)	1 medium, sliced sautéed	3–5
Potatoes	1 medium	20–25, sliced; 90, baked, 350°F
	3 small new	20–25, whole
Potatoes (sweet) or yams	1 medium, sliced	30–35
Spinach	½ pound	5
Squash (summer) or zucchini	½ pound, sliced, boiled, or sautéed	5–10
Tomatoes	½ pound, sliced	5–10 (without water)
Turnips	⅓ pound, cubed	25–30

* Boiled or steamed unless otherwise noted.

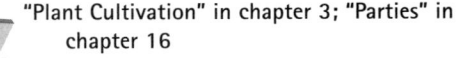

"Plant Cultivation" in chapter 3; "Parties" in chapter 16

Go to

COOKING FRESH FRUIT

To cook any of the fruits below, prepare the fruit according to the directions and add to the proper amount of boiling water. Add sugar and cook for the appropriate time.

Fruit	Amount[1]	How to Prepare	Amount of Boiling Water (cups)	Amount of Sugar (cups)	Cooking Time After Adding Fruit (in minutes)
Apples	8 medium	Pare and slice	½	¼	8 to 10 (slices) 12 to 15 (sauce)
Apricots	15	Halve; pit and peel if desired	½	¾	5
Cherries	1 quart	Remove pits	1	⅔	5
Cranberries	1 pound	Sort	1 or 2, as desired[2]	2	5
Peaches	6 medium	Pare, pit, and halve or slice	¾	¾	5
Pears	6 medium	Pare, core, and halve or slice	⅔	⅓	10 (soft varieties); 20 to 25 (firm varieties)
Plums	8 large	Halve, pit	½	⅔	5
Rhubarb	1½ pounds	Slice	¾	⅔	2 to 5

[1] Makes 6 servings, about ½ cup each.   [2] Cranberries make 6 servings with 1 cup water; 8 servings with 2 cups water.

SERVING LARGER GROUPS

Here's how much to buy when you need to feed a crowd.

Type	8 Servings	12 Servings	16 Servings
Meat/Poultry/Fish			
Boneless	2–3 lbs.	3–4 lbs.	5–6 lbs.
Chops, roasts	3–5 lbs.	5–7 lbs.	7–9 lbs.
Ribs	6–8 lbs.	9–12 lbs.	12–15 lbs.
Whole birds	8–10 lbs.	12–14 lbs.	16–20 lbs.
Greens			
Lettuce	1–2 heads	2–3 heads	4–5 heads
Cooked leafy greens, peas	4 lbs.	6 lbs.	8 lbs.
Other vegetables	2 lbs.	3 lbs.	4 lbs.
Frozen, in 1-lb. bags	2 bags	3 bags	4 bags
Starches			
Potatoes	2–3 lbs.	4–5 lbs.	6–7 lbs.
Rice (uncooked)	3 cups	4½ cups	6 cups
Pasta (uncooked)	1 lb.	1½ lbs.	2 lbs.
Potato or pasta salad	1 quart	2 quarts	3 quarts
Dessert			
Cakes	1	1	2
Pies	1	2	3
Ice cream	2 pints	4 pints	6 pints
Drinks			
Iced drinks	2 liters	4 liters	6 liters
Coffee (ground)	¼ lb.	½ lb.	1 lb.

A
Closer
Look

Recommended Maximum Food Storage Times

Food	Maximum	Type of Storage	Food	Maximum	Type of Storage
Beef	1–3 days	Refrigerator	Flour	8 months	Pantry
Butter	2 weeks	Refrigerator	Ground meat	1–2 days	Refrigerator
Canned goods	1 year	Pantry	Milk	1 week	Refrigerator
Cereal	2–3 months	Pantry	Dried pasta	2 years	Pantry
Cheese	1–3 weeks	Refrigerator	Poultry	1–2 days	Refrigerator
Eggs	1–2 weeks	Refrigerator	Rice	2 years	Pantry
Fish	1 day	Refrigerator			

A
Closer
Look

Temperature of Food for Control of Bacteria

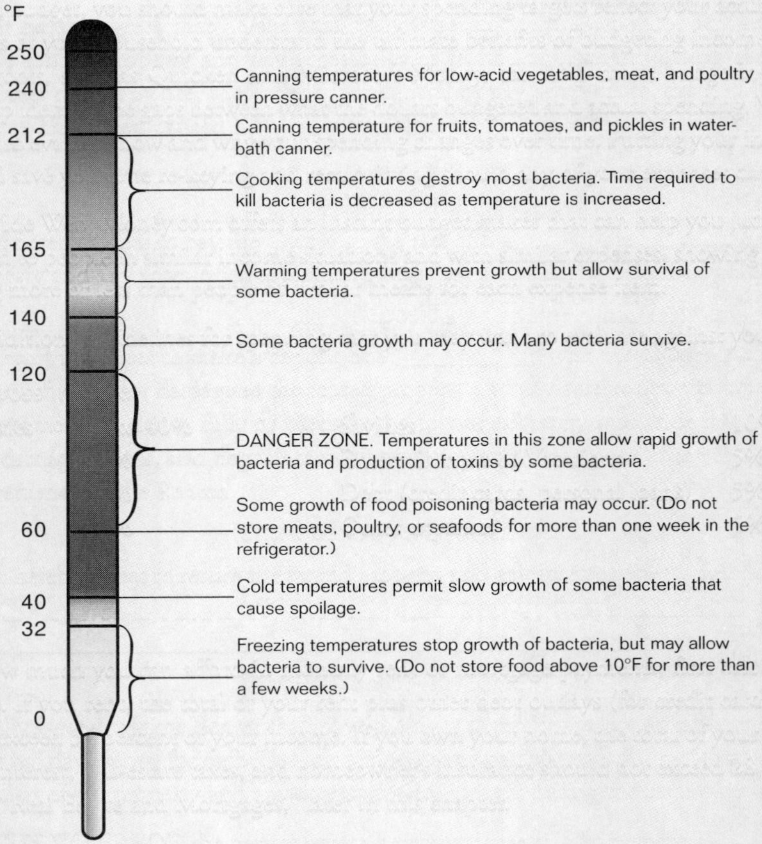

°F

- 250
- 240 — Canning temperatures for low-acid vegetables, meat, and poultry in pressure canner.
- 212 — Canning temperature for fruits, tomatoes, and pickles in water-bath canner.
  — Cooking temperatures destroy most bacteria. Time required to kill bacteria is decreased as temperature is increased.
- 165 — Warming temperatures prevent growth but allow survival of some bacteria.
- 140 — Some bacteria growth may occur. Many bacteria survive.
- 120 — DANGER ZONE. Temperatures in this zone allow rapid growth of bacteria and production of toxins by some bacteria.
- 60 — Some growth of food poisoning bacteria may occur. (Do not store meats, poultry, or seafoods for more than one week in the refrigerator.)
- 40 — Cold temperatures permit slow growth of some bacteria that cause spoilage.
- 32 — Freezing temperatures stop growth of bacteria, but may allow bacteria to survive. (Do not store food above 10°F for more than a few weeks.)
- 0

Household Tips

"Temperature Conversions" in chapter 12

Go to

FOOD HOT LINES

To provide consumers with information on cooking, health, and nutrition, several organizations have established toll-free telephone services.

Nutrition Hot Line
American Institute for Cancer Research
800-843-8114
e-mail: aicrweb@aicr.org

Center for Food Safety and Applied Nutrition
888-723-3366

Turkey Talk-Line
Butterball
800-323-4848 (November–December only)

Meat and Poultry Hot Line
Department of Agriculture
800-535-4555
800-256-7072 (TDD/TTY)

Holiday Bake-Line
Land-O-Lakes
800-782-9606 (November–December only)

Nutrition Information Line
American Dietetic Association
800-366-1655

PANTRY BASICS

Certain ingredients are used so frequently by the typical home cook that they should always be ready. Keep the following basics on hand at all times to simplify weekly and daily shopping and cooking.

Canned goods   fruit juice, soft drinks, tomato sauce, soups, canned beans, peanut butter, tuna fish

Condiments   ketchup, prepared mustard, mayonnaise, maple syrup, Tabasco® sauce, soy sauce, Worcestershire sauce®, horseradish, salad dressing, tahini

Dry goods   coffee, tea, breakfast cereal, rice, pasta, dried beans, flour, bread crumbs, baking soda, baking powder, yeast, cornstarch, cream of tartar

Fats and oils   butter, olive oil, vegetable oil

Fresh foods   bread, milk, eggs, cheese, yogurt, celery, carrots, potatoes, garlic, onions, lemons, limes

Seasonings   sugar, salt, black pepper, paprika, oregano, basil, bay leaves, cayenne pepper, dry mustard, curry powder, chili powder, cumin, coriander, thyme, sage, rosemary, dill, tarragon, ginger, cinnamon, nutmeg, cloves, cocoa, vanilla extract, honey, wine vinegar, balsamic vinegar

HERBS AND SPICES

Herbs can provide creative, flavorful alternatives to salt for seasoning foods. Through the skillful use of herbs and spices, you can create imaginative flavors and turn simple foods into gourmet delights.

Employees at the Ivory Soap company overmixed a batch of soap, causing it to be filled with excess bubbles. As a result, the soap floated. Customers loved it, and Ivory soap has been floating ever since.

Herbs and spices differ only in that most herbs grow in temperate areas while most spices grow in tropical regions. Many people like to grow their own herbs in order to have a fresh supply throughout the growing season. Professional cooks also prefer fresh herbs. Because fresh herbs are less concentrated, two to three times as much of them should be used if a recipe calls for dried herbs.

Here are some tips for cooking with herbs and spices.

- In general, the weaker the flavor of the main staple item, the lower the level of added seasoning required to achieve a satisfactory balance of flavor in the end product.
- Dried herbs are stronger than fresh, and powdered herbs are stronger than crumbled. A useful formula is ¼ teaspoon powdered herb = ¾ to 1 teaspoon crumbled = 2 teaspoons fresh.

Household Tips

- Leaves should be finely chopped because the more cut surface exposed, the more flavor will be absorbed.
- A mortar and pestle can be used to powder dry herbs when necessary.
- Scissors are often the best utensil for cutting fresh herbs.
- Be conservative with amounts until you are familiar with the strength of an herb. The aromatic oils can be too strong if a great deal is used.
- The flavoring of herbs is lost by extended cooking. Add herbs to soups or stews about 45 minutes before completing the cooking. For cold foods such as dips, cheeses, vegetables, and dressings, herbs should be added several hours, or even overnight, before using.
- For casseroles and hot sauces, add finely chopped fresh or dried herbs directly to the mixture.
- To become familiar with the specific flavor of an herb, try mixing it with butter and/or cream cheese, letting it set for at least an hour, and then spreading it on a plain cracker.
- Dried herbs should be stored in plastic bags, boxes, or tins rather than cardboard containers. They should be out of direct sunlight and away from the stove.

As a world commodity, coffee is second only to crude oil.

Household Tips

SELECTING HERBS AND SPICES TO GO WITH FOODS

Food	Herbs and Spices
Beef	Bay leaf, chives, cloves, cumin, garlic, hot pepper, marjoram, rosemary, savory
Bread	Allspice, caraway, cardamom, curry powder, marjoram, oregano, poppy seed, rosemary, thyme
Cakes	Allspice, cardamom, ginger
Cheese	Anise, basil, chervil, chives, curry, dill, fennel, garlic, marjoram, oregano, parsley, sage, thyme
Fish	Sweet basil, chervil, dill, fennel, French tarragon, garlic, parsley, thyme
Fruit	Anise, cinnamon, coriander, cloves, ginger, lemon verbena, mint, rose geranium, sweet cicely
Lamb	Garlic, marjoram, oregano, rosemary, thyme
Pork	Coriander, cumin, garlic, ginger, hot pepper, pepper sage, savory, thyme
Poultry	Garlic, oregano, rosemary, sage, savory
Salads	Anise, basil, chives, dill, French tarragon, garlic chives, marjoram, mint, oregano, parsley, savory, sorrel, tarragon (many are best used fresh or added to salad dressing; otherwise, use herb vinegars for extra flavor)
Sauces	Allspice, basil, cardamom, chili powder, chives, cumin, curry, fennel, ginger, marjoram, oregano, parsley, rosemary
Soups	Bay leaf, chervil, French tarragon, marjoram, parsley, savory, rosemary
Stews	Allspice, basil, cardamom, chili powder, curry, dill, ginger, parsley, sage
Vegetables	Basil, chervil, chives, dill, French tarragon, marjoram, mint, parsley, pepper, thyme

Herbal Salt Substitutes

A Closer Look

These can be placed in shakers and used instead of salt.

Basic salt substitute   Use 2 teaspoons garlic powder and 1 teaspoon each of basil, oregano, and powdered lemon rind (or dehydrated lemon juice). Put ingredients into a blender and mix well. Store in a glass container and add rice to prevent caking.

Tangy salt substitute   Mix well 3 teaspoons basil; 2 teaspoons each of savory (summer is best), celery seed, ground cumin seed, sage, and marjoram; and 1 teaspoon lemon thyme. Powder with a mortar and pestle.

Spicy seasoning   Mix in a blender 1 teaspoon each of cloves, pepper, and coriander seed (crushed); 2 teaspoons paprika; and 1 tablespoon rosemary. Store in an airtight container.

CHEMICAL ADDITIVES

Additives are substances not naturally found in foods that are introduced during processing to improve flavor, appearance, or consistency or to preserve freshness.

COMMON ADDITIVE TERMS

Antioxidants retard the oxidation of unsaturated fats and oils, colorings, and flavorings. Oxidation leads to rancidity, flavor changes, and loss of color. Most of these effects are caused by the reaction of oxygen in the air with fats.

Chelating agents trap trace amounts of metal atoms that would otherwise cause food to discolor or go rancid.

Emulsifiers keep oil and water mixed together.

Flavor enhancers contribute little or no flavor of their own, but accentuate the natural flavor of foods. They are most often used when very little of a natural ingredient is present.

Thickening agents are natural or chemically modified carbohydrates that absorb some of the water present in food, thereby making the food thicker. Thickening agents "stabilize" factory-made foods by keeping the complex mixtures of oils, water, acids, and solids well mixed.

TYPES OF ADDITIVES

The information on the following pages comes from the Center for Science in the Public Interest and is available from the organization as a color chart entitled "Chemical Cuisine." The address is 1875 Connecticut Ave., NW, Suite 300, Washington, DC 20009-5728 or call 202-332-9110.

Following each entry is a letter that corresponds to one these three categories:

(A) *Avoid.* The additive is unsafe in the amounts normally consumed or is poorly tested.

(C) *Caution.* The additive may be unsafe, is poorly tested, or is used in foods that people tend to eat too much of.

(S) *Safe.* The additive appears to be safe.

CHEMICAL ADDITIVES

ALGINATE; PROPYLENE GLYCOL ALGINATE Thickening agent, foam stabilizer *Ice cream, cheese, candy, yogurt*	Alginate, an apparently safe derivative of seaweed (kelp), maintains the desired texture in dairy products, canned frosting, and other factory-made foods. Propylene glycol alginate, a chemically modified algin, thickens acidic foods (soda pop, salad dressing) and stabilizes the foam in beer. (S)
ALPHA TOCOPHEROL (vitamin E) Antioxidant, nutrient *Vegetable oil*	Vitamin E is abundant in whole wheat, rice germ, and vegetable oils. It is destroyed by the refining and bleaching of flour. Vitamin E prevents oils from turning rancid. (S)
ARTIFICIAL COLORINGS	Most artificial colorings are synthetic chemicals that do not occur in nature. Though some are safer than others, colorings are not listed by name on labels. Colorings are used almost solely in foods of low nutritional value (candy, soda pop, gelatin desserts, etc.). Several dyes have caused allergic reactions (Yellow No. 5) or promoted cancer, and there is evidence that colorings may cause hyperactivity in some sensitive children. The use of coloring usually indicates that fruit or other natural ingredients have not been used. (A)
ARTIFICIAL FLAVORINGS *Soft drinks, candy, breakfast cereals, gelatin desserts, other food items.*	Hundreds of chemicals are used to create flavors; many may be used in a single flavoring, as in cherry soda pop. Most flavoring chemicals also occur in nature and are probably safe, but they may cause hyperactivity in some children. (A)

continues

Chemical Additives, Continued

ASCORBIC ACID (vitamin C); ERYTHORBIC ACID Antioxidant, nutrient, color stabilizer *Oily foods, cereals, soft drinks, cured meats*	Ascorbic acid helps maintain the red color of cured meats and prevents the formation of nitrosamines (see also SODIUM NITRITE). It helps prevent loss of color and flavor by reacting with unwanted oxygen. It is used as a nutrient additive in drinks and breakfast cereals. Sodium ascorbate is a more soluble form of ascorbic acid. Erythorbic acid (sodium erythorbate) serves the same functions as ascorbic acid but has no value as a vitamin. (S)
ASPARTAME Artificial sweetener *Drink mixes, gelatin, desserts, other foods*	Aspartame, made up of two amino acids, was thought to be the perfect artificial sweetener, but questions have arisen about the quality of the cancer tests done on it. In addition, some individuals have reported severe behavioral effects after drinking diet soda. People with PKU should avoid it. (C)
BETA CAROTENE Coloring, nutrient *Margarine, shortening, non-dairy whiteners, butter*	Beta carotene is used as an artificial coloring and a nutrient supplement. The body converts it to vitamin A, which is part of the light-detection mechanism of the eye. (S)
BROMINATED VEGETABLE OIL (BVO) Emulsifier, clouding agent *Soft drinks*	BVO keeps flavor oils in suspension and gives a cloudy appearance to citrus-flavored soft drinks. The residues of BVO found in body fat are cause for concern. Safer substitutes are available. (A)
BUTYLATED HYDROXYANISOLE (BHA) Antioxidant *Cereals, chewing gum, potato chips, vegetable oil*	BHA retards rancidity in fats, oils, and oil-containing foods. While most studies indicate it is safe, a 1982 Japanese study demonstrated that it causes cancer in rats. This synthetic chemical often can be replaced by safer chemicals. (A)
BUTYLATED HYDROXYTOLUENE (BHT) Antioxidant *Cereals, chewing gum, potato chips, oils, other edibles*	BHT retards rancidity in oils. It both increased and decreased the risk of cancer in various animal studies. Residues of BHT occur in human fat. BHT is unnecessary or is easily replaced by safe substitutes. (A)
CAFFEINE Stimulant *Coffee, tea, cocoa (natural), soft drinks (additive)*	Caffeine may cause miscarriages or birth defects and should be avoided by pregnant women. It also keeps many people from sleeping. New evidence indicates that caffeine may cause fibrocystic breast disease in some women. (A)
CALCIUM (OR SODIUM) PROPIONATE Preservative *Bread, rolls, pies, cakes*	Calcium propionate prevents mold on bread and rolls. The calcium is a beneficial mineral; the propionate is safe. Sodium propionate is used in pies and cakes because calcium alters the action of chemical leavening agents. (S)
CALCIUM (OR SODIUM) STEAROLYL LACTYLATE Dough conditioner, whipping agent *Bread dough, cake fillings, artificial whipped cream, processed egg white*	This additive strengthens bread dough so that it can be used in bread-making machinery for more uniform grain and volume. It acts as a whipping agent in dried, liquid, or frozen egg white and artificial whipped cream. Sodium stearoyl fumerate serves the same purpose. (S)
CARRAGEENAN Thickening and stabilizing agent *Ice cream, jelly, chocolate milk, infant formula*	Carrageenan is obtained from seaweed. Large amounts of carrageenan have harmed test animals' colons; the small amounts in food are probably safe. Better tests are needed. (C)

"Vitamin/Mineral Food Chart" in chapter 18

Go to

CASEIN; SODIUM CASEINATE Thickening and whitening agent *Ice cream, ice milk, sherbet, coffee creamers*	Casein, the principal protein in milk, is a nutritious protein that contains adequate amounts of all the essential amino acids. (S)
CITRIC ACID; SODIUM CITRATE Acid flavoring, chelating agent *Ice cream, sherbet, fruit drinks, candy, carbonated beverages, instant potatoes*	Citric acid is versatile, widely used, cheap, and safe. It is an important metabolite in virtually all living organisms and is especially abundant in citrus fruits and berries. It is used as a strong acid, a tart flavoring, and an antioxidant. Sodium citrate, also safe, is a buffer that controls the acidity of gelatin desserts, jam, ice cream, candy, and other foods. (S)
CORN SYRUP Sweetener, thickener *Candy, toppings, syrups, snack foods, imitation dairy foods*	Corn syrup is a sweet, thick liquid made by treating cornstarch with acids or enzymes. It may be dried and used as corn syrup solids in coffee whiteners and other dry products. Corn syrup contains no nutritional value other than calories, promotes tooth decay, and is used mainly in low-nutrition foods. (C)
DEXTROSE (GLUCOSE, CORN SUGAR) Sweetener, coloring agent *Bread, caramel, soda pop, cookies, other foods*	Dextrose is an important chemical in every living organism. A sugar, it is a source of sweetness in fruits and honey. Added to foods as a sweetener, it represents empty calories and contributes to tooth decay. Dextrose turns brown when heated and contributes to the color of bread crust and toast. (C)
DIGLYCERIDES	*See* MONOGLYCERIDES and DIGLYCERIDES.
ETHYLENEDIAMINE TETRA-ACETIC ACID (EDTA) Chelating agent *Salad dressing, margarine, sandwich spreads, mayonnaise, processed fruits and vegetables, canned shellfish, soft drinks*	Modern food-manufacturing technology, which involves metal rollers, blenders, and containers, results in trace amounts of metal contamination in food. EDTA traps metal impurities, which would otherwise promote rancidity and the breakdown of artificial colors. (S)
FERROUS GLUCONATE Coloring, nutrient *Black olives, vitamin pills*	Used by the olive industry to generate a uniform jet-black color and in pills as a source of iron, this substance is safe. (S)
FUMARIC ACID Tartness agent *Powdered drinks, pudding, pie, fillings, gelatin desserts*	A solid at room temperature, inexpensive, and highly acidic, fumaric acid is the ideal source of tartness and acidity in dry food products. However, it dissolves slowly in cold water, a drawback cured by adding dioctyl sodium sulfosuccinate (DSS), a poorly tested, detergentlike additive. (S)
GELATIN Thickening and gelling agent *Powdered dessert mix, yogurt, ice cream, cheese spreads, beverages*	Gelatin is a protein obtained from animal bones, hooves, and other parts. It has little nutritional value because it contains little or none of several essential amino acids. (S)
GLYCERIN (GLYCEROL) Maintainer of water content *Marshmallows, candy, fudge, baked goods*	Glycerin forms the backbone of fat and oil molecules and is quite safe. The body uses it as a source of energy or as a starting material in making more complex molecules. (S)
GUMS (ARABIC, FURCELLERAN, GHATTI, GUAR, KARAYA, LOCUST BEAN, TRAGACANTH) Thickening agents, stabilizers *Beverages, ice cream, frozen puddings, salad dressings, dough, cottage cheese, candy, drink mixes*	Gums derive from natural sources (bushes, trees, or seaweed) and are poorly tested. They are used to thicken foods, prevent sugar crystals from forming in candy, stabilize beer foam (arabic), form gel in pudding (furcelleran), encapsulate flavor oils in powdered drink mixes, and keep oil and water mixed in salad dressings. Tragacanth sometimes causes severe allergic reactions. (S)

Household Tips

continues

Chemical Additives, Continued

HEPTYL PARABEN Preservative *Beer, noncarbonated soft drinks*	Heptyl paraben—short for the heptyl ester of parahydroxybenzoic acid—is a preservative. Studies suggest that this chemical is safe, but, like other additives in alcoholic beverages, it has never been tested in the presence of alcohol. (C)
HYDROGENATED VEGETABLE OIL Source of oil or fat *Margarine, processed foods*	Vegetable oil, usually a liquid, can be made into a semisolid by treating it with hydrogen. Hydrogenation reduces levels of polyunsaturated oils. Many people eat too much oil and fat of all kinds, natural and hydrogenated. High-fat diets promote obesity, heart disease, and possibly cancer. (C)

HYDROLYZED VEGETABLE
   PROTEIN (HVP)
Flavor enhancer
*Instant soups, frankfurters, sauce
   mixes, beef stew*
	HVP consists of vegetable (usually soybean) protein that has been chemically broken down into the amino acids of which it is composed. HVP is used to bring out the natural flavor of food. (S)

INVERT SUGAR Sweetener *Candy, soft drinks, many other foods*	Invert sugar, an even mixture of dextrose and fructose (two sugars), is sweeter and more soluble than sucrose (table sugar). Invert sugar forms when sucrose is split in two by an enzyme or acid. It contributes to tooth decay. (C)
LACTIC ACID Acidity regulator *Spanish olives, cheese, frozen desserts, carbonated beverages*	This safe acid occurs in almost all living organisms. It inhibits spoilage in Spanish-type olives, balances the acidity in cheese making, and adds tartness to frozen desserts, carbonated fruit-flavored drinks, and other goods. (S)
LACTOSE Sweetener *Whipped topping mix, breakfast pastry*	Lactose is a carbohydrate found only in milk. One-sixth as sweet as table sugar, it is added to food as a slightly sweet source of carbohydrate. Milk turns sour when bacteria convert lactose to lactic acid. Worldwide, more people are lactose-intolerant than tolerant. Many people not of northern European descent have trouble digesting lactose. (S)
LECITHIN Emulsifier, antioxidant *Baked goods, margarine, chocolate, ice cream*	A common constituent of animal and tissues, lecithin is a source of the nutrient choline. It keeps oil and water from separating, retards rancidity, reduces spattering in a frying pan, and leads to fluffier cakes. Major sources are egg yolks and soybeans. (S)
MANNITOL Sweetener, other uses *Chewing gum, low-calorie foods*	Not quite as sweet as sugar and poorly absorbed by the body, mannitol contributes only half as many calories as sugar. Used as the "dust" on chewing gum, it prevents gum from absorbing moisture and becoming sticky. (S)

MONOGLYCERIDES and
   DIGLYCERIDES
Emulsifiers
*Baked goods, margarine, candy,
   peanut butter*
	These substances make bread softer, improve the stability of margarine, and make caramel less sticky. They prevent staleness and keep the oil in peanut butter from separating. Monoglycerides and diglycerides are safe, though most foods they are used in are high in refined flour, sugar, or fat. (S)

MONOSODIUM
   GLUTAMATE (MSG)
Flavor enhancer
*Soup, seafood, poultry, cheese,
   sauces, stews, other foods*
	This amino acid brings out the flavor of protein-containing foods. Large amounts of MSG fed to infant mice destroyed nerve cells in the brain. Public pressure forced baby food companies to stop using MSG. MSG can cause a burning sensation in the back of the neck and forearms, tightness of the chest, and headaches in some people. (C)

PHOSPHORIC ACID;
   PHOSPHATES
Acidulant, chelating agent,
   buffer, emulsifier, nutrient,
   discoloration inhibitor
*Baked goods, cheese, powdered
   foods, cured meats, soft drinks,
   cereals, dehydrated potatoes*
	Phosphoric acid acidifies and flavors cola beverages. Phosphate salts are in hundreds of processed foods for many purposes. Calcium and iron phosphates act as mineral supplements. Sodium aluminum phosphate is a leavening agent. Calcium and ammonium phosphates serve as food for yeast in bread. Sodium acid pyrophosphate prevents discoloration. Phosphates are not toxic, but their widespread use has led to dietary imbalances that may contribute to osteoporosis. (C)

POLYSORBATE 60 Emulsifier *Baked goods, frozen desserts,* * imitation dairy products*	Polysorbate 60 is short for polyoxyethylene-(20)-sorbitan monostearate. Like its close relatives polysorbate 65 and 80, it works the same way that diglycerides do, but smaller amounts are needed. They keep baked goods from going stale, keep dill oil dissolved in bottled dill pickles, help coffee whiteners dissolve in coffee, and prevent oil from separating out of artificial whipped cream. (S)
PROPYL GALLATE Antioxidant *Vegetable oils, meat products,* * potato sticks, chicken soup* * base, chewing gum*	This substance retards the spoilage of fats and oils and is often used with BHA and BHT because of the synergistic effect these additives have. The best long-term feeding study on this additive was peppered with suggestions but not proof of cancer. (A)
QUININE Flavoring *Tonic water, quinine water,* * bitter lemon*	This drug can cure malaria and is used as a bitter flavoring in a few soft drinks. There is a slight chance that quinine may cause birth defects, so pregnant women should avoid quinine-containing beverages and drugs. It has been very poorly tested. (A)
SACCHARIN Synthetic sweetener *Diet products*	Saccharin is 350 times sweeter than sugar. Studies have not shown that saccharin helps people lose weight. In 1977, the FDA proposed that saccharin be banned because of repeated evidence that it causes cancer. It is gradually being replaced by aspartame. (A)
SALT (SODIUM CHLORIDE) Flavoring *Most processed foods*	Salt is used liberally in many processed foods. Other additives contribute additional sodium. A diet high in sodium may cause high blood pressure, which increases the risk of heart attack and stroke. (A)
SODIUM BENZOATE Preservative *Fruit juices, carbonated drinks,* * pickles, preserves*	Manufacturers have used sodium for over 70 years to prevent the growth of microorganisms in acidic foods. (S)
SODIUM CARBOXY- ** METHYL-CELLULOSE** ** (CMC)** Thickening and stabilizing agent *Ice cream, beer, pie fillings, icings,* * diet foods, candy*	CMC is made by reacting cellulose with derivative of acetic acid. Studies indicate that CMC is safe. (S)
SODIUM NITRITE; ** SODIUM NITRATE** Preservative, coloring, flavoring *Bacon, ham, frankfurters,* * luncheon meats, smoked fish,* * corned beef*	Nitrite can lead to the formation of small amounts of potent cancer-causing chemicals (nitrosamines), particularly in fried bacon. Nitrite is tolerated in foods because it can prevent the growth of bacteria that cause botulism poisoning. Nitrite also stabilizes the red color in cured meats and gives a characteristic flavor. Companies should find safer methods of preventing botulism. Sodium nitrate is used in dry-cured meats because it slowly breaks down into nitrite. (A)
SORBIC ACID; ** POTASSIUM SORBATE** Prevents growth of mold *Cheese, syrup, jelly, cakes,* * wines, dry fruits*	These additives occur naturally in many plants and are safe under normal circumstances. (S)
SORBITAN ** MONOSTEARATE** Emulsifier *Cakes, candy, frozen desserts,* * puddings, icings*	Like monoglycerides, diglycerides, and polysorbates, this additive keeps oil and water mixed. In chocolate candy, it prevents the discoloration that occurs when the candy is warmed up, then cooled down. (S)

continues

Household Tips

Chemical Additives, Continued

SORBITOL
Sweetener, thickening agent,
    maintainer of moisture
*Dietetic drinks and foods, candy,
    shredded coconut, chewing gum*
	Sorbitol occurs naturally in fruits and berries and is a close relative of the sugars; however, it is half as sweet as sugar. It is used in noncariogenic chewing gum because oral bacteria do not metabolize it well. Large amounts of sorbitol (2 ounces for adults) have a laxative effect, but otherwise it is safe. Diabetics use sorbitol because it is absorbed slowly and does not cause blood sugar to increase rapidly. (S)

STARCH; MODIFIED STARCH Thickening agent *Soups, gravies, baby foods*	Starch, the major component of flour, potatoes, and corn, is used as a thickening agent. It does not, however, dissolve in cold water. Chemists have solved this problem by reacting starch with various chemicals. These modified starches are added to some foods to improve their consistencies and to keep the solids suspended. Starch and modified starches make foods look thicker and richer than they really are. (S)
SUGAR (SUCROSE) Sweetener *Table sugar, sweetened foods*	Sucrose, ordinary table sugar, occurs naturally in fruit, sugar cane, and sugar beets. Americans consume about 65 pounds of refined sugar per person per year. Sugar, corn syrup, and other refined sweeteners make up about one-eighth of the average diet, but they contain no vitamins, minerals, or protein. (A)

SULFUR DIOXIDE; SODIUM
    BISULFITE
Preservative, bleach
*Dried fruits, wines, processed
    potatoes*
	Sulfiting agents prevent discoloration (in dried fruits, some "fresh" shrimp, and some dried, fried, and frozen potatoes) and bacterial growth (in wines). They also destroy vitamin B_1 and can cause severe reactions in asthmatics. This additive has caused at least seven deaths. (A)

VANILLIN; ETHYL VANILLIN Substitute for vanilla *Ice cream, baked goods, beverages, chocolate, candy, gelatin desserts*	Vanilla flavoring is derived from a bean, but vanillin, the major flavor component of vanilla, is cheaper to produce in a factory. A derivative, ethyl vanillin, comes closer to matching the taste of real vanilla. Both chemicals are safe. (S)

OUTLAWED ADDITIVES

Name	Year Outlawed	Use
Cobalt salts	1966	Beer foam stabilizer
Cyclamate	1960	Artificial sweetener
Dulcin	1950	Artificial sweetener
Green No. 1	1965	Coloring agent
Orange B	1978	Coloring agent
Red No. 2	1976	Coloring agent
Safrole	1960	Root beer flavoring
Violet No. 1	1973	Coloring agent

Go to "Consumer Information and Protection" in chapter 22; "Treatment for Health Emergencies" in chapter 17; "Home Remedies" in chapter 18

BEVERAGES

Selecting and serving beverages, especially alcoholic beverages, can often be confusing. The information below is intended to aid hosts and hostesses serve their guests responsibly and pleasurably.

AMOUNT OF LIQUOR NEEDED FOR NUMBER OF DRINKS SERVED

Liquor is commonly sold in 750-milliliter and 1-liter bottles. A 750-milliliter bottle is equivalent to 25.4 fluid ounces. One liter is equivalent to 33.8 fluid ounces.

Champagne Bottle Sizes

Name	Capacity	Bottles
Bottle	0.75 liter	1
Magnum	1.5 liters	2
Jeroboam	3 liters	4
Rehoboam	4.5 liters	6
Methuselah	6 liters	8
Salmanazar	9 liters	12
Balthazar	12 liters	16
Nebuchadnezzar	15 liters	20

Number of People	Number of Drinks	Amount Needed
For cocktails		
4	10 to 16	one 750-ml bottle
6	15 to 22	two 750-ml bottles
8	18 to 24	two 750-ml bottles
12	20 to 40	three 750-ml bottles
20	40 to 65	three 1-liter bottles
For buffet or dinner		
4	8 cocktails	one 750-ml bottle
	8 glasses of wine	two 1-liter bottles
	4 liqueurs	one 750-ml bottle
	10 highballs	one 750-ml bottle
6	12 cocktails	one 750-ml bottle
	12 glasses of wine	three 1-liter bottles
	8 liqueurs	one 750-ml bottle
	16 highballs	two 750-ml bottles
8	16 cocktails	one 750-ml bottle
	16 glasses of wine	three 1-liter bottles
	16 liqueurs	one 750-ml bottle
	18 highballs	two 750-ml bottles
20	40 cocktails	three 750-ml bottles
	40 glasses of wine	seven 1-liter bottles
	25 liqueurs	two 750-ml bottles
	50 highballs	three 1-liter bottles
For after-dinner party		
4	12 to 16	one 750-ml bottle
6	18 to 26	two 750-ml bottles
8	20 to 34	two 750-ml bottles
12	25 to 45	three 750-ml bottles
20	45 to 75	three 1-liter bottles plus one 750-ml bottle

Household Tips

MIXING DRINKS

Always be sure of your ingredients and measure them accurately. A jigger is 1½ ounces; a pony, ¾ ounce; a bar spoon, ½ teaspoon; and a dash, 7 to 10 drops.

Ice should always be the first ingredient that goes into the glass. Use new ice for every drink and do not let drinks stand too long before serving. The best bartenders chill cocktail glasses in the refrigerator before serving.

Drinks containing fruit juices, eggs, or other dissimilar ingredients should always be shaken fast and vigorously. The ingredients will mix more readily and completely in a shaker or an electric blender. Never shake drinks mixed with carbonated water or ginger ale. Stir them smoothly and not too vigorously for about half a minute. This will keep the drink sparkling and prevent a flat taste. It also will chill the drink properly and thoroughly.

When a drink calls for fruit juice, use fresh juice if possible. The juice is put into the mixing glass with the proper amount of sugar or other sweetener before the liquor.

Fine granulated sugar can be used for sweetening in most cases. Many people prefer simple syrup, which can easily be made by dissolving 2 cups of granulated sugar in 1 cup of boiling water. One teaspoon of simple syrup is equivalent to one teaspoon of sugar.

For drinks requiring a twist of lemon, orange, or lime, use a piece of peel about 1½ inches long and ¼ inch wide. Twist this over the drink to extract a bit of oil, and then drop in the peel.

ALCOHOLIC DRINK RECIPES

Except where otherwise indicated, *shake* means to shake with cracked ice and then strain into a glass; *stir* means to stir over ice in the glass; and *straight up* means served without ice.

"Alcohol Consumption" and "Precautions During Pregnancy" in chapter 18

Go to

Alexander   Shake 1 oz. brandy, 1 oz. crème de cacao, and 1 oz. cream.

B & B   Stir ½ oz. benedictine and ½ oz. brandy (or cognac); B & B may also be served straight up.

Black Russian   Stir 1½ oz. vodka and ¾ oz. Kahlua®.

Black Velvet   Pour equal parts Guinness® stout and champagne over ice in a tall glass.

Bloody Mary   Shake or stir 1½ oz. vodka, 3 oz. tomato juice, the juice of ½ lemon, a dash each of Worcestershire® and Tabasco® sauce, and a pinch each of salt, pepper, and celery salt.

Bronx Cocktail   Shake 1 oz. gin, ½ oz. dry vermouth, ½ oz. sweet vermouth, and ½ oz. orange juice.

Bullshot   Substitute consommé for tomato juice and follow the directions for Bloody Mary.

Champagne Cocktail   Mix 1 lump sugar, 2 dashes angostura bitters, and 1 oz. brandy; top with chilled champagne.

Cosmopolitan   Shake 1¼ oz. Absolut Citron®, ¼ oz. Rose's® lime juice, ¼ oz. Cointreau® or triple sec, ¼ cup cranberry juice, 1 cup ice cubes; garnish with lime.

Cuba Libre (Rum and Coke®)   Over ice in a tall glass, pour 1 oz. light rum and the juice of ½ lime; top with cola.

Daiquiri   Shake 1½ oz. light rum, the juice of 1 lime, and 1 teaspoon powdered sugar (often served with the addition of crushed fruit or fruit juice as strawberry daiquiri, peach daiquiri, etc.; blended with crushed ice, it becomes a frozen daiquiri).

Gibson   A martini with the addition of a pearl onion instead of the traditional olive.

Gimlet   Shake 1 oz. gin and 1 oz. Rose's® lime juice or the juice of 1 lime.

Gin and Tonic   Pour 2 oz. gin over ice in a tall glass; top with tonic water.

Gin Fizz   Shake 2 oz. gin, the juice of ½ lemon, and 1 teaspoon powdered sugar; top with soda water in a tall glass.

Grasshopper   Shake ½ oz. crème de menthe, ½ oz. white crème de cacao, and ½ oz. cream.

Harvey Wallbanger   Add 1 oz. Galliano® to a Screwdriver.

Jack Rose   Shake 1½ oz. apple brandy, the juice of ½ lime, and 1 teaspoon grenadine.

Kir   To a glass of chilled white wine, add 1 teaspoon crème de cassis.

Mai Tai   Shake 2 oz. rum, 1 oz. curaçao, the juice of ½ lime, ½ oz. grenadine, ½ oz. almond-flavored syrup, and ½ teaspoon powdered sugar; serve over crushed ice.

Manhattan   Stir with cracked ice 1½ oz. whiskey, ¾ oz. sweet vermouth, and a dash of angostura bitters; serve over ice or straight up with a maraschino cherry.

Margarita   Shake 1½ oz. tequila, ½ oz. Cointreau® or triple sec, and the juice of ½ lime; serve in a chilled, salt-rimmed glass.

Martini   Stir gin and dry vermouth; strain into a chilled glass. The original ratio of gin to vermouth was 2:1, but contemporary tastes tend toward "drier" ratios of 3:1, 5:1, and even 7:1. Serve straight up with an olive or, less traditionally, over ice or with a lemon twist. Made with a pearl onion, it is called a Gibson; with vodka, a vodka martini or Vodkatini.

Mint Julep   Mix in a tall glass 1 lump sugar, 1 tablespoon water, and 4 sprigs of mint; fill the glass with crushed ice; add 2 oz. bourbon, and serve with straws, without stirring.

Old-Fashioned   Mix in a short glass ½ lump sugar, 2 dashes angostura bitters, and 1 dash water; stir in ice cubes and 2 oz. whiskey.

Orange Blossom   Shake 1 oz. gin and 1 oz. orange juice.

Pimm's Cup   Over ice in a tall glass, pour 1 oz. Pimm's No. 1 Cup®; top with lemonade, 7-Up®, or ginger ale.

Piña Colada   Over crushed ice in a tall glass, pour ½ oz. light rum; ½ oz. dark rum; 1 oz. each of orange, lime, and pineapple juice; and 1 dash of grenadine. Top with coconut milk.

Before refrigerators, ice was cut from frozen lakes in the winter, put aboard ships, and transported around the world.

Pink Gin   Add 1 dash angostura bitters to 2 oz. gin. Pink Gin may be served straight up or with water or soda and ice.

Planter's Punch   Over crushed ice in a tall glass, pour 2 oz. soda water, the juice of 2 limes, and 2 teaspoons powdered sugar; stir to frost glass; add 2 dashes angostura bitters and 2 oz. rum.

Rickey   Over cracked ice, pour 2 oz. gin and the juice of ½ lime; top with soda water. This traditional gin rickey is often modified by substituting other spirits—hence, Scotch rickey, Irish rickey, etc.

Rob Roy   Using Scotch whiskey, follow the directions for a Manhattan.

Rusty Nail   Stir 2 oz. Scotch whiskey with 1 oz. Drambuie®.

Salty Dog   Stir 2 oz. gin, 2 oz. grapefruit juice, and ¼ teaspoon salt.

Sangre   A Bloody Mary made with tequila instead of vodka.

Screwdriver   Over ice in a tall glass, pour 2 oz. vodka; top with orange juice.

7 & 7   Over ice, pour 1½ oz. Seagram's® whiskey; top with 7-Up.®

Sidecar   Shake 1 oz. brandy, ½ oz. Cointreau® or triple sec, and the juice of ½ lemon.

Household Tips

Singapore Sling   Shake 2 oz. gin, ½ oz. cherry brandy, the juice of ½ lemon, and 1 teaspoon powdered sugar; pour over ice cubes in a tall glass and top with soda water.

Stinger   Shake or stir 1 oz. brandy and 1 oz. white crème de menthe.

Tequila Sunrise   Shake or stir in a tall glass 1½ oz. tequila and 3 oz. orange juice; add 1 oz. grenadine; do not stir.

Toddy   Dissolve 1 lump sugar in a little water in a short glass; add 2 oz. spirits (brandy, gin, rum, or whiskey) and top with water (with boiling water, the drink is a hot toddy).

Tom Collins   Shake 2 oz. gin, the juice of ½ lemon, and 1 teaspoon powdered sugar; pour over ice cubes in a tall glass and top with soda water (made with vodka in place of gin, this is a Vodka Collins).

Whiskey Sour   Shake 2 oz. whiskey, the juice of ½ lemon, and ½ teaspoon powdered sugar.

White Lady   Shake 1½ oz. gin, 1 teaspoon powdered sugar, 1 teaspoon cream, and 1 egg white.

Zombie   Blend with cracked ice 3 oz. rum, ½ oz. apricot brandy, 1 oz. pineapple juice, the juice of 1 lime and 1 orange, and 1 teaspoon powdered sugar. Strain into a tall frosted glass; float ½ oz. rum (151 proof) on top before serving with straws.

WINES AND THEIR SERVICE

Red table wines should be served cool or at room temperature. Room temperature means about 65 to 68°F, so some cooling may be necessary. Red wines go well with all foods with the possible exception of seafood. White table wines, rosé wines, and all sparkling wines—both red and white—should be served well chilled. Dry wines should not be served with sweet dishes.

So that corks stay moist and tight, store wines on their sides. If the cork is removed an hour or two before serving, red wines will expand a bit and give off a delightful scent. Smell the cork to see if it is sour-smelling; if so, the wine has started to turn to vinegar and should not be served; it can, however, be kept for cooking.

Many good wines will contain a small amount of sediment. This is harmless and will settle on the bottom of the bottle if it is stood upright for about two hours before serving. When serving champagne, hold the bottle at a slight angle for a few seconds after the cork is removed. This reduces the amount of frothing and maintains a maximum amount of sparkle.

Wineglasses should be placed to the right of the water goblet; they are arranged according to their use, the first wineglass being closest to the water goblet. If more than one wine is served, the glasses used first are removed when the course is through.

The person serving should fill his or her own glass one-quarter full and then taste the wine to check the quality and flavor. Then the other glasses should be filled half to three-quarters full but never to the very top. Wine is poured as soon as a course is served. The person pouring should not lift the glasses from the table.

When more than one wine is served, remember that light wine comes before heavy or full wine, dry white wine precedes sweet red wine, and dry red wine is served before white sweet wine. The "correct" wine is always the one you like best; however, certain wines complement certain foods. The following wine and food list is a guide to what people generally like. One's own taste should be the final judge.

SELECTING WINES TO GO WITH FOODS

After Dinner   Brandy, Cointreau, benedictine, crème de menthe.

Canapés, Crackers, Olives, Cheese Dips, Other Hors d'Oeuvres   Sherry, vermouth, or champagne.

Cheese or Nuts   Port, sherry, red Burgundy, muscatel, zinfandel, Barbera.

How to Store Coffee

Bean form	Room temperature	4–5 weeks
	Freeze	5–6 months (grind amount needed only)
	Refrigerator	Avoid
Ground	Room temperature	7–10 days
	Freezer	5–6 weeks
	Refrigerator	Up to 3 weeks

Desserts   Sweet sauterne, champagne, port, muscatel, Tokay.

Fowl   Rhine wine, dry sauterne, champagne, Bordeaux, white or red Burgundy (with game).

Meats   Claret, red Burgundy, rosé (with cold cuts).

Seafood   Chablis, Rhine wine, Moselle, dry sauterne, white Burgundy.

Soups   Sherry or Madeira.

PRIME WINE VINTAGES BY REGION/VARIETY

The years of prime wine vintages are given in descending order of quality.

Australia

Coonawarra: 1990, 1997, 1991, 1998/99
Hunter Valley: 1991, 1998, 1999, 1996

Chile

1999, 1997, 1996, 1994

California

Cabernet Sauvignon: 1994, 1997, 1991, 1992
Chardonnay: 1997, 1995, 1992, 1991
Pinot Noir: 1997, 1994, 1991, 1999
Zinfandel: 1994, 1996, 1993, 1991

France

Alsace: 1997, 1990, 1996, 1998
Bordeaux, red: 1990, 1995, 1998, 1994
Bordeaux, white: 1990, 1999, 1997, 1998
Burgundy, red: 1990, 1996, 1995, 1997
Burgundy, white: 1990, 1996, 1995, 1992
Loire: 1996, 1995, 1990, 1999
Rhone: 1998, 1990, 1995, 1999

Germany

Mosel: 1990, 1996, 1995, 1994
Rhine: 1996, 1990, 1994, 1999

Italy

Piedmont: 1990, 1998, 1996, 1997
Tuscany: 1997, 1990, 1995, 1999
Veneto/Amarone: 1997, 1990, 1995, 1998

Spain

Ribera del Duero: 1996, 1995, 1991, 1994
Rioja: 1995, 1994, 1999, 1990

CLOTHING

The following section contains instructions about properly washing clothing, removing stains, and choosing the right size.

WASHING INSTRUCTIONS FOR DIFFERENT FABRIC TYPES

Cottons and Linens   Separate whites and colors. Pretreat and soak heavily soiled articles. Load washer about 3 pounds lighter than manufacturer's recommendation. Wash whites and colorfast items in very hot water with all-purpose detergent for a full washer cycle. Extremely dirty articles should be washed separately. Use cool water for colors that are likely to bleed, with a shorter cycle for lightly soiled loads. For lightweight and sheer cottons, wash whites in warm water and colors in cool water with an all-purpose detergent for a shortened washing cycle.

Synthetics   Wash white nylon separately from other synthetics, as it picks up color easily. A 3- or 4-pound load of easy-care fabrics washes and dries with fewer wrinkles than a capacity load. Wash in warm

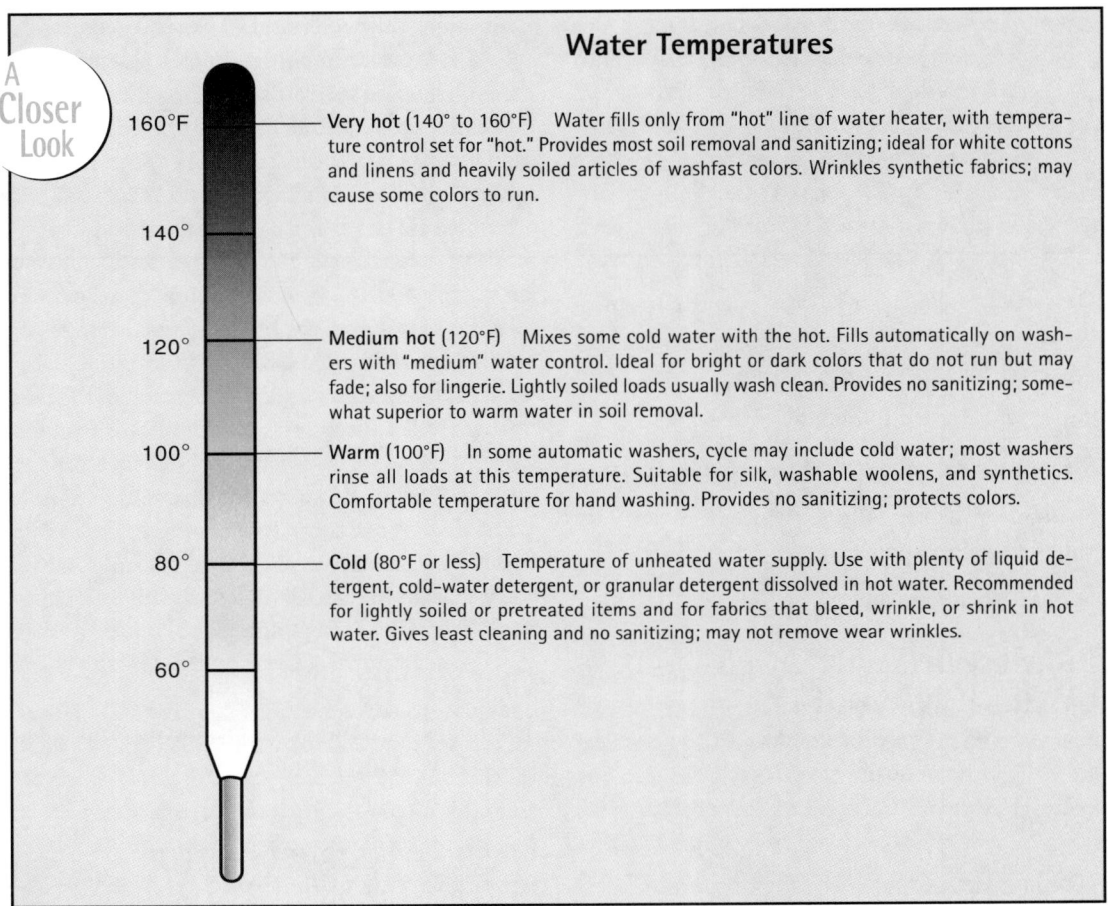

Water Temperatures

Very hot (140° to 160°F)   Water fills only from "hot" line of water heater, with temperature control set for "hot." Provides most soil removal and sanitizing; ideal for white cottons and linens and heavily soiled articles of washfast colors. Wrinkles synthetic fabrics; may cause some colors to run.

Medium hot (120°F)   Mixes some cold water with the hot. Fills automatically on washers with "medium" water control. Ideal for bright or dark colors that do not run but may fade; also for lingerie. Lightly soiled loads usually wash clean. Provides no sanitizing; somewhat superior to warm water in soil removal.

Warm (100°F)   In some automatic washers, cycle may include cold water; most washers rinse all loads at this temperature. Suitable for silk, washable woolens, and synthetics. Comfortable temperature for hand washing. Provides no sanitizing; protects colors.

Cold (80°F or less)   Temperature of unheated water supply. Use with plenty of liquid detergent, cold-water detergent, or granular detergent dissolved in hot water. Recommended for lightly soiled or pretreated items and for fabrics that bleed, wrinkle, or shrink in hot water. Gives least cleaning and no sanitizing; may not remove wear wrinkles.

160°F

140°

120°

100°

80°

60°

or cool water with an all-purpose detergent and a shortened washing cycle. Use hot water for badly soiled articles.

Woolens and Delicates   Hand wash in cold water with Woolite® or a similar detergent and rinse thoroughly. Roll woolens tightly in a towel to remove excess water (do not wring) and dry flat on a drying rack. Allow delicates to drip-dry. Follow manufacturer's instructions when "dry clean only" appears on the care label.

TECHNIQUES FOR WASHING FABRICS

Soaking   To help loosen stains and dirt, soak heavily soiled articles, dusty curtains and draperies, and certain stained fabrics before washing. Agitate the items for a few minutes in the washer with warm

water and detergent, using about half the detergent needed for washing. Extract the water before washing as usual. If you have to soak only a few items, use a small container such as a bucket. Submerge the fabric in a warm detergent solution for 15 minutes or until stains diminish. Agitate with your hands and extract excess water before washing as usual.

Loading   A washer load made up of two large sheets or tablecloths with a variety of smaller articles washes more effectively than one made up of all large articles. Bulky pieces such as blankets, bedspreads, and throw rugs should be washed individually.

Rinsing   To maximize effective rinsing, do not overload your washer or add more detergent than recommended by the manufacturer. If the machine does not extract water efficiently, have its spinning mechanism checked.

To reach out-of-the-way places with your vacuum cleaner, use an empty wrapping paper tube as an extension. Flatten the end of the tube to reach into tight crevices.

Using Fabric Softener   Fabric softeners make textiles softer and fluffier while minimizing wrinkles and deep creases. Softeners also reduce the static electricity that builds up on some fabrics when they rub against each other. Add fabric softener to the final rinse water in proportion to the weight of the clothes rather than the volume of water. Some softeners come in sheets that you can add to the dryer. To keep fabrics soft, use a softener each time you wash, as washing removes any softener added to previous loads.

STAIN REMOVAL

Many common stains fall into one of three categories: greasy, nongreasy, and combination. These stains can be removed by following the appropriate method for each given below. When necessary, separate directions are given for washable and nonwashable articles. Directions for nonwashables are for articles made of fabrics that are not damaged by the application of small amounts of water.

GREASY STAINS

Washable Articles   Regular washing, either by hand or by machine, removes some greasy stains. Some stains can be removed by rubbing soap or detergent into the stain and then rinsing with warm water. On some wash-and-wear or permanent-press fabrics, it may be necessary to rub soap or detergent thoroughly into the stain and allow it to stand for several hours, or overnight, before rinsing. Often, however, a grease solvent is necessary; this is effective even after an article has been washed. Sponge the stain thoroughly with the grease solvent and dry. Repeat if necessary. It often takes extra time to remove greasy stains from a fabric with a special finish.

A yellow stain may remain after a solvent treatment if the stain has been set by age or heat. To remove a yellow stain, use a chlorine or peroxygen bleach. If it is safe for the fabric, a strong sodium perborate treatment is usually the most effective.

Nonwashable Articles   Sponge stains well with grease solvent and dry. Repeat if necessary. It may take extra time to remove greasy stains from fabrics with a special finish.

A yellow stain may remain after a solvent treatment if the stain has been set by age or heat. To remove a yellow stain, use a chlorine or peroxygen bleach. If safe for the fabric, a strong sodium perborate treatment is usually the most effective.

NONGREASY STAINS

Many fresh stains can be removed by simple treatments. Stains set by heat or age may be difficult or impossible to remove.

Washable Articles   Sometimes, regular laundry methods will remove nongreasy stains; in other cases, laundering will actually set the stains. Sponge the stain with cool water or soak it in cool water for 30 minutes or longer; some stains require an overnight soak. If the stain persists after sponging or soaking, work a soap or detergent into it and then rinse. If the stain remains after detergent treatment, use a chlorine or peroxygen bleach.

Nonwashable Articles   Sponge the stain with cool water. If it remains, rub soap or detergent on the stain and work it into the fabric. Rinse. A final sponging with rubbing alcohol helps to remove the soap or detergent and to dry the fabric more quickly. Test alcohol on the fabric first to be sure it does not affect the dye. Dilute the alcohol with 2 parts of water before using it on acetate. If the stain remains after rinsing, use a chlorine or peroxygen bleach.

Household Tips

COMBINATION STAINS

Combination stains are caused by materials that contain both greasy and nongreasy substances.

Washable Articles Sponge the stain with cool water or soak in cool water for 30 minutes or longer. If the stain persists, work soap or detergent into it and then rinse thoroughly. Allow the article to dry. If a greasy stain remains, sponge with a grease solvent. Allow the article to dry. Repeat if necessary. If a colored stain remains after the fabric dries, use a chlorine or peroxygen bleach.

Nonwashable Articles Sponge the stain with cool water. If it remains, rub soap or detergent on the stain and work it into the fabric. Rinse the spot well with water. Allow the article to dry. If a greasy stain remains, sponge with a grease solvent. Allow to dry. Repeat if necessary. If a colored stain remains after the fabric dries, use a chlorine or peroxygen bleach.

SPECIFIC STAINS

Adhesive Tape Scrape gummy matter from stains carefully with a dull table knife; avoid damaging fabric. Sponge with a grease solvent.

Early mattresses were filled with straw and held up with a rope stretched across the bed frame. If the rope was tight, sleep was comfortable. Hence the phrase, "sleep tight."

Alcoholic Beverages Follow directions for nongreasy stains. An alternative method, if alcohol does not affect the color of the fabric, is to sponge the stain with rubbing alcohol. Dilute alcohol with 2 parts of water before using on acetate. If a stain remains, use a chlorine or peroxygen bleach.

The alcohol in alcoholic beverages will cause bleeding of some dyes, which results in loss of color or formation of a dye ring around the edge of the stain. When either change occurs, the original appearance of the fabric cannot be restored.

Antiperspirants and Deodorants Wash or sponge the stain thoroughly with soap or detergent and warm water. Rinse. If the stain is not removed, use a chlorine or peroxygen bleach. Antiperspirants that contain such substances as aluminum chloride are acid; they may cause fabric damage and change the color of some dyes. Fabric color may be restored by sponging with ammonia. Dilute ammonia with an equal volume of water for use on wool or silk. Rinse.

Blood Follow directions for nongreasy stains, with one variation. If the stain is not removed by soap or detergent, put a few drops of ammonia on it and repeat the treatment with detergent. Rinse. Follow with a bleach treatment if necessary. Bloodstains that have been set by heat will be difficult to remove.

Candy and Syrup For chocolate candy and syrup, follow directions for combination stains. For other candy and syrup, follow directions for nongreasy stains.

Carbon Paper Work soap or detergent into the stain; rinse well. If the stain is not removed, put a few drops of ammonia on it and repeat the treatment; rinse well. Repeat again if necessary.

Chewing Gum Scrape gum off without damaging fabric. The gum can be scraped off more easily if it is first hardened by rubbing it with ice. If a stain remains, sponge thoroughly with a grease solvent.

Chlorine Bleach Use one of the following treatments to remove yellow chlorine bleach stains from fabrics with resin finishes, or to prevent such stains from appearing. Always treat the fabric before ironing it. On some fabrics, the yellow stains form before ironing; on others, after ironing. In either case, ironing before the chlorine is removed weakens the fibers.

Yellow stains caused by the use of chlorine bleach on wool and silk cannot be removed. White or faded spots caused by use of chlorine bleach on colored fabrics cannot be restored to the original color.

Treatment for any fabric: Rinse fabric thoroughly with water. Then soak for 30 minutes or longer in a solution containing 1 teaspoon of sodium thiosulfate to each quart of warm water. Rinse thoroughly. To strengthen the treatment, make the sodium thiosulfate solution as hot as is safe for the fabric.

Treatment for white or colorfast fabrics: Rinse the fabric thoroughly with water. Then use a color remover, following the directions given on the package for removing stains.

Coffee and Tea   *With cream:* Follow directions for combination stains.

Without cream: Follow directions for nongreasy stains.

Alternatively, for both types of stains, and if safe for the fabric, pour boiling water through the spot from a height of 1 to 3 feet.

Correction Fluid   Sponge the stain with acetone or amyl acetate. Use amyl acetate on acetate, Arnel®, Dynel®, and Verel®; use acetone on other fabrics.

Cosmetics and Crayon   *Washable articles:* Apply undiluted liquid detergent to the stain, or dampen the stain and rub in soap or detergent until thick suds are formed. Work in until the outline of the stain is gone; then rinse well. Repeat if necessary. It may help to dry the fabric between treatments.

Nonwashable articles: Sponge with a grease solvent until no more color is removed. If the stain is not removed, use the method given for washable articles.

Dyes   Follow directions for nongreasy stains; if bleach is needed, use chlorine bleach or color remover. A long soak in sudsy water often is effective on fresh dye stains.

Fish Slime, Mucus, Vomit   Follow directions for nongreasy stains or treat the stain with a lukewarm solution of salt and water—¼ cup salt to each quart of water. Sponge the stain with the solution or soak the stain in it. Rinse well.

Fruit, Fruit Juices   Follow directions for nongreasy stains or, if it is safe for the fabric, pour boiling water through the spot from a height of 1 to 3 feet. When any fruit juice is spilled on a fabric, it is a good idea to sponge the spot immediately with cool water. Some fruit juices, citrus among them, are invisible on the fabric after they dry but turn yellow on aging or heating. This yellow stain may be difficult to remove.

Furniture Polish   Follow directions for greasy stains or, if the polish contains wood stain, follow directions given for paint.

Glue and Mucilage   *Airplane glue, household cement:* Follow directions for correction fluid.

Casein glue: Follow directions for nongreasy stains.

Plastic glue: Wash the stain with soap or detergent and water before the glue hardens; some types of glues cannot be removed after they have hardened.

To remove some dried plastic glue stains, immerse the stain in a hot 10-percent acetic acid solution or hot vinegar. Keep acid or vinegar at or near the boiling point until the stain is removed. This may take 15 minutes or longer. Rinse with water.

Other types of glues and mucilage: Follow directions for nongreasy stains, but soak the stain in hot water instead of cool.

Grass, Flowers, Foliage   *Washable articles:* Work soap or detergent into the stain; then rinse. If it is safe for the dye, sponge the stain with alcohol. Dilute the alcohol with 2 parts of water for use on acetate. If the stain remains, use a chlorine or peroxygen bleach.

Nonwashable articles: Use the methods for washable articles, but try alcohol first if it is safe for the dye.

Ink, Ballpoint   Sponge the stain repeatedly with acetone or amyl acetate, or spray it with hair spray. This will remove fresh stains. Old stains may also require bleaching. Washing removes some types of ballpoint ink stains but sets other types. To see whether the stain will wash out, mark a scrap of similar material with the ink and wash it.

Household Tips

Ink, Black (India ink) Treat the stain as soon as possible. These stains are very hard to remove if dry.

Washable articles: Force water through the stain until all loose pigment is removed; otherwise, the stain will spread when treated. Wash with soap or detergent, several times if necessary. Then soak the stain in warm suds containing 1 to 4 tablespoons of ammonia to a quart of water. Dried stains may need to be soaked overnight. An alternative method is to force water through the stain until all loose pigment is removed, wet the spot with ammonia, and then work soap or detergent into it. Rinse. Repeat if necessary.

The first vacuum cleaner was so large it had to be drawn by horses and required a team of men to use it.

Nonwashable articles: Force water through the stain until all loose pigment is removed; otherwise, the stain will spread when you treat it. Sponge stain with a solution of water and ammonia (1 tablespoon of ammonia per 1 cup of water). Rinse with water. If stain remains, moisten it with ammonia and then work soap or detergent into it. Rinse. Repeat if necessary. If ammonia changes the color of the fabric, sponge first with water and then moisten with vinegar. Rinse well.

Ink, Drawing (colors other than black) Follow directions for nongreasy stains. If bleach is needed, use a color remover if it is safe for the dye. If a color remover is not safe, try other bleaches.

Ink, Writing *Washable articles.* Follow directions for nongreasy stains. Because writing inks vary greatly in composition, it may be necessary to try more than one kind of bleach. Try a chlorine bleach on all fabrics for which it is safe. For other fabrics, try peroxygen bleach. A few types of inks require treatment with color removers. A strong bleach treatment may be needed. A strong bleach, however, may leave a faded spot on some colored fabrics. If a yellow stain remains after bleaching, treat it as a rust stain.

Nonwashable articles: If possible, use a blotter (for small stains) or absorbent powder to remove excess ink before it soaks into the fabric. Then follow directions for washable articles.

Iodine *Washable articles:* Three methods for removing iodine stains are given below. If the method you try first does not remove the stain, try another.

Water: Soak in cool water until the stain is removed; some stains require soaking overnight. If the stain remains, rub it with soap or detergent and wash it in warm suds. If the stain is not removed, soak the fabric in a solution containing 1 tablespoon of sodium thiosulfate to each pint of warm water, or sprinkle the crystals on the dampened stain. Rinse well as soon as the stain is removed.

Steam: Moisten the stain with water; then hold it in the steam from a boiling teakettle.

Rubbing alcohol: If alcohol is safe for the dye, cover the stain with a pad of cotton soaked in it. If necessary, keep the pad wet for several hours. Dilute with 2 parts water for use on acetate.

Nonwashable articles: Try the steam or alcohol methods given above.

Mildew *Washable articles:* Treat mildew spots while they are fresh, before the mold growth has a chance to weaken the fabric. Wash the mildewed article thoroughly and dry it in the sun. If the stain remains, treat it with a chlorine or peroxygen bleach.

Nonwashable articles: Send the article to a dry cleaner promptly.

Mud Let the stain dry; then brush well. If the stain remains, follow directions for nongreasy stains. Stains from iron-rich clays not removed by this method should be treated as rust stains.

Mustard *Washable articles:* Rub soap or detergent into the dampened stain; rinse. If the stain is not removed, soak the article in a hot detergent solution for several hours, or overnight if necessary. If the stain remains, use a bleach.

Nonwashable articles: If alcohol is safe for the dye, sponge the stain with it. Dilute the alcohol with 2 parts of water for use on acetate. If alcohol cannot be used, or if it does not remove the stain completely, follow the treatment for washable articles but omit the soaking.

Nail Polish   Follow directions for correction fluid. Nail polish removers also can be used to remove stains. Before using nail polish remover on acetate, Arnel®, Dynel®, or Verel®, test it on a scrap of material to make sure it will not damage the fabric.

Computer printer toner powder should be wiped off fabric with a clean, dry cloth, then rinsed out with cold water.

Paint, Varnish   Treat stains promptly, as they are always harder—and sometimes impossible—to remove after they have dried on fabric. Because there are so many different kinds of paints and varnishes, no one method will remove all stains. Read the label on the container; if a certain solvent is recommended as a thinner, it may be more effective in removing stains than the other solvents recommended.

Washable articles: To remove fresh stains, rub soap or detergent into the stain and wash. If the stain has dried or is only partially removed by washing, sponge it with turpentine until no more paint or varnish is removed (for aluminum paint stains, dry cleaning may be more effective than turpentine). While the stain is still wet with the solvent, work soap or detergent into it, put the article in hot water, and soak it overnight. Thorough washing will remove most types of paint stains. If the stain remains, repeat the treatment.

Nonwashable articles: Sponge fresh stains with turpentine until no more paint is removed (for aluminum paint stains, dry cleaning may be more effective than turpentine). If the stain remains, put

a drop of liquid detergent on it and work it into the fabric with the edge of the bowl or a spoon. Alternatively, sponge the stain with turpentine and treat with detergent as many times as necessary. If alcohol is safe for the dye, sponge the stain with it to remove turpentine and detergent. Dilute the alcohol with 2 parts of water for use on acetate. If alcohol is not safe for the dye, sponge the stain first with warm soap or detergent solution, then with water.

Pencil   A soft eraser will remove pencil marks from some fabrics. If the marks cannot be erased, follow directions for carbon paper.

Perfume   Follow directions for alcoholic beverages.

Perspiration   Wash or sponge the stain thoroughly with soap or detergent and warm water. Work carefully because some fabrics are weakened by perspiration; silk is the fiber most easily damaged. If perspiration has changed the color of the fabric, try to restore it by treating it with ammonia or vinegar. Apply ammonia to fresh stains and apply vinegar to old stains; rinse with water.

If an oily stain remains, follow directions for greasy stains. Remove any yellow discoloration with a chlorine or peroxygen bleach. If it is safe for the fabric, the strong sodium perborate treatment recommended for greasy-stain removal is often the most effective for these stains.

Rust   *Oxalic-acid method:* PRECAUTION: OXALIC ACID IS POISONOUS IF SWALLOWED. Moisten the stain with oxalic-acid solution (1 tablespoon of oxalic-acid crystals in 1 cup warm water). If the stain is not removed by a single treatment, heat the solution and repeat. If the stain is stubborn, place oxalic-acid crystals directly on it. Moisten the stain with water as hot as is safe for the fabric; allow it to stand a few minutes, or dip it in hot water. Repeat if necessary. Do not use this method on nylon. Rinse the article thoroughly. If it is allowed to dry in the fabric, oxalic acid will cause damage.

Household Tips

Cream-of-tartar method: If the treatment is safe for the fabric, boil the stained article in a solution containing 4 teaspoons of cream of tartar to each pint of water. Boil until the stain is removed. Rinse thoroughly.

Lemon-juice method: Spread the stained portion over a pan of boiling water and squeeze lemon juice on it; or sprinkle salt on the stain, squeeze lemon juice on it, and spread the fabric in the sun to dry. Rinse thoroughly. Repeat if necessary.

Color removers can be used to remove rust stains from white fabrics.

Scorch Stains   If the article is washable, follow the directions for nongreasy stains. To remove light scorch stains from an article that is nonwashable, apply hydrogen peroxide. The strong treatment may be needed to remove the stains. Repeat if necessary. Severe scorch stains cannot be removed, however, because the fabric already has been damaged.

Shellac   Using alcohol, sponge or soak the stain. Dilute the alcohol with 2 parts water for use on acetate. If alcohol bleeds the dye, try turpentine.

Shoe Polish   Because there are many different kinds of shoe polish, no one method will remove all stains. It may be necessary to try more than one of the methods given below.

1. Follow directions for cosmetics.
2. Sponge the stain with alcohol if it is safe for the dye in the fabric. Dilute the alcohol with 2 parts water for use on acetate.
3. Sponge the stain with grease solvent or turpentine. If turpentine is used, remove it by sponging with a warm soap or detergent solution or with alcohol.

If the stain is not removed by any of these methods, use a chlorine or peroxygen bleach. If safe for the fabric, the strong sodium perborate treatment recommended for greasy-stain removal is often the most effective.

Soft Drinks   Follow directions for nongreasy stains. When any soft drink is spilled on a fabric, sponge the spot immediately with cool water. Some soft drinks are invisible after they dry but turn yellow on aging or heating. The yellow stain may be difficult to remove.

Natural gas is naturally odorless. The odor is added to make its fumes detectable.

Soot, Smoke   Follow directions for cosmetics.

Tar   Follow directions for greasy stains. If the stain is not removed by this method, sponge it with turpentine.

Urine   To remove stains caused by normal urine, follow directions for nongreasy stains. If the color of the fabric has been changed, sponge the stain with ammonia. If this treatment does not restore the color, sponging with acetic acid or vinegar may help. If the stain is not removed by one or both of these methods, see directions for medicines and yellowing.

Yellowing, Brown Stains   To remove storage stains—or unknown yellow or yellow-brown stains—from fabrics, use as many of the following treatments as necessary, if safe for the fabric, in the order given.

1. Wash.
2. Use a mild treatment of a chlorine or peroxygen bleach.
3. Use the oxalic-acid method for treating rust stains.
4. Use a strong treatment of a chlorine or per-oxygen bleach.

CLOTHING SIZE CONVERSION TABLES

WOMEN

Blouses and sweaters

U.S.	32	34	36	38	40	42	44
British	34	36	38	40	42	44	46
European	38	40	42	44	46	48	50

Coats and dresses

U.S.	4	6	8	10	12	14	16	18
British	6	8	10	12	14	16	18	20
European	34	36	38	40	42	44	46	48

Shoes

U.S.	5–5½	6–6½	7–7½	8–8½	9
British	3½–4	4½–5	5½–6	6½–7	7½
European	37	38	39	40	41

Stockings

U.S. and British	8	8½	9	9½	10	10½
European	0	1	2	3	4	5

MEN

Hats

U.S.	6⅝	6¾	6⅞	7	7⅛	7¼	7⅜	7½
British	6½	6⅝	6¾	6⅞	7	7⅛	7¼	7⅜
European/Japanese	53	54	55	56	57	58	59	60

Shirts

U.S. and British	14	14½	15	15½	16	16½	17
European/Japanese	36	37	38	39	41	42	43

Shoes

U.S.	7	7½	8	8½	9	9½	10	10½	11
British	5½	6	6½	7	7½	8	8½	9	9½
European	39	40	41	42	43	43	44	44	45

Socks

U.S. and British	9½	10	10½	11	11½	12	12½
European	39	40	41	42	43	44	45

Suits and coats

U.S. and British	34	36	38	40	42	44	46
European	44	46	48	50	52	54	56

STANDARD SIZES OF MATERIALS AND TOOLS

Most materials and tools used in household repairs and improvements are sold in standardized sizes. The charts below list sizes commonly encountered in hardware and home supply stores.

INTERIOR MATERIALS

WALLS

Type	Thicknesses	Lengths	Widths
Decorative hardboard (embossed surface)	1/4″	4′ to 16′	4′
Fiberboard (burlap or cork-surfaced)	15/32″	8′, 10′, 12′, 14′	4′
Gypsum board (plain or vinyl-surfaced)	1/4″, 3/8″, 1/2″	6′ to 16′	2′, 4′
Hardboard (tempered or untempered)	3/8″, 3/16″, 1/4″, 5/16″	6′ to 16′	4′
Hardwood plywood (prefinished)	5/32″, 3/16″, 1/4″, 7/16″	7′, 8′	4′
Hardwood plywood (veneered paneling)	1/8″ to 3/4″	7′, 8′, 9′, 10′	4′
Particle-core plywood	3/4″, 7/16″	7′, 8′, 9′, 10′	4′
Plastic-surfaced hardboard	1/8″, 3/16″, 1/4″	6′, 7′, 8′, 10′	16″, 4′
Prefinished hardboard	1/8″, 3/16″, 1/4″	6′ to 16′	16″, 4′
Textured plywood (rough-sawn, brushed, grooved)	3/8″, 5/8″	8′, 9′, 10′	4′
Unfinished plywood	3/4″ to 1 7/8″	8′, 9′, 10′	4′
Vinyl-surfaced plywood	3/16″, 1/4″, 5/16″	7′, 8′	4′
Wood-grained hardboard	3/16″, 1/4″	7′, 8′, 9′, 10′	4′

CEILINGS

Type	Thicknesses	Lengths	Widths
Acoustical panels	1/2″, 3/4″, 1″	2′, 8′, 10′, 12′, 14′	2′, 4′
Acoustical tiles	1/2″	12″	12″
Decorative acoustical tile (embossed, textured, etc.)	1/2″	12″, 2′, 4′	12″, 2′
Fiberglass acoustical panels	2″	8′, 10 1/2′, 12 1/2′, 14′, 16′	4′
Plastic-surfaced hardboard blocks	1/4″	16″	16″
Wood-grained planks	1/2″	4′	5 3/16″, 6 3/8″, 8 3/16″

FLOORS

Type	Thicknesses	Lengths	Widths
Asphalt (or asphalt-asbestos) tile	1/8″, 3/16″	9″	9″
Ceramic-tile sheets	1/8″, 1/4″	12″	12″
Indoor-outdoor carpet	N/A	As desired	3′, 6′, 9′, 12′, 15′
Indoor-outdoor carpet tile	N/A	9″, 12″	9″, 12″
Sheet vinyl	N/A	As desired	6′, 9′, 12′
Vinyl and vinyl-asbestos tile	1/2″ to 1/8″	9″, 12″, 18″, 36″	4″, 9″, 12″, 18″, 36″
Wood parquet blocks	5/16″, 7/16″	9″, 10″	9″, 10″
Wood strips	3/8″	2″	1′ to 8′

BATHROOM FIXTURES

Types	Lengths	Depths	Heights
Bathtubs	4′6″, 5′, 5′6″	2′, 2′6″, 2′7″, 2′8″	1′2″, 1′3″, 1′4″
Compact corner tubs	3′2″, 3′6″, 4′	3′3″, 3′10″, 4′1½″	12″
One-piece fiberglass recessed shower units	3′, 4′, 5′	3′	6′1½″
One-piece fiberglass tub/shower units	5′	2′8⅞″	6′1½″
Shower stalls	2′6″ to 3′6″	2′6″ to 3′6″	6′3″ to 6′5″
Sinks	19″ to 30″	16″ to 20″	2′7″ (counter height)
Toilets (tank size)	18″ to 23½″	25″ to 30″	18½″ to 40″

KITCHEN EQUIPMENT

Type	Widths	Depths	Heights
Built-in ovens (set in cabinet)	23¾″ to 36″	23½″	29¾″
Built-in ranges (set in countertop)	12″ to 42″	19″ to 22″	34″ to 36″
Dishwashers	24″	24¼″ to 30″	34″ to 36″
Double sinks (set in counters)	32″	20″	2′7″
Drop-in ranges and ovens (recessed into base cabinets)	30″	24″ to 27¼″	34″ to 36″
Freestanding ranges and ovens	20″ to 42″	24¾″ to 26⅝″	35″ to 36″
Freezers (chest)	46½″ to 72″	29″, 32″	36″, 37″
Freezers (upright)	24″ to 32″	26″ to 32″	57″ to 71″
Ranges and eye-level ovens	30″	27⅛″ to 28¾″	59⅛″, 64⅛″
Refrigerators	28″ to 35″	25″ to 30″	61″ to 36″
Single sinks (set in counters)	24″, 30″	21″	2′7″
Slide-in ranges and ovens (set between base cabinets)	20″ to 36″	24″ to 26⅞″	34″ to 36″
Triple sinks (set in counters)	42″, 45″	21″, 22″	2′7″

EXTERIOR MATERIALS

SIDING

Type	Thicknesses	Lengths	Widths
Aluminum (horizontal)	N/A	9′4½″, 10′, 12′6″, 16′	8″, 10″
Hardboard lap (horizontal)	⅜″, ⁷⁄₁₆″	12′, 16′	6″, 8″, 9″, 10″, 12″
Hardboard panels (vertical)	¼″, ⁵⁄₁₆″, ⅜″, ⁷⁄₁₆″	6′, 7′, 8′, 9′, 10′, 16′	4′
Plywood panels	⅜″, ½″, ⅝″	8′, 9′, 10′, 12′	4′
Prefinished steel (horizontal)	N/A	12′6″	8″, 9½″
Vinyl lap (horizontal)	N/A	12½′	8″, 12″
Vinyl V-grooved (vertical)	N/A	10′	10″
Wood lap (horizontal)	½″, ⅝″, ¾″	3′ to 20′	6″, 8″, 10″, 12″

Household Tips

continues

Exterior Materials, Continued

DOORS AND WINDOWS

Type	Thicknesses	Heights	Widths
Bifold, 2-door units	1⅛″, 1⅜″	6′8″	2′, 2′8″, 3′
Bifold, 4-door units	1⅛″, 1⅜″	6′8″	3′, 4′, 5′, 6′
Flush (hollow, solid)	1⅜″, 1¾″, 2¼″	6′8″, 7′	6″
Louvered	1⅛″, 1⅜″	6′6″, 6′8″, 7′	1′3″ to 3′
Panel	1⅜″, 1¾″	6′8″, 7′	1′2″ to 3′4″
Sash (with one or more glass panels)	1⅜″, 1¾″	6′8″, 7′	2′ to 3′6″
Sliding glass, 2-panel units	N/A	6′8″	5′, 6′, 6′2¼″, 8′8¼″
Sliding glass, 3-panel units	N/A	6′8″	9′, 9′¾″, 12′, 12′2¾″
Steel entry (single, double, sidelight)	1¾″	6′8″	2′8″, 3′

DISPOSAL OF HAZARDOUS HOUSEHOLD CHEMICALS

Many of the ordinary household cleaners and other materials we use every day must be disposed of properly to avoid endangering ourselves, our pets, and our environment. Never throw containers of flammable, reactive, or corrosive liquids such as paint, solvents, or automotive fluid in the trash, where they might leak or evaporate dangerously. Read the label for disposal information and adhere to community regulations regarding the disposal of these substances. The following methods are recommended for the safe disposal of toxic household waste.

Method A   For small amounts, dilute with lots of water and pour down the drain. For large amounts, use method D.

Method B   In a well-ventilated place away from pets and people, allow to evaporate, or combine it with an absorbent material such as cat litter and

Material	Method A	Method B	Method C	Method D
Antifreeze	■			
Brake fluid			■	■
Car batteries			■	■
Contact cement		■		
Degreasers			■	
Diesel fuel			■	■
Furniture polish				■
Kerosene			■	
Motor oil			■	■
Paint—latex		■		
Paint—oil base				■
Paint stripper	■			
Paint thinner				■
Paintbrush cleaner—phosphate	■			
Paintbrush cleaner—solvent				■
Power-steering fluid			■	■
Rust remover	■			
Solvent-based glue, adhesive, sealant				■
Transmission fluid			■	■
Water-based glue, adhesive, sealant		■		
Wood finish				■
Wood preservative				■

Indoor Light Bulbs

A Closer Look

Lumens measure how much light a bulb puts out. Watts measure the amount of power a bulb uses. Both measurements appear on light bulb packaging. Use the chart below to find right bulb for the purpose.

Type	Watts	Lumens	Hours
Soft white incandescent	40	445	750–1,500
	100	1,710	
Halogen spot or floodlight	50	600	2,500–3,000
	90	1,300	
Halogen bulb	60	960	2,250–3,000
	100	1,850	
Compact fluorescent	11	600	8,000–10,000
	15	925	
	23	1,580	
Compact fluorescent reflector	15	725	10,000
	20	1,000	

---

allow to solidify. Wrap thoroughly in plastic and discard in trash.

Method C   Recycle at a local center set up for this purpose, or use method D.

Method D   Save for special collection by local authorities or call your local health department, cooperative extension service, or environmental protection agency for instructions.

RECYCLING

You can help protect the environment by taking three steps to limit the amount of garbage sent to landfills and incinerators:

1. Reduce the amount of disposable material you use in the form of shopping bags, paper towels, product packaging, and so on.
2. Reuse as many items as possible (such as coffee cans to hold nails, newspaper as packing material, old sheets as drop cloths).
3. Recycle as much of the rest as possible.

Many organic materials, such as food and yard waste, can go into a compost pile (see next section), and a growing number of other items are now recycled through community programs. Follow your city's recycling laws and make the most of voluntary recycling centers that take up the slack. To make recycling easier, post a list of recyclables in your kitchen or garage and set up separate containers to sort them according to local regulations. Rinse out containers before discarding and, where applicable, return deposit cans and bottles. Most municipalities have facilities to recycle the following items.

Paper	Newspaper, magazines, catalogs, corrugated cardboard, smooth (gray) cardboard, egg and produce cartons, beverage cartons, paper bags, wrapping paper, office paper, junk mail, paperback books, telephone books
Plastic	Bottles and jugs
Glass	Bottles and jars
Metal	Cans, aluminum foil and trays, utensils, pots and pans, appliances, furniture, machine parts, tools, nuts and bolts

COMPOSTING

Composting is a great way to recycle certain biodegradable materials to the benefit of your yard and garden. In a compost heap, you may dispose of fruit and vegetable peels, stems, leaves and cores, pulp from your juicing machine, crushed egg-shells, coffee grounds, cut flowers, woodstove ashes, sawdust,

Household Tips

Stop Blowing Fuses!

A Closer Look

Electrical overloads—trying to draw too much electricity through a circuit—causes fuses to blow and circuit breakers to trip. To prevent this, be aware of how much electricity common appliances use and avoid having too many on at one time on one circuit. Two or more of the following appliances will overload a 15-amp circuit.

Appliance	Amps
Clothes washer	10
Hair dryer	10
Iron	9
Microwave	6–12
Portable heater	10
Refrigerator	6–15
Table saw	13–15
Toaster	7–10
Window air conditioner	8–16

chicken and rabbit droppings, grass clippings, hedge trimmings, small wood chips, leaves, pine needles, sod, and dirt. Finished compost can be worked into yard and garden soil to enrich it and make your plantings thrive. Here's how to make compost:

1. Collect equal parts wet or green material and dried or brown material, making sure both have been reduced to fairly small pieces.
2. Using alternating layers of green and brown, build a pile roughly 3′ × 3′ × 3′. This pile can be freestanding, or you can use one of the many compost containers on the market. Dampen the pile as you build, and sprinkle in some fresh soil or compost starter (available at garden stores) as a catalyst.
3. For the first month, turn the pile once a week to aerate and to blend decomposed material with fresh material. Use a pitchfork for this job and wet the compost if necessary.
4. After the first month, insert a compost thermometer into the pile to monitor its temperature. Decomposing compost will heat up to the 120° to 160°F range; turn the pile whenever it cools below this temperature. The compost is ready to use when it no longer heats up.

HOW TO BUILD A FIRE

Before starting a fire in your fireplace, make sure you have a screen to keep sparks and coals inside. For best results, use a rack to elevate the fire and allow air to flow underneath. Keep fireplace tools handy for tending the fire as it burns.

1. Remove most of the soot and ashes from previous fires, leaving larger coals and charred logs.
2. Crumple or loosely roll several sheets of newspaper and arrange on top of the coals.
3. Lay short, dry kindling over the newspaper in a crisscross or side-by-side pattern. If the logs or wood pieces you will use are damp or green, place fire-starters beneath the kindling.
4. Put a few small to medium logs atop the kindling. Larger pieces can be added after the fire has established itself.
5. Open the flue. Use long fireplace matches to light the fire in several places, from below.

BABY-SITTER CHECKLIST

Whenever you leave your children with a baby-sitter, it is important to provide the sitter with the basic information he or she will need to care for your children and to handle any emergencies. Show the sitter around your home, explaining door locks, alarm systems, and fire extinguishers; point out first-aid supplies and telephones; and indicate the location of your children's toys, clothing, and food. In addition, leave the following list of phone numbers and vital data by the telephone.

Your home address and phone number(s)
Children's names, ages, heights, and weights
Mother's name, location, and phone number(s)
Father's name, location, and phone number(s)
Fire department/paramedics phone number(s)
Police department phone number(s)
Poison-control center phone number(s)
Children's doctor's name, address, and phone number
Nearest hospital/emergency room, address, and phone number
Taxi or car service name and phone number(s)
Nearest reliable neighbor's name, address, and phone number

Household Tips

Reliable friends/relatives' names, addresses, and
  phone numbers
Children's school name(s) and phone number(s):
Children's health-insurance-plan number
  and insurer's phone number(s)
Children's health problems (allergies, asthma, etc.)
Mealtimes and bedtimes
Children's duties
Children's food and play preferences
Baby-sitter's duties

CAR-MAINTENANCE CHECKLIST

You can keep your car running longer and better by
following a few simple maintenance routines. Your
owner's manual indicates how often you should
change fluids, tune the engine, rotate the tires, etc.
Follow the manufacturer's recommendations, increasing the frequency of maintenance for cars that
see heavy use or lots of stop-and-go driving. If you
or your car's monitoring systems detect problems,
maintenance should be performed as needed. Your
maintenance schedule should include a number of
basic procedures.

Fluids

Change motor oil and filter
Replace antifreeze/coolant
Replace automatic-transmission fluid and filter
Refill windshield-washer fluid and change blades

Engine

Change spark plugs
Check alternator and starter
Clean battery and terminals
Clean/replace air filter
Check timing
Check intake manifold
Check/replace PCV (positive crankcase ventilation)
Check/replace belts

Tires

Check air pressure
Check treads, replace tire if less than 1/16″
Rotate tires
Check brakes/pads
Check wheel alignment

ADDITIONAL SOURCES OF INFORMATION

ORGANIZATIONS AND SERVICES

Auto Safety Hot Line
U.S. Department of Transportation
400 7th St., SW, Room 5326
Washington, DC 20580
800-424-9393
http://www.nhtsa.dot.gov

This hot line provides information on air bags, seat
belts, child seats, auto recalls, and other safety issues.
Open 8 A.M. to 10 P.M. EST.

Genova Plumbers Hot Line
7034 E. Court St.
Davison, MI 48423
800-521-7488

The staff can suggest solutions to plumbing problems
involving gutters and plastic fittings as well as more
technical problems. The hotline operates weekdays between 8 A.M. and 5 P.M., EST.

Major Appliance Consumer Action Panel
  (MACAP)
20 N. Wacker Dr.
Chicago, IL 60606
312-984-5858

MACAP responds to inquiries about problems with
major appliances. Call for further instructions. It is
open weekdays from 8:30 A.M. to 5 P.M., CST.

Shopsmith, Inc.
6530 Poe Ave.
Dayton, OH 45414
800-543-7586

Shopsmith answers questions related to woodworking.
If they cannot answer your question, they will research
the information and call back. Call weekdays between
8 A.M. and 9 P.M. and Saturdays between 9 A.M. and
1 P.M., EST.

Soap and Detergent Association
1500 K Street, NW, Ste. 300
Washington, DC 20005
202-347-2900
E-mail: info@sdahq.org

This association answers questions on all aspects of
soaps and detergents. They also have free publications. Call Monday through Friday from 9 A.M. to
4:45 P.M., EST.

Household Tips

MAGAZINES

COOKING AND DINING

Bon Appetit
6300 Wilshire Blvd.
Los Angeles, CA 90048
http://www.bonappetit.com

Food and Wine
1120 Avenue of the Americas
New York, NY 10036
http://www.foodandwine.com

Gourmet
4 Times Square
New York, NY 10036
http://eat.epicurious.com/gourmet

HOME AND GARDENING

Architectural Digest
6300 Wilshire Blvd.
Los Angeles, CA 90048
http://www.archdigest.com

Better Homes and Gardens
1716 Locust St.
Des Moines, IA 50309
http://www.bhglive.com

Country Living
P.O. Box 7138
Red Oak, IA 51591
http://www.countryliving.com

The Family Handyman
2915 Commerce Drive
Eagen, MN 55121
http://www.familyhandyman.com

Horticulture
98 N. Washington St.
Boston, MA 02114

House Beautiful
1700 Broadway, 36th floor
New York, NY 10019
http://homearts.com

Metropolitan Home
1633 Broadway
New York, NY 10019
http://www.methome.com

Southern Living
2100 Lakeshore Dr.
Birmingham, AL 35209
http://www.southernliving.com

BOOKS

Bernstein, Peter, and Christopher Ma. *The Practical Guide to Practically Everything.* Random House, 1998.

Brody, Jane. *Jane Brody's Good Food Book.* Bantam, 1987.

Bykofsky, Sheree, and Paul Fargis, eds. *The Big Book of Life's Instructions.* Galahad Books, 1999.

Cunningham, Marion, et al. *Fannie Farmer Cookbook.* Knopf, 1996.

Dadd, Debra Lynn. *Home Safe Home.* Tarcher/Putnam, 1997.

Family Circle editors. *The Family Circle Good Cook's Book.* Simon & Schuster, 1993.

Green, Mark. *The Consumer Bible.* Workman, 1998.

Heloise. *All-New Hints from Heloise.* Perigee, 1989.

Hufnagel, James A., et al. *The Stanley Complete Step-by-Step Book of Home Repair and Improvement.* Simon & Schuster, 2000.

Johnson, Hugh. *Hugh Johnson's Pocket Encyclopedia of Wine 2001.* Fireside/Simon & Schuster, 2000.

Kaplan, Leon. *Keep This Book in Your Glove Compartment.* Berkley Books, 1997.

Mendelson, Cheryl. *Home Comforts: The Art and Science of Keeping House.* Scribner, 1999.

Mr. Boston Official Bartender's and Party Guide. Warner, 2000.

Reader's Digest Association. *Ask the Family Handyman.* Reader's Digest Association, 1999.

Rombauer, Irma S., et al. *The Joy of Cooking.* Rev. ed. Simon & Schuster, 1997.

Rosso, Julee, and Sheila Lukins. *The New Basics Cookbook.* Workman, 1989.

Satin, Morton. *Food Alert! The Ultimate Sourcebook for Food Safety.* Facts on File, 1999.

20

PERSONAL FINANCES

Personal finances are often a mystifying subject. The objective of making more from your income than just enough to live on is shared by many. But faced with a huge assortment of possible investments, insurance plans, real-estate ventures, and retirement plans, how can you, as an individual, decide on the best course of action?

This chapter provides a starting point. It contains information on making a budget, the types of insurance available, loans, real estate, and mortgages. Social Security and retirement planning are covered, and glossaries of financial and real-estate terms are included. You should consult some of the many reputable sources on the World Wide Web, books and periodicals devoted to financial planning, or professional financial planners, however, before you create a master plan for your personal finances.

The most fortunate 1% of households have accumulated more wealth than the bottom 95%.

TABLES OF COMMON INTEREST

SIMPLE INTEREST

Simple interest is computed on the amount of the principal (total amount borrowed) of a loan. To calculate simple interest: Dollar amount × Interest rate × Length of time (in years) = Amount of Interest.

SIMPLE INTEREST ON A $100 LOAN

Time	Annual Rate							
	5%	6%	7%	8%	9%	10%	15%	20%
1 month	.4167	.5000	.5833	.6667	.7500	.8333	1.2500	1.6667
6 months	2.5000	3.0000	3.5000	4.0000	4.5000	5.0000	7.5000	10.0000
12 months	5.0000	6.0000	7.0000	8.0000	9.0000	10.0000	15.0000	20.0000
24 months	10.0000	12.0000	14.0000	16.0000	18.0000	20.0000	30.0000	40.0000
36 months	15.0000	18.0000	21.0000	24.0000	27.0000	30.0000	45.0000	60.0000

COMPOUND INTEREST

Compound interest means earning interest on the interest in addition to interest on the principal. To calculate compound interest: (Original dollar amount + Earned interest) × Interest rate × Length of time = Amount of Compound Interest. To determine the approximate number of years it will take for the principal to double, divide the interest rate percent into 72.

COMPOUND INTEREST ON $100 PRINCIPAL, COMPOUNDED ANNUALLY

Time	Annual Rate					
	5%	6%	7%	8%	9%	10%
6 months	2.50	3.00	3.50	4.00	4.50	5.00
1 year	5.00	6.00	7.00	8.00	9.00	10.00
2 years	10.25	12.36	14.49	16.64	18.81	21.00
3 years	15.76	19.10	22.50	25.97	29.50	33.10
4 years	21.55	26.25	31.08	36.05	41.16	46.41
5 years	27.63	33.82	40.26	46.93	53.86	61.05

MORTGAGE AMORTIZATION FACTORS

Monthly mortgage payments include a percentage of the principal plus interest on the principal. The size of the monthly payment reflects the amount of the loan, the term of the loan, and the interest rate that applies—whether fixed or variable.

MONTHLY PRINCIPAL + INTEREST PAYMENT ON A $100,000 LOAN

Term	_ Interest rate _							
	4%	5%	6%	7%	8%	9%	10%	15%
5 years	1841.65	1887.12	1933.28	1980.12	2027.64	2075.84	2124.71	2379.00
10 years	1012.45	1060.66	1110.21	1161.08	1213.28	1266.76	1321.51	1613.35
15 years	739.69	790.79	843.86	898.83	955.65	1014.27	1074.61	1399.59
20 years	605.98	659.96	716.43	775.30	836.44	899.72	965.03	1316.79
25 years	527.84	584.59	644.30	706.80	771.82	839.20	908.71	1280.84
30 years	477.42	536.82	599.55	665.30	733.76	804.62	877.58	1264.45
35 years	442.77	504.69	570.19	638.86	710.26	783.99	859.67	1256.81
40 years	417.94	482.20	550.21	621.43	695.31	771.36	849.16	1253.22

MAKING A BUDGET

The first step in personal financial planning is to get a clear picture of where you currently stand. An inventory of expected income and expenses projected on both a monthly and an annual basis will allow individuals and families to create a budget. A budget helps to keep expenses within the boundaries of income while also showing what amount, if any, is available for investments.

Following are outlines of income and expense categories that you should include in any personal budget. Note that expenses include fixed obligations and flexible or discretionary outlays, which you can change as circumstances and objectives change.

Income

    Salaries (total in household)   _____

    Bonuses, tips   _____

    Investments (interest, dividends, capital gains, real-estate income)   _____

TOTAL INCOME   _____

Expenses

    Housing (rent or mortgage payments)   _____

    Utilities (gas, electric, water, telephone)   _____

    Taxes (federal, state, and local income; local real estate;   _____
      Social Security)

    Interest payments (car, bank loan, credit card, other loans)   _____

    Principal payments (amount of borrowed principal repaid)   _____

    Insurance (health, life, property)   _____

    Education (tuition, supplies, room and board)   _____

    Personal expenses   _____

    Contributions   _____

    Food   _____

    Transportation   _____

      TOTAL FIXED OUTLAYS   _____

Clothing   _____
Entertainment   _____
Vacations and recreation   _____
Furniture, appliances, and home improvements   _____
Health and beauty   _____
Savings (general or specific for future purchases or objectives)   _____
Miscellaneous   _____
    TOTAL VARIABLE OUTLAYS   _____

TOTAL EXPENSES   _____

    AMOUNT AVAILABLE FOR INVESTING   _____
        (total income minus total expenses)

Budgets are useful only when the amounts specified in each category are not regularly exceeded. If you have trouble keeping a budget, you should make sure that your spending targets reflect your actual expenses and that the members of your household understand the ultimate benefits of budgeting income and expenses. Many software tools, such as Quicken and Microsoft Money, can help make budgeting easier. These programs will help identify the gaps between what the dollars budgeted and actual spending. With these programs, you can also evaluate how and why your spending changes over time. Putting your information into a spreadsheet will save you time re-keying and recalculating should any of your expenses change.

On the World Wide Web, Money.com offers an instant budget maker that can help you judge your spending in comparison to people in similar income situations and with similar expenses, showing whether or not you are spending more or less than people of similar means for each expense item.

Here are some additional guidelines for spending that you may want to evaluate against your own:

Average % of Gross Income

Housing & Utilities	25 to 40%	Savings	10% plus
Taxes	20%	Entertainment & Vacations	5%
Transportation	15%	Debt (credit cards, personal loans)	5%
Food	10%	Other expenses	5%
Clothing	5%		

HOW MUCH CAN YOU SPEND ON HOUSING?

To figure out how much you can afford in monthly rent or mortgage payments, first calculate your total monthly income. If you rent, the total of your rent plus other debt outlays (for credit cards, school loans, etc.) should not exceed 36 percent of your income. If you own your home, the total of your mortgage principal, mortgage interest, real-estate taxes, and homeowner's insurance should not exceed 28 percent of your income. *See also* "Real Estate and Mortgages," later in this chapter.

AVERAGE COST OF RAISING A CHILD

The Agricultural Research Service of the U.S. Department of Agriculture calculates that it costs a two-parent, two-child family $121,230–$241,770 to raise a child to the age of 18. The cost per child increases by a factor of 1.26 for a family with only one child, while it decreases by a factor of 0.78 for a family with three children.

TOTAL SPENDING IN DOLLARS FOR CHILD REARING OVER 18 YEARS

Yearly Income	Yearly Expense (0–2 years)	Housing	Food	Transport	Clothes	Health Care	Education & Child Care	Misc.	Total Expenditures
$38,000 or less	$ 6,280	$39,900	$17,550	$ 9,120	$ 8,970	$ 9,480	$12,390	$17,540	$121,230
$38,000–$64,000	8,740	55,170	28,650	24,420	10,680	11,640	16,560	18,510	165,630
More than $64,000	13,000	89,580	35,670	32,760	13,770	13,380	26,250	30,090	241,770

If you plan on sending that child to a 4-year private college, in 2002 it will cost you about $30,000 a year. If your child is an infant in 2002, by the time he or she reaches 18 the cost is projected to reach $75,000 a year.

CALCULATING YOUR NET WORTH

Use the following chart to calculate your current net worth. Be sure to include amounts held individually and jointly to evaluate your family's net worth.

Assets

Cash on hand and liquid assets
>   Checking and savings accounts   _____
>   Cash value of life insurance   _____
>   U.S. savings bonds   _____
>   Equity in pension funds   _____
>   Money-market funds   _____
>   Brokerage funds   _____
>   Trusts   _____
>   Debts owed you   _____
>   Other   _____
>   TOTAL   _____

Personal Holdings

>   Car(s) (current value)   _____
>   Home(s)   _____
>   Boat(s)   _____
>   Major appliances   _____
>   Furs and jewelry   _____
>   Antiques and collectibles   _____
>   Art   _____
>   Other   _____
>   TOTAL   _____

Investments

>   Common stocks   _____
>   Preferred stocks   _____
>   Corporate and municipal bonds   _____
>   Mutual funds   _____
>   Certificates of deposit   _____
>   Business investments   _____
>   Real-estate investments   _____

IRAs	_____	
Other	_____	
TOTAL		_____

TOTAL ASSETS _____

Liabilities

Bills due	_____
Revolving charge and bank-card debts	_____
Taxes due	_____
Outstanding mortgage	_____
Outstanding loans (bank, insurance, etc.)	_____
Stock margin accounts payable	_____
Other debts	_____

TOTAL LIABILITIES _____

NET WORTH (Assets minus liabilities) _____

INSURANCE

Life is full of risks. One way you can minimize the effects of these risks is to obtain insurance. By insuring your health, your life, your property, and your car, as well as getting coverage for loss of income in the event of a disability, you can ensure that you and your family remain financially stable even if catastrophe strikes. Additionally, you can use some types of insurance to further your personal financial goals.

HEALTH INSURANCE

Health insurance covers the costs of medical care. It is available to individuals and families through private insurers, health maintenance organizations (HMOs), and preferred provider organizations (PPOs). Although many Americans are covered by one of these plans (paid for by or organized through employers, unions, or other groups), you can buy individual policies to provide additional coverage or to replace the group benefits. For the self-employed, individual policies are often the only choice available.

PRIVATE INSURANCE

Health insurance obtained from a private company can cover a wide variety of services and may pay for these services directly or through reimbursements to the insured individual. Patients are free to select their own doctors under these plans.

FEE FOR SERVICE

Under fee-for-service plans, the individual pays a percentage of medical costs, called coinsurance, usually around 20 percent, and the insurance company pays the rest, usually 80 percent. With fee-for-service insurance, a patient sees a doctor of his or her choice, then the patient or medical care provider submits a claim to the insurance company for reimbursement. Such plans frequently pay according to a predetermined fee schedule. Any amounts in excess of the scheduled fee are considered to be over the limits of reasonable expenses and will not be reimbursed. In addition, fee-for-service plans include deductibles normally ranging from $100 to $500 annually. The insured is responsible for paying all medical costs up to the deductible; then insurance pays 80 percent of covered expenses. Fee-for-service policies usually have an annual out-of-pocket maximum, meaning that once the maximum expense limit is reached, the insured is responsible for paying the rest of the medical expenses for that year. These policies may also have lifetime benefit maximums to protect themselves against severe loss should an insured become very ill and need expensive treatment. It is best to choose a policy with a lifetime limit of $1 million or more, to protect yourself in the event of catastrophic injury.

The manual for IRS employees includes provisions for collecting taxes after a nuclear war.

MANAGED CARE

The three major types of managed care plans are HMOs, PPOs, and POS plans. Managed care plans generally provide comprehensive health benefits to members and often offer incentives to patients to use the providers within their network. Instead of paying separately for each service rendered, coverage is paid for in advance. These plans minimize out-of-pocket medical expenses when you receive coverage from providers within the plan.

HEALTH MAINTENANCE ORGANIZATIONS (HMOs)

HMOs provide medical care to those who pay a quarterly or monthly fee. HMOs are oriented toward preventive health care, and people who pay the premium are entitled to medical, surgical, and hospital care. Some plans also cover the costs of some prescription medicines and provide partial coverage of dental services. Some HMOs provide the services of several doctors at a single location connected with a hospital. Others allow subscribers to receive care from doctors in their individual offices; the doctors then are reimbursed by the HMO on a fee-for-service basis. Important aspects of an HMO that you should scrutinize are the patient-to-physician ratio, the services for which deductibles or additional fees are charged, the availability of maternity benefits, and the relationship of the HMO or participating doctor to a hospital.

PREFERRED PROVIDER ORGANIZATIONS (PPOs)

PPOs resemble HMOs in most respects, cutting the cost of health care by negotiating lower rates with selected providers. But you have more freedom of choice with a PPO, because it covers care not only by selected providers but by professionals outside the network. Some plans, however, require that you apply for preapproval of treatment by nonnetwork providers. Even when treatment is pre-approved, a lower percentage of your costs is reimbursed than for care by preferred providers. You generally must pay out-of-network providers up front and submit a claim to the PPO to get your money back. They offer more flexibility than an HMO, however, the premiums are higher and, as with fee-for-service plans, you may have to pay coinsurance when selecting doctors outside of the network.

POINT-OF-SERVICE (POS)

Point-of-service coverage is similar to PPO, however, with this type of plan you usually select a primary care physician who coordinates all of your medical care.

MEDICARE

Medicare is the federal program of hospital and medical insurance primarily for those over 65 years of age and who are no longer covered by an employer's plan. With the high cost of healthcare these days, many elderly people have to purchase supplemental insurance to cover expenses that Medicare does not cover. These programs, called Medigap or MedSup, are private insurance policies that help cover the gaps in Medicare coverage.

LONG-TERM HEALTH CARE INSURANCE

This type of insurance is a must today for anyone nearing or in retirement. People are living longer and their needs, as they age, are greater. This type of insurance can help protect the assets that you have accumulated over your lifetime should you require long-term healthcare, such as going into a nursing home. A long-term care policy can cover the medical care, nursing care, and other assistance that you may need if you have a chronic illness or disability, when you are not well enough to care for yourself over an extended period of time. Long-term care can be expensive but, with life expectancy on the rise, it can be well worth the expense.

Personal Finances

LIFE INSURANCE

The purpose of life insurance is to provide future financial security for your family. Life insurance provides an immediate estate that will enable your family to maintain the household after you die. You also can use life insurance to build up cash reserves for future expenses, such as retirement or college tuition.

By purchasing a life-insurance policy, you are buying into a risk-sharing group. Although no one can predict with any reliability when any individual is going to die, it is possible to predict with great accuracy the number of nonsmoking 32-year-old women who exercise regularly and are not overweight who will die at any given point over the next 40 years. The costs of premiums for people of different ages in various risk categories then can be calculated on the basis of how much the insurance company will pay in benefits to each group's beneficiaries. Buy when you are young and healthy and when you have dependents. Older people and those not in the best of health pay much higher rates.

You have six types of life insurance to choose from, all but one of which (term insurance) fall into the category of cash-value insurance. Term insurance works the same way automobile or homeowner's insurance works—the insured item being your life. Cash-value plans add investment to the picture, crediting a portion of your premiums to an interest-bearing account. You can borrow against the account while you are alive, and the cash value is paid out tax-free to your beneficiaries upon your death.

term insurance   Provides a death benefit to beneficiaries for a specified period of time. It can be renewable or convertible to whole life and features a low initial premium that rises with each new term. Term life typically has no cash value.

whole life insurance   Offers protection for life at a fixed premium. It provides a fixed death benefit and a cash value that can be borrowed against and increases over the years. These policies are more expensive.

"Life Expectancy in 1995 by Race, Sex, and Age" in chapter 18; "Government Benefits" in **Go to** chapter 25

universal life insurance   Offers permanent protection, flexible premiums and death benefits, and a cash value based on premiums paid to date and current interest rates. They usually have higher yields than plain whole life but they generally don't guarantee a certain rate.

excess interest whole life insurance   Provides permanent protection, a fixed premium that the insurer may adjust after the policy is issued, a fixed death benefit, a cash value that grows depending on market conditions, and the possibility that premiums may be reduced or dispensed with for one or more years if investments are sufficiently profitable.

variable life insurance   Offers permanent protection; fixed or flexible premiums; policyholder control over the investment of the policy's cash value; and variable death benefits and cash values, depending on the investment performance of the underlying assets in the account. Policy owners can choose among several investment options for these assets, mainly among bond and stock funds.

adjustable life insurance   Gives permanent protection that can be reduced to a shorter term if desired, a death benefit that can be raised or lowered, and premiums that can be increased or decreased.

The American Council of Life Insurance recommends that you evaluate your life-insurance needs, buy from a company licensed in your state, select a trustworthy insurance agent, compare costs of similar policies, ask about lower premium rates for nonsmokers, and read your policies and understand them. After selecting coverage that is right for you, inform your beneficiaries about the kind and amount of life insurance you own, keep your policy in a safe place at home, keep the company's name and policy number in a safe deposit box, and check your coverage periodically to be sure it meets your current needs.

DISABILITY INSURANCE

Disability insurance provides coverage for loss of income when an illness or injury prevents you from working. Compulsory temporary disability insurance is provided in California, Hawaii, New Jersey, New York, Rhode Island, and Puerto Rico. Social Security also provides disability coverage at varying levels, depending on family size and the recipient's age and usually only to those who are severely disabled.

Long-term disability insurance usually covers between 50 to 70 percent of your income. In addition, three types of disability insurance are available through private companies:

noncancelable   Policies that protect your income as long as you continue to make premium payments. Coverage may be increased as income increases.

guaranteed renewable   Policies that are less expensive than noncancellable ones, because insurers can increase premium rates. The insurer is not permitted to cancel or amend the policy benefits during the period that the policy is guaranteed renewable.

optionally or conditionally renewable   Policies that can be renewed or not renewed each year, for reasons stated in the policy, with variable premium rates. They are the least expensive private option.

More information about disability insurance can be obtained from the Health Insurance Association of America, 555 13th Street NW, Suite 600 East, Washington, D.C. 20004.

PROPERTY AND LIABILITY INSURANCE

The purchase of a home is the largest investment most individuals will make in their lifetimes. The home also represents the largest portion of their total financial worth. It therefore makes sense to insure against its possible damage or loss. Even renters stand to lose a substantial amount of money if the uninsured contents of their apartments or houses are destroyed. Determining the cost of rebuilding or refurnishing your home will enable you to properly select the amount of coverage you will need.

A wide array of homeowner's insurance policies is available, including coverage for renters and apartment dwellers. The type of coverage most appropriate for you depends on the sort of risks your property is exposed to and the value of the property. Some policies cover only specific causes of damage or loss, while others provide "all-risk" coverage that pays for any loss or damage except that specifically excluded by the policy. Available homeowner's policies follow:

homeowner's 1   Covers damage caused by fire, lightning, extended perils (such as windstorms, hail, smoke damage, explosions, riots, and vehicular and aircraft damage), vandalism, malicious mischief, theft, and personal liability. This very limited policy is seldom sold or purchased.

homeowner's 2   Adds extended coverage for a variety of other potential problems—such as broken water pipes, freezing of plumbing fixtures, and building collapse—to the coverage offered in homeowner's 1.

homeowner's 3   An "all risks" policy for buildings that is more extensive than either 1 or 2. It also can cover personal property to a limited extent. The only events it excludes are flood, earthquake, war, and nuclear accident.

homeowner's 4   Covers personal property only. The extent of coverage is generally the same as in 2, but the policy is designed for renters.

homeowner's 5   Provides the most comprehensive "all risks" coverage for homes and personal property.

homeowner's 6   Designed for condominium owners. It covers loss of personal property and loss of use of the dwelling.

homeowner's 8   More limited than homeowner's 1. Homeowner's 8 is a named-perils policy designed for owners of older homes where the cost of reconstructing the home in the event of a catastrophic loss exceeds the market value of the home.

Ask for replacement cost coverage, which will help you replace what you lost even if the value of those items has risen. Otherwise, the insurer will pay you only the depreciated value. You can also purchase an inflation guard, which increases your premium with the rate of building cost inflation.

Homeowner's policies cover more than just a home and its contents. Most types include the main dwelling, any other structures on the property, personal belongings that are kept in the dwelling or elsewhere, costs of additional living expenses, and comprehensive personal liability—including medical payments and damage to others' property.

Comprehensive personal liability insurance protects against the loss of your home or property in the event that someone is injured accidentally, whether the injury occurs at the home or elsewhere (such as on a golf course or during a softball game). This type of insurance pays up to a set amount for each occurrence of personal liability (injury and property damage) and up to set amounts for medical payments to others and damage to others' property. Excluded from the comprehensive personal liability insurance provisions of most homeowner's policies are losses resulting from business or professional activities; use of boats, ships, and planes; intentional injury or damage; acts of war or nuclear accidents; and liabilities covered by other insurance policies, such as workers' compensation. Additional liability insurance is available for some of these situations. If you are looking for a comprehensive plan, umbrella liability coverage, for those with substantial net worth, covers both auto and homeowner's liability limits above the underlying coverage.

AUTOMOBILE INSURANCE

When you are evaluating the risks to which you are regularly exposed, driving a car is one risk you must consider. The possibility of an accident involving your car is so great that most states have made at least limited automobile insurance mandatory.

Automobile insurance covers three broad risk categories:

liability insurance   Covers personal injuries and property damage resulting from ownership, maintenance, or use of a vehicle. Separate limits for payments apply to each person involved in an accident and to the property damage incurred.

medical insurance   Covers the medical costs incurred in an accident up to a set amount per person per accident.

collision insurance   Pays the costs of having a car repaired after it has been damaged in an accident.

Additional automobile insurance, such as comprehensive insurance, also is available to pay for damages resulting from fire or theft. Insurance also is available for damages resulting from an uninsured driver, towing and labor, and transportation needed while a damaged car is repaired. Many states mandate the inclusion of no-fault personal injury insurance in any automobile insurance policy; this provides benefits for those injured in an accident, regardless of who was responsible for the accident.

The types of coverage and the monetary limits of the policy, the driver's age, the frequency of use of the vehicle, the driver's accident history, and the place where the vehicle is kept are considered in determining the cost of liability insurance. Costs for coverage of damage to a vehicle are calculated on the purchase price of the vehicle and its age. When evaluating insurance policies, it is important to compare what is *not* covered by a given policy—its exclusions—as well as what *is* covered and how much it will cost. Comparative shopping and a trustworthy insurance agent can help you choose wisely when buying insurance for your vehicles.

CREDIT AND LOANS

One key to enhancing personal finances is credit. With loans, credit cards, revolving-charge plans at department stores, and other methods of delaying payment, people obtain goods and services for which they otherwise would have to wait. Of course, use of credit results in debts and interest charges that must be paid to maintain a good credit rating and ensure the availability of more credit.

Getting credit is a fairly straightforward procedure. You can apply to a bank for a loan or a bank credit card—such as VISA® or MasterCard®—or to a department store or gasoline company for a revolving charge account by filling out an application form. These companies will ask about your income, employment history, length and type of residence, credit history, and major assets (car, home, etc.) to determine your creditworthiness.

As of 1998, 44 percent of families in America had credit card balances, holding a median balance of $1,700, paying a median interest rate of 15 percent.

A positive credit history—meaning that you have received credit and made payments on time—is one of the strongest recommendations for further credit. If you have never had credit before, a good first step is to obtain a department-store or gasoline-company credit card (these types of cards are often easier to get than bank credit cards) or to take out a small loan at a bank where you keep a savings and/or checking account. Having a reasonably large amount of money in the bank also can help persuade issuers to provide you with credit.

When you want to obtain credit, especially once you have established creditworthiness, comparison shopping is very important. Different states have different limits on the amount of interest that can be charged on consumer loans and bank cards. Interest rates on loans can range from less than 2 percent per month to 36 percent per year or more. Credit-card rates range from less than 11 percent to 22 percent or more per year. You do not need to be a resident of a state to get credit from lending institutions headquartered there, and you can apply by mail.

The amount of indebtedness you should assume is not easy to calculate. Credit-granting institutions base their decisions on your gross income and expenses. Your own decision about how much credit you should use is harder to evaluate. Calculating the amount of money you have available from your income after deducting monthly expenses will give you some idea of what you can afford, although other factors—such as ever-decreasing balances in your checking and savings accounts, use of overdrafts or credit to cover regular expenses, and difficulty making payments on credit lines you already have—may suggest that additional credit is not a good idea.

If you find yourself overwhelmed with debt and getting into trouble with too many outstanding credit card bills, you may wish to consolidate your debt. By obtaining a consolidation loan, you can pay off several bills with the proceeds from the loan and then make one payment a month instead of several to various creditors. This is also advantageous if the interest rate on the loan is less than the interest rates of your other bills.

Consumer credit counseling services are good sources of advice. These organizations help consumers find a way to repay debts through careful budgeting and management of funds. Often, these nonprofit organizations are funded by creditors. The counseling services can sometimes negotiate with your creditors to get them to accept a longer pay-off period.

If you own a home you may be able to obtain a home equity loan to use for various purposes, including paying down your debt. A home equity loan is based on the difference between the amount of equity paid on a home and its current market value.

Problems that can arise from credit, such as billing errors or unfair denial of credit, can be remedied under federal regulations. The Fair Credit Billing Act requires that, if you notify a creditor in writing about an error on a bill, your complaint must be acknowledged within 30 days and resolved within 90 days. The Equal Credit Opportunity Act requires creditors to give you a reason if you are denied credit and prohibits discrimination based on race, gender, age, marital status, religion, national origin, or receipt of public assistance.

If you are denied credit on the basis of a negative report from a credit bureau, you can obtain the information that agency supplied to the creditor free of charge if you request it within 30 days of being turned down, or for a small fee at any time. You can

Personal Finances

challenge the accuracy of any item in your credit file; this forces the credit bureau to investigate the item and remove it if it cannot be substantiated. If there is negative information on your credit report that is factual, you can take certain steps to help your situation, such as paying any balances due and having the creditors update your file. In seven years, negative information, except for bankruptcies (which may take ten years), will be removed from your report. Any item in your file also can be amended at your request to include a 100-word explanation that will be added to your file. For assistance in dealing with credit problems, contact the nonprofit National Foundation for Credit Counseling, 800-388-CCCS (2227), http://www.nfcc.org

Many banks now issue debit cards. (Increasingly, ATM cards can function as debit cards as well.) Usually, the only requirement for obtaining a debit card is a checking account. Be aware that the cost of any item that you purchase with a debit card will be automatically deducted from your checking account immediately. It is easy to confuse debit and credit cards because they look alike. However, if you use a debit card and do not realize that the money is being withdrawn automatically from your checking account you may lose track off how much money you have in your account to pay your bills. Immediately keep track of all withdrawals made with your debit card in order to keep your checkbook balanced.

Hundreds of credit bureaus exist throughout the United States, but three companies predominate nationally. Contact one of the following for information on your credit rating:

Equifax Inc.
P.O. Box 105873
Atlanta, GA 30348
800-233-7654 for Maryland residents
800-548-4548 for Vermont residents
800-997-2493 for all 50 states
http://www.equifax.com

TransUnion LLC
Consumer Disclosure Center
P.O. Box 1000
Chester, PA 19022

800-888-4213
800-916-8800
http://www.transunion.com

Experian Credit Bureau, Inc.
Attn: Consumer Assistance Department
P.O. Box 596
Pittsburgh, PA 15230
888-EXPERIAN
888-397-3742
http://www.experian.com

REAL ESTATE AND MORTGAGES

American society is geared toward home ownership. The desire to own a home, and the labyrinthine process of purchasing one, can have a tremendous impact on an individual's or a family's finances. A home represents the single largest financial commitment most people will make in their lifetimes. It therefore requires a careful, reasoned decision based on a thorough examination of the steps involved in the purchase. What follows are some of the basics involved in buying a home and obtaining a mortgage. Potential home buyers are cautioned to seek out as much additional information as is practical from specialized books, real-estate professionals, and friends who have made similar purchases.

THE DECISION TO BUY A HOME

Owning their own home is something most people believe to be desirable regardless of their financial circumstances. They think that owning a home is a perfect investment and that renting is akin to throwing money away. This is not always the case. Home ownership often includes a great many hidden expenses, while renters take care of the basic need for shelter at a set monthly cost without having to deal with headaches such as various taxes, sewage disposal, or sidewalk repairs.

You need to consider a number of factors when deciding whether to buy your own home. First among these should be the way you lead your life. Home ownership can provide greater space, a chance to set down roots, the option to make any alterations you choose, the possibility of providing yard space and better schools for your children, and the pride of having a home of your own. Renters have greater flexibility about when they can move, generally pay less of their income for shelter, avoid the ancillary costs and added work of maintaining a residence, and can use any excess funds for investments that offer a guaranteed rate of return.

Also of great importance in the decision to buy a home is your current financial situation. Home ownership requires enough money to make a down payment (generally at least 10 percent of the purchase price, and often 20 or 25 percent) to obtain a mortgage and to make payments on that mortgage for many years to come. Renters need to have enough money to make some sort of security deposit and to pay the rent each month.

AFFORDABILITY

It is best to shop for a mortgage before you shop for a home so that you know how much money is available to you. A long-standing rule of thumb is that the annual cost of a home should not exceed 25 percent of your gross annual income. If you can manage monthly payments that do not exceed 25 percent of your income, you will probably have little trouble obtaining a mortgage or making the payments.

A penny minted in 1727 was the first U.S. coin to have the words "United States of America." It also bore the motto, "Mind Your Own Business."

But even if mortgage payments come to 25 percent of your income, the cost of a home will be substantially more. You will need funds to cover utilities, water and sewage costs, various taxes, repairs, improvements, and even garbage cans and yard equipment. Additional costs may include commuting expenses. It is wise to set aside an additional 10 percent of the basic annual costs for unseen expenses.

A careful evaluation of present and projected income and expenses—including money spent on nonessen-

tial interests, hobbies, and pastimes—will give you some idea of what you can afford to pay for a home on a monthly basis. From there, you can look at mortgage-payment schedules to find out how much of a mortgage you can afford.

One thing to keep in mind when deciding what you can afford is that many experts advise against buying the most expensive house in a given neighborhood. A lower-priced home in a higher-priced neighborhood offers greater security and a better likelihood of seeing the property value increase.

See also "How Much Can You Spend on Housing?", earlier in this chapter.

AN OLD HOME OR A NEW ONE?

If you have a choice between buying a new home or one that has been occupied, you must weigh the pluses and minuses of each. The value of similar new and used homes in similar neighborhoods will go up about equally, but other aspects of each type of home may make you choose one over the other.

New homes have more modern amenities, are often less likely to suffer system breakdowns (that is, plumbing, heating, and water supply), should not require much upkeep or many repairs, and often can be mortgaged for a greater percentage of the price over a longer term. Older homes frequently are less expensive, have larger rooms, are better built, have finished landscaping, and are closer to the center of town. The individual merits of the actual houses you look at will guide you in making a final choice.

THE DOWN PAYMENT

Among the many decisions to be made in the home-buying process is whether to make a large or small down payment.

While a higher down payment can reduce your monthly payments or the term of the mortgage, there are a number of advantages in making as small a down payment as possible: You retain access to your money; the money you pay in later years will be less valuable, because of inflation, than money spent now; and the interest included in your mortgage payments is tax deductible, so the more you borrow, the more you can deduct. However, with a down payment of less than 20 percent, the lender may require you to purchase private mortgage insurance (PMI), which protects the bank should you default.

THE MORTGAGE

At one time, the only mortgages widely available in the United States were fixed-rate mortgages that required fixed monthly payments for a specific period, usually 25 or 30 years. Recently, however, a wide variety of mortgage options has become available. A hybrid loan, for instance, offers a fixed rate initially for the first 5 to 7 years and then converts to an adjusted rate for the rest of the term. Here are some others:

graduated payment mortgage (GPM)   Has a fixed rate of interest but varying payments. Payments begin at a low amount and are increased at a fixed rate each year, rising to a level higher than on a fixed-rate mortgage. Initial payments may be lower than the cost of interest, in which case the unpaid interest is added to the principal. This type of mortgage is good for first-time buyers who expect their incomes to rise during the course of the mortgage. These loans are available in 15- and 30-year amortization schedules. They work well in markets where real estate appreciation is expected to be rapid.

pledged-account mortgage (PAM)   A variation of the GPM based on the difference between payments and the accrued interest from a savings account pledged to that purpose by the borrower. A pledged account mortgage allows the borrower to obtain 100 percent financing if a relative agrees to pledge a savings account or a certificate of deposit as collateral for the loan. The pledged money continues to earn interest, eventually payable to the person who pledged the money. When the borrower has sufficient equity in the property, the pledge money is returned.

adjustable-rate mortgage (ARM)   Has a flexible interest rate that varies according to a selected interest-rate index. The rate may go up when the index goes up, and most rates go down when the index goes down. This type of mortgage may contain limitations on the maximum and minimum rates. The changing rate can affect the monthly payment, the term, or the outstanding principal. Some plans change the rate more frequently than they change the payments. This can result in underpayments on interest that then are added to the outstanding balance.

balloon mortgage   Requires that the loan be paid off in full or refinanced at the end of the mortgage term, usually 5 to 7 years. The advantage of the balloon mortgage is that monthly payments during the term are generally lower than they would be for a traditional 30-year mortgage. These are good for first or starter homebuyers.

convertible ARM   A combination of both fixed rate and adjustable rate mortgages, allowing the borrower to convert to a fixed rate mortgage after a set period of time.

graduated-payment adjustable-rate mortgage (GPARM)   Combines features of GPMs and ARMs. Some plans defer interest in the early years, others set rising payments during the first several years, and still others fix low payments early on. Countless variations are possible.

wraparound mortgage   Allows the buyer to assume the balance of a lower-rate mortgage from the seller, making payments to amortize both that original mortgage and the additional amount being borrowed at prevailing rates. This mortgage reduces the overall interest rate on the total amount. Wraparound mortgages are very rare and allow buyers to purchase a home without qualifying for a loan or paying closing costs.

shared-appreciation mortgage (SAM)   In return for a reduced interest rate for the borrower, the lender receives a set portion of the amount by which the home has appreciated when it is sold or the loan is paid. Because the final value of the home cannot be determined in advance, additional interest can be due if the value has not appreciated sufficiently. Be aware, however, that should your home appreciate significantly, the lender may benefit more than you do. You should make sure that this type of arrangement is in your best interest.

Federal Housing Administration Loans   These loans are insured by the U.S. Department of Housing and Urban Development. They are designed to make housing affordable for those with low to moderate incomes. Offered at both fixed and adjustable rates, they may require down payments of as little as 3 percent.

reverse mortgage   Really not a mortgage at all, but a way of getting monthly payments in return for some of the equity in a house. It is advantageous for people over the age of 75 with significant equity and insufficient cash.

points   Charged by many lenders in addition to the mortgage payments themselves. These additional amounts—each point is equal to 1 percent of the loan—are paid by the buyer at the time the mortgage goes into effect (at the closing). They represent a portion of the interest that you pay up front in exchange for a lower rate later. The longer you plan on staying in the house, the more points you should consider paying.

See also "Mortgage Amortization Factors," earlier in this chapter.

GOING TO CONTRACT

Anything and everything can and possibly will go wrong when it comes time to draw up a contract and close the deal to buy a home. No list of potential pitfalls could be considered all-inclusive. The best advice is to obtain a lawyer who is familiar with the kind of property purchase you are making and to read every word in every document presented to you with your lawyer.

COMMON REAL-ESTATE TERMS

amortization   A gradual paying off of a mortgage by periodic installments.

appraisal   An estimation of a property's value, often made by lenders before deciding the amount of a mortgage.

assessed valuation   A value placed on a property as a basis for taxation.

assumable mortgage   A mortgage taken over from the seller of a property by the buyer.

balloon payment   The final payment on a loan or mortgage, usually larger than the previous payments.

binder   An agreement by the buyer to cover the down payment on the purchase of real estate before a final contract is drawn up.

broker   Usually a licensed agent who acts on behalf of the seller of a property, making arrangements for the sale.

closing   The meeting of a buyer, a seller, a banker, and attorneys for all parties at which a real-estate sale is completed with the writing of checks. It usually takes place 30 to 60 days after the signing of the contract.

commission   The amount paid to a real-estate broker for services rendered.

condominium   A multiple-unit dwelling, townhouse, or detached house; the owner buys a title to a single unit and an undivided interest in common areas (the land, roof, elevator, etc.).

contract   A binding agreement between parties to transact real estate under agreed-upon terms.

cooperative apartment   A multiple-unit dwelling; buyers purchase individual shares in a cooperative corporation that owns the building. Each share entitles the holder to a proprietary lease on an apartment in the building.

deed   A written document that conveys ownership of real property.

equity   The value of an owner's real property after deducting mortgages and liens.

escrow A written agreement or something of value placed in the care of someone else and, once conditions are met, delivered to a designated party. Often used for payment of taxes along with mortgage payments.

Fannie Mae The Federal National Mortgage Association—the largest secondary mortgage agency.

Federal Housing Administration (FHA) A division of the federal government's Department of Housing and Urban Development that insures mortgages.

foreclosure A legal procedure in which real estate is sold by the lender to pay a defaulting borrower's debt.

Freddie Mac The Federal Home Loan Mortgage Corporation, which buys mortgages from lenders, allowing the lenders to make new mortgages.

Ginnie Mae The Government National Mortgage Association (GNMA), which buys FHA-insured loans from lenders.

indexing A means of adjusting the interest rate on a loan or mortgage according to an agreed-upon index or indicator.

interest Money paid to a lender for use of borrowed principal.

LIBOR An average of rate quotes from five major international banks. Fannie Mae and Freddie Mac use LIBOR as an index of loans they purchase.

lien A claim on the property of another granted as security for the payment of a loan or mortgage.

lock The commitment of a borrower to a mortgage rate some time between the application and the closing date; obtaining a lock may require a payment by the borrower.

mortgage A written instrument that creates a lien on a given property in return for a loan.

mortgage insurance (MI) Also called Private Mortgage Insurance (PMI), typically required by the lender when the loan-to-value ratio is above 80 per-

cent on a conforming loan. FHA loans always require mortgage insurance.

point An amount equal to 1 percent of a loan, charged to the borrower by the lender.

prepayment penalty An additional fee charged for paying off a mortgage before it is due.

principal The amount of money borrowed from a lender for a mortgage, upon which interest is computed.

qualifying ratio The ratio of the borrower's fixed monthly expenses to his or her gross monthly income. Conforming ratios are often expressed as two numbers such as 28/36 where 28 would be the gross debt service ratio and 36 would be the total debt service ratio. These ratios help lenders determine a potential borrower's creditworthiness.

title A written document that gives evidence of property ownership.

title insurance Insurance against loss resulting from defects of title to a specifically described parcel of real estate.

INVESTMENTS AND RETIREMENT

If you are like most people, your main source of income for the greater part of your life is the salary or fees you earn from working. This income may or may not be adequate to support the lifestyle you want to maintain. If you would like to increase your income, you might consider making investments. Even if your earned income is enough for the present, you might want to invest now to plan for a secure retirement.

SETTING GOALS

There is little point in considering investments without developing the goals you hope to reach by making those investments. Investing is a means to an end. That end generally can be described as financial security—having enough income to live on after you retire. But a more specific set of goals is essential.

You must develop short-term and long-term strategies. Calculate the amounts you have available to invest now and those you can make available in the future. Then figure the rate of return you require from your investments, taking into account the amount of income you will need those investments to produce in the future after factoring in inflation. You also need to evaluate your need for access to the principal or profit on short notice, along with whether you are willing to take greater risks for a potentially higher return or will accept lower profits in return for greater security.

France had the first supermarket in the world. It was started by relatives of the people who started the Texas Big Bear supermarket chain.

Other aspects you should consider when creating short- and long-term goals are diversification of your investments to reduce risks, the tax status of the income your investments will produce, and the availability of loans using your investments as collateral.

Setting goals is a continual process. Your current goals should be based on how you envision your future.

CHOOSING YOUR INVESTMENTS

Once you have decided on your investment goals, you must answer the most difficult question of all: What should you invest in? The possibilities are almost limitless.

It is unwise to select an investment without close scrutiny. Selecting a stock because someone—even a stockbroker—tells you "it's a good bet" is not a good way to handle your money. You can select the types of investments you believe will be most effective in helping you reach your short- and long-term goals. But you then should seek professional assistance from an appropriate source: bankers for information about money-market accounts, individual retirement accounts (IRAs), or certificates of deposit

(CDs); or stockbrokers for information about stocks and bonds.

Be aware, however, that these investment professionals stand to profit from the advice they give. The less ethical may try to steer you toward investments that are not ideal for you.

The first and best investment you can make, one that guarantees a return and does not put your money at risk, is to pay off your debts. Investing $2,000 in a mutual fund that pays 10 percent does not make sense if you are paying 18 percent interest on a $2,000 credit-card balance. Using the money to pay off the debt will put you 8 percent ahead of the game.

Here are the most widely used investment vehicles:

bank accounts   These investments involve virtually no risk (they are insured by the federal government up to $100,000) and are very liquid (they allow for easy access to your money), but they offer low returns. Checking and savings accounts usually require a minimum balance if you want to avoid fees. Keep enough money in your accounts to avoid fees, and if the account does not pay interest, put the remainder in a savings account that does. Bank accounts are good short-term investments for money that you need to keep on hand. Banks have different rates of interest and fees. Shop around for the bank that requires the lowest minimums, charges the lowest fees, and yields the highest rates of interest.

life insurance   Cash-value life-insurance policies invest a portion of your premiums in an account that bears interest at a moderate rate and grows over time. While low-risk, this investment is relatively expensive when you consider the unspectacular rate of return. You can borrow against the value of your policy while you are alive, but you cannot withdraw funds or the interest you earn. Cash-value life insurance does pay a tax-free death benefit to your heirs when you die, but that savings is minimal unless you are in a high tax bracket. A better choice for low-risk investing would be bonds, and for long-term investing, stocks.

annuities   Offered by insurance companies, annuities resemble a combination of cash-value life insurance and individual retirement accounts (IRAs). You contribute to the plan during the accumulation phase, it grows and compounds without taxation, and you receive distributions after age 59½. Penalties apply for early withdrawal, and if you die before the pay-out phase begins, your beneficiaries receive a sum equal to your investment. Although they are tax-deferred, annuities include high fees to make up for high operating expenses. Annuities can provide peace of mind, guaranteeing an income stream in retirement that continues throughout a lifetime. You pay more for this insurance, but, for some, the benefits are well worth the extra cost. A fixed annuity pays out fixed installments, whereas a variable annuity can allow the investor to capture market returns by varying the payment with the investment value of the account. (See "Planning for Retirement," later in this chapter, for more viable investments.)

bonds   When you purchase a bond, you lend money to the issuer of the bond. Bonds are safe investments—you get back your investment plus interest when the bond matures—but lose value relative to other investments when interest rates rise. Depending on the type of bond, this investment can tie up your money for one week to 30 years. Bonds offer a moderate return on your investment, which in some cases will be tax-free. The different types of bonds are issued by banks (certificates of deposit), state governments (municipal bonds), the federal government (treasuries), mortgage holders (Ginnie Maes), and corporations (corporate bonds). Bank CDs generally require a minimum $500 investment and mature in one week to five years, penalizing early withdrawal of your money. Municipal bonds and treasuries may require as little as $25 to invest and mature in an average of 10 years. Treasury bills, one type of U.S. bond, are six-month instruments in $10,000 denominations. These bills offer market interest rates with high security, can easily be sold, and are not subject to state and local income taxes. A minimum investment of $500 or more is required by various Ginnie Maes, which mature after a period of up to 30 years. Corporate bonds may require a minimum deposit of $1,000 and mature in one to 30 years, but they can be cashed in easily before they mature. Bonds represent a stable vehicle for the short- to long-term investment of money that you will not need in the interim. You can purchase bonds individually or through diversified bond funds (see "Mutual Funds," later in this chapter).

stocks   A share of stock is a small piece of a publicly held company, so its performance as an investment depends on the fortunes of that company. Some stocks pay dividends that reflect the company's profitability, and they grow or decline in capital value according to the financial health of the company. As a result, stocks may fluctuate greatly in value and yield unreliable dividends, making them a poor short-term investment choice. And because companies may fail at any time, the funds you invest in stocks may disappear completely. Thus, you should not invest in stocks unless you can afford to lose the money you put into them, you have the stomach to ride out the company's hard times, and you can stand to put your money at risk. In return for your patience and intestinal fortitude, however, stocks can offer phenomenal returns over the long run, making them an excellent way to build wealth for the future. Investing in individual stocks requires time-consuming research into companies, detailed reporting to the IRS, and the payment of transaction fees to a broker. To avoid these drawbacks, as well as to minimize risk through diversification, invest in a stock fund that consists of a portfolio of various stocks and is managed by an investment professional (see "Mutual Funds," later in this chapter). Stocks are a good way to invest disposable income for the long term.

real estate   In terms of risk and return, real estate is comparable to stock as an investment. The value of real estate goes up and down with the local economy, and the capital investment is substantial, but in the long term, owning real estate is a superb way to build wealth. If you own your home, you build equity as you pay off your mortgage, which increases your net worth (you also may borrow against your equity if necessary). You will pay real-estate taxes and the various expenses of home ownership, but you also will receive tax breaks to offset that expense. You can achieve the same results and bring in rent money by investing in real estate other than your home, but being a landlord brings many headaches. Only the very wealthy can afford to hold nonrental property other than their primary residence, because they pay taxes on it, tie up large sums of capital, and do not see a penny of profit until they sell (and profit is not guaranteed). Real-estate oddities such as limited partnerships and time shares most often offer high risk without high returns while they tie up your money. But owning your home is a very worthwhile long-term investment if you buy wisely. Another way to invest in real estate without owning property is to invest in real estate investment trust (REIT) mutual funds. This strategy enables you to capture the returns of the real estate market without the hassle of taking care of the property or putting up a large down payment. It also helps to lessen the risk by spreading your investment across a number of different properties held within the portfolio.

small business   Given the rate at which small businesses fail, investing in a small business is not for the faint of heart. The returns, however, can be staggering if careful research and management combine with good luck. You can minimize your risk by starting your own business instead of buying out someone or investing in an ongoing enterprise. That way, you have complete control over your investment, even if you do have to put in long hours to make it pay off. As with stock, you should be prepared to lose your money, and as with real estate, you should view a small business as a long-term investment.

miscellaneous   Precious metal received a lot of attention as an investment in the 1970s and 1980s, but the rapid growth in value of precious metals at that time is uncharacteristic. More typically, precious metals represent a hedge against inflation, but they do not outpace inflation as an investment. Collectibles such as coins, stamps, antiques, or wine are not good investments. The risk is very high, and the potential returns are disproportionately mediocre; it is also quite difficult to turn these investments into cash.

WORTH THE RISK?

All investments involve risk. As you plan your investment strategy, you must decide what kinds of risks you are willing to take. The rule of thumb is that lower-risk investments yield lower returns and higher-risk investments yield higher returns, but this oversimplifies the picture. In addition to weighing the historical performance of a potential investment, you must consider your investment goals and timeline.

If you want to make long-term investments to finance your retirement, for instance, you will do better putting money into a volatile vehicle like stocks than into a stable but low-yielding one like a money-market account. When all is said and done, your investment probably will grow more over the years—despite the risks. Nevertheless, it is unwise to put your entire nest egg into one volatile basket. Always keep a portion of your investments in lower-risk vehicles such as bonds, and diversify your high-risk investments across several different vehicles. That way, if one investment collapses, you won't go broke.

You can put about $50 in pennies in a half-gallon milk container.

For shorter-term goals like saving up for a new car, you are better off with lower-risk investments that are unlikely to lose value in the near future. Emergency money or money you will need within the next five years should not go into risky investments.

Who you are should come into play as well. If you like to play it safe with your money, accept that your investment results will be solid but not spectacular. If you are attracted by the prospect of big money, accept that you will have to take some risks. Older investors, those with limited funds to invest, or people with greater financial and family commitments should take fewer risks; while younger, wealthier, and unmarried investors can afford to venture into the unknown.

MUTUAL FUNDS

Mutual funds are professionally managed portfolios of investment vehicles like stocks and bonds. When you invest in a mutual fund, your money goes into a large pool with that of many other investors. With that large pool of cash, money managers can invest in a portfolio geared to meet specific goals, such as stability or growth. Many investors find mutual funds an attractive way to go, because the legwork is done by a professional, they can achieve diversification even with a small investment, and their transaction costs are reduced.

When choosing a mutual fund, consider the individual fund's historical performance as well as the performance of other, similar funds managed by the same firm. You should choose a fund that fits in with your financial picture and investment goals and consider the possible tax impact of its dividends and capital-gains distributions. And don't forget to figure in the cost of the fund—both the up-front load, or commission, charged by the broker (many no-load funds are available) and the ongoing operating fees charged by the fund. Operating fees can take a significant bite out of your returns.

Mutual funds fall into several categories based on the types of investments you make:

money-market funds   The safest type of fund, money-market accounts are virtually identical to bank savings accounts from the investor's standpoint, except they require a minimum deposit to open ($1,000–$25,000) and they offer check-writing privileges. Money-market funds also pay higher interest, yet they keep your money as safe as money in savings accounts by investing it in conservative vehicles such as short-term bank certificates of deposit (CDs), U.S. Treasury bonds, and corporate bonds. The interest on some funds is tax-free.

Money-market funds are good short-term investments for funds that you need to keep liquid.

bond funds   The manager of a bond fund assembles a portfolio of bonds that mature at about the same rate. Short-term funds feature bonds with a maturity cycle of 2 to 3 years, intermediate-term funds focus on bonds that mature in 7 to 10 years, and long-term funds include 20-year instruments. As the bonds come due, managers reinvest in similar bonds. Bond funds emphasize dividends, or income, over capital growth and are reasonably safe.

stock funds   Specializing in small, medium, or large companies, stock funds may focus on capital growth or value. **Value-oriented funds** are portfolios of stocks that are well priced in relation to the size and profitability of the company. **Growth-oriented funds** feature companies whose revenues and profits are growing quickly. Growth and small-company orientation translate into higher risk and return, while value and large-company orientation make a fund safer relative to other stock investments. Stock funds may specialize in overseas companies, in certain industries, or in socially responsible or environmentally conscious companies. **Index funds** select a portfolio meant to mirror the performance of a stock-market index, such as the *Standard and Poor's 500* (an index of the stocks of America's 500 largest corporations). Index funds often outperform the market, because they cost less to manage, using computers rather than people to select stocks.

hybrid funds   These mutual funds combine investment in a variety of vehicles, usually stocks and bonds. They are safer and slower growing than stock funds, but riskier and higher yielding than bond funds. If your investment strategy is middle-of-the-road, but you don't have enough money to invest in separate stock funds and bond funds, a hybrid fund offers a good alternative.

funds of funds   Investment companies sell mutual-fund packages that consist of funds that invest in other funds. This can simplify your investment strategy even further than conventional mutual funds, allowing you to buy into a diversified portfolio that includes both stock funds and bond funds. It is essential to shop carefully to find a high-quality fund of funds, or the benefits of simplicity may be canceled out by poor performance.

MAJOR MUTUAL FUND COMPANIES

American Century
800-345-6488
http://www.americancentury.com

Charles Schwab & Company
800-526-8600
http://www.schwab.com

Dreyfus Service Corp.
800-443-9792
http://www.dreyfus.com

Fidelity Investments
800-544-6666
http://www.fidelity.com

Franklin Templeton Investments
800-342-5236
http://www.franklintempleton.com

Janus
888-223-0351
http://www.janus.com

Scudder Investments
800-SCUDDER
http://www.myscudder.com

Strong Funds
800-368-1480
http://www.estrong.com

T. Rowe Price
800-638-5660
http://www.troweprice.com

Transamerica
800-89-ASK-US
http://www.transamerica.com

Vanguard Group
800-662-7447
http://www.vanguard.com

PLANNING FOR RETIREMENT

Although few working people require income from their investments to meet routine expenses, most people will require income from outside sources in order to retire in security and comfort. There are three potential providers of retirement income: pension plans funded by an employer, government retirement funds, and an individual's own retirement fund. The best way to ensure your financial security after retirement is to arrange for retirement income from at least two or even all three of these sources. With life expectancy on the increase, retirees today are living a lot longer and are staying active, thus spending more money in retirement. Today, you must plan on having your retirement savings last 30 years or more.

employer-funded retirement plans   Can be pension plans, profit-sharing plans, or a combination of the two. Most pension plans define the benefits due and eligibility qualifications required of each employee in advance. They are designed to provide employees with a guaranteed income after they reach a certain age, generally 65, and retire. Some plans allow for early retirement at reduced benefits. In addition to providing income after retirement, many plans also provide vested benefits for employees who stop working for the company before they reach the minimum retirement age, death benefits, medical benefits, and a pension for surviving spouses.

employer-sponsored plans   Include 401(k) plans, in which you contribute a percentage of your paycheck before taxes and reduce your taxable income (and sometimes the employer matches your contribution), and 403(b) plans, which are like 401(k)s but are available to employees of not-for-profit and public-sector organizations. Many financial advisors recommend contributing the maximum allowed to these accounts, if you can afford to do so. You save on your taxes and benefit more from compounding returns.

profit-sharing plans   Differ from pension plans in that an employer's contributions to the fund are dependent on company profits. Profit-sharing plans also may have provisions for vesting at an earlier age and withdrawal and loan privileges.

If you are self-employed or own a small business with fewer than 20 employees, you have two options for setting up a retirement plan for your business. **Simplified employee pension individual retirement accounts** (SEP-IRAs) let you save up to 13.05 percent of pretax income, up to $24,000 a year. **Keogh plans** allow for the contribution of up to 20 percent of pretax income, to a maximum of $30,000 annually. Under a Keogh, you can establish a vesting schedule that requires employees to remain with the company a certain number of years before they are entitled to their entire savings.

Social Security The basic retirement plan provided by the government. More than 90 percent of the workers in the United States are earning benefits under Social Security through contributions they and their employers make in the form of Social Security taxes. Social Security provides monthly payments to qualified workers who retire at age 62 or older; health insurance for the elderly under Medicare; and monthly payments to disabled workers and to spouses and children of workers who retire, become disabled, or die. However, if you retire at 62 you will receive a smaller amount of Social Security then if you wait until full retirement age at 65—or 67, for those born in 1960 or later. If you put off retirement until age 70, you stand to benefit even more with special credits you receive from Social Security for delaying your retirement. The dollar amount of benefits is dependent on the rate set by the government as well as on other sources of income the retiree has available. People qualify for Social Security benefits on the basis of "quarters of coverage." Workers earn one credit toward coverage for a set amount of income they earn, up to four credits each calendar year. A worker is eligible for retirement benefits if he or she has earned as many credits as the number of calendar years between age 21 (or since 1950) and retirement. Visit the Social Security Administration at www.ssa.gov to calculate your future benefits.

The future of Social Security, however, is uncertain. By 2013, benefits will start to exceed payroll revenues as millions of baby boomers start retiring. By 2030, every two people working will have to produce enough tax revenue to support one retiree. This imbalance will make it impossible for such a small work force to support the current Social Security system. Securing your own financial retirement by investing wisely may not only be your best bet but also your only bet toward a secure retirement.

individual retirement plans Can be created according to needs and financial resources using many of the investments outlined above. The most popular individual plan, the **individual retirement account** (IRA), allows some individuals to deduct contributions of up to $2,000 a year from their income taxes. Married couples who file taxes jointly can take the full deduction if their adjusted gross income (AGI) is less than $40,000 or if one or both spouses are not covered by an employer-sponsored retirement plan. A single taxpayer with an income of less than $25,000 also is eligible for the full deduction. Single taxpayers earning between $25,000 and $40,000 and married joint-filers earning between $40,000 and $60,000 can take a partial deduction, depending on their income. If you are investing for the long term, it may make sense to maintain an IRA even if you cannot deduct your contributions. Many IRAs are simply mutual funds tailored to the needs of retirement-minded investors, so they can be used in much the same way and may better meet your retirement investing goals than other funds. In addition, conventional IRAs are tax-free until they pay out in your retirement years. A Roth IRA, which allows for contributions of up to $2,000 a year as long as your income is less than $110,000 (for singles) or $160,000 (for couples), is a nondeductible IRA in which your money grows tax free. You pay income on your money up front but when you withdraw the money in retirement those withdrawals are not taxed.

Several online tools can help you determine what you need to do now to secure your financial future. You can also opt to seek the advice of a financial planner, who for a fee or a commission can aid you in building a solid financial future.

COMMON INVESTMENT TERMS

accrued interest   Interest earned by a bond since the last payment was made.

Alternative Trading System (ATS)   An electronic system that allows securities to be traded even after the markets have closed, often for a more reasonable price than attainable by trading on an exchange. Some ATSs are also called electronic communication networks or ECNs.

AMEX   The American Stock Exchange.

appreciation   The increase in value of an investment.

asset   Something you own or that is owed to you.

bear market   A declining stock market.

bid and asked price   The highest price offered for a security at a given time *(bid)* and the lowest price accepted for that security at that time *(asked)*.

Big Board   The New York Stock Exchange.

blue chip   The stock of a top-rated company known for the quality of its products and the security and return on investment of its stock; also the company itself.

bond   A corporation's note acknowledging indebtedness for a certain amount and promising to pay interest at a given rate on that amount as well as to pay back the principal on a certain date. *See also* **junk bond; Treasury bond.**

book value   The theoretical worth of a share of stock as shown on a company's balance sheet. This has little relationship to the stock's market value.

bull market   A rising stock market.

capital gain or capital loss   The gain or loss resulting from the sale of an asset.

capital stock   All shares of stock in a company, both common and preferred.

capitalization   All securities issued by a company, including bonds, common and preferred stock, and debentures.

collateral   Property or securities used by a borrower to secure a loan.

convertible securities   Securities that can be exchanged by the holder for common stock or another security.

coupon bond   A bond with coupons attached that are clipped by the holder and presented for payment of interest due.

current assets   The total amount of cash, securities, inventory, and receivables expected during the normal business cycle of a company, usually one year.

current liabilities   The total amount of debt and other payments that will be due during the normal business cycle of a company, usually one year.

debenture   An unsecured promissory note backed by a company's general credit.

discount   The amount of money below the issuing price of a stock or bond at which it sells.

discretionary account   A securities account that leaves some or all decisions about purchases and sales to the discretion of a broker.

dividend   A payment by a company equally divided among its stockholders. *See also* **stock dividend.**

Dow Jones average   The average price of selected stocks, used as an indicator of the stock market's performance.

equity   The interest stockholders have in a company, or the amount of property a property holder actually has paid for as opposed to the portion held by a mortgage.

ex-dividend   A stock that does not pay a recently declared dividend to its new purchaser.

Federal Deposit Insurance Corporation (FDIC)   The federal agency that insures amounts of up to $100,000 deposited in qualified banks.

fiduciary   Someone who acts on behalf of another in financial matters.

gilt-edged security A high-grade preferred stock or bond issued by a company with a strong performance record.

income fund A mutual fund designed to provide current income.

individual retirement account (IRA) A tax-sheltered and sometimes tax-deductible retirement plan.

interest The money paid by a borrower to a lender for the use of the borrowed money.

investment The use of money to make more money.

junk bond A high-risk, high-yielding corporate bond.

Keogh plan A tax-sheltered retirement plan for self-employed people with no pension plans.

liabilities All claims against and amounts owed by a person or company.

listed stock Stock traded on a securities exchange.

margin The portion of a stock's price paid by the buyer when the broker arranges for the remainder to be purchased on credit.

market order An order to buy or sell at the current market price of a security.

maturity The date on which a bond or loan is to be paid off.

money-market fund A mutual fund that invests in short-term financial securities.

municipal bond A bond issued by a local government.

mutual fund An investment company that continually offers new stock and redeems outstanding shares on demand.

Nasdaq The electronic market for trading over-the-counter securities. Companies on Nasdaq are predominately growth-oriented securities, many of which are technology stocks.

odd lot An amount of stock bought or sold in units other than 10 shares or 100 shares.

offer The price at which someone is willing to sell.

over-the-counter market The arena in which stocks not listed on exchanges are bought and sold.

par The issuing value of a share of common stock.

preferred stock Stock that must receive its share of earnings before payment is made on common stock.

premium The amount over par value by which a preferred stock is sold.

puts and calls Options that give the right to sell or buy a specified number of shares of stock at a specified price within a specified time.

red herring A preliminary prospectus issued to gauge interest in a new stock issue.

Securities and Exchange Commission (SEC) The federal agency that oversees securities trading.

stock Ownership shares in a company.

stock dividend Shares distributed to current shareholders in a company in proportion to those they hold.

stock split The division of currently outstanding shares into a larger number of shares.

tax shelter A way in which taxes on income may be legally decreased, eliminated, or deferred.

tender offer An offer by one company to purchase shares of stock in another company directly from its stockholders.

Treasury bill A short-term U.S. government security sold at a discount in competitive bidding.

Treasury bond A long-term U.S. government bond issued in $1,000 denominations.

yield The amount of dividend or interest expressed as a percentage of the selling price.

zero-coupon bonds Bonds that are sold at a discount from their face value but do not pay interest.

TIPPING

"Domestic Travel" and "Foreign Travel" in chapter 24 **Go to**

The following list suggests what are generally considered to be adequate amounts to tip various people for services rendered. Keep in mind that tips are a way of expressing satisfaction. Larger tips should be given to those who provide extraordinarily good service; smaller tips or no tip at all should be given when service is poor.

Location	Person	Amount
Airport	Skycap	$1–$2 per bag
	In-flight personnel	None
Barbershop	Haircutter	15% of the cost, generally a minimum of $1
Beauty shop	One operator	15% of bill
	Person who washes hair	$2 or more depending on bill
	Manicurist	$2–3 or more depending on cost
	Spa services	15–20% of bill
Cruise ship	Staff	Expect to spend between $65 and $100 per person, per week on gratuities.
	Cabin Steward	$3–3.50 per person, per day
	Dining Room Waiter	$3–3.50 per person, per day
	Dining Room Busboy	$1.50–2.00 per day
	Wine Steward	$1.50 per person, per day of wine service
	Maitre d'/Head Waiter	$5.00 per person for entire cruise if exceptional service
	Room Service Waiter	$1–2 per order
	Bar Tab	On most cruise ships a 15% gratuity is automatically added to your bill at the end of the cruise
Deliveries	Pizza	$1–2 if short distance, $2–3 for longer distance or $5 or more for large delivery.
	Furniture	$5–10 per person, perhaps $20 if it is heavy or requires assembly
Driver	Taxi	15–20% of fare
	Limousine	20% of fare
Hotel	Housekeeping	$2–5 a night, consider more if you stay longer than one week
	Bellhop	$1–2 per bag, an additional $1 or more for showing the room
	Concierge	$5–10 (for restaurant reservations, theater tickets, etc.)
	Room-service waiter	15% of bill
	Lobby attendant	None for opening door or calling taxi from stand; $1 or more for help with luggage or finding a taxi on the street
	Desk clerk	None unless special service is given during long stay; then, $5
Restaurant	Waiter	15–20% of bill
	Headwaiter/maitre d'	None, unless special services are provided; then, about $5
	Wine steward	15% of wine bill
	Bartender	10–15% of bar bill
	Busperson	None
	Server at counter	15% of bill
	Coat check	$1–2 per coat
	Rest-room attendant	50 cents if provided with a handtowel only. $1 or more if special services are provided
	Car-park attendant	$1–2 given when car is brought to you
Sports arena	Usher	$1 per party if shown to your seat
Tour	Guide	$1–2 per day/per person
	Driver	$1–2 per day/per person
Train	Dining-car waiter	15% of bill
	Steward/bar-car waiter	15% of bar bill
	Redcap or porter	Posted rate plus 50¢

Personal Finances

ADDITIONAL SOURCES OF INFORMATION

ORGANIZATIONS AND SERVICES

Consult the following organization for referrals to reputable planners:

Financial Planning Association
Atlanta—Denver—Washington D.C.
800-322-4237
404-845-0011
Fax: 404-845-3660
http://www.fpanet.org

MAGAZINES AND NEWSPAPERS

The following publications offer substantial coverage of events and trends that affect personal finances. Addresses and phone numbers are for subscriptions.

Barron's National Business Weekly
200 Burnett Rd.
Chicopee, MA 01020
800-544-0422
www.barrons.com

Business Week
1221 Avenue of the Americas
New York, NY 10020
800-635-1200
http://www.businessweek.com

Forbes
60 Fifth Ave.
New York, NY 10011
800-888-9896
http://www.forbes.com

Fortune
Time Life Building
Rockefeller Center
New York, NY 10020
800-621-8000
http://www.fortune.com

Kiplinger's Personal Finance Magazine
The Kiplinger Washington Editors, Inc.
1729 H St., NW
Washington, DC 20006
800-544-0155
http://kiplinger.com

Money
Time Life Building
Rockefeller Center
New York, NY 10020
http://www.money.com

The Wall Street Journal
84 2nd Ave
Chicopee, MA 01020
800-568-7625
http://www.wsj.com

BOOKS

Chilton, David. *The Wealthy Barber*, 3rd ed. Prima Publishing, 1998.

Clifford, Denis, and Cora Johnson. *Plan Your Estate*, 5th ed. Nolo Press, 2000.

Dunnan, Nancy. *Dun and Bradstreet Guide to Your Investments 1999*. HarperCollins, 1999.

Eisenberg, Richard. *The Money Book of Personal Finance*. Warner, 1998.

Garner, Robert J., et al. *Ernst & Young's Personal Financial Planning Guide*, 3rd ed. Wiley, 1999.

Good-Garton, Julie. *All About Mortgages: Insider Tips for Financing Your Home*, 2nd ed. Dearborn Publishing, 1999.

Hunt, Mary. *The Complete Cheapskate: How to Get Out of Debt, Stay Out and Break Free from Money Worries Forever*. Broadman & Holman, 1998.

Kiplinger's Buying & Selling a Home, 6th ed. Kiplinger Books, 1999.

Patterson, Martha P. *The New Working Woman's Guide to Retirement Planning: Saving and Investing Now for a Secure Future*, 2nd ed. University of Pennsylvania Press, 1999.

Rowland, Mary. *The New Commonsense Guide to Mutual Funds,* revised. Bloomberg Press, 1998.

Siegel, Alan M., et al. *The Wall Street Journal Guide to Planning Your Financial Future: The Easy-To-Read Guide to Planning for Retirement*. Fireside, 1998.

Tyson, Eric. *Personal Finances for Dummies*, 3rd ed. Hungry Minds, Inc., 2000.

Tyson, Eric, and Ray Brown. *Mortgages for Dummies*. Hungry Minds, Inc., 1999.

Personal Finances

21

LEGAL INFORMATION

FORMS AND CONTRACTS

The documents in the following sections are fairly standard versions of simple agreements, requests, or statements. They are meant to demonstrate the basic content of similar documents. Because laws vary from state to state (and because agreements can have their own special circumstances, terms, or other complexities), it is always a good idea to consult with a lawyer before drawing up or signing a contract. For additional legal forms and contracts, consult the Internet Legal Resource Guide: http://www.ilrg.com/forms.

BILL OF SALE

Bill of Sale
of

_____

STATE OF _____   )
)   ss:

COUNTY OF _____   )

KNOW YE ALL MEN BY THESE PRESENTS,

That I, _____ , of

_____ ,

    Street Address   *City*   *State*   *Zip*

for and in consideration of payment of the sum of $ _____ , the receipt of which is hereby acknowledged, do hereby grant, bargain, sell, and convey to:

_____ , of

_____ ,

    Street Address   *City*   *State*   *Zip*

and his/her heirs, executors, administrators, successors, and assigns the following property:

_____

_____

_____

_____

    I hereby warrant that I am the lawful owner of said property and that I have full legal right, power, and authority to sell said property. I further warrant said property to be free of all encumbrances and that I will warrant and defend said property hereby sold against any and all persons whomsoever.

    IN WITNESS WHEREOF, I, the seller, have hereto set my hand and seal this _____ day of _____ , 20_____ .

(Signed) _____

                                          Seller

CERTIFICATE OF NOTARY

A certificate of notary often accompanies agreements or statements; it may be required in some localities. A certificate of notary might be useful with the following documents in this section:

- Bill of Sale
- Declaration of Gift
- Living Will
- Power of Attorney
- Privacy Act/Freedom of Information Act Request
- Request for Reason for Adverse Credit Action

Certificate of Notary

STATE OF   )
)   ss:
COUNTY OF   )

On this _____ day of _____ , 20___ , before me personally came and appeared _____ , known, and known to me, to be the individual described in and who executed the foregoing instrument, and who duly acknowledged to me that he/she executed same for the purpose therein contained.

IN WITNESS WHEREOF, I hereunto set my hand and official seal.

_____

Notary Public

My commission expires:_____

CONTRACT

Agreement Between Owner and Contractor

THIS AGREEMENT is hereby entered into this _____ day of _____ , 20_____ , between _____ , of

_____

| *Street Address* | *City* | *Street* | *Zip* | *Phone* |

hereinafter called Owner, and _____ , of

_____

| *Street Address* | *City* | *Street* | *Zip* | *Phone* |

hereinafter called the Contractor.

The said parties, for the considerations hereinafter mentioned, hereby agree to the following:

Description of the Work

1. The Contractor shall provide all materials and labor required to perform all of the work for:

as shown on the drawing(s), and set forth in the specifications and/or description(s) prepared by _____ , which drawing(s) and specifications and/or description(s) are identified by the signatures of the parties to this agreement, and which form a part of this agreement and are incorporated by reference herein for all purposes.

Payment

2. Under the terms of this agreement, the Owner agrees to pay the Contractor, for materials to be furnished and work to be done, the sum of _____ ($ _____), subject to any additions or deductions as hereinafter provided for in this agreement, and to make the following payments:

_____

_____

_____

and that the final payment shall be made subject to the hereinafter stated conditions of this agreement.

It is agreed that no payment made under this agreement shall be considered conclusive evidence of full performance of this contract, either wholly or in part by the Contractor, and that acceptance of payment shall not be considered by the Contractor to be acceptance by the Owner of any defective materials or workmanship.

Liens

3. Final payment shall not be due until such time as the Contractor has provided the Owner with a release of any liens arising from this agreement; or receipts for payment in full for all materials and labor

for which a lien could be filed; or a bond satisfactory to the Owner indemnifying the Owner against any lien.

Timely Completion of the Work

4. The Contractor agrees that the various portions of the work shall be completed on or before the following dates:

_____

_____

_____

and the entire work shall be completed on or before the _____ day of _____ , 20_____.

In the event the work is not completed by the aforementioned date, the Owner shall be entitled to receive as damages from the Contractor, the sum of _____ ($ _____) per _____ , it being agreed that the aforementioned sum is reasonable, taking into account the difficulty in determining the exact amount of damages the Owner would sustain in the event of said delay, and that the agreed sum shall be considered as liquidated damages.

If the Contractor is delayed in the completion of the work by any changes ordered in the work, by acts of God, fire, flood, or any other unavoidable casualties; or by labor strikes, late delivery of materials; or by neglect of the Owner, his agents or representatives; or by any subcontractor employed by the Contractor; the time for completion of the work shall be extended for the same period as the delay occasioned by any of the aforementioned causes.

Surveys and Easements

5. The Owner shall provide and pay for all surveys. All easements for access across the property of another, and for permanent changes, and for the construction or erection of structures shall also be obtained and paid for by the Owner.

Licenses, Permits, and Building Codes

6. The Contractor shall obtain and pay for all permits and licenses required for the prosecution and timely completion of the work. The Contractor shall comply with all appropriate regulations relating to the conduct of the work and shall advise the Owner of any specifications or drawings which are at variance therewith.

Materials and Equipment

7. The Contractor shall provide and pay for all materials, tools, and equipment required for the prosecution and timely completion of the work. Unless otherwise specified in writing, all materials shall be new and of good quality.

Samples

8. Whenever the Owner may require, the Contractor will furnish for approval all samples as directed, and the work shall be in accordance with approved samples.

Labor and Supervision

9. In the prosecution of the work the Contractor shall at all times keep a competent foreman and a sufficient number of workers skilled in their trades to suitably perform the work.

continues

Legal Information

The foreman shall represent the Contractor and, in the absence of the Contractor, all instructions given by the Owner to the foreman shall be binding upon the Contractor as though given to the Contractor. Upon request of the foreman, instructions shall be in writing.

Alterations and Changes

10. All changes and deviations in the work ordered by the Owner must be in writing, the contract sum being increased or decreased accordingly by the Contractor. Any claims for increases in the cost of the work must be presented by the Contractor to the Owner in writing, and written approval of the Owner shall be obtained by the Contractor before proceeding with the ordered change or revision.

In the event that additional work, not shown on the drawings and/or not described in the specifications, is required to comply with laws, regulations, or building codes, such additional work shall be considered as done under the terms of this agreement.

Correction of Deficiencies

11. The Contractor agrees to reexecute any work that does not conform to the drawings and specifications, warrants the work performed, and further agrees that he shall remedy any defects resulting from faulty materials or workmanship that shall become evident during a period of one year after completion of the work. This provision shall apply with equal force to all work performed by subcontractors as to work that is performed by direct employees of the Contractor.

Protection of the Work

12. It shall be the responsibility of the Contractor to reasonably protect the work, the property of the Owner, and adjacent property and the public; and the Contractor shall be responsible for any damage, injury, or death resulting from his negligence or from any intentional act of the Contractor or the Contractor's employees, agents, or subcontractors.

Cleaning Up

13. The Contractor shall keep the premises free from the accumulation of waste and, upon completion of the work, shall remove all waste, equipment, and other materials and leave the premises in broom-clean condition.

Contractor's Liability Insurance

14. The Contractor shall obtain insurance to protect himself against claims for property damage arising out of his or any subcontractor's performance of this contract; and to protect himself against claims under provisions of Workman's Compensation and any similar employee benefit acts, and from claims for bodily injury, including death, due to performance of this contract by the Contractor or any subcontractor employed for the performance of this contract.

Owner's Liability Insurance

15. It shall be the responsibility of the Owner, at the Owner's option, to obtain insurance to protect himself from the contingent liability of claims for property damage and bodily injury, including death, that may arise from the performance of this contract.

Fire Insurance with Extended Coverage

16. The Owner shall obtain fire insurance with extended coverage at 100 percent of the value of the entire structure, including materials and labor related to the work described in this agreement. Certificates of insurance shall be filed with the Contractor if he so requests. The aforesaid fire insurance need

not include tools, equipment, scaffolding, or forms owned or rented by the Contractor, any subcontractor, or their respective employees.

Owner's Right to Terminate the Agreement

17. In the event the Contractor shall fail to meet the provisions of this agreement, the Owner shall, after seven (7) days' written notice to the Contractor and his surety, have the right to take possession of the premises in order to complete the work as specified in the agreement. The Owner may deduct the cost thereof from any payment then and thereafter due to the Contractor or may, at his option, terminate the agreement, take possession of any materials, and complete the work as he deems appropriate. If the unpaid balance of the contracted sum exceeds the Owner's expenses of completing the work, such excess shall be paid to the Contractor. If such expense shall exceed the unpaid balance, the Contractor shall pay the difference to the Owner.

Contractor's Right to Terminate the Agreement

18. In the event the Owner shall fail to pay the Contractor within seven (7) days after the date upon which payment shall become due, the Contractor shall have the right, after seven (7) days' written notice to the Owner, to stop work and may, at his option, terminate the agreement and recover from the Owner payment for all work executed, plus any loss sustained, plus a reasonable profit, plus damages.

In the event the work is stopped by any court or other public authority for a period of thirty (30) days through no fault of the Contractor, the Contractor shall have the right to stop work and may, at his option, terminate the agreement and recover from the Owner payment for all work executed, plus any loss sustained, plus a reasonable profit, plus damages.

Assignment of Rights

19. Neither the Owner nor Contractor shall have the right to assign any rights or interest occurring under this agreement without the written consent of the other; nor shall the Contractor assign any sums due, or to become due, to him under the provisions of this agreement.

Access and Inspection

20. The Owner, Owner's representative, and public authorities shall at all times have access to the work.

An appropriately licensed representative of the Owner, whose authority shall be set forth in writing by the Owner, shall have the authority to direct the removal of any materials and the taking down of any portions of the work failing to meet drawings, specifications, laws, regulations, or building codes; the reexecution of said work deemed as being done under the provisions of Article 11 of this agreement.

Any other removal of materials or taking down of any portions of the work as directed by the Owner's representative shall be in writing and at the sole expense of the Owner.

Attorney Fees

21. Attorney fees and court costs shall be paid by the defendant in the event that judgment must be obtained, and is, to enforce this agreement or any breach thereof.

IN WITNESS WHEREOF, the parties hereto set their hands and seals the day and year written above.

_____   _____
Witness as to Owner   *Owner*

_____   _____
Witness as to Contractor   *Contractor*

DECLARATION OF GIFT

Declaration of Gift

TO ALL TO WHOM THESE PRESENTS SHALL COME OR MAY CONCERN, KNOW THAT on this _____ day of _____ , 20___ , I, _____ , of _____ ,

| Street | City | State | Zip |

being of sound and disposing mind and memory, do hereby irrevocably give, bestow, and deliver up to _____ , of _____ ,

| Street | City | State | Zip |

all of my right, title, and interest in the following described property valued at _____ _____ ($ _____):

_____

_____

_____

_____

_____

_____

_____

IN WITNESS WHEREOF, I hereunto set my hand and seal on the date above mentioned.

_____

LEASES

"Open" Rental Agreement

THIS AGREEMENT is made this _____ day of _____ , 20_____ ,
between _____ , of

_____

| Street Address | City | State | Zip |

hereinafter called "Owner," and _____ , of

_____

| Street Address | City | State | Zip |

hereinafter called "Renter."

Property

_____

_____

_____

_____

_____

| Year | Make | Model/Type |

_____

| Capacity | Horsepower | Serial No. |

The Owner warrants that to the best of his/her knowledge and belief, the aforesaid property is free of any known faults or deficiencies which would affect its safe and dependable operation under normal and prudent usage.

Rental Period

The Owner agrees to rent the above-described property to the Renter for a period of _____ beginning _____ and ending _____ .

Use of Property

_____

_____

_____

_____

_____

The Renter further agrees that the rented property (A) shall not be used beyond any rated capacity; (B) shall not be used for any illegal purpose; (C) shall not be used in any manner for which it was not designed, built, or designated by the manufacturer; (D) will not be used in a negligent manner; (E) will not be

continues

operated by any other person without the written permission of the Owner; and (F) will not be removed from the designated area of use or operation.

Area of Use or Operation

The Renter agrees to operate/use the above-described property only at the following location or within the following described area(s):

_____

_____

_____

Insurance

The Renter hereby agrees that he/she shall fully indemnify the Owner for any and all damage to or loss of the rented property and any accessories or related equipment during the term of this Agreement whether caused by fire, theft, flood, vandalism, or any other cause, except that which shall be determined to have been caused by a fault or deficiency of the rented property, accessories, or equipment.

Rental Rate

The Renter hereby agrees to pay the Owner at the rate of $ _____ per _____ for the use of said property and any accessories/equipment. Any fuel used shall be paid for by the Renter.

Deposit

The Renter further agrees to make a deposit of $ _____ with the Owner, said deposit to be used, in the event of loss of or damage to the rented property and any accessories/equipment during the term of this Agreement, to defray fully or partially the cost of necessary repairs or replacement. In the absence of any damage or loss, said deposit shall be credited toward payment of the rental fee, and any excess shall be returned to the Renter.

Return of Property to Owner

The Renter hereby agrees to return the rented property and any accessories/equipment to the Owner at _____ no later than _____ .

Termination of Agreement

It is mutually agreed that the Renter shall have the right to terminate this Agreement at any time by payment of one full day's rental for each 24-hour period or any part thereof, during which the Renter has retained possession of the property and any accessories/equipment during the term of this Agreement.

IN WITNESS WHEREOF, the parties hereto hereby execute this Agreement.

(Signed) _____
Renter

(Signed) _____
Owner

Seasonal Lease Agreement—Furnished Country/Seashore House

Landlord_____

Address   *Phone*

Managing Agent _____

_____

Address   *Phone*

Premises _____

_____

Address   *Phone*

Tenant _____

_____

Address   *Phone*

Tenant _____

_____

Address   *Phone*

1. The LANDLORD hereby leases to _____ (and) _____ , hereinafter termed TENANT, the premises described above for a term of _____ beginning _____ and ending _____ , at a monthly rate of $_____ , making a total rental amount payable under this lease of $_____ .

2. The tenant agrees to pay the rent in the following manner:_____ (Landlord specify if payments are to be made by mail, and if so, to what address. If payments are to be made to the landlord or his agent in person, state the place where, and the person to whom, payments should be made.)

3. The tenant, in addition to rent, agrees to pay all charges for water, gas, fuel oil, and electricity used during the term of the lease, such charges to be paid monthly in addition to rent.

4. Upon receipt of any payment for rent or utilities in cash, the landlord agrees to issue a receipt stating the tenant's name, a description of the premises, the amount paid, the date paid, and the period for which rent or utilities is paid.

5. The tenant agrees to place a security deposit of $ _____ , to be used by the landlord at the termination of this lease for the cost of replacing or repairing damage, if any, to the premises or furnishings caused by the intentional or negligent acts of the tenant.

6. The landlord agrees to return said security deposit to the tenant upon the tenant's vacating the premises subject to the terms and conditions herein.

7. The tenant agrees to take good care of the premises and of the furnishings therein, and at the end of the term of this lease to deliver up to the landlord the premises and furnishings in good order, normal wear and tear excepted.

8. The landlord covenants that the leased premises are, to the best of his or her knowledge, clean, safe, sound, and healthful and that there exists no violation of any applicable housing code, law, or

continues

Seasonal Lease Agreement, Continued

regulation of which he or she is aware, and that no such violation will be permitted to exist during the term of this lease or any extension thereof.

9. The tenant shall promptly comply with all laws, orders, ordinances, and regulations pertaining to his or her use of the premises, and the tenant shall not keep therein any article or thing of a dangerous, flammable, or explosive nature that might be pronounced "hazardous" or "extra hazardous" by any responsible insurance company.

10. The tenant shall, in case of fire, give immediate notice to the proper authorities and to the landlord, who will cause the damage to be promptly repaired; but if the premises be so damaged that the landlord shall decide to terminate this lease, then upon 10 days' personal or written notice to the tenant, this lease shall terminate and the accrued rent shall be paid up to the time of the fire.

11. The tenant shall do no cooking in any room used for sleeping purposes, but shall have the right to use jointly with any other tenants a room set aside by the landlord for that purpose.

12. The tenant shall, at reasonable times, give access to the landlord or his agents for any reasonable and lawful purpose. Except in situations of compelling emergency, the landlord shall give the tenant at least 24 hours' notice of intention to seek access, the date and time at which access will be sought, and the reason therefor.

13. In the event of default by the tenant, the tenant shall remain liable for all rent due or to become due during the term of this lease. The landlord shall have the obligation to relet the premises in the landlord's name for the balance of the term, or longer, and will apply proceeds of such reletting toward the reduction of the tenant's obligations enumerated herein.

14. The tenant shall permit the landlord or his agents to show the premises at reasonable hours, to persons desiring to rent or purchase same, 30 days prior to the expiration of this lease, and will permit the notice "To Let" or "For Sale" to be placed on said premises and remain thereon without hindrance or molestation after said date.

15. The tenant shall not assign this lease, nor underlet or underlease the premises, or any part thereof, nor make any alterations to the premises, nor permit same to be used at any time during the term of this lease for any other purpose than a private residence.

16. This lease, and any attached List of Furnishings signed by both parties and dated, and incorporated herein by reference for all purposes, constitutes the entire agreement between the parties hereto. No changes shall be made herein except by writing, signed by each party and dated.

17. In the event legal action is required to enforce any provision of this agreement, the prevailing party shall be entitled to recover reasonable attorney's fees and costs.

18. This lease, when filled out and signed, is a binding legal obligation.

IN WITNESS WHEREOF, the parties hereto have executed this agreement.

_____
Witness as to landlord

_____   *Landlord*
Witness as to landlord   By _____

_____   *Landlord*
_____
          Tenant

_____   Dated this _____ day of _____ , 20_____ .
Witness as to landlord

Lease Agreement—Unfurnished Apartment

Landlord _____

_____
            Address   *Phone*

Managing Agent _____

_____
            Address   *Phone*

Premises _____

_____
            Address   *Apt. No.*

Tenant _____

Tenant _____

1. The LANDLORD hereby leases to _____ (and) _____ , hereinafter termed TENANT, the premises described above for a term of beginning and ending _____ , at a monthly rate of $ _____ , making a total rental amount payable under this lease of $ _____ .

2. The tenant agrees to pay the rent herein provided subject to the terms and conditions set forth herein.

3. Rent shall be payable in equal monthly installments to be paid in advance on the _____ day of each month.

4. Rent shall be payable in the following manner:
(Specify above if payments are to be made by mail, and if so, to what address. If payments are to be made to the landlord or the landlord's agent in person, state the place where, and the person to whom, payments are to be made.)

5. Upon receiving any payment of rent in cash, the landlord agrees to issue a receipt stating the tenant's name, a description of the premises, the amount of rent paid, the date paid, and the period for which rent is paid.

6. The landlord covenants that the leased premises are, to the best of his or her knowledge, clean, safe, sound, and healthful and that there exists no violation of any applicable housing code, law, or regulation of which he or she is aware.

7. The tenant agrees to comply with all sanitary laws, ordinances, and rules, and all orders of the Board of Health or other authorities affecting the cleanliness, occupancy, and preservation of the premises during the term of this lease.

8. The tenant shall use the leased premises exclusively as a private residence for no more than _____ persons, and the tenant will not make alterations therein without the written consent of the landlord.

9. The tenant shall keep fixtures in said apartment in good order and repair, and the tenant shall cause to be made, at the tenant's expense, all required repairs to heating and air-conditioning apparatus, refrigerator, range, electric and gas fixtures, and plumbing work whenever such damage shall have resulted from misuse, waste, or neglect, it being understood that the landlord is to have same in good order and repair when giving possession.

continues

Lease Agreement—Unfurnished Apartment, Continued

10. The tenant shall not keep or have in the leased premises any article or thing of a dangerous, flammable, or explosive nature that might be pronounced "hazardous" or "extra hazardous" by any responsible insurance company.

11. The tenant shall give prompt notice to the landlord of any dangerous, defective, unsafe, or emergency condition in the leased premises, said notice being given by any suitable means. The landlord shall repair and correct said conditions promptly upon receiving notice thereof from the tenant.

12. The landlord covenants that all essential services are now provided and shall be provided at all times during the term of this lease and any extension, renewal, or continuation thereof, except where any interruption of essential services shall be for maintenance or for cause beyond control of the landlord such as strike, storm, civil insurrection, fire, or acts of God. "Essential services" hereunder are defined as heat, hot and cold running water, a properly functioning toilet, light in public areas, and suitable building security.

13. The _____ shall pay for gas and electricity except to the extent otherwise set forth herein.

14. The landlord covenants that consumption of electricity for the public halls and other common areas and use and consumption of gas for heat or hot water in public areas are recorded on separate meters, and that said electricity and gas are and will at all times be billed to and paid by the landlord.

15. The tenant covenants that during the last 30 days of this lease, or any renewal thereof, the landlord or his agents, with reasonable notice, and at reasonable hours, have the privilege of showing the premises to prospective buyers or tenants.

16. The tenant shall, at reasonable times, give access to the landlord or his agents for any reasonable and lawful purpose. Except in situations of compelling emergency, or to show the premises for rental or sale, the landlord agrees to give the tenant 24 hours' notice, stating the time and date when access will be sought, and the reason therefor.

17. The landlord covenants that the tenant and the tenant's family shall have, hold, and enjoy the leased premises for the term of this lease, subject to the provisions and conditions set forth herein.

18. The tenant covenants that he shall not commit nor permit a nuisance in or upon the premises, that he shall not maliciously or by reason of gross negligence damage the premises, and that he shall not engage in conduct so as to interfere substantially with the comfort and safety of occupants of adjacent apartments or buildings.

19. The tenant agrees to place a security deposit with the landlord in the amount of $ _____ , to be used by the landlord for the cost of replacing and/or repairing damage, if any, to the premises caused by the intentional or negligent acts of the tenant.

20. The landlord agrees, within 10 days of receiving said security deposit, to deposit same in an interest-bearing account in a banking organization, in which said deposit shall earn interest at a rate which shall be the prevailing rate earned by other such deposits made with banking organizations in such circumstances.

21. The landlord agrees, within 10 days of making such deposit, to notify the tenant, in writing, of the name and address of the banking organization in which the deposit of security money has been made.

22. The landlord shall be entitled to receive, as administrative expenses, an amount equal to 1 percent per annum upon the security payment so deposited, which shall be in lieu of all other administrative and custodial expenses. The balance of the interest paid by the banking organization shall be the money of

the tenant and shall be paid to the tenant on each anniversary of this lease or any extension or renewal thereof.

23. The landlord agrees to return said security deposit to the tenant within 10 days of the tenant's vacating the leased premises subject to the terms and conditions set forth herein.

24. In the event of any breach by the tenant of any of the tenant's covenants or agreements herein, the landlord may give the tenant five days' notice to cure said breach, setting forth in writing which covenants or agreements have been breached. If any breach is not cured within said five-day period, or reasonable steps to effectuate said cure are not commenced and diligently pursued within said five-day period and thereafter until said breach has been cured, the landlord may terminate this lease upon five days' additional notice to the tenant, with said notice being in lieu of a Notice to Quit, which tenant hereby waives. The tenant shall then become liable for the cost of landlord's normal redecorating and cleaning expenses related to preparation of the premises for rental to a succeeding tenant.

Said termination shall be ineffective if the tenant cures said breach or commences and diligently pursues reasonable steps to effectuate such cure at any time prior to the expiration of said five-day termination. Upon terminating this lease as provided herein, the landlord or his agent may commence proceedings against the tenant for his removal as provided for by law.

25. In the event of any breach by the landlord of any of the landlord's covenants or agreements herein, the tenant may give the landlord 10 days' notice to cure said breach, setting forth in writing the manner in which said covenants and agreements have been breached. If said breach is not cured within said 10-day period, or reasonable steps to effectuate said cure are not commenced and diligently pursued within said 10-day period and thereafter until said breach has been cured, rent hereunder shall be fully abated from the time at which said 10 days' notice expired until such time as the landlord has fully cured the breach set forth in the notice provided for in this paragraph.

26. In no case shall any abatement of rent hereunder be effected where the condition set forth in the notice provided for herein was created by the intentional or negligent act of the tenant, but the landlord shall have the burden of proving that rent abatement may not be effected for the foregoing reason.

27. The landlord agrees to deliver possession of the leased premises at the beginning of the term provided for herein. In the event of the landlord's failure to deliver possession at the beginning of said term, the tenant shall have the right to rescind this lease and to recover any consideration paid under terms of this agreement.

28. The tenant agrees that this lease shall be subject to and subordinate to any mortgage or mortgages now on said premises or which any owner of said premises may hereafter at any time elect to place on said premises.

29. Unless otherwise provided for elsewhere in this lease, any notice required or authorized herein shall be given in writing, one copy of said notice mailed via U.S. certified mail, return receipt requested, and one copy of said notice mailed via U.S. first-class mail.

Notice to the tenant shall be mailed to him at the leased premises. Notice to the landlord shall be mailed to him, or to the managing agent, at their respective addresses as set forth herein, or at such new address as to which the tenant has been duly notified.

30. This lease constitutes the entire agreement between the parties hereto. No changes shall be made herein except by writing, signed by each party and dated. The failure to enforce any right or remedy

continues

Lease Agreement—Unfurnished Apartment, Continued

hereunder, and the payment and acceptance of rent hereunder, shall not be deemed a waiver by either party of such right or remedy in the absence of a writing as provided for herein.

31. In the event legal action is required to enforce any provision of this agreement, the prevailing party shall be entitled to recover reasonable attorney's fees and costs.

32. The landlord and tenant agree that this apartment lease, when filled out and signed, is a binding legal obligation.

IN WITNESS WHEREOF, the parties hereto have executed this agreement.

_____

Landlord

By _____

_____
Witness as to landlord

_____
Witness as to landlord

_____

Tenant

_____
Witness as to tenant

_____
Witness as to tenant

_____

Tenant

_____
Witness as to tenant

_____
Witness as to tenant

Dated this _____ day of _____ , 20____ .

LIVING WILL

Living Will

Directive to Physicians:

I, _____ , of

_____ ,

| *Street Address* | *Apt. No.* | *City* | *State* | *Zip* |

being of sound mind, do hereby willfully and voluntarily make known my desire that my life not be prolonged under any of the following conditions, and do hereby further declare:

1. If I should, at any time, have an incurable condition caused by any disease or illness, or by any accident or injury, and be determined by any two or more physicians to be in a terminal condition whereby the use of "heroic measures" or the application of life-sustaining procedures would only serve to delay the moment of my death, and where my attending physician has determined that my death is imminent whether or not such "heroic measures" or life-sustaining measures are employed, I direct that such measures and procedures be withheld or withdrawn and that I be permitted to die naturally.

2. In the event of my inability to give directions regarding the application of life-sustaining procedures or the use of "heroic measures," it is my intention that this directive shall be honored by my family and physicians as my final expression of my right to refuse medical and surgical treatment, and my acceptance of the consequences of such refusal.

3. I am mentally, emotionally, and legally competent to make this directive and I fully understand its import.

4. I reserve the right to revoke this directive at any time.

5. This directive shall remain in force until revoked.

IN WITNESS WHEREOF, I have hereunto set my hand and seal this _____ day of _____ , 20_____ .

(Signed) _____

Declaration of Witness:

The declarant is personally known to me and I believe him/her to be of sound mind and emotionally and legally competent to make the herein-contained **Directive to Physicians**. I am not related to the declarant by blood or marriage, nor would I be entitled to any portion of the declarant's estate upon his/her decease, nor am I an attending physician of the declarant, nor an employee of the attending physician, nor an employee of a health-care facility in which the declarant is a patient, nor a patient in a health-care facility in which the declarant is a patient, nor am I a person who has any claim against any portion of the estate of the declarant upon his/her decease.

(Signed) _____   (Signed) _____

Witness   *Witness*

_____   _____

Address   *Address*

POWER OF ATTORNEY

Power of Attorney

STATE OF _____)
)   ss:

COUNTY OF _____)

KNOW YE ALL MEN BY THESE PRESENTS,

That I, _____ , of

_____ ,

    Street Address   *Apt. No.*   *City*   *State*   *Zip*

do hereby make, constitute, and appoint _____ , of

_____ ,

    Street Address   *Apt. No.*   *City*   *State*   *Zip*

as my true and lawful Attorney-in-Fact, for me and in my name, place, and stead to:

_____

_____

_____

_____

_____

    I further give and grant to my said Attorney-in-Fact full power and authority to do and perform every act necessary and proper to be done in the exercise of any of the foregoing powers as fully as I might or could do if personally present, with full power of substitution and revocation, hereby ratifying and confirming all that my said Attorney-in-Fact shall lawfully do, or cause to be done by virtue hereof.

    This instrument may not be changed orally.

    IN WITNESS WHEREOF, I have hereunto set my hand and seal this day of _____ , 20__ .

                                 (Signed) _____

PRIVACY ACT/FREEDOM OF INFORMATION ACT REQUEST

Attn: _____

    This is a request under provisions of Title 5 USC, Sec. 552, the Freedom of Information Act, and Title 5 USC, Sec. 552a, the Privacy Act.

    Please furnish me with copies of all records on me retrievable by the use of an individual identifier and by the use of any combination of identifiers (e.g., name + date of birth + Social Security number, etc.) that are contained in the following systems of records:

_____

_____

_____

_____

    In order to identify myself and to facilitate your search of records systems, I provide the following information:

_____

     Last Name   *First*   *Middle*

_____

    Street   *City*   *State*   *Zip*

_____

   Date of Birth   *Place of Birth*   *Sex*   *Social Security Number*

    In the event that any part or all of my records are withheld, I request a complete list of all records being withheld and the specific exemption being claimed for the withholding of each.

    In the event that search and copying fees are estimated to exceed $ _____ , I request an opportunity to review such records, or to have a duly authorized representative review such records, in order to select those to be copied.

    If you have any questions regarding this request, please telephone me at _____ weekdays between _____ and _____ or write to me at the above address.

    As provided for by Sec. 552(a)(6)(i) of the Freedom of Information Act, I shall expect to receive a reply within twenty (20) business days.

                                  Sincerely,

                               _____

PROMISSORY NOTE

Promissory Note

$ _____

Date _____

_____ after the above date I promise to pay to the order of _____
(*number of days*)

the sum of _____ ($ _____),
together with interest at _____ percent per annum, payable at
_____.

    The maker and endorser of this note further agree to waive demand, notice of nonpayment and protest, and in case suit shall be brought for the collection hereof, or the same has to be collected upon demand of an attorney, to pay reasonable attorney's fees for making such collection. Deferred interest payments to bear interest from maturity at _____ percent per annum, payable semiannually.

(Signed) _____
                                         Maker

(Signed) _____
                                        Endorser

Due _____

REQUEST FOR REASON FOR ADVERSE CREDIT ACTION

Request for Reason for Adverse Credit Action

Date: _____

Dear _____

    On _____ , I was notified that my application for credit dated _____ was denied based upon information received by you from a source other than a consumer credit reporting agency.

    Pursuant to my right under the Fair Credit Reporting Act, Title 15 USC, Sec. 1681m(b), I hereby request that the nature of the information received by you be disclosed to me.

    Please forward such information to me at the above address.

    Thank you for your prompt attention to this matter.

Sincerely,

_____

SECURITY AGREEMENT

Security Agreement

STATE OF   )
)   ss:
COUNTY OF   )

KNOW YE ALL MEN BY THESE PRESENTS,

That I, _____ , of

_____ ,

Street Address   *Apt. No.*   *City*   *State*   *Zip*

hereinafter called "Debtor," hereby grant to _____ , of

_____ ,

Street Address   *Apt. No.*   *City*   *State*   *Zip*

hereinafter called the "Secured Party," a security interest in the following described property as collateral to secure payment of the obligation described herein.

Collateral

_____

_____

_____

_____

Obligation

_____

_____

_____

_____

Default in the payment of all or any part of the obligation described is a default under this Agreement. Upon such default, the Secured Party may declare all of the above-described obligation(s) immediately due and payable and shall have the remedies of a secured party under provisions of the Uniform Commercial Code. In the event legal action is required to enforce any provision of this Agreement, the prevailing party shall be entitled to recover reasonable attorney's fees and costs.

The Debtor hereby agrees to exercise reasonable caution and care in use of the herein-described collateral; to adequately insure or keep insured the described collateral; not to attempt to sell, assign, or dispose of said collateral or his/her interest therein; not to encumber nor to permit any encumbrance against same; and not to remove said collateral from the county where the Debtor resides without written permission of the Secured Party.

continues

Security Agreement, Continued

> EXECUTED this _____ day of _____ , 20___ .
>
> (Signed) _____
> *Debtor*
>
> (Signed) _____
> *Secured Party*

STATUTE OF LIMITATIONS

A statute of limitations defines the time span after an alleged offense during which legal action may be brought. After that time has elapsed, legal proceedings cannot be initiated, regardless of a case's merits.

If you angrily shake your fist at someone, it's legally considered "assault." If you follow up your actions by punching the person in the nose, the offense is "assault and battery."

FEDERAL STATUTE OF LIMITATIONS

CAPITAL OFFENSES

There is no limitation on prosecution in cases punishable by death and in the crime of murder, even when the death penalty is not prescribed.

NONCAPITAL OFFENSES

The limitation on noncapital offenses is five years, although Congress may make specific exceptions.

STATE STATUTE OF LIMITATIONS

This varies by crime and by state. On the World Wide Web, check http://www.findlaw.com/11stategov/ for links to Web pages for all 50 states. Each state Web page has extensive links to legal resources within that state, including legislative information, state constitution, statutes, and court opinions.

COPYRIGHTS

The copyright law protects works of authorship, published or unpublished, in any tangible medium of expression. Under this law, creators of—among other things—books, theatrical works, computer programs, videotapes, movies, music, lyrics, choreography, pantomimes, and recordings can secure exclusive rights to perform, display, or reproduce their works. These individuals have a property right for their work and may license it for reproduction or other use.

However, anyone may make "fair use" of copyrighted material. The definition of this term depends on who is using the material, how much is used, the percentage of the entire work that the excerpt used constitutes, the purpose of the use, and the effect such use may have on the ability of the copyright holder to derive income from his or her creation. For example, a teacher may be able to photocopy a few pages of a book for use in a classroom, but an advertising firm may be entitled to quote no more than a few lines from the same book in an ad without obtaining permission from the copyright holder. And while it may be lawful to quote 200 words from a novel without asking permission, the same would not be true in the case of a poem if the 200 words constituted the whole poem.

The term of copyright for a work depends on when it was created. Works created on or after January 1, 1978, are protected as soon as the work is fixed in a tangible means of expression, for the life of the author plus 70 years. In cases of joint authorship, the term is measured by the life of the longest surviving author, plus 70 years. If the work is of corporate au-

The Death Penalty

A Closer Look

States That Have Capital Punishment			States and Districts That Do Not Have Capital Punishment
Alabama	Kentucky	Ohio	Alaska
Arizona	Louisiana	Oklahoma	District of Columbia
Arkansas	Maryland	Oregon	Hawaii
California	Mississippi	Pennsylvania	Iowa
Colorado	Missouri	South Carolina	Maine
Connecticut	Montana	South Dakota	Massachusetts
Delaware	Nebraska	Tennessee	Michigan
Florida	Nevada	Texas	Minnesota
Georgia	New Hampshire	Utah	North Dakota
Idaho	New Jersey	Virginia	Rhode Island
Illinois	New Mexico	Washington	Vermont
Indiana	New York	Wyoming	West Virginia
Kansas	North Carolina		Wisconsin

thorship, a work for hire, anonymous or pseudonymous, it is protected for 95 years after publication or 120 years after creation, whichever is shorter. Works created before January 1, 1978, but not published, are protected from January 1, 1978 through the life of the author plus 70 years or until December 31, 2002, whichever is longer. Works created before January 1, 1978, but published between January 1, 1978 and December 31, 2002, are protected for the life of the author plus 70 years or December 31, 2047, whichever is longer.

Works published before 1923 are in the public domain; they are no longer protected by copyright. Works published with an effective copyright notice between 1923 and 1963 were protected for 28 years. If their copyright was renewed, they were protected for 47 additional years. Later legislation added an automatic 20 years to this term; thus, they could be protected for 28 years plus 67 years. If the copyright was not renewed, they are in the public domain. Works published from 1964 through 1977, when published with a copyright notice, are protected for 28 years, with an automatic extension of 67 years for a second term.

On March 1, 1989, the United States joined the Berne Convention for the Protection of Literary and Artistic Works, an international copyright treaty.

Under this convention, works are copyrighted from the moment they are fixed, or notated in some tangible form, such as in writing or on audiotape.

Under the 1909 Copyright Act, works published without notice went into the public domain upon publication. Works published without a copyright notice between January 1, 1978, and March 1, 1989, effective date of the Berne Convention Implementation Act, retained copyright only if copyright registration was made within five years of publication. A copyright notice is not required for works published as of March 1, 1989, but it is still recommended.

A copyright notice includes the word "Copyright" or the abbreviation "Copr." the year the work was first published, and the name of the owner of the copyright. The copyright symbol, a "C" in a circle (except for recordings, which use a circled "P"), also must be displayed.

Displaying the notice of copyright is sufficient to establish exclusive rights to an original work. In many cases, however, formal registration of a copyright claim is a prerequisite for filing suit for infringement for works whose country of origin is the United States. In addition, subject to certain exceptions, the remedies of statutory damages and attorneys' fees are not available for those infringements occurring before registration.

In 1992, Congress passed legislation that applies the same principles of fair use governing published works to unpublished works created between 1964 and 1977 (inclusive). The legislation also prescribes more stringent criminal sanctions for copyright infringement, designating certain violations as felonies.

A copy of any work registered for copyright must be deposited with the Library of Congress. Works that are not registered for copyright also may need to be deposited there.

In addition to the Berne Convention, the United States is a member of the Universal Copyright Convention, another multilateral agreement. Most countries of the world belong to one or both of these conventions, offering international copyright protection to all authors' registered works. The basic feature of this protection is "national treatment," under which the alien author is treated by a country in the same manner that it treats its own authors.

The international implementation of *General Agreement on Tariffs and Trade* (GATT) restored copyright protection to certain foreign works that had entered the public domain in the U.S. GATT also criminalized the production and distribution of pirated sound recordings and music videos.

The Digital Millennium Copyright Act of 1998 sought to update U.S. copyright law for the digital age. The Act makes it a crime under most circumstances for an individual to circumvent access-protection technology built into software or other media or for an individual to manufacture, sell, or distribute code-cracking devices used to illegally copy software or other media.

Currently, filing for copyright registration costs $30. For more information and application forms, write to

Register of Copyrights
The Library of Congress
101 Independence Ave.
Washington, DC 20559
http://lcweb.loc.gov/copyright

PATENTS

Congressional grants of patents and copyrights are based on Article I, Section 8 of the Constitution, which states that "Congress shall have power . . . to promote the progress of science and useful arts, by securing for limited times to authors and inventors the exclusive rights to their respective writings and discoveries."

A patent is the grant of a property right to an inventor, excluding others from making, using, or selling his or her invention. The invention may consist of "any new and useful process, machine, manufacture, or composition of matter, or any new and useful improvements thereof . . ." This patent law also covers ornamental designs, plants, and new forms of animal life. But no one can patent printed matter or a way of doing business.

In addition to being useful, the invention must be new. If the inventor describes the invention in a printed publication, uses the invention publicly, or places it on sale, he or she must apply for a patent before one year goes by; otherwise, any right to a patent is lost.

The Patent and Trademark Office currently receives more than 150,000 applications for patents each year, and it has granted more than 5 million patents since 1790. The agency grants new patents only after a diligent search of the records to make sure that the patent is original. Inventors may use the agency's Search Room (patent-research library) in Washington or any of the many patent-depository libraries throughout the United States to conduct their own searches before filing.

Although inventors can handle their own applications, the agency advises that the process is complex enough to require a patent attorney—a lawyer who also has a degree in engineering or physical science.

Only the inventor may apply for a patent. If the inventor is dead or incapacitated, a legal representative or guardian may apply. If two or more persons shared the ideas for the invention, they may apply jointly. But if one person had the idea and the other financed its development, only the person with the original idea may apply.

The application consists of a written description of the invention, with "claims" relating its distinguishing features—ways in which it does things in an entirely novel manner or improves significantly on previous inventions. If applicable, diagrams must accompany the description. Models usually are unnecessary. The Patent Office keeps all documents submitted in application for a patent strictly confidential during the process.

It is not uncommon for some or all of the claims to be rejected on the first action by the patent examiner; relatively few applications are allowed as filed. The applicant responds to the examiner's objections with clarification and explanation. If the Patent Office finally rejects the application, the inventor can take the case to the Board of Patent Appeals and Interferences. If the board turns down the application, the inventor has recourse through the Court of Appeals for the Federal Circuit or a civil suit in U.S. District Court in Washington, D.C.

About 1 percent of all patent applications encounter a problem because two or more applications are filed by different inventors claiming substantially the same patentable invention. Only one of the inventors can receive a patent, and the procedure to determine that one is called an *interference*. Each party to such a proceeding must submit evidence proving when the invention was made. As in the case of the rejection of any other patent, the decision of the examiners can be appealed.

If a patent applied for before June 8, 1995, is granted, it is good for 17 years. Under the terms of the GATT international treaty, most patents applied for after that date have a term of 20 years if granted (patents on ornamental designs have a term of 14 years).

Small entities—individual inventors, small businesses, and not-for-profit organizations—pay a filing fee of $370 for most patents and an additional fee of $640 if the patent is issued. For ornamental designs, the fees are $165 (filing fee) and $460 (upon issue of patent), and for plant varieties, the fees are $255 and $310. Large entities such as corporations pay twice these amounts. Inventors also must pay maintenance fees after 3½, 7½, and 11½ years. Currently, these fees for small entities are $440, $1,010, and $1,550. For large entities, fees are $880, $2,020, and $3,100.

Once a patent is granted, all documents relating to it become available for public inspection. The Patent Office can keep such information secret, however, if its commissioner decides that such information is vital to the national security.

As with any other property, patents may be sold or assigned in whole or in part to someone else. The patent holder also may license others to use the process or produce the product under specific conditions. The Patent Office cautions that a part owner of a patent—no matter how small his or her interest—may make, use, and sell the invention for his or her own profit without regard to the other owner. He or she also may sell the interest (or any part of it) or license others to use or make it. Therefore, inventors should be very careful when agreeing to sell a part interest in their patent.

Patented articles must be marked with the word "Patent" and the number of the patent. Some people use "Patent Pending" or "Patent Applied For" to inform others of the status of a patent claim, but such words have no legal effect. To combat infringement of a patent, the person holding the patent may bring a civil suit.

Patents granted by the Patent and Trademark Office protect inventions in the United States only. However, the United States is a signatory of several treaties that facilitate applications for patent protection in other countries. For further information, write to

Patent Assistance Center
Crystal Plaza 3
Washington, D.C. 20231
800-786-9199
http://www.uspto.gov

"Significant Inventions, Technological Advances, and Scientific Discoveries" **Go to** in chapter 5

"Significant Inventions, Technological Advances, and Scientific Discoveries" in chapter 5

Legal Information

FEDERAL JUDICIAL SYSTEM

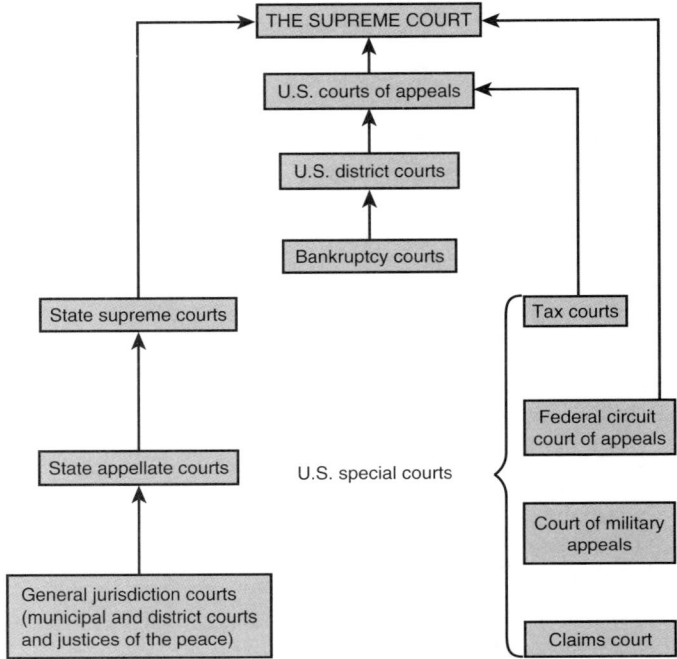

SUPREME COURT JUSTICES

This section lists all the Supreme Court justices in U.S. history. The first date for each justice is the year when the justice took the oath of office. The second date is the last year the person served as a Supreme Court justice. Some justices were appointed in the preceding year but actually assumed office during the first year listed.

Justice	Term	Justice	Term	Justice	Term
John Jay*	1789–95	Alfred Moore	1800–04	James M. Wayne	1835–67
James Wilson	1789–98	John Marshall*	1801–35	Roger B. Taney*	1836–64
John Blair, Jr.	1790–96	William Johnson	1804–34	Philip P. Barbour	1836–41
William Cushing	1790–1810	Henry Brockholst	1807–23	John Catron	1837–65
John Rutledge	1790–91	Livingston		John McKinley	1838–52
James Iredell	1790–99	Thomas Todd	1807–26	Peter V. Daniel	1842–60
Thomas Johnson	1792–93	Gabriel Duval	1811–35	Samuel Nelson	1845–72
William Paterson	1793–1806	Joseph Story	1812–45	Levi Woodbury	1845–51
John Rutledge*	†1795	Smith Thompson	1823–43	Robert C. Grier	1846–70
Oliver Ellsworth*	1796–1800	Robert Trimble	1826–28	Benjamin R. Curtis	1851–57
Samuel Chase	1796–1811	John McLean	1830–61	John A. Campbell	1853–61
Bushrod Washington	1798–1829	Henry Baldwin	1830–44	Nathan Clifford	1858–81

* Chief Justice
† John Rutledge took the oath of office as Chief Justice in 1795 as a recess appointee. However, the Senate rejected his appointment later that year.

Justice	Term	Justice	Term	Justice	Term
David Davis	1862–77	Charles E. Hughes	1910–16	Fred M. Vinson*	1946–53
Samuel F. Miller	1862–90	Horace H. Lurton	1910–14	Thomas C. Clark	1949–67
Noah H. Swayne	1862–81	Joseph R. Lamar	1911–16	Sherman Minton	1949–56
Stephen J. Field	1863–97	Willis Van Devanter	1911–37	Earl Warren*	1953–69
Salmon P. Chase*	1864–73	Mahlon Pitney	1912–22	John Marshall	1955–71
Joseph P. Bradley	1870–92	James C. McReynolds	1914–41	Harlan II	
William Strong	1870–80	Louis D. Brandeis	1916–39	William J. Brennan, Jr.	1956–90
Ward Hunt	1873–82	John H. Clarke	1916–22	Charles E. Whittaker	1957–62
Morrison R. Waite*	1874–88	William H. Taft*	1921–30	Potter Stewart	1958–81
John M. Harlan	1877–1911	George Sutherland	1922–38	Byron R. White	1962–93
William B. Woods	1881–87	Pierce Butler	1923–39	Arthur J. Goldberg	1962–65
Stanley Matthews	1881–89	Edward T. Sanford	1923–30	Abe Fortas	1965–69
Samuel Blatchford	1882–93	Harlan F. Stone	1925–41	Thurgood Marshall	1967–91
Horace Gray	1882–1902	Charles E. Hughes*	1930–41	Warren E. Burger*	1969–86
Melville W. Fuller*	1888–1910	Owen J. Roberts	1930–45	Harry A. Blackmun	1970–94
Lucius Q. C. Lamar	1888–93	Benjamin N. Cardozo	1932–38	Lewis F. Powell, Jr.	1972–87
David J. Brewer	1890–1910	Hugo L. Black	1937–71	William H. Rehnquist	1972–86
Henry B. Brown	1891–1906	Stanley F. Reed	1938–57	John Paul Stevens	1975–
George Shiras, Jr.	1892–1903	Felix Frankfurter	1939–62	Sandra Day O'Connor	1981–
Howell E. Jackson	1893–95	William O. Douglas	1939–75	William H. Rehnquist*	1986–
Edward D. White	1894–1910	Frank Murphy	1940–49	Antonin Scalia	1986–
Rufus W. Peckham	1896–1909	Harlan F. Stone*	1941–46	Anthony M. Kennedy	1988–
Joseph McKenna	1898–1925	James F. Byrnes	1941–42	David H. Souter	1990–
Oliver W. Holmes	1902–32	Robert H. Jackson	1941–54	Clarence Thomas	1991–
William R. Day	1903–22	Wiley B. Rutledge	1943–49	Ruth Bader Ginsburg	1993–
William H. Moody	1906–10	Harold H. Burton	1945–58	Stephen Gerald Breyer	1994–
Edward D. White*	1910–21				

*Chief Justice

SUPREME COURT DECISIONS

The following Supreme Court decisions are among the most significant in the 19th and 20th centuries.

1803 *Marbury v. Madison.* For the first time, the Court ruled an act of Congress unconstitutional, establishing the principle of judicial review.

1819 *McCullock v. Maryland.* The Court's ruling upheld the constitutionality of the creation of the Bank of the United States and denied to the states the power to tax such an institution because, as Justice John Marshall put it, "the power to tax is the power to destroy."

1819 *Trustees of Dartmouth College v. Woodward.* The Court ruled that a state could not arbitrarily alter the terms of a contract. Although this case applied to a college, its implications widened in later years when the same principle was used to limit the ability of states to interfere with business contracts.

1857 *Dred Scott v. Sanford.* The Missouri Compromise was declared unconstitutional because it deprived a person (a slave) of his property without due process of law. This was only the second time the Court had asserted the power of judicial review. The decision also stated that slaves are not citizens of any state or of the United States.

1877 *Munn v. Illinois.* States were allowed to regulate businesses when "a public interest" was involved. This principle was weakened by rulings in other cases in the late 19th century.

1896 *Plessy v. Ferguson.* The Court ruled that state laws enforcing segregation by race are constitutional if accommodations are equal as well as separate. This ruling was overturned by the Court's 1954 *Brown v. Board of Education of Topeka* decision.

1904 *Northern Securities Co. v. U.S.* The Court backed government action against big businesses that restrained trade, in effect putting teeth in the Sherman Act.

1908 *Muller v. Oregon.* The Court ruled that a state could legislate maximum working hours based on evidence compiled by future Supreme Court Justice Louis D. Brandeis.

1911 *Standard Oil Co. of New Jersey et al. v. U.S.* The Court dissolved the Standard Oil Trust—not because of its size, but because of its unreasonable restraint of trade. The principle involved is called "the rule of reason."

1919 *Schenck v. U.S.* The Court upheld the World War I Espionage Act. In a landmark decision dealing with free speech, Justice Oliver W. Holmes said that a person who encourages draft resistance during a war is a "clear and present danger."

1935 *Schechter v. U.S.* Invalidating the National Industrial Recovery Act of the New Deal, the Court declared that Congress could not delegate its powers to the president.

1951 *Dennis et al. v. U.S.* The Court ruled the 1946 Smith Act constitutional. The act made it a crime to advocate the overthrow of the government by force. In its 1957 *Yates v. U.S.* decision, the Court tempered this ruling by permitting such advocacy in the abstract if it is not connected to action to achieve the goal.

1954 *Brown v. Board of Education of Topeka.* In an example of sociological jurisprudence, the Court held that laws enforcing segregated schools were unconstitutional. It called for desegregation of schools "with all deliberate speed."

1957 *Roth v. U.S.* This ruling based obscenity decisions on whether a publication appeals to "prurient interests." The Court also said that obscene material is that which lacks any "redeeming social importance."

1961 *Mapp v. Ohio.* The Court extended the federal exclusionary rule to the states. This rule prevented prosecutors from using illegally obtained evidence in a criminal trial.

1962 *Baker v. Carr.* The Court held that state legislatures must be apportioned to provide equal protection under the law (14th Amendment). A follow-up decision applied the same principle to the size of congressional districts, insisting that they be approximately equal in population.

1966 *Miranda v. Arizona.* The Court declared that before questioning suspects, police must inform them of their right to remain silent; that any statements they make can be used against them; and that they have the right to remain silent until they have an attorney, which the state will provide if they cannot afford one.

1972 *Furman v. Georgia.* The Court found unconstitutional all death-penalty statutes then in force in the states. However, it held out the possibility that if these statutes were rewritten to be less subjective and randomly imposed, they might be constitutional (as the Court has subsequently held in many instances).

1973 *Roe v. Wade.* The Court ruled state laws prohibiting abortion unconstitutional, except as they apply to the last trimester of pregnancy, on the basis that the 14th Amendment provides for a woman's freedom to make a private decision about her reproductive practices.

1978 *University of California v. Bakke.* The ruling allowed a university to admit students on the basis of race if the school's goal is to combat discrimination. Subsequent decisions of the Court have filled in the details of how government and business may use quotas to make up for racism in the past.

1986 Bowers v. Hardwick. In a case involving the enforcement of Georgia's law against sodomy, the Court ruled that states have the power to regulate sexual relations in private between consenting adults.

The U.S. Supreme Court traditionally begins its sessions on the first Monday in October.

1989 Webster v. Reproductive Health Services. The Court upheld a Missouri law forbidding public employees to perform most abortions, prohibiting the use of public buildings for abortions, and requiring a fetal-viability test prior to abortions after the 20th week of pregnancy. This case set a precedent allowing other states to restrict access to abortions.

1993 Harris v. Forklift Systems, Inc. In a suit brought by a Tennessee woman against her former employer, the Court found that workers may claim sexual harassment even when severe economic or emotional damage does not result. The decision broadened Title VII civil-rights protections against sexual discrimination in the workplace and enlarged the legal definition of sexual harassment.

1996 Romer v. Evans The Court struck down an amendment to Colorado's state constitution that barred homosexuals from seeking civil-rights protection against discrimination.

1999 Reno v. ACLU The Court struck down two provisions of the Communications Decency Act of 1996 that criminalized the "knowing" transmission of "obscene or indecent" messages on the Internet to any recipient under 18 years of age, ruling that the statute abridged the First Amendment guarantee of freedom of speech.

2000 Bush v. Gore In a 5–4 decision in a suit arising out of the disputed 2000 presidential election results in Florida, brought by George W. Bush against Albert Gore, Jr., the court ruled that the manual recounts ordered by the Florida Supreme Court violated the U.S. Constitution's equal protection and due process clauses.

COMMON LEGAL TERMS

accessory An accessory *before* the fact helps another person commit or try to commit a crime but is not present at the commission of the crime. An accessory *during* the fact witnesses a crime but does not do what he or she could do to prevent it. An accessory *after* the fact helps another avoid arrest for the commission of a crime.

accomplice An individual who joins with another to commit a crime. The accomplice bears equal responsibility under the law.

actus reus A wrongful act, as opposed to *mens rea*—thoughts and intentions behind the act. For example, in a murder, *homicide* is the *actus reus,* and *malice aforethought* is the *mens rea.*

adjudication A final judgment in a legal proceeding.

affidavit A written statement sworn or affirmed to be true before a person legally authorized to administer an oath.

age of consent The minimum age for marrying without parental consent; also, the minimum age for consensual sexual relations. Sexual intercourse with someone below the age of consent can result in a charge of assault or statutory rape, even if both people participate willingly.

alibi An assertion or fact placing the defendant at the time of the crime in another location than the scene of that crime.

amicus curiae Latin for "friend of the court." A person or organization not party to a case who submits information useful to the court in that proceeding. Amicus curiae briefs generally are submitted when the suit involves matters of wide public interest.

amnesty An act of government forgiving members of a group, such as unregistered gun owners or illegal aliens, who normally would be subject to prosecution.

appeal   A request to a superior court to reverse the decision of a lower court or government agency or to grant a new trial.

appellate court   A court whose jurisdiction is confined to reviewing decisions of lower courts or agencies.

arraignment   A court procedure in which formal charges are brought against a defendant, who is advised of his or her constitutional rights and may have the opportunity to offer a plea.

assault   A threatened or attempted physical attack in which the attacker appears to have the ability to bring about bodily harm if not stopped. *Aggravated assault* involves an attack perpetrated with recklessness and intent to injure seriously or an assault with a deadly weapon. *Battery* is an assault in which the assailant makes physical contact with the victim.

attachment   A court writ authorizing legal authorities to seize property that may be needed for the payment of a judgment in a judicial proceeding. *See also* **writ.**

bail   Security provided to ensure the presence of a defendant in court during the course of a case. Defendants raising this security are said to "make bail"; those fleeing and forfeiting the security have "jumped bail." The actual document securing the defendant's release is the "bail bond."

bar   A collective term for all lawyers practicing in a particular court system.

battery   *See* **assault.**

bench warrant   A court order authorizing a public official to arrest a person and bring that individual to court.

bequest   Personal property bequeathed (given as a gift) in a will. *Devise* is the term for handing down real property (land and what is built upon it or affixed to it) through a will.

beyond a reasonable doubt   The degree to which jurors must be convinced before they may convict a person of a crime. The jurors must find the prosecution's case proven beyond the point at which a reasonable, average, prudent person would be convinced before returning a verdict of guilty.

bill of particulars   The specific events to be dealt with in a criminal trial, presented to the defendant so that he or she may effectively prepare a defense.

binding over   The action of a lower court shifting a case to a grand jury or superior court when the inferior court believes that a crime has been committed. Also, a court order to jail a defendant during the course of a proceeding.

boilerplate   Language uniformly found in certain types of documents—for instance, the "small print" in a contract that people often neglect to read.

breach of contract   Failure to do something required in a contract. *See also* **contract.**

breaking and entering   The illegal entrance into premises with criminal intent. Simply pushing a door open and walking in may constitute breaking and entering.

brief   A document in which a lawyer makes his or her client's case by raising legal points and citing authorities.

burden of proof   In a civil case, the requirement that a plaintiff or defendant must show that the majority of evidence is on his or her side in order to win a suit. In a criminal case, the prosecutor's burden of proof is to prove every fact involved in a charge.

burglary   Unlawful presence in a building with the intent of committing a felony or taking something of value. *See also* **robbery.**

capacity   The ability to understand the facts and significance of one's behavior. A defendant cannot be convicted of a crime in which he or she did not have the legal capacity to comprehend it.

cease and desist order A legal order preventing a person or organization from continuing a specific activity. A *mandatory injunction,* on the other hand, orders the performance of a specified act.

certiorari A writ in which a superior court commands an inferior court to deliver the records of a proceeding to the superior body so that it may decide whether there is basis for appeal.

The guarantee that each state will have an equal number of votes in the Senate is the only provision in the Constitution that cannot be amended. (Article V.)

character witness *See* **witness.**

chattel Personal, rather than real, property. A *chattel mortgage,* for example, is a loan to buy an expensive item, such as a car, in which the item, or chattel, is security for the debt.

circumstantial evidence Evidence based not on direct observation or knowledge but implied from things already known.

civil contempt *See* **contempt of court.**

class action A lawsuit brought by a group of people with a shared purpose.

clemency A reduction of criminal punishment, often granted to prevent the execution of a prisoner.

codicil An addition to a will altering it.

common-law marriage A relationship in which two people live together as husband and wife without formally getting married.

community property Property owned by a husband and wife jointly.

competency hearing A procedure to determine legal capacity (for example, of a defendant in a criminal case), understand the charges, and cooperate with a lawyer in preparing a defense. *Compos mentis* is a finding of competence to stand trial; *non compos mentis* is the finding of a lack of competence to go to trial.

complaint The first statement of facts (in a civil proceeding) or accusation (in a criminal case).

compos mentis *See* **competency hearing.**

consent decree An agreement between two parties sanctioned by the court—for example, between a company and the government, involving allegations of violations of antitrust laws. In the consent decree, the company would agree to cease such practices without formally admitting guilt.

conspiracy The plotting by two or more people to break the law.

contempt of court Anything done to hinder the work of the court. *Civil contempt* involves failure to follow a court order benefiting another party in a case, as in the failure to pay court-ordered damages; *criminal contempt* consists of the obstruction of justice.

contract A commitment between two or more parties, enforceable by law.

corpus delicti The object upon which a crime has been committed. The term does not necessarily refer to a body, although a corpse with a knife in its back would be an example in a homicide.

corroborating evidence Additional evidence of a different character to the same point that backs up proof already offered in a proceeding.

criminal contempt *See* **contempt of court.**

criminal negligence *See* **negligence.**

cross-examination The interrogation of a witness to discredit or show in a new light testimony that was offered by that person during direct examination.

custody In a divorce case, the right to house, care for, and discipline a child.

damages A court-ordered monetary award to someone who has suffered loss or injury by another.

de facto   Actually exercising power though not legally or officially established. A practice sanctioned by custom, as opposed to *de jure,* a practice formally backed by law.

de jure   *See* **de facto.**

decree   A court's decision in a case; its judgment.

defamation   The damaging of another person's reputation through writing (*libel*) or speech (*slander*).

default judgment   A court determination made against a defendant who fails to show up in court or fails to take some other court-required action.

defendant   A person or institution being sued or accused in a legal proceeding.

deposition   A pretrial interrogation of a witness, usually in a lawyer's office.

devise   *See* **bequest.**

directed verdict   A verdict declared by the court in a civil trial before the jury gets the case. Judges render this verdict when the facts and the law in a case point to a definite conclusion. There cannot be a directed verdict of guilty in a criminal trial, since that would violate a defendant's right to trial by jury.

discovery   A pretrial process that enables one side in a litigation to elicit information from the other side relating to the facts in the case.

disorderly conduct   A broad spectrum of offenses, such as drunkenness or fighting, that disturb the public peace.

district attorney   *See* **prosecutor.**

docket   A list of cases to be tried by a court—its calendar. Also, a summary of a court's activities.

double jeopardy   The condition of being tried a second time for a crime after the first case has been decided. Double jeopardy is prohibited by the 5th Amendment of the U.S. Constitution.

due process   The general doctrine that legislation must promote the legitimate aims of government (*substantive due process*) and that nobody can be deprived of liberty or property through unfair procedures (*procedural due process*).

easement   The right to use another person's land.

emancipation   The parental yielding of authority over, control over, and responsibility for a minor.

eminent domain   The right of the state to convert private property to public property.

entrapment   A defense by which a defendant seeks to show that he or she would not have committed an unlawful act if not tricked into doing it by law-enforcement officials.

equal protection   The 14th-Amendment requirement that all groups of people be treated equally by the legal system.

estate   Everything an individual owns.

eviction   The dispossessing of a tenant from land or premises he or she has occupied.

evidence   Testimony, documents, and objects used to prove matters of fact at a trial.

exclusionary rule   A rule preventing introduction at a criminal trial of evidence obtained in violation of the 4th Amendment's prohibition against unreasonable searches and seizures, even if that evidence otherwise would be admissible. *See also* **search and seizure.**

executor/executrix   A man or woman, respectively, appointed to administer the provisions of a will.

eyewitness   A person who can testify as to what happened because he or she was there when it happened and saw it. Technically, a person who offers testimony of something overheard is an *earwitness.*

fair hearing   A special administrative procedure set up to ensure that a person will not be harmed or denied his or her rights without due process of law before a court can intervene. Examples of extraordinary circumstances calling for a fair hearing include loss of welfare benefits and deportation.

fair use   The conditions under which a person can use material copyrighted by another.

false imprisonment   *See* **kidnapping.**

false pretenses   The means to take another's property through trickery. This crime involves the intent to secure the title to the property through some seemingly legal transaction. *See also* **larceny.**

fee   An interest in which land is or may become possessory; *freehold* is land held in fee.

felony   A serious crime, as opposed to a *misdemeanor.* The distinction often is made in terms of the applicable punishment; felonies are punishable by a certain minimum prison term—under federal law, one year.

felony murder   A homicide committed in the course of another crime, such as a burglary.

fiduciary   A person in a position of trust who acts for the benefit of another person. Examples are executors, corporate directors, and infant guardians.

finding   The basis in fact or law for a judgment. *See also* **judgment.**

fraud   The injury of a person or group of persons through deceit.

freehold   *See* **fee.**

frisk   *See* **stop and frisk.**

garnishment   The legal impoundment of funds by which a creditor sends notices through the court to the debtor's employer, thus seizing the debtor's salary to pay off the debt owed to the creditor.

grand jury   A jury of from 12 to 23 people empowered to look into possible criminal activity in an area, report on it, and indict individuals when it finds evidence that they have committed a crime.

grand larceny   *See* **larceny.**

grandfather clause   A provision in some laws allowing people who had legally engaged in an activity prior to its restriction by law to continue to engage in that activity.

guardian   A person entrusted to look out for the interests of a minor or an incompetent person. The specific fiduciary relationship is defined by law and court orders.

habeas corpus   The order by a judge to have a prisoner brought to court to determine the legality of the imprisonment.

harmless error   An error in a trial that had no effect on the outcome of the case. An appeals court will not overturn a judgment if it determines that errors made in the original trial were unimportant.

hearsay evidence   Statements made outside of court attesting to some fact; therefore the person making the statements may not be cross-examined or otherwise scrutinized. For example, if A testifies in court that he heard B say something, in most cases, B's statement will not be admissible as evidence.

homicide   An act in which one person causes the death of another. *See also* **manslaughter; murder.**

hung jury   A jury that is unable to reach a verdict.

immunity from prosecution   The exemption of a witness from prosecution to thwart a refusal to testify based on constitutional rights. The witness cannot be prosecuted on the basis of anything he or she says while testifying under such immunity.

impanel   To select a jury.

in camera   A judicial proceeding from which the public is excluded. Although the term literally means "in chambers," the proceeding can be held anywhere outside of open court.

in loco parentis   A person or institution acting toward a minor "in place of parents" without a formal adoption procedure—for example, the relationship between a school and a student.

Legal Information

in rem A proceeding involving property without reference to the claims of people on that property.

indictment A document delivered to a grand jury in which a public prosecutor accuses one or more persons of committing a crime. If the grand jury thinks the evidence submitted is sufficient to warrant a trial, it endorses the indictment as a true bill.

infant A person who has not reached the age of majority (usually 18), at which he or she enjoys the full rights of citizenship and is legally responsible for his or her acts.

information A prosecuting attorney's written accusation of criminal activity, similar to an indictment but not presented to a grand jury. Information may be used to initiate proceedings against defendants in state, but not federal, courts.

infringement A violation of a law or right.

injunction A court order preventing someone from doing a specific act.

injury The violation of a person's rights to the point where he or she suffers any kind of damage, including financial.

inquest A coroner's investigation into the cause of death.

insanity A mental state in which a person lacks legal responsibility.

intestate Without a will.

judgment A court's final decision in a case. *See also* **verdict.**

jury A representative group of people who determine issues of fact at a trial. The Constitution guarantees the right to trial by jury for all crimes punishable by imprisonment for more than six months. In civil trials, juries range in number from 6 to 12 people. State trial juries do not need a unanimous vote to convict (with the exception of six-person juries), but federal juries do.

kidnapping The illegal seizure and removal of a person without his or her consent. *False imprisonment* involves illegally confining a person against his or her will without moving that person and may be committed by police officers who fail to make arrests properly.

larceny The act of gaining the use or possession of property through an overtly illegal act, as in stealing a car. *Grand larceny* involves the theft of an object worth more than a specified amount. *See also* **robbery.**

leading question A lawyer's question to a witness that predetermines the answer, thus putting words in the witness's mouth. Such questions are legitimate during cross-examination but not during direct examination.

libel *See* **defamation.**

magistrate An official, such as a justice of the peace, who performs low-level judicial functions.

majority, age of *See* **infant.**

malfeasance Wrongful conduct by a public official. *Misfeasance* is the misperforming of a proper act. *Nonfeasance* is the nonperformance of an act that a person has agreed to or is duty-bound to do.

malice aforethought An antisocial state of mind, often at issue in a murder trial, marked by cruelty and recklessness for which there is no justification. *See also* **manslaughter.**

malpractice Wrongful conduct by a professional, either through negligence or lack of ethics.

mandamus A writ commanding someone, often a public official, to perform some act. Mandamus frequently is issued when time is of the essence. *See also* **writ.**

mandatory injunction *See* **cease and desist order.**

manslaughter Homicide without malice aforethought. *Voluntary manslaughter* is homicide with mitigating circumstances—for example, a fight in which one person kills another. *Involuntary manslaughter* is killing through criminal negligence, as in drunk driving.

material witness   *See* **witness.**

mens rea   *See* **actus reus.**

Miranda rule   The obligation of the police, when interrogating someone after an arrest, to read to that person his or her constitutional rights. These rights include the right to a lawyer, to remain silent until advised by counsel, and to know that anything he or she say may be used as evidence.

misdemeanor   *See* **felony.**

misfeasance   *See* **malfeasance.**

mistrial   The ending of a trial before the rendering of a verdict. Possible causes include a hung jury or the incapacity of the judge, jurors, or attorneys.

mitigating circumstances   Conditions under which a crime was committed that tend to reduce the punishment in a case—for example, the circumstances leading to a crime of passion.

moral turpitude   Baseness, depravity, vileness, or extreme antisocial behavior. A person's moral turpitude is sometimes taken into account by a judge when sentencing.

murder   Homicide with malice aforethought. Murder in the second degree generally involves less premeditation than the same crime in the first degree. *See also* **malice aforethought; premeditation.**

negligence   Carelessness, acting without reasonable caution, putting another person at risk of injury, or not performing an act that one is obliged to do, with the same consequences. In *criminal negligence,* there is the added element of recklessness.

next of kin   Closest blood relatives or, lacking them, the next closest relations, even if they are related only by marriage.

nolo contendere   A defendant's statement that the charges in a case will not be contested.

non compos mentis   *See* **competency hearing.**

nonfeasance   *See* **malfeasance.**

notary public   A person with the authority to administer oaths, witness documents, and accept depositions.

on the merits   A court judgment resting on the facts in the case rather than on a legal technicality.

open court   Judicial proceedings fully accessible to the public.

pardon   An act by which a governor or the president can excuse a person from punishment and restore his or her civil rights; however, a pardon usually does not wipe out a conviction.

parole   The release of a person from prison under controlled conditions. The parolee must fulfill certain requirements, such as reporting regularly to a parole officer.

perjury   The act of lying while under oath.

plaintiff   The person who initiates a lawsuit.

plea   A defendant's answer to a complaint.

Bexley, Ohio's Ordinance No. 223 (1919) prohibits the installation and usage of slot machines in outhouses.

plea bargain   A deal between the prosecutor and the accused, in which the accused pleads guilty in return for lesser punishment than might be received at the end of a trial.

polling the jury   A proceeding in which the judge asks each juror, after the verdict has been rendered, to restate his or her decision in the case.

power of attorney   A document in which one person authorizes another to act as an agent on his or her behalf.

preliminary hearing   A proceeding held after an arrest but before an indictment to see whether there is sufficient evidence to continue holding the prisoner and proceed with a case. *See also* **indictment.**

premeditation   The degree of planning and forethought sufficient to show intent to commit an act—often a factor in determining the degree of guilt in a murder case.

preponderance of evidence   The standard of proof used to settle civil lawsuits—determining which side's evidence has greater weight.

presentment   A grand jury's accusation, based not on material presented to it by a prosecutor, but on its own investigation.

preventive detention   The holding of a prisoner without bail; also accomplished by setting bail so high that the prisoner cannot meet it.

In Hartford, Connecticut, you can be arrested for walking across a street on your hands.

pro bono   Meaning "for the good"—the taking of a case by an attorney without a fee. Pro bono cases often are defended on behalf of groups backing important causes.

probable cause   The rule under which police need to have a reasonable belief that someone has committed a crime before making an arrest, or that the object for which they are searching in connection with a crime is at a specific location before they search for and seize it. *See also* **search and seizure.**

probate   The process by which the legitimacy of a will is established.

probation   The suspension of a person's sentence, leaving that individual at liberty but under court supervision.

process   A writ requiring that a person appear in court.

prosecutor   The person responsible for bringing the accused to justice. Depending on the level on which he or she functions, the prosecutor usually is

called a *district attorney, county prosecutor, federal prosecutor,* or, if appointed by a legislature to conduct an investigation, a *special prosecutor.*

protective custody   The imprisonment of an individual for his or her own protection.

public defender   A lawyer provided by the state to an accused person who cannot afford or refuses counsel.

punitive damages   An award to a plaintiff in a civil suit that exceeds actual losses, thereby punishing the defendant for his actions.

real property   Land and what is built on it, growing upon it, and affixed to it.

reasonable doubt   *See* **beyond a reasonable doubt.**

release on one's own recognizance   To free the accused on a promise to appear in court rather than on bail.

resident alien   A foreign citizen who intends to live in the United States permanently. Immigration authorities must approve the status of a resident alien.

restraining order   A temporary order granted to prevent some action until a hearing can be held on that action.

robbery   The use of violence or intimidation to seize another person's property. *See also* **burglary.**

search and seizure   A law-enforcement procedure involving the search of a person or premises when police have probable cause to suspect they will find and be able to seize criminal evidence. *See also* **probable cause; search warrant.**

search warrant   A court order authorizing law-enforcement officials to look for objects or people involved in the commission of a crime and to produce them in court. The order stipulates the places that the officials may search.

self-defense   A plea by which a person may justify the use of force to ward off an attack if the attack was unprovoked, retreat was impossible, and the threat of harm seemed imminent.

self-incrimination   An act in a legal proceeding by which a person says something that causes him or her to appear guilty of some type of crime. Under the 5th Amendment, a person cannot be forced to make such a statement.

sequester   To prevent a jury from having outside contacts until a trial is finished.

show cause order   A court order, issued at the request of one party, requiring a second party to convince the court, usually within a matter of days, that a specific act should not be carried out or allowed.

slander   *See* **defamation.**

statute of limitations   The period of time during which a person may initiate a legal action. See "Statute of Limitations," earlier in this chapter.

statutory rape   A criminal offense involving sex with a boy or girl under the age of consent; the age differs in various states.

stay   A court order preventing some act or proceeding until a specific condition is met or the stay is lifted.

stop and frisk   A procedure in which police who believe a suspect may be carrying a weapon with the intent to use it can stop that person and search the suspect's outer layer of clothing for a weapon.

subpoena   A court writ requiring a person to appear to testify at a judicial proceeding at a specific time and place under penalty of law.

Celebrated attorney Clarence Darrow (1857–1938) spent only one year in law school, opting to learn the law at a Youngstown, Ohio, law office.

summary judgment   A procedure by which a party in a civil dispute, if it believes that the other side's argument is without merit, can move to have a case resolved before going to trial.

summons   A notice to appear in court as a defendant in a suit.

testament   *See* **will.**

tort   A violation of legal duty, not involving a contract, that results in harm to another person or another person's property—for example, an act of libel that damages a person's reputation.

true bill   *See* **indictment.**

venue, change of   The transfer of a trial to another location, usually on the grounds that a fair trial is improbable in the original jurisdiction.

verdict   A judge or jury's finding of fact. The *judgment*, not the verdict, is the final determination in a case. For example, a judge can declare a jury's verdict *false*—that is, invalid—because it is not based on the evidence.

voir dire   A term usually applied to the interrogation of people to determine their competency as jurors. The term, which is French for "speak the truth," also describes a trial hearing without the jury present to determine a matter of fact or law, such as the validity of a confession.

waiver   The conscious forgoing of a legal right.

warrant   A court writ directing a public employee to do something—for example, to make an arrest.

will   A document specifying the disposition of a person's property after his or her death. Most states require two or three people to witness a will. Although *will* generally means the same thing as *testament*, the latter applies only to the distribution of personal property, as opposed to real property.

witness   A person who testifies in court under oath. A *material witness* is one whose testimony is central to a case; a *character witness* testifies to the character of an individual.

writ   A written order from a judicial body commanding a law-enforcement officer to do something specified.

wrongful death statute   A law that enables survivors or the person administering an estate to sue for monetary compensation for a death caused by some person or persons. The law is based on the fact that the death deprives survivors or the estate of the services or income of the deceased.

youthful offender   One who, at a judge's discretion, may be sentenced with special consideration given to his or her age. The category applies to defendants older than juveniles (no longer minors) but not yet, in the opinion of the judge, adults. Offender is usually between the ages of 18 and 25.

ADDITIONAL SOURCES OF INFORMATION

ORGANIZATIONS AND SERVICES

American Bar Association (ABA)
541 N. Fairbanks St.
Chicago, IL 60611
312-988-5522
http://www.abanet.org

The ABA publishes the *Directory of Lawyer Referral Services*, which lists services located throughout the United States and covers a range of general and special-interest needs. The office is open from 9 A.M. to 5 P.M., CST.

American Civil Liberties Union (ACLU)
125 Broad St.
New York, NY 10004
212-549-2500
http://www.aclu.org

The ACLU monitors civil-rights issues and incidents across the country and files lawsuits against parties whose actions violate the U.S. Constitution. Through a variety of publications and activities, its educational arm seeks to raise the public's awareness of constitutional topics. The office is open weekdays from 9 A.M. to 5:30 P.M., EST.

Lamba Legal Defense and Education Fund
120 Wall Street
Suite 1500
New York, NY 10005
212-809-8585
http://www.lambdalegal.org

This is the nation's oldest and largest organization working for the civil rights of gay men, lesbians, and people with HIV/AIDS. For the telephone numbers and hours of operation of Lamda's regional legal help desks, consult the website or call the general telephone number above.

NAACP Legal Defense and Education Fund
99 Hudson St.
16th Floor
New York, NY 10013
212-219-1900

The staff at the NAACP Legal Defense Fund will put individuals or groups who feel that they have been discriminated against in touch with an attorney who can help. The office is open weekdays from 9:30 A.M. to 5 P.M., EST.

National Center for Youth Law
405 14th St.
15th Floor
Oakland, CA 94612
510-835-8098
http://www.youthlaw.org

This organization provides counseling and referrals related to legal matters affecting young people, including juvenile justice and child welfare. The office is open from 9 A.M. to 5 P.M., PST.

National Legal Aid & Defender Association
1625 K St., NW
Suite 800
Washington, DC 20006
202-452-0620
http://www.nlada.org

This association acts as a clearinghouse of organizations providing legal services for those without the means to pay. The office is open from 9 A.M. to 5:30 P.M., EST.

NOW Legal Defense and Education Fund
395 Hudson St.
New York, NY 10014
212-925-6635
http://www.nowldef.org

This organization provides referrals for legal issues related to women's rights, such as economic inequality, pregnancy discrimination, and problems with changing one's surname. The office is open weekdays from 9:30 A.M. to 1:00 P.M., EST.

BOOKS

American Bar Association. *Consumers' Guide to Getting Legal Help.* ABA, nd.

Belli, Melvin, and Allen P. Wilkinson. *Everybody's Guide to the Law.* Harper Perennial, 1987.

Black, Henry C. *Black's Law Dictionary,* 7th ed. West, 1999.

Bove, Alexander A., Jr. *The Complete Book of Wills and Estates,* 2nd ed. Henry Holt, 2000.

Coughlin, George Gordon, Jr. *Your Handbook of Everyday Law.* HarperCollins, 1993.

Elias, Stephen, and Susan Levinkind. *Legal Research: How to Find and Understand the Law,* 9th ed. Nolo Press, 2001.

Feinman, Jay M. *Law 101: Everything You Need to Know about the American Legal System.* Oxford, 2000.

Gifis, Steven H. *Law Dictionary.* Barron's, 1996.

Hall, Kermit L., ed. *The Oxford Companion to the Supreme Court.* Oxford, 1992.

Hall, Kermit L., ed. *The Oxford Guide to United States Supreme Court Decisions.* Oxford, 2001.

Jordan, Cora. *Neighbor Law: Fences, Trees, Boundaries & Noise.* Nolo, 2001.

Pressman, David. *Patent It Yourself,* 8th ed. Nolo Press, 2000.

Ventura, John. *Law for Dummies,* IDG Books, 1996.

Wilson, Lee. *The Copyright Guide, Revised.* Allworth Press, 2000.

WEB SITES

http://www.findlaw.com
Provides a comprehensive listing of legal resources.

http://www.ilrg.com
Provides a categorized index of legal websites

http://www.lawyers.com
Provides legal information and resources, such as a lawyer locator.

http://www.law.cornell.edu/lii.html
Provides a starting point for finding legal information online; maintained by the Legal Information Institute at Cornell Law School.

http://www.lectlaw.com/inll/1.htm
Provides links to a large number of topics of legal issues for federal, state, and foreign laws.

Legal Information

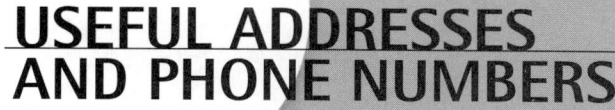

USEFUL ADDRESSES AND PHONE NUMBERS

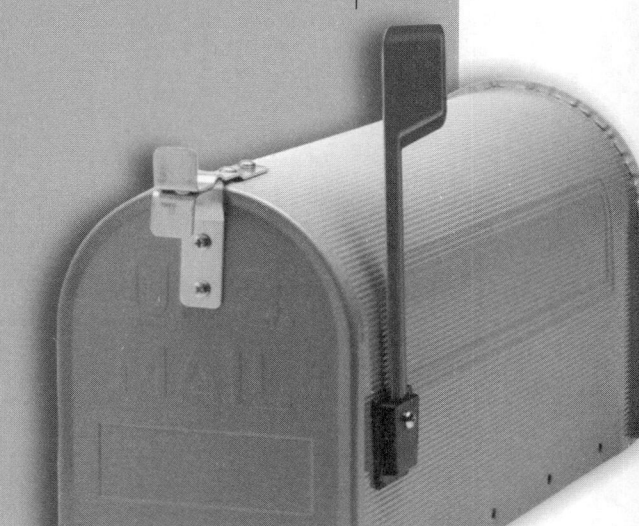

AGING

PRIVATE ORGANIZATIONS

American Association of Retired Persons
601 E St. NW
Washington, DC 20049
800-424-3410
http://www.aarp.org

American Society on Aging
833 Market St., Suite 511
San Francisco, CA 94103
415-974-9600
http://www.asaging.org

Andrus Gerontology Center
University of Southern California
Ethel Percy Andrus Gerontology Center
3715 McClintock Ave.
Los Angeles, CA 90089-0191
213-740-6060
http://www.usc.edu/dept/gero

Associacion Nacional por Personas Mayores
(National Association for Hispanic Elderly)
234 E. Colorado Blvd.
Suite 300
Pasadena, CA 91101
626-564-1988
http://www.aoa.gov/directory/139.html

Associacion Nacional por Personas Mayores
(National Association for Hispanic Elderly)
Job Placement Center
1452 West Temple St.
Suite 100
Los Angeles, CA 90026
213-202-5900

National Senior Citizens Law Center
1101 14th St., NW, Suite 400
Washington, DC 20005
202-289-6976
http://www.nsclc.org

Self-Help for the Elderly
407 Sansome St.
San Francisco, CA 94111-3112
415-982-9171
http://www.selfhelpfortheelderly.com

STATE COMMISSIONS AND OFFICES

State commissions and offices on aging are responsible for coordinating services for older Americans.

They can provide information on programs, services, and opportunities for the aging.

Alabama

Department of Senior Services
770 Washington Ave.
RSA Plaza, Suite 470
Montgomery, AL 36130
334-242-5743
877-425-2243
800-243-5463 (Alabama only)
http://adss.state.al.us

Alaska

Commission on Aging
Division of Senior Services
Department of Administration
P.O. Box 110209
Juneau, AK 99811-0209
907-465-3250
907-465-2205 (TTY)
http://www.alaskaaging.org

Arizona

Aging and Adult Administration
Department of Economic Security
1789 W. Jefferson, 950A
Phoenix, AZ 85007
602-542-4446
http://www.de.state.az.us.aaa

Arkansas

Division of Aging and Adult Services
Department of Human Services
P.O. Box 1437, Slot S-530
Little Rock, AR 72203-1437
501-682-2441
800-482-8049 (Arkansas only)
http://www.state.ar.us/dhs/aging

California

Department of Aging
1600 K St.
Sacramento, CA 95814
916-322-3887
800-510-2020 (Information line)
800-735-2929 (TDD)
http://www.aging.ca.gov

Go to "Investments and Retirement" in chapter 20

Colorado

Division of Aging and Adult Services
Office of Adult and Veterans Services
Colorado Department of Human Services
1575 Sherman St.
Denver, CO 80203-1714
303-866-2800
http://www.cdhs.state.co.us/oss/aas

Connecticut

Elderly Services Division
Department of Social Services
25 Sigourney St., 10th Floor
Hartford, CT 06106-5033
860-424-5277
800-994-9422
http://www.stelderlyservices.state.ct.us

Delaware

**Division of Services for Aging and Adults with
   Physical Disabilities**
1901 N. DuPont Highway
1st Floor Annex
New Castle, DE 19720
302-577-4791
800-223-9074 (Delaware only)
http://dsaapd.com

District of Columbia

D.C. Office on Aging
441 4th St., NW, Suite 900 South
One Judiciary Sq.
Washington, DC 20001
202-724-5622
http://www.dcoa.dc.gov

Florida

Department of Elder Affairs
4040 Esplanade Way, Suite 315
Tallahassee, FL 32399-7000
850-414-2000
http://elderaffairs.state.fl.us

Georgia

Office of Aging Services
2 Peachtree St., NW, 9th Fl.
Atlanta, GA 30303
404-657-5258
http://www2.state.ga.us/departments/dhr/aging.html

Hawaii

Executive Office on Aging
250 South Hotel, Room 406
Honolulu, HI 96813
808-586-0100
http://www.state.hi.us/eoa

Idaho

Idaho Commission on Aging
3380 Americana Terrace
Suite 120
Boise, ID 83706
208-334-3833
http://www.idahoaging.com

Illinois

Department on Aging
421 E. Capitol Ave., #100
Springfield, IL 62701-1789
217-785-2870
800-252-8966 (voice/TDD inside Illinois)
http://www.state.il.us/aging

Indiana

Bureau of Aging/In-Home Care Services Division
Department of Human Services
P.O. Box 7083, MS-21
Indianapolis, IN 46207-7083
317-232-7020
800-986-3505
800-532-3213 (Inside Iowa only)
http://www.in.gov/fssa/elderly/aging

Iowa

Department of Elder Affairs
200 10th St., 3rd Fl.
Des Moines, IA 50309-3609
515-281-5187
800-532-3213 (Iowa only)
http://www.state.ia.us/elderaffairs

Kansas

Department on Aging
New England Building
503 S. Kansas Ave.
Topeka, KS 66603-3404
785-296-4986
785-291-3167 (TTY)
800-432-3535 (Kansas only)
http://www.agingkansas.org/kdoa

Kentucky
Office of Aging Services
Department for Social Services
275 E. Main St., 5C-D
Frankfort, KY 40601
502-564-6930
http://chs.state.ky.us/aging/

Louisiana
Governors Office of Elder Affairs
P.O. Box 80374
Baton Rouge, LA 70898-0374
225-342-7100
http://www.gov.state.la.us/depts/elderly/htm

Maine
Bureau of Elder and Adult Services
11 Statehouse Station
35 Anthony Ave.
Augusta, ME 04333-0011
207-624-5335
800-262-2232
207-624-5442 (TTY)
888-720-1925 (TTY)
http://www.state.me.us/dhs/beas/welcome.htm

Maryland
Office on Aging
301 W. Preston St., Suite 1007
Baltimore, MD 21201
410-767-1100
410-767-1083 (TDD)
800-243-3425 (Maryland only)
http://www.mdoa.state.md.us/

Massachusetts
Executive Office of Elder Affairs
1 Ashburton Pl., 5th Floor
Boston, MA 02111
617-727-7750
800-882-2003 (Massachusetts only)
800-872-0166 (TDD Massachusetts only)
http://www.state.ma.us/elder

Michigan
Office of Services to the Aging
P.O. Box 30676
Lansing, MI 48909
517-373-8230
http://www.miseniors.net

Minnesota
Minnesota Board on Aging
444 Lafayette Rd.
St. Paul, MN 55155-3843
651-296-2770
800-882-6262
800-652-9747 (Minnesota only)
http://www.mnaging.org

Mississippi
Council on Aging
Division of Aging and Adult Services
750 N. State St.
Jackson, MS 39202
601-359-4929
800-948-3090 (Mississippi only)
http://www.mdhs.state.ms.us/aas.html

Missouri
Department of Health and Senior Services
P.O. Box 570
Jefferson City, MO 65102
573-751-6400
800-235-5503
http://www.health.state.mo.us/

Montana
Senior and Long Term Care Division
Bureau of Aging Services
Department f Health and Human Services
P.O. Box 4210
Helena, MT 59604
406-444-4077
800-332-2272 (Montana only)
http://www.dphhs.state.mt.us/sltc

Nebraska
Nebraska Department on Aging
Department of Health and Human Services
P.O. Box 95044
Lincoln, NE 68509
402-471-2306
http://www.hhs.state.ne.us/ags/agsindex.htm

Nevada
Division for Aging Services
Department of Human Resources
3100 West Sahara Avenue, Suite 103
Las Vegas, NV 89102
702-486-3545
http://www.nvaging.net

New Hampshire

Division of Elderly and Adult Services
Brown Building
129 Pleasant St.
Concord, NH 03301
603-271-4680
800-351-1888 (New Hampshire only)
http://www.dhhs.state.nh.us

New Jersey

Division of Senior Affairs
Department of Health and Senior Services
P.O. Box 807
Trenton, NJ 08625-0807
609-943-3437
800-792-8820 (New Jersey only)
http://www.state.nj.us/health/senior/sraffair.htm

New Mexico

State Agency on Aging
228 E. Palace Ave.
Santa Fe, NM 87501
505-827-7640
800-432-2080 (New Mexico only)
http://www.nmaging.state.nm.us

New York

New York State Office for the Aging
2 Empire State Plaza
Albany, NY 12223-1251
518-474-5731
800-342-9871 (New York only)
http://aging.state.ny.us/

North Carolina

Division of Aging
Department of Human Resources
2101 Mail Service Center
Raleigh, NC 27699-2101
919-733-3983
800-662-7030 (voice/TDD in North Carolina only)
http://www.dhhs.state.nc.us/aging/home.htm

North Dakota

Department of Human Service
Aging Services Division
600 South 2nd Street, Suite 1C
Bismarck, ND 5854-5729
701-328-8910
701-328-8968 (TDD)
800-451-8693
http://lnotes.state.nd.us/dhs/dhsweb.nsf/ServicePages/
  AgingServices

Ohio

Ohio Department of Aging
50 W. Broad St., 9th Floor
Columbus, OH 43215
614-466-5500
614-466-6191 (TDD)
800-282-1206 (Ohio only—nursing home information)
http://www.state.oh.us/age/

Oklahoma

Aging Services
312 NE 28th Street
Oklahoma City, OK 3105
405-521-2281
405-236-5513 (TDD)
http://www.okdhs.org/aging/index.html

Oregon

Seniors and People with Disabilities
Department of Human Services
500 Summer St., NE 97301
Salem, OR 97310-0105
503-945-5811
800-232-3020 (voice/TDD in Oregon)
http://www.sdsd.hr.state.or.us

Pennsylvania

Department of Aging
555 Walnut St., 5th Fl.
400 Market St., 7th Floor
Harrisburg, PA 17101-1919
717-783-1549
http://www.aging.state.pa.us/aging/site/default.asp

Rhode Island

Department of Elderly Affairs
160 Pine St.
Providence, RI 02903
401-222-2858
800-322-2880 (Rhode Island only)
http://www.dea.state.ri.us

South Carolina

Division on Aging
Office of the Governor
202 Arbor Lake Dr., #301
Columbia, SC 29223-4535
803-898-2850
800-868-9095
http://www.state.sc.us/dss

South Dakota

Office of Adult Services and Aging
700 Governors Dr.
Pierre, SD 57501
605-773-3656
http://www.state.sd.us

Tennessee

Commission on Aging
Andrew Jackson Bldg.
500 Deaderick St., 9th Floor
Nashville, TN 37243-0860
615-741-2056
http://www.state.tn.us

Texas

Texas Department on Aging
4900 N. Lamar Blvd.
P.O. Box 12786, Capitol Station
Austin, TX 78751
512-424-6840
http://www.tdoa.state.tx.us

Utah

Division of Aging and Adult Services
P.O. Box 45500
Salt Lake City, UT 84145-0500
801-538-3910
http://www.hsdaas.state.ut.us

Vermont

Department of Aging and Disabilities
103 S. Main St.
Waterbury, VT 05671-2301
802-241-2400 (voice/TDD)
http://www.dad.state.vt.us

Virginia

Department for the Aging
1600 Forest Ave., Suite 102
Richmond, VA 23229
804-662-9333
800-552-4464 (Virginia only)
800-552-3402 (Virginia only—Ombudsman Hotline)
http://www.aging.state.va.us

Washington

Aging and Adult Services Administration
P.O. Box 45050
Olympia, WA 98504-5050
800-422-3263
800-737-7931 (TDD)
http://www.aasa.dshs.wa.gov/

West Virginia

Commission on Aging
Holly Grove Capitol Complex
1900 Kanawha Blvd. East
Charleston, WV 25305-0160
304-558-3317
http://www.state.wv.us

Wisconsin

Bureau of Aging and Long Term Care Resources
1 West Wilson St., Room 450
P.O. Box 7851
Madison, WI 53707-7851
608-266-2536
http://www.dhfs.state.wi.us/aging/

Wyoming

Division on Aging
6101 Yellowstone Road, Room 259B
Cheyenne, WY 82002-0480
307-777-7986
800-442-2766 (Wyoming only)
http://wdhfs.state.wy.us/aging/index.htm

American Samoa

Territorial Administration on Aging
Government of American Samoa
Pago Pago, AS 96799
011-684-633-1251
http://www.government.as/aging.htm

Guam

Division of Senior Citizens
Department of Public Health and Social Services
Government of Guam
P.O. Box 2816
Agana, GU 96910
011-671-475-0263
http://ns.gov.gu/government.html

Puerto Rico

Oficina para los Asuntos de la Vejez
Comisión de Derechos Ciudadanos (CODECI)
PO Box 50063
Cobians Plaza Piso U M Ofic C
Ave. Ponce de León
Puerto Rico
787-721-6121
http://www.gobierno.pr

Virgin Islands
Virgin Islands: Senior Citizens Affairs
Department of Human Services
Knud Hansen Complex
Building A 1303 Hospital Ground
St. Thomas, VI 00840
340-774-0930
http://www.usvi.gov/humanservices/

ALCOHOLISM AND DRUG ABUSE

Al-Anon Family Group Headquarters
1600 Corporate Landing Parkway
Virginia Beach, VA 23454-5617
757-563-1600
http://www.al-anon.alateen.org

Alcohol and Drug Problems Association of North America
307 North Main
St. Charles, MO 63301
314-589-6702
http://www.adpana.com

Substance Abuse and Mental Health Service Administration
U.S. Department of Health and Human Services
Center for Substance Abuse Prevention
5600 Fishers Lane
Rockville, MD 20857
301-443-0365
http://www.os.dhhs.gov

Alcoholics Anonymous World Services
475 Riverside Dr.
New York, NY 10115
212-870-3400
http://www.aa.org

American Council on Alcoholism
3900 North Fairfax Drive
Suite 401
Arlington, VA 22203
703-248-9005
http://www.aca-usa.org

American Council on Alcohol Problems
2376 Lakeside Dr.
Birmingham, AL 35244
205-989-8177
http://www.american councilonalcoholproblems.com

"Safe Alcohol Consumption" in chapter 18

Go to

Association of Halfway House Alcoholism Programs of North America
5 Ridgeview Road
P.O. Box 610
Kerhonkson, NY 12446
845-626-2684
http://www.ahhap.org

BACCHUS and GAMMA
Peer Education Network
P.O. Box 100430
Denver, CO 80250-0430
303-871-0901
http://www.bacchusgamma.org

Cocaine Helpline
800-COCAINE

Do It Now Foundation
P.O. Box 27568
Tempe, AZ 85285-7568
480-736-0599
http://www.doitnow.org

Families Anonymous
P.O. Box 3475
Culver City, CA 90231-3475
800-736-9805
http://www.familiesanonymous.org

Narcotics Anonymous
P.O. Box 9999
Van Nuys, CA 94109
818-773-9999
http://www.na.com

National Association for Children of Alcoholics
11426 Rockville Pike, Suite 100
Rockville, MD 20852
301-468-0985
888-554-COAS (888-554-2627)
http://www.nacoa.org

National Association of Alcoholism and Drug Abuse Counselors
901 N. Washington St.
Suite 600
Alexandria, VA 22314
703-741-7686
800-548-0497
http://www.naadac.org

National Association on Drug Abuse Problems
355 Lexington Ave.
New York, NY 10017
212-986-1170
http://www.nadap.com

National Cocaine Hotline
800-992-9239

National Council on Alcoholism and Drug Dependence
20 Exchange Place
Suite 2902
New York, NY 10005
212-269-7797
800-NCA-CALL (800-622-2255)
http://www.ncadd.org

National Families in Action
2957 Clairmont Rd.
Suite 150
Atlanta, GA 30345
770-934-6364
http://www.nationalfamilies.org

National Family Partnership
(formerly National Federation of Parents for Drug-Free Youth)
2490 Coral Way
Suite 501
Miami, FL 33145
305-856-4886
800-705-8997
http://www.nfp.org

National Parents Resource Institute for Drug Education
166 St. Charles St.
Bowling Green, KY 42101
800-279-6361
http://www.prideusa.org

Odyssey Center
Substance Abuse Training For Professionals
7475 Dakin St.
Suite 601
Denver, CO 80221
303-657-0996

Women in Need, Inc.
115 W. 31st St.
New York, NY 10001
212-695-7330
http://women-in-need.org/

CHILDREN

CHILD ABUSE

American Association for Protecting Children
c/o American Humane Association
63 Inverness Dr. East
Englewood, CO 80112

800-227-4645
http://www.americanhumane.org

American Professional Society on the Abuse of Children
National Office
P.O. Box 26901
CHO 3B-3406
Oklahoma City, OK 73190
405-271-8202
http://www.apsac.org

Child Welfare League of America
Headquarters
440 First St. NW, 3rd Fl.
Washington, DC 20001-2085
202-638-2952
http://www.cwla.org/

The Children's Defense Fund
25 E Street NW
Washington, DC 20001
202-628-8787
cdfinfo@childrensdefense.org

Clearinghouse on Child Abuse and Neglect Information
330 C Street SW
Washington, DC 20447
703-385-7656
800-FYI-3366
http://www.calib.com/nccanch

Klaas Kids Foundation
P.O. Box 925
Sausalito, CA 94966
415-331-6867
http://www.klaaskids.org/

National Association of Child Advocates
1522 K Street NW
Suite 600
Washington, DC 20005-1202
http://www.childadvocacy.org

National Children's Alliance
1612 K Street, NW, Suite 500
Washington, DC 20006
202-452-6001
800-239-9950
http://www.nncac.org/

Parents Anonymous
675 W. Foothill Blvd., Suite 220
Claremont, CA 91711
909-621-6184
http://www.parentsanonymous.org

"Traveling Tips for the Disabled" in chapter 24  **Go to**

Prevent Child Abuse America
200 S. Michigan Ave., 17th Fl.
Chicago, IL 60604
312-663-3520
800-CHILDREN (800-244-5373)
http://www.preventchildabuse.org

DISABLED CHILDREN

Association for Children with Retarded Mental Development/Lifespire
345 Hudson St., 3rd Fl.
New York, NY 10014
212-741-0100
http://www.acrmd.com

ERIC Clearinghouse of Disabilities and Gifted Education
Department of Education
1110 N. Glebe Rd.
Arlington, VA 22201-5704
800-328-0272
http://www.ericec.org

National Center for Learning Disabilities
381 Park Ave. South, Suite 1401
New York, NY 10016
212-545-7510
888-575-7373
http://www.ld.org

National Information Center for Children and Youth with Handicaps
P.O. Box 1492
Washington, DC 20013
202-884-8200
800-695-0285
http://www.nichcy.org

RUNAWAYS

American Youth Work Center & Youth Today
1200 17th St., NW, 4th Fl.
Washington, DC 20036
202-785-0764
800-599-2455
http://www.youthtoday.org

Focus Adolescent Services
1-877-FOCUS
http://www.focusas.com/

National Center for Missing and Exploited Children
Charles B. Wang International Children's Bureau
699 Prince Street
Alexandria, VA 22314-3175

703-274-3900
800-THE-LOST
http://www.missingkids.com/

National Network for Youth
1319 F St., NW, 4th Fl.
Washington, DC 20004
202-783-7949
http://www.nn4youth.org

National Runaway Switchboard
3080 N. Lincoln Ave.
Chicago, IL 60657
800-621-4000
http://www.nrscrisisline.org

CONSUMER INFORMATION AND PROTECTION

BETTER BUSINESS BUREAUS

Some locations are serviced by local bureaus in adjoining states. To locate the bureau nearest you, use the zip code search or state directory at http://www.bbb.org/bureaus/index.html.

UNITED STATES—NATIONAL HEADQUARTERS

Council of Better Business Bureaus
4200 Wilson Blvd., Suite 800
Arlington, VA 22203
703-276-0100
http://www.bbb.org

STATE, COUNTY, AND CITY GOVERNMENT CONSUMER PROTECTION OFFICES

Listed below are consumer protection offices that are part of state, county, and city governments. Some are located in governors' offices, state attorney generals' offices, or mayors' offices. Check in your state to see which office can help resolve complaints, furnish information or helpful publications, or provide other services. As a general rule, the first place to go for help with a consumer problem is the local office nearest your home. If you are having a problem with a business outside your state, however, contact the consumer office in the state in which you made the purchase. Because most offices require that complaints be in writing, you might save time by writing, rather than calling, with your initial complaint.

Alabama—State Office

Director
Consumer Protection Division
Office of the Attorney General
11 S. Union St.
Montgomery, AL 36130
334-242-7334
800-392-5658 (Alabama only)
http://www.ago.state.al.us/consumer.cfm

Alaska

Attorney General's Office
1031 W. 4th Ave.
Suite 200
Anchorage, AK 99501
907-465-2133
http://www.law.state.ak.us/consumer/

Arizona—State Offices

Consumer Protection Office of the Attorney General
1275 W. Washington St., Room 259
Phoenix, AZ 85007
602-542-3702
602-542-5763
800-352-8431 (Arizona only)
http://ag.state.az.us/consumer/index.html

Assistant Attorney General
Consumer Protection Office of the Attorney General
402 W. Congress St., Suite 315
Tucson, AZ 85701
520-628-6504
800-352-8431

Arizona—SELECTED County Offices

County Attorney
Apache County Attorney's Office
P.O. Box 637
St. Johns, AZ 85936
520-337-4364

County Attorney
Cochise County Attorney's Office
P.O. Drawer CA
Bisbee, AZ 85603
520-432-9377

County Attorney
Coconino County Attorney's Office
Coconino County Courthouse

100 E. Birch
Flagstaff, AZ 86001
520-779-6518

County Attorney
Gila County Attorney's Office
1400 E. Ash St.
Globe, AZ 85501
520-425-3231

County Attorney
Graham County Attorney's Office
Graham County Courthouse
800 W. Main
Safford, AZ 85546
520-428-3620

County Attorney
Greenlee County Attorney's Office
P.O. Box 1717
Clifton, AZ 85533
520-865-4108

County Attorney
La Paz County Attorney's Office
1320 Kofa Avenue
P.O. Box 709
Parker, AZ 85344
520-669-6118

County Attorney
Mohave County Attorney's Office
P.O. Box 7000
Kingman, AZ 86402
520-753-0719

County Attorney
Navajo County Attorney's Office
P.O. Box 668
Holbrook, AZ 86025
520-524-4026

County Attorney
Pima County Attorney's Office
1400 Legal Services Building
32 N. Stone
Tucson, AZ 85701
520-740-5600

County Attorney
Pinal County Attorney's Office
P.O. Box 887
Florence, AZ 85232
520-868-6271

County Attorney
Santa Cruz County Attorney's Office
2100 N. Congress Dr., Suite 201

Nogales, AZ 85621
520-761-7800 x3121

County Attorney
Yavapai County Attorney's Office
Yavapai County Courthouse
255 E. Gurley
Prescott, AZ 86301
520-771-3344

County Attorney
Yuma County Attorney's Office
168 S. Second Ave.
Yuma, AZ 85364
520-329-2270

Arizona—City Office
Consumer Affairs Division
Tucson City Attorney's Office
1501 N. Oracle Annex
Tucson, AZ 85705
520-791-4886

Arkansas—State Office
Consumer Protection Division
Office of Attorney General
200 Tower Bldg.
323 Center St.
Little Rock, AR 72201
501-682-2341 (voice/TDD)
800-482-8982 (voice/TDD in Arkansas)

California—State Offices
California Department of Consumer Affairs
400 R St., Suite 1080
Sacramento, CA 95814
916-445-1254 (consumer information)
916-522-1700 (TDD)

Office of the Attorney General
Public Inquiry Unit
P.O. Box 944255
Sacramento, CA 94244-2550
916-322-3360

Bureau of Automotive Repair
California Department of Consumer Affairs
10220 Systems Parkway
Sacramento, CA 95827
916-255-4200

California—SELECTED County Offices
District Attorney
Alameda County District Attorney's Office
1225 Fallon St., Room 900

Oakland, CA 94612
510-272-6222

District Attorney
Contra Costa County District Attorney's Office
725 Court St., 4th Floor
Martinez, CA 94553
925-646-4500

Business Affairs
Fresno County District Attorney's Office
2220 Tulare St., Suite 1000
Fresno, CA 93721
559-488-3133

Consumer and Major Business Fraud Section
Kern County District Attorney's Office
1215 Truxtun Ave.
Bakersfield, CA 93301
661-868-2340

Los Angeles County Department of Consumer Affairs
500 W. Temple St.
Room B-96
Los Angeles, CA 90012-2706
213-974-1452

Consumer and Environmental Protection Unit
Marin County District Attorney's Office
3501 Civic Center Dr., Room 130
San Rafael, CA 94903
415-499-6450

District Attorney
Mendocino County District Attorney's Office
P.O. Box 1000
Uklah, CA 95482
707-463-4211

Consumer Protection Division
Monterey County District Attorney's Office
P.O. Box 1131
Salinas, CA 93902
831-755-5073
831-647-7773

Consumer Affairs Division
Napa County District Attorney's Office
931 Parkway Mall
Napa, CA 94559
707-253-4211

Consumer Protection Division
Orange County District Attorney's Office
401 Civic Center Dr. West, Suite 120
Santa Ana, CA 92701
714-834-3600

Economic Crime Division
Riverside County District Attorney's Office
4075 Main St.
Riverside, CA 92501
909-955-5400

Consumer and Environmental Protection Division
Sacramento County District Attorney's Office
901 G Street
Sacramento, CA 95814
916-874-6218

Consumer Fraud Division
San Diego County District Attorney's Office
Hall of Justice
330 West Broadway
San Diego, CA 92101
619-531-4040

Consumer and Environmental Protection Unit
San Francisco County District Attorney's Office
880 Bryant Street
San Francisco, CA 94103
415-552-6400
415-553-1752

If you want to send a letter to the North Pole, the correct address is North Pole, AK 99705.

Consumer and Business Affairs Division
San Joaquin County District Attorney's Office
Courthouse
Stockton, CA 95202
209-468-2400

Consumer Fraud Department
San Luis Obispo County District Attorney's Office
County Government Center
1050 Monterey St., Room 450
San Luis Obispo, CA 93408
805-781-5800

Consumer Fraud and Environmental Protection Unit
San Mateo County District Attorney's Office
401 Marshall St.
Hall of Justice and Records
Redwood City, CA 94063
650-363-4636

Consumer Mediation Program
Santa Barbara County District Attorney's Office
1105 Santa Barbara St.
Santa Barbara, CA 93101
805-568-2390

Consumer Fraud Unit
Santa Clara County District Attorney's Office
70 W. Hedding St., West Wing
San Jose, CA 95110
408-299-7400

Division of Consumer Affairs
Santa Cruz County District Attorney's Office
701 Ocean St., Room 200
Santa Cruz, CA 95060
831-424-2050

Consumer Affairs Unit
Solano County District Attorney's Office
600 Union Ave.
Fairfield, CA 94533
707-421-6859

Consumer Fraud Unit
Stanislaus County District Attorney's Office
800 11th Street, Room 200
Modesto, CA 95354
209-525-5550

Consumer and Environmental Protection Division
Ventura County District Attorney's Office
800 S. Victoria Ave.
Ventura, CA 93009
805-654-3110

Special Services Unit—Consumer/Environmental
Yolo County District Attorney's Office
301 Second Street
Woodland, CA 95695
530-666-8180

California—City Offices

Consumer Protection Division
Los Angeles City Attorney's Office
200 N. Main St.
1600 City Hall East
Los Angeles, CA 90012
213-485-4515

Consumer Division
Santa Monica City Attorney's Office
1685 Main St., Room 310
Santa Monica, CA 90401
310-458-8336

Colorado—State Offices

Consumer Protection Unit
Office of the Attorney General
1525 Sherman St., 7th Fl.
Denver, CO 80203
303-866-4500

Inspection and Consumer Services
Department of Agriculture
Main Offices
2331 West 31st Ave.
Denver, Colorado 80211
303-477-0093

Colorado—County Offices

District Attorney
Archuleta, LaPlata, and San Juan Counties District
 Attorney's Office
1060 East 2nd Ave.
Durango, CO 81301
970-247-8850

District Attorney
Boulder County District Attorney's Office
P.O. Box 471
Boulder, CO 80306
303-441-3700

Denver County District Attorney's Economic Crime
 and Fraud Office
Second Judicial District
303 W. Colfax Ave., Suite 1300
Denver, CO 80204
720-913-9179

Economic Crime Division
El Paso and Teller Counties District Attorney's Office
105 East Vermijo
Colorado Springs, CO 80903
719-520-6002

District Attorney
Pueblo County District Attorney's Office
201 W. 8th St., Suite 801
Pueblo, CO 81003
719-583-6030

Consumer Fraud Investigator
Weld County District Attorney's Consumer Office
P.O. Box 1167
Greeley, CO 80632
970-356-4010

Connecticut—State Offices

Department of Consumer Protection
State Office Bldg.
165 Capitol Ave.
Hartford, CT 06106
860-713-6300
800-842-2649

Antitrust/Consumer Protection
Office of Attorney General
55 Elm St.
Hartford, CT 06106
860-808-5318

Connecticut—City Office

Middletown Office of Consumer Protection
245 deKoran Dr.
Middletown, CT 06457
860-344-3491

Delaware—State Offices

Consumer Protection Unit
Office of Attorney General
Carvel State Building, 5th Fl.
820 N. French St.
Wilmington, DE 19801
302-577-8600

District of Columbia

Department of Consumer and Regulatory Affairs
941 North Capital St. NE
Washington, DC 20002
202-282-DCRA

Florida—State Offices

Department of Agriculture and Consumer Services
Division of Consumer Services
407 South Calhoun St.
Mayo Building
Tallahassee, FL 32399-0800
850-488-2221
800-435-7352 (Florida only)
800-352-9832 (in Spanish)

Consumer Division
Office of the Attorney General
The Capital, Suite PL01
Hollywood, FL 32399-1050
850-487-1963

Florida—SELECTED County Offices

Broward County Consumer Affairs Division
115 S. Andrews Ave., Room A-460
Fort Lauderdale, FL 33301
954-765-5350

Consumer Advocate
Metropolitan Dade County Consumer Protection
 Division
140 W. Flagler St., 9th Floor
Miami, FL 33130
305-375-4222

Dade County Economic Crime Unit
Office of the State Attorney
1469 Northwest 13th Terrace, Room 600
Miami, FL 33125
305-324-3030

Hillsborough County Department of Consumer Affairs
8900 N. Armenia Ave., Suite 222
Tampa, FL 33602
813-272-6750

Orange County Consumer Fraud Unit
415 N. Orange Ave.
P.O. Box 1673
Orlando, FL 32802
407-836-2490

Citizens Intake
Palm Beach County Office of State Attorney
401 North Dixie Highway
West Palm Beach, FL 33401
561-355-7100

Palm Beach County Division of Consumer Affairs
50 South Military Trail, Suite 201
West Palm Beach, FL 33405
561-712-6600

Pasco County Consumer Affairs Division
West Pasco Government Center
7530 Little Rd., Suite 140
New Port Richey, FL 34654
727-847-8110

Pinellas County Office of Consumer Affairs
15251 Roosevelt Boulevard, Suite 209
Clearwater, FL 33760
727-464-6200

Florida—City Offices
Chief of Consumer Affairs
City of Jacksonville Division of Consumer Affairs
117 W. Duval St.
Jacksonville, FL 32202
904-630-1212 Ext. 4090

Tamarac Board of Consumer Affairs
7525 NW 88th Ave.
Tamarac, FL 33321
954-724-1346

Georgia—State Office
Governors Office of Consumer Affairs
2 Martin Luther King, Jr. Dr., Suite 356
Atlanta, GA 30334

404-651-8600
404-656-3790
800-869-1123 (Georgia only)

Hawaii—State Offices
Office of Consumer Protection
Department of Commerce and Consumer Affairs
Honolulu Office
Leiopapa A. Kamehama Building
235 S. Beretania St., Suite 801
Honolulu, HI 96813
808-586-2630

Office of Consumer Protection
Department of Commerce and Consumer Affairs
Hilo Office
345 Kekuanaoa St., Suite 12
75 Aupuni St.
Hilo, HI 96720
808-933-0910

Office of Consumer Protection
Department of Commerce and Consumer Affairs
Wailuku Office
1063 Lower Main St.
Suite c-216
Wailuku, HI 96793
808-984-8244

Idaho—State Office
Office of the Attorney General
Consumer Protection Unit
700 W. Jefferson St.
P.O. Box 83720
Boise, ID 83720
208-334-2424
800-432-3545 (Idaho only)

Illinois—State Offices
Governors Office of Citizens Assistance
222 S. College
Springfield, IL 62706
217-782-0244
800-252-8666 (Illinois only)

Consumer Protection Division
Office of the Attorney General
100 W. Randolph, 12th Floor
Chicago, IL 60601
312-814-3000
800-386-5438 (Illinois only)

Useful Addresses

Consumer Protection Division
Office of the Attorney General
500 S. Second St.
Springfield, IL 62706
217-782-9011
800-243-0618 (Illinois only)

Illinois—Regional Offices

Assistant Attorney General
Carbondale Regional Office
Office of the Attorney General
1001 East Main St.
Carbondale, IL 62901
618-529-6400
800-243-0607 (Illinois only)

Assistant Attorney General
East Central Regional Office
Office of the Attorney General
1776 E. Washington St.
Urbana, IL 61802
217-278-3366

Assistant Attorney General
Kankakee Regional Office
Office of the Attorney General
1012 N. 5th Ave.
Kankakee, IL 60901
815-935-8500

Assistant Attorney General
Metro–East Illinois
201 West Pointe Dr., Suite 7
Belleville, IL 62226
618-236-8616
618-236-8619 (TTY)

Assistant Attorney General
Northern Illinois Regional Office
7230 Argus Drive
Rockford, IL 61107
815-484-8100
815-484-8113 (TTY)

Assistant Attorney General
Peoria County
Office of the State's Attorney
324 Main St., Room 111
Peoria County Courthouse
Peoria, IL 61602
309-672-6900

Assistant Attorney General
Quincy Regional Office
Office of the Attorney General
628 Main St.
Quincy, IL 62301

217-223-2221 (voice/TDD)
217-223-2254 (TTY)

Illinois—SELECTED County Offices

Adams County Office of the State's Attorney
521 Vermont St.
Quincy, IL 62301
217-277-2225

Calhoun County Office of the State's Attorney
County Courthouse
P.O. Box 187
Hardin, IL 62047
618-576-9013

Clark County Office of the State's Attorney
2nd Floor Courthouse
501 Archer
Marshall, IL 62441
217-826-6142

You can have a birthday greeting sent from the President of the United States to anyone 80-years-old or older. Send your request a few months in advance to your local congressman or senator.

Consumer Fraud Division
Cook County Office of the State's Attorney
303 Daley Center
Chicago, IL 60602
312-603-5440
312-603-7605 (TDD)

State's Attorney
Madison County Office of the State's Attorney
Madison County Administration Building
157 N. Main St., Suite 402
Edwardsville, IL 62025
618-692-6280

Director
Consumer Protection Division
Rock Island County Office of the State's Attorney
County Courthouse
210 15th St.
Rock Island, IL 61201
309-786-4451, ext. 229

Illinois—City Offices

Chicago Department of Consumer Services
121 N. LaSalle St., Room 808
Chicago, IL 60602
312-744-4006
312-744-9385 (TTY)
312-744-9400 (complaint line)

Des Plaines Consumer Protection Commission
1420 Miner St., 6th Fl.
Des Plaines, IL 60016
847-391-5300

Indiana—State Office

Consumer Protection Division
Office of the Attorney General
Indiana Government Center South, 5th Fl.
402 W. Washington St.
Indianapolis, IN 46204
317-232-6330
800-382-5516 (Indiana only)

Indiana—SELECTED County Offices

Consumer Protection Division
Lake County Prosecutor's Office
2293 N. Main St.
Crown Point, IN 46307
219-755-3300

Marion County Prosecuting Attorney
560 City-County Bldg.
200 E. Washington St.
Indianapolis, IN 46204-3363
317-327-3522

Vanderburgh County Prosecuting Attorney
Administration Bldg., Room 108
Civic Center Complex
Evansville, IN 47708
812-435-5150

Indiana—City Office

Director
Gary Office of Consumer Affairs
401 Broadway B2
Gary, IN 46402
219-881-5297

Iowa—State Office

Consumer Protection Division
Office of the Attorney General
1305 E. Walnut St., 2nd Floor
Des Moines, IA 50319
515-281-5926

Kansas—State Office

Consumer Protection Division
Office of the Attorney General
120 SW 10th Ave., 2nd Fl.
Kansas Judicial Center
Topeka, KS 66612-3751
785-296-3751
800-432-2310 (Kansas only)

Kansas—SELECTED County Offices

Consumer Fraud Division
Johnson County District Attorney's Office
Johnson County Courthouse
P.O. Box 728
Olathe, KS 66051
913-715-3000

Consumer Fraud and Economic Crime Division
Sedgwick County District Attorney's Office
535 North Main
Wichita, KS 67203
316-383-7921

Assistant District Attorney
Shawnee County District Attorney's Office
200 SE 7th St.
Topeka, KS 66603
785-233-8200 Ext. 4330

Kentucky—State Offices

Consumer Protection Division
Office of the Attorney General
The Capitol, Suite 118
700 Capitol Avenue
Frankfort, KY 40601
502-696-5389

Consumer Protection and Education Division
Kentucky Department of Insurance
P.O. Box 517
Louisville, KY 40602
502-564-6034
800-432-9257 (Kentucky only)

Louisiana—State Office

Office of the Attorney General
One American Place
301 Main St., 12th Fl.
P.O. Box 94095
Baton Rouge, LA 70804-9005
225-342-7900
800-351-4889 (consumer hotline)

Louisiana—SELECTED County Office

Consumer Protection Division
Jefferson Parish District Attorney's Office
Gretna Courthouse
Annex Building, 5th Fl.
Gretna, LA 70053
504-368-1020

Maine—State Offices

Department of Financial and Professional Regulation
Bureau of Consumer Credit Protection
State House Station No. 35
Augusta, ME 04333-0035
207-624-8527
800-965-5235

Department of the Attorney General
Public Protection Division
Consumer Information and Mediation Service
6 State House Station
Augusta, ME 04333-0006
207-626-8849

Number 10 Downing Street in London still has the 23 chairs used by Gladstone and Disraeli during Queen Victoria's reign. Only one of the chairs has arms.

Maryland—State Offices

Consumer Protection Division
Office of the Attorney General
200 St. Paul Pl.
Baltimore, MD 21202
410-528-8662
410-576-6550
888-743-0023

Licensing & Consumer Services
Motor Vehicle Administration
6601 Ritchie Highway, NE
Glen Burnie, MD 21062
410-768-7536

Consumer Affairs Specialist
Eastern Shore Branch Office
Consumer Protection Division
Office of the Attorney General
Salisbury District Court/Multiservice Center
201 Baptist St., Suite 30
Salisbury, MD 21801-4976
301-543-6620

Maryland—SELECTED County Offices

Howard County Office of Consumer Affairs
6751 Gateway Drive, 2nd fl.
Columbia, MD 21046
410-313-6420
410-313-6401

Montgomery County Division of Consumer Affairs
100 Maryland Ave., 3rd Floor
Rockville, MD 20850
240-7773636

Massachusetts—State Offices

Consumer Protection Division
Department of the Attorney General
200 Portland St.
Boston, MA 02114
617-727-8400 (consumer hotline)

New Bedford Office of the Attorney General
105 William St., 1st fl.
New Bedford, MA 02740
508-990-9700

Fair Labor and Business Practices
Pittsfield Office of the Attorney General
160 North St.
Pittsfield, MA 01201
413-447-7324 ext. 218

Worcester Office of the Attorney
One Exchange Place
Worcester, MA 01608
508-792-7600

Western Massachusetts Consumer Protection Division
Department of the Attorney General
1350 Main St., 4th Fl.
Springfield, MA 01103
413-784-1240

Massachusetts—SELECTED County Offices

Consumer Fraud Prevention
Franklin County District Attorney's Office
238 Main St.
Greenfield, MA 01301
413-774-5102 Ext. 226

Consumer Protection
Northwestern District Attorney's Office
1 Gleason Plaza
Northhampton, MA 01060
413-586-9225

City Offices
Mayor's Office of Consumer Affairs and Licensing
Boston City Hall, Room 817
Boston, MA 02201
617-635-3834

Michigan—State Offices

Consumer Protection Division
Office of the Attorney General
P.O. Box 30213
Lansing, MI 48909
517-373-1140
517-335-1935

Bureau of Automotive Regulation
Michigan Department of State
Mutual Building, 2nd Fl.
208 N. Capitol Ave.
Lansing, MI 48918
517-373-0964

Michigan—SELECTED County Offices

Bay County Consumer Protection Unit
1230 Washington Ave.
Suite 768
Bay City, MI 48708
989-895-4185

Consumer Protection Department
Macomb County Office of the Prosecuting Attorney
One South Main
Mt. Clemens, MI 48043
586-469-5350

Michigan—City Office

City of Detroit
Consumer Affairs Department
65 Cadillac Square
Suite 1600
Detroit, MI 48226
313-224-6995

Minnesota—State Offices

Office of Consumer Services
Office of the Attorney General
1400 NCL Tower
445 Minnesota St.
St. Paul, MN 55101
651-296-3353
800-657-3787
651-297-7206 (TTY)
800-366-4812 (TTY)

Minnesota—SELECTED County Office

Citizen Protection Unit
Hennepin County Attorney's Office
C-2000 County Government Center
Minneapolis, MN 55487
612-348-5550

Minnesota—City Office

Consumer Affairs Division
Minneapolis Department of Licenses & Consumer Services
City Hall, Room 1C
350 S. Fifth St.
Minneapolis, MN 55415
612-673-2080

Mississippi—State Offices

Office of the Secretary Of State
Regulation and Enforcement Division
P.O. Box 136
Jackson, MS 34205-0136
601-359-1350

Office of the Attorney General
Consumer Protection Division
P.O. Box 220
Jackson, MS 39205-0220
601-359-3680

Missouri

Office of the Attorney General
Consumer Protection Division
Supreme Court Building
P.O. Box 899
207 West High Street
Jefferson City, MO 65102
573-751-3321

Montana-State Offices

Department of Justice
Office of Attorney General
Consumer Protection Division
P.O. Box 201401
Helena, MT 59620-1401
406-444-2026

Montana Department of Commerce
Consumer Affairs Unit
P.O. Box 200501
Helena, MT 59620-0501
406-444-3797

Nebraska—State Office

Office of the Attorney General
Consumer Protection Division
2115 State Capitol
Lincoln, NE 68509
402-471-2682
800-727-6432

Nevada

Nevada Attorney General
Consumer Affairs Division
Carson City Office
100 North Carson Street
Carson City, NV 89701-4717
775-684-1100

Telemarketing, Securities and Deceptive Trade
  Practices
Consumer Affairs Division
555 East Washington St., Suite 3900
Las Vegas, NV 89101
702-486-3777

Bureau of Consumer Protection
Office of the Attorney General
1000 East William St., Suite 200
Carson City, NV 89710
775-687-6300

New Hampshire—State Office

Chief Consumer Protection and Antitrust Bureau
Office of the Attorney General
33 Capital St.
State House Annex
Concord, NH 03301
603-271-3591

New Jersey—State Offices

Division of Consumer Affairs
Office of Consumer Protection
124 Halsey St.
Newark, NJ 07101
973-504-6200
800-242-5846
973-504-6588 (TDD)

Office of the Attorney General
Division of Consumer Affairs
P.O. Box 080
Trenton, NJ 08625-0080
609-292-4925

New Jersey—Selected County Offices

Atlantic County Division of Consumer Affairs
Department of Law
1333 Atlantic Avenue
Atlantic City, NJ 08401
609-343-2376

Burlington County Department of Consumer Affairs
County Office Building
3rd Floor, Room 354
49 Rancocas Road
PO Box 6000
Mount Holly, NJ 08060-6000
609-265-5054

Camden City Attorney
Office of the City Attorney
Suite 419—City Hall
P.O. Box 95120
Camden, NJ 08101
856-757-7170

Cape May County Consumer Affairs
4 Moore Rd.
Cape May Courthouse, NJ 08210-1601
609-463-6475

Cumberland County Consumer Affairs
788 E. Commerce St.
Bridgeton, NJ 08302
856-453-2203

Essex County
Division of Community Action/Consumer Services
50 South Clinton St., 3rd floor
East Orange, NJ 07018
973-395-8350

Gloucester County
Department of Consumer Protection/Weights &
  Measures
152 N. Broad St.
Woodbury, NJ 08096
856-853-3349

Hudson County Consumer Affairs
Administration Bldg.
595 Newark Ave.
4th floor, Room 407
Jersey City, NJ 07306
201-795-6295

Hunterdon County Consumer Affairs
P.O. Box 2900
Flemington, NJ 08822
908-806-5174

Livingston Division of Consumer Affairs
357 S. Livingston Ave.
Livingston, NJ 07039
973-535-7976

Mercer County
Office of Consumer Affairs
640 S. Broad St., Rm. 404
Trenton, NJ 08650-0068
609-989-6671

Middlesex County
Consumer Affairs
Middlesex County Administration Bldg.
J.F.K. Square, 2nd floor, Suite 290
New Brunswick, NJ 08901
732-745-3875

Monmouth County
Department of Consumer Affairs
50 E. Main St.
P.O. Box 1255
Freehold, NJ 07728
732-431-7900

North Bergen Consumer Affairs
Municipal Bldg.
4233 Kennedy Blvd.
North Bergen, NJ 07047
201-330-7292

Ocean County Consumer Affairs
1027 Hooper Ave. Bldg. 2
P.O. Box 2191
Toms River, NJ 08754
732-929-2105

Passaic County Department of Law and Public Safety
Division of Weights and Measures
Consumer Protection
1310 Route 23, North
Wayne, NJ 07470
973-305-5881

Perth Amboy Division of Consumer Affairs
City Hall
260 High St,
Perth Amboy, NJ 08861
732-826-0290

Secaucus Department of Consumer Affairs
203 Patterson Plank Road
Secaucus, NJ 07091
201-330-2008

Somerset County Consumer Affairs
Administration Bldg.
20 Grove Street

P.O. Box 3000
Somerville, NJ 08876-1262
908-231-7000

Union County Consumer Affairs
300 North Ave., East
P.O. Box 186
Westfield, NJ 07091
908-654-9840

Wayne Township Division of Consumer Affairs
475 Valley Road
Wayne, NJ 07470
973-694-1800

New Mexico—State Office

Santa Fe Office of Attorney General
Consumer Protection Division
407 Galisteo St.
Bataan Memorial Building, Rm. 260
P.O. Drawer 1508
Santa Fe, NM 87501
505-827-6060
800-678-1508

New Mexico
Albuquerque Regional Office
Consumer Protection Division
111 Lomas NW, Suite 300
Albuquerque, NM 87102
505-222-9000
800-300-2020

New York—State Offices

Office of the Attorney General
Albany Executive Offices
State Capitol, Room 220
Albany, NY 12224-0341
518-474-7330

Consumer Fraud Bureau
Office of the Attorney General
New York Executive Offices
120 Broadway
New York, NY 10271
212-416-8345
800-771-7755

New York State Consumer Protection Board
5 Empire State Plaza, Suite 2101
Albany, NY 12223-1556
518-474-8583

Department of Insurance
Consumer Services Bureau
25 Beaver St.
New York, NY 10004

212-480-6400
800-342-3736

Department of Law
Office of the Attorney General
Bureau of Investor Protection and Securities
120 Broadway, 23rd Fl.
New York, NY 10271
212-416-8200

Bureau of Weights and Measures
Department of Agriculture and Markets
1 Winners Circle
Albany, NY 12235
518-457-3452

New York—Regional Offices
Buffalo Regional Office
Office of Attorney General
Consumer Affairs Division
107 Delaware Ave. 4th Fl.
Buffalo, NY 14202
800-771-7755 (toll free in NY)

Office Wagon Number 123 was the address for the Ringling Brothers and Barnum and Bailey Circus main office and ticket wagon.

Poughkeepsie Regional Office
Office of Attorney General
Consumer Affairs Division
235 Main St. 3rd Fl.
Poughkeepsie, NY 12601
800-771-7755 (toll free in NY)

Rochester Regional Office
Office of Attorney General
Consumer Affairs Division
144 Exchange Blvd.
Rochester, NY 14614-2175
716-546-7430
800-771-7755 (toll free in NY)
716-327-3249 (TDD)

Suffolk Regional Office
Office of the Attorney General
300 Motor Parkway
Hauppauge, NY 11788-5127
631-231-2401

Syracuse Regional Office
Office of Attorney General
Consumer Affairs Division
615 Erie Blvd. West, Ste. 102

Syracuse, NY 13210-2339
315-448-4848
800-771-7755 (toll free in NY)

Utica Regional Office
Office of Attorney General
Consumer Affairs Division
207 Genesee St. Rm. 504
Utica, NY 13501
315-793-2225
800-771-7755 (toll free in NY)

New York—SELECTED County Offices
Broome County District Attorney's Office
The Press Building, 7th Fl.
19 Chenango St.
Binghamton, NY 13901
607-778-8000

Dutchess County Department of Consumer Affairs
98 Peach Road
Poughkeepsie, NY 12601
845-486-2949

Erie County District Attorney's Office
Consumer Fraud Bureau
25 Delaware Ave.
Buffalo, NY 14202
716-858-2424

Nassau County Office of Consumer Affairs
160 Old Country Rd.
Mineola, NY 11501
516-571-2600

Orange County District Attorney's Office
255 Main St.
Goshen, NY 10924
845-291-2050

Orange County Department of Weights and Measures
County Government Center
255 Main St.
Goshen, NY 10924
845-291-2400

Putnam County Department of Consumer Affairs
110 Old Route 6, Building 3
Carmel, NY 10512
845-225-2039

Rockland County Office of Consumer Protection
50 Sanitarium Road
Pomona, NY 10970
845-364-2680

Steuben County Department of Weights, Measures, and Consumer Affairs
3 E. Pulteney Square
Bath, NY 14810
607-776-9631

Suffolk County Department of Consumer Affairs
North County Complex, Building 340
Hauppauge, NY 11788
631-853-4600

Ulster County Consumer Fraud Bureau
20 Lucas Avenue
Kingston, NY 12401
845-340-3260

Westchester County District Attorney's Office
111 Dr. Martin Luther King, Jr. Blvd.
White Plains, NY 10601
914-285-3303

Westchester County Department of Consumer Protection
112 East Post Road, 4th Fl.
White Plains, NY 10601
914-995-2155

New York—City Offices

Babylon Consumer Protection Board
Town Hall
200 East Sunrise Highway
Lindenhurst, NY 11757
631-957-3005

Town of Colonie Consumer Protection Board
Memorial Town Hall
Newtonville, NY 12128
518-783-2704

Mt. Vernon Office of Consumer Affairs
City Hall, 11th Fl.
Mt. Vernon, NY 10550
914-665-2433

New York City Department of Consumer Affairs
42 Broadway
New York, NY 10004
212-487-4444

Queens Neighborhood Office
New York City Department of Consumer Affairs
120-55 Queens Blvd., Room 301A
Kew Gardens, NY 11424
718-286-2990

Staten Island Neighborhood Office
New York City Department of Consumer Affairs
Staten Island Borough Hall, Room 422

Staten Island, NY 10301
212-487-4444

City of Oswego Office of Consumer Affairs
City Hall
West Oneida St.
Oswego, NY 13126
315-342-7245

Ramapo Consumer Protection Board
Ramapo Town Hall
237 Route 59
Suffern, NY 10901-5399
845-357-5100

Schenectady Bureau of Consumer Protection
City Hall
Jay St., Room 204
Schenectady, NY 12305
518-382-5061

Yonkers Office of Consumer Protection,
Weights and Measures
87 Nepperhan Ave.Yonkers, NY 10703
914-377-6807

North Carolina—State Office

Consumer Protection Section
Office of the Attorney General
North Carolina Department of Justice
P.O. Box 629
Raleigh, NC 27602
919-716-6400

North Dakota—State Offices

Office of the Attorney General
State Capitol Bldg.
Bismarck, ND 58505
701-328-2210
800-472-2600 (North Dakota only)

North Dakota—SELECTED County Offices

Quad County Community Action Agency
27½ South Third Street
Grand Forks, ND 58201
701-746-5431

Ohio—State Offices

Consumer Protection Section
Ohio Attorney General
30 E. Broad St., 25th Floor
Columbus, OH 43215-3428
614-466-4320
800-282-0515 (toll free in Ohio)

Office of Consumers' Counsel
10 West Broad Street, Suite 1800
Columbus, OH 43215-3485
614-466-9467
877-742-5622 (toll-free in Ohio)

Ohio–SELECTED County Offices

Economic Crime Division
Franklin County Office of Prosecuting Attorney
369 South High Street
Columbus, OH 43215
614-462-3555.

Montgomery County Fraud and Economic Crimes Division
Dayton Montgomery County Fraud Section
301 West 3rd Street
Dayton, OH 45402
513-225-4747

Portage County Office of Prosecuting Attorney
466 South Chestnut Street
Ravenna, OH 44266-3000
330-296-4593

Summit County Office of Prosecuting Attorney
53 University Avenue
Akron, OH 44308-1680
330-643-2800
330-643-8277 (TDD/TTY)

Ohio–City Office

Neighborhood Services Department
Cincinnati Office of Consumer Affairs
Division of Human Services
City Hall, Room 126
Cincinnati, OH 45202
513-352-6146

Oklahoma–State Offices

Consumer Protection Unit
Office of the Attorney General
4545 N. Lincoln Blvd., #260
Oklahoma City, OK 73105
(405) 521-3921

Department of Consumer Credit
4545 N. Lincoln Blvd., Suite 260
Oklahoma City, OK 73105
405-521-3653

Oregon–State Offices

Financial Fraud Section
Department of Justice
1162 Court St. NE

Salem, OR 97310
503-378-4732
503-378-4320 (hotline)
503-229-5576 (in Portland only)

Pennsylvania–State Offices

Office of Attorney General
Strawberry Square, 14th Floor
Harrisburg, PA 17120
717-787-9707
800-441-2555 (toll free in PA)

Office of Consumer Advocate
Office of Attorney General
Forum Place, 5th Floor
555 Walnut Street
Harrisburg, PA 17101-1921
717-783-5048 (for utilities only)

Pennsylvania—Branch Offices

Bureau of Consumer Services
Pennsylvania Public Utility Commission
PO Box 3265
Harrisburg, PA 17105-3265
717-783-1740
800-782-1110 (general complaints)

Bureau of Consumer Protection
Office of Attorney General
1001 State Street, 1009
Erie, PA 16501
814-871-4371
800-441-2555 (toll free in PA)

Bureau of Consumer Protection
Office of Attorney General
301 Chestnut Street, Suit 105
Harrisburg, PA 17101
717-787-7109
800-441-2555 (toll free in PA)

Bureau of Consumer Protection
Office of Attorney General
171 Lovell Avenue, Suite 202
Ebensburg, PA 15931
814-471-1831
800-441-2555 (toll free in PA)

Bureau of Consumer Protection
Office of Attorney General
21 South 12th Street, 2nd Floor
Philadelphia, PA 19107
215-560-2414
800-441-2555 (toll free in PA)

Bureau of Consumer Protection
Office of Attorney General
Manor Complex, 6th Floor
564 Forbes Avenue
Pittsburgh, PA 15219
412-565-5135
800-441-2555 (toll free in PA)

Bureau of Consumer Protection
Office of Attorney General
Samter Building, Room 214
101 Penn Avenue
Scranton, PA 18503-2025
570-963-4913
800-441-2555 (toll free in PA)

Pennsylvania—SELECTED County Offices

Bucks County Consumer Protection/Weights and
  Measures
50 North Main Street
Doylestown, PA 18901
215-348-7442
Toll free in PA: 1-800-441-2555

Chester County Weights and Measures/
  Consumer Affairs
Government Services Center, Suite 390
601 Westtown Road
West Chester, PA 19382-4547
610-344-6150
800-441-2555 (toll free in PA)

Cumberland County Consumer Affairs
Weights and Measures
One Courthouse Square
Carlisle, PA 17013-3330
717-240-6180
800-441-2555 (toll free in PA)

Delaware County Office of Consumer Affairs
Media Courthouse
201 West Front Street
Media, PA 19063
610-891-4865
800-441-2555 (toll free in PA)

Montgomery County Department of Consumer
  Affairs
Human Services Center
1430 Dekalb Street, P.O. Box 311
Norristown, PA 19404-0311
610 2783565
717-963-4913
800-441-2555 (toll free in PA)

Economic Crime Unit
Philadelphia District Attorney's Office
1421 Arch Street
Philadelphia, PA 19102
215-686-8750

Rhode Island—State Offices

Attorney General
Consumer Protection Unit
150 South Main Street
Providence, RI 02903
401-274-4400

South Carolina—State Offices

Consumer Protection Office
Office of the Attorney General
P.O. Box 11549
Columbia, SC 29211
888-95-FRAUD (Insurance fraud)
888-662-4328 (Medicaid fraud)
877-BE-ALERT (Securities Fraud)

State Ombudsman Office of Executive Policy and
  Program
1205 Pendleton Street, Room 308
Columbia, South Carolina 29201
803-734-0457

South Dakota—State Offices

Office of The Attorney General
Division of Consumer Protection
500 East Capitol Ave
Pierre, SD 57501-5070
605-773-4400
800-300-1986 (South Dakota only)

Tennessee—State Offices

Office of the Attorney General
Consumer Protection Division
425 5th Ave. North, 2nd Floor
Nashville, TN 37243
615-741-4737
800-342-8385

Division of Consumer Affairs
Department of Commerce and Insurance
500 James Robertson Parkway
Nashville, TN 37243-0600
800-342-8385 (inside Tennessee)
615-741-4737

Texas—State Offices

Consumer Protection Division
Office of Attorney General
1600 Pacific Ave., Ste. 1700
Dallas, TX 75201
214-742-8944

Consumer Protection Division
Office of Attorney General
310 N. Mesa, Ste.900
El Paso, TX 79901-1301
915-542-4800/1596

Consumer Protection Division
Office of Attorney General
808 Travis, Ste. 812
Houston, TX 77002
713-223-5886
713-223-5821

Consumer Protection Division
Office of Attorney General
916 Main St., Ste. 806
Lubbock, TX 79401-2905
806-747-5238

Consumer Protection Division
Office of Attorney General
3201 North McColl Rd., Ste. B
McAllen, TX 78501
956-682-4547

Consumer Protection Division
Office of Attorney General
115 East Travis St., Ste. 925
San Antonio, TX 78205-1607
210-225-4191

25 Main St. in Cooperstown,
New York, is the site of the famous
National Baseball Hall of Fame.

Office of Consumer Credit Commissioner
2601 N. Lamar Blvd.
Austin, Texas 78705
512-936-7600
800-538-1579

Texas—SELECTED County Offices

Dallas County District Attorney's Office
Specialized Crime Division
133 North Industrial Blvd., LB 19
Dallas, TX 75207-4399
214-653-3820

Harris County Consumer Fraud Division
Office of District Attorney
1201 Franklin, Ste. 600
Houston, TX 77002
713-755-5836

Utah—State Office

Division of Consumer Protection
Department of Commerce
160 East 300 South
Box 146704
Salt Lake City, UT 84114-6704
801-530-6601
800-721-7233 (toll free in Utah)

Consumer Protection Division
Office of the Attorney General
Utah State Capitol Office
111 State Capitol
Salt Lake City, UT 84114
801-530-6601

Vermont—State Offices

Public Protection Division
Office of the Attorney General
109 State Street
Montpelier, VT 05602
802-828 3171

Consumer Assurance Section
Department of Agriculture, Food and Market
116 State Street
Montpelier, VT 05602
802-828-3456

Virginia—State Offices

Antitrust and Consumer Litigation Section
Office of the Attorney General
900 East Main Street
Richmond, VA 23219
804-786-2116
804-786-0122

Office of Consumer Affairs
Department of Agriculture and Consumer Services
Washington Building, Suite 100
P.O. Box 1163
Richmond, VA 23219
804-786-2042
800-552-9963 (Toll free in VA)
804-371-6344 (TDD)

Virginia—SELECTED County Offices

Office of Citizen and Consumer Affairs
2100 Clarendon Blvd, Suite 314
Arlington, VA 22201
703-228-3260
703-228-4611 (TTY)

**Fairfax County Department of Cable
Communications and Consumer Protection**
12000 Government Center Parkway, Suite 433
Fairfax, VA 22035
703-324-5949

**Prince William County
Office of Consumer Affairs**
1 County Complex Court
Prince William, Virginia 22192
703-792-4660

Virginia—City Offices

**Carmen Gonzales, Consumer Affairs Administrator
Alexandria Office of Consumer Affairs**
City Hall
301 King Street, room 1900
P.O. Box 178
Alexandria, VA 22313
703-838-4350
703-838-5056 (TDD)

**Consumer Affairs Division
Virginia Beach Office of the Commonwealth
  Attorney
Consumer Affairs Division**
2425 Nimmo Parkway
Virginia Beach, VA 23456-9060
757-426-5836

Washington—State Offices

**Consumer and Business Fair Practices Division
Office of the Attorney General**
900 Fourth Ave. Suite 2000
Seattle, WA 98164-1012
206-464-6684
800-551-4636 (toll free in Washington)

**Consumer and Business Fair Practices Division
Office of the Attorney General**
West 1116 Riverside
Spokane, WA 99201-1194
509-456-3123

**Consumer and Business Fair Practices Division
Office of the Attorney General**
1019 Pacific Ave S. 3rd Floor
Tacoma, WA 98402-4411
253-593-2904

Washington—City Offices

**Chief Deputy Prosecuting Attorney
Fraud Division**
900 4th Ave., #1002
Seattle, WA 98164
206-296-9010

**Revenue and Consumer Affairs Division
Department of Finance**
Key Tower
700 5th Avenue, Room 4250
Seattle, WA 98104
206-684-8484

West Virginia—State Offices

**Consumer Protection Division
Office of the Attorney General**
812 Quarrier Street, 6th Floor
P.O. Box 1789
Charleston, WV 25326-1789
304-558-8986
800-368-8808 (in WV only)

**Divisions of Weights and Measures
Department of Labor**
570 McCorkle Ave.
St. Albans, WV 25177
304-722-0602

**City of Charleston
Department of Consumer Protection**
P.O. Box 2749
Charleston, WV 25330
304-348-6439

Wisconsin—State Offices

**Director, Consumer Protection
Department of Agriculture, Trade and Consumer
  Protection**
2811 Agriculture Dr.
P.O. Box 8911
Madison, WI 53708
608-224-4921
800-422-7128 (toll free in WI)

**Director, Consumer Protection
Department of Agriculture, Trade and Consumer
  Protection**
3610 Oakwood Hills Parkway
Eau Claire, WI 53701-7754
715-839-3848

**Director, Consumer Protection
Department of Agriculture, Trade and Consumer
  Protection**
200 N. Jefferson Street, Suite 146-A

Green Bay, WI 54301
920-448-5110

Director, Consumer Protection
Department of Agriculture, Trade and Consumer Protection
10930 W. Potter Road, Suite C
Milwaukee, WI 53226-3450
414-266-1231

Wyoming—State Offices
Office of the Attorney General
123 Capitol Building
200 W. 24th Street
Cheyenne, WY 82002
307-777-7841
307-777-5351 (TDD)

Office of Consumer Protection and Citizen Advocacy
Department of Justice
Office of the Attorney General
P.O. Box 7857
Madison, WI 53707-7857
608-266-1221
800-422-7128 (in WI)

Wisconsin—SELECTED County Offices
District Attorney
Marathon County District Attorney's Office
Marathon County Courthouse
Wausau, WI 54401
715-847-5555

Assistant District Attorney
Milwaukee County District Attorney's Office
Consumer Fraud Unit
821 West State Street, Room 412
Milwaukee, WI 53233-2485
414-278-4585

Consumer Fraud Investigator
Racine County Sheriff's Department
717 Wisconsin Avenue
Racine, WI 53403
414-636-3125
800-242-4202, ext. 3125 (Toll free)

American Samoa
Assistant Attorney General
Consumer Protection Bureau
Office of the Attorney General
Executive Office Building, Utulei
P. O. Box 7
Pago Pago, AS 96799
684- 633-4163

Puerto Rico
Secretary
Department of Justice
Apartado 9020192
San Juan, Puerto Rico 00902
787-721-2900

Virgin Islands
Department of Licensing and Consumer Affairs
Property & Procurement Bldg.,
1 Sub Base, Rm 205
St. Thomas, USVI 00802
340-774-3130
809-721-2900

DISABILITIES

TELECOMMUNICATIONS DEVICE FOR THE DEAF

Hearing- and speech-impaired people who use a telecommunications device for the deaf (known as TDD or TTY) can get help with calls made from a TDD to a TDD by using the following service:

TDD/TTY Operator Services
800-855-1155

The TDD operator can help you if you have telecommunications devices for the deaf to make:

- Credit card calls (if you have a telephone credit card)
- Collect calls (calls paid for by the person you are calling)
- Third-number telephone calls (calls billed to a number other than the one you are calling to or from)
- Person-to-person calls (calls to a specific person)
- Calls from a hotel or motel
- Calls from a coin phone (credit card, collect, or bill to third-number calls only)

The TDD operator can also help you:

- Get the number if you have a problem with a call
- Get assistance for problems with calls

"Sign Language" and "Braille Alphabet, Numbers, and Punctuation" in chapter 12
Go to

- Get telephone numbers that you cannot find in the telephone book
- Report problems with your telephone

The TDD operator cannot interpret voice to TDD or TDD to voice.

Remember, most calls made with the help of an operator are more expensive, so dial calls yourself when you can to save money.

BOOKS FOR BLIND AND PHYSICALLY HANDICAPPED PERSONS

The Library of Congress has a free reading program for blind and physically handicapped individuals and offers publications in Braille and recorded books and magazines to persons who cannot hold a book or see well enough to read regular print. Special playback equipment is available on a loan basis from the Library of Congress, and cassettes and recordings on discs can be ordered from about 158 cooperating libraries. Anyone who is medically certified as unable to hold a book or read ordinary print because of a visual handicap can borrow these materials postage-free and return them in the same manner. For more information, contact:

> **National Library Service for the Blind and Physically Handicapped**
> The Library of Congress
> Washington, DC 20542
> 202-707-5100
> 800-424-9100

Recording for the Blind and Dyslexic (RFB) is a national nonprofit service organization that provides free cassettes of educational textbooks and other resources to medically certified individuals. Eligibility extends to visually, physically, and perceptually handicapped individuals. One of RFB's special services is a collection of cassettes of a wide variety of consumer publications from the federal government. There is a one-time registration fee. For more information and an application, contact:

Recording for the Blind and Dyslexic
20 Roszel Rd.
Princeton, NJ 08540
609-452-0606
800-221-4792 (toll free outside New Jersey)
http://www.rfbd.org

DOMESTIC VIOLENCE RESOURCES

Below is a partial listing of domestic violence resources in the United States. Where possible, a statewide, toll-free hot line is listed; for states that do not have one, there is an organization that can refer you to legal assistance, crisis counseling, and shelters in your area.

National

Domestic Violence Resource Center
National Criminal Justice Resource Center
Box 6000-AIQ
Rockville, MD 20850
301-251-5063
800-627-6872
http://www.ncjrs.org

National Coalition Against Domestic Violence
P.O. Box 18749
Denver, CO 80218
303-839-1852
http://www.ncadv.org

National Coalition Against Domestic Violence Public Policy Office
1532 16th Street, NW
Washington, DC 20036
202-745-1211
http://www.ncadv.org

National Coalition on Child Abuse and Family Violence
800-222-2000

National Domestic Violence Hot Line
800-799-7233

Alabama

Alabama Coalition Against Domestic Violence
334-832-4842

Alaska

Alaska Network on Domestic Violence and Sexual Assault
907-586-3650

Arizona

Arizona Coalition Against Domestic Violence
602-279-2900

Arkansas

Arkansas Coalition Against Violence to Women and Children
501-812-0571

California

California Alliance Against Domestic Violence
916-444-7163
800-524-4765

California Alliance Against Domestic Violence-Southern Office
310-649-2479

Statewide California Coalition for Battered Women
562-981-1202
888-722-2952

Colorado

Colorado Coalition Against Domestic Violence
303-831-9632

Connecticut

Connecticut Coalition Against Domestic Violence
860-282-7892
800-281-1481 (in CT)
888-774-2900 (in-state Hotline)

Delaware

Family Violence Program
Battered Women's Hot Line
302-762-6110

Delaware Coalition Against Domestic Violence
302-658-2958

District of Columbia

DC Coalition Against Domestic Violence
202-299-1181

Domestic Violence Clinic
International Woman's Human Rights Clinic
At Georgetown Law Center
202-662-9640

Florida

Florida Coalition Against Domestic Violence
850-425-2749
800-500-1199 (in FL)

Georgia

Georgia Coalition on Family Violence
770-984-0085
800-334-2836 (in GA)

Hawaii

Hawaii State Coalition Against Domestic Violence
808-486-5072

Idaho

Idaho Coalition Against Sexual and Domestic Violence
208-384-0419

Illinois

Illinois Coalition Against Domestic Violence
217-789-2830 (9 A.M.–5 P.M.)

Indiana

Indiana Coalition Against Domestic Violence
317-543-3908
800-332-7385

Iowa

Iowa Coalition Against Domestic Violence
515-244-8028
800-942-0333 (in IA)

Kansas

Safe House
620-231-8251

Kansas Coalition Against Sexual and Domestic Violence
785-232-9784

Kentucky

Kentucky Domestic Violence Association
502-695-2444

Lincoln Trail Domestic Violence Program
(Elizabethtown County)
800-767-5838

Louisiana

Louisiana Coalition Against Domestic Violence
225-752-1296

Maine

Maine Coalition to End Domestic Violence
207-941-1194

Caring Unlimited
207-324-1802
800-239-7298

Maryland

Maryland Network Against Domestic Violence
301-352-4574
800-MD-HELPS

Massachusetts

Battered Women Fight Back, Inc.
617-971-0131

Battered Women's Hotline
617-661-7203

Domestic Violence Initiative
617-424-6456

Massachusetts Coalition of Battered Women's Services
617-248-0922

Michigan

Michigan Coalition Against Domestic and Sexual Violence
517-347-7000

Minnesota

Minnesota Coalition for Battered Women
651-646-6177
651-646-0994 (emergency hot line, call collect 24 hours)

Mississippi

Mississippi State Coalition Against Domestic Violence
601-981-9196
800-898-3234

Missouri

Missouri Coalition Against Domestic Violence
573-634-4161

Montana

Montana Network Against Domestic Violence and Sexual Assault
406-586-0263
406-586-4111
800-655-7867

Nebraska

Nebraska Domestic Violence and Sexual Assault Coalition
402-476-6256
800-876-6238 (in Nebraska)

Nevada

Nevada Network Against Domestic Violence
775-828-1115
800-230-1955

New Hampshire

New Hampshire Coalition Against Domestic and Sexual Violence
603-224-8893
800-852-3388 (in NH)

New Jersey

New Jersey Coalition for Battered Women
609-584-8107
800-572-7233

New Mexico

New Mexico State Coalition Against Domestic Violence
505-246-9240
800-773-3645 (state hot line)

Women's Community Association
505-247-4219 (24 hours)

New York

New York State Coalition Against Domestic Violence
518-432-4864
800-942-6906

Poder
800-942-6908 (Spanish)

North Carolina

North Carolina Coalition Against Domestic Violence
919-956-9124

North Dakota

North Dakota Council on Abused Women's Services
701-255-6240
800-472-2911 (in ND)

Ohio

Ohio Domestic Violence Network
614-784-0023
800-934-9840

Oklahoma

Oklahoma Coalition on Domestic Violence and Sexual Assault
405-848-1815
800-522-7233

Oregon

Oregon Coalition Against Domestic and Sexual Violence
503-365-9644

Pennsylvania

Pennsylvania Coalition Against Domestic Violence
717-545-6400
800-932-4632

Rhode Island

Rhode Island Council on Domestic Violence
401-467-9940
800-494-8100 (in RI)

South Carolina

South Carolina Coalition Against Domestic Violence and Sexual Assault
803-750-1222
800-260-9293

South Dakota

South Dakota Coalition Against Domestic Violence and Sexual Assault
605-945-0869
800-572-9196

Tennessee

Tennessee Coalition Against Domestic and Sexual Violence
615-386-9406
800-289-9018 (info line)

Statewide Domestic Violence and Child Abuse Hotline
800-356-6767

Texas

Council On Family Violence
512-794-1133

Utah

Domestic Violence Advisory Council
801-538-4635
800-897-5465 (in UT)

Vermont

Vermont Network Against Domestic Violence and Sexual Assault
802-223-1302 (weekdays, daytime)

Virginia

Virginians Against Domestic Violence
757-221-0990
800-838-VADV

Washington

Washington State Domestic Violence Hot Line
800-562-6025

Washington State Coalition Against Domestic Violence
360-407-0756

West Virginia

West Virginia Coalition Against Domestic Violence
304-965-3552

Wisconsin

Wisconsin Coalition Against Domestic Violence
608-255-0539 (9 A.M.–5 P.M. weekdays)

Wyoming

Wyoming Coalition Against Domestic Violence and Sexual Assault
307-755-5481

FAMILY PLANNING

Family Planning Council
260 S. Broad St., Suite 1000
Philadelphia, PA 19102
215-985-2600
http://www.familyplanning.org

International Planned Parenthood Federation
Western Hemisphere Region
120 Wall St., 9th Fl.
New York, NY 10005
212-248-6400
http://www.ippf.org/

National Family Planning and Reproductive Health Association
1627 K St. NW, 12th Fl.
Washington, DC 20006
202-293-3114
http://www.nfprha.org

"Precautions During Pregnancy" in chapter 18; "Average Cost of Raising a Child" in chapter 20

Go to

Planned Parenthood Federation of America
810 Seventh Ave.
New York, NY 10019
212-541-7800
http://www.plannedparenthood.org

Population Institute
107 2nd St., NE
Washington, DC 20002
202-544-3300
http://www.populationinstitute.org

Resolve: The National Infertility Association
1310 Broadway
Somerville, MA 02144-1779
617-643-2424
http://www.resolve.org

FEDERAL GOVERNMENT AGENCIES AND BUREAUS

Here is a selection of federal agencies that offer a wide range of information, enforcement, and/or complaint-handling services for products and services used by the general public. Many offices also have telecommunications devices for the deaf (TDDs). Voice users can call 800-877-8339 for the help of a relay operator from the Federal Information Relay Service.

Agriculture Department
Consumer and Community Affairs Director
Park Center, Rm. 912
Park Center Drive
Alexandria, VA 22302
703-305-2000
http://www.usda.gov

Civil Rights Commission
Congressional Affairs Unit
624 9th St. NW
Washington, DC 20425
202-376-8317
http://www.usccr.gov

Commerce Department
Public Affairs
1401 Constitution Ave., NW
Washington, DC 20230
202-482-5151
http://www.doc.gov

Commodity Futures Trading Commission
Office of Governmental Affairs
Headquarters Office
Three Lafayette Centre
1155 21st Street, NW
Washington DC 20581
Phone: (202) 418-5000
http://www.cftc.gov

Federal Consumer Information Center
Pueblo, CO 81009
800-FED-INFO
http://www.pueblo.gsa.gov/

Education Department
U.S. Department of Education
Consumer Affairs Staff
400 Maryland Avenue, SW
Washington, DC 20202-0498
800-USA-LEARN (1-800-872-5327)
http://www.ed.gov/index.jsp

U.S. Department of Energy
Office of Consumer and Public Liaison
1000 Independence Ave., SW
Washington, DC 20585
800-dial-DOE
http://www.energy.gov/

Environmental Protection Agency
Public Information Center
US EPA Headquarters
Ariel Rios Building
1200 Pennsylvania Ave., N.W.
Washington, DC 20460
212-637-3660
212-637-3675 (community relations)
212-637-3671 (environmental education)
http://www.epa.gov

Environmental Protection Agency
Main Regional Office
290 Broadway
New York, NY 10007-1866
212-637-5000
http://www.epa.gov

Environmental Protection Agency
Edison Laboratories
2890 Woodbridge Ave.
Edison, NJ 08837-3679
732-321-6754
http://www.epa.gov

Environmental Protection Agency
Niagara Falls Public Information Center
345 Third Street, Suite 530

Niagara Falls, NY 14303
716-285-8842
http://www.epa.gov

Federal Communications Commission
Consumer Assistance and Small Business Office
445 12th Street SW
Washington, DC 20554
888-CALL-FCC (225-5322)
888-TELL-FCC (835-5322) (TYY)
http://www.fcc.gov

Federal Deposit Insurance Corporation
Division of Finance
550 17th Street, NW
Washington, DC 20429-9990
800-759-6596
202-736-0000
Call Center Numbers:
877-ASKFDIC (877-275-3342)
800-925- 4618 (TDD)

Federal Housing Finance Board
1777 F Street, NW
Washington, DC 20006-5210
202-408-2500
http://www.fhfb.gov/

Federal Maritime Commission
Office of Informal Inquiries and Complaints
Main Offices
800 North Capitol Street, N.W.
Washington, D.C. 20573
202-523-5807
http://www.fmc.gov

Federal Maritime Commission
Los Angeles Area Representative
P.O. Box 230
839 South Beacon Street, Room 320
San Pedro, CA 90733-0230
310-514-4905

Federal Maritime Commission
Miami Area Representative
Customs Management Center
909 S.E., 1st Avenue, Room 705
Miami, Florida 33131
305-536-4316

Federal Maritime Commission
New Orleans Area Representative
U.S. Customs House
423 Canal Street, Room 309B
New Orleans, Louisiana 70130
504-589-6662

Federal Maritime Commission
New York Area Representative
Federal Maritime Commission
Building No. 75, Room 205B
JFK International Airport
Jamaica, NY 11430
718-553-2228

Federal Maritime Commission
Seattle Area Representative
c/o U.S. Customs
7 South Nevada Street, Suite 100
Seattle, Washington 98134
206-553-0221

Federal Reserve
Board of Governors
Division of Consumer and Community Affairs
20th Street and Constitution Avenue, NW,
Washington, DC 20551
202-452-3819
202-452-3102
http://www.federalreserve.gov/

Health and Human Services Department
Consumer Affairs and Information
200 Independence Avenue, SW
Washington, DC 20201
877-696-6775
http://www.hhs.gov/

Health and Human Services Department
Food and Drug Administration
5600 Fishers Lane
Rockville, MD 20857-0001
888-INFO-FDA (888-463-6332)
http://www.fda.gov/

Department of Health and Human Services
National Health Information Center
P.O. Box 1133
Washington, DC 20013-1133
800-336-4797 (toll-free) or
301-565-4167 (in the Washington, D.C., area)
http://www.health.gov/nhic/

Office of Inspector General
Small Business Administration
Investigations Division
Mail Code: 4113
409 Third Street, SW
Washington, DC 20416
OIG Fraud Line
800-767-0385
202-205-7151
http://www.sba.gov/ig/

U.S. Department of Housing and Urban Development
451 7th Street S.W.
Washington, DC 20410
202-708-1112
202-708-1455 (TTY)
http://www.hud.gov

U.S. Department of the Interior
Consumer Affairs Administrator
1849 C. Street N.W.
Washington, DC 20240
202-208-3100
http://www.doi.gov/

U.S. Department of Transportation
400 7th Street, S.W.
Washington D.C. 20590
202-366-4000
http://www.dot.gov/

Department of Labor
Consumer Affairs Department
200 Constitution Avenue, NW
Washington, DC 20210
866-4-USA-DOL
877-889-5627 (TTY)
http://www.dol.gov

National Credit Union Administration
1775 Duke Street
Alexandria VA 22314
703-518-6300
http://www.ncua.gov

National Institute of Standards and Technology
100 Bureau Drive, Stop 3460
Gaithersburg, MD 20899-3460
301-975-NIST (6478)
301-975-8295 (TTY)
http://www.nist.gov/

National Labor Relations Board
1099 14th Street
Washington, D.C. 20570-0001
202-273-1770
http://www.nlrb.gov/

U.S. Nuclear Regulatory Commission
Office of Public Affairs (OPA)
Washington, D.C. 20555
800-368-5642 (toll free)
301-415-8200
301-415-5575 (TDD)
http://www.nrc.gov/

"Federal Judicial System" in chapter 21; "Federal Government" in chapter 25

Go to

Peace Corps
The Paul D. Coverdell Peace Corps Headquarters
1111 20th Street NW
Washington, D.C. 20526
800-424-8580 or
202-695-1857 (TTY)
http://www.peacecorps.gov/

Postal Rate Commission
Office of the Consumer Advocate
1333 H Street, NW
Suite 300
Washington, DC 20268-0001
202-789-6800
202-789-6881 (TTY)
http://www.prc.gov/

Security and Exchange Commission
SEC Headquarters
450 Fifth Street, NW
Washington, DC 20549
Office of Education and Assistance
800-SEC-0330
202-942-8088
202-942-7114 (TTY)
202-942-9634 (complaint center)
http://www.sec.gov/

Security and Exchange Commission
Northeast Regional Office
233 Broadway
New York, NY 10279
646-428-1500

Security and Exchange Commission
Southeast Regional Office
1401 Brickell Avenue, Suite 200
Miami, FL 33131
305-536-4700

Security and Exchange Commission
Midwest Regional Office
175 W. Jackson Boulevard
Suite 900
Chicago, IL 60604
312-353-7390

Security and Exchange Commission
Central Regional Office
1801 California Street, Suite 4800
Denver, CO 80202-2648
303-844-1000

Security and Exchange Commission
Pacific Regional Office
5670 Wilshire Boulevard, 11th Floor
Los Angeles, CA 90036-3648
323-965-3998

Hot Lines and Information Services

A Closer Look

Air safety hot line	800-FAA-SURE (800-322-7873)
Auto safety hot line	800-424-9393
Child abuse hot line	800-4-A-CHILD (800-422-4453)
Domestic violence hot line	800-799-SAFE (800-799-7233)
Drug hot line	800-662-HELP (800-662-4357)
Gay/lesbian youth hotline	800-347-TEEN (800-347-8336)
National Center for Missing and Exploited Children	800-843-LOST (800-843-5678)
National Organization for Victim Assistance (NOVA)	800-879-NOVA (800-879-6682)
National Runaway Switchboard	800-621-4000
Parents who have kidnapped their children hot line	800-A-WAY-OUT (800-292-9688)
Product safety hot line	800-638-2772

Social Security Administration
Office of Public Inquiries
Windsor Park Building
6401 Security Blvd.
Baltimore, MD 21235
800-772-1213
410-965-8882 (HQ only)
800-325-0778 (TTY)
http://www.ssa.gov/

U.S. Small Business Administration
SBA Answer Desk
6302 Fairview Road, Suite 300
Charlotte, North Carolina 28210
800-UASK-SBA (1-800-827-5722)
704-344-6640 (TTY)
hhtp://www.sba.gov

U.S. Small Business Administration
Office of Advocacy
409 3rd St., SW
Washington, DC 20416
202-205-6533
http://www.sba.gov/ADVO/

United States Postal Service
Office of Inspector General
ATTN: HOTLINE
1735 N. Lynn Street
Arlington, VA 22209-2020
888-USPS-OIG
888-877-7644
866-OIG-TEXT (TTY)
888-644-8398 (TTY)
http://www.uspsoig.gov/
http://www.usps.com/

Veterans Health Administration
810 Vermont Ave. NW
Washington, DC 20420
202-273-5400
http://www.va.gov/

FEDERAL INFORMATION CENTERS

The Federal Information Center (FIC) offers information about federal government services, programs, and regulations. The FIC can also tell you which federal agency to contact for help with specific problems.

Their toll-free number is 800-688-9889 (800-326-2996 for TDD users). The FIC is open for public inquiries from 9:00 A.M. to 8:00 P.M., Eastern time, Monday through Friday, except federal holidays. They can also be reached on the World Wide Web at http://fic.info.gov/.

PARENTING

ADOPTION

Adoptive Families of America
3333 Highway 100 North
Minneapolis, MN 55422
612-535-4829
http://www.adoptivefam.org

National Adoption Center
1500 Walnut St., Suite 701
Philadelphia, PA 19102
215-735-9988
800-TO-ADOPT
http://www.adopt.org

National Adoption Information Clearinghouse
330 C St. SW
Washington, DC 20447
703-352-3488
http://www.calib.com/naic

North American Council on Adoptable Children
970 Raymond Ave., Suite 106
St. Paul, MN 55114
612-644-3036
http://www.ncac.org

Orphan Voyage
1122 Marco Place
Jacksonville, FL 32207
904-398-4269

Orphan Voyage
Gay Swearington
13906 Pepperrell Drive
Tampa, FL 33624
904-468-2622

SINGLE-PARENT FAMILIES

Big Brothers/Big Sisters of America
230 N. 13th St.
Philadelphia, PA 19107
215-567-7000
http://www.bbbsa.org

Parents Without Partners
1650 South Dixie Highway, Suite 510
Boca Raton, FL 33432
561-391-8833
http://www.parentswithoutpartners.org

Single Mothers By Choice
P.O. Box 1642
New York, NY 10028
212-988-0993

RADIO AND TELEVISION NETWORKS

ABC, Inc.
77 W. 66th St.
New York, NY 10023
212-456-7777
http://www.abc.com

ABC, Inc.
500 S. Buena Vista St.
Burbank, CA 91521-4551
818-560-1000

American Movie Classics (AMC)
530 Fifth Ave., 6th Fl.
New York, NY 10036
212-382-5200

American Movie Classics (AMC)
Viewer Mail
200 Jericho Quadrangle
Jericho, NY 11753
516-803-3000
http://www.amctv.com

Arts & Entertainment Television Network (A&E)
235 E. 45th St.
New York, NY 10017
212-210-1400
http://www.AandE.com

Associated Press Broadcast Services
1825 K St., NW, Suite 800
Washington, DC 20006
800-821-4747
202-736-1105 or 800-527-7234 (Radio Division)
202-736-1155 (Television Division)
202-736-9500 (Broadcast News Center)
202-736-1116 or 800-342-5147 (Customer Service)
http://www.apbroadcast.com

Black Entertainment Television (BET)
2000 M St. NW
Washington, DC 20036
202-533-1990
http://www.bet.com

Black Entertainment Television (BET)
West Coast Headquarters
1840 Century Park E. #600
Los Angeles, CA 90067
310-552-8400
http://www.bet.com

Bravo Networks
200 Jericho Quadrangle
Jericho, NY 11753
800-531-0002
516-803-3000
http://www.bravotv.com

Cable News Network (CNN)
One CNN Center
Box 105366
Atlanta, GA 30348-5366
404-827-1700
http://www.cnn.com

Cable News Network (CNN)
New York Office
5 Penn Plaza, 20th Floor
New York, NY 10001
212-714-7800
http://www.cnn.com

Cable News Network Financial News (CNNFN)
Cable News Network (CNN)
5 Penn Plaza, 20th Floor
New York, NY 10001
800-959-4228
212-714-7800
http://www.cnnfn.com

Cable Satellite Public Affairs Network (C-Span)
400 N. Capitol St., NW, Suite 650
Washington, DC 20001
202-737-3220-765-464-3080 (viewer services)
http://www.c-span.org

Cartoon Network
1050 Techwood Dr., NW
Atlanta, GA 30318
4040-885-4390
http://cartoonnetwork.com

CBS Corporation
51 W. 52nd St.
New York, NY 10019-6188
212-975-4321
http://www.cbs.com

CBS Corporation
7800 Beverly Blvd.
Los Angeles, CA 90036
323-575-2345
http://www.cbs.com

Cinemax
1100 Avenue of the Americas
New York, NY 10036
212-512-1000
http://www.cinemax.com

Comedy Central
1775 Broadway
New York, NY 10019
212-767-8600
http://www.comcentral.com

Consumer News and Business Channel (CNBC)
2200 Fletcher Ave.
Fort Lee, NJ 07024
800-788-2622
877-251-5685 (viewer services)
http://www.cnbc.com

Consumer News and Business Channel (CNBC)
3000 W. Alameda Ave. #C296
Burbank, CA 91523
818-840-3214

Court TV
600 Third Ave.
New York, NY 10016
212-973-2800
http://www.courtv.com

The Discovery Channel
641 Lexington Ave., 8th Fl.
New York, NY 10022
212-751-2220
859-342-8439 (viewer relations)
http://www.discovery.com

Every year, thousands of people visit 12305 Fifth Helena Dr. in Brentwood, California. It's the first house that Marilyn Monroe owned and the house where she died.

The Disney Channel
3800 W. Alameda Ave.
Burbank, CA 91505
818-569-7500
http://disneychannel.disney.go.com/disneychannel

The Disney Channel
500 Park Ave., 7th Fl
New York, NY 10022
212-735-5380
http://disneychannel.disney.go.com/disneychannel

E! Entertainment Television, Inc.
11 W. 42nd St., 19th Floor
New York, NY 10036
212-852-5100
and
5750 Wilshire Blvd.
Los Angeles, CA 90036
323-954-2400
http://www.eonline.com

Entertainment and Sports Programming Network (ESPN)
935 Middle St.
Bristol, CT 06010
860-766-2000
http://www.espn.com

Fox Broadcasting Company
10201 W. Pico Blvd.
Los Angeles, CA 90035
310-369-1000
http://www.fox.com

Fox Broadcasting Company
P.O. Box 900
Beverly Hills, CA 90213
310-369-1000
http://www.fox.com

fX Network
10000 Santa Monica Boulevard
Los Angeles, CA 90067
310-286-3800
http://www.fxnetworks.com

fX Network
P.O. Box 900
Beverly Hills, CA 90213
http://www.fxnetworks.com

Game Show Network
550 Madison Ave.
New York, NY 10022
212-833-8500
http://www.gameshownetwork.com

The Golf Channel
90 Park Ave., #1700
New York, NY 10016
212-984-1056
http://www.golf.com/golfchannel

Home Box Office, Inc. (HBO)
1100 Avenue of the Americas
New York, NY 10036
212-512-1000
http://www.hbo.com

Home and Garden TV
9721 Sherrill Blvd.
Knoxville, TN 37932
865-694-2700 (corporate headquarters)
865-694-7879 (consumer questions)
http://www.hgtv.com

Home Shopping Networks
1 HSN Drive
St. Petersburg, FL 33729
727-872-1000
http://www.hsn.com

Independent Film Channel
11 Penn Plaza
New York, NY 10001
646-273-7200
http://www.ifctv.com

Independent Film Channel
Rainbow Media Holdings, Inc.
200 Jericho Quadrangle
Jericho, NY 11753

516-803-3000
http://www.ifctv.com

The Learning Channel
7700 Wisconsin Ave.
Bethesda, MD 20814-3522
301-986-1999
http://www.tlc.discovery.com

Lifetime Television
309 W. 49th St.
New York, NY 10019
212-474-7000
http://www.lifetimetv.com

Madison Square Garden Network (MSG)
Two Pennsylvania Plaza
New York, NY 10021
212-465-5926
http://www.msgnetwork.com

MSNBC
MSNBC TV
One MSNBC Plaza
Secaucus, NJ 07094
201-583-5000
201-583-5012 (MSNBC Cable)
http://www.msnbc.com

MTV Networks
MTV Studios
1515 Broadway
New York, NY 10036
212-258-8000
http://www.mtv.com/

MTV Networks
2600 Colorado Avenue
Santa Monica, CA 90404
310-752-8000
http://www.mtv.com/

TNN Networks
(The National Network, formerly The Nashville Network)
1515 Broadway #4228
New York, New York 10036
212-846-2566
888-POP-1090 (toll-free)
http://www.thenewtnn.com/

National Public Radio (NPR)
635 Massachusetts Avenue N.W.
Washington, D.C. 20001
202-513-2000
http://www.npr.org

NBC Cable Networks
2200 Fletcher Avenue
Fort Lee, NJ 07024
201-346-2314
http://www.nbc.com

NBC Studios/NBC News
30 Rockefeller Plaza
New York, N.Y. 10112
212-664-4444
212-664-3700 (tours)
http://www.nbc.com

NBC Entertainment
3000 West Alameda Avenue
Burbank, CA 91523
818-840-4444
http://www.nbc.com/

Nickelodeon/Nick at Night
1515 Broadway
New York City, NY 10036
212-258-7500
212-258-8000
800-NICK-NET
http://nick.com

Nickelodeon/Nick at Night
231 West Olive Ave.
Burbank, CA 91502
818-736-3000
http://nick.com

Hallmark Channel
12700 Ventura Blvd.
Studio City, CA 91604
212-930-1947
http://www.hallmarkchannel.com

OVATION—The Arts Network
5801 Duke Street
Suite D-112
Alexandria, VA 22304
800-OVATION
http://www.ovationtv.com/

The Playboy Channel
Corporate Headquarters
680 North Lake Shore Drive
Chicago, Illinois 60611
312-751-8000
http://www.playboy.com/

The Playboy Channel
New York Office
730 Fifth Avenue
New York, New York 10019

212-261-5000
http://www.playboy.com/

The Playboy Channel
Playboy Enterprises International, Inc.
9242 Beverly Boulevard
Beverly Hills, California 90210
310-246-4000
http://www.playboy.com/

Public Broadcasting Service (PBS)
Public Broadcasting Service
1320 Braddock Place
Alexandria, Virginia 22314
703-739-5000
http://www.pbs.org/

QVC
1200 Wilson Drive
West Chester, PA
888-81LOCAL
http://qvc.com

Reuters Information Services, Inc.
1700 Broadway
New York, NY 10019
212-273-1700

Reuters America
3 Times Sq.
New York, NY 10036
646-223-4000

The SciFi Channel
USA Networks
1230 Avenue of the Americas, 18th Floor
New York, NY 10020
212-413-5000
http://www.scifi.com/

Sheridan Broadcasting Corporation and American Urban Radio Network
960 Penn. Ave. #200
Pittsburgh, PA 15222
412-456-4000

Showtime
1633 Broadway, 17th Floor
NY, NY 10019
212-708-1275
http://www.sho.com/

The Travel Channel
7700 Wisconsin Avenue
Bethesda, MD 20814-3522
888-892-3484
http://travel.discovery.com/

Turner Classic Movies (TCM)
1050 Techwood Dr.
Atlanta, GA 30318.
404-827-1500
http://www.turnerclassicmovies.com

Turner Network Television (TNT)
One CNN Center
Box 105366
Atlanta, GA 30348-5366
404-827-1500
http://www.tnt.tv/

TV Food Network
1180 Avenue of the Americas, 12th Fl.
New York, NY 10036
212-398-8836
http://www.foodtv.com/

United Paramount Network (UPN)
11800 Wilshire Blvd
Los Angeles, CA 90025-6602
310-575-7000
http://www.upn.com/

United Press International (UPI)
World Headquarters
1510 H St.
Washington, DC 20005
202-898-8000
http://www.upi.com/

USA Network
1230 6th Ave
New York, NY 10020
212-408-9100
http://www.usanetwork.com/

VH1
1515 Broadway, 12th Floor
New York, NY 10036
212-258-8000
http://www.vh1.com/

Viewer's Choice
18 Bay St.
Box 787, Suite 100
Toronto, Ontario
M5J 2T3
416-965-2010
800-565-MOVIE (6684)
416-956-2083 (TTY/TDD)
800-661-6674 (TTY/TDD)

Warner Brothers Network
411 Hollywood Blvd.
Burbank, CA 91505

818-977-5000
http://wb.com

The Weather Channel
300 Interstate North Pkwy.
Atlanta, GA 30339-2404
800-471-5544
770-226-0000
http://www.weather.com/

Westwood One Inc.
9540 Washington Boulevard
Culver City, CA 90232
310-840-4000
http://www.westwoodone.com/

UNITED STATES SERVICE ACADEMIES

The Air Force Academy
Colorado Springs, CO 80840
719-333-3070 (Admissions)
719-472-0102 (Visitors Center)
http://www.usafa.af.mil/

The Merchant Marine Academy
300 Steamboat Rd
Kings Point, NY 11024
516-773-5000
http://www.usmma.edu/

US Military Academy
West Point, N.Y. 10996
Phone: (845) 938-4011
http://www.usma.edu/

US Naval Academy
121 Blake Road Annapolis,
Maryland 21402-5000
410-293-1000
410-236-6933 (Information and Tours)
800-778-4260 (Visitor Center)
http://www.usna.edu

ADDITIONAL SOURCES OF INFORMATION

MAGAZINES

AFRICAN AMERICAN INTEREST

Ebony
820 S. Michigan Ave.
Chicago, IL 60605
312-322-9200
http://ebony.com

Go to
"Newspapers" in chapter 25

Essence
1500 Broadway
New York, NY 10036
212-642-0600
http://www.essence.com

Jet
820 S. Michigan Ave.
Chicago, IL 60605-2103
312-322-9200
http://www.jetmag.com

Upscale
P.O. Box 10798
Atlanta, GA 30310
404-758-7467
http://www.upscalemagazine.com

AGING

Modern Maturity
American Association of Retired Persons
601 E St. NW
Washington, DC 20049-0001
202-434-6880
http://www.modernmaturity.org
http://www.aarp.org

My Generation
780 Third Ave.
New York, NY 10017
212-826-8877
http://www.mygeneration.org

New Choices
Reader's Digest Road
Pleasantlville, NY 10570-7000
914-238-1000
http://www.newchoices.com

CONSUMER INFORMATION AND PROTECTION

Consumer Reports
Consumers Union of the U.S., Inc.
101 Truman Ave.
Yonkers, NY 10703-1044
914-378-2200
http://www.consumerreports.org

GAY/LESBIAN

The Advocate
P.O. Box 4371
Los Angeles, CA 90078-4371

323-871-1225
http://www.advocate.com

Out Magazine
80 8th Ave., Suite 315
New York, NY 10011
http://www.out.com

GENERAL INTEREST

American Heritage
90 Fifth Ave,
New York, NY 10011
212-367-3100
http://www.americanheritage.com

The Atlantic Monthly
77 N. Washington St., Ste. 5
Boston, MA 02117
617-854-7700
http://www.theatlantic.com

Harpers
666 Broadway
New York, NY 10012
212-420-5720
http://www.harpers.org

National Geographic
1145 17th St., NW
Washington, DC 20036
202-857-7000
http://www.nationalgeographic.com

The New Yorker
4 Times Square
New York, NY 10036
212-286-2860
http://www.newyorker.com

People
1271 Avenue of the Americas
New York, NY 10020
212-522-1212
http://www.people.com

Reader's Digest
Reader's Digest Rd.
Pleasantville, NY 10570
914-238-1000
http://www.readersdigest.com

Smithsonian
750 9th St. NW
Suite 710MRC
Washington, DC 20560
202-275-2000
http://www.smithsonianmag.com

Utne Reader
1624 Harmon Place
Suite 330
Minneapolis, MN 55403
612-338-5040
http://www.utne.com

Vanity Fair
4 Times Square
New York, NY 10036
212-286-8180
http://www.vanityfair.com

HISPANIC AMERICAN INTEREST

Latina Magazine
1500 Broadway, 7th Fl.
New York, NY 10036
212-642-0200
http://www.latina.com

MEN'S INTERESTS

Details
7 West 34th St., 4th Fl.
New York, NY 10001
212-630-4000
http://www.details.com

Esquire
250 West 55th St., 7th Fl.
New York, NY 10019
212-649-4020
http://www.esquire.com

FHM—For Him Magazine
110 Fifth Ave.
New York, NY 10011
212-886-3600
http://www.fhmus.com

Gear
450 West 15th St.
New York, NY 10011
212-771-7000

GQ
4 Times Square
New York, NY 10036
212-286-2860
http://www.qc.com

Maxim
1040 Avenue of the Americas, 14th Fl.
New York, NY 10018
212-302-2626
http://www.maximonline.com

Men's Health
733 Third Ave., 15th Fl.
New York, NY 10017
212-697-2040
http://www.menshealth.com

Men's Journal
1290 Avenue of the Americas
New York, NY 10104
212-484-1616
http://www.mensjournal.com

Penthouse
11 Penn Plaza
New York, NY 10001
212-702-6000
http://www.penthouse.com

Playboy
680 N. Lake Shore Dr.
Chicago, IL 60611
312-751-8000
http://www.playboy.com

Stuff Magazine
1040 Avenue of the Americas
New York, NY 10018
212-372-3889
http://www.stuff-mag.com

PARENTING AND FAMILY

American Baby
1440 Broadway, 14th Fl.
New York, NY 10018
212-204-4200
http://www.americanbaby.com

Baby Talk
530 Fifth Ave.
New York, NY 10036
212-522-8989
http://www.parenting.com

Child Magazine
375 Lexington Ave.
New York, NY 10017
212-499-2000
http://www.child.com

Family
51 Atlantic Ave., Ste. 200
Floral Park, NY 11001
516-616-1930
http://www.familymedia.com

Family Digest
P.O. Box 3368
Danville, CA 94526-9568

925-838-4800
http://www.familydigest.com

Healthy Kids
1440 Broadway
New York, NY 10018
212-204-4200
http://www.healthykids.com

Lamaze Parents Magazine
9 Old Kings Highway S.
Darien, CT 06820-4505
203-656-3600
http://www.lamaze.com

Parenting Magazine
530 Fifth Ave.
New York, NY 10036
212-522-8989
http://www.parenting.com

Parents Magazine
375 Lexington Ave.
New York, NY 10017
212-499-2000
http://www.parents.com

Working Mother
135 West 50th St., 6th Fl.
New York, NY 10020-1208
212-445-6100
http://www.workingmother.com

WOMEN'S INTERESTS

Allure
4 Times Square
New York, NY 10036
212-286-7441
http://www.allure.com

Cosmopolitan
224 W. 57th St.
New York, NY 10019
212-649-3570
http://www.cosmomag.com

Elle
1633 Broadway
New York, NY 10019
212-767-5800
http://www.elle.com

Family Circle
375 Lexington Ave.
New York, NY 10017
212-499-2000
http://www.familycircle.com

Good Housekeeping
959 8th Ave.
New York, NY 10019
212-649-2200
http://www.goodhousekeeping.com

Harpers Bazaar
1700 Broadway
New York, NY 10019
212-903-5000
http://www.harpersbazaar.com

InStyle
1271 Avenue of the Americas
New York, NY 10020
212-522-1212
http://www.instyle.com

Jane
7 West 34th St.
New York, NY 10001
212-630-3900
http://www.janemag.com

Marie Claire
1790 Broadway
New York, NY 10019
212-649-5000
http://www.marieclaire.com

More
125 Park Ave.
New York, NY 10017
212-557-6600
http://www.more.com

Ms.
20 Exchange Place, 22nd Fl.
New York, NY 10005-509-2092
212-509-2092
http://www.msmagazine.com

O, The Oprah Magazine
1700 Broadway
New York, NY 10019
212-903-5000
http://www.oprah.com

Rosie
375 Lexington Ave.
New York, NY 10017
212-499-1772
http://www.rosie.com

Seventeen
850 Third Ave., 9th Fl.
New York, NY 10022
212-407-9700
http://www.seventeen .com

Vogue
4 Times Square
New York, NY 10036
212-286-286
http://www.vogue.com

W
7 West 34th St.
New York, NY 10001
212-630-4000
http://www.wmagazine.com

Woman's Day
1633 Broadway
New York, NY 10019
212-767-6000
http://www.womansday.com

Woman's World
270 Sylvan Ave.
Englewood Cliffs, NJ 07632
201-569-6699

YM
15 East 26th St.
New York, NY 10010
646-758-0555
http://www.ym.com

BOOKS

AGING

Beers, Mark & Steven Urice. *Aging in Good Health: A Complete Essential Medical Guide for Men and Women over Fifty and their Families.* Pocket Books, 1992.

Binstock, Robert H. and Linda K. George, eds. *Handbook of Aging and the Social Sciences,* 4th ed. Academic Press, 1995.

ALCOHOLISM AND DRUG ABUSE

Evans, Glen, et al. *The Encyclopedia of Alcoholism.* 2nd ed. Facts on File, 1991.

National Directory of Drug Abuse and Alcoholism Treatment and Prevention Programs. Gordon Press, 1991.

Sabroe, Knud-Erik. *Alcohol and Society: Patterns and Attitudes.* Coronet Books, 1994.

CONSUMER INFORMATION AND PROTECTION

Consumer Reports Buying Guide. Consumer Reports, annual.

Consumer Resource Handbook. U.S. Office of Consumer Affairs, annual.

DISABILITIES

Bondo, Bruce E. *Tax Options & Strategies: A State by State Guide for Persons with Disabilities, Senior Citizens, Veterans and their Families.* Demos Vermande, 1995.

Doyle, Brian. *Disability, Discrimination and Equal Opportunities: A Comparative Study of the Employment Rights of Disabled Persons.* Mansell, 1995.

Witt, Melanie A. *Job Strategies for People with Disabilities: Enable Yourself for Today's Job Market.* Peterson's Guides, 1992.

DOMESTIC VIOLENCE

Berry, Dawn Bradley. *Domestic Violence Sourcebook: Everything You Need to Know.* Lowell House, 1996.

FAMILY PLANNING

Freeman, Sarah and Vern Bullough. *The Complete Guide to Fertility and Family Planning.* Prometheus Books, 1992.

Pocket Guide for Family Planning Service Providers. J. H. Piego, 1995.

PARENTING

Casey, Eileen. *Maternity Leave: The Working Woman's Guide to Combining Pregnancy, Motherhood and Career.* Avon, 1995.

Starer, Dan. *Who to Call: The Parent's Sourcebook.* Quill, 1992.

GENERAL

Berkman, Robert L. *Find It Fast.* HarperPerennial, 1997.

The World Almanac and Book of Facts. World Almanac Books, annual.

V

RECREATION

23

SPORTS AND GAMES

AUTO RACING

Track races are held on oval asphalt tracks that are rectangular in shape with straightaways and banked (curved and sloped upward) corners. Road races are held on courses that include straight sections, hills, and various types of turns, such as hairpins and doglegs. Drag races are held on a drag strip, a straight paved track usually about 440 yards long.

Stock cars are late-model American-made production sedans (with front-mounted engines, doors, fenders, and a windshield) that have been modified to increase their power and speed. They typically race 200 to 600 miles on oval tracks.

Formula 1 cars are custom-built according to specifications that govern such elements as body design and engine size. The basic vehicle has a smooth contour to decrease air resistance, a low driver's seat in an open cockpit, no fenders, a spoiler near the back to hold the car to the road, and a rear-mounted engine. Formula 1 cars are used in Grand Prix races that are held on road courses up to 200 miles long.

When Barney Oldfield became the first man to drive a car 60 mph, most doctors claimed that such speed would cause deafness.

Indy cars are similar to Formula 1 cars but have different engine sizes, chassis (frame) formats, and transmission configurations. Such cars race on oval tracks for 150 miles or longer.

Drag-racing vehicles include *pro stock* (modified production cars) and *dragsters* (long, narrow-framed single seaters with large rear wheels).

AUTO RACING FLAGS

Flag	Message
Solid green	Indicates the start of an event: a race, a practice, etc. Signals that laps are being counted
Red and yellow, divided diagonally	Indicates the race must be restarted; usually shown after a yellow flag if the first lap has not been completed.
Blue with diagonal orange stripe	Signals a driver to let a faster driver overtake. Also called the "move over" flag.
Solid yellow	Signals drivers to proceed with caution; usually indicates an accident or debris on the track. In certain shorter races the lap count is suspended, in others such as NASCAR, Formula I, and Indy car, the laps are still counted
Solid red	Indicates danger. The race must stop and all drivers should turn off their engines. The lap count is suspended.
Solid black	Indicates a penalty on a particular car, which must leave the track. If the driver has broken a rule, a penalty is assessed. If the car is unfit to race, repairs must be made before the car can return to the track.
Solid white	Signals one lap remaining in a race. Displayed when the race leader crosses the finish line at the beginning of the final lap, and to all remaining cars until the leader again crosses the finish line
Black and white checkered	Signals the finish of the event: a race, a practice, etc. Waved when the leader passes the finish line.

INDIANAPOLIS 500

A major auto race in the United States for many years has been the Indianapolis 500, which consists of 250 laps around the 2½-mile-long oval track at the Indianapolis Motor Speedway in Indiana. The winners since 1911 follow.

Date	Driver	Car	Average m.p.h.
1911	Ray Harroun	Marmon	74.602
1912	Joe Dawson	National	78.719
1913	Jules Goux	Peugeot	75.933
1914	Rene Thomas	Delage	82.474
1915	Ralph DePalma	Mercedes	89.840
1916	Dario Resta	Peugeot	84.001[1]
1917	No race held		
1918	No race held		
1919	Howard Wilcox	Peugeot	85.050
1920	Gaston Chevrolet	Monroe	88.618
1921	Tommy Milton	Frontenac	89.621
1922	Jimmy Murphy	Murphy Special	94.484
1923	Tommy Milton	H.C.S. Special	90.954
1924	L. L. Corum–Joe Boyer	Duesenberg Special	98.234
1925	Peter DePaolo	Duesenberg Special	101.127
1926	Frank Lockhart	Miller Special	95.904[2]
1927	George Souders	Duesenberg Special	97.545
1928	Louis Meyer	Miller Special	99.482
1929	Ray Keech	Simplex Piston Ring Special	97.585
1930	Billy Arnold	Harry Hartz Special	100.448
1931	Louis Schneider	Bowes Seal Fast Special	96.629
1932	Fred Frame	Miller-Hartz Special	104.144
1933	Louis Meyer	Tydol Special	104.162
1934	William Cummings	Boyle Products Special	104.863
1935	Kelly Petillo	Gilmore Speedway Special	106.240
1936	Louis Meyer	Ring Free Special	109.069
1937	Wilbur Shaw	Shaw-Gilmore Special	113.580
1938	Floyd Roberts	Burd Piston Ring Special	117.200
1939	Wilbur Shaw	Bolye Special	115.035
1940	Wilbur Shaw	Bolye Special	114.277
1941	Floyd Davis–Mauri Rose	Noc-Out Hose Clamp Special	115.117
1942	No race held		
1943	No race held		
1944	No race held		
1945	No race held		
1946	George Robson	Thorne Engineering Special	114.820
1947	Mauri Rose	Blue Crown Spark Plug Special	116.338
1948	Mauri Rose	Blue Crown Spark Plug Special	119.814
1949	Bill Holland	Blue Crown Spark Plug Special	121.327
1950	Johnny Parsons	Kurtiss-Kraft Wynns Special	124.001[3]
1951	Lee Wallard	Belanger Special	126.244
1952	Troy Ruttman	Agajanian Special	128.922
1953	William Vukovich	Fuel Injection Special	128.740
1954	William Vukovich	Fuel Injection Special	130.840
1955	Robert Sweikert	Zink Special	128.209
1956	Pat Flaherty	Zink Special	128.490
1957	Sam Hanks	Belond Exhaust Special	135.601
1958	Jimmy Bryan	Belond Special	133.791
1959	Rodger Ward	Leader CARD Special	135.856
1960	Jim Rathmann	Ken-Paul Special	138.767
1961	A. J. Foyt	Bowes Special	139.130
1962	Rodger Ward	Leader Card Special	140.292

[1] 300 miles [2] 400 miles [3] 345 miles

continues

Indianapolis 500 Winners, Continued

Date	Driver	Car	Average m.p.h.
1963	Parnelli Jones	Agajanian Special	143.137
1964	A. J. Foyt	Sheraton-Thompson Special	147.350
1965	Jim Clark	Lotus-Ford	150.686
1966	Graham Hill	Lola-Ford	144.317
1967	A. J. Foyt	Coyote Ford	151.207
1968	Bobby Unser	Offenhauser-Eagle	152.882
1969	Mario Andretti	Hawk-Ford	156.867
1970	Al Unser	P. J. Colt-Ford	155.749
1971	Al Unser	Johnny Lightning Special	157.735
1972	Mark Donohue	Sunoco McLaren-Offy	162.962
1973	Gordon Johncock	Eagle-Offenhauser	159.036[4]
1974	Johnny Rutherford	McLaren-Offenhauser	158.589
1975	Bobby Unser	Eagle-Offenhauser	149.213[5]
1976	Johnny Rutherford	McLaren-Offenhauser	148.725[6]
1977	A. J. Foyt	Coyote-Foyt	161.331
1978	Al Unser	Lola-Cosworth	161.363
1979	Rick Mears	Penske-Cosworth	158.899
1980	Johnny Rutherford	Chaparral	142.862
1981	Bobby Unser	Penske-Cosworth	138.085
1982	Gordon Johncock	Wildcat-Cosworth	162.026
1983	Tom Sneva	March-Cosworth	162.117
1984	Rick Mears	March-Cosworth	163.612
1985	Danny Sullivan	March-Cosworth	152.982
1986	Bobby Rahal	March-Cosworth	170.722
1987	Al Unser	March-Cosworth	162.175
1988	Rick Mears	Penske-Chevrolet	149.809
1989	Emerson Fittipaldi	Penske-Chevrolet	167.581
1990	Arie Luyendyk	Lola-Chevrolet	185.981
1991	Rick Mears	Penske-Chevrolet	176.460
1992	Al Unser, Jr.	Galmer-Chevrolet	134.479
1993	Emerson Fittipaldi	Penske-Chevrolet	157.207
1994	Al Unser, Jr.	Penske-Ilmor Mercedes	160.872
1995	Jacques Villeneuve	Reynard-Ford Cosworth	153.616
1996	Buddy Lazier	Reynard-Ford Cosworth	147.956
1997	Arie Luyendyk	G-Force Aurora	145.827
1998	Eddie Cheever Jr.	Dallara-Aurora	145.155
1999	Kenny Brack	Dallara-Aurora	153.176
2000	Juan Montoya	G. Force-Aurora	167.607
2001	Helio Castroneves	Dallara-Aurora	153.601

[4] 332.5 miles   [5] 435 miles   [6] 255 miles

BASEBALL

Baseball, named for the three bases and home plate that are parts of the playing field, has 9 or 10 players on each side. The offensive team sends to home plate one batter at a time, who uses a wooden or metal bat to try to hit a small cowhide-covered ball thrown from the pitcher to the catcher, two members of the defensive team. The defensive team also consists of four infielders and three outfielders. If the batter hits the ball on the ground, he must run to-

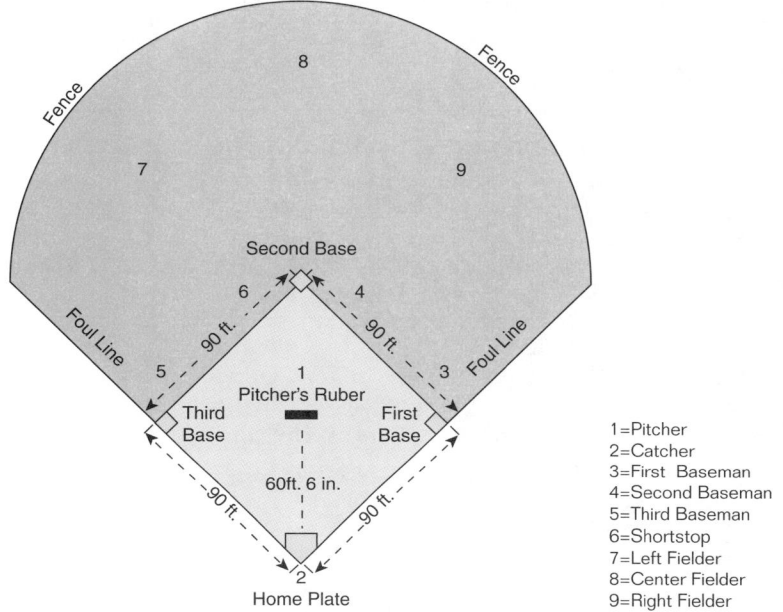

Baseball Field

1=Pitcher
2=Catcher
3=First Baseman
4=Second Baseman
5=Third Baseman
6=Shortstop
7=Left Fielder
8=Center Fielder
9=Right Fielder

ward first base; he is out if a defensive player throws the ball to a teammate standing on first base before the runner reaches the base. The batter is also out if the ball he hits is caught by a defensive player before it hits the ground. A strike is called if the batter in a swing fails to strike the pitched ball, fails to swing at a pitch determined by the umpire to be a strike, or hits the ball into foul territory. Three strikes put the batter out (a strikeout). Outs may also be made when a defensive player who has the ball tags a base runner when the runner is between bases, or when a defensive player who has the ball steps on second base, third base, or home plate if the runner is forced to move to that base because the batter or another base runner is moving to occupy the preceding base.

The offensive team attempts to score runs by causing offensive base runners to go around all four bases and cross home plate safely. The offensive team scores runs by accumulating hits, which are balls hit between the two foul lines that go uncaught, allowing a batter to safely reach first base (a single), second base (a double), or third base (a triple), thus driving runners ahead of him to circle the bases. Batters can also reach base and move the runners ahead a base by obtaining a walk, four pitches that the batter does not swing at and that are determined by the umpire not to be strikes. Runs also can be scored with a home run, whereby a batter hits the ball over the outfield fence or far enough that he can circle the bases. The game is divided into nine innings, with three outs for each team in each inning. The batting, or offensive, team takes the field (defensive positions) after making three outs, when the opponents become batters. At the end of nine innings, the team that has accumulated the most runs is the winner. If both teams have scored the same number of runs at the end of nine innings, extra innings are played until the tie is broken.

Cleveland Indians star Lou Boudreau blew his nose and blew a game. He forgot that putting a towel to his face was the "steal" sign.

U.S. AND CANADIAN MAJOR LEAGUE BASEBALL TEAMS

AMERICAN LEAGUE (AL)

Eastern Division	Central Division	Western Division
Baltimore Orioles	Chicago White Sox	Anaheim Angels
Boston Red Sox	Cleveland Indians	Oakland Athletics
New York Yankees	Detroit Tigers	Seattle Mariners
Tampa Bay Devil Rays	Kansas City Royals	Texas Rangers
Toronto Blue Jays	Minnesota Twins	

NATIONAL LEAGUE (NL)

Eastern Division	Central Division	Western Division
Atlanta Braves	Chicago Cubs	Arizona Diamondbacks
Florida Marlins	Cincinnati Reds	Colorado Rockies
Montreal Expos	Houston Astros	Los Angeles Dodgers
New York Mets	Milwaukee Brewers	San Diego Padres
Philadelphia Phillies	Pittsburgh Pirates	San Francisco Giants
	St. Louis Cardinals	

WORLD SERIES

After each major league team plays a regular-season schedule of 162 games, the three division winners in each league plus a wild-card team (the second-place division team with the best won-lost record) meet in a series of playoffs to determine the league pennant winner. The American League pennant winner then meets the National League pennant winner in October in a best-of-seven-games World Series for the major league championship that has been played since 1903 (except for the years 1904 and 1994). A best-of-nine-games World Series was played in 1903, 1919, 1920, and 1921. Tied games were played in 1907 and 1912. Winners and losers of the World Series follow.

Year	Winner	League	Loser	League	Games
1903	Boston Red Sox	AL	Pittsburgh Pirates	NL	5–3
1904	No series				
1905	New York Giants	NL	Philadelphia Athletics	AL	4–1
1906	Chicago White Sox	AL	Chicago Cubs	NL	4–2
1907	Chicago Cubs	NL	Detroit Tigers	AL	4–0–1
1908	Chicago Cubs	NL	Detroit Tigers	AL	4–1
1909	Pittsburgh Pirates	NL	Detroit Tigers	AL	4–3
1910	Philadelphia Athletics	AL	Chicago Cubs	NL	4–1
1911	Philadelphia Athletics	AL	New York Giants	NL	4–2
1912	Boston Red Sox	AL	New York Giants	NL	4–3–1
1913	Philadelphia Athletics	AL	New York Giants	NL	4–1
1914	Boston Braves	NL	Philadelphia Athletics	AL	4–0
1915	Boston Red Sox	AL	Philadelphia Phillies	NL	4–1
1916	Boston Red Sox	AL	Brooklyn Dodgers	NL	4–1
1917	Chicago White Sox	AL	New York Giants	NL	4–2
1918	Boston Red Sox	AL	Chicago Cubs	NL	4–2
1919	Cincinnati Reds	NL	Chicago White Sox	AL	5–3

Sports/Games

Year	Winner	League	Loser	League	Games
1920	Cleveland Indians	AL	Brooklyn Dodgers	NL	5–2
1921	New York Giants	NL	New York Yankees	AL	5–3
1922	New York Giants	NL	New York Yankees	AL	4–0
1923	New York Yankees	AL	New York Giants	NL	4–2
1924	Washington Senators	AL	New York Giants	NL	4–3
1925	Pittsburgh Pirates	NL	Washington Senators	AL	4–3
1926	St. Louis Cardinals	NL	New York Yankees	AL	4–3
1927	New York Yankees	AL	Pittsburgh Pirates	NL	4–0
1928	New York Yankees	AL	St. Louis Cardinals	NL	4–0
1929	Philadelphia Athletics	AL	Chicago Cubs	NL	4–1
1930	Philadelphia Athletics	AL	St. Louis Cardinals	NL	4–2
1931	St. Louis Cardinals	NL	Philadelphia Athletics	AL	4–3
1932	New York Yankees	AL	Chicago Cubs	NL	4–0
1933	New York Giants	NL	Washington Senators	AL	4–1
1934	St. Louis Cardinals	NL	Detroit Tigers	AL	4–3
1935	Detroit Tigers	AL	Chicago Cubs	NL	4–2
1936	New York Yankees	AL	New York Giants	NL	4–2
1937	New York Yankees	AL	New York Giants	NL	4–1
1938	New York Yankees	AL	Chicago Cubs	NL	4–0
1939	New York Yankees	AL	Cincinnati Reds	NL	4–0
1940	Cincinnati Reds	NL	Detroit Tigers	AL	4–3
1941	New York Yankees	AL	Brooklyn Dodgers	NL	4–1
1942	St. Louis Cardinals	NL	New York Yankees	AL	4–1
1943	New York Yankees	AL	St. Louis Cardinals	NL	4–1
1944	St. Louis Cardinals	NL	St. Louis Browns	AL	4–2
1945	Detroit Tigers	AL	Chicago Cubs	NL	4–3
1946	St. Louis Cardinals	NL	Boston Red Sox	AL	4–3
1947	New York Yankees	AL	Brooklyn Dodgers	NL	4–3
1948	Cleveland Indians	AL	Boston Braves	NL	4–2
1949	New York Yankees	AL	Brooklyn Dodgers	NL	4–1
1950	New York Yankees	AL	Philadelphia Phillies	NL	4–0
1951	New York Yankees	AL	New York Giants	NL	4–2
1952	New York Yankees	AL	Brooklyn Dodgers	NL	4–3
1953	New York Yankees	AL	Brooklyn Dodgers	NL	4–2
1954	New York Giants	NL	Cleveland Indians	AL	4–0
1955	Brooklyn Dodgers	NL	New York Yankees	AL	4–3
1956	New York Yankees	AL	Brooklyn Dodgers	NL	4–3
1957	Milwaukee Braves	NL	New York Yankees	AL	4–3
1958	New York Yankees	AL	Milwaukee Braves	NL	4–3
1959	Los Angeles Dodgers	NL	Chicago White Sox	AL	4–2
1960	Pittsburgh Pirates	NL	New York Yankees	AL	4–3
1961	New York Yankees	AL	Cincinnati Reds	NL	4–1
1962	New York Yankees	AL	San Francisco Giants	NL	4–3
1963	Los Angeles Dodgers	NL	New York Yankees	AL	4–0
1964	St. Louis Cardinals	NL	New York Yankees	AL	5–3
1965	Los Angeles Dodgers	NL	Minnesota Twins	AL	4–3
1966	Baltimore Orioles	AL	Los Angeles Dodgers	NL	4–0
1967	St. Louis Cardinals	NL	Boston Red Sox	AL	4–3
1968	Detroit Tigers	AL	St. Louis Cardinals	NL	4–3
1969	New York Mets	NL	Baltimore Orioles	AL	4–1
1970	Baltimore Orioles	AL	Cincinnati Reds	NL	4–1
1971	Pittsburgh Pirates	NL	Baltimore Orioles	AL	4–3

Sports/Games

continues

World Series Winners, Continued

Year	Winner	League	Loser	League	Games
1972	Oakland Athletics	AL	Cincinnati Reds	NL	4–3
1973	Oakland Athletics	AL	New York Mets	NL	4–3
1974	Oakland Athletics	AL	Los Angeles Dodgers	NL	4–1
1975	Cincinnati Reds	NL	Boston Red Sox	AL	4–3
1976	Cincinnati Reds	NL	New York Yankees	AL	4–0
1977	New York Yankees	AL	Los Angeles Dodgers	NL	4–2
1978	New York Yankees	AL	Los Angeles Dodgers	NL	4–2
1979	Pittsburgh Pirates	NL	Baltimore Orioles	AL	4–3
1980	Philadelphia Phillies	NL	Kansas City Royals	AL	4–2
1981	Los Angeles Dodgers	NL	New York Yankees	AL	4–2
1982	St. Louis Cardinals	NL	Milwaukee Brewers	AL	4–3
1983	Baltimore Orioles	AL	Philadelphia Phillies	NL	4–1
1984	Detroit Tigers	AL	San Diego Padres	NL	4–1
1985	Kansas City Royals	AL	St. Louis Cardinals	NL	4–3
1986	New York Mets	NL	Boston Red Sox	AL	4–3
1987	Minnesota Twins	AL	St. Louis Cardinals	NL	4–3
1988	Los Angeles Dodgers	NL	Oakland Athletics	AL	4–1
1989	Oakland Athletics	AL	San Francisco Giants	NL	4–0
1990	Cincinnati Reds	NL	Oakland Athletics	AL	4–1
1991	Minnesota Twins	AL	Atlanta Braves	NL	4–3
1992	Toronto Blue Jays	AL	Atlanta Braves	NL	4–3
1993	Toronto Blue Jays	AL	Philadelphia Phillies	NL	4–2
1994	No series				
1995	Atlanta Braves	NL	Cleveland Indians	AL	4–2
1996	New York Yankees	AL	Atlanta Braves	NL	4–2
1997	Florida Marlins	NL	Cleveland Indians	AL	4–3
1998	New York Yankees	AL	San Diego Padres	NL	4–0
1999	New York Yankees	AL	Atlanta Braves	NL	4–0
2000	New York Yankees	AL	New York Mets	NL	4–1
2001	Arizona Diamondbacks	NL	New York Yankees	AL	4–3

BASKETBALL

Basketball usually is played indoors on a rectangular wooden court by two teams, each with five players. At both ends of the court are suspended two goals, or baskets (18 inches in diameter), consisting of a circular metal rim 10 feet above the floor attached to a square backboard made of wood, plastic, or fiberglass. A cord net is hung below the rim. The object is to shoot the ball so that it goes through the basket from above and to prevent your opponents from doing the same. Basketball uses a large rubber ball covered with leather.

Play begins with a jump ball. The official throws the ball upward at the center circle between two opposing players. The two players try to tip or slap the ball to a teammate and thus gain possession of the ball. Each team defends one goal. There are offensive and defensive halves of the court for each team, divided by the midcourt line. A player advances the ball down the court by passing to a teammate, dribbling (bouncing the ball while walking or running), or shooting the ball at the basket. Running or walking while holding the ball is not permitted. If a shot goes in the basket, two points are awarded to the shooting team. If a shot is missed (usually hitting the rim or backboard), a defensive player may rebound the ball (catch it as it bounces away from the basket). He then may begin to advance the ball to the other end of the court in preparation for a shot by his team. An offensive player may also rebound a missed shot and shoot again. A shot made from beyond the three-point line (22 feet from the center of the basket on NBA courts) scores three points instead of the usual two.

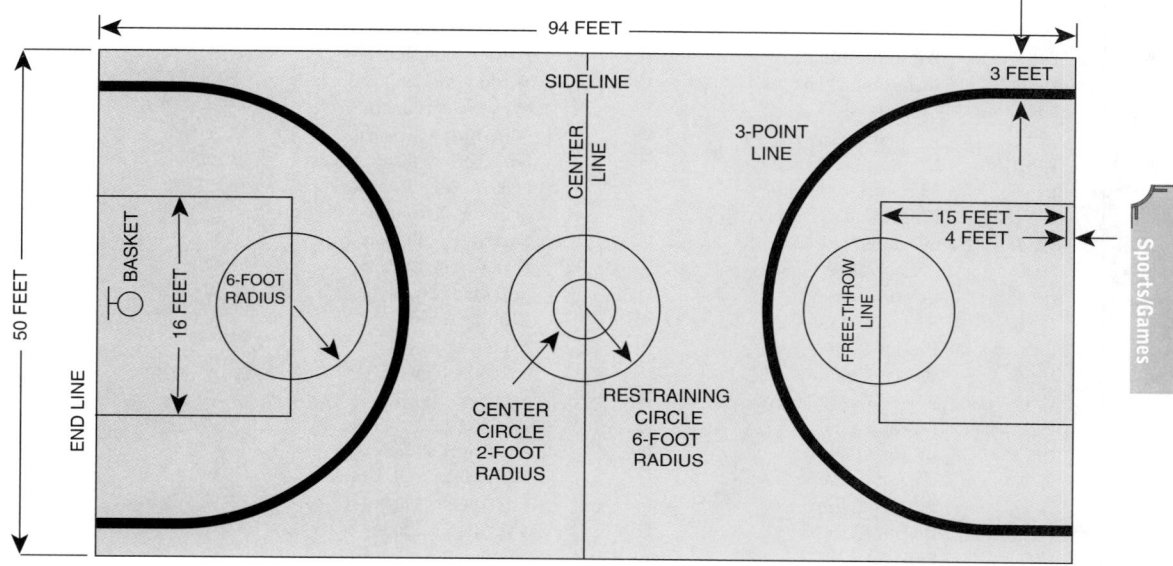

Basketball Court

Holding, pushing, grabbing, and similar types of body contact are not permitted; these are called fouls. They may result in a foul shot or free throw, an unimpeded shot taken by the offended player from a line on the court 15 feet from the basket. A successful free throw scores one point.

Professional basketball games are divided into four 12-minute quarters; the team with more points at the end of that time wins the game.

NATIONAL BASKETBALL ASSOCIATION (NBA) TEAMS
EASTERN CONFERENCE

Atlantic Division	Central Division
Boston Celtics	Atlanta Hawks
Miami Heat	Chicago Bulls
New Jersey Nets	Cleveland Cavaliers
New York Knicks	Detroit Pistons
Orlando Magic	Indiana Pacers
Philadelphia 76ers	Milwaukee Bucks
Washington Wizards	New Orleans Hornets
	Toronto Raptors

WESTERN CONFERENCE

Midwest Division	Pacific Division
Dallas Mavericks	Golden State Warriors
Denver Nuggets	Los Angeles Clippers
Houston Rockets	Los Angeles Lakers
Minnesota Timberwolves	Phoenix Suns
San Antonio Spurs	Portland Trail Blazers
Utah Jazz	Sacramento Kings
Vancouver Grizzlies	Seattle SuperSonics

NATIONAL BASKETBALL ASSOCIATION CHAMPIONS

After each National Basketball Association (NBA) team plays a regular-season schedule of 82 games, the eight teams in each conference with the best won-lost records meet in a series of play-offs to determine the conference champion. The Eastern Conference champion then meets the Western Conference champion in the spring in a best-of-seven-games series for the NBA championship. Winners and losers of the NBA championship series are listed on the next page.

Year	NBA Winners	Conference	Losers	Conference	Games
1947	Philadelphia Warriors	E	Chicago Stags	W	4–1
1948	Baltimore Bullets	W	Philadelphia Warriors	E	4–2
1949	Minneapolis Lakers	W	Washington Capitols	E	4–2
1950	Minneapolis Lakers	W	Syracuse Nationals	E	4–2
1951	Rochester Royals	W	New York Knickerbockers	E	4–3
1952	Minneapolis Lakers	W	New York Knickerbockers	E	4–3
1953	Minneapolis Lakers	W	New York Knickerbockers	E	4–1
1954	Minneapolis Lakers	W	Syracuse Nationals	E	4–3
1955	Syracuse Nationals	E	Fort Wayne Pistons	W	4–3
1956	Philadelphia Warriors	E	Fort Wayne Pistons	W	4–1
1957	Boston Celtics	E	St. Louis Hawks	W	4–3
1958	St. Louis Hawks	W	Boston Celtics	E	4–2
1959	Boston Celtics	E	Minneapolis Lakers	W	4–0
1960	Boston Celtics	E	St. Louis Hawks	W	4–3
1961	Boston Celtics	E	St. Louis Hawks	W	4–1
1962	Boston Celtics	E	Los Angeles Lakers	W	4–3
1963	Boston Celtics	E	Los Angeles Lakers	W	4–2
1964	Boston Celtics	E	San Francisco Warriors	W	4–1
1965	Boston Celtics	E	Los Angeles Lakers	W	4–1
1966	Boston Celtics	E	Los Angeles Lakers	W	4–3
1967	Philadelphia 76ers	E	San Francisco Warriors	W	4–2
1968	Boston Celtics	E	Los Angeles Lakers	W	4–2
1969	Boston Celtics	E	Los Angeles Lakers	W	4–3
1970	New York Knickerbockers	E	Los Angeles Lakers	W	4–3
1971	Milwaukee Bucks	W	Baltimore Bullets	E	4–0
1972	Los Angeles Lakers	W	New York Knickerbockers	E	4–1
1973	New York Knickerbockers	E	Los Angeles Lakers	W	4–1
1974	Boston Celtics	E	Milwaukee Bucks	W	4–3
1975	Golden State Warriors	W	Washington Bullets	E	4–0
1976	Boston Celtics	E	Phoenix Suns	W	4–2
1977	Portland Trail Blazers	W	Philadelphia 76ers	E	4–2
1978	Washington Bullets	E	Seattle Supersonics	W	4–3
1979	Seattle Supersonics	W	Washington Bullets	E	4–1
1980	Los Angeles Lakers	W	Philadelphia 76ers	E	4–2
1981	Boston Celtics	E	Houston Rockets	W	4–2
1982	Los Angeles Lakers	W	Philadelphia 76ers	E	4–2
1983	Philadelphia 76ers	E	Los Angeles Lakers	W	4–0
1984	Boston Celtics	E	Los Angeles Lakers	W	4–3
1985	Los Angeles Lakers	W	Boston Celtics	E	4–2
1986	Boston Celtics	E	Houston Rockets	W	4–2
1987	Los Angeles Lakers	W	Boston Celtics	E	4–2
1988	Los Angeles Lakers	W	Detroit Pistons	E	4–3
1989	Detroit Pistons	E	Los Angeles Lakers	W	4–0
1990	Detroit Pistons	E	Portland Trail Blazers	W	4–1
1991	Chicago Bulls	E	Los Angeles Lakers	W	4–1
1992	Chicago Bulls	E	Portland Trail Blazers	W	4–2
1993	Chicago Bulls	E	Phoenix Suns	W	4–2
1994	Houston Rockets	W	New York Knickerbockers	E	4–3
1995	Houston Rockets	W	Orlando Magic	W	4–0
1996	Chicago Bulls	E	Seattle Supersonics	W	4–2
1997	Chicago Bulls	E	Utah Jazz	W	4–2
1998	Chicago Bulls	E	Utah Jazz	W	4–2
1999	San Antonio Spurs	W	New York Knicks	E	4–1
2000	Los Angeles Lakers	W	Indiana Pacers	E	4–2
2001	Los Angles Lakers	W	Philadelphia 76ers	E	4–1

BICYCLE RACING

Road-racing bicycles have a free front wheel, multiple gears on the rear wheel, and a brake for each wheel. Track-racing bicycles have a single fixed gear on the rear wheel and no brakes. Cyclo-cross bicycles have typical road gears but have stronger rims and fatter tires.

The basic types of road races are (1) *time trials,* in which cyclists start at intervals and race either over a fixed distance (generally between 10 and 100 miles) to achieve the fastest time, or for a fixed time (generally 12 or 24 hours) to achieve the longest distance; (2) *criteriums,* in which cyclists ride a predetermined number of laps (covering a total distance ranging from 10 to 60 miles) on a closed circuit of 1 to 3 miles; (3) *road races,* in which cyclists ride from point to point, around several long circuits, or complete a combination of the two over a course that features long, steep climbs; and (4) *multiday stage races,* lasting from three days to three weeks, that include a combination of time trials, criteriums, and road races and whose winner is the cyclist with the lowest accumulated time for all stages.

Track races are held on steeply banked tracks either outdoors or inside buildings called *velodromes.* The basic types of track races are (1) *sprints,* in which two or more cyclists compete over a short distance (generally 1,000 meters for men and 500 meters for women); (2) *handicaps,* a massed-start event where the order in which each cyclist starts is determined by past proven speed; and (3) *pursuits,* in which two cyclists or teams start directly opposite from each other and then try to catch up to one another (over a distance of 4 to 5 kilometers) before reaching the finish.

In cyclo-cross races (generally 1 to 15 kilometers long), cyclists race off-road and encounter such obstacles as fences, streams, mud, sand, forests, ditches, fallen trees, gates, creek beds, and artificial hurdles, forcing them to dismount occasionally and carry their bicycles.

TOUR DE FRANCE

The most famous stage race is the Tour de France, a three-week event held annually in France and portions of other European countries in late June and early July and ranging in length from 2,500 to 3,000 miles. The course is changed each year and includes steep mountain climbs. Winners of the Tour de France follow.

Year	Cyclist	Home Country
1903	Maurice Garin	France
1904	Henri Cornet	France
1905	Louis Trousselier	France
1906	Rene Pottier	France
1907	Lucien Petit-Breton	France
1908	Lucien Petit-Breton	France
1909	Francois Faber	France
1910	Octave Lapize	France
1911	Gustave Garrigou	France
1912	Odile Defraye	Belgium
1913	Phillippe Thys	Belgium
1914	Phillippe Thys	Belgium
1915	*Race not held*	
1916	*Race not held*	
1917	*Race not held*	
1918	*Race not held*	
1919	Firmin Lambot	Belgium
1920	Philippe Thys	Belgium
1921	Leon Scieur	Belgium

Year	Cyclist	Home Country
1922	Firmin Lambot	Belgium
1923	Henri Pelissier	France
1924	Ottavio Bottecchia	Italy
1925	Ottavio Bottecchia	Italy
1926	Lucien Buysse	Belgium
1927	Nicolas Frantz	Luxembourg
1928	Nicolas Frantz	Luxembourg
1929	Maurice Dewaele	Belgium
1930	Andre Leducq	France
1931	Antonin Magne	Italy
1932	Andre Leducq	France
1933	Georges Speicher	France
1934	Antonin Magne	Italy
1935	Romain Maes	Belgium
1936	Sylvere Maes	Belgium
1937	Roger Lapebie	France
1938	Gino Bartali	Italy
1939	Sylvere Maes	Belgium
1940	*Race not held*	

continues

Tour de France Winners, Continued

Year	Cyclist	Home Country
1941	*Race not held*	
1942	*Race not held*	
1943	*Race not held*	
1944	*Race not held*	
1945	*Race not held*	
1946	*Race not held*	
1947	Jean Robic	France
1948	Gino Bartali	Italy
1949	Fausto Coppi	Italy
1950	Fredi Kubler	Switzerland
1951	Hugo Koblet	Switzerland
1952	Fausto Coppi	Italy
1953	Louison Bobet	France
1954	Louison Bobet	France
1955	Louison Bobet	France
1956	Roger Walkowiak	France
1957	Jacques Anquetil	France
1958	Charly Gaul	Luxembourg
1959	Fredrico Bahamontes	Spain
1960	Gastone Nencimi	Italy
1961	Jacques Anquetil	France
1962	Jacques Anquetil	France
1963	Jacques Anquetil	France
1964	Jacques Anquetil	France
1965	Felice Gimondi	Italy
1966	Lucien Aimar	France
1967	Roger Pingeon	France
1968	Jan Janssen	Holland
1969	Eddy Merckx	Belgium
1970	Eddy Merckx	Belgium
1971	Eddy Merckx	Belgium

Year	Cyclist	Home Country
1972	Eddy Merckx	Belgium
1973	Luis Ocana	Spain
1974	Eddy Merckx	Belgium
1975	Bernard Thevenet	France
1976	Lucien Van Impe	Belgium
1977	Baernard Thevenet	France
1978	Bernard Hinault	France
1979	Bernard Hinault	France
1980	Joop Zoetemelk	Holland
1981	Bernard Hinault	France
1982	Bernard Hinault	France
1983	Laurent Fignon	France
1984	Laurent Fignon	France
1985	Bernard Hinault	France
1986	Greg LeMond	United States
1987	Stephen Roche	Ireland
1988	Pedro Delgado	Spain
1989	Greg LeMond	United States
1990	Greg LeMond	United States
1991	Miguel Indurain	Spain
1992	Miguel Indurain	Spain
1993	Miguel Indurain	Spain
1994	Miguel Indurain	Spain
1995	Miguel Indurain	Spain
1996	Bjarne Riis	Denmark
1997	Jan Ullrich	Germany
1998	Marco Pantani	Italy
1999	Lance Armstrong	United States
2000	Lance Armstrong	United States
2001	Lance Armstrong	United States

BOWLING

Bowling, or tenpins, is an indoor sport in which a player attempts to knock down 10 wooden pins that are arranged in a triangular formation. The player accomplishes this by rolling a ball down a wooden lane, or alley. The ball, which weighs at most about 16 pounds, is fitted with three holes for thumb and finger grips. Each game is divided into 10 frames, and the bowler is allowed a maximum of two rolls per frame, except for the last frame, where he is allowed three. If a player knocks down all 10 pins with one roll, it is called a strike; the second roll of the frame is not used, except for the 10th frame, where three strikes are possible. If a player knocks down all 10 pins using both rolls of the frame, it is called a spare. The number of pins knocked down by the end of the game determines the score, with spares scoring 10 plus the number of pins knocked down on the next roll, and strikes scoring 10 plus the number of pins knocked down on the next two rolls. A perfect game of 12 consecutive strikes scores 300.

FOOTBALL

American football has 11 players on each team and is played on a large rectangular field. At each end of the field is an end zone, where the goalposts are placed. The object is to gain possession of an inflated leather or pigskin ball and move it across the opponents' goal line by running or passing, thus scoring a touchdown, which is worth six points.

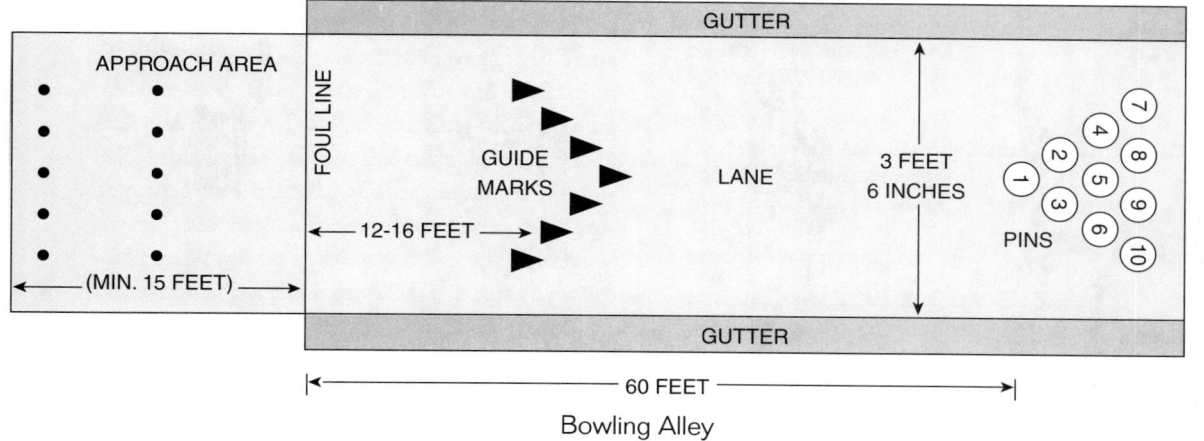

Bowling Alley

Passing the ball is usually done by the quarterback. Players also score points by kicking the ball through the goalposts. This opportunity is given automatically after a touchdown; the point is called a point after touchdown, or extra point. A field goal scores three points. The defensive team can score by downing an offensive player in his own end zone. This is called a safety and scores two points.

The term "down" in football has been used since the late 19th century. When a ball carrier was tackled, he would yell "down" to keep opponents from piling on top of him.

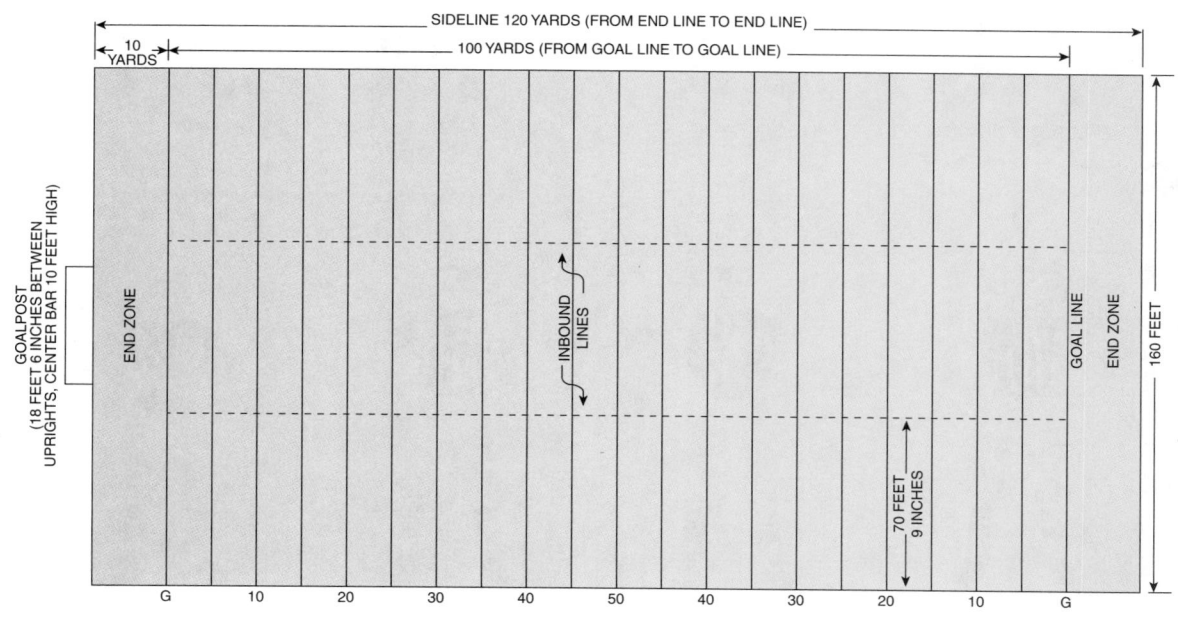

Football Field

Sports/Games

Official Football Signals

TOUCHDOWN, FIELD GOAL, or SUCCESSFUL TRY

ILLEGAL FORWARD PASS
If followed by raised hand flung downward: INTENTIONAL GROUNDING OF PASS.

FIRST DOWN

DEAD BALL or NEUTRAL ZONE ESTABLISHED
With raised fist closed: FOURTH DOWN.

LOSS OF DOWN

ILLEGAL CHUCKING

NO TIME-OUT or TIME-IN WITH WHISTLE

DELAY OF GAME or EXCESS TIME-OUT
If followed by forearms rotated over and over in front of body: ILLEGAL FORMATION.

PERSONAL FOUL

HOLDING

ILLEGAL USE OF HANDS

PENALTY REFUSED, INCOMPLETE PASS, PLAY OVER, or MISSED GOAL

Sports/Games

DOUBLE TOUCH

PASS JUGGLED IN-
BOUNDS AND CAUGHT
OUT OF BOUNDS

SAFETY

INTERFERENCE WITH
FORWARD PASS or
FAIR CATCH

INVALID FAIR
CATCH SIGNAL

INELIGIBLE RECEIVER, or IN-
ELIGIBLE MEMBER OF KICK-
ING TEAM DOWNFIELD

TIME-OUT
If followed by placing one hand on
top of cap: REFEREE'S TIME-
OUT; if followed by arm swung at
side: TOUCHBACK.

OFFSIDE, ENCROACHING,
or FREE KICK VIOLATION

ILLEGAL MOTION AT SNAP

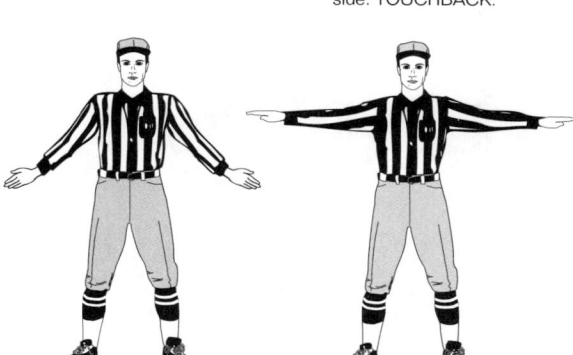

CRAWLING, PUSHING, or
HELPING RUNNER

UNSPORTSMANLIKE
CONDUCT

ILLEGAL CUT

The offensive team must gain 10 yards in four tries, called downs, or give up possession of the ball. If 10 or more yards are gained, the offense has four more downs to advance the ball. If on the fourth down (or, rarely, before) it seems unlikely that the 10-yard minimum will be reached, the offense has the option of kicking the ball to the opponents. This is called a punt, and the defensive team, after catching the ball, goes on offense. The defensive team may also gain possession of the ball, and thus become the offense, by catching a ball passed by the quarterback that was intended for a teammate (interception), or by recovering the ball after it has been dropped by an offensive player (fumble). The defense hinders the attempts of the offense to gain yardage by tackling the ball carrier and pulling him to the ground. Because blocking and tackling can be very rough, football players wear protective helmets and substantial padding.

In 1950 the Los Angeles Rams were the first professional football team to put an insignia on their helmets. They painted yellow horns on their blue leather helmets.

The game is divided into four 15-minute periods; the team with the most points after the end of that time is the winner.

NATIONAL FOOTBALL LEAGUE (NFL) TEAMS

NATIONAL FOOTBALL CONFERENCE (NFC)

Eastern Division	Central Division	Western Division
Arizona Cardinals	Chicago Bears	Atlanta Falcons
Dallas Cowboys	Detroit Lions	Carolina Panthers
New York Giants	Green Bay Packers	New Orleans Saints
Philadelphia Eagles	Minnesota Vikings	San Francisco 49ers
Washington Redskins	Tampa Bay Buccaneers	St. Louis Rams

AMERICAN FOOTBALL CONFERENCE (AFC)

Eastern Division	Central Division	Western Division
Buffalo Bills	Baltimore Ravens	Denver Broncos
Indianapolis Colts	Cincinnati Bengals	Kansas City Chiefs
Miami Dolphins	Cleveland Browns	Oakland Raiders
New England Patriots	Jacksonville Jaguars	San Diego Chargers
New York Jets	Pittsburgh Steelers	Seattle Seahawks
	Tennessee Titans	

THE SUPER BOWL

After each National Football League (NFL) team plays a regular-season schedule of 16 games, the three division winners in each conference plus wild-card teams (the three teams with the best won-lost records in the rest of the conference) meet in a series of playoff games to determine the conference champion. The National Football Conference (NFC) champion then meets the American Football Conference (AFC) champion in January in the Super Bowl game for the NFL championship. The first four Super Bowls were played between the champions of the National Football League and the American Football League (AFL); the leagues then merged. Winners and losers of the Super Bowl are listed on the next page.

SUPER BOWL WINNERS

Bowl	Year	Winner	Conference	Loser	Conference	Score
I	1967	Green Bay Packers	NFL	Kansas City Chiefs	AFL	35–10
II	1968	Green Bay Packers	NFL	Oakland Raiders	AFL	33–14
III	1969	New York Jets	AFL	Baltimore Colts	NFL	16–7
IV	1970	Kansas City Chiefs	AFL	Minnesota Vikings	NFL	23–7
V	1971	Baltimore Colts	AFC	Dallas Cowboys	NFC	16–13
VI	1972	Dallas Cowboys	NFC	Miami Dolphins	AFC	24–3
VII	1973	Miami Dolphins	AFC	Washington Redskins	NFC	14–7
VIII	1974	Miami Dolphins	AFC	Minnesota Vikings	NFC	24–7
IX	1975	Pittsburgh Steelers	AFC	Minnesota Vikings	NFC	16–6
X	1976	Pittsburgh Steelers	AFC	Dallas Cowboys	NFC	21–17
XI	1977	Oakland Raiders	AFC	Minnesota Vikings	NFC	32–14
XII	1978	Dallas Cowboys	NFC	Denver Broncos	AFC	27–10
XIII	1979	Pittsburgh Steelers	AFC	Dallas Cowboys	NFC	35–31
XIV	1980	Pittsburgh Steelers	AFC	Los Angeles Rams	NFC	31–19
XV	1981	Oakland Raiders	AFC	Philadelphia Eagles	NFC	27–10
XVI	1982	San Francisco 49ers	NFC	Cincinnati Bengals	AFC	26–21
XVII	1983	Washington Redskins	NFC	Miami Dolphins	AFC	27–17
XVIII	1984	Los Angeles Raiders	AFC	Washington Redskins	NFC	38–9
XIX	1985	San Francisco 49ers	NFC	Miami Dolphins	AFC	38–16
XX	1986	Chicago Bears	NFC	New England Patriots	AFC	46–10
XXI	1987	New York Giants	NFC	Denver Broncos	AFC	39–20
XXII	1988	Washington Redskins	NFC	Denver Broncos	AFC	42–10
XXIII	1989	San Francisco 49ers	NFC	Cincinnati Bengals	AFC	20–16
XXIV	1990	San Francisco 49ers	NFC	Denver Broncos	AFC	55–10
XXV	1991	New York Giants	NFC	Buffalo Bills	AFC	20–19
XXVI	1992	Washington Redskins	NFC	Buffalo Bills	AFC	37–24
XXVII	1993	Dallas Cowboys	NFC	Buffalo Bills	AFC	52–17
XXVIII	1994	Dallas Cowboys	NFC	Buffalo Bills	AFC	30–13
XXIX	1995	San Francisco 49ers	NFC	San Diego Chargers	AFC	49–26
XXX	1996	Dallas Cowboys	NFC	Pittsburgh Steelers	AFC	27–17
XXXI	1997	Green Bay Packers	NFC	New England Patriots	AFC	35–21
XXXII	1998	Denver Broncos	AFC	Green Bay Packers	NFC	31–24
XXXIII	1999	Denver Broncos	AFC	Atlanta Falcons	NFC	34–19
XXXIV	2000	St. Louis Browns	AFC	Tennessee Titans	AFC	23–16
XXXV	2001	Baltimore Ravens	AFC	New York Giants	NFC	34–7
XXXVI	2002	New England Patriots	AFC	St. Louis Rams	NFC	20–17

GOLF

Golf is an outdoor game in which players hit a small hard ball with specially designed clubs that consist of a metal shaft and a wooden or metal club head. The object is to strike the ball with the club so that the ball goes into a cup that is sunk in the ground and marked with a flag. A standard golf course is divided into 18 holes, each with a tee, where the initial stroke is made; a grass fairway; and a green, a smooth grass surface where the cup is located. Each player attempts to reach the green and hit the ball into the cup using as few strokes as possible. Obstacles—such as water,

tall grass called rough, or traps filled with sand—may be found near the green or fairway. As many as 14 different types of clubs may be used depending on the length of shot required or the terrain. The distance from tee to cup varies greatly, but generally the distance is from 100 to 600 yards. The length and difficulty of the hole determine the par, the number of strokes that a good golfer would need to put the ball into the cup. After 18 holes, the player with the lowest number of strokes is the winner of that round. Golf tournaments are typically won by the player with the best (lowest) cumulative score after four rounds.

THE MASTERS

Four major golf tournaments carry the most important titles in professional golf. They are the Masters, the Professional Golfer's Association (PGA) Tournament, the U.S. Open, and the British Open. The Masters, played at the Augusta National Golf Club in Augusta, Georgia, is the title most sought in professional golf. The winners of the Masters Tournament follow.

Year	Winner	Score
1934	Horton Smith	284
1935	Gene Sarazen*	282
1936	Horton Smith	285
1937	Byron Nelson	283
1938	Henry Picard	285
1939	Ralph Guldahl	279
1940	Jimmy Demaret	280
1941	Craig Wood	280
1942	Byron Nelson*	280
1943	No tournament held	
1944	No tournament held	
1945	No tournament held	
1946	Herman Keiser	282
1947	Jimmy Demaret	281
1948	Claude Harmon	279
1949	Sam Snead	282
1950	Jimmy Demaret	283
1951	Ben Hogan	280
1952	Sam Snead	286
1953	Ben Hogan	274
1954	Sam Snead*	289
1955	Cary Middlecoff	279
1956	Jack Burke	289
1957	Doug Ford	283
1958	Arnold Palmer	284
1959	Art Wall, Jr.	284
1960	Arnold Palmer	282
1961	Gary Player	280
1962	Arnold Palmer*	280
1963	Jack Nicklaus	286
1964	Arnold Palmer	276
1965	Jack Nicklaus	271
1966	Jack Nicklaus*	288
1967	Gay Brewer	280
1968	Bob Goalby	277

Year	Winner	Score
1969	George Archer	281
1970	Billy Casper*	279
1971	Charles Coody	279
1972	Jack Nicklaus	286
1973	Tommy Aaron	283
1974	Gary Player	278
1975	Jack Nicklaus	276
1976	Ray Floyd	271
1977	Tom Watson	276
1978	Gary Player	277
1979	Fuzzy Zoeller*	280
1980	Severiano Ballesteros	275
1981	Tom Watson	280
1982	Craig Stadler*	284
1983	Severiano Ballesteros	280
1984	Ben Crenshaw	277
1985	Bernhard Langer	282
1986	Jack Nicklaus	279
1987	Larry Mize*	285
1988	Sandy Lyle	281
1989	Nick Faldo	283
1990	Nick Faldo	278
1991	Ian Woosnam	277
1992	Fred Couples	275
1993	Bernhard Langer	277
1994	Jose Maria Olazabal	279
1995	Ben Crenshaw	274
1996	Nick Faldo	276
1997	Tiger Woods	270
1998	Mark O'Meara	279
1999	Jose Maria Olazabal	280
2000	Vijay Singh	278
2001	Tiger Woods	272
2002	Tiger Woods	276

*Won in a playoff.

HORSE RACING

Horses are raced either under saddle (by a jockey) or in harness (with a driver). Saddle racing occurs either on flat courses or involves jumping over artificial obstructions such as ditches, hedges, and walls (steeplechases) or framelike barriers (hurdles). In harness races, a horse trained as a trotter or pacer is driven from a small two-wheeled vehicle called a sulky.

Thoroughbred saddle racing, run on flat courses, involves purebred (pedigreed) horses bred especially for racing. Thoroughbred horses originated from a cross between Arabian stallions and English mares. Competitions differ according to distance, horse age, weight to be carried, and other considerations. In *sweepstakes,* owners pay a stake (fee) for their horses to be eligible. In *handicaps,* horses are given different weights, based on their past performance, to equalize their chances to win. Top weights are assigned to better horses; lesser weights are assigned to those horses considered inferior.

A horse's age is established by January 1st in the year in which it is born. Horses must be at least two years old to run in flats, three years old to run in steeplechases, and four years old to run in hurdles.

Flat races are run counterclockwise on oval tracks; thus the horses turn left. Distances are measured in furlongs (1 furlong = ⅛ mile = 220 yards).

THE TRIPLE CROWN

The best-known horse races in the United States are the Kentucky Derby (1¼ miles; at Churchill Downs in Louisville, KY), the Preakness Stakes (1¹³⁄₁₆ miles; at Pimlico Race Course in Baltimore, MD), and the Belmont Stakes (1½ miles; at Belmont Park in Elmont, NY). These three races for three-year-olds make up horse racing's Triple Crown. Eleven horses have won all three events.

Year	Horse	Year	Horse
1919	Sir Barton	1946	Assault
1930	Gallant Fox	1948	Citation
1935	Omaha	1973	Secretariat
1937	War Admiral	1977	Seattle Slew
1941	Whirlaway	1978	Affirmed
1943	Count Fleet		

WINNING HORSES IN THE KENTUCKY DERBY

Year	Horse	Year	Horse	Year	Horse
1875	Aristides	1901	His Eminence	1927	Whiskery
1876	Vagrant	1902	Alan-a-Dale	1928	Reigh Count
1877	Baden Baden	1903	Judge Himes	1929	Clyde Van Dusen
1878	Day Star	1904	Elwood	1930	Gallant Fox
1879	Lord Murphy	1905	Agile	1931	Twenty Grand
1880	Fonso	1906	Sir Huon	1932	Burgoo King
1881	Hindoo	1907	Pink Star	1933	Brokers Tip
1882	Apollo	1908	Stone Street	1934	Cavalcade
1883	Leonatus	1909	Wintergreen	1935	Omaha
1884	Buchanan	1910	Donau	1936	Bold Venture
1885	Joe Cotton	1911	Meridian	1937	War Admiral
1886	Ben Ali	1912	Worth	1938	Lawrin
1887	Montrose	1913	Donerail	1939	Johnstown
1888	Macbeth II	1914	Old Rosebud	1940	Gallahadion
1889	Spokane	1915	Regret	1941	Whirlaway
1890	Riley	1916	George Smith	1942	Shut Out
1891	Kingman	1917	Omar Khayyam	1943	Count Fleet
1892	Azra	1918	Exterminator	1944	Pensive
1893	Lookout	1919	Sir Barton	1945	Hoop Jr.
1894	Chant	1920	Paul Jones	1946	Assault
1895	Halma	1921	Behave Yourself	1947	Jet Pilot
1896	Ben Brush	1922	Morvich	1948	Citation
1897	Typhoon II	1923	Zev	1949	Ponder
1898	Plaudit	1924	Black Gold	1950	Middleground
1899	Manuel	1925	Flying Ebony	1951	Count Turf
1900	Lieutenant Gibson	1926	Bubbling Over	1952	Hill Gail

continues

Winning Horses in the Kentucky Derby, Continued

Year	Horse
1953	Dark Star
1954	Determine
1955	Swaps
1956	Needles
1957	Iron Liege
1958	Tim Tam
1959	Tomy Lee
1960	Venetian Way
1961	Carry Back
1962	Decidedly
1963	Chateaugay
1964	Northern Dancer
1965	Lucky Debonair
1966	Kauai King
1967	Proud Clarion
1968	Forward Pass*
1969	Majestic Prince

Year	Horse
1970	Dust Commander
1971	Canonero II
1972	Riva Ridge
1973	Secretariat
1974	Cannonade
1975	Foolish Pleasure
1976	Bold Forbes
1977	Seattle Slew
1978	Affirmed
1979	Spectacular Bid
1980	Genuine Risk
1981	Pleasant Colony
1982	Gato del Sol
1983	Sunny's Halo
1984	Swale
1985	Spend a Buck
1986	Ferdinand

Year	Horse
1987	Alysheba
1988	Winning Colors
1989	Sunday Silence
1990	Unbridled
1991	Strike the Gold
1992	Lil E. Tee
1993	Sea Hero
1994	Go for Gin
1995	Thunder Gulch
1996	Grindstone
1997	Silver Charm
1998	Real Quiet
1999	Charismatic
2000	Fusaichi Pegasus
2001	Monarchos
2002	War Emblem

*In 1968, Dancer's Image finished first but was disqualified.

ICE HOCKEY

Ice hockey is played on a rectangular rink that is surrounded by a wooden wall. At each end of the ice is placed a netted goal. Six skaters make up each team, including the goalie, whose job it is to protect the goal. By using wooden sticks, the players attempt to propel a rubber disc, called the puck, across the ice and into the opponents' goal. This scores a point.

The game begins with a faceoff in the center of the ice. The official drops the puck between two players, one from each team. Both teams try to gain control of the puck and to advance it toward the opponent's goal by skating with the puck, passing it to a teammate, or shooting it directly toward the goal. The defense tries to hinder this advance by deflecting or intercepting a pass or shot or by bodychecking an opposing player. This is physically blocking an opponent with a hip or shoulder.

There is a wide range of penalties for which an offending player may be removed from the ice for a stated number of minutes. During this time, the penalized team plays with one fewer player than its opponents, giving a power play to the fully manned team. Penalty times range from two minutes for minor violations to ejection from the game for the most serious fouls. Holding on to the puck or to an opponent, checking from behind, tripping, using the stick illegally, and fighting all normally result in penalties. The offensive player in control of the puck must cross his own blue line before any of his teammates. In moving down the ice and attacking the opponent's end, if an attacking player without the puck crosses that line first, he is offside. This is a violation, leading to a resetting of the puck and a new faceoff.

There are only 2 days in the entire year without games played in one of the 4 major professional sports (football, hockey, basketball, and baseball)—the day before and the day after the Major League All-Star game.

Hockey is a rough sport and players wear hip pads, shoulder pads, padded gloves, and helmets. The game consists of three 20-minute periods with rest periods in between. The team with more goals at the end of that time wins the game.

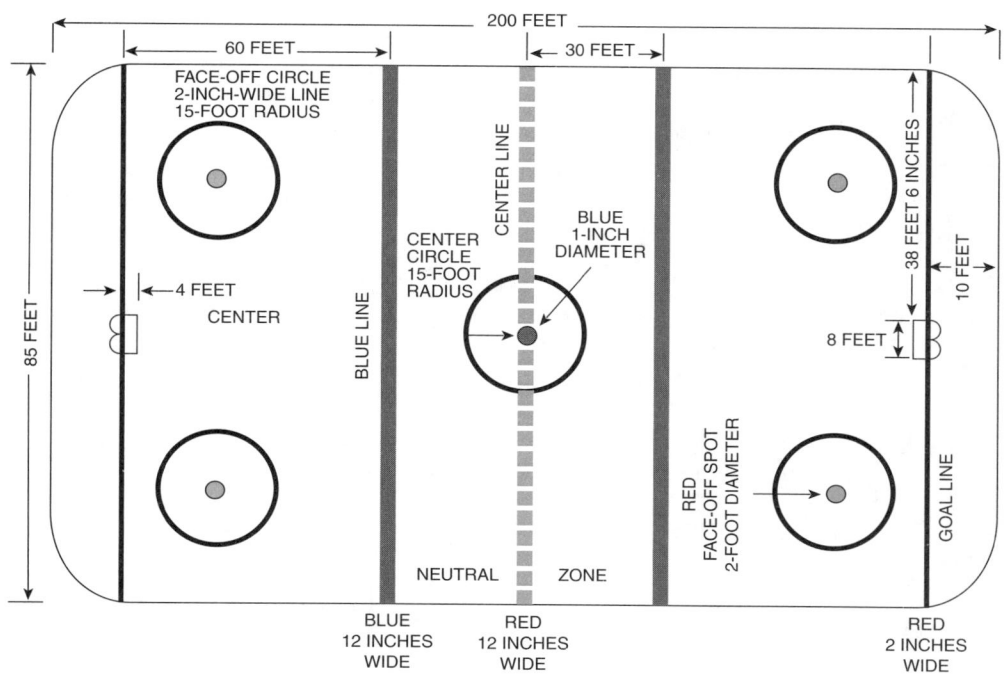

Ice Hockey Rink

NATIONAL HOCKEY LEAGUE (NHL) TEAMS
WESTERN CONFERENCE

Pacific Division
Anaheim Mighty Ducks
Dallas Stars
Los Angeles Kings
Phoenix Coyotes
San Jose Sharks

Northwest Division
Calgary Flames
Colorado Avalanche
Edmonton Oilers
Minnesota Wild
Vancouver Canucks

Central Division
Chicago Blackhawks
Columbus Blue Jackets
Detroit Red Wings
Nashville Predators
St. Louis Blues

EASTERN CONFERENCE

Northeast Division
Boston Bruins
Buffalo Sabres
Montreal Canadiens
Ottawa Senators
Toronto Maple Leafs

Southeast Division
Atlanta Thrashers
Carolina Hurricanes
Florida Panthers
Tampa Bay Lightning
Washington Capitals

Atlantic Division
New Jersey Devils
New York Islanders
New York Rangers
Philadelphia Flyers
Pittsburgh Penguins

THE STANLEY CUP

In 1893 the governor-general of Canada, Lord Stanley of Preston, presented a cup (then called the Dominion Challenge Trophy) to be awarded annually to the country's amateur hockey champion. After two professional leagues, the National Hockey Association (NHA) and the Pacific Coast Hockey Association (PCHA), began a playoff in 1911, the winner was awarded the cup. In 1917 the NHA disbanded, and the NHL was formed. From 1923 to 1926 the Western Canada Hockey League (WCHL) champion also participated in the Stanley Cup playoffs. After 1926 the Stanley Cup has been awarded exclusively to the NHL champion.

Under the present system each National Hockey League (NHL) team plays a regular-season schedule of 82 games. The eight teams in each conference with the highest point total (two points are awarded for each win, and one point for each tie) then meet in a series of playoffs to determine the conference champion. The West-

THE STANLEY CUP WINNERS

Season	Winner	Loser	Games
1926–27	Ottawa Senators	Boston Bruins	2–0
1927–28	New York Rangers	Montreal Maroons	3–2
1928–29	Boston Bruins	New York Rangers	2–0
1929–30	Montreal Canadiens	Boston Bruins	2–0
1930–31	Montreal Canadiens	Chicago Black Hawks	3–2
1931–32	Toronto Maple Leafs	New York Rangers	3–0
1932–33	New York Rangers	Toronto Maple Leafs	3–1
1933–34	Chicago Black Hawks	Detroit Red Wings	3–1
1934–35	Montreal Maroons	Toronto Maple Leafs	3–0
1935–36	Detroit Red Wings	Toronto Maple Leafs	3–1
1936–37	Detroit Red Wings	New York Rangers	3–2
1937–38	Chicago Black Hawks	Toronto Maple Leafs	3–1
1938–39	Boston Bruins	Toronto Maple Leafs	4–1
1939–40	New York Rangers	Toronto Maple Leafs	4–2
1940–41	Boston Bruins	Detroit Red Wings	4–0
1941–42	Toronto Maple Leafs	Detroit Red Wings	4–3
1942–43	Detroit Red Wings	Boston Bruins	4–0
1943–44	Montreal Canadiens	Chicago Black Hawks	4–0
1944–45	Toronto Maple Leafs	Detroit Red Wings	4–3
1945–46	Montreal Canadiens	Boston Bruins	4–1
1946–47	Toronto Maple Leafs	Montreal Canadiens	4–2
1947–48	Toronto Maple Leafs	Detroit Red Wings	4–0
1948–49	Toronto Maple Leafs	Detroit Red Wings	4–0
1949–50	Detroit Red Wings	New York Rangers	4–3
1950–51	Toronto Maple Leafs	Montreal Canadiens	4–1
1951–52	Detroit Red Wings	Montreal Canadiens	4–0
1952–53	Montreal Canadiens	Boston Bruins	4–1
1953–54	Detroit Red Wings	Montreal Canadiens	4–3
1954–55	Detroit Red Wings	Montreal Canadiens	4–3
1955–56	Montreal Canadiens	Detroit Red Wings	4–1
1956–57	Montreal Canadiens	Boston Bruins	4–1
1957–58	Montreal Canadiens	Boston Bruins	4–2
1958–59	Montreal Canadiens	Toronto Maple Leafs	4–1
1959–60	Montreal Canadiens	Toronto Maple Leafs	4–0
1960–61	Chicago Black Hawks	Detroit Red Wings	4–2
1961–62	Toronto Maple Leafs	Chicago Black Hawks	4–2
1962–63	Toronto Maple Leafs	Detroit Red Wings	4–1
1963–64	Toronto Maple Leafs	Detroit Red Wings	4–3
1964–65	Montreal Canadiens	Chicago Black Hawks	4–3

Season	Winner	Loser	Games
1965–66	Montreal Canadiens	Detroit Red Wings	4–2
1966–67	Toronto Maple Leafs	Montreal Canadiens	4–2
1967–68	Montreal Canadiens	St. Louis Blues	4–0
1968–69	Montreal Canadiens	St. Louis Blues	4–0
1969–70	Boston Bruins	St. Louis Blues	4–0
1970–71	Montreal Canadiens	Chicago Black Hawks	4–3
1971–72	Boston Bruins	New York Rangers	4–2
1972–73	Montreal Canadiens	Chicago Black Hawks	4–2
1973–74	Philadelphia Flyers	Boston Bruins	4–2
1974–75	Philadelphia Flyers	Buffalo Sabres	4–2
1975–76	Montreal Canadiens	Philadelphia Flyers	4–0
1976–77	Montreal Canadiens	Boston Bruins	4–0
1977–78	Montreal Canadiens	Boston Bruins	4–2
1978–79	Montreal Canadiens	New York Rangers	4–1
1979–80	New York Islanders	Philadelphia Flyers	4–2
1980–81	New York Islanders	Minnesota North Stars	4–1
1981–82	New York Islanders	Vancouver Canucks	4–0
1982–83	New York Islanders	Edmonton Oilers	4–0
1983–84	Edmonton Oilers	New York Islanders	4–1
1984–85	Edmonton Oilers	Philadelphia Flyers	4–1
1985–86	Montreal Canadiens	Calgary Flames	4–1
1986–87	Edmonton Oilers	Philadelphia Flyers	4–3
1987–88	Edmonton Oilers	Boston Bruins	4–0
1988–89	Calgary Flames	Montreal Canadiens	4–2
1989–90	Edmonton Oilers	Boston Bruins	4–1
1990–91	Pittsburgh Penguins	Minnesota North Stars	4–2
1991–92	Pittsburgh Penguins	Chicago Black Hawks	4–0
1992–93	Montreal Canadiens	Los Angeles Kings	4–1
1993–94	New York Rangers	Vancouver Canucks	4–3
1994–95	New Jersey Devils	Detroit Red Wings	4–0
1995–96	Colorado Avalanche	Florida Panthers	4–0
1996–97	Detroit Red Wings	Philadelphia Flyers	4–0
1997–98	Detroit Red Wings	Washington Capitals	4–1
1998–99	Dallas Stars	Buffalo Sabres	4–2
1999–2000	New Jersey Devils	Dallas Stars	4–2
2001–2002	Detroit Red Wings	Carolina Hurricanes	4–1

ern Conference champion then meets with the Eastern Conference champion in the spring in a best-of-seven-games series for the NHL championship.

SOCCER

Soccer, often referred to as "football" outside the United States, is played by two opposing teams of 11 players each on a rectangular field. At either end of the field is a goal, constructed of a pair of upright 8-foot-high posts with a 24-foot-long crossbar. The object of the game is for one set of players to force the ball into the goal defended by the opposing team.

At the beginning of a game, the choice of field ends and the opportunity to kick off are decided by a coin toss. Once play has started, players may not touch the ball with their hands with two exceptions: Goalkeepers within their areas may touch the ball with their hands, and when the ball goes out of bounds by crossing the touch lines, it is thrown back by hand. The team in possession of the ball is the offensive team. By kicking the ball or using their heads, members of the offensive team try to move the ball down the field until one of its members is in a position to shoot the ball into the goal of the opposing team.

The defending team may gain possession of the ball by intercepting passes or by tackling opposing play-

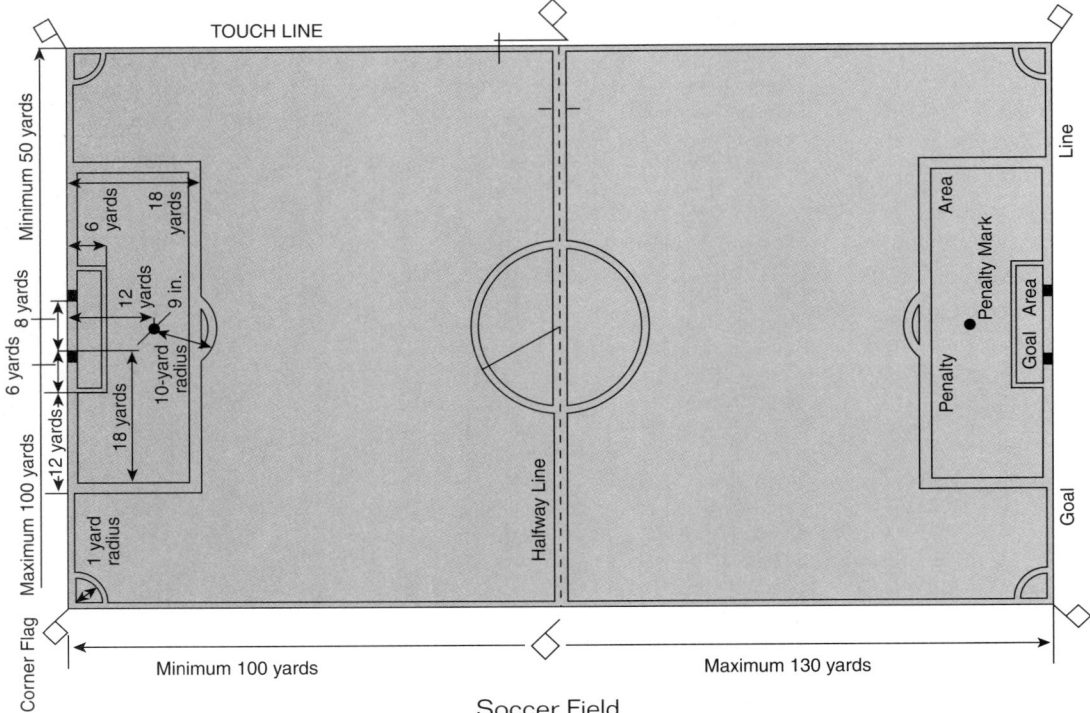

Soccer Field

ers. A tackle can be either a use of the feet or a charge against an opponent's shoulder. The penalty for a violent or dangerous tackle is a direct free kick at the ball by the opposing side.

When the ball goes out of play by passing over the goal line beyond the goalposts, it is restarted by the opposing team. The defending team kicks the ball back into play from within that half of the goal area nearest to where the ball crossed the line; the offensive team kicks it back from the corner circle at the nearest corner flag. As with free kicks, generally, the ball may not be touched again by the kicker until it has been touched by another player. A goal may be scored from a direct corner kick.

When a goal is scored, the game is restarted with a kickoff by the team conceding the goal. A match consists of two 45-minute periods. At the end of the match, the team scoring the greater number of goals is the winner. If no goals are scored, or an equal number of goals is scored by both teams, the game is considered a draw.

THE WORLD CUP

The World Cup championship, the contest for international soccer supremacy, is played every four years at different locations throughout the world.

WORLD CUP WINNERS		
Year	Winner	Loser
1930	Uruguay	Argentina
1934	Italy	Czechoslovakia
1938	Italy	Hungary
1942	*No competition*	
1946	*No competition*	
1950	Uruguay	Brazil
1954	West Germany	Hungary
1958	Brazil	Sweden
1962	Brazil	Czechoslovakia
1966	England	West Germany
1970	Brazil	Italy
1974	West Germany	Netherlands
1978	Argentina	Netherlands
1982	Italy	West Germany
1986	Argentina	West Germany
1990	West Germany	Argentina
1994	Brazil	Italy
1998	France	Brazil
2002	Brazil	Germany

TENNIS

Tennis is played either indoors or outdoors on a rectangular court, which may be grass, clay, or synthetic. A small felt-covered rubber ball is hit back and forth over a net with wooden or metal rackets, which are fitted with strings made of lamb's gut, nylon, or synthetic material. The net, which is 3 feet above the court's surface at its midpoint, is stretched across the court. Tennis may be played either as singles, with one player on each side, or as doubles, with two players on each side. In doubles, the court is 9 feet wider than in singles, because of the addition of two doubles alleys.

To initiate play, the server stands behind the baseline and to the right of the center mark and hits the ball with the racket so that the ball lands in the diagonally opposite service court of the opponent. If this first serve does not land in this service area because it is hit too long or too wide, or hits the net, the server may try again with a second serve. If this second serve is not a legal serve, the receiver scores a point. At each point, the serve alternates left to right, with the server always serving from behind the baseline to the diagonally opposite service court. The receiver attempts to return a legal serve by hitting the ball anywhere into the opponent's court, which in-cludes the alleys in doubles. Play continues until one player (or one team, in doubles) fails to make a legal return. A point is then scored by the opponent.

Four points, designated as 15, 30, 40, and game, constitute a game; a player must win each game by at least two points. Thus, if after six points in any game, each player has scored three, the score is 40–40 (this is called deuce). One player must then score two consecutive points to win the game; this player has the advantage after winning the first of these two points. Having the advantage, if the player wins the second consecutive point, he or she wins the game; but if the opponent wins that point, the score goes back to 40–40, or deuce. Play then continues until one player wins the game by scoring two consecutive points.

Each player (or team, in doubles) alternates by serving one game and receiving the next. The first to win six games wins a set, provided the margin of victory is two games or more. Thus, if the score reaches six games to four, the set is over, but at six to five, play continues. If the score reaches six to six, a tiebreaker is usually employed. A match consists of the best two out of three sets in women's play and usually the best three out of five in men's play.

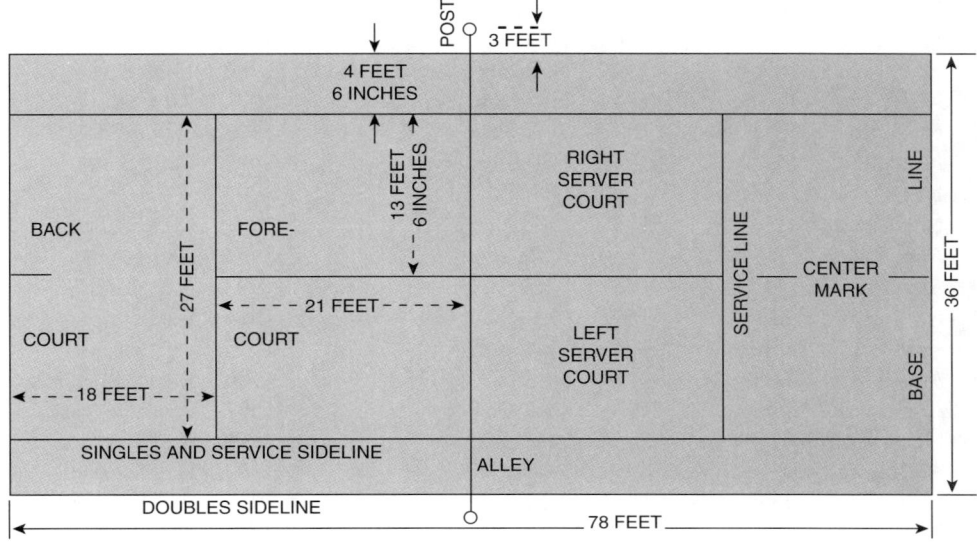

Tennis Court

WIMBLEDON

There are four major championships in professional tennis that make up the Grand Slam: the French Open; the Australian Open; the U.S. Open; and the All-England Lawn Tennis Championships, better known as Wimbledon. Wimbledon is the oldest and most prestigious tournament of the four. The winners since 1877 follow.

MEN'S SINGLES CHAMPIONS

1877	Spencer W. Gore	1919	Gerald Patterson	1961	Rod Laver
1878	P. F. Hadow	1920	Bill Tilden	1962	Rod Laver
1879	J. T. Hartley	1921	Bill Tilden	1963	Chuck McKinley
1880	J. T. Hartley	1922	Gerald Patterson	1964	Roy Emerson
1881	William Renshaw	1923	William Johnston	1965	Roy Emerson
1882	William Renshaw	1924	Jean Borotra	1966	Manuel Santana
1883	William Renshaw	1925	Jean Rene Lacoste	1967	John Newcombe
1884	William Renshaw	1926	Jean Borotra	1968	Rod Laver
1885	William Renshaw	1927	Henri Cochet	1969	Rod Laver
1886	William Renshaw	1928	Jean Rene Lacoste	1970	John Newcombe
1887	Herbert Lawford	1929	Henri Cochet	1971	John Newcombe
1888	Ernest Renshaw	1930	Bill Tilden	1972	Stan Smith
1889	William Renshaw	1931	Sidney Wood	1973	Jan Kodes
1890	Willoughby Hamilton	1932	Ellsworth Vines	1974	Jimmy Connors
1891	Wilfred Baddeley	1933	Jack Crawford	1975	Arthur Ashe
1892	Wilfred Baddeley	1934	Fred Perry	1976	Bjorn Borg
1893	Joshua Pim	1935	Fred Perry	1977	Bjorn Borg
1894	Joshua Pim	1936	Fred Perry	1978	Bjorn Borg
1895	Wilfred Baddeley	1937	Donald Budge	1979	Bjorn Borg
1896	Harold Mahoney	1938	Donald Budge	1980	Bjorn Borg
1897	Reginald Doherty	1939	Bobby Riggs	1981	John McEnroe
1898	Reginald Doherty	1940	No tournament held	1982	Jimmy Connors
1899	Reginald Doherty	1941	No tournament held	1983	John McEnroe
1900	Reginald Doherty	1942	No tournament held	1984	John McEnroe
1901	Arthur Gore	1943	No tournament held	1985	Boris Becker
1902	H. Laurence Doherty	1944	No tournament held	1986	Boris Becker
1903	H. Laurence Doherty	1945	No tournament held	1987	Pat Cash
1904	H. Laurence Doherty	1946	Yvon Petra	1988	Stefan Edberg
1905	H. Laurence Doherty	1947	Jack Kramer	1989	Boris Becker
1906	H. Laurence Doherty	1948	Bob Falkenburg	1990	Stefan Edberg
1907	Norman Brookes	1949	Ted Schroeder	1991	Michael Stich
1908	Arthur Gore	1950	Budge Patty	1992	Andre Agassi
1909	Arthur Gore	1951	Dick Savitt	1993	Pete Sampras
1910	Anthony F. Wilding	1952	Frank Sedgman	1994	Pete Sampras
1911	Anthony F. Wilding	1953	Vic Seixas	1995	Pete Sampras
1912	Anthony F. Wilding	1954	Jaroslav Drobny	1996	Richard Krajicek
1913	Anthony F. Wilding	1955	Tony Trabert	1997	Pete Sampras
1914	Norman Brookes	1956	Lew Hoad	1998	Pete Sampras
1915	No tournament held	1957	Lew Hoad	1999	Pete Sampras
1916	No tournament held	1958	Ashley Cooper	2000	Pete Sampras
1917	No tournament held	1959	Alex Olmedo	2001	Goran Ivanisevic
1918	No tournament held	1960	Neale Fraser	2002	Lleyton Hewitt

WOMEN'S SINGLES CHAMPIONS

1884	Maud Watson	1921	Suzanne Lenglen	1962	Karen Susman
1885	Maud Watson	1922	Suzanne Lenglen	1963	Margaret Smith
1886	Blanche Bingley	1923	Suzanne Lenglen	1964	Maria Bueno
1887	Lottie Dod	1924	Kitty McKane	1965	Margaret Smith
1888	Lottie Dod	1925	Suzanne Lenglen	1966	Billie Jean King
1889	Blanche Bingley Hillyard	1926	Kitty McKane Godfree	1967	Billie Jean King
1890	L. Rice	1927	Helen Wills	1968	Billie Jean King
1891	Lottie Dod	1928	Helen Wills	1969	Ann Jones
1892	Lottie Dod	1929	Helen Wills	1970	Margaret Smith Court
1893	Lottie Dod	1930	Helen Wills Moody	1971	Evonne Goolagong
1894	Blanche Bingley Hillyard	1931	Cilly Aussem	1972	Billie Jean King
1895	Charlotte Cooper	1932	Helen Wills Moody	1973	Billie Jean King
1896	Charlotte Cooper	1933	Helen Wills Moody	1974	Chris Evert
1897	Blanche Bingley Hillyard	1934	Dorothy Round	1975	Billie Jean King
1898	Charlotte Cooper	1935	Helen Wills Moody	1976	Chris Evert
1899	Blanche Bingley Hillyard	1936	Helen Jacobs	1977	Virginia Wade
1900	Blanche Bingley Hillyard	1937	Dorothy Round	1978	Martina Navratilova
1901	Charlotte Cooper Sterry	1938	Helen Wills Moody	1979	Martina Navratilova
1902	Muriel Robb	1939	Alice Marble	1980	Evonne Goolagong
1903	Dorothea Douglass	1940	No tournament held	1981	Chris Evert Lloyd
1904	Dorothea Douglass	1941	No tournament held	1982	Martina Navratilova
1905	May Sutton	1942	No tournament held	1983	Martina Navratilova
1906	Dorothea Douglass	1943	No tournament held	1984	Martina Navratilova
1907	May Sutton	1944	No tournament held	1985	Martina Navratilova
1908	Charlotte Cooper Sterry	1945	No tournament held	1986	Martina Navratilova
1909	Dora Boothby	1946	Pauline Betz	1987	Martina Navratilova
1910	Dorothea Douglass Chambers	1947	Margaret Osborne	1988	Steffi Graf
		1948	A. Louise Brough	1989	Steffi Graf
1911	Dorothea Douglass Chambers	1949	A. Louise Brough	1990	Martina Navratilova
		1950	A. Louise Brough	1991	Steffi Graf
1912	Ethel Larcombe	1951	Doris Hart	1992	Steffi Graf
1913	Dorothea Douglass Chambers	1952	Maureen Connolly	1993	Steffi Graf
		1953	Maureen Connolly	1994	Conchita Martinez
1914	Dorothea Douglass Chambers	1954	Maureen Connolly	1995	Steffi Graf
		1955	A. Louise Brough	1996	Steffi Graf
1915	No tournament held	1956	Shirley Fry	1997	Martina Hingis
1916	No tournament held	1957	Althea Gibson	1998	Jana Novotna
1917	No tournament held	1958	Althea Gibson	1999	Lindsay Davenport
1918	No tournament held	1959	Maria Bueno	2000	Venus Williams
1919	Suzanne Lenglen	1960	Maria Bueno	2001	Venus Williams
1920	Suzanne Lenglen	1961	Angela Mortimer	2002	Serena Williams

VOLLEYBALL

Volleyball is played either outdoors or indoors on a rectangular court, with six players to a side. An inflated ball is hit back and forth over a net; the players try to prevent the ball from hitting the court on their own side. The net's top is 8 feet above the floor (7½ feet in women's play). To initiate play, a player serves the ball by hitting it with the hand or fist and thereby sending it over the net toward the opponent's court. After the serve, the ball may be hit with any part of the body. The ball may be hit a maximum of three times by each team, the final hit sending the ball over the net. Catching or holding the ball is not permitted.

If the receiving team allows the ball to hit the floor on its side, or hits the ball out of bounds, the serving team scores a point and serves again. If the serving team allows the ball to hit the floor, hits it out of bounds, or fails to make a legal serve, the serve is transferred to the opponents, but no point is scored. The first team to reach 15 points wins the game, provided the margin of victory is at least two points. In championship play, a match is won by winning three out of five games.

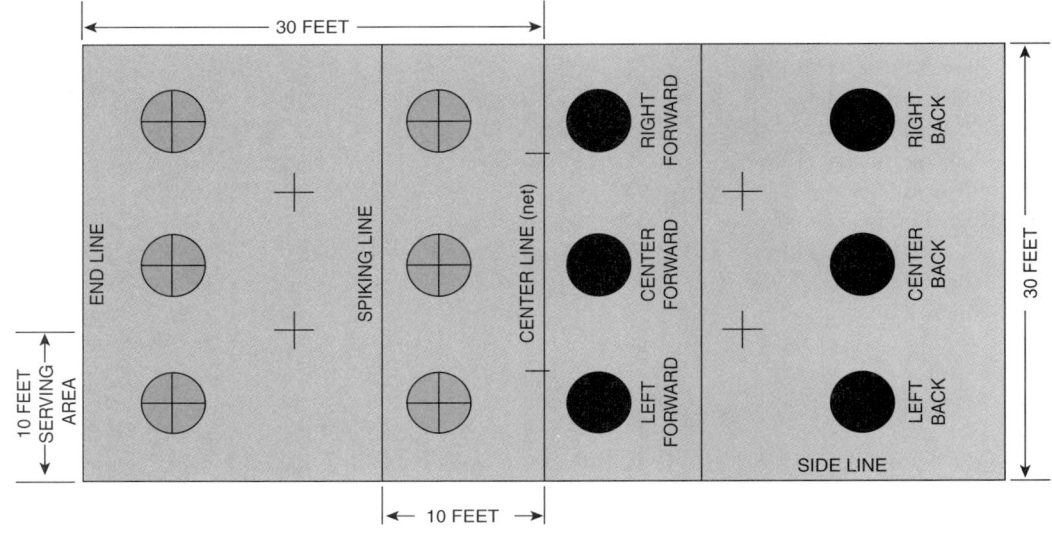

Volleyball Court

OLYMPIC GAMES

The modern Olympic Games began in Athens in 1896, to promote greater international understanding through athletics. The games originated in ancient Greece sometime prior to 776 B.C., but were discontinued after 392 A.D. The Olympic Games competition is held every four years at different locations throughout the world. Since 1994 winter and summer games have been played in alternating four-year cycles. Winter games occurred in 1994, 1998, and so on; summer games occurred in 1996, 2000, and so on.

LOCATIONS
SUMMER GAMES

1896	Athens, Greece	1932	Los Angeles, California
1900	Paris, France	1936	Berlin, Germany
1904	St. Louis, Missouri	1940	No games held
1908	London, England	1944	No games held
1912	Stockholm, Sweden	1948	London, England
1920	Antwerp, Belgium	1952	Helsinki, Finland
1924	Paris, France	1956	Melbourne, Australia
1928	Amsterdam, The Netherlands	1960	Rome, Italy

1964	Tokyo, Japan
1968	Mexico City, Mexico
1972	Munich, West Germany
1976	Montreal, Canada
1980	Moscow, USSR
1984	Los Angeles, California

1988	Seoul, South Korea
1992	Barcelona, Spain
1996	Atlanta, Georgia
2000	Sydney, Australia
2004	Athens, Greece

WINTER GAMES

1924	Chamonix, France
1928	St. Moritz, Switzerland
1932	Lake Placid, New York
1936	Garmisch-Partenkirchen, Germany
1940	No games held
1944	No games held
1948	St. Moritz, Switzerland
1952	Oslo, Norway
1956	Cortina, Italy
1960	Squaw Valley, California

1964	Innsbruck, Austria
1968	Grenoble, France
1972	Sapporo, Japan
1976	Innsbruck, Austria
1980	Lake Placid, New York
1984	Sarajevo, Yugoslavia
1988	Calgary, Canada
1992	Albertville, France
1994	Lillehammer, Norway
1998	Nagano, Japan
2002	Salt Lake City, Utah

2000 SUMMER OLYMPIC EVENTS

Men and Women		Men	Women
Archery	Modern pentathlon	Baseball (team)	Rhythmic gymnastics
Badminton	Rowing	Boxing	Softball (team)
Basketball (team)	Shooting	Wrestling—Freestyle	Synchronized swimming (team)
Beach volleyball	Soccer (team)	Wrestling—Greco-Roman	
Canoeing/Kayaking	Table tennis		
Cycling	Taekwando		
Diving	Tennis		
Equestrian*	Triathlon		
Fencing	Volleyball		
Field hockey (team)	Water polo (team)		
Gymnastics	Weight lifting		
Handball (team)	Yachting		
Judo			

Men's Swimming	Women's Swimming
50m, 100m, 200m, 400m, 1,500m freestyle	50 m, 100m, 200m, 400m, 800m freestyle
100m, 200m backstroke	100m, 200m backstroke
100m, 200m breaststroke	100m, 200m breaststroke
100m, 200m butterfly	100m, 200m butterfly
200m, 400m individual medley	200m, 400m individual medley
400m, 800m freestyle relay	400m, 800m freestyle relay
400m medley relay	400m medley relay

continues

2000 Summer Olympic Events, Continued

Men's Track and Field	Women's Track and Field
100m, 200m, 400m dash	100m, 200m, 400m dash
800m, 1,500m, 5,000m, 10,000m run	800m, 1,500m, 5,000m, 10,000m run
110m, 400m hurdles	100m, 400m hurdles
400m relay (4 × 100)	400m relay (4 × 100)
1,600m relay (4 × 400)	1,600m relay (4 × 400)
3,000m steeplechase	20km walk
20km, 50km walk	Marathon
Marathon	High jump
High jump	Long jump
Long jump	Triple jump
Triple jump	Discus
Discus	Hammer throw
Hammer throw	Javelin
Javelin	Pole vault
Pole vault	Shot put
Shot put	Heptathlon
Decathlon	

* In equestrian events, men and women competed against one another; in shooting, they competed separately, as well as against one another.

2002 WINTER OLYMPIC GAMES

Except for ski jumping, all winter sports at the 2002 Olympic games were divided into two classes, one for men and the other for women. Only men competed in ski jumping events. In pairs figure skating and ice dancing, men and women performed together.

Alpine skiing	Downhill Slalom Giant slalom Super giant slalom Combined			Pairs Ice dancing
			Freestyle skiing	Moguls Aerials

Biathlon	*Men:* 20km individual, 10km
	    sprint, 12.5km pursuit, 30km
	    relay (4 × 7.5)
	Women: 15km individual, 7.5km
	    sprint, 10km pursuit, 30km relay
	    (4 × 7.5)
			Ice hockey (team)	

			Luge	Singles Doubles (one competition, open to men and women)
			Nordic combined	Individual Sprint Team
Bobsledding	*Men:* 2-man, 4-man *Women:* 2-woman		**Ski jumping**	90m, 120m (individual) 120m (team)

**Cross-country
    skiing**
	Men: 15km and 50km classic,
	    combined pursuit start, 30km
	    freestyle, 40km relay (4 × 10),
	    1.5km sprint
	Women: 10km and 30km classic,
	    combined pursuit, 15km
	    freestyle, 20km relay (4 × 5)
	    1.5km sprint
			Snowboarding	Parallel giant slalom
				Halfpipe

			**Short track
			    speed skating**
				Men: 500m, 1,000m, 1,500m,
				    5,000m relay
				Women: 500m, 1,000m, 1,500m,
				    3,000m relay

Curling			**Skeleton speed
			    skating**
				Men: 500m, 1,000m, 1,500m,
				    5,000m, 10,000m
				Women: 500m, 1,000m, 1,500m,
				    3,000m, 5,000m

Figure skating	Men's singles Women's singles			

MAJOR SPORTS FIGURES

The following list of leading sports personalities is not meant to be comprehensive. The athletes selected have made notable contributions to their respective sports or the world of sports at large. Many are popular contemporary figures whose current accomplishments only hint at their long-term potential, or who have achieved a measure of notoriety through their individual style. Every effort has been made to include American and international athletes, men and women, and figures from as wide a variety of sports as possible.

Each figure is an American unless otherwise noted. All are listed by the name under which they are best known; bracketed names indicate that the athlete began his or her career under that name. If an individual was or is involved in a team sport, the team or teams with which that person is most closely associated are included as well.

Aaron, Henry (Hank) (1934–   ). Baseball player (outfielder); Milwaukee-Atlanta Braves, Milwaukee Brewers. He holds numerous major league records, including career home runs (755) and runs batted in (2,297).

Abdul-Jabbar, Kareem [Lew Alcindor] (1947–   ). Basketball player (center); Milwaukee Bucks, Los Angeles Lakers. The NBA's all-time leading scorer (38,387 points), he won most valuable player honors six times.

Ali, Muhammed [Cassius Clay] (1942–   ). Boxer, noted for his wit. Ali won the heavyweight championship three times. During the Vietnam War, he refused induction into the military and was suspended and stripped of his title.

Ashe, Arthur (1943–93). Tennis player. He won the U.S. Open (1968) and Wimbledon (1975) singles championships. After contracting AIDS, he became a leading spokesperson in the fight against that disease.

Bannister, Roger (1929–   ). British middle-distance runner. He was the first person to run a mile in under 4 minutes (May 6, 1954).

Blair, Bonnie (1964–   ). Speed skater. She won gold medals in three consecutive Olympics (1988, 1992, 1994) and was the recipient of the 1992 Sullivan Award.

The University of Alabama football team was originally called the Red Elephants. After they won the 1920 Rose Bowl, a sportswriter said, "they washed over their opponents like a crimson tide." The team has been known as the Crimson Tide ever since.

Bird, Larry (1956–   ). Basketball player (forward); Boston Celtics. A three-time NBA most valuable player (1984–86), he is credited (with Magic Johnson) for the sharp increase in the sport's popularity in the mid-1980s.

Borg, Bjorn (1956–   ). Swedish tennis player. A five-time Wimbledon singles champion, he led Sweden to its first Davis Cup title (1975). He was noted for his strong base-line play and dazzling shots.

Brown, Jim (1936–   ). Football player (fullback); Cleveland Browns. During his career, he gained 12,312 yards and was named the NFL's most valuable player three times. He retired after the 1965 season to become an actor.

Bryant, Paul ("Bear") (1913–83). College football coach; various universities. He led Alabama to 25 winning seasons and 6 national championships. His career total of 323 victories is third on the all-time list.

Bubka, Sergei (1963–   ). Ukrainian pole vaulter. The first to clear the 20-foot barrier (both indoors and outdoors), he holds the world record in this event. He won a gold medal at the 1988 Olympics.

Butkus, Dick (1942–   ). Football player (linebacker); Chicago Bears. An eight-time NFL Pro

Bowl selection, he was noted for his aggressive, relentless style of play and bruising tackles.

Button, Dick (1929–   ). Figure skater. Twice an Olympic gold medalist (1948, 1952), he won the world championship five consecutive years (1948–52). He later became famous for his commentary during televised skating events.

Chamberlain, Wilt (1936–99). Basketball player (center); Philadelphia–San Francisco Warriors, Philadelphia 76ers, Los Angeles Lakers. He led the NBA in scoring seven times, setting a single-game record with 100 points (1962).

Cobb, Ty (1886–1961). Baseball player (outfielder); Detroit Tigers. Cobb won 12 batting titles during his 24-year career, and his lifetime batting average of .367 is the highest in major league history.

Comaneci, Nadia (1961–   ). Romanian gymnast. She achieved seven perfect scores while winning gold medals in the all-around, balance-beam, and uneven-bar competitions at the 1976 Olympics.

Connors, Jimmy (1952–   ). Tennis player. Noted for his on-court tantrums and powerful service, he is the all-time leader among men, with 109 tournament titles, including five U.S. Open and two Wimbledon championships.

Cooper, Cynthia (1963–   ). Basketball player (forward). A two-time WNBA MVP (1997–98) and three-time scoring leader (1997–99), she led the Houston Comets to the first four WNBA championships (1997–2000).

Corbett, James J. ("Gentleman Jim") (1866–1933). Boxer. Considered to have been the first "scientific" fighter, Corbett was heavyweight champion from 1892 to 1897. His 1891 bout with Peter Jackson went 61 rounds, ending in a draw.

DiMaggio, Joe (1914–99). Baseball player (outfielder); New York Yankees. He hit safely in a major league record 56 consecutive games (1941). Known as the "Yankee Clipper" for his graceful style, he won

the American League most valuable player award three times.

Earnhardt, Dale (1952–2001). Race car driver. A seven-time NASCAR national champion (1980, 1986–87, 1990–91, 1993–94), Earnhardt died in a final-lap crash at the 2001 Daytona 500.

Ederle, Gertrude (1906–   ). Swimmer. In 1926, she became the first woman to swim the English Channel, breaking the existing men's record for the crossing.

Evert, Chris (1954–   ). Tennis player. Second among women in all-time tournament victories with 157, she captured six U.S. Open championships and three Wimbledon titles. She was noted for her cool, unflappable on-court demeanor.

Faldo, Nick (1957–   ). British golfer. Winner of the Masters tournament in 1989, 1990, and 1996, he also won three British Open titles (1987, 1990, 1992) and led the European team to victory in the 1995 Ryder Cup.

Fleming, Peggy (1948–   ). Figure skater. She was U.S. champion for five consecutive years (1964–68) and also captured three straight world titles (1966–68). After winning a gold medal in the 1968 Winter Olympics, she starred with the Ice Follies and Holiday on Ice.

Foreman, George (1948–   ). Boxer. He twice held a heavyweight title (1973–74, 1994–95). At 45, he was the oldest fighter ever to win a championship bout.

Fosbury, Dick (1947–   ). High jumper. A gold medalist in the 1968 Olympics, he invented the technique known as the "Fosbury flop."

Foyt, A. J. (1935–   ). Race car driver. A four-time winner of the Indianapolis 500, he also captured seven U.S. Auto Club championships. His 67 lifetime victories in Indy car racing are a record.

Gehrig, Lou (1903–41). Baseball player (first baseman); New York Yankees. He set the major league record for consecutive games played (2,130;

broken, 1995) and career grand-slam home runs (23), and he still holds the American League single-season record for runs batted in (184; set 1931). His career was prematurely ended by amyotrophic lateral sclerosis (ALS), now widely known as Lou Gehrig's disease.

Gibson, Althea (1927–). Tennis player. She won both the U.S. Open and Wimbledon singles championships in consecutive years (1957–58). She was the first African American to compete in either event and the first to be named Associated Press female athlete of the year.

Graf, Steffi (1969–). German tennis player. In 1988, at the age of 19, she won the coveted Grand Slam of tennis (Australian, French, U.S. Open, Wimbledon). She has captured five U.S. Open and seven Wimbledon championships.

Gretzky, Wayne (1961–). Canadian hockey player (center); Edmonton Oilers, other teams. The leading scorer in NHL history, he received the Hart Trophy as the league's most valuable player nine times (1980–87, 1989). His smooth, dominant ice style earned him the nickname "The Great One."

Griffey, Ken, Jr. (1969–). Baseball player (outfielder); Seattle Mariners, Cincinnati Reds. Noted for his charismatic personality and acrobatic fielding, Griffey twice led the American League in home runs (1994, 1997).

Halas, George ("Papa Bear") (1895–1983). Football executive and coach. He founded the Chicago Bears in 1920 and led the team to five NFL championships during his 40 years as its head coach. His 324 career victories are second on the all-time list.

Hamilton, Scott (1958–). Figure skater. He reigned as U.S. and world champion four consecutive years (1981–84) and won an Olympic gold medal in 1984.

Hamm, Mia (1972–). Soccer player. The all-time leading scorer in women's international soccer (81 goals), she starred on two World Cup champions

(1991, 1999) and two U.S. Olympic teams (gold medal, 1996; silver medal, 2000).

Heiden, Eric (1958–). Speed skater. He won all five gold medals in men's events at the 1980 Olympics and was world champion three consecutive years (1977–79). He was the 1980 Sullivan Award winner.

Henderson, Rickey (1958–). Baseball player (outfielder); Oakland A's, New York Yankees, other teams. He holds the major league single-season record for stolen bases (130), set in 1982, and is the all-time career stolen-base leader (still active).

Henie, Sonja (1912–69). Norwegian figure skater. She won 10 consecutive world championships (1927–36) and earned 3 Olympic gold medals (1928, 1932, 1936). Henie transformed the sport by introducing ballet movements into her routines.

Hogan, Ben (1912–97). Golfer. He won four U.S. Open titles and captured both the PGA and the Masters championships twice. He survived serious injuries sustained in a 1949 car crash and returned to win the 1950 U.S. Open.

Jackson, Reggie (1946–). Baseball player (outfielder); Oakland A's, New York Yankees, other teams. Noted for his flamboyant style, he led the American League in home runs four times, and hit five round-trippers (including three in the final game) in the 1977 World Series. His many World Series heroics earned him the nickname "Mr. October."

Johnson, Earvin ("Magic") (1959–). Basketball player (guard); Los Angeles Lakers. With Larry Bird, he helped bring the sport to a new level of popularity in the mid-1980s. He won NBA most valuable player honors three times and ranks second in career assists. He retired after announcing that he had contracted the HIV virus but returned to lead the "Dream Team" to a gold medal in the 1992 Olympics.

Johnson, Randy (1963–). Baseball player (pitcher); Seattle Mariners, Arizona Diamondbacks

He led the American League in strikeouts four consecutive seasons (1992–95). At 6'10", his imposing mound presence has earned him the nickname "Big Unit."

Jones, Marion (1975–). Track and field competitor. A two-time world champion in the 100m dash (1997, 1999), she won five medals (3 gold, 2 bronze) at the 2000 Olympics.

Jordan, Michael (1963–). Basketball player (guard); Chicago Bulls. A ten-time NBA leading scorer (1987–93, 1996–98) and five-time winner of the league's most-valuable-player award, Jordan led the Bulls to six championships in eight seasons (1991–93, 1996–98). He is regarded by many as the greatest player in the history of the game for his dazzling moves and clutch performances.

Joyner-Kersee, Jackie (1962–). Track and field performer. Twice an Olympic gold-medal winner in the heptathlon (1988, 1992), she is widely considered to be one of world's greatest female athletes.

Killy, Jean Claude (1943–). French skier. He won three gold medals in Alpine events (downhill, slalom, giant slalom) in the 1968 Olympics and twice took the World Cup overall championship (1967, 1968).

King, Billie Jean (1943–). Tennis player. King won the U.S. Open singles championship 4 times and captured 6 Wimbledon titles. Her 39 Grand Slam titles (including doubles and mixed-doubles play) is third on the all-time list. In 1973 she defeated Bobby Riggs in the "Battle of the Sexes" tennis exhibition.

Kiraly, Karch (1960–). Volleyball player. He led the U.S. Olympic team to two gold medals (1984, 1988) and won the gold medal in the first Olympic beach volleyball competition (1996).

Laver, Rod (1938–). Australian tennis player. He twice won tennis's Grand Slam (1962, 1969) and earned four Wimbledon titles (1961–62, 1968–69).

Lemieux, Mario (1965–). Canadian hockey player; Pittsburgh Penguins. He led the NHL in scoring five times (1988–89, 1992–93, 1996) and earned the league's most valuable player award three times (1988, 1993, 1996). Despite recuperating from Hodgkin's disease, he was the NHL's scoring champ in 1993.

Leonard, Sugar Ray (1956–). Boxer. He held titles in five different weight classes (welterweight, junior middleweight, middleweight, light heavyweight, super middleweight) over his 14-year career.

Lewis, Carl (1961–). Track and field performer. He won nine gold medals in running events (4 × 100m relay; 100m and 200m dashes) and the long jump in the 1988 and 1992 Olympics.

Lombardi, Vince (1913–70). Football coach; Green Bay Packers, Washington Redskins. He led the Packers to five NFL championships and victories in Super Bowls I and II. The trophy awarded to the Super Bowl champion is named in his honor.

Louganis, Greg (1960–). Diver. He twice won Olympic gold medals in springboard and platform diving (1984, 1988). He remained competitive despite having contracted the HIV virus.

Louis, Joe (1914–81). Boxer. Nicknamed the "Brown Bomber," he held the world heavyweight championship from 1937 to 1949.

Mantle, Mickey (1931–95). Baseball player (outfielder); New York Yankees. He won the American League triple crown in 1956 and hit a record 18 World Series home runs. He was named the AL's most-valuable-player three times.

Marciano, Rocky (1923–69). Boxer. The world heavyweight champion from 1952 to 1956, he retired undefeated with 49 victories (43 by knockouts).

Marino, Dan (1961–). Football player (quarterback); Miami Dolphins. Among the NFL's all-time leading quarterbacks, he is third in passing efficiency and first in both touchdown passes and passing yardage. He is considered one of the greatest passers in league history, despite never having won a Super Bowl.

Mays, Willie (1931–). Baseball player (outfielder); New York–San Francisco Giants, New York Mets. Third on the all-time career home-run list (660), his enthusiastic play and effervescent personality led to his nickname "Say Hey Kid."

McEnroe, John (1959–). Tennis player. Third on the all-time tournament victory list with 77, he won four U.S. Open singles championships (1979–81, 1984) and three Wimbledon singles titles (1981, 1983–84). He was noted for his short temper on court.

McGwire, Mark (1963–). Baseball player (first baseman); Oakland Athletics, St. Louis Cardinals. He hit 70 home runs in 1998, breaking Roger Maris's season home-run record (61).

Messier, Mark (1961–). Canadian hockey player (center); Edmonton Oilers, New York Rangers. Twice chosen the NHL's most valuable player (1990, 1992), he led the Rangers to the team's first Stanley Cup championship in 54 years (1994).

Montana, Joe (1956–). Football player (quarterback); San Francisco 49ers, Kansas City Chiefs. Montana ranks in the top ten in career passing percentage, yardage, completions, and touchdowns. He is the only player to win the Super Bowl MVP award three times (1982, 1985, 1990).

Morceli, Noureddine (1970–). Algerian middle-distance runner. He held world records in four events (1,500 meter, mile, 2,000 meter, and 3,000 meter).

Moser-Proll, Annemarie (1953–). Austrian skier. She won six World Cup Alpine overall championships (1971–75, 1979) and took the gold medal in the women's downhill at the 1980 Olympics.

Namath, Joe (1943–). Football player (quarterback); New York Jets. He led the Jets to victory over the heavily favored Baltimore Colts in Super Bowl III after guaranteeing a win, putting the upstart AFL on an equal footing with the older, established NFL. His flamboyant off-field personality led to his nickname "Broadway Joe."

Navratilova, Martina (1956–). Tennis player (born Czechoslovakia). She won nine Wimbledon championships and four U.S. Open titles (1983–84, 1986–87) on her way to 56 career Grand Slam titles (singles and doubles) and a record 161 victories in all.

Nicklaus, Jack ("Golden Bear") (1940–). Golfer. The leading money winner on the PGA tour eight times, he captured six Masters tournaments among his 70 career wins, second on the all-time list.

Nurmi, Paavo (1897–1973). Finnish distance runner. He won six Olympic gold medals (1920, 1924, 1928) and broke numerous world records in the 1,500m, 5,000m, and cross-country events.

Owens, Jesse (1913–80). Track and field competitor. He broke four world records in one afternoon of competition (May 25, 1935) and won four gold medals in the 1936 Olympics.

Palmer, Arnold (1929–). Golfer. In 1968 he became the first to earn $1 million on the PGA tour. He captured four Masters (1958, 1960, 1962, 1964) and two British Opens (1961–62) on his way to over 70 career tournament wins.

Payton, Walter (1954–99). Football player (running back); Chicago Bears. The NFL's career rushing leader (16,726 yards), he led the league five consecutive seasons (1976–80).

Pelé [Edson Arantes do Nascimento] (1940–). Brazilian soccer player. He scored 1,281 goals during his 22-year career, and led Brazil to three World Cup championships (1958, 1962, 1970). His speed and acrobatic skills earned him an international following.

Petty, Richard (1937–). Race car driver. The winner of seven NASCAR national championships,

Petty achieved seven Daytona 500 victories and a record 200 career wins.

Plante, Jacques (1929–86). Canadian hockey player (goalie); Montreal Canadiens. He won the Vezina Trophy (awarded to the NHL's top goalie) seven times. He was the first goalie to wear a protective mask in a game (1959).

Rice, Jerry (1962–   ). Football player (receiver); San Francisco 49ers. He holds NFL records for career touchdowns (156) and receptions (942). Rice was the most valuable player in Super Bowl XXIII (1989).

Richard, Maurice ("Rocket") (1921–2000). Canadian hockey player (right wing); Montreal Canadiens. He scored 544 regular-season and 82 playoff goals and starred on eight Stanley Cup champions.

Rickey, Branch (1881–1965). Baseball executive; St. Louis Cardinals, Brooklyn Dodgers, Pittsburgh Pirates. Known for his innovative ideas, he signed Jackie Robinson to a major league contract with the Dodgers, thus breaking baseball's so-called color barrier (1947). He also established the sport's first farm system (Cardinals, 1919).

Ripken, Cal, Jr. (1960–   ). Baseball player (infielder); Baltimore Orioles. Twice the American League's most valuable player (1983, 1991), he broke Lou Gehrig's record for consecutive games played in 1995.

Robinson, Jackie (1919–72). Baseball player (infielder); Brooklyn Dodgers. The first African American to play in the major leagues (1947), he was selected the National League's most valuable player in 1949.

Rockne, Knute (1888–1931). Football coach; Notre Dame (college). Rockne helped to modernize the game by introducing the platoon system and stressing the forward pass. He built Notre Dame into a perennial college-football powerhouse.

Roy, Patrick (1965–   ). Canadian hockey player (goalie); Montreal Canadiens; Colorado Avalanche. He holds several major NHL records, including career regular-season victories and career playoff victories.

Ruth, Babe [George Herman] (1895–1948). Baseball player (outfielder, pitcher); Boston Red Sox, New York Yankees. Ruth set major league records for home runs in a season (60, in 1927) and career (714); both were later eclipsed.

Ryan, Nolan (1947–   ). Baseball player (pitcher); various teams. He holds numerous major league records, including strikeouts in a season (383, in 1973), career strikeouts (5,714), and career no-hit games (7).

Rudolph, Wilma (1940–94). Sprinter. She took three gold medals in the 1960 Olympics (100m and 200m dashes, 4 x 10m relay). She was the Sullivan Award winner in 1961.

Sampras, Pete (1971–   ). Tennis player. He has won more Grand Slam singles titles (13), including four at the U.S. Open and seven at Wimbledon, than any other male player.

Secretariat (1970–1989). Race horse. He captured horse racing's coveted Triple Crown in 1973, winning the Belmont Stakes by an astounding 31 lengths. He sired and grandsired notable thoroughbreds (Risen Star, Charismatic).

Shoemaker, Willie (1931–   ). Jockey. He rode four Kentucky Derby and five Belmont Stakes champions and retired as horse racing's leading career money winner.

Shula, Don (1930–   ). Football coach; Baltimore Colts, Miami Dolphins. He led six teams to the Super Bowl, winning twice (with the Dolphins). His 1972 Miami team went 17–0. He retired as the NFL's all-time leader in victories (347).

Simpson, O(renthal) J(ames) (1947–   ). Football player (running back); Buffalo Bills. Simpson set the NFL single-season rushing record with 2,003 yards (1974; broken 1984) and led the league in rushing four times. In his 1995 criminal trial, Simpson was found not guilty of the murders of his ex-wife, Nicole Brown Simpson and her friend, Ronald Goldman. In 1997 he was found liable for the murders in a subsequent civil trial.

Smith, Dean (1931–   ). Basketball coach; North Carolina (college). He led his teams to 25 NCAA tournament appearances and won national championships in 1982 and 1993. He is college basketball's all-time "winningest" coach.

Spitz, Mark (1950–   ). Swimmer. Spitz won seven gold medals in the 1972 Olympics, setting world records in each event. His 11 career medals (9 gold, 1 silver, 1 bronze) in two Olympic appearances (1968, 1972) are the most by an American (tied with Matt Biondi).

Stengel, Casey [Charles Dillon] (1890–1975). Baseball manager; various teams. He led the New York Yankees to 10 American League pennants (1949–53, 1955–58, 1960) and 7 World Series titles (1949–53, 1956, 1958) and was the first manager of the expansion New York Mets (1962). He was famous for his eccentric use of language, termed "Stengelese."

Summitt, Pat (1952–   ). Women's basketball coach. Tennessee (college). She has led the Lady Vols to 6 NCAA championships (1987, 1989, 1991, 1996–98) and ranks second in career victories.

Thorpe, Jim (1888–1953). Multisport athlete. He won both the pentathlon and the decathlon in the 1912 Olympics but was later disqualified for a prior loss of his amateur status. His medals were restored in 1982. He also played professional baseball (1913–19) and football (1919–26). Thorpe is considered the greatest Native American athlete of all time.

Tyson, Mike (1966–   ). Boxer. At 19, he became the youngest fighter to win a heavyweight championship (1986). The undisputed champion from 1987 to 1990, he was stripped of his crown after a felony rape conviction (1992). He regained the title in 1996 but lost it to Evander Holyfield in 1997.

Weissmuller, Johnny (1904–84). Swimmer. He won 52 national championships and 5 Olympic gold medals and set 67 world records. After retiring, he earned fame as the lead actor in a series of Tarzan films.

Williams, Venus (1980–   ). Tennis player. She won two Grand Slam tournaments in 2000 (Wimbledon, U.S. Open) and captured gold medals in singles and doubles (with sister Serena) at the 2000 Olympics.

Witt, Katarina (1965–   ). German figure skater. She twice won Olympic gold medals (1984, 1988) and captured four world championships (1984–85, 1987–88).

Wooden, John (1910–   ). Basketball coach; UCLA (college). He won a record 10 national championships (1964–65, 1967–73, 1975). His UCLA team set an NCAA record with 88 consecutive wins (1971–74).

Woods, Tiger (1975–   ). Golfer. He was the first player to win three consecutive U.S. Amateur titles (1994–96) and the youngest golfer to win the Masters (1997, with a record low score of 270 and a record margin of 12 strokes). His early professional successes and enthusiastic followers have created a popular phenomenon known as "Tiger-mania."

Young, Cy (1867–1955). Baseball player (pitcher); various teams. He holds the major league records for career wins (511) and losses (316). The annual award given to the best pitcher in each league is named in his honor.

Zaharias, Babe Didrikson (1914–56). Multisport athlete. She captured two gold medals in the 1932 Olympics (80m hurdles, javelin), earned All-America honors in basketball (1930–32), and won numerous amateur and professional golf tournaments (in the 1940s and 1950s). She is considered one of the greatest female athletes of all time.

BOARD GAMES

BACKGAMMON

Backgammon is a board game played by two players, each with 15 markers, or stones, which at the beginning of the game are placed in a standard initial configuration (see diagram) on the board. The board is divided into two tables, each with 12 triangular spaces, or points. Each player rolls two dice to determine the number of points moved by the stones, with black moving around the board in one direction and white moving in the opposite direction. The numbers on each die can be combined to move one stone the total amount indicated, or each die's value can be applied separately to single stones. If "doubles" are thrown (such as two 6s), the player can move twice as many points as are shown on the dice—in this case, four stones can move 6 spaces each, one can move 6 spaces and one 18 spaces, two can move 12 spaces each, or one stone can move 24 spaces. The object of the game is to be the first person to move his or her stones around the board and then off, called bearing off. A player may begin bearing off only when all of his or her stones are on the table opposite his or her beginning table. Each number on the die must correspond exactly with the number of the point a stone is on in order to bear the stone off. However, when all the stones are off

the six point, a roll of 6 may bear off a stone on the five point; when all stones are off the six and five points, a roll of 6 or 5 may bear off a stone on the four point, and so on.

A university study found that people spend more on refreshments at tractor pulls than they do at football games.

Any number of stones of the same color may stay on one point, but stones of the opposite color may not occupy the same point. A point occupied by two or more stones of the same color is said to be closed; it prevents the opponent from landing there. A point occupied by one marker (or none) is open. A single stone on any point is called a blot, and the opponent may land there with a hit. The opponent then places the blot on the bar, thereby sending it back to the owner's beginning table. The blot can reenter the game only when the owner rolls a number on one of the dice corresponding to an open point or one occupied by stones of the owner's color on his or her beginning table. All blots on the bar must reenter the table before the owner makes another move.

Backgammon depends on the roll of the dice and is therefore partially a game of chance, but it can also involve complex strategy and tactics. The game may

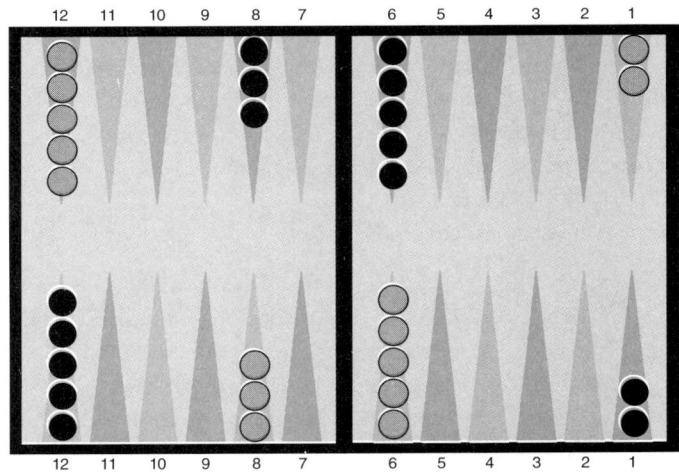

Backgammon Starting Position

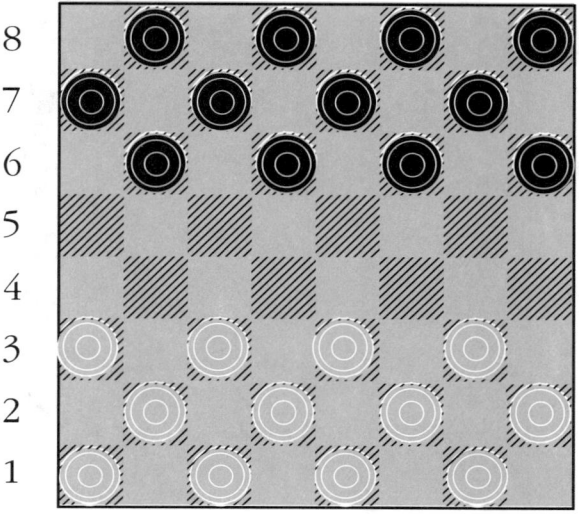

Checkers Starting Position

make use of the doubling cube, which is a die with a number on each face (2, 4, 8, 16, 32, 64). Using this cube, either player can at any point in the game double the stakes, whether they be points, as in tournament play, or money, as in the gambling version.

CHECKERS

Checkers is played by two players on a board with 64 squares alternating light and dark. Only the dark squares of the board are used. The board is eight squares wide and eight squares long. Each player uses 12 wooden discs called checkers, usually red for one player and black for the other. The pieces are set up on the dark squares of the first three ranks, four in each rank. Black moves first, and the players alternate turns by moving one checker forward diagonally toward the opposing player's checkers. The object is to jump over the opponent's pieces, which are then removed from play. A player wins when all the opponent's pieces have been removed. If a player manages to advance a piece to the last rank on the opposite end of the board, that piece becomes a king and thereby acquires the capability of moving backward as well as forward.

CHESS

Chess is a game for two players, one directing the white pieces and one directing the black pieces. It is played on a board with 64 squares of alternating colors, black and white. The board is eight squares wide and eight long. Squares on the board are normally referred to by coordinates, using numbered ranks and lettered files. (See illustration, p. 728.) Each player has 16 pieces: eight pawns, two rooks, two knights, two bishops, a queen, and a king. To start the game, the pieces are set up using the 32 spaces of ranks 1 and 2 (for one color) and 7 and 8 (for the other color). Rooks occupy the outermost files (a and h), with knights placed next to them (b and g); next to them are the bishops (c and f). Toward the center of the board (d and e) the king and queen are placed, with the white queen on a white square and the black queen on a black square. The pawns are placed in front of these pieces, using ranks 2 and 7.

The object of the game is to capture the opponent's king by placing him in checkmate. In this position, the king is under attack by an opposing piece (check), and wherever the king moves, it remains under attack by that or another opposing piece. The attacking side thus wins the game. If a player feels

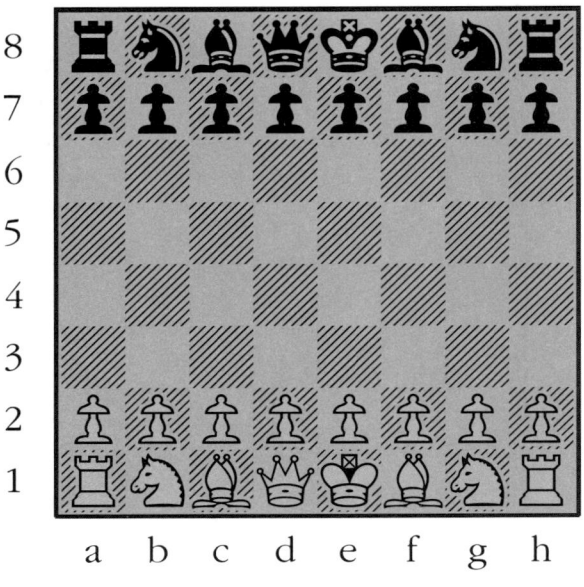

Chess Starting Position

that checkmate is unavoidable, he or she may give up, or resign. If neither white nor black is able to checkmate the opponent or force resignation, a draw may be agreed upon. If the king is not in check and if a player can make no moves, or if all otherwise legal moves would expose his king to check, the game ends in a stalemate.

Any piece may capture, or take, an opponent's piece by landing on the square occupied by that piece. The king, however, cannot be captured and is instead put into check when attacked. If a piece is captured, it is removed from the board. If a pawn reaches the last rank (1 or 8), it is immediately "promoted" to a queen, rook, bishop, or knight at its owner's wish, without regard to the number of them the owner already has.

Each type of piece moves in a prescribed way. A rook moves forward or back, left or right as many squares in one direction as is desired. Knights move two squares in one direction (forward, back, left, or right) and one square at right angles to the first direction—or one square in one direction and two squares at right angles to the first move—resulting in an L-shaped move. The knight is the only piece that

may jump over another piece. Bishops move diagonally any number of spaces in one direction. The queen moves forward, back, left, right, or diagonally any number of spaces in one direction. The king moves as the queen does, but one space at a time. Pawns move forward only, one space at a time, except for the first move, which may be two spaces. Pawns capture pieces by moving diagonally. There are only two instances in which pieces may move in other than these prescribed ways:

1. *Castling* is a two-part move involving the king and a rook. If neither of these pieces has moved previously, if there are no pieces between them, and if the king is neither in check nor would move through or to a guarded square, the king may move two spaces toward the rook, and the rook may move to the square on the other side of the king.

2. If, by moving ahead two squares on its first move, a black pawn lands next to a white pawn on the same rank, the white pawn may capture the black pawn by moving diagonally to the square immediately behind the black pawn. This is called taking *en passant,* or capturing in

passing. Of course, a black pawn may capture a white pawn in the same way.

MONOPOLY®

Monopoly® uses a board with 40 spaces around the perimeter. Players, starting with a fixed amount of money, roll two dice and, in turn, advance their tokens around the board the number of spaces indicated by the dice. If a player lands on any of 22 properties, that player may buy it at a stated price. This money goes into the bank. The player then receives a deed for that property, which states the rent that an opposing player must pay the owner if the player lands on it. The object of the game is to accumulate the properties and, by charging rent when an opponent lands there, to drive opposing players into bankruptcy. Properties are grouped by colors, with two or three to a group. If a player acquires all the properties within a single color, that player may develop those properties by purchasing houses and hotels. These dramatically increase the rent.

In addition to the color-coded properties, which are given street names, there are also four railroads and two utility companies that may be purchased. These also carry rents, but they may not be developed. If a player lands on any of six spaces, three called "Chance" and three "Community Chest," that player must pick up a card from two piles placed in the center of the board and follow its instructions. These involve monetary transactions either beneficial or harmful to the player. There is a neutral space called "Free Parking," a "Jail" space, two tax spaces, and a space called "Go." Play begins on the Go space, and the players collect $200 each time they circle the board and pass it.

In informal play, Monopoly® may involve considerable negotiation and trading among players. The game ends when all but one player has gone bankrupt; the remaining player is the winner.

SCRABBLE®

Scrabble® is a word game for two, three, or four players. The game uses a Scrabble® board with 225 spaces, 100 lettered tiles, 2 blank tiles, and a tile rack for each player. Each player, starting with seven letters, attempts to form words on the board using letters from his or her own hand and from words on the board. Words may read from left to right or from top to bottom. Usually a new word uses one letter from a word already on the board, with which it interlocks at right angles, as in a crossword. Letters may be added to an existing word to form a new one.

Each player, after using some or all of his or her tiles to form a word on the board, replenishes the playing hand from the pool of remaining tiles, which are facedown. Thus, each player always has seven tiles with which to form words, except toward the end of the game, when the pool runs out.

Each letter has a numerical value associated with it; this number is marked on the tile. Players score for each word formed, based on the value of each letter in the word. Scores are recorded with pencil and paper. Players may augment scores by using certain

---

A Closer Look

The Most Landed-On Spaces on the Monopoly® Game Board

According to Irvin R. Hertzel of Iowa State University, there are 10 spaces on the Monopoly® game board you can count on landing on more than the others. Using a computer, Hertzel, a mathematician, was able to figure out the overall probability of landing on each square. The following are the 10 most landed-on spaces.

1. Illinois Avenue
2. Go
3. B. & O. Railroad
4. Free Parking
5. Tennessee Avenue
6. New York Avenue
7. Reading Railroad
8. St. James Place
9. Water Works
10. Pennsylvania Railroad

94 Acceptable Two–Letter Scrabble® Words

aa	be	fa	lo	om	ti
ad	bi	go	ma	on	to
ae	bo	ha	me	op	uh
ag	by	he	mi	or	um
ah	da	hi	mm	os	un
ai	de	hm	mo	ow	up
al	do	ho	mu	ox	us
am	ef	id	my	oy	ut
an	eh	if	na	pa	we
ar	el	in	ne	pe	wo
as	em	is	no	pi	xi
at	en	it	nu	re	xu
aw	er	jo	od	sh	ya
ax	es	ka	oe	si	ye
ay	et	la	of	so	
ba	ex	li	oh	ta	

premium spaces on the board. These special spaces result in doubling or tripling the values of single letters or complete words. When no player is able to form additional words, each player's score is tallied. Values of unplayed letters for each player are subtracted. The highest score wins the game.

CARD GAMES

BLACKJACK

Blackjack is a gambling game that uses a standard 52-card deck. Ace counts as 1 or 11 points; king, queen, jack, and 10 count as 10 each; all other cards count as their face number. The object is to hold two or more cards totaling 21 or as close to 21 as possible without going over. Cards are dealt one at a time, clockwise, starting with the player at the dealer's left. Each player receives one card facedown and one card faceup. After this initial deal, each player may stand and refuse more cards or take additional cards faceup. For example, having been dealt a king down and a 6 up (totaling 16), if the player chooses to take an additional card and receives another 6, that player is out with 22. An ace and a picture card or a 10 is called blackjack; it totals 21 and beats all other hands.

Various betting methods are used, but usually bets are made before and after the initial deal and after each subsequent deal. All players play against the dealer, and bets are settled depending on which hands are closest to but not over 21; if the dealer has the same count as a given player, the hand is considered a standoff.

BRIDGE

Contract bridge uses a standard 52-card deck and is a game for four players, in partnerships of two. The teams are designated North–South and East–West. Cards in each suit rank ace (high), king, queen, jack, 10, 9, . . . 2 (low); and suits rank spades (high), hearts, diamonds, and clubs (low). Each player receives cards, dealt one at a time clockwise, starting at the dealer's left.

Each player in turn gets a chance to make a bid, which is a statement of the intention to win more than six tricks. At the same time, the player either declares a high-ranking suit (trump) or declares no trump. If a player chooses not to bid, he or she may pass. Bids go around the table in clockwise rotation, with each bid being higher than any preceding bid. A bid may be doubled by an opponent or redoubled by a partner. These double the scoring value of a bid if it is played. This bidding segment of the game is called the auction, and the highest bid becomes the contract. One member of the contracting team declares the trump and becomes the declarer. That person's partner spreads his or her hand faceup on the table and becomes the dummy.

The object of the game is to win tricks in order to fulfill the contract or to defeat the opponent's attempt to fulfill it. The player to the declarer's left leads, and all players must follow suit if possible. A trick is won by the highest card of the suit led if no trump is played, or by the highest trump played.

When all 13 tricks have been taken, the result is scored. There is a complicated scoring system depending primarily on whether the contract was made and by how much. The two members of a partnership score their combined tricks as a single unit. Extra points may be scored in several ways. A bonus is scored if a doubled or redoubled bid is made. One of two types of slams is scored if the contracting team wins 12 tricks or all 13. Honor points are scored when a player receives certain cards in the deal (ace, king, queen, jack, 10 of trump, or the four aces if no trump has been declared).

When a side accumulates 100 or more points in trick scores, the game is over. The side that first wins two out of three games wins a rubber. After each rubber, partnerships may change and play may begin again.

PINOCHLE

Pinochle is played by two to four players and uses a 48-card deck, which includes two of each rank from 9 to ace in all four suits. The rank of cards in each suit is ace (high), 10, king, queen, jack, 9. Cards are dealt three at a time, clockwise, starting to the dealer's left. In two-hand pinochle, both players receive 12 cards; in three-hand (auction pinochle), each receives 15; and in four-hand (partnership pinochle), each receives 12 cards. The remaining cards, if any, form the stock. After an ad hoc high-ranking suit, called trump, has been determined, the

player to the left of the dealer leads by placing a card in the middle, followed by each player in rotation. Tricks are won by the high trump or by the higher card of the suit led if no trump is played. The winner of the trick leads for the next trick. Except in two-hand pinochle, a player must always follow the suit that is led, if possible.

Cards taken in tricks determine the scoring, with each ace counting 11, each ten 10, each king 4, each queen 3, and each jack 2. Nines do not score. A player can also score points by winning the last trick. In addition, certain combinations of cards, called melds, have scoring value. These include the flush (ace, 10, king, queen, jack in the same suit); the marriage (king and queen in the same suit); groups of cards of the same rank (four aces, four kings, etc.); and two special melds, the nine of trump and the pinochle (queen of spades and jack of diamonds).

Points taken in tricks are added to those accumulated by melding. Usually the player or team that first reaches 1,000 points wins the game.

POKER

Poker is a popular card game that uses a standard 52-card deck, with cards ranking ace (high), king, queen, jack, 10, 9, ... 2 (low). The ace can also rank low if used as part of ace-2-3-4-5. Jokers are sometimes used as wild cards, which can stand for any card the holder chooses. There are hundreds of forms of poker, but invariably the cards are dealt clockwise, one at a time, starting with the player to the dealer's left. Usually each player receives five cards facedown, but depending on the type of poker, more cards may be dealt, or some may be dealt faceup.

Poker is a gambling game that uses chips of different monetary value. Bets by players go into a pile of chips called the pot. The object is to win the pot, either by showing the best hand or by making a bet that no one is willing to match. The rank of poker hands without wild cards is as follows. The top six hands are illustrated on the next page.

Sports/Games

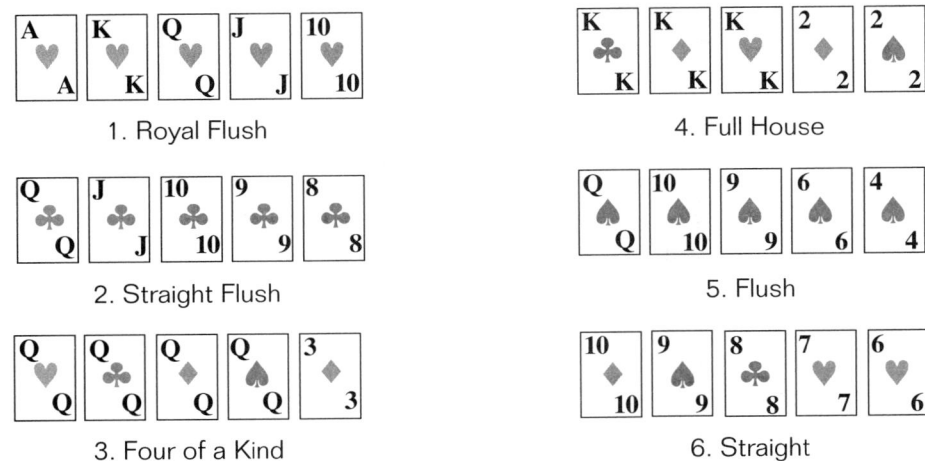

1. Royal Flush   4. Full House

2. Straight Flush   5. Flush

3. Four of a Kind   6. Straight

Top Six Winning Poker Hands

1. *Royal flush:* a sequence of ace, king, queen, jack, 10 of the same suit
2. *Straight flush:* five cards in sequence in the same suit
3. *Four of a kind:* four cards of the same rank
4. *Full house:* three of a kind and a pair
5. *Flush:* five cards of the same suit
6. *Straight:* five cards in sequence, regardless of suit
7. *Three of a kind:* three cards of the same rank
8. *Two pair:* two cards of the same rank and two others of a different rank
9. *One pair:* two cards of the same rank
10. *High card:* five unmatched cards, one with the highest rank of the five

RUMMY

Rummy uses a regular deck of 52 cards. The cards rank king (high), queen, jack, 10, . . . 2, ace (low). Cards are dealt one at a time, clockwise, starting at the dealer's left. The number of cards dealt to each player depends on the number of players in the game: with two players, 10 cards each; with three or four players, 7 cards each; with five or six players, 6 cards each. The undealt remainder of the deck is placed facedown, forming the stock. Its top card is turned up next to the stock, forming the discard pile. The object is to form groups (three or more cards of the same rank) or sequences (three or more cards of the same suit in sequence of rank). Forming groups or sequences is called melding.

One at a time and proceeding clockwise, players draw one card from the top of the stack or the top of the discard pile. If melding is possible, groups or sequences are placed faceup in front of the player. A player may also lay off, or add to his or her own or an opponent's melds. A player's turn ends by his placing one card faceup on the discard pile. When one player melds all the cards remaining in a hand, that player goes out, thus ending that deal, which is then scored. The player going out scores his or her own melds plus the points left in the opponents' hands. The other players score just their own melds. Aces count as 1; all picture cards count as 10; and the rest of the cards count as their face number. High score wins.

Except when going out, a player must discard one card after each play, whether or not that player has melded or laid off.

SOLITAIRE

Solitaire, or Patience, refers to a group of card games played by one person. The most popular and best known of these games is Klondike. Using a standard 52-card deck, the player deals a tableau or layout, consisting of seven piles of cards. The first pile on the far left has one card, the second pile two, and so on to the far right pile, which has seven cards. These cards are dealt facedown except for the top card in each pile. On these piles, descending sequences are built in alternating colors. For example, a red 9 may be placed on a black 10. Entire sequences or individual cards may be moved from pile to pile, provided correct colors and sequences are maintained. If a down card in a pile is revealed, it is turned faceup and may then become part of a sequence. When a pile is exhausted, a king may replace it.

When they become available, aces are placed above the original layout. The object is to build sequences in suit from the four aces (the foundations) up to the four kings, thus using all cards of the original layout as well as the remaining cards, which form the stock. From the stock, the player turns up one card at a time, forming a waste pile. The top card of the waste pile is available for play on the layout or foundations. The player goes through the stock only once and wins the game if he or she successfully places the entire deck on the foundations. Many players employ alternative, more liberal methods of dealing the stock.

ADDITIONAL SOURCES OF INFORMATION

ORGANIZATIONS AND SERVICES

GENERAL

Amateur Athletic Union of the U.S.
c/o The Walt Disney World Resort
P.O. Box 10000
Lake Buena Vista, FL 32830-1000
407-934-7200
http://aausports.org

National Collegiate Athletic Association (NCAA)
700 W. Washington Street
P.O. Box 6222
Indianapolis, IN 46206-6222
http://www.ncaa.org

AUTO RACING

American Hot Rod Association (AHRA)
N. 101 Hayford Rd.
Spokane, WA 99204
509-244-2372

Championship Auto Racing Teams (CART)
755 W. Big Beaver, Ste. 00
Bloomfield Hills, MI 48084
248-362-8800
http://www.cart.com

National Association for Stock Car Racing
http://www.nascar.com/index.html

National Hot Rod Association (NHRA)
2035 Financial Way
Glendora, CA 91740
626-914-4761
http://www.nhra.com

BASEBALL

American League (AL)
245 Park Ave.
New York, NY 10022
212-931-7600
http://www.majorleaguebaseball.com/al/

Baseball Hall of Fame
P.O. Box 590
Cooperstown, NY 13326
607-547-7200
http://www.baseballhalloffame.org

Major League Baseball Commissioner's Office
245 Park Ave.
New York, NY 10022
212-931-7800
http://www.majorleaguebaseball.com

National Association of Professional Baseball Leagues
(minor league clubs)
P.O. Box A
St. Petersburg, FL 33731
727-822-6937
http://www.minorleaguebaseball.com

National League (NL)
245 Park Ave.
New York, NY 10022
212-931-7700
http://www.majorleaguebaseball.com/nl/

BASKETBALL

Basketball Hall of Fame
P.O. Box 179
1150 West Columbus Ave.
Springfield, MA 01101-0179
413-781-6500
http://www.hoophall.com

National Basketball Association (NBA)
645 Fifth Ave.
New York, NY 10022
212-826-7000
http://www.nba.com

BICYCLE RACING

United States Cycling Federation (USCF)
(amateur)
c/o USOC
1 Olympic Plaza
Colorado Springs, CO 80909
719-578-4581

BOWLING

National Bowling Association
377 Park Ave. South
7th Floor
New York, NY 10016
212-689-8308
http://www.tnbainc.org

Professional Bowler's Association of America (PBA)
1720 Merriman Rd.
P.O. Box 5118
Akron, OH 44334-0118
330-836-5568
http://www.pba.org

FOOTBALL

National Football Foundation and College Hall of Fame
22 Maple Ave.
Morristown, NJ 07960
973-829-1933
http://www.footballfoundation.com

National Football League (NFL)
280 Park Ave.
New York, NY 10017
212-450-2000
http://www.nfl.com

Pro Football Hall of Fame
2121 George Halas Dr., NW
Canton, OH 44708
330-456-8207
http://www.profootballhof.com

GOLF

Ladies Professional Golf Association (LPGA)
100 International Golf Dr.
Daytona Beach, FL 32124-1092
904-274-6200
http://www.lpga.com

Professional Golfer's Association of America (PGA)
100 Avenue of the Champions
P.O. Box 109601
Palm Beach Gardens, FL 33410-9601
561-624-8400
http://www.pga.com

U.S. Golf Association (USGA)
Liberty Corner Rd.
P.O. Box 708
Far Hills, NJ 07931-0708
908-234-2300
http://www.usga.org

U.S. Golf Association Museum and Library
Golf House
Far Hills, NJ 07931-0708
908-234-2300
http://www.usga.org/golfhouse/index.html

HORSE RACING

National Museum of Racing and Hall of Fame
191 Union Ave.
Saratoga Springs, NY 12866-3566
518-584-0400
http://www.racingmuseum.org

U.S. Trotting Association
750 Michigan Ave.
Columbus, OH 43215-1191
614-224-2291
http://www.ustrotting.com

ICE HOCKEY

American Hockey League (AHL)
1 Monarch Place
Suite 2400
Springfield, MA 01103
413-781-2030
http://www.canoe.ca/AHL/home.html

Hockey Hall of Fame
BCE Place
30 Yonge St.
Toronto, Ontario MSE 1X8
Canada
416-360-7735
http://www.hhof.com

National Hockey League (NHL)
1251 Avenue of the Americas
New York, NY 10020
212-789-2000
http://www.nhl.com

SOCCER

U.S. Soccer Federation
1801 South Prairie Ave.
Chicago, IL 60616
312-808-1300
http://www.US-Soccer.com/

TENNIS

International Tennis Hall of Fame and Museum
Newport Casino
194 Bellevue Ave.
Newport, RI 02840
401-849-3990
800-457-1144
http://www.tennisfame.org

U.S. Tennis Association (USTA)
70 West Red Oak Ln.
White Plains, NY 10604
914-696-7000
http://www.usta.com

TRACK AND FIELD

Intercollegiate Association of Amateur Athletes of America (IC4A)
P.O. Box 3
Centerville, MA 02632
508-771-5060

International Amateur Athletics Federation
17 rue Princesse Florestine
BP 359
MC 98007 Monaco Cedex
(011) 33 377 93 10 88 88
http://www.iaaf.org

USA Track and Field
P.O. Box 120
Indianapolis, IN 46206-0120
317-261-0500
http://www.usatf.org

VOLLEYBALL

USA Volleyball
715 S. Circle Road
Colorado Springs, CO 80910
719-228-6800
http://www.usavolleyball.org

OLYMPIC GAMES

United States Olympic Committee (USOC)
Olympic Plaza
Colorado Springs, CO 80909-5760
719-632-5551
http://www.usoc.org

BOARD AND CARD GAMES

American Contract Bridge League (ACBL)
2990 Airways Blvd.
Memphis, TN 38116-3847
901-332-5586
http://www. acbl.org

National Scrabble Association (NSA)
c/o Williams & Co.
P.O. Box 700
Greenport, NY 11944
631-477-0033
http://www. scrabble-assoc.com

United States Chess Federation (US Chess)
3054 NYS Route 9W
New Windsor, NY 12553
845-562-8350
http://www.uschess.org

MAGAZINES

ESPN: The Magazine
19 E. 34th Street
New York, NY 10016

The Sporting News
P.O. 51575
Boulder, CO 80323

Sports Illustrated
1271 Avenue of the Americas
New York, NY 10020

BOOKS

GENERAL

Diagram Group. *Rules of the Game: The Complete Illustrated Encyclopedia of All the Sports of the World.* Rev ed. St. Martin's, 1995.

Donavan, Michael Leo. *The Name Game: Football, Baseball, Hockey & Basketball——How Your Favorite Sports Teams Were Named.* Warwick, 1997.

Kent, Michael, ed. *The Oxford Dictionary of Sports Science and Medicine.* Oxford University Press, 1998.

Palmatier, Robert S., and Harold L. Ray. *Dictionary of Sports Idioms.* NTC, 1993.

Porter, David L., ed. *Biographical Dictionary of American Sports.* 4 vols. Greenwood, 1987–89.

AUTO RACING

Golenbock, Peter, and Greg Fielden. *The Stock Car Racing Encyclopedia.* Hungry Minds, 1997.

Gunnell, John A., ed. *Race Car Flashback: A Celebration of America's Affair with Auto Racing from 1900 to the 1980s.* Krause Publications, 1994.

Popely, Rick, and L. Spencer Riggs. *Indianapolis 500 Chronicle.* Publications International, 1998.

BASEBALL

The Baseball Encyclopedia: The Complete and Definitive Record of Major League Baseball. 10th ed. Macmillan General Reference, 1996.

Bjarkman, Peter C., ed. *Encyclopedia of Major League Baseball: American League Team Histories.* Carroll & Graf, 1993.

Bjarkman, Peter C., ed. *Encyclopedia of Major League Baseball: National League Team Histories.* Carroll & Graf, 1993.

Dewey, Donald, et al. *Encyclopedia of Major League Baseball Teams.* HarperCollins, 1993.

Dickson, Paul. *The New Dickson Baseball Dictionary.* Harcourt Brace, 1999.

Lorimer, Lawrence. *The National Baseball Hall of Fame Baseball Desk Reference.* Dorling Kindersley, 2002.

Neft, David S., Richard M. Cohen, and Michael L. Neft. *The Sports Encyclopedia: Baseball.* 21st ed. St. Martin's, 2001.

Nemec, David. *The Great Encyclopedia of 19th Century Major League Baseball.* Donald I. Fine, 1997.

Pietrusza, David. *Major Leagues: The Formation, Sometimes Absorption and Mostly Inevitable Demise of 18 Professional Baseball Organizations, 1871 to Present.* McFarland, 1991.

Riley, James A. *The Biographical Encyclopedia of the Negro Baseball Leagues.* Carroll & Graf, 1994.

Solomon, Burt. *The Baseball Timeline.* Dorling Kindersley, 2001.

Thorn, John, et al., eds. *Total Baseball: The Official Encyclopedia of Major League Baseball.* 7th ed. Total Sports, 2001.

Ward, Geoffrey C., and Ken Burns. *Baseball: An Illustrated History.* Knopf, 1994.

BASKETBALL

Douchant, Mike. *Encyclopedia of College Basketball.* Gale Research, 1994.

Hubbard, Jan, ed. *The Official NBA Basketball Encyclopedia.* 3rd ed. Doubleday, 2000.

Neft, David S., and Richard M. Cohen. *The Sports Encyclopedia: Pro Basketball.* St. Martin's, 1992.

Savage, Jim. *Encyclopedia of the NCAA Basketball Tournament: The Complete Independent Guide to College Basketball's Championship Event.* Dell, 1990.

Vancil, Mark. *The NBA at Fifty.* Park Lane, 1996.

BICYCLE RACING

Abt, Samuel. *Pedaling for Glory: Victory and Drama in Professional Bicycle Racing.* Motorbooks International, 1997.

Nye, Peter. *Heart of Lions: The History of American Bicycle Racing.* W. W. Norton, 1989.

Ritchie, Andrew. *Bicycle Racing Record Book.* Motorbooks International, 1998.

Sutherland, Sandra W. *No Brakes!: Bicycle Track Racing in the United States.* Iris, 1996.

BOWLING

Allen, George, and Dick Ritger. *Complete Guide to Bowling Principles: The Encyclopedia.* Technical Education, 1994.

FOOTBALL

Carroll, Bob, et al., eds. *Total Football II: The Official Encyclopedia of the National Football League.* HarperCollins, 1999.

Maher, Tod, and Bob Gill, eds. *The Pro Football Encyclopedia: The Complete and Definitive Record of Professional Football.* Hungry Minds, 1997.

Neft, David S., Richard M. Cohen, and Rich Korch. *The Sports Encyclopedia: Pro Football.* 17th ed. St. Martin's, 1999.

Ours, Robert. *College Football Encyclopedia: The Authoritative Guide to 124 Years of College Football.* Prima, 1993.

GOLF

Campbell, Malcolm. *Random House International Encyclopedia of Golf: The Definitive Guide to the Game.* Random House, 1991.

Glenn, Rhonda. *The Illustrated History of Women's Golf.* Taylor, 1991.

Peper, George. *Golf Magazine's Encyclopedia of Golf: The Complete Reference.* HarperCollins, 1993.

United States Golf Association. *The Official Rules of Golf.* Triumph Books, 2000.

HORSE RACING

Ainslie, Tom. *Ainslie's Complete Guide to Thoroughbred Racing.* Fireside, 1988.

Bowen, Edward L. *The Jockey Club's Illustrated History of Thoroughbred Racing in America.* Bullfinch, 1994.

Stout, Nancy. *Homestretch: A Celebration of America's Greatest Tracks.* Running Press, 2000.

ICE HOCKEY

Diamond Dan, et al. eds. *Total Hockey: The Official Encyclopedia of the National Hockey League.* Total Sports, 2000.

Fischler, Stan. *Fischler's Illustrated History of Hockey.* Warwick, 1993.

SOCCER

Lablanc, Michael L., and Richard Henshaw. *The World Encyclopedia of Soccer.* Gale Research, 1993.

Murray, Bill. *The World's Game: A History of Soccer.* University of Illinois Press, 1998.

Pickering, David. *Cassell Soccer Companion: History, Facts, and Anecdotes.* Continuum, 1999.

Radnedge, Keir. *The Complete Encyclopedia of Soccer 2000–2001.* Carleton Books, 2000.

Sports/Games

TENNIS

Collins, Bud, and Zander Hollander, eds. *Bud Collins's Tennis Encyclopedia*. 3rd ed. Visible Ink Press, 1997.

Gillmeister, Heiner. *Tennis: A Cultural History.* Cassell Academic, 1997.

Savage. Jim. *The Grand Slam Tennis Encyclopedia: The Definitive Record of Wimbledon, the Australian Open, the French Open, and the U.S. Open.* Macmillan General Reference, 1996.

TRACK AND FIELD

Lawson, Gerald. *World Record Breakers in Track & Field Athletics.* Human Kinetics, 1997.

VOLLEYBALL

Kessel, John. *Volleyball Encyclopedia.* Sports Support Syndicate, 1996.

Shewman, Byron. *Volleyball Centennial: The First 100 Years.* Masters, 1996.

OLYMPIC GAMES

Wise, Michael T., et al., eds. *Chronicle of the Olympics, 1896–1996.* Dorling-Kindersley, 1996.

Young, David C. *The Modern Olympics: A Struggle for Revival.* Johns Hopkins University Press, 1996.

BOARD AND CARD GAMES

Mohr, Merilyn Simonds. *The New Games Treasury: More Than 500 Indoor and Outdoor Favorites with Strategies, Rules and Traditions.* Houghton Mifflin, 1997.

WEB SITES

CBS SportsLine
A major online sports information network
www.cbs.sportsline.com

CNN/SI
Comprehensive online site from Cable News Network and Sports Illustrated
sportsillustrated.cnn.com

ESPN SportsZone
The online site of the cable sports giant
www.espn.go.com

Sporting News
Online counterpart to the long-running print publication
www.sportingnews.com

USA Today
Online site of the nationwide daily newspaper
www.usatoday.com

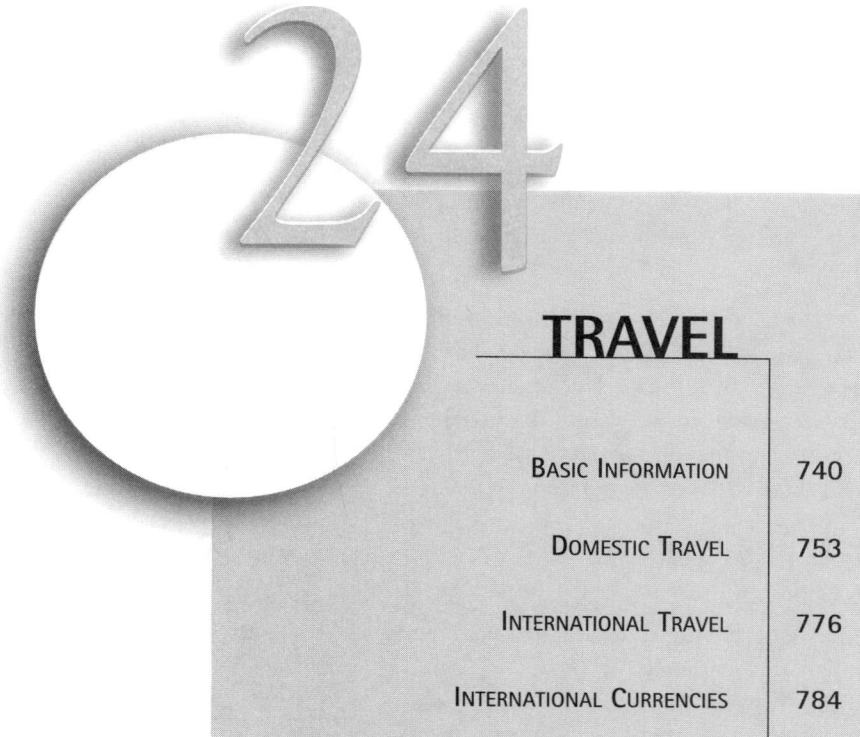

24

TRAVEL

BASIC INFORMATION

Whether you're planning a weekend getaway nearby or an extended stay on another continent, careful preparation is essential for a safe and successful trip.

Airline security and increased antiterrorism procedures after September 11, 2001, created tight carry-on restrictions and longer delays at airports. Air travelers are advised to call their airline carrier or check up-to-date web sites before traveling to stay informed about the latest alerts and procedures.

TRAVELERS' CHECKLIST

Things to Do

- ✓ Arrange for the post office to hold your mail, or have someone collect it daily.
- ✓ Stop all deliveries to your home.
- ✓ Arrange for the care of your animals, plants, and lawn.
- ✓ Put your valuables in a safety-deposit box.
- ✓ Notify your neighbors and the police of absence and let them know how you can be reached.
- ✓ Leave a key with a neighbor.
- ✓ Arrange for travelers' insurance coverage, if needed.
- ✓ Notify your travel agent of any special needs you might have, such as the use of an airport wheelchair.
- ✓ Reconfirm your airline ticket and other reservations.
- ✓ Tag your luggage for easy identification.
- ✓ Set timers or leave a light on.
- ✓ Empty the refrigerator and turn it on low.
- ✓ Turn off the hot water.
- ✓ Lock all doors and windows.

Things to Bring

- ✓ Government-issued photo I.D.
- ✓ Airline or other tickets and travel documents.
- ✓ Auto registration, if driving.
- ✓ Passport, visas, and health certificates.
- ✓ Medical information and doctor's name and telephone number.

Travelers' First-Aid Kit

A Closer Look

Antiseptic lotion or ointment
Aspirin or acetaminophen
Cold and cough remedies
Gauze bandages and adhesive tape, elastic bandages
Heating pad
Ice pack
Identification bracelet
Insect repellent and insect-bite medication
Medical information regarding condition, allergies, medications, blood type, and special needs
Milk of magnesia and diarrhea medication
Moleskin for blisters and calluses
Physician's name, address, and telephone number
Prescription medications and refills
Sunscreen and sunburn-relief lotion
Telephone numbers of emergency contacts
Thermometer
Throat lozenges
Vitamins

- ✓ Special over-the-counter or prescription medications.
- ✓ Insurance papers.
- ✓ Credit cards.
- ✓ Travelers' checks and personal checks.
- ✓ Cash, including some in the currency of the country to which you are traveling.
- ✓ Names and addresses of people to contact in an emergency.
- ✓ Names, addresses, phone numbers, reservation numbers, and dates for places where you will be staying.
- ✓ Lightweight fold-up tote bag for purchases.
- ✓ Addresses of friends and family to whom to send mail.
- ✓ Extra pair of eyeglasses (or contacts) and your eyeglass (or contact) prescription.

TIPS FOR TRAVELERS WITH DISABILITIES

Good planning is key to enjoyable travel by people with disabilities. Since the passage of the Americans with Disabilities Act in 1990, travel in the United States is much more accessible for those with disabilities. Airports, railroads, and public and private transportation systems all must provide access for the disabled. Cruise ships have increasing numbers of cabins and ramps designed for disabled travelers. However, it is still advisable to consult with a travel agent who specializes in handling travelers with disabilities or to research facilities beforehand by calling the carrier or via the Internet, especially when traveling outside the United States.

FURTHER INFORMATION

Access-Able Travel Source
http://www.access-able.com/

Mobility International
541-343-1284
Fax 541-343-6812

National Park Service
(for information on U.S. highway rest areas)
202-208-6843

Society for the Advancement of Travel for the Handicapped (SATH)
212-447-7284
Fax 212-725-8253

CAR-RENTAL AGENCY TOLL-FREE NUMBERS AND WEB SITES

Alamo
(U.S. and international)
800-462-5266
800-522-9292 TDD
http://www.goalamo.com

AutoEurope
(U.S. and Europe)
800-223-5555
http://www.auto-europe.com/

Avis
(U.S. and international)
800-331-1212 domestic
800-331-1084 international
800-331-2323 TDD
http://www.avis.com/

Budget
(U.S. and international)
800-527-0700 domestic
800-472-3325 international
800-826-5510 TDD
http://www.budgetrentacar.com/

Dollar/EuroDollar
(U.S. and international)
800-800-4000 domestic
800-800-6000 international
800-232-3301 TDD
http://www.dollarcar.com/

Enterprise
(U.S. and Canada)
800-736-8227
http://www.pickenterprise.com/

Europe by Car
(Europe)
800-223-1516
http://www.europebycar.com/

Hertz
(U.S. and international)
800-654-3131 domestic
800-654-3001 international
800-654-2280 TDD
http://www.hertz.com/

Kemwel Holiday Autos
(U.S. and international)
800-678-0678
http://www.kemwel.com/

National
(U.S. and international)
800-227-7368 domestic
800-227-3876 international
800-328-6323 TDD
http://www.nationalcar.com/

Many businesses provide TDD lines, which are telecommunication devices for the deaf.

Payless
(U.S. and international)
800-729-5377
http://www.paylesscar.com/

Rent-a-Wreck
(U.S. and international)
800-535-1391
http://rentawreck.com/raw/

Thrifty
(U.S. and international)
800-847-4389
http://www.thrifty.com/

"Symbols to Guide the Traveler" in chapter 12

Go to

Travel

Traveling with Pets

A Closer Look

Although most travelers leave home without them, vacationing with pets is possible; if you plan carefully, taking your pet along can save on guilt, worry, and even money. It's easier to leave the goldfish in the care of friends, but the family dog can go with you almost anywhere. Information and suggestions to make this easier appear below.

Travel Checklist

- ✓ Proper identification (name and address tag)
- ✓ Thermos of water
- ✓ Plastic bowls
- ✓ Proof of up-to-date immunizations
- ✓ Pet carrier
- ✓ First-aid kit, including bandages, antiseptic, and medications (including tranquilizers) prescribed by your veterinarian
- ✓ Food (and can opener, if needed)
- ✓ Certificate of good health signed by your veterinarian
- ✓ Leash and muzzle
- ✓ Flea powder or flea collar
- ✓ Blanket
- ✓ Pet toys
- ✓ Grooming tools

Pretravel Suggestions

Introduce your pet to car travel with trial runs.

Allow your pet to become familiar with the pet carrier before your trip.

Do not feed your pet for several hours before the trip.

Exercise your pet right before leaving.

Travel Restrictions

Automobile No restrictions.

Bus Except for Seeing Eye dogs, pets are prohibited on buses in interstate travel.

Train Pets may be taken only in private compartments or in the baggage car.

Airplane Pets can come on board in pet carriers or can remain in the baggage compartment. Restrictions vary, so inquire of individual airlines in advance.

National park Pets are allowed on leashes except in bathing areas.

State and private parks Restrictions vary, so check with the individual facility.

Hotel, motel, and campground Most do accept pets; notify the owner ahead of time.

International Travel (Including Hawaii)

Most countries require a recent certificate of good health and proof of immunizations. In addition, the following places may require a quarantine (at the owner's expense) for the number of days indicated. The number of days in quarantine may vary according to the type of pet and its state of health. Check with individual embassies or consulates for specific requirements.

Hawaii	180		Norway	120
Hong Kong	180		Panama	180
Jamaica	180		Singapore	30
Jordan	42		Sweden	120
Korea	21		Trinidad and Tobago	180
Malta	180		United Kingdom	180
Mauritius	180			

Returning Home

Upon your return, a quarantine officer at customs will check documents and inspect your animal. The official may require confinement of any animal that you have purchased abroad; typically confinement is in your own home rather than in an official quarantine. Pets purchased abroad also will require proof of immunization, certificates of good health, and payment of an import duty.

HOTEL/MOTEL CHAIN TOLL-FREE NUMBERS AND WEB SITES

American Historic Inns, Inc.
(U.S.) 800-379-4887
http://www.bnbinns.com

Best Western
(U.S. and international)
800-780-7234
800-528-2222 TDD
http://www.bestwestern.com/

Clarion
(U.S. and international)
800-252-7466
800-228-3323 TDD
http://www.clarioninn.com/

Comfort Inn
(U.S. and international)
800-228-5150
800-228-3323 TDD
http://www.comfortinn.com/

Days Inn
(U.S. and international)
800-329-7155
800-228-3323 TDD
http://www.daysinn.com/

Delta
(U.S. and international)
800-268-1133
http://www.deltahotels.com/

Doubletree
(U.S. and Mexico)
800-222-8733
800-528-9898 TDD
http://www.hilton.com/doubletree

EconoLodge
(U.S. and Canada)
800-553-2666
800-228-3323 TDD
http://www.econolodge.com

Embassy Suites
(U.S. and international)
800-362-2779
http://www.embassy-suites.com/

Hampton Inn
(U.S. and international)
800-426-7866
http://www.hampton-inn.com/

Hilton
(U.S. and international)
800-445-8667
http://www.hilton.com/

Holiday Inn
(U.S. and international)
800-465-4329
http://www.holiday-inn.com/

Howard Johnson
(U.S. and international)
800-446-4656
800-654-8442 TDD
http://hojo.com/

Hyatt
(U.S. and international)
800-233-1234
http://www.hyatt.com/

LaQuinta
(U.S.)
800-531-5900
800-426-3101 TDD
http://www.laquinta.com/

Marriott
(Includes Marriott Hotels, Renaissance, Courtyard Marriott, Residence Inn, Fairfield Inn, TownPlace Suites, Spring Hill Suites)
(U.S. and international)
888-236-2427
http://www.marriott.com/

Quality Inn
(U.S. and international)
800-228-5151
800-228-3323 TDD
http://www.qualityinn.com

Radisson
(U.S. and international)
800-333-3333
800-906-2200 TDD
http://www.radisson.com/

Ramada Inn
(U.S. and Canada)
800-272-6232
800-228-3232 TDD
http://www.ramada.com/

Red Lion
(U.S. and Mexico)
800-733-5466
800-528-9898 TDD
http://www.redlion.com

Travel

Rodeway Inn
(U.S. and international)
800-228-2000
800-228-3323 TDD
http://www.rodeway.com

Sheraton
(U.S. and international)
800-325-3535
http://www.sheraton.com/

Sleep Inn
(U.S. and international)
800-753-3746
800-228-3323 TDD
http://www.hotelchoice.com

Summit International
(U.S. and international)
800-457-4000
http://www.summithotels.com/

Westin
(U.S. and international)
800-228-3000
800-325-1717 TDD
http://www.westin.com/

AIRLINE CODES, TOLL-FREE NUMBERS, AND WEB SITES

Airline (Home Country)	Code	Toll-Free Number(s)	Web Site
ACES (Colombia)	VX	800-846-2237	http://www.aces.com.co/index2.htm
Aer Lingus (Ireland)	EI	800-223-6537	http://www.aerlingus.ie/
Adria Airways (Slovenia)	JP		http://www.adria.si/eng/index.htm
Aeroflot Russian International Airlines (Russia)	SU	800-995-5555	http://www.aeroflot.com/
Aerolineas Argentinas (Argentina)	AR	800-333-0276	http://www.aerolineas.com.ar/english
Aeromexico (Mexico)	AM	800-237-6639	http://www.aeromexico.com/
Aeroperu (Peru)	PL	800-777-7717	http://www.travelx.com/aeroperu.html
Air Afrique (Côte d'Ivoire)	RK	800-456-9192	http://www.sinergia.it/airafrique.htm
Air Caledonie/Air Calin (New Caledonia)	SB	800-677-4277	http://www.pacificislands.com/airlines/caledonie.html
Air Canada (Canada)	AC	800-776-3000 800-361-8071 TDD	http://www.aircanada.ca/
Air China (China)	CA	800-882-8122	http://www.airchina.org.cn/english/index.htm
Air Fiji (Fiji Islands)	PC	800-677-4277	http://www.airfiji.net
Air France/Air Inter Europe (France)	AF	800-237-2747	http://www.airfrance.fr/
Air India (India)	AI	800-223-2250	http://www.airindia.com/
Air Jamaica (Jamaica)	JM	800-523-5585	http://www.airjamaica.com
Air Madagascar (Madagascar)	MD	800-821-3388	http://www.air-mad.com
Air Malawi			http://www.africaonline.co.ke/airmalawi/
Air Malta	KM		http://www.airmalta.com
Air Mauritius (Mauritius)	MK	800-537-1182	http://www.airmauritius.int.en/
Air Nauru (Nauru)	ON	800-677-4277	http://www.pacificislands.com/airlines/nauru.html
Air New Zealand (New Zealand)	NZ	800-926-7255	http://www.airnewzealand.com
Air Seychelles (Seychelles)	HM	800-677-4277	http://www.airseychelles.net
Air Slovenia			http://www.adria.si/eng/index.htm
Air Ukraine (Ukraine)	6U		http://www.airukraine.com
Air Vanuatu (Micronesia)	NF	800-677-4277	http://www.pacificislands.com/airlines/vanuatu.html
Air Zimbabwe (Zimbabwe)	UM	800-742-3006	http://www.airzimbabwe.com

Airline (Home Country)	Code	Toll–Free Number(s)	Web Site
Air Tran Airways (U.S.)	J7	800-247-8726	http://www.airtran.com/
Alaska Airlines (U.S.)	AS	800-252-7522	http://www.alaska-air.com/
Alitalia (Italy)	AZ	800-223-5730	http://www.alitalia.it/english/index.html
All Nippon Airways/ANA (Japan)	NH	800-235-9262	http://www.metrotel.co.uk/travlog/ana.html
Aloha Airlines (U.S.)	AQ	800-367-5250 800-554-4833 TDD	http://www.alohaair.com/
American Airlines (U.S.)	AA	800-433-7300 800-543-1586 TDD	http://www.aa.com
American Trans Air/ATA (U.S.)	TZ	800-225-2995 800-293-6194 TDD	http://www.ata.com
American West Airlines (U.S.)	HP	800-235-9292 800-526-8077 TDD	http://www.americanwest.com
Ansett Australia (Australia)	AN	800-366-1300	http://www.ansett.com.au/
Asiana Airlines (South Korea)	OZ	800-227-4262	http://www.us.flyasia.com
Austrian Airlines (Austria)	OS	800-843-0002	http://www.aua.com/
Avianca Colombia (Colombia)	AV	800-284-2622	http://www.avianca.com/
Aviateca (Guatemala)	GU	800-327-9832	http://www.grupotaca.com
Bahamasair (Bahamas)	UP		http://www.bahamasair.com
Balkan Bulgarian Airlines (Bulgaria)	LZ	800-852-0944	http://www.balkan-air.com/
Bangkok Airways	PG		http://www.bkkair.co.th
British Airways (United Kingdom)	BA	800-247-9297	http://www.us.british-airways.com/
British Midland (United Kingdom)	BD	800-788-0555	http://www.flybmi.com
BWIA International (Trinidad and Tobago)	BW	800-538-2942	http://www.bwee.com/caribbean
Cathay Pacific Airways (Hong Kong)	CX	800-233-2742	http://www.cathay-usa.com/
Cayman Airways	KX	800-422-9626	http://www.caymanairways.com
China Airlines (Taiwan)	CI	800-227-5118	http://www.china-airlines.com/
China Eastern Air (China)	MU	800-200-5118	http://www.cea.online.sh.cn/html/enindex.html
Comair—a subsidiary of Delta Airlines (U.S.)	DL	800-354-9822	http://www.fly-comair.com/
Continental Airlines (U.S.)	CO	800-525-0280 (domestic) 800-231-0856 (international)	http://www.continental.com/
Copa (Panama)	CM	800-892-2672	http://www.copaair.com/
Croatia Airlines (Croatia)	OU	800-247-5353	http://www.croatiaairlines.com
Cyprus Airways (Cyprus)	CY	800-333-2977	http://www.cyprusairways.com
Czech Airlines/CSA (Czech Republic)	OK	800-223-2365	http://www.csa.cz/
Delta Airlines (U.S.)	DL	800-221-1212	http://www.delta-air.com/
Egypt Air (Egypt)	MS	800-334-6787	http://www.egyptair.com.eg/dos/home.asp
El Al Israel Airlines (Israel)	LY	800-223-6700	http://www.elal.com
Emirates Air (United Arab Emirates)	EK	800-777-3999	http://www.emiratesairline.com
Ethiopian Airlines (Ethiopia)	ET	800-445-2733 (Eastern U.S.) 800-433-9677 (Midwestern and Western U.S.)	http://www.ethiopianairlines.com
EVA Airways (Taiwan)	BR	800-695-1188	http://www.evaair.com

Travel

continues

Airline Codes, Toll–Free Numbers, and Web Sites, Continued

Airline (Home Country)	Code	Toll–Free Number(s)	Web Site
Finnair (Finland)	AY	800-950-5000	http://www.finnair.fi
Frontier Airlines (U.S.)	F9	800-432-1359	http://www.flyfrontier.com/
Garuda Indonesia (Indonesia)	GA	800-342-7832	http://garudaindonesia.com
Greenlandair			http://www.greenland-guide.dk/gla/default.htm
Gulf Air (Persian Gulf)	GF	888-359-4853	http://www.gulfairco.com/
Guyana Airways (Guyana)	GY	800-242-4210	http://www.turq.com/guyana/guyana.html
Hawaiian Airlines (U.S.)	HA	800-367-5320	http://www.hawaiianair.com/
Horizon Air—a subsidiary of Alaska Airlines (U.S.)	AS	800-547-9308	http://www.horizonair.com/
Iberia Airlines (Spain)	IB	800-772-4642	http://www.iberia.com
Icelandair (Iceland)	FI	800-223-5500	http://www.icelandair.com/
Japan Airlines/JAL (Japan)	JL	800-525-3663	http://www.japanairlines.com
Kenya Airways (Kenya)	KQ	800-343-2506	http://www.kenya-airways.com
KLM Royal Dutch Airlines (The Netherlands)	KL	800-374-7747	http://www.klm.nl/
Korean Air (South Korea)	KE	800-438-5000	http://www.koreanair.com
Kuwait Airways (Kuwait)	KU	800-424-1128	http://www.kuwait-airways.com
LACSA Airlines (Costa Rica)	LR	800-225-2272	http://www.lacsa.com
Lan Chile (Chile)	LA	800-735-5526	http://www.lanchile.com/
Lauda Air (Austria)	NG	800-645-3880	http://www.laudaair.com
LOT Polish Airlines (Poland)	LO	800-223-0593	http://www.lot.com
LTU International Airways (Germany)	LT	800-888-0200	http://www.ltu.de/
Lufthansa Airlines (Germany)	LH	800-645-3880	http://www.lufthansa.com/
Malaysia Airlines		888-359-8655	http://www.malaysiaair.com
MALEV Hungarian Airlines (Hungary)	MA	800-223-6884	http://www.malev.hu/ew/angol/default.asp
Martinair Holland (The Netherlands)	MP	800-627-8462	http://www.martinair.com
Mesa Airlines (U.S.)	YV	800-637-2247	http://www.mesa_air.com/
Mexicana Airlines (Mexico)	MX	800-531-7921	http://www.mexicana.com.mx/mxz/english/home.asp
Midway Airlines (U.S.)	JI	800-446-4392 or 888-226-4392	http://www.midwayair.com
Midwest Express Airlines (U.S.)	YX	800-452-2022	http://www.midwestexpress.com/
New England Airlines (U.S.)	EJ	800-243-2460	http://www.ids.net/flybi/nea/
Nica Airlines (Nicaragua)	6Y	800-831-6422	http://www.grupotaca.com
Northwest Airlines (U.S.)	NW	800-225-2525 (domestic) 800-447-4747 (international)	http://www.nwa.com/
Olympic Airways (Greece)	OA	800-223-1226	http://www.olympic-airways.gr
Pacific Coastal Airlines (U.S.)	8P	800-663-2872	http://www.pacific-coastal.com/
Peninsula Airways/Penair (U.S.)	KS	800-448-4226	http://www.penair.com/
Philippine Airlines (The Philippines)	PR	800-435-9725	http://www.philippinesair.com
Polynesian Airlines (Western Samoa)	PH	800-677-4277	http://www.polynesianair.com

Airline (Home Country)	Code	Toll–Free Number(s)	Web Site
Qantas Airways (Australia)	QF	800-227-4500	http://www.qantas.com/au/index.html
Reno Air (U.S.)	QQ	800-736-6247	http://www.renoair.com/
Royal Air Maroc (Morocco)	AT	800-344-6726	http://www.royalairmaroc.com
Royal Jordanian Airlines (Jordan)	RJ	800-223-0470	http://www.rja.com.jo/
Royal Nepal Airlines (Nepal)	RA	800-266-3725	http://www.royalnepal.com
Royal Tonga Airline (Tonga)	WR	800-486-6426	http://www.tongatapu.net.to/tonga/islands/royalt/default.htm
Sabena Belgian World Airlines (Belgium)	SN	800-950-1000	http://www.sabena.com/
Saudi Arabian Airlines (Saudi Arabia)	SV	800-472-8342	http://www.saudiairlines.com
Scandinavian Airlines/SAS (Scandinavia)	SK	800-221-2350	http://www.sas.se/
Singapore Airlines (Singapore)	SQ	800-742-3333	http://www.singaporeair.com/
Solomon Airlines (Solomon Islands)	IE	800-677-4277	http://www.solomonairlines.com/english/
South African Airways/SAA (South Africa)	SA	800-722-9675	http://www.saa.co.za/1024.html
Southwest Airlines (U.S.)	WN	800-435-9792	http://www.iflyswa.com/
Sun Air			http://www.fiji.to/
Sunflower Airlines (Fiji Islands)	PI	800-707-3454	http://www.fijiguide.com/Sunflower/sunad.html
SWISS (Switzerland)	SR	877-359-7947	http://www.swiss.com/
TACA International Airlines (El Salvador)	TA	800-535-8780	http://www.grupotaca.com
TAP Air Portugal (Portugal)	TP	800-221-7370	http://www.tap-airportugal.pt/en/index1.html
Thai Airways International (Thailand)	TG	800-221-2500	http://www/thaiair.com
Transbrasil Airlines (Brazil)	TR	800-872-3153	http://www.transbrasil.com.br/
Travel Air (Costa Rica)	8T	800-924-2727	http://www.centralamerica.com/cr/tran/travlair.htm
Turkish Airlines/THY/Turk Hava Yollari (Turkey)	TK	800-874-8875	http://www.turkishairlines.com/
Trans World Airlines/TWA (U.S.)	TW	800-221-2000 (domestic) 800-892-4141 (international)	http://www.twa.com/
United Airlines (U.S.)	UA	800-241-6522	http://www.ual.com/
Ukraine International Airlines (Ukraine)	PS	800-876-0114	http://www.ukraine-international.com/eng/index.html
USAirways/USAir (U.S.)	US	800-428-4322	http://www.usairways.com/
Varig Brazilian Airlines (Brazil)	RG	800-468-2744 or 800-262-1706	http://www.varig.com.br
VASP Brazilian Airlines (Brazil)	VP	800-732-8277	http://www.vasp.com.br/
Virgin Atlantic Airways (U.K.)	VS	800-862-8621	http://www.virgin-atlantic.com
WestJet Airlines (Canada)	WJ	800-538-5696	http://www.westjet.com/
World Airways (U.S.)	WO	800-967-5350	http://www.worldair.com/

Travel

AIRPORT CODES, NAMES, AND LOCATIONS

UNITED STATES AIRPORTS

Code	U.S. Airport	Location
ABQ	Albuquerque International Airport	Albuquerque, NM
ACY	Atlantic City International Airport	Atlantic City, NJ
ANC	Anchorage International Airport	Anchorage, AK
ATL	Hartsfield International Airport	Atlanta, GA
AUS	Robert Mueller/Bergstrom International Airport	Austin, TX
BDL	Bradley International Airport	Hartford, CT
BHM	Birmingham International Airport	Birmingham, AL
BNA	Nashville International Airport	Nashville, TN
BOS	Logan International Airport	Boston, MA
BRO	Brownsville/South Padre Island International Airport	Brownsville, TX
BUR	Burbank/Pasadena/Glendale Airport	Burbank, CA
BWI	Baltimore/Washington International Airport	Baltimore, MD
CAE	Columbia Metropolitan Airport	Columbia, SC
CHS	Charleston International Airport	Charleston, SC
CLE	Hopkins International Airport	Cleveland, OH
CLT	Charlotte/Douglas International Airport	Charlotte, NC
CMH	Port Columbus International Airport	Columbus, OH
CVG	Greater Cincinnati International Airport	Covington, KY/Cincinnati, OH
DCA	Ronald Reagan Washington National Airport	Washington, DC
DEN	Denver International Airport	Denver, CO
DFW	Dallas/Ft. Worth International Airport	Dallas, TX
DTW	Detroit Metropolitan Airport	Detroit, MI
EWR	Newark International Airport	Newark, NJ
FLL	Ft. Lauderdale/Hollywood International Airport	Ft. Lauderdale, FL
GPT	Gulfport/Biloxi Regional Airport	Biloxi, MS
HNL	Honolulu International Airport	Honolulu, HI
HOU	William P. Hobby Airport	Houston, TX
HSV	Huntsville International Airport	Huntsville, AL
IAD	Dulles International Airport	Washington, DC
IAH	Houston Intercontinental Airport	Houston, TX
JAN	Jackson International Airport	Jackson, MS
JAX	Jacksonville International Airport	Jacksonville, FL
JFK	John F. Kennedy International Airport	New York, NY
LAS	McCarran International Airport	Las Vegas, NV
LAX	Los Angeles International Airport	Los Angeles, CA
LGA	La Guardia Airport	New York, NY
MCI	Kansas City International Airport	Kansas City, MO
MCO	Orlando International Airport	Orlando, FL
MEM	Memphis International Airport	Memphis, TN
MIA	Miami International Airport	Miami, FL
MKE	General Mitchell International Airport	Milwaukee, WI
MOB	Mobile Regional Airport	Mobile, AL
MSP	Minneapolis/St. Paul International Airport	Minneapolis, MN
MSY	Moisant International Airport	New Orleans, LA
MYR	Myrtle Beach International Airport	Myrtle Beach, SC
OAK	Metropolitan Oakland International Airport	Oakland, CA

Travel

Code	U.S. Airport	Location
OKC	Will Rogers World Airport	Oklahoma City, OK
ORD	O'Hare International Airport	Chicago, IL
PDX	Portland International Airport	Portland, OR
PHL	Philadelphia International Airport	Philadelphia, PA
PHX	Sky Harbor International Airport	Phoenix, AR
PIT	Greater Pittsburgh International Airport	Pittsburgh, PA
RDU	Raleigh-Durham International Airport	Raleigh, NC
RIC	Richmond International Airport	Richmond, VA
RNO	Reno-Cannon International Airport	Reno, NV
SAN	San Diego International Airport	San Diego, CA
SAT	San Antonio International Airport	San Antonio, TX
SAV	Savannah International Airport	Savannah, GA
SDF	Standiford Field	Louisville, KY
SEA	Seattle/Tacoma International Airport	Seattle, WA
SFO	San Francisco International Airport	San Francisco, CA
SJC	San Jose International Airport	San Jose, CA
SLC	Salt Lake City International Airport	Salt Lake City, UT
SMF	Sacramento Metropolitan Airport	Sacramento, CA
SRQ	Sarasota/Bradenton International Airport	Sarasota, FL
STL	Lambert–St. Louis International Airport	St. Louis, MO
TPA	Tampa International Airport	Tampa, FL
TUL	Tulsa International Airport	Tulsa, OK

INTERNATIONAL AIRPORTS

Code	International Airport	Location
ACA	General Juan N. Alvarez Airport	Acapulco, Mexico
AEP	Jorge Newbery Airpark	Buenos Aires, Argentina
AKL	Auckland International Airport	Auckland, New Zealand
ALA	Almaty International Airport	Almaty, Kazakhstan
AMS	Schiphol International Airport	Amsterdam, The Netherlands
ANR	Deurne Airport	Antwerp, Belgium
ANU	V. C. Bird/Coolidge International Airport	Antigua Island, Antigua
ARN	Arlanda International Airport	Stockholm, Sweden
ASU	Silvio Pettirossi Airport	Asuncion, Paraguay
ATH	Hellinikon International Airport	Athens, Greece
AUA	Queen Beatrix International Airport	Oranjestad, Aruba
AUH	Abu Dhabi International Airport	Abu Dhabi, United Arab Emirates
BAH	Bahrain International Airport	Bahrain, Bahrain
BAK	Baku Bina International Airport	Baku Bina, Azerbaijan
BBU	Baneasa Airport	Bucharest, Romania
BCN	Barcelona Transoceanic Airport	Barcelona, Spain
BDA	Kindley Field	Bermuda
BEY	Beirut International Airport	Beirut, Lebanon
BFN	JBM Hertzog Airport	Bloemfontein, South Africa
BFS	Belfast International Airport	Belfast (Northern Ireland), United Kingdom
BGI	Grantley Adams International Airport	Bridgetown, Barbados
BIM	South Bimini International Airport	Bimini, Bahamas

continues

Travel

Airport Codes, Names, and Locations, Continued

Code	International Airport	Location
BJS	Beijing International Airport	Beijing, China
BJX	Leon International Airport	Leon, Mexico
BKK	Don Muang International Airport	Bangkok, Thailand
BNE	Brisbane International Airport	Brisbane (Queensland), Australia
BOG	Eldorado Airport	Bogotá, Colombia
BOM	Bombay International Airport	Bombay, India
BRU	Brussels Airport	Brussels, Belgium
BSL	Basel/Mulhouse EuroAirport	Basel, Switzerland
BUD	Budapest Ferihegyi Airport	Budapest, Hungary
BZE	Belize International Airport	Belize City, Belize
CAI	Cairo International Airport	Cairo, Egypt
CAN	Baiyun Airport	Guangzhou, China
CAS	Casablanca Airport	Casablanca, Morocco
CCS	Simon Bolivar Airport	Caracas, Venezuela
CCU	Dum Dum International Airport	Calcutta, India
CDG	Charles de Gaulle Airport	Paris (Roissy), France
CGH	São Paulo Congonhas Airport	São Paulo, Brazil
CGK	Joekarno-Hatta International Airport	Jakarta, Indonesia
CGN	Cologne/Bonn Airport	Cologne, Germany
CHC	Christchurch International Airport	Christchurch, New Zealand
CJU	Cheju International Airport	Cheju, South Korea
CPH	Copenhagen International Airport	Copenhagen, Denmark
CPT	Capetown International Airport	Capetown, South Africa
CRL	Charleroi Brussels South Airport	Brussels, Belgium
CUN	Cancun International Airport	Cancun, Mexico
CUR	Hato Airport	Curacao, Netherlands Antilles
DBV	Hrvastka Airport	Dubrovnik, Croatia
DEL	Delhi International Airport	New Delhi, India
DOH	Doha Airport	Doha, Qatar
DUB	Dublin Airport	Dublin, Ireland
DUR	Louis Botha International Airport	Durban, South Africa
DUS	Dusseldorf Airport	Dusseldorf, Germany
EBB	Entebbe International Airport	Entebbe, Uganda
EZE	Ezeiza International Airport	Buenos Aires, Argentina
FCO	Fiumicino (Leonardo da Vinci) Airport	Rome, Italy
FLR	Peretola Airport	Florence, Italy
FPO	Freeport International Airport	Freeport, Bahamas
FRA	Frankfurt International Airport	Frankfurt, Germany
FRU	Bishkek/Frunze Manas International Airport	Bishkek (Chuy), Kyrgyzstan
GCM	Owen Roberts International Airport	Grand Cayman, Cayman Islands
GDL	Miguel Hidalgo y Costilla Airport	Guadalajara, Mexico
GEN	Gardermoen Airport	Oslo, Norway
GIG	Rio de Janeiro/Galeao International Airport	Rio de Janeiro, Brazil
GLA	Glasgow Airport	Glasgow (Scotland), United Kingdom
GND	PT Saline Airport	Grenville, Grenada
GVA	Geneva International Airport	Geneva, Switzerland
GYE	Simon Bolivar Airport	Guayaquil, Ecuador
HAM	Fuhlsbuttel International Airport	Hamburg, Germany

Code	International Airport	Location
HEL	Helsinki-Vantaa International Airport	Helsinki, Finland
HIJ	Hiroshima Airport	Hiroshima, Japan
HKG	Kai Tek (Chek Lap Kok) International Airport	Hong Kong, China
HND	Haneda International Airport	Tokyo, Japan
INN	Kranebitten Airport	Innsbruck, Austria
IST	Ataturk/Yesilkov International Airport	Istanbul, Turkey
JAV	Ilulissat Airport	Jakobshavn, Greenland
JCN	Inchon International Airport	Inchon, South Korea
JFJ	Kangerlussuaq (Sondre Stromfjord) Airport	Kangerslussuaq, Greenland
JNB	Johannesburg/Grand Central International Airport	Johannesburg, South Africa
JRS	Atarot Airport	Jerusalem, Israel
KBL	Kabul Airport	Kabul, Afghanistan
KDL	Kärdla Airport	Kärdla, Estonia
KHI	Quaid-e-Azam International Airport	Karachi, Pakistan
KIN	Norman Manley Airport	Kingston, Jamaica
KIX	Kansai International Airport	Osaka, Japan
KTP	Kingston Airport	Kingston, Jamaica
KUL	Sultan Abdul Aziz Shah, Subang International Airport	Kuala Lumpur, Malaysia
KWI	Kuwait Airport	Kuwait
LED	Pulkovo II International Airport	St. Petersburg (Leningrad), Russia
LGW	Gatwick Airport	London (England), United Kingdom
LHR	Heathrow International Airport	London (England), United Kingdom
LIM	Jorge Chavez International Airport	Lima, Peru
LIS	Lisbon Airport	Lisbon, Portugal
LPA	Las Palmas/Gran Canaria Airport	Las Palmas/Gran Canaria (Canary Islands), Spain
LPB	J. F. Kennedy/El Alto Airport	La Paz, Bolivia
LUX	Findel Airport	Luxembourg
MAD	Madrid Barajas Airport	Madrid, Spain
MAN	Ringway International Airport	Manchester (England), United Kingdom
MBJ	Sangster Airport	Montego Bay, Jamaica
MCT	Seeb Airport	Muscat, Oman
MEL	Tullamarine International Airport	Melbourne (Victoria), Australia
MEX	Benito Juarez International Airport	Mexico City, Mexico
MFM	Macau International Airport	Macau, Macao
MGA	A. C. Sandino Airport	Managua, Nicaragua
MLA	Malta International Airport	Malta
MLE	Hulele International Airport	Malé, Maldives
MNL	Ninoy Aquino International Airport	Manila, Philippines
MRX	Caribe Santiago Mariño International Airport	Margarita Island, Venezuela
MUC	Strauss International Airport	Munich, Germany
MVD	Carrasco Airport	Montevideo, Uruguay
MXP	Milano-Malpensa International Airport	Milan, Italy
NAP	Capodichino International Airport	Naples, Italy
NAS	Nassau International Airport	Nassau, Bahamas
NBO	Jomo Kenyatta International Airport	Nairobi, Kenya
NEV	Nevis Airport	Charlestown, Nevis
NRT	Narita International Airport	Tokyo, Japan

continues

Airport Codes, Names, and Locations, Continued

Code	International Airport	Location
OHD	Ohrid Airport	Ohrid, Republic of Macedonia
ORY	Orly Airport	Paris (Orly), France
OST	Ostend Airport	Oostende, Belgium
OTP	Otopeni International Airport	Bucharest, Romania
PAP	Mais Gate Airport	Port-au-Prince, Haiti
PEK	Beijing (Peking) Capital Airport	Beijing (Peking), China
PER	Perth International Airport	Perth (Western Australia), Australia
PMI	Palma de Mallorca Airport	Balearic Islands, Spain
POP	La Union Airport	Puerto Plata, Dominican Republic
POS	Piarco International Airport	Port of Spain (Trinidad Island), Trinidad
PRG	Ruzyne Airport	Prague, Czech Republic
PTP	Le Raizet Airport	Pointe-a-Pitre, Guadeloupe
PTY	Tocumen Airport	Panama City, Panama
PVR	Ordaz International Airport	Puerto Vallarta, Mexico
QCA	Makkah Airport	Mecca (Makkah), Morocco
RAD	Beef Island Airport	Tortola, British Virgin Islands
REK	Reykjavik Airport	Reykjavik, Iceland
RIX	Riga International Airport	Riga, Latvia
RUH	King Khalid Airport	Riyadh, Saudi Arabia
SAL	San Salvador International Airport	San Salvador, El Salvador
SCL	Comodoro Arturo Merino Benite Airport	Santiago, Chile
SDA	Saddam International Airport	Baghdad, Iraq
SDQ	Airport of the Americas	Santo Domingo, Dominican Republic
SEL	Kimpo International Airport	Seoul, South Korea
SHA	Hongqiao Airport	Shanghai, China
SHJ	Sharjah International Airport	Sharjah, United Arab Emirates
SIN	Changi International Airport	Singapore
SIP	Simferopol International Airport	Adygea, Ukraine
SJO	Juan Santamaria International Airport	San Jose, Costa Rica
SJU	Marin International Airport	San Juan, Puerto Rico
SKB	Golden Rock Airport	Basseterre, St. Kitts
SLL	Salalah International Airport	Salalah, Oman
SLU	Vigie Airport	Castries, St. Lucia
SOF	Sofia Airport	Sofia, Bulgaria
STT	Cyril E. King Airport	Charlotte Amalie (St. Thomas), U.S. Virgin Islands
STX	Alexander Hamilton Airport	Christensted (St. Croix), U.S. Virgin Islands
SVO	Sheremetyevo International Airport	Moscow, Russia
SXF	Schönefeld Airport	Berlin, Germany
SXM	Princess Juliana Airport	Philipsburg (St. Martin), Netherlands Antilles
SYD	Kingsford-Smith International Airport	Sydney (New South Wales), Australia
TAS	Tashkent International Airport	Tashkent, Uzbekistan
TLV	Ben Gurion Airport	Tel Aviv, Israel
TPE	Chiang Kai Shek Airport	Taipei, Taiwan
TRN	Caselle International Airport	Turin, Italy
TXL	Tegel Airport	Berlin, Germany
UIO	Mariscal Airport	Quito, Ecuador
ULN	Ulan Bator Airport	Ulan Bator, Mongolia

Code	International Airport	Location
VIE	Wien-Schwechat International Airport	Vienna, Austria
VNO	Vilnius International Airport	Vilnius, Lithuania
VVI	Viru Viru International Airport	Santa Cruz, Bolivia
WAW	Okçecie Airport	Warsaw, Poland
WQX	Gander International Airport	Gander (Newfoundland), Canada
XPL	Comayagua Airport	Comayagua, Honduras
YAP	Yap International Airport	Yap Island, Micronesia
YEG	Edmonton International Airport	Edmonton (Alberta), Canada
YHZ	Halifax International Airport	Halifax (Nova Scotia), Canada
YOW	Ottawa International Airport	Ottawa (Ontario), Canada
YUL	Dorval International Airport	Montreal (Quebec), Canada
YVR	Vancouver International Airport	Vancouver (British Columbia), Canada
YWG	Winnipeg International Airport	Winnipeg (Manitoba), Canada
YXU	Greater London International Airport	London (Ontario), Canada
YYC	Calgary International Airport	Calgary (Alberta), Canada
YYJ	Victoria International Airport	Victoria (British Columbia), Canada
YYZ	Pearson International Airport	Toronto (Ontario), Canada
ZAG	Zagreb Airport	Zagreb, Croatia
ZAZ	Zaragoza International Airport	Zaragoza, Spain
ZRH	Zurich-Kloten Airport	Zurich, Switzerland

Travel

DOMESTIC TRAVEL

STATE TOURISM OFFICES

Alabama Bureau of Tourism and Travel
P.O. Box 492
401 Adams Ave.
Montgomery, AL 36103-4927
800-252-2262 or 334-242-4169
http://www.touralabama.org

Alaska Tourism Division
2600 Cordova St., Ste. 201
Anchorage, AK 99503-2745
907-929-2200
http://www.travelalaska.com

Arizona Office of Tourism
2702 N. 3rd St., Ste. 4015
Phoenix, AZ 85004
888-520-3433
http://www.arizonaguide.com

Arkansas Department of Parks and Tourism
One Capitol Mall
Little Rock, AR 72201
800-628-8725 or 501-682-7777
http://arkansas.com

California Office of Tourism
P.O. Box 1499
Sacramento, CA 95812-1499

800-862-2543
http://gocalif.ca.gov

Colorado Tourism Office
1625 Broadway, Ste. 1700
Denver, CO 80202
800-265-6723
http://colorado.com

The Boston University Bridge is the only place in the world where it is possible for a boat to sail under a train running under a car driving under an airplane.

Connecticut Office of Tourism
Department of Economic and Community
   Development
505 Hudson St.
Hartford, CT 06106
800-282-6863 or 860-270-8080
http://www.tourism.state.ct.us

Delaware Tourism Office
99 Kings Hwy.
Dover, DE 19901
866-284-7483 or 302-739-4271
http://www.visitdelaware.net

Visit Florida
661 E. Jefferson St., Ste. 300
Tallahassee, FL 32301
888-737-2872 or 941-922-3575
http://www.flausa.com

Georgia Department of Industry,
   Trade and Tourism
P.O. Box 1776
Atlanta, GA 30301
800-847-4842 or 404-656-3590
http://www.georgia.org

Hawaii Visitors and Convention Bureau
2270 Kalakaua Ave., Ste. 801
Honolulu, HI 96815
800-GO-HAWAII or 808-923-1811
http://www.visithawaii.org

Idaho Department of Commerce
Tourism Division
700 West State St.
P.O. Box 83720
Boise, ID 83720-0093
800-842-5858 or 208-334-2470
http://www.visitid.org

Illinois Bureau of Tourism
100 W. Randolph St., Suite 3-400
Chicago, IL 60601
800-226-6632 or 217-785-6334
http://www.enjoyillinois.com

Indiana Tourism Department
One N. Capitol Ave., Ste. 700
Indianapolis, IN 46204-2288
800-289-6646 or 317-232-4685
http://www.in.gov/tourism/

Iowa Division of Tourism
200 E. Grand Ave.
Des Moines, IA 50309
888-472-6035 or 515-242-4705
http://www.traveliowa.com/index.htm

Kansas Department of Commerce and Housing
Division of Travel and Tourism
700 SW Harrison St., Ste. 1300
Topeka, KS 66603-3712
800-252-6727 or 785-296-2009
http://www.travelks.com

Kentucky Department of Travel Development
500 Mero St., Ste. 2200
Frankfort, KY 40601
800-225-8747 (TDD equipped) or 502-564-4930
http://www.kytourism.com

Louisiana Office of Tourism
P.O. Box 94291
Baton Rouge, LA 70804-9291
800-677-4082 or 225-342-8119
http://www.crt.state.la.us/crt/tourism.htm

Maine Office of Tourism
29 State House Station
Augusta, ME 04330
888-624-6345 or 207-287-5711
http://www.visitmaine.com

Maryland Office of Tourist Development
217 E. Redwood St., 9th Fl.
Baltimore, MD 21202
800-543-1036 or 800-634-7386
http://www.mdisfun.org

Massachusetts Office of Travel and Tourism
10 Park Plaza, Ste. 4510
Boston, MA 02116
800-227-6277 or 617-973-8500
http://www.mass-vacation.com

Travel Michigan
4225 Miller Rd., Ste. 4
Flint, MI 48507-9821
888-784-7328 or 517-373-0670
http://travel.michigan.org

Minnesota Travel Information Center
100 Metro Square
121 7th Pl. East
St. Paul, MN 55101
800-657-3700 or 651-296-5029
http://www.exploreminnesota.com

Mississippi Development Authority
Division of Tourism
P.O. Box 849
Jackson, MS 39205
800-927-6378 or 610-359-3297
http://www.visitmississippi.org

Missouri Division of Tourism
P.O. Box 1055
Jefferson City, MO 65102
800-877-1234 or 573-751-4133
http://www.missouritourism.com

Travel Montana
Department of Commerce
1424 9th Ave.
P.O. Box 200533
Helena, MT 59620-0533
800-847-4868 or 406-444-2654
http://travelmontana.state.mt.us

Travel

Nebraska Division of Travel and Tourism
P.O. Box 98907
Lincoln, NE 68509-9807
800-228-4307
http://www.visitnebraska.org

Nevada Commission on Tourism
401 North Carson St.
Carson City, NV 89701
800-638-2328 or 775-687-4322
http://www.travelnevada.com

**New Hampshire Division of Travel and
   Tourism Development**
172 Pembroke Rd.
P.O. Box 1856
Concord, NH 03302-1856
800-386-4664
http://www.visitnh.gov

**New Jersey Commerce and Economic
   Growth Commission**
Division of Travel and Tourism
P.O. Box 820
20 W. State St.
Trenton, NJ 08625
800-847-4865 or 609-777-0885
http://www.state.nj.us/travel

New Mexico Department of Tourism
491 Old Santa Fe Trail
Santa Fe, NM 87503
800-733-6396 (ext. 0643) or 505-827-7400
http://www.newmexico.org

New York Division of Tourism
30 S. Pearl St., 2nd Fl.
Albany, NY 12245
800-225-5697 or 518-474-4116
http://iloveny.state.ny.us

**North Carolina Division of Tourism,
   Film and Sports Development**
4324 Mail Service Center
Raleigh, NC 27699-4324
800-847-4862 or 919-715-5900
http://www.visitnc.com

North Dakota Tourism
Liberty Memorial Bldg.
604 East Blvd.
Bismarck, ND 58505-0825
800-435-5663 or 701-328-2525
http://www.ndtourism.com

Ohio Division of Travel and Tourism
P.O. Box 1001
Columbus, OH 43216-0101
800-282-5393
http://www.ohiotourism.com

Oklahoma Tourism and Recreation Department
15 N. Robinson, Ste. 100
Oklahoma City, OK 73102
800-652-6552 or 405-521-2406
http://www.otrd.state.ok.us

Oregon Tourism Commission
775 Summer St., NE
Salem, OR 97310
800-547-7842
http://www.traveloregon.com

*The interstate highway system
requires that one mile in every five
be straight. These sections can be
used as airstrips in time of war or
other emergencies.*

Pennsylvania Office of Tourism
Commonwealth Keystone Bldg.
400 North St., 4th Fl.
Harrisburg, PA 17120-0225
800-847-4872 or 717-232-8880
http://www.experiencepa.com

Rhode Island Tourism Division
One W. Exchange St.
Providence, RI 02903
800-556-2484 or 401-222-2601
http://visitrhodeisland.com

**South Carolina Department of Parks,
   Recreation, and Tourism**
1205 Pendleton St., Ste. 106
Columbia, SC 29201
800-868-2492 or 803-734-1700
http://www.travelsc.com

South Dakota Department of Tourism
Capitol Lake Plaza
711 E. Wells Ave.
c/o 500 E. Capitol Ave.
Pierre, SD 57501-5070
800-732-5682 or 605-773-3301
http://www.travelsd.com

"States and Territories" in chapter 25; "United
   States" in the atlas

Go to

Tennessee Department of Tourist Development
Rachel Jackson Bldg., 5th Fl.
320 6th Ave. N
Nashville, TN 37202-3170
800-836-6200 or 615-741-2159
http://www.state.tn.us/tourdev/

Texas Department of Economic Development
Tourism Division
P.O. Box 141009
Austin, TX 78714
800-888-8839 or 512-478-0098
http://traveltex.com

Utah Travel Council
P.O. Box 147420
Salt Lake City, UT 84114-7420
800-200-1160 or 801-538-1030
http://www.utah.com

Vermont Department of Tourism and Marketing
6 Baldwin St., Drawer 33
Montpelier, VT 05633-1301
800-837-6668 or 802-828-3237
http://www.1-800-vermont.com

Virginia Tourism Corporation
901 E. Byrd St.
Richmond, VA 23219-2048
800-847-4882 or 800-326-3244
http://www.virginia.org

Washington Department of Tourism
P.O. Box 42500
Olympia, WA 98504
800-544-1800 or 360-725-5050
http://www.tourism.wa.gov

Washington, D.C., Convention and Visitors Association
1212 New York Ave. NW, Ste. 600
Washington, DC 20005
800-422-8644 or 202-789-7000
http://www.washington.org

West Virginia Division of Tourism
2101 Washington St. E
Charleston, WV 25305
800-225-5982 or 304-558-2200
http://www.state.wv.us/tourism/

Wisconsin Department of Tourism
201 W. Washington
P.O. Box 7976
Madison, WI 53707-7976
800-432-8747 or 608-266-2161
http://www.travelwisconsin.com

Wyoming Business Council—Tourism
Interstate 25 at College Dr.
Cheyenne, WY 82002
800-225-5996 or 307-777-7777
http://www.wyomingtourism.org

"Time Adjustments: Daylight Savings Time in the United States" in chapter 1

Go to

PRECIPITATION CHART

AVERAGE PRECIPITATION FOR SELECTED STATES AND CITIES (IN INCHES)

State	City	Jan/Feb	Mar/Apr	May/Jun	Jul/Aug	Sep/Oct	Nov/Dec
Alabama	Mobile	5.1	5.4	5.4	6.9	4.4	4.7
Alaska	Juneau	4.1	3.0	3.3	4.7	7.3	4.7
Arizona	Phoenix	0.7	0.6	0.1	0.9	0.8	0.8
California	Los Angeles	2.5	1.4	0.1	0.1	0.3	1.7
	San Francisco	3.8	2.2	0.1	0.04	0.7	3.0
Colorado	Denver	0.6	1.5	2.1	1.7	1.1	0.8
Connecticut	Hartford	3.3	3.7	3.9	3.4	3.7	4.0
Delaware	Wilmington	3.0	3.4	3.7	3.8	3.2	3.4
District of Columbia	Washington	2.7	2.9	3.5	3.9	3.2	3.1
Florida	Jacksonville	3.6	3.2	4.6	6.8	5.0	2.5
	Miami	2.0	2.6	7.7	6.6	6.6	2.2
Georgia	Atlanta	4.8	5.0	3.9	4.3	3.2	4.1

AVERAGE PRECIPITATION FOR SELECTED STATES AND CITIES (IN INCHES)

State	City	Jan/Feb	Mar/Apr	May/Jun	Jul/Aug	Sep/Oct	Nov/Dec
Hawaii	Honolulu	2.9	1.9	0.8	0.5	1.5	3.4
Idaho	Boise	1.3	1.3	0.9	0.4	0.8	1.4
Illinois	Chicago	1.4	3.2	3.6	3.9	3.1	2.7
Indiana	Indianapolis	2.4	3.4	3.7	4.0	2.8	3.3
Iowa	Des Moines	1.0	2.8	4.1	4.0	3.1	1.6
Kansas	Dodge City	0.5	1.7	3.2	2.8	1.6	0.7
Kentucky	Louisville	3.1	4.4	4.0	4.0	2.9	3.7
Louisiana	New Orleans	5.5	4.7	5.2	6.1	4.3	5.1
Maine	Portland	3.4	3.9	3.5	3.0	3.5	4.7
Massachusetts	Boston	3.6	3.6	3.2	3.0	3.2	4.1
Michigan	Detroit	1.8	2.8	3.3	3.3	2.5	2.7
Minnesota	Duluth	1.0	2.1	3.4	3.8	3.2	1.5
	Minneapolis	0.9	2.2	3.7	3.6	2.5	1.3
Mississippi	Jackson	5.0	5.7	4.1	4.1	3.4	5.4
Missouri	Kansas City	1.1	2.8	4.9	4.2	4.1	1.8
	St. Louis	2.0	3.5	3.8	3.4	2.9	3.2
Montana	Helena	0.6	0.9	1.9	1.1	0.8	0.6
Nebraska	Omaha	0.8	2.4	4.2	3.4	3.0	1.3
Nevada	Reno	1.0	0.5	0.6	0.3	0.4	0.9
New Jersey	Atlantic City	3.3	3.6	3.0	4.0	2.9	3.5
New Mexico	Albuquerque	0.5	0.5	0.6	1.5	0.9	0.5
New York	Albany	2.3	3.0	3.5	3.3	2.9	3.1
	Buffalo	2.5	2.8	3.3	3.6	3.3	3.8
	New York	3.3	4.0	4.0	4.2	3.7	4.2
North Carolina	Raleigh	3.6	3.2	3.8	4.0	3.0	3.1
North Dakota	Bismarck	0.4	1.2	2.5	1.9	1.2	0.5
Ohio	Cleveland	2.1	3.0	3.6	3.5	3.0	3.1
	Columbus	2.2	3.2	4.0	4.0	2.6	3.0
Oklahoma	Oklahoma City	1.3	2.7	4.8	2.6	3.5	1.7
Oregon	Portland	4.6	3.0	1.8	0.9	2.2	5.7
Pennsylvania	Philadelphia	3.0	3.5	3.7	4.0	3.0	3.4
	Pittsburgh	2.5	3.3	3.7	3.5	2.7	2.9
Rhode Island	Providence	3.7	4.1	3.5	3.4	3.6	4.4
South Carolina	Charleston	3.4	3.5	5.5	6.9	3.9	2.7
South Dakota	Huron	0.6	1.6	3.0	2.2	1.4	0.6
Tennessee	Memphis	4.0	5.4	4.3	3.6	3.3	5.4
	Nashville	3.7	4.6	4.2	3.7	3.0	4.4
Texas	Dallas–Ft. Worth	2.0	3.1	3.9	2.3	3.5	2.1
	Houston	3.1	3.1	5.1	3.5	4.6	3.6
Utah	Salt Lake City	1.2	2.0	1.4	0.8	1.4	1.3
Vermont	Burlington	1.7	2.5	3.3	3.9	3.1	2.8
Virginia	Norfolk	3.6	3.4	3.8	4.0	3.5	3.0
	Richmond	3.2	3.3	3.7	4.7	3.4	3.2
Washington	Seattle-Tacoma	4.7	2.9	1.6	1.0	2.6	5.9
Wisconsin	Milwaukee	1.5	3.1	3.0	3.5	2.9	2.4
Wyoming	Lander	0.6	1.4	2.1	0.6	1.1	0.7

Travel

AIR MILEAGE FROM NEW YORK CITY—DOMESTIC

Albuquerque	1,810
Atlanta	747
Baltimore	170
Boston	188
Chicago	711
Denver	1,628
Detroit	483
Kansas City, MO	1,097
Los Angeles	2,446
Memphis	953
Miami	1,095
Nashville	758
New Orleans	1,173
Omaha	1,144
Philadelphia	83
Phoenix	2,142
Portland, OR	2,455
St. Louis	873
Salt Lake City	1,972
San Francisco	2,568
Seattle	2,419
Washington, D.C.	204

NATIONAL PARK DIRECTORY

For detailed information on the National Parks, write to the Superintendent of Documents at the Government Printing Office in Washington, D.C., 20402, or call 202-512-1800. The GPO's *The National Parks: Index* describes each park. Or go to http://www.nps.gov for online information about National Parks.

Acadia National Park, Bar Harbor, Maine
Area: 47,633 acres
Open: Year-round
Major attractions: Mountains (highest point on Atlantic coast) showing marine erosion and glaciation, lakes, forests, marine life
Activities: Camping, fishing, hiking, biking, horseback riding, cross-country skiing, swimming, nature walks

Arches National Park, Moab, Utah
Area: 76,519 acres
Open: Year-round
Major attractions: Huge rock formations caused by erosion, mountains, Colorado River gorge
Activities: Camping, climbing, hiking, nature walks

Badlands National Park, Interior, South Dakota
Area: 242,755 acres
Open: Year-round
Major attractions: Multicolored peaks and spires caused by erosion, fossil sites, wildlife, Pine Ridge Indian Reservation near site of Wounded Knee battleground.
Activities: Camping, fishing, hiking, biking, bird watching, horseback riding, cross-country skiing

Big Bend National Park, Big Bend National Park, Texas
Area: 801,163 acres
Open: Year-round
Major attractions: Mountains, canyons, desert, U.S. and Mexican flowers, trees, wildlife.
Activities: Camping, boating, fishing, hiking, horseback riding, biking, stargazing, whitewater rafting

Biscayne National Park, Homestead, Florida
Area: 172,924 acres
Open: Year-round
Major attractions: Underwater coral reefs, marine life.
Activities: Boating, snorkeling, scuba diving, camping, kayaking, swimming, wildlife viewing

Black Canyon of the Gunnison National Park, Montrose, Colorado
Area: 27,705 acres
Open: Year-round
Major attractions: Monolithic rock walls rising 2,000 feet above the Gunnison River.
Activities: Camping, boating, climbing, fishing, hiking, stargazing, mountaineering, snowshoeing, skiing, kayaking

Bryce Canyon National Park, Bryce Canyon, Utah
Area: 35,836 acres
Open: Year-round
Major attractions: Multi-colored rock erosions.
Activities: Camping, hiking, horseback riding, biking, museum tours, cross country skiing

Canyonlands National Park, Moab, Utah
Area: 337,570 acres
Open: Year-round
Major attractions: Rock formations, ancient cliff dwellings, Green River and Colorado River canyons.
Activities: Camping, boating, climbing, fishing, hiking, stargazing, white-water rafting, nature walks

Capitol Reef National Park, Torrey, Utah
Area: 241,905 acres
Open: Year-round
Major attractions: Colorful rock formations, desert plays and wildlife, pioneer exhibits (including a one-room schoolhouse).

Activities: Camping, boating, climbing, fishing, hiking, stargazing, mountaineering, nature walks, horseback riding

Carlsbad Caverns National Park, Carlsbad, New Mexico
Area: 46,775 acres
Open: Year-round
Major attractions: Nation's deepest limestone cavern with spectacular underground formations, above-ground desert plants, rock formations
Activities: Cavern tours, hiking, wildlife viewing

Channel Islands National Park, Ventura, California
Area: 249,561 acres
Open: Year-round
Major attractions: Marine life, sea birds
Activities: Boating, hiking, fishing, scuba diving, snorkeling, camping, kayaking, nature walks

Crater Lake National Park, Crater Lake, Oregon
Area: 183,224 acres
Open: Year-round
Major attractions: Deepest lake in the United States (2,000 feet) in crater of extinct volcano, multicolored rocks, forests, mountain flowers, wildlife
Activities: Camping, boating, fishing, hiking, stargazing, biking, nature walks, snowshoeing, bird-watching

Death Valley National Park, Death Valley, California
Area: 3,367,627 acres
Open: Year-round
Major attractions: Spectacular desert scenery, rare desert wildlife, historical sites and remnants of mining.
Activities: Biking, bird-watching, camping, hiking, swimming, nature walks, horseback riding

Denali National Park and Preserve, Denali, Alaska
Area: 4,740,912 acres
Open: Year-round
Major attractions: Peaks of Alaska Range, including Mount McKinley (20,320 feet—highest point in North America), rare wildlife and subarctic plant life, huge Denali fault, break in earth's crust.
Activities: Camping, dogsledding, fishing, hiking, stargazing, mountaineering, snowshoeing, snowmobiling, cross-country skiing, nature walks

Everglades National Park, Homestead, Florida
Area: 1,399,078 acres
Open: Year-round
Major attractions: Immense subtropical wilderness, mangrove swamps, wild animals, rare birds
Activities: Camping, boating, fishing, hiking, nature walks, biking

Gates of the Arctic National Park and Preserve, Fairbanks, Alaska
Area: 7,523,898 acres
Open: Year-round
Major attractions: Snow-covered peaks of Brooks Range north of the Arctic Circle, tundra wilderness, wildlife
Activities: Hunting, camping, fishing, hiking, mountaineering, snowshoeing, dogsledding, cross-country skiing

Glacier Bay National Park, Gustavus, Alaska
Area: 3,224,840 acres
Open: Year-round (Visitor center open only during the summer months)
Major attractions: Great Mendenhall Glacier, iceberg formations from glaciers, dense coastal rain forests, wildlife, nearby, Mount Logan, highest point in Canada (19,850 feet)
Activities: Camping, hiking, hunting, fishing, kayaking, boating

Gateway National Recreation Area New York City, New York (Brooklyn, Queens, and Staten Island), and Monmouth County, New Jersey
Area: 26,600 acres
Open: Year-round; several visitor centers
Major attractions: Jamaica Bay Wildlife Refuge, Jacob Riis and Sandy Hook beaches, Floyd Bennett Field Campground
Activities: Auto touring, biking, bird-watching, boating, camping, fishing, hiking, horseback riding, nature walks, stargazing, swimming, wildlife viewing

Glacier National Park, West Glacier, Montana
Area: 1,013,572 acres
Open: Year-round (Most park services and facilities are available from late May through October. In late fall, winter, and spring there are very limited services available in the park.)
Major attractions: Rugged mountain peaks of Continental Divide, glaciers, numerous alpine lakes and streams, rare wildflowers, wildlife, ancient Blackfoot hunting grounds
Activities: Hiking, horseback riding, camping, fishing, cross-country skiing, boating

Grand Canyon National Park, Grand Canyon, Arizona
Area: 1,217,403 acres
Open: Year-round
Major attractions: Mile-deep, 1.5-billion-year-old canyon of Colorado River, showing geologic features with fossil plants and animals, multicolored rocks, wide range of plants and animals, Havasupai Indian reservation

continues

Activities: Camping, horseback riding, hiking, boating, nature walks, white-water rafting

Grand Teton National Park, Moose, Wyoming
Area: 309,994 acres
Open: Year-round
Major attractions: Mountains, trails of famous early explorers, perennial snowfields, wild plants, animals, and birds
Activities: Camping, boating, fishing, hiking, snowshoeing, horseback riding, snowmobiling

Great Basin National Park, Baker, Nevada
Area: 77,180 acres
Open: Year-round
Major attractions: The South Snake Range (example of a desert mountain island), Wheeler Peak (13,063 feet), Lehman Caves, alpine lakes, ancient bristlecone-pine groves
Activities: Camping, biking, hiking, snowshoeing, horseback riding, caving

Great Smoky Mountains National Park, Gatlinburg, Tennessee
Area: 521,621 acres
Open: Year-round
Major attractions: Highest mountains in the eastern United States (6,500 feet), wide range of plants, wildlife
Activities: Camping, fishing, hiking, nature walks, biking, horseback riding

Guadalupe Mountains National Park, Salt Flat, Texas
Area: 86,416 acres
Open: Year-round
Major attractions: Desert wilderness, limestone fossil reef, wildlife, highest point in Texas (8,749 feet)
Activities: Camping, hiking, nature walks, bird-watching

Haleakala National Park, Makawao, Maui, Hawaii
Area: 29,824 acres
Open: Year-round
Major attractions: Haleakala crater, scenic pools, rare wildlife, semitropical vegetation
Activities: Camping, hiking, nature walks, horseback riding, swimming, stargazing

Hawaii Volcanoes National Park, Hawaii National Park, Hawaii
Area: 209,695 acres
Open: Year-round
Major attractions: Volcano activity, semitropical plants, birds
Activities: Camping, hiking, nature walks, bird-watching, hunting, museums, stargazing

Hot Springs National Park, Hot Springs, Arkansas
Area: 5,550 acres
Open: Year-round
Major attractions: Ancient hot springs for bathing with reputed therapeutic benefits
Activities: Camping, hiking, bathing, museums, bird-watching

Isle Royale National Park, Houghton, Michigan
Area: 571,790 acres
Open: April through October
Major attractions: Historic fisheries, hardwood and evergreen forests, pre-Columbian copper mines, wildlife, lighthouses, shipwrecks
Activities: Camping, hiking, fishing, kayaking, boating, swimming, scuba diving, stargazing

Joshua Tree National Park, Twentynine Palms, California
Area: 1,017,748 acres
Open: Year-round
Major attractions: Meeting point of the Colorado and Mojave Deserts, natural oases, Joshua tree forests, geological formations
Activities: Camping, hiking, nature walks, biking, bird-watching, horseback riding

Katmai National Park, King Salmon, Alaska
Area: 3,674,530 acres
Open: June through September
Major attractions: Varied subarctic environment, Alagnak Wild River, Valley of 10,000 Smokes, wildlife
Activities: Camping, hiking, mountaineering, fishing, kayaking, wildlife viewing

Kenai Fjords National Park, Seward, Alaska
Area: 670,000 acres
Open: Year-round
Major attractions: Mountains, ice fields, fjord system, varied marine life
Activities: Camping, hiking, fishing, boating, kayaking, wildlife viewing

Kings Canyon National Park, Three Rivers, California
Area: 461,901 acres
Open: May through October
Major attractions: High Sierra peaks, giant sequoia trees, mile-deep canyon, alpine lakes, glaciers and snowfields, wildlife
Activities: Camping, hiking, horseback riding, fishing, cross-country skiing, mountaineering

Kobuk Valley National Park, Kotzbue, Alaska
Area: 1,750,737 acres
Open: Year-round

Major attractions: Baird Mountain peaks, forests, tundra, great sand dunes, prehistoric archaeological sites, arctic wildlife

Activities: Camping, hiking, boating, fishing, dogsledding, cross-country skiing

Lake Clark National Park and Preserve, Anchorage, Alaska

Area: 2,619,733 acres

Open: Year-round

Major attractions: Aleutian Range peaks, Cook Inlet, live volcanoes, fossils, forests, wildlife

Activities: Camping, hiking, boating, fishing, hunting, bird-watching, white-water rafting, kayaking, mountaineering

Lassen Volcanic National Park, Mineral, California

Area: 106,372 acres

Open: Year-round (Access is difficult in winter and spring.)

Major attractions: Live volcano (intermittent eruptions from 1914 to 1921), hot springs

Activities: Camping, hiking, boating, fishing, snowshoeing, cross-country skiing

Mammoth Cave National Park, Mammoth Cave, Kentucky

Area: 52,830 acres

Open: Year-round

Major attractions: Large cavern (330 miles of passageways), underground river

Activities: Camping, hiking, boating, fishing, nature walks, cave tours, horseback riding

Mesa Verde National Park, Mesa Verde National Park, Colorado

Area: 52,122 acres

Open: May through October

Major attractions: Pre-Colombian cliff dwellings, lookout showing six mountain ranges in four states

Activities: Camping, hiking, cliff-dwelling tours, stargazing, bird-watching

Mount Rainier National Park, Ashford, Washington

Area: 235,625 acres

Open: Year-round

Major attractions: Mountain terrain (summit is 14,400 feet) featuring glaciers, forests, and subalpine meadows

Activities: Hiking, camping, guided climbs, horseback riding, snowshoeing, skiing, wildlife viewing

North Cascades National Park, Marblemount, Washington

Area: 504,781 acres

Open: Year-round

Major attractions: Alpine wilderness area featuring mountains, lakes, forests, glaciers, wildlife

Activities: Camping, hiking, boating, fishing, horseback riding, kayaking, mountaineering, white-water rafting

Olympic National Park, Port Angeles, Washington

Area: 922,651 acres

Open: Year-round

Major attractions: Rain forests of giant evergreens, mountains (including Hurricane Ridge), rocky beaches on peninsula between Pacific Ocean and Puget Sound, indigenous plants and wildlife

Activities: Camping, hiking, boating, fishing, bird watching, stargazing, mountaineering, kayaking

Petrified Forest National Park, Petrified Forest National Park, Arizona

Area: 93,533 acres

Open: Year-round

Major attractions: Petrified logs now in form of multicolored quartz, prehistoric Native American rock carvings, part of the Painted Desert

Activities: Hiking, nature walks, biking, horseback riding, museums

Redwood National Park, Crescent City, California

Area: 112,598 acres

Open: Year-round

Major attractions: Redwood forests, including tallest known tree in the world, Pacific Ocean coastline

Activities: Camping, hiking, fishing, white-water rafting, kayaking, biking, scuba diving, snorkeling

Rocky Mountain National Park, Crescent City, California

Area: 265,723 acres

Open: Year-round

Major attractions: Mountains, lakes, streams, forests, wildflower meadows, wild animals

Activities: Camping, hiking, fishing, horseback riding, cross-country skiing, mountaineering, snowshoeing

Saguaro National Park, Tucson, Arizona

Area: 91,446 acres

Open: Year-round

Major attractions: Giant Saguaro cacti, wildlife

Activities: Hiking, nature walks, wildlife viewing

Sequoia National Park, Three Rivers, California

Area: 402,510 acres

Open: Year-round

Major attractions: High Sierra peaks, including Mount Whitney (14,494 feet), sequoia forests, wildlife

continues

Activities: Camping, hiking, fishing, caving, horse-back riding, climbing, mountaineering, wildlife viewing

Shenandoah National Park, Luray, Virginia
Area: 199,014 acres
Open: Year-round
Major attractions: Blue Ridge Mountains, hardwood forests, wildflowers
Activities: Camping, hiking, horseback riding, nature walks, biking, climbing

Theodore Roosevelt Memorial National Park, Medora, North Dakota
Area: 70,447 acres
Open: Year-round
Major attractions: Little Missouri River badlands, site of former President Theodore Roosevelt's ranch, wildlife
Activities: Camping, hiking, kayaking, horseback riding, bird-watching, nature walks

Virgin Islands National Park, St. John, U.S. Virgin Islands
Area: 14,689 acres
Open: Year-round
Major attractions: Tropical plant and animal life, marine life, sandy beaches, colonial plantations, early Carib relics
Activities: Camping, hiking, fishing, nature walks, swimming, diving, kayaking, snorkeling

Voyageurs National Park, International Falls, Minnesota
Area: 218,200 acres
Open: Year-round
Major attractions: Evergreen forests, ancient rock outcroppings, bogs, glacial lakes, wildlife
Activities: Boating (access to interior is mainly by boat), camping, fishing, hiking, swimming, skiing

Wind Cave National Park, Hot Springs, South Dakota
Area: 28,295 acres
Open: Year-round
Major attractions: Limestone caverns, bison herds, wildlife
Activities: Camping, hiking, nature walks, caving, horseback riding, stargazing

Wrangell-St.Elias National Park and Preserve, Glennallen, Alaska
Area: 8,323,618 acres
Open: Year-round
Major attractions: Largest U.S. national park, greatest concentration of peaks over 14,000 feet in North America, rugged coastline, boreal forests, alpine tundra, wildlife

Activities: Climbing, hunting, fishing, mountaineering, camping, boating, kayaking, wildlife viewing, white-water rafting, horseback riding

Yellowstone National Park, Yellowstone National Park, Wyoming
Area: 2,219,791 acres
Open: Year-round
Major attractions: Oldest national park, spectacular wilderness, Old Faithful geyser, hot springs, lakes, streams, and waterfalls, wildlife, the Grand Canyon of the Yellowstone
Activities: Camping, hiking, fishing, cross-country skiing, boating, nature walks, horseback riding

Yosemite National Park, Yosemite National Park, California
Area: 761,266 acres
Open: Year-round
Major attractions: Mountain peaks over 10,000 feet, spectacular granite domes and monoliths, highest waterfall in the United States, sequoia groves, wildlife
Activities: Camping, hiking, rock climbing, mountaineering, fishing, horseback riding, biking, nature walks, swimming, skiing

Zion National Park, Springdale, Utah
Area: 146,592 acres
Open: Year-round (Visitor center open from Memorial Day through Labor Day)
Major attractions: Huge canyons and gorges carved by mountain rivers, colorful rock cliffs, wildlife
Activities: Camping, hiking, horseback riding, climbing, skiing

NATIONAL WILDLIFE REFUGES LOCATIONS AND FACILITIES

This is not a listing of the entire Refuge System, but of only those refuges that offer visitor centers or visitor contact stations. The address given is that of the office that administers the refuge; it does not necessarily reflect the location of the refuge.

Refuge conditions, regulations, and activities are varied and subject to change. Please check with the refuge manager regarding conditions, regulations, and facilities for persons with disabilities before taking a trip to a refuge. Check http://refuges.fws.gov for more information.

"The Animal Kingdom" and "The Plant Kingdom" in chapter 3

Go to

continues

ACTIVITIES / **WILDLIFE VIEWING SEASONS**

Columns (left to right): Food/lodging nearby · Hunting · Fishing · Nonmotorized boating · Motorized boating · Archaeological sites · Auto-tour route · Hiking trails · Wildlife viewing sites · Educational programs · Visitor contact station · Visitor center · Winter · Fall · Summer · Spring

Alabama

Refuge	Food/lodging	Hunting	Fishing	Nonmot. boating	Mot. boating	Archaeol. sites	Auto-tour	Hiking trails	Wildlife viewing	Educ. programs	Visitor contact	Visitor center	Winter	Fall	Summer	Spring
Bon Secour NWR, 12295 State Hwy. 180, Gulf Shores, AL 36542	■							■			■			■		■
Choctaw NWR, P.O. Box 808, Jackson, AL 36545		■	■								■			■		■
Eufaula NWR, 509 Old Hwy. 165, Eufaula, AL 36027	■	■	■	■	■		■	■	■		■			■		■
Wheeler NWR, 2700 Refuge Hq. Rd., Decatur, AL 35603	■	■	■	■	■		■	■	■	■	■	■	■	■	■	■

Alaska

Refuge	Food/lodging	Hunting	Fishing	Nonmot. boating	Mot. boating	Archaeol. sites	Auto-tour	Hiking trails	Wildlife viewing	Educ. programs	Visitor contact	Visitor center	Winter	Fall	Summer	Spring
Alaska Maritime NWR, 2355 Kachemak Bay Dr., Suite 101, Homer, AK 99603	■	■	■	■	■	■					■		■	■	■	■
Aleutian Islands Unit, PCS 486, Box 5251, FPO AP, Adak, AK 96506-5251						■										■
Alaska Peninsula NWR, P.O. Box 277, King Salmon, AK 99613		■	■	■	■						■			■	■	■
Arctic NWR, 101 12th Ave., Box 20, Fairbanks, AK 99701		■	■	■	■			■			■					■
Becharof NWR, P.O. Box 277, King Salmon, AK 99613		■	■								■					
Innoko NWR, P.O. Box 69, McGrath, AK, 99627		■	■	■					■		■		■	■	■	
Izembek NWR, #1 Izembek Dr., P.O. Box 127, Cold Bay, AK 99571		■	■	■							■			■		
Kanuti NWR, 101 12th Ave., Box 11, Room 262, Fairbanks, AK 99701		■	■	■							■					
Kenai NWR, P.O. Box 2139, Soldotna, AK 99669-2139	■	■	■	■	■		■	■	■		■	■				
Kodiak NWR, 1390 Buskin River Rd., Kodiak, AK 99615		■	■			■		■			■			■		■
Koyukuk NWR, P.O. Box 287, Galena, AK 99741		■	■	■				■			■			■		■
Nowitna NWR, P.O. Box 287, Galena, AK 99742		■	■					■	■		■					
Tetlin NWR, P.O. Box 779, Tok, AK 99780		■	■	■							■			■		
Togiak NWR, P.O. Box 270, Dillingham, AK 99576		■	■					■	■		■	■				
Yukon Delta NWR, P.O. Box 346, Bethel, AK 99559-0346	■	■	■	■					■		■			■		
Yukon Flats NWR, 101 12th Ave., Room 264, Fairbanks, AK 99701		■	■	■						■	■					

Travel

National Wildlife Refuges Locations and Facilities, *Continued*

ACTIVITIES	Bill Williams NWR, 60911 Hwy. 95, Parker, AZ 85344	Buenos Aires, NWR, P.O. Box 109, Sasabe, AZ 85633	Cabeza Prieta NWR, 1611 North Second Ave., Ajo, AZ 85321	Cibola NWR, Route 2, Box 138, Cibola, AZ 85328-9609	Imperial NWR, P.O. Box 72217, Yuma, AZ 85365	Kofa NWR, 356 W. 1st St., P.O. Box 6290, Yuma, AZ 85366-6290	Big Lake NWR, P.O. Box 67, Manila, AR 72006	Felsenthal NWR, P.O. Box 1157, Crossett, AR 71635	Holla Bend NWR, Rt. 1, Box 59, Dardanelle, AR 72834-9704	Wapanocca NWR, P.O. Box 279, Turrell, AR 72384-0279	White River NWR, 321 West 7th St., P.O. Box 308, DeWitt, AR 72042-0308	Don Edwards San Francisco Bay NWR, P.O. Box 524, Newark, CA 94560-0524	Havasu NWR, P.O. Box 3009, Needles, CA 92363	Humbolt Bay NWR, 1020 Ranch Rd., Loleta, CA 95551-9633	Kern NWR, P.O. Box 670, Delano, CA 93216-0670	Lower Klamath NWR, Rt. 1, Box 74, Tulelake, CA 96134-9715	Modoc NWR, P.O. Box 1610, Alturas, CA 96101-1610	Sacramento NWR, 752 County Rd. 99W, Willows, CA 95988-9639	Salton Sea NWR, 906 W. Sinclair Rd., Calipatria, CA 92233-0120
Food/lodging nearby	■	■	■		■			■	■	■		■			■	■	■	■	■
Hunting	■	■	■	■		■		■	■	■	■		■		■	■	■	■	■
Fishing	■			■	■			■	■	■	■						■	■	
Nonmotorized boating				■	■			■	■	■	■				■	■	■		
Motorized boating				■	■			■		■	■				■				
Archaeological sites													■						
Auto-tour route	■		■	■	■			■	■						■	■	■	■	■
Hiking trails		■	■		■	■						■						■	
Wildlife viewing sites	■	■	■	■				■	■	■		■			■	■	■	■	■
Educational programs		■	■		■			■		■		■						■	
Visitor contact station	■		■			■		■		■		■			■				
Visitor center			■	■					■			■		■		■	■	■	
WILDLIFE VIEWING SEASONS — Winter	■	■	■	■	■			■	■	■		■	■		■	■	■	■	■
Fall	■	■	■	■	■			■	■	■		■	■		■	■	■	■	■
Summer			■								■				■				■
Spring	■	■	■	■	■			■	■	■		■	■		■	■	■	■	■

Arizona

Bill Williams NWR, 60911 Hwy. 95, Parker, AZ 85344
Buenos Aires, NWR, P.O. Box 109, Sasabe, AZ 85633
Cabeza Prieta NWR, 1611 North Second Ave., Ajo, AZ 85321
Cibola NWR, Route 2, Box 138, Cibola, AZ 85328-9609
Imperial NWR, P.O. Box 72217, Yuma, AZ 85365
Kofa NWR, 356 W. 1st St., P.O. Box 6290, Yuma, AZ 85366-6290

Arkansas

Big Lake NWR, P.O. Box 67, Manila, AR 72006
Felsenthal NWR, P.O. Box 1157, Crossett, AR 71635
Holla Bend NWR, Rt. 1, Box 59, Dardanelle, AR 72834-9704
Wapanocca NWR, P.O. Box 279, Turrell, AR 72384-0279
White River NWR, 321 West 7th St., P.O. Box 308, DeWitt, AR 72042-0308

California

Don Edwards San Francisco Bay NWR, P.O. Box 524, Newark, CA 94560-0524
Havasu NWR, P.O. Box 3009, Needles, CA 92363
Humbolt Bay NWR, 1020 Ranch Rd., Loleta, CA 95551-9633
Kern NWR, P.O. Box 670, Delano, CA 93216-0670
Lower Klamath NWR, Rt. 1, Box 74, Tulelake, CA 96134-9715
Modoc NWR, P.O. Box 1610, Alturas, CA 96101-1610
Sacramento NWR, 752 County Rd. 99W, Willows, CA 95988-9639
Salton Sea NWR, 906 W. Sinclair Rd., Calipatria, CA 92233-0120

Travel

Sweetwater Marsh NWR, 301 Caspian Way, Imperial Beach, CA 91932-3149

Tijuana Slough NWR, 301 Caspian Way, Imperial Beach, CA 91932-3149

Tule Lake NWR, Rt. 1, Box 74, Tulelake, CA 96134-9715

Colorado

Alamosa NWR, 9383 El Rancho Ln., Alamosa, CO 81101-9003

Arapaho NWR, P.O. Box 457, Walden, CO 80480-0457

Browns Park NWR, 1319 Hwy. 318, Maybell, CO 81640

Rocky Mountain Arsenal NWR, Bldg. 111, Commerce City, CO 80022-1748

Connecticut

Stewart B. McKinney NWR, 730 Old Clinton Rd., P.O. Box 1030, Westbrook, CT 06498-1030

Delaware

Bombay Hook NWR, 2591 Whitehall Neck Rd., Smyrna, DE 19977-9764

Prime Hook NWR, RD 3, Box 195, Milton, DE 19968-9751

Florida

Arthur R. Marshall Loxahatchee NWR, 10216 Lee Road, Boynton Beach, FL 33437-4796

Cedar Keys NWR, 16450 NW 31st Pl., Chiefland, FL 32626

Chassahowitzka NWR, 1502 S.E. Kings Bay Dr., Crystal River, FL 34429

Crystal River NWR, 1502 S.E. Kings Bay Dr., Crystal River, FL 34429

Egmont Key NWR, 1502 S.E. Kings Bay Dr., Crystal River, FL 34429

Great White Heron NWR, P.O. Box 430510, Big Pine Key, FL, 33043-0510

Hobe Sound NWR, P.O. Box 645, Hobe Sound, FL 33475-0645

J.N. "Ding" Darling NWR, 1 Wildlife Dr., Sanibel, FL 33957

Key West NWR, P.O. Box 430510, Big Pine Key, FL 33043-0510

Lake Woodruff NWR, 4490 Grand Ave., P.O. Box 488, DeLeon Springs, FL 32130-0488

Lower Suwannee NWR, 16450 NW 31st Pl., Chiefland, FL 32626

Merritt Island NWR, P.O. Box 6504, Titusville, FL 32782

National Key Deer Refuge, P.O. Box 430510, Big Pine Key, FL 33043-0510

St. Marks NWR, P.O. Box 68, St. Marks, FL 32355

St. Vincent NWR, 479 Market St., P.O. Box 447, Apalachicola, FL 32329-0447

continues

Travel

National Wildlife Refuges Locations and Facilities, *Continued*

Travel

	Food/lodging nearby	Hunting	Fishing	Nonmotorized boating	Motorized boating	Archaeological sites	Auto-tour route	Hiking trails	Wildlife viewing sites	Educational programs	Visitor contact station	Visitor center	Winter	Fall	Summer	Spring
Georgia																
Banks Lake NWR, Route 2, Box 3330, Folkson, GA 31537			●	●	●				●		●			●		●
Harris Neck NWR, 1000 Business Center Dr., Suite 10, Savannah, GA 31405	●	●	●	●					●					●	●	●
Okefenokee NWR, Route 2, Box 3330, Folkson, GA 31405	●	●		●	●			●	●	●		●		●		●
Piedmont NWR, Route 1, Box 670, Juliette Rd., Round Oak, GA 31038	●	●	●					●	●	●		●				
Hawaii																
Hakalau Forest NWR, 32 Kinoole St., Suite 101, Hilo, HI 96720-2469		●														
Kealia Pond NWR, P.O. Box 1042, Kihei, HI 96753-1042	●								●	●			●	●	●	●
Kilauea Point NWR, P.O. Box 1128, Kilauea, Kauai, HI 96754-1128	●		●			●			●	●		●	●	●	●	●
Midway Atoll NWR, P.O. Box 29460, Midway Island Station #4, Lihue, HI 96820-1860					●	●		●	●	●	●	●		●	●	●
Idaho																
Bear Lake NWR, 370 Webster, P.O. Box 9, Montpelier, ID 83254-1019	●	●	●	●	●		●		●	●	●			●	●	●
Camas NWR, 2150 East 2350 North, Hamer, ID 83425-5030									●						●	
Deer Flat NWR, 13751 Upper Embankment Rd., Nampa, ID 83686-8046					●		●		●	●	●			●	●	●
Grays Lake NWR, 74 Grays Lake Rd., Wayan, ID 83285-5006									●							
Kootenai NWR, HCR 60, Box 283 (Westside Rd.), Bonners Ferry, ID 83805-9518	●	●	●						●					●		
Minidoka NWR, 961 E. Minidoka Dam, Rupert, ID 83350-9414	●	●	●		●				●							
Illinois																
Brussels District, HCR, Box 107, Brussels, IL 62013-0107	●											●		●		
Chautauqua NWR, 19031 E. County Rd. 2015 N, Havana, IL, 62644	●	●	●	●	●		●		●	●	●		●	●	●	●
Clarence Cannon NWR, 1704 North 24th St., Quincy, IL 62301	●	●	●	●	●		●	●	●	●	●			●		●

Crab Orchard NWR, 8588 Rte. 148, Marion, IL, 62959
Cypress Creek NWR, 0137 Rustic Campus Dr, Ullin, IL 62992
Mark Twain NWR Complex, 1704 N. 24th St., Quincy, IL 62301
Savanna District, P.O. Box 336, Savanna, IL 61074

Indiana
Muscatatuck NWR, 12985 E. U.S. Hwy. 50, Seymour, IN 47274

Iowa
DeSoto NWR, 1434 316th Ln., Missouri Valley, IA 51555-7033
McGregor District, P.O. Box 460, McGregor, IA 52157
Neal Smith NWR, P.O. Box 399, Prairie City, IA 50228
Union Slough NWR, 1710 360th St., Titonka, IA 50480
Wapello District, 10728 County Rd. X61, Wapello, IA 52653-9477

Kansas
Flint Hills NWR, P.O. Box 128, 530 West Maple, Hartford, KS 66854
Kirwin NWR, R.R. 1, Box 103, Kirwin, KS 67644
Quivira NWR, R.R. #3, Box 48A, Stafford, KS 67578

Louisiana
Atchafalaya NWR, 1010 Gause Blvd., Bldg. 936, Slidell, LA 70458
Cameron Prairie NWR, 1428 Hwy. 27, Bell City, LA 70630
Catahoula NWR, P.O. Drawer Z, Rhinehart, LA 71363-0201
D'Arbonne NWR, Route 2, Box 401-A, Farmerville, LA 71241
Delta NWR, 1010 Gause Blvd., Bldg. 936, Slidell, LA 70458
Grande Cote NWR, 401 Island Rd., Marksville, LA 71351
Lacassine NWR, 209 Nature Rd., Lake Arthur, LA 70549
Lake Ophelia NWR, 401 Island Rd., Marksville, LA 71351
Sabine NWR, 3000 Holly Beach Hwy., Hackberry, LA 70645
Tensas River NWR, Route 2, Box 295, Tallulah, LA 71282
Upper Quachita NWR, Route 2, Box 401-A, Farmerville, LA 71241

Maine
Mooshorn NWR, RR 1, Box 202, Ste. 1, Baring, ME 04694-9703
Petit Manan NWR, P.O. Box 279, Millbridge, ME 04658-0279

continues

Travel

Travel

National Wildlife Refuges Locations and Facilities, Continued

Location	Food/lodging nearby	Hunting	Fishing	Nonmotorized boating	Motorized boating	Archaeological sites	Auto-tour route	Hiking trails	Wildlife viewing sites	Educational programs	Visitor contact station	Visitor center	Winter	Fall	Summer	Spring
Maine, continued																
Rachel Carson NWR, 321 Port Rd., Wells, ME 04090	■	■						■	■		■			■	■	■
Sunhaze Meadows NWR, 1033 S. Main St., Old Town, ME 04468-2023		■	■	■	■			■		■	■		■	■	■	■
Maryland																
Blackwater NWR, 2145 Key Wallace Dr., Cambridge, MD 21613-9536	■							■	■	■		■	■	■	■	■
Eastern Neck NWR, 1730 Eastern Neck Rd., Rock Hall, MD 21661-1815	■	■	■						■						■	■
Patuxent Research Refuge, 12100 Beech Forest Rd., Suite 138, Laurel, MD 20708-4036																
Massachusetts																
Great Meadows NWR, Weir Hill Rd., Sudbury, MA 01776-1427	■		■					■	■	■	■	■	■	■	■	■
Monomoy NWR, Wikis Way, Morris Island, Chatham, MA 02633-2556	■		■					■	■					■	■	■
Parker River NWR, 261 Northern Blvd., Plum Island, Newburyport, MA 01950-4315	■		■		■		■		■			■		■	■	■
Silvio O. Conte National Fish and Wildlife Refuge, 28 Avenue A, Turner Falls, MA 01376												■				
Michigan																
Seney NWR, HCR #2, Box 1, Seney, MI 49883	■							■	■	■	■	■	■	■	■	■
Shiawassee NWR, 6975 Mower Rd., Saginaw, MI 48601					■				■						■	
Minnesota																
Agassiz NWR, Route 1, Box 74, Middle River, MN 56737		■							■	■	■	■	■	■	■	■
Big Stone NWR, RR 1, Box 25, Odessa, MN 56276	■	■	■				■		■	■	■	■	■	■	■	■
Fergus Falls WMD, Route 1, Box 76, Fergus Falls, MN 56537	■	■			■				■	■					■	■
Hamden Slough NWR, Route 1, Box 32, Audubon, MN 56511-9713								■							■	
Litchfield WMD, 971 East Frontage Rd., Litchfield, MN 55355	■	■	■	■					■						■	

Minnesota Valley NWR, 3815 East 80th St., Bloomington, MN 55425-1600

Morris WMD, Route 1, Box 877, Morris, MN 56267

Rice Lake NWR, Route 2, Box 67, McGregor, MN 55760

Rydell NWR, Route 3, Box 105, Erskine, MN 56535

Tamarac NWR, HC 10, Box 145, Rochert, MN 56578-9735

Upper Mississippi River Wildlife & Fish Refuge, 51 E. 4th St., Rm. 1010, Winona, MN 55987

Winona District, 51 E. 4th St., Room 203, Winona, MN 55987

Mississippi

Mississippi Sandhill Crane NWR, 7200 Crane Ln., Gautier, MS 39553-2500

Mississippi WMD, P.O. Box 1070, 16736 Highway 8 West, Grenada, MS 38902-1070

Noxubee NWR, Route #1, Box 142, Brooksville, MS 39739

St. Catherine Creek NWR, P.O. Box 117, Sibley, MS 39165

Yazoo NWR, Route 1, Box 286, 728 Yazoo Refuge Rd., Hollandale, MS 38748

Missouri

Annada District, P.O. Box 88, Annada, MO 63330-0088

Mingo NWR, 24279 State Hwy 51, Puxico, MO 63960

Squaw Creek NWR, P.O. Box 158, Mound City, MO 64470

Swan Lake NWR, Route 1, Box 29A, Summer, MO 64681-0068

Montana

Benton Lake NWR, 922 Bootlegger Tr., Great Falls, MT 59404-6133

Bowdoin NWR, HC 65 Box 570, Malta, MT 59538

Charles M. Russell NWR, P.O. Box 110, Lewistown, MT 59457-0110

Lee Metcalf NWR, P.O. Box 247, Stevensville, MT 59870

Medicine Lake NWR, 223 North Shore Rd., Medicine Lake, MT 59247-9600

National Bison Range, 132 Bison Range Rd., Moiese, MT 59824

Red Rock Lakes NWR, Monida Star Route, Box 15, Lima, MT 59739

Nebraska

Fort Niobrara NWR, HC 14, Box 67, Valentine, NE 69201

Rainwater Basin WMD, P.O. Box 1686, Kearney, NE 68848-1686

Nevada

Ash Meadows NWR, P.O. Box 115, Amargosa Valley, NV 89020

Ruby Lake NWR, HC 60, Box 860, Ruby Valley, NV 89833-9802

continues

Travel

Travel

National Wildlife Refuges Locations and Facilities, Continued

Activities key: FL = Food/lodging nearby, Hu = Hunting, Fi = Fishing, NB = Nonmotorized boating, MB = Motorized boating, Ar = Archaeological sites, AT = Auto-tour route, HT = Hiking trails, WV = Wildlife viewing sites, EP = Educational programs, VCS = Visitor contact station, VC = Visitor center. Wildlife Viewing Seasons: Wi = Winter, Fa = Fall, Su = Summer, Sp = Spring.

Refuge	FL	Hu	Fi	NB	MB	Ar	AT	HT	WV	EP	VCS	VC	Wi	Fa	Su	Sp
New Hampshire																
Great Bay NWR, 336 Nimble Hill Rd., Newington, NH 03801		■						■			■			■	■	
Lake Umbagog NWR, P.O. Box 240, Errol, NH 03579			■	■	■				■		■					■
Wapack NWR, Weir Hill Rd., Sudbury, MA 01776-1427	■							■						■	■	
New Jersey																
Cape May NWR, 24 Kimbles Beach Rd., Cape May Courthouse, NJ 08210-4207	■		■	■				■	■		■			■		■
Edwin B. Forsythe NWR-Barnegat, 70 Collingstown Rd., P.O. Box 544, Barnegat, NJ 08005-0544		■														■
Edwin B. Forsythe NWR-Brigantine, P.O. Box 72, Great Creek Rd., Oceanville, NJ 08231-0072	■	■	■	■	■		■		■	■	■			■		■
Great Swamp NWR, 152 Pleasant Plains Rd., Basking Ridge, NJ 07920		■	■				■	■	■	■	■					■
Wallkill River NWR, P.O. Box 383, Sussex, NJ 07461-0383		■		■												■
New Mexico																
Bitter Lake NWR, P.O. Box 7, Roswell, NM 88202-0007	■		■				■	■	■	■				■		■
Bosque del Apache NWR, P.O. Box 1246, Socorro, NM 87801-1246		■					■	■	■	■	■	■	■	■		■
Las Vegas NWR, Route 1, Box 399, Las Vegas, NM 87701	■	■						■		■		■	■	■		■
Maxwell NWR, P.O. Box 276, Maxwell, NM 87728-0276	■		■		■									■		
New York																
Jamaica Bay WR, Public Affairs Office, 210 New York Avenue, Staten Island, NY 10305	■						■	■	■	■	■	■	■	■	■	■
Iroquois NWR, P.O. Box 517, 1101 Casey Rd., Alabama, NY 14003-0517		■	■													■
Montezuma NWR, 3395 Routes 5/20 East, Seneca Falls, NY 13148-9778	■		■	■			■	■	■	■	■	■	■	■	■	■
Wertheim NWR, P.O. Box 21, Smith Rd., Shirley, NY 11967-0021	■	■	■	■	■			■		■			■	■	■	■

North Carolina

Mackay Island NWR, P.O. Box 39, Knotts Island, NC 27950-0039

Mattamuskeet NWR, Route 1, Box N-2, Swan Quarter, NC 27885

Pea Island NWR, P.O. Box 1969, Manteo, NC 27954-1969

Pee Dee NWR, Rt. 1, Box 92, Wadesboro, NC 28170

Roanoke River NWR, P.O. Box 430, Windsor, NC 27983

North Dakota

Arrowwood NWR, 7745 11th St. SE, Pingree, ND 58476-8308

Arrowwood WMD, 7745 11th St. SE, Pingree, ND 58476-8308

Audubon NWR, RR 1, P.O. Box 16, Coleharbor, ND 58531

Chase Lake Prairie Project WMD, 5924 19th St. SE, Woodworth, ND 58496

Des Lacs NWR, P.O. Box 578, Kenmare, ND 58746-0578

Devils Lake WMD, P.O. Box 908, Devils Lake, ND 58301-0908

J. Clark Sayler NWR, P.O. Box 66, Upham, ND 58789

Kulm WMD, P.O. Box E, Kulm, ND 58456-0170

Lake Ilo NWR, P.O. Box 127, Dunn Center, ND, 58626-0127

Long Lake NWR, 12000 353rd St. SE, Moffitt, ND 58560-9740

Sullys Hill National Game Preserve, P.O. Box 908. Devils Lake, ND 58301-0908

Tewaukon NWR, 9754 143½ Ave. SE. Cayuga, ND 58013

Upper Souris NWR, 17705 212th Ave. NW, Berthold, ND 58718-9666

Valley City WMD, 11515 River Rd., Valley City, ND 58072-9619

Ohio

Ottawa NWR, 14000 West State Rt. 2, Oak Harbor, OH 43449

Oklahoma

Salt Plains NWR, Route 1, Box 76, Jet, OK 73749-9722

Sequoyah NWR, Route 1, Box 18A, Vian, OK 74962

Tishomingo NWR, Route 1, Box 151, Tishomingo, OK 73460

Washita NWR, Route 1, Box 68, Butler, OK 73625-9744

Wichita Mountains Wildlife Refuge, RR 1, Box 448, Indiahoma, OK 73552

Oregon

Ankeny NWR, 2301 Wintel Rd., Jefferson, OR 97352-9758

Hart Mountain National Antelope Refuge, P.O. Box 111, Lakeview, OR 97630-0107

Klamath Forest NWR, HC 63, Box 303, Chiloquin, OR 97624-9616

Malheur NWR, HC 72, Box 245, Princeton, OR 97721-9505

continues

Travel

National Wildlife Refuges Locations and Facilities, Continued

Travel

Key: ■ = feature/activity available. Seasons under WILDLIFE VIEWING SEASONS.

Location	Food/lodging nearby	Hunting	Fishing	Nonmotorized boating	Motorized boating	Archaeological sites	Auto-tour route	Hiking trails	Wildlife viewing sites	Educational programs	Visitor contact station	Visitor center	Winter	Fall	Summer	Spring
Oregon, *continued*																
McNary NWR, P.O. Box 1700, Umatilla, OR 97882-0700		■	■					■	■	■	■	■		■		■
Sheldon, NWR, P.O. Box 111, Lakeview, OR 97630-0107		■	■					■	■	■				■	■	■
Umatilla NWR, P.O. Box 700, Umatilla, OR 97882-0700	■	■	■	■		■	■	■	■	■	■			■		■
William L. Finley NWR, 26208 Finley Refuge Rd., Corvallis, OR 97333-9533	■	■	■	■	■								■	■		■
Pennsylvania																
Erie NWR, 11296 Wood Duck Ln., Guys Mills, PA 16327	■	■	■							■		■	■	■	■	■
John Heinz NWR at Tinicum, Ste. 104, Scott Plaza 2, Philadelphia, PA 19113			■		■				■	■	■			■		■
Rhode Island																
Ninigret NWR, P.O. Box 307, Shoreline Plaza, Rte. 1A, Charlestown, RI 02813-0317	■		■					■			■	■			■	
Sachuest Point NWR, P.O. Box 307, Shoreline Plaza, Rte. 1A, Charlestown, RI 02813-0317	■		■					■								
South Carolina																
ACE Basin NWR, P.O. Box 848, Hollywood, SC 29449-0848	■	■	■	■		■	■	■	■	■	■	■	■	■	■	■
Cape Romain NWR, 5801 Hwy. 17 North, Awendaw, SC 29429	■	■	■		■			■		■						
Carolina Sandhills NWR, Rte. 2, Box 100, McBee, SC 29101	■	■	■					■								
Santee NWR, Rte. 2, Box 370, Summerton, SC 29148																
South Dakota																
Lacreek NWR, HC 5, Box 114, Martin, SD 57551	■	■	■		■	■	■	■			■	■	■	■	■	■
Lake Andes NWR, 38672 291st St., Lake Andes, SD 57356-6838	■	■	■		■			■		■						

continues

Travel

Madison WMD, P.O. Box 48, Madison, SD 57042-0048

Sand Lake NWR, 39650 Sand Lake Dr., Columbia, SD 57433

Waubay NWR, RR1, Box 39, Waubay, SD 57273-9910

Tennessee

Chickasaw NWR, 1505 Sand Bluff Rd., Ripley, TN 38063

Cross Creeks NWR, 643 Wildlife Rd., Dover, TN 37058

Hatchie NWR, 4172 Hwy. 76 South, Brownsville, TN 38012-8332

Reelfoot NWR, 4343 Hwy. 157, Union City, TN 38261

Tennessee NWR, P.O. Box 849, 810 East Wood St., Paris, TN 38242-0849

Texas

Anahuac NWR, P.O. Box 278, Anahuac, TX 77514-0278

Aransas NWR, P.O. Box 100, Austwell, TX 77950-0100

Attwater Prairie Chicken NWR, P.O. Box 519, Eagle Lake, TX 77434-0519

Brazoria NWR, 1212 North Velasco, Ste. 200, Angleton, TX 77515

Buffalo Lake NWR, P.O. Box 179, Umbarger, TX 79091-0179

Hagerman NWR, 6465 Refuge Rd., Sherman, TX 75092-5817

Laguna Atascosa NWR, P.O. Box 450, Rio Hondo, TX 78583-0450

McFaddin NWR, P.O. Box 609, Sabine Pass, TX 77655-0609

Muleshoe NWR, P.O. Box 549, Muleshoe, TX 79347-0549

San Bernard NWR, 1212 North Velasco, Ste. 200, Angleton, TX 77515

Santa Ana NWR, Rte. 2, Box 202A, Alamo, TX 78516

Utah

Bear River Migratory Bird Refuge, 58 South 950 West, Brigham City, UT 84302

Fish Springs NWR, P.O. Box 568, Dugway, UT 84022-0568

Ouray NWR, 266 West 100 North, Ste. 2, Vernal, UT 84078

Vermont

Missisquoi NWR, P.O. Box 163, Swanton, VT 05488-0163

Virginia

Back Bay NWR, 4005 Sandpiper Rd., Virginia Beach, VA 23456-2412

Chincoteague NWR, P.O. Box 62, Chincoteague, VA 23336-0062

Eastern Shore of Virginia NWR, 5003 Hallett Circle, Cape Charles, VA 23310

Presquile NWR, P.O. Box 189, Prince George, VA 23875

National Wildlife Refuges Locations and Facilities, Continued

Refuge column key:

1. **Washington** — Columbia NWR, P.O. Drawer F, 735 E. Main St., Othello, WA 99344-0227
2. Conboy Lake NWR, Box 5, 100 Wildlife Refuge Rd., Glenwood, WA 98619-0005
3. Little Pend Oreille NWR, 1310 Bear Creek Rd., Colville, WA 99114-9713
4. McNary NWR, P.O. Box 1700, Umatilla, OR 97882-0700
5. Nisqually NWR, 100 Brown Farm Rd., Olympia, WA 98516-2302
6. Ridgefield NWR, P.O. Box 457, 301 N. Thrid St., Ridgefield, WA 98642-0457
7. Turnbull NWR, 26010 South Smith Rd., Cheney, WA 99004-9326
8. **West Virginia** — Ohio River Islands NWR, P.O. Box 1811, Parkersburg, WV 26102-1811
9. **Wisconsin** — Horicon NWR, W4279 Headquarters Rd., Mayville, WI 53050
10. Leopold WMD, W4279 Headquarters Rd., Mayville, WI 53050
11. Necedah NWR, W7996 20th St. West, Necedah, WI 54646-7531
12. St. Croix WMD, 1764 95th St., New Richmond, WI 54017
13. Trempealeau NWR, W28488 Refuge Rd., Trempealeau, WI 54661-8272
14. **Wyoming** — National Elk Refuge, 675 E. Broadway, P.O. Box C, Jackson, WY 83001
15. Seedskadee NWR, P.O. Box 700, Green River, WY 82935-0700
16. **Puerto Rico** — Cabo Rojo NWR, P.O. Box 510, Boqueron, PR 00622-0510
17. Culebra NWR, P.O. Box 190, Culebra, PR 00775

		1	2	3	4	5	6	7	8	9	10	11	12	13	14	15	16	17
ACTIVITIES	Food/lodging nearby	■	■			■	■	■		■				■	■		■	■
	Hunting	■	■			■	■		■	■	■				■	■		
	Fishing	■	■	■		■	■	■	■	■	■				■	■	■	■
	Nonmotorized boating	■				■			■	■	■							
	Motorized boating	■							■			■						
	Archaeological sites															■		
	Auto-tour route	■				■	■	■	■	■								
	Hiking trails									■	■	■			■		■	■
	Wildlife viewing sites	■				■	■		■	■	■							
	Educational programs	■				■	■	■	■	■	■	■		■	■		■	■
	Visitor contact station	■				■	■	■	■	■					■		■	■
	Visitor center									■	■			■	■		■	■
WILDLIFE VIEWING SEASONS	Winter					■									■	■		
	Fall	■	■			■	■		■	■	■				■	■		
	Summer			■		■	■		■	■	■	■				■		■	■
	Spring	■				■	■	■	■	■	■	■				■		

ANIMAL HIGHLIGHTS OF SOME POPULAR NATIONAL WILDLIFE REFUGES

State	Refuge	Wildlife
Alabama	Wheeler	Ducks, geese, alligators
Alaska	Kenai	Moose, wolf, bear, swan, caribou
Arizona	Imperial	Yuma clapperrail, bald eagle
Arkansas	Felsenthal	American alligator, eagle, red-cockaded woodpecker, waterfowl
California	San Francisco Bay	Waterfowl, harbor seals
Colorado	Brown's Park	Antelope, mule deer, elk, waterfowl
Florida	St. Mark's	Alligator, otter, various toads, black bear, woodpecker, gopher tortoise
Georgia	Okefenokee	Alligator, sandhill crane, owl, woodstork
Idaho	Bear Lake	White-faced ibis
Illinois	Crab Orchard	Beaver, deer, bald eagle, wild turkey, Canadian geese
Iowa	De Soto	Snow and Canadian geese, eagles, many duck species
Kansas	Kirwin	Deer, quail, wild turkey, river otter
Louisiana	Tensas River	Deer, black bears, waterfowl, raptors
Maine	Moosehorn	Black bear, beaver, porcupine, American woodcock, bald eagle, waterfowl
Maryland	Blackwater	Deer, waterfowl, Delmarva fox squirrel, bald eagles
Massachusetts	Monomoy	Shorebird, waterfowl, harbor and gray seals
Michigan	Seney	Black bear, beaver, white-tailed deer, eagle, osprey, otter
Minnesota	Tamarac	White-tailed deer, black bear, river otter, moose, eagle, waterfowl, wild turkey, porcupine, beaver
Mississippi	Noxubee	White-tailed deer, alligator, red-cockaded woodpecker, wild turkey
Missouri	Mingo	White-tailed deer, coyote, fox, weasel, bobcat, waterfowl
Montana	Charles M. Russell	Antelope, bighorn sheep, sharp-tailed grouse, bobcat, coyote
Nebraska	Fort Niobrara	Buffalo, elk, Texas longhorn, white-tailed deer, sharp-tailed grouse, prairie chicken, meadowlark, sandpiper
Nevada	Stillwater	Long-billed dowitcher, black-necked stilt, American white pelican, double-crested cormorant, white-faced ibis
New Jersey	Forsythe (Brigantine Division)	Otter, red fox, bald eagle, peregrine falcon, hawk, owl, snowgeese
New Mexico	Bosque del Apache	Coyote, snow geese, sandhill and white whooping crane, mule deer, porcupine, badger, mountain lion
New York	Iroquois	White-tailed deer, beaver, muskrat, fox, mink, raccoon, turkey, waterfowl, eagle
North Carolina	Alligator River	Waterfowl, American woodcock, raptors, black bears, American alligators, white-tailed deer, raccoons, rabbits, quail, river otters, red wolves, red-cockaded woodpeckers
North Dakota	Des Lacs	Snow geese, ducks, sparrow
Oklahoma	Wichita Mountains	Bison, elk, buffalo, deer, longhorn cattle, coyote, red-tailed hawk, prairie dog
Oregon	Malheur	Tundra swan, sandhill crane, owl, hawk, egret, heron
Pennsylvania	Erie	Eagle, owl, sandpiper, beaver
Rhode Island	Ninigret	Raptors, waterfowl, songbirds, osprey, coyote, white-tailed deer, opossum, hawk
South Carolina	Cape Romain	Alligator, raccoon, loggerhead sea turtle, deer, waterfowl, shorebirds
South Dakota	Lacreek	Eagle, falcon, whooping crane, owl, hawk, trumpeter swans, geese
Tennessee	Reelfoot	Ducks, geese, raptors, wading birds, shorebirds, bald eagle, osprey
Texas	Hagerman	Bobwhite quail, mourning dove, white-tailed deer, bobcat, geese, ducks
Utah	Fish Springs	Heron, egret, white-faced ibis, coyote, raven, gopher snake

continues

State	Refuge	Wildlife
Vermont	Missisquoi	Deer, raccoon, muskrat, waterfowl
Virginia	Chinocteague	Wild pony, deer, more than 100 species of birds
Washington	Columbia	Coyote, hawk, owl, duck, geese
Wisconsin	Horicon	Mink, raccoon, coyote, red fox, white-tailed deer, crane, heron, ducks
Wyoming	National Elk	Elk, moose, bighorn sheep, mule deer, coyote, badger, porcupine, weasel

A Closer Look

Best Theme Parks

Although the traditional American tourist attractions—from Mount Rushmore to the Grand Canyon to the Statue of Liberty to the Golden Gate Bridge—are still high on many travelers' itineraries, since the 1950s the greatest volume of visitors has been seen at "theme" amusement parks modeled on the pioneering, enormously successful Disneyland. U.S. amusement parks entertain more than 170 million visitors a year. These are the top 10 according to *Amusement Business Magazine*.

1. **Magic Kingdom, Walt Disney World, Buena Vista, Florida**
   http://disneyworld.disney.go.com/waltdisneyworld/parksandmore/parkindex?id=TPMagicKingdomPrk
2. **Disneyland, Anaheim, California**
   http://www.disneyland.disney.go.com/disneylandresort/disneyland/index?id=227
3. **Epcot Center, Walt Disney World, Buena Vista, Florida**
   http://disneyworld.disney.go.com/waltdisneyworld/parksandmore/parkindex?id=TPEpcotPrk
4. **Disney MGM Studios, Walt Disney World, Buena Vista, Florida**
   http://disneyworld.disney.go.com/waltdisneyworld/parksandmore/parkindex?id=TPDisneyMGMStudiosPrk
5. **Animal Kingdom, Disney-MGM-Studios, Walt Disney World, Buena Vista, Florida**
   http://disneyworld.disney.go.com/waltdisneyworld/parksandmore/parkindex?id=TPAnimalKingdomPrk/
6. **Universal Studios, Orlando, Florida**
   http://www.universalstudios.com/themeparks/html/orlando/univstudios/sfamily/
7. **Universal Islands of Adventure, Orlando, Florida**
   http://www.universalstudios.com/themeparks/html/orlando/islands/
8. **Universal Studios, Hollywood, California**
   http://www.universalstudios.com/themeparks/html/hollywood/main.html
9. **Sea World, Orlando, Florida**
   http://www.seaworld.com/seaworld/sw_florida/swfframe.html
10. **Busch Gardens, Tampa Bay, Florida**
    http://www.4adventure.com/buschgardens/bg_tampa/frame.html

INTERNATIONAL TRAVEL

GOVERNMENT TOURIST INFORMATION CENTERS

The following list includes the U.S. locations (and/or English-language web sites when available) for official tourist information centers of other nations. Tourist information also may be obtained by contacting the appropriate embassy (*see* "Requirements Before Proceeding Abroad: Individual Country Requirements," later in this chapter, for embassy addresses, telephone numbers, and web sites).

Additional information for certain countries may be obtained from the following regional associations:

European Travel Commission
(Members: Austria, Belgium, Croatia, Cyprus, Czech Republic, Denmark, Estonia, Finland, France, Germany, Great Britain, Greece, Hungary, Iceland, Ireland, Italy, Luxembourg, Malta, Monaco, Netherlands, Norway, Poland, Portugal, Romania, Slovenia, Spain, Sweden, Switzerland, and Turkey)
One Rockefeller Plaza, Suite 214
New York, NY 10020
212-218-1200
http://www.visiteurope.com

Scandinavian Tourist Board
(Members: Denmark, Finland, Iceland, Norway,
   and Sweden)
655 Third Ave.
New York, NY 10017
800-346-4636 or 212-885-9700
http://www.goscandinavia.com

The following list includes national tourist offices
and associated web sites:

Anguilla Tourist Board
http://www.net.ai

Antigua and Barbuda Department of Tourism
610 Fifth Ave., Suite 311
New York, NY 10020
888-268-4227 or 212-541-4117
http://www.antigua-barbuda.org/

Argentina National Tourist Council
12 W. 56th St.
New York, NY 10019
212-603-0443
http://www.sectur.gov.ar/homepage.htm

Aruba Tourism Authority
1000 Harbor Blvd.
Weehawken, NJ 07087
800-862-7822 or 201-330-0800
http://www.interknowledge.com/aruba/index.html

Australian Tourist Commission
2049 Century Park East, Suite 1920
Los Angeles, CA 90067
310-229-4870
http://www.atc.net.au

Austrian National Tourist Office
P.O. Box 1142
New York, NY 10108-1142
212-944-6880
http://www.anto.com/

Bahamas Ministry of Tourism
150 E. 52nd St., 28th Floor North
New York, NY 10022
800-327-7678 or 212-758-2777
http://www.bahamas.com

Consulate General of Bangladesh
10850 Wilshire Blvd., Suite 1250
Los Angeles, CA 90024
310-441-9399
http://www.bangladeshconsulatela.com

"Major Zoos and Aquariums" and "Major Botanical Gardens and Arboretums" in chapter 11

Go to

Barbados Tourism Authority
800 Second Ave., 2nd Floor
New York, NY 10017
800-221-9831 or 212-986-6516
http://www.barbados.org/

Belgian National Tourist Office
780 Third Ave., Suite 1501
New York, NY 10017
212-758-8130
http://www.visitbelgium.com

Belize Tourist Board
800-624-0686
http://www.travelbelize.org

Bermuda Department of Tourism
205 E. 42nd St., 16th Floor
New York, NY 10017
800-223-6106 or 212-818-9800
http://www.bermudatourism.com/

Bhutan
Far Fung Places
1914 Fell St.
San Francisco, CA 94117
415-386-8306
http://www.farfungplaces.com

*If you walked the entire length
of China's Great Wall, you would
be walking farther than the
distance between New York City
and Miami, Florida.*

Tourism Corporation of Bonaire
10 Rockefeller Plaza, Suite 900
New York, NY 10020
800-266-2473 or 212-956-5912
http://www.infobonaire.com

Brazilian Tourism Center
16 W. 46th St.
New York, NY 10036
212-730-0515

British Virgin Islands Tourist Board
370 Lexington Ave., Suite 1605
New York, NY 10017
800-835-8530 or 212-696-0400
http://www.bviwelcome.com

Travel

Canadian Tourism Commission
http://www.canadatourism.com

Cayman Islands Department of Tourism
420 Lexington Ave., Suite 2733
New York, NY 10170
212-682-5582
http://www.caymanislands.ky

Chilean National Tourism Board
800-244-5366
http://www.visit-chile.org

China National Tourist Office
350 Fifth Ave., Suite 6413
New York, NY 10118
212-760-8218
http://www.cnto.org

Cook Islands Tourism Corporation
http://www.cook-islands.com

Costa Rican National Tourist Board
800-343-6332
http://www.tourism-costarica.com

Curaçao Tourist Board
475 Park Ave. South, Suite 2000
New York, NY 10016
800-270-3350 or 212-683-7660
http://www.curacao-tourism.com

Cyprus Tourism Organization
13 E. 40th St.
New York, NY 10016
212-683-5280
http://www.cyprustourism.org/

Czech Center New York
1109 Madison Ave.
New York, NY 10028
212-288-0971
http://www.czech.cz/new_york/

The Danish Tourist Board
655 Third Ave., 18th Floor
New York, NY 10017
212-885-9700
http://www.dt.dk/

Dominica Tourist Office
800 Second Ave., Suite 1802
New York, NY 10017
212-949-1711
http://www.dominica.dm/tourism.htm

Dominican Republic Tourist Office
136 E. 57th St., Suite 803
New York, NY 10022
888-358-9599 or 888-374-6361 or 212-575-4966

Egyptian Tourist Authority
630 Fifth Ave., Suite 1706
New York, NY 10111
212-332-2570
http://touregypt.net/

Estonian Tourist Board
http://www.tourism.ee

Fiji Visitors Bureau
5777 W. Century Blvd., Suite 220
Los Angeles, CA 90045
800-932-3454 or 310-568-1616
http://www.bulafiji.com

Finnish Tourist Board
655 Third Ave.
New York, NY 10017
800-346-4636 or 212-885-9700
http://www.finland-tourism.com

French Government Tourist Office
44 Madison Ave., 16th Floor
New York, NY 10022
212-838-7800
http://www.francetourism.com

French Polynesia
Tahiti Tourist Promotion Board
300 Continental Blvd., Suite 160
El Segundo, CA 90245
900-365-4949 or 310-414-8484
http://www.gototahiti.com

German National Tourist Office
122 E. 42nd St., 52nd Floor
New York, NY 10168-0072
212-661-7200
http://www.visits-to-germany.com

Gibraltar Tourist Board
http://www.gibraltar.gi/tourism/

Greek National Tourism Organization
Olympic Tower
645 Fifth Ave.
New York, NY 10022
212-421-5777
http://www.gnto.gr/

"The Atlas" on pages 945–952

Go to

Travel

Greenland
http://www.greenland-guide.gl/

Grenada Board of Tourism
800 Second Ave., Suite 400-K
New York, NY 10017
800-927-9554 or 212-687-9554
http://www.grenada.org

Guam Visitors Bureau
1336-C Park St.
Alameda, CA 94501
800-873-4826 or 510-865-0366
http://www.visitguam.org

Guatemala Tourist Commission
300 Sevilla Ave., Suite 210-A
Coral Gables, FL 33134
305-443-0343
http://www.inguat.net/indexe.html

Haiti
http://www.haititourisme.org

Honduras Tourism Institute
299 Alhambra Circle
Coral Gables, FL 33114
305-461-0600
http://www.turq.com/honduras.html

Hong Kong Tourism Board
115 E. 54th St., 2nd Floor
New York, NY 10022-4512
800-282-4582 or 212-421-3382
http://www.hkta.org

Hungarian National Tourist Office
150 E. 58th St.
New York, NY 10155-3398
212-355-0240
http://www.gotohungary.com

Icelandic Tourist Board
655 Third Ave.
New York, NY 10017
212-949-9700
http://www.goiceland.org

Government of India Tourist Office
1270 Avenue of the Americas, Suite 1808
New York, NY 10020
212-586-4901
http://www.tourindia.com/

Indonesian Council of Tourism Partners
22660 Pacific Coast Highway #108
Malibu, CA 90265
866-INDONESIA or 877-717-7700 or
    808-638-8500 or 310-338-2217
http://www.ictpindonesia.com

Irish Tourist Board
345 Park Ave.
New York, NY 10154
800-223-6470 or 212-418-0800
http://www.irelandvacations.com

Israel Ministry of Tourism Information Center
800 Second Ave., 16th Floor
New York, NY 10017
888-774-7723 or 212-499-5650
http://www.goisrael.com/

Italian Government Tourist Board
630 Fifth Ave., Suite 1565
New York, NY 10111
212-245-5618 or 212-245-4822
http://www.italiantourism.com/html/welcome.html

Jamaica Tourist Board
801 Second Ave., 20th Floor
New York, NY 10017
800-233-4582 or 212-856-9727
http://www.jamaicatravel.com/

Japanese National Tourist Organization
One Rockefeller Plaza, Suite 1250
New York, NY 10020
212-757-5640
http://www.jnto.go.jp/

Jordan Tourism Board
Court House Place
2000 N. 14th St., Suite 770
Arlington, VA 22201
877-SEE-JORDAN or 703-243-7404
http://www.tourism.com.jo

Kenya Tourist Office/Consulate
424 Madison Ave.
New York, NY 10017
212-486-1300
http://www.kenyatourism.org

Korea, Republic of (South Korea)
    Korea National Tourism Office
One Executive Dr., Suite 100
Fort Lee, NJ 07024
800-868-7567 or 201-585-0909
http://www.knto.or.kr/english/index.html

Travel

Lebanon Ministry of Tourism
http://www.lebanon-tourism.gov.lb/main.htm

Lithuania Department of Tourism
C/o Vytis Tours
40-24 235th St.
Douglaston, NY 11363
718-423-6161
http://www.tourism.lt

Luxembourg National Tourist Office
17 Beekman Pl.
New York, NY 10022
212-935-8888
http://www.ont.lu/address.htm

Macau Government Tourist Office
Integrated Travel Resources, Inc.
5757 W. Century Blvd., Suite 660
Los Angeles, CA 90045-6407
310-568-0009
http://www.macautourism.gov.mo

Malaysia Tourism Promotion Board
120 E. 56th St., Suite 804
New York, NY 10022
800-558-6787 or 212-754-1113
http://tourism.gov.my/

Maldives Tourist Promotion Board
http://www.visitmaldives.com

Malta Tourist Office
300, Lanidex Plaza
Parsippany, NJ 07054
887-466-2582 or 973-884-0899
http://visitmalta.com

Mauritius Tourism Promotion Authority
http://www.mauritius.net

Mexican Government Tourist Office
1911 Pennsylvania Ave.
Washington, DC 20006
800-446-3942 or 202-728-1750
http://mexico-travel.com

Federated States of Micronesia Visitors Board
http://www.visit-fsm.org

**Monaco Government Tourist and
    Convention Bureau**
565 Fifth Ave., 23rd Floor
New York, NY 10017
800-753-9696 or 212-286-3330
http://www.monaco-tourism.com

Moroccan National Tourist Office
20 E. 46th St., Suite 120
New York, NY 10017
212-557-2520
http://www.tourism-in-morocco.com

Nepal Tourism Board
http://www.welcomenepal.com

The Netherlands Board of Tourism
355 Lexington Ave.
New York, NY 10017
888-464-6552 or 212-370-7360
http://www.holland.com/us/

New Zealand Tourism Board
501 Santa Monica Blvd., Suite 300
Santa Monica, CA 90401
800-388-5494 or 310-395-7480
http://www.nztb.org.nz

Niue Tourism Office
http://www.niueisland.com

Norfolk Island Tourism
http://www.norfolkisland.com.au

Northern Ireland Tourist Board
551 Fifth Ave., Suite 701
New York, NY 10176
212-922-0101
http://www.ni-tourism.com

Norwegian Tourist Board
655 Third Ave., Suite 1810
New York, NY 10022
212-885-9700
http://www.visitnorway.com

Palau Visitors Authority
http://www.visit-palau.com

Papua New Guinea Tourism Promotion Authority
Los Angeles, CA
949-752-5440
http://www.paradiselive.org.pg

Philippine Tourism Center
556 Fifth Ave.
New York, NY 10036
212-575-7915

Polish National Tourist Office
275 Madison Ave., Suite 1711
New York, NY 10016
212-338-9412
http://www.polandtour.org/

ICEP—Portuguese Trade & Investment Commission
590 Fifth Ave., 3rd Floor
New York, NY 10036
800-767-8842 or 212-354-4610
http://www.portugal.org/tourism/index.html

Puerto Rico Tourism Company
666 Fifth Ave., 15th Floor
New York, NY 10103
800-866-7827 or 212-586-6262
http://www.prtourism.com

Romania National Tourist Office
342 Madison Ave., Suite 210
New York, NY 10173
800-621-8687 or 212-545-7118
http://www.romaniatouristoffice.com

Russian National Tourist Office
130 W. 42nd St., Suite 412
New York, NY 10036
877-221-7120 or 212-575-3431
http://www.russia-travel.com

Rwandan Office of Tourism and National Parks
http://usembkigali.net/pas/tourism.htm

Saba Tourist Office
http://www.sabatourism.com

St. Eustatias Tourist Office
http://www.turq.com/statia

St. Kitts and Nevis Department of Tourism
414 E. 75th St., Suite 5
New York, NY 10021
800-582-6208 or 212-535-1234
http://www.interknowledge.com/stkitts-nevis/
    knacc01.htm

St. Lucia Tourist Board
820 Second Ave., 9th Floor
New York, NY 10017
800-456-3984 or 212-867-2950
http://www.interknowledge.com/st-lucia/index.html

St. Maarten Tourist Office
675 Third Ave., Suite 1806
New York, NY 10017
800-786-2278 or 212-953-2084
http://www.st-maarten.com

"Foreign Dialing Codes" in chapter 26

Go to

St. Martin Tourist Office
French West Indies Tourist Board
444 Madison Ave.
New York, NY 10022
900-990-0040 (95 cents per minute)
http://www.interknowledge.com/st-martin/
    index.html

St. Vincent and the Grenadines Tourist Office
801 Second Ave.
New York, NY 10017
800-729-1726 or 212-687-4981
http://www.turq.com/stvincent/

Scottish Tourist Board (*See also* **United Kingdom—British Tourist Authority**)
http://www.visitscotland.com

Senegal Tourism Office
http://www.senegal-tourism.com

National Tourism Organization of Serbia
http://www.serbia-tourism.org/

Seychelles Tourist Office
235 E. 40th St., Suite 24A
New York, NY 10016
212-687-9766

Singapore Tourism Board
590 Fifth Ave., 12th Floor
New York, NY 10036
212-302-4861
http://www.singapore-usa.com

Slovak Tourist Board
345 E. 12th St.
New York, NY 10003
212-358-9686
http://www.sacr.sk/

Slovenian Travel Inc.
345 E. 12th St.
New York, NY 10003
212-358-9024
http://www.sloveniatravel.com/

South African Tourism Board
500 Fifth Ave., 20th Floor, Suite 2040
New York, NY 10110
800-822-5368 or 212-730-2929
http://www.satour.org

Tourist Office of Spain
666 Fifth Ave., 35th Floor
New York, NY 10103
212-265-8822
http://www.okspain.org/

Travel

Sri Lanka Tourist Board
111 Wood Avenue South
Iselin, NJ 08830
732-516-9800
http://www.lanka.net/ctb/

Swedish Travel and Tourism Council
P.O. Box 4649, Grand Central Station
New York, NY 10163-4649
212-885-9700
http://www.gosweden.org

Switzerland Tourism
Swiss Center
608 Fifth Ave.
New York, NY 10020
800-794-7795
http://www.myswitzerland.com

Taiwan Visitors Association
405 Lexington Ave., 37th Floor
New York, NY 10174
212-867-1632
http://www.tva.org.tw/

Tanzania Tourist Board
http://www.tanzania-web.com

Tourism Authority of Thailand
351 E. 52nd St.
New York, NY 10222
212-754-1770
http://www.tat.or.th/

Tonga Visitors Bureau
4805 Driftwood Ct.
El Sobrante, CA 94803-1805
510-233-1381 or 510-768-6227

Trinidad and Tobago Tourism Development Authority
25 W. 43rd St., Suite 1508
New York, NY 10036
800-748-4224 or 888-595-4868 or 212-719-0540
http://www.visittnt.com

Tunisian Tourism Office
1575 Massachusetts Ave., NW
Washington, DC 20005
202-466-2546
http://tourismtunisia.com

Turkish Tourism and Information Office
821 United Nations Plaza
New York, NY 10017
212-687-2194
http://www.turkey.org

Turks and Caicos Tourist Office
1146 Biscayne Blvd., Suite 302
North Miami, FL 33181
305-891-4117
http://www.turksandcaicostourism.com

Uganda Tourist Board
http://www.visituganda.com

United Kingdom—British Tourist Authority
551 Fifth Ave., 7th Floor
New York, NY 10176
800-462-2748
http://www.travelbritain.org

U.S. Virgin Islands, Divisions of Tourism (St. Croix, St. John, St. Thomas)
http://www.usvi.net

Vanuatu National Tourism Office
http://www.vanuatutourism.com/intro.htm

Venezuelan Tourism Association
P.O. Box 3010
Sausalito, CA 94966
800-331-0100 or 415-331-0100

Wales Tourist Board (*See also* United Kingdom-British Tourist Authority)
http://www.visitwales.com

Zambia National Tourist Board
237 E. 52nd St.
New York, NY 10022
212-308-2155
http://www.zamnet.zm/zamnet/zntb/zntb.html

INTERNATIONAL AUTO REGISTRATION MARKS

Abu Dhabi	UAE	Fiji	FJI	Mexico	MEX
Afghanistan	AFG	Finland	FIN	Moldova	MD
Albania	AL	France	F	Monaco	MC
Alderney	GBA	Gambia	WAG	Mongolia	MGL
(Channel Islands)		Georgia	GE	Morocco	MA
Algeria	DZ	Germany, Federal	D	Mozambique	MOC
Andorra	AND	Republic of		Myanmar	BUR
Argentina	RA	Ghana	GH	Namibia	NAM
Australia	AUS	Gibraltar	GBZ	Nauru	NAU
Austria	A	Great Britain	GB	Nepal	NEP
Bahamas	BS	Greece	GR	Netherlands	NL
Bahrain	BRN	Grenada	WG	Netherlands Antilles	NA
Bangladesh	BD	Guatemala	GCA	New Zealand	NZ
Barbados	BDS	Guernsey	GBG	Nicaragua	NIC
Belarus	BY	Guyana	GUY	Niger	RN
Belgium	B	Haiti	RH	Nigeria	WAN
Belize	BZ	Hong Kong	HK	Norway	N
Benin	DY	Hungary	H	Pakistan	PK
Bolivia	BL	Iceland	IS	Panama	PA
Bosnia	BIH	India	IND	Papua New Guinea	PNG
Botswana	RB	Indonesia	RI	Paraguay	PY
Brazil	BR	Iran	IR	Peru	PE
Brunei	BRU	Iraq	IRQ	Philippines	RP
Bulgaria	BG	Ireland	IRL	Poland	PL
Burkina Faso	BF	Isle of Man	GBM	Portugal	P
Burundi	RU	Israel	IL	Qatar	Q
Cambodia	K	Italy	I	Romania	RO
Cameroon	RVC	Ivory Coast	CI	Russian Federation	RUS
Canada	CDN	Jamaica	JA	Rwanda	RWA
Central African	RCA	Japan	J	St. Lucia	WL
Republic		Jersey	GBJ	St. Vincent	WV
Chad	TCH	Jordan	HKJ	Samoa	WS
Chile	RCH	Kazakhstan	KZ	San Marino	RSM
Colombia	CO	Kenya	EAK	Saudi Arabia	SA
Congo, Republic	RCB	Krygyzstan	KS	Senegal	SN
of the		Kuwait	KWT	Seychelles	SY
Congo, Democratic	ZRE	Laos	LAO	Sierre Leone	WAL
Republic of		Latvia	LV	Singapore	SGP
Costa Rica	CR	Lebanon	RL	Slovakia	SK
Croatia	HR	Lesotho	LS	Slovenia	SLO
Cuba	C	Liberia	LB	Somalia	SO
Curaçao	NA	Libya	LAR	South Africa	ZA
Cyprus	CY	Liechtenstein	FL	South Korea	ROK
Czech Republic	CZ	Lithuania	LT	Spain	E
Denmark	DK	Luxembourg	L	Sri Lanka	CL
Dominican Republic	DOM	Macedonia	MK	Sudan	SUD
Ecuador	EC	Madagascar	RM	Suriname	SME
Egypt	ET	Malawi	MW	Swaziland	SD
El Salvador	ES	Malaysia	MAL	Sweden	S
Eritrea	ER	Mali	RMM	Switzerland	CH
Estonia	EST	Malta	M	Syria	SYR
Ethiopia	ETH	Mauritania	RIM	Taiwan	RC
Faroe Islands	FO	Mauritius	MS	Tajikistan	TJ

continues

International Auto Registration Marks Continued

Tanzania	EAT	Turkmenistan	TM	Venezuela	YV
Thailand	T	Uganda	EAU	Vietnam	VN
Togo	TG	Ukraine	UA	Yemen	AND
Trinidad and Tobago	TT	United States	USA	Zambia	Z
Tunisia	TN	Uruguay	ROU	Zimbabwe	ZW
Turkey	TR	Vatican City	SCV		

AIR MILEAGE FROM NEW YORK CITY—INTERNATIONAL

Acapulco	2,260
Amsterdam	3,639
Antigua	1,783
Aruba	1,963
Athens	4,927
Barbados	2,100
Beijing	6,844
Bermuda	771
Bogotá	2,487
Bombay	7,808
Brussels	3,662
Buenos Aires	5,302
Caracas	2,123
Copenhagen	3,849
Curaçao	1,993
Frankfurt	3,851
Geneva	3,859
Glasgow	3,211
Hamburg	3,806
Hong Kong	8,095
Johannesburg	7,964
Kingston	1,583
Kuwait City	6,366
Lima	3,651
Lisbon	3,366
London	3,456
Madrid	3,588
Manchester	3,336
Mexico City	2,086
Milan	4,004
Moscow	4,680
Nassau	1,101
Oslo	3,671
Paris	3,628
Reykjavík	2,600
Rio de Janeiro	4,816
Rome	4,280
St. Croix	1,680
San Juan	1,609
Santo Domingo	1,560
Sydney	9,932
Tel Aviv	5,672
Tokyo	6,755
Zurich	3,926

INTERNATIONAL CURRENCIES

The table on the opposite page lists the official names for selected currencies around the world. Colonial legacies have made certain names—dollar, peso, franc, and pound, for example—widespread. The traveler should not assume equivalency in value, or transferability, among units sharing a name; that is, one cannot spend Central African francs in France or Turkish lira in Rome.

The column titled "Smaller Monetary Unit" lists the anglicized form of the plural—e.g., Czech 100 halers—followed by the native language plural in parentheses (haleru). When no smaller unit is given, the traveler may assume none exists. Where more than one term is used locally for the same unit, both names are given, separated by *or*. Units of measurement with the word *new* preceding them are the current international exchange unit. There may be an older unit of currency still in circulation that is not to be confused with the new unit.

The abbreviations used are as follows:

CFA   Communauté financieére africaine (African Financial Community)

CFP   Communauté financieére pacific (Pacific Financial Community)

European currency changed on January 1, 2002, when Austria, Belgium, Finland, France, Germany, Greece, Ireland, Italy, Luxembourg, the Netherlands, Portugal, and Spain—12 of the 15 nations of the European Union—began using the euro throughout their economies. (The other three EU members, the United Kingdom, Sweden, and Denmark, retained their own currency.) Old national currencies appear in ( ) for the 12 euro nations. Old currencies were in use alongside the euro for two months, until February 28, 2002. After that date, commercial banks can continue to accept the old currencies in exchange for euros, but other businesses do not.

INTERNATIONAL CURRENCIES

Location	Currency	Smaller Monetary Unit
Albania	lek	100 qindarka
Angola	kwanza	100 lwei
Argentina	peso	10,000 australes
Armenia	dram	100 louma
Australia	Australian dollar	100 cents
Austria	euro (schilling)	100 cents (100 groschen)
Bahamas	Bahamian dollar	100 cents
Bahrain	Bahraini dinar	1,000 fils
Barbados	Barbadian dollar	100 cents
Belarus	rouble	100 kopeks (rarely used)
Belgium	euro (Belgian franc)	100 cents (100 centimes)
Belize	Belize dollar	100 cents
Bermuda	Bermudan dollar	100 cents
Bosnia and Herzegovina	convertible marka	——
Burundi	Burundi franc	100 centimes
Canada	Canadian dollar	100 cents
Cape Verde	Escudo caboverdiano	100 centavos
Cayman Islands	Cayman dollar	100 cents
Chile	Chilean peso	100 centavos
China	renminbi yuan	10 jiao or 100 fen
Comoros	Comorian franc	100 centimes
Congo, Democratic Republic of (formerly Zaire)	Congolese franc	100 centimes
Costa Rica	colon	100 céntimos
Czech Republic	koruna	100 haléū
Denmark	Danish kroner	100 øre
Djibouti	Dijbouti franc	100 centimes
Egypt	pound	100 piastres
Eritrea	nafka	100 cents
Estonia	kroon	100 sents
Ethiopia	Ethiopian birr	100 cents
Faroe Islands	Denmark krone	100 øre
Fiji	Fiji dollar	100 cents
Finland	euro (markka)	100 cents (100 penniä)
France	euro (French franc)	100 centimes
Georgia	lari	100 tetri
Germany	euro (Deutsche mark)	100 cents (100 pfennig)
Ghana	Cedi	100 pesewas
Greece	euro (Drachma)	100 cents (100 leptae)
Greenland	Denmark krone	100 øre
Guinea	Guinea franc	100 centimes
Guyana	Guyana dollar	100 cents
Hungary	Forint	100 fillér

continues

International Currencies, Continued

Location	Currency	Smaller Monetary Unit
Iceland	Icelandic króna	100 aurar
India	Indian rupee	100 paisa
Indonesia	rupiah	100 sen
Iran	rial	——
Ireland	euro (punt or pound)	100 cents (100 puigin or pence)
Israel	shekel	100 agora
Italy	euro (lira)	100 cents (100 centesimi)
Jamaica	Jamaican dollar	100 cents
Japan	yen	——
Kenya	Kenyan shilling	100 cents
Kuwait	Kuwaiti dinar	1,000 fils
Laos	kip	100 at
Lebanon	Lebanese pound	100 piastres
Liberia	Liberian dollar	100 cents
Libya	Libyan dinar	1,000 dirhams
Liechtenstein	Swiss franc	100 rappen or centimes
Lithuania	lita	100 centu
Luxembourg	euro (Luxembourg franc)	100 cents (100 centimes)
Macedonia	dinar	100 paras
Madagascar	Franc Malgache	100 centimes
Malaysia	Malaysia dollar or ringitt	100 sen
Maldives	rufiyaa	100 laaris
Malta	Maltese lira	100 cents or 1,000 mils
Mexico	peso	100 centavos
Moldova	lei	——
Mongolia	tughrik	100 möngö
Namibia	Namibian dollar	100 cents
Nepal	Nepalese rupee	100 paisa
Netherlands	euro (guilder or florin)	100 cents (100 cents)
New Zealand	New Zealand dollar	100 cents
Nicaragua	córdoba	100 centavos
Oman	rial Omani	1,000 baisas
Pakistan	Pakistani rupee	100 paisa
Panama	balboa	100 centésimos
Paraguay	guaraní	100 céntimos
Peru	new sol	100 cénts
Philippines	Philippines peso	100 centavos
Poland	zlory	100 groszy
Portugal	euro (escudo)	100 cents (100 centavos)
Russia	new rouble	100 kopeks
Rwanda	Rwanda franc	100 centimes
St. Helena	St. Helena pound	100 pence
São Tomé and Princípé	dobra	100 centavos
Saudi Arabia	Saudi Arabian riyal	100 halala
Seychelles	Seychelles rupee	100 cents
Singapore	Singapore dollar	100 cents
Slovakia	koruna	100 halierov
Slovenia	tolar	100 stotins
Solomon Islands	Solomon Island dollar	100 cents

Location	Currency	Smaller Monetary Unit
Somalia	Somali shilling	100 cents
Spain	euro (peseta)	100 cents (100 céntimos)
Sri Lanka	Sri Lanka rupee	100 cents
Sudan	Sudanese dinar	10 pounds
Suriname	Suriname guilder	100 cents
Swaziland	Lilangeni	100 cents
Sweden	Swedish krona	100 öre
Switzerland	Swiss franc	100 centimes or rappen
Syria	Syrian pound	100 piastres
Taiwan	new Taiwan dollar	100 cents
Tajikistan	Tajikistan rouble	100 tanga
Tanzania	Tanzanian shilling	100 cents
Thailand	baht	100 satang
Togo	franc CFA	100 centimes
Trinidad and Tobago	Trinidad dollar	100 cents
Tunisia	Tunisian dinar	1,000 millimes
Turkey	Turkish lira	100 kurus
Ukraine	hryvna	100 kopiykas
United Arab Emirates	UAE dirham	100 fils
United States	U.S. dollar	100 cents
Uzbekistan	sum	100 tiyin
Venzuela	bolívar	100 céntimos
Vietnam	dông	10 hào or 100 xu
Yemen	riyal	100 fils
Zimbabwe	Zimbabwe dollar	100 cents

REQUIREMENTS BEFORE PROCEEDING ABROAD

This listing is prepared solely for the information of U.S. citizens traveling as tourists and does not apply to persons planning to immigrate to foreign countries. A visa is generally an endorsement or stamp placed by officials of a foreign country on a U.S. passport that allows the bearer to visit that country.

PASSPORTS

Persons who travel to a country where a U.S. passport is not required should have documentary evidence of their U.S. citizenship and identity to facilitate reentry into the United States. Countries that do not require a passport to enter or depart frequently require this evidence. Documentary evidence of U.S. citizenship may be an expired passport, a certified birth certificate, a certificate of naturalization, a certificate of citizenship, or a report of birth abroad of a citizen of the United States.

IMPORTANT

Travelers should check passport and visa requirements with the consular officials of the countries to be visited well in advance of their departure dates, because such information is subject to change.

Documentary evidence of identity may be a valid driver's license or government identification provided they identify you by physical description or photograph.

Some Arab and African countries will not issue visas or allow entry if your passport gives evidence of travel to Israel. If this applies to you, consult the nearest U.S. passport agency for guidance.

In addition to the passport agencies listed below, passport applications and information are available at approximately 4,500 public facilities in the United States. If an automated appointment number is listed, please call that number in advance to make an appointment. Have your Social Security number available when calling.

"Countries of the World" in chapter 26

Boston Passport Agency
Thomas P. O'Neill Federal Bldg.
10 Causeway St., Suite 247
Boston, MA 02222-1094
Automated appointment #: 617-878-0900
Services provided to Maine, Massachusetts, New Hampshire, Rhode Island, upstate New York, and Vermont

Chicago Passport Agency
Kluczynski Federal Bldg.
230 S. Dearborn St., Suite 380
Chicago, IL 60604-1564
Automated appointment #: 312-341-6020
Services provided to Illinois and Michigan

Honolulu Passport Agency
Prince Kuhio Federal Bldg.
300 Ala Moana Blvd., Suite 1-330
Honolulu, HI 96850
Recorded information #: 808-522-8283
Services provided to American Samoa, the Federated States of Micronesia, Guam, Hawaii, and the Northern Mariana Islands

Houston Passport Agency
Mickey Leland Federal Bldg.
1919 Smith St., Suite 1400
Houston, TX 77002-8049
Automated appointment #: 713-751-0294
Services provided to Kansas, Oklahoma, New Mexico, and Texas

Los Angeles Passport Agency
Federal Bldg.
11000 Wilshire Blvd., Suite 1000
Los Angeles, CA 90024-3615
Automated appointment #: 310-575-5700
Services provided to southern California (all counties south of and including San Luis Obispo, Kern and San Bernardino) and Nevada (Clark County only)

Miami Passport Agency
Claude Pepper Federal Office Bldg.
51 SW First Ave., 3rd Floor
Miami, FL 33130
Automated appointment #: 305-539-3600
Services provided to Florida, South Carolina, and the U.S. Virgin Islands

National Passport Center
31 Rochester Avenue
Portsmouth, NY 03801-2900
Services provided: Passport by mail (Form DSP-82) applications accepted

New Orleans Passport Agency
One Canal Place
365 Canal St., Suite 1300
New Orleans, LA 70130-6508
Automated appointment #: 504-412-2600
Services provided to Alabama, Arkansas, Georgia, Iowa, Indiana, Kentucky, Louisiana, Mississippi, Missouri, North Carolina, Ohio, Puerto Rico, Tennessee, Virginia, (except District of Columbia suburbs), and Wisconsin

New York Passport Agency
376 Hudson St.
New York, NY 10014-3621
Automated appointment #: 212-206-3500
Services provided to New York City and Long Island

Philadelphia Passport Agency
U.S. Custom House
200 Chestnut St., Room 103
Philadelphia, PA 19106-2970
Automated appointment #: 215-418-5937
Services provided to Delaware, New Jersey, Pennsylvania, and West Virginia

San Francisco Passport Agency
95 Hawthorne St., 5th Floor
San Francisco, CA 94105-3901
Automated appointment #: 415-538-2700
Services provided to Arizona, northern California (all counties north of and including Monterey, Kings, Tulare, and Mono), Nevada (except Clark County), and Utah

Seattle Passport Agency
Henry Jackson Federal Bldg.
915 Second Ave., Suite 992
Seattle, WA 98174-1091
Automated appointment #: 206-808-5700
Services provided to Alaska, Colorado, Idaho, Minnesota, Montana, Nebraska, North Dakota, Oregon, South Dakota, Washington, and Wyoming

Stamford Passport Agency
One Landmark Square
Broad and Atlantic Sts.
Stamford, CT 06901-2667
Automated appointment #: 203-969-9000
Services provided to Connecticut and New York (Westchester County only)

Washington Passport Agency
1111 19th St. NW
Washington, DC 20524

Automated appointment #: 202-647-0578
Services provided to Maryland, northern Virginia (including Alexandria and Arlington, Fairfax, Loudon, Stafford, and Prince William Counties)

Special Issuance Agency
1111 19th St., NW Room 350
Washington, DC 20524
Services provided: Applications accepted for diplomatic, official, and no-fee passports

Call the National Passport Information Center's passport information number 900-225-5674 (TDD 900-225-7778) (charges incurred per minute) or 888-362-8668 (TDD 888-498-3648) (flat rate charge) to obtain more information, to request a passport application or to check on the status of a passport application. Automated information is available 24 hours a day, 7 days a week. Operators can be reached Monday through Friday (excluding federal holidays) from 8:00 A.M. to 8:00 P.M. Eastern standard time. Services are provided in English and Spanish.

Visit the U.S. State Department at its web site for information about Passport Services: http://travel.state.gov/passport_services.html

VISAS

IMPORTANT

It is the responsibility of the traveler to obtain a visa, where required, from the appropriate embassy or nearest consulate of the country to be visited before proceeding abroad.

Allow sufficient time for processing your visa application, especially if you apply by mail. Most foreign consular representatives are located in principal cities, particularly Chicago, New Orleans, New York, San Francisco, and Washington, D.C. In many instances, a traveler may be required to obtain visas from the consular office in the area of his or her residence. You can obtain addresses of foreign consular offices in the United States by consulting the *Congressional Directory* (available in most libraries), by accessing the U.S. State Department's online list of foreign consular offices in the U.S. (http://www.state.gov/www/travel/consular_offices/fco_index.html), or by visiting the web sites listed below and in the "Government Tourist Information Centers" and "Additional Sources of Information" sections of this chapter.

For further assistance, you can also contact travel agents and visa information services such as World Wide Visa Services (800-527-1861), World Travel Guide Online Services (http://www.wtgonline.com), and Travel Document Systems (800-874-5100; Washington, D.C., local number 202-638-3800; fax 202-638-4674; http://www.traveldocs.com). In addition, the U.S. State Department's Bureau of Consular Affairs (http://travel.state.gov) offers a wealth of information for travelers, including health and safety advisories.

IMMUNIZATIONS

Under the International Health Regulations adopted by the World Health Organization, a country may require certificates of immunization against yellow fever. A few countries still require a cholera immunization as well. Check with health-care providers or your records to ensure other immunizations (for example, tetanus and polio) are up to date. Prophylactic medication for malaria and certain other preventive measures are advisable for some travelers. No immunizations are required to return to the United States. Pertinent information is included in Health Information for International Travel (the "Yellow Book"), available from the U.S. Government Printing Office, Washington, DC 20402, http://www.bookstore.gpo.gov, or you can obtain it from your local health department or physician, or by contacting the Public Health Foundation at http://bookstore.phf.org.

An increasing number of countries have established regulations regarding AIDS testing, particularly for long-term visitors. Check with the embassy or consulate of the country you plan to visit for the latest information on whether this is a requirement for entry.

CONTACT INFORMATION FOR INDIVIDUAL COUNTRIES—ONLINE SOURCES

Country	Supplemental Web Site
Afghanistan, Islamic State of	http://www.afghan-web.com
Albania, Republic of	http://www.albinfo.com
Algeria, Democratic and Popular Republic of	http://www.algeria-tourism.org
Andorra	http://www.andorra.com
Angola, Republic of	http://www.africavacationguide.com/travel/Angola_Practical_Info.html
Anguilla	http://www.travelnotes.org/LatinAmerica/Anguilla/anguilla_tourism.htm
Antigua and Barbuda	http://www.travelnotes.org/LatinAmerica/Antigua/antigua_tourism.htm
Argentina	http://www.consuladoargentino-losangeles.org/argentina_tourism_online.htm
Armenia, Republic of	http://www.tourismarmenia.com
Aruba	http://www.aruba.com
Australia	http://www.australia.com
Austria	http://www.touristnet.at/englisch/index.htm
Azerbaijan, Republic of	http://www.friends-partners.org/oldfriends/azerbaijan
Bahamas, Commonwealth of	http://www.bahamatravelnet.com/home.html
Bahrain, State of	http://www.bahraintourism.com
Bangladesh, People's Republic of	http://www.bangladesh.com/travel/
Barbados	http://www.funbarbados.com
Belarus, Republic of	http://www.belarusguide.com
Belgium	http://www.trabel.com
Belize	http://www.belize.com
Benin, Republic of	http://www.sas.upenn.edu/African_Studies/Country_Specific/Benin.html
Bermuda	http://www.bermuda.com
Bhutan	http://www.bhutan-info.org
Bolivia	http://www.boliviaweb.com
Bosnia and Herzegovina, Republic of	http://www.bosnet.org/bosnia/
Botswana, Republic of	http://www.botswana-online.com
Brazil	http://www.lonelyplanet.com/destinations/south_america/brazil/
British Virgin Islands (includes Anegarda, Jost van Dyke, Tortola, and Virgin Gorda)	http://www.britishvirginislands.com
Brunei Darussalam, State of	http://www.brunei.bn
Bulgaria, Republic of	http://www.travel-bulgaria.com
Burkina Faso	http://www.worldskip.com/burkinafaso/
Burundi, Republic of	http://www.burundi.org
Cambodia, Kingdom of	http://www.cambodia-web.net
Cameroon, Republic of	http://www.adminet.com/world/cm/
Canada	http://canada.worldweb.com
Cape Verde, Republic of	http://www.traveldocs.com/cv/
Cayman Islands	http://cayman.com.ky
Central African Republic	http://www.africaguide.com/country/car/
Chad, Republic of	http://www.africavacationguide.com/travel/Chad_Practical_Info.html
Chile	http://www.lonelyplanet.com/destinations/south_america/chile_and_easter_island/
China, People's Republic of China	http://www.chinasite.com
Colombia	http://www.drcomputer.com/colombia/guide01.htm
Comoros Islands (Federal Islamic Republic of the Comoros)	http://www.ksu.edu/sasw/comoros/comoros.html

Country	Supplemental Web Site
Congo, Democratic Republic of (formerly Zaire)	http://www.africaguide.com/country/zaire
Congo, Republic of the	http://www.sas.upenn.edu/African_Studies/Country_Specific/Congo.html
Cook Islands	http://cookpages.com
Costa Rica	http://www.amerisol.com
Côte d'Ivoire, Republic of (Ivory Coast)	http://www.africaguide.com/country/ivoryc/
Croatia	http://www.hr/
Cuba	http://lonelyplanet.com/destinations/caribbean/cuba/
Curaçao	http://www.curacao.com
Cyprus, Republic of	http://www.windowoncyprus.com
Czech Republic	http://czech-tourism.com
Denmark, Kingdom of (including Greenland and the Faroe Islands)	http://www.alltraveldenmark.com
Djibouti, Republic of	http://www.tuttinsieme.it/tutti/tut/af/djibouti/djidir.htm
Dominica, Commonwealth of	http://www.delphis.dm/basics.htm
Dominican Republic	http://www.dr1.com
Ecuador (including Galapagos Islands)	http://www.tuttinsieme.it/tutti/tut/souame/ecuador/eqdir.htm
Egypt, Arab Republic of	http://www.tourism.egnet.net/culture.htm
El Salvador	http://www.latinworld.com/centro/elsalvador/index.html
Equatorial Guinea, Republic of	http://www.lonelyplanet.com/destinations/africa/equatorial_guinea/
Eritrea	http://www.africavacationguide.com/travel/Eritrea_Practical_Info.html
Estonia	http://www.tuttinsieme.it/tutti/tut/eur/estonia/tourism.htm
Ethiopia, Federal Democratic Republic of	http://tour.ethiopiaonline.net
European Union	http://europa.eu.int/index_en.htm
Fiji	http://www.fijivision.com/tourist.html
Finland	http://www.travelmad.com/html/finland.htm
Former Yugolsav Republic of Macedonia (FYROM)	http://www.middleeastnews.com/Macedonia.html
France	http://www.franceway.com/welcome.htm
French Guiana	http://www.lonelyplanet.com/destinations/south_america/french_guiana/
French Polynesia	http://www.tahiti-explorer.com
French West Indies	http://www.cieux.com/fwi.html
Gabonese Republic (Gabon)	http://dmoz.org/Regional/Africa/Gabon/Travel_and_Tourism/
Gambia	http://www.gambia.com
Georgia, Republic of	http://dmoz.org/Regional/Asia/Georgia/Travel_and_Tourism/Lodging/
Germany, Federal Republic of	http://www.deutschland-tourismus.de/e/dest_con_main_e.html
Ghana	http://www.ghana.com/republic/tourism
Greece	http://www.greek-tourism.gr
Greenland	http://www.lonelyplanet.com/destinations/europe/greenland/
Grenada	http://www.turq.com/grenada.html
Guam	http://www.guam.net/home/bjohns/guamlinks.html
Guatemala	http://www.lonelyplanet.com/destinations/central_america/guatemala/
Guinea, Republic of	http://www.ware.it/Africa/Guinea/1guinea.htm
Guinea-Bissau, Republic of	http://www.west-africa.com/Guinea-Bissau/Guinea-Bissau.htm
Guyana, Co-operative Republic of	http://www.turq.com/guyana.html
Haiti	http://www.haititourisme.org
Holy See, Apostolic Nunciature of the (the Vatican)	http://www.vatican.va

continues

Contact Information, Continued

Country	Supplemental Web Site
Honduras	http://www.latinworld.com/centro/honduras/index.html
Hong Kong (Special Administrative Region of the People's Republic of China)	http://www.e-hongkong.com
Hungary, Republic of	http://www.miwo.hu/index-en.phtml
Iceland	http://www.travelnet.is/
India	http://india-tourism.de/english/
Indonesia, Republic of	http://www.indonesiatourism.com
Iran	http://www.salamiran.org
Iraq	http://www.undp.org/missions/iraq
Ireland	http://www.goireland.com
Israel and the Occupied Territories (Jerusalem, Gaza, Golan Heights, and the West Bank)	http://www.infotour.co.il
Italy	http://www.italytourism.it
Jamaica	http://www.jamaica-irie.com
Japan	http://www.japan-guide.com
Jordan, Hashemite Kingdom of	http://www.seejordan.org
Kazakstan	http://www.asiatour.org
Kenya	http://www.seekenya.com
Kiribati, Republic of (formerly Gilbert Islands)	http://www.tskl.net.ki/kiribati/
Korea, Democratic People's Republic of (North Korea)	http://www.lonelyplanet.com/destinations/north_east_asia/north_korea/
Korea, Republic of (South Korea)	http://www.lonelyplanet.com/destinations/north_east_asia/south_korea/
Kuwait, State of	http://www.undp.org/missions/kuwait
Kyrgyz Republic (Kyrgyzstan)	http://www.bishkek.su/KyrgyzstanTourism/
Laos (Lao People's Democratic Republic)	http://www.visit-laos.com
Latvia	http://www.tvnet.lv/en/
Lebanon	http://www.lol.com.lb/tourism/index.shtml
Lesotho, Kingdom of	http://www.undp.org/missions/lesotho/
Liberia, Republic of	http://www.liberia.net
Liechtenstein	http://www.tourismus.li/
Lithuania	http://www.baltic.ws/lithuania/tourism.html
Luxembourg, Grand Duchy of	http://www.alltravelluxembourg.com
Macau	http://www.macau.gov.mo
Madagascar, Democratic Republic of	http://www.madagascar-guide.com/top/HP_Fr1Eng.html
Malawi	http://malawi.tripod.com/
Malaysia (and the Borneo States, Sarawak, and Sabah)	http://www.interknowledge.com/malaysia/index.html
Maldives	http://www.tuttinsieme.it/tutti/tut/as/maldives/tourism.htm
Mali, Republic of	http://www.traveldocs.com/ml
Malta	http://visitmalta.com
Marshall Islands, Republic of the	http://travel.state.gov/marshall_islands.html
Mauritania, Republic of	http://www.arab.net/mauritania/mauritania_contents.html
Mauritius	http://www.mauritius-info.com
Mexico	http://www.go2mexico.com

Country	Supplemental Web Site
Micronesia, Federated States of (Kosrae, Yap, Pohnpei, and Chuuk)	http://www.lonelyplanet.com/destinations/pacific/federated_states_of_micronesia/
Moldova, Republic of	http://www.net.md/tourism/
Monaco, Principality of	http://www.monte-carlo.mc/
Mongolia	http://www.mol.mn
Morocco	http://www.arab.net/morocco/morocco_contents.html
Mozambique, Republic of	http://www.mozambique.mz
Myanmar, Union of	http://www.myanmar.com
Namibia	http://www.iwwn.com.na/namtour/
Naura, Republic of	http://www.traveldocs.com/nr/
Nepal, Kingdom of	http://www.undp.org/missions/nepal
Netherlands	http://www.goholland.com
Netherlands Antilles	http://www.islandconnoisseur.com/abc/
New Zealand	http://www.tourism.net.nz
Nicaragua	http://www.latinworld.com/centro/nicaragua/index.html
Niger, Republic of	http://www.txdirect.net/~jmayer/fon.html#LiNiger
Nigeria, Republic of	http://www.nigeria.com
Niue	http://www.hideawayholidays.com.au/niue_.htm
Norfolk Island	http://www.ni.net.nf/
Northern Mariana Islands, Commonwealth of the	http://www.mariana-islands.gov.mp/
Norway, Kingdom of	http://www.alltravelnorway.com
Oman, Sultanate of	http://www.omanet.com/back.htm
Pakistan	http://www.pak.gov.pk
Palau, Republic of	www.lonelyplanet.com/destinations/pacific/palau/
Panama	http://www.panamainfo.com
Papua New Guinea	http://lonelyplanet.com/destinations/australasia/papua_new_guinea/
Paraguay	http://www.latinworld.com/sur/paraguay/index.html
Peru	http://www.peru-explorer.com
Philippines	http://www.tourism.gov.ph
Poland, Republic of	http://www.pl-info.net/en/tourism/index.shtml
Portugal (including Azores and the Madeira Islands)	http://portugal-info.net
Qatar, State of	http://www.arab.net/qatar/qatar_contents.html
Romania	http://www.ici.ro/romania/tourism/index.html
Russia	http://russia-tourism.com
Rwanda, Republic of	http://www.bcr-rwanda.com/index1024.html
Saba	http://www.reefrainfrst.com/saba.htm
St. Eustatius	http://travel.discovery.com/dest/weisdb/caribbean/saba/over.html
St. Kitts and Nevis	http://www.geographia.com/stkitts-nevis/index.htm
St. Lucia	http://www.turq.com/stlucia.html
St. Marteen	http://www.gobeach.com/page3.htm
St. Martin	http://www.gobeach.com/page3.htm
St. Vincent and the Grenadines	http://www.turq.com/stvincent/
San Marino, Republic of	http://inthenet.sm/rsm/intro.htm
São Tome and Principé	http://www.traveldocs.com/st/
Saudi Arabia, Kingdom of	http://www.arabia.com
Scotland	http://www.electricscotland.com/tourist/
Senegal, Republic of	http://www.senegal-tourism.com

continues

Contact Information, Continued

Country	Supplemental Web Site
Serbia and Montenegro ("Federal Republic of Yugoslavia")	http://www.travelnotes.org/Europe/serbia.htm
Seychelles	http://www.sey.net
Sierra Leone	http://www.sierra-leone.org
Singapore	http://www.newasia-singapore.com
Slovak Republic	http://www.slovakia.org/tourism/
Slovenia, Republic of	http://www.ntz-nta.si/
Solomon Islands	http://www.commerce.gov.sb/
Somali Democratic Republic (Somalia)	http://www.arab.net/somalia/somalia_contents.html
South Africa	http://www.southafrica.net
Spain	http://www.tourspain.es/turespai/marcoi.htm
Sri Lanka	http://www.lonelyplanet.com/destinations/indian_subcontinent/sri_lanka/
Sudan, Republic of	http://www.sudan.net/tourism.shtml
Suriname, Republic of	http://www.surinam.net
Swaziland, Kingdom of	http://www.swazi.com
Sweden	http://www.europeanvacationguide.com/travel/Sweden_Practical_Info.html
Switzerland	http://www.traveling.ch/
Syrian Arab Republic	http://www.arab.net/syria/syria_contents.html
Taiwan, Republic of China on	http://www.taipei.org
Tajikistan	http://www.lonelyplanet.com/destinations/central_asia/tajikistan/
Tanzania, United Republic of (Zanzibar)	http://www.newafrica.com/travel/highlights/details.asp?countryid=49
Thailand, Kingdom of	http://www.thailandtravelsearch.com/thailand/tourism_travel_directory/index.shtml
Togo, Republic of	http://www.republicoftogo.com
Tonga	http://www.tongaonline.com
Trinidad and Tobago	http://discovertrinidad.com
Tunisia	http://www.arab.net/tunisia/tunisia_contents.html
Turkey, Republic of	http://www.exploreturkey.com
Turkmenistan	http://www.turkmenistan.com
Tuvalu Island	http://www.emulateme.com/tuvalu.htm
Uganda, Republic of	http://www.africa-insites.com/uganda/default.htm
Ukraine	http://www.un.int/ukraine/
United Arab Emirates (UAE) (Abu Dabi, Dubai, Sharjah, Ras Al Khaimah, Fujairah, Ajman, and Umm Al Quwain)	http://www.emirates.org
United Kingdom (England, Northern Ireland, Scotland, and Wales)	http://www.great-britain.org
Uruguay	http://www.visit-uruguay.com/colonia.htm
U.S. Virgin Islands	http://www.virginisles.com/facts/tourism.html
Uzbekistan, Republic of	http://www.tourism.uz
Vanuatu	http://www.tourismvanuatu.com/welcome.htm
Venezuela	http://www.lonelyplanet.com/destinations/south_america/venezuela/
Vietnam	http://www.gocvietnam.com
Western Samoa	http://public-www.pi.se/~orbit/samoa/welcome.html
Yemen, Republic of	http://www.al-bab.com/yemen/
Zambia, Republic of	http://www.zambia.co.zm/
Zimbabwe	http://www.travelnotes.org/Africa/Zimbabwe/zimbabwe_tourism.htm

CONTACT INFORMATION FOR INDIVIDUAL COUNTRIES

The following lists contact information for embassies and consulates of individual countries in the United States. Wherever possible, the contact information provided is for the Consular Division of the embassy, which is the division handling visas, passports, and other such services. Contact information for United Nations Missions in the United States is provided for countries that do not have an embassy or a consulate in America.

IMPORTANT

International travelers should always visit the U.S. State Department web site at http://travel.state.gov for up-to-date travel warnings and advisories for U.S. citizens and residents. A number of countries listed on the following pages are on the State Department's list of countries where unnecessary travel is discouraged or where all travel is advised against. As political situations can be volatile, always check with the State Deparment before traveling abroad.

Afghanistan, Islamic State of   Inquiries should be addressed to the Permanent Mission of the Islamic State of Afghanistan to the United Nations, 360 Lexington Ave., 11th Fl., New York, NY 10017 (212-972-1212) or the Consulate General in New York at 212-972-2276.

Albania, Republic of   Contact the Embassy of the Republic of Albania, 2100 S St. NW, Washington, DC 20005 (202-223-4942, fax 202-628-7342) or the Permanent Mission of the Republic of Albania to the United Nations at 212-249-2059.

Algeria, Democratic and Popular Republic of Contact the Embassy of the Democratic and Popular Republic of Algeria, Consular Section, 2118 Kalorama Rd. NW, Washington, DC 20008 (202-265-2800, fax 202-667-2174), http://www.algeria-us.org, or the Permanent Mission of the Democratic and Popular Republic of Algeria to the United Nations at 212-750-1960.

Andorra   Contact the Permanent Mission of Andorra to the United Nations, Two United Nations Plaza, 25th Fl., New York, NY 10017 (212-750-8064, fax 212-750-6630).

Angola, Republic of   Contact the Embassy of the Republic of Angola, Consular Section, 1615 M St. NW, Suite 900, Washington, DC 20036 (202-785-1156, fax 202-785-1258), http://www.angola.org or the Permanent Mission of the Republic of Angola to the United Nations at 212-861-5656.

Anguilla. *See* **British West Indies.**

Antigua and Barbuda   Contact the Embassy of Antigua and Barbuda, 3216 New Mexico Ave. NW, Washington, DC 20016 (202-362-5122, fax 202-362-5225) or the Consulate General in Miami at 305-381-6762.

Argentina   Contact the Embassy of Argentina, Consular Section, 1811 Q St. NW, Washington, DC 20009 (202-238-6460, fax 202-332-3171), http://embajadaargentina-usa.org or the nearest Consulate General: Atlanta (404-880-0805), Chicago (312-819-2606), Houston (713-871-8935), Los Angeles (323-954-9155), Miami (305-373-7794), or New York (212-603-0400).

Armenia, Republic of   Contact the Embassy of the Republic of Armenia, 2225 R St., NW, Washington, DC 20008 (202-319-1976, fax 203-319-2982), http://www.armeniaemb.org or the Consulate General in Los Angeles at 310-657-3817.

Aruba   Contact the Embassy of the Netherlands, 4200 Linnean Ave. NW, Washington, DC 20008 (202-244-5300, fax 202-362-3430), http://www.netherlands-embassy.org or the nearest Consulate General: Chicago (312-856-0110), Houston (713-622-8000), Los Angeles (310-268-1598), or New York (212-246-1429). *See also* **Netherlands.**

Australia   Contact the Embassy of Australia, 1601 Massachusetts Ave., NW, Washington, DC 20036 (202-797-3000, fax 202-797-3168), http://www.austemb.org or the nearest Consulate General: Atlanta (404-760-3400), Honolulu (808-524-5050),

Los Angeles (310-229-4800), New York (212-351-6500), or San Francisco (415-536-1970).

Austria Contact the Embassy of Austria, Consular Section, 3524 International Ct. NW, Washington, DC 20008 (202-895-6767, fax 202-895-6773), http://www.austria.org or the nearest Consulate General: Chicago (312-222-1515), Los Angeles (310-444-9310), or New York (212-737-6400).

Azerbaijan, Republic of Contact the Embassy of the Republic of Azerbaijan, 927 15th St. NW, Suite 700, Washington, DC 20005 (202-842-0001, fax 202-842-0004), http://www.azembassy.com or to the Permanent Mission of the Republic of Azerbaijan to the United Nations at 212-371-2559.

Azores. *See* **Portugal.**

Bahamas, Commonwealth of Contact the Embassy of the Commonwealth of the Bahamas, 2220 Massachusetts Ave. NW, Washington, DC 20008 (202-319-2660, fax 202-319-2668) or the nearest Consulate General: Miami (305-373-6295) or New York (212-421-6420).

Bahrain, State of Contact the Embassy of the State of Bahrain, 3502 International Dr. NW, Washington, DC 20008 (202-342-0741, fax 202-362-2192), http://www.bahrainembassy.org or the Consulate General in New York at 212-223-6200.

Bangladesh, People's Republic of Contact the Embassy of the People's Republic of Bangladesh, 3510 International Dr., NW, Washington, DC 20007 (202-244-2745, fax 202-244-5366), http://www.bangladoot.org or the Consulate General in Los Angeles (310-441-9399) or New York (212-599-6767).

Barbados Contact the Embassy of Barbados, 2144 Wyoming Ave. NW, Washington, DC 20008 (202-939-9200, fax 202-332-7467) or the Consulate General: Miami (305-442-1994) or New York (212-867-8435).

Belarus, Republic of Contact the Embassy of the Republic of Belarus, 1619 New Hampshire Ave. NW, Washington, DC 20008 (202-986-1606, fax 202-986-1805).

Belgium Contact the Embassy of Belgium, 3330 Garfield St., NW, Washington, DC 20008 (202-333-6900, fax 202-333-3079), http://www.diplobel.org/usa or the nearest Consulate General: Atlanta (404-659-2150), Chicago (312-263-6624), Los Angeles (323-857-1244), or New York (212-586-5110).

Belize Contact the Embassy of Belize, 2535 Massachusetts Ave. NW, Washington, DC 20008 (202-332-9636, fax 202-332-6888) or the Consulate General in Hollywood, CA at 213-469-7343.

Benin, Republic of Contact the Embassy of the Republic of Benin, 2124 Kalorama Rd. NW, Washington, DC 20008 (202-232-6656, fax 202-265-1996) or the Permanent Mission of the Republic of Benin to the United Nations at 212-249-6014.

Bermuda. *See* **United Kingdom.**

Bhutan, Kingdom of Contact the Permanent Mission of the Kingdom of Bhutan to the United Nations, Two United Nations Plaza, 27th Floor, New York, NY 10017 (212-826-1919, fax 212-826-2998).

Bolivia Contact the Embassy of the Republic of Bolivia, Consular Division, 1819 H St. NW, Suite 240, Washington, DC 20006 (202-232-4827, fax 202-232-8017), http://www.bolivia-usa.org or the nearest Consulate General: Miami (305-358-3450), New York (212-687-0530), or San Francisco (415-495-5173).

Bonaire. *See* **Netherlands Antilles.**

Bosnia and Herzegovina, Republic of Contact the Embassy of Bosnia and Herzegovina, 2109 E St. NW, Washington, DC 20037 (202-337-1500, fax 202-337-1502), http://www.bosnianembassy.org or the Consulate General in New York at 212-593-1042.

Botswana, Republic of Contact the Embassy of the Republic of Botswana, 1531–1533 New Hampshire Ave. NW, Washington, DC 20036 (202-244-4990, fax 202-244-4164) or the Permanent Mission of the Republic of Botswana to the United Nations at 212-889-2277.

Brazil Contact the Embassy of Brazil, Consular Services, 3009 Whitehaven St. NW, Washington, DC 20008 (202-338-2828, fax 202-238-2818), http://www.brasilemb.org or the nearest Consulate General: Boston (617-542-4000), Chicago (312-464-0244), Houston (713-961-3063), Los Angeles (323-651-2664), Miami (305-285-6200), New York (917-777-7777), or San Francisco (415-981-8170).

British Virgin Islands (including **Anegarda, Jost van Dyke, Tortola,** and **Virgin Gorda**). *See* **United Kingdom.**

British West Indies (including **Anguilla, Cayman Islands, Montserrat,** and **Turks and Caicos Islands**). *See* **United Kingdom.**

Brunei Darussalam, State of Contact the Embassy of the State of Brunei Darussalam, 3520 International Ct. NW, Washington, DC 20008 (202-237-1838, fax 202-885-0560), http://www.bruneiembassy.org or the Permanent Mission of the State of Brunei Darussalam to the United Nations at 212-697-3465.

Bulgaria, Republic of Contact the Embassy of the Republic of Bulgaria, 1621 22nd St. NW, Washington, DC 20008 (202-387-0174, fax 202-234-7973), http://www.bulgaria-embassy.org or the Consulate General in New York at 212-935-4646.

Burkina Faso Contact the Embassy of Burkina Faso, 2340 Massachusetts Ave. NW, Washington, DC 20008 (202-332-5577, fax 202-667-1882), http://www.burkinaembassy-usa.org or the Permanent Mission of Burkina Faso to the United Nations at 212-288-7515.

Burundi, Republic of Contact the Embassy of the Republic of Burundi, 2233 Wisconsin Ave. NW, Suite 212, Washington, DC 20007 (202-342-2574, fax 202-342-2578) or the Permanent Mission of the Republic of Burundi to the United Nations at 212-499-0001.

Cambodia, Kingdom of Contact the Royal Embassy of Cambodia, 4500 16th St. NW, Washington, DC 20011 (202-276-7742, fax 202-726-8381) or the Permanent Mission of the Kingdom of Cambodia to the United Nations at 212-223-0676.

Cameroon, Republic of Contact the Embassy of the Republic of Cameroon, 2349 Massachusetts Ave. NW, Washington, DC 20008 (202-265-8790, fax 202-387-3826) or the Honorary Consulate in Houston at 713-774-7693.

Canada Contact the Embassy of Canada 501 Pennsylvania Ave. NW, Washington, DC 20001 (202-682-1740, fax 202-682-7726), http://www.canadianembassy.org or the nearest Consulate General: Atlanta (404-532-2000), Boston (617-262-3760), Buffalo (716-858-9500), Chicago (312-616-1860), Dallas (214-922-9806), Detroit (313-567-2340), Los Angeles (213-346-2700), Miami (305-579-1600), Minneapolis (612-332-7486), New York (212-596-1628), or Seattle (206-443-1777).

Cape Verde, Republic of Contact the Embassy of the Republic of Cape Verde, 3415 Massachusetts Ave. NW, Washington, DC 20007 (202-965-6820, fax 202-965-1207) or the Consulate General in Boston at 617-353-0014.

Cayman Islands. *See* **British West Indies.**

Central African Republic Contact the Embassy of the Central African Republic, 1618 22nd St. NW, Washington, DC 20008 (202-483-7800, fax 202-332-9893) or the Honorary Consulate in New York at 212-983-0330.

Chad, Republic of Contact the Embassy of the Republic of Chad, 2002 R St. NW, Washington, DC 20009 (202-462-4009, fax 202-265-1937), http://www.chadembassy.org or the Permanent Mission of the Republic of Chad to the United Nations at 212-986-0980.

Chile Contact the Embassy of Chile, 1732 Massachusetts Ave. NW, Washington, DC 20036 (202-785-1746, fax 202-887-5579), http://www.chile-usa.org or the nearest Consulate General: Chicago (312-654-8780), Houston (713-621-5853), Los Angeles (310-785-0047), Miami (305-373-8623), New York (212-355-0612), or San Francisco (415-982-7662).

China, People's Republic of Contact the Embassy of the People's Republic of China, 2300 Connecticut Ave. NW, Washington, DC 20008 (202-328-2500, fax 202-588-0032), http://www.china-embassy.org or the nearest Consulate General: Chicago (312-803-0098), Houston (713-524-0780), Los Angeles (213-807-8088), New York (212-330-7400), or San Francisco (415-674-2900).

China, Republic of. *See* **Taiwan.**

Colombia Contact the Embassy of Colombia, Consular Division, 1857 Connecticut Ave. NW, Suite 524, Washington, DC 20008 (202-332-7476, fax 202-332-7180), http://www.colombiaemb.org or the nearest Consulate General: Atlanta (404-255-3038), Boston (617-536-6222), Chicago (312-923-1196), Houston (713-527-8919), Los Angeles (323-653-4299), Miami (305-448-5558), New Orleans (504-525-5580), New York (212-949-9898), San Francisco (415-495-7195), San Juan, PR (787-754-6885), or Seattle (202-332-7476).

Comoros Islands (Federal Islamic Republic of the Comoros) Contact the Embassy of the Federal Islamic Republic of Comoros, 420 E. 50th St., New York, NY 10022 (212-972-8010, fax 212-983-4712).

Congo, Democratic Republic of (formerly Zaire) Contact the Zairian Embassy, 1800 New Hampshire Ave. NW, Washington, DC 20009 (202-234-7690, fax 202-237-0748) or the Permanent Mission of the Democratic Republic of Congo to the United Nations at 201-812-1636.

Congo, Republic of the Contact the Embassy of the Republic of the Congo, 4891 Colorado Ave. NW, Washington, DC 20011 (202-726-5500, fax 202-726-1860) or the Permanent Mission of the Republic of Congo to the United Nations at 212-744-7840.

Cook Islands Contact the Embassy of New Zealand, 37 Observatory Circle NW, Washington, DC 20008 (202-328-4800, fax 202-667-5227), http://www.nzemb.org, the Consulate General in Los Angeles (310-207-1605) or New York (212-832-4038).

Costa Rica Contact the Embassy of Costa Rica, Consular Division, 2114 S St. NW, Washington, DC 20008 (202-234-2945), http://www.costarica-embassy.org or the nearest Consulate General: Atlanta (770-951-7025), Chicago (312-263-2772), Fremont, CA (510-790-0785), Houston (713-266-1527), Los Angeles (213-380-7915), Miami (305-871-7485), New Orleans (504-581-6800), New York (212-509-3066), or San Juan, PR (787-723-6227).

Côte d'Ivoire, Republic of (Ivory Coast) Contact the Embassy of the Republic of Côte d'Ivoire, 2424 Massachusetts Ave. NW, Washington, DC 20008 (202-797-0300) or the Honorary Consulate in San Francisco at 415-391-0176.

Croatia, Republic of Contact the Embassy of the Republic of Croatia, 2343 Massachusetts Ave. NE, Washington, DC 20008 (202-588-5899, fax 202-588-8936), http://www.croatiaemb.org or the nearest Consulate General: Chicago (312-482-9902), Los Angeles (310-477-1009), or New York (212-599-3066).

Cuba   Travel to Cuba is restricted by U.S. Department of Treasury regulations requiring that citizens obtain a license to visit Cuba. Contact the Licensing Division, Office of Foreign Assets Control, U.S. Department of the Treasury, 1500 Pennsylvania Ave. NW, Treasury Annex, Washington, DC 20220 (202-622-2480, fax 202-622-1657, info-by-fax service 202-622-0077). There is no Cuban embassy in the United States, as the U.S. does not maintain diplomatic relations with Cuba. For more information about entry requirements and visas, contact the Embassy of Switzerland, Cuban Interests Section, 2360 16th St. NW, Washington, DC 20009 (202-797-8518, fax 202-797-8521).

Curaçao. *See* **Netherlands Antilles.**

Cyprus, Republic of   Contact the Embassy of the Republic of Cyprus, 2211 R St. NW, Washington, DC 20008 (202-462-5772, fax 202-483-6710) or the Consulate General in New York at 212-686-6016.

Czech Republic   Contact the Embassy of the Czech Republic, Consular Department, 3900 Spring of Freedom St. NW, Washington, DC 20008 (202-274-9121, fax 202-363-6308), http://www.mzv.cz/washington/ or the Consulate General in Los Angeles (310-473-0889) or New York (212-717-5643).

Denmark, Kingdom of (including **Greenland** and the **Faroe Islands**) Contact the Royal Danish Embassy, 3200 Whitehaven St. NW, Washington, DC 20008 (202-234-4300, fax 202-328-1470), http://www.denmarkemb.org or the nearest Consulate General: Chicago (312-787-8780), Los Angeles (310-443-2090), or New York (212-223-4545).

Djibouti, Republic of   Contact the Embassy of the Republic of Djibouti, 1156 15th St. NW, Suite 515, Washington, DC 20005 (202-331-0270, fax 202-331-0302) or the Permanent Mission of the Republic of Djibouti to the United Nations at 212-753-3163.

Dominica, Commonwealth of   Contact the Embassy of the Commonwealth of Dominica, 3216 New Mexico Ave. NW, Washington, DC 20016 (202-364-6781, fax 202-364-6791) or the Consulate General in New York at 212-599-8478.

Dominican Republic   Contact the Embassy of the Dominican Republic, 1715 22nd St. NW, Washington, DC 20008 (202-332-6280, fax 202-265-8057), http://www.domrep.org or the nearest Consulate General: Baltimore (410-719-8788), Boston (617-482-8121), Chicago (312-486-8400), Houston (713-266-0165), Miami (305-358-3220), New Orleans (504-522-1843), New York (212-768-2480), Philadelphia (215-923-3006), or San Francisco (415-982-5144).

Ecuador (including the **Galapagos Islands**)   Contact the Embassy of Ecuador, Consular Section, 2535 15th St. NW, Washington, DC 20009 (202-234-7166, fax 202-265-9325), http://www.ecuador.org or the nearest Consulate General: Jersey City, NJ (201-985-1700), New Orleans (504-523-3229), New York (212-808-0170), or San Francisco (415-957-5921).

Egypt, Arab Republic of   Contact the Embassy of the Arab Republic of Egypt, 3521 International Ct. NW, Washington, DC 20008 (202-895-5400, fax 202-244-4319), http://www.embassyofegypt washingtondc.org or the nearest Consulate General: Chicago (312-828-9162), Houston (713-961-4915), New York (212-759-7120), or San Francisco (419-346-9700).

El Salvador   Contact the Embassy of El Salvador, Consular Affairs, 1424 16th St. NW, 2nd Floor, Washington, DC 20036 (202-331-4032) or the nearest Consulate General: Boston (617-577-9111), Chicago (312-322-1393), Houston (713-270-6239), Dallas (214-637-0732), Los Angeles (213-383-5776), Miami (305-371-8850), New York (212-889-5608), or San Francisco (415-781-7924).

England. *See* **United Kingdom.**

Equatorial Guinea, Republic of   Contact the Embassy of the Republic of Equatorial Guinea, 2020 16th St. NW, Washington, DC 20009 (202-518-5700, fax 202-518-5252) or the Permanent Mission to the Republic of Equatorial Guinea to the United Nations at 914-664-1882.

Eritrea   Contact the Embassy of Eritrea, 1708 New Hampshire Ave. NW, Washington, DC 20009 (203-319-1991, fax 202-319-1304) or the Permanent Mission of Eritrea to the United Nations at 212-687-3390.

Estonia   Contact the Embassy of Estonia, 2131 Massachusetts Ave. NW, Washington, DC 20008 (202-588-0101, fax 202-588-0108), http://www.estemb.org or the Consulate General in New York at 212-883-0636.

Ethiopia, Federal Democratic Republic of   Contact the Embassy of Ethiopia, Consular Affairs, 3506 International Dr. NW, Washington, DC 20008 (202-274-4555), http://www.ethiopianembassy.org or the Permanent Mission of Ethiopia to the United Nations at 212-421-1830.

European Union (**Belgium, Denmark, Finland, France, Germany, Greece, Ireland, Italy, Luxembourg, the Netherlands, Portugal, Spain, Sweden** and **the United Kingdom**)   Established to promote cooperation between the United States and the member states of the Union, the European Union's Delegation of the European Commission to the United States offers helpful information on trade agreements, international policies, justice matters, and many other topics of interest to prospective travelers in Europe. For more information, contact the European Union, Delegation of the European Commission to the United States, 2300 M St., NW, Washington, DC 20007 (202-862-9500, fax 202-429-1766), http://www.eurunion.org.

Faroe Islands. *See* **Denmark.**

Federal Republic of Yugoslavia. *See* **Serbia and Montenegro.**

Fiji   Contact the Embassy of Fiji, 2233 Wisconsin Ave. NW, Suite 240, Washington, DC 20007 (202-337-8320, fax 202-337-1996) or the Permanent Mission of Fiji to the United Nations at 212-687-4130.

Finland   Contact the Embassy of Finland, 3301 Massachusetts Ave. NW, Washington, DC 20008 (202-298-5800, fax 202-298-6030), http://www.finland.org or the Consulate General in Los Angeles (310-203-9903) or New York (212-750-4400).

Former Yugoslav Republic of Macedonia (FYROM)   Contact the Embassy of the Former Yugoslav Republic of Macedonia, 3050 K St. NW, Washington, DC 20007 (202-337-3063, fax 202-337-3093) or the Consulate General in New York at 212-317-1727.

France (including **French Guiana, French Polynesia,** and **French West Indies**)   Contact the Embassy of France, 4101 Reservoir Rd. NW, Washington, DC 20007 (202-944-6000, fax 202-944-6148), http://www.info-france-usa.org or the nearest Consulate General: Atlanta (404-495-1660), Boston (617-542-7374), Chicago (312-787-5359), Houston (713-572-2799), Los Angeles (310-235-3200), Miami (305-372-9799), New Orleans (504-523-5772), New York (212-606-3689), or San Francisco (415-397-4330).

French Guiana. *See* **France.**

French Polynesia (including **Society Islands, French Southern** and **Antarctic Lands, Tuamotu, Gambier, French Austral, Marquesas, Kerguelen, Crozet, New Caldeonia, Tahiti,** and **Wallis** and **Futuna Islands**). *See* **France.**

French West Indies (including **Guadeloupe, Isles des Saintes, La Desirade, Marie Galante, Martinique, St. Barthelemy,** and **St. Martin**). *See* **France.**

Gabonese Republic (Gabon)   Contact the Embassy of the Gabonese Republic, 2034 20th St. NW, Washington, DC 20009 (202-797-1000, fax 202-332-0668) or the Permanent Mission of the Gabonese Republic to the United Nations at 212-686-9720.

Galapagos Islands. *See* **Ecuador.**

Gambia   Contact the Embassy of Gambia, 1155 15th St. NW, Washington, DC 20005 (202-785-1399, fax 202-785-1430) or the Honorary Consulate in Beverly Hills, CA at 310-274-5084.

Georgia, Republic of   Contact the Embassy of the Republic of Georgia, Consular Office, 1615 New Hampshire Ave. NW, Suite 300, Washington, DC 20009 (202-393-6060, fax 202-393-4537), http:// www.georgiaemb.org or the nearest Honorary Consulate: Boston (617-492-0727), Houston (281-633-3500), or San Juan, PR (787-724-8070).

Germany, Federal Republic of   Contact the German Consulate at the Embassy of the Federal Republic of Germany, 4645 Reservoir Rd. NW, Washington, DC 20007 (202-298-4393, fax 202-471-5558), http://www.germany-info.org or the nearest Consulate General: Atlanta (404-659-4760), Boston (617-536-4414), Chicago (312-580-1199), Houston (713-627-7770), Los Angeles (323-930-2703), Miami (305-358-0290), New York (212-610-9700), or San Francisco (415-775-1061).

Ghana   Contact the Embassy of Ghana, 3512 International Dr., NW, Washington, DC 20008 (202-686-4520, fax 202-686-4527), http://www. ghanaembassy.org or the Consulate General in New York at 212-832-1300.

Gibraltar. *See* **United Kingdom.**

Great Britain. *See* **United Kingdom.**

Greece   Contact the Embassy of Greece, Consular Section, Massachusetts Ave. NW, Washington, DC 20008 (202-939-5818, fax 202-234-2803), http:// www.greekembassy.org or the nearest Consulate General: Boston (617-543-0100), Chicago (312-225-3915), Los Angeles (310-826-5555), New York (212-988-5500), or San Francisco (415-775-2102).

Greenland. *See* **Denmark.**

Grenada   Contact the Embassy of Grenada, 1701 New Hampshire Ave. NW, Washington, DC 20009 (202-265-2561) or the Consulate General in New York at 212-599-0301.

Guadeloupe (French West Indies). *See* **France.**

Guatemala   Contact the Embassy of Guatemala, Consular Section, 2220 R St. NW, Washington, DC 20008 (202-745-4952, fax 202-745-1908), http:// www.guatemala-embassy.org or the nearest Consulate General: Chicago (312-332-1587), Houston (713-953-9531), Los Angeles (213-365-9251), Miami (305-679-9945), New York (212-686-3837), or San Francisco (415-788-5651).

Guinea, Republic of   Contact the Embassy of the Republic of Guinea, 2112 Leroy Pl. NW, Washington, DC 20008 (202-483-9420, fax 202-483-8688) or the Permanent Mission of the Republic of Guinea to the United Nations at 212-687-8115.

Guinea-Bissau, Republic of   Contact the Embassy of the Republic of Guinea-Bissau, 15929 Yukon Lane, Rockville, MD 20855 (301-947-3958) or the Permanent Mission of the Republic of Guinea-Bissau to the United Nations at 212-338-9380.

Guyana, Republic of   Contact the Embassy of the Republic of Guyana, 2490 Tracy Pl. NW, Washington, DC 20008 (202-265-6900, fax 202-232-1297), http://www.guyana.org/govt/embassy.html or the Consulate General in New York at 212-527-3215.

Haiti, Republic of   Contact the Embassy of the Republic of Haiti, 2311 Massachusetts Ave. NW, Washington, DC 20008 (202-332-4090, fax 202-745-7215), http://www.haiti.org or the nearest Consulate General: Boston (617-266-3660), Chicago (312-922-4004), Miami (305-859-2003), or New York (212-697-9767).

Holy See, Apostolic Nunciature of the (the Vatican) Contact the Holy See Nunciature, 3339 Massachusetts Ave. NW, Washington, DC 20008 (202-333-7121) or the Permanent Observer Mission of the Holy See to the United Nations at 212-370-7885. *See also* **Italy.**

Honduras Contact the Embassy of Honduras, Consular Section, 1528 K St. NW, 2nd Floor, Washington, DC 20005 (202-737-2972, fax 202-737-2907) or the nearest Consulate General: Chicago (773-342-8281), Houston (713-622-7911), Los Angeles (213-383-9244), Miami (305-447-8927), New York (212-269-3611), San Francisco (315-392-0076), or Tampa (813-209-3249).

Point Roberts, Washington, is cut off from the rest of the state by British Columbia, Canada. To travel between Point Roberts and the rest of the state, you must pass through both Canadian and U.S. customs.

Hong Kong (Special Administrative Region of the People's Republic of China). *See* **China, People's Republic of.**

Hungary, Republic of Contact the Embassy of the Republic of Hungary, 3910 Shoemaker St. NW, Washington, DC 20008 (202-362-6730, fax 202-966-8135), http://www.hungaryemb.org or the Consulate General in Los Angeles (310-473-9344) or New York (212-752-0669).

Iceland Contact the Embassy of Iceland, 1156 15th St. NW, Suite 1200, Washington, DC 20005 (202-265-6653, fax 202-265-6656), http://www.iceland.org or the Consulate General in New York at 212-593-2700.

India Contact the Embassy of India, Consular Wing, 2536 Massachusetts Ave. NW, Washington, DC 20008 (202-939-9806, fax 202-797-4693), http://www.indianembassy.org or the nearest Con-

sulate General: Chicago (312-595-0405), Houston (713-626-2148), New York (212-774-0600), or San Francisco (415-668-0662).

Indonesia, Republic of Contact the Embassy of the Republic of Indonesia, 2020 Massachusetts Ave. NW, Washington, DC 20036 (202-775-5200, fax 202-775-5365) or the nearest Consulate General: Chicago (312-345-9300), Houston (713-785-1691), Los Angeles (213-383-5126), New York (212-879-0600), or San Francisco (415-474-9571).

Iran, Islamic Republic of The United States does not maintain diplomatic or consular relations with Iran. Inquiries should be addressed to the Embassy of Pakistan, Interest Section of the Islamic Republic of Iran, 2209 Wisconsin Ave. NW, Washington, DC 20007 (202-965-4990, fax 202-965-1073) or to the Permanent Mission of the Islamic Republic of Iran to the United Nations at 212-682-2020.

Iraq The United States suspended diplomatic and consular operations in Iraq in 1990. Since February 1991, U.S. passports are not valid for travel in, to, or through Iraq without authorization from the Department of State. Passport validation requests should be forwarded in writing to Deputy Assistant Secretary for Passport Services, Office of Passport Policy and Advisory Services—US Dept. of State, 2401 E St. NW, 9th Floor, Washington, DC 20522. For more information, contact the Embassy of Algeria, Iraqi Interests Section, 1801 P St. NW, Washington, DC 20036 (202-483-7500, fax 202-462-5066).

Ireland Contact the Embassy of Ireland, 2234 Massachusetts Ave. NW, Washington, DC 20008 (202-462-3939, fax 202-232-5993), http://www.irelandemb.org or the nearest Consulate General: Boston (617-267-9330), Chicago (312-337-1868), New York (212-319-2555), or San Francisco (415-392-4214).

Israel and the Occupied Territories (Jerusalem, Gaza, Golan Heights, and the **West Bank)** Contact the Embassy of Israel, Consular Section, 3514

International Dr. NW, Washington, DC 20008 (202-364-5557, fax 202-364-5429), http://www.israelemb.org or the nearest Consulate General: Atlanta (404-487-6500), Boston (617-535-0200), Chicago (312-297-4800), Houston (713-627-3780), Los Angeles (323-852-5500), Miami (305-925-9400), New York (212-499-5410), Philadelphia (215-546-5556), or San Francisco (415-844-7500).

Italy   Contact the Embassy of Italy, 3000 Whitehaven St. NW, Washington, DC 20008 (202-612-4400, fax 202-518-2154), http://www.italyemb.org or the nearest Consulate General: Boston (617-542-0483), Chicago (312-467-1550), Houston (713-850-7520), Los Angeles (310-820-0622), Miami (305-374-6322), New York (212-737-9100), Philadelphia (215-592-7329), or San Francisco (415-292-9210).

Ivory Coast. *See* **Côte d'Ivoire.**

Jamaica   Contact the Embassy of Jamaica, 1520 New Hampshire Ave. NW, Washington, DC 20036 (202-452-0660, fax 202-452-0081), http://www.emjam-usa.org or the Consulate General in Miami (305-374-8431) or New York (212-935-9000).

Japan   Contact the Embassy of Japan, 2520 Massachusetts Ave. NW, Washington, DC 20008 (202-238-6700, fax 202-328-2187), http://www.embjapan.org or the nearest Consulate General: Anchorage (907-562-8424), Atlanta (404-892-2700), Boston (617-973-9772), Chicago (312-280-0400), Denver (305-534-1151), Detroit (313-567-0120), Guam (671-646-1290), Honolulu (808-543-3111), Houston (713-652-2977), Kansas City, MO (816-471-0111), Los Angeles (213-617-6700), Miami (305-530-9090), New Orleans (504-529-2101), New York (212-371-8222), Portland, OR (503-221-1811), San Francisco (415-777-3533), or Seattle (206-682-9107).

Jordan, Hashemite Kingdom of   Contact the Embassy of the Hashemite Kingdom of Jordan, Consular Section, 3504 International Dr. NW, Washington, DC 20008 (202-966-2861, fax 202-686-4491), http://www.jordanembassyus.org or the Consulate in New York at 212-832-0119.

Kazakhstan, Republic of   Contact the Embassy of the Republic of Kazakhstan, 1401 16th St. NW, Washington, DC 20008 (202-387-6101, fax 202-462-3829), http://www.president.kz or the Consulate in New York at 212-888-3024.

Kenya   Contact the Embassy of Kenya, 2249 R St. NW, Washington, DC 20008 (202-387-6101, fax 202-462-3829), http://www.kenyaembassy.com or the Permanent Mission of Kenya to the United Nations at 212-486-1985.

Kiribati, Republic of (formerly **Gilbert Islands**) Contact the British Embassy, Consular Section, 3100 Massachusetts Ave. NW, Washington, DC 20008 (202-588-7800, fax 202-588-7850).

Korea, Democratic People's Republic of (North Korea) The United States currently does not maintain diplomatic or consular relations with North Korea. The Swedish Embassy in Cambodia is acting as the consular protecting power for the U.S. government in North Korea. A U.S. Treasury Department license must be obtained for any U.S. citizen to engage in any travel-related transaction, whether travel will be to or within North Korea. Before planning any travel to North Korea, contact the Licensing Division, Office of Foreign Assets Control, U.S. Department of the Treasury, 1500 Pennsylvania Ave. NW, Treasury Annex, Washington, DC 20220 (202-622-2480, fax 202-622-1657, info-by-fax service 202-622-0077). Visa information must be obtained from a consulate in a country that maintains diplomatic relations with North Korea, such as France.

Korea, Republic of (South Korea)   Contact the Embassy of Korea, Consular Division, 2320 Massachusetts Ave. NW, Washington, DC 20008 (202-939-5663, fax 202-342-1597), http://emb.dsdn.net or the nearest Consulate General: Atlanta (404-522-1611), Boston (617-641-2830), Chicago (312-822-9485), Honolulu (808-595-6109), Houston (713-961-0186), Los Angeles (213-385-9300), New York

(646-674-6000), San Francisco (415-921-2251), or Seattle (206-441-1011).

Kuwait, State of Contact the Embassy of the State of Kuwait, 2940 Tilden St. NW, Washington, DC 20008 (202-966-0702, fax 202-966-0517) or the Permanent Mission of the State of Kuwait to the United Nations at 212-973-4300.

Kyrgyz Republic (Kyrgyzstan) Contact the Embassy of the Kyrgyz Republic, 1732 Wisconsin Ave. NW, Washington, DC 20007 (202-338-5141, fax 202-338-5139), http://www.kyrgyzstan.org or the Consulate General in New York at 212-319-2836.

Laos (Lao People's Democratic Republic) Contact the Embassy of Lao People's Democratic Republic, Consular Section, 2222 S St. NW, Washington, DC 20008 (202-332-6416, fax 202-332-4923), http://www.laoembassy.com or the Permanent Mission of the Lao People's Democratic Republic to the United Nations at 212-832-2734.

Latvia Contact the Embassy of Latvia, 4325 17th St. NW, Washington, DC 20011 (202-726-8213, fax 202-726-6785), http://www.latvia-usa.org or the nearest Honorary Consulate: Houston (713-888-0404), Palos Verdes, CA (310-377-1784), or Willoughby, OH (216-951-6665).

Lebanon Contact the Embassy of Lebanon, 2560 28th St. NW, Washington, DC 20008 (202-939-6300, fax 202-939-6324), http://www.lebanon embassy.org or the nearest Consulate General: Detroit (313-567-0233), Los Angeles (323-467-1253), or New York (212-744-7905).

Lesotho, Kingdom of Contact the Embassy of the Kingdom of Lesotho, 2511 Massachusetts Ave. NW, Washington, DC 20008 (202-797-5533, fax 202-234-6815) or the Honorary Consulate in New Orleans at 504-524-6908.

Liberia, Republic of Contact the Embassy of the Republic of Liberia, 5201 16th St. NW, Washington, DC 20011 (202-723-0437, fax 202-723-0436),

http://www.liberiaemb.org or the Consulate General in New York (212-687-1025).

Libya Since December 1981, U.S. passports are not valid for travel in, to, or through Libya without authorization from the Department of State. Application for exemption to this restriction should be submitted in writing to Passport Services, U.S. Department of State, 1111 19th St. NW, Washington, DC 20524, Attn: CA/PPT/PAS. In addition, U.S. citizens need a Treasury Department license in order to engage in any transactions related to travel to and within Libya. Before planning any travel to Libya, U.S. citizens should contact the Licensing Division, Office of Foreign Assets Control, U.S. Department of the Treasury, 1500 Pennsylvania Ave. NW, Treasury Annex, Washington, DC 20220 (202-622-2480, fax 202-622-1657, info-by-fax service 202-622-0077). Application and inquiries for visas must be made through a country that maintains diplomatic relations with Libya.

Liechtenstein Contact the Embassy of Switzerland, 2900 Cathedral Ave. NW, Washington, DC 20008 (202-745-7900, fax 202-387-2564), http://www.swissemb.org or the nearest Consulate General: Atlanta (404-870-2000), Chicago (312-915-0061), Houston (713-650-0000), Los Angeles (310-575-1145), New York (212-758-2560), or San Francisco (415-788-2272).

Lithuania Contact the Embassy of Lithuania, 2622 16th St. NW, Washington, DC 20009 (202-234-5860, fax 202-328-0466), http://www.lt embassyus.org or the Consulate General in Chicago (312-397-0382) or New York (212-354-7849).

Luxembourg, Grand Duchy Contact the Embassy of the Grand Duchy of Luxembourg, 2200 Massachusetts Ave. NW, Washington, DC 20008 (202-265-4171, fax 202-328-8270), http://www. luxembourg-usa.org or the Consulate General in New York (212-888-6664) or San Francisco (415-788-0816).

Travel

Macau (Macau became a Special Administrative Region of the People's Republic of China in December 1999.) Contact the Embassy of the People's Republic of China, 2300 Connecticut Ave. NW, Washington, DC 20008 (202-328-2500, fax 202-588-0032) or the nearest Consulate General of China: Chicago (312-803-0098), Houston (713-524-0780), Los Angeles (213-807-8088), New York (212-330-7400), or San Francisco (415-674-2900). Or contact the American Consulate General in Hong Kong (852-2523-9011).

Macedonia. *See* **Former Yugoslav Republic of Macedonia (FYROM).**

Madagascar, Republic of Contact the Embassy of the Republic of Madagascar, 2374 Massachusetts Ave. NW, Washington, DC 20008 (202-265-5525, fax 202-265-3034), http://www.embassy.org/madagascar.

Malawi Contact the Embassy of Malawi, 2408 Massachusetts Ave. NW, Washington, DC 20008 (202-797-1007) or the Honorary Consulate in Vista, CA (760-598-1836).

Malaysia (and the **Borneo States, Sarawak,** and **Sabah**) Contact the Embassy of Malaysia, Consular Division, 1900 24th St. NW, Washington, DC 20008 (202-328-2700, fax 202-483-7669) or the Consulate General in Los Angeles (213-892-1238) or New York (212-490-2722).

Maldives Contact the Permanent Mission of the Republic of Maldives to the United Nations, 800 2nd Ave., Suite 400E, New York, NY 10017 (212-599-6195).

Mali, Republic of Contact the Embassy of the Republic of Mali, 2130 R St. NW, Washington, DC 20008 (202-332-2249, fax 202-332-6603), http://www.maliembassy.org or the Permanent Mission of the Republic of Mali to the United Nations at 212-737-4150.

Malta Contact the Embassy of Malta, 2017 Connecticut Ave. NW, Washington, DC 20008 (202-462-3611), http://www.magnet.mt or the Consulate in New York at 212-725-2345.

Marshall Islands, Republic of Contact the Embassy of Marshall Islands, 2433 Massachusetts Ave. NW, Washington, DC 20008 (202-234-5414, fax 202-232-3236), http://www.rmiembassyus.org or the Consulate General in Honolulu at 808-545-7767).

Martinique (French West Indies). *See* **France.**

Santa Fe, New Mexico, founded in 1607, is the oldest continuously occupied state capital. It has no regularly scheduled airline service and no passenger train service.

Mauritania, Republic of Contact the Embassy of the Republic of Mauritania, 2129 Leroy Pl. NW, Washington, DC 20008 (202-232-5700, fax 202-319-2623) or the Permanent Mission of the Republic of Mauritania to the United Nations at 212-986-7963.

Mauritius Contact the Embassy of Mauritius, 4301 Connecticut Ave. NW, Suite 441, Washington, DC 20008 (202-244-1491, fax 202-966-0983), http://www.idsonline.com/usa/embassydc.html or the nearest Honorary Consulate: Atlanta (404-264-1700), Los Angeles (310-557-2009), or San Francisco (415-693-9233).

Mayotte Island. *See* **France.**

Mexico Contact the Embassy of Mexico, Consular Division, 2827 16th St. NW, Washington, DC 20009 (202-736-1000, fax 202-797-8458), http://www.embassyofmexico.org or contact the nearest Consulate General: Albuquerque (505-247-2147), Atlanta (404-266-2233), Austin, TX (512-478-2866), Boston (617-426-4181), Calexico, CA (760-357-3863), Chicago (312-855-0066), Dallas (214-630-7341), Denver (303-331-1110), El Paso,

TX (915-533-3644), Fresno, CA (559-233-9770), Houston (713-271-6800), Los Angeles (213-351-6800), Miami (305-716-4977), New Orleans (504-522-3698), New York (212-217-6400), Philadelphia (215-922-3834), Phoenix (602-242-7398), Portland, OR (503-274-1442), Sacramento, CA (916-441-3287), San Antonio, TX (210-227-1085), San Bernardino, CA (909-889-9836), San Diego, CA (619-231-8414), San Jose, CA (408-294-3414), or Santa Ana, CA (714-835-3069).

Micronesia, Federated States of (Kosrae, Yap, Panape, and **Truk)**   Contact the Embassy of the Federated States of Micronesia, 1725 N St. NW, Washington, DC 20036 (202-223-4383, fax 202-223-4391), http://www.fsmembassy.org or the nearest Consulate General: Guam (671-646-9154) or Honolulu (808-836-4775).

Miquelon Island. *See* **France.**

Moldova, Republic of   Contact the Embassy of the Republic of Moldova, 2101 S St. NW, Washington, DC 20008 (202-667-1130, fax 202-667-1204), http://www.moldova.org or the Permanent Mission of the Republic of Moldova to the United Nations at 212-682-3523.

Monaco, Principality of   Contact the Consulate General of Monaco, 565 Fifth Ave., New York, NY 10017 (212-759-5227) or the nearest Honorary Consulate: Chicago (312-642-1242), Los Angeles (213-655-8970), New Orleans (504-522-5700), New York (212-759-5227), San Francisco (415-362-5050), or San Juan, PR (787-721-4215).

Mongolia   All foreigners are required to be registered with the police at the Citizen's Information and Registration Center in Mongolia upon arrival and are warned to do so in order to avoid being denied exit and/or fined upon departure. Contact the Embassy of Mongolia, 2833 M St. NW, Washington, DC 20007 (202-333-7117, fax 202-298-7117), http://www.monemb.org or the Permanent Mission of Mongolia to the United Nations at 212-861-9460.

Montenegro. *See* **Serbia and Montenegro.**

Montserrat. *See* **British West Indies.**

Morocco, Kingdom of   Contact the Embassy of the Kingdom of Morocco, 1601 21st St. NW, Washington, DC 20009 (202-462-7979, fax 202-265-0161) or the Consulate General in New York at 212-758-2625.

Mozambique, Republic of   Contact the Embassy of the Republic of Mozambique, 1990 M St. NW, Suite 570, Washington, DC 20036 (202-293-7146, fax 202-835-0245), http://www.embamoc-usa.org or the Permanent Mission of the Republic of Mozambique to the United Nations at 212-644-5965.

Myanmar, Union of   Contact the Embassy of the Union of Myanmar, 2300 S St. NW, Washington, DC 20008 (202-332-9044, fax 202-332-9046) or the Permanent Mission of the Union of Myanmar to the United Nations at 212-535-1310.

Namibia   Contact the Embassy of Namibia, 1605 New Hampshire Ave. NW, Washington, DC 20009 (202-986-0540, fax 202-986-0443) or the Honorary Consulate in Detroit at 313-259-0054.

Nepal, Kingdom of   Contact the Royal Nepalese Embassy, 2131 Leroy Pl. NW, Washington, DC 20008 (202-667-4550, fax 202-667-5534), http://www.newweb.net/nepal_embassy or the Consulate General in New York at 212-370-3988.

Netherlands, the, and **Netherlands Antilles** (including **Bonaire, Curaçao, Saba, St. Maarten,** and **Statia [St. Eustatius]**)   Contact the Embassy of the Netherlands, 4200 Linnean Ave. NW, Washington, DC 20008 (202-244-5300, fax 202-362-3430), http://www.netherlands-embassy.org or the nearest Consulate General: Chicago (312-856-0110), Houston (713-622-8000), Los Angeles (310-268-1598), or New York (212-246-1429).

New Caledonia (French Polynesia). *See* **France.**

New Zealand   Contact the Embassy of New Zealand, 37 Observatory Circle NW, Washington, DC 20008 (202-328-4800, fax 202-667-5227), http://www.nzemb.org or the Consulate General in Los Angeles (310-207-1605) or New York (212-832-4038).

Nicaragua   Contact the Embassy of Nicaragua, 1627 New Hampshire Ave. NW, Washington, DC 20009 (202-939-6531, fax 202-939-6574) or the nearest Consulate General: Houston (713-272-9628), Los Angeles (213-252-1170), Miami (305-220-6900), New Orleans (504-523-1507), New York (212-986-6562), or San Francisco (415-765-6821).

Niger, Republic of   Contact the Embassy of the Republic of Niger, 2204 R St. NW, Washington, DC 20008 (202-483-4224, fax 202-683-3169) or the Permanent Mission of the Republic of Niger to the United Nations at 212-421-3260.

Nigeria, Republic of   The U.S. State Department has issued the following entry-requirement-related information for Nigeria: "A visa is required and must be obtained in advance; airport visas are not available. Promises of entry into Nigeria without a visa are credible indicators of a fraudulent commercial scheme in which the perpetrators seek to exploit the foreign traveler's illegal presence in Nigeria with threats of extortion or bodily harm. U.S. citizens cannot legally depart Nigeria unless they can prove, by presenting their entry visas, that they entered Nigeria legally." Contact the Embassy of the Federal Republic of Nigeria, 1333 16th St. NW, Washington, DC 20036 (202-986-8400, fax 202-775-1385), http://www.nigeria-government.com/faqframe.html or the Consulate General in New York at 212-808-0301.

Niue. *See* **New Zealand.**

Norfolk Island. *See* **Australia.**

Northern Ireland. *See* **United Kingdom.**

Northern Mariana Islands, Commonwealth of the   Self-governing commonwealth in political union with the U.S.; no restrictions on entry or travel for U.S. citizens.

North Korea. *See* **Korea, Democratic People's Republic of.**

Norway, Kingdom of   Contact the Royal Norwegian Embassy, 2720 34th St. NW, Washington, DC 20008 (202-333-6000, fax 202-337-0870), http://www.norway.org or contact the nearest Consulate General: Houston (713-521-2900), Miami (305-358-4386), Minneapolis (612-332-3338), New York (212-421-7333), or San Francisco (415-986-0766).

Oman, Sultanate of   Contact the Embassy of the Sultanate of Oman, 2535 Belmont Rd. NW, Washington, DC 20008 (202-387-1980, fax 202-745-4933) or the Permanent Mission of the Sultanate of Oman to the United Nations at 212-355-3505.

Pakistan, Islamic Republic of   Contact the Embassy of the Islamic Republic of Pakistan, 2315 Massachusetts Ave. NW, Washington, DC 20008 (202-939-6200, fax 202-387-0484), http://www.pakistan-embassy.com or the Consulate General in Los Angeles (310-441-5114) or New York (212-879-5800).

Palau, Republic of   Contact the Embassy of the Republic of Palau, 1150 18th St. NW, Suite 750, Washington, DC 20036 (202-452-6814, fax 202-452-6281), http://www.ropembassy.org or the Consulate in Guam (671-646-9281).

Panama   Contact the Embassy of Panama, 2862 McGill Terrace NW, Washington, DC 20008 (202-483-1407, fax 202-387-6141) or the nearest Consulate General: Atlanta (404-522-4114), Coral Gables, FL (305-447-3700), Houston (713-622-4451), New Orleans (504-525-3458), New York (212-840-2450), Philadelphia (215-574-2994), San Francisco (415-391-4268), or Tampa, FL (305-447-3700).

Travel

Papua New Guinea Contact the Embassy of Papua New Guinea, 1779 Massachusetts Ave. NW, Suite 805, Washington, DC 20036 (202-745-3680, fax 202-745-3679), http://www.pngembassy.org or contact the Consulate General in Honolulu (808-623-8144).

Paraguay Contact the Embassy of Paraguay, 2400 Massachusetts Ave. NW, Washington, DC 20008 (202-483-6960, fax 202-234-4508) or the Consulate General in Miami (305-374-9090) or New York (212-682-9441).

Charles Lindbergh was not the first person to fly across the Atlantic. Eight years before Lindbergh's flight, two men copiloted a twin-engine plane from Newfoundland to Ireland. Lindbergh's achievement was doing it alone.

Peru Contact the Embassy of Peru, 1700 Massachusetts Ave. NW, Washington, DC 20036 (202-833-9860, fax 202-659-8124), http://www.peruemb.org or the nearest Consulate General: Chicago (312-782-1599), Houston (713-781-5000), Los Angeles (213-252-5910), Miami (305-374-1305), Paterson, NJ (973-278-3324), New York (212-481-7410), or San Francisco (415-362-5185).

Philippines Contact the Embassy of the Philippines, 1600 Massachusetts Ave. NW, Washington, DC 20036 (202-467-9300, fax 202-467-9417), http://www.embassyonline.com or the nearest Consulate General: Chicago (312-332-6458), Guam (671-646-4620), Honolulu (808-595-6316), Los Angeles (213-639-0980), New York (212-764-1330), or San Francisco (415-433-6666).

Poland, Republic of Contact the Consular Division of the Embassy of the Republic of Poland, 2224 Wyoming Ave. NW, Washington, DC 20008 (202-234-3800, fax 202-328-2152), http://www.polishworld.com/polemb or the nearest Consulate

General: Boston (617-357-1980), Chicago (312-337-8166), Los Angeles (310-442-8500), New York (646-237-2100), or San Juan, PR (809-721-0495).

Portugal (including **Azores and the Madeira Islands**) Contact the Embassy of Portugal at 2125 Kalorama Rd. NW, Washington, DC 20008 (202-328-8610, fax 202-462-3726), http://www.portugalemb.org or the nearest Consulate General: Boston (617-536-8740), Newark (973-643-4200), New York (212-246-4580), or San Francisco (415-346-3400).

Qatar, State of Contact the Embassy of the State of Qatar, 4200 Wisconsin Ave. NW, Suite 200, Washington, DC 20016 (202-274-1600, fax 202-237-0061) or the Consulate General in Houston at 713-355-8221.

Reunion Island. *See* **France.**

Romania Contact the Embassy of Romania, Consular Section, 1607 23rd St. NW, Washington, DC 20008 (202-332-2879, fax 202-232-4748), http://www.roembus.org or the nearest Consulate General: Chicago (312-573-1315), Los Angeles (310-444-0043), or New York (212-682-9122).

Russian Federation Contact the Embassy of the Russian Federation, Consular Division, 2641 Tunlaw Rd. NW, Washington, DC 20007 (202-939-8907, fax 202-483-7579), http://www.russianembassy.org or the nearest Consulate General: New York (212-348-0926), San Francisco (415-928-6878), or Seattle (206-728-1910).

Rwanda, Republic of Contact the Embassy of the Republic of Rwanda, 1714 New Hampshire Ave. NW, Washington, DC 20009 (202-232-2882, fax 202-232-4544), http://www.rwandemb.org or the Consulate General in San Francisco at 415-772-9181.

Saba. *See* **Netherlands Antilles.**

St. Barthelemy (French West Indies). *See* **France.**

St. Eustatius (Statia). *See* **Netherlands Antilles.**

St. Kitts and Nevis Contact the Embassy of St. Kitts and Nevis, 3216 New Mexico Ave. NW, Washington, DC 20016 (202-686-2636, fax 202-686-5740) or the Permanent Mission of St. Kitts and Nevis to the United Nations at 212-535-1234.

St. Lucia Contact the Embassy of St. Lucia, 3216 New Mexico Ave., Washington, DC 20016 (202-364-6792, fax 202-364-6723) or the Consulate in New York at 212-697-9360.

St. Maarten. *See* **Netherlands Antilles.**

St. Martin (French West Indies). *See* **France.**

St. Pierre. *See* **France.**

St. Vincent and the Grenadines Contact the Embassy of St. Vincent and the Grenadines, 3216 New Mexico Ave., Washington, DC 20016 (202-364-6730, fax 202-364-6736) or the Honorary Consulate in Malibu, CA (310-457-8111) or New Orleans (504-523-1385).

Samoa, Independent State of Contact the Embassy to the United States and Permanent Mission of the Independent State of Samoa to the United Nations, 800 Second Ave., Suite 400J, New York, NY 10017 (212-599-6196, fax 212-599-0797) or the Honorary Consulate in Honolulu at 808-677-7197.

San Marino, Republic of Contact the Permanent Mission of the Republic of San Marino to the United Nations, 327 East 50th St., New York, NY 10022 (212-751-1234, fax 212-751-1436).

São Tome and Principé Contact the Permanent Mission of São Tome and Principé to the United Nations, 400 Park Ave., 7th Floor, New York, NY 10022 (212-317-0533, fax 212-317-0580).

Saudi Arabia, Kingdom of Contact the Royal Embassy of Saudi Arabia, 601 New Hampshire Ave. NW, Washington, DC 20037 (202-342-3800), http://www.saudiembassy.net or the nearest Consulate General: Houston (713-785-5577), Los Angeles (310-479-6000), or New York (212-752-2740).

Scotland. *See* **United Kingdom.**

Senegal, Republic of Contact the Embassy of the Republic of Senegal, 2112 Wyoming Ave. NW, Washington, DC 20008 (202-234-0450, fax 202-332-6315) or the Honorary Consulate General in Miami (305-371-4286) or Newton, MA (617-964-9641).

Serbia and Montenegro (Federal Republic of Yugoslavia) The Federal Republic of Yugoslavia currently has no consular office issuing visas in the United States. The Embassy of Yugoslavia in Ottawa, Canada, will accept applications from the U.S. (613-233-6289).

Seychelles Contact the Embassy and Permanent Mission of Seychelles to the United Nations, 800 Second Ave., Suite 400C, New York, NY 10017 (212-972-0785, fax 212-972-1786).

Sierra Leone Contact the Embassy of Sierra Leone, 1701 19th St. NW, Washington, DC 20009 (202-939-9261, fax 202-483-1793) or the Permanent Mission of Sierra Leone to the United Nations at 212-688-1656.

Singapore, Republic of Contact the Embassy of the Republic of Singapore, 3501 International Pl. NW, Washington, DC 20008 (202-537-3100, fax 212-537-0876).

Slovak Republic Contact the Embassy of the Slovak Republic, 2201 Wisconsin Ave. NW, Suite 250, Washington, DC 20007 (202-965-5160, fax 202-965-5166), http://www.slovakemb.com or the nearest Honorary Consulate: Broadview Heights, OH (440-838-4949), Chicago (630-548-1944), Denver (303-692-8833), Eden Prairie, MN (612-937-9006), or Pittsburgh (412-531-2990).

Slovenia, Republic of Contact the Embassy of the Republic of Slovenia, 1525 New Hampshire Ave. NW, Washington, DC 20036 (202-667-5363, fax 202-667-4563), http://www.embassy.org/slovenia or the Consulate General in New York at 212-370-3006).

Travel

Solomon Islands   Contact the Embassy to the United States and Permanent Mission of the Solomon Islands to the United Nations, 800 Second Ave., Suite 400L, New York, NY 10017 (212-599-6192, fax 212-661-8925).

Somali Democratic Republic (Somalia)   Contact the Consulate of the Somali Democratic Republic in New York (212-688-9410).

South Africa   Contact the Embassy of South Africa, Consular Section, Suite 220, Van Ness Center, 4301 Connecticut Ave. NW, Washington, DC 20008 (202-232-4400, fax 202-244-9417), http://usaembassy.southafrica.net or the Consulate General in Los Angeles (323-651-0902) or New York (212-213-4880).

South Korea. *See* **Korea, Republic of.**

Spain   Contact the Embassy of Spain, Consulate General, 2375 Pennsylvania Ave. NW, Washington, DC 20037 (202-728-2330, fax 202-728-2302), http://www.spainemb.org or the nearest Consulate General: Boston (617-536-2506), Chicago (312-782-4588), Houston (713-783-6200), Los Angeles (323-938-0158), Coral Gables, FL (305-446-5511), New Orleans (504-525-4951), New York (212-355-4080), San Juan, PR (787-758-6090), or San Francisco (415-922-2995).

Sri Lanka   Contact the Embassy of Sri Lanka, 2148 Wyoming Ave. NW, Washington, DC 20008 (202-483-4025, fax 202-232-7181), or the Consulate General in Los Angeles at 323-624-0479.

Statia (St. Eustatius). *See* **Netherlands Antilles.**

Sudan, Republic of the   Contact the Embassy of the Republic of the Sudan, 2210 Massachusetts Ave. NW, Washington, DC 20008 (202-338-8565, fax 202-667-2406), http://www.sudanembassyus.org or the Consulate General in New York at 212-573-6033.

Suriname, Republic of   Contact the Embassy of the Republic of Suriname, 4301 Connecticut Ave. NW, Suite 460, Washington, DC 20008 (202-244-

7488, fax 202-244-5878) or the Consulate in Miami at 305-593-2697.

Swaziland, Kingdom of   Contact the Embassy of the Kingdom of Swaziland, 3400 International Dr. NW, Washington, DC 20008 (202-362-6683, fax 202-244-8059) or the Permanent Mission of the Kingdom of Swaziland to the United Nations at 212-371-8910.

Sweden   Contact the Embassy of Sweden, 1501 M St. NW, Washington, DC 20005 (202-467-2600, fax 202-467-2699), http://www.swedenemb.org or the nearest Consulate General: Chicago (312-781-6262), Los Angeles (310-445-4008), New York (212-583-2550), or San Francisco (415-788-2631).

Switzerland   Contact the Embassy of Switzerland, 2900 Cathedral Ave. NW, Washington, DC 20008 (202-745-7900, fax 202-387-2564), http://www.swissemb.org or the nearest Consulate General: Atlanta (404-870-2000), Chicago (312-915-0061), Houston (713-650-0000), Los Angeles (310-575-1145), New York (212-599-5700), or San Francisco (415-788-2272).

Syrian Arab Republic (Syria)   The U.S. State Department cautions travelers that "Entry to Syria is not granted to persons with passports bearing an Israeli visa or entry/exit stamps, or to persons born in the Gaza region or of Gazan descent. Foreigners who wish to stay 15 days or more in Syria must register with Syrian Immigration by their fifteenth day in Syria. Americans between the ages of 18 and 45 who are of Syrian birth or recent descent are subject to the Syrian compulsory military service requirement, unless they receive an exemption from the Syrian Embassy in the United States prior to their entry into Syria." Contact the Embassy of the Syrian Arab Republic, 2215 Wyoming Ave. NW, Washington, DC 20008 (202-232-6313, fax 202-234-9548), http://www.embassyofsyria-usa.org or the Honorary Consulate General in Houston (713-622-8860) or Newport Beach, CA (949-640-9888).

Tahiti (French Polynesia). *See* **France.**

Taiwan, Republic of China on Contact the Taipei Economic and Cultural Representative Office (TECRO), 4201 Wisconsin Ave. NW, Washington, DC 20016 (202-895-1800, fax 202-966-0825) or the Representative Office in New York at 212-486-0088.

Tajikistan Contact the Embassy of the Russian Federation, Consular Division, 2641 Tunlaw Rd. NW, Washington, DC 20007 (202-939-8907, fax 202-483-7579), http://www.russianembassy.org or the nearest Consulate General: New York (212-348-0926), San Francisco (415-928-6878), or Seattle (206-728-1910).

Tanzania, United Republic of (Zanzibar) Contact the Embassy of the United Republic of Tanzania, 2139 R St. NW, Washington, DC 20008 (202-939-6125, fax 202-797-7408) or the Permanent Mission of the United Republic of Tanzania to the United Nations at 212-972-9160.

Thailand, Kingdom of Contact the Royal Thai Embassy, 1024 Wisconsin Ave. NW, Washington, DC 20007 (202-944-3600, fax 202-944-3611), http://www.thaiembdc.org or the nearest Consulate General: Chicago (312-236-2447), Los Angeles (213-962-9574), or New York (212-754-1770).

Togo, Republic of Contact the Embassy of the Republic of Togo, 2208 Massachusetts Ave. NW, Washington, DC 20008 (202-234-4212, fax 202-232-3190) or the Honorary Consulate in Miami at 305-371-4286.

Tonga Contact the Consulate General of Tonga, 360 Post St., Suite 604, San Francisco, CA 94108 (415-781-0365, fax 415-781-3964).

Trinidad and Tobago Contact the Embassy of Trinidad and Tobago, 1708 Massachusetts Ave. NW, Washington, DC 20036 (202-467-6490, fax 202-785-3130), http://tradepoint.tidco.co.tt/trademission/washington.html or the Consulate in Miami (305-374-2199) or New York (212-682-7272).

Tunisia The U.S. State Department cautions travelers that "Americans born in the Middle East or with Arabic names have experienced delays in clearing Immigration at airports upon arrival. American citizens of Tunisian origin are expected to enter Tunisia as Tunisians, on their Tunisian passports. If the Tunisian/American succeeds in entering on an American passport, there is a high probability that a Tunisian passport will be required before exiting the country." Contact the Embassy of Tunisia, 1515 Massachusetts Ave. NW, Washington, DC 20005 (202-862-1850, fax 202-862-1858) or the nearest Honorary Consulate: Miami (305-375-6195), New York (212-272-6962), or San Francisco (415-922-9222).

Japan's New Tokyo International Airport is only 40 miles from Tokyo; however, due to traffic, it typically takes four hours or more to catch a flight.

Turkey, Republic of Contact the Embassy of the Republic of Turkey, Consular Section, 2525 Massachusetts Ave. NW, Washington, DC 20008 (202-612-6740, fax 202-319-1639), http://www.turkey.org or the nearest Consulate General: Chicago (312-263-0644, ext. 28), Houston (713-622-5849), Los Angeles (323-937-0118), or New York (212-949-0160).

Turkmenistan Contact the Embassy of Turkmenistan, 2207 Massachusetts Ave. NW, Washington, DC 20008 (202-588-1500, fax 202-588-0697), http://www.turkmenistanembassy.org or the Permanent Mission of Turkmenistan to the United Nations at 212-486-8908.

Turks and Caicos Islands. *See* **British West Indies.**

Tuvalu Island Contact the British Embassy, 3100 Massachusetts Ave. NW, Washington, DC 20008 (202-588-6500, fax 202-588-7870).

Uganda, Republic of   Contact the Embassy of the Republic of Uganda, 5911 16th St. NW, Washington, DC 20011 (202-726-7100, fax 202-726-1727), http://ugandaweb.com/ugaembassy/ or the Permanent Mission of the Republic of Uganda to the United Nations at 212-949-0110.

Ukraine   Contact the Embassy of Ukraine, 3350 M St. NW, Washington, DC (202-333-0606, fax 202-333-0817), http://www.ukremb.com or the Consulate General in Chicago (312-642-4388) or New York (212-371-5690).

United Arab Emirates (UAE) (Abu Dabi, Dubai, Sharjah, Ras Al Khaimah, Fujairah, Ajman, and **Umm Al Quwain)**   Contact the Embassy of the United Arab Emirates, 1255 W. 22nd St. NW, Washington, DC 20037 (202-955-7999) or the Permanent Mission of the United Arab Emirates to the United Nations at 212-371-0480.

United Kingdom (England, Northern Ireland, Scotland, and **Wales)**   Contact the British Embassy, 3100 Massachusetts Ave. NW, Washington, DC 20008 (202-588-6500, fax 202-588-7870), http://www.britainusa.com or the nearest Consulate General: Atlanta (404-954-7700), Boston (617-248-9555), Chicago (415-617-1300), Houston (713-659-6270), Los Angeles (310-477-3322), New York (212-745-0200), or San Francisco (415-981-3030).

Uruguay   Contact the Embassy of Uruguay, Consular Office, 2715 M St., 3rd Floor NW, Washington, DC 20007 (202-331-4219, fax 202-331-8142) or the nearest Consulate General: Chicago (312-867-3893), Los Angeles (310-394-5777), Miami (305-443-9764), or New York (212-753-8581).

Uzbekistan, Republic of   Contact the Embassy of the Republic of Uzbekistan, Consular Section, 1746 Massachusetts Ave. NW, Washington, DC 20036 (202-530-7291, fax 202-293-6804), http://www.uzbekistan.org or the Consulate General in New York at 212-754-7403.

Vanuatu, Republic of   Contact the British Embassy, Consular Section, 3100 Massachusetts Ave.

NW, Washington, DC 20008 (202-588-6500, fax 202-588-7870) or the Permanent Mission of the Republic of Vanuatu to the United Nations at 212-593-0144.

Vatican. *See* **Holy See, Apostolic Nunciature of the.**

Venezuela   Contact the Embassy of Venezuela, 1099 30th St. NW, Washington, DC 20007 (202-342-2214, fax 202-342-6820), http://www.embavenez-us.org or the nearest Consulate General: Boston (617-266-9475), Chicago (312-236-9655), Houston (713-974-0028), Miami (305-577-4214), New Orleans (504-522-3284), New York (212-826-1660), San Francisco (415-955-1982), or San Juan, PR (787-766-4250).

Vietnam   Contact the Embassy of Vietnam, 1233 20th St. NW, Suite 400, Washington, DC 20037 (202-861-0737, fax 202-861-0917), http://www.vietnamembassy-usa.org or the Consulate in San Francisco at 415-922-1577.

Wales. *See* **United Kingdom.**

Yemen, Republic of   Contact the Embassy of the Republic of Yemen, 2600 Virginia Ave. NW, Washington, DC 20037 (202-965-4760, fax 202-337-2017), http://www.nusacc.org/yemen or the Permanent Mission of the Republic of Yemen to the United Nations at 212-355-1730.

Zaire. *See* **Congo, Democratic Republic of.**

Zambia, Republic of   Contact the Embassy of the Republic of Zambia, 2419 Massachusetts Ave. NW, Washington, DC 20008 (202-265-9717, fax 202-332-0876) or the Permanent Mission of the Republic of Zambia to the United Nations at 212-972-7200.

Zanzibar. *See* **Tanzania.**

Zimbabwe   Contact the Embassy of Zimbabwe, 1608 New Hampshire Ave. NW, Washington, DC 20009 (202-332-7100, fax 202-483-9326) or the Permanent Mission of Zimbabwe to the United Nations at 212-980-9511.

CUSTOMS INFORMATION

At reentry into the United States, you must declare all articles in your possession that you have acquired abroad, stating their actual purchase price or, if they were not purchased, their market value in the country where you acquired them. You must fill out a declaration form before reaching customs to show to U.S. customs inspectors.

If you were out of the country for 48 hours or more, you will be exempt from paying duty and federal tax on the first $400 worth of goods. Generally, values above that amount are subject to duty at a straight 10 percent. For example, if you bring in $600 worth of goods, you will pay about $20 in duty. If you are traveling with your family, remember that each family member is allowed the same $400 exemption.

The items brought into the United States must be for your own use or for personal gifts. You may not resell them for profit.

If you leave the United States with foreign-made goods already in your possession, be sure to register them, using their serial numbers, with the customs office *before* leaving, or bring proof (sales slips, for example) with you that you bought them in the United States. If you lack proof of domestic purchase or registration, you may be charged duty upon reentry.

There are customs restrictions on bringing in certain plants, animals, medications, and foods, and children may not bring in alcohol. You can get a list of restricted items from the U.S. Department of Agriculture, Washington, DC 20205.

For further information, contact the local office of the Treasury Department or the U.S. Customs Service, P.O. Box 7407, Washington, DC 20004, 202-566-8195, http://www.customs.ustreas.gov/travel/index.html (a comprehensive web site that may answer all your questions).

ADDITIONAL SOURCES OF INFORMATION

WEB SITES

Access-Able Travel
http://www.access-able.com/
Especially for travelers with disabilities, contains
    links to many other helpful sites

All of the Embassies of Washington, D.C.
TeleDiplomacy, Inc.
http://www.embassy.org/embassies.index.html
Contact information for foreign government offices
    in the United States

All the Hotels on the Web
Internet Marketing Service, Ltd.
http://www.all-hotels.com

Breezner's Guide to Airport Rental Cars
http://www.bnm.com/rcar.htm

The Centers for Disease Control
Home Travel Information Page
http://www.cdc.gov/travel/index.htm

How Far Is It?
Bali Online
http://www.indo.com/distance/

National Park Service
http://www.nps.gov

Travel Document Systems
http://www.traveldocs.com/
Country-by-country information plus downloadable
    passport and visa applications and services online

Travelocity
http://www.travelocity.com
Information about destinations and booking travel

U.S.-based Embassies and Consulates
InfoCatch
http://www.embassyweb.com
Links to foreign embassies on-line

The U.S. State Department's Travel Warnings Site
http://travel.state.gov/travel_warnings.html

**Washington Post's International Information
    Online**
The Washington Post Company
http://www.washingtonpost.com/wp-srv/inatl/
    front.htm

Travel

World Travel Guide Online Services
Columbus Group
http://www.wtgonline.com/

MAGAZINES

Condé Nast Traveler
4 Times Square
New York, NY 10036
http://www.condenast.co.uk

Travel & Leisure
1120 Avenue of the Americas
New York, NY 10036
http://www.traveleisure.com

BOOKS

Audubon Guide to the National Wildlife Refuges (series). Griffin, 2000.

Axtell, Roger E. *Do's and Taboo's of Using English Around the World.* Wiley, 1995.

Berlitz Pocket Guides (series). Berlitz Travel Guides. See most recent editions.

Birnbaum, Stephen. *Birnbaum's Travel Guides* (series). Houghton-Mifflin. See most recent editions.

Colwell, Stephen D., and Ann R. Shulman. *Trouble-Free Travel: And What to Do When Things Go Wrong.* Nolo Press, 1996.

Fodor's Guides (series). See most recent editions. Prentice-Hall.

Goode, J. Paul. *Goode's World Atlas.* 20th ed. Rand McNally, 1999.

Hostelling International Guidebook (series). International Youth Hostel Federation. See most recent editions.

Hostelling Experience: North America 2001. America Youth Hostels, 2001.

Lonely Planet Guides (series). Lonely Planet. See most recent editions.

Mobil Travel Guides (series). Fodor's Travel Publications. See most recent editions.

National Geographic's Guide to the Interstates: Crossing America. National Geographic Society, 2001.

National Geographic's Guide to the National Parks of the United States. National Geographic Association, 2001.

Nwanna, Gladson I., Ph.D. *Americans Traveling Abroad: What You Should Know Before You Go.* 2nd ed. World Travel Institute Press, 1995.

Safro, Jill, ed. *Birnbaum's Walt Disney World for Kids, by Kids.* Hyperion, 2001.

Sakach, Deborah. *Bed & Breakfasts and Country Inns.* 12th ed. American Historic Inns, Inc., 2001.

Simony, Maggy, ed. *The Traveler's Reading Guide: Ready-Made Reading Lists for the Armchair Traveler.* Facts on File, 1993.

Traveling with Your Pet—The AAA Petbook. AAA Publishing, 2001.

Wade, Betsy. *The New York Times Practical Traveler Handbook: An A–Z Guide to Getting There and Back.* Times Books, 1994.

THE POLITICAL WORLD

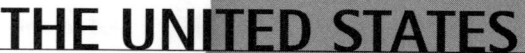

25

THE UNITED STATES

IMPORTANT DATES IN AMERICAN HISTORY

For significant science and technology advances, refer to the time line in chapter 5; for important dates and events in sports, refer to chapter 23.

20,000 B.C.E.	*Homo sapiens* first appears in the Americas (soon after its appearance in Europe). Archaeologists theorize that Asians migrate to America over the Bering Strait land bridge during the next ten millennia (Beringian Theory).
7000 B.C.E.	Native Americans develop agriculture independent of the Eastern Hemisphere.
700s	First Puebloan towns (Pueblos) appear in the American Southwest.
985	Bjarni Hejolfsson is the first European to sight the Americas from his boat in the North Atlantic.
1000	Leif Erikson explores Labrador.
1004	Norse settlements founded in Labrador and Newfoundland. Internal squabbling and conflicts with Skraelings (Native Americans) lead to their disappearance.
1150	Hopi Pueblo of Oraibi founded in what is now northeastern Arizona. Keresan Pueblo of Akoma (Acoma) is founded in what is now western New Mexico. They are the oldest continuously inhabited communities in the modern United States.
1350	Mohawk Hiawatha ("He Makes Rivers") and Huron Deganawidah ("Two River Currents Flowing Together") establish the Iroquois League of Nations. It is the oldest functioning government still in existence in North America.
1470s	English fishermen begin working off the northeastern Canadian coast.
1492	In the name of Spain, Italian Cristobol Colon (Christopher Columbus) lands on a Caribbean island (exact location unknown). Columbus makes three more voyages to the Americas.
1497	Italian Giovanni Caboto (John Cabot) explores the Canadian coast in the name of England.
1499	Italian Amerigo Vespucci sails to South America. A cartographer calls the continents of the New World "America," based on Vespucci's first name.
1513	Spain's Juan Ponce de Leon searches for the Fountain of Youth in Florida.
1524	Italian Giovanni de Verrazano maps the Atlantic coast from Maine to South Carolina in the name of France.
1534	Spain's Cabeza de Vaca ventures from Florida to Texas over a two-year period.
1534	France's Jacques Cartier explores the St. Lawrence River and Canada over a seven-year period.
1539	Spain's Hernan de Soto explores the South from the Carolinas to Mississippi.
1540	Spain's Francisco Vasquez de Coronado pillages the southwestern Pueblos, venturing as far as the southern Great Plains.
1542	Spain's Juan Rodriguez de Cabrillo sails up the California coast to Oregon.
1565	Spain establishes the colony of San Agustin (St. Augustine) in Florida.
1576	Martin Frobisher explores Canada on behalf of England.
1585	Sir Walter Raleigh establishes the Roanoke colony in Virginia in the name of England; the colonists return to England by year's end.
1587	Second Roanoke colony established in Virginia. Virginia Dare becomes the first baby born in North America to English parents, but soon afterward the colony disappears.
1598	Don Juan de Onate conquers the Pueblos of the Southwest in the name of Spain.
1500s	European, African, and Asian diseases and Spanish conquests kill more than 90 percent of all indigenous peoples in the Western Hemisphere.
1600	France establishes small, short-lived settlements along the St. Lawrence River.
1602	France's Samuel de Champlain begins explorations of New England and the St. Lawrence River.
1607	The Virginia Company of Plymouth establishes the colony of Sagadahoc, on the Kennebec River of Maine; it lasts less than a year.

1607   The Virginia Company of London establishes a colony at Jamestown, Virginia.

1608   France's first successful colony is established at Quebec.

1609   Englishman Henry Hudson explores Canada and New York for the Netherlands.

1610   Spain establishes Santa Fe, New Mexico.

1613   Holland's Dutch East India Company establishes New Amsterdam (later New York).

1614   In Virginia, Indian chief Powhatan forges an alliance with the English by marrying his daughter Pocahontas to colonist John Rolfe.

1617   Pocahontas dies of disease during a trip to England; Powhatan dies the next year.

1619   First meeting of the Virginia Assembly (House of Burgesses). Twenty indentured servants are the first black Africans sold in Britain's North American colonies.

1620   The Virginia Company of Plymouth establishes the Plymouth colony in present-day Massachusetts; settlers sign the Mayflower Compact establishing their local government.

1620   New Amsterdam is named the capital of New Netherlands.

1628   The Company of New France builds a fur trading network with Algonquin and Cree peoples that stretches from the Great Lakes to the Mississippi Valley.

1630   The Massachusetts Bay Colony is established.

1634   Lord Baltimore establishes Maryland colony, which permits the practice of Catholicism.

1636   Roger Williams is expelled from Massachusetts and founds Rhode Island colony. Harvard University is founded to train Christian ministers.

1637   In the Pequot War (begun 1636), New England colonists massacre Native American women and children and sell the survivors into slavery in the Caribbean.

1639   The Fundamental Order of Connecticut is the first written constitution in the British colonies.

1640   The New Netherlands Charter of Freedoms and Exemptions is written.

1654   Spanish Sephardim arriving in New Amsterdam are the first Jews in America.

1651   England passes the first Navigation Act affecting the colonial economy.

1663   England establishes colonies in the Carolinas and New Jersey.

1664   England captures New Amsterdam, renaming it New York.

1676   New England colonists win King Philip's War against Native Americans. Twenty-five percent of New England's Native Americans are dead.

1680   Pueblos revolt and drive the Spanish from the Southwest.

1681   William Penn establishes Pennsylvania colony.

1682   La Salle explores the Mississippi River from Minnesota to the Gulf of Mexico for France.

1689   The English reform their colonial policy after colonial rebellions in Massachusetts, New York, and Maryland.

1689   The French establish colonies at Mobile, New Orleans, and Pensacola.

1692   Spain reconquers the Pueblos of the Southwest.

1692   In Salem, Massachusetts, 19 people are convicted of witchcraft and executed.

1701   The French establish Fort Detroit.

1712   After a slave rebellion in New York City, 21 Africans are executed and 6 more commit suicide.

1718   The Spanish establish San Antonio, Texas.

1723   Abenaki (Indian) Wars rage in Maine and Vermont for more than four years.

1731   The first American circulating library is founded in Philadelphia.

1732   James Oglethorpe establishes the colony of Georgia.

1732   Benjamin Franklin publishes the first *Poor Richard's Almanac*.

1739   The religious revival known as the Great Awakening begins.

1741   After another slave rebellion in New York City, 26 Africans are publicly executed and another 71 are sold and deported.

1754	The French establish Fort Duquesne near present-day Pittsburgh. They defeat a force from British Virginia led by George Washington, beginning the French and Indian War.
1756	England and France declare war.
1757	French troops capture Fort William Henry in New York.
1758	British and American troops capture Fort Duquesne, rename it Fort Pitt.
1759	British troops capture Quebec City, the French capital in Canada, in the last major battle of the war.
1763	The Treaty of Paris ends the French and Indian War; France gives up nearly all its American territories. Spain cedes Florida to the British.
1764	Britain imposes the Revenue Act taxes (the Sugar Act) on the colonies to pay for the French and Indian War.
1765	Britain passes the Stamp Act tax and the Quartering (British troops) Act; colonists organize the Sons of Liberty and the Stamp Act Congress in opposition.
1766	The Stamp Act is repealed, but the Declaratory Act affirms the King's power over the colonies.
1767	The Townshend Acts impose British duties on many goods imported to the colonies.
1768	England closes the Massachusetts Assembly and the British Army occupies Boston. The colonists resist by agreeing not to buy or import items that are taxed.
1770	The Townshend Acts are repealed, but England taxes tea. Five Americans are killed by British soldiers in the Boston Massacre.
1770	Spain establishes Monterey, California.
1773	Americans dump $10,000 worth of tea into Boston Harbor in the Boston Tea Party.
1774	The Coercive (Intolerable) Acts close Boston Harbor and bring trade to a standstill.
1774	The first Continental Congress meets in Philadelphia and draws up a Declaration of Rights and Grievances.
1775	"The shot heard 'round the world" at the Battle of Lexington and Concord begins the Revolutionary War.
1775	The Second Continental Congress meets and raises an army, appointing George Washington as its commander. King George III declares the colonies to be in rebellion.
1776	Thomas Paine publishes *Common Sense*; the British Army evacuates Boston; the Continental Congress signs the Declaration of Independence on July 4.
1776	The British Army captures New York City; the British execute Nathan Hale for spying; the Continental Army attacks British forces in New Jersey at Princeton and Trenton.
1777	The British Army occupies Philadelphia. Americans stop British general Burgoyne's southward march through New York at Saratoga and win a resounding victory. The American Army winters at Valley Forge.
1777	Continental Congress drafts the Articles of Confederation, a plan for a united government after independence.
1778	France sends military aid to the colonies; the British Army evacuates Philadelphia.
1778	Britain's Captain James Cook sails to Alaska and Hawaii.
1779	The British Army captures Savannah.
1780	British capture Charleston and defeat Americans at Camden, South Carolina. American traitor Benedict Arnold escapes to England.
1781	American and French troops and the French fleet surround the British army of General Cornwallis at Yorktown, Virginia. Cornwallis surrenders, ending Britain's hopes for victory.
1781	Maryland is the 13th state to ratify the Articles of Confederation, establishing an independent confederacy of American states.
1783	In the Treaty of Paris, Britain recognizes American independence and cedes Florida back to Spain. George Washington resigns as commander of the Continental Army.
1787	Congress passes the Northwest Ordinance, organizing territories in the Great Lakes region.

A Closer Look

Admission of 13 Original States

	State	Date of Admission		State	Date of Admission
1.	Delaware	December 7, 1787	8.	South Carolina	May 23, 1788
2.	Pennsylvania	December 12, 1787	9.	New Hampshire	June 21, 1788
3.	New Jersey	December 18, 1787	10.	Virginia	June 25, 1788
4.	Georgia	January 2, 1788	11.	New York	July 26, 1788
5.	Connecticut	January 9, 1788	12.	North Carolina	November 21, 1789
6.	Massachusetts	February 6, 1788	13.	Rhode Island	May 29, 1790
7.	Maryland	April 28, 1788			

1787   A constitutional convention meets in Philadelphia to discuss revisions to the Articles of Confederation. Instead it writes a new Constitution establishing a more powerful central government, subject to acceptance by 9 of the 13 colonies.

1787   The new Constitution is fiercely debated; Delaware is the first state to ratify.

1788   New Hampshire is the ninth state to ratify the constitution, putting it into effect. Three other states ratify in 1788, and Rhode Island—after 12 "no" votes—ratifies in 1790.

1789   First federal elections: George Washington is elected president and inaugurated in the federal capital, New York City. John Adams is elected vice president.

1790   Congress approves the first ten amendments to the Constitution, the Bill of Rights, and submits them to the states for ratification.

1790   Congress selects a site between northern and southern states, on the Potomac River, for the new national capital, to be called the District of Columbia.

1791   The Bill of Rights is ratified; Vermont becomes the 14th state, splitting off from New York State.

1792   George Washington is elected to a second term as president.

1793   Eli Whitney and others invent the cotton gin, increasing cotton production and the demand for slaves in the South; the Fugitive Slave Act makes it illegal to harbor escaped slaves.

1793   Captain Robert Gray establishes the U.S. claim to the Columbia River in the wilderness of the Northwest.

1794   Washington uses federal troops to crush the Whiskey Rebellion in Pennsylvania.

1796   Washington refuses to run for a third term and publishes his farewell address. John Adams is elected president. Thomas Jefferson is vice president.

1798   President Adams signs the Alien and Sedition Acts, which impose harsh restrictions on non-citizens and curtail freedom of the press. Thomas Jefferson leads opposition to the acts, and all expire or are repealed by 1802.

1799   George Washington dies at his home in Mount Vernon.

1800   Thomas Jefferson wins the presidential election and is inaugurated in the new capital, which has been named for George Washington, already considered "the father of his country."

1801   John Marshall is appointed Chief Justice of the Untied States Supreme Court, which he will help make into an important branch of the federal government.

1801   Spain, which gained the Louisiana Territory from France in 1763, cedes it back to France.

1803   The Supreme Court, in *Marbury v. Madison*, overturns a congressional act because it violates the Constitution.

1803   Thomas Jefferson agrees to buy the Louisiana Territory from France, nearly doubling the area of the United States.

1804   Jefferson supports the Lewis and Clark expedition to explore the vast northern reaches of the Louisiana Purchase.

United States

1804	Bitter rivals Aaron Burr and Alexander Hamilton fight a duel; Hamilton, the architect of early U.S. economic policy, dies of his wounds.
1806	Lewis and Clark return to St. Louis after traveling overland to the Pacific and back, bringing descriptions of the native peoples, rugged landscape, and wildlife of the West.
1807	Robert Fulton invents the first practical steamboat.
1808	In accordance with the Constitution, the importation of slaves becomes illegal.
1811	American troops attack and defeat Shawnee Indians at Tippacanoe in Indiana. The Shawnee will fight for Britain in the War of 1812, which begins next year.
1812	The U.S. declares war on Britain, beginning the War of 1812.
1813	U.S. Captain Oliver Hazard Perry wins the naval Battle of Lake Erie, then writes his superior: "We have met the enemy and they are ours."
1814	British forces capture Washington, D.C., and burn down the White House, the Capitol, and the Library of Congress. Americans defeat the British on Lake Champlain, however, ending the British threat of an invasion from Canada.
1815	The War of 1812 ends in December 1814; before word reaches America, General Andrew Jackson routs the British in the Battle of New Orleans—with the help of pirate Jean Laffitte.
1816	Efforts begin to repatriate free African-Americans to Liberia, West Africa. Some 22,000 will return to Africa over the next 45 years.
1817	New York begins building the Erie Canal.
1818	The 49th parallel becomes the U.S.-Canadian border from Minnesota to the Rocky Mountains; England and the U.S. occupy Oregon Territory jointly.
1819	Spain sells Florida to the U.S.
1820	The Missouri Compromise mandates that states enter the union in pairs, one slave and one free, to maintain the political balance between slave states and free states.
1821	Sequoia creates a written syllabary for the Cherokee language; Emma Willard founds the first American college for women.
1823	President James Monroe issues the Monroe Doctrine, declaring the preeminence of the United States in the Western Hemisphere.
1825	The Erie Canal is completed, providing rapid transport of Midwestern goods to the Atlantic through the port of New York City.
1825	Andrew Jackson receives the most popular votes in the presidential election but lacks a majority in the electoral college; the House of Representatives elects John Quincy Adams.
1826	The American Temperance Society is founded, devoted to outlawing the manufacture and sale of alcoholic beverages.
1827	The Cherokee Nation adopts a written constitution. The governor of Georgia vows to seize all Cherokee lands by 1830.
1828	The Baltimore-Ohio Railroad begins passenger service.
1830	The United States Postal Service is the nation's single largest employer, with one post office per 1,500 Americans nationwide.
1830	The Mexican government tries but fails to stem the flood of U.S. immigrants to Texas.
1830	The Indian Removal Act authorizes the removal of Native Americans from the South.
1831	Cyrus McCormick's invention of the automatic reaper for harvesting wheat is the first of many labor-saving devices that will revolutionize farming.
1831	William Lloyd Garrison begins publishing the abolitionist newspaper *The Liberator*.
1831	The religious movement known as the Second Great Awakening begins.
1831	Nat Turner leads a slave rebellion in Virginia; he is eventually caught and executed. The price of cotton triples in the next five years, further entrenching slavery in the South.
1832	The Supreme Court upholds Cherokee land claims, but Georgia sells the land anyway.

United States

1835	President Andrew Jackson signs a treaty justifying the removal of Cherokees from the South; the Second Seminole War begins in Florida.
1835	American immigrants in Texas begin war to secede from Mexico; the Mexican army crushes rebel forces at the Alamo and Goliad.
1836	Sam Houston's rebel army defeats the Mexican army at the San Jacinto River. The Republic of Texas becomes an independent nation.
1837	The first modern public school system is created in Massachusetts.
1838	The U.S. Army begins the removal of Cherokees. The journey to Indian Territory west of the Mississippi is known as the Trail of Tears. A third of Cherokees die on the way.
1840	The Whig Party elects its first presidential candidate, William Henry Harrison.
1841	Harrison catches pneumonia at his inauguration and dies after one month in office.
1843	Former slave Sojourner Truth begins giving abolitionist lectures.
1844	Mormon leader Joseph Smith is killed by a lynch mob in Carthage, Illinois. Mormons are driven out of nearby Nauvoo, Illinois, and begin migrating to Utah.
1844	Three days of anti-immigrant riots erupt in Philadelphia.
1844	The anti-immigrant, anti-Catholic American Republican Party (the Know Nothings) is founded in New York City.
1844	Samuel F. B. Morse invents the telegraph.
1845	Former slave Frederick Douglass publishes "Narrative" of his life.
1845	Congress annexes Texas; Mexico severs diplomatic ties to the U.S.
1846	Hostilities break out between the U.S. and Mexico; Congress declares war.
1846	A treaty with Britain sets the U.S.-Canadian border from the Rockies to the Pacific.
1847	A potato famine in Ireland results in large waves of Irish immigrants to the U.S.
1847	Mormon leader Brigham Young establishes Salt Lake City.
1847	American troops capture Mexico City. In a treaty ending the war, Mexico cedes vast territories in present-day southwestern U.S.
1848	The Seneca Falls (NY) Convention on women's rights is held.
1849	Thousands of gold seekers known as 49ers rush to California by land and sea after reports of a gold strike the previous year. The territory becomes a state in 1850.
1850	The Compromise of 1850 provides that new states south of the 36'30″ line of latitude will be slave states; former slave Harriet Tubman begins helping fugitive slaves escape to Canada on her "Underground Railroad."
1852	*Uncle Tom's Cabin* by Harriet Beecher Stowe gains huge popularity in the North, sensitizing millions to the evils of slavery.
1854	The Kansas-Nebraska Act overturns the Compromise of 1850 and provides that Kansas will determine its stance on slavery by popular vote.
1854	The Republican Party is founded to oppose extension of slavery to western territories.
1856	Kansas Territory has competing proslavery and antislavery governments. More than 200 die in the ensuing violence known as Bleeding Kansas.
1857	In the Dred Scott case, the Supreme Court declares that slaves are property with no citizenship rights.
1858	Senate candidates Abraham Lincoln and Stephen Douglas debate slavery in Illinois. Douglas wins the Senate campaign; Lincoln will run for president in 1860.
1859	Antislavery fanatic John Brown raids the U.S. armory at Harper's Ferry, Virginia. He is convicted of treason and executed, but antislavery activists consider him a hero.
1859	The Comstock Lode silver-mining boom begins in Nevada.
1860	Republican candidate Abraham Lincoln is elected president. South Carolina secedes from the U.S. State militia forces seize federal armories throughout the South.

A Closer Look

Secession of American States

	State	Date of Secession		State	Date of Secession
1.	South Carolina	December 20, 1860	7.	Texas	February 1, 1861
2.	Mississippi	January 9, 1861	8.	Virginia	April 17, 1861
3.	Florida	January 10, 1861	9.	Arkansas	May 6, 1861
4.	Alabama	January 11, 1861	10.	North Carolina	May 20, 1861
5.	Georgia	January 19, 1861	11.	Tennessee	June 8, 1861
6.	Louisiana	January 26, 1861			

1860   The short-lived Pony Express begins delivering mail between Missouri and California.

1861   Ten more Southern states secede and form the Confederate States of America. Confederate troops fire on Ft. Sumter in Charleston Bay; Congress (now without all its Southern representatives) declares war.

1861   Bull Run (Manassas), the first pitched battle of the war, is a Confederate victory.

1861   The transcontinental telegraph is completed, ending operation of the Pony Express.

1862   In major battles at Shiloh (TN), Second Bull Run (VA), Antietam (MD), and Fredericksburg (VA), both armies sustain huge losses. Confederate armies, undermanned and undersupplied, fight the Union to a standstill.

1862   An Indian uprising in Minnesota leads to 1,000 dead on both sides; 38 Dakota Sioux are hanged. In Colorado, U.S. militias massacre 300 Cheyenne at Sand Creek.

1863   President Lincoln issues the Emancipation Proclamation, declaring all slaves in the Confederacy free. Union armies win major battles at Gettysburg (PA) and Vicksburg (MS). Hundreds die in draft riots and race riots in Northern cities.

1864   Union General Grant drives through Confederate lines in northern Virginia and besieges Richmond (the Confederate capital). General Sherman captures Atlanta, then marches across Georgia to the sea.

1865   Grant's army captures Richmond and forces the surrender of the Confederate army at Appomattox, Virginia, ending the war. Days later, Southern patriot John Wilkes Booth assassinates President Lincoln in Washington.

1865   Congress passes the 13th Amendment, outlawing slavery.

1866   Congress passes the 14th Amendment, giving citizenship rights to former slaves.

1867   The Reconstruction Act establishes a federal military presence in the Southern states.

1868   Lieutenant Colonel George Custer's 7th Cavalry massacres Cheyenne civilians at the Washita River.

1868   Hard-line Republicans in Congress impeach (accuse) President Johnson. In his trial, the Senate is one vote short of removing him from office.

1869   The first transcontinental railroad is linked at Promontory Point, Utah.

1869   Elizabeth Cady Stanton and Susan B. Anthony establish the National Women's Suffrage Association.

1872   John D. Rockefeller founds Standard Oil, which extracts and refines oil; its first major product is kerosene for home lighting.

1876   Custer and his 7th Cavalry, on a mission to attack Native Americans in the Dakota Territory, are wiped out in a surprise counterattack, later known as Custer's Last Stand.

1876   Alexander Graham Bell invents the telephone.

1876   In the presidential election, neither Rutherford Hayes nor Samuel Tilden gains an electoral college majority, leaving the election to be decided by Congress.

Readmission of American States

State	Date of Readmission		State	Date of Readmission
1. Tennessee	July 24, 1866		7. North Carolina	June 25, 1868
2. Arkansas	June 22, 1868		8. South Carolina	June 25, 1868
3. Alabama	June 25, 1868		9. Virginia	January 26, 1870
4. Florida	June 25, 1868		10. Mississippi	February 23, 1870
5. Georgia	June 25, 1868*		11. Texas	March 30, 1870
6. Louisiana	June 25, 1868			

*Readmitted a second time on July 15, 1870

1877	Southern congressmen help elect Hayes in return for promises that he will end Reconstruction. Federal troops are withdrawn from the South.
1877	The Great Railroad Strike of 1877 sparks widespread sympathy strikes across the nation, but President Hayes uses federal troops to crush the strike.
1878	New Haven, Connecticut, is the site of the first working telephone system.
1879	The first electric lighting system is installed in Cleveland, Ohio.
1880	Large waves of immigrants begin arriving from Eastern Europe.
1881	The Federation of Organized Trades and Labor Unions (later the American Federation of Labor) is founded.
1882	The first Chinese Exclusion Act, banning Chinese immigrants, is passed.
1883	The Pendleton Act creates the federal civil service system.
1884	The first skyscraper is designed in Chicago by architect Louis Sullivan.
1886	Police in Chicago fire into a group of strikers. During a protest demonstration three days later, a bomb kills policemen and many demonstrators are killed in the Haymarket Riot.
1886	The last major Indian war ends with the surrender of chief Geronimo in Arizona.
1889	Jane Addams opens Hull House in Chicago, a "settlement house" where immigrants and the poor can receive education and emergency assistance.
1890	Indian reservation police capture and kill chief Sitting Bull; two weeks later, army cavalry massacre 300 Lakotas at Wounded Knee Creek, South Dakota.
1890	The Sherman Anti-Trust Act is passed to restrain the power of business trusts and monopolies.
1890	The Mississippi legislature establishes a literacy test to keep African-Americans from voting. Other Southern states follow suit.
1892	Telephone lines between New York and Chicago are completed.
1892	The federal government establishes Ellis Island as its official immigration arrival site.
1893	A financial panic brings widespread business failure and unemployment.
1894	Federal troops are sent to Illinois to force an end to railway workers' strike against wage cuts at the Pullman Car Co.
1895	Once numbering more than 40,000,000, there are now fewer than 1,000 bison in the world.
1896	The Supreme Court rules in *Plessy v. Ferguson* that racial segregation is constitutional if facilities (such as schools) are "separate but equal."
1898	The U.S. battleship *Maine* is destroyed by explosions in Havana in January; the U.S. soon declares war on Spain. Fighting ends in August; the U.S. gains possession of Cuba, Puerto Rico, the Philippine Islands, and Guam.
1898	The U.S. annexes the Hawaiian Islands.
1900	The U.S. becomes the world's leading industrial nation in terms of population involved in industry, industrial output, and percentage of gross national product.

United States

1901	U.S. Steel is founded by Andrew Carnegie.
1901	President McKinley is assassinated; Vice President Theodore Roosevelt is sworn in, becoming the youngest president to serve. Theodore Roosevelt establishes the national parks system during his presidency.
1903	The Wright brothers fly the first power-driven airplane in Kitty Hawk, North Carolina.
1904	The U.S. begins building the Panama Canal.
1906	A major earthquake and fire devastate San Francisco.
1908	Henry Ford produces the first Model T automobile.
1910	The National Association for the Advancement of Colored People (NAACP) is founded.
1911	The Triangle Shirt Waist Company fire in New York City kills 146 workers.
1913	The Ford Motor Company uses the first moving assembly line.
1913	The 17th Amendment provides for direct election of Senators (previously chosen by state legislatures.
1914	World War I begins in Europe; the U.S. remains neutral.
1914	The National Guard kills families of striking coal miners in Ludlow, Colorado. The miners take over the coal fields until driven out by federal troops.
1915	The ocean liner *Lusitania* is sunk by a German submarine; nearly 1,200 people die, including 128 Americans. The U.S. moves toward aiding Allied nations.
1916	Mexican general Pancho Villa raids New Mexico settlements; U.S. forces pursue him into Mexico.
1916	Jeanette Rankin of Montana is the first woman elected to the House of Representatives.
1917	The U.S. enters World War I on April 4; U.S. forces begin arriving in France.
1918	U.S. forces see heavy fighting; World War I ends with an armistice in November.
1919	President Wilson urges U.S. Senate to ratify the Treaty of Versailles, ending the world war, and join the League of Nations; the Senate refuses. Wilson suffers a stroke and is disabled.
1920	The 18th Amendment prohibits manufacture or sale of alcoholic beverages (Prohibition); it will be repealed in 1933. The 19th Amendment gives women the right to vote.
1920	The first commercial radio station, KDKA in Pittsburgh, reports the results of the presidential election: Warren Harding will be the new president.
1921	Margaret Sanger founds the American Birth Control League (later Planned Parenthood).
1923	President Harding, whose administration has been tarnished by rumors of corruption, dies unexpectedly; straight arrow Vice President Calvin Coolidge is sworn in.
1924	Congress establishes quotas to limit immigration, especially from Asia, Latin America, and Africa.
1925	The sensational Scopes Monkey Trial in Dayton, Tennessee, tests a state law banning the teaching of evolution. Famed attorney Clarence Darrow defends Scopes; the prosecution is led by William Jennings Bryan, a three-time candidate for president.
1925	Nellie Tayloe Ross of Wyoming becomes the first female governor.
1927	Charles Lindbergh makes the first solo nonstop trans-Atlantic flight, from New York to Paris.
1927	The first Academy Awards are presented.
1927	*The Jazz Singer*, the first motion picture with synchronized sound, is released.
1927	Anarchists Nicola Sacco and Bartolomeo Vanzetti, convicted as "radicals" for murders in a 1920 shoe factory robbery, are executed despite international pleas claiming their innocence.
1928	Amelia Earhart is the first woman to fly solo across the Atlantic.
1929	The stock market crashes, marking the beginning of the Great Depression.
1931	More than one-quarter of all Americans are unemployed. Another quarter have only part-time work.
1931	The Empire State Building in New York opens; it is the tallest structure in the world.

United States

1932	Thousands of World War I veterans march on Washington, demanding early payment of a bonus voted by Congress. The U.S. Army disperses the marchers, using tanks and cavalry.
1932	Franklin Roosevelt is elected president in a landslide, promising "a new deal for the American people," who are suffering from the deepening Depression.
1933	During his first 100 days in office, President Roosevelt and Congress enact a wide range of economic recovery programs.
1935	The Social Security Act creates a federal system to provide support for retired and unemployed workers through taxes paid by employers and employees.
1936	The Great Sit Down Strike against General Motors in Flint, Michigan, leads to the recognition of the United Auto Workers union by GM.
1936	African-American track star Jesse Owens wins four gold medals at the summer Olympics in Adolf Hitler's Berlin, calling Nazi beliefs of racial superiority into question.
1938	The first federal minimum wage is implemented.
1939	Germany invades Poland, beginning World War II in Europe; the U.S. is officially neutral but secretly provides assistance to the Allies.
1940	The U.S. rapidly increases aid to Britain and introduces the first peacetime draft.
1941	Japan attacks the Pearl Harbor naval base in Hawaii on December 7; the U.S. declares war on Japan and Germany, entering World War II.
1942	In the Philippines, 10,000 Allied troops surrender to the Japanese. U.S. Naval forces defeat the Japanese fleet in the battles of the Coral Sea and Midway. Allies invade North Africa.
1943	The Allies invade Italy, capture Guadalcanal from Japan, and begin sustained bombing of German cities.
1944	The Allies invade the Normandy coast of France, liberate Paris, and drive the German army back toward its borders. In the Pacific, forces win naval battle of the Philippine Sea and capture Guam and Saipan.
1945	President Roosevelt dies in April; Harry Truman becomes president.
1945	Germany surrenders as Soviet and U.S. troops converge on Berlin; Hitler commits suicide.
1945	The U.S. captures Iwo Jima and Okinawa from Japan and firebombs Tokyo. In August, the first atomic bombs are dropped on cities of Hiroshima and Nagasaki. Japan surrenders, ending World War II.
1945	Nazi leaders are put on trial by the Allies in the Nuremberg Tribunal. Allied nations approve the charter of the United Nations.
1946	A Cold War between superpowers—the U.S. and the Soviet Union—begins.
1947	The U.S. appropriates billions under the Marshall Plan to help its European allies rebuild and to limit the spread of Communism.
1947	African-American Jackie Robinson plays for the Brooklyn Dodgers, becoming the first of his race to play in major league baseball since before 1900.
1948	President Truman ends desegregation in the U.S. armed forces by executive order.
1949	The North Atlantic Treaty Organization (NATO) is established.
1950	Communist-led North Korea invades U.S. ally South Korea. U.S. and other United Nations troops intervene, beginning the Korean Conflict.
1950	Former State Department official Alger Hiss, suspected of sending secrets to the Soviet Union, is convicted of perjury. Senator Joseph McCarthy of Wisconsin claims to have lists of other Communists in the government.
1951	Julius and Ethel Rosenberg are convicted of treason for giving the USSR atomic secrets during World War II and are sentenced to death.
1951	The first nuclear power plant is built in the U.S.

United States

1952	Former general Dwight Eisenhower is elected president on the Republican ticket, ending 20 years of Democratic presidents.
1952	The U.S. detonates the first hydrogen bomb at Eniwetok Atoll in the mid-Pacific.
1953	An armistice agreement ends the Korean conflict; North and South Korea remain divided.
1954	In *Brown v. Board of Education*, the Supreme Court declares "separate but equal" schools for white and black students unconstitutional.
1954	Congress censures Senator McCarthy, ending his "witch-hunt" for Communists in the government.
1955	African-American Rosa Parks is arrested in Montgomery, Alabama, for refusing to give up her seat to a white person; next year, local minister Martin Luther King, Jr. helps organize a boycott of buses, beginning a new era of civil rights demonstrations.
1956	USSR premier Nikita Khruschev tells Western ambassadors, "We will bury you!"; the Cold War intensifies.
1956	Passage of the Federal Aid Highway Act inaugurates the first interstate highway system.
1957	Federal troops enforce the desegregation of Little Rock Central High School in Arkansas.
1957	The USSR launches *Sputnik,* the first man-made satellite, shocking Americans and beginning the "Space Race"; the U.S. launches its first satellite the following year.
1959	Alaska and Hawaii become the 49th and 50th states.
1959	USSR premier Khrushchev visits the U.S.
1960	Cuban leader Fidel Castro expropriates U.S.-owned businesses, begins creating a communist regime, and accepts aid from the USSR.
1960	An American U-2 spy plane is shot down over the USSR.
1960	Civil rights demonstrators sit in at lunch counters in Greensboro, North Carolina, to force integration of public accommodations.
1960	Presidential candidates John Kennedy and Richard Nixon appear in the first televised presidential debates; Kennedy wins a close election.
1961	U.S.-supported fighters invade Cuba at the Bay of Pigs; they are defeated and captured.
1961	Civil rights workers begin Freedom Rides to integrate interstate buses in the South.
1961	Alan Shepard is the first American astronaut in space.
1962	The U.S. detects Soviet nuclear missiles in Cuba and demands their removal; after tense discussions, the Soviets dismantle the missiles and remove them.
1962	James Meredith is the first African-American to register at the University of Mississippi.
1962	John Glenn is the first American astronaut to orbit the earth.
1962	Rachel Carson publishes *Silent Spring,* about chemical pollution in the environment.
1963	Martin Luther King, Jr. is jailed in Birmingham, Alabama, for civil rights activity; King gives his "I Have a Dream" speech before 250,000 civil rights marchers in Washington, D.C.
1963	President Kennedy is assassinated in Dallas, Texas; Lyndon Johnson becomes president.
1964	Congress passes the Gulf of Tonkin Resolution, escalating the Vietnam War.
1964	Congress passes the Civil Rights Act, challenging racial segregation and discrimination in the public sector.
1965	The U.S. begins bombing of North Vietnam as involvement in war escalates.
1965	Congress passes the Voting Rights Act, striking down restrictions faced by African-Americans in the South. Black leader Malcolm X is assassinated in New York's Harlem.
1965	President Johnson announces new Great Society programs to help the poor.
1965	Riots in the Watts section of Los Angeles begin years of racial violence in cities, including Cleveland and Chicago (1966) and Newark and Detroit (1967).
1966	The National Organization for Women is founded.

United States

1966   U.S. troops in Vietnam approach 400,000.

1966   In *Miranda v. Arizona*, the U.S. Supreme Court requires that suspects be read their rights to remain silent and to have legal counsel.

1967   Hundreds of thousands oppose the Vietnam War in demonstrations around the country.

1967   Hippie culture in San Francisco flowers during the "Summer of Love."

1967   Boxing champion Muhammad Ali refuses induction into the army; his title is taken away.

1968   A major offensive by Vietcong during the Tet holiday shakes public confidence in the war.

1968   Martin Luther King, Jr. is assassinated in Memphis.

1968   President Johnson decides not to run for reelection; Democratic presidential hopeful Robert Kennedy is assassinated; protesters and police clash violently at the Democratic convention in Chicago; Vice President Humphrey is nominated.

1968   Republican Richard Nixon is elected president.

1969   The U.S. bombs Vietcong strongholds in Cambodia; U.S. troop strength reaches 534,000.

1969   U.S. astronauts land on the moon; millions watch on television as Neil Armstrong is the first human being to walk on its surface.

1970   U.S. and South Vietnamese troops invade Cambodia, setting off hundreds of antiwar demonstrations; at Kent State University in Ohio, four demonstrators are killed by National Guard.

1970   Earth Day is celebrated for the first time; President Nixon signs the Clean Air Act.

1971   The *New York Times* publishes the Pentagon Papers, government documents that reveal official disagreement about the Vietnam War in the 1960s.

1971   The 26th Amendment lowers the voting age from 21 to 18.

1972   President Nixon visits China and meets with Mao Zedong.

1972   As U.S. troops leave Vietnam, North Vietnamese troops advance; the U.S. resumes the bombing of North Vietnam's cities.

1972   Men paid by Nixon's reelection campaign are caught after breaking into Democratic Party offices in the Watergate apartment complex. The White House denies any involvement.

1973   A cease-fire is concluded in Vietnam, but the U.S. continues bombing.

1973   In *Roe v. Wade*, the Supreme Court establishes the right of women to abortion.

1973   Nixon's staff is implicated in the Watergate burglary and cover-up in Senate hearings; secret taping of White House conversations is revealed.

1974   The Supreme Court orders Nixon to give tapes to the prosecutors; the tapes reveal Nixon's involvement in Watergate scandal. Faced with impeachment, he resigns August 9.

1974   President Gerald Ford pardons Nixon for any crimes he may have committed in office.

1974   Oil prices skyrocket; the cost of living rises rapidly.

1975   The North Vietnamese capture Saigon as last Americans evacuate; Vietnam is unified under a Communist government.

1975   Teamsters leader James Hoffa, suspected of ties with organized crime, disappears and is presumed dead. His body is never found.

1976   Georgia Democrat Jimmy Carter defeats Gerald Ford for the presidency; he is the first southerner elected since before the Civil War.

1977   President Carter pardons 10,000 draft resisters from the Vietnam era.

1977   The Alaska oil pipeline opens, carrying oil nearly 800 miles from Prudhoe Bay to Valdez.

1978   The U.S. agrees to return the Panama Canal to Panama in December 1999.

1978   Residents evacuate Love Canal, near Niagara Falls, New York, because the landfill on which their houses are built is filled with toxic wastes.

1979   President Carter negotiates the Camp David Accords, a peace treaty between Israel and Egypt.

United States

1979   A nuclear accident at Three Mile Island, Pennsylvania, causes little damage but prompts concern about the safety of nuclear power plants.

1979   Militant nationalists in Iran take 66 hostages at the U.S. embassy in Tehran.

1980   The U.S. boycotts the summer Olympics in Moscow because Soviets have invaded Afghanistan.

1980   An attempt by U.S. forces to rescue the hostages in Iran ends in disaster.

1980   Conservative Ronald Reagan wins the Republican presidential nomination and defeats Jimmy Carter in the general election.

1980   Mount Saint Helens, a volcano in Washington State, erupts continuously for nine hours on May 18, killing 57 and causing billions of dollars of property damage

1981   U.S. hostages are released by Iran soon after President Reagan's inauguration.

1981   Reagan is seriously wounded in an assassination attempt.

1981   Sandra Day O'Connor becomes the first woman appointed to the Supreme Court.

1982   The Equal Rights Amendment to the Constitution, approved by Congress in 1972, fails to gain ratification by two-thirds of the states.

1982   Federal antitrust action breaks up AT&T, which controls most local telephone systems.

1982   The Vietnam War Memorial is dedicated in Washington.

1983   President Reagan proposes the Strategic Defense Initiative, a plan to shoot down incoming long-range missiles.

1983   A suicide bomber kills 246 at a U.S. Marines barracks in Lebanon; U.S. troops invade Grenada.

1984   The U.S. mines harbors in Nicaragua to pressure its leftist government; Congress votes to cut off funds aimed at toppling the Nicaraguan government.

1984   President Reagan is reelected; Democratic nominee Geraldine Ferraro is the first woman nominated for vice president by a major party.

1985   President Reagan meets with new Soviet leader Mikhail Gorbachev; they agree to pursue talks on arms control.

1986   The space shuttle *Challenger* explodes after liftoff, killing seven.

1986   White House aides resign in the Iran-Contra affair; it is revealed they secretly sold weapons to Iran and used the proceeds to support opposition Contras in Nicaragua.

1987   After congressional hearings, Reagan admits that "policy went astray" in Iran-Contra.

1987   The Dow Jones stock average loses nearly a quarter of its value in one day, October 19.

1987   President Reagan's nomination of conservative Robert Bork to the Supreme Court is defeated by a 58–42 vote in the Senate after bruising confirmation hearings.

1988   Vice President George Bush is elected president, carrying 40 states.

1989   The USSR begins to break apart, as many of its republics declare independence; these changes end the Cold War and leave the U.S. as the single world superpower.

1989   The oil tanker *Exxon-Valdez* runs aground and spills 11 million gallons of oil into Prince William Sound, Alaska, causing widespread environmental damage.

1989   Chinese soldiers massacre student demonstrators in Beijing's Tiananmen Square; relations between the U.S. and China are strained.

1989   The U.S invades Panama and arrests President Manuel Noriega; he is later tried and convicted for his role in international smuggling of cocaine.

1990   The Americans with Disabilities Act offers new protections for the disabled.

1990   Iraq attacks neighboring Kuwait; with U.N. support, the U.S. plans a military response.

1991   U.S.-dominated United Nations forces defeat Iraq in the Persian Gulf War.

1991   Los Angeles police are videotaped beating African-American suspect Rodney King.

1991   Conservative Clarence Thomas is named to the Supreme Court after contentious confirmation hearings.

1992   Police are acquitted in the Rodney King beating, setting off the city's worst riots in history.

1992	Hurricane Andrew strikes south Florida, leaving 250,000 homeless and $20 billion in damage.
1992	Democrat Bill Clinton is elected president, defeating President Bush's run for reelection.
1993	Federal agents attack the Branch Davidian cult complex near Waco, Texas; a fire kills leader David Koresh and at least 70 others, including women and children.
1993	A bomb explodes under the World Trade Center in New York, killing six and injuring hundreds. Islamic militants are caught and later convicted.
1993	Massive flooding of the Mississippi River and its tributaries causes $10 billion in damage.
1993	The North American Free Trade Agreement, sponsored by the Clinton administration, passes in Congress.
1994	A major earthquake kills 50 and causes widespread damage northeast of Los Angeles.
1994	Republicans gain control of the House of Representatives for the first time since 1952 and the Senate for the first time since 1986; Newt Gingrich is named Speaker of the House.
1995	Republicans propose conservative Contract with America legislation.
1995	A federal office building in Oklahoma City is blown up, killing 169; Timothy McVeigh and Terry Nichols are arrested and later convicted.
1995	Congress forces a shutdown of federal offices in a budget dispute with the Clinton administration.
1996	Unabomber Theodore Kaczinski, who mailed lethal bombs to victims, is arrested.
1996	Congress reforms the federal welfare system; Clinton signs the changes into law.
1996	President Clinton is elected to a second term; Republicans keep control of Congress.
1997	The House of Representatives fines Speaker Newt Gingrich $300,000 for ethics violations.
1997	Tobacco companies agree to pay states for medical costs of some tobacco-related illnesses.
1998	Bill Clinton is accused of an improper relationship with a White House intern; he denies, then later admits indiscretion. The House impeaches (charges) him with perjury and obstruction of justice.
1998	U.S. Embassies in Tanzania and Kenya are bombed by terrorists.
1999	The Senate acquits President Clinton of impeachment charges.
1999	Serbian troops invade Kosovo. The U.S. leads NATO bombing of Serbia; after 11 weeks, Serbia agrees to withdraw.
2000	After reaching historic highs, the stock market begins a long decline as investors lose faith in dot-com and high-tech companies.
2000	Republican George W. Bush wins the presidency; the election is decided by results in Florida, where vote-counting disputes are ultimately resolved by the Supreme Court.
2000	In congressional elections, Republicans have a slim lead in the House; the Senate is divided 50–50. First Lady Hillary Clinton is elected senator from New York.
2001	Timothy McVeigh is executed for the Oklahoma City bombing.
2001	On September 11, terrorist hijackers crash airliners into New York's World Trade Center and the Pentagon in Washington. Nearly 3,000 are killed, including hundreds of police and firemen, when the Trade Center towers collapse.
2001	Letters containing deadly anthrax are received by news organizations and by U.S. senators, causing five deaths. The source of the letters cannot be determined.
2001	The U.S. identifies Islamic militant Osama bin Laden's terrorist organization as the culprit in the September 11 attacks. President Bush declares a "War on Terror," and the U.S. begins bombing in Afghanistan, where bin Laden is in hiding.
2001	The Taliban regime in Afghanistan collapses; U.S. troops and Afghan allies carry out search-and-destroy missions against the terrorists, but do not find bin Laden.
2002	The Enron corporation declares bankruptcy, the largest in U.S. history. Revelations of accounting improprieties prompt congressional investigation.

HISTORIC DOCUMENTS AND PRONOUNCEMENTS

THE DECLARATION OF INDEPENDENCE

IN CONGRESS, JULY 4, 1776

The unanimous Declaration of the thirteen united States of America

When in the Course of human events, it becomes necessary for one people to dissolve the political bands which have connected them with another, and to assume among the powers of the earth, the separate and equal station to which the Laws of Nature and of Nature's God entitle them, a decent respect to the opinions of mankind requires that they should declare the causes which impel them to the separation.

We hold these truths to be self-evident, that all men are created equal, that they are endowed by their Creator with certain unalienable rights, that among these are life, liberty and the pursuit of happiness. That to secure these rights, governments are instituted among men, deriving their just powers from the consent of the governed,—That whenever any form of government becomes destructive of these ends, it is the Right of the People to alter or to abolish it, and to institute a new government, laying its foundation on such principles and organizing its powers in such form, as to them shall seem most likely to effect their safety and happiness. Prudence, indeed, will dictate that governments long established should not be changed for light and transient causes; and accordingly all experience hath shown, that mankind are more disposed to suffer, while evils are sufferable, than to right themselves by abolishing the forms to which they are accustomed. But when a long train of abuses and usurpations, pursuing invariably the same object evinces a design to reduce them under absolute despotism, it is their right, it is their duty, to throw off such government, and to provide new guards for their future security.—Such has been the patient sufferance of government. The history of the present King of Great Britain is a history of repeated injuries and usurpations, all having in direct object the establishment of an absolute tyranny over these States. To prove this, let facts be submitted to a candid world.

He has refused his assent to laws, the most wholesome and necessary for the public good.

He has forbidden his Governors to pass laws of immediate and pressing importance, unless suspended in their operation till his assent should be obtained; and when so suspended, he has utterly neglected to attend to them.

He has refused to pass other laws for the accommodation of large districts of people, unless those people would relinquish the right representation in the legislature, a right inestimable to them and formidable to tyrants only.

He has called together legislative bodies at places unusual, uncomfortable, and distant from the depository of their public records, for the sole purpose of fatiguing them into compliance with his measures.

He has dissolved Representative Houses repeatedly, for opposing with manly firmness his invasions on the rights of the people.

He has refused for a long time, after such dissolutions, to cause others to be elected; whereby the legislative powers, incapable of annihilation, have returned to the people at large for their exercise; the State remaining in the mean time exposed to all the dangers of invasion from without, and convulsions within.

He has endeavoured to prevent the population of these States; for that purpose obstructing the laws for naturalization of foreigners; refusing to pass others to encourage their migrations hither, and raising the conditions of new appropriations of lands.

He has obstructed the administration of justice, by refusing his assent to laws for establishing judiciary powers.

He has made judges dependent on his will alone, for the tenure of their offices, and the amount and payment of their salaries.

He has erected a multitude of new offices, and sent hither swarms of officers to harass our people, and eat out their substance.

He has kept among us, in times of peace, standing armies without the consent of our legislatures.

He has affected to render the military independent of and superior to the civil power.

He has combined with others to subject us to a jurisdiction foreign to our constitution, and unacknowledged by our laws; giving his assent to their acts of pretended legislation:

For quartering large bodies of armed troops among us:

For protecting them, by a mock trial, from punishment for any murders which they should commit on the inhabitants of these States:

For cutting off our trade with all parts of the world:

For imposing taxes on us without our consent:

For depriving us in many cases, of the benefits of trial by jury:

For transporting us beyond seas to be tried for pretended offenses:

For abolishing the free system of English laws in a neighbouring province, establishing therein an arbitrary government, and enlarging its boundaries so as to render it at once an example and fit instrument for introducing the same absolute rule into these colonies:

For taking away our charters, abolishing our most valuable laws, and altering fundamentally the forms of our governments:

For suspending our own legislatures, and declaring themselves invested with power to legislate for us in all cases whatsoever.

He has abdicated government here, by declaring us out of his protection and waging war against us.

He has plundered our seas, ravaged our coasts, burnt our towns, and destroyed the lives of our people.

He is at this time transporting large armies of foreign mercenaries to complete the works of death, desolation and tyranny, already begun with circumstances of cruelty and perfidy scarcely paralleled in the most barbarous ages, and totally unworthy of the head of a civilized nation.

He has constrained our fellow citizens taken captive on the high seas to bear arms against their country, to become the executioners of their friends and brethren, or to fall themselves by their hands.

United States

continues

The Declaration of Independence, Continued

He has excited domestic insurrections amongst us, and has endeavoured to bring on the inhabitants of our frontiers, the merciless Indian savages, whose known rule of warfare is an undistinguished destruction of all ages, sexes and conditions.

In every stage of these oppressions we have petitioned for redress in the most humble terms: Our repeated petitions have been answered only by repeated injury. A prince, whose character is thus marked by every act which may define a tyrant, is unfit to be the ruler of a free people.

Nor have we been wanting in attentions to our British brethren. We have warned them from time to time of attempts by their legislature to extend an unwarrantable jurisdiction over us. We have reminded them of the circumstances of our emigration and settlement here. We have appealed to their native justice and magnanimity, and we have conjured them by the ties of our common kindred to disavow these usurpations, which, would inevitably interrupt our connections and correspondence. They too have been deaf to the voice of justice and of consanguinity. We must, therefore, acquiesce in the necessity which denounces our separation, and hold them, as we hold the rest of mankind, enemies in war, in peace friends.

WE, THEREFORE, the Representatives of the United States of America, in General Congress, Assembled, appealing to the Supreme Judge of the world for the rectitude of our intentions, do, in the name, and by authority of the good people of these Colonies, solemnly publish and declare, That these United Colonies of the British Crown, and that all political connection between them and the State of Great Britain, is and ought to be totally dissolved; and that as free and independent States, they have full power to levy war, conclude peace, contract alliances, establish commerce, and to do all other acts and things which independent States may of right do. And for the support of this Declaration, with a firm reliance on the protection of Divine Providence, we mutually pledge to each other our lives, our fortunes and our sacred honor.

Georgia

BUTTON GWINNETT   GEO. WALTON
LYMAN HALL

North Carolina

WM. HOOPER   JOHN PENN
JOSEPH HEWES

South Carolina

EDWARD RUTLEDGE   THOMAS LYNCH JUNR.
THOS. HEYWARD JUNR.   ARTHUR MIDDLETON

Maryland

SAMUEL CHASE   CHARLES CARROLL
WM. PACA   OF CARROLLTON
THOS. STONE

Virginia

GEORGE WYTHE

RICHARD HENRY LEE

TH. JEFFERSON

BENJA. HARRISON

THOS. NELSON JR.

FRANCIS LIGHTFOOT LEE

CARTER BRAXTON

Pennsylvania

ROBT. MORRIS

BENJAMIN RUSH

BENJA. FRANKLIN

JOHN MORTON

GEO. CLYMER

JAS. SMITH

GEO. TAYLOR

JAMES WILSON

GEO. ROSS

Delaware

CAESAR RODNEY

GEO. READ

THO. M'KEAN

New York

WM. FLOYD

PHIL. LIVINGSTON

FRANS. LEWIS

LEWIS MORRIS

New Jersey

RICHD. STOCKTON

JNO. WITHERSPOON

FRAS. HOPKINSON

JOHN HART

ABRA CLARK

New Hampshire

JOSIAH BARTLETT

WM. WHIPPLE

MATTHEW THORNTON

Massachusetts Bay

JOHN HANCOCK

SAML. ADAMS

JOHN ADAMS

ROBT. TREAT PAINE

ELBRIDGE GERRY

Rhode Island

STEP. HOPKINS

WILLIAM ELLERY

Connecticut

ROGER SHERMAN

SAML. HUNTINGTON

WM. WILLIAMS

OLIVER WOLCOTT

United States

THE CONSTITUTION OF THE UNITED STATES OF AMERICA

PREAMBLE

WE THE PEOPLE of the United States, in order to form a more perfect Union, establish justice, insure domestic tranquility, provide for the common defense, promote the general welfare, and secure the blessings of liberty to ourselves and our posterity, do ordain and establish this Constitution for the United States of America.

ARTICLE I

SECTION 1. All legislative powers herein granted shall be vested in a Congress of the United States, which shall consist of a Senate and House of Representatives.

SECTION 2. The House of Representatives shall be composed of members chosen every second year by the people of the several States, and the electors in each State shall have the qualifications requisite for electors of the most numerous branch of the State Legislature.

No person shall be a Representative who shall not have attained to the age of twenty-five years, and been seven years a citizen of the United States, and who shall not, when elected, be an inhabitant of that State in which he shall be chosen.

Representatives and direct taxes shall be apportioned among the several States which may be included within this Union, according to their respective numbers, which shall be determined by adding to the whole number of free persons, including those bound to service for a term of years, and excluding Indians not taxed, three-fifths of all other persons. The actual enumeration shall be made within three years after the first meeting of the Congress of the United States, and within every subsequent term of ten years, in such manner as they shall by law direct. The number of representatives shall not exceed one for every thirty thousand, but each State shall have at least one Representative; and until such enumeration shall be made, the State of New Hampshire shall be entitled to choose three, Massachusetts eight, Rhode Island and Providence Plantations one, Connecticut five, New York six, New Jersey four, Pennsylvania eight, Delaware one, Maryland six, Virginia ten, North Carolina five, South Carolina five, and Georgia three.

When vacancies happen in the representation from any State, the executive authority thereof shall issue writs of election to fill such vacancies.

The House of Representatives shall choose their Speaker and other officers; and shall have the sole power of impeachment.

SECTION 3. The Senate of the United States shall be composed of two Senators from each State, chosen by the legislature thereof, for six years and each Senator shall have one vote.

Immediately after they shall be assembled in consequence of the first election, they shall be divided as equally as may be into three classes. The seats of the Senators of the first class shall be vacated at the expiration of the second year, of the second class at the expiration of the fourth year, and of the third class at the expiration of the sixth year, so that one-third may be chosen every second year; and if vacancies happen by resignation, or otherwise, during the recess of the legislature of any State, the executive thereof may make temporary appointments until the next meeting of the legislature, which shall then fill such vacancies.

No person shall be a Senator who shall not have attained to the age of thirty years, and been nine years a citizen of the United States, and who shall not, when elected, be an inhabitant of that State for which he shall be chosen.

The Vice President of the United States shall be President of the Senate, but shall have no vote, unless they be equally divided.

The Senate shall choose their other officers, and also a President pro tempore, in the absence of the Vice President, or when he shall exercise the office of President of the United States.

The Senate shall have the sole power to try all impeachments. When sitting for that purpose, they shall be on oath or affirmation. When the President of the United States is tried, the Chief Justice shall preside: and no person shall be convicted without the concurrence of two thirds of the members present.

Judgment in cases of impeachment shall not extend further than to removal from office, and disqualification to hold and enjoy any office of honor, trust or profit under the United States: but the party convicted shall nevertheless be liable and subject to indictment, trial, judgment and punishment, according to law.

SECTION 4. The times, places and manner of holding elections for Senators and Representatives, shall be prescribed in each State by the legislature thereof; but the Congress may at any time by law make or alter such regulations, except as to the places of choosing Senators.

The Congress shall assemble at least once in every year, and such meeting shall be on the first Monday in December, unless they shall by law appoint a different day.

SECTION 5. Each House shall be the judge of the elections, returns and qualifications of its own members, and a majority of each shall constitute a quorum to do business; but a smaller number may adjourn from day to day, and may be authorized to compel the attendance of absent members, in such manner, and under such penalties as each House may provide.

Each House may determine the rules of its proceedings, punish its members for disorderly behavior, and, with the concurrence of two-thirds, expel a member.

Each House shall keep a journal of its proceedings, and from time to time publish the same, excepting such parts as may in their judgment require secrecy; and the yeas and the nays of the members of either house on any question shall, at the desire of one-fifth of those present, be entered on the journal.

Neither House, during the session of Congress, shall, without the consent of the other, adjourn for more than three days, nor to any other place than that in which the two Houses shall be sitting.

SECTION 6. The Senators and Representatives shall receive a compensation for their services, to be ascertained by law, and paid out of the Treasury of the United States. They shall in all cases, except treason, felony and breach of the peace, be privileged from arrest during their attendance at the session of their respective Houses, and in going to and returning from the same; and for any speech or debate in either House, they shall not be questioned in any other place.

No Senator or Representative shall, during the time for which he was elected, be appointed to any civil office under the authority of the United States, which shall have been created, or the emoluments whereof shall have been increased during such time; and no person holding any office under the United States, shall be a member of either House during his continuance in office.

SECTION 7. All bills for raising revenue shall originate in the House of Representatives; but the Senate may propose or concur with amendments as on other bills.

Every bill which shall have passed the House of Representatives and the Senate, shall, before it becomes a law, be presented to the President of the United States; if he approves he shall sign it, but if not he shall return it, with his objections to that House in which it shall have originated, who shall enter the objections at large on their journal, and proceed to reconsider it. If after such reconsideration two thirds of that House shall agree to pass the bill, it shall be sent, together with the objections, to the other House, by which it shall likewise be reconsidered, and if approved by two thirds of that House, it shall become a law. But in all such cases the votes of both Houses shall be determined by yeas and nays, and the names of the persons voting for and against the bill shall be entered on the journal of each House respectively. If any bill shall not be returned by the President within ten days (Sundays excepted) after it shall have been presented to him, the same shall be a law, in like manner as if he had signed it, unless the Congress by their adjournment prevent its return, in which case it shall not be a law.

United States

Every order, resolution, or vote to which the concurrence of the Senate and House of Representatives may be necessary (except on a question of adjournment) shall be presented to the President of the United States; and before the same shall take effect, shall be approved by him, or being disapproved by him, shall be repassed by two thirds of the Senate and House of Representatives, according to the rules and limitations prescribed in the case of a bill.

SECTION 8. The Congress shall have power to lay and collect taxes, duties, imposts and excises, to pay the debts and provide for the common defense and general welfare of the United States; but all duties, imposts and excises shall be uniform throughout the United States;

To borrow money on the credit of the United States;

To regulate commerce with foreign nations, and among the several States, and with the Indian tribes;

To establish a uniform rule of naturalization, and uniform laws on the subject of bankruptcies throughout the United States;

To coin money, regulate the value thereof, and of foreign coin, and fix the standard of weights and measures;

To provide for the punishment of counterfeiting the securities and current coin of the United States;

To establish post offices and post roads;

To promote the progress of science and useful arts, by securing for limited times to authors and inventors the exclusive right to their respective writings and discoveries;

To constitute tribunals inferior to the Supreme Court;

To define and punish piracies and felonies committed on the high seas, and offenses against the law of nations;

To declare war, grant letters of marque and reprisal, and make rules concerning captures on land and water;

To raise and support armies, but no appropriation of money to that use shall be for a longer term than two years;

To provide and maintain a navy;

To make rules for the government and regulation of the land and naval forces;

To provide for calling forth the militia to execute the laws of the Union, suppress insurrections and repel invasions;

To provide for organizing, arming, and disciplining the militia, and for governing such part of them as may be employed in the service of the United States, reserving to the States respectively, the appointment of the officers, and the authority of training the militia according to the discipline prescribed by Congress;

To exercise exclusive legislation in all cases whatsoever, over such district (not exceeding ten miles square) as may, by cession of particular States, and the acceptance of Congress, become the seat of the Government of the United States, and to exercise like authority over all places purchased by the consent of the legislature of the State in which the same shall be, for the erection of forts, magazines, arsenals, dock-yards, and other needful buildings;—And

To make all laws which shall be necessary and proper for carrying into execution the foregoing powers, and all other powers vested by this Constitution in the Government of the United States, or in any department or officer thereof.

SECTION 9. The migration or importation of such persons as any of the States now existing shall think proper to admit, shall not be prohibited by the Congress prior to the year one thousand eight hundred and eight, but a tax or duty may be imposed on such importation, not exceeding ten dollars for each person.

The privilege of the writ of habeas corpus shall not be suspended, unless when in cases of rebellion or invasion the public safety may require it.

No bill of attainder or ex post facto law shall be passed.

No capitation, or other direct, tax shall be laid, unless in proportion to the census or enumeration herein before directed to be taken.

No tax or duty shall be laid on articles exported from any State.

No preference shall be given by any regulation of commerce or revenue to the ports of one State over those of another: nor shall vessels bound to, or from, one State, be obliged to enter, clear, or pay duties in another.

No money shall be drawn from the Treasury, but in consequence of appropriations made by law; and a regular statement and account of the receipts and expenditures of all public money shall be published from time to time.

No title of nobility shall be granted by the United States: And no person holding any office of profit or trust under them, shall, without the consent of the Congress, accept of any present, emolument, office, or title, of any kind whatever, from any King, Prince, or foreign State.

SECTION 10. No State shall enter into any treaty, alliance, or confederation; grant letters of marque and reprisal; coin money; emit bills of credit; make any thing but gold and silver coin a tender in payment of debts; pass any bill of attainder, ex post facto law, or law impairing the obligation of contracts, or grant any title of nobility.

No State shall, without the consent of the Congress, lay any imposts or duties on imports or exports, except what may be absolutely necessary for executing its inspection laws: and the net produce of all duties and imposts, laid by any state on imports or exports, shall be for the use of the Treasury of the United States; and all such laws shall be subject to the revision and control of the Congress.

No State shall, without the consent of Congress, lay any duty of tonnage, keep troops, or ships of war in time of peace, enter into any agreement or compact with another State, or with a foreign power, or engage in war, unless actually invaded, or in such imminent danger as will not admit of delay.

ARTICLE II

SECTION 1. The executive power shall be vested in a President of the United States of America. He shall hold his office during the term of four years, and together with the Vice President, chosen for the same term, be elected, as follows:

Each State, shall appoint, in such manner as the legislature thereof may direct, a number of electors, equal to the whole number of Senators and Representatives to which the State may be entitled in the Congress; but no Senator or Representative, or person holding an office of trust or profit under the United States, shall be appointed an elector.

The electors shall meet in their respective States, and vote by ballot for two persons, of whom one at least shall not be an inhabitant of the same State with themselves. And they shall make a list of all the persons voted for, and of the number of votes for each; which list they shall sign and certify, and transmit sealed to the seat of the Government of the United States, directed to the President of the Senate. The President of the Senate shall, in the presence of the Senate and House of Representatives, open all the certificates, and the votes shall then be counted. The person having the greatest number of votes shall be the President, if such number be a majority of the whole number of electors appointed; and if there be more than one who have such majority, and have an equal number of votes, then the House of Representatives shall immediately choose by ballot one of them for President; and if no persons have a majority, then from the five highest on the list the said House shall in like manner choose the President. But in choosing the President, the votes shall be taken by States, the representation from each State having one vote; a quorum for this purpose shall consist of a member or members from two-thirds of the States, and a majority of all the States shall be necessary to a choice. In every case, after the choice of the President, the person having the greatest number of votes of the electors shall be the Vice President. But if there should remain two or more who have equal votes, the Senate shall choose from them by ballot the Vice President.

United States

The Congress may determine the time of choosing the electors, and the day on which they shall give their votes; which day shall be the same throughout the United States.

No person except a natural born citizen, or a citizen of the United States, at the time of the adoption of this Constitution, shall be eligible to the office of President; neither shall any person be eligible to that office who shall not have attained to the age of thirty-five years, and been fourteen years a resident within the United States.

In case of the removal of the President from office, or of his death, resignation, or inability to discharge the powers and duties of the said office, the same shall devolve on the Vice President, and the Congress may by law provide for the case of removal, death, resignation, or inability, both of the President and Vice President, declaring what officer shall then act as President, and such officer shall act accordingly, until the disability be removed, or a President be elected.

The President shall, at stated times, receive for his services, a compensation, which shall neither be increased nor diminished during the period for which he shall have been elected, and he shall not receive within that period any other emolument from the United States, or any of them.

Before he enter on the execution of his office, he shall take the following oath or affirmation:—"I do solemnly swear (or affirm) that I will faithfully execute the office of President of the United States, and will to the best of my ability, preserve, protect and defend the Constitution of the United States."

SECTION 2. The President shall be Commander in Chief of the Army and Navy of the United States, and of the militia of the several States, when called into the actual service of the United States; he may require the opinion, in writing, of the principal officer in each of the executive departments, upon any subject relating to the duties of their respective offices, and he shall have power to grant reprieves and pardons for offenses against the United States, except in cases of impeachment.

He shall have power, by and with the advice and consent of the Senate, to make treaties, provided two-thirds of the Senators present concur; and he shall nominate, and by and with the advice and consent of the Senate, shall appoint ambassadors, other public ministers and consuls, Judges of the Supreme Court, and all other officers of the United States, whose appointments are not herein otherwise provided for, and which shall be established by law: but the Congress may by law vest the appointment of such inferior officers, as they think proper, in the President alone, in the courts of law, or in the heads of departments.

The President shall have power to fill up all vacancies that may happen during the recess of the Senate, by granting commissions which shall expire at the end of their next session.

SECTION 3. He shall from time to time give to the Congress information of the State of the Union, and recommend to their consideration such measures as he shall judge necessary and expedient; he may, on extraordinary occasions, convene both Houses, or either of them, and in case of disagreement between them, with respect to the time of adjournment, he may adjourn them to such time as he shall think proper; he shall receive ambassadors and other public ministers; he shall take care that the laws be faithfully executed, and shall commission all the officers of the United States.

SECTION 4. The President, Vice President and all civil officers of the United States, shall be removed from office on impeachment for, and conviction of, treason, bribery, or other high crimes and misdemeanors.

ARTICLE III

SECTION 1. The judicial power of the United States, shall be vested in one Supreme Court, and in such inferior courts as the Congress may from time to time ordain and establish. The judges, both of the Supreme and inferior Courts, shall hold their offices during good behavior, and shall, at stated times, receive for their services, a compensation, which shall not be diminished during their continuance in office.

SECTION 2. The judicial power shall extend to all cases, in law and equity, arising under this Constitution, the laws of the United States, and treaties made, or which shall be made, under their authority;—to all cases affecting ambassadors, other public ministers and consuls;—to all cases of admiralty and maritime jurisdiction;—to controversies to which the United States shall be a party;—to controversies between two or more States;—between a State and citizens of another State;—between citizens of different States,—between citizens of the same State claiming lands under grants of different States, and between a State, or the citizens thereof, and foreign States, citizens or subjects.

In all cases affecting ambassadors, other public ministers and consuls, and those in which a State shall be a party, the Supreme Court shall have original jurisdiction. In all the other cases before mentioned, the Supreme Court shall have appellate jurisdiction, both as to law and fact, with such exceptions, and under such regulations as the Congress shall make.

The trial of all crimes, except in cases of impeachment, shall be by jury; and such trial shall be held in the State where the said crimes shall have been committed; but when not committed within any State, the trial shall be at such place or places as the Congress may by law have directed.

SECTION 3. Treason against the United States, shall consist only in levying war against them, or in adhering to their enemies, giving them aid and comfort. No person shall be convicted of treason unless on the testimony of two witnesses to the same overt act, or on confession in open court.

The Congress shall have power to declare the punishment of treason, but no attainder of treason shall work corruption of blood, or forfeiture except during the life of the person attainted.

ARTICLE IV

SECTION 1. Full faith and credit shall be given in each State to the public acts, records, and judicial proceedings of every other State. And the Congress may by general laws prescribe the manner in which such acts, records, and proceedings shall be proved, and the effect thereof.

SECTION 2. The citizens of each State shall be entitled to all privileges and immunities of citizens in the several States.

A person charged in any State with treason, felony, or other crime, who shall flee from justice, and be found in another State, shall on demand of the executive authority of the State from which he fled, be delivered up, to be removed to the State having jurisdiction of the crime.

No person held to service or labor in one State, under the laws thereof, escaping into another, shall, in consequence of any law or regulation therein, be discharged from such service or labor, but shall be delivered up on claim of the party to whom such service or labor may be due.

SECTION 3. New States may be admitted by the Congress into this Union; but no new State shall be formed or erected within the jurisdiction of any other State; nor any State be formed by the junction of two or more States, or parts of States, without the consent of the legislatures of the States concerned as well as of the Congress.

The Congress shall have power to dispose of and make all needful rules and regulations respecting the Territory or other property belonging to the United States; and nothing in this Constitution shall be so construed as to prejudice any claims of the United States, or of any particular State.

SECTION 4. The United States shall guarantee to every State in this Union a republican form of Government, and shall protect each of them against invasion; and on application of the legislature, or of the executive (when the legislature cannot be convened) against domestic violence.

ARTICLE V

The Congress, whenever two thirds of both Houses shall deem it necessary, shall propose amendments to this Constitution, or on the application of the legislatures of two thirds of the several States, shall call a convention for proposing amendments, which, in either case, shall be valid to all intents and purposes, as part of this Constitution, when ratified by the legislatures of three fourths of the several States, or by conventions in three fourths thereof, as the one or the other mode of ratification may be proposed by the Congress; provided that no amendment which may be made prior to the year one thousand eight hundred and eight shall in any manner affect the first and fourth clauses in the Ninth Section of the First Article; and that no State, without its consent, shall be deprived of its equal suffrage in the Senate.

George Washington was not the first president of the United States. In 1781 John Hanson of Maryland was named the first "president of the United States in Congress assembled," and seven others followed.

ARTICLE VI

All debts contracted and engagements entered into, before the adoption of this Constitution, shall be as valid against the United States under this Constitution, as under the Confederation.

This Constitution, and the laws of the United States which shall be made in pursuance thereof; and all treaties made, or which shall be made, under the authority of the United States, shall be the supreme law of the land; and the judges in every State shall be bound thereby, any thing in the Constitution or laws of any State to the contrary notwithstanding.

The Senators and Representatives before mentioned, and the members of the several State legislatures, and all executive and judicial officers, both of the United States and of the several States, shall be bound by oath or affirmation, to support this Constitution; but no religious test shall ever be required as a qualification to any office or public trust under the United States.

ARTICLE VII

The ratification of the conventions of nine States shall be sufficient for the establishment of this Constitution between the States so ratifying the same.

Done in convention by the unanimous consent of the States present the seventeenth day of September

in the year of our Lord one thousand seven hundred and eighty seven and of the independence of the United States of America the twelfth. In witness whereof we have hereunto subscribed our names,

GEO. WASHINGTON—*President* and deputy from Virginia

Attest WILLIAM JACKSON *Secretary*

New Hampshire

JOHN LANGDON	NICHOLAS GILMAN

Massachusetts

NATHANIEL GORHAM	RUFUS KING

Connecticut

WM. SAML. JOHNSON	ROGER SHERMAN

New York

ALEXANDER HAMILTON

New Jersey

WIL. LIVINGSTON	WM. PATERSON
DAVID BREARLEY	JONA. DAYTON

Pennsylvania

B. FRANKLIN	THOS. FITZSIMONS
THOMAS MIFFLIN	JARED INGERSOLL
ROBT MORRIS	JAMES WILSON
GEO. CLYMER	GOUV. MORRIS

Delaware

GEO. READ	RICHARD BASSETT
GUNNING BEDFORDJUN	JACO. BROOM
JOHN DICKINSON	

Maryland

JAMES MCHENRY	DANL. CARROLL
DAN OF ST. THOS. JENIFER	

Virginia

JOHN BLAIR	JAMES MADISON JR.

North Carolina

WM. BLOUNT	HU. WILLIAMSON
RICHD. DOBBS SPAIGHT	

South Carolina

J. RUTLEDGE	CHARLES PINCKNEY
CHARLES COTESWORTH PINCKNEY	PIERCE BUTLER

Georgia

WILLIAM FEW	ABR. BALDWIN

Amendments

[The first ten amendments to the Constitution are called the *Bill of Rights*.]

AMENDMENT I (1791)

Congress shall make no law respecting an establishment of religion, or prohibiting the free exercise thereof; or abridging the freedom of speech, or of the press; or the right of the people peaceably to assemble, and to petition the Government for a redress of grievances.

AMENDMENT II (1791)

A well regulated militia, being necessary to the security of a free State, the right of the people to keep and bear arms, shall not be infringed.

AMENDMENT III (1791)

No soldier shall, in time of peace be quartered in any house, without the consent of the owner, nor in time of war, but in a manner to be prescribed by law.

AMENDMENT IV (1791)

The right of the people to be secure in their persons, houses, papers, and effects, against unreasonable searches and seizures, shall not be violated, and no warrants shall issue, but upon probable cause, supported by oath or affirmation, and particularly describing the place to be searched, and the persons or things to be seized.

AMENDMENT V (1791)

No person shall be held to answer for a capital, or otherwise infamous crime, unless on a presentment or indictment of a Grand Jury, except in cases arising in the land or naval forces, or in the militia, when in actual service in time of war or public danger; nor shall any person be subject for the same offense to be twice put in jeopardy of life or limb; nor shall be compelled in any criminal case to be a witness against himself, nor be deprived of life, liberty, or property, without due process of law; nor shall private property be taken for public use, without just compensation.

AMENDMENT VI (1791)

In all criminal prosecutions, the accused shall enjoy the right to a speedy and public trial, by an impartial jury of the State and district wherein the crime shall have been committed, which district shall have been previously ascertained by law, and to be informed of the nature and cause of the accusation; to be confronted with the witnesses against him; to have compulsory process for obtaining witnesses in his favor, and to have the assistance of counsel for his defense.

AMENDMENT VII (1791)

In suits at common law, where the value in controversy shall exceed twenty dollars, the right of trial by jury shall be preserved, and no fact tried by a jury, shall be otherwise reexamined in any Court of the United States, than according to the rules of the common law.

AMENDMENT VIII (1791)

Excessive bail shall not be required, nor excessive fines imposed, nor cruel and unusual punishments inflicted.

AMENDMENT IX (1791)

The enumeration in the Constitution, of certain rights, shall not be construed to deny or disparage others retained by the people.

AMENDMENT X (1791)

The powers not delegated to the United States by the Constitution, nor prohibited by it to the States, are reserved to the States respectively, or to the people.

AMENDMENT XI (1798)

The judicial power of the United States shall not be construed to extend to any suit in law or equity, commenced or prosecuted against one of the United States by citizens of another State, or by citizens or subjects of any foreign State.

United States

AMENDMENT XII (1804)

The electors shall meet in their respective States, and vote by ballot for President and Vice President, one of whom, at least, shall not be an inhabitant of the same State with themselves; they shall name in their ballots the person voted for as President, and in distinct ballots the person voted for as Vice President, and they shall make distinct lists of all persons voted for as President, and of all persons voted for as Vice President, and of the number of votes for each, which lists they shall sign and certify, and transmit sealed to the seat of the government of the United States, directed to the President of the Senate;—The President of the Senate shall, in the presence of the Senate and House of Representatives, open all the certificates and the votes shall then be counted;—The person having the greatest number of votes for President, shall be the President, if such number be a majority of the whole number of electors appointed; and if no person have such majority, then from the persons having the highest numbers not exceeding three on the list of those voted for as President, the House of Representatives shall choose immediately, by ballot, the President. But in choosing the President, the votes shall be taken by States, the representation from each State having one vote; a quorum for this purpose shall consist of a member or members from two-thirds of the States, and a majority of all the States shall be necessary to a choice. And if the House of Representatives shall not choose a President whenever the right of choice shall devolve upon them, before the fourth day of March next following, then the Vice President shall act as President, as in the case of the death or other constitutional disability of the President.—The person having the greatest number of votes as Vice President, shall be the Vice President, if such number be a majority of the whole number of electors appointed, and if no person have a majority, then from the two highest numbers on the list, the Senate shall choose the Vice President; a quorum for the purpose shall consist of two-thirds of the whole number of Senators, and a majority of the whole number shall be necessary to a choice. But no person constitu-tionally ineligible to the office of President shall be eligible to that of Vice President of the United States.

AMENDMENT XIII (1865)

SECTION 1. Neither slavery nor involuntary servitude, except as a punishment for crime whereof the party shall have been duly convicted, shall exist within the United States, or any place subject to their jurisdiction.

SECTION 2. Congress shall have power to enforce this article by appropriate legislation.

AMENDMENT XIV (1868)

SECTION 1. All persons born or naturalized in the United States, and subject to the jurisdiction thereof, are citizens of the United States and of the State wherein they reside. No State shall make or enforce any law which shall abridge the privileges or immunities of citizens of the United States; nor shall any State deprive any person of life, liberty, or property, without due process of law; nor deny to any person within its jurisdiction the equal protection of the laws.

SECTION 2. Representatives shall be apportioned among the several States according to their respective numbers, counting the whole number of persons in each State, excluding Indians not taxed. But when the right to vote at any election for the choice of electors for President and Vice President of the United States, Representatives in Congress, the executive and judicial officers of a State, or the members of the legislature thereof, is denied to any of the male inhabitants of such State, being twenty-one years of age, and citizens of the United States, or in any way abridged, except for participation in rebellion, or other crime, the basis of representation therein shall be reduced in the proportion which the number of such male citizens shall bear to the whole number of male citizens twenty-one years of age in such State.

SECTION 3. No person shall be a Senator or Representative in Congress, or elector of President and Vice President, or hold any office, civil or military, under the United States, or under any State, who, having previously taken an oath, as a member of

Congress, or as an officer of the United States, or as a member of any State legislature, or as an executive or judicial officer of any State, to support the Constitution of the United States, shall have engaged in insurrection or rebellion against the same, or given aid or comfort to the enemies thereof. But Congress may by a vote of two-thirds of each house, remove such disability.

SECTION 4. The validity of the public debt of the United States, authorized by law, including debts incurred for payment of pensions and bounties for services in suppressing insurrection or rebellion, shall not be questioned. But neither the United States nor any State shall assume or pay any debt or obligation incurred in aid of insurrection or rebellion against the United States, or any claim for the loss or emancipation of any slave; but all such debts, obligations and claims shall be held illegal and void.

SECTION 5. The Congress shall have power to enforce, by appropriate legislation, the provisions of this article.

AMENDMENT XV (1870)

SECTION 1. The right of citizens of the United States to vote shall not be denied or abridged by the United States or by any State on account of race, color, or previous condition of servitude.

SECTION 2. The Congress shall have power to enforce this article by appropriate legislation.

AMENDMENT XVI (1913)

The Congress shall have power to lay and collect taxes on incomes, from whatever source derived, without apportionment among the several States, and without regard to any census or enumeration.

AMENDMENT XVII (1913)

SECTION 1. The Senate of the United States shall be composed of two Senators from each State, elected by the people thereof, for six years; and each Senator shall have one vote. The electors in each State shall have the qualifications requisite for electors of the most numerous branch of the State legislatures.

SECTION 2. When vacancies happen in the representation of any State in the Senate, the executive authority of such State shall issue writs of election to fill such vacancies: *Provided,* that the legislature of any State may empower the executive thereof to make temporary appointments until the people fill the vacancies by election as the legislature may direct.

SECTION 3. This amendment shall not be so construed as to affect the election or term of any Senator chosen before it becomes valid as part of the Constitution.

AMENDMENT XVIII (1919)

SECTION 1. After one year from the ratification of this article the manufacture, sale, or transportation of intoxicating liquors within, the importation thereof into, or the exportation thereof from the United States and all territory subject to the jurisdiction thereof for beverage purposes is hereby prohibited.

SECTION 2. The Congress and the several States shall have concurrent power to enforce this article by appropriate legislation.

SECTION 3. This article shall be inoperative unless it shall have been ratified as an amendment to the Constitution by the legislatures of the several States, as provided in the Constitution, within seven years from the date of the submission hereof to the States by the Congress.

AMENDMENT XIX (1920)

SECTION 1. The right of citizens of the United States to vote shall not be denied or abridged by the United States or by any State on account of sex.

SECTION 2. Congress shall have power to enforce this article by appropriate legislation.

AMENDMENT XX (1933)

SECTION 1. The terms of the President and Vice President shall end at noon on the 20th day of January, and the terms of Senators and Representatives at noon on the 3d day of January, of the years in which such terms would have ended if this article had not been ratified; and the terms of their successors shall then begin.

SECTION 2. The Congress shall assemble at least once in every year, and such meeting shall begin at noon on the 3d day of January, unless they shall by law appoint a different day.

SECTION 3. If, at the time fixed for the beginning of the term of the President, the President elect shall have died, the Vice President elect shall become President. If a President shall not have been chosen before the time fixed for the beginning of his term, or if the President elect shall have failed to qualify, then the Vice President elect shall act as President until a President shall have qualified; and the Congress may by law provide for the case wherein neither a President elect nor a Vice President elect shall have qualified, declaring who shall then act as President, or the manner in which one who is to act shall be selected, and such person shall act accordingly until a President or Vice President shall have qualified.

SECTION 4. The Congress may by law provide for the case of the death of any of the persons from whom the House of Representatives may choose a President whenever the right of choice shall have devolved upon them, and for the case of the death of any of the persons from whom the Senate may choose a Vice President whenever the right of choice shall have devolved upon them.

SECTION 5. Sections 1 and 2 shall take effect on the 15th day of October following the ratification of this article.

SECTION 6. This article shall be inoperative unless it shall have been ratified as an amendment to the Constitution by the legislatures of three-fourths of the several States within seven years from the date of its submission.

AMENDMENT XXI (1933)

SECTION 1. The eighteenth article of amendment to the Constitution of the United States is hereby repealed.

SECTION 2. The transportation or importation into any State, Territory, or possession of the United States for delivery or use therein of intoxicating liquors, in violation of the laws thereof, is hereby prohibited.

SECTION 3. This article shall be inoperative unless it shall have been ratified as an amendment to the Constitution by conventions in the several States, as provided in the Constitution, within seven years from the date of the submission hereof to the States by the Congress.

AMENDMENT XXII (1951)

SECTION 1. No person shall be elected to the office of the President more than twice, and no person who has held the office of President, or acted as President, for more than two years of a term to which some other person was elected President shall be elected to the office of the President more than once. But this article shall not apply to any person holding the office of President when this article was proposed by the Congress, and shall not prevent any person who may be holding the office of President, or acting as President, during the term within which this article becomes operative from holding the office of President or acting as President during the remainder of such term.

SECTION 2. This article shall be inoperative unless it shall have been ratified as an amendment to the Constitution by the legislatures of three-fourths of the several States within seven years from the date of its submission to the States by the Congress.

AMENDMENT XXIII (1961)

SECTION 1. The District constituting the seat of Government of the United States shall appoint in such manner as the Congress may direct:

A number of electors of President and Vice President equal to the whole number of Senators and Representatives in Congress to which the District would be entitled if it were a State, but in no event more than the least populous State; they shall be in addition to those appointed by the States, but they shall be considered, for the purposes of the election of President and Vice President, to be electors appointed by a State; and they shall meet in the District and perform such duties as provided by the twelfth article of amendment.

SECTION 2. The Congress shall have power to enforce this article by appropriate legislation.

AMENDMENT XXIV (1964)

SECTION 1. The right of citizens of the United States to vote in any primary or other election for President or Vice President, for electors for President or Vice President, or for Senator or Representative in Congress, shall not be denied or abridged by the United States or any State by reason of failure to pay any poll tax or other tax.

SECTION 2. The Congress shall have power to enforce this article by appropriate legislation.

AMENDMENT XXV (1967)

SECTION 1. In case of the removal of the President from office or of his death or resignation, the Vice President shall become President.

SECTION 2. Whenever there is a vacancy in the office of the Vice President, the President shall nominate a Vice President who shall take office upon confirmation by a majority vote of both Houses of Congress.

SECTION 3. Whenever the President transmits to the President pro tempore of the Senate and the Speaker of the House of Representatives his written declaration that he is unable to discharge the powers and duties of his office, and until he transmits to them a written declaration to the contrary, such powers and duties shall be discharged by the Vice President as Acting President.

SECTION 4. Whenever the Vice President and a majority of either the principal officers of the executive departments or of such other body as Congress may by law provide, transmit to the President pro tempore of the Senate and the Speaker of the House of Representatives their written declaration that the President is unable to discharge the powers and duties of his office, the Vice President shall immediately assume the powers and duties of the office as Acting President.

Thereafter, when the President transmits to the President pro tempore of the Senate and the Speaker of the House of Representatives his written declaration that no inability exists, he shall resume the powers and duties of his office unless the Vice President and a majority of either the principal officers of the executive department or of such other body as Congress may by law provide, transmit within four days to the President pro tempore of the Senate and the Speaker of the House of Representatives their written declaration that the President is unable to discharge the powers and duties of his office. Thereupon Congress shall decide the issue, assembling within forty-eight hours for that purpose if not in session. If the Congress, within twenty-one days after receipt of the latter written declaration, or, if Congress is not in session, within twenty-one days after Congress is required to assemble, determines by two-thirds vote of both Houses that the President is unable to discharge the powers and duties of his office, the Vice President shall continue to discharge the same as Acting President; otherwise, the President shall resume the powers and duties of his office.

AMENDMENT XXVI (1971)

SECTION 1. The right of citizens of the United States who are eighteen years of age or older, to vote shall not be denied or abridged by the United States or by any State on account of age.

SECTION 2. The Congress shall have power to enforce this article by appropriate legislation.

AMENDMENT XXVII (1992)

No law, varying the compensation for the services of the Senators and Representatives, shall take effect, until an election of Representatives shall have intervened.

The U.S. has signed more than 300 treaties with Native American nations. According to U.S. Constitution Article VI, such treaties "shall be the supreme law of the land."

THE EMANCIPATION PROCLAMATION

President Abraham Lincoln's Emancipation Proclamation took effect on January 1, 1863. Although it did not actually free any slaves, it made clear for the first time that slavery would be abolished when the Union won the Civil War.

By the President of the United
States of America:

A Proclamation.

Whereas on the 22d day of September, A.D. 1862, a proclamation was issued by the President of the United States, containing, among other things, the following, to wit:

"That on the 1st day of January, A.D. 1863, all persons held as slaves within any State or designated part of a State the people whereof shall then be in rebellion against the United States shall be then, thenceforward, and forever free; and the executive government of the United States, including the military and naval authority thereof, will recognize and maintain the freedom of such persons and will do no act or acts to repress such persons, or any of them, in any efforts they may make for their actual freedom.

"That the executive will on the 1st day of January aforesaid, by proclamation, designate the States and parts of States, if any, in which the people thereof, respectively, shall then be in rebellion against the United States; and the fact that any State or the people thereof shall on that day be in good faith represented in the Congress of the United States by members chosen thereto at elections wherein a majority of the qualified voters of such States shall have

participated shall, in the absence of strong countervailing testimony, be deemed conclusive evidence that such State and the people thereof are not then in rebellion against the United States."

Now, therefore, I, Abraham Lincoln, President of the United States, by virtue of the power in me vested as Commander-in-Chief of the Army and Navy of the United States in time of actual armed rebellion against the authority and government of the United States, and as a fit and necessary war measure for suppressing said rebellion, do, on this 1st day of January, A.D. 1863, and in accordance with my purpose so to do, publicly proclaimed for the full period of one hundred days from the first day above mentioned, order and designate as the States and parts of States wherein the people thereof, respectively, are this day in rebellion against the United States the following, to wit:

Arkansas, Texas, Louisiana (except the parishes of St. Bernard, Plaquemines, Jefferson, St. John, St. Charles, St. James, Ascension, Assumption, Terrebonne, Lafourche, St. Mary, St. Martin, and Orleans, including the city of New Orleans), Mississippi, Alabama, Florida, Georgia, South Carolina, North Carolina, and Virginia (except the forty-eight counties designated as West Virginia, and also the counties of Berkeley, Accomac, Northampton, Elizabeth City, York, Princess Anne, and Norfolk, including the cities of Norfolk and Portsmouth), and which excepted parts are for the present left precisely as if this proclamation were not issued.

And by virtue of the power and for the purpose aforesaid, I do order and declare that all persons held as slaves within said designated States and parts of States are, and henceforward shall be, free; and that the Executive Government of the United States, including the military and naval authorities thereof, will recognize and maintain the freedom of said persons.

And I hereby enjoin upon the people so declared to be free to abstain from all violence, unless in necessary self-defense; and I recommend to them that, in all cases when allowed, they labor faithfully for reasonable wages.

And I further declare and make known that such persons of suitable condition will be received into the armed service of the United States to garrison forts, positions, stations, and other places, and to man vessels of all sorts in said service.

And upon this act, sincerely believed to be an act of justice, warranted by the Constitution upon military necessity, I invoke the considerate judgment of mankind and the gracious favor of Almighty God.

THE GETTYSBURG ADDRESS

President Abraham Lincoln wrote the Gettysburg Address on the back of an envelope during a train ride from Washington, D.C., to Pennsylvania. The event of its presentation was the dedication of the battlefield as a memorial. Several longer speeches preceded Lincoln's, and were much better received by the crowd, although now long forgotten. Upon delivering the Gettysburg Address, President Lincoln received a polite response. Few present at the time realized they had just heard what many now consider the greatest presidential address of all time. The following is the Nicolay draft from the Library of Congress, thought to be the earliest surviving copy of the speech.

Four score and seven years ago our fathers brought forth, upon this continent, a new nation, conceived in liberty, and dedicated to the proposition that "all men are created equal"

Now we are engaged in a great civil war, testing whether that nation, or any nation so conceived, and so dedicated, can long endure. We are met on a great battle field of that war. We come to dedicate a portion of it, as a final resting place for those who died here, that the nation might live. This we may, in all propriety do. But, in a larger sense, we can not dedicate—we can not consecrate—we can not hallow, this ground—The brave men, living and dead, who struggled here, have hallowed it, far above our poor power to add or detract. The world will little note, nor long remember what we say here; while it can never forget what they did here.

It is rather for us, the living, we here be dedicated to the great task remaining before us—that, from these honored dead we take increased devotion to that cause for which they here, gave the last full measure of devotion—that we here highly resolve these dead shall not have died in vain; that the nation, shall have a new birth of freedom, and that government of the people, by the people, for the people, shall not perish from the earth.

THE U.S. FLAG

As English settlers populated the colonies, each territory adopted a flag. By 1707, each colony had its own flag, the forerunners of the individual state flags today. The first colonial flag representing all the colonies, however, was believed to have been raised on Prospect Hill in Boston at the Battle of Bunker Hill in 1775. The "Continental Colors" bore the cross of the British flag in the upper left corner with 13 alternating red and white stripes extending horizontally to represent the 13 colonies. In 1777, the first Continental Congress "Resolved, that the Flag of the United States be thirteen stripes alternate red and white, that the Union be thirteen stars white on a blue field, representing a constellation."

This flag was flown at Fort McHenry, Maryland, during the War of 1812 and was the inspiration for Francis Scott Key's "Star-Spangled Banner." By 1818, five more states had joined, and on April 4, Congress voted to keep the number of stripes at 13 and to add a star to the field for every new state, the stars for the new states being added on July 4 after each state's admission to the Union.

The table on page 850 shows the order in which states joined the Union and the number of revisions the flag went through before arriving at its current design. *See also* "Admission of the 13 Original States" in this chapter.

THE PLEDGE OF ALLEGIANCE

"I pledge allegiance to the flag of the United States of America, and to the Republic for which it stands, one nation under God, indivisible, with liberty and justice for all."

The phrase "under God" was added to the pledge by an Act of Congress in 1954. The original pledge, written in 1892 by Francis Bellamy, contained the phrase "my flag."

United States

THE U.S. FLAG: 1777–1960

Date Introduced	Number of Stars	Design Number	New States
June 14, 1777	13	1	Original 13 colonies
May 1, 1795	15	2	Vermont, Kentucky
July 4, 1818	20	3	Tennessee, Ohio, Louisiana, Indiana, Mississippi
July 4, 1819	21	4	Illinois
July 4, 1820	23	5	Alabama, Maine
July 4, 1822	24	6	Missouri
July 4, 1836	25	7	Arkansas
July 4, 1837	26	8	Michigan
July 4, 1845	27	9	Florida
July 4, 1846	28	10	Texas
July 4, 1847	29	11	Iowa
July 4, 1848	30	12	Wisconsin
July 4, 1851	31	13	California
July 4, 1858	32	14	Minnesota
July 4, 1859	33	15	Oregon
July 4, 1861	34	16	Kansas
July 4, 1863	35	17	West Virginia
July 4, 1865	36	18	Nevada
July 4, 1867	37	19	Nebraska
July 4, 1877	38	20	Colorado
July 4, 1890	43	21	North Dakota, South Dakota, Montana, Washington, Idaho
July 4, 1891	44	22	Wyoming
July 4, 1896	45	23	Utah
July 4, 1908	46	24	Oklahoma
July 4, 1912	48	25	New Mexico, Arizona
July 4, 1959	49	26	Alaska
July 4, 1960	50	27	Hawaii

CARE AND USE

Many Americans see the flag as a sacred article representing their devotion to the nation. On the other end of the spectrum, the U.S. Supreme Court has upheld flag burning as a constitutionally protected right. The following conventions concern the care and use of flags.

The U.S. flag should be flown on holidays and special occasions, but only in good weather. The flag is flown from sunrise to sunset, and at night only if well lit. The flag is flown at half-mast to commemorate the deaths of state officials and until noon on Memorial Day. The flag should not touch the ground while being handled, and it should be hoisted and lowered during the playing of "Taps." It should appear prominently above any other flags and be to its own right (stars to the left). In a group of flags, it should be in the center. The United Nations flag and the Navy Chaplain church pennant may fly above it.

If the flag is hung on a pole extending from a building, the union (the field of stars) should be away from the building; when the flag is hung over the center of a street, the union should be to the north in an east-west street and to the east in a north-south street.

On a platform, the flag may be hung flat against the wall behind and above the speaker with the field of stars to the audience's left. In a church or public auditorium, the flag on its staff should be to the speaker's right as he or she faces the audience and all other flags to the speaker's left. If the flag is flown anywhere else in the chancel or on a platform, it should be to the right of the audience as they face the platform.

Salute when the flag passes in a parade or review, is being raised or lowered, is present at the playing of the national anthem, or is present at the saying of the Pledge of Allegiance.

Civilians should salute the flag by standing at attention and placing their right hands over their hearts. Men should remove their hats and hold them over their left shoulders with their right hands. Military personnel in uniform should give the military salute. Noncitizens should stand at attention.

The flag at the White House is flown only when the president is in residence and only from sunrise to sunset. At the Capitol building, the flag flies over the appropriate wing when the House or Senate is in session. The flag is flown all night long and is lit by lights from the Capitol dome. Other special national monuments also fly the flag at night, notably Fort McHenry National Monument in Baltimore, Maryland, where Francis Scott Key was inspired to write "The Star-Spangled Banner."

The United States is the only country that does not tip its flag to honor the host nation during the opening ceremonies of the Olympics.

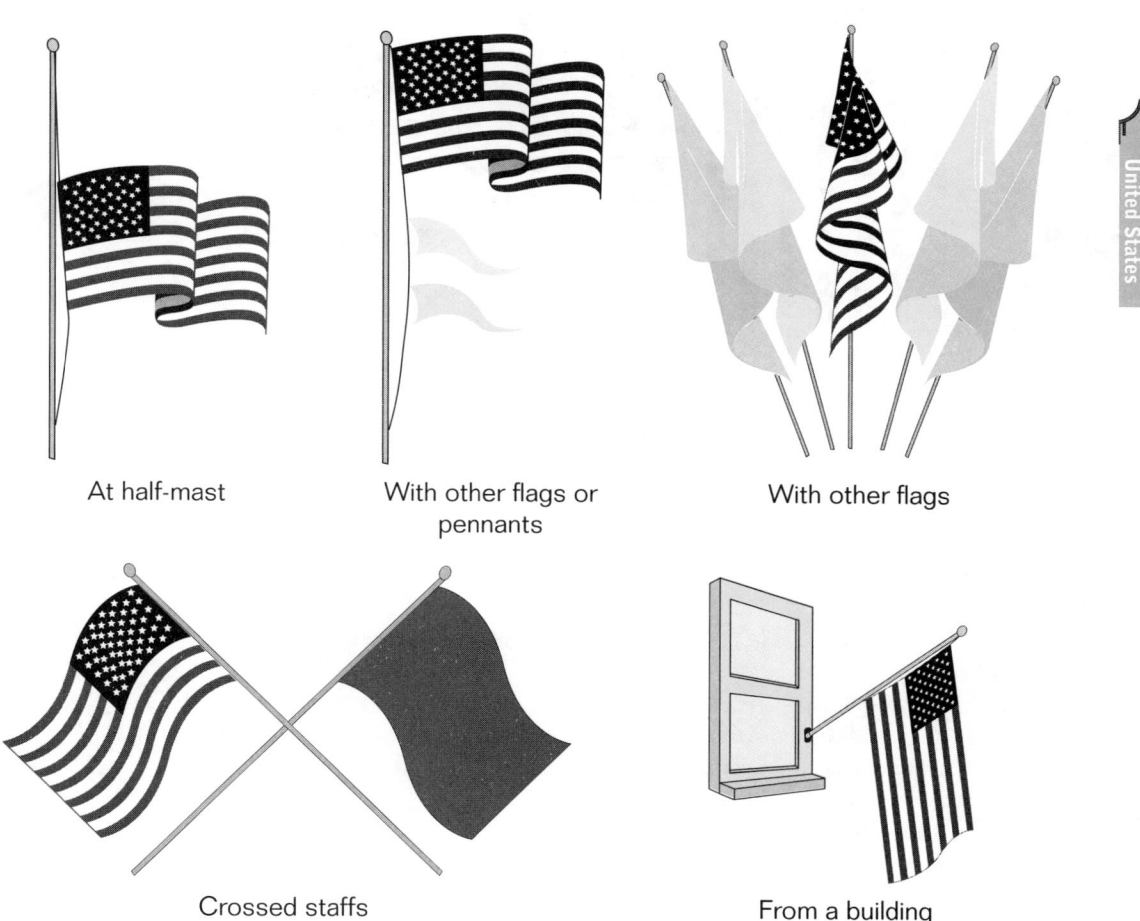

At half-mast

With other flags or pennants

With other flags

Crossed staffs

From a building

United States

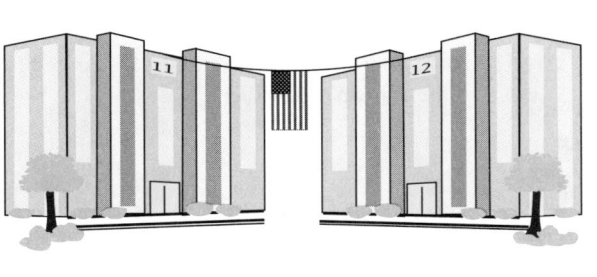

Over a street

On a platform

Against a wall

FEDERAL GOVERNMENT

While the total size of the federal government has grown considerably since 1789, its relationship to the size of the country has actually decreased during that time, employing a smaller percentage of the nation's workers and constituting a smaller percentage of the economy.

The chart on p. 853 shows the structure of the U.S. government, along with its departments and agencies. The tripartite system of government features checks and balances. The president must sign all congressional legislation, unless Congress overrides his veto. Congress may impeach and remove the president. The senate must approve presidential appointees (including U.S. Supreme Court Justices) and ratify all treaties signed by the president. Although appointed by the president and approved by the senate, the U.S. Supreme Court may overturn any federal legislation it deems unconstitutional and rule against unconstitutional actions or inactions by the executive branch.

Croatia was the first country to recognize the United States as an independent country in 1776.

United States

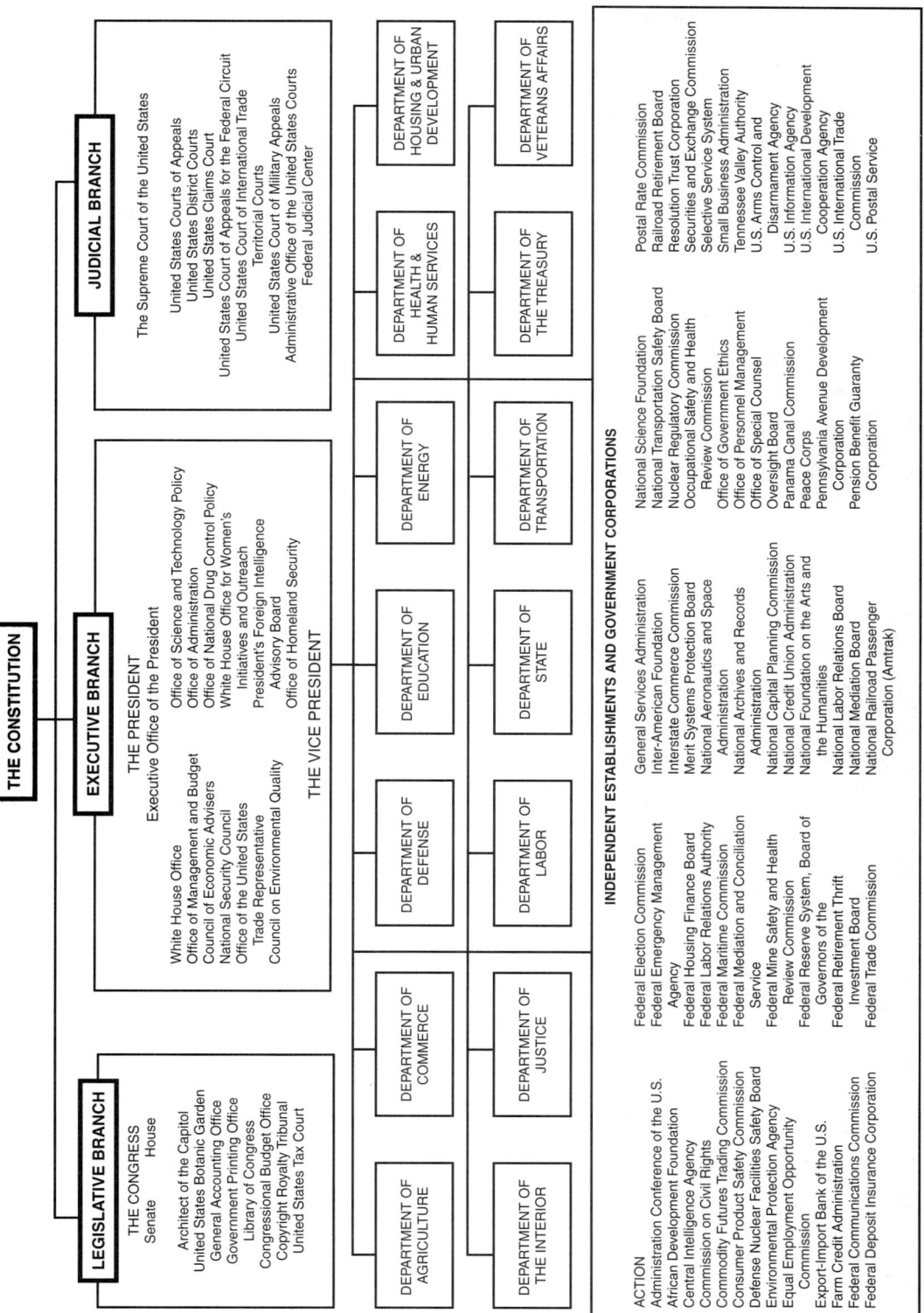

Federal Government Structure

THE CONSTITUTION

LEGISLATIVE BRANCH

THE CONGRESS
Senate   House

Architect of the Capitol
United States Botanic Garden
General Accounting Office
Government Printing Office
Library of Congress
Congressional Budget Office
Copyright Royalty Tribunal
United States Tax Court

EXECUTIVE BRANCH

THE PRESIDENT
Executive Office of the President

White House Office
Office of Management and Budget
Council of Economic Advisers
National Security Council
Office of the United States
Trade Representative
Council on Environmental Quality

Office of Science and Technology Policy
Office of Administration
Office of National Drug Control Policy
White House Office for Women's
Initiatives and Outreach
President's Foreign Intelligence
Advisory Board
Office of Homeland Security

THE VICE PRESIDENT

JUDICIAL BRANCH

The Supreme Court of the United States

United States Courts of Appeals
United States District Courts
United States Claims Court
United States Court of Appeals for the Federal Circuit
United States Court of International Trade
Territorial Courts
United States Court of Military Appeals
Administrative Office of the United States Courts
Federal Judicial Center

DEPARTMENT OF AGRICULTURE

DEPARTMENT OF THE INTERIOR

DEPARTMENT OF COMMERCE

DEPARTMENT OF JUSTICE

DEPARTMENT OF DEFENSE

DEPARTMENT OF LABOR

DEPARTMENT OF EDUCATION

DEPARTMENT OF STATE

DEPARTMENT OF ENERGY

DEPARTMENT OF TRANSPORTATION

DEPARTMENT OF HEALTH & HUMAN SERVICES

DEPARTMENT OF THE TREASURY

DEPARTMENT OF HOUSING & URBAN DEVELOPMENT

DEPARTMENT OF VETERANS AFFAIRS

INDEPENDENT ESTABLISHMENTS AND GOVERNMENT CORPORATIONS

ACTION
Administration Conference of the U.S.
African Development Foundation
Central Intelligence Agency
Commission on Civil Rights
Commodity Futures Trading Commission
Consumer Product Safety Commission
Defense Nuclear Facilities Safety Board
Environmental Protection Agency
Equal Employment Opportunity
Commission
Export-Import Bank of the U.S.
Farm Credit Administration
Federal Communications Commission
Federal Deposit Insurance Corporation

Federal Election Commission
Federal Emergency Management
Agency
Federal Housing Finance Board
Federal Labor Relations Authority
Federal Maritime Commission
Federal Mediation and Conciliation
Service
Federal Mine Safety and Health
Review Commission
Federal Reserve System, Board of
Governors of the
Federal Retirement Thrift
Investment Board
Federal Trade Commission

General Services Administration
Inter-American Foundation
Interstate Commerce Commission
Merit Systems Protection Board
National Aeronautics and Space
Administration
National Archives and Records
Administration
National Capital Planning Commission
National Credit Union Administration
National Foundation on the Arts and
the Humanities
National Labor Relations Board
National Mediation Board
National Railroad Passenger
Corporation (Amtrak)

National Science Foundation
National Transportation Safety Board
Nuclear Regulatory Commission
Occupational Safety and Health
Review Commission
Office of Government Ethics
Office of Personnel Management
Office of Special Counsel
Oversight Board
Panama Canal Commission
Peace Corps
Pennsylvania Avenue Development
Corporation
Pension Benefit Guaranty
Corporation

Postal Rate Commission
Railroad Retirement Board
Resolution Trust Corporation
Securities and Exchange Commission
Selective Service System
Small Business Administration
Tennessee Valley Authority
U.S. Arms Control and
Disarmament Agency
U.S. Information Agency
U.S. International Development
Cooperation Agency
U.S. International Trade
Commission
U.S. Postal Service

PRESIDENTS AND VICE PRESIDENTS OF THE UNITED STATES

President	Term	Year of Birth–Death	Party	Vice President	Year of Birth–Death	Congresses
1. George Washington	4/30/1789–3/3/1797	1732–1799	I	John Adams	1735–1826	1, 2, 3, 4
2. John Adams	3/4/1797–3/3/1801	1735–1826	F	Thomas Jefferson	1743–1826	5, 6
3. Thomas Jefferson	3/4/1801–3/3/1805	1743–1826	D-R	Aaron Burr	1756–1836	7, 8
	3/4/1805–3/3/1809			George Clinton	1739–1812	9, 10
4. James Madison	3/4/1809–3/3/1813	1751–1836	D-R	George Clinton	1739–1812	11, 12
	3/4/1813–3/3/1817			Elbridge Gerry	1744–1814	13, 14
5. James Monroe	3/4/1817–3/3/1825	1758–1835	D-R	Daniel D. Tompkins	1774–1825	15, 16, 17, 18
6. John Quincy Adams	3/4/1825–3/3/1829	1767–1848	D-R	John C. Calhoun	1782–1850	19, 20
7. Andrew Jackson	3/4/1829–3/3/1833	1767–1845	D	John C. Calhoun	1782–1850	21, 22
	3/4/1833–3/3/1837			Martin Van Buren	1782–1862	23, 24
8. Martin Van Buren	3/4/1837–3/3/1841	1782–1862	D	Richard M. Johnson	1780–1850	25, 26
9. William Henry Harrison	3/4/1841–4/4/1841	1773–1841	W	John Tyler	1790–1862	27
10. John Tyler	4/6/1841–3/3/1845	1790–1862	W	—	—	27, 28
11. James K. Polk	3/4/1845–3/3/1849	1795–1849	D	George M. Dallas	1792–1864	29, 30
12. Zachary Taylor	3/4/1849–7/9/1850	1784–1850	W	Millard Fillmore	1800–1874	31
13. Millard Fillmore	7/10/1850–3/3/1853	1800–1874	W	—	—	31, 32
14. Franklin Pierce	3/4/1853–3/3/1857	1804–1869	D	William R. King	1786–1853	33, 34
15. James Buchanan	3/4/1857–3/3/1861	1791–1868	D	John C. Breckinridge	1821–1875	35, 36
16. Abraham Lincoln	3/4/1861–3/3/1865	1809–1865	R	Hannibal Hamlin	1809–1891	37, 38
	3/4/1865–4/15/1865			Andrew Johnson	1808–1875	39
17. Andrew Johnson	4/15/1865–3/3/1869	1808–1875	NU	—	—	39, 40
18. Ulysses S. Grant	3/4/1869–3/3/1873	1822–1885	R	Schuyler Colfax	1823–1885	41, 42
	3/4/1873–3/3/1877			Henry Wilson	1812–1875	43, 44
19. Rutherford B. Hayes	3/4/1877–3/3/1881	1822–1893	R	William A. Wheeler	1819–1887	45, 46
20. James Garfield	3/4/1881–9/19/1881	1831–1881	R	Chester A. Arthur	1829–1886	47
21. Chester A. Arthur	9/20/1881–3/3/1885	1829–1886	R	—	—	47, 48
22. Grover Cleveland	3/4/1885–3/3/1889	1837–1908	D	Thomas A. Hendricks	1819–1885	49, 50
23. Benjamin Harrison	3/4/1889–3/3/1893	1833–1901	R	Levi P. Morton	1824–1920	51, 52
24. Grover Cleveland	3/4/1893–3/3/1897	1837–1908	D	Adlai E. Stevenson	1835–1914	53, 54
25. William McKinley	3/4/1897–3/3/1901	1843–1901	R	Garret A. Hobart	1844–1899	55, 56
	3/4/1901–9/14/1901			Theodore Roosevelt	1858–1919	57
26. Theodore Roosevelt	9/14/1901–3/3/1905	1858–1919	R	—	—	57, 58
	3/4/1905–3/3/1909			Charles W. Fairbanks	1852–1918	59, 60
27. William H. Taft	3/4/1909–3/3/1913	1857–1930	R	James S. Sherman	1855–1912	61, 62
28. Woodrow Wilson	3/4/1913–3/3/1921	1856–1924	D	Thomas R. Marshall	1854–1925	63, 64, 65, 66
29. Warren G. Harding	3/4/1921–8/2/1923	1865–1923	R	Calvin Coolidge	1872–1933	67, 68
30. Calvin Coolidge	8/3/1923–3/3/1925	1872–1933	R	—	—	68
	3/4/1925–3/3/1929			Charles G. Dawes	1865–1951	69, 70
31. Herbert C. Hoover	3/4/1929–3/3/1933	1874–1964	R	Charles Curtis	1860–1936	71, 72
32. Franklin D. Roosevelt	3/4/1933–1/20/1941	1882–1945	D	John N. Garner	1868–1967	73, 74, 75, 76
	1/20/1941–1/20/1945			Henry A. Wallace	1888–1965	77, 78
	1/20/1945–4/12/1945			Harry S Truman	1884–1972	79
33. Harry S Truman	4/12/1945–1/20/1949	1884–1972	D	—	—	79, 80
	1/20/1949–1/20/1953			Alben W. Barkley	1877–1956	81, 82
34. Dwight D. Eisenhower	1/20/1953–1/20/1961	1890–1969	R	Richard M. Nixon	1913–1994	83, 84, 85, 86

F = Federalist; D-R = Democratic-Republican; D = Democrat; W = Whig; R = Republican; NU = National Union Party, a coalition of Republicans and War Democrats (Andrew Johnson was a Democrat); I = Independent

President	Term	Year of Birth–Death	Party	Vice President	Year of Birth–Death	Congresses
35. John F. Kennedy	1/20/1961–11/22/1963	1917–1963	D	Lyndon B. Johnson	1908–1973	87, 88
36. Lyndon B. Johnson	11/22/1963–1/20/1965	1908–1973	D	—	—	88
	1/20/1965–1/20/1969			Hubert H. Humphrey	1911–1978	89, 90
37. Richard M. Nixon	1/20/1969–1/20/1973	1913–1994	R	Spiro T. Agnew*	1918–1996	91, 92
	1/20/1973–8/9/1974			Gerald R. Ford	1913–	93
38. Gerald R. Ford	8/9/1974–1/20/1977	1913–	R	Nelson A. Rockefeller	1908–1979	93, 94
39. James (Jimmy) Carter	1/20/1977–1/20/1981	1924–	D	Walter F. Mondale	1928–	95, 96
40. Ronald Reagan	1/20/1981–1/20/1989	1911–	R	George Bush	1924–	97, 98, 99, 100
41. George H. W. Bush	1/20/1989–1/20/1993	1924–	R	J. Danforth Quayle	1947–	101, 102
42. William Clinton	1/20/1993–1/20/2001	1946–	D	Albert A. Gore, Jr.	1948–	103, 104, 105
43. George W. Bush	1/20/2001–	1946–	R	Richard B. Cheney	1941–	106

* Spiro T. Agnew resigned on October 10, 1973. Gerald R. Ford was inaugurated December 6, 1973.

UNITED STATES SUPREME COURT JUSTICES

Justices to the U.S. Supreme Court are nominated by the president, subject to hearings by the senate judiciary committee, and confirmed by a majority vote of the senate. In the following chart, Chief Justices are italicized.

Justice	Term	Justice	Term	Justice	Term
John Jay	1789–1795	Robert C. Grier	1846–1870	Horace H. Lurton	1910–1914
John Rutledge	1789–1791	Benjamin R. Curtis	1851–1857	Charles E. Hughes	1910–1916
William Cushing	1789–1810	John A. Cambell	1853–1861	Willis Van Devanter	1911–1937
James Wilson	1789–1798	Nathan Clifford	1858–1881	Joseph R. Lamar	1911–1916
John Blair	1789–1796	Noah H. Swayne	1862–1881	*Edward D. White*	1910–1921
Robert H. Harrison	1789–1790	Samuel F. Miller	1862–1890	Mahlon Pitney	1912–1922
James Iredell	1790–1799	David Davis	1862–1877	James C. McReynolds	1914–1941
*John Rutledge**	1795	Stephen J. Field	1863–1897	Louis D. Brandeis	1916–1939
Samuel Chase	1796–1811	*Salmon P. Chase*	1864–1873	John H. Clarke	1916–1922
Oliver Ellsworth	1796–1800	William Strong	1870–1880	*William H. Taft*	1921–1930
Bushrod Washington	1798–1829	Joseph P. Bradley	1870–1892	George Sutherland	1922–1938
Alfred Moore	1799–1804	Ward Hunt	1873–1882	Pierce Butler	1922–1939
John Marshall	1801–1835	*Morrison R. Waite*	1874–1888	Edward T. Sanford	1923–1930
William Johnson	1804–1834	John M. Harlan	1877–1911	Harlan F. Stone	1925–1941
H. Brockholst Livingston	1806–1833	William B. Woods	1880–1887	*Charles E. Hughes*	1930–1941
Thomas Todd	1807–1826	Stanley Mathews	1881–1889	Owen J. Roberts	1930–1945
Joseph Story	1811–1845	Horace Gray	1882–1902	Benjamin N Cardozo	1932–1938
Gabriel Duval	1811–1835	Samuel Blatchford	1882–1893	Hugo L. Black	1937–1951
Smith Thompson	1823–1843	Lucius Q. C. Lamar	1888–1893	Stanley F. Reed	1938–1957
Robert Trimble	1826–1828	*Melville Fuller*	1888–1910	Felix Frankfurter	1939–1962
John McClean	1829–1861	David J. Brewer	1890–1910	William O. Douglas	1939–1975
Henry Baldwin	1830–1844	Henry B. Brown	1890–1906	Frank Murphy	1940–1949
James M. Wayne	1835–1867	George Shiras, Jr.	1892–1903	*Harlan F. Stone*	1941–1946
Roger B. Taney	1836–1864	Howell E. Jackson	1893–1895	James F. Byrnes	1941–1942
Philip P. Barbour	1836–1841	Edward D. White	1894–1910	Robert H. Jackson	1941–1954
John Catron	1837–1865	Rufus W. Peckham	1895–1909	Wiley B. Rutledge	1943–1949
John McKinley	1837–1852	Joseph McKenna	1898–1925	Harold H. Burton	1945–1958
Peter V. Daniel	1841–1860	Oliver W. Holmes	1902–1932	*Fred M. Vison*	1946–1953
Samuel Nelson	1845–1872	William D. Day	1903–1922	Tom C. Clark	1949–4967
Levi Woodbury	1845–1851	William H. Moody	1906–1910	Sherman Minton	1949–1956

*Rutledge was appointed Chief Justice and served one term, but he was not confirmed in that position by the Senate.

continues

United States Supreme Court Justices, Continued

Justice	Term	Justice	Term	Justice	Term
Earl Warren	1953–1969	Abe Fortas	1965–1969	Sandra Day O'Connor	1981–
John Marshall Harlan	1955–1971	Thurgood Marshall	1967–1991	Antonin Scalia	1986–
William J. Brennan, Jr.	1956–1990	*Warren C. Burger*	1967–1986	Anthony M. Kennedy	1988–
Charles E. Whitaker	1957–1962	Harry A. Blackmun	1970–1994	David H. Souter	1990–
Potter Stewart	1958–1981	Lewis F. Powell, Jr.	1972–1987	Clarence Thomas	1991–
Byron R. White	1962–1993	*William H. Rehnquist*	1972–	Ruth Bader Ginsberg	1993–
Arthur J. Goldberg	1962–1965	John P. Stevens III	1975–	Stephen Breyer	1994–

WHERE TO WRITE YOUR SENATORS AND REPRESENTATIVES

Constituents can write to their senators and representatives at the following addresses:

> **Senator's name**
> United States Senate
> Washington, DC 20510

> **Representative's name**
> United States House of Representatives
> Washington, DC 20515

Listings of specific addresses of members of Congress are in the most current edition of *The Congressional Staff Directory* or *Congressional Quarterly's Washington Directory*, both of which are available in local libraries. These books also list the home offices of members of Congress. Local telephone directories may also be consulted.

Both the Senate and the House have offices in the Capitol Building, and additional offices are housed at the following buildings:

SENATE OFFICES

> **Dirksen Senate Office Building**
> Constitution Avenue between 1st and
>   2nd Streets, NE

> **Hart Senate Office Building**
> 2nd Street and Constitution Avenue, NE

> **Russell Senate Office Building**
> Constitution Avenue between Delaware Avenue and
>   1st Street, NE

HOUSE OFFICES

> **Cannon House Office Building**
> Independence Avenue between C and
>   1st Streets, SE

> **Longworth House Office Building**
> Independence Avenue between C and South
>   Capitol Streets, SE

> **Rayburn House Office Building**
> Independence Avenue between South Capitol and
>   1st Streets, SE

Four pairs of U.S. presidents have been related: John and John Quincy Adams (father/son), Benjamin and William Henry Harrison (grandfather/grandson), Theodore and Franklin Delano Roosevelt (cousins), and George H. W. Bush and George W. Bush (father/son).

COMMON LEGISLATIVE TERMS

Many terms below are defined in the context of the U.S. Congress. Some of the terms may be applicable as well, with some variation, to state legislatures.

act   A bill that has been approved by both the Senate and the House of Representatives and has been signed by the president or passed over his veto, thus becoming law. Acts are sometimes reviewed by the Supreme Court to determine their constitutionality.

Go to   "Business Protocols and Forms of Address" in chapter 15

The Electoral College

A Closer Look

The president and vice president of the United States are elected not by popular vote but by the Electoral College, as stipulated in Article II, Section 1, of the U.S. Constitution. On Election Day, each state selects a number of electors equal to that of its U.S. senators and representatives; these electors are all affiliated with the party that has received the highest popular vote in their districts. Including the District of Columbia's three electoral votes, the total is 538, with a majority of 270 votes needed to win. The votes are counted in a joint session of Congress on January 6. If no candidate for president has won a majority, the House selects one of the three leading candidates, with all members from a state voting in a bloc; if no vice presidential candidate has a majority, the Senate, voting as individuals, choose one from the top two candidates.

In four presidential elections, the winners of the largest number of popular votes failed to win the presidency:

1824 None of the four major Democratic candidates (John Quincy Adams, Andrew Jackson, Henry Clay, William H. Crawford) received a majority of electoral votes, thereby sending the election to the House of Representatives. Despite his overwhelming advantage in the popular vote (43.1%), Andrew Jackson was bypassed by the House in favor of John Quincy Adams, the second highest recipient of popular votes (30.5%). John C. Calhoun was chosen Vice President by the Electoral College.

1876 The Democratic presidential nominee Samuel J. Tilden (NY) initially led in both popular votes (4,284,020–4,036,572) and electoral votes (184–165) over Republican Rutherford B. Hayes (OH). However, this did not include the electoral tallies of Florida, South Carolina, and Louisiana. Their combined 20 electoral votes could swing the election either way. Early indications gave these states to Tilden. Republicans challenged on the grounds of corrupt balloting procedures. Two sets of electors from each of the states emerged, one from each party. A 15-member commission of 8 Republicans and 7 Democrats (5 senators, 5 representatives, 5 Supreme Court justices) negotiated the infamous Compromise of 1877. Democrats agreed to accept the Republican electors from the three states, thereby giving Hayes the presidency 185–184. In return, the Republicans agreed to withdraw all union troops from the South and put an end to Reconstruction. As a result, the federal government would no longer attempt to guarantee the civil, legal, or human rights of African-Americans, and the South would soon witness the rise of a de facto state of apartheid known as Jim Crow.

1888 Democrat Grover Cleveland won the popular vote, 5,540,050–5,444,337, but lost the electoral vote (233–168) and presidency to Republican Benjamin Harrison.

2000 Democrat Al Gore won the popular vote, 50,996,582–50,456,062, but lost the electoral vote (271–266) and presidency to Republican George Bush, Jr.

amendment A change or revision in the wording of a pending bill or other measure by striking out existing language, by inserting new language, or both.

appropriate act A legislative act authorizing the expenditure of federal funds for a specific purpose or purposes.

bill A measure proposing legislation to create a new act or to amend or repeal existing law.

budget A statement of future federal-government expenses and revenues initially formulated by the president and the executive branch. Congress considers the proposed budget in a series of appropriation acts initially introduced in the House of Representatives.

caucus An informal group of legislators that exists to promote issues of common interest (based, for example, on regional, political, ideological, ethnic, or economic concerns) and that possibly shares research staff.

cloture A parliamentary maneuver in the Senate to force the end of a filibuster, thus permitting a measure, amendment, or motion to come to a vote. Cloture, which limits consideration of a pending matter to an additional 30 hours, can be invoked only by an affirmative vote of three-fifths (normally 60 members) of the full Senate.

coalition   A combination of individuals or parties, usually needed to gain a majority vote.

committee of the whole   The legislative forum in which the entire membership of the House of Representatives meets under special rules of procedure (most notably limiting individual debate to five minutes instead of the usual hour) in order to expedite their deliberations on particular categories of legislation.

George Washington is the only Independent president: he never belonged to a political party.

committee   A legislative group in either house of Congress that considers bills, resolutions, and other legislative matters over which the committee has jurisdiction. Committees are fact-finding bodies that hold hearings and listen to witnesses as well as investigate and debate issues, and then prepare a piece of legislation or a bill to present to the whole body for debate. *See also* **conference committee; joint committee; standing committee.**

conference committee   A temporary group of members of both houses of Congress assigned to reconcile differing versions of the same bill passed in the House and Senate. *See also* **joint committee.**

Congressional Record   A substantially verbatim account of the daily proceedings of Congress, kept since 1873.

deficit   The amount by which expenditures (outlays) exceed revenues (receipts) in a given fiscal period. Deficit spending occurs when the government borrows money to cover the difference between income and spending. *See also* **surplus.**

filibuster   A procedural strategy by which a senator controls the floor and debates a bill at length in order to block or delay Senate action on it. *See also* **cloture.**

impeachment   The formal presentation of charges against a public official accused of misconduct in order to bring about his or her trial and removal from office, if convicted. The House of Representatives can vote for impeachment of federal officials; the Senate is responsible for trying them.

initiative   The procedure by which voters petition a state legislature for a new law. Typically, the legislature rejects the initiative and puts it out to a referendum by the voters. *See also* **referendum.**

joint committee   A committee that includes members of both the Senate and the House and that can publish studies and background reports within its specified jurisdictions, but normally lacks authority to report legislation.

line-item veto   The power of a chief executive to veto particular parts of a bill rather than reject the bill as a whole.

lobbyist   A person representing a special interest who seeks to influence lawmakers or a regulatory agency by pressing the views of a group, organization, or industry on issues under consideration.

majority leader   The leader of the party holding the majority of members in the House or Senate. The majority leader plans strategy, guides debate, maintains party discipline, and speaks for the party either in support of or in criticism of the president. The Senate majority leader also leads the Senate as a whole and must negotiate the agenda with the minority party.

majority party   The party holding the majority of the seats in a legislative body.

mandate   A vote of confidence from the people, often used loosely to indicate broad support for a party's policy initiative.

minority leader   The leader of the party holding a minority of seats in a legislative body, who serves as the party's principal spokesperson and strategist.

minority party   The party holding a minority of seats in a legislative body.

override   Congress's negation of a president's vote by voting for a bill with a two-thirds majority.

pocket veto   The indirect veto of a bill by the president. A pocket veto occurs when the president has not signed a bill within ten days of its presentation to him and Congress has adjourned within those ten days.

United States

political action committee (PAC) A group formed outside of political parties in order to raise money for donation to lawmakers who support the group's policies and aims.

president pro tempore The constitutionally recognized officer of the Senate who presides over the chamber when the vice president of the United States, who also functions as president of the Senate, is absent. Normally, however, the president pro tempore appoints a succession of other senators to serve as the presiding officer.

quorum A predetermined minimum number of members of a legislative assembly who must be present in order for the assembly to conduct business.

reapportionment A change or adjustment in the size or boundaries of legislative districts based on population increases or decreases.

recall A special popular vote held in order to consider removing an elected official before he or she has completed his or her term of office.

referendum A legislative issue on which voters can vote directly, usually at the time of an election. *See also* **initiative.**

representative Any elected official who represents voters in a legislative body; the term most often refers to a member of the House of Representatives, the lower house of Congress. States elect differing numbers of representatives to Congress, depending on their population as determined by the federal census. Representatives serve two-year terms.

rider An attempt to secure passage of a controversial proposal by attaching it as an amendment to a nonrelated bill whose passage is otherwise considered essential.

senator A member of the Senate, the upper house of Congress. Each state elects two senators, who serve overlapping terms of six years.

Speaker of the House The presiding officer in the House, elected by the consensus of the majority party.

standing committee A permanent committee in either the House or the Senate that is assigned jurisdiction over particular issues.

surplus The amount by which revenues (receipts) exceed expenditures (outlays) in a given fiscal period. *See also* **deficit.**

veto The power given to the president under the Constitution to refuse to sign a bill and so prevent it from becoming law. The president may return it to the Congress with notes on his objections. *See also* **line-item veto; override; pocket veto.**

whip An elected representative who serves as an assistant to the majority or minority leader and who is responsible for gathering members of his or her party and making sure they are present when a crucial partisan vote occurs.

HOW A BILL BECOMES LAW
FIRST READING

To become law, a bill is introduced by a senator or representative in the Senate or House and is assigned a number or title by the clerk of the House. The bill is then assigned to the committee of the Senate or House that is responsible for the particular area the bill relates to (for example, a bill providing aid to farmers would go to the Committee on Agriculture). The committee debates the bill, listens to the opinions of interested people and members of Congress, and sometimes offers amendments to the bill. The bill is then voted on by the committee and, if passed, is sent back to the clerk of the House. If the bill is unacceptable to the committee when they receive it, they may table it, killing consideration of the bill. This process is called the first reading of the bill.

SECOND AND THIRD READINGS

In the second reading, the clerk of the House reads the bill to the House, which then debates it and suggests amendments. At the third reading, after the bill is debated, a vote is called for and the title of the bill is read before the vote.

PASSAGE

If the bill passes, it is sent to the other house, where it is again debated, amendments are added, and a vote is taken. If it passes with amendments, a joint congressional committee (composed of members of both the House and the Senate) tries to reach a compromise between the two versions of the bill. If not passed by the second house, the bill dies.

Only four women have appeared on U.S. currency: Martha Washington, Pocahontas, Susan B. Anthony, and Sacagawea.

PRESIDENTIAL ACTION

When the bill is passed, it is sent to the president. If he signs it, it becomes law. If he holds the bill for ten days (not including Sundays), it automatically becomes law without his signature, unless Congress has adjourned during that time, in which case the bill is automatically killed in a process known as a *pocket veto*. If the president disapproves of the bill, he vetoes it, sending it back to the house that originally produced it, along with his objections.

Once back in the house, the bill is debated again in light of the president's comments and a roll-call vote is taken. To remain an active bill, it must receive at least a two-thirds vote from that house. If it does not, it is defeated. If the bill does get the support of two-thirds of that house, it is sent to the other house, where it again must receive a vote of two-thirds to override a presidential veto.

FEDERAL SPENDING AS A PERCENTAGE OF THE BUDGET

As the U.S. government has grown in size over the years, so has its spending and its accumulation of debt. The following chart outlines that growth and the directions it has taken since 1790.

Year	Defense	Veterans Benefits	Social Security	Health/ Medicare	Education	Interest on Debt	Federal Debt in Millions
1790	14.9	4.1	N/A	N/A	N/A	55.0	75.463
1800	55.7	0.6	N/A	N/A	N/A	31.3	82.976
1810	48.4 (1814 = 79.9)	1.0	N/A	N/A	N/A	34.9	53.173
1820	38.4	17.6	N/A	N/A	N/A	28.1	91.016
1830	52.9	9.0	N/A	N/A	N/A	12.6	48.565
1840	54.3 (1847 = 80.7)	10.7	N/A	N/A	N/A	0.7	3.573
1850	43.8	4.7	N/A	N/A	N/A	1.0	63.543
1860	44.2 (1865 = 88.9)	1.7	N/A	N/A	N/A	5.0	64.844
1870	25.7	9.2	N/A	N/A	N/A	41.7	2,436.453
1880	19.3	21.2	N/A	N/A	N/A	35.8	2,090.909
1890	20.9 (1899 = 48.6)	33.6	N/A	N/A	N/A	11.4	1,222.397
1900	36.6	27.0	N/A	N/A	N/A	7.7	1,263.417
1910	45.1 (1919 = 59.5)	23.2	N/A	N/A	N/A	3.1	1,146.940
1920	37.1	3.4	N/A	N/A	N/A	16.0	24,299.321
1930	25.3	6.6	N/A	N/A	N/A	19.9	16,185.310
1940	17.5 (1945 = 89.4)	6.0	0.3	0.5	20.8	9.4	42,967.531
1950	32.2	20.3	1.8	0.6	0.6	11.3	256,853.0
1960	52.2	5.9	12.6	0.9	1.0	7.5	290,525.0
1970	41.8	4.4	15.5	6.2	4.4	7.3	308,927.0
1980	22.7	3.6	20.1	9.4	5.4	8.9	909,050.0
1990	23.9	2.3	19.8	12.4	3.1	14.7	3,266,073.0
2000	16.2	2.5	22.9	19.6	3.3	14.7	5,686,000.0

STATES, DISTRICT OF COLUMBIA, AND TERRITORIES

America comprises 50 states, the District of Columbia, and 9 territories. State and territorial governments are independent of each other but subordinate to the federal government. The following chart provides basic information concerning all of them.

State	Entry Date (Rank)	Capital	Flower	Bird	Motto	Nickname
Alabama	12/14/1819 (22)	Montgomery	Camellia	Yellow Hammer	We dare defend our rights	Heart of Dixie; Camelia State
Alaska	1/3/1959 (49)	Juneau	Forget-me-not	Willow Ptarmigan	North to the future	The Last Frontier
Arizona	2/14/1912 (48)	Phoenix	Saguaro	Cactus Wren	*Diat Deus* (God enriches)	Grand Canyon State
Arkansas	6/16/1836 (25)	Little Rock	Apple Blossom	Mockingbird	*Regnat populus* (The people rule)	Land of Opportunity
California	9/9/1850 (31)	Sacramento	Golden Poppy	California Valley Quail	*Eureka!* (I found it)	Golden State
Colorado	8/1/1876 (38)	Denver	Blue Columbine	Lark Bunting	*Nil sine numine* (Nothing without providence)	Centennial State
Connecticut	1/9/1788 (5)	Hartford	Mountain Laurel	American Robin	*Qui transtulet sustinet* (He who transplanted still sustains)	Constitution State; Nutmeg State
Delaware	12/7/1787 (1)	Dover	Peach Blossom	Blue Hen Chicken	Liberty and independence	First State; Diamond State
District of Columbia	U.S Capital 12/1/1800	Washington	American Beauty Rose	Wood Thrush	*Justia Omnibus* (Justice for all)	Capital City
Florida	3/3/1845 (27)	Tallahassee	Orange Blossom	Mockingbird	In God we trust	Sunshine State
Georgia	1/2/1788 (4)	Atlanta	Cherokee Rose	Brown Thrasher	Wisdom, justice, and moderation	Empire State of the South; Peach Tree State
Hawaii	8/21/1959 (50)	Honolulu	Hibiscus	Nene Goose	The life of the land is perpetuated in righteousness	Aloha State
Idaho	7/3/1890 (43)	Boise	Syringa	Mountain Bluebird	*Esto perpetua* (It is eternal)	Gem State
Illinois	12/3/1818 (21)	Springfield	Native Violet	Cardinal	State sovereignty—national union	Prairie State; Land of Lincoln
Indiana	12/11/1816 (19)	Indianapolis	Peony	Cardinal	Crossroads of America	Hossier State
Iowa	12/28/1846 (29)	Des Moines	Wild Rose	Goldfinch	Our liberties we prize and our rights we will maintain	Hawkeye State
Kansas	1/29/1861 (34)	Topeka	Sun Flower	Western Meadowlark	*Ad astr per aspera* (To the stars through difficulties)	Sunflower State
Kentucky	6/1/1792 (15)	Frankfort	Goldenrod	Kentucky Cardinal	United we stand, divided we fall	Bluegrass State
Louisiana	4/30/1812 (18)	Baton Rouge	Magnolia	Eastern Brown Pelican	Union, justice, and confidence	Pelican State

States, District of Columbia, and Territories, Continued

State	Entry Date (Rank)	Capital	Flower	Bird	Motto	Nickname
Maine	3/15/1820 (23)	Augusta	Pine Cone and Tassel	Chickadee	*Dirigo* (I Direct)	Pine Tree State
Maryland	4/28/1788 (7)	Annapolis	Black-eyed Susan	Baltimore Oriole	*Fati maschii, parole femine* (Manly deeds, womanly words)	Old Line State; Free State
Massachusetts	2/6/1788 (6)	Boston	Mayflower	Chickadee	*Ense petit placidam sub liberate quietem* (By the sword we seek peace but peace only under liberty)	Bay State; Colony State
Michigan	1/26/1837 (26)	Lansing	Apple Blossom	Robin	*Si quaeris peninulam amoenam circumspice* (If you seek a pleasant peninsula, look about you)	Great Lakes State; Wolverine State
Minnesota	5/11/1858 (32)	St. Paul	Showy Lady Slipper	Common Loon	*L'etoile du nord* (Star of the north)	North Star State
Mississippi	12/10/1817 (20)	Jackson	Magnolia	Mockingbird	*Virtute et armis* (By valor and arms)	Magnolia State
Missouri	8/10/1821 (24)	Jefferson City	Hawthorn	Bluebird	*Salus populi suprema lex esto* (The welfare of the people shall be the supreme law)	Show-Me State
Montana	11/8/1889 (41)	Helena	Bitterroot	Western Meadowlark	*Oro y plata* (Gold and silver)	Treasure State
Nebraska	3/1/1867 (37)	Lincoln	Goldenrod	Meadowlark	Equality before the law	Cornhusker State
Nevada	10/3/1864 (36)	Carson City	Sagebrush	Mountain Bluebird	All for our country	Sagebrush State; Battle Born State
New Hampshire	6/21/1788 (9)	Concord	Purple Lilac	Purple Finch	Live free or die	Granite State
New Jersey	12/18/1787 (3)	Trenton	Purple Violet	Eastern Goldfinch	Liberty and prosperity	Garden State
New Mexico	1/6/1912 (47)	Santa Fe	Yucca	Roadrunner	*Crescit eundo* (It grows as it goes)	Land of Enhancement
New York	7/26/1788 (11)	Albany	Rose (any color)	Bluebird	*Excelsior* (Ever upward)	Empire State
North Carolina	11/21/1789 (12)	Raleigh	Dogwood	Cardinal	*Esse quam videri* (To be rather than to seem)	Tar Heel State; Old North State
North Dakota	11/2/1889 (39)	Bismark	Wild Prairie Rose	Western Meadowlark	Liberty and union, now and forever one and inseparable	Peace Garden State
Ohio	3/1/1803 (17)	Columbus	Scarlet Carnation	Cardinal	With God, all things are possible	Buckeye State
Oklahoma	11/16/1907 (46)	Oklahoma City	Mistletoe	Scissor-tailed Flycatcher	*Labor omnia vincit* (Labor conquers all things)	Sooner State

State	Entry Date (Rank)	Capital	Flower	Bird	Motto	Nickname
Oregon	2/14/1859 (33)	Salem	Oregon Grape	Western Meadowlark	The union	Beaver State
Pennsylvania	12/12/1787 (2)	Harrisburg	Mountain Laurel	Ruffed Grouse	Virtue, liberty, and independence	Keystone State
Rhode Island	5/29/1790 (13)	Providence	Violet	Rhode Island Hen	Hope	Little Rhody; Ocean State
South Carolina	5/23/1788 (8)	Columbia	Carolina Jessamine	Carolina Wren	*Dum spiro spero* (While I breath, I hope)	Palmetto State
South Dakota	11/2/1889 (40)	Pierre	Pasque Flower	Pheasant	Under God, the people rule	Coyote State; Sunshine State
Tennessee	6/1/1796 (16)	Nashville	Iris	Mockingbird	Agriculture and commerce	Volunteer State
Texas	12/29/1845 (28)	Austin	Blue Bonnet	Mockingbird	Friendship	Lone Star State
Utah	1/4/1896 (45)	Salt Lake City	Sego Lily	Seagull	Industry	Beehive State
Vermont	3/4/1791 (14)	Montpelier	Red Clover	Thrush	Freedom and unity	Green Mountain State
Virginia	6/25/1788 (10)	Richmond	Flowering Dogwood	Cardinal	*Sic semper tyrannis* (Thus always to tyrants)	Old Dominion
Washington	11/11/1889 (42)	Olympia	Rhododendron	Willow Goldfinch	*Alki* (By and by)	Evergreen State
West Virginia	6/20/1863 (35)	Charleston	Big Rhododendron	Cardinal	*Montani semper liberi* (Mountaineers are always free)	Mountain State
Wisconsin	5/29/1848 (30)	Madison	Wood Violet	Robin	Forward	Badger State
Wyoming	7/0/1890 (44)	Cheyenne	Indian Paintbrush	Meadowlark	Equal Rights	Equality State

Territories	Year Acquired	Capital	Flower	Bird	Motto	
American Samoa	1899	Pago Pago	Paog (Ua-Fla)	—	*Samoa Muamua le Atua* (In Samoa God is first)	
Federated States of Micronesia	1947	Pohnpei	—	—	—	
Guam	1950	Agana	Puti Tai Nobio (Bougainvillea)	Toto (Fruit Dove)	Where America's day begins	
Marshall Islands	1947	Majuro	—	—	Joannes est monem eius (John is his name)	
Midway Islands	1867	N/A	—	—	—	
Northern Mariana Islands	1947	Saipan	—	—	—	
Palu	1947	Koror	—	—	—	
Puerto Rico	1898	San Juan	Mega	Reinita	—	
Virgin Islands	1927	Charlotte Amalie	Yellow Elder	Yellow Breast	—	

United States

STATE NAME ORIGINS

The etymologies of some state names are more well established than others.

Alabama From the Muskogee Indian language, perhaps meaning "town."

Alaska A Russian corruption of the Aleutian word *alashak,* meaning "mainland."

Arizona Origin unknown; perhaps a Spanish corruption of either the Pima word *arizonac,* meaning "small spring," or the Aztec word *arizuma,* meaning "silver-bearing."

Arkansas A French corruption of *Quapaw,* the name of the people indigenous to the region.

Nebraska is the only state in the nation with a unicameral (one-house) state legislature.

California The name of a fictitious earthly paradise in the 16th-century Spanish romance *Las Serged de Explandian* by Montalvo.

Colorado Spanish for "red."

Connecticut English corruption of *Quinnehtukqut,* the name of the people indigenous to the region.

Delaware Corruption of the nickname of a former English governor of Virginia, Lord de La Warr.

Washington, District of Columbia named for George Washington and Christopher Columbus.

Florida Spanish for "flowery Easter."

Georgia Named for King George II of England.

Hawaii English corruption of *owhyhee* or *awaiki,* indigenous words meaning "homeland."

Idaho Origin unknown; possibly an English corruption of *idahi,* the Na-i-shan Dine (a.k.a Plains Apache, Lipan Apache, or Kiowa-Apache) name for the Comanche people. Possibly a fabricated word.

Illinois From *Illini,* the French corruption of the Piwarea (a.k.a Peoria) word for "men."

Indiana English place name reflective of the word "Indian."

Iowa English corruption of the name of the Paxoje (a.k.a Ioway) people who are indigenous to the region.

Kansas English corruption of the name of the Kaw (a.k.a Kansa) people who are indigenous to the region.

Kentucky Origin unknown; perhaps from the Haudenosaunee (a.k.a Iroquois) word *ken-ta-ten,* meaning "meadow."

Louisiana Named for King Louis XIV of France.

Maine Origin unknown; perhaps archaic French term meaning "province," or named for the French province of Mayne.

Maryland Named for Queen Henrietta Maria of England, wife of King Charles I.

Massachusetts The name of the people indigenous to the region.

Michigan French corruption of the Anishinabe (a.k.a Ojibwa or Chippewa) word *micigama,* meaning "great water."

Minnesota English corruption of the Dakota (a.k.a Sioux) words *mni sosha,* meaning "muddy water."

Montana The Latin word for "mountainous."

Nebraska English corruption of the UmoN'hoN (a.k.a Omaha) word for "flat water."

Lake Superior is the second-largest freshwater lake in the world.

Nevada Spanish for "snow-clad."

New Hampshire Named for the English county of Hampshire.

New Jersey   Named for the Isle of Jersey off the coast of England.

New Mexico   Named for the Spanish territory of northern Mexico, originally a Spanish corruption of *Mexika,* a Nauhuatl-speaking nation indigenous to the region.

New York   Originally New Netherlands, named for England's Duke of York after English conquest.

North Carolina   Named for King Charles I of England, from the Latin *Carolus* meaning "Charles."

North Dakota   The name of the people indigenous to the region (a.k.a Lakota, Nakota, and Sioux).

Ohio   Origin unknown; perhaps an English corruption of a Haudenosuanee (a.k.a Iroquois) word meaning "great water."

Oklahoma   A word coined in the 19th century to mean "Indian" by Choctaw-speaking Reverend Allen Wright.

Oregon   Origin unknown; perhaps an English corruption of an unknown indigenous word.

Pennsylvania   Named for the colony's founder, Sir William Penn, and the English word "sylvan," an adjective referring to forests.

Rhode Island   Origin unknown; perhaps an English corruption of an earlier Dutch name, *Roode Elandt,* meaning "red island," or named by the English for the Greek island of Rhodes.

South Carolina   see North Carolina.

South Dakota   see North Dakota.

Tennessee   Originally the state of Franklin, in honor of Benjamin Franklin. Renamed in 1788, an English corruption of *Tanasi,* the name of a Cherokee town.

Texas   English corruption of the Spanish name *Tejas,* itself a corruption of the name of peoples indigenous to the region who spoke a language in the Caddoan family.

➜ **"North America" and "United States" in the atlas**

Go to

Utah   English corruption of *Ute,* the collective name of several peoples indigenous to the region who speak dialects of the Numic language, which is part of the Uto-Aztecan family.

Vermont   English corruption of the French *vert,* meaning "green," and *mont,* meaning "mountains."

Virginia   Named for Queen Elizabeth I of England, also known as the Virgin Queen.

Washington   Named for George Washington.

West Virginia   See Virginia.

Wisconsin   English corruption of *ouisconsin,* an Anishinabe (a.k.a Ojibwa or Chippewa) word meaning "grassy place."

The Mississippi River is the world's third longest (behind the Amazon and the Nile). However, the Missouri River from its mouth to the Gulf of Mexico is the world's longest unbroken riverine waterway.

Wyoming   From the Wyoming Valley in Pennsylvania. Origin unknown, perhaps an English corruption of a word from one of the languages in the Algonquin family, spoken by the peoples indigenous to Pennsylvania.

TERRITORIAL ACQUISITION

The United States' territorial expansion across the American continent involved two processes: gaining recognition of exclusive rights to land from the its imperial rivals (mostly European), and then seizing actual control of the land in question from its indigenous inhabitants, the various Native nations who lived there. Both processes involved negotiations and occasionally open wars of aggression instigated by the U.S. The following chart reflects the various phases by which the U.S. gained the rights to its present territory exclusive from other imperial rivals.

United States

Territory	Date Acquired	Sq. Miles	How Acquired
Original 13 States	1783	888,685	Treaty of Paris with Great Britain
Louisiana Purchase	1803	827,192	Purchase from France
Florida	1819	72,003	Adams-Onis Treaty with Spain
Texas	1845	390,143	Annexation of Independent Texas
Oregon Territory	1846	285,580	Oregon Boundary Treaty with Great Britain
Mexican Cession	1848	529,017	Conquest of Mexico/Treaty of Guadalupe-Hidalgo
Gadsden Purchase	1853	29,640	Purchase from Mexico
Midway Islands	1867	2	Annexed Uninhabited Islands
Alaska	1867	589,757	Purchase from Russia
Wake Island	1898	3	Annexed Uninhabited Island
Hawaii	1898	6,450	Conquest of Independent nation
The Philippines	1899	115,600	Conquest of Spain/Treaty of Paris (independent 1946)
Puerto Rico	1899	3,435	Conquest of Spain/Treaty of Paris
Guam	1899	212	Conquest of Spain/Treaty of Paris
American Samoa	1900	76	Treaty with Germany, Great Britain
Panama Canal Zone	1904	553	Hay-Nunau-Varilla Treaty with Panama (Returned 1978)
Corn Islands	1914	4	Treaty with Nicaragua (Returned 1978)
Virgin Islands	1917	133	Purchase from Denmark
Trust Territory of Pacific Islands	1947	717	United Nations Trusteeship. Now independent: Federated States of Micronesia (1990), Marshall Islands (1991), and Palau (1994)

THE AMERICAN PEOPLE

The population of the United States has grown and its demographic composition has changed much since the republic's inception. The following chart traces that growth and dynamic change since 1790.

Year	No. of States	Population	Percent Increase	Percent Urban/Rural	Percent White/ Non–White	Persons per Household	Birth Rate per 1,000 people	Death Rate per 1,000 people
1790	13	3,929,214	—	5.1/94.9	80.7/19.3	5.79	N/A	N/A
1800	16	5,308,483	35.1	6.1/93.9	81.1/18.9	N/A	55.0	N/A
1810	17	7,239,881	36.4	7.3/92.7	81.0/19.0	N/A	54.3	N/A
1820	23	9,638,543	33.1	7.2/92.8	81.6/18.4	N/A	55.2	N/A
1830	24	12,866,020	33.5	8.8/91.2	81.9/18.1	N/A	51.4	N/A
1840	26	17,069,543	32.7	10.8/89.2	83.2/16.8	N/A	51.8	N/A
1850	31	23,191,876	35.9	15.3/84.7	84.3/15.7	5.5	43.3	N/A
1860	33	31,443,321	35.6	19.8/80.2	85.6/14.4	5.28	44.3	N/A
1870	37	39,818,449	26.6	25.7/74.3	86.2/13.8	5.09	38.3	N/A
1880	38	50,155,783	26.0	28.2/71.8	86.5/13.5	5.04	39.8	N/A
1890	44	62,947,714	25.5	35.1/64.9	87.5/12.5	4.93	31.5	N/A
1900	45	75,994,575	20.7	39.6/60.4	87.9/12.1	4.76	32.3	17.2
1910	46	91,972,266	21.0	45.6/54.4	88.9/11.1	4.54	30.1	14.7
1920	48	105,710,620	14.9	51.2/48.8	89.7/10.3	4.34	27.7	13.0
1930	48	122,755,046	16.1	56.1/43.9	89.8/10.2	4.11	21.3	11.3
1940	48	131,669,275	7.2	56.5/43.5	89.8/10.2	3.76	19.4	10.8
1950	48	150,697,361	14.5	64.0/36.0	89.5/10.5	3.37	24.1	9.6
1960	50	179,323,175	18.5	69.9/31.1	88.6/11.4	3.33	23.7	9.5
1970	50	203,302,031	13.4	73.6/26.4	87.6/12.4	3.14	18.4	9.5
1980	50	226,542,199	11.4	73.7/26.3	85.9/14.1	2.75	15.9	8.8
1990	50	248,718,301	9.8	75.2/24.8	83.9/16.1	2.63	16.6	8.6
2000	50	281,421,906	13.2	80.2/19.8	75.1/24.9	2.59	14.4	8.5

United States

U.S. POPULATION BY STATE: 2000

State	Population	% change since 1990	Persons per sq. mile	State	Population	% change since 1990	Persons per sq. mile
Alabama	4,447,100	10.1	87.6	Montana	902,195	12.9	6.2
Alaska	626,932	14.0	1.1	Nebraska	1,711,263	8.4	22.3
Arkansas	2,673,400	13.7	51.3	Nevada	1,998,257	66.3	18.2
California	33,871,648	13.6	217.1	New Hampshire	1,235,786	11.4	137.8
Colorado	4,301,261	30.6	41.5	New Jersey	8,414,350	8.6	1,134.5
Connecticut	3,405,565	03.6	702.9	New Mexico	1,819,046	20.1	15.0
Delaware	783,600	17.6	401.0	New York	18,976,457	5.5	401.9
District of Columbia	572,059	−5.7	9,378.0	North Carolina	8,049,313	21.4	165.2
Florida	15,982,378	23.5	296.4	North Dakota	642,200	0.5	9.3
Georgia	8,186,453	26.4	141.4	Ohio	11,353,140	4.7	277.3
Hawaii	1,211,537	9.9	188.6	Oklahoma	3,450,654	9.7	50.3
Idaho	1,293,953	28.5	15.6	Oregon	3,421,399	20.4	35.6
Illinois	12,419,293	8.6	223.4	Pennsylvania	12,281,054	3.4	274.0
Indiana	6,080,485	9.7	169.5	Rhode Island	1,048,319	4.5	1,003.2
Iowa	2,926,324	5.4	52.4	South Carolina	4,012,012	15.1	133.2
Kansas	2,688,418	8.5	32.9	South Dakota	754,844	8.5	9.9
Kentucky	4,041,769	9.6	101.7	Tennessee	5,689,283	16.7	138.0
Louisiana	4,468,976	5.9	102.6	Texas	20,851,820	22.8	79.6
Maine	1,274,923	3.8	41.3	Utah	2,233,169	29.6	27.2
Maryland	5,296,486	10.8	541.9	Vermont	608,827	8.2	65.8
Massachusetts	6,349,097	5.5	809.8	Virginia	7,078,515	14.4	178.8
Michigan	9,938,444	6.9	175.0	Washington	5,894,121	21.1	88.6
Minnesota	4,919,479	12.4	61.8	West Virginia	1,808,344	0.8	75.1
Mississippi	2,844,658	10.5	60.6	Wisconsin	5,363,675	9.6	98.8
Missouri	5,595,211	9.3	81.2	Wyoming	493,782	8.9	5.1
				United States	**281,421,906**	**13.1**	**79.6**

IMMIGRATION TO THE UNITED STATES

Immigration has played an integral role in the expansion of the United States since its inception. During the antebellum era, there were no restrictions on immigration. By the end of the 19th century, restrictive legislation such as the Chinese Exclusion Act (1882) affected various sources of immigration. Today, individual nations are assigned quotas for the number of legal emigrants they may send to the U.S. (Note: not all nations have the same quotas.) Immigrants who can prove political persecution should they be returned to their home country are not counted in their country's quotas. The sole exception is Cuba, whose refugees do not have to prove political persecution. The following chart shows the broad geographic sources of U.S. immigrants in millions.

Decade	Europe	Americas	Asia
1820s	0.106	0.012	N/A
1830s	0.496	0.033	N/A
1840s	1.597	0.062	N/A
1850s	2.453	0.075	0.042
1860s	2.065	0.167	0.065
1870s	2.272	0.404	0.070
1880s	4.735	0.427	0.070
1890s	3.555	0.039	0.075
1900s	8.065	0.362	0.324
1910s	4.332	1.144	0.247
1920s	2.463	1.517	0.112
1930s	0.348	0.160	0.016
1940s	0.621	0.355	0.032
1950s	1.326	0.997	0.150
1960s	1.123	1.716	0.590
1970s	0.800	1.983	1.588
1980s	0.762	3.616	2.738
1990s	1.291	4.530	5.547

United States

AMERICAN WORKERS

As the historical processes of urbanization, immigration, and the Industrial Revolution steadily expanded during the 19th century, the face of the American workforce began to change. The following numbers chart many of those changes.

Year	No. of workers in millions	Male percent of workers	Female percent of workers	Percent of married females working	Percent unemployed	Farmers as a percent of workers	Percent of workers in unions
1810	2.330	N/A	N/A	N/A	N/A	84	N/A
1840	5.660	N/A	N/A	N/A	N/A	75	N/A
1860	11.110	N/A	N/A	N/A	N/A	53	N/A
1870	12.506	85	15	N/A	N/A	53	N/A
1880	17.392	85	15	N/A	N/A	52	N/A
1890	23.318	83	17	19	4 (1894 = 18)	43	N/A
1900	19.073	82	18	21	5	40	3
1910	38.167	79	21	25	6	31	6
1920	41.614	79	21	24	5 (1921 = 12)	26	12
1930	48.830	78	22	25	9 (1933 = 25)	22	7
1940	53.011	76	24	27	15 (1944 = 1)	17	27
1950	62.208	72	28	31	5.3	12	25
1960	69.628	67	33	38	5.5	8	26
1970	82.771	62	38	43	4.9	4	25
1980	106.940	58	42	52	7.1	3	23
1990	125.840	55	45	58	5.6	3	16
2000	137.673	54	46	60	4.5	3	15

U.S. POSTAL SERVICE

ZIP CODES

Five-digit ZIP (Zone Improvement Plan) codes were introduced in 1964 to identify each postal delivery area in the United States. In some areas, two cities may share a ZIP code; in others, such as New York City, one geographic area may have many ZIP codes, including separate ZIP codes for each major office building. In this book, the Zip codes are representative rather than specific for the larger cities. In New York City, for example, the indicated ZIP code is 10199, which is the ZIP code for the Manhattan borough postmaster. In 1983, the USPS introduced the ZIP +4 code, an expanded version of ZIP codes. Use of the four-digit add-on is voluntary, and it is primarily intended for the use of businesses and bulk mailers. For the ZIP code for a specific address in any area served by the U.S. Postal Service, the reader should consult a copy of the *U.S. Postal Service National Five-Digit ZIP Code & Post Office Directory*, available at any local post office and revised yearly, or use the U.S. Postal Service online ZIP code service at http://www.usps.gov/ncsc.

Aberdeen, SD	57401	Allentown, PA	18101	Anniston, AL	36201
Abilene, TX	79604	Alton, IL	62002	Antioch, CA	94509
Addison, IL	60101	Altoona, PA	16601	Appleton, WI	54911
Akron, OH	44309	Amarillo, TX	79120	Arcadia, CA	91006
Alameda, CA	94501	Ames, IA	50010	Arlington, TX	76010
Albany, GA	31706	Anaheim, CA	92803	Arlington Heights, IL	60004
Albuquerque, NM	87101	Anchorage, AK	99501	Artesia, CA	90701
Alexandria, LA	71301	Anderson, IN	46011	Arvada, CO	80004
Alexandria, VA	22313	Anderson, SC	29621	Asheville, NC	28810
Alhambra, CA	91802	Annapolis, MD	21401	Ashland, KY	41101
Allen Park, MI	48101	Ann Arbor, MI	48106	Aspen, CO	81611

Athens, GA	30601	Blue Springs, MO	64015	Champaign, IL	61820
Atlanta, GA	30304	Boca Raton, FL	33432	Chandler, AZ	85224
Atlantic City, NJ	08401	Boise, ID	83708	Chapel Hill, NC	27514
Attleboro, MA	02703	Bolingbrook, IL	60439	Charleston, SC	29423
Auburn, AL	36830	Bossier City, LA	71111	Charleston, WV	25301
Auburn, NY	13021	Boston, MA	02205	Charlotte, NC	28228
Auburn, WA	98002	Boulder, CO	80302	Charlottesville, VA	22906
Augusta, GA	30901	Bountiful, UT	84010	Chattanooga, TN	37421
Aurora, GA	80010	Bowie, MD	20715	Chelsea, MA	02150
Aurora, IL	60504	Bowling Green, KY	42101	Chesapeake, VA	23320
Austin, TX	78710	Bowling Green, OH	43402	Chester, PA	19013
Azusa, CA	91702	Boynton Beach, FL	33435	Cheyenne, WY	82001
Bakersfield, CA	93302	Bradenton, FL	34206	Chicago, IL	60607
Baldwin Park, CA	91706	Brattleboro, VT	05301	Chicago Heights, IL	60411
Baltimore, MD	21233	Brea, CA	92621	Chico, CA	95926
Bangor, ME	04401	Bremerton, WA	98310	Chicopee, MA	01020
Barberton, OH	44203	Bridgeport, CT	06602	Chula Vista, CA	91910
Bartlesville, OK	74003	Bristol, CT	06010	Cicero, IL	60650
Baton Rouge, LA	70821	Brockton, MA	02401	Cincinnati, OH	45234
Battle Creek, MI	49016	Broken Arrow, OK	74012	Claremont, CA	91711
Bay City, MI	48706	Brookfield, WI	53045	Clarksville, TN	37040
Bayonne, NJ	07002	Brookline, MA	02146	Clearwater, FL	34618
Baytown, TX	77520	Brooklyn Center, MN	55429	Cleveland, OH	44101
Beaumont, TX	77707	Brooklyn Park, MN	55443	Cleveland, TN	37311
Beavercreek, OH	45434	Brook Park, OH	44142	Cleveland	44118
Beaverton, OR	97005	Brownsville, TX	78520	Heights, OH	
Bell, CA	90201	Brunswick, OH	44212	Clifton, NJ	07015
Belleville, IL	62220	Bryan, TX	77801	Clifton, IA	52732
Belleville, NJ	07109	Buena Park, CA	90622	Clovis, CA	93612
Bellevue, WA	98009	Buffalo, NY	14240	Clovis, NM	88101
Bellflower, CA	90706	Burbank, CA	91505	Coconut Grove, FL	33233
Bell Gardens, CA	90201	Burlingame, CA	94010	College Station, TX	77840
Bellingham, WA	98225	Burlington, IA	52601	Colorado	80901
Beloit, WI	53511	Burlington, NC	27215	Springs, CO	
Bergenfield, NJ	07621	Burlington, VT	05401	Columbia, MO	65201
Berkeley, CA	94704	Burnsville, MN	55337	Columbia, SC	29292
Berwyn, IL	60402	Burton, MI	48509	Columbia, TN	38401
Bessemer, AL	35020	Butte, MT	59701	Columbus, GA	31908
Bethel Park, PA	15102	Calumet City, IL	60409	Columbus, IN	47201
Bethesda, MD	20814	Camarillo, CA	93010	Columbus, MS	39701
Bethlehem, PA	18016	Cambridge, MA	02140	Columbus, OH	43216
Bettendorf, IA	52722	Camden, NJ	08101	Compton, CA	90220
Beverly, MA	01915	Campbell, CA	95008	Concord, CA	94520
Beverly Hills, CA	90210	Canton, OH	44711	Concord, NH	03301
Billings, MT	59101	Cape Coral, FL	33910	Coon Rapids, MN	55433
Biloxi, MS	39530	Cape Girardeau, MO	63701	Coral Gables, FL	33114
Binghamton, NY	13902	Carbondale, IL	62901	Coral Springs, FL	33065
Birmingham, AL	35203	Carlsbad, CA	92008	Corona, CA	91720
Bismarck, ND	58501	Carlsbad, NM	88220	Corpus Christi, TX	78469
Blacksburg, VA	24060	Carrollton, TX	75006	Corvallis, OR	97333
Blaine, MN	55434	Carson, CA	90745	Costa Mesa, CA	92626
Bloomfield, NJ	07003	Carson City, NV	89701	Council Bluffs, IA	51501
Bloomington, IL	61701	Casper, WY	82601	Covina, CA	91722
Bloomington, IN	47401	Cedar Falls, IA	50613	Covington, KY	41011
Bloomington, MN	55420	Cedar Rapids, IA	52401	Cranston, RI	02910

Crystal, MN	55428	Elmira, NY	14901	Galesburg, IL	61401
Culver City, CA	90230	El Monte, CA	91731	Galveston, TX	77550
Cumberland, MD	21502	El Paso, TX	79910	Gardena, CA	90247
Cupertino, CA	95014	Elyria, OH	44035	Garden City, MI	48135
Cuyahoga Falls, OH	44222	Emporia, KS	66801	Garden Grove, CA	92642
Cypress, CA	90630	Englewood, CO	80110	Garfield, NJ	07026
Dallas, TX	75260	Enid, OK	73701	Garfield Heights, OH	44125
Daly City, CA	94015	Erie, PA	16515	Garland, TX	75040
Danbury, CT	06810	Escondido, CA	92025	Gary, IN	46401
Danville, IL	61832	Euclid, OH	44112	Gastonia, NC	28052
Danville, VA	24541	Eugene, OR	97401	Glendale, AZ	85301
Davenport, IA	52802	Evanston, IL	60201	Glendale, CA	91209
Davis, CA	95616	Evansville, IN	47708	Glendora, CA	91740
Dayton, OH	45401	Everett, MA	02149	Glenview, IL	60025
Daytona Beach, FL	32114	Everett, WA	98203	Gloucester, MA	01930
Dearborn, MI	48120	Fairborn, OH	45324	Goldsboro, NC	27530
Dearborn Heights, MI	48127	Fairfield, CA	94533	Grand Forks, ND	58201
Decatur, AL	35602	Fairfield, OH	45014	Grand Island, NE	68802
Decatur, IL	62521	Fair Lawn, NJ	07410	Grand Junction, CO	81501
Deerfield Beach, FL	33441	Fall River, MA	02720	Grand Prairie, TX	75051
De Kalb, IL	60115	Fargo, ND	58102	Grand Rapids, MI	49501
Delray Beach, FL	33444	Farmington, NM	87401	Granite City, IL	62040
Del Rio, TX	78840	Fayetteville, AR	72701	Great Falls, MT	59401
Denton, TX	76201	Fayetteville, NC	28302	Greeley, CO	80631
Denver, CO	80201	Ferndale, MI	48220	Green Bay, WI	54303
Des Moines, IA	50318	Findlay, OH	45839	Greenfield, WI	53220
Des Plaines, IL	60018	Fitchburg, MA	01420	Greensboro, NC	27420
Detroit, MI	48233	Flagstaff, AZ	86001	Greenville, MS	38701
Dothan, AL	36303	Flint, MI	48502	Greenville, NC	27834
Downers Grove, IL	60515	Florence, AL	35631	Greenville, SC	29602
Downey, CA	90241	Florence, SC	29501	Gresham, OR	97030
Dubuque, IA	52001	Florissant, MO	63033	Grosse Pointe, MI	48230
Duluth, MN	55806	Fond du Lac, WI	54935	Gulfport, MS	39503
Duncanville, TX	75138	Fontana, CA	92335	Hackensack, NJ	07602
Dunedin, FL	32132	Fort Collins, CO	80521	Hagerstown, MD	21740
Durham, NC	27701	Fort Dodge, IA	50501	Hallandale, FL	33009
East Chicago, IN	46312	Fort Lauderdale, FL	33110	Haltom City, TX	76117
East Cleveland, OH	44112	Fort Lee, NJ	07024	Hamilton, OH	45011
East Detroit, MI	48021	Fort Myers, FL	33906	Hammond, IN	46320
East Lansing, MI	48823	Fort Pierce, FL	34981	Hampton, VA	23670
Easton, PA	18042	Fort Smith, AR	72901	Hanover Park, IL	60103
East Orange, NJ	07019	Fort Wayne, IN	46802	Harlingen, TX	78550
East Providence, RI	02914	Fort Worth, TX	76161	Harrisburg, PA	17107
East St. Louis, IL	62201	Frankfort, KY	40601	Hartford, CT	06101
Eau Claire, WI	54703	Frederick, MD	21701	Harvey, IL	60426
Edina, MN	55424	Fredericksburg, VA	22404	Hattiesburg, MS	39402
Edmond, OK	73034	Freeport, IL	61032	Haverhill, MA	01831
Edmonds, WA	98020	Freeport, NY	11520	Hawthorne, CA	90250
El Cajon, CA	92020	Fremont, CA	94538	Hayward, CA	94544
El Dorado, AR	71730	Fresno, CA	93706	Hazleton, PA	18201
Elgin, IL	60120	Fridley, MN	55432	Hempstead, NY	11551
Elizabeth, NJ	07207	Fullerton, CA	92634	Hialeah, FL	33010
Elk Grove, IL	60007	Gadsden, AL	35901	Highland, IN	46322
Elkhart, IN	46515	Gainesville, FL	32608	Highland Park, IL	60035
Elmhurst, IL	60126	Gaithersburg, MD	20877	Highland Park, MI	48203

High Point, NC	27260	Killeen, TX	76541	Long Branch, NJ	07740
Hillsboro, OR	97123	Kingsport, TN	37660	Longmont, CO	80501
Hilo, HI	96720	Kingston, NC	38501	Longview, TX	75602
Hobbs, NM	88240	Kingsville, TX	78363	Longview, WA	98632
Hoboken, NJ	07030	Kirkwood, MO	63122	Lorain, OH	44052
Hoffman Estates, IL	60195	Knoxville, TN	37950	Los Altos, CA	94022
Holland, MI	49423	Kokomo, IN	46902	Los Angeles, CA	90052
Hollywood, FL	33022	La Crosse, WI	54601	Los Gatos, CA	95030
Holyoke, MA	01040	Lafayette, IN	47901	Louisville, KY	40231
Honolulu, HI	96820	Lafayette, LA	70501	Loveland, CO	80538
Hopkinsville, KY	42240	La Habra, CA	90631	Lowell, MA	01853
Hot Springs, AR	71901	Lake Charles, LA	70601	Lubbock, TX	79402
Houma, LA	70360	Lakeland, FL	33805	Lufkin, TX	75901
Houston, TX	77201	Lakewood, CA	90714	Lynchburg, VA	24506
Huber Heights, OH	45424	Lakewood, CO	80215	Lynn, MA	01901
Huntington, WV	25704	Lakewood, OH	44107	Lynwood, CA	90262
Huntington Beach, CA	92647	Lake Worth, FL	33461	Macon, GA	31213
		La Mesa, CA	91941	Madison, WI	53714
Huntington Park, CA	90255	La Mirada, CA	90638	Madison Heights, MI	48071
Huntsville, AL	35813	Lancaster, CA	93534	Malden, MA	02148
Hurst, TX	76053	Lancaster, OH	43130	Manchester, NH	03103
Hutchinson, KS	67501	Lancaster, PA	17604	Manhattan, KS	66502
Idaho Falls, ID	83401	Lansing, IL	60438	Manhattan Beach, CA	90266
Independence, MO	64050	Lansing, MI	48924	Manitowoc, WI	54220
Indianapolis, IN	46206	La Puente, CA	91747	Mankato, MN	56001
Inglewood, CA	90311	Laredo, TX	78041	Mansfield, OH	44901
Inkster, MI	48141	Largo, FL	34640	Maple Heights, OH	44137
Iowa City, IA	52240	Las Cruces, NM	88001	Maplewood, MN	55109
Irvine, CA	92713	Las Vegas, NV	89199	Marietta, GA	30060
Irving, TX	75015	Lawrence, IN	46226	Marion, IN	46952
Irvington, NJ	07111	Lawrence, KS	66044	Marion, OH	43302
Ithaca, NY	14850	Lawrence, MA	04842	Marlborough, MA	01752
Jackson, MI	49201	Lawton, OK	73501	Marshalltown, IA	50158
Jackson, MS	39205	Leavenworth, KS	66048	Mason City, IA	50401
Jackson, TN	38301	Lebanon, PA	17042	Massillon, OH	44646
Jacksonville, FL	32203	Lee's Summit, MO	64063	Maywood, IL	60153
Jamestown, NY	14701	Leominster, MA	01453	McAllen, TX	78501
Janesville, WI	53545	Lewiston, ID	83501	McKeesport, PA	15134
Jefferson City, MO	65101	Lewiston, ME	04240	Medford, MA	02155
Jersey City, NJ	07303	Lexington, KY	40511	Medford, OR	97501
Johnson City, TN	37601	Lima, OH	45802	Melbourne, FL	32901
Johnstown, PA	15901	Lincoln, NE	68501	Melrose, MA	02176
Joliet, IL	60436	Lincoln Park, MI	48146	Memphis, TN	38101
Jonesboro, AR	72401	Linden, NJ	07036	Menlo Park, CA	94025
Joplin, MO	64801	Lindenhurst, NY	11757	Menomonee Falls, WI	53051
Kalamazoo, MI	49001	Little Rock, AR	72231	Mentor, OH	44060
Kankakee, IL	60901	Littleton, CO	70220	Merced, CA	95340
Kansas City, KS	66106	Livermore, CA	94550	Meriden, CT	06450
Kansas City, MO	64108	Livonia, MI	48150	Meridian, MS	39301
Kearny, NJ	07032	Lodi, CA	95240	Merrillville, IN	46410
Kenner, LA	70062	Logan, UT	84321	Mesa, AZ	85201
Kennewick, WA	99336	Lombard, IL	60148	Mesquite, TX	75149
Kenosha, WI	53140	Lompoc, CA	93436	Miami, FL	33152
Kent, OH	44240	Long Beach, CA	90809	Miami Beach, FL	33139
Kettering, OH	45429	Long Beach, NY	11561	Middletown, CT	06457

United States

Middletown, OH	45042	New Orleans, LA	70113	Oxnard, CA	93030
Midland, MI	48640	Newport, RI	02840	Pacifica, CA	94044
Midland, TX	79711	Newport Beach, CA	92660	Paducah, KY	42001
Midwest City, OK	73130	Newport News, VA	23607	Palatine, IL	66067
Milford, CT	06460	New Rochelle, NY	10802	Palm Springs, CA	92263
Milpitas, CA	95035	Newton, MA	02158	Palo Alto, CA	94303
Milwaukee, WI	53203	New York, NY	10199	Panama City, FL	32401
Minneapolis, MN	55401	Niagara Falls, NY	14302	Paramount, CA	90723
Minnetonka, MN	55345	Niles, IL	60648	Paramus, NJ	07652
Minot, ND	58701	Norfolk, VA	23501	Paris, TX	75460
Mishawaka, IN	46544	Normal, IL	61761	Parkersburg, WV	26101
Missoula, MT	59801	Norman, OK	73069	Park Ridge, IL	60068
Mobile, AL	36601	Norristown, PA	19401	Parma, OH	44129
Modesto, CA	95350	Northampton, MA	01060	Pasadena, CA	91109
Moline, IL	61265	Northbrook, IL	60062	Pasadena, TX	77501
Monroe, LA	71203	North Charleston, SC	29406	Pascagoula, MS	39567
Monroeville, PA	15146	North Chicago, IL	60064	Passaic, NJ	07055
Monrovia, CA	91016	North Las Vegas, NV	89030	Paterson, NJ	07510
Montclair, NJ	07042	North Little Rock, AR	72114	Pawtucket, RI	02860
Montebello, CA	90640	North Miami, FL	33261	Peabody, MA	01960
Monterey, CA	93940	North Miami	33160	Pembroke Pines, FL	33024
Monterey Park, CA	91754	Beach, FL		Pensacola, FL	32501
Montgomery, AL	36119	North Olmsted, OH	44070	Peoria, IL	61601
Moore, OK	73160	North Richland	76180	Perth Amboy, NJ	08861
Moorhead, MN	56560	Hills, TX		Petaluma, CA	94952
Morgantown, WV	26505	North Tonawanda, NY	14120	Petersburg, VA	23804
Mountainview, CA	94042	Norwalk, CA	90650	Phenix City, AL	36867
Mount Prospect, IL	60056	Norwalk, CT	06856	Philadelphia, PA	19104
Mount Vernon, NY	10551	Norwich, CT	06360	Phoenix, AZ	85027
Muncie, IN	47302	Norwood, OH	45212	Pico Rivera, CA	90660
Murfreesboro, TN	37130	Novato, CA	94947	Pine Bluff, AR	71601
Murray, UT	84107	Nutley, NJ	07110	Pinellas Park, FL	34665
Muskegon, MI	49440	Oak Forest, IL	60452	Pittsburgh, CA	94565
Muskogee, OK	74401	Oaklando, CA	94615	Pittsburgh, PA	15290
Nacogdoches, TX	75961	Oak Lawn, IL	60455	Pittsfield, MA	01201
Nampa, ID	83651	Oak Park, IL	60301	Placentia, CA	92670
Napa, CA	94558	Oak Park, MI	48237	Plainfield, NJ	07061
Naperville, IL	60540	Oak Ridge, TN	37830	Plano, TX	75074
Nashua, NH	03060	Ocala, FL	32678	Plantation, FL	33318
Nashville, TN	37229	Oceanside, CA	92054	Pleasant Hill, CA	94523
National City, CA	91950	Odessa, TX	79761	Pleasanton, CA	94566
Naugatuck, CT	06770	Ogden, UT	84401	Plum, PA	15239
New Albany, IN	47150	Oklahoma City, OK	73125	Plymouth, MN	55447
Newark, CA	94560	Olathe, KS	66061	Pocatello, ID	83201
Newark, DE	19711	Olympia, WA	98501	Pomona, CA	91766
Newark, NJ	07102	Omaha, NE	68108	Pompano Beach, FL	33060
Newark, OH	43055	Ontario, CA	91761	Ponca City, OK	74601
New Bedford, MA	02740	Orange, CA	92613	Pontiac, MI	48343
New Berlin, WI	53151	Orange, NJ	07051	Portage, IN	46368
New Britain, CT	06050	Orem, UT	84057	Port Arthur, TX	77640
New Brunswick, NJ	08901	Orlando, FL	32802	Port Huron, MI	48060
New Castle, PA	16108	Oshkosh, WI	54901	Portland, ME	04101
New Haven, CT	06511	Ottumwa, IA	52501	Portland, OR	97208
New Iberia, LA	70560	Overland Park, KS	66204	Portsmouth, NH	03801
New London, CT	06320	Owensboro, KY	43201	Portsmouth, OH	45662

Portsmouth, VA	23707	St. Cloud, MN	56301	Silver Springs, MD	20907
Poughkeepsie, NY	12601	St. Joseph, MO	64501	Simi Valley, CA	93065
Providence, RI	02904	St. Louis, MO	63155	Sioux City, IA	51101
Provo, UT	84601	St. Louis Park, MN	55426	Sioux Falls, SD	57101
Pueblo, CO	81003	St. Paul, MN	55101	Skokie, IL	60076
Quincy, IL	62301	St. Petersburg, FL	33730	Slidell, LA	70458
Quincy, MA	02269	Salem, MA	01970	Somerville, MA	02143
Racine, WI	53403	Salem, OR	97301	Somerville, NJ	08876
Rahway, NJ	07065	Salina, KS	67401	South Bend, IN	46624
Raleigh, NC	27611	Salinas, CA	93907	South Euclid, OH	44121
Rancho Cucamonga, CA	91730	Salt Lake City, UT	84199	Southfield, MI	48037
		San Angelo, TX	76902	South Gate, CA	90280
Rancho Palos Verdes, CA	90274	San Antonio, TX	78284	Southgate, MI	48195
		San Bernardino, CA	92403	South San Francisco, CA	94080
Rapid City, SD	57701	San Bruno, CA	94066		
Raytown, MO	64133	San Buenaventura (Ventura), CA	93001	Sparks, NV	89431
Reading, PA	19612			Spartanburg, SC	29301
Redding, CA	96001	San Clemente, CA	92672	Spokane, WA	99210
Redlands, CA	92373	San Diego, CA	92199	Springfield, IL	62703
Redondo Beach, CA	90277	Sandusky, OH	44870	Springfield, MA	01101
Redwood City, CA	94064	Sandy, UT	84070	Springfield, MO	65801
Reno, NV	89510	San Francisco, CA	94188	Springfield, OH	45501
Renton, WA	98058	San Gabriel, CA	91776	Springfield, OR	97477
Revere, MA	02151	San Jose, CA	95101	Stamford, CT	06904
Rialto, CA	92376	San Leandro, CA	94577	State College, PA	16801
Richardson, TX	75080	San Luis Obispo, CA	93401	Sterling Heights, MI	48311
Richfield, MN	55423	San Mateo, CA	94402	Steubenville, OH	43952
Richland, WA	99352	San Rafael, CA	94901	Stillwater, OK	74074
Richmond, CA	94802	Santa Ana, CA	92799	Stockton, CA	95208
Richmond, IN	47374	Santa Barbara, CA	93102	Stow, OH	44224
Richmond, VA	23232	Santa Clara, CA	95051	Strongsville, OH	44136
Ridgewood, NJ	07450	Santa Cruz, CA	95060	Suffolk, VA	23434
Riverside, CA	92507	Santa Fe, NM	87501	Sunnyvale, CA	94086
Riviera Beach, FL	33404	Santa Maria, CA	93454	Sunrise, FL	33345
Roanoke, VA	24022	Santa Monica, CA	90406	Superior, WI	54880
Rochester, MI	48308	Santa Rosa, CA	95402	Syracuse, NY	13220
Rochester, MN	55901	Sarasota, FL	34230	Tacoma, WA	98413
Rochester, NY	14692	Saratoga, CA	95070	Tallahassee, FL	32301
Rockford, IL	61125	Savannah, GA	31402	Tamarac, FL	33320
Rock Hill, SC	29730	Sayreville, NJ	08872	Tampa, FL	33630
Rock Island, IL	61201	Schaumburg, IL	60194	Taunton, MA	02780
Rockville, MD	20850	Schenectady, NY	12305	Taylor, MI	48180
Rockville Center, NY	11570	Scottsdale, AZ	85251	Tempe, AZ	85282
Rocky Mount, NC	27801	Scranton, PA	18505	Temple, TX	76501
Rome, GA	30161	Seal Beach, CA	90740	Terre Haute, IN	47808
Rome, NY	13440	Seaside, CA	93955	Texarkana, TX	75501
Rosemead, CA	91770	Seattle, WA	98109	Texas City, TX	75590
Roseville, MI	48066	Selma, AL	36701	Thornton, CO	80229
Roseville, MN	55113	Shaker Heights, OH	44120	Thousand Oaks, CA	91360
Roswell, NM	88201	Shawnee Mission, KS	66202	Tinley Park, IL	60477
Royal Oak, MI	48068	Shawnee, OK	74801	Titusville, FL	32780
Sacramento, CA	95813	Sheboygan, WI	53081	Toledo, OH	43601
Saginaw, MI	48065	Shelton, CT	06484	Topeka, KS	66603
St. Charles, MO	63301	Sherman, TX	75090	Torrance, CA	90510
St. Clair Shores, MI	48080	Shreveport, LA	71102	Torrington, CT	06790

United States

Trenton, NJ	08650	Walnut Creek, CA	94596	Wheaton, IL	60187
Troy, MI	48099	Waltham, MA	02154	Wheat Ridge, CO	80033
Troy, NY	12180	Warner Robins, GA	31093	Wheeling, WV	26003
Tucson, AZ	85726	Warren, MI	48090	White Plains, NY	10602
Tulsa, OK	74103	Warren, OH	44481	Whittier, CA	90605
Turlock, CA	95380	Warwick, RI	02886	Wichita, KS	67276
Tuscaloosa, AL	35401	Washington, DC	20013	Wichita Falls, TX	76307
Tustin, CA	92680	Waterbury, CT	06701	Wilkes-Barre, PA	18701
Twin Falls, ID	83301	Waterloo, IA	50701	Williamsport, PA	17701
Tyler, TX	75712	Watertown, NY	13601	Wilmette, IL	60091
Union City, CA	94587	Waukegan, IL	60085	Wilmington, DE	19850
Union City, NJ	07087	Waukesha, WI	53186	Wilmington, NC	28402
University City, MO	63130	Wausau, WI	54401	Wilson, NC	27893
Upland, CA	91786	Wauwatosa, WI	53213	Winona, MN	55987
Upper Arlington, OH	43221	Weirton, WV	26062	Winston-Salem, NC	27102
Urbana, IL	61801	West Allis, WI	53214	Woburn, MA	01801
Utica, NY	13504	West Covina, CA	91793	Woodland, CA	95695
Vacaville, CA	95688	Westfield, MA	01085	Woonsocket, RI	02895
Valdosta, GA	31601	Westfield, NJ	07090	Worcester, MA	01613
Vallejo, CA	94590	West Haven, CT	06516	Wyandotte, MI	48192
Valley Stream, NY	11580	West Jordan, UT	84084	Wyoming, MI	49509
Vancouver, WA	98661	Westland, MI	48185	Yakima, WA	98903
Vicksburg, MS	39180	West Lafayette, IN	47906	Yonkers, NY	10702
Victoria, TX	77901	West Memphis, AR	72301	Yorba Linda, CA	92686
Vineland, NJ	08360	West Mifflin, PA	15122	York, PA	17405
Virginia Beach, VA	23450	Westminster, CA	92683	Youngstown, OH	44501
Visalia, CA	93277	Westminster, CO	80030	Ypsilanti, MI	48197
Vista, CA	92083	West New York, NJ	07093	Yuma, AZ	85364
Waco, TX	76702	West Orange, NJ	07052	Zanesville, OH	43701
Walla Walla, WA	99362	West Palm Beach, FL	33406		

TWO-LETTER STATE AND TERRITORY ABBREVIATIONS

Alabama	AL	Kentucky	KY	Ohio	OH
Alaska	AK	Louisiana	LA	Oklahoma	OK
American Samoa	AS	Maine	ME	Oregon	OR
Arizona	AZ	Marshall Islands	MH	Palau	PW
Arkansas	AR	Maryland	MD	Pennsylvania	PA
California	CA	Massachusetts	MA	Puerto Rico	PR
Colorado	CO	Michigan	MI	Rhode Island	RI
Connecticut	CT	Minnesota	MN	South Carolina	SC
Delaware	DE	Mississippi	MS	South Dakota	SD
District of Columbia	DC	Missouri	MO	Tennessee	TN
Federated States of	FM	Montana	MT	Texas	TX
Micronesia		Nebraska	NE	Utah	UT
Florida	FL	Nevada	NV	Vermont	VT
Georgia	GA	New Hampshire	NH	Virginia	VA
Guam	GU	New Jersey	NJ	Virgin Islands	VI
Hawaii	HI	New Mexico	NM	Washington	WA
Idaho	ID	New York	NY	West Virginia	WV
Illinois	IL	North Carolina	NC	Wisconsin	WI
Indiana	IN	North Dakota	ND	Wyoming	WY
Iowa	IA	Northern Mariana	MP		
Kansas	KS	Islands			

GEOGRAPHIC DIRECTIONAL ABBREVIATIONS

North	N	West	W	Southwest	SW
East	E	Northeast	NE	Northwest	NW
South	S	Southeast	SE		

STREET DESIGNATORS (STREET SUFFIXES)

Alley	ALY	Forge	FRG	Path	PATH
Annex	ANX	Fork	FRK	Pike	PIKE
Arcade	ARC	Forks	FRKS	Pines	PNES
Avenue	AVE	Fort	FT	Place	PL
Bayou	BYU	Freeway	FWY	Plains	PLNS
Beach	BCH	Gardens	GDNS	Plaza	PLZ
Bend	BND	Gateway	GTWY	Point	PT
Bluff	BLF	Glen	GLN	Port	PRT
Bottom	BTM	Green	GRN	Prairie	PR
Boulevard	BLVD	Grove	GRV	Radial	RADL
Branch	BR	Harbor	HBR	Ranch	RNCH
Bridge	BRG	Haven	HVN	Rapids	RPDS
Brook	BRK	Heights	HTS	Rest	RST
Burg	BG	Highway	HWY	Ridge	RDG
Bypass	BYP	Hill	HL	River	RIV
Camp	CP	Hills	HLS	Road	RD
Canyon	CYN	Hollow	HOLW	Row	ROW
Cape	CPE	Inlet	INLT	Run	RUN
Causeway	CSWY	Island	IS	Shoal	SHL
Center	CTR	Islands	ISS	Shoals	SHLS
Circle	CIR	Isle	ISLE	Shore	SHR
Cliffs	CLFS	Junction	JCT	Shores	SHRS
Club	CLB	Key	KY	Spring	SPG
Corner	COR	Knolls	KNLS	Springs	SPGS
Corners	CORS	Lake	LK	Spur	SPUR
Course	CRSE	Lakes	LKS	Square	SQ
Court	CT	Landing	LNDG	Station	STA
Courts	CTS	Lane	LN	Stream	STRM
Cove	CV	Light	LGT	Street	ST
Creek	CRK	Loaf	LF	Summit	SMT
Crescent	CRES	Locks	LCKS	Terrace	TER
Crossing	XING	Lodge	LDG	Trace	TRCE
Dale	DL	Loop	LOOP	Track	TRAK
Dam	DM	Mall	MALL	Trail	TRL
Divide	DV	Manor	MNR	Trailer	TRLR
Drive	DR	Meadows	MDWS	Tunnel	TUNL
Estates	EST	Mill	ML	Turnpike	TPKE
Expressway	EXPY	Mills	MLS	Union	UN
Extension	EXT	Mission	MSN	Valley	VLY
Fall	FL	Mount	MT	Viaduct	VIA
Falls	FLS	Mountain	MTN	View	VW
Ferry	FRY	Neck	NCK	Village	VLG
Field	FLD	Orchard	ORCH	Ville	VL
Fields	FLDS	Oval	OVAL	Vista	VIS
Flats	FLT	Park	PARK	Walk	WALK
Ford	FRD	Parkway	PKY	Way	WAY
Forest	FRST	Pass	PASS	Wells	WLS

United States

MAJOR DAILY NEWSPAPERS

NATIONAL

Christian Science Monitor
One Norway St.
Boston, MA 02115-3195
http://www.csmonitor.com

USA Today
1000 Wilson Blvd.
Arlington, VA 22209
http://www.usatoday.com

Wall Street Journal
200 Liberty St.
New York, NY 10281
http://www.wsj.com

LOCAL (BY STATE)

Alabama
Birmingham News
2200 4th Ave. N.
Birmingham, AL 35203

Birmingham Post-Herald
P.O. Box 2553
Birmingham, AL 35202-2553

Montgomery Advertiser
P.O. Box 1000
Montgomery, AL 36101-1000

Alaska
Anchorage Daily News
P.O. Box 149001
Anchorage, AK 99514-9001

Arizona
Arizona Republic
P.O. Box 1950
Phoenix, AZ 85001-1950

Arizona Daily Star
P.O. Box 26807
Tucson, AZ 85726-6807

Phoenix Gazette
P.O. Box 1950
Phoenix, AZ 85001-1950

Arkansas
Arkansas Democrat-Gazette
Capitol Avenue and Scott
P.O. Box 2221
Little Rock, AR 72203

California
Fresno Bee
3425 N. 1st St.
Fresno, CA 93726-6819

Los Angeles Times
Times Mirror Square
Los Angeles, CA 90012

Sacramento Bee
2100 Q St.
P.O. Box 15779
Sacramento, CA 95852

San Diego Union-Tribune
350 Camino de la Reina
San Diego, CA 92108

San Francisco Chronicle
901 Mission St.
San Francisco, CA 94103

San Francisco Examiner
110 Fifth St.
San Francisco, CA 94103

Colorado
Denver Post
1560 Broadway
Denver, CO 80202

Rocky Mountain News
400 West Colfax Ave.
Denver, CO 80201

Connecticut
Hartford Courant
285 Broad St.
Hartford, CT 06115-2510

New Haven Register
40 Sargent Dr.
New Haven, CT 06511

Delaware
News-Journal
P.O. Box 19850
Wilmington, DE 19850

District of Columbia

Washington Post
1150 15th St., NW
Washington, DC 20071

Florida

Florida Times Union
One Riverside Ave.
Jacksonville, FL 32202-4924

Fort Lauderdale Sun-Sentinel
200 E. Las Olas Blvd.
Ft. Lauderdale, FL 33301-2293

Miami Herald
One Herald Plaza
Miami, FL 33132-1693

Orlando Sentinel
633 N. Orange Ave.
Orlando, FL 32801

St. Petersburg Times
P.O. Box 1121
St. Petersburg, FL 33701

Georgia

Atlanta Journal and Constitution
72 Marietta St., NW
Atlanta, GA 30303

Hawaii

Honolulu Advertiser
605 Kapiolani Blvd.
Honolulu, HI 96813

Honolulu Star Bulletin
P.O. Box 3080
Honolulu, HI 96802

Idaho

Idaho Statesman
1200 N. Curtis Rd.
Boise, ID 83707

Illinois

Chicago Sun-Times
401 N. Wabash Ave.
Chicago, IL 60611

Chicago Tribune
435 N. Michigan Ave.
Chicago, IL 60611

Indiana

Indianapolis Star News
307 N. Pennsylvania St.
Indianapolis, IN 46204-1811

Post-Tribune
1065 Broadway St.
Gary, IN 46402-2998

South Bend Tribune
225 W. Colfax Ave.
South Bend, IN 46626-0001

Iowa

Des Moines Register
P.O. Box 957
Des Moines, IA 50304

Kansas

Topeka Capital-Journal
616 Jefferson St.
Topeka, KS 66607-1197

Wichita Eagle
825 E. Douglas St.
Wichita, KS 67201

Kentucky

Courier-Journal
525 W. Broadway
Louisville, KY 40202-2137

Herald-Leader
100 Midland Ave.
Lexington, KY 40508

Louisiana

The Advocate
525 Lafayette St.
Baton Rouge, LA 70821

Times-Picayune
3800 Howard Ave.
New Orleans, LA 0140

Maine

Daily News
491 Main St.
Bangor, ME 04402

Portland Press Herald
P.O. Box 1460
390 Congress St.
Portland, ME 04101

Maryland

The Baltimore Sun
501 N. Calvert St.
Baltimore, MD 21278-0001

Massachusetts

Boston Globe
135 Morrissey Blvd.
Boston, MA 02107

Boston Herald
1 Herald Square
Boston, MA 02106

Michigan

Detroit Free Press
321 W. Lafayette Blvd.
Detroit, MI 48226

Detroit News
615 W. Lafayette Blvd.
Detroit, MI 48226

Republican Gerald Ford is the only unelected president. President Nixon appointed him vice president after Spiro Agnew resigned. Ford then assumed the presidency after Nixon's resignation.

Minnesota

St. Paul Pioneer Press
345 Cedar St.
St. Paul, MN 55101-1057

Star Tribune
425 Portland Ave.
Minneapolis, MN 55488-0001

Mississippi

Clarion Ledger
311 E. Pearl St.
Jackson, MS 39205

Missouri

Kansas City Star
1729 Grand Ave.
Kansas City, MO 64108

Post-Dispatch
900 N. Tucker Blvd.
St. Louis, MO 63101

Montana

Billings Gazette
401 N. Broadway
Billings, MT 59101-1243

Great Falls Tribune
P.O. Box 5468
Great Falls, MT 59403

Nebraska

Lincoln Journal
926 P St.
Lincoln, NE 68501

Lincoln Star
926 P St.
Lincoln, NE 68508

World-Herald
World-Herald Square
Omaha, NE 68102

Nevada

Las Vegas Review-Journal
1111 W. Bonanza
Las Vegas, NV 89125

Las Vegas Sun
800 S. Valley View
Box 4275
Las Vegas, NV 89127

Reno Gazette Journal
P.O. Box 22000
Reno, NV 89520-2000

New Hampshire

Union-Leader
P.O. Box 9555
Manchester, NH 03108

United States

New Jersey

Asbury Park Press
3601 Hwy. 66
Neptune, NJ 07754

Record
150 River St.
Hackensack, NJ 07601

Star-Ledger
Star-Ledger Plaza
Newark, NJ 07102-1200

Why is American paper currency known as "greenbacks"? During the Civil War, the cash-strapped federal government selected the distinctive green color in use today because it was cheapest ink available.

New Mexico

Albuquerque Journal
7777 Jefferson NE
Albuquerque, NM 87109

Albuquerque Tribune
7777 Jefferson NE
Albuquerque, NM 87109

New York

Buffalo News
One News Plaza
P.O. Box 100
Buffalo, NY 14240

Newsday
235 Pinelawn Rd.
Melville, NY 11747-4250

New York Daily News
450 W. 33rd St.
New York, NY 10001

New York Post
1211 Sixth Ave.
New York, NY 10036

New York Times
229 W. 43rd St.
New York, NY 10036-3913

North Carolina

Observer
P.O. Box 32188-28232
Charlotte, NC 28232

News & Observer
215 S. McDowell St.
Raleigh, NC 27602

North Dakota

Bismark Tribune
P.O. Box 1498
707 E. Front Ave.
Bismark, ND 58502-1498

Ohio

Akron Beacon Journal
44 E. Exchange St.
Akron, OH 44328-0001

Blade
541 Superior St.
Toledo, OH 43660-0001

Cincinnati Enquirer
312 Elm St.
Cincinnati, OH 45202-2410

Cincinnati Post
125 E. Court St.
Cincinnati, OH 45202-1211

Cleveland Plain Dealer
1801 Superior Ave.
Cleveland, OH 44114-2198

Columbus Dispatch
34 S. Third St.
Columbus, OH 43215

Daily News
Fourth and Ludlow Sts.
Dayton, OH 45401

Oklahoma

Oklahoman
9000 N. Broadway
Oklahoma City, OK 73114

Tulsa World
P.O. Box 1770
Tulsa, OK 74102

United States

Oregon

The Oregonian
1320 SW Broadway
Portland, OR 97201-3469

Pennsylvania

Philadelphia Daily News
400 N. Broad St.
Philadelphia, PA 19101

Philadelphia Inquirer
400 N. Broad St.
Philadelphia, PA 19101

Pittsburgh Post-Gazette
P.O. Box 957
50 Boulevard of Allies
Pittsburgh, PA 15222

Pittsburgh Press
34 Boulevard of Allies
Pittsburgh, PA 15230

Rhode Island

Journal-Bulletin
75 Fountain St.
Providence, RI 02902

South Carolina

Post & Courier
134 Columbus St.
Charleston, SC 29403-4800

The State
P.O. Box 1333
Columbia, SC 29202

South Dakota

Argus Leader
P.O. Box 5034
Sioux Falls, SD 57117-5034

Tennessee

Commercial Appeal
495 Union Ave.
Memphis, TN 38103-3221

Nashville Banner
1100 Broadway
Nashville, TN 37203-3116

News-Sentinel
204 W. Church Ave.
Knoxville, TN 37902-1612

Tennessean
1100 Broadway
Nashville, TN 37203-3116

Texas

Austin American-Statesman
P.O. Box 670
Austin, TX 78767

Dallas Morning News
Communications Center
Dallas, TX 75265

Express-News
P.O. Box 2171
San Antonio, TX 78297

Fort Worth Star-Telegram
400 W. 7th St.
Fort Worth, TX 76102

Houston Chronicle
801 Texas Ave.
Houston, TX 7700

Houston Post
4747 Southwest Fwy.
Houston, TX 77027

Utah

Deseret News
30 E. First St.
Salt Lake City, UT 84110

Salt Lake Tribune
143 S. Main St.
Salt Lake City, UT 84111

Vermont

Free Press
191 College St.
Burlington, VT 05401

Virginia

Virginian-Pilot
150 W. Brambleton Ave.
Norfolk, VA 23510

Richmond Times-Dispatch
P.O. Box 85333
Richmond, VA 23293-1000

United States

Washington

Seattle Post-Intelligencer
101 Elliott Ave., W
Seattle, WA 98119

Seattle Times
P.O. Box 70
Seattle, WA 98111-1070

West Virginia

Herald Dispatch
P.O. Box 2017
946 Fifth Ave.
Huntington, WV 25720

News-Register
1500 Main St.
Wheeling, WV 26003

Wisconsin

Milwaukee Journal Sentinel
333 W. State St.
Milwaukee, WI 53203-1305

State Journal
P.O. Box 8058
Madison, WI 53708

Wyoming

Wyoming Tribune-Eagle
702 W. Lincolnway
Cheyenne, WY 82001

ADDITIONAL SOURCES OF INFORMATION

MAGAZINES

NEWSMAGAZINES

Newsweek
251 W. 57th St.
New York, NY 10019
http://www.newsweek.com

Time
1271 Avenue of the Americas
New York, NY 10020
http://www.pathfinder.com

U.S. News & World Report
2400 N St., NW
Washington, DC 20037
http://www.usnews.com

Harper's Magazine
666 Broadway, 11th Floor
New York, NY 10012
http://www.harpers.org

PUBLIC, SOCIAL, AND POLITICAL AFFAIRS

Mother Jones
731 Mission St.
San Francisco, CA 94103
http://www.motherjones.com

The Nation
72 Fifth Ave.
New York, NY 10011
http://www.thenation.com

The New Republic
1220 19th St., NW
Washington, DC 20036
http://www.enews.com/magazines/tnr

BOOKS

Ayers, Edward L., et al. *American Passages: The History of the United States,* 2 vols. New York: Harcourt Inc., 2000.

Barone, Michael, Grant Ujifusa, and Richard E. Cohen. *The Almanac of American Politics 1998.* Times Books, 1997.

Congress and the Nation. Congressional Quarterly, published every four years.

Congressional Quarterly Almanac. Congressional Quarterly, annual.

Congressional Quarterly Weekly. Congressional Quarterly, weekly.

Consumer's Resource Handbook. U.S. Office of Consumer Affairs, latest edition.

Flags of America. 2nd ed. National Flag Foundation, 1994.

Foner, Eric, and John A. Garraty, eds. *The Reader's Companion to American History.* Houghton Mifflin, 1991.

Garwood, Alfred N. *Almanac of the Fifty States.* Information Publication, 1987.

Hatch, Jane M. *The American Book of Days.* 3rd ed. H. W. Wilson, 1978.

Henretta, James A., et al. *America's History,* 4th edition, 2 vols. New York: Bedford/St. Martin's, 2000.

Kane, Joseph Nathan. *Nicknames and Sobriquets of U.S. Cities, States, and Countries.* 3rd ed. Scarecrow Press, 1979.

Lesko, Matthew. *Information U.S.A.* Viking, 1986.

Norton, Mary Beth, et al. *A People and a Nation,* 6th edition, 2 vols. New York: Houghton Mifflin, 2001.

Schlesinger, Arthur M., Jr., ed. *The Almanac of American History.* Putnam, 1984.

Shearer, Benjamin F., and Barbara S. Shearer. *State Names, Seals, Flags and Symbols: A Historical Guide.* Greenwood, 1994.

Statistical Abstract of the United States. U.S. Bureau of the Census, annual.

Urdang, Laurence, ed. *The Timetables of American History.* Touchstone, 1996.

United States

26

THE WORLD

COUNTRIES OF THE WORLD

Afghanistan
Area: 647,500 km² (249,999 mi²)
Capital: Kabul
Government: In transition
Population: 25,888,797
Languages: Pushtu, Afghan Persian, Turkic
Religions: Sunni Muslim, Shi'a Muslim

Albania
Area: 28,750 km² (11,100 mi²)
Capital: Tirana
Government: Republic
Population: 3,490,435
Languages: Albanian, Greek
Religions: Muslim, Albanian Orthodox, Roman
   Catholic

Algeria
Area: 2,381,740 km² (919,590 mi²)
Capital: Algiers
Government: Republic
Population: 31,193,917
Languages: Arabic, French, Berber dialects
Religion: Sunni Muslim

Andorra
Area: 450 km² (174 mi²)
Capital: Andorra la Vella
Government: Coprincipality of France and Spain
Population: 66,824
Languages: Catalan, French, Castilian
Religion: Roman Catholic

Angola
Area: 1,246,700 km² (481,351 mi²)
Capital: Luanda
Government: Republic
Population: 10,145,267
Languages: Portuguese, Bantu dialects
Religions: Indigenous beliefs, Roman Catholic,
   Protestant

Anguilla
Area: 91 km² (35 mi²)
Capital: The Valley
Government: Dependent territory of United Kingdom
Population: 11,797
Language: English
Religions: Anglican, Methodist

Antarctica
Area: 14,000,000 km² (5,500,000 mi²)
Capital: None
Government: Various nations—including Argentina,
   Australia, Chile, France, New Zealand, Norway, and
   United Kingdom—claim areas of the continent;
   Antarctic Treaty of 1959, signed by 42 nations, places
   these claims in abeyance and stipulates peaceful uses
   of Antarctica.
Population: No indigenous inhabitants; seasonal
   population of researchers averages about 4,000 in
   summer and 1,000 in winter.

Antigua and Barbuda
Area: 440 km² (170 mi²)
Capital: Saint John's
Government: Parliamentary democracy affiliated with
   United Kingdom
Population: 66,464
Languages: English, local dialects
Religions: Anglican, Methodist, Roman Catholic

Argentina
Area: 2,766,890 km² (1,068,296 mi²)
Capital: Buenos Aires
Government: Republic
Population: 36,955,182
Languages: Spanish, English, Italian
Religions: Roman Catholic, Protestant, Jewish

Armenia
Area: 29,283 km² (11,306 mi²)
Capital: Yerevan
Government: Presidential republic
Population: 3,344,336
Languages: Armenian, Russian
Religion: Armenian Orthodox

Aruba
Area: 193 km² (75 mi²)
Capital: Oranjestad
Government: Independent territory of the Netherlands
Population: 69,539
Languages: Dutch, Papiamento, Spanish, English
Religions: Roman Catholic, Protestant

Australia
Area: 7,686,850 km² (2,967,893 mi²)
Capital: Canberra
Government: Federal parliamentary state affiliated with
   Great Britain
Population: 19,164,620
Languages: English, aboriginal languages
Religions: Anglican, Roman Catholic, other Protestant
   faiths

Austria
Area: 83,850 km² (32,374 mi²)
Capital: Vienna
Government: Federal republic
Population: 8,131,111
Language: German
Religions: Roman Catholic, Protestant

The World

Azerbaijan
Area: 86,506 km² (33,400 mi²)
Capital: Baku
Government: Parliamentary republic
Population: 7,748,163
Languages: Azeri, Russian
Religions: Muslim, Orthodox

If there were only 100 people in the world, half would live in just 5 countries: 21 in China, 15 in India, 5 in the former Soviet Union, 5 in the United States, and 4 in Indonesia.

Bahamas
Area: 13,940 km² (5,382 mi²)
Capital: Nassau
Government: Independent commonwealth affiliated with United Kingdom
Population: 294,982
Languages: English, Creole
Religions: Baptist, Anglican, Roman Catholic, other Protestant faiths

Bahrain
Area: 620 km² (239 mi²)
Capital: Manama
Government: Monarchy
Population: 634,137
Languages: Arabic, English, Farsi, Urdu
Religions: Shi'a Muslim, Sunni Muslim

Bangladesh
Area: 144,000 km² (55,598 mi²)
Capital: Dhaka
Government: Republic
Population: 129,194,224
Languages: Bangla, English
Religions: Muslim, Hindu

Barbados
Area: 460 km² (166 mi²)
Capital: Bridgetown
Government: Parliamentary democracy affiliated with United Kingdom
Population: 274,059
Language: English
Religions: Anglican, Pentecostal, Methodist, Roman Catholic

Barbuda
See **Antigua and Barbuda.**

Belarus
Area: 207,718 km² (80,200 mi²)
Capital: Minsk
Government: Constitutional republic
Population: 10,366,719
Languages: Byelorussian, Russian
Religions: Russian Orthodox, Baptist

Belgium
Area: 30,520 km² (11,784 mi²)
Capital: Brussels
Government: Constitutional monarchy
Population: 10,241,506
Languages: Flemish, French
Religions: Roman Catholic, Protestant

Belize
Area: 22,960 km² (8,865 mi²)
Capital: Belmopan
Government: Parliamentary democracy affiliated with United Kingdom
Population: 249,183
Languages: English, Spanish, Maya, Garifuna
Religions: Roman Catholic, Anglican, Methodist

Benin
Area: 112,620 km² (43,483 mi²)
Capital: Porto-Novo
Government: Multiparty democracy
Population: 6,395,919
Languages: French, Fon, Yoruba, tribal dialects
Religions: Indigenous beliefs, Muslim, Christian

Bermuda
Area: 50 km² (19 mi²)
Capital: Hamilton
Government: Dependent territory of United Kingdom
Population: 63,022
Language: English
Religions: Anglican, Roman Catholic, African Methodist

Bhutan
Area: 47,000 km² (18,147 mi²)
Capital: Thimphu
Government: Monarchy
Population: 2,005,222
Languages: Dzongkha, other Tibetan dialects, Nepalese dialects
Religions: Lamaistic Buddhist, Hindu

Bolivia
Area: 1,098,580 km² (424,162 mi²)
Capitals: La Paz and Sucre
Government: Republic
Population: 8,152,620
Languages: Spanish, Quechua, Aymara
Religions: Roman Catholic, Protestant

Bosnia and Herzegovina
Area: 51,129 km² (19,741 mi²)
Capital: Sarajevo
Government: Republic
Population: 3,835,777
Languages: Serbo-Croatian
Religions: Muslim, Serbian Orthodox, Roman Catholic

Botswana
Area: 600,370 km² (231,803 mi²)
Capital: Gaborone
Government: Parliamentary republic
Population: 1,576,470
Languages: English, Setswana
Religions: Indigenous beliefs, Christian

Brazil
Area: 8,511,970 km² (3,286,472 mi²)
Capital: Brasília
Government: Federal republic
Population: 172,860,370
Languages: Portuguese, Spanish, English, French
Religion: Roman Catholic

British Virgin Islands
Area: 150 km² (58 mi²)
Capital: Road Town
Government: Dependent territory of United Kingdom
Population: 20,353
Language: English
Religions: Methodist, Anglican, other Protestant faiths, Roman Catholic

Brunei
Area: 5,770 km² (2,228 mi²)
Capital: Bandar Seri Begawan
Government: Constitutional sultanate
Population: 336,376
Languages: Malay, English, Chinese
Religions: Muslim, Buddhist, Christian, indigenous beliefs

Bulgaria
Area: 110,910 km² (42,822 mi²)
Capital: Sofia
Government: Emerging democracy
Population: 7,796,694
Language: Bulgarian
Religions: Bulgarian Orthodox, Muslim, Jewish, Roman Catholic

Burkina Faso
Area: 274,200 km² (105,869 mi²)
Capital: Ouagadougou
Government: Parliamentary republic
Population: 11,946,065
Languages: French, Sudanic tribal dialects
Religions: Muslim, indigenous beliefs, Christian

Burma
See **Myanmar.**

Burundi
Area: 27,830 km² (10,745 mi²)
Capital: Bujumbura
Government: Republic
Population: 6,054,714
Languages: Kirundi, French, Swahili
Religions: Roman Catholic, indigenous beliefs, Protestant, Muslim

Cambodia
Area: 181,040 km² (69,900 mi²)
Capital: Phnom Penh
Government: Constitutional monarchy
Population: 12,212,306
Languages: Khmer, French
Religions: Theravada Buddhist

Cameroon
Area: 475,440 km² (183,567 mi²)
Capital: Yaoundé
Government: Unitary republic
Population: 15,421,937
Languages: English, French, African languages
Religions: Indigenous beliefs, Christian, Muslim

Canada
Area: 9,976,140 km² (3,851,788 mi²)
Capital: Ottawa
Government: Confederation, with parliamentary democracy
Population: 31,278,097
Languages: English, French
Religions: Roman Catholic, United Church, Anglican

Cape Verde
Area: 4,030 km² (1,556 mi²)
Capital: Praia
Government: Republic
Population: 401,343
Languages: Portuguese, Crioulo
Religions: Roman Catholic and indigenous beliefs

Cayman Islands
Area: 260 km² (100 mi²)
Capital: George Town
Government: Dependent territory of United Kingdom
Population: 34,763
Language: English
Religions: United Church, Anglican, Baptist, Roman Catholic

Central African Republic
Area: 622,980 km² (240,533 mi²)
Capital: Bangui
Government: Military republic
Population: 3,512,751
Languages: French, Sangho, Arabic, Hunsa, Swahili
Religions: Christian (with animist beliefs), indigenous beliefs, Muslim

Chad
Area: 1,284,000 km² (495,752 mi²)
Capital: N'Djamena
Government: Republic
Population: 8,824,504
Languages: French, Arabic, Sara, Sango
Religions: Muslim, Christian, indigenous beliefs/animism

Chile
Area: 756,950 km² (292,258 mi²)
Capital: Santiago
Government: Republic
Population: 15,152,797
Language: Spanish
Religions: Roman Catholic, Protestant

China
Area: 9,596,960 km² (3,705,386 mi²)
Capital: Beijing
Government: Communist
Population: 1,261,832,482
Languages: Mandarin, Yue, Wu, Minbei, Minnan, Xiang, Gan, Hakka dialects, minority languages
Religions: Officially atheist; Confucianist, Taoist, Buddhist, Muslim, Christian

Christmas Island
Area: 135 km² (52 mi²)
Capital: The Settlement
Government: Territory of Australia
Population: 2,195
Language: English
Religions: Buddhist, Muslim, Christian

Colombia
Area: 1,138,910 km² (439,733 mi²)
Capital: Bogotá
Government: Republic
Population: 39,685,655
Language: Spanish
Religion: Roman Catholic

Comoros
Area: 2,170 km² (838 mi²)
Capital: Moroni
Government: Independent republic
Population: 578,400

Languages: Arabic, French, Cormorian
Religions: Sunni Muslim, Roman Catholic

Congo, Democratic Republic of (formerly Zaire)
Area: 2,345,410 km² (905,563 mi²)
Capital: Kinshasa
Government: Republic
Population: 51,964,999
Languages: French, Lingala, Swahili, Kingwana, Kikongo, Tshiluba
Religions: Roman Catholic, Protestant, Kimbanguist, Muslim, indigenous beliefs

Congo, Republic of the
Area: 342,000 km² (132,046 mi²)
Capital: Brazzaville
Government: Republic
Population: 2,830,961
Languages: French, Lingala, Kikongo
Religions: Christian, animist, Muslim

Cook Islands
Area: 240 km² (93 mi²)
Capital: Avarua
Government: Self-governing in association with New Zealand
Population: 19,989
Language: English
Religion: Cook Islands Christian Church

Costa Rica
Area: 51,100 km² (19,730 mi²)
Capital: San José
Government: Democratic republic
Population: 3,710,558
Languages: Spanish, English
Religion: Roman Catholic

Croatia
Area: 56,524 km² (21,824 mi²)
Capital: Zagreb
Government: Republic
Population: 4,282,216
Language: Serbo-Croatian
Religion: Roman Catholic

Cuba
Area: 110,860 km² (42,803 mi²)
Capital: Havana
Government: Communist
Population: 11,141,997
Language: Spanish
Religions: Roman Catholic, Orthodox

Cyprus
Area: 9,250 km² (3,571 mi²)
Capital: Nicosia

Government: Republic; northern part administered
by Turkey
Population: 758,363
Languages: Greek, Turkish, English
Religions: Greek Orthodox, Muslim, Armenian,
Maronite

The Czech Republic
Area: 78,864 km² (30,342 mi²)
Capital: Prague
Government: Parliamentary democracy
Population: 10,272,179
Languages: Czech, Slovak
Religions: Roman Catholic, Czech Brethren

Denmark
Area: 43,070 km² (16,629 mi²)
Capital: Copenhagen
Government: Constitutional monarchy
Population: 5,336,394
Languages: Danish, Faroese, Greenlandic, German
Religions: Evangelical Lutheran, other Protestant faiths,
Roman Catholic

Djibouti
Area: 22,000 km² (8,494 mi²)
Capital: Djibouti
Government: Republic
Population: 451,442
Languages: French, Arabic, Somali, Afar
Religions: Muslim, Christian

Dominica
Area: 750 km² (290 mi²)
Capital: Roseau
Government: Parliamentary democracy
Population: 71,540
Languages: English, French patois
Religions: Roman Catholic, Methodist, Pentecostal,
Seventh-Day Adventist, Baptist

Dominican Republic
Area: 48,730 km² (18,815 mi²)
Capital: Santo Domingo
Government: Republic
Population: 8,442,533
Language: Spanish
Religion: Roman Catholic

Ecuador
Area: 283,560 km² (109,483 mi²)
Capital: Quito
Government: Republic
Population: 12,920,092
Languages: Spanish, Indian languages (especially
Quechua)
Religion: Roman Catholic

Egypt
Area: 1,001,450 km² (386,660 mi²)
Capital: Cairo
Government: Republic
Population: 68,359,979
Languages: Arabic, English, French
Religions: Muslim, Coptic Christian

El Salvador
Area: 21,040 km² (8,124 mi²)
Capital: San Salvador
Government: Republic
Population: 6,122,515
Languages: Spanish, Nahua
Religions: Roman Catholic, Protestant Evangelical

Equatorial Guinea
Area: 28,050 km² (10,830 mi²)
Capital: Malabo
Government: Republic
Population: 474,214
Languages: Spanish, French, Fang, Bubi, Ibo
Religion: Roman Catholic

Eritrea
Area: 123,300 km² (45,754 mi²)
Capital: Asmara
Government: In transition
Population: 4,135,933
Languages: Afar, Bilen, Kunama, Nara, Arabic,
Tobedawi, Saho, Tigre, Tigrinya
Religions: Muslim, Eritrean Orthodox Christian

Estonia
Area: 45,100 km² (17,413 mi²)
Capital: Tallinn
Government: Republic
Population: 1,431,471
Languages: Estonian, Russian
Religions: Lutheran, Russian Orthodox

Ethiopia
Area: 1,133,380 km² (437,600 mi²)
Capital: Addis Ababa
Government: Constitutional republic
Population: 64,117,452
Languages: Amharic, Tigrinya, Orominga, Guaraginga,
Somali, Arabic, English
Religions: Muslim, Ethiopian Orthodox, animist

Falkland Islands
Area: 12,170 km² (4,699 mi²)
Capital: Stanley
Government: Dependent territory of United Kingdom
Population: 2,805
Language: English
Religions: Anglican, Roman Catholic

Faroe Islands
Area: 1,400 km² (541 mi²)
Capital: Tórshavn
Government: Self-governing overseas administrative division of Denmark
Population: 45,296
Languages: Faroese, Danish
Religion: Evangelical Lutheran

Fiji
Area: 18,270 km² (7,054 mi²)
Capital: Suva
Government: Military republic
Population: 832,494
Languages: English, Fijian, Hindustani
Religions: Christian, Hindu, Muslim

Finland
Area: 337,030 km² (130,127 mi²)
Capital: Helsinki
Government: Republic
Population: 5,167,486
Languages: Finnish, Swedish, Lapp, Russian
Religions: Evangelical Lutheran, Greek Orthodox

France
Area: 547,030 km² (211,208 mi²)
Capital: Paris
Government: Republic
Population: 59,329,691
Languages: French, regional dialects
Religions: Roman Catholic, Protestant, Jewish, Muslim

French Guiana
Area: 83,534 km² (32,253 mi²)
Capital: Cayenne
Government: Overseas department of France
Population: 172,605
Language: French
Religion: Roman Catholic

French Polynesia
Area: 4,000 km² (1,544 mi²)
Capital: Papeete
Government: Overseas territory of France
Population: 249,110
Languages: French, Tahitian
Religions: Protestant, Roman Catholic

Gabon
Area: 267,670 km² (103,347 mi²)
Capital: Libreville
Government: Republic
Population: 1,208,436
Languages: French, Fang, Myene, Bateke, Bapounou/Eschira, Bandjabi
Religions: Christian, animist, Muslim

The Gambia
Area: 11,300 km² (4,363 mi²)
Capital: Banjul
Government: Republic
Population: 1,367,124
Languages: English, Mandinka, Wolof, Fula, local dialects
Religions: Muslim, Christian, indigenous beliefs

Georgia
Area: 69,699 km² (26,911 mi²)
Capital: Tbilisi
Government: Republic
Population: 5,019,538
Languages: Georgian, Russian
Religions: Georgian Orthodox

Germany
Area: 356,910 km² (137,803 mi²)
Capital: Berlin
Government: Federal republic
Population: 82,797,408
Language: German
Religions: Protestant, Roman Catholic

Ghana
Area: 238,540 km² (92,100 mi²)
Capital: Accra
Government: Republic
Population: 19,533,560
Languages: English, Akan, Moshi-Dagomba, Ewe, Ga-Adangbe
Religions: Indigenous beliefs, Muslim, Christian

Gibraltar
Area: 6.5 km² (2.5 mi²)
Capital: Gibraltar
Government: Dependent territory of United Kingdom
Population: 27,578
Languages: English, Spanish, Italian, Portuguese, Russian
Religions: Roman Catholic, Anglican, Muslim, Jewish

Greece
Area: 131,940 km² (50,942 mi²)
Capital: Athens
Government: Presidential parliamentary
Population: 10,601,527
Languages: Greek, English, French
Religions: Greek Orthodox, Muslim

Greenland
Area: 2,175,600 km² (839,999 mi²)
Capital: Nuuk (Godthåb)
Government: Self-governing overseas administrative division of Denmark
Population: 56,309

Languages: Eskimo dialects, Danish
Religion: Evangelical Lutheran

Grenada
Area: 340 km² (131 mi²)
Capital: St. George's
Government: Parliamentary democracy affiliated with
 United Kingdom
Population: 89,312
Languages: English, French patois
Religions: Roman Catholic, Anglican, other Protestant
 faiths

Guadeloupe
Area: 1,780 km² (687 mi²)
Capital: Basse-Terre
Government: Overseas department of France
Population: 426,493
Languages: French, Creole
Religions: Roman Catholic, Hindu, pagan African

Guatemala
Area: 108,890 km² (42,042 mi²)
Capital: Guatemala City
Government: Republic
Population: 12,639,939
Languages: Spanish, Quiche, Cakchiquel, Kekchi, other
 Indian dialects
Religions: Roman Catholic, Protestant, traditional
 Mayan

Guernsey
Area: 64 km² (25 mi²)
Capital: St. Peter Port
Government: British crown dependency
Population: 65,386
Languages: English, French, Norman-French
Religions: Anglican, Roman Catholic, other Protestant
 faiths

Guinea
Area: 245,860 km² (94,927 mi²)
Capital: Conakry
Government: Republic
Population: 7,466,200
Languages: French, tribal languages
Religions: Muslim, Christian, indigenous beliefs

Guinea-Bissau
Area: 36,120 km² (13,948 mi²)
Capital: Bissau
Government: Republic
Population: 1,285,715
Languages: Portuguese, Criolo, African languages
Religions: Indigenous beliefs, Muslim, Christian

Guyana
Area: 214,970 km² (83,000 mi²)
Capital: Georgetown
Government: Republic
Population: 697,286
Languages: English, Amerindian dialects
Religions: Christian, Hindu, Muslim

Haiti
Area: 27,750 km² (10,714 mi²)
Capital: Port-au-Prince
Government: Republic
Population: 6,867,995
Languages: French, Creole
Religions: Roman Catholic/voodoo, Protestant

Honduras
Area: 112,090 km² (43,278 mi²)
Capital: Tegucigalpa
Government: Republic
Population: 6,249,598
Languages: Spanish, Amerindian dialects
Religions: Roman Catholic, Protestant

Hong Kong
Area: 1,077 km² (416 mi²)
Capital: None
Government: Special administrative region of China
Population: 7,120,000
Languages: Cantonese, English
Religions: Local religions, Christian

Hungary
Area: 93,030 km² (35,919 mi²)
Capital: Budapest
Government: Republic
Population: 10,138,844
Language: Hungarian (Magyar)
Religions: Roman Catholic, Calvinist, Lutheran

Iceland
Area: 103,000 km² (39,768 mi²)
Capital: Reykjavík
Government: Republic
Population: 276,365
Languages: Icelandic
Religions: Evangelical Lutheran, other Protestant faiths,
 Roman Catholic

India
Area: 3,287,590 km² (1,269,338 mi²)
Capital: New Delhi
Government: Federal republic
Population: 1,014,003,817
Languages: Hindi, English, Bengali, Telugu, Marathi,
 Tamil, Urdu, Gujarati, Malayalan, Kannada, Oriya,

Punjabi, Assamese, Kashmiri, Sindhi, Sanskrit, Hindustani
Religions: Hindu, Muslim, Christian, Sikh, Buddhist, Jains

Indonesia
Area: 1,904,570 km² (735,272 mi²)
Capital: Jakarta
Government: Republic
Population: 224,784,210
Languages: Bahasa Indonesian, Javanese, English, Dutch
Religions: Muslim, Protestant, Roman Catholic, Hindu, Buddhist

Iran
Area: 1,648,000 km² (636,293 mi²)
Capital: Teheran
Government: Theocratic republic
Population: 65,619,636
Languages: Farsi, Turk, Kurdish, Arabic, Luri, Baloch
Religions: Shi'a Muslim, Sunni Muslim, Zoroastrian, Jewish, Christian, Baha'i

Iraq
Area: 434,920 km² (167,923 mi²)
Capital: Baghdad
Government: Republic
Population: 22,675,617
Languages: Arabic, Kurdish, Assyrian, Armenian
Religions: Shi'a Muslim, Sunni Muslim, Christian

Ireland
Area: 70,280 km² (27,135 mi²)
Capital: Dublin
Government: Republic
Population: 3,797,257
Languages: English, Irish (Gaelic)
Religions: Roman Catholic, Anglican

Israel
Area (excluding occupied territories): 20,770 km² (8,019 mi²)
Capital: Jerusalem
Government: Parliamentary democracy
Population: 5,842,454 (excluding occupied territories)
Languages: Hebrew, Arabic, English
Religions: Jewish, Muslim, Christian, Druze
See also **West Bank and Gaza Strip.**

Italy
Area: 301,230 km² (116,305 mi²)
Capital: Rome
Government: Republic
Population: 57,634,827
Languages: Italian, German, French, Slovene
Religion: Roman Catholic

Ivory Coast
Area: 322,460 km² (124,502 mi²)
Capital: Abidjan (also Yamoussoukro)
Government: Republic
Population: 15,980,950
Languages: French, Dioula, tribal languages
Religions: Muslim, indigenous beliefs, Christian

Jamaica
Area: 10,990 km² (4,243 mi²)
Capital: Kingston
Government: Parliamentary democracy affiliated with United Kingdom
Population: 2,652,689
Languages: English, Creole
Religions: Protestant, Roman Catholic, spiritualist cults

Japan
Area: 377,835 km² (145,882 mi²)
Capital: Tokyo
Government: Constitutional monarchy
Population: 126,549,976
Language: Japanese
Religions: Shinto, Buddhist, Christian

Jersey
Area: 117 km² (45 mi²)
Capital: Saint Helier
Government: British crown dependency
Population: 89,721
Languages: English, French, Norman-French
Religions: Anglican, other Protestant faiths, Roman Catholic

Jordan
Area: 91,880 km² (35,475 mi²) (excluding West Bank)
Capital: Amman
Government: Constitutional monarchy
Population: 4,998,564 (excluding West Bank)
Languages: Arabic, English
Religions: Sunni Muslim, Christian

Kazakhstan
Area: 2,717,428 km² (1,049,200 mi²)
Capital: Alma Alta
Government: Constitutional republic
Population: 16,733,227
Languages: Kazakh, Russian
Religions: Muslim, Russian Orthodox

Kenya
Area: 582,650 km² (224,961 mi²)
Capital: Nairobi
Government: Republic
Population: 30,339,770
Languages: English, Swahili, local languages
Religions: Protestant, Roman Catholic, indigenous beliefs, Muslim

Kiribati
Area: 710 km² (274 mi²)
Capital: Tarawa
Government: Republic
Population: 91,985
Languages: English, Gilbertese
Religions: Roman Catholic, Protestant, Seventh-Day
   Adventist, Baha'i

*There are two independent nations
smaller than New York City's
Central Park: Vatican City and
Monaco. Each is less than one
square mile.*

**Korea, Democratic People's Republic of
(North Korea)**
Area: 120,540 km² (46,540 mi²)
Capital: Pyongyang
Government: Communist
Population: 21,687,550
Language: Korean
Religions: Buddhist, Confucianist, Ch'ondogyo

Korea, Republic of (South Korea)
Area: 98,480 km² (38,023 mi²)
Capital: Seoul
Government: Republic
Population: 47,470,969
Language: Korean
Religions: Confucianist, Christian, Buddhist, Shamanist,
   Ch'ondogyo

Kuwait
Area: 17,820 km² (6,880 mi²)
Capital: Kuwait City
Government: Nominal constitutional monarchy
Population: 1,973,572
Languages: Arabic, English
Religions: Sunni Muslim, Shi'a Muslim, Christian,
   Hindu, Parsi

Kyrgyzstan
Area: 198,509 km² (76,642 mi²)
Capital: Bishkek
Government: Constitutional republic
Population: 4,685,230
Languages: Kirghiz, Russian
Religions: Muslim, Russian Orthodox

Laos
Area: 236,800 km² (91,428 mi²)
Capital: Vientiane
Government: Communist

Population: 5,497,459
Languages: Lao, French, English
Religions: Buddhist, animist

Latvia
Area: 63,701 km² (24,595 mi²)
Capital: Riga
Government: Republic
Population: 2,404,926
Languages: Lettish, Lithuanian, Russian
Religions: Lutheran, Russian Orthodox, Catholic

Lebanon
Area: 10,400 km² (4,015 mi²)
Capital: Beirut
Government: Republic
Population: 3,578,036
Languages: Arabic, French, Armenian, English
Religions: Muslim and Christian, each divided into sects
   (17 in all)

Lesotho
Area: 30,350 km² (11,718 mi²)
Capital: Maseru
Government: Modified constitutional monarchy
Population: 2,143,141
Languages: Sesotho, English, Zulu, Xhosa
Religions: Christian, indigenous beliefs

Liberia
Area: 111,370 km² (43,000 mi²)
Capital: Monrovia
Government: Republic
Population: 3,164,156
Languages: English, Niger-Congo languages
Religions: Indigenous beliefs, Christian, Muslim

Libya
Area: 1,759,540 km² (679,358 mi²)
Capital: Tripoli
Government: Military dictatorship
Population: 5,115,450
Languages: Arabic, Italian, English
Religion: Sunni Muslim

Liechtenstein
Area: 160 km² (62 mi²)
Capital: Vaduz
Government: Constitutional monarchy
Population: 32,204
Languages: German, Alemannic
Religions: Roman Catholic, Protestant

Lithuania
Area: 65,190 km² (25,170 mi²)
Capital: Vilnius
Government: Republic

Population: 3,620,756
Languages: Lithuanian, Polish, Russian
Religions: Roman Catholic

Luxembourg
Area: 2,586 km² (998 mi²)
Capital: Luxembourg
Government: Constitutional monarchy
Population: 437,389
Languages: Luxembourgish, German, French, English
Religions: Roman Catholic, Protestant

Macau
Area: 16 km² (6 mi²)
Capital: Macau
Government: Overseas territory of Portugal until 1999
Population: 496,837
Languages: Portuguese, Cantonese
Religions: Buddhist, Roman Catholic

Macedonia
Area: 25,713 km² (9,928 mi²)
Capital: Skopje
Government: Republic
Population: 2,041,467
Languages: Macedonian, Albanian, Serbo-Croatian
Religions: Eastern Orthodox, Muslim

Madagascar
Area: 587,040 km² (226,656 mi²)
Capital: Antananarivo
Government: Republic
Population: 15,506,472
Languages: French, Malagasy
Religions: Indigenous beliefs, Christian, Muslim

Malawi
Area: 118,480 km² (45,745 mi²)
Capital: Lilongwe
Government: Constitutional republic
Population: 10,385,849
Languages: English, Chichewa, Tombuka
Religions: Protestant, Roman Catholic, Muslim,
    indigenous beliefs

Malaysia
Area: 329,750 km² (127,316 mi²)
Capital: Kuala Lumpur
Government: Constitutional monarchy with hereditary
    rulers in peninsular states
Population: 21,793,293
Languages: Malay, English, Chinese dialects, Tamil,
    Hakka dialects, tribal languages
Religions: Muslim, Buddhist, Hindu, Confucianist,
    Christian

Maldives
Area: 300 km² (116 mi²)
Capital: Male
Government: Republic
Population: 301,475
Languages: Divehi, English
Religion: Sunni Muslim

Mali
Area: 1,240,000 km² (478,764 mi²)
Capital: Bamako
Government: Republic
Population: 10,685,948
Languages: French, Bambara
Religions: Muslim, indigenous beliefs, Christian

Malta
Area: 320 km² (124 mi²)
Capital: Valletta
Government: Parliamentary democracy
Population: 391,670
Languages: Maltese, English
Religion: Roman Catholic

Man, Isle of
Area: 588 km² (227 mi²)
Capital: Douglas
Government: British crown dependency
Population: 73,112
Languages: English, Manx Gaelic
Religions: Anglican, other Protestant faiths, Roman
    Catholic

Martinique
Area: 1,100 km² (425 mi²)
Capital: Fort-de-France
Government: Overseas department of France
Population: 414,516
Languages: French, Creole patois
Religions: Roman Catholic, Hindu, pagan African

Mauritania
Area: 1,030,700 km² (397,953 mi²)
Capital: Nouakchott
Government: Republic
Population: 2,667,859
Languages: Hasaniya Arabic, French, Toucouleur,
    Fula, Sarakole, Wolof
Religion: Muslim

Mauritius
Area: 1,860 km² (718 mi²)
Capital: Port Louis
Government: Parliamentary democracy affiliated with
    United Kingdom
Population: 1,179,368

Languages: English, Creole, French, Hindi, Urdu, Hakka, Bojpoori
Religions: Hindu, Roman Catholic, Anglican, Muslim

Mayotte
Area: 375 km² (145 mi²)
Capital: Dzaoudzi
Government: Territorial collectivity of France
Population: 155,911
Languages: Mahorian, French
Religions: Muslim, Christian

Mexico
Area: 1,972,550 km² (761,602 mi²)
Capital: Mexico City
Government: Federal republic
Population: 100,349,766
Language: Spanish, Mayan dialects
Religions: Roman Catholic, Protestant

Moldova
Area: 33,701 km² (13,012 mi²)
Capital: Kishinev
Government: Republic
Population: 4,430,654
Languages: Romanian, Russian
Religions: Russian Orthodox, Seventh-Day Adventist

Monaco
Area: 1.9 km² (.7 mi²)
Capital: Monaco
Government: Constitutional monarchy
Population: 31,693
Languages: French, English, Italian, Monegasque
Religion: Roman Catholic

Mongolia
Area: 1,565,000 km² (604,247 mi²)
Capital: Ulaanbaatar
Government: Republic
Population: 2,616,383
Languages: Khalkha Mongol, Turkic, Russian, Chinese
Religions: Tibetan Buddhist, Muslim

Montserrat
Area: 100 km² (39 mi²)
Capital: Plymouth
Government: Dependent territory of United Kingdom
Population: 6,409
Language: English
Religions: Anglican, other Protestant faiths, Roman Catholic

Morocco
Area: 446,550 km² (172,413 mi²)
Capital: Rabat
Government: Constitutional monarchy

Population: 30,122,350
Languages: Arabic, French, Berber dialects
Religions: Muslim, Christian, Jewish

Mozambique
Area: 801,950 km² (309,633 mi²)
Capital: Maputo
Government: Republic
Population: 19,104,696
Languages: Portuguese, indigenous languages
Religions: Indigenous beliefs, Christian, Muslim

Myanmar (formerly Burma)
Area: 676,550 km² (261,216 mi²)
Capital: Yangon (Rangoon)
Government: Military
Population: 41,734,853
Languages: Burmese, ethnic languages
Religions: Buddhist, Christian, Muslim, animist beliefs

Namibia
Area: 824,290 km² (318,258 mi²)
Capital: Windhoek
Government: Republic
Population: 1,771,327
Languages: Afrikaans, German, English, indigenous languages
Religions: Christian, indigenous beliefs

Nauru
Area: 20 km² (8 mi²)
Capital: Yaren
Government: Republic
Population: 11,845
Languages: Nauruan, English
Religions: Protestant, Roman Catholic

Nepal
Area: 140,800 km² (54,363 mi²)
Capital: Kathmandu
Government: Constitutional monarchy
Population: 24,702,119
Languages: Nepali, local languages
Religions: Hindu, Buddhist, Muslim

The Netherlands
Area: 41,526 km² (16,033 mi²)
Capital: Amsterdam and The Hague
Government: Constitutional monarchy
Population: 15,892,237
Language: Dutch
Religions: Roman Catholic, Protestant

Netherlands Antilles
Area: 800 km² (313 mi²)
Capital: Willemstad (on Curacao)
Government: Autonomous territory of the Netherlands

Population: 207,827
Languages: Dutch, Papiamento, English, Spanish
Religions: Roman Catholic, Protestant, Jewish, Seventh-Day Adventist

New Caledonia
Area: 19,060 km² (7,359 mi²)
Capital: Nouméa
Government: Overseas territory of France
Population: 201,816
Languages: French, Melanesian-Polynesian dialects
Religions: Roman Catholic, Protestant

New Zealand
Area: 268,680 km² (103,737 mi²)
Capital: Wellington
Government: Parliamentary democracy affiliated with United Kingdom
Population: 3,819,762
Languages: English, Maori
Religions: Anglican, Presbyterian, Roman Catholic

Nicaragua
Area: 129,494 km² (49,998 mi²)
Capital: Managua
Government: Republic
Population: 4,812,569
Languages: Spanish, English, Amerindian dialects
Religion: Roman Catholic

Niger
Area: 1,267,000 km² (489,189 mi²)
Capital: Niamey
Government: Republic (under military control)
Population: 10,075,571
Languages: French, Hausa, Djerma
Religions: Muslim, indigenous beliefs, Christian

Nigeria
Area: 923,770 km² (356,668 mi²)
Capital: Lagos
Government: Republic
Population: 123,337,822
Languages: English, Hausa, Yoruba, Ibo, Fulani
Religions: Muslim, Christian, indigenous beliefs

Niue
Area: 260 km² (100 mi²)
Capital: Alofi
Government: Self-governing territory affiliated with New Zealand
Population: 1,837
Languages: Polynesian (Tongan-Samoan dialect), English
Religions: Ekalesia Nieu, Mormon

Norfolk Island
Area: 36 km² (13 mi²)
Capital: Kingston
Government: Territory of Australia
Population: 2,285
Languages: English, Norfolk
Religions: Anglican, other Protestant faiths, Roman Catholic, Seventh-Day Adventist

Norway
Area: 324,220 km² (125,181 mi²)
Capital: Oslo
Government: Constitutional monarchy
Population: 4,481,162
Languages: Norwegian, Lapp, Finnish
Religions: Evangelical Lutheran, other Protestant faiths, Roman Catholic

Oman
Area: 212,460 km² (82,031 mi²)
Capital: Muscat
Government: Absolute monarchy
Population: 2,533,389
Languages: Arabic, English, Baluchi, Urdu
Religions: Ibadhi Muslim, Sunni Muslim, Shi'a Muslim, Hindu

Pakistan
Area: 803,940 km² (310,401 mi²)
Capital: Islamabad
Government: Federal republic
Population: 141,553,775
Languages: Urdu, English, Punjabi, Sindhi, Pushtu, Baluchi
Religions: Muslim, Christian, Hindu

Palau
Area: 458 km² (177 mi²)
Capital: Koror
Population: 18,766
Government: Parliamentary republic
Languages: English, Palauan
Religions: Christian, Modekngei

Panama
Area: 78,200 km² (30,193 mi²)
Capital: Panama City
Government: Centralized republic
Population: 2,808,268
Languages: Spanish, English
Religions: Roman Catholic, Protestant

Papua New Guinea
Area: 461,690 km² (178,259 mi²)
Capital: Port Moresby
Government: Parliamentary democracy affiliated with United Kingdom

The World

Population: 4,926,984
Languages: English, Motu, local dialects
Religions: Roman Catholic, Protestant, indigenous
  beliefs

Paraguay
Area: 406,750 km² (157,046 mi²)
Capital: Asunción
Government: Republic
Population: 5,585,828
Languages: Spanish, Guarani
Religions: Roman Catholic, Mennonite, other
  Protestant faiths

Peru
Area: 1,285,220 km² (496,223 mi²)
Capital: Lima
Government: Republic
Population: 27,012,899
Languages: Spanish, Quechua, Aymara
Religion: Roman Catholic

Philippines
Area: 300,000 km² (115,830 mi²)
Capital: Manila
Government: Republic
Population: 81,159,644
Languages: Philipino (Tagalog), English
Religions: Roman Catholic, Muslim, Buddhist

Poland
Area: 312,680 km² (120,727 mi²)
Capital: Warsaw
Government: Democratic state
Population: 36,646,023
Language: Polish
Religions: Roman Catholic, Russian Orthodox, Catholic

Portugal
Area: 92,080 km² (35,552 mi²)
Capital: Lisbon
Government: Republic
Population: 10,048,232
Language: Portuguese
Religions: Roman Catholic, Protestant

Qatar
Area: 11,000 km² (4,247 mi²)
Capital: Doha
Government: Traditional monarchy
Population: 744,483
Languages: Arabic, English
Religion: Muslim

Réunion
Area: 2,510 km² (969 mi²)
Capital: Saint-Denis

Government: Overseas department of France
Population: 720,934
Languages: French, Creole
Religion: Roman Catholic

Romania
Area: 237,500 km² (91,699 mi²)
Capital: Bucharest
Government: Republic
Population: 22,411,121
Languages: Romanian, Hungarian, German
Religions: Romanian Orthodox, Roman Catholic,
  Protestant, Muslim, Jewish

Russia
Area: 17,075,352 km² (6,592,800 mi²)
Capital: Moscow
Government: Constitutional republic
Population: 146,001,176
Language: Russian
Religions: Russian Orthodox, Baptist, Jewish, Muslim

Rwanda
Area: 26,340 km² (10,170 mi²)
Capital: Kigali
Government: Republic (under military control)
Population: 7,229,129
Languages: Kinyarwanda, French, Kiswahili, English
Religions: Roman Catholic, Protestant, indigenous
  beliefs, Muslim

St. Helena
Area: 122 km² (47 mi²)
Capital: Jamestown
Government: Dependent territory of the United
  Kingdom
Population: 7,197
Language: English
Religions: Anglican, other Protestant faiths, Roman
  Catholic

St. Kitts and Nevis
Area: 269 km² (104 mi²)
Capital: Basseterre
Government: Constitutional monarchy affiliated with
  United Kingdom
Population: 38,819
Language: English
Religions: Anglican, other Protestant faiths, Roman
  Catholic

St. Lucia
Area: 620 km² (239 mi²)
Capital: Castries
Government: Parliamentary democracy affiliated with
  United Kingdom
Population: 156,260

Languages: English, French patois
Religions: Roman Catholic, Protestant, Anglican

St. Pierre and Miquelon
Area: 242 km² (93 mi²)
Capital: Saint-Pierre
Government: Territorial collectivity of France
Population: 6,896
Language: French
Religion: Roman Catholic

St. Vincent and the Grenadines
Area: 340 km² (131 mi²)
Capital: Kingstown
Government: Constitutional monarchy affiliated with
    United Kingdom
Population: 115,461
Languages: English, French patois
Religions: Anglican, other Protestant faiths, Roman
    Catholic, Seventh-Day Adventist

Samoa
Area: 2,860 km² (1,104 mi²)
Capital: Apia
Government: Constitutional monarchy
Population: 179,466
Languages: Samoan, English
Religions: Congregational, Roman Catholic, other
    Protestant faiths

San Marino
Area: 60 km² (23 mi²)
Capital: San Marino
Government: Republic
Population: 26,937
Language: Italian
Religion: Roman Catholic

São Tome and Princípe
Area: 960 km² (371 mi²)
Capital: São Tome and Princípe
Government: Republic
Population: 159,883
Language: Portuguese, Fang
Religions: Roman Catholic, Evangelical Protestant,
    Seventh-Day Adventist

Saudi Arabia
Area: 2,149,690 km² (829,995 mi²)
Capital: Riyadh
Government: Monarchy
Population: 22,023,506
Language: Arabic
Religion: Muslim

"The World's Major Religions" in chapter 9;
"Frequently Used Foreign Words and
Phrases" in chapter 13
Go to

Senegal
Area: 196,190 km² (75,748 mi²)
Capital: Dakar
Government: Republic
Population: 9,987,494
Languages: French, Wolof, Pulaar, Diola, Mandingo
Religions: Muslim, indigenous beliefs, Christian

Seychelles
Area: 455 km² (176 mi²)
Capital: Victoria
Government: Republic
Population: 79,326
Languages: English, French, Creole
Religions: Roman Catholic, Anglican

Sierra Leone
Area: 71,740 km² (27,699 mi²)
Capital: Freetown
Government: Republic
Population: 5,232,624
Languages: English, Mende, Krio, Temne
Religions: Muslim, indigenous beliefs, Christian

Singapore
Area: 633 km² (244 mi²)
Capital: Singapore
Government: Republic
Population: 4,151,720
Languages: Chinese, Tamil, Malay, English
Religions: Buddhist, Muslim, Christian, Hindu, Sikh,
    Taoist Confucianist

Slovakia
Area: 49,035 km² (18,928 mi²)
Capital: Bratislava
Government: Parliamentary democracy
Population: 5,407,956
Languages: Slovak, Hungarian
Religions: Roman Catholic, Protestant, Orthodox,
    Uniate

Slovenia
Area: 20,246 km² (7,817 mi²)
Capital: Ljubljana
Government: Republic
Population: 1,927,593
Languages: Slovene, Serbo-Croatian
Religions: Roman Catholic, Protestant

Solomon Islands
Area: 28,450 km² (10,985 mi²)
Capital: Honiara
Government: Independent parliamentary state within
    British Commonwealth
Population: 466,194

Languages: Melanesian, English, local dialects
Religions: Anglican, Roman Catholic, other Protestant faiths

Somalia
Area: 637,660 km² (246,201 mi²)
Capital: Mogadishu
Government: In transition
Population: 7,253,137
Languages: Somali, Arabic, Italian, English
Religion: Sunni Muslim

South Africa
Area: 1,221,040 km² (471,444 mi²)
Capital: Pretoria, Cape Town, and Bloemfontein
Government: Republic
Population: 42,421,021
Languages: Afrikaans, English, Zulu, Xhosa, Tswana
Religions: Christian, Hindu, Muslim

Spain
Area: 504,750 km² (194,884 mi²)
Capital: Madrid
Government: Parliamentary monarchy
Population: 39,996,671
Languages: Castilian Spanish, Catalan, Galician, Basque
Religion: Roman Catholic

Sri Lanka
Area: 65,610 km² (25,332 mi²)
Capital: Colombo
Government: Republic
Population: 19,238,575
Languages: Sinhala, Tamil, English
Religions: Buddhist, Hindu, Christian, Muslim

Sudan
Area: 2,505,810 km² (967,493 mi²)
Capital: Khartoum
Government: Republic, with military
Population: 35,079,814
Languages: Arabic, Nubian, Ta Bedawie, Nilotic and Nilo-Hamitic dialects, Sudanic dialects, English
Religions: Sunni Muslim, indigenous beliefs, Christian

Suriname
Area: 163,270 km² (63,039 mi²)
Capital: Paramaribo
Government: Republic
Population: 431,303
Languages: Dutch, English, Sranan Tongo, Javanese
Religions: Hindu, Muslim, Roman Catholic, Protestant

Svalbard
Area: 62,049 km² (23,597 mi²)
Capital: Longyearbyen
Government: Territory of Norway

Population: 3,231
Languages: Russian, Norwegian
Religion: Evangelical Lutheran

Swaziland
Area: 17,360 km² (6,703 mi²)
Capital: Mbabane
Government: Independent monarchy within British commonwealth
Population: 1,083,289
Languages: English, siSwati
Religions: Christian, indigenous beliefs

Sweden
Area: 449,960 km² (173,729 mi²)
Capital: Stockholm
Government: Constitutional monarchy
Population: 8,873,052
Languages: Swedish, Lapp, Finnish
Religions: Evangelical Lutheran, Roman Catholic

Switzerland
Area: 41,290 km² (15,942 mi²)
Capital: Bern
Government: Federal republic
Population: 7,262,372
Languages: German, French, Italian, Romansch
Religions: Roman Catholic, Protestant, Jewish

Syria
Area: 185,180 km² (71,498 mi²)
Capital: Damascus
Government: Military republic
Population: 16,305,659
Languages: Arabic, Kurdish, Armenian, Aramaic, Circassian, French
Religions: Sunni Muslim, Alawite, Druze, other Muslim sects, Christian

Taiwan
Area: 35,980 km² (13,892 mi²)
Capital: Taipei
Government: Republic
Population: 22,191,087
Languages: Mandarin Chinese, Taiwanese and Hakka dialects
Religions: Buddhist, Confucianist, Taoist, Christian

Tajikistan
Area: 139,909 km² (54,019 mi²)
Capital: Dushanbe
Government: Republic
Population: 6,440,732
Languages: Tadzhik, Russian
Religion: Muslim

The World

Tanzania
Area: 945,090 km² (364,899 mi²)
Capital: Dar es Salaam (scheduled to move to Dodoma, 2005)
Government: Republic
Population: 35,306,126
Languages: Swahili, English
Religions: Christian, Muslim, indigenous beliefs

Thailand
Area: 514,000 km² (198,455 mi²)
Capital: Bangkok
Government: Constitutional monarchy
Population: 61,230,874
Languages: Thai, English, local dialects
Religions: Buddhist, Muslim

Togo
Area: 56,790 km² (21,927 mi²)
Capital: Lomé
Government: One-party republic
Population: 5,018,502
Languages: French, Ewe, Mina, Dagomba, Kabyè
Religions: Indigenous beliefs, Christian, Muslim

Tokelau
Area: 10 km² (4 mi²)
Capital: None (various local government agencies)
Government: Territory of New Zealand
Population: 1,503
Languages: Tokelauan, English
Religions: Congregational Christian Church, Roman Catholic

Tonga
Area: 748 km² (289 mi²)
Capital: Nuku'alofa
Government: Constitutional monarchy
Population: 102,321
Languages: Tongan, English
Religions: Free Wesleyan, Roman Catholic, Mormon

Trinidad and Tobago
Area: 5,130 km² (1,981 mi²)
Capital: Port-of-Spain
Government: Parliamentary democracy
Population: 1,175,523
Languages: English, Hindi, French, Spanish
Religions: Roman Catholic, Hindu, Protestant, Muslim

Tunisia
Area: 163,610 km² (63,170 mi²)
Capital: Tunis
Government: Republic
Population: 9,593,402
Languages: Arabic, French
Religions: Muslim, Christian, Jewish

Turkey
Area: 780,580 km² (301,382 mi²)
Capital: Ankara
Government: Republican parliamentary democracy
Population: 65,666,677
Languages: Turkish, Kurdish, Arabic
Religion: Muslim (mostly Sunni)

Turkmenistan
Area: 488,000 km² (188,417 mi²)
Capital: Ashkhabad
Government: Republic
Population: 4,518,268
Languages: Turkmen, Russian
Religion: Sunni Muslim, Eastern Orthodox

Turks and Caicos Islands
Area: 500 km² (193 mi²)
Capital: Grand Turk (Cockburn Town)
Government: Dependent territory of United Kingdom
Population: 17,502
Language: English
Religions: Baptist, Methodist, Anglican, Seventh-Day Adventist

Tuvalu
Area: 26 km² (10 mi²)
Capital: Funafuti
Government: Democracy affiliated with United Kingdom
Population: 10,838
Languages: Tuvaluan, English
Religion: Protestant

Uganda
Area: 236,040 km² (91,135 mi²)
Capital: Kampala
Government: One-party republic
Population: 23,317,560
Languages: English, Luganda, Swahili, Bantu and Nilotic languages
Religions: Roman Catholic, Protestant, Muslim, indigenous beliefs

Ukraine
Area: 603,729 km² (233,100 mi²)
Capital: Kiev
Government: Republic
Population: 49,153,027
Languages: Ukrainian, Russian
Religions: Russian Orthodox, Baptist, Roman Catholic, Jewish

United Arab Emirates
Area: 83,600 km² (32,278 mi²)
Capital: Abu Dhabi
Government: Federation of seven emirates

The World

Population: 2,369,153
Languages: Arabic, Farsi, English, Hindi, Urdu
Religions: Muslim, Christian, Hindu

United Kingdom

Area: 244,820 km² (94,525 mi²)
Capital: London
Government: Constitutional monarchy
Population: 59,508,382
Languages: English, Welsh, Scottish Gaelic
Religions: Anglican, other Protestant faiths, Roman
Catholic, Jewish, Muslim

United States

Area: 9,629,046 km² (3,717,796 mi²)
Capital: Washington, D.C.
Government: Federal republic
Population: 275,562,673
Languages: English, Spanish
Religions: Protestant, Roman Catholic, Jewish

Uruguay

Area: 176,220 km² (68,039 mi²)
Capital: Montevideo
Government: Republic
Population: 3,334,074
Language: Spanish
Religions: Roman Catholic, Protestant, Jewish

Uzbekistan

Area: 447,293 km² (172,700 mi²)
Capital: Tashkent
Government: Republic
Population: 24,755,519
Languages: Uzbek, Russian
Religions: Muslim, Eastern Orthodox

Vanuatu

Area: 14,760 km² (5,699 mi²)
Capital: Port-Vila
Government: Republic
Population: 189,618
Languages: English, French, Bislama
Religions: Protestant, Roman Catholic, indigenous
beliefs

Vatican City

Area: 0.438 km² (108.7 acres)
Capital: Vatican City
Government: Independent papal state
Population: 870
Languages: Italian, Latin
Religion: Roman Catholic

Venezuela

Area: 912,050 km² (352,143 mi²)
Capital: Caracas

Government: Republic
Population: 23,542,649
Languages: Spanish, Amerindian dialects, Portugeuse,
Italian
Religion: Roman Catholic

Vietnam

Area: 329,560 km² (127,243 mi²)
Capital: Hanoi
Government: Communist
Population: 78,773,873
Languages: Vietnamese, French, Chinese, English,
Khmer, tribal dialects
Religions: Buddhist, Confucianist, Taoist, Roman
Catholic, indigenous beliefs, Muslim, Protestant

Wallis and Futuna

Area: 274 km² (106 mi²)
Capital: Mata-Utu
Government: Overseas territory of France
Population: 15,283
Languages: French, Wallisian
Religion: Roman Catholic

West Bank and Gaza Strip

Area: 6,240 km² (2,410 mi²)
Capital: None
Government: Israeli military rule
Population: 1,427,741 (excluding Israeli settlers)
Languages: Arabic, Hebrew, English
Religions: Muslim, Jewish, Christian

Western Sahara

Area: 2,860 km² (1,097 mi²)
Capital: None
Government: Moroccan administrative protectorate
Population: 222,631
Languages: Hassaniya Arabic, Moroccan Arabic
Religion: Muslim

Yemen

Area: 527,970 km² (203,849 mi²)
Capital: Sanaa
Government: Republic
Population: 17,479,206
Language: Arabic
Religions: Muslim, Christian, Hindu

Yugoslavia, Federal Republic of

(Consists of Serbia, the largest republic of
preindependence Yugoslavia, and Montenegro, the
smallest republic) This country has not been
recognized by the United States.
Area: 102,173 km² (39,449 mi²)
Capital: Belgrade
Government: Federal republic

The World

Population: 10,662,087
Languages: Serbo-Croatian, Hungarian (Vojvodina),
    Albanian (Kosovo), Montenegrin
Religions: Serbian Orthodox, Muslim, Roman Catholic

Zambia
Area: 752,610 km² (290,583 mi²)
Capital: Lusaka
Government: Multiparty state
Population: 9,582,418
Languages: English, indigenous languages and dialects
Religions: Christian, Muslim, Hindu, indigenous beliefs

Zimbabwe
Area: 390,580 km² (150,803 mi²)
Capital: Harare
Government: Parliamentary democracy
Population: 11,342,521
Languages: English, Shona, Sindebele
Religions: Indigenous/Christian beliefs, Christian,
    indigenous beliefs, Muslim

GREAT EVENTS IN WORLD HISTORY

Throughout prehistory, antiquity, and the early Middle Ages, it is often difficult to place exact dates. Therefore, most of the dates in this time line up to the year A.D. *1000 should be considered approximate.*

1,600,000 B.C. Earliest humanlike ancestors.
250,000 B.C. Earliest Homo sapiens.
70,000 B.C. Neanderthals use stone tools and fire.
40,000 B.C. Ice Age ends; Cro-Magnons migrate into Europe.
30,000 B.C. Neanderthals disappear.
28,000 B.C. Asians cross land bridge between Asia and America.
20,000 B.C. European cave art exists.
12,000 B.C. Dog domesticated from Asian wolf.
8000 B.C. Agriculture develops in Near East.
6500 B.C. Wheel invented by Sumerians.
6000 B.C. First true pottery made.
5000 B.C. Copper, first shapable metal, smelted in Persia.
4236 B.C. Earliest date on Egyptian calendar.
3760 B.C. Earliest date on Jewish calendar.
3600 B.C. Bronze made in southwestern Asia.
3100 B.C. Egypt united under first dynasty.

3000 B.C. Phoenicians migrate to eastern Mediterranean.
2780 B.C. First Egyptian pyramid built.
2700 B.C. Cheops builds Great Pyramid at Giza.
2697 B.C. Huang-ti becomes "Yellow Emperor" of China.
2640 B.C. Legendary Empress Si Ling-chi introduces silk production in China.
2340 B.C. Sargon establishes Semitic and Sumerian civilizations.
2150 B.C. Aryans invade Indus Valley.
2000 B.C. Bronze Age begins in Europe.
1760 B.C. Shang dynasty is founded in China.
1750 B.C. Hammurabi, Babylonian king, issues code of laws.
1400 B.C. Iron Age begins in Asia.
1250 B.C. Exodus of Israelites from Egypt.
1193 B.C. Greeks destroy city of Troy.
1100 B.C. Pa-out-She, Chinese scholar, compiles first dictionary.
1000 B.C. Hebrews establish Jerusalem as capital of Israel.
994 B.C. Teutons migrate to Rhine River area.
850 B.C. Epic poems of the Greek poet Homer are the first great works of Western literature.
815 B.C. Carthage is founded by Phoenicians.
776 B.C. First Olympic Games are held in Greece.
753 B.C. Rome is founded.
580 B.C. King Nebuchadnezzar builds Hanging Gardens of Babylon.
563 B.C. Buddha is born.
559 B.C. Cyrus establishes Persian Empire.
551 B.C. Confucius is born.
460 B.C. Pericles establishes democracy in Athens, beginning a golden age that will make Greek culture a predominant influence in the Mediterranean for 1,000 years.
450 B.C. Herodotus' *History* surveys the known world; he is later called "the father of history."
426 B.C. Demosthenes leads Athenians to victories in the Peloponnesian War.
424 B.C. Sophocles' play *Oedipus Rex* is performed in Athens.

399 B.C. Athenian philosopher Socrates is put to death for his teachings. His students Plato and Aristotle are the first great Western philosophers.

336 B.C. Alexander III, king of Macedonia, begins conquests that will include Egypt, the Mediterranean, and the Middle East by his death in 323 B.C.

300 B.C. Meng-Tse spreads the philosophy of Confucius in Orient.

270 B.C. Rome conquers the Italian peninsula.

236 B.C. Asoka, emperor of India, becomes a Buddhist missionary.

218 B.C. North African city-state Carthage sends Hannibal through Spain and over the Alps to attack Rome; he retreats in 207 B.C.

215 B.C. China builds Great Wall to protect against invasions from central Asia.

201 B.C. Carthage surrenders to Rome.

146 B.C. Greece becomes a Roman province.

64 B.C. Rome captures Jerusalem.

54 B.C. Roman general Julius Caesar conquers Gaul (France), invades Britain.

48 B.C. Caesar returns to Rome, becomes Dictator for Life; is assassinated in 44 B.C.

28 B.C. Octavian defeats rivals and becomes the first Roman emperor under the name Caesar Augustus.

5 B.C. Jesus Christ is born.

A.D. 30 Jesus is executed.

A.D. 32 Saul of Tarsus (Paul) begins early Christian missionary work.

A.D. 64 Rome under Nero is partly destroyed by fire.

A.D. 70 A Roman force destroys the great Jewish Temple in Jerusalem.

A.D. 79 Eruption of Vesuvius destroys Pompeii.

A.D. 135 The Romans destroy Jerusalem, scatter Jews to the four corners of the empire.

A.D. 177 Persecution drives Christians in Rome to worship in catacombs.

A.D. 268 Goths, tribes from northern Europe, invade Greece.

A.D. 312 Constantine becomes first Christian emperor of Rome.

A.D. 330 Constantine moves the capital of the empire from Rome to Constantinople (present-day Istanbul, Turkey).

"Significant Dates in the History of Religion" Go to in chapter 9; "Philosophical Movements and Schools of Thought" in chapter 10

A.D. 370 Asian Huns invade Europe.

A.D. 395 The Roman Empire divides into two—East and West.

A.D. 399 *Confessions* by the North African bishop Augustine tells the story of his conversion to Christianity.

A.D. 406 Vandals from central Europe invade Gaul (France); Romans leave Britain.

A.D. 410 Goths sack Rome.

A.D. 425 Germanic tribes including Angles and Saxons invade Britain.

A.D. 433 Mongol leader Attila the Hun begins conquests in Asia and Europe.

A.D. 476 The Goths depose Western Roman emperor, the Western Roman Empire comes to an end.

A.D. 550 Eastern emperor Justinian codifies Roman law in Corpus Juris Civilis.

A.D. 570 Muhammad is born at Mecca.

A.D. 627 Emperor Tai Zong of Tang Dynasty begins a golden age in China.

A.D. 632 Muhammad dies, having established the Muslim faith, which will grow to be a major world religion.

A.D. 634 Muslims begin conquest of Near East and Africa.

A.D. 711 Moors (Muslims from North Africa) invade Spain from North Africa.

A.D. 768 Charlemagne (Charles the Great), becomes king of the Franks. He will be crowned Holy Roman Emperor in 800.

A.D. 862 Vikings, tribes originating in Scandinavia, seize control of northern Russia, raid France.

A.D. 874 Vikings settle Iceland.

A.D. 900 Spain begins to drive out Moors.

A.D. 932 Printed books from woodblocks are developed in China.

A.D. 936 German Otto I becomes Holy Roman Emperor.

A.D. 995 Fugiware Michiaga founds Japanese golden age.

A.D. 1000 Vikings begin exploration of North America.

1054 Eastern (Byzantine) and Western (Roman) churches separate. Muslim (Islamic) culture spreads in Africa.

1066 Normans, Viking tribe settled in western France, conquer Britain.

1096 Pope and European kings launch First Crusade to oust Muslims from Holy Land.

1148 Second Crusade begins.

1156 Civil wars are fought in Japan.

1161 Chinese use explosives in warfare.

1162 Thomas á Becket becomes archbishop of Canterbury. He is murdered in 1170.

1189 Last recorded Viking voyage to North America.

1190 Genghis Khan begins conquest of Asia.

1192 Crusaders reach Jerusalem but fail to capture the city.

1202 Arabic numerals introduced to Europe.

1204 Crusaders capture and sack Constantinople.

1210 Mongol leader Genghis Khan invades China.

1210 Francis of Assisi founds Franciscan religious order.

1215 The Magna Carta, limiting royal power, is signed by England's King John.

1228 Sixth Crusade results in capture of Jerusalem.

1240 Mongols capture Moscow, destroy Kiev.

1244 Muslim forces recapture Jerusalem.

1259 Thomas Aquinas develops a systematic theology that will prevail in the Western (Roman) Church.

1260 Kublai Khan, grandson of Genghis Khan, founds Yuan dynasty in China.

1271 Venetian Marco Polo travels to China; he returns in 1295.

1274 Mongols' invasion of Japan fails.

1291 Crusades end as Muslims rout Christians in Palestine.

1295 King Edward I summons first representative English Parliament.

1336 Civil war lasting until 1392 begins in Japan.

1337 Hundred Years' War between England and France begins.

1347 Plague spreads from China to Cyprus.

1348 Plague spreads to England.

1351 Plague reaches Russia; more than 25 million Europeans die.

1363 Tamerlane, leader of a Mongol tribe, begins conquest of western Asia.

1368 Mongol dynasty ends in China; Ming dynasty begins.

1402 Tamerlane conquers Ottoman Empire centered in Turkey.

1419 Henry the Navigator of Portugal begins period of African explorations.

1429 Joan of Arc leads a victorious French army against the English at Orleans; she is executed as a witch in 1431.

1453 Ottoman Turks conquer Constantinople, ending the Byzantine Empire.

1453 The Hundred Years' War ends; England loses all territories in France.

1454 Printing press using movable metal type is introduced.

1455 England's Wars of the Roses begin.

1478 Spanish Inquisition to punish heretics (especially Muslims and Jews) begins.

1482 Portuguese colonize African Gold Coast.

1492 Christopher Columbus discovers "the Indies," actually islands in the unknown Western Hemisphere.

1507 First world map showing "America."

1517 German monk Martin Luther protests against Church abuses, beginning the Protestant Reformation in northern Europe.

1519 Hernan Cortés conquers Aztecs and claims Mexico for Spain.

1522 Crew under Ferdinand Magellan circumnavigates the world.

1531 Francisco Pizarro begins conquest of Peru for Spain.

1534 Henry VIII is excommunicated and declares himself head of the Church of England. Ignatius Loyola founds the Jesuits, a monastic order opposing the Reformation.

1542 French theologian John Calvin establishes Protestant government in Geneva.

1547 Ivan IV becomes first czar of united Russia.

1557 Portuguese establish colony at Macao.

1558 Elizabeth I becomes queen of England.

1582 More accurate Gregorian calendar is introduced in western Europe.

Go to "Art Movements and Styles" and "Architectural Styles and Movements" in chapter 7; "Literary Movements, Periods, and Styles" in chapter 8

The World

1588   An armada of Spanish warships attacks England, is defeated by the English fleet.

1603   England's Queen Elizabeth dies; her reign has been a golden age for British arts and letters.

1604   Russia begins settlement in Siberia.

1607   English found North American colony of Virginia.

1618   Thirty Years' War begins as a conflict between Europe's Protestants and Catholics.

1620   English Pilgrims reach Cape Cod, found Plymouth Colony.

1626   Dutch found New Amsterdam (New York).

1637   Russian explorers reach Pacific coast of Siberia.

1642   English Puritans under Oliver Cromwell wage war against King Charles I; Charles is captured and beheaded in 1649.

1654   Portuguese take Brazil from Dutch.

1660   England's monarchy is restored.

1661   English take control of Bombay in India.

1664   Manchu dynasty is founded in China.

1683   Turkish army overruns Vienna.

1696   Peter the Great leads Russian modernization program.

1715   French king Louis XIV, the Sun King, dies; during his long reign, French manners and styles have been admired and imitated throughout Europe.

1733   English weaver John Kay invents the flying sewing shuttle, an early advance in the Industrial Revolution.

1763   British defeat French in North America, gain control of Canada.

1775   American colonists revolt against the British government, beginning the American Revolution.

1776   Colonists publish the Declaration of Independence.

1781   British army surrenders to Americans and French at Yorktown, Virginia.

1783   Treaty of Paris recognizes independence of American colonies.

1788   First English convicts are transported to Australia.

1789   French Revolution begins.

1789   U.S. Constitution takes effect; George Washington is elected first president.

"Significant Inventions, Technological Advances, and Scientific Discoveries" **Go to** in chapter 5

1792   France is declared a republic.

1793   France's King Louis XVI is beheaded. A Reign of Terror leads to many executions.

1793   Toussaint L'Ouverture leads a revolt, ending slavery in French Haiti.

1793   First free settlers migrate to Australia.

1796   French commander Napoleon Bonaparte invades Italy.

1798   Napoleon occupies Rome and invades Egypt but is defeated in the Battle of the Nile by British admiral Horatio Nelson.

1799   Napoleon become first consul of France.

1803   France, in need of money, sells Louisiana territory to the United States.

1804   Bonaparte becomes Napoleon I, emperor of France; the Napoleonic Code establishes a new legal framework for all territories controlled by France.

1805   The French lose the naval battle of Trafalgar to Britain but win on land at Austerlitz against Austria and Russia.

1806   Napoleon dissolves Holy Roman Empire.

1807   England abolishes slave trade.

1808   Napoleon overruns Spain.

1812   Napoleon invades Russia and occupies Moscow but is forced to retreat, losing most of his army to cold and starvation.

1812   The U.S. declares war on Britain.

1813   French armies suffer losses in Germany and Spain; in 1814, Napoleon abdicates.

1815   Napoleon returns to power; British and Prussian armies defeat him decisively at Waterloo, ending the Napoleonic wars.

1819   Spain cedes Florida to the United States.

1821   Mexico, together with many South and Central American countries, declares independence from Spain.

1823   U.S. President Monroe issues the Monroe Doctrine, a warning against European colonization in the Americas.

1830   Revolutions depose the French king, gain Belgium's independence from the Netherlands.

1833   England bans slavery and child labor in factories.

The World

1836 Texas secedes from Mexico, declares independence as the Republic of Texas.

1837 Queen Victoria succeeds to the British throne at age 18.

1846 Famines begin in Ireland. More than 1 million die; many emigrate to the U.S.

1848 Mexico cedes California and New Mexico territories to the U.S. after defeat in the Mexican-American War.

1848 *The Communist Manifesto* by Marx and Engels helps fan revolutions in France, Belgium, Austria, and Poland.

1849 A gold strike in California attracts thousands of adventurers from around the world.

1851 Louis Napoleon declares himself emperor of France.

1854 Britain and France begin Crimean War against Russia; treaty in 1856 guarantees free access to the Black Sea.

1854 Japan ends isolation, signs commercial treaty with the U.S.

1858 Czar Alexander begins emancipating the serfs in Russia.

1861 U.S. Civil War begins.

1861 A unified Kingdom of Italy is established.

1865 Northern states win U.S. Civil War, abolish slavery; President Lincoln is assassinated.

1867 United States acquires Alaska from Russia; Dominion of Canada gains independence from Britain.

1868 Japan ends 700-year shogun rule, begins modernization.

1869 Suez Canal is completed, shortening trade routes between Asia and Europe; the first transcontinental railroad is completed across the U.S.

1870 Prussia invades France and captures Paris; the French government of Louis Napoleon falls.

1871 Germany is united under Kaiser Wilhelm of Prussia.

1881 Russia's Czar Alexander is assassinated by terrorists.

1894 Sun Yat-sen begins move to end Manchu dynasty in China.

1895 European nations complete colonization of Africa, extend colonies and commercial concessions in Asia.

1898 Spain cedes Cuba, Puerto Rico, the Philippines, and Guam to the U.S. after defeat in the Spanish-American War.

1899 Occupying U.S. forces begin a three-year war against insurgents in the Philippines.

1899 Britain defeats Dutch settlers in South Africa.

1900 In China, the Boxer Rebellion against European traders, is put down by an international (European) force.

1901 U.S. President McKinley is assassinated. Theodore Roosevelt becomes president.

1903 Panama secedes from Colombia, agrees with U.S. plan to build Panama Canal.

1903 Americans Orville and Wilbur Wright make the first powered heavier-than-air flight.

1905 Japan gains concessions from Russia in Asia after victories in Russo-Japanese War.

1905 Russian protests against repressive government lead to violence; put down by the czarist government in 1906.

1906 Mohandas Gandhi begins nonviolent protests in South Africa against segregation of East Indians.

1908 William d'Arcy discovers oil in Persian Gulf region.

1908 Japan begins long occupation of Korea.

1909 The first moving assembly line is introduced at a Ford Motor plant in Detroit.

1910 South Africa gains independence from Britain.

1910 Chinese revolution ends Manchu dynasty, and republic is formed under president Sun Yat-Sen.

1912 Passenger ship *Titanic* sinks; 1,513 lives are lost.

1914 Germany and Austria declare war on France, Britain, and Russia (the Allied Powers) and invade Belgium, beginning the Great War (later called World War I).

1914 The Panama Canal opens.

1915 German submarines disrupt shipping in the Atlantic. Germans use poison gas on the battlefield.

The World

1916 England uses tanks for first time. Battle of the Somme (July–November) causes more than 1.3 million casualties.

1917 The United States declares war on Germany and Austria, joins the Allied Powers (Allies).

1917 In Russia, revolutionaries overthrow the czar; Bolsheviks seize power; Russia withdraws from the war.

1918 The Allies drive Germans back. Kaiser Wilhelm of Germany abdicates; Germany signs armistice ending World War I.

1919 Allies impose heavy penalties on Germany in the Treaty of Versailles and form the League of Nations.

1919 Sinn Fein declares independence for Ireland; civil war against British rule begins, leading to independent Irish state declared in 1921.

1922 Union of Soviet Socialist Republics (USSR) is established; Fascist Benito Mussolini gains power in Italy.

1923 Adolf Hitler forms National Socialist (Nazi) Party in Germany. Turkey becomes a republic, ending the 600-year-old Ottoman Empire.

1924 Joseph Stalin succeeds Lenin as leader of USSR.

1927 Leader Chiang Kai-shek purges Communists in Chinese government, beginning a long civil war.

1929 A worldwide depression begins; the U.S. stock market crashes in October.

1929 Fighting begins between Jews and Arabs in Palestine.

1930 Mohandas Gandhi begins civil disobedience campaign, protesting British political and commercial control in India.

1931 The Great Depression deepens; banks fail, millions in Europe and U.S. are unemployed.

1931 The Japanese occupy Manchuria.

1932 Franklin Roosevelt is elected U.S. president.

1933 Nazi Adolf Hitler is named chancellor of Germany, purges opposition; Great Purges begin in USSR.

1934 Chinese Nationalist armies drive Communists, led by Mao Zedong, on 6,000-mile "Long March" to remote Yunan Province.

1935 Italy invades Ethiopia. Hitler begins open rearmament; German Jews lose citizenship, civil rights.

1936 Germany makes alliances with Italy and Japan; Spanish Fascist leader Franco begins Spanish Civil War.

1936 Britain's King Edward VIII abdicates to marry an American divorcee.

1937 Japanese invade China, capturing Peking and Shanghai; German aircraft bomb Spain in support of Franco.

1938 Germany annexes Austria; Munich Pact grants Czechoslovakia's Sudentenland to Germany.

1939 Franco captures Madrid, ending the Spanish Civil War; Italy invades Albania; Germany invades Poland September 1; Britain and France (the Allies) declare war, beginning World War II.

1940 German armies overrun France, Belgium, Denmark, and Norway; British pilots defeat German bombers in the Battle of Britain. Japan and Italy join war against Britain and France.

1941 Germany invades Russia; Italy and Germany invade Egypt; Japanese attack Pearl Harbor in Hawaii; U.S. declares war, joins Allies.

1942 Japanese capture Philippines and most of Southeast Asia; U.S. defeats Japan in the naval Battle of Midway. Allies invade North Africa.

1943 Allies invade Italy; Italian government surrenders; USSR defeats Germans at Stalingrad; Allied bombing raids devastate German cities. Allies begin recapture of Japanese Pacific bases.

1944 Allies invade France, liberate Paris, Brussels, and Rome; Allies defeat Japanese in Philippine Sea and Saipan. Germans bombard London with V-2's, first long-range missiles.

1945 Allies close in on Berlin; Hitler commits suicide; Germany surrenders.

1945 U.S. drops atom bombs on Japanese cities Hiroshima and Nagasaki; Japan surrenders, ending the war.

The World

"Supreme Court Decisions" in chapter 21; Go to
"Important Dates in American History"
in chapter 25

1946 The United Nations is established.

1946 German war crime trials are held in Nuremburg.

1946 The Philippines become independent after 48 years as a U.S. possession.

1947 Marshall Plan provides U.S. aid for European war recovery.

1947 Britain grants independence to Indian subcontinent, forming nations of India and Pakistan.

1948 Nation of Israel is established; war begins between Israel and Arab League.

1948 Gandhi is assassinated by a Hindu extremist.

1948 Communists gain control of Czechoslovakia; Korea is divided into communist North and capitalist South; the USSR blockades Berlin; Allies defeat blockade by airlifting food to Berlin.

1949 Mao Zedong's communists gain control of China; defeated Nationalists set up government on island of Taiwan.

1949 Germany is divided into Communist East Germany and capitalist West; U.S. and its allies form the North Atlantic Treaty Organization (NATO).

1950 North Korean troops, supported by USSR and China, invade South Korea. U.S.-led UN troops are sent to defend South Korea.

1951 Chinese Communists occupy Tibet.

1952 Jawaharlal Nehru is elected first prime minister of India; Elizabeth II ascends to the British throne; World War II general Eisenhower is elected U.S. president.

1953 USSR leader Josef Stalin dies; USSR announces development of hydrogen bomb.

1953 An armistice ends Korean War, leaving borders between North and South unchanged.

1954 Vietnamese defeat French at Dien Bien Phu, French withdraw; Vietnam is divided into communist North Vietnam and capitalist South Vietnam. Algeria begins war against French colonial rule.

1955 European communist states sign Warsaw Pact in opposition to NATO.

1956 Soviets crush anti-Russian uprising in Hungary; Egypt nationalizes Suez Canal, and British withdraw; Israel invades Egypt.

1957 Russia launches first artificial satellite, *Sputnik 1*; U.S. launches *Explorer 1* the next year.

1957 European Common Market is formed.

1958 Army overthrows French government over Algerian war; General de Gaulle becomes premier.

1959 Revolutionary Fidel Castro overthrows Cuban government, becomes premier.

1960 First sub-Saharan African colonies become independent.

1960 Castro aligns Cuba with the USSR.

1961 U.S.-supported invasion of Cuba at Bay of Pigs fails. U.S. sends military advisers to South Vietnam.

1961 USSR sends first human, Yuri Gagarin, into space. The U.S. puts John Glenn into orbit the next year.

1961 East Germany builds the Berlin Wall to prevent East Germans from escaping to the west.

1962 Discovery of Soviet missiles in Cuba and U.S. blockade threaten nuclear war; Soviets agree to remove missiles.

1962 Nelson Mandela is imprisoned for activities against South Africas's apartheid (racial separation) laws.

1962 Algeria gains independence from France.

1963 U.S. President Kennedy is assassinated.

1963 The United States, Great Britain, and Soviet Union sign nuclear test ban treaty.

1963 The U.S. sends military advisers to South Vietnam to resist guerrilla attacks from communist North.

1964 The U.S. begins bombing of North Vietnam.

1965 The U.S. sends combat troops to Vietnam. Antiwar protests begin.

1966 China undergoes "Cultural Revolution."

1967 In Six-Day War, Israel occupies Jerusalem and West Bank of Jordan River.

The World

1968 North Vietnam launches Tet offensive against South Vietnam; U.S. troop deployment in Vietnam passes 500,000. Soviets crush Czech uprising.

1968 Martin Luther King, Jr., and U.S. presidential candidate Robert Kennedy are assassinated; Richard Nixon is elected president.

1968 Student demonstrations close universities in France and U.S.; Mexican police fire on student protesters.

1969 U.S. astronauts land on the moon.

1969 Peace talks to end Vietnam War begin in Paris; the U.S. begins gradual reduction of troop strength.

1970 U.S. troops invade Cambodia.

1971 Communist China replaces Taiwan in United Nations.

1972 U.S. president Nixon travels to China to renew relations.

In Paraguay, dueling is legal provided both parties are registered blood donors.

1973 A U.S.-supported coup overthrows Chile's elected Marxist government; General Augusto Pinochet becomes president.

1973 Syria and Egypt attack Israel in October War.

1973 A cease-fire in Vietnam ends involvement of U.S. ground troops.

1974 Accused of serious crimes in the Watergate scandal, U.S. president Nixon resigns to avoid impeachment.

1975 North Vietnamese troops storm Saigon, last Americans are evacuated. Vietnam is unified under communist government.

1976 Mao Zedong, chairman of the People's Republic of China, dies.

1976 Riots in Soweto township increase racial tensions in South Africa.

1978 U.S. president Carter helps negotiate the Camp David Accords, a peace treaty between Israel and Egypt.

1979 Muslim leader Ayatollah Khomeini gains control of Iran; Iranians seize U.S. Embassy in Tehran and hold hostages until early 1980.

1979 Soviet Union invades Afghanistan, beginning a nine-year war.

1979 Nicaraguan dictator Somoza is driven into exile; the leftist Sandinista party takes power.

1980 Iraq invades Iran, beginning an eight-year war. The Solidarity trade union confronts communists in Poland.

1981 Ronald Reagan takes office as U.S. president; he is wounded by an assassination attempt but recovers.

1981 Egyptian president Sadat is assassinated.

1983 Soviets shoot down South Korean airliner, and 269 are killed.

1983 Terrorists in Lebanon destroy U.S. embassy, bomb U.S. and French military barracks; more than 350 are killed.

1984 Peacekeepers withdraw from Lebanon; Indian prime minister Indira Gandhi is assassinated.

1985 Mikhail Gorbachev becomes leader of the USSR.

1986 Corazon Aquino is elected president of Philippines, replacing longtime dictator Ferdinand Marcos.

1986 U.S. space shuttle *Challenger* explodes in flight, killing crew of seven.

1986 U.S. aircraft raid Libya in retaliation for terrorist bombing in Germany.

1986 A nuclear accident at Chernobyl near Kiev in the Ukraine causes widespread damage and injury.

1987 Gorbachev introduces economic and social reforms in the USSR; U.S. and USSR agree to reduce nuclear arms.

1988 USSR begins withdrawal from Afghanistan. Iran and Iraq sign a cease-fire. Jordan's King Hussein cedes land and authority to Palestine Liberation Organization (PLO).

1989 Chinese massacre protesters in Beijing's Tiananmen Square.

1989 U.S. troops invade Panama and take General Manuel Noriega into custody.

1989 The Berlin Wall is opened; Czechoslovakia elects a noncommunist government; Romanian leader Nicolae Ceaùsescu is overthrown and executed; Pinochet regime ends in Chile.

1990 Black leader Nelson Mandela is released from South African prison after 27 years.

1990 Iraq invades Kuwait; UN approves military action against Iraq.

1990 East German regime falls, Germany reunites; Poland elects Solidarity leader Lech Walesa president.

1991 A U.N. force led by the U.S. drives Iraqis from Kuwait in 100-hour Operation Desert Storm.

1991 Soviet communist coup fails; the Soviet Union is dissolved; Boris Yeltsin becomes Russian president.

1991 Croatia and Slovenia declare independence from Yugoslavia; communist government of Albania falls.

1992 South African whites vote to end white minority rule.

1992 Serbian nationalists begin "ethnic cleansing" of Muslims in Bosnia.

1992 Hindu extremists destroy a mosque in Ayodhya, India.

1993 South Africa adopts a constitution providing equal rights for black citizens.

1993 Maastricht Treaty and North American Free Trade Agreement (NAFTA) establish free trade blocs in Europe and North America.

1993 World Trade Center in New York is evacuated after terrorist bomb explodes in underground garage; six are killed.

1994 Nelson Mandela is elected first black president of South Africa.

1994 The Hutu majority kill more than 500,000 Tutsi in Rwanda.

1994 Israel signs peace treaty with Jordan, extends Palestinian self-rule.

1994 Russian forces invade the breakaway republic of Chechnya.

1995 Earthquake in Kobe, Japan, kills 5,000.

1995 NATO forces bomb Serb positions in Bosnia; a peace treaty ends the fighting in December.

1995 Israeli prime minister Itzhak Rabin is assassinated.

1996 Israel cracks down on terrorists in response to suicide bombings.

1996 UN tribunal indicts Serbs and Croats for war crimes.

1996 Russians and Chechens sign peace treaty.

1997 Insurgents in Zaire overturn dictator, change country name to Democratic Republic of Congo.

1997 Hong Kong reverts to Chinese control after 156 years as British colony.

1998 Peace treaty signed between Ireland and Northern Ireland.

1998 Indonesian riots overthrow longtime President Suharto.

1998 India and Pakistan test nuclear weapons for the first time.

1998 Serb forces massacre civilians in Kosovo.

1999 U.S. president Clinton is acquitted of impeachment charges.

1999 NATO bombs Serbia; Serbs agree to withdraw troops from Kosovo.

1999 Russia troops reenter Chechnya.

2000 Vladimir Putin is elected Russian president.

2000 Israel withdraws troops from Lebanon, ending long occupation.

2000 Yugoslav president Slobodan Milosevic loses election, is driven from office by mass protests.

2001 Israeli-Palestinian violence increases; Ariel Sharon becomes Israeli prime minister.

2001 Terrorists highjack passenger jets in U.S., crash them into World Trade Center in New York, Pentagon in Washington; almost 3,000 are killed.

2001 U.S. and Britain bomb Afghanistan, where Osama bin Laden, presumed leader of terrorists, is in hiding.

2001 Muslim fundamentalist regime in Afghanistan collapses; U.S. ground troops continue search for bin Laden.

2002 Israel invades the West Bank and Gaza Strip; Palestinian suicide bombings intensify.

MAJOR WARS, BATTLES, AND OTHER ARMED CONFLICTS

Simultaneous wars that were part of one general conflict but that had different names depending on the continent where they were fought are grouped together.

War, Battle, or Conflict	Date
Trojan War (Achaeans and other Greek peoples)	12th century B.C.
Persian Wars (Persians vs. Greek city-states)	499–494, 490, 480–479 B.C.
Marathon, Battle of	490 B.C.
Salamis, Battle of (naval)	480 B.C.
Thermopylae, Battle of	480 B.C.
Plataea, Battle of	479 B.C.
Pelopennesian War (Athens vs. Sparta)	431–404 B.C.
Sparta-Thebes conflict in Greece	
Leuctra, Battle of	371 B.C.
Greece vs. Macedonia	
Chaeronea, Battle of	338 B.C.
Alexander the Great, conquests of	334–323 B.C.
Wars between Alexander's successors	315–280 B.C.
Punic Wars (Carthage vs. Rome)	
First	264–241 B.C.
Second (Hannibalic)	218–201 B.C.
Third	149–146 B.C.
Social War (Marsic or Marsian War) (Rome vs. Samnites and Marsi)	90–88 B.C.
Mithridatic Wars (Rome vs. Pontus)	88–84, 82–81, 74–63 B.C.
Gallic Wars (Julius Caesar's conquest of Gaul for Rome)	58–51 B.C.
Roman civil wars	49–31 B.C.
Pharsalus, Battle of	48 B.C.
Philippi, Battle of	42 B.C.
Actium, Battle of (naval)	Sept. 2, 31 B.C.
Rome vs. Germans (under Arminius)	
Teutoburg Forest, Battle of	A.D. 9
Rome vs. Visigoths	
Adrianople, Battle of	378
Rome vs. Franks	
Soissons, Battle of	486
Franks (under Charles Martel) vs. Saracen Muslims	
Tours, Battle of	Oct. 732
Normans (under William the Conqueror) vs. Saxons	
Hastings, Battle of	Oct. 14, 1066
Crusades (attempts by Western Christians to free Holy Land from Muslims)	
First	1096–99
Second	1147–49
Third	1187–92
Fourth	1202–04
Fifth	1217–21
Sixth (Diplomatic)	1228–29
Seventh	1248–50
Eighth	1270
Genghis Khan, conquests of	1198–1227

War, Battle, or Conflict	Date
Scottish struggle for independence from England	
Bannockburn, Battle of	June 24, 1314
Hundred Years' War (France vs. England)	1337–1453
Crécy, Battle of	Aug. 26, 1346
Calais, Siege of	1346–47
Poitiers, Battle of	1356
Agincourt, Battle of	Oct. 25, 1415
Orléans, Siege of	1428–May 1429
Roses, Wars of the (English civil wars)	1455–99
Bosworth Field, Battle of	Aug. 22, 1485
Scotland and France vs. England	
Flodden Field, Battle of	Sept. 9, 1513
Spain and Venice vs. Turkey	
Lepanto, Battle of (naval)	Oct. 7, 1571
Spain vs. England	
Armada, the Spanish, defeat of (naval)	July 31–Aug. 8, 1588
Catholic League vs. France	
Ivry, Battle of	Mar. 14, 1590
Thirty Years' War (conflict among various European countries)	1618–48
English Civil War	1642–52
Edgehill, Battle of	Oct. 23, 1642
Marston Moor, Battle of	July 2, 1644
Dunbar, Battle of	Sept. 3, 1650
England vs. the Netherlands	1652–54, 1665–67
Devolution, War of (France vs. Spain)	1667–68
Dutch War (France and England vs. the Netherlands)	1672–78
King Philip's War (New England colonies vs. Wampanoag, Narragansett, and Nipmuck Indians)	July 4, 1675–Aug. 12, 1676
English Civil War	
Monmouth Rebellion	1685
Grand Alliance, War of the (War of the League of Augsburg) (France vs. England, Holy Roman Empire, Germany, Austria, Spain, Sweden, the Netherlands, and Brandenburg)	1688–97
King William's War (French vs. English colonies in America)	1689–97
Great Northern War (Sweden vs. Russia, Poland, and Denmark)	1700–21
Spanish Succession, War of the (France vs. England, Holland, Austria, Prussia, Portugal, and Savoy)	1701–14
Queen Anne's War (French vs. English colonies in America)	1702–13
Jenkins' Ear, War of (Great Britain vs. Spain)	Oct. 1739–41
Austrian Succession, War of the (Austria, England, the Netherlands, and Saxony vs. Prussia, Spain, France, and Bavaria)	1740–48
King George's War (British vs. French colonies in North America)	1744–48
Stuart attempt to regain the British throne	
Culloden Moor, Battle of	April 16, 1746
Seven Years' War (Prussia and Great Britain vs. Austria, France, Sweden, Russia, Saxony, Spain, and Kingdom of the Two Sicilies)	1756–63
French and Indian War (British vs. French colonies in North America)	1756–63
Cherokee War (Cherokee Indians vs. settlers on the western borders of Virginia and the Carolinas)	1759–61

The World

continues

Major Wars, Battles, and Other Armed Conflicts, Continued

War, Battle, or Conflict	Date
American Revolution	1775–81
Lexington and Concord, Battles of	Apr. 19, 1775
Fort Ticonderoga, Battle of	May 10, 1775
Bunker Hill, Battle of	June 17, 1775
Canada Expedition	Sept. 1775–June 1776
Long Island, Battle of	Aug. 27, 1776
Trenton, Battle of	Dec. 26, 1776
Princeton, Battle of	Jan. 2–3, 1777
Bennington, Battle of	Aug. 15, 1777
Saratoga, Battle of	Oct. 7, 1777
Brandywine, Battle of the	Sept. 11, 1777
Germantown, Battle of	Oct. 4, 1977
Monmouth, Battle of	June 28, 1778
Wyoming Valley Massacre	Summer 1778
Savannah, Battle of	Dec. 23–29, 1778
Bonhomme Richard and *Serapis,* naval battle between	Sept. 23, 1779
Savannah, Siege of	Sept.–Oct. 1779
Charleston, Siege of	Feb.–May 1780
Camden, Battle of	Aug. 16, 1780
Kings Mountains, Battle of	Oct. 7, 1780
Cowpens, Battle of	Jan. 17, 1781
Yorktown, Siege of	Sept.–Oct. 19, 1781
French Revolution (French civil war and war against most European countries)	1789–99
Bastille, storming of the	July 14, 1789
Reign of Terror	Sept. 1793–July 1794
Franco-American Naval War	1798–1800
Napoleon I, campaigns of and wars against	1796–1815
(France vs. various European countries)	
Italian campaign	Mar. 1796–Apr. 1797
Nile, Battle of the (naval)	Aug. 1, 1798
Marengo, Battle of	June 14, 1800
Hohenlinden, Battle of	Dec. 3, 1800
Copenhagen, Battle of (naval)	Apr. 2, 1801
Trafalgar, Battle of (naval)	Oct. 21, 1805
Austerlitz, Battle of	Dec. 2, 1805
Jena and Auerstädt, Battles of	Oct. 14, 1806
Eylau, Battle of	Feb. 8, 1807
Friedland, Battle of	June 14, 1807
Aspern, Battle of	1809
Wagram, Battle of	1809
Borodino, Battle of	Sept. 7, 1812
Leipzig, Battle of	Oct. 16–19, 1813
Waterloo, Battle of	June 18, 1815
Barbary Wars (United States vs. Morocco, Algiers, Tunis, and Tripoli)	1801–05, 1815
War of 1812 (United States vs. Great Britain)	1812–15
Detroit, Surrender of	Aug. 18, 1812
Frenchtown, Battle of	Jan. 22, 1813
Lake Erie, Battle of (naval)	Sept. 10, 1813
Thames, Battle of the	Oct. 5, 1813

War, Battle, or Conflict	Date
War of 1812 (United States vs. Great Britain), *cont.*	
Chippewa, Battle of	July 5, 1814
Bladensburg, Battle of	Aug. 24, 1814
Lake Champlain, Battle of (naval)	Sept. 11, 1814
New Orleans, Battle of	Jan. 8, 1815
Creek War (United States vs. Creek Indians)	1813–14
Greek War of Independence (from Turkey)	1821–29
Navarino, Battle of (naval)	Oct. 20, 1827
Anglo-Burman Wars	1824–26, 1852–53, 1885
Java War (Java vs. the Netherlands)	1825–30
Russo-Turkish Wars	1828–29, 1853–56, 1877–78
Texas struggle for independence from Mexico	1836
Alamo, Siege of the	Feb. 23–Mar. 6, 1836
San Jacinto, Battle of	Apr. 21, 1836
Anglo-Chinese (Opium) War	1839–42
Anglo-Afghan Wars	1839, 1878–79
Sikh Wars (Great Britain vs. India)	1845, 1849
Mexican War (United States vs. Mexico)	1846–48
Taiping Rebellion (Chinese rising against Manchu Dynasty)	1850–64
Crimean War (Russia vs. Ottoman Empire, Great Britain, France, and Sardinia)	1853–56
Sevastopol, Siege of	Sept. 14, 1854–Sept. 9, 1855
Second Opium War (Great Britain and France vs. China)	1856–60
Sepoy Mutiny (revolt of Indian soldiers against British rule)	1857–59
Austro-Sardinian War (War of Italian Liberation) (Austria vs. France and Sardinia)	1859
Magenta, Battle of	June 4, 1859
Solferino, Battle of	June 24, 1859
Civil War, U.S.	1861–1865
Eastern Theater	
Fort Sumter, attack on	Apr. 12–14, 1861
Bull Run (Manassas), First Battle of	July 21, 1861
Ball's Bluff, Battle of	Oct. 21, 1861
Monitor and *Merrimack*, naval battle between	Mar. 9, 1862
Fair Oaks (Seven Pines), Battle of	May 31–June 1, 1862
Seven Days' Battles	June 25–July 1, 1862
Cedar Mountain, Battle of	Aug, 9, 1862
Bull Run (Manassas), Second Battle of	Aug. 29–30, 1862
Antietam, Battle of	Sept. 17, 1862
Fredericksburg, Battle of	Dec. 13, 1862
Chancellorsville, Battle of	May 1–5, 1863
Gettysburg, Battle of	July 1–3, 1863
Charleston, Sieges of	July–Aug. 1863
Fort Pillow Massacre	Apr. 12, 1864
Wilderness, Battle of the	May 5–6, 1864
Spotsylvania, Battle of	May 8–18, 1864
Cold Harbor, Battle of	June 1–3, 1864
Petersburg, Siege of	June 1864–Apr. 2, 1865
Cedar Creek, Battle of	Oct. 19, 1864
Sherman's March to the Sea	Nov. 15–Dec. 25, 1864

continues

The World

Major Wars, Battles, and Other Armed Conflicts, Continued

War, Battle, or Conflict	Date
Civil War, U.S., *cont.*	
Fort Fisher, Battle of	Jan. 15, 1865
Five Forks, Battle of	Apr. 1, 1865
Appomattox Court House	Apr. 9, 1865
Western Theater	
Boonville, Battle of	June 17, 1861
Fort Henry, Battle of	Feb. 6, 1862
Fort Donelson, Battle of	Feb. 13–16, 1862
Shiloh (Pittsburg Landing), Battle of	Apr. 6–7, 1862
Island No. 10, Battle of	Apr. 7–8, 1862
Corinth, Battle of	Oct. 3–4, 1862
Murfreesboro (Stones River), Battle of	Dec. 31, 1862–Jan. 2, 1863
Vicksburg, Siege of	May 19–July 3, 1863
Chickamauga, Battle of	Sept. 19–20, 1863
Chattanooga, Battle of	Nov. 23–25, 1863
Lookout Mountain, Battle of	Nov. 24, 1863
Missionary Ridge, Battle of	Nov. 24–25, 1863
Kennesaw Mountain, Battle of	June 27, 1864
Atlanta, Siege of	July 20–Sept. 2, 1864
Franklin, Battle of	Nov. 30, 1864
Nashville, Battle of	Dec. 15–16, 1864
Off Cherbourg, France	
Alabama and *Kearsarge*, naval battle between	June 19, 1864
War of the Triple Alliance (Brazil, Argentina, and Uruguay vs. Paraguay)	1864–70
Seven Weeks' War (Prussia vs. Austria)	June 14–July 1866
Ten Years' War (Cuba vs. Spain)	1868–78
Franco-Prussian War	July 19, 1870–Feb. 1, 1871
Gravelotte, Battle of	Aug. 18, 1870
Metz, Siege of	Aug. 19–Oct. 27, 1870
Sedan, Battle of	Sept. 1, 1970
Russo-Turkish War	1877–78
Zulu War (Great Britain vs. Zulus)	1879
First South African War (Great Britain vs. Transvaal)	1881
War of the Pacific (Chile vs. Peru and Bolivia)	1879–84
Mahdist War (revolt of followers of the Mahdi against Egyptian rule)	1881–90
Khartoum, Siege of	Jan. 1885
Sino-French War	1884–85
Sino-Japanese War	1894–95
Spanish-American War	1898
Manila Bay, Battle of (naval)	May 1, 1898
San Juan Hill, Battle of	July 1, 1898
Santiago, Battle of (naval)	July 3, 1898
Boer War (South African War, Anglo-Boer War, or Second War of Freedom) (Great Britain vs. Transvaal and Orange Free State)	1899–1902
Boxer Rebellion (China vs. foreign powers involved in the country)	1900–01
Russo-Japanese War	Feb. 5, 1904–Sept. 5, 1905
Japan Sea (Tsushima), Battle of the (naval)	May 27, 1905
Mexican Civil War	1910–20

War, Battle, or Conflict	Date
Balkan Wars	
First (Turkey vs. Serbia, Montenegro, Greece, and Bulgaria)	Oct. 8, 1912–May 30, 1913
Second (Bulgaria vs. Serbia, Greece, Turkey, Montenegro, and Romania)	June 29–Aug. 10, 1913
World War I (Austria, Germany, Turkey, and Bulgaria vs. Russia, France, Great Britain, Serbia, Italy, and United States)	July 28, 1914–Nov. 11, 1918
Charleroi, Battle of	Aug. 22–23, 1914
Tannenberg, Battle of	Aug. 26–30, 1914
Marne, First Battle of the	Sept. 5–14, 1914
Ypres, First Battle of	Oct. 20 and 31, Nov. 11, 1914
Coronel, Battle of (naval)	Nov. 1, 1914
Falklands, Battle of the (naval)	Dec. 8, 1914
Dogger Bank, Battle of (naval)	Jan. 24, 1915
Ypres, Second Battle of	Apr. 22–May 24, 1915
Gallipoli Expedition (Dardanelles Campaign)	Apr. 25, 1915–Jan. 9, 1916
Verdun, Siege of	Feb. 21–Dec. 1916
Kut al Imara, Battle of	Apr. 1916
Asiago, Battle of	May 14–June 1916
Jutland, Battle of (naval)	May 31–June 1, 1916
Somme, Battle of the	July–Nov. 1916
Arras, Battle of	Apr. 4–May 4, 1917
Ypres (Passchendaele), Third Battle of	July 31–Nov. 10, 1917
Caporetto, Battle of	Oct.–Dec. 1917
Cambrai, Battle of	Nov. 20–Dec. 7, 1917
St. Quentin, Battle of	Mar. 21, 1918
Belleau Wood, Battle of	June 3–9, 1918
Chateau-Thierry, Battle of	July 15–21, 1918
Marne, Second Battle of the	July 18–Aug. 7, 1918
Amiens, Battle of	Aug. 8, 1918
St. Mihiel, Battle of	Sept. 12–21, 1918
Argonne, Battle of the	Sept. 26–Nov. 11, 1918
Vittorio Veneto, Battle of	Oct. 1918
October (Bolshevik) Revolution and counterrevolutionary movements (Russian civil war)	1917–20
Polish-Soviet War	1920–21
Greco-Turkish War	1921–22
Chinese Civil War	1927–36, 1946–50
Chaco War (Paraguay-Bolivia)	Dec. 1928–Nov. 1935
Japanese invasion of Manchuria and other parts of China	1931–37
Italian invasion of Ethiopia	Oct. 3, 1935–May 5, 1936
Spanish Civil War	1936–39
World War II (Germany, Italy, and Japan vs. United States, England, France, Russia, and other countries)	1939–45
Western European Theater	
Poland, German conquest of	Sept. 1–17, 1939
Norway and Denmark, fall of	Apr.–June 1940
Western Europe, German conquest of	May–June 1940
Britain, Battle of (air)	June 19–Oct. 12, 1940
Bismarck, sinking of the (naval)	May 1941
Normandy invasion	June 6, 1944
Rhine River, Allied advance toward the (Operation Market Garden)	Fall 1944
Bulge, Battle of the	Dec. 16, 1944–Jan. 21, 1945

The World

continues

Major Wars, Battles, and Other Armed Conflicts, Continued

War, Battle, or Conflict	Date
World War II (Germany, Italy, and Japan vs. United States, England, France, Russia, and other countries), *cont.*	
Russian Front	
Finland, Soviet attack on	Nov. 30, 1939–Mar. 13, 1940
Soviet Union, initiation of German attack on	June 22, 1941
Stalingrad, Siege of	July 1942–Feb. 2, 1943
Kursk, Battle of	July 12–19, 1943
Dniepr River, Soviet offensive across the	Summer–fall 1943
Ukraine, Soviet liberation of	Winter 1944
Berlin, fall of	Apr. 16–May 2, 1945
Mediterranean Theater	
Tobruk, Battles of	Dec. 1940, June and Nov. 1942
Greece, German conquest of	Apr.–May 1941
El Alamein, First Battle of	July 2–4, 1942
El Alamein, Second Battle of	Aug. 30–Nov. 4, 1942
North Africa, Allied invasion of (Operation Torch)	Nov. 8, 1942–May 11, 1943
Sicily, Allied invasion of	July 10–Aug. 16, 1943
Italy, Allied invasion of	Sept.–Oct. 1943
Anzio, operation at	Jan.–June 1944
Pacific Theater	
Pearl Harbor, bombing of (air/naval)	Dec. 7, 1941
Malaya and Dutch East Indies, Japanese conquest of	Dec. 7, 1941–Feb. 15, 1942
Philippines, Japanese conquest of the	Dec. 22, 1941–May 6, 1942
Burma, Japanese invasion of	Jan.–May 1942
Lombok Strait, Battle of (naval)	Feb. 19–20, 1942
Java Sea, Battle of the (naval)	Feb. 27, 1942
Tokyo, Doolittle bombing of	Apr. 18, 1942
Coral Sea, Battle of the (naval)	May 7–8, 1942
Midway, Battle of (naval)	June 4–5, 1942
Savo Sea, Battle of the (naval)	Aug. 1942
Guadacanal, Battle of (land/naval)	Aug. 7, 1942–Feb. 7, 1943
Eastern Solomons, Battle of the (naval)	Aug. 23–25, 1942
Santa Cruz Island, Battle of (naval)	Oct. 26, 1942
Gilbert Islands, conquest of the	Nov. 1943
Marshall Islands, invasion of the	Jan. 1944
New Guinea, conquest of	Apr.–July 1944
Leyte Gulf, Battle of (naval)	Oct. 24, 1944
Iwo Jima, conquest of	Feb. 19–Mar. 16, 1945
Okinawa, invasion of	Mar. 31, 1945
Hiroshima and Nagasaki, atomic bombing of	Aug. 6 and 9, 1945
Algerian war for independence from France	1945–62
Indonesian war for independence from the Netherlands	1945–49
Vietnamese war for independence from France	1946–54
Dien Bien Phu, fall of	May 7, 1954
Arab-Israeli War	1948–49
Korean War (North Korea and Communist China vs. South Korea and United Nations forces)	1950–53
38th parallel, initial North Korean attack across the	June 25, 1950
Inchon, UN landing at	Sept. 15, 1950
Manchurian border, Chinese Communist crossing of	Nov. 26, 1950

War, Battle, or Conflict	Date
Hungary, uprising in and Soviet invasion of	Oct. 23–Nov. 1956
Suez War (Israel, Great Britain, and France vs. Egypt)	Oct. 29–Dec. 1956
Revolutionary guerrilla warfare in Cuba (against Batista regime)	1956–59
Vietnam War (South Viet Nam and United States vs. North Vietnam)	1960–75
Tet Offensive, beginning of	Jan. 31, 1968
Bay of Pigs invasion (United States vs. Cuba)	Apr. 17–19, 1961
India-Pakistan war	1965
Six Day War (Israel vs. Egypt, Jordan, and Syria)	June 5–10, 1967
Nigerian civil war	1967–70
Bangladesh war (India vs. Pakistan)	1971–72
Yom Kippur War (Israel vs. Egypt and Syria)	Oct. 1973
Lebanon, civil war and Syrian and Israeli occupation of	1973–85
Soviet intervention in Afghanistan	1979–89
Persian Gulf War (Iran vs. Iraq)	1980–88
Salvadoran civil war	1980–92
Falklands War (Argentina vs. Great Britain)	Apr. 2–June 14, 1982
Grenada, United States intervention in	Oct. 25–27, 1983
Yugoslavian civil war	1987–99
Panama, United States invasion of	1989
Persian Gulf War (Iraq vs. United States and coalition of numerous countries)	1990–91
Rwandan civil war	1994
Chechnya, Russian invasion of	1994–96
Yugoslavia, NATO intervention in	1999
Afghanistan, intervention in	2001–2002

WORLD EXPLORATION AND DISCOVERY

40,000 B.C. Cro-Magnons migrate to Europe from Near East.

28,000 B.C. Humans migrate from Asia to Americas over land bridge.

5000 B.C. Sumerians migrate to Mesopotamia.

2300 B.C. Semites migrate from Arabia to Mesopotamia.

2000 B.C. Israelites migrate from Euphrates Valley to Canaan.

1000 B.C. Phoenician sailors explore Britain and western Africa.

700 B.C. Central Asian tribes migrate to Persia.

640 B.C. Greek explorer Colaeus reaches Gibraltar and Spain.

600 B.C. Egyptian pharaoh Necho circumnavigates Africa; Greek explorer Midacritus finds tin in England or Brittany.

510 B.C. Greek traveler Scylax explores Indus River, Red Sea, and Arabia.

500 B.C. Bantu tribes migrate through eastern Africa; Greek explorer Hekataios travels to Spain and North Africa; Carthaginian explorer Himlico visits French Atlantic Coast.

480 B.C. Carthaginian admiral Hanno explores west coast of Africa.

424 B.C. Greek traveler Herodotus visits North Africa, Italy, and Arabia.

400 B.C. Greek explorer Ctesias travels to Ganges River in India.

345 B.C. Greek explorer Pythias explores northwest European coastline.

327 B.C. Alexander the Great leads army to Indus Valley of India.

325 B.C. Greek admiral Nearchus attempts to circumnavigate Arabia.

302 B.C. Greek traveler Megasthenes visits India, Tibet, and Ceylon.

218 B.C. Hannibal leads army with elephants from Spain to Italy.

138 B.C. Decimus Brutus becomes first Roman to reach west coast of Spain.

128 B.C. Chinese explorer of central Asia has contact with Greeks.

112 B.C. Greek explorer Eudoxus sails to India and western Africa.

100 B.C. Greek explorer Hippalus finds direct ocean route to India.

55 B.C. Julius Caesar leads Roman army to Britain.

A.D. 20 King Juba of Morocco explores Canary Islands.

Cleopatra was part Macedonian, part Greek, and part Iranian. She was not an Egyptian.

A.D. 80 Gnaeus Agricola explores Atlantic coast of Britain.

A.D. 100 Roman explorer Julius Maternus crosses Sahara to Sudan; Alexander, Greek trader, sails to Vietnam and Cambodia; Chinese explorer Kan Ying reaches Black Sea.

A.D. 370 Huns, nomadic Mongols, invade Europe and reach Gaul.

A.D. 400 Chinese monk Fa Hsien visits India, Ceylon, and Java.

A.D. 407 Northern European Goths and Vandals spread to Mediterranean.

A.D. 431 Gunavarman, prince of Kashmir, travels to Java and China.

A.D. 570 Brendan, Irish monk, reportedly discovers America.

A.D. 620 Vikings explore Ireland.

A.D. 645 Chinese monk Yuan Chuang travels overland to India and returns.

A.D. 861 Vikings discover Iceland.

A.D. 872 Iraqi traveler Ibn Wahab visits China.

A.D. 900 Mayans migrate from Central America to Yucatan Peninsula; Arab traveler Ibn Rosteh explores Malay Peninsula and Java.

A.D. 921 Arabian diplomat Ahmad Ibn Fodhlan explores Russia and Poland.

A.D. 950 Maori sailors discover New Zealand.

A.D. 980 Arabs migrate to east coast of Africa.

A.D. 981 Eric the Red discovers Greenland.

A.D. 986 Viking sailor Bjarne Herjulfsson sights North America.

A.D. 1000 Leif Ericsson explores Atlantic coast of North America.

1002 Thorwald Ericsson explores American coast below New England.

1007 Viking Thorfinn Karlsefni establishes North American colony.

1150 Polynesian Toi Kai Rakan opens settlement of New Zealand.

1165 Spanish rabbi Benjamin visits synagogues of Asia and Near East.

1245 Franciscan monk Giovanni Carpini travels to Mongol capital.

1271 Marco Polo begins 24-year journey to Orient and Near East.

1291 Vivaldi brothers try sailing Atlantic from Genoa to India; Italian explorer Malocello discovers Canary Islands.

1337 Josef Faquin circumnavigates known world of 14th century.

1350 Polynesian chief Marutuahu establishes colony in New Zealand.

1419 Portuguese King Henry begins African exploration.

1431 Portuguese explorer discovers Azores.

1440 Italian explorer Niccolò Conti travels in Indonesia and Malaya.

1446 Portuguese explorer Nuno Tristao is lost on second trip to Africa.

1455 Venetian sailor Cadamosto discovers Cape Verde Islands.

1482 Portuguese navigator Diego Cao explores Congo River; Portugal establishes African Gold Coast settlements.

1488 Portuguese explorer Bartholomeu Dias sails around Cape of Good Hope.

1492 Christopher Columbus discovers the West Indies; German navigator Martin Behaim shows Earth is spherical.

1493 Pope Alexander VI divides New World between Spain and Portugal.

1494 Bartolome Colon, brother of Columbus, explores Haiti.

1495 Francisco de Almeida establishes Portuguese naval bases in eastern Africa.

1497 Italian John Cabot discovers Newfoundland for England.

1498 Columbus discovers South America and Trinidad; Portuguese navigator Vasco da Gama finds sea route to India.

1499 Spanish explorer Vincent Yañez Pinzon discovers mouth of Amazon River.

1500 Portuguese explorer Pedro Cabral discovers Brazil.

1501 Amerigo Vespucci explores coast of Brazil; Spanish explorer Rodrigo Bastidas discovers Colombia.

1502 Columbus discovers Nicaragua; Spaniard Alonso de Ojeda explores Haiti, Guiana, and Venezuela.

1504 Portuguese explorer Pacheco Pereira visits India.

1505 Portuguese establish settlements in Mozambique; Portuguese nobleman Tristão da Cunha leads expedition to India.

1507 German maps by Martin Waldseemuller identify New World as "America."

1510 Afonso de Albuquerque establishes Portuguese base in India at Goa.

1512 Spanish priest Bartolomé Las Casas is missionary to Cuban Indians.

1513 Balboa, in Panama, discovers Pacific Ocean; Ponce de Leon explores Florida and West Indies; Portuguese reach Canton, China.

1514 Spanish explorer Francisco de Montejo travels to West Indies.

1516 Spanish explorer Juan Diaz de Solís discovers Rio de la Plata, Uruguay.

1517 Spanish explorer Fernandez de Cordoba discovers Mayan ruins.

1518 Pedro Alvarado explores Southeast Mexico for Spain; Spanish conquistador Juan de Grijalva discovers Aztec Empire.

1519 Hernán Cortés conquers Mexico for Spain.

1521 Ferdinand Magellan dies in an attempt to circumnavigate Earth.

1522 Spanish navigator Juan Sebastián del Cano is first to circumnavigate Earth.

1524 Italian explorer Giovanni da Verrazano discovers New York harbor; Francisco Pizarro explores the west coasts of Panama and Peru.

1526 Italian Sebastian Cabot explores Rio de la Plata, Uruguay.

1527 Cabeza de Vaca begins trek from Florida to Mexican west coast.

1528 Spanish explorer Panfilo de Narvaez dies near mouth of Mississippi.

1530 German adventurer Nikolaus Federmann explores Venezuela, Colombia, and the Andes.

1533 Spanish conquistador Francisco Pizarro conquers Peru; Spanish conquistador Sebastián de Benalcázar conquers Ecuador.

1535 Jacques Cartier explores Saint Lawrence River; Spanish explore Chile; Spanish explorer Don Pedro de Mendoza establishes settlement of Buenos Aires.

1536 Spaniard Jiménez de Quesada explores Colombia and Orinoco River; Spanish conquistador Domingo de Irala explores Parana and Paraguay rivers.

1540 Vásquez de Coronado explores Arizona and New Mexico; Spanish monk Andres Urdaneta explores Philippine Islands.

1541 Hernando de Soto discovers Mississippi River; Francisco de Orellana travels Amazon River from source in Peru to mouth; Gonzalo Pizarro crosses the Andes from Ecuador to the Amazon River.

1542 Portuguese explorer Mendes Pinto is first European in Japan.

1544 Spanish conquistadors explore coast of Oregon.

1553 English explorer Richard Chancellor establishes Russian trade route.

1554 English explorer Sir Hugh Willoughby dies seeking Northeast Passage.

1557 Portuguese establish Chinese base at Macao.

1562 French explorer Jan Ribault establishes colony in South Carolina.

1564 Miguel López de Legazpi claims Marianas and Philippines for Spain and founds Manila.

1569 Spanish explorer Alvaro Bazan crosses Chaco of South America.

1576 English explorer Sir Martin Frobisher searches for Northwest Passage.

1581 Cossack Timofeevich extends Russian territory into Siberia.

1582 Cossack Koltso aids Timofeevich in exploration of Siberia; Spanish explorer Berrio navigates Orinoco River.

1584 Sir Walter Raleigh explores Virginia and North Carolina.

1592 Explorer Cornelis de Houtman discovers Dutch route to East Indies.

1594 Dutch explorer Willem Barents searches for Northeast Passage.

1595   Dutch establish settlements on Guinea Coast.

1598   Van Neck leads second Dutch expedition to East Indies; English explorer Will Adams travels to Japan.

1602   Englishman Bartholomew Gosnold explores New England coast.

1603   Samuel de Champlain explores Saint Lawrence River as "route to China."

1607   Englishman John Smith helps establish Jamestown, Virginia.

1608   Champlain founds city of Quebec; John Smith explores Cape Cod and Chesapeake Bay.

1610   Henry Hudson discovers Hudson Bay and River; Dutch navigator Willem Schouten sails around Cape Horn.

1613   Dutch colonist Jan Coen establishes factories in Indonesia; English explorer William Baffin discovers Baffin Bay and Island.

1614   Dutch captain Christianssen establishes fort at Albany, New York.

1615   Champlain explores lakes Huron and Ontario.

1617   Dutch explorers Jakob LeMaire and Willem Schouten start trip around world.

1618   French explorer Imbert discovers Timbuktu in Africa.

1620   English Pilgrims reach Cape Cod.

1626   French establish settlements in Madagascar; Dutch settle New Amsterdam in North America; French missionary Jean de Brébeuf explores Lake Huron region.

1631   English captain Thomas James explores James Bay in Canada.

1637   Russian explorers reach Pacific coast of Siberia.

1642   French explorer Sieur de Maisonneuve founds city of Montreal; Dutch explorer Abel Tasman discovers Van Dieman's Land (Tasmania).

1645   Capuchin monks explore Congo River.

1646   French missionary Isaac Jogues discovers Lake George.

1649   Cossack Dezhnev explores Siberia and Alaska for Russia; Cossack Stadukhin explores the Lena and Kolyma rivers in Siberia.

1652   Dutch colonist Jan van Riebeek founds Cape of Good Hope settlement.

1659   French fur trader Pierre Radisson explores Minnesota.

1670   French fur trader Perrot explores upper Mississippi region.

1673   French explorers Louis Joliet and Jacques Marquette navigate the length of the Mississippi.

1675   Belgian explorer Louis Hennepin discovers Niagara Falls and Mississippi River source.

1679   Frenchman Daniel Duluth explores Minnesota and Great Lakes.

1681   Sieur de La Salle explores Mississippi and names delta area Louisiana; English buccaneer William Dampier explores South Pacific islands.

1682   Buero da Silva explores Central Mountains region of Brazil; Pieres de Campos explores rivers of South America.

1683   Dutch explorer Aerssen establishes colony of Suriname; German naturalist Kaempfer visits Java, Thailand, and Japan.

1685   French missionary Claude Allouez explores western Lake Superior.

1697   Cossack Atlasov explores Kamchatka Peninsula for Russia.

1699   William Dampier explores northwest coast of Australia.

1721   Norwegian missionary Hans Egede is first European in Greenland in 200 years.

1723   Russian adventurer Fedorov explores northwest coast of America.

1732   Gvozdev explores Bering Sea and Alaska coastline for Russia.

1741   Russian explorer Chrikov discovers some Aleutian Islands.

1744   Frenchman Charles La Condamine measures arc of meridian in Andes.

1745   Basov explores Aleutian Islands for Russia.

1770   English navigator James Cook explores east coast of Australia.

1772   English explorer Samuel Hearne is first European to reach Arctic Ocean; Frenchman Yves Kerguélen-Trémarec discovers Antarctic islands; James Cook searches for possible continent of Antarctica.

1776 Cook searches for possible Atlantic–Pacific maritime passage.

1784 Daniel Boone explores Appalachian and Ozark areas.

1789 Scottish fur trader Sir Alexander Mackenzie explores western Canada.

Guam has no sand, only ground coral, which is used to make its roads.

1790 Russian fur trader Aleksandr Baranov explores Alaska; American explorer Robert Gray discovers Columbia River.

1797 German adventurer Hornemann explores caravan routes of Sahara Desert.

1798 British explorer George Bass circumnavigates Tasmania.

1799 German explorer Alexander von Humboldt tours North and South America.

1802 English explorer Matthew Flinders circumnavigates Australia; Portuguese explorers cross Africa.

1804 Lewis and Clark begin exploration of Louisiana Purchase; Russian Lisyanskii explores Pacific from Hawaii to Alaska.

1805 Canadian Fraser explores Canada west of Rocky Mountains; Russian navigator Adam Krusenstern maps Sakhalin, discovers mouth of Amur River.

1815 Russian navigator Otto Kotzebue discovers many Pacific islands.

1818 French explorer René Caillé crosses Sahara, reaching Timbuktu.

1819 English explorer Sir William Parry finds Northwest Passage in Arctic.

1820 American Nathaniel Palmer discovers Palmer Peninsula of Antarctica.

1821 Russian Fabian Bellinghausen leads South Pole expedition.

1825 British explorer Sir John Franklin surveys Canadian Arctic region.

1828 German physicist Georg Erman circumnavigates Earth, studying magnetic fields.

1829 English explorer Freemantle founds West Australia colony.

1830 British Lander brothers explore Niger River and Delta.

1831 American Benjamin Bonneville explores Rocky Mountains and California; British explorer James Ross finds North Magnetic Pole.

1835 British colonist Bourke explores new areas of Australia; American pioneer Jim Bowie explores U.S. Southwest.

1837 American trapper Joseph Walker explores Sierra Mountains.

1840 Frenchman Dumont d'Urville discovers Antarctic islands.

1842 John Fremont begins exploration west of Rockies.

1843 British colonist Edward Eyre explores South and West Australia; Scottish explorer Sir James Ross proves Antarctica has ice barrier.

1846 German explorer Friedrich Leichhardt disappears crossing Australia.

1847 French naturalist Comte de Castelnau crosses South America west to east.

1848 American explorer Elisha Kane surveys Gulf of Mexico.

1850 English naval officer Sir Robert McClure discovers Northwest Passage.

1851 German explorer Heinrich Barth crosses Sahara Desert twice; American explorer Savage rediscovers Yosemite Valley.

1853 Englishman Sir Richard Burton is first non-Muslim to visit Mecca and Medina; American explorer Elisha Kane leads Arctic expedition.

1854 U.S. Commodore Matthew Perry ends isolation of Japan; German Schlagintweit brothers explore Central Asia; Portuguese explorer Silva Porto crosses South Africa, west to east.

1855 Russian adventurer Nevelskoi explores Amur and proves Sakhalin is an island.

1856 Scottish missionary David Livingstone explores Africa; English explorers Richard Burton and John Speke discover Lake Tanganyika; English explorer Gregory crosses Australia east to west.

1857 English explorer John Speke discovers Lake Victoria.

1860 Irish explorer Robert Burke is first to cross Australia south to north; German explorer Karl Decken leads Kilimanjaro Mountain expedition; John Speke and James Grant prove Lake Victoria is source of Nile; American Isaac Hayes searches for "open sea" above Arctic Circle.

1863 Frenchman Louis Faidherbe explores Senegal and Niger River in Africa.

1864 Hermann Schlagintweit is first European to cross Kuenlun range.

1866 Doudart explores Mekong River route to source for France.

1871 Russian naturalist Aleksi Fedchenko explores Asian mountain ranges; British journalist Henry Stanley finds missing Livingstone; American Charles Hall is first to explore above 82 degrees north latitude.

1872 French colonist Francis Garnier searches for China–Tibet river route.

1874 John and Alexander Forrest survey western Australia.

1878 German Eduard Schnitzer (Emin Pasha) explores African lake country; English explorer Sir George Nares surveys Magellan Strait; Russian Grigori Potanin explores Gobi Desert of Mongolia.

1879 Swedish explorer Nils Nordenskjöld discovers Northeast Passage; Russian Nikolai Przhevalski is first to cross Tibet's Humboldt Mountains; Joseph Thompson explores Great Rift Valley of Africa.

1880 French colonist Pierre Brazza explores African river routes to sea.

1882 French explorer Pierre Bonvalot discovers ancient cities of Asia.

1883 French officer Foucauld explores Algerian oases and Morocco.

1885 Portuguese explorer Capelo crosses South Africa.

1888 Norwegian Fridtjof Nansen explores Greenland ice cap; French explorer Louis Binger leads African scientific expedition.

1889 German explorer Hans Meyer is first to scale Kilimanjaro peak; Austrian Oskar Baumann explores African rivers and lakes.

1891 German Erich von Drygalski explores West Greenland.

1892 Scottish oceanographer William Bruce explores Antarctic coastline; Englishman William Conway is first to scale 23,000-foot Himalayan peaks; American Robert Peary explores Greenland and proves it is an island.

1893 Swedish engineer Andre explores Arctic by balloon; German explorer Goetzen crosses Africa east to west.

1894 Englishwoman Mary Kingsley explores Ogowe River in Africa.

1895 French explorer Charles Bonin crosses Tibet and Mongolia; Englishman Frederick Jackson explores Franz Josef Land in Arctic.

1897 Gerlache de Gomery leads Belgian Antarctic expedition.

1899 Sweden's Sven Hedin finds sources of Bramaputra and Indus rivers.

1900 Norwegian Carsten Borchgrevink is early Antarctic explorer.

1906 Norwegian Roald Amundsen is first to navigate Northwest Passage.

1908 British explorer Sir Ernest Shackleton nearly reaches South Pole.

1909 American explorer Robert Peary is first to reach North Pole.

1910 Bavarian officer Wilhelm Filchner leads German Antarctic expedition.

1911 Norwegian explorer Roald Amundsen reaches South Pole; American explorer Bingham discovers Machu Picchu in Peru; British explorer Sir Douglas Mawson leads Antarctic expedition.

1912 British explorer Robert Scott reaches South Pole.

1913 Theodore Roosevelt explores central Brazilian rivers.

1926 Americans Floyd Bennett and Richard Byrd fly over North Pole; American Lincoln Ellsworth flies over North Pole; Italian engineer Umberto Nobile flies over North Pole, from Norway to Alaska.

1927 American Charles Lindbergh is first to fly solo across Atlantic Ocean.

1929 American explorer Richard Byrd is first to fly over South Pole; German Hugo Eckener makes round-the-world flight.

1931 Eckener flies over North Pole.

1932 British explorer St. John Philby crosses Arabia's Rub-al-Kali Desert; French explorer Jean Piccard explores stratosphere in balloon gondola.

1935 Lincoln Ellsworth flies over South Pole.

1937 Russian aviator Valeri Chkalov is first to fly from USSR to America over North Pole.

1947 Norwegian Thor Heyerdahl sails balsa raft from Peru to Polynesia.

1953 British mountaineer Sir Edmund Hillary and Tenzing Norgay of Nepal scale Mount Everest.

1956 Heyerdahl explores Easter Island and eastern Pacific.

1957 (July 1957–Dec. 1958) As part of the International Geophysical Year, 67 nations cooperate in scientific exploration of the Earth and its environment.

1957 Soviet Union launches *Sputnik 1*, the world's first artificial earth satellite.

1958 *Explorer 1*, first U.S. satellite, is launched and discovers Van Allen radiation belts around Earth; U.S. nuclear submarine *Nautilus* passes under ice cap at North Pole.

1959 Soviet probes *Lunas 1, 2, and 3*, respectively, fly by, impact, and photograph the moon.

1960 U.S. submarine *Triton* completes first circumnavigation of the globe under water; U.S. Navy Lieutenant Don Walsh and French explorer Jacques Piccard dive in the bathyscaphe *Trieste* to a record 35,000 feet to the floor of the Mariana Trench, the deepest point in the Pacific Ocean; NASA weather satellite *TIROS 1* transmits television pictures of cloud cover.

1961 Soviet cosmonaut Yuri Gagarin, in *Vostok 1*, is first person to orbit Earth.

1962 John Glenn, in *Freedom 7*, is first U.S. astronaut to orbit around the Earth; NASA's *Mariner 2* becomes first space probe to fly by another planet (Venus).

1964 NASA's *Ranger 7* returns close-up photographs of the Moon just prior to impacting the lunar surface.

1965 NASA's *Mariner 4* space probe, as it flies by the planet Mars, transmits first close-up pictures of the planet's surface.

1966 Soviet Union's *Luna 9* and NASA's *Surveyor 1* make first soft landings on lunar surface.

1968 U.S. astronauts Frank Borman, James Lovell, and William Anders, in *Apollo 8*, are first persons to orbit the moon.

1969 U.S. astronauts Neil Armstrong and Edwin "Buzz" Aldrin, in *Apollo 11*'s lunar landing module *Eagle*, are first persons to step onto the lunar surface.

1970 Soviet Union's unmanned probe *Luna 16* returns from the Moon with rock samples; its *Luna 17* mission lands a self-propelled vehicle on the Moon; its *Venera 7* space probe lands on Venus.

1971 NASA's *Mariner 9* becomes first space probe to orbit another planet (Mars).

1973 NASA's *Pioneer 10* becomes first space probe to fly by the planet Jupiter.

1974 NASA's *Mariner 10* space probes takes first close-up photographs of the planets Venus and Mercury.

1976 NASA's *Vikings 1* and *2* become first spacecraft to land on surface of Mars.

1978 Italian Reinhold Messner and Austrian Peter Habeler make the first conquest of Mount Everest without artificial oxygen supplies; Japanese explorer Naomi Uemura becomes the first person to make a solo journey to the North Pole.

1979 NASA's *Voyager 1*, during flyby of Jupiter, discovers ring, erupting volcanoes on the Jovian satellite Io, and three new satellites; NASA's *Pioneer 11*, becomes first space probe to fly by the planet Saturn.

1980 During flyby of the planet Saturn, *Voyager 1* discovers six new satellites.

1981 NASA scientists report that two meteorites found in the Antarctic may have originated on the planet Mars.

1982 Soviet space probes *Veneras 13* and *14* land on Venus and transmit first color photos.

1983 *Pioneer 10* becomes first spacecraft to leave solar system.

1984 Soviet engineers drill 7.5 miles to reach the Earth's lower crust.

1985 Deep oceanic vents are found in the Mid-Atlantic Ridge; U.S. oceanographer Robert Ballard leads French-American team, using sonar and a robot submarine, that discovers wreck of British ocean liner *Titanic* .

1986 NASA's *Voyager 2* space probe flies by the planet Uranus and discovers ten new satellites; European Space Agency's *Giotto* space probe photographs nucleus of Halley's comet.

1989 *Voyager 2* flies by the planet Neptune and discovers six new satellites and five rings.

1995 NASA's *Galileo* space probe releases entry probe into Jupiter's atmosphere and becomes first craft to orbit the planet.

1997 NASA's *Pathfinder* space probe lands on the surface of Mars, and its *Sojourner* rover carries out first mobile exploration of another planet.

1998 Former *Mercury* astronaut Senator John Glenn (77) becomes the oldest person ever to fly in space; assembly of International Space Station begins; *Lunar Prospector* becomes first NASA moon launch in 25 years.

1999 Bertrand Picard and Brian Jones become the first people to circumnavigate Earth nonstop in a balloon; Air Force Lieutenant Colonel Eileen Collins becomes the first woman to command a NASA space shuttle mission; spacecraft *Stardust* is launched to gather dust samples from Comet Wild-2 and return them to Earth.

2000 The first cargo ship docks with the International Space Station; the first official crew reaches the station. Rendezvous spacecraft reaches the asteroid Eros, the first spacecraft to orbit an asteroid.

2001 The *Mir* space station—the largest manmade object in space—falls into the South Pacific Ocean; the first citizen "space tourist," Dennis Tito, visits the International Space Station; Claudie Haigneré becomes the first European woman astronaut to visit the International Space Station.

2002 Mark Shuttleworth becomes the second space tourist to visit the International Space Station; Mars Odyssey, which reached Mars in 2001, begins its science mapping mission at the red planet; scientists are still able to contact *Pioneer 10,* a spacecraft launched 30 years ago.

POPULATION OF MAJOR WORLD CITIES

An asterisk (*) indicates that the population figure is for the metropolitan area.

City	Description	Population
Addis Ababa, Ethiopia	Capital since 1896	2,639,000
Ahmedabad, India	Founded in 1411	3,298,000
Alexandria, Egypt	Founded by Alexander the Great, 332 B.C.	3,431,000
Algiers, Algeria	Founded in 10th century on Roman site	1,885,000
Amman, Jordan	Site of biblical city of Ammonites	1,300,000
Amsterdam, the Netherlands	Founded in 1300	1,101,000
Ankara, Turkey	Capital of Galacia around 300 B.C.	3,028,000
Athens, Greece	Ancient Greek city-state in 700 B.C.	772,000
Auckland, New Zealand	Founded in 1840, original capital	346,000
Baghdad, Iraq	Center of Islamic culture since 813	4,797,000
Baku, Azerbaijan	Founded in 9th century	1,149,000
Bandung, Indonesia	Founded in 1810	2,368,000
Bangalore, India	Founded in 16th century	4,087,000*
Bangkok, Thailand	Capital since 1782	5,876,000
Barcelona, Spain	Founded by Carthaginians around 300 B.C.	2,819,000*
Barranquilla, Colombia	Inland seaport since 1935	1,157,000
Beijing, China	Founded around 1122 B.C. as Peking; renamed in 1949	10,839,000
Beirut, Lebanon	Site of ancient Phoenician settlement	1,900,000*
Belgrade, Serbia	Site of Singidunum, ancient Roman camp	1,555,000
Belo Horizonte, Brazil	Cattle and cotton-trading center	4,170,000*

City	Description	Population
Berlin, Germany	Founded in 13th century; capital of Germany 1871–1945, of United Germany since 1990	3,471,000*
Birmingham, England	Market town since before 13th century	1,020,000
Bogotá, Colombia	Founded by conquistadors in 1538	5,699,000
Bombay, India	Established in early Christian era	12,572,000*
Brisbane, Australia	Founded in 1824 as a penal colony	1,146,000
Brussels, Belgium	Capital since 1530	948,000
Bucharest, Romania	Capital since 1861	2,054,000
Budapest, Hungary	Site of Aquincum, 2nd-century Roman camp	2,011,000
Buenos Aires, Argentina	Settled by conquistadors in 1536	2,961,000
Cairo, Egypt	Site of 7th-century Arab military camp	6,790,000
Calcutta, India	Developed from 1690 English factory site	4,400,000
Calgary, Alberta, Canada	Originally (1875) Northwest Mounted Police post	899,000*
Cali, Colombia	Founded by conquistadors in 1536	2,710,000*
Cape Town, South Africa	Founded in 1652 as Dutch naval base	855,000
Caracas, Venezuela	Founded by conquistadors in 1567	3,153,000*
Casablanca, Morocco	Site of ancient city of Anfa	3,541,000*
Chicago, Illinois, United States	Originally portage site for fur traders	2,896,000
Chittagong, Bangladesh	Portuguese trading post in 1600s	2,041,000*
Chongqing, China	Former capital of Nationalist China	3,870,000
Cologne, Germany	Site of Roman (A.D. 50) Colonia Agrippina	964,000
Copenhagen, Denmark	Capital since 1443	1,338,000*
Córdoba, Argentina	Founded in 1573; university founded in 1613	1,434,000*
Damascus, Syria	City of Egyptians and Hittites before 1000 B.C.	2,335,000*
Delhi, India	Capital of northern India in 13th century	7,207,000
Dhaka, Bangladesh	Capital since 1971 secession from Pakistan	6,105,000*
Dnepropetrovsk, Ukraine	Founded in 1787 at Cossack village site	1,190,000
Donetsk, Ukraine	Founded in 1870, called Stalino until 1961	1,121,000
Dresden, Germany	Originally (A.D. 922) a Slavonic settlement	491,000
Dublin, Ireland	Originally a 9th-century Viking base	985,000*
Düsseldorf, Germany	Rhine River port since 11th century	576,000
Edmonton, Alberta, Canada	Originally (1795) Hudson Bay trading post	617,000
Essen, Germany	Ruhr Valley city founded in 9th century	627,000
Frankfurt, Germany	Site of ancient Roman military camp	651,000
Fukuoka, Japan	Seaport on Hakata Bay founded in 13th century	1,285,000
Genoa, Italy	Roman settlement in 3rd century B.C.	678,000
Glasgow, Scotland	Founded by 6th-century missionaries	663,000
Guadalajara, Mexico	Originally founded in 1530	1,646,000
Guangzhou, China	Inland seaport since 3rd century B.C.	3,114,000
Guatemala City, Guatemala	Founded as capital in 1776	1,167,000
Guayaquil, Ecuador	Founded by conquistadors in 1535	1,877,000
Hamburg, Germany	Founded in 9th century by Charlemagne	1,707,000
Harbin, China	Village until linked by railroad in 1898	2,505,000
Havana, Cuba	Founded in 1519 as Spanish navy base	2,256,000
Ho Chi Minh City, Vietnam	Formerly Saigon, ancient Khmer village	4,322,000*
Hyderabad, India	Founded as Golconda; capital in 1589	3,045,000
Hyderabad, Pakistan	Founded in 1768 as capital of Sind	1,151,000*
Ibadan, Nigeria	Founded around 1830 as military camp	1,731,000
Istanbul, Turkey	Until A.D. 300, Byzantium; until 1930, Constantinople	7,490,000
Jakarta, Indonesia	Founded in 1619 as Batavia; renamed 1971	8,228,000

continues

The World

Population of Major World Cities, Continued

City	Description	Population
Jerusalem, Israel	Capital of ancient kingdoms of Israel and Judah	592,000
Johannesburg, South Africa	Founded as gold-mining camp in 1886	1,196,000
Kanpur, India	Village until ceded to British in 1801	2,111,000
Karachi, Pakistan	Founded in 1725 as Hindu trading center	11,794,000*
Kharkov, Ukraine	Founded in 1654 as outpost of Moscow	1,555,000
Kiev, Ukraine	"Mother of Russian Cities," founded in A.D. 882	2,670,000
Kinshasa, Democratic Republic of Congo	Founded in 1881 as Leopoldville; renamed 1966	5,064,000
Kobe, Japan	Ancient fishing village until 1868	1,477,000
Kuala Lumpur, Malaysia	Founded as tin-mining settlement in 1857	1,378,000
Lagos, Nigeria	Former slave trading center; now the capital	5,195,000*
Lahore, Pakistan	Capital of Mogul sultans in 11th century	6,040,000*
La Paz, Bolivia	Founded in 1548; capital since 1898	1,001,000
Leipzig, Germany	Founded in 11th century; Bach was organist here	511,000
Lima, Peru	Site of oldest university in Americas (1551)	7,443,000*
Lisbon, Portugal	Ancient Phoenician, Carthaginian trading center	818,000
Liverpool, England	Chartered in 1207 by King John	482,000
Lodz, Poland	Founded in 1423; belonged to Russia until 1919	849,000
London, England	Established in A.D. 43 as Roman town of Londinium	7,074,000
Los Angeles, California, United States	Founded in 1781 as capital of Spanish colony	3,598,000
Madras, India	Founded in 1640 as British outpost	5,361,000*
Madrid, Spain	A Moorish fortress until 932	3,029,000
Managua, Nicaragua	Established as capital in 1855 to end feud	959,000
Manila, Philippines	Founded by Spanish in 1571	1,655,000
Marseilles, France	Originally Massilia, Ionian Greek colony, in 600 B.C.	1,087,000
Mecca, Saudi Arabia	Birthplace of Muhammad in 570	630,000
Medellín, Colombia	Coffee, drugs, mining center founded in 1675	1,970,000*
Melbourne, Australia	Founded 1835 by Tasmanian settlers	3,217,000
Mexico City, Mexico	Aztec capital until captured by Cortés in 1521	8,605,000
Milan, Italy	Ancient Celtic town captured by Romans in 222 B.C.	1,371,000
Minsk, Belarus	City on Moscow-Warsaw rail link founded in 11th century	1,772,000
Monterrey, Mexico	Founded in 1579; invaded by U.S. troops in 1846	1,110,000
Montevideo, Uruguay	Settled by Spanish in 1726; capital since 1828	1,378,000
Montreal, Quebec, Canada	Site of Indian encampment, founded by French in 1642	3,337,000
Moscow, Russia	Founded in 1147; became capital around 1340	9,233,000
Munich, Germany	Founded in 1158; birthplace of Nazi movement, 1923	1,240,000
Nagoya, Japan	Buddhist temple site in 2nd century; now an industrial city	2,155,000
Nanjing, China	Founded in 1368; twice capital in 20th century	2,211,000
Naples, Italy	Named Neapolis (New City) by Greek settlers around 600 B.C.	1,369,000
New York City, New York, United States	Founded in 1609 as New Amsterdam by Dutch; renamed 1664	7,420,000
Nizhni Novgorod, Russia	Founded in 1221; called Gorky after Maxim Gorky during Soviet era	1,458,000
Novosibirsk, Russia	"Chicago of Siberia," founded in 1893 on Trans-Siberian Railway	1,478,000
Odessa, Ukraine	Founded by Tartars in 14th century	1,096,000

City	Description	Population
Osaka, Japan	Founded in 16th century as capital city	2,624,000
Ottawa, Ontario, Canada	Selected as capital in 1858 by Queen Victoria	323,000
Palermo, Italy	Founded by Phoenicians in 8th century B.C.	698,000
Paris, France	Grew from pre-Roman settlement named Lutetia Parisiorum	2,152,000
Port-au-Prince, Haiti	Founded by sugar planters in 1749; capital since 1804	917,000
Pôrto Alegre, Brazil	Founded in 1742 by settlers from Azores	1,288,000
Prague, Czech Republic	Grew from 10th-century trading center	1,226,000
Pusan, South Korea	Originally a fishing village; opened to trade in 1443	3,830,000
Pyongyang, North Korea	Existed as Heijo, Korean cultural center, in 1100 B.C.	2,639,000
Quebec City, Quebec, Canada	Site of Indian settlement visited by Cartier in 1535	168,000
Quezon City, Philippines	Founded in 1940 as site of future capital	1,989,000
Quito, Ecuador	Originally Quito Indian camp; captured by Incas in 1470	1,487,000
Recife, Brazil	Settled by Portuguese in 1535	1,346,000
Rio de Janeiro, Brazil	Founded by Portuguese in 1502; capital since 1889	5,851,000
Riyadh, Saudi Arabia	Onetime center of classic Arabic architecture	2,776,000*
Rome, Italy	According to legend, founded in 753 B.C. by Romulus	2,775,000
Rosario, Argentina	City in La Pampa region; founded in 1730	1,118,000
Rotterdam, the Netherlands	North Sea port chartered in 1328	593,000
St. Petersburg, Russia	Founded in 1703; named Leningrad from 1924 to 1991	5,113,000
Salvador, Brazil	Founded in 1549 as Bahia	2,211,000
Samara, Russia	Founded in 1586; formerly Kuibyshev	1,232,000
Santiago, Chile	Founded in 1541 by conquistadors	5,067,000
Santo Domingo, Dominican Republic	Oldest continuous European settlement in Americas, founded in 1496	2,135,000
São Paulo, Brazil	Founded in 1554 by Jesuit missionaries on Indian campsite	9,786,000
Sapporo, Japan	Founded in 1869 in government plan to develop Hokkaido Island	1,774,000
Seoul, South Korea	Originally named Keijo, a Korean capital since 1392	10,776,000
Seville, Spain	Originally Hispalis, a Phoenician trading center	719,000
Shanghai, China	Existed as Hu-tsen in Sung dynasty, 11th century	7,551,000
Shenyang, China	Formerly Mukden, capital city of 12th-century Tartars	3,860,000
Singapore, Singapore	Originally Singhapura, destroyed in 1365; refounded in 1819	3,462,000
Sofia, Bulgaria	Founded as Sardica by 2nd-century Romans; capital since 1879	1,192,000
Stockholm, Sweden	Originally a fishing village, founded in 13th century	736,000
Surabaja, Indonesia	Grew from 17th-century Javanese trading post	2,701,000
Sydney, Australia	First British settlement in Australia, 1788	3,770,000
Taipei, Taiwan	Settled in 18th century by Chinese mainland immigrants	2,596,000
Tashkent, Uzbekistan	Ancient central Asian city; existed in 1st century B.C.	2,148,000
Tbilisi, Georgia	Also called Tiflis; settled in 4th century B.C.	1,310,000
Tehran, Iran	Settled in 13th century by refugees from Mongol invasion	6,750,000
Tianjin, China	Also called Tientsin, ancient trading center	4,575,000
Tokyo, Japan	Founded in 12th century as fortress for warlord	8,164,000
Toronto, Ontario, Canada	Originally Fort Rouille, 1749; York, 1793; renamed 1834	4,344,000*
Tripoli, Libya	Founded as Oea by Phoenicians in 7th century B.C.	591,000
Tunis, Tunisia	Pre-Carthaginian city with access to Mediterranean	1,897,000*
Turin, Italy	Ancient Roman city of Augusta Taurinorum	962,000

continues

The World

Population of Major World Cities, Continued

City	Description	Population
Valencia, Spain	Former city of Romans, Visigoths, Moors	764,000
Vancouver, British Columbia, Canada	Originally settled in 1875 as Granville; renamed 1886	1,831,000*
Vienna, Austria	Capital of the Austro-Hungarian Empire 1278–1918; now capital of the Austrian republic	1,595,000
Volgograd, Russia	Founded in 1589 as Tsaritsyn; later Stalingrad; renamed Volgograd in 1961	1,003,000
Warsaw, Poland	Settled in 11th century; capital since 1596	1,651,000
Washington, District of Columbia, United States	Founded in 1790 on site selected by George Washington	607,000
Wellington, New Zealand	Founded in 1840; replaced Auckland as capital in 1865	166,000
Yangon, Myanmar	Existed as fishing village in 6th century	4,196,000
Yekaterinburg, Russia	Founded in 1721; called Sverdlovsk during Soviet era	1,351,000
Yokohama, Japan	Feudal fishing village until opened to foreign trade in 1859	3,307,000

THE UNITED NATIONS

The United Nations organization was established during World War II as an outgrowth of an agreement among 26 countries fighting the Germany-Italy-Japan Axis. It replaced the League of Nations as an instrument for the promotion of international peace and security.

The name was suggested by U.S. President Franklin D. Roosevelt in 1941 and was officially adopted the following year. The United Nations was formally organized on June 26, 1945, following an initial San Francisco conference to draft a charter.

The basic charter contains 19 chapters, divided into 111 articles, and provides for the support of a number of international organs and agencies (see chart).

THE SIX OFFICIAL LANGUAGES OF THE UNITED NATIONS

Arabic	French
Chinese	Russian
English	Spanish

SECRETARIES-GENERAL OF THE UNITED NATIONS

Name	Trygve Lie
Country	Norway
Term of Office	1946–1952

Name	Dag Hammarskjöld
Country	Sweden
Term of Office	1953–1961

Name	U Thant
Country	Myanmar (formerly Burma)
Term of Office	1961–1971

Name	Kurt Waldheim
Country	Austria
Term of Office	1972–1981

Name	Javier Pérez de Cuellar
Country	Peru
Term of Office	1982–1991

Name	Boutros Boutros-Ghali
Country	Egypt
Term of Office	1992–1996

Name	Kofi Annan
Country	Ghana
Term of Office	1997–

THE UNITED NATIONS SYSTEM

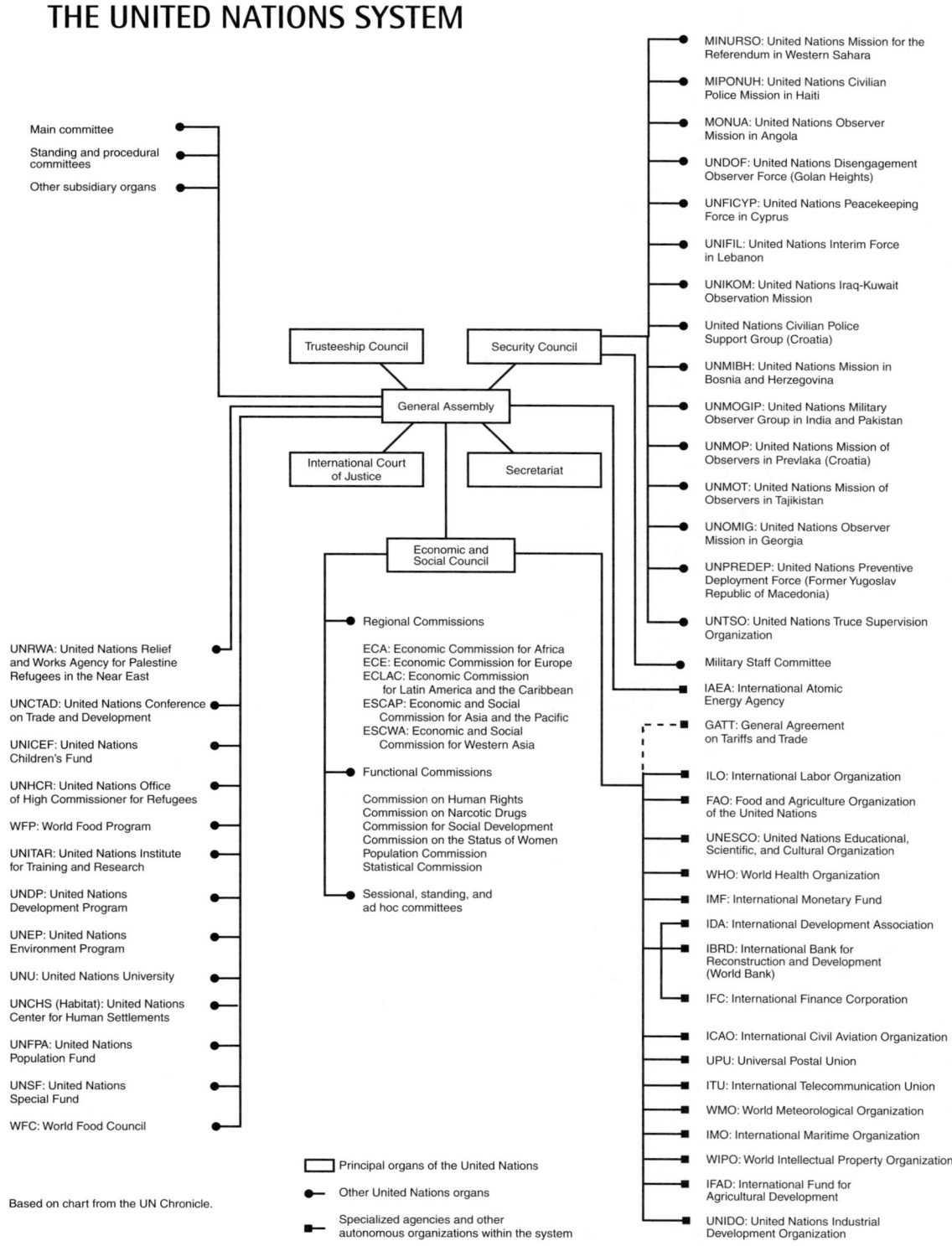

Main committee

Standing and procedural committees

Other subsidiary organs

Trusteeship Council

Security Council

General Assembly

International Court of Justice

Secretariat

Economic and Social Council

MINURSO: United Nations Mission for the Referendum in Western Sahara

MIPONUH: United Nations Civilian Police Mission in Haiti

MONUA: United Nations Observer Mission in Angola

UNDOF: United Nations Disengagement Observer Force (Golan Heights)

UNFICYP: United Nations Peacekeeping Force in Cyprus

UNIFIL: United Nations Interim Force in Lebanon

UNIKOM: United Nations Iraq-Kuwait Observation Mission

United Nations Civilian Police Support Group (Croatia)

UNMIBH: United Nations Mission in Bosnia and Herzegovina

UNMOGIP: United Nations Military Observer Group in India and Pakistan

UNMOP: United Nations Mission of Observers in Prevlaka (Croatia)

UNMOT: United Nations Mission of Observers in Tajikistan

UNOMIG: United Nations Observer Mission in Georgia

UNPREDEP: United Nations Preventive Deployment Force (Former Yugoslav Republic of Macedonia)

UNTSO: United Nations Truce Supervision Organization

Military Staff Committee

IAEA: International Atomic Energy Agency

GATT: General Agreement on Tariffs and Trade

ILO: International Labor Organization

FAO: Food and Agriculture Organization of the United Nations

UNESCO: United Nations Educational, Scientific, and Cultural Organization

WHO: World Health Organization

IMF: International Monetary Fund

IDA: International Development Association

IBRD: International Bank for Reconstruction and Development (World Bank)

IFC: International Finance Corporation

ICAO: International Civil Aviation Organization

UPU: Universal Postal Union

ITU: International Telecommunication Union

WMO: World Meteorological Organization

IMO: International Maritime Organization

WIPO: World Intellectual Property Organization

IFAD: International Fund for Agricultural Development

UNIDO: United Nations Industrial Development Organization

UNRWA: United Nations Relief and Works Agency for Palestine Refugees in the Near East

UNCTAD: United Nations Conference on Trade and Development

UNICEF: United Nations Children's Fund

UNHCR: United Nations Office of High Commissioner for Refugees

WFP: World Food Program

UNITAR: United Nations Institute for Training and Research

UNDP: United Nations Development Program

UNEP: United Nations Environment Program

UNU: United Nations University

UNCHS (Habitat): United Nations Center for Human Settlements

UNFPA: United Nations Population Fund

UNSF: United Nations Special Fund

WFC: World Food Council

Regional Commissions

ECA: Economic Commission for Africa
ECE: Economic Commission for Europe
ECLAC: Economic Commission for Latin America and the Caribbean
ESCAP: Economic and Social Commission for Asia and the Pacific
ESCWA: Economic and Social Commission for Western Asia

Functional Commissions

Commission on Human Rights
Commission on Narcotic Drugs
Commission for Social Development
Commission on the Status of Women
Population Commission
Statistical Commission

Sessional, standing, and ad hoc committees

☐ Principal organs of the United Nations

● Other United Nations organs

■ Specialized agencies and other autonomous organizations within the system

Based on chart from the UN Chronicle.

The World

UNITED NATIONS MEMBER STATES

Member	Year of Admission	Member	Year of Admission	Member	Year of Admission
Afghanistan	1946	Cyprus	1960	Korea, Republic of	1991
Albania	1955	Czech Republic	1993	Kuwait	1963
Algeria	1962	Denmark	1945	Kyrgyzstan	1992
Andorra	1993	Djibouti	1977	Lao People's	1955
Angola	1976	Dominica	1978	Democratic Republic	
Antigua and Barbuda	1981	Dominican Republic	1945	Latvia	1991
Argentina	1945	Ecuador	1945	Lebanon	1945
Armenia	1992	Egypt	1945	Lesotho	1966
Australia	1945	El Salvador	1945	Liberia	1945
Austria	1955	Equatorial Guinea	1968	Libyan Arab Jamahiriya	1955
Azerbaijan	1992	Eritrea	1993	Liechtenstein	1990
Bahamas	1973	Estonia	1991	Lithuania	1991
Bahrain	1971	Ethiopia	1945	Luxembourg	1945
Bangladesh	1974	Fiji	1970	Macedonia (the former	1993
Barbados	1966	Finland	1955	Yugoslav Republic of)	
Belarus	1945	France	1945	Madagascar	1960
Belgium	1945	Gabon	1960	Malawi	1964
Belize	1981	Gambia	1965	Malaysia	1957
Benin	1960	Georgia	1992	Maldives	1965
Bhutan	1971	Germany	1973	Mali	1960
Bolivia	1945	Ghana	1957	Malta	1964
Bosnia and	1992	Greece	1945	Marshall Islands	1991
Herzegovina		Grenada	1974	Mauritania	1961
Botswana	1966	Guatemala	1945	Mauritius	1968
Brazil	1945	Guinea	1958	Mexico	1945
Brunei Darussalam	1984	Guinea-Bissau	1974	Micronesia	1991
Bulgaria	1955	Guyana	1966	(Federated States of)	
Burkina Faso	1960	Haiti	1945	Moldova	1992
Burundi	1962	Honduras	1945	Monaco	1993
Cambodia	1955	Hungary	1955	Mongolia	1961
Cameroon	1960	Iceland	1946	Morocco	1956
Canada	1945	India	1945	Mozambique	1975
Cape Verde	1975	Indonesia	1950	Myanmar	1948
Central African	1960	Iran (Islamic	1945	Namibia	1990
Republic		Republic of)		Nauru	1999
Chad	1960	Iraq	1945	Nepal	1955
Chile	1945	Ireland	1955	Netherlands	1945
China	1945	Israel	1949	New Zealand	1945
Colombia	1945	Italy	1955	Nicaragua	1945
Comoros	1975	Jamaica	1962	Niger	1960
Congo, Democratic	1960	Japan	1956	Nigeria	1960
Republic of		Jordan	1955	Norway	1945
Congo, Republic of the	1960	Kazakhstan	1992	Oman	1971
Costa Rica	1945	Kenya	1963	Pakistan	1947
Côte d'Ivoire	1960	Kirbati	1999	Palau	1994
Croatia	1992	Korea, Democratic	1991	Panama	1945
Cuba	1945	People's Republic of		Papua New Guinea	1975

Member	Year of Admission	Member	Year of Admission	Member	Year of Admission
Paraguay	1945	Slovakia	1993	Uganda	1962
Peru	1945	Slovenia	1992	Ukraine	1945
Philippines	1945	Solomon Islands	1978	United Arab Emirates	1971
Poland	1945	Somalia	1960	United Kingdom of	1945
Portugal	1955	South Africa	1945	Great Britain and	
Qatar	1971	Spain	1955	Northern Ireland	
Romania	1955	Sri Lanka	1955	United Republic of	1961
Russian Federation	1945	Sudan	1956	Tanzania	
Rwanda	1962	Suriname	1975	United States of	1945
Saint Kitts and Nevis	1983	Swaziland	1968	America	
Saint Lucia	1979	Sweden	1946	Uruguay	1945
Saint Vincent and	1980	Syrian Arab Republic	1945	Uzbekistan	1992
the Grenadines		Tajikistan	1992	Vanuatu	1981
Samoa	1976	Thailand	1946	Venezuela	1945
San Marino	1992	Togo	1960	Viet Nam	1977
São Tomé and Principe	1975	Tonga	1999	Yemen	1947
Saudi Arabia	1945	Trinidad and Tobago	1962	Yugoslavia	1945
Senegal	1960	Tunisia	1956	Zambia	1964
Seychelles	1976	Turkey	1945	Zimbabwe	1980
Sierra Leone	1961	Turkmenistan	1992		
Singapore	1965	Tuvalu	2000		

INTERNATIONAL ORGANIZATIONS

ADB	African Development Bank
AL	Arab League (League of Arab States)
ANZUS	ANZUS Council; treaty signed by Australia, New Zealand, and the United States
APC	African Peanut (Groundnut) Council
AsDB	Asian Development Bank
ASEAN	Association of Southeast Asian Nations
BENELUX	Belgium, Netherlands, Luxembourg Economic Union
CACM	Central American Common Market
CARICOM	Caribbean Community and Common Market
CCC	Customs Cooperation Council
CDB	Caribbean Development Bank
CE	Council of Europe
CEAO	West African Economic Community
CENTO	Central Treaty Organization
CFA	African Financial Community
CE	Council of Europe
CIS	Commonweath of Independent States (12 members of former Soviet Union)
CP	Colombo Plan
EC	European Community
ECA	Economic Commission for Africa (UN)
ECE	Economic Commission for Europe (UN)
ECLAC	Economic Commission for Latin America and the Caribbean (UN)
ECOSOC	Economic and Social Council (UN)
ECOWAS	Economic Community of West African States
ESCWA	Economic and Social Commission for Western Asia (UN)
EFTA	European Free Trade Association
EIB	European Investment Bank
ENTENTE	Political-Economic Association of Ivory Coast, Benin, Niger, Burkina Faso, and Togo
ESA	European Space Agency
ESCAP	Economic and Social Commission for Asia and the Pacific (UN)
EU	European Union
FAO	Food and Agriculture Organization (UN)
G-77	Group of 77
GA	General Assembly (UN)
GCC	Gulf Cooperation Council

IAEA	International Atomic Energy Agency (UN)
IBEC	International Bank for Economic Cooperation
IBRD	International Bank for Reconstruction and Development ("World Bank," UN)
ICAO	International Civil Aviation Organization (UN)
ICJ	International Court of Justice (UN)
IDA	International Development Association (IBRD affiliate, UN)
IDB	Inter-American Development Bank
IDB	Islamic Development Bank
IEA	International Energy Agency (associated with OECD)
IFAD	International Fund for Agricultural Development (UN)
IFC	International Finance Corporation (IBRD affiliate, UN)
IIB	International Investment Bank
ILO	International Labor Organization (UN)
IMF	International Monetary Fund (UN)
IMO	International Maritime Organization (UN)
INTELSAT	International Telecommunications Satellite Organization
INTERPOL	International Criminal Police Organization
IOC	International Olympic Committee
IOM	International Organization for Migration
ITU	International Telecommunications Union (UN)
LAIA	Latin American Integration Association
NAFTA	North American Free Trade Agreement
NAM	Nonaligned Movement
NATO	North Atlantic Treaty Organization
OAPEC	Organization of Arab Petroleum Exporting Countries
OAS	Organization of American States
OAU	Organization of African Unity
ODECA	Organization of Central American States

OECD	Organization for Economic Cooperation and Development
OIC	Organization of the Islamic Conference
OIEC	Organization for International Economic Cooperation
OPEC	Organization of Petroleum Exporting Countries
PAHO	Pan American Health Organization
SAARC	South Asian Association for Regional Cooperation
SADC	Southern African Development Community
SC	Security Council (UN)
SELA	Latin American Economic System
SPC	South Pacific Commission
SPF	South Pacific Forum
TC	Trusteeship Council (UN)
TDB	Trade and Development Board (UN)
UDEAC	Economic and Customs Union of Central Africa
UEAC	Union of Central African States
UNCTAD	UN Conference on Trade and Development
UNDP	UN Development Program
UNESCO	UN Educational, Scientific, and Cultural Organization
UNICEF	UN Children's Fund
UNIDO	UN Industrial Development Organization
UPU	Universal Postal Union (UN)
WEU	Western European Union
WFC	World Food Council (UN)
WFTU	World Federation of Trade Unions
WHO	World Health Organization (UN)
WIPO	World Intellectual Property Organization (UN)
WMO	World Meteorological Organization (UN)
WTO	World Tourism Organization
WTO	World Trade Organization

The World

SEVEN WONDERS OF THE ANCIENT WORLD

Artemision at Ephesus   This temple of the Greek goddess Artemis (also the Roman goddess Diana) was begun in 541 B.C. at Ephesus (now a site in Turkey) and completed 220 years later. The temple was 425 feet long and 220 feet wide with 127 marble columns, each 60 feet tall. The gates were made of cypress and the ceiling of cedar. The temple was destroyed by the Goths in A.D. 262.

The Colossus of Rhodes   This 100-foot-tall bronze statue of the sun god Helios was erected between 292 and 280 B.C. in the harbor at Rhodes. According to legend, it appeared to stand astride the harbor but was actually on a promontory overlooking it. The statue was toppled by an earthquake around 224 B.C. and lay in ruins until A.D. 653, when the remains were sold as scrap metal.

The Hanging Gardens of Babylon   This series of five terraces of glazed brick, each 50 feet above the next, was erected by King Nebuchadnezzar for his wife, Amytis, in 562 B.C. The terraces, featuring rare and exotic plants, were connected by a winding stairway. A pumping device supplied water so the gardens could be irrigated by fountains.

The Mausoleum at Halicarnassus This 140-foot-high white marble structure was built in 352 B.C. at Halicarnassus (now a site in Turkey) in memory of King Mausolus of Caria. Its massive base contained the sarcophagus and supported 36 columns crowned with a stepped pyramid on which was constructed a marble chariot. It was destroyed for the use of stone to build a castle for the Knights of Saint John in 1402.

Olympian Zeus This statue of the supreme god in Greek mythology was executed in gold and ivory for the temple at Olympia. The figure of the seated Zeus was 40 feet tall and rested on a base that was 12 feet high. The portions of the statue representing the flesh of the god were covered with marble, and his cloak was made of gold. Golden lions rested near his feet.

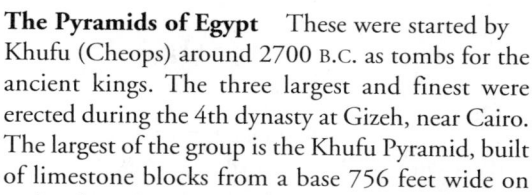

"Major World Philosophers" in chapter 10; "Cultural Symbols" in chapter 12

The Pyramids of Egypt These were started by Khufu (Cheops) around 2700 B.C. as tombs for the ancient kings. The three largest and finest were erected during the 4th dynasty at Gizeh, near Cairo. The largest of the group is the Khufu Pyramid, built of limestone blocks from a base 756 feet wide on each side and covering an area of 13 acres. It is 482 feet high. Smaller pyramids were built for wives and other members of the royal families.

The Tower of Pharos This was a great lighthouse built on the island of Pharos, at Alexandria, Egypt, during the reign of Ptolemy Philadelphus, 285 B.C. Also called the Pharos, it was 500 feet tall with a ramp leading to the top. Light was produced with a fire and reflectors and could be seen from a distance of 42 miles.

ROYAL RULERS OF EUROPE AND ASIA

CHINA

Major Chinese Dynasties

Hsia	c.1994–c.1523 B.C.
Shang	c.1523–c.1027 B.C.
Zhou	c.1027–256 B.C.
Western Zhou	c.1027–771 B.C.
Eastern Zhou	770–256 B.C.
Spring and Autumn Period	722–481 B.C.
Warring States Period	403–222 B.C.
Qin	221–206 B.C.
Han, Former (Western)	202 B.C.–A.D. 8
Hsin	A.D. 9–23
Han, Later (Eastern)	25–220
Period of Disunion	220–589
Three Kingdoms Period	220–265
Wei	220–265
Shu	221–263
Wu	222–280
Jin	265–420
Western Jin	265–317
Eastern Jin	317–420
Northern Dynasties	386–581
Northern Wei	386–534
Eastern Wei	534–550
Northern Ch'i	550–577
Western Wei	535–557
Northern Zhou	557–581
Southern Dynasties	420–589
Song	420–479
Ch'i	479–502
Liang	502–557
Ch'en	557–589
Sui	581–618
Tang	618–906
Five Dynasties (Wu Tai)	907–960
Later Liang	907–923
Later Tang	923–936
Later Jin	936–946
Later Han	947–950
Later Zhou	951–960
Ten Kingdoms	902–979
Liao	947–1125
Western Xia	990–1227
Jin	1115–1234

The World

Major Chinese Dynasties, *continued*

Sung	960–1279
Northern Sung	960–1127
Southern Sung	1127–1279
Yüan (Mongol)	1260–1368
Ming	1368–1644

Qing (Manchu) Dynasty Rulers

Shun Chih	1644–1661
K'ang Hsi	1661–1722
Yung Cheng	1722–1735
Ch'ien Lung	1735–1796
Chia Ch'ing	1796–1820
Tao Kuang	1820–1851
Hsien Feng	1851–1861
T'ung Chi	1861–1875
Kuang Hsu	1875–1898
Tzu Hsi (empress dowager)	1898–1908
Hsiian T'ung	1908–1912

ENGLAND/GREAT BRITAIN

Saxon

Egbert	829–839
Ethelwulf	839–858
Ethelbald	858–860
Ethelbert	860–866
Ethelred I	866–871
Alfred	871–899
Edward (the Elder)	899–924
Athelstan	924–940
Edmund I	940–946
Edred	946–955
Edwy	955–959
Edgar	959–975
Edward (the Martyr)	975–978
Ethelred II	978–1016
Edmund II	1016

Danish

Canute	1017–1035
Harold I	1035–1040
Hardicanute	1040–1042

Saxon

Edward (the Confessor)	1042–1066
Harold II	1066

Norman

William I (the Conqueror)	1066–1087
William II (Rufus)	1087–1100
Henry I (Beauclerc)	1100–1135
Stephen	1135–1154

Plantagenet

Henry II	1154–1189
Richard I (Coeur de Lion)	1189–1199
John (Lackland)	1199–1216
Henry III	1216–1272
Edward I	1272–1307
Edward II	1307–1327
Edward III	1327–1377
Richard II	1377–1399

Lancaster

Henry IV (Bolingbroke)	1399–1413
Henry V	1413–1422
Henry VI	1422–1461

York

Edward IV	1461–1470

Lancaster

Henry VI (restored)	1470–1471

York

Edward IV (restored)	1471–1483
Edward V	1483
Richard III	1483–1485

Tudor

Henry VII	1485–1509
Henry VIII	1509–1547
Edward VI	1547–1553
Mary I	1553–1558
Elizabeth	1558–1603

Stuart

James I	1603–1625
Charles I	1625–1649
[Commonwealth	1649–1653;
Oliver Cromwell, Lord Protector, 1653–1658; Richard Cromwell, Lord Protector, 1658–1659; military rule until the Restoration]	

The World

Charles II	1660–1685
James II	1685–1688
William III and Mary II	1689–1702
Anne	1702–1714

Hanover

George I	1714–1727
George II	1727–1760
George III	1760–1820
George IV	1820–1830
William IV	1830–1837
Victoria	1837–1901

Saxe-Coburg

Edward VII	1901–1910

Windsor

George V	1910–1936
Edward VIII	1936
George VI	1936–1952
Elizabeth II	1952–

FRANCE

Henri I	1031–1060
Philip I	1060–1108
Louis VI	1108–1137
Louis VII	1137–1180
Philip II	1180–1223
Louis VIII	1223–1226
Louis IX	1226–1270
Philip III	1270–1285
Philip IV	1285–1314
Louis X	1314–1316
John I	1316
Philip V	1316–1322
Charles IV	1322–1328
Philip VI	1328–1350
John II	1350–1364
Charles V	1364–1380
Charles VI	1380–1422
Charles VII	1422–1461
Louis XI	1461–1483
Charles VIII	1483–1498
Louis XII	1498–1515
François I	1515–1547
Henri II	1547–1559
François II	1559–1560
Charles IX	1560–1574

Henri III	1574–1589
Henri IV	1589–1610
Louis XIII	1610–1643
Louis XIV	1643–1715
Louis XV	1715–1774
Louis XVI	1774–1792
(First Republic)	1792–1804
Napoleon I	1804–1814
Louis XVIII	1814–1824
Charles X	1824–1830
Louis Philippe	1830–1848
(Second Republic)	1848–1852
Napoleon III	1852–1870

GERMANY

Frederick I	1701–1713
Frederick William I	1713–1740
Frederick II	1740–1786
Frederick William II	1786–1797
Frederick William III	1797–1840
Frederick William IV	1840–1861
William I	1861–1888
Frederick III	1888
William II	1888–1918

JAPAN

Tokugawa Shogun rule	1603–1868
(Meiji) Mutsuhito	1868–1912
Taisho (Yoshihito)	1912–1926
Shōwa (Hirohito)	1926–1989
Heisei (Akihito)	1989–

RUSSIA

Ivan III	1462–1505
Vasilly III	1505–1533
Ivan IV	1533–1584
Theodore I	1584–1598
Boris Godunov	1598–1605
Theodore II	1605
Demetrius I	1605–1606
Basil IV	1606–1610
Wladyslaw (Polish Prince)	1610–1613
Mikhail Romanov	1613–1645
Alexis I	1645–1676
Theodore III	1676–1682
Ivan V and Peter I	1682–1689
Peter I (alone)	1689–1725

Russia, *cont.*

Catherine I	1725–1727
Peter II	1727–1730
Anna	1730–1740
Ivan VI	1740–1741
Elizabeth	1741–1762
Peter III	1762

Catherine II	1762–1796
Paul I	1796–1801
Alexander I	1801–1825
Nicholas I	1825–1855
Alexander II	1855–1881
Alexander III	1881–1894
Nicholas II	1894–1917

ORDER OF BRITISH PEERAGE

Titles of nobility, or peerages, are granted by the king or queen of Great Britain upon the recommendation of the prime minister. In most *hereditary peerages,* the title passes on to a peer's eldest son, or to his closest male heir if the peer has no son (the other children are considered commoners). The title becomes extinct if there is no male heir. There are some ancient peerages that allow the title to be passed to a daughter if the holder leaves no male descendant. The last hereditary peerage was granted in 1964.

Life peerages are created each year by the British monarch for several distinguished persons. Life peers hold the rank for their own lives only; the titles do not pass on to their children. Both men and women may be granted life peerages, and the titles given to them are baron or baroness.

The following are the five grades of peers, ranked from the highest to the lowest, and the dates they were created. (Duke is the highest hereditary rank below that of prince.)

1. duke   *or*   duchess (1337)
2. marquess,   *or*   marchioness (1385)
    marquis
3. earl   *or*   countess (c. 800–1000)
4. viscount   *or*   viscountess (1440)
5. baron   *or*   baroness (c. 1066)

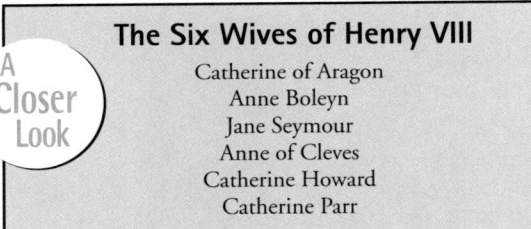

A Closer Look

The Six Wives of Henry VIII

Catherine of Aragon
Anne Boleyn
Jane Seymour
Anne of Cleves
Catherine Howard
Catherine Parr

GENEALOGY CHARTS OF THE BRITISH MONARCHY

Before the Conquest (827–1066)

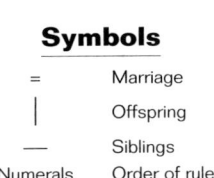

Symbols

=	Marriage
		Offspring
—	Siblings
Numerals	Order of rule

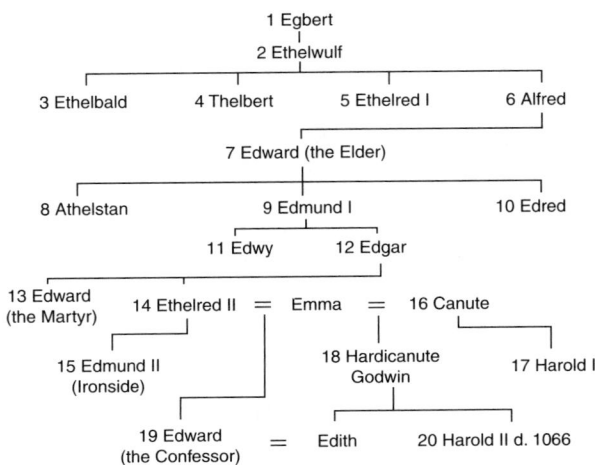

Norman Line (1066–1154)
Union of English and Norman Lines in Henry II

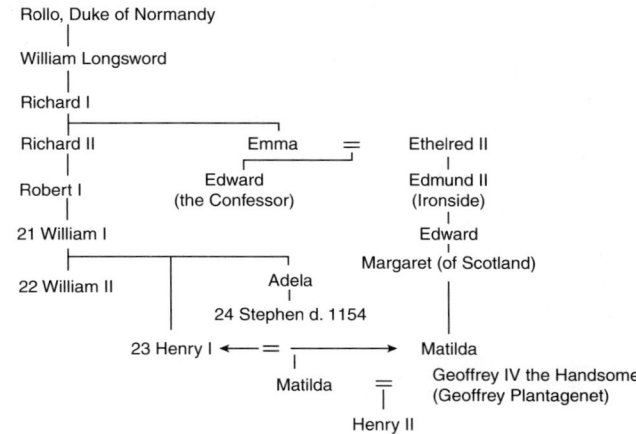

Plantagenet Line (1154–1399)

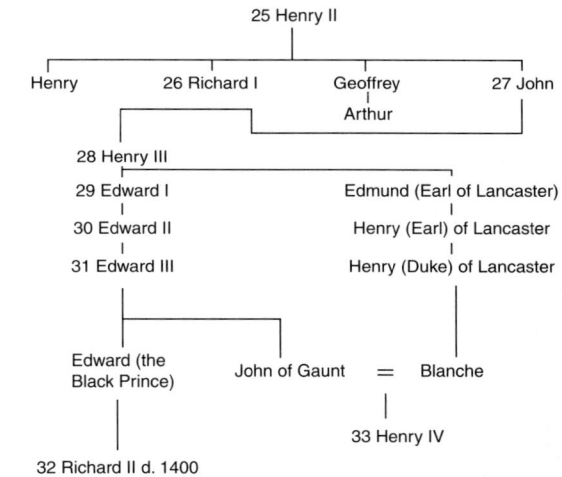

House of Lancaster (1399–1461)
House of York (1461–1485)

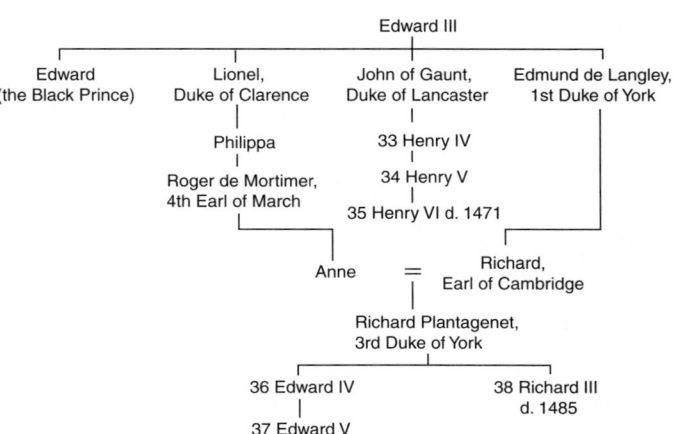

The World

House of Tudor (1485–1603)

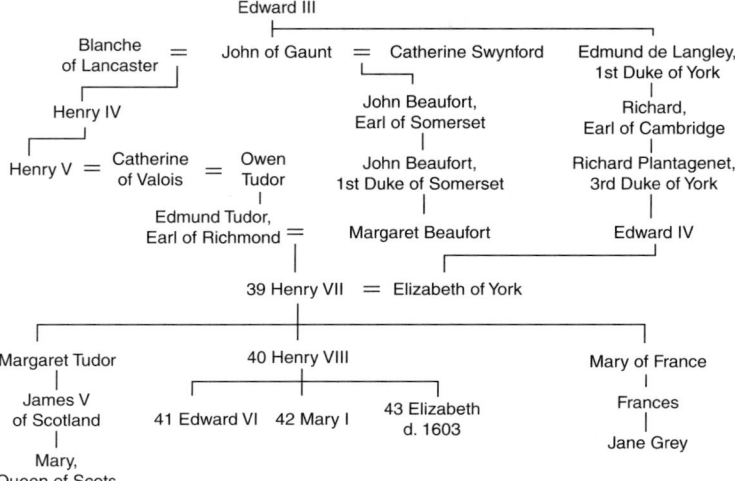

House of Stuart (1603–1714)

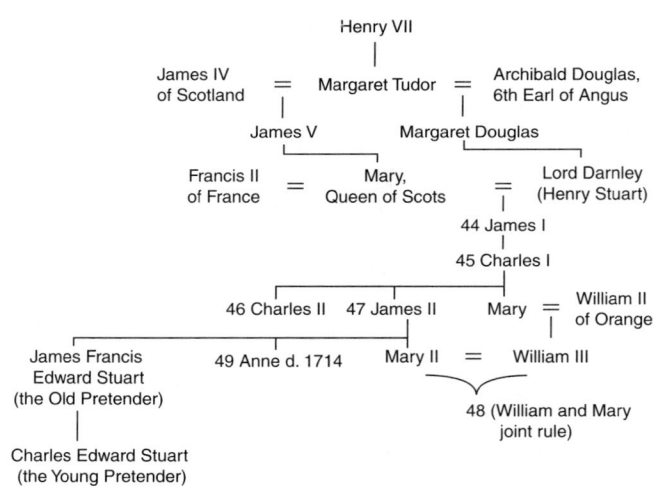

Houses of Hanover, Saxe-Coburg, and Windsor (1714–

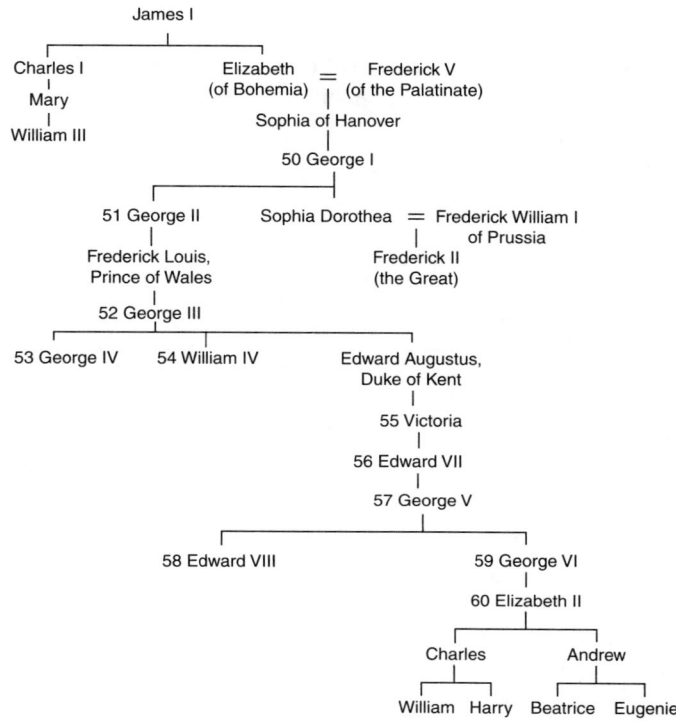

CONNECTIONS BETWEEN ROYAL FAMILIES

In the following charts, the notations (V1), (V2), and so on indicate the first, second, etc., child of Victoria, Queen of England.

ENGLAND, DENMARK, AND RUSSIA

Connections Between the Royal Families
of England, Denmark, and Russia

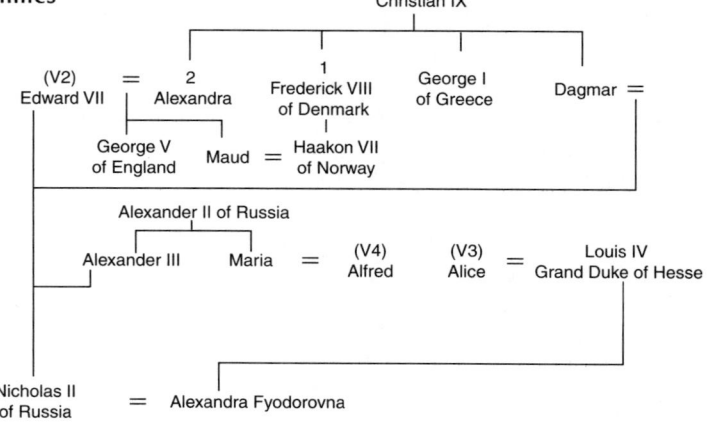

ENGLAND, GERMANY, AND SPAIN

Connections Between the Royal Families
of England, Germany, and Spain

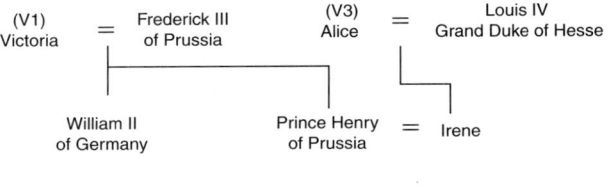

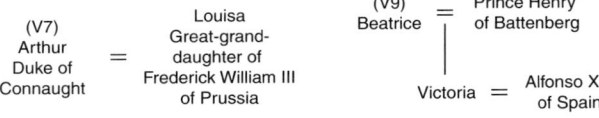

PRIME MINISTERS

AUSTRALIA

Sir Edmund Barton	1901–1903
Alfred Deakin	1903–1904
John Christian Watson	1904
George Houston Reid	1904–1905
Alfred Deakin	1905–1908
Andrew Fisher	1908–1909
Alfred Deakin	1909–1910
Andrew Fisher	1910–1913
Sir Joseph Cook	1913–1914
Andrew Fisher	1914–1915
William Morris Hughes	1915–1923
Stanley Melbourne Bruce	1923–1929
James Henry Scullin	1929–1932
Joseph Aloysius Lyons	1932–1939
Earle Page	1939
Robert Gordon Menzies	1939–1941
Arthur William Fadden	1941
John Curtin	1941–1945
Francis M. Forde (served 6 days)	1945
Joseph Benedict Chifley	1945–1949
Robert Gordon Menzies	1949–1966
Harold E. Holt	1966–1967
John McEwan (served 22 days)	1967–1968
John G. Gorton	1968–1971
William McMahon	1971–1972
(Edward) Gough Whitlam	1972–1975
Malcolm Fraser	1975–1983
Bob Hawke	1983–1991
Paul Keating	1991–1996
John Winston Howard	1996–

CANADA

John Alexander Macdonald	1867–1873
Alexander Mackenzie	1873–1878
John Alexander Macdonald	1878–1891
Sir John J. Abbott	1891–1892
Sir John S. D. Thompson	1892–1894
Sir Mackenzie Bowell	1894–1896
Sir Charles Tupper	1896
Sir Wilfrid Laurier	1896–1911
Sir Robert Laird Borden	1911–1920
Arthur Meighen	1920–1921
W. L. Mackenzie King	1921–1926
Arthur Meighen	1926
W. L. Mackenzie King	1926–1930
Richard Bedford Bennett	1930–1935
W. L. Mackenzie King	1935–1948
Louis Stephen Saint Laurent	1948–1957
John George Diefenbaker	1957–1963
Lester Bowles Pearson	1963–1968
Pierre Elliott Trudeau	1968–1979
Charles Joseph (Joe) Clark	1979–1980
Pierre Elliott Trudeau	1980–1984
John Napier Turner	1984
Brian Mulroney	1984–1993
Kim Campbell	1993
Jean Chretien	1993–

ENGLAND/GREAT BRITAIN

Sidney Godolphin (Earl of Godolphin)	1700–1701
Charles Howard (Earl of Carlisle)	1701–1702
Sidney Godolphin (Earl of Godolphin)	1702–1710

John Poulett (Earl Poulett)	1710–1711
Robert Harley (Earl of Oxford)	1711–1714
Charles Talbot (Duke of Shrewsbury)	1714
Charles Montagu (Earl of Halifax)	1714–1715
Charles Howard (Earl of Carlisle)	1715
Robert Walpole (Earl of Oxford)	1715–1717
James Stanhope (Earl Stanhope)	1717–1718
Charles Spencer (3rd Earl of Sunderland)	1718–1721
Robert Walpole (Earl of Oxford)	1721–1742
Spencer Compton (Earl of Wilmington)	1742–1743
Henry Pelham	1743–1754
Duke of Newcastle (Thomas Pelham-Holles)	1754–1756
William Cavendish (Duke of Devonshire)	1756–1757
Duke of Newcastle (Thomas Pelham-Holles)	1757–1762
John Stuart (Earl of Bute)	1762–1763
George Grenville	1763–1765
Marquis of Rockingham (Charles Watson-Wentworth)	1765–1766
William Pitt (Earl of Chatham)	1766–1768
Augustus Henry Fitzroy (Duke of Grafton)	1768–1770
Frederick North (Earl of Guilford)	1770–1782
Marquis of Rockingham (Charles Watson-Wentworth)	1782
Earl of Shelburne (William Petty)	1782–1783
William Henry Cavendish Bentinck (Duke of Portland)	1783
William Pitt	1783–1801
Henry Addington (Viscount Sidmouth)	1801–1804
William Pitt	1804–1806
William Wyndham Grenville (Baron Grenville)	1806–1807
William Henry Cavendish Bentinck (Duke of Portland)	1807–1809
Spencer Perceval	1809–1812
Robert Banks Jenkinson (Earl of Liverpool)	1812–1827
George Canning	1827
Frederick John Robinson (Viscount Goderich)	1827–1828
Duke of Wellington (Arthur Wellesley)	1828–1830
Charles Grey (Earl Grey)	1830–1834
William Lamb (Viscount Melbourne)	1834
Sir Robert Peel	1834–1835
William Lamb (Viscount Melbourne)	1835–1841
Sir Robert Peel	1841–1846
Lord John Russell	1846–1852
Edward George Geoffrey Smith Stanley (Earl of Derby)	1852
George Hamilton Gordon (Earl of Aberdeen)	1852–1855
Viscount Palmerston (Henry John Temple)	1855–1858
Edward George Geoffrey Smith Stanley (Earl of Derby)	1858–1859
Viscount Palmerston (Henry John Temple)	1859–1865
Earl (formerly Lord John) Russell	1865–1866
Edward George Geoffrey Smith Stanley (Earl of Derby)	1866–1868
Benjamin Disraeli (Earl of Beaconsfield)	1868
William Ewart Gladstone	1868–1874
Benjamin Disraeli (Earl of Beaconsfield)	1874–1880
William Ewart Gladstone	1880–1885
Robert Arthur Talbot Gascoyner-Cecil (Marquis of Salisbury)	1885–1886
William Ewart Gladstone	1886
Robert Arthur Talbot Gascoyner-Cecil (Marquis of Salisbury)	1886–1892
William Ewart Gladstone	1892–1894
Earl of Rosebery (Archibald Philip Primrose)	1894–1895
Robert Arthur Talbot Gascoyner-Cecil (Marquis of Salisbury)	1895–1902
Arthur James Balfour	1902–1905
Sir Henry Campbell-Bannerman	1905–1908
Herbert Henry Asquith (Earl of Oxford and Asquith)	1908–1916
David Lloyd George (Earl of Dwyfor)	1916–1922
Andrew Bonar Law	1922–1923
Stanley Baldwin (Earl Baldwin of Bewdley)	1923–1924

James Ramsay MacDonald	1924	Sir Anthony Eden	1955–1957
Stanley Baldwin (Earl Baldwin of Bewdley)	1924–1929	Harold Macmillan	1957–1963
		Sir Alec Douglas-Home	1963–1964
James Ramsay MacDonald	1929–1935	Harold Wilson	1964–1970
Stanley Baldwin (Earl Baldwin of Bewdley)	1935–1937	Edward Heath	1970–1974
		Harold Wilson	1974–1976
Neville Chamberlain	1937–1940	James Callaghan	1976–1979
Winston Churchill	1940–1945	Margaret Thatcher	1979–1990
Clement Attlee	1945–1951	John Major	1990–1997
Winston Churchill	1951–1955	Tony Blair	1997–

FOREIGN DIALING CODES

Note: For international telephone calls automatically routed through AT&T, dial 011 and then dial the code for that country, the city code if one is indicated, and the subscriber telephone number to be reached. Other long-distance telephone services may have other procedures and should be consulted for their specific instructions.

Algeria	213	Denmark	45	Guantanamo Bay	
American Samoa	684	(Copenhagen 1 or 2)		U.S. naval base	53
Andorra	376	Ecuador	593	(all points 99)	
(all points 628)		(Guayaquil 4)		Guatemala	502
Argentina	54	(Quito 2)		(Guatemala City 2)	
(Buenos Aires 1)		Egypt	20	Guyana	592
Australia	61	(Alexandria 3)		(Georgetown 2)	
(Melbourne 39)		(Cairo 2)		Haiti	509
(Sydney 2)		El Salvador	503	(Port-au-Prince 1)	
Austria	43	England. *See* United		Honduras	504
(Vienna 1)		Kingdom.		Hong Kong	852
Bahrain	973	Ethiopia	251	(Hong Kong 9)	
Bangladesh	880	(Addis Ababa 1)		Hungary	36
Belgium	32	Fiji	679	(Budapest 1)	
(Brussels 2)		Finland	358	Iceland	354
(Antwerp 3)		(Helsinki 9)		(Akureyri 6)	
Belize	501	France	33	(Reykjavík 1)	
Bolivia	591	(Marseille 491)		India	91
(La Paz 2)		(Nice 492 or 493)		(Bombay 22)	
Brazil	55	(Paris 1)		(Calcutta 33)	
(Brasília 61)		French Antilles	596	(New Delhi 11)	
(Rio de Janeiro 21)		French Antilles-	590	Indonesia	62
Cameroon	237	Guadeloupe		(Jakarta 21)	
Chile	56	French Polynesia	689	Iran	98
(Santiago 2)		Gabon	241	(Teheran 21)	
China	86	Germany	49	Iraq	964
(Beijing 10)		(Frankfurt 69)		(Baghdad 1)	
(Shanghai 21)		(Munich 89)		Ireland	353
Colombia	57	(Berlin 30)		(Dublin 1)	
(Bogotá 1)		(other areas of former		(Galway 91)	
Costa Rica	506	East Germany 37)		Israel	972
Cyprus	357	Greece	30	(Haifa 4)	
Czech Republic	42	(Athens 1)		(Jerusalem 2)	
(Prague 2)		Guam	671	(Tel Aviv 3)	

The World

Italy	39	New Zealand	64	Spain	34
(Florence 55)		(Auckland 9)		(Barcelona 3)	
(Rome 6)		(Wellington 4)		(Madrid 1)	
(Venice 41)		Nicaragua	505	(Seville 54)	
Ivory Coast	225	(Managua 2)		Sri Lanka	94
Japan	81	Nigeria	234	(Columbo 1)	
(Tokyo 3)		(Lagos 1)		Suriname	597
(Osaka 6)		Norway	47	Sweden	46
(Yokohama 45)		(Bergen 5)		(Göteborg 31)	
Jordan	962	(Oslo 2)		(Stockholm 8)	
(Amman 6)		Oman	968	Switzerland	41
Kenya	254	Pakistan	92	(Geneva 22)	
Korea, South	82	(Islamabad 51)		(Bern 31)	
(Pusan 51)		(Karachi 21)		(Zurich 1)	
(Seoul 2)		Panama	507	Taiwan	886
Kuwait	965	Papua New Guinea	675	(Tainan 6)	
Liberia	231	Paraguay	595	(Taipei 2)	
Libya	218	(Asuncion 21)		Thailand	66
(Tripoli 21)		Peru	51	(Bangkok 2)	
Liechtenstein	423	(Lima 1)		Tunisia	216
(all points 75)		Philippines	63	(Tunis 1)	
Luxembourg	352	(Manila 2)		Turkey	90
Malawi	265	Poland	48	(Istanbul 1)	
(Domasi 531)		(Warsaw 22)		United Arab Emirates	971
Malaysia	60	Portugal	351	(Abu Dhabi 2)	
(Kuala Lumpur 3)		(Lisbon 1)		(Dubai 4)	
Mexico	52	Qatar	974	United Kingdom	44
(Mexico City 5)		Romania	40	(Belfast 1232)	
(Guadalajara 3)		(Bucharest 1)		(Glasgow 141)	
Monaco	377	Russia	7	(London 207 or 208)	
(Casablanca 2)		(Moscow 095)		Uruguay	598
Morocco	212	Saipan	670	(Montevideo 2)	
(Agadir 8)		San Marino	39	Vatican City	39
Namibia	264	(all points 541)		(all points 6)	
Netherlands	31	Saudi Arabia	966	Venezuela	58
(Amsterdam 20)		(Riyadh 1)		(Caracas 2)	
(Rotterdam 10)		Senegal	221	(Maracaibo 61)	
(The Hague 70)		Singapore	65	Yemen Arab Republic	967
Netherlands Antilles	599	South Africa	27	Yugoslavia	381
Netherlands Antilles-Aruba	297	(Cape Town 21)		(Belgrade 11)	
(Aruba 8)		(Johannesburg 11)			
New Caledonia	687	(Pretoria 12)			

ADDITIONAL SOURCES OF INFORMATION

ORGANIZATIONS AND SERVICES

The Asia Foundation
465 California St., 14th Fl.
San Francisco, CA 94104

Bureau of Public Affairs
U.S. Department of State
2201 C St., NW
Washington, DC 20520

Carnegie Endowment for International Peace
1779 Massachusetts Ave. NW
Washington, DC 20036

Central Intelligence Agency
Public Affairs Director
Washington, DC 20505

European Union Office of Press and Public Affairs
2300 M St., NW
Washington, DC 20037

Middle East Institute
1761 N St., NW
Washington, DC 20036

Organization of American States
17th Street and Constitution Avenue, NW
Washington, DC 20006

United Nations Headquarters
United Nations Plaza
New York, NY 10017

United Nations Information Center
1775 K St., Suite 400
Washington, DC 20006

United States Mission to the United Nations
799 United Nations Plaza
New York, NY 10017

BOOKS

Banks, Arthur S., and Muller, Thomas C., eds. *Political Handbook of the World, 2000*, CSA, 2000.

Barzun, Jacques, *From Dawn to Decadence, 500 Years of Western Cultural Life*, HarperPerennial, 2001.

Black, Jeremy, ed. *The DK Atlas of World History*, DK Publishers, 2000.

Central Intelligence Agency, *The World Factbook*, U.S. Government Printing Office, annual.

Chandler, David. *Macmillan Encyclopedia of Military History*. 2 vols, Macmillan, 1996.

Clements, John, ed. *Clements' Encyclopedia of World Government*, Political Research, 2000.

Commire, Anne, ed. *Women in World History*, 11 vols. Gale, 2000.

DK Publishing Staff, *World Desk Reference*, DK Publishers, 2000.

Hammond staff, *Hammond World Atlas*, 3rd ed. Hammond, 2000.

Hulme, F. Edward. *Flags of the World: Their History, Blazonry, and Associations*. Gordon Press, 1977.

Krieger, Joel, ed. *The Oxford Companion to Politics of the World*, Oxford, 2001

Maps on File 2000. Facts on File, 2000.

Oxford staff, *Oxford Desk Reference Atlas*, 3rd ed. Oxford, 2000.

Schraepler, Hans-Albrecht. *Dictionary of International Economic Organizations*. Georgetown University Press, 1999.

Simony, Maggy. *The Traveler's Reading Guide: Ready-Made Reading Lists for the Armchair Traveler*. Rev. ed. Holt, Rinehart and Winston, 1994.

Wetterau, Bruce. *The New York Public Library Book of Chronologies*. Prentice Hall, 1994.

Williamson, David. *The Kings and Queens of England*, Lund Humphries, 1998.

World Almanac Staff. *The World Almanac and Book of Facts*. Pharo Books, annual.

WEB SITES

Comparative Analysis of Major World Religions
www.comparativereligion.com

Atlapedia—Key facts and statistics on all countries of the world as well as physical and political maps.
http://www.atlapedia.com

The CIA World Factbook—Comprehensive facts about the world's countries complied by the CIA (see book listed above).
http://www.cia.gov/cia/publications/factbook

Ragz International World History—Covers wide variety of topics from prehistory through World War II.
http://www.ragz-international.com/index1.htm

World History—E-texts, maps, and links on a variety of history topics from antiquity to the twentieth century.
http://www.fsmitha.com

City Population—Statistics and maps about the population of the major agglomerations of the world.
http://www.citypopulation.de

ATLAS

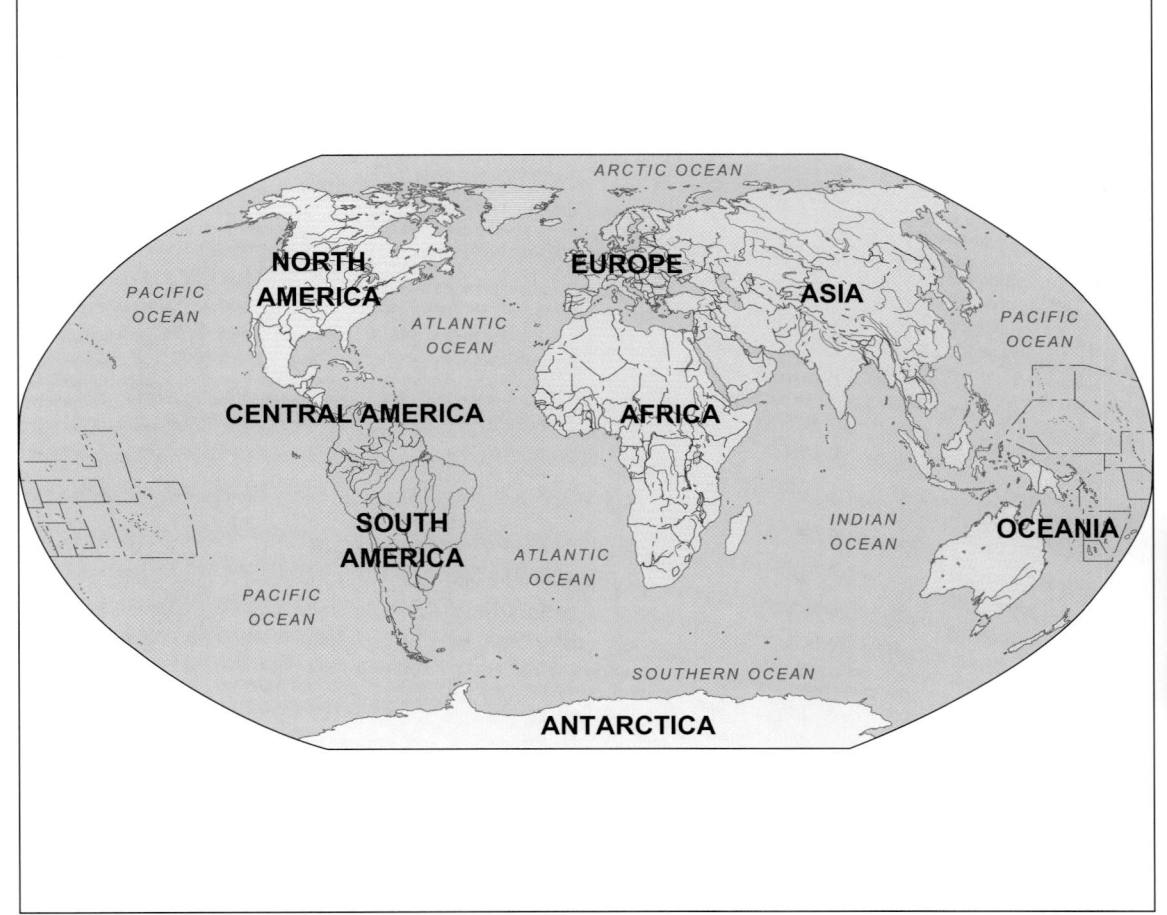

ATLANTIC

OCEAN

Gulf of Biscay

EUROPE

ASIA

Volga

Aral Sea

Danube

Black Sea

Caspian Sea

Sardinia I.

MEDITERRANEAN SEA

Sicily I.

Str. of Gibraltar

Melilla (Sp.)

Oran

Algiers

Tunis

C. Bon

Crete I.

Cyprus I.

Euphrates

Tigris

Persian Gulf

Madeira Islands (Por.)

Rabat

Ceuta (Sp.)

TUNISIA

Gulf of Gabès

Tripoli

Bengasi

Alexandria

Cairo

El-Giza

Casablanca

MOROCCO

Marrakech

Canary Islands (Sp.)

Agadir

El Aaiún

ALGERIA

LIBYA

EGYPT

Aswân

Red Sea

Waha

Western Sahara

Tamanrasset

Ras Nouâdhibou

MAURITANIA

Djado

Zouar

Port Sudan

Nouakchott

MALI

Tombouctou

Gao

NIGER

CHAD

Omdurman

Khartoum

Asmera

ERITREA

Socotra I. (Yemen)

SENEGAL

C. Vert

Dakar

Niger

BURKINA FASO

Niamey

Kano

L. Chad

Ndjamena

SUDAN

White Nile

Blue Nile

Djibouti

DJIBOUTI

Ras Asir

Gulf of Aden

GAMBIA

Banjul

Bamako

GUINEA-BISSAU

Bissau

Conakry

GUINEA

Bobo Dioulasso

Ouagadougou

BENIN

Abuja

Freetown

SIERRA LEONE

Kumasi

IVORY COAST

TOGO

NIGERIA

CENTRAL AFRICAN REPUBLIC

ETHIOPIA

Addis Ababa

SOMALI REPUBLIC

Monrovia

GHANA

Accra

Porto Novo

Lomé

Lagos

Bangui

Juba

LIBERIA

Abidjan

CAMEROON

Isiro

L. Albert

UGANDA

Mogadishu

Gulf of Guinea

Malabo

Douala

Yaoundé

Kampala

KENYA

Bioko I.

EQUATORIAL GUINEA

Libreville

CONGO

DEMOCRATIC REPUBLIC OF THE CONGO

RWANDA

Kigali

Nairobi

SÃO TOMÉ & PRINCIPE

São Tomé

GABON

Brazzaville

Bujumbura

BURUNDI

L. Victoria

Mombasa

Pemba I.

Pagalu I. (Ec. G.)

Pointe-Noire

Kinshasa

L. Tanganyika

TANZANIA

Zanzibar I.

Dar es Salaam

Mafia I.

Ascension I. (U.K.)

Luanda

Cosmoledo Islands (Sey.)

L. Malawi

COMOROS

Moroni

Mayotte I. (Fr.)

ANGOLA

ZAMBIA

MALAWI

Lilongwe

St. Helena I. (U.K.)

Lusaka

MOZAMBIQUE

Zambezi

Harare

Antananarivo

NAMIBIA

ZIMBABWE

Mozambique Channel

MAURITIUS

Porto Luis

Windhoek

BOTSWANA

Bulawayo

MADAGASCAR

Réunion Is. (Fr.)

ATLANTIC

OCEAN

Gaborone

Pretoria

Maputo

Johannesburg

Mbabane

SWAZILAND

Vereeniging

LESOTHO

Durban

INDIAN

OCEAN

Cape Town

SOUTH AFRICA

Maseru

C. of Good Hope

Port Elizabeth

Population:

ANGOLA Country

● Luanda Capital

• Pointe Noire Other cities

– – – Natinal Border

Scale: 1:40.000.000

0   300   600   900 km

CAPE VERDE

Praia

SEYCHELLES

Victoria

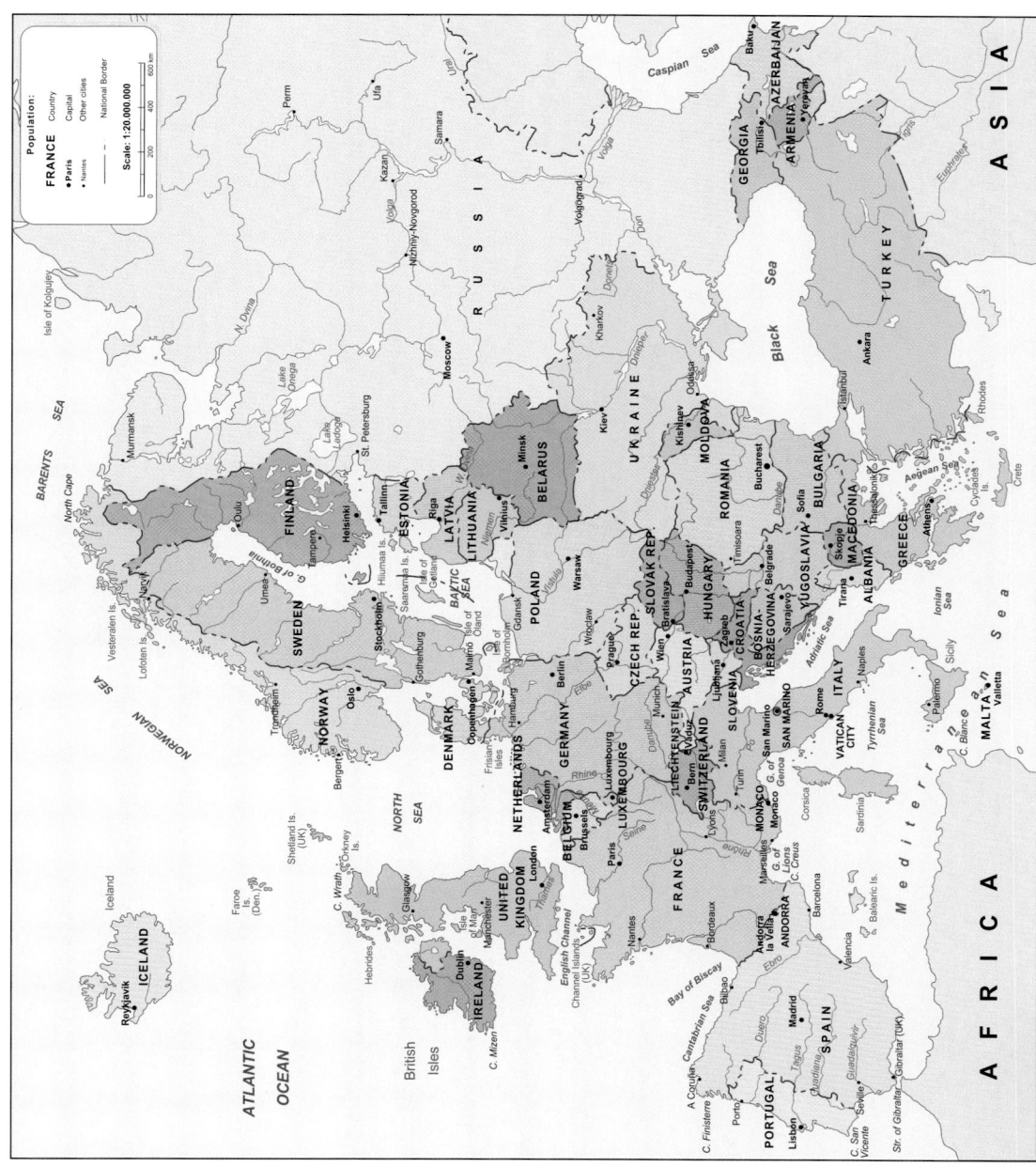

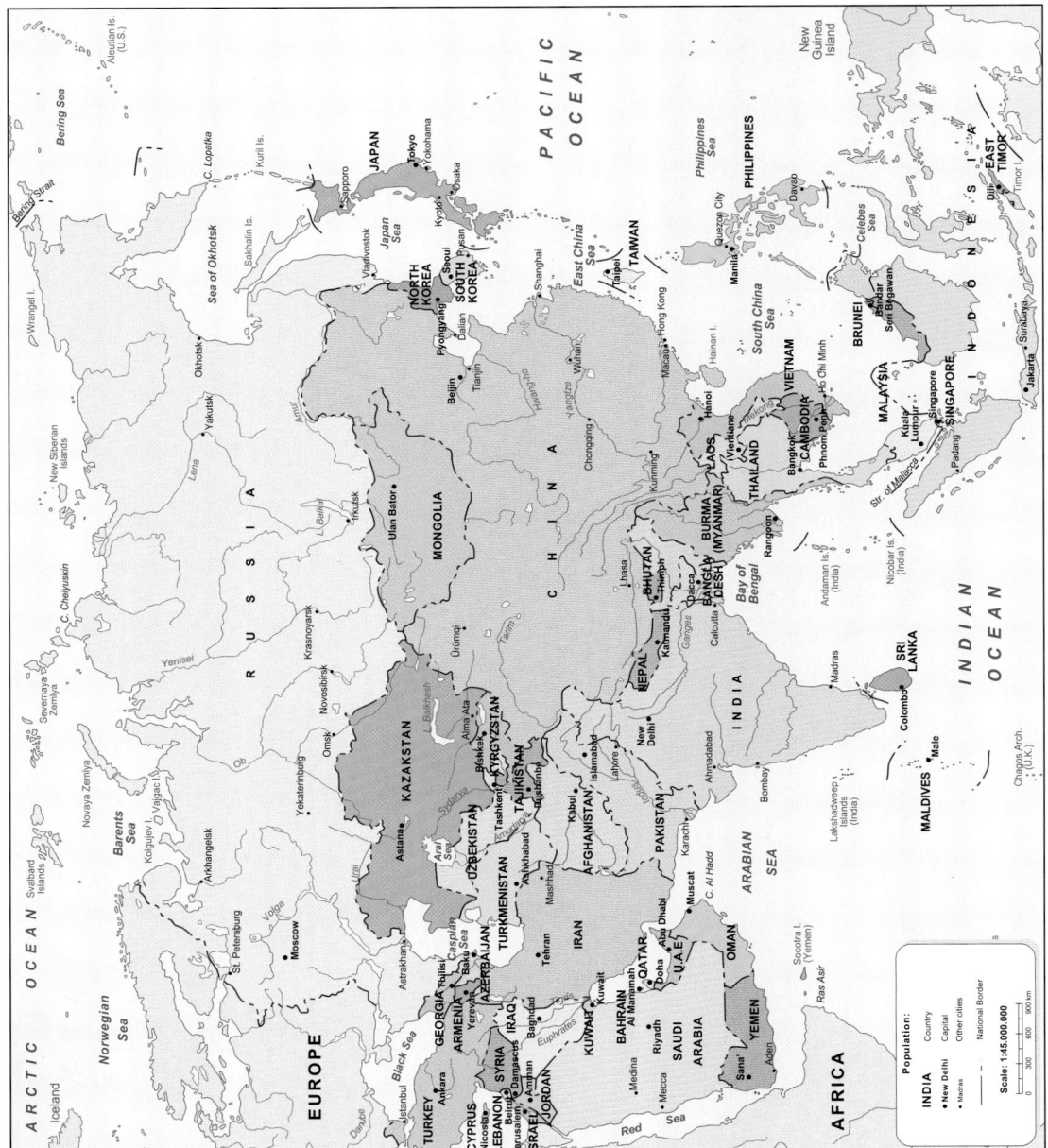

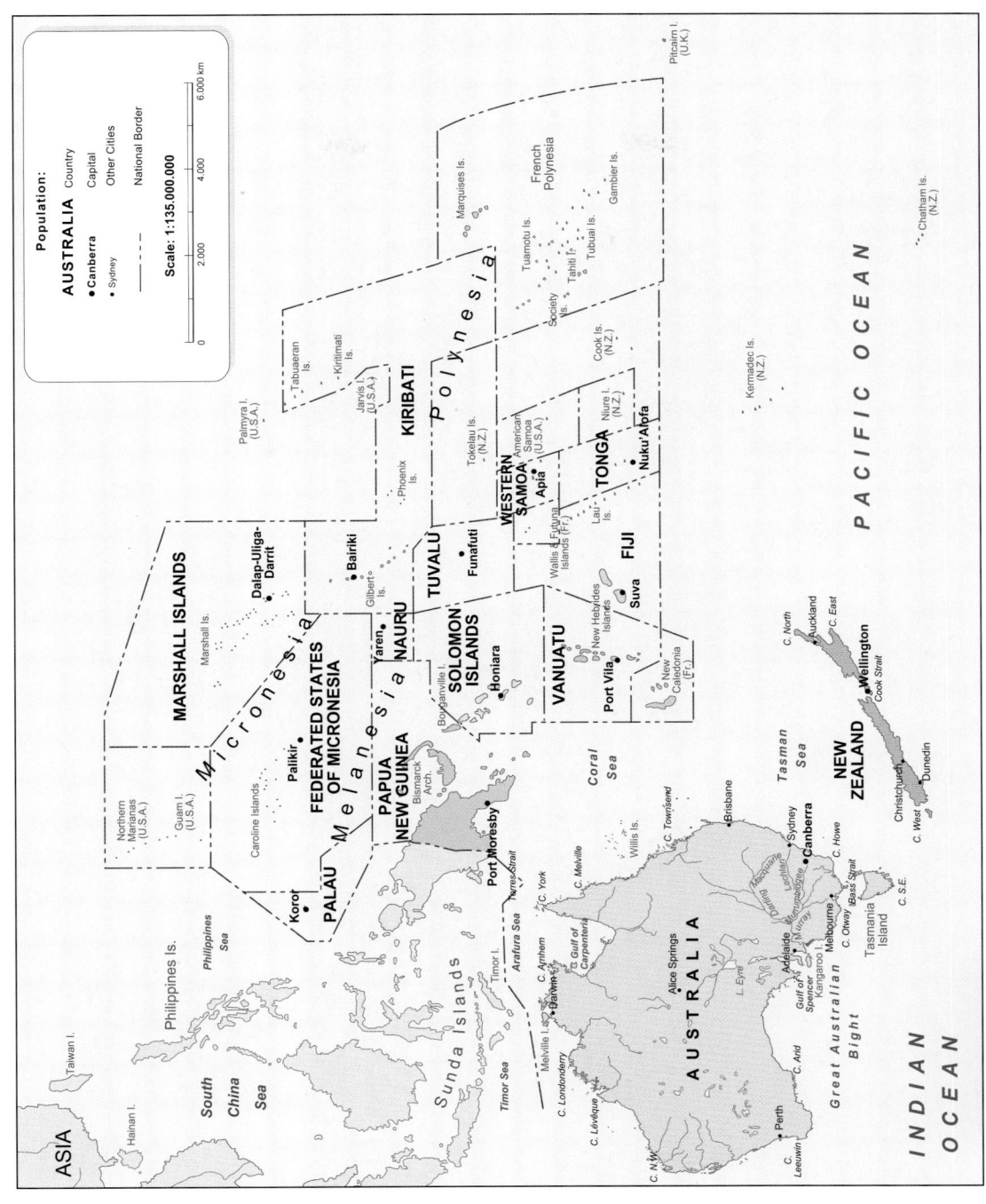

Gulf of
México

Yucatan
Channel

Gulf of
Honduras

Greater Antilles

Lesser Antilles

Caribbean Sea

ATLANTIC

OCEAN

CENTRAL

AMERICA

Nicaragua

C. de la Aguja   Venezuela
Margarita I.
Cartagena   Maracaibo   Gulf of
Gulf of   L. Maracaibo
Darien   **Caracas**
Orinoco
VENEZUELA
Medellín   Georgetown
Coco I.   **GUYANA**   Paramaribo
(C. Rica)   Gulf of   Cayenne
Panama   **SURINAM**   C. Orange
Malpelo I.   Cali   **•Bogotá**   **FRENCH**
(Colombia)   **GUIANA**
C. San Francisco   **COLOMBIA**   Maracá I.
Amazon
River Delta
Marajó I.
•Quito
ECUADOR
Galapagos   Gulf of   Guayaquil   Manaus
Islands   Guayaquil   Belém
(Ec.)   Amazon
Pto.   Marañón   Fernando de
Baquerizo   Noronha I.
Moreno   Fortaleza
C. San Roque
Pta. Negra
Recife
Trujillo
PERU
B R A Z I L
Lima
Callao   Salvador
Todos
los Santos
Bay
Titicaca   **•La Paz**   **BOLIVIA**
Brasília
PACIFIC   **Sucre**
Iquique   •Potosi
Gulf   Grande
OCEAN   of   **PARAGUAY**   Belo Horizonte
Arica   Rio de Janeiro
C. Frio   Trinidad I.
San Félix I.   San   **•Asunción**   São Paulo
Ambrosio I.   Sao Francisco I.
Sta. Catarina I.
Pôrto
Alegre
CHILE   Santa Fe   **URUGUAY**
Córdoba
Juan Fernández   Rosario   **Montevideo**
Arch.   **Santiago**   **Buenos**
(Chile)   **Aires**
La Plata   Rio de la Plata
ARGENTINA   C. San Antonio
Pta. Lavapie
Blanca Bay   ATLANTIC
Gulf of San Matias
OCEAN
Chiloé I.
Chonos Arch.   Gulf of San Jorge
C. Tres Puntas
Gulf of Penas
Falkland I.
(U.K.)
C. San Diego
Magellan's Str.   South
C. Horn   Georgia I.
Drake Str.   (U.K.)

Population:

PERU   Country
• **Lima**   Capital
• Callao   Other Cities
─ ─ ─   National Border

Scale: 1:35.000.000
0   300   600   900 km

ASIA

ARCTIC OCEAN

Wrangel I.

Bering Sea

St. Lawrence I.

Bering Strait

Barrow Pt.

Greenland Island

Iceland

Queen Elizabeth Islands

Baffin Bay

Nunivak I.

Yukon

ALASKA (U.S.A.) Fairbanks

Porcupine

C. Bathurst

Melville I.

Banks I.

Somerset I.

Devon I.

Prince of Wales

Baffin Island

Davis Strait

Anchorage

Victoria I.

Gulf of Amundsen

Gulf of Boothia

Kodiak I.

Great Bear Lake

Gulf of Alaska

Great Slave Lake

Southampton I.

C. Wolstenholme

Hudson Strait

C. Chidley

Labrador Sea

Alexander Arch.

Lake Athabasca

Hudson Bay

C. Charles

Newfoundland Island

Queen Charlotte Islands

C A N A D A

Belcher Is.

C. Henrietta Maria

James Bay

Eastmain

Gulf of St. Lawrence

C. Race

St.-Pierre et Miquelon (Fr.)

Edmonton

Reindeer Lake

Lake Winnipeg

Vancouver Island

Vancouver

Calgary

C. Flattery Seattle

Regina

Winnipeg

Lake Superior

Lake Huron

Quebec

Montreal

Ottawa

St. John

Bay of Fundy

C. Sable

Portland

Columbia

UNITED

Lake Michigan

Lake Ontario

Toronto

Boston

C. Cod

C. Blanco

STATES OF

Minneapolis

Detroit

Lake Erie

New York

Long I.

C. Mendocino

Pt. Arena

AMERICA

Chicago

Cleveland

Philadelphia

San Francisco

Denver

Kansas City

St. Louis

Washington

Chesapeake Bay

Bermuda I. (U.K.)

Las Vegas

Ohio

C. Hatteras

Pt. Concepción

Los Angeles

Phoenix

Gila

Arkansas

Tennessee

Memphis

Atlanta

ATLANTIC OCEAN

Dallas

PACIFIC

OCEAN

Houston

Colorado

New Orleans

Mississippi River Delta

Miami

C. Sable

Straits of Florida

Gulf of California

Monterrey

Gulf of Mexico

MEXICO

Yucatan Channel

Greater Antillas

C. San Lucas

C. Catoche

Gulf of Campeche

Gulf of Honduras

Caribbean Sea

C. Corrientes

Guadalajara

Revilla Gigedo Is.

México

CENTRAL AMERICA

L. Maracaibo

Gulf of Tehuantepec

C. Gracias a Dios

L. Nicaragua

Gulf of Mosquitos

Population:

CANADA Country

● **Ottawa** Capital

• Calgary Other cities

– – – National Border

Scale: 1:37.500.000

0   300   600   900 km

Atlas

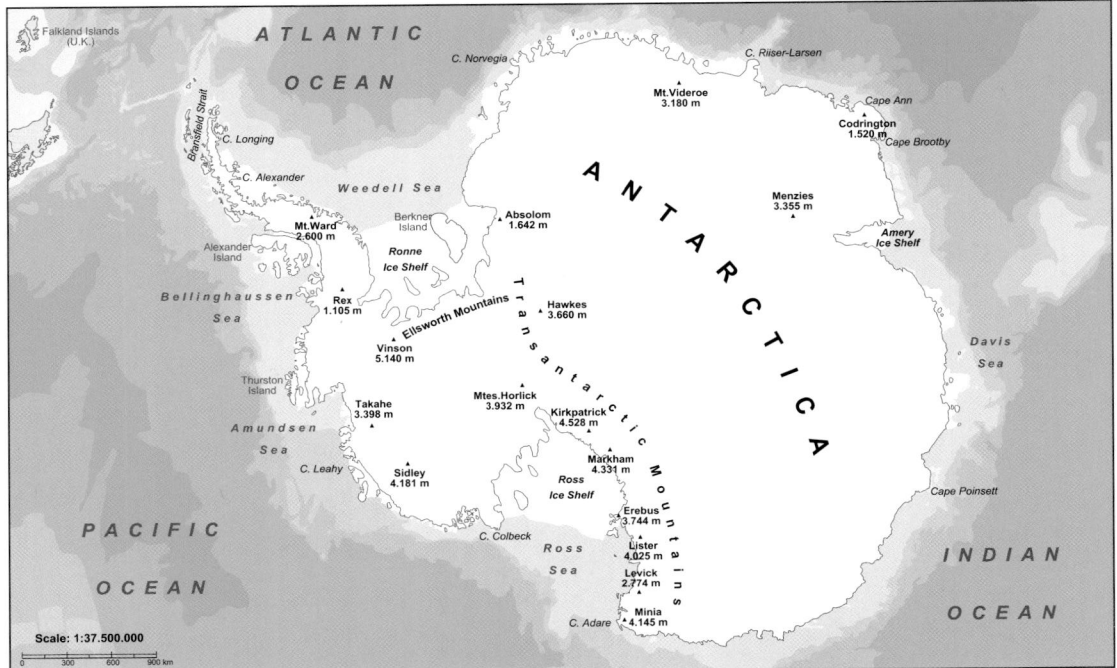

Falkland Islands
(U.K.)

ATLANTIC

OCEAN

C. Norvegia

C. Riiser-Larsen

Mt.Videroe
3.180 m

Cape Ann

Codrington
1.520 m
Cape Brootby

Bransfield Strait

C. Longing

C. Alexander

Weddell Sea

Menzies
3.355 m

Amery
Ice Shelf

Berkner
Island

Absolom
1.642 m

A   N   T   A   R   C   T   I   C   A

Ronne
Ice Shelf

Mt.Ward
2.600 m

Alexander
Island

Bellinghaussen
Sea

Rex
1.105 m

Ellsworth Mountains

Hawkes
3.660 m

Davis
Sea

Vinson
5.140 m

Thurston
Island

Takahe
3.398 m

Mtes.Horlick
3.932 m

Transantarctic Mountains

Kirkpatrick
4.528 m

Amundsen
Sea

C. Leahy

Sidley
4.181 m

Markham
4.331 m

Ross
Ice Shelf

Erebus
3.744 m

Cape Poinsett

PACIFIC

OCEAN

C. Colbeck

Ross
Sea

Lister
4.025 m

Levick
2.774 m

INDIAN

OCEAN

Minia
4.145 m

C. Adare

Scale: 1:37.500.000

0   300   600   900 km

INDEX

Index

U